Contract Law in Focus

Focus Casebook Series

Contract Law in Focus

Michael B. Kelly
Professor of Law
University of San Diego School of Law

Lucille M. Ponte
Professor of Law
Florida Coastal School of Law

Published by Wolters Kluwer in New York.

Wolters Kluwer Legal & Regulatory US serves customers worldwide with CCH, Aspen Publishers, and Kluwer Law International products. (www.WKLegaledu.com)

To contact Customer Service, e-mail customer.service@wolterskluwer.com, call 1-800-234-1660, fax 1-800-901-9075, or mail correspondence to:

Wolters Kluwer
Attn: Order Department
PO Box 990
Frederick, MD 21705

Printed in the United States of America.

1 2 3 4 5 6 7 8 9 0

ISBN 978-1-4548-7850-6

Library of Congress Cataloging-in-Publication Data

Names: Kelly, Michael B., (Law teacher) author. | Ponte, Lucille M., 1958- author.
Title: Contract law in focus / Michael B. Kelly, Professor of Law, University of San Diego School of Law, Lucille M. Ponte, Professor of Law, Florida Coastal School of Law.
Description: New York : Wolters Kluwer, [2016] | Series: Focus casebook series
Identifiers: LCCN 2016019963 | ISBN 9781454878506
Subjects: LCSH: Contracts — United States. | LCGFT: Casebooks.
Classification: LCC KF889.85 .K45 2016 | DDC 346.7302/2 — dc23
LC record available at https://lccn.loc.gov/2016019963

About Wolters Kluwer Legal & Regulatory US

Wolters Kluwer Legal & Regulatory US delivers expert content and solutions in the areas of law, corporate compliance, health compliance, reimbursement, and legal education. Its practical solutions help customers successfully navigate the demands of a changing environment to drive their daily activities, enhance decision quality and inspire confident outcomes.

Serving customers worldwide, its legal and regulatory portfolio includes products under the Aspen Publishers, CCH Incorporated, Kluwer Law International, ftwilliam.com and MediRegs names. They are regarded as exceptional and trusted resources for general legal and practice-specific knowledge, compliance and risk management, dynamic workflow solutions, and expert commentary.

To Christine, Marguerite, and Dolores—

with love and gratitude for honoring the unspoken contract of our sister bond.

L.M.P.

In loving memory of Leverett H. Kelly,

to whom I owe so much.

M.K.

Summary of Contents

Table of Contents

PART I. FORMATION

Chapter 2. Offer and Definiteness 31

PART III. REMEDIES

Chapter 16. Equitable Remedies 755

The Focus Casebook Series

Help students reach their full potential with the fresh approach of the Focus Casebook Series. Instead of using the "hide the ball" approach, selected cases illustrate key developments in the law and show how courts develop and apply doctrine. The approachable manner of this series provides a comfortable experiential environment that is instrumental to student success.

Students perform best when applying concepts to real-world scenarios. With assessment features, such as Real Life Applications and Applying the Concepts, the Focus Casebook Series offers many opportunities for students to apply their knowledge.

Focus Casebook Features Include:

Case Previews and Post-Case Follow-Ups — To succeed, law students must know how to deconstruct and analyze cases. Case Previews highlight the legal concepts in a case before the student reads it. Post-Case Follow-Ups summarize the important points.

In re Hlavin

As the hypothetical of Mary Jones and her loaves of bread illustrates, the number of potential disputes about the kinds of debt that are or are not to be considered consumer debts is simply limitless. The lawyer has to recognize when the issue matters and can be contested. As you read In re Hlavin, a case involving the 11 U.S.C §707(b) dismissal for abuse provision, consider the following questions:

1. Why is it the debtors and not the bankruptcy trustee who are arguing that their home mortgage is not a consumer debt?
2. What does this court s
gage is or isn't a consu

Post-Case Follow-Up

Is this opinion making a distinction between the repossessor himself disturbing the peace and his committing an act that motivates another to disturb the peace once the repossessor is gone? Would the result in this case have been different if the activities of the repossessors had awakened the debtor or the neighbor and the one awakened had shouted at them out of a window something like, "Stop, thief! I've called the police"? See Robinson v. Citicorp National Services, Inc., 921 S.W.2d 52 (Mo. Ct. App. 1996), and Chrysler Credit Corp. v. Koontz, 661 N.E.2d 1171 (1996). If the debtor's husband had raced outside with a firearm while the repossessors were pulling away from the property? If he or the neighbor had fired a firearm at the fleeing repossessors? If a sleeping child had been in the car unseen by the repossessor when the car was driven off? See Chapa v. Traciers & Associates, 267 S.W.3d 386 (Tex. App. 2008)? If the repossessor had violated a driving ordinance in the course of repos-

The Focus Casebook Series

Real Life Applications — Every case in a chapter is followed by Real Life Applications, which present a series of questions based on a scenario similar to the facts in the case. Real Life Applications challenge students to apply what they have learned in order to prepare them for real-world practice. Use Real Life Applications to spark class discussions or provide them as individual short-answer assignments.

In re Hlavin: Real Life Applications

1. Would the result in *Hlavin* have been different if the loans secured by their home had originally been taken out to fund a failed business venture? What if they had been taken out for home improvement or a vacation but then actually used to fund a business venture? Would it matter if they told the bank the money was being borrowed for home improvement or vacation but intended it to be used to fund a business venture? What if the home loans had been taken out for mixed personal/business reasons?
2. If the debtors in *Hlavin* had 30 different consumer debts totaling $75,000 and only one business debt totaling $76,000, would that court find that they had "primarily consumer debts" under §707(b)(1)? What would be the result if a court utilized one of the alternative approaches to this question mentioned in *Hlavin*?

Applying the Concepts — These end-of-chapter exercises encourage students to synthesize the chapter material and apply relevant legal doctrine and code to real-world scenarios. Students can use these exercises for self-assessment or the professor can use them to promote class interaction.

Applying the Concepts

1. Assume you are consulted by the following potential bankruptcy clients. Which of these appear at first blush to be candidates for a consumer bankruptcy filing as opposed to a non-consumer or business filing?
   a. The individual owners of an unincorporated video rental store whose business has plummeted due to the popularity of Internet movie-streaming services.
   b. A married couple both employed but who have abused their credit card spending and now owe more than they make together in a year.
   c. A recently divorced woman with two children whose ex-husband is unemployed and not contributing child support and who is having trouble paying her monthly living expenses.
   d. A married couple, one of whom has suffered major health problems resulting in medical expenses in excess of what they can expect to earn in ten years.

Preface

Ensure student success with the Focus Casebook Series.

FOCUS APPROACH

In a law office, when a new associate attorney is being asked to assist a supervising attorney with a legal matter in which the associate has no prior experience, it is common for the supervising attorney to provide the associate with a recently closed case file involving the same legal issues so that the associate can see and learn from the closed file to assist more effectively with the new matter. This experiential approach is at the heart of the ***Focus Casebook Series***.

Additional hands-on features, such as Real Life Applications, Application Exercises, and Applying the Concepts provide more opportunities for critical analysis and application of concepts covered in the chapters. Professors can assign problem-solving questions as well as exercises on drafting documents and preparing appropriate filings.

CONTENT SNAPSHOT

The introduction discusses the structure and sources of contract law, noting its origins in state-level, common law decisions. It also addresses some of the ways the law divides contract law, defining goods that are regulated by the Article 2 of the Uniform Commercial Code.

Chapter 1 provides an overview of three things: the important role contracts play in the economy and society; the elements a party must prove in order to obtain relief from breach of contract and the general framework of remedies available to the prevailing party; and some of the themes that recur in later chapters of the book and in other courses.

Chapter 2 begins the discussion of Assent: the requirement that all parties to a contract agree to the same terms. It focuses on how to determine whether an offer has been made that would allow the other party to create a contract by accepting.

Chapter 3 concludes the discussion of Assent by identifying the ways that a party may accept an offer: usually in words, but sometimes by performance or by silence. It also addresses some of the ways agreements change during the process of reaching assent.

Chapter 4 introduces the concept of consideration and reviews the classical "benefit-detriment" approach and the Holmesian modern "bargain" theory.

Common challenges to consideration, such as gratuitous promises, conditional gifts, sham consideration, illusory promises, and adequacy of consideration are discussed.

Chapter 5 reviews instances in which promises are enforced without consideration, including promissory estoppel and promissory restitution and the attendant application of the material benefit rule. Issues of past consideration, moral obligation, the preexisting duty rule, and modifications made in good faith are addressed.

Chapter 6 examines the role and burden of proof for contract defenses in defeating claims of breach. The contract defenses of incapacity, physical and economic duress, and undue influence are considered.

Chapter 7 continues the discussion of contract defenses, focusing on the ways inaccurate information may allow one party to avoid a contract, beginning with deceptive information provided by the other party or, sometimes, a third party (misrepresentation). It also addresses situations where one party's mistake might justify refusing to enforce the contract even if the other party did not cause the mistake.

Chapter 8 surveys limits on the enforceability of contracts taking into account the protection of both societal and individual interests. The policy constraints of unconscionability, illegality, statute of frauds, and exceptions to the statute of frauds are explored.

Chapter 9 addresses the techniques of interpretation, examining the kinds of information lawyers use to interpret contracts and the ways they use that information. Particular attention to problems that arise when one party objects that a written contract does not accurately reflect the agreement the parties reached.

Chapter 10 looks at conflicts which may arise when party rights and duties are not explicitly addressed in their contracts. Implied terms grounded in good faith and fair dealing, commercial reasonableness, and UCC gap fillers are reviewed. The chapter also discusses express and implied warranties and output and requirements contracts under the UCC.

Chapter 11 discusses conditions, which define whether one party's duty to perform has become due. It addresses both express conditions (specified by the parties) and conditions implied by the law, including circumstances when one party's breach may excuse the other party from needing to perform.

Chapter 12 addresses instances when a party may lawfully repudiate a contract, even if the other party has substantially performed their contract duties, or if a party raises concerns about whether or not contract duties will be performed when due. This chapter considers the UCC's perfect tender rule and efforts to cure in goods transactions. The concepts of anticipatory repudiation, retraction of a repudiation, and demands of adequate assurances of due performance are probed.

Chapter 13 recognizes that the failure to perform due to changed circumstances, after the contract was entered into, may allow parties to be excused from their contract duties. This chapter explores excuses that arise from changed circumstances, such as impossibility, impracticability, and frustration of purpose, and addresses the role of force majeure clauses in contracts.

Chapter 14 discusses third party contract rights, including agreements creating rights and duties for those who are not parties to the original contract or instances when a party to a contract transfers their contract rights or duties to another party.

The chapter reviews intended and incidental third party beneficiaries, the assignment of rights, the delegation of duties, and the use of novations.

Chapter 15 discusses the damages a party may collect for breach of contract, including market measures, incidental damages, and consequential damages. It introduces several doctrines that limit damages (avoidability, foreseeability, and uncertainty) and the ways the parties may limit damages by agreement in the contract itself.

Chapter 16 addresses additional remedies parties might seek for breach of contract, primarily court orders compelling a party to perform all or part of what was promised. It also addresses relief for unjust enrichment, an alternative to damages for breach, allowing a monetary recovery even if courts refuse to enforce the contract.

RESOURCES

Casebook: The casebook is structured around text, cases, and application exercises. Highlighted cases are introduced with a *Case Preview,* which sets up the issue and identifies key questions. *Post-Case Follow-ups* expand on the holding in the case. *Real Life Applications* present opportunities to challenge students to apply concepts covered in the case to realistic hypothetical cases. *Application Exercises* offer a mix of problem solving and research activities to determine the law of the state where the student plans to practice. State law application exercises better prepare the student to actually handle cases. *Applying the Concepts* feature provides occasions for critical analysis and application of concepts covered in the chapter.

Other resources to enrich your class include Practice Skills Exercises, or supplementary material such as *Examples & Explanations: Contracts, Sixth Edition* by Brian A. Blum. Ask your Wolters Kluwer sales representative or go to WKLegaledu.com to learn more about building the product package that's right for you.

Acknowledgments

The authors wish to acknowledge and thank Carol McGeehan, Kim Crowley, Developmental Editor, Betsy Kenny, Developmental Editor, and David J. Herzig, Associate Publisher—Legal Education at Wolters Kluwer, Andrew Blevins of The Froebe Group, and all of our external reviewers for their efforts and support for this book, as well as Ann Okerson, LIBLICENSE creator and owner, for use of contract language from Model License Agreement with Commentary (Version 5.0) at the **Center for Research Libraries.** We also wish to thank Major League Baseball and the Major League Baseball Players Association for their kind permission to reprint contract language from the American League Standard Baseball Players Contract.

Contract Law in Focus

Introduction to the Study of Contracts

Welcome to law school. The study of law offers incredible rewards. The insights it allows into policy making and implementation prepare you for any career path you might elect. Your ability to help others achieve their objectives will be intensely fulfilling and intellectually challenging. We hope you find the study of law as exciting as we did.

The study of contract law is one of the most fascinating courses in the curriculum. We know that some of you will find that a little hard to believe. But keep an open mind. It is not all (or even mostly) numbers. Contract is the way people make choices and improve their lives, taking what they have and exchanging it for things they want more. This field of study is all about how people establish relationships and achieve their goals. Contracts are a tool for personal fulfillment.

This introduction sets the stage for the study of contract law. It lays down basic information about the way contracts are governed in the United States. It does not introduce you to the substance of contract doctrine, which starts in Chapter 1. But it does introduce you to the legal system that regulates contracts. It identifies where contract rules originate and introduces some of the sources referred to repeatedly throughout the book. It also discusses some of the ways contract law is subdivided.

A. THE STRUCTURE OF CONTRACT LAW

You can learn about the law from many sources. This book is a secondary source. It draws together rules that were created by primary sources: the bodies of government responsible for creating and enforcing the laws governing contracts. The primary sources of contract law are divided in at least three ways, with rules (1) created by the judiciary, legislature, or treaty; (2) at the state or federal level; (3) relating to contracts in general or to contracts of a specific type. As the American legal system evolved, it made various choices in its approach to contract law. This section introduces you to those choices.

First, contract rules emerged primarily from court decisions. Thus, you may need to read a series of decisions to understand the nuances of a legal rule, its exceptions, and its application to different settings. Second, contract law is primarily state law, which may require you to study different approaches taken in different states. Third, a state may apply different rules to different types of contracts. Sales of **goods** (things, other than money, that can be moved, such as newspapers, groceries, cattle, iron ore, refrigerators, airplanes, or printing presses) may have different rules from sales of **services** (work people do for others, such as employment contracts or construction contracts), sales of **securities** (such as stocks and bonds), sales of **real estate** (land), or sales of **intangibles** (other things, such as insurance policies, patents, or rights to sue). Even though the distinctions are often minor, the structure of contract law requires you to understand various sources of contract law.

1. Common Law

Contract law initially emerged from **common law**, decisions made by courts, not statutes passed by legislatures. Courts created the doctrines of contract law by deciding individual disputes and explaining why they reached a particular outcome. Under the doctrine of **stare decisis**, subsequent courts were bound to respect earlier decisions, treating them as the law. Thus, later courts tried to apply the rationale of the earlier decisions when they faced similar issues. Variations on the facts produced different results. New situations also might have led a court to refine or create exceptions to the rules applied in prior cases.

In a common law system, like the U.S. system, the cases are the law. Courts do not just apply rules generated by others; rather, they generate the rules through legal decisions and, when appropriate, amend the rules. Judges, not legislatures, created and refined contract law. Until relatively recently, legislatures devoted their attention to other matters, such as criminal law and taxes, rarely enacting statutes governing contracts. Recently, legislatures have enacted more laws applicable to contracts. These range from attempts to codify all of contract law (such as the California Civil Code) to regulations aimed at specific contract practices (such as credit card fees). These statutes are important. However, no single codified body of contract doctrine exists that one can read and apply. The rules often are found in cases.

2. State Law

In general, contract law is a matter left to the states. Each state may regulate contracts as it sees fit. On the whole, states take remarkably similar approaches to the problems of contract law. They face the same issues and sometimes find wisdom in the way other states resolved the problems in the past. Still, each state court may phrase a rule a little differently, leaving room for subtle differences in contract law from state to state.

Some matters of contract law are federally regulated. For example, the federal government promulgates the rules governing the contracts it makes. Government Contracts is an entirely separate field of study. While government contracts start with normal contract principles, the government alters the rules somewhat, usually in a way that favors the government or the taxpayers. Federal law regulates the sale of securities, contracts with labor unions, and the warranties on automobiles, among other things. Despite federal legislation, state law governs most contract issues addressed in an introductory course in contract law.

3. Different Types of Contracts

The principles of contract law are often broad-based in their application. They can work well when applied to any kind of contract. Yet different kinds of contracts produce special problems that may justify specific solutions. In some cases, the specific solution simply restates the general principle in language appropriate for that particular setting. In other situations, the nature of the contracts or the structure of the industry requires slightly different rules. For example, states heavily regulate insurance policies. Federal labor law provides special rules for some employment contracts. Sales of stock and other securities have been regulated by the federal government since the 1929 stock market crash. Heavily regulated areas such as these receive almost no attention in the first-year contracts course. The principles you study this year provide the foundation concepts of contract law, subject to changes made by statutes and other regulations.

This book frequently will address one distinction based on the type of contract: comparing the rules governing sales of goods to the rules governing other contracts, particularly services and real estate. In many cases, you will see how similar they are. In others, however, you will note the way legislators have adopted slightly different rules for sales of goods.

4. Reasons, Not Just Rules

The varied sources of contract law make it difficult to announce any rule as black letter law. The similarities among the states allow some generalizations. But the distinctions make it critical to focus on the factors that justify a rule, not just a rule itself. In any case, a common law court may decide to change the rule previously announced because it no longer seems to suit the needs of the state. You must understand the reasons courts shape the rules one way or another in order to persuade a court to change a rule (or not to change it), to interpret a rule in favor of your client, or to craft an exception to a rule that helps your client. The language of the rules may vary, but the reasons for preferring a particular resolution apply more broadly. The rules presented in this book are not written in stone. Some types of problem recur over and over, producing renewed efforts to find a balance between conflicting interests. Understanding those interests and how past efforts to resolve them have succeeded or failed is essential to understanding contract law — both as it exists today and as it will evolve in the future.

B. THE SOURCES OF CONTRACT LAW

Contract law emerges from the courts and the legislatures of 50 states, several territories, and the federal government. Naturally, this book will not include every statute or every decision that might be applied to a contract issue. Instead, it tries to identify the central core of contract law, the approaches that have been adopted widely. In that regard, it relies heavily on a few key sources that deserve some introduction here, before we jump into the doctrines themselves. The general rules laid out in the chapters that follow largely are derived from the following sources. Cases in the book illustrate how the principles are applied.

1. The Uniform Commercial Code (UCC) and Sales of Goods

The **Uniform Commercial Code** is a comprehensive body of statutes governing common business transactions, such as sales of goods, checks, and **security interests** (creditors' rights to take property if a debt is not paid). Because businesses often sell across state lines, it helps to have rules that apply nationwide. Every state, except Louisiana, has adopted the UCC to govern some contract issues.

Article 2 of the UCC governs sales of goods. When this book refers to the UCC, it almost always means Article 2. Article 2 does not apply to contracts for services, real estate, or intangibles. Still, a large number of contracts involve sales of goods. For example, consumer transactions involving goods include sales at grocery stores, clothing stores, and appliance stores (or their websites). Business contracts involving goods are equally common. Almost every purchase of raw materials involves the sale of goods: an iron mine sells ore to a smelter, who sells iron to a steel company, who sells steel to an auto part manufacturer, who sells a hood to an auto manufacturer, who sells a car to a dealership, who sells it to a consumer, and every step involves a sale governed by the UCC. This book will not try to cover every detail of the UCC. A separate course in the UCC (or perhaps just Article 2) will allow you to study the code in more detail. But some provisions of Article 2, as well as a few provisions and definitions from Article 1 of the UCC, offer useful comparisons to the rest of contract law. You will encounter UCC provisions throughout the book.

The UCC is a primary source of law because it has the full force and effect of law. It is statutory law, passed by the state legislature and signed by the governor. Courts may interpret the UCC, but cannot amend it (the way they can amend their own earlier pronouncements under the common law). When a contract deals with goods, the UCC governs.

You need to identify when a contract involves sales of goods in order to decide if the UCC applies or whether to look elsewhere for the appropriate rule. The definition of goods — things moveable at the time of identification to the contract — will produce an obvious result in most cases. Watch out for a few traps.

- Goods can be really big. An airplane is a good. A construction crane is a good.
- Goods can be intended for permanent installation. A machine to be installed in a factory is a good; it moves to the factory before it is installed. A chandelier is a good. Once installed, they become **fixtures**, things that are attached to and become part of land or buildings.
- Goods can be attached to the land, if they will be severed from the land for delivery. Crops are goods. Ore, minerals, timber, oil, and gas are goods.
- Goods include the unborn young of animals (with apologies to those who find it objectionable to treat animals as property). Even though the unborn animal may not be severable from the mother at the time they are identified the contract, a contract to sell a calf is a sale of goods, even if the calf is not yet born.

A few things that look like goods are not. Money is not a good if it is the price. But money can be a good, if it is being bought and sold. A currency exchange or the sale of a coin collection is a sale of goods. Securities (such as stocks) are not goods. They represent ownership of a company, not a tangible thing. The certificate is tangible and moveable, but the ownership is not. Debt instruments and insurance policies are not goods, for the same reason.

not goods

Similarly, admission tickets (say, to a concert) are not goods. The concert, a service, is the core of that sale; the ticket is a symbol of your right to hear it (or perhaps a very short lease of a particular seat). Transportation tickets also represent a right to claim a service; the tickets are not goods in themselves. Depending on the nature of the transaction, courts differ on whether digital assets, such as downloaded software or music, are considered goods or services.

Some contracts involve a mix between goods and services. For example, construction contracts involve both supplying the materials for the building and providing labor to use them to erect the structure. The UCC applies if the predominant purpose of the contract is a sale as opposed to services. For an entire building, construction services are likely to be the predominant factor, even though the contractor supplies the materials. Installation can be a smaller part of a contract that essentially is a sale of goods. For instance, when a factory buys a machine, installation may be incidental. The sale is predominant. Similarly, a homeowner who buys a furnace may receive free installation; the sale of the furnace, not the installation, seems the predominant factor in this contract. Some sellers remove all doubt by creating two contracts. A store that sells hardwood flooring may offer installation, but enter a separate contract for installation. That ensures that the sale of the goods remains under the UCC, even though the contract for installation may be governed by different rules.

Currency Exchange

In a currency exchange, each currency is the good and each the price, depending on the party's perspective. An American seeking euros pays the price in U.S. dollars. She sees the euro as the good. But the person selling euros is also buying dollars, paying the price in euros. Each thinks it is a buyer of goods, paying the price. Each is right. That makes each a seller, from the other's perspective. The UCC applies either way; it is a sale of goods, even if the parties disagree about which currency is the good.

We live in interesting times. In 2001, the National Conference of Commissioners on Uniform State Laws (NCCUSL) proposed changes to Article 1. Those changes have been adopted in 40 states and seem likely to be adopted in more states. Not all states, however, passed the revisions as written. Rather than a uniform state law, lawyers now face the original Article 1 (in about ten states) and several variations of revised Article 1. One variation involves the definition of good faith, requiring all parties to a contract to behave honestly—though how much honesty varies with the definition. Good faith is covered in Chapter 10.

You may encounter some mention of revisions to Article 2, proposed by NCCUSL in 2003. Those revisions received no support and have been withdrawn. Thus, original Article 2 remains the law in the 49 states that adopted it.

2. The Convention on International Sales of Goods

The global economy requires rules that apply to parties in different nations. **The United Nations Convention on Contracts for the International Sale of Goods** (**CISG** or, sometimes, the Vienna Convention), sets forth the law governing sales of goods (excluding household purchases) if the buyer and seller are in different countries and both (or sometimes only one) of those countries have ratified the treaty. At least 84 nations, including the United States, have ratified the CISG. Under the U.S. Constitution, **treaties** (agreements between nations) supersede any U.S. law, except the Constitution itself. Therefore, the CISG supplants both federal and state laws that are inconsistent with it. Unless the contract says otherwise, states must apply the CISG, not the UCC, when dealing with certain international sales of goods to which the treaty applies.

Hierarchy of Law

Within the United States, some laws take priority over others. The list below shows the pattern of priority. Laws higher on the list will override inconsistent laws lower on the list.

1. U.S. Constitution
2. Treaties (such as CISG)
3. Federal statutes
4. State constitution
5. State statutes (such as the UCC)

The CISG illustrates alternative ways to address contract issues. Occasionally, we will introduce different approaches taken by the CISG. But detailed study of the CISG needs to await an upper level course on the topic. For now, the CISG helps to keep us from becoming too insular in our point of view.

International treaties also affect choice of law: the decision of which nation's law should govern when a dispute involves international conduct or parties. Sometimes a contract will specify which nation's law should apply to a dispute. Treaties govern when to honor those provisions and what to do if no provision exists. (Within the United States, the decision of which state's law should apply to a contract also involves choice of law, though not governed by treaties.)

3. The Restatement (Second) of Contracts

The **Restatement (Second) of Contracts** is an effort to identify the general rules of contract law as revealed by the rulings of state courts. It was created by the **American**

Law Institute—a body of renowned lawyers, jurists, and scholars. The Restatement is not a statute or any kind of law, but a secondary source that describes the law. The three-volume work resembles the structure of a statutory code. Each section is written as a rule of law, but it has no binding effect and it has not been enacted by any state government. Its power to persuade judges lies in the force of its reasoning and the credibility of its authors.

While the Restatement (Second) of Contracts is not law, it is a very good summary of the law. The states often have taken remarkably similar approaches to many problems posed by contracts. The Restatement (Second) of Contracts reports that consensus relatively accurately. It reports a single rule, which will not capture every minor variation in wording between courts of different states. As a framework for resolving contract disputes, however, the second Restatement is very reliable. Because it is a very good summary of state practice, states confronting an issue for the first time often elect to follow the approach announced in the second Restatement. Thus, the discussion in the chapters that follow often begins with the rules as formulated in the Restatement (Second) of Contracts. Be alert, however, for states that have adopted a different rule by statute or judicial decision. Also be alert for cases that quote or refer to the first Restatement, published in 1932. Some states prefer a few of those rules. You may find them persuasive. But the older rules often differ from the second Restatement. Be sure you know which one you are quoting when you use these rules.

4. The Restatement (Third) of Restitution and Unjust Enrichment

One of the newest developments affecting contract law is the approval of the Restatement (Third) of Restitution and Unjust Enrichment. This newest Restatement identifies several refinements to contract law, particularly relating to **remedies** (relief a court can grant the winning party) and **defenses** (justifications for refusing to perform). This book will introduce a few of the more interesting observations made in this new Restatement.

As with the Restatement (Second) of Contracts, the Restatement (Third) of Restitution and Unjust Enrichment is not law. Rather, it represents an effort to identify common threads in the common law as it continues to develop. The quality of the work makes it likely that state courts will find it persuasive, adopting some of the refinements. To the extent that the new Restatement correctly identifies the rationale for decided cases, those cases may persuade other courts to adopt similar approaches.

5. Private Rules

A contract makes its own rules. The parties, by agreement, make a rule that applies to them. This private rule-making is obviously true of promises: the parties have no obligation to perform at all until they create that duty by making a contract. The parties may define those duties in any way they wish, within some limits. In short, the parties can make their own rules.

The vast majority of statutes and cases involving contracts create **default rules**: rules that apply unless the parties have agreed to something different. For instance, the UCC includes rules governing how to calculate damages. Nonetheless, the parties to a contract are free to provide a different way to measure damages if they prefer. Some rules are regulatory. The parties cannot disclaim the duty of good faith and fair dealing. Similarly, public policies, such as the rule prohibiting penalty clauses, are imposed on parties regardless of any agreement to the contrary. With few exceptions, the parties can make their own rules to govern their dealings.

6. Cases

Judicial decisions are another primary source of law. These decisions by judges represent the law of the state in action. In some cases, judges apply rules that were created before the case arose. In others, judges find it necessary to select or define a rule before deciding how the rule applies to a given case. In any event, the decisions of courts are law in their own right. Even when applying statutes, courts may interpret the statutes to provide additional clarity to those governed by them.

The cases in this book have been edited, sometimes rather significantly. In part, editing allows us to present only the issues pertinent to the chapter at hand. Many cases involve a number of issues, some of them not related to contract law at all. Procedural issues abound in cases, including discussions of which state's contract law should apply. Disputes often raise more than one issue of contract law. Instead of asking you to read the entire opinion, we have chosen the portion of the opinion that illustrates the point being made in that section.

In some cases, even that portion has been edited. Judges sometimes address issues at length. That approach may be appropriate to explain to a party why it lost the case (or to explain to a reviewing court why it should not reverse the decision). A detailed discussion of each pertinent precedent may make the opinion more persuasive. But often you can understand the court's point without all of that elaboration. In those situations, we abbreviate the discussion — always noting omissions. You should feel free to read the entire opinion online or in the official reporters. Particularly if an ellipsis (. . .) occurs at a point where you find the discussion puzzling, it may pay to revisit the original source and see the court's full discussion.

Another way we have kept the opinions shorter is by deleting some of the citations courts provided. Governed by stare decisis, courts often cite to earlier cases to support their statements about the rule and how it applied to similar situations in the past. Those citations are an important part of legal writing. You will need to cite support to the court in order to persuade it that your position is consistent with prior law. But in some instances, the citations will not enhance your appreciation of the points made in the case. In those circumstances, we may omit citations.

We also regularly omit citations to the trial record. A court relying on the facts of the case may cite to affidavits or testimony provided. Those citations are useful to the parties and a reviewing court, showing that the court was relying of the evidence adduced by the parties, not just making up facts on its own. But citations to the trial record are of no use in this book. Unlike cases, where you might look up the cited opinion, you cannot easily find transcripts of the trial testimony to verify that the court accurately stated the facts. Nor is there any particular reason to do that in this course.

While upper level practice courses may require you to develop a record and evaluate the evidence, here the goal is to help you understand contract doctrine and how it applies. The facts that the court states are what matters. Citations to the source will be omitted, sometimes without noting the omission.

C. CONCLUSION

This book draws on wealth of materials to help introduce you to contract law. The variety of materials and the variety of problems to which it applies should help keep the study of contracts fresh. We hope you find as much enthusiasm for the course as we do. Be ready for an interesting tour through the law of contracts. We hope to set the stage for a stimulating career in the law. No matter what area of the law you choose to pursue, you will encounter contracts. We look forward to helping guide you through the basic tenets of contract law.

1

Introduction to Contract Doctrine

An overview of contract doctrine provides useful context for the detailed rules addressed in subsequent chapters. Contract rules overlap and intertwine, making it easier to understand each doctrine if you have a sense of the overall framework. An overview of the substance and themes of contract law will help make sense of the details encountered later. Many discussions of contract rules reflect these themes, but they sometimes remain a subtext. Identifying them explicitly will help you see them at work throughout the course.

A. EXCHANGES, CONTRACTS, AND SOCIETAL WEALTH

A **contract** is a promise that the law will enforce or, at least, that creates a duty the law will recognize. Primarily, the law enforces promises that are part of voluntary exchanges. Voluntary exchanges serve a vital role for society, allowing people to exchange what they have now for things they would prefer to have. Enforcing exchange promises helps people rely on these promises. Enforcement offers some reassurance to a party who performs first that it really will receive the promised return performance when the time for that performance arrives.

Key Concepts

- The value of exchanges to society
- The elements required to prove breach of contract
- The consequences of breach
- The elements required to recover for unjust enrichment (or quasi-contract)
- The difference between objective and subjective approaches to legal issues
- The balance between freedom of contract and protection from unwise contracts

1. The Value of Exchanges

Exchanges offer people a way to improve their current situation. They are the most common way people can obtain something that they want, but don't already have. The choices are limited: make it yourself; steal it; wait for someone to give it to you; or offer someone an exchange. Offering an exchange—promising to give another something she wants if she will give you what you want—offers a way to improve both your situation and hers. Each of you gives up something you want less in exchange for something you want more, a classic win-win situation.

In this way, voluntary exchanges increase people's utility, whether measured in dollars (increasing societal wealth) or joy (when gains bring happiness, not monetary profit). By making both parties better off after the exchange, society as a whole benefits—with the exception of antisocial contracts, such as sale of controlled substances or murder for hire. For the vast majority of exchanges, two people improve without any harm to others.

The entire economy runs on exchanges. Workers exchange time and skill for income, and then exchange income for food, clothing, shelter, and other things that make their lives better. Businesses exchange money for equipment, materials, and labor necessary to produce their goods and services, and then exchange their finished goods or services for money. Students exchange tuition for education, and then use their education to produce income. Each exchange improves the position of both parties. Each prefers what it receives to what it gives up.

Mutual benefit is built into voluntary exchanges. A person who expects to be worse off after an exchange will refuse to deal. Willingness to enter an exchange shows that both parties prefer the exchange to their current situation.

Consider an example of a mutually beneficial exchange. Sam's bike is worth $1,000 to Sam, but Bobby likes it more than that (say, $2,000). The table shown in Exhibit 1.1 examines how each would fare if Sam sold the bike to Bobby (at three different prices). The fourth column in the table adds their values, showing how much society (here, the two of them together) has.

EXHIBIT 1.1 A Mutually Beneficial Exchange

If the price is:	Sam has:	Bobby has:	Society has:
no deal	bike ($1,000)	$2,000	$3,000
$1,500	$1,500	$500 + bike (valued at $2,000)	$4,000
$1,001	$1,001	$999 + bike (valued at $2,000)	$4,000
$1,999	$1,999	$1 + bike (valued at $2,000)	$4,000

At each price, both Sam and Bobby benefit. At any price below $1,000 or above $2,000, one of them would refuse to agree. The total (Bobby's holdings plus Sam's holdings) does not depend on the price. Price determines who gets a bigger share of the gain, not the total gain. Is Bobby paying $1,500 for a bike that is only worth $1,000? No. Items don't have worth; they have worth to a person for a purpose. To Sam, the bike may be a tired old thing worth only $1,000. But to Bobby the bike has attributes that offer more joy than anything else he could get for $2,000. Bobby is not overpaying; Sam is not undercharging. Each improves after the deal.

2. The Value of Commitment

When you buy a cup of coffee with cash, you don't need to make promises.
baranq/Shutterstock.com

Because exchanges improve societal well-being, the law supports and even encourages exchanges. By enforcing exchange promises, contract law protects people who rely on those promises. A person who performs first faces some risk that the other party will refuse to perform — will keep the price and the bike. Contract law reduces that risk by giving the performing party a way to enforce the promise. The possibility of enforcement makes it less profitable to break a promise. Instead of keeping the other party's performance, the promise breaker ends up paying the price and paying a lawyer. The law makes it easier to commit to an exchange today, even though performance will occur at a later time.

People could make those exchanges without promises, entering exchanges as needs arise instead of making commitments in advance. Present needs could be paid for today (rather than making a promise to pay in the future); future needs could be dealt with when the time comes. When you buy a cup of coffee with cash, you don't need to make promises. Both you and the coffee shop perform almost simultaneously; you hand over the money, they hand over the coffee.

Enforceable promises can assist even simple transactions like the coffee shop. If you use a credit card, the exchange depends on promises: your promise to pay the credit card bill and the credit card company's promise to pay the coffee shop. If the shop makes the coffee fresh when you order it, one of you needs to perform first.

For many transactions immediate exchanges just do not work. An annual lease (promising payments every month) allows stability that day-to-day leases lack. A mortgage (promising payments in advance) works much better than saving until a buyer can pay cash for a home. Imagine a law school run on a day-to-day basis, with neither school nor students committing to teach or to pay for classes beyond today.

Promises reduce uncertainty. Lessees want to know they will not have to find a new place to live the next day; the lessor wants to know how much rent to expect each month. Neither would be happy with such temporary arrangements — or with the hassle involved in making and collecting daily rent payments. Instead, each side wants a promise that lasts at least a month, usually longer. (Hotels offer shorter-term leases, but at higher prices that compensate for the uncertainty.) The ability to plan for the future almost requires everyone to enter contracts.

The need for planning makes it troubling for people to change their minds after agreeing to an exchange. One party might regret the promise, preferring not to perform. But the other may have relied on that performance, expecting to attend classes, live in the apartment, or receive a weekly paycheck. In order for promises to reduce uncertainty, promises must be reliable — even if one party no longer finds the exchange beneficial.

3. Commitment Despite Errors

If exchanges always improved both parties' positions, contract law might be unnecessary. People would perform without any compulsion. A desire to withdraw from an exchange suggests a lack of mutual benefit, undermining the rationale for enforcement. A mutual benefit that seemed to exist at the time the agreement was made may have disappeared.

People sometimes agree to exchanges that are not mutually beneficial. Sometimes people buy on impulse, regretting their choice almost immediately. We even have a name for it: buyer's remorse. Sometimes the remorse, too, is fleeting; given a little time, they are happy with the exchange. But in other cases regrets persist. Some decisions to enter exchanges result from cognitive errors, as people misunderstand their own desires or miscalculate the costs or risks involved. Other decisions may reflect choices people should not make. They want the exchange, but it is not really good for them. Society's benefit from these exchanges is less clear.

Individual autonomy may justify enforcing contracts even in these cases. People need to be able to make their own mistakes. Otherwise, they never learn from their mistakes. More important, honoring a person's stated preferences probably results in fewer mistakes. In part, enforcement offers people a reason to think before they act. Equally important, individual decisions seem less likely to produce mistakes than any alternative. Who could make a better decision about whether you should go to law school, business school, or medical school — or which one to attend? Anyone else trying to decide what is best for you seems likely to make more mistakes (or worse mistakes) than you would make. Your decisions deserve deference, despite the possibility of error, because they are the best decisions society can expect.

Human nature suggests another reason to enforce contracts despite errors that might undermine mutual benefit. Parties might try to back out of a deal even if it is mutually beneficial, if they thought backing out would allow them to capture a bigger share of the benefits for themselves. This can border on theft, as where a buyer receives the goods and then refuses to pay the price. The value of the goods may exceed the price, but keeping both is better still (for the thief, not the other party).

In some cases, the withdrawal is strategic rather than dishonest. Having agreed to one price, a party might immediately wonder if the other would have agreed to a better deal. If a party could back out freely, she could then try to renegotiate for a better price. (Once renegotiated, she might try again for a still better price.) Each time, a mutually beneficial deal is revoked, then replaced by a different mutually beneficial deal—unless the person asks too much and the entire deal falls apart. Society cares more about the net benefit than about how the parties divide the benefit. Thus, the original deal serves society as well as the substitute—and much better than the risk that the deal disintegrates.

A person might try to withdraw from a deal that was mutually beneficial when made because subsequent events undermine the benefit of the deal. In effect, a party made a mistake in predicting the benefits of the deal. Consider a sale of stock. The buyer expects the stock's value to increase; the seller may expect it to fall. The buyer would rather pay the price today than take the risk that it will cost more later. The seller would rather agree to the price today than bear the risk that it will fall later. The deal is mutually beneficial when formed. After the stock price changes, one party may regret the deal. But that risk (of a change in stock value) is the reason for the contract. The contract was designed to allocate the risk of a change in price. The change does not undermine the mutual benefit of the contract as formed.

The ability of contracts to limit future risks offers an important reason people enter promises instead of just immediate exchanges. A store that needs a steady supply of tomatoes could buy them one week at a time, taking advantage of any price decrease in the future. However, that would involve risking a price increase or, worse, a shortage that made tomatoes unavailable. A contract, if enforceable, provides assurance that supplies will be available at a price the store can accept. Similarly, the seller guards against future price decreases or declines in demand by locking in the sale today. But if either party can avoid the contract on the ground that the deal no longer is beneficial, the contract would serve no function.

Promises would lose much of their value if a state decided that a party's attempt to withdraw from the deal showed that the promise was not mutually beneficial (and, thus, not worthy of enforcement). Contracts would lose their reliability. Contract law attributes significance to the assent as of the time the contract is made. A party concerned about subsequent changes undermining the benefit should not enter a contract. If she makes the contract, a claim it should not be enforced will require more than just her preference to withdraw from the deal.

B. THE GENERAL FRAMEWORK OF CONTRACT LAW

Contract law is interrelated; the reasons for one doctrine often make sense because of the way it fits with other doctrines. An introduction to the other doctrines may help you appreciate the way contract doctrines work together.

A cause of action for breach of contract requires proof of three basic elements:

1. that an enforceable promise was made;
2. that the defendant's performance was due; and
3. that the defendant failed to perform without excuse.

To recover more than **nominal damages** (a modest amount, usually $1, that acknowledges the plaintiff was right), a plaintiff also must show that it suffered an actual loss as a result of the breach.

1. Enforceability

To be enforceable, a promise must satisfy three requirements. First, **mutual assent** limits enforcement to promises where both of the parties (or all of the parties) have agreed to the terms. The assent of both parties bolsters the assumption that the contract is mutually beneficial. Typically, courts evaluate mutual assent by looking for an offer by one party and acceptance of that offer by the other. That two-step model may not always describe the series of communications that go into negotiating a deal. But most transactions ultimately come down to each party, one at a time, signaling willingness to live by the terms agreed.

Second, **consideration** requires that the promise be part of an exchange. For reasons discussed above, contract law starts with the principle of limiting enforcement to bargained-for exchanges. As with most rules, exceptions exist, particularly when one party relies to its detriment on a promise made by the other. Even without a bargain, allowing the promisor to back out of the deal after the other party has incurred costs may produce injustice.

Third, **definiteness** requires that the promise be sufficiently detailed to allow a court to identify a breach and to formulate a suitable remedy. If a promise is so vague that a court cannot tell whether conduct was performance or breach, a court cannot enforce the deal. In some cases, vagueness suggests the parties were not finished negotiating the deal, intending to be bound only after they finalized the additional terms.

In some cases, parties may regret agreeing to an exchange. If that regret reflects nothing more than the party's own bad judgment, the law will enforce the contract anyway. But sometimes a party's ability to exercise good judgment is impaired by forces that undermine the legitimacy of the agreement itself. In those cases, courts may refuse to enforce a deal despite the existence of assent, consideration, and definiteness. This outcome primarily occurs when a party can prove a **defense** to the contract, a reason that it should not be enforced despite assent, consideration, and definiteness. The most common defenses include:

1. **Incapacity**—attributes of an individual that impaired the ability to make a rational decision, such as youth, mental illness, or intoxication;
2. **Misrepresentation and Mistake**—misinformation (usually, but not always, provided by others) that impaired a person's ability to make a rational decision;
3. **Duress and Undue Influence**—improper pressure (including threats) others apply that impaired a person's ability to make or to express a rational decision;
4. **Unconscionability**—primarily, terms so outrageous that they should not be enforced even if a party appears to have assented to them.

Exhibit 1.2 demonstrates the relationship between the components that make a contract enforceable.

EXHIBIT 1.2 Decision Tree for Enforceability of Contracts

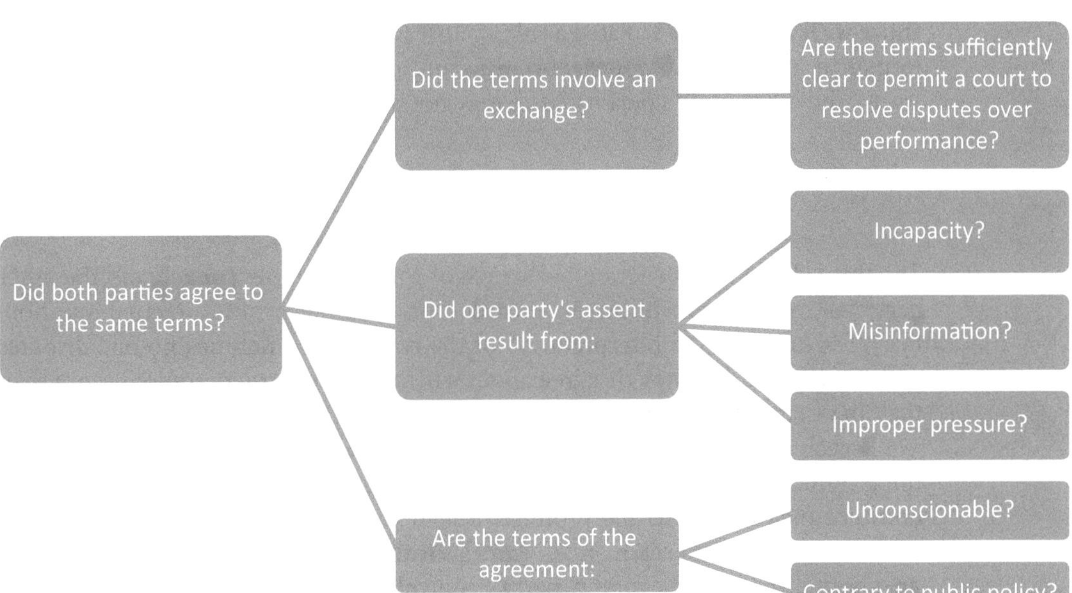

To be enforceable, the top row of questions must be answered "Yes," and all the questions below the top row must be answered "No."

In addition, some contract terms may harm others in society or contradict important societal values or policies, making them unacceptable even if both parties were willing to agree to those terms. Public policy precludes enforcement of such terms—sometimes even if neither party raises the defense.

2. Performance Due

The second element of an action for breach of contract asks whether performance is due. Many contracts include **conditions**, events that trigger the duty to perform. For example, fire insurers promise to perform if an insured event (such as a fire) occurs; a fire is a condition of their duty to perform. If the insured property does not suffer fire damage, then the insurer owes no duty to pay anything to the insured. Performance comes due when all the conditions have been met.

Even where contracts do not specify conditions, a party may be entitled to withhold performance until certain events occur. Commonly, one party's performance may need to occur first. Until that person performs, the other's performance does not become due. For example, employment contracts usually require the work to occur first; an employer's duty to pay comes due after the employee works for a month or a week. If the employee does not work, failure to pay is not breach because duty to pay never came due. Performance usually becomes due when the other party provides **substantial performance**—providing the recipient with the important aspects of performance, even if some details of performance fall short. Thus, an employer's duty to pay probably comes due if the employee worked the entire week, even if she violated a rule against smoking in the workplace. If nonperformance amounts to a **material breach** (failure to perform a significant part of the work), the other party's performance may not come due.

3. Unexcused Nonperformance

The third element of an action for breach of contract defines **breach**: did the other party fail to perform without an excuse? Failure to perform is a factual question, but often turns on the interpretation of the contract. Sometimes no one disputes what each party did; they disagree about whether the contract required more than that. In other cases, parties may dispute what the parties actually did.

Breach depends on nonperformance, not culpability. A party that does everything humanly possible in an effort to perform still breaches if the performance does not measure up to the promise. But in some extraordinary circumstances, courts excuse nonperformance. **Impracticability** excuses nonperformance if unexpected disasters beyond a party's control preclude performance. For example, a seller may be excused from delivering goods if its factory burned down or a new law prohibited delivering the goods. **Frustration** applies when unanticipated circumstances arise that make the other party's performance nearly useless. For example, a contract to rent a limo for prom night might be frustrated if the prom is postponed due to an outbreak of H1N1 flu. Both excuses work from the premise that circumstances have changed so seriously that parties probably would have agreed that the contract should not remain in force, at least if they had had the foresight to anticipate this situation and provide for it in the contract.

4. Remedies

If a claim for breach succeeds, the plaintiff is entitled to a remedy: an award from the court to prevent, cure, or compensate for the losses caused by the breach. Remedy often is the primary concern. "Is he liable?" is only a prelude to "What can I get?"

Contract remedies generally pursue a party's **expectation interest**, seeking to place the victim of a breach (we'll call that person the plaintiff) in the position that she would have occupied if the breach had not occurred (that is, if the promise had been performed). A court can achieve that directly by issuing an order of **specific performance**—an injunction compelling a breaching party to perform the promise. A plaintiff might obtain relief sooner by arranging for a substitute performance (sometimes called **cover**) instead of asking the court to make the defendant perform. Suing for **damages**—an amount of money necessary to produce the equivalent of performance—would allow recovery of any extra cost incurred in connection with the substitute arrangements. Damages are more common than injunctions.

Occasionally, courts may award a less generous recovery. Damages based on the **reliance interest** seek to place the victim in the position that she would have occupied if the promise had never been made. This allows recovery of expenses incurred in reliance on the contract, but does not include any gains that would have been realized if the defendant had performed. This remedy can be critical when the gains are difficult to measure or to predict. Awarding the expenses allows some recovery (so plaintiff at least breaks even) even though full expectation is impractical.

Vitally, courts limit damages in contract actions to compensation for losses suffered due to the breach. In part because breach can be innocent, moral outrage has little or no place in contract recoveries. Thus, for breach of contract, courts refuse to award **punitive damages**, intended to punish willful wrongdoers and to make an example of them in order to deter others. The law also resists efforts to inflate compensatory damages for breach of contract. Plaintiffs cannot recover for losses that they could have avoided by reasonable efforts. Plaintiffs must prove damages with reasonable certainty. Courts rarely award damages for emotional distress. Remedies for breach of contract target the loss, but no more.

Limiting remedies also serves to encourage mutually beneficial exchanges. If remedies were too severe, the risk of serious sanctions might discourage people from making enforceable promises. Even if the chance of breach seemed slight, the cost of breach might outweigh the gains. At the extreme, if the law imposed capital punishment for breach, how often would people make enforceable promises? But even modest sanctions might deter some transactions. Society benefits from voluntary exchanges. Policies that discourage exchanges reduce those benefits. By limiting remedies to compensation, society imposes the least deterrent to contract that seems justifiable.

5. Unjust Enrichment (or Quasi-Contract)

Because some promises are not enforceable, courts sometimes need to address cases in which people began performing their side of a deal before realizing

Revolutionizing Damage Remedies

Until 1936, courts spoke only of seeking the plaintiff's position if the contract had been performed. In that year, Lon L. Fuller and William R. Perdue, Jr., produced what has become the most famous law review article in the field of contract law: *The Reliance Interest in Contract Damages* (pts. 1 & 2), 46 Yale L.J. 52, 373 (1936-1937). This remarkable work forever changed the way courts talk about damages, introducing the terms "expectation interest" and "reliance interest." You may wish to read the article to see how carefully, thoroughly, and insightfully these academic observers analyzed the landscape of judicial opinions and offered improved ways to address damage issues.

Deterring Promises

Would you promise to umpire a Little League baseball game if breach involved a $1,000 (or even a $100) penalty? You probably won't forget or write down the wrong time or get stuck in traffic. But one misstep and your pay for several weeks of games disappears. The price of umpires will rise (either because supply declines or because umpires charge more to cover the risk). That means the fees parents have to pay to join Little League teams will rise — perhaps reducing the number of children who can participate, perhaps just decreasing the number of other things their parents can afford. (And soccer referees would face the same tradeoff.) Life might be better for a lot of people without penalties.

that the other party will not need to perform its side of the exchange. For example, a buyer may make a down payment on a house before the seller, with justification, decides to cancel the deal. No one suggests the seller can keep the down payment and the house. Nevertheless, if the contract was unenforceable, buyer cannot sue for breach of contract.

At several points in the contracts course, you will encounter a second cause of action: **unjust enrichment**. It has two elements:

1. Defendant received a benefit (usually at the expense of plaintiff); and
2. Retaining the benefit would be unjust, unless plaintiff is compensated for the benefit.

Plaintiff must establish both elements to prevail. The second element, though worded vaguely, seeks to exclude liability in cases where the defendant has a right to keep the benefit. This certainly applies if the benefit was a gift. It also applies if the defendant had a valid contract right to the performance. (Unjust enrichment will not change contract rights that are enforceable; it comes into play if the contract fails to establish peoples' rights.) Less obviously, a defendant may keep benefits bestowed by **volunteers**: those who provide unsolicited benefits in circumstances where they should bargain before performing. For example, tree trimmers should negotiate the price with homeowners, not just trim the trees and then submit bills. Homeowners may have received benefits. Trimmers who expected to be paid are not donors. Yet because they should have bargained first, they will be treated as volunteers, who (like donors) have no right to recover for unjust enrichment.

If the plaintiff prevails in an unjust enrichment action, she is entitled to recover **restitution** (sometimes called the **restitution interest**): an amount needed to place the party that received the benefit (typically the defendant, a party who did not perform the alleged contract) in the position it would have occupied if the contract had not been made. In effect, the defendant must return any benefits it received as a result of the promises (or their fair market value, if the benefit itself cannot be returned). This can work both ways: if a contract for sale of land is held unenforceable after both parties have performed, the seller is entitled to a return of the land, just as the buyer is entitled to a return of the price.

Unjust Enrichment, Quasi-Contract, Contract Implied-in-Law, and Restitution

Unjust enrichment has many names. Courts frequently refer to **quasi-contract** or **contract implied-in-law**, two ways to say unjust enrichment. Both terms reflect the recognition that recoveries here are not based on an actual enforceable promise, but on obligations the law imposes. When a person should make restitution, the law infers a promise to do so, but distinguishes that inference from promises a person actually made. (Beware of the similarity to **contract implied-in-fact**, which is an actual promise a party makes, but one inferred from conduct that signals a promise instead of from words expressing a promise.) Sometimes courts use restitution, a name for the remedy, to describe the basis for the remedy. While the words differ, each term describes a category of situations in which a defendant should return benefits received from the plaintiff. The general category encompasses a number of more specific causes of action, such as **quantum meruit** (an action seeking to recover the value of services rendered), **quantum valebat** (an action seeking to recover the value of goods delivered), and **money had and received** (an action seeking to recover payments made). For simplicity, this text strives to use the term "unjust enrichment."

6. Seeing the Outline

Such a brief description of contract law cannot do justice to the intricacy. At best, it shows the skeleton of the law. But the skeleton gives the body much of its shape. By keeping remedies from being excessive, the law avoids discouraging too many promises. The harsher the consequences of breach, the more likely people will decide not to make promises in order to avoid facing sanctions for breach. Keeping penalties low also fits with the relatively strict definition of breach. Remedies that punish seem inapt where breach may be blameless. Other systems are possible. The law could impose harsher sanctions on breach, but limit breach to blameworthy conduct. Perhaps the limited definition of breach would allay fears of people considering whether to make a promise. But it might reduce the willingness of people to rely on promises once made. If some promisors could avoid liability because they breached without blame, the people to whom they made promises would receive nothing. They would get neither performance nor remedy, just an empty promise. The skeleton outlines a different system, where more promises are made, where any breach produces compensation, but where compensation is limited and punishment virtually nonexistent.

C. INTRODUCTION TO THE THEMES OF CONTRACT LAW

Behind important contract doctrines lie some issues that arise over and over again in the law — not just in contract law, but in all aspects of the law. The answers will not always be the same, but the problems will be very similar and the language and arguments nearly identical. This section identifies some of these themes.

Two themes recur in different parts of contract law. One addresses how the law deals with individual intent. Because it is hard to prove (or even to know) what an individual is thinking, intent poses problems for the law. Those problems grow larger in situations where the law seeks to encourage people to think more carefully. A second theme explores the relative value of individual freedom. Contract offers individuals an opportunity to make their own choices. Some of those choices may be poor, even disastrous. The inclination to rescue people from poor choices can be strong, even though this involves negating their own choices. The extent to which society should interfere with those choices arises in several areas of contract law.

1. Subjective versus Objective Tests

Courts can interpret words in at least three ways: (1) according to the intent of the speaker; (2) according to the understanding of the listener; or (3) according to what a reasonable listener would have understood. The first two are **subjective**. They refer to what a person actually thought: what the speaker actually intended or what the listener actually thought the speaker intended. The last is **objective**. It refers to what reasonable people under the circumstances would have understood. It relies not on the hidden intent of the individual, but infers intent from **manifestations**

Subjective versus Objective

You probably have experienced this debate since you were a child. Every time your parents said, "You should have known better," they implied you deserved blame for not living up to a reasonable person test. Every time you said, "But I didn't know," you implied that blame should depend on what you actually knew, not what your parents thought you should have known.

(words or actions). An objective test also pays less heed to a party who claims he misunderstood the words if that person should have known what was meant.

Contract law confronts interpretations of this sort at several levels. Contract formation may occur when a person's words seem (objectively) to assent to a promise, even if the person says that she never intended (subjectively) to assent at all. The court may interpret promises in a contract in the way (objective) reasonable observers would understand them, even if one party alleges she (subjectively) intended a different meaning—and never would have agreed in the first place if she had known the contract would be interpreted to mean that.

Objective and subjective compete in a second, perhaps more familiar, way. Sometimes contracts require efforts, not results. For example, doctors usually promise to try to treat a condition, rather than promising to cure it. Real estate agents promise to try to sell your house, rather than promising to sell it for a certain price. Proving a breach of an obligation to try raises a question: how much effort did the contract require? Parties may make the efforts that they honestly think (subjectively) are appropriate. But the efforts may seem unreasonable from an objective perspective—say, that of a reasonable person, perhaps in the same occupation. Whether the efforts breach the contract or perform it depends on whether the contract calls for an objective test (reasonable efforts) or a subjective test (good faith efforts, the efforts a person honestly believes are sufficient).

An objective test serves as a hedge against disingenuous claims of subjective intent. Sometimes a person who really did know better (or really did intend one thing) hopes to avoid adverse consequences by pretending that she did not, even though that makes her seem unreasonable. An objective test makes what she actually thought irrelevant, preventing the person from avoiding the just consequences. However, an objective test also would apply to people who really did not know better (or did not intend that thing). If what really matters is the actual intent, an objective test will miss the mark in some cases.

Real estate agents promise to try to sell your house, rather than promising to sell it for a certain price.
rSnapshot Photos/Shutterstock.com

The law confronts this problem in almost every setting. Criminal law often requires subjective intent, using terms like **malice** (intent to harm). Alternatively, some crimes settle for an objective test, such as negligent homicide. Tort law uses both subjective and objective tests, depending on the situation: negligence involves an objective test, while intentional torts are subjective.

Case Preview

Luebbert v. Simmons

This case presents a straightforward choice between an objective and subjective approach to contract formation. The defendant in this case signed a promissory note, promising to repay money she had borrowed. But she contends she did not intend to promise to repay the money. The court must decide whether her subjective intent determines whether mutual assent occurred.

As you read *Luebbert v. Simmons*, look for the following:

1. Did Ms. Simmons and Mr. Luebbert reach a "meeting of the minds" here?
2. Does the court hold that Ms. Simmons did intend (subjectively) to make a serious promise or that her intent does not matter, given her words?
3. Does Ms. Simmons contend that she never intended to repay the loans? Or only that she did not intend to repay $12,200, the amount of the note? Does this make any difference to the court?
4. If Ms. Simmons was not serious about intending to pay the note, why did she sign it?

Luebbert v. Simmons

98 S.W.3d 72 (Mo. Ct. App. 2003)

HOWARD, Judge.

Respondent, Charles Luebbert, filed a three-count lawsuit against Appellant, Mary Simmons, in which he sought recovery on Count I for money due on a promissory note allegedly executed by Ms. Simmons. . . .

. . .

FACTS

Viewed in a light most favorable to the trial court's judgment, the evidence adduced at trial showed as follows [footnote omitted]:

Mr. Luebbert and Ms. Simmons, who both lived in homes on Lake Lotowana in Jackson County, Missouri, began dating in the fall of 1994. In March of 1995, Ms. Simmons arranged to rent her lake home to Royals' manager Bob Boone and moved with her two daughters into Mr. Luebbert's lake home. At this time, Ms. Simmons was in the middle of a divorce and had filed for bankruptcy. Thus, Ms. Simmons often borrowed money from Mr. Luebbert during their relationship. She occasionally paid

him back from the commissions she received as a real estate agent. Nonetheless, Mr. Luebbert repeatedly reminded her of the money she owed him.

One March evening, as they sat having drinks on Mr. Luebbert's deck overlooking the lake, Ms. Simmons, using a fill-in-the-blank form, sloppily wrote Mr. Luebbert a promissory note stating that she owed him $12,200 "at 10% due by Dec[ember] 30, 1995." Shortly thereafter, on March 29, 1995, she gave him a second, more-legible promissory note, which, except for the better handwriting, did not vary from the first note she had written. Mr. Luebbert never received payment on the note.

Ms. Simmons and her daughters moved out of Mr. Luebbert's home on June 1, 1995. At this time, she wrote two post-dated $1,000 checks to Mr. Luebbert. Because they remained friends after she moved out, Mr. Luebbert repeatedly honored her request that he hold off on cashing the checks. When he finally did try to cash them, payment had been stopped on the checks.

. . .

A one-day trial to the court was had on August 10, 2001. . . . After Mr. Luebbert and Ms. Simmons testified and counsel presented closing argument to the court, the trial court took the case under advisement.

On September 10, 2001, the court entered judgment against Ms. Simmons on Count I of Mr. Luebbert's claim in the sum of $12,200, plus interest of $8,153.13, plus costs. . . . This appeal follows.

. . .

Point II

In her second point on appeal, Ms. Simmons contends that the trial court erred in entering judgment against her on Mr. Luebbert's promissory note claim. She contends that "such decision is against the weight of the evidence and misapplied Missouri Contract law in that the evidence showed that the parties did not intend to enter into any agreement for [her] repayment of any 'loans.' "

"A promissory note is a written contract for the payment of money." *Merz v. First Nat'l Bank*, 682 S.W.2d 500, 501 (Mo. App. 1984). "The basic elements of a contract are offer, acceptance and consideration." *Beck v. Shrum*, 18 S.W.3d 8, 10 (Mo. App. 2000). In support of her contention that the parties did not intend to enter into an agreement for her to repay any supposed loans made to her by Mr. Luebbert, Ms. Simmons cites *Klamen v. Genuine Parts Co.*, 848 S.W.2d 38, 40 (Mo. App. 1993), and *New Medico Associates, Inc. v. Snadon*, 855 S.W.2d 489, 491 (Mo. App. 1993), for the general requirement a valid contract requires a "meeting of the minds," characterized by the objective manifestations of the parties through expressed promises, and a showing that the parties have assented to all essential terms. She then argues that "[t]he overwhelming evidence in this case showed that [she] did not seriously intend to accept a loan repayment obligation for the arbitrary amount of $12,200." In support of her argument, she complains that Mr. Luebbert did not successfully explain how the arbitrary $12,200 figure coincided with any alleged loans he made to her.

In cases such as this, a party's intent to form a contract "is usually established by circumstantial evidence," so we consider the evidence offered at trial. [Citation omitted.] Although Ms. Simmons testified that she was drunk and just joking around when she jokingly filled the first promissory note out for $12,200, Mr. Luebbert's testimony demonstrated otherwise. With the aid of his supporting Exhibits 17 through 24 [footnote omitted], Mr. Luebbert itemized for the court the loans that he had made to Ms. Simmons and money she had paid him back. He insisted that each time he loaned her money to help her out, it was with the understanding that she would pay him back. His itemization demonstrated that she owed him $12,200—the amount of the promissory note. Mr. Luebbert also testified that the note came into being after he had begun to question Ms. Simmons concerning when she was ever going to repay him. He explained that Ms. Simmons insisted on giving him the promissory note because she had promised to pay him back the money he loaned her.

With regard to Ms. Simmons' insistence that they were both drunk, Mr. Luebbert testified that, although they had been drinking, neither of them were drunk at the time. In fact, Ms. Simmons also testified that she was not so drunk at the time that she could not recall what happened. *See Lucy v. Zehmer*, 196 Va. 493, 84 S.E.2d 516, 520 (1954) ([T]he court found that "[t]he record is convincing that [Defendant] was not intoxicated to the extent of being unable to comprehend the nature and consequences of the instrument he executed, and hence that instrument is not to be invalidated on that ground.").

With regard to Ms. Simmons's insistence that the promissory note was just a joke, Mr. Luebbert said otherwise. He loaned her the money and expected her to pay it back, and she filled out the promissory note in response to his insistence that she do so. *Lucy v. Zehmer* is also instructive on this claim that the promissory note was a joke; the court explains:

> An agreement or mutual assent is of course essential to a valid contract but the law imputes to a person an intention corresponding to the reasonable meaning of his words and acts. If his words and acts, judged by a reasonable standard, manifest an intention to agree, it is immaterial what may be the real but unexpressed state of his [or her] mind.
>
> So a person cannot set up that he was merely jesting when his conduct and words would warrant a reasonable person in believing that he intended a real agreement.

Id. at 522 [citations omitted]. Ms. Simmons' conduct and insistence that she would pay Mr. Luebbert back after he questioned her about the money he loaned her suggest that she intended a real agreement.

This was a credibility call, and the trial court was free to believe Mr. Luebbert's account of these dealings. The trial court's finding that Ms. Simmons had the necessary intent in signing the promissory note and that she was bound thereby is supported by Mr. Luebbert's testimony, supporting documentation, and other circumstantial evidence; it is not against the weight of the evidence.

Point II is denied.

CONCLUSION

The trial court did not err in . . . rendering judgment in Mr. Luebbert's favor on his promissory note claim. Accordingly, we affirm the judgment.

The court says that a meeting of the minds is shown through objective manifestations, such as expressed promises. The signature on the note expressed a promise to repay, an expression that others could witness in a way that no one could witness what Ms. Simmons secretly was thinking. This comes down squarely on the side of an objective test, relying on the observable conduct to determine whether assent occurred. The court goes further, suggesting that Ms. Simmons probably did seriously intend to make this promise, even though she now denies it. If the objective test truly prevails, the comments about what Ms. Simmons really intended are irrelevant—dicta unrelated to the legal rule at play.

Luebbert v. Simmons: Real Life Application

1. You have been consulted by Sean Sullivan, the local Catholic bishop. At a recent charity event, Vincent Este (a wealthy parishioner) offered to make a substantial donation to the church in exchange for one of the local parish churches. The bishop jokingly signed an agreement to sell the church and accepted the donation, never intending to relinquish the property, believing the parishioner was just making a gift to the church. The bishop's statement that he never intended to sell the church is corroborated by a polygraph test, a functional MRI test, and testimony of 20 other clergymen of various faiths who swear that Msgr. Sullivan always tells the truth, even when the truth is not to his advantage. Should you litigate the case or advise the bishop to deliver the deed?

2. Terry saw a magazine ad for a very attractive watch. To find out how much it might cost, Terry visited a website offering the particular brand. Terry added a watch to the shopping cart and filled in the information necessary to make the purchase, but before clicking to submit the order, Terry began to reconsider the price. At that point, Terry's cat jumped onto the desk. Trying to catch the cat to keep it off the keyboard, Terry's elbow accidently bumped the mouse, moving it over the Submit box and clicking it. Terry immediately notified the company of the error via their Contact Us tool. Did Terry assent to a contract? If the company charges Terry's credit card and ships the watch, can Terry persuade a court to award a refund?

Contract law employs both objective and subjective tests. Assent employs an objective test, but with subjective exceptions. Interpretation starts with a subjective test (if the parties intended the same thing), moving to objective tests to resolve cases where the parties had different intents. In interpreting the efforts required under a contract, either a subjective or an objective test might apply, depending on the contract language and context. A clause allowing a party to refuse to pay if dissatisfied might apply if he is actually dissatisfied (a subjective test), but might be limited to situations where he has reason to be dissatisfied (an objective test). At several points during the course, you may need to discuss whether an objective or subjective test would be more appropriate under the circumstances.

2. Individual Freedom versus Societal Control

Contract is the means by which people improve their situation. They give up something they want less and, in exchange, bargain to receive something they want more. Because each person knows (better than anyone else, at least) how much he values the things he has and the things he wants, these decisions belong in the hands of each individual. Contract is intensely democratic. Obligations arise by the unanimous consent of the people affected by them (that is, the parties to the contract, all of whom must assent to the duties it creates). A majority does not impose its preferences on the rest; all the parties to a contract must agree.

When outsiders interfere with contracts, they impede people's ability to achieve their goals. As a result, rules limiting people's power to make and enforce contracts should be kept to a bare minimum. The law should protect people's choices, not constrain them.

Not everyone sees contract in this rosy light. Where some see contract as liberating, others see it as a means by which the powerful exploit the powerless. The powerful can withhold their assent to a contract unless the powerless give up far more than they receive. The powerful can demand all kinds of unfair terms, hiding them in fine print or relying on people's resignation; knowing that the terms cannot be changed, people may sign them without even reading them to know what they might be promising away. The result is a huge transfer of wealth from the underprivileged to the elite, exacerbating differences in wealth and perpetuating the powerlessness of the victims.

Neither the utopian nor dystopian view caricatured above provides a completely accurate view of contract in practice. Each probably captures a piece of the truth, at least in regard to some contracts. Trying to negotiate with a credit card or cell phone company may seem dystopian. On the other hand, it seems unlikely that your contract with the law school is designed to keep you from moving up in the world. Many of the most important contracts you will make — for example, buying or leasing a home or a car — improve your situation.

These two views of contract law compete in many ways. Sometimes they offer differing explanations for the same doctrines. Sometimes they offer criticisms of doctrines that seem to reflect the others' view of contract.

In the end, one must admit that contract starts as an individualistic field. Contracts are made by individuals, not by the state. The law starts out by trusting people to make their own decisions. The divide occurs over how far people should be allowed to make their own mistakes or be protected from them. As you study contract law, watch for ways in which reliance on individuals to protect their own interests either fails or works.

Chapter Summary

- Voluntary exchanges benefit society. Contract law seeks to optimize that benefit by protecting and promoting exchanges.
- An action for breach of contract requires an enforceable promise, performance of which has come due, but which has not been performed (without excuse).
- To be enforceable, a promise requires mutual assent to a voluntary exchange (consideration) on terms that a court can ascertain well enough to act (definiteness).
- While parties cannot avoid their commitments merely because they regret them, when circumstances surrounding the transaction preclude a person from exercising sound judgment, a defense may permit a party to refuse to perform. Common problems include incapacity (youth, mental illness, intoxication); misinformation (misrepresentation or mistake); improper pressure (duress or undue influence); unconscionability (usually concealed terms); and public policies limiting enforcement.
- Remedies include injunctions and damages aimed at securing the benefit of the bargain to the nonbreaching party. Damages may seek to grant a party the benefit of the bargain (the expectation interest) or may seek to prevent any harm caused by the promise itself (the reliance interest).
- Unjust enrichment is a cause of action available when a party has gained a benefit at the expense of another and it would be unjust to allow the party to retain the benefit without compensating the other for it.
- Contract law frequently must decide whether objective manifestations (words and actions) should govern even if subjective intentions differed from the manifestations. Similarly, contract frequently has to decide whether the minimum requirements of the law are satisfied by objectively reasonable efforts or by subjectively honest efforts (even if unreasonable).
- Allowing people to make their own contracts includes allowing them to make their own mistakes. When enforcing a contact would enforce a mistake, society sometimes seeks to protect people from their own mistakes.

PART I

Formation

Unless society is willing to enforce every promise, the law must define which promises deserve enforcement. The chapters that follow identify the limitations on enforceability.

Mutual assent is the first step, and is covered in Chapters 2 and 3. Promises, and therefore contracts, involve things people voluntarily undertake to do. These chapters address difficulties that arise in determining whether assent exists and whether it was mutual. These chapters also discuss definiteness, which may affect the court's assessment of whether the parties had finished negotiating a deal (that is, reached assent), but also may affect a court's ability to enforce a contract.

Even if voluntary, society's interest in enforcing promises is limited. Consideration, discussed in Chapter 4, focuses on exchanges, which generally benefit society. Chapter 5 addresses exceptions, where society elects to enforce promises that are not part of bargained-for exchanges.

2

Offer and Definiteness

Individuals create the obligation to perform promises. Their mutual assent to the terms they specify creates an obligation where no duty to act would exist without the promises. But willingness to assent may vary over time; a party who seemed to agree to a bargain at one point later may indicate unwillingness to enter or to perform the bargain. The doctrines relating to assent help determine whether a party's change of heart is breach (a contract already had been formed) or negotiation (the parties were still considering whether to enter the deal).

A thorough understanding of assent is needed. At the negotiation stage, understanding the doctrines of assent will help you clarify when and whether the negotiations reach the stage of commitment to the transaction. When negotiators have been less careful, some parties will use technical applications of the assent doctrines to avoid liability on agreements they really tried to make, but now regret. A thorough study of assent will help you to rebuff these efforts. Other doctrines pose the risk that parties who never intended to agree to an exchange find themselves bound to perform. Understanding these doctrines will help you to protect your client when others seek to enforce agreements he never made. Finally, doctrines of assent can help you identify the terms to which the parties agreed, vital when negotiations include several communications with varying terms.

Key Concepts

- The structure of assent (offer and acceptance)
- The objective approach to assent
- Distinguishing offers from preliminary negotiations
- The role of definiteness in formation and offer
- Promises to prolong offers (options)
- Elements of revocation

A. OFFER AND ACCEPTANCE

An **offer** proposes an agreement on specific terms, giving another person the power to conclude the transaction by agreeing to those terms.[1] The person making a proposal is called the **offeror**; the person to whom the proposal is made is the **offeree**. The offeree's response may accept, reject, or propose changes. (A fourth possibility—"I'll think about it"—may precede, but does not replace, the three basic possibilities.) An **acceptance** requires an unequivocal expression of assent to the terms of an offer (all of them) in a manner authorized by the offer.[2] Anything less than an acceptance is a **rejection**, a refusal to enter the agreement—though a manifest intention to consider an offer further (such as saying "I'll think about it") may not be a rejection.[3] A rejection may include a **counteroffer**, a proposal to deal on different terms.[4] A counteroffer not only rejects the original offer, but also creates a new offer. The roles are reversed; the first party now gets to respond.

Offeror and Offeree

Rules of assent often use the terms "offeror" and "offeree." If negotiations go back and forth, each party may make an offer at some point. For each communication, the party proposing a deal on certain terms is the offeror. The party invited to accept is the offeree. If the offeree proposes different terms (a counteroffer), she becomes an offeror and the original offeror is now the offeree of the counteroffer. As you work through facts of a problem, you may find it helpful to use offer as a verb rather than a noun: "Brandy offered to pay $15" is clearer than "The offeree counteroffered with $15."

A contract becomes binding on both parties at the moment an offer is accepted. Until that point, either party may reopen or withdraw from negotiations without liability (with some exceptions). After that point, each party is bound to the terms of the transaction (assuming the other elements of contract formation are satisfied). Assent may not end negotiations. The parties can agree to a **modification**, adding new terms to the contract or changing old ones, or a **rescission**, canceling the deal altogether. But these changes require the assent of both parties—an offer to modify or rescind and an acceptance of that offer. Without the other's consent, conduct that falls short of that promised in the agreement is nonperformance and, unless excused, will constitute **breach**.

Assent could be even simpler. For sales of **goods**—things that are moveable, such as cars, casebooks, cats, cattle, Cessnas, coal, coffee, computers, copiers, corn, and so on—Article 2 of the **Uniform Commercial Code** (**UCC**) recognizes assent from any words or conduct that to show agreement between the parties.[5]

This open-ended standard does not require identifying a specific offer or acceptance. Any conduct indicating intent to enter a contract will permit a court to find assent to a sale of goods. Parties may show agreement via offer and acceptance, but are not limited to that traditional mode of analysis.

Despite the admirable simplicity of the UCC, offer and acceptance remain the dominant mode for analyzing assent. This common law doctrine continues to govern except where displaced by statute. Thus, contracts for services (such as construction or employment), real estate, and **intangibles** (such as insurance policies)

---

[1] RESTATEMENT (SECOND) OF CONTRACTS §24.
[2] *Id.* §58.
[3] *Id.* §38(2).
[4] *Id.* §39.
[5] UCC §2-204.

arise when an offer has been accepted. Even for sales of goods, the traditional rules often influence the way courts talk about assent. For international transactions, the **United Nations Convention on Contracts for the International Sale of Goods (CISG)**, a treaty governing sales of goods between parties in different nations, codified offer and acceptance as the means of analyzing assent.[6] Familiarity with the intricacies of offer and acceptance remains essential. The remainder of this chapter focuses on that approach.

Even a simple rule can produce complex problems. Lawyers confront a range of situations, requiring attention to the nuances of the rules and of the contexts in which they arise. The rules and definitions governing assent have subtle implications that help resolve cases.

As you read the sections below, it may help to keep in mind three different questions that these doctrines may need to answer.

1. Did the parties agree at all?
2. When did their agreement take effect?
3. To what terms did they agree?

Finding offer and acceptance establishes the assent of the parties, even if one party later argues that it did not agree to the deal. While some parties really contend they never agreed at all, more often, arguments of this sort arise because one party tried to back out of the deal at about the same time that the other tried to assent to it. The agreement takes effect when the acceptance becomes effective. Determining whether the offer closed before the offeree accepted it can be vital. Acceptance agrees to the terms of the offer, making it vital to identify the offer, especially when several offers move between the parties before one is accepted. Even after that point, a later offer to modify the deal, if accepted by the other party, might change the terms. But this, too, involves identifying an offer and acceptance. As you encounter problems, consider which of these questions require an answer. It may help you focus on the issues that require attention.

B. THE OBJECTIVE APPROACH AND ITS IMPLICATIONS

The objective approach dominates analysis of assent. The law attaches significance to the things that people say and do, regardless of what they secretly were thinking at the time. Rules of assent often refer to "manifestations of assent"[7] to clarify the focus on observable conduct. While courts sometimes refer to a "meeting of the minds," modern courts do not recognize a contract based on uncommunicated decisions to agree. Assent requires a meeting of the words — or deeds that communicate as effectively as words.

---

[6]CISG arts. 14-24.

[7]*See, e.g.*, Restatement (Second) of Contracts §3 (defining agreement).

The objective approach influences the law's response to several types of problems. It is not just a theory, but has practical implications for several situations when assent might be contested.

Traditionally, the objective approach assigns meaning to words and deeds based on how an objective, reasonable person would have understood them under the circumstances. The fact that one party thought the words signified acceptance carries no more weight than that the other party thought the words signified rejection. Courts ask what a disinterested person perceiving the words or deeds would have understood them to mean.

1. Jest

Jest arises when one party claims that she was joking: her words, taken literally, appeared to agree to a deal, but she did not mean them to be taken seriously. In effect, she contends that she meant "no" even though she said "yes." Allowing a party to agree to a contract and then escape his obligations by contending that he was joking poses serious risks. If unenforceable, a party might pretend it was joking in an effort to avoid a contract that proved less profitable than expected — or just to see if the other side might be persuaded to offer more than the original bargain. Even if confident the person really was joking, courts may choose to enforce the agreement to protect the other party's reliance on the existence of a contract. The objective approach to assent minimizes these problems.

Jest negates assent if a reasonable person would have realized the words were not serious (or if the listener actually did realize the words were not serious). If a reasonable person would have believed the speaker was serious, then the words constitute assent. In effect, the risk lies on the party intending a joke: unless she lets the other party in on the jest, a court may take the transaction seriously. The rule does not require absolute clarity of intention: the joker need not shout "Not!" or "I'm joking!" A wink, a grin, or a poke in the ribs to let the other party know you are not serious would help. A dense person who misses the clues cannot enforce the agreement, as long as a reasonable person would have recognized the jest.

The rule flows naturally from the requirement of a promise. "A promise is a manifestation of intention to act . . . in a specified way, so made as to justify a promisee in understanding that a commitment has been made."[8] The focus is on what the listener is justified in believing, not on what the speaker intended. Where a reasonable person would recognize a jest, the promisee would not be justified in believing that a commitment had been made. Where the words reasonably seemed serious, however, understanding a commitment would be justified.

---

[8] *Id.* §2.

Case Preview

Lucy v. Zehmer

Although the objective approach seems fairly intuitive, it sometimes requires a court to hold someone to a contract even though she never intended to make it—or, at least, it seems plausible that she never had that intent. *Lucy* offers an example where the seller's action seems understandable, and yet the court finds it necessary to enforce the deal.

As you read *Lucy v. Zehmer*, look for the following:

1. Did the court conclude that Zehmer (seller) really was serious and only pretended to be joking? Or does the court believe that Zehmer really was joking, but must be held to the deal anyway?
2. Before the paper was signed, did Zehmer (seller) give Lucy (buyer) any indication that Zehmer would refuse to go through with the deal? Should Lucy have recognized Zehmer was jesting?
3. Could Zehmer have called Lucy's bluff without signing the paper?
4. Does it matter that Zehmer believed Lucy was joking?

Lucy v. Zehmer

196 Va. 493 (1954)

BUCHANAN, J.

. . . The instrument sought to be enforced was written by A. H. Zehmer on December 20, 1952, in these words: "We hereby agree to sell to W. O. Lucy the Ferguson Farm complete for $50,000.00, title satisfactory to buyer," and signed by the defendants, A. H. Zehmer and Ida S. Zehmer.

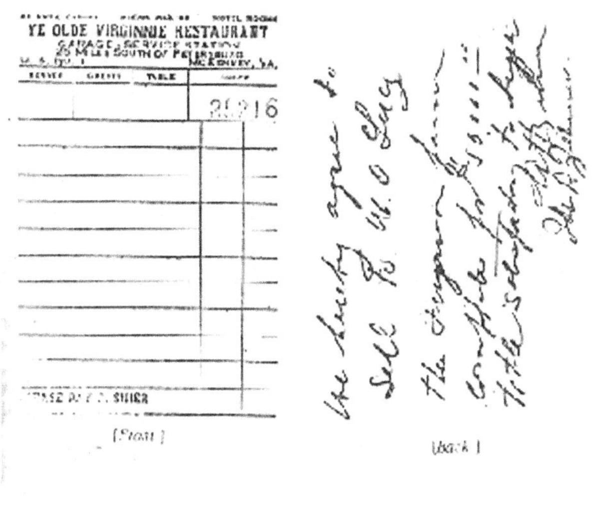

The answer of A. H. Zehmer admitted that . . . Lucy offered him $50,000 cash for the farm, but that he, Zehmer, considered that the offer was made in jest; that so thinking, and both he and Lucy having had several drinks, he wrote out "the memorandum" quoted above and induced his wife to sign it; that he did not deliver the memorandum to Lucy, but that Lucy picked it up, read it, put it in his pocket, attempted to offer Zehmer $5 to bind the bargain, which Zehmer refused to accept, and realizing for the first time that Lucy was serious, Zehmer

assured him that he had no intention of selling the farm and that the whole matter was a joke. Lucy left the premises insisting that he had purchased the farm.

. . .

[The court recounted the testimony of Lucy, Mr. Zehmer, Mrs. Zehmer, and a waitress in detail. They differ in details but are largely consistent with Zehmer's testimony that] [h]e bought this farm more than ten years ago for $11,000. He had had twenty-five offers, more or less, to buy it, [but] had given them all the same answer, that he was not interested in selling it. On this Saturday night before Christmas . . . Lucy . . . offered him a drink [from a bottle Lucy brought with him for this purpose]. "I was already high as a Georgia pine, and didn't have any more better sense than to pour another great big slug out and gulp it down, and he took one too."

. . . Lucy asked whether he still had the Ferguson farm. He replied that he had not sold it and Lucy said, "I bet you wouldn't take $50,000.00 for it." Zehmer asked him if he would give $50,000 and Lucy said yes. Zehmer replied, "You haven't got $50,000 in cash." Lucy said he did and Zehmer replied that he did not believe it. They argued "pro and con for a long time," mainly about "whether he had $50,000 in cash that he could put up right then and buy that farm."

Finally, said Zehmer, Lucy told him if he didn't believe he had $50,000, "you sign that piece of paper here and say you will take $50,000.00 for the farm." [He did.]

. . . Lucy said, "Get your wife to sign it." Zehmer walked over to where she was and she at first refused to sign but did so after he told her that he "was just needling him [Lucy], and didn't mean a thing in the world, that I was not selling the farm."

. . .

. . . The record is convincing that Zehmer was not intoxicated to the extent of being unable to comprehend the nature and consequences of the instrument he executed, and hence that instrument is not to be invalidated on that ground.

. . .

The appearance of the contract, the fact that it was under discussion for forty minutes or more before it was signed; Lucy's objection to the first draft because it was written in the singular, and he wanted Mrs. Zehmer to sign it also; the rewriting to meet that objection and the signing by Mrs. Zehmer; the discussion of what was to be included in the sale, the provision for the examination of the title, the completeness of the instrument that was executed, the taking possession of it by Lucy with no request or suggestion by either of the defendants that he give it back, are facts which furnish persuasive evidence that the execution of the contract was a serious business transaction rather than a casual, jesting matter as defendants now contend.

. . .

In the field of contracts, as generally elsewhere, "We must look to the outward expression of a person as manifesting his intention rather than to his secret and unexpressed intention. 'The law imputes to a person an intention corresponding to the reasonable meaning of his words and acts.'" *First Nat. Bank v. Roanoke Oil Co.*, 169 Va. 99, 114, 192 S.E. 764, 770.

At no time prior to the execution of the contract had Zehmer indicated to Lucy by word or act that he was not in earnest about selling the farm. They had argued about it and discussed its terms, as Zehmer admitted, for a long time. Lucy testified that if there was any jesting it was about paying $50,000 that night. The contract and the evidence show that he was not expected to pay the money that night. . . . Not until Lucy [offered $5 in earnest money] was anything said or done to indicate that the matter was a joke. Both of the Zehmers testified that when Zehmer asked his wife to sign he whispered that it was a joke so Lucy wouldn't hear and that it was not intended that he should hear.

The mental assent of the parties is not requisite for the formation of a contract. If the words or other acts of one of the parties have but one reasonable meaning, his undisclosed intention is immaterial except when an unreasonable meaning which he attaches to his manifestations is known to the other party. . . .

An agreement or mutual assent is of course essential to a valid contract but the law imputes to a person an intention corresponding to the reasonable meaning of his words and acts. If his words and acts, judged by a reasonable standard, manifest an intention to agree, it is immaterial what may be the real but unexpressed state of his mind.

So a person cannot set up that he was merely jesting when his conduct and words would warrant a reasonable person in believing that he intended a real agreement.

Whether the writing signed by the defendants and now sought to be enforced by the complainants was the result of a serious offer by Lucy and a serious acceptance by the defendants, or was a serious offer by Lucy and an acceptance in secret jest by the defendants, in either event it constituted a binding contract of sale between the parties.

Reversed and remanded.

Lucy holds parties to their words and acts, regardless of any secret intention. The rule applies to those who never intended to accept, not just to those who changed their minds later and raised jest as a pretext to back out of a deal. The approach protects people who rely on what seem to be perfectly serious indications of assent. No one needs to read another's mind in order to determine assent, but may rely on the normal meaning of the person's words and actions. It puts the onus on jesters to reveal their jest to others before (or perhaps as) they signal assent. In effect, the court holds that if it looks like a promise and sounds like a promise and smells like a promise, it is a promise — and, like any promise, should be taken seriously.

Lucy v. Zehmer: Real Life Applications

1. What if Lucy really knew that Zehmer was joking, that he agreed just to call Lucy's bluff, with no intention of actually selling the farm? Does it matter that a reasonable person would have interpreted the writing as serious if Lucy knew better than the ordinary reasonable person?
2. If what Lucy actually knew matters, how could you find evidence to prove that Lucy knew Zehmer was joking? Do you have to get Lucy to admit it under oath?

Or might other sources offer insight into what Lucy knew at the time? (Don't limit yourself to what might have been done in 1954. Where would you look if a similar case arose today?)

3. A very successful musician lost a laptop computer. The musician offered a $1 million reward for the return of the laptop. When the laptop was returned — by someone who found it, not by someone who stole it — the musician offered $1,000 and backstage passes to a concert, but said the $1 million reward was obviously a joke. Should the person who returned the computer receive the $1 million?

4. As part of a reality TV show, actors offer unsuspecting members of the public money to do embarrassing things. Initial refusals are met with goading by the actors and steadily increasing offers, until the mark complies. The amounts normally total a few thousand dollars and the network usually pays the amount the performers promise. The highest payment actors are allowed to offer without advance permission (over a headset) is $50,000. Filming one episode, repeated refusals made an actor so sure that the person would refuse that the actor offered $1 million without advance approval — much more than the show could pay. The person surprised the actor by starting to perform the embarrassing act. Before the person completed the act, the actor repudiated the offer as a joke. Is the person entitled to the $1 million?

5. During a television ad for a soft drink, a producer offered items bearing the soft drink logo if consumers submitted a certain number of points earned by purchasing the soft drinks. In addition to t-shirts, sunglasses, and jackets, the producer offered a military jet aircraft for seven million points. A customer submitted the requisite number of points. The producer argued that the offer of the jet was a jest, not a serious offer. Should the producer succeed? You can see the ad at https://www.youtube.com/watch?v=U_n5SNrMaL8. *See Leonard v. Pepsico*, 88 F. Supp. 2d 116 (S.D.N.Y. 1999).

---

2. Misunderstood Assent

Jest involves people who want their words to differ from their actual intent. The joke requires pretending to be serious. In other situations, the difference is unintentional: one party may intend to reject a deal and seek to communicate that intent, but choose words or deeds that the other understands to signify assent to the contract. This rarely is as simple as meaning "no" but instead saying "yes" or signing on the dotted line — though that can happen. On rare occasions, universities have sent out acceptance letters to applicants they intended to reject — in one case, accepting 28,000 people who should have received rejections. That does not sound like fraud by the university. But it raises the same concern for reliance by parties who took the letters seriously. Allowing a party to avoid enforcement based on undisclosed reservations might rescue mistaken universities, but create a risk of manipulation by others. Parties might pretend they meant to reject the deal in order to avoid contracts they now regret. Indeed, an escape on this basis might encourage people to be unclear in the hope that ambiguity would justify escape based on misunderstanding.

If a party reasonably understood the communication as an assent, the contract is formed on that basis, regardless of what the other party intended. The law again looks to the words and actions, as a reasonable observer would have understood them, without any concern for what the party meant (or now claims to have meant).

Consider *Embry v. Hargadine, McKittrick Dry Goods Co.*[9] An employee stated he would quit unless he received a one-year extension on his contract, to which the employer responded "Go ahead [back to work], you're all right." The employee interpreted this reassurance as agreement to the extension, though the employer said he intended the words to postpone the conversation until they were less busy. The court concluded that a reasonable person would understand this as assent, holding the employer to the contract.

Juries will not always reach decisions that seem intuitive. In *Trademark Properties Inc. v. A & E Television Networks*,[10] the creator of the show *Flip This House* entered extended discussions pitching the show to a representative of the A & E network. After the creator laid out the terms, the executive responded, "Okay, okay, I get it." The creator understood this as assent to the terms proposed. Despite the network's claim that the remark merely reflected an understanding of the terms, not agreement to them, a jury concluded that, in context, a reasonable person in the position of the creator reasonably would understand the words as assent.

Intoxication and Assent

An intoxicated person may not intend to agree to a contract. But his or her words still might indicate assent to a reasonable observer. The objective approach does not negate assent because the intoxication prevented a subjective intent to agree.

Intoxication can be so severe that it destroys the capacity to enter a contract. Incapacity is a defense covered in Chapter 6. The court in *Lucy* notes how severe intoxication must be to establish the incapacity defense. The facts there fall short of that level. In fact, Lucy may have been more intoxicated than Zehmer. Mrs. Zehmer suggested that her husband should drive Lucy home to keep Lucy from getting behind the wheel.

3. Perfectly Understood Assent

Occasionally, words that a reasonable person would misunderstand are understood perfectly by the parties involved. In these cases, it seems odd to substitute a reasonable misunderstanding for the parties' actual and accurate understanding of what each intended.

Consider two variations on the facts of *Embry*: (1) If the employee understood that the employer rejected the offer, a court slavishly adhering to the objective approach might enforce a deal that neither party thought was made because a reasonable person would have understood the words as assent. (2) If both parties understood the words to signify assent, but a reasonable person would have

[9] 127 Mo. App. 383 (1907).

[10] 422 Fed. Appx. 199 (4th Cir. 2011).

misunderstood them as a rejection, a purely objective approach might refuse to enforce a contract both parties intended to make.

If both parties correctly interpret each other's words, their shared understanding should govern. Interpreting the words any other way frustrates legitimate expectations derived from effective communication. Even if an objective observer might misinterpret the words, neither party was misled. The objective approach resolves conflicting understandings, but need not override shared understanding.

Parties rarely admit they understood communications that a reasonable observer would misunderstand, producing relatively few decided cases to support either approach in these settings. That also makes it hard to predict how courts might respond when such cases arise.

Cases sometimes arise in which it seems likely that the other party understood words that, on their face, do not express agreement. Thus, in *Lim v. The TV Corporation International*,[11] defendant auctioned off the rights to the name "golf.tv." Plaintiff's bid of $1,010 was accepted in an e-mail that referred to it as "——golf.tv." Technically, this is not the name plaintiff bid on—and is an impossible name, because the web does not recognize dashes in names. For purposes of overcoming a demurrer, the court held that, in context, the acceptance referred to "golf.tv," the only bid plaintiff submitted. But not every court reaches the same result. In *United States v. Braunstein*,[12] the government received a bid of ten cents per pound for surplus raisins, but responded with a telegram accepting the bid of "ten cents per box." Each box held 25 pounds, making this a 96 percent reduction from the price bid. Buyer did not try to take advantage of this error, but also did not treat it as an acceptance of its bid, refusing to go forward with the sale even after seller clarified its acceptance. Seller urged "that the defendants knew perfectly well what the" acceptance meant. The court held that a reasonable person would be confused by the response, unsure whether it really was an acceptance. The court granted summary judgment for buyer without discussing whether buyer actually understood the response as an acceptance.

4. Form Contracts

An enormous number of modern transactions involve form contracts. One party drafts terms in advance and offers them to the other. Many forms are **contracts of adhesion**, offered on a take-it-or-leave-it basis. The offeror will do business only on the terms of the form; it will not negotiate changes. Other forms allow more room for negotiation, either filling in blanks or adding or changing terms to supplement or replace those in the basic form.

If a person signs a form (or clicks "I Agree"), he manifests assent to the agreement. The outward signs justify the other person in believing that the signer agrees to the terms on the form. The manifestation may not represent subjective assent.

[11] 99 Cal. App. 4th 684, 121 Cal. Rptr. 2d 333 (2002).
[12] 75 F. Supp. 137 (S.D.N.Y. 1947).

But the signature provides an objective manifestation of assent. The words and deeds govern, not the private intent.

Some explain this result in terms of a duty to read. It applies even to those who cannot read (for example, the blind or illiterate). Aware of one's own inability, a person can have the terms read to her if the terms matter. Technically, this is not a legal duty to read. People are free to sign agreements without reading them. But the risk of not learning the terms falls on the party who did not read them.

By clicking Sign Up, you agree to our Terms and that you have read our Data Use Policy, including our Cookie Use.

Online agreement form: Contract of Adhesion

Even if everyone knows the signer did not read the terms, the signature may indicate assent. Failure to read does not signal an objection. Rather, signing without reading implies acceptance of whatever the terms say—a willingness to take the risk that the terms are unfavorable.

Partial Assent

Subjective assent often is partial rather than complete. Parties may intend to agree to the terms they know the contract contains (the price, the delivery date, perhaps the warranty), but have no intent regarding other, less salient terms (a forum selection or arbitration clause). If subjective assent mattered, parties might argue that they assented to some terms but not others.

Signing a contract, however, does not communicate partial assent to the other party (or to a reasonable observer). A signature looks like complete assent to either the drafter or an objective observer. People can express divided assent, but inferring it from words of complete assent stretches credulity. Without some indication that the signature does not apply to certain terms, the rules here preclude efforts to treat assent as making some but not all of the terms binding.

Giving weight to the subjective intent of one party (the signer) usually involves ignoring the other party's subjective intent. Including a clause in a written form reflects the drafting party's subjective intent to include that term in the bargain. The drafting party did not intend to agree to a transaction without the term, even if the signing party did not intend to agree to that term. There seems no particular reason to treat the signing party's subjective intent (to enter a contract without that term) more favorably than the drafting party's subjective intent (to enter a contract with that term). The alternative—to find no contract at all, given the difference in intentions—might void huge numbers of contracts both parties seriously tried to enter.

The objective approach prevents frustrating the parties' intent to enter a binding agreement. Because assent turns on objective manifestations, the failure to reach subjective agreement on all the points of the contract does not preclude formation. A party that wishes to avoid a particular term may raise it during the negotiations. Courts are reluctant to reward parties who bypass negotiations by signing a document, but then seek to avoid objectionable terms on the basis of subjective assent.

Objectively Unacceptable Terms

In extreme cases, a signature may not indicate assent: if the drafter has reason to know that the signer would reject the whole contract if she knew it contained a term, courts may exclude that term.[13] A reasonable person in the other party's position would realize that the signature does not reflect assent to that unacceptable term. In effect, the drafter knows that the signature is a counteroffer, not an acceptance. In going through with the contract, the drafter implicitly accepts the counteroffer.

Excluding the objectionable term, rather than negating assent to the entire agreement, makes this provision look more like a sanction for drafting outrageous terms than an assent provision. It effectively divides assent, rather than finding none existed.

The rule will protect against truly egregious terms, those that the drafter has reason to know would make the entire contract unacceptable. For example, in *Lowey v. Watt*,[14] a filing service agreed to represent individuals pursuing gas leases from the government. The form agreement the service prepared included a term that would invalidate any lease that the clients obtained. The court held that the term was not part of the contract because the filing service knew that clients would never agree to a term that, in effect, negated the entire purpose of the contract.

Reason to know that the signer would prefer a different term will not satisfy this rule. For example, termination charges in cell phone contracts, even if concealed, probably survive this rule (even if other objections you will study in later chapters might prevail). Buyers might prefer to exclude them, but usually would not refuse the entire contract rather than face the potential termination fee.

Reason to know might be specific or general. Rarely, a term may be so objectionable that the drafting party has reason to know that anyone would refuse the contract if aware of the term. Any term that bad may violate public policy or prove unconscionable. Alternatively, a party may have given specific indications that the term is unacceptable. This might arise if a party requested a different term and was told that term would be included. Those negotiations offer some reason to know that the requesting party would reject the deal without the term.

C. OFFERS

The definition of offer can be broken down into four required parts:

1. a manifestation of willingness
2. to enter a bargain

[13] Restatement (Second) of Contracts §211(3).

[14] 684 F.2d 957, 971 (D.C. Cir. 1982), *abrogated on other grounds by National Fuel Gas Supply Corp. v. F.E.R.C.*, 811 F.2d 1563 (D.C. Cir. 1987).

3. that justifiably appears to invite an offeree's acceptance,
4. and that acceptance justifiably appears to conclude the transaction.[15]

These requirements make an offer a conditional **promise** (expressed commitment to act): a promise, because the offeror commits to the terms proposed; conditional, because the commitment will become binding only if a specified event occurs — the offeree agrees to the terms by accepting the offer. (When dealing with exchanges, this usually means the offeree commits to provide the offeror something in return for the promise.) The offeror lacks the power to withdraw after the offeree's acceptance. An offer not only invites the offeree to accept, but also gives the offeree the power to conclude the negotiations by accepting.

Each component of an offer deserves a brief discussion. You may recognize the objective approach in the requirements for an offer: *manifestation* of willingness; *justifiably* appear. The definition focuses on what the offeror says (or what others hear), not on what the offeror thinks. His unwillingness to act does not matter if the words or conduct manifest a willingness to act. Nor does it matter whether the offeror in fact wants another's acceptance or intends for that acceptance to conclude the transaction. If the words justify the other in believing that her assent is invited and will conclude the bargain, then the private thoughts will not prevent a court from finding an offer.

Any words or conduct that manifests an intention to enter a bargain may be an offer. Manifestation necessarily implies communication to the offeree. A secret manifestation is almost an oxymoron. While an offer is a conditional promise, it does not require the incantation of special words, such as "I offer" or "I promise." Any manifestation of willingness serves to make an offer or a promise.

The manifestation must convey the terms the offeror proposes. This may require proposing a **bargain**, an exchange of performances. That requirement is central to the issue of **consideration** (the return a promisor receives for a promise). Most offers will in fact propose bargains. But as used here, the word bargain may just mean a proposal, one that the promisor expects the other to accept or reject. Thus, a proposal that lacks consideration probably qualifies as an offer.

No Magic Words

Children sometimes think promises are a special kind of statement. They may say: "I said I would, but I didn't promise." In defining promise, the law does not allow adults such leeway. "I will" is all it takes to make a promise, without special incantations such as "I promise," "I give you my word," or "On my honor, I will." Consider all the magic in the words "I do."

A proposal is an offer only if the recipient justifiably believes his assent is invited. This permits an offeror to limit who may accept an offer, as long as she does so clearly. Parents might offer to sell a car to their child on different terms than they would offer to anyone else. Someone overhearing that offer has no power to accept — unless something in the context justifies a belief that the parents invited the eavesdropper's assent. Offerors may extend their offers to as many or as few people as they wish. However, their offers should include any limitations; if others

[15] RESTATEMENT (SECOND) OF CONTRACTS §24.

justifiably believe that they are included among the offerees, they have the power to accept. For example, if a coach at a Little League baseball game offers an ice cream cone to "anyone who can point to right field," that might be broad enough that parents, other coaches, or members of the other team reasonably could believe they can accept the offer. While the context may make it clear that only players on the team could accept, starting the offer with "Tigers" seems a safer way to limit the scope of the offer.

An offer must justify the other in understanding that its assent will conclude the deal. A proposal may explore the possibility of a deal instead of seeking to conclude it. For instance, haggling about the price of a car may not end the discussions. Either party may want to settle other terms before committing: the seller may want to limit the warranty; the buyer may want to discuss financing. Communications might justify one to believe the other was inviting an assent that would conclude the deal. But some proposals will not have that aspect of finality and, thus, will not be considered offers.

The law distinguishes offers from **preliminary negotiations**, proposals that a party makes with the expectation that she can reconsider before becoming bound. If one party knows or has reason to know that the other party does not intend to commit to a proposal until a future expression, then the terms proposed were not an offer.[16] In effect, this is the opposite of the last component of offer: you cannot justifiably believe that your assent will conclude the transaction if you know or have reason to know that the other party does not intend to be bound yet. Only if the communication reasonably seems like the final stage of the negotiations will the communication be treated as an offer.

Try your hand at applying this rule to the following situation. Terry wants a new dining table in time for Thanksgiving. At a furniture store, Terry sees a table she likes and says to the salesperson, "I'll buy this table, if it comes in teak." The salesperson replies, "Sold!" Terry then asks whether the table can be delivered by Thanksgiving, at which time the salesperson says that teak needs to be ordered from the factory and cannot arrive in time. Can Terry keep shopping or has a contract already been formed?

The definitions here — and the objective approach generally — place the risk of unclear communication on the party who did not intend to assent. That party may preclude assent by expressing that intent. Absolute clarity is not required; even subtle indications of reservation may make it unreasonable to believe that assent will conclude the deal. The party whose reservations are unclear risks finding itself bound despite an intention to reserve judgment on the deal.

While many factors may limit an offeree's justification for believing its assent will conclude negotiations, two examples commonly arise:

1. the expectation that the agreement will be reduced to writing (or to a more complete writing);
2. the incompleteness of the proposal.

[16] *Id.* §26.

Either fact might make it unreasonable to believe the other party intends to be bound by an acceptance. These problems are sufficiently common that each is discussed separately in subsections 3 and 4 below.

1. The Master of the Offer

An offer bestows considerable power on the offeree. She may create a contract (by accepting) or reject it (by doing nothing). If the offer remains open long enough, she can wait to see whether it will be a good deal before accepting. As long as the offer remains open, the offeror cannot prevent a contract from being formed. The offeree controls whether a contract arises.

The offeree's power is constrained by the offeror's power to frame the offer. That power is both substantive and procedural. Substantively, the offeree's power is limited to the terms proposed by the offeror. The offeree can accept these terms or reject them, but cannot create a contract on different terms. The offeree can propose different terms. That proposal is not an acceptance, but a counteroffer. The offeree then becomes the offeror of the new offer.

Procedurally, the offeror can specify several aspects of how the offeree may accept. One detail, limiting the identity of the offeree(s), has been noted above. Offering Amanda $20 an hour to babysit Logan does not give Andrew any ability to accept, even if he overheard the offer to Amanda. Other procedural details an offer may specify include the time allowed for acceptance, the manner of signifying acceptance, and the time when acceptance takes effect.

Limiting the time within which acceptance is possible can be critical. Imagine an offer to sell land in which the offeree could wait a few months to see whether the price went up or down before deciding whether to accept. Those deals exist; they are called **option contracts** and involve an enforceable promise to keep the offer open for a period of time. A seller could specify a much shorter duration for an offer, perhaps ending before the conclusion of the phone call in which the offer was made.

The offeror also can specify the medium of communication. A careful offeror may choose to specify a means of acceptance that will be reasonably reliable and prompt, reducing the risk of slow or misdirected acceptances. Requiring e-mail instead of snail mail might serve the offeror's desire for speed. Requiring a writing rather than a phone call provides a record some offerors might find important.

Unless the offer specifies a particular medium, an offer invites any reasonable form of communication.[17] Usually, an offeree may reply by the same medium that the offeror used to convey the offer, barring specifications in the offer to the contrary.[18] The offeror can require acceptance by performance. If so, the only way to create a contract is to perform. (An offer of $100 to anyone who returns a lost dog typically requires acceptance by returning the dog; promising to return the dog has no effect.) An offeror may authorize acceptance by silence, allowing the absence of

[17] *Id.* §30.
[18] *Id.* §65.

a rejection to signal assent. The offeror could specify that acceptance must be signified by smashing a cream pie into your own face. If so, the offeree cannot accept the offer without performing the specified act. An offeror may place any number of limitations on an offeree's ability to accept the offer. An offeror need not constrain acceptance in any of these ways, but she can.

The offeror even can alter the rules governing when acceptance becomes binding. For example, an offer can specify that acceptance will be binding only when it is received by the offeror.

2. Advertisements

Advertisements, with some exceptions, are not offers. Ads inform the public of opportunities and invite them to make offers, which the advertiser then may accept or reject as it sees fit. That traditional interpretation extended to any kind of advertising: leaflets, posters, mailers, displays in a store window, even prices posted on the shelves. These are not offers that a consumer can accept. Rather, they invite the consumer to make an offer (at the cash register) that the store can accept — or, less commonly, reject. The rule may have originated as a way to protect sellers if acceptances exceed supply. Rather than holding that the additional acceptances created contracts that the seller cannot perform, courts treated the customers' responses as offers. The rationale has less force in some settings (say, price tags on the goods at a grocery store), but probably explains the origin of the rule.

Because advertisers usually accept offers from consumers on the terms advertised, the rule here makes little practical difference. The contract arises a few seconds later when the advertiser accepts the consumer's offer (instead of the other way around). The difference becomes more significant if the advertiser refuses to honor the terms in the ad. Several factors might cause refusal, including an error in the ad, a change in the advertiser's ability to perform (as when supplies run out), or a change in market conditions that make the terms unfavorable to the advertiser. The rule protects the advertiser from being bound by the consumer's acceptance.

Faced with unwarranted refusals to honor their ads, courts sometimes hold an ad to be an offer if it is so clear, definite, and explicit that it leaves nothing open for negotiation. In *Lefkowitz v. Great Minneapolis Surplus Store*,[19] a store advertised a lapin stole for $1, specifying "first come, first served." Lefkowitz came first, but the store refused to sell him the stole based on a house rule limiting special offers to women. The ad did not mention that rule. If the ad merely invited offers, the store had a right to reject Lefkowitz's offer (for that reason or for no reason at all). The court held the ad was so complete that it left nothing to negotiation, making it an offer. Lefkowitz had accepted the offer, forming a contract, before the store invoked the house rule.

Both the rule and the exception lack much justification in today's world. As an application of the definition of offer, this rule seems outdated. Nineteenth-century

[19] 86 N.W.2d 689 (Minn. 1957).

courts explained that the public does not justifiably believe that their assent to an advertisement will conclude a transaction. Whatever its validity at the time, the advent of laws governing truth in advertising and unfair business practices substantially increase the public's justification in believing that the advertiser invites and will be bound by the consumer's acceptance. In any event, the rule persists.

The exception is difficult to apply. Ads never really state all the terms. Even in *Lefkowitz,* the ad did not specify the time or place of delivery, payment or credit terms, and several other details. If the store refused Lefkowitz's check, demanding cash, the ad was not sufficiently complete to say which one breached. The court could fill in terms. But the exception purportedly applies when there is nothing to negotiate—that is, where neither the parties nor the court need to address an open term.

The exception, combined with statutes governing truth in advertising, has changed advertising practice, if not litigation outcomes. Advertisers now include disclaimers or exclusions to prevent both claims (that their ads are offers and that their failure to honor them constitutes false advertising). By including terms such as "offer subject to change without notice," "quantities limited," or "while supplies last," advertisers alert consumers that their assent will not conclude the deal, thus not qualifying as an offer. That language would protect them even if the rule made all ads offers. On any rule, careful drafting can help protect advertisers. The existing rules tend to pollute the airwaves, as more broadcast commercials include eight seconds of fast-talking disclaimers.

Consumer Power and Ads

Can a store really advertise a price, and when you get there, refuse to honor the ad? Under contract law, yes. The store has not made an offer. When you make an offer, it is free to reject it. Even if contract law called ads "offers," stores could revoke the offer (as discussed below), perhaps by a big sign at the front door. However, laws regulating false advertising and unfair business practices offer some protection. Marketplace competition also provides protection. A store that refuses to honor its advertised prices will lose customers to its competitors who don't behave so badly. Don't underestimate consumer power.

3. Written Memorial Contemplated and Preliminary Agreements

During negotiations, parties may indicate that they anticipate recording their agreement in writing. Even if the parties already consider the deal final, they may want a written record of a deal to help them perform or to resolve disputes. In other situations, parties may want to review the final document before committing to the transaction (typically, by signing the document). The law gives effect to either intent.

If a party has reason to know the other does not intend to be bound until a final writing has been signed, then no offer exists for that party to accept. She cannot justifiably believe that her assent will conclude the deal. If, however, the parties intend to enter an oral contract, that oral assent suffices even though they also intend to prepare a written version later.

Both situations are common. Employment frequently is offered and accepted orally, then followed with confirming letters and signed employment agreements. But in this setting parties often consider the writing a mere formality, recording a deal already entered orally. When a landlord shows an apartment to prospective renters, they may agree on rent and other terms while viewing the apartment. Both parties commonly understand that signing the lease marks the point at which they become bound.

Sometimes the first agreement may be an informal writing rather than an oral agreement. The same questions arise concerning whether the parties intended the first agreement to conclude the contract or whether they intended to remain free to reconsider after they review the final, more formal writing. If one party tries to pull out after the oral (or informally written) agreement but before signing the (formal) written agreement, a court must determine the effect the parties intended for their oral agreement to have.

This discussion does not involve a new rule, but an application of the definition of offer. The issue remains whether one party knew or had reason to know that the other did not intend to be bound until the writing (or a more final writing) was signed. Because oral agreements usually are enforceable,[20] refusing to enforce an oral agreement would be odd—unless there was no assent in the first place (because no offer was made).

Written Memorial Contemplated

If the parties offer and accept terms, assent exists without regard to whether the expressions are oral or in writing. Indeed, the law does not even require words, sometimes giving effect to assent expressed by actions or by silence. Conduct after an oral agreement does not change the effect of the parties' assent. Creating a writing to record their agreement does no harm, but is not necessary. They were bound from the moment of oral acceptance—and would be even if they did not create the writing. Even if, during negotiations, they each signaled a desire to record the agreement in writing, the failure to do so would not negate the oral contract they created. Subsequent events may not unfold exactly as the parties expected, but their original assent is unaffected.

An oral proposal, however, might not be an offer. The party making the proposal might signal that its assent will not be final until a writing is signed. An adequate signal would give the other party reason to know that the first does not intend to be bound until some further expression of assent (signing a final written agreement). Reason to know this prevents negotiations up to that point from being offers. They are preliminary negotiations. If the parties eventually sign a writing, the first signer makes an offer, the second accepts it. Cases with a writing signed by both parties rarely raise issues of assent.

If every suggestion to record the agreement in writing signaled a reservation of assent until signing occurs, none of these cases would involve offers. If suggestions

[20]Chapter 8 discusses the statute of frauds, which rejects enforcement of some contracts without some written evidence that they were agreed upon. Even in those cases, the contract itself may not need to be written.

for a writing never signaled a reservation of assent until the writing was signed, then offers would always be found. However, people vary both in which situation they intend to apply and how well they signal their intent. Rather than attempt to force people to adopt one approach or the other, the law seeks to determine which approach the parties intended. Both motivations are understandable. Some people might want to lock in the deal today, but still want the advantages of a record for proving the existence of the agreement and the terms that it contains. Others might want time to reflect on the deal after they see it in writing before they commit. The result is a mix of cases that differ primarily in whether a reservation was intended and, if so, whether it was adequately communicated to the other party.

As with other rules relying on the objective approach, unclear expressions create a risk that obligations will be imposed on a party who intended to remain free to withdraw from the deal. The relatively safe course is for a party wishing to postpone the binding event to manifest that intention clearly.

Case Preview

Trademark Properties Inc. v. A & E Television Networks

This case involves a substantial business deal that the parties never reduced to a written agreement. The parties produced an entire season of the television show before their disagreement over how to compensate the creator of the series led to a parting of the ways. The court had to decide whether the creator's proposal to split net revenues evenly was accepted by the network. That depends on whether the parties intended the binding event to be the written contract they contemplated or the oral understanding they reached on the phone.

As you read *Trademark Properties Inc. v. A & E Television Networks*, look for the following:

1. How did the court evaluate whether the parties intended to be bound before signing a formal writing? What was important?
2. How was the court able to discern what the parties actually intended? Was it limited to the parties' own statements regarding what they had in mind?
3. Which if any aspect(s) of the four-factor test did the court apply here? Was one factor decisive? Or did it take more than one factor to support the result?

Trademark Properties Inc. v. A & E Television Networks

422 Fed. Appx. 199 (4th Cir. 2011)

Baldock, Senior Circuit Judge:

Plaintiff Richard C. Davis approached Defendant A & E Television Networks with the concept that he maintains became the reality television series "Flip This

House." This dispute arises out of the parties' disagreement over an alleged oral agreement to split equally net revenues of the show. Plaintiff sued . . . demanding approximately $7.5 million in damages, *i.e.*, half of the net revenues from the three seasons that had completed filming prior to trial. [A] jury returned a verdict awarding Plaintiff a little over $4 million, essentially half of the first season's net revenues. [W]e affirm the district court's denial of Defendant's motions for judgment as a matter of law and a new trial.

. . .

. . . Plaintiff is a South Carolina real estate broker who buys underpriced properties to renovate and sell, . . . a process . . . commonly known as "flipping." In 2003, Plaintiff conceived of the idea of a television show to document the flipping process and later developed a pilot episode of the show. In 2004, Plaintiff submitted the pilot to multiple television networks, including Defendant. . . .

After Nordlander [director of lifestyle programming for Defendant] viewed the pilot, the two spoke over the phone for a little less than an hour on June 3, 2004 about turning the show into a series. Essentially, Plaintiff proposed that he would assume all of the financial risk relating to the purchase and resale of the real estate but that they would otherwise equally split the net revenues of the television show. In response to Plaintiff's offer, Plaintiff maintains Nordlander said "Okay, okay, I get it." Thus, Plaintiff argues that by the end of this June 3 telephone conversation he and Defendant, via Nordlander, had entered into an oral contract to produce a television series based on Plaintiff's pilot and to share all resulting net revenues equally, subject to approval by Defendant's board of directors.

[The directors approved the series. Defendant hired a production company.]

The parties never reduced any oral agreement to writing. Nonetheless, they filmed thirteen episodes of "Flip this House." By all accounts, the show was a commercial success. But . . . [t]he parties could not resolve the matter of Plaintiff's compensation. Defendant offered to pay Plaintiff an appearance fee per episode and a five percent share of incremental revenue attributable to the show. Plaintiff rejected that offer and signed a talent agreement with another television network. Defendant went on to produce three more seasons of "Flip this House" without Plaintiff's participation. Defendant never paid Plaintiff any money, let alone half of the series' net revenue, for his role in its production. At trial, Defendant denied ever entering into any contract with Plaintiff.

. . .

Absent prohibition by the statute of frauds, oral contracts are just as binding as written contracts under New York law. . . . However, where an alleged contract is oral, the party asserting its enforceability bears an even heavier burden of proving more than agreement on or acceptance of all material terms, but also overall agreement to be bound by the oral agreement without a writing. . . .

. . .

Defendant contends that New York law holds that contracts that are sufficiently novel and complex must be in writing to be enforceable and that this agreement is one such contract. In addition, Defendant maintains that Plaintiff's repeatedly-asserted expectation that their agreement be reduced to writing proves that the parties only intended to be bound by a writing.

Defendant's statement of New York law is not entirely correct. We can find no case, nor has Defendant cited one, in which a New York court declared that as a matter of law a contract was so novel and complex that it had to have been in writing to be enforced. Instead, under New York law whether an oral agreement in the absence of a writing is binding depends on the parties' objectively-manifested intent. And, the sole case Defendant cites on this point makes clear that to discern that intent, we consider a number of factors, including:

> (1) whether a party has made an "explicit statement that it reserves the right to be bound only when a written agreement is signed," (2) "whether one party has partially performed," (3) "whether there was literally nothing left to negotiate or settle, so that all that remained to be done was to sign what had already been fully agreed to," and (4) *"whether the agreement concerns those complex and substantial business matters where requirements that contracts be in writing are the norm rather than the exception."*

Braun v. CMGI, Inc., 64 Fed. Appx. 301, 303 (2d Cir. 2003) (quoting *R.G. Group*, 751 F.2d at 75-76 (applying New York law)) (emphasis added). "No single factor is decisive, but each provides significant guidance." Therefore, contrary to Defendant's assertion, "whether the agreement concerns those complex and substantial business matters where requirements that contracts be in writing are the norm" is just one factor the fact-finder considers in deciding whether the parties intended to be bound without a written document.

First, Defendant contends because the alleged contract in this case "involved potentially millions of dollars, was a sharp departure from [its own] and industry practice . . . and by [Plaintiff's] own account could run for decades . . . [a] writing therefore was legally necessary to bind the parties." We agree that the contract involved a "substantial business matter" and it may well not have been Defendant's typical practice to split revenues. But we also note a reasonable jury could find that the contract at issue was not so complex. Hiring a third-party production company, adding all revenue, subtracting all reasonable expenses, splitting the remainder in two, and renewing each year depending on the show's ratings are easy enough concepts to understand. The jury could have also considered Defendant's demonstrated willingness to produce, pay for, and air a television series — a substantial business matter even without any agreement to share revenue — without a written contract.

Second, Defendant argues "[t]he evidence that the parties intended and attempted to reach a written agreement strongly confirms that the purported oral agreement was unenforceable" without a writing. Again, Defendant cannot escape the fact that by its own admission it undertook to develop and air a television series featuring Plaintiff without a written contract. It is not such a far leap from that fact to infer that Defendant and Plaintiff also intended to be bound by their oral agreement as to how to compensate Plaintiff without a written contract. There is also no evidence that Nordlander or any other of Defendant's representatives ever stated Defendant would not be obligated to Plaintiff without a formally executed document. Furthermore, we agree with the district court that the jury could have reasonably concluded from the trial testimony that Plaintiff "thought he had an oral contract, but expected a written contract . . . . [M]ost people feel more comfortable with a written contract than with an oral contract. And I think that based upon his

testimony, which the jury could have believed, he was promised a written contract by Mr. Nordlander, and he thought he was going to get one." That a party wants an oral contract reduced to writing does not necessarily mean the parties did not intend to be bound until such reduction; it may just reveal that the party wants to avoid a "he said, she said" argument down the road as to what the parties orally agreed.

. . .

For the reasons herein, we affirm the district court's denial of Defendant's motions for a judgment as a matter of law and a new trial.

Post-Case Follow-Up

After identifying a four-factor test, the court noted that no one factor is decisive. In the case, this meant that the fourth factor did not override the others; the fact that A & E (like other networks) usually entered written agreements when acquiring series did not prevent them from making an oral agreement this time. On the other hand, partial performance — for an entire TV season — may have been decisive, demonstrating some intent by each party to be bound on some terms, if not the ones plaintiff alleged. Concluding that all essential terms were agreed seems a stretch given the dispute over the payment term. But if the network agreed to the term orally, perhaps this dispute involved more an effort to renegotiate a term than to finish negotiating a term not yet agreed. The court did not mention an express reservation of right to review the final writing before committing to the deal. Should the presence (or absence) of a reservation have played a larger role in the analysis?

Trademark Properties Inc. v. A & E Television Networks: Real Life Applications

1. Assume that the *TPI* case could be appealed to a higher court to determine the appropriate test for whether an oral agreement could be enforced even though the parties never reduced it to written form, as planned. Could A & E benefit from persuading the court to adopt the Restatement (Second) of Contracts §§26-27 instead of the four-factor test? Or are the court's four factors just another way to express the Restatement test?

2. Even the dissent believed that plaintiff deserved something. If the contract is not enforceable, is there any basis for recovery? If the contract is not enforceable, how does A & E have any right to produce and air the series? How can the court sort out a full year of performance under an unenforceable agreement?

3. Suppose Nordlander carefully informed Davis that the discussions would not be final until a signed writing was executed. All other facts remain the same — including production of 13 episodes. What is A & E's best argument for refusing to perform the oral agreement alleged by Davis? (Consider writing out

the argument and exchanging papers with a classmate, offering comments on his or her response.)

4. Wright threatened to sue Ringer for copyright infringement. Ringer orally agreed to settle the claim by stopping the infringing activity and paying Wright $50,000. Wright submitted a formal document recording the terms of the settlement, but Ringer never signed the agreement. Ringer renewed its infringing activity and never paid Wright. Wright sued for breach of the settlement agreement. At no time did either party suggest to the other that it intended to remain free to reconsider the deal until the settlement agreement had been signed, nor did either indicate explicitly that it intended the oral agreement to be the binding event. Should the court enforce the settlement agreement? If not, how should Wright proceed?

Preliminary Agreements

Preliminary agreements pose a more difficult problem. Unlike oral agreements, which may include all the terms the parties ever intend to make, preliminary agreements generally include only the core terms of the deal. These core terms may be written and signed. The agreement is preliminary because the parties explicitly intend to address additional details and to produce a subsequent written agreement covering the entire transaction.

If parties intend to bind themselves to the transaction at the time of the preliminary agreement (sometimes called a letter of intent), courts will enforce the preliminary agreement. Often parties intend to retain the power to walk away from the deal until they sign a final writing. Like two people engaged to be married, they understand the wedding itself occurs when they sign the final writing (the marriage license), marking the point at which their union becomes legally effective. But just as some states still recognize suits for breach of a promise of marriage, some courts infer an intent to make the preliminary agreement binding from the circumstances surrounding its creation.

Enforcing a preliminary agreement faces two problems, both related to finding an offer. First, parties often reserve the right to back out until they sign

Flip This House

Flip This House is still under production, though it appears that several spinoffs use varying names. You can find episodes of seasons 1, 3, 4 and 5 at A & E: http://www.aetv.com/the-big-fix/video/. Richard Davis appeared in *The Real Estate Pros* on TLC. The show no longer airs, but you can see a short video with Richard Davis at http://www.tlc.com/tv-shows/other-shows/videos/the-real-estate-pros-richards-rule-for-real-estate-in/.

Determining the Binding Event

How can you tell whether an oral agreement was binding and the writing just a formality, or the written memorial was to be the binding event? Start by asking the parties. They may tell you different things, now that one wants out of the deal. Try ex-employees involved in the deal. Look for other witnesses to the deal. Look at the parties' conduct. Did they act as if the deal was already concluded without a signed writing? Did either expressly reserve the right not to be bound until the writing was signed? If so, that should end the inquiry. Everything was preliminary negotiation. Did one party start performing and the other accept the performance as if it was its right? That implies the recipient thought the contract was already final. Is this the kind of deal that usually isn't finalized without a signed writing? If so, the parties probably understood that signing was the binding event. The facts will vary with the context. Basically, you must look for ways to tell a persuasive story showing that the parties really did (or did not) think the deal was done already.

the final writing. Sometimes the reservation is explicit and unambiguous. Second, the agreement may lack important terms. A court could supply the missing terms if it appeared that the parties intended their agreement to be final. Unlike a gap in a final agreement, however, the parties often intend to continue to negotiate those terms themselves. They have not invited the court to fill the gaps. Thus, both the indefiniteness and the express reservations suggest that the parties know that commitment has been reserved until the signing of the final agreement. On both scores, finding an offer in the preliminary agreement poses problems.

Once, courts simply rejected these "agreements to agree" out of hand, refusing to enforce them until the parties reached a final agreement. The parties may have signed the same writing, but because it was not an offer, it failed to create any power to conclude the deal by accepting. Some courts continue to follow that approach. In *Empro Manufacturing v. Ball-Co Manufacturing*,[21] the parties expressly reserved the right to withdraw from the deal until the final agreement was signed. The court treated this reservation as conclusive. The preliminary agreement itself stated that it had no binding effect.

Other courts enforce preliminary agreements if it appears the parties intended the preliminary agreement to be binding. Courts infer that the time and effort the parties invested in negotiating and signing a preliminary agreement suggests they intended it to have some effect. Even in the face of an express reservation of the right to withdraw, a court might find the parties intended a binding preliminary agreement. In *Texaco v. Pennzoil*,[22] a court applying New York law identified four factors to consider:

(1) whether a party expressly reserved the right to be bound only when a written agreement is signed;
(2) whether there was any partial performance by one party that the party disclaiming the contract accepted;
(3) whether all essential terms of the alleged contract had been agreed upon; and
(4) whether the complexity or magnitude of the transaction was such that a formal, executed writing would normally be expected.[23]

You may recall that the *Trademark Properties Inc.* court used similar factors in deciding whether an oral agreement was the final agreement of the parties or merely preliminary negotiations. While these four factors seem reasonable on their face, much may depend on the way in which a court interprets and applies them.

If the preliminary agreement does not contain an express reservation, the last three factors help evaluate whether the parties intended the preliminary agreement to be binding. Accepting the other party's performance implies that a party believed it had a right to that performance — which would be true only under a binding preliminary agreement. If omitted details seem essential to the deal, then it is less likely that the parties intended to be bound until the parties reached agreement on those details. On the other hand, where the remaining terms seem less significant, courts

[21] 870 F.2d 423 (7th Cir. 1989).
[22] 729 S.W.2d 768 (Tex. App. 1987), *cert. dismissed*, 485 U.S. 994 (1988).
[23] 729 S.W.2d at 788-789.

show some willingness to enforce the preliminary agreement, filling open terms with default terms as needed. In more complex transactions, parties might think an express reservation unnecessary because everyone understands that the deal becomes final only after the final agreement. In really big deals, parties probably state the effect of the preliminary agreement expressly.

Even if the parties include an express reservation, the four-factor test may permit a court to conclude that the preliminary agreement was binding (as happened in *Texaco*). An express reservation is only one factor. For instance, in *Texaco*, the court found the express reservation insufficient in light of a press release that repeatedly used the verb "will" without attaching the qualification "if a final agreement is reached." This language created an impression that the agreement already was final. Under this modern approach, parties entering preliminary agreements cannot be confident that a court will find that an express reservation postpones the binding event until the final writing is signed.

Overriding an express reservation may be plausible in some cases. Accepting the other party's performance as if it was due sends mixed signals, undermining an express reservation. A party that demanded the other's performance sends an even stronger signal that it considered the agreement binding. Agreement on the essential terms reduces problems with definiteness. Still, a reservation suggests the parties viewed the remaining terms as sufficiently important to negotiate them, rather than simply to rely on the court to fill the gaps. Finally, the complexity of the deal suggests more reason to expect the parties to realize that the final agreement is the binding event — and more reason to doubt the ability of gap fillers to achieve an agreement the parties would accept.

The uncertainty created by courts has affected the way lawyers draft preliminary agreements. Instead of specifying that the agreements have no binding effect, they may include a **liquidated damages clause**, a term specifying how much money a party must pay as damages if it breaches. The price for backing out of the negotiations prematurely is in the preliminary agreement. Technically, any remedy provision suggests the parties did intend the agreement to be binding. Those favoring easy withdrawal specify a smaller amount, as a token of damages.

4. Definiteness

The requirement of **definiteness**, sometimes referred to as **certainty**, prevents enforcement of a contract when the terms proposed were so unclear or incomplete that enforcement would be impossible or inappropriate. Definiteness plays a double role in contract formation. As noted above, indefiniteness may prevent a communication from being an offer. A communication may be so incomplete that the other party could not justifiably believe that its assent would conclude the deal. In addition, definiteness is a separate requirement of contract formation. Even if the parties did assent, terms may be so indefinite that the court finds enforcement unfeasible. These two aspects of definiteness are intertwined, making it useful to address them together here.

Definiteness as a Requirement of an Offer

An incomplete proposal may signal that the party does not intend to be bound until more of the details are negotiated. If so, a party receiving the proposal cannot justifiably believe that its assent will conclude the transaction. The signal that further discussions are expected before a commitment is made—not the intent, but the outward signs of that intent—prevents the proposal from being an offer at all. An offer need not specify every conceivable term; modest gaps, even on important terms such as price, may not prevent an offeree from reasonably understanding that her assent will conclude the deal. In some circumstances, however, the significance or number of missing terms provides ample indication that the proposal is not an offer.

For example, consider the following conversation.

Homeowner: I'd like to hire you to paint my house for $5,000.
Painter: I accept.
Homeowner: I insist you use Glidden paint.
Painter: That's fine.
Homeowner: I need the job finished by July 10.
Painter: That won't work. I am booked until August 1. I'll start then.
Homeowner: That's unacceptable. If you can't finish by July 10, I need to find another painter who can.

If the homeowner's first statement was an offer, the contract became binding when the painter accepted. Everything after that involved modifications of the original contract, filling in the gaps.

The first line, however, may not be an offer. It seems to open negotiations, not invite another to conclude them. The statement lacked many of the terms parties usually discuss in this type of contract—so many that it might be unreasonable for either party to believe that the other's statements invited an assent that would conclude the deal. A court could fill the gaps with reasonable terms, allowing it to ascertain whether a breach occurred. But perhaps the court should not find an offer and, thus, not find assent.

Definiteness or Certainty?

Some sources (including the second Restatement) use the term "certainty" to describe the requirement that the terms of a contract be sufficiently clear to allow enforcement. Others, including this book, call this requirement "definiteness." By either name, the rule (like a rose) has the same substance. "Certainty," however, is the name of another doctrine involving a limitation on damages. Using definiteness to describe the formation requirement may reduce the risk of confusing the two doctrines. Whatever name you use, be sure to keep the substance distinct.

Efforts to fill gaps in a contract have no merit if the parties are still negotiating. Gap filling occurs after the court concludes that the parties intended their agreement to be binding. Until then, the parties remain free to specify their own terms and, if they fail to agree, to break off negotiations and deal with others instead. Otherwise, filling in a gap might produce a contract to which neither party would have agreed. In the painting hypothetical above, a court might infer that performance needed to be completed within a reasonable time and find that, factually, that required completion by July 20. Neither party would have agreed to that term. That would have been unacceptably late for the homeowner, but unacceptably early for the painter.

Issues of definiteness depend heavily on the facts. In house painting, time for performance may be important enough that people know the deal will not be final until that is discussed. In other kinds of contracts, timing may be less important. Even if timing usually is important, it might not be important to these parties. For instance, if the conversation had ended after the first two lines (or the first four), either party would have difficulty claiming the deal was not yet complete. Once they agree on the details important to them and end the negotiations, reopening them with afterthoughts seems unlikely to jeopardize the original agreement.

The rules here set the framework for the arguments; they do not easily resolve the arguments. Where the parties intended a contract, the court will enforce the agreement, filling in gaps as needed—unless the agreement is so vague that enforcement would be impractical. Where neither party reasonably could believe the other's words invited an assent that would conclude the transaction, the court will not find an offer (making acceptance superfluous). Subsequent negotiations may provide a basis for finding a contract, but only once one party is justified in believing that its assent will conclude the deal.

Definiteness as a Requirement of Formation

As a separate requirement of contract formation, definiteness requires two things:

1. A promise must be sufficiently clear to provide a court with a reasonable basis for determining whether it has been performed or breached; and
2. A promise must be sufficiently clear to provide a court with a reasonable basis for awarding a remedy for breach.[24]

Each imposes an important requirement, although neither prong prevents enforcement of promises very often. If a court cannot tell whether a promise has been performed or breached, it has no basis upon which to hold a party liable. Similarly, if it can find a breach, but has no way to assess a remedy, it cannot provide relief. The requirement, in effect, states that if a court cannot find any practical way to resolve the case, it should rule that the contract was void for indefiniteness.

How could a promise be so vague that the court could not tell whether it had been breached? Consider the famous case of *Hoffman v. Red Owl Stores*,[25] usually studied in a different context. Red Owl promised Hoffman a franchise grocery store. The agreement never specified the size of the store or even the city in which it would be located. If Red Owl had tendered a small store in a remote and tiny village, would that perform the contract or breach it? The agreement was so vague

[24]Restatement (Second) of Contracts §33(2).
[25]133 N.W.2d 267 (Wis. 1965).

Red Owl grocery store

that it provided no basis upon which to determine whether this was breach. In fact, Red Owl did not tender any store to Hoffman. Even if the exact nature of the store it needed to tender could not be ascertained, the court might have sufficient basis for determining that tendering no store breached the bargain.

If breach can be ascertained, the remedy often will be apparent. The normal remedy seeks to put the plaintiff in the position she would have occupied if the contract had been performed. If the promise is sufficiently definite to allow a court to ascertain a breach, often a court can assess how performance would have benefited the recipient, providing a reasonable basis for calculating a remedy. In some cases, however, ascertaining breach will differ from ascertaining performance. In *Hoffman*, tendering no store was breach. But performance might have been quite minimal. Without knowing the size or location of a store that would comply with the contract, it is difficult to ascertain how much plaintiff would have benefited if the contract had been performed.

Even that problem might not be fatal to a contract. Definiteness does not require that every detail of a contract be specified by the parties. If courts conclude that the parties intended a binding contract, they will interpret the agreement to include details not expressly stated by the parties. The parties' silence might mean that they failed to agree, but it also might mean that the missing terms were not important enough to mention. In effect, the parties' silence may indicate that they would be satisfied with any reasonable term on that issue. As long as the court can supply a reasonable term, it can enforce the contract.

For instance, suppose a homeowner and a house painter agree on terms, including price, color, and almost every other term the contract would need, but fail to specify when the job should be done. Consider three ways a court might handle the gap: (1) A court could reject the contract as indefinite. That fails to give effect to the deal they made. It also risks strategic behavior. A party that regrets agreeing to a deal often can identify some detail the contract did not mention. Unless the court can supply these missing terms by interpretation, every contract may be vulnerable. No matter how long and thorough a document becomes, a clever lawyer may find some additional detail that the parties could have included. (2) A court could interpret the agreement to give the painter an indefinite amount of time to perform. If so, no matter how long the painter delays, it never breaches any express term. It has not performed yet, but was not required to perform yet. It seems unlikely that the parties intended to give the painter discretion to perform years later. (3) A court could infer a deadline that seems consistent with the parties' intentions. Usually, this would require completion within a reasonable time.[26] With this addition, the court has a basis for determining whether a breach occurred. At some point, the delay will become unreasonable, constituting a breach. The remedy—any increased cost incurred to hire a substitute painter—poses no difficulty either.

The UCC codifies this approach. The sections numbered 2-3xx[27] include a number of specific terms that courts should use when parties do not specify a term for themselves. These terms include promises relating to quality (warranties), timing, place for performance, and even the price. (If you do not have to ask, you must have meant to pay the going rate.)

The courts' willingness to fill gaps in a contract with default terms eliminates most of the problems with indefinite contracts. Where the parties intended a contract to be formed, the court can enforce that agreement. Parties still may express their duties in terms so vague or incomplete that a court cannot fill the gaps, but these cases are increasingly rare.

Case Preview

Chavez v. McNeely

This case involves a consent decree—an agreement between the parties settling their divorce litigation that the court incorporated into its judgment, making it a court order. The parties left the amount of support McNeely would receive flexible, leaving room for it to vary if McNeely's needs or Chavez's ability to pay changed over time. That flexibility required some interpretation in order to decide whether the amount of support actually paid satisfied the requirements of the agreement.

As you read *Chavez v. McNeely*, look for the following:

1. Did the court decide that the terms were so vague that no offer had been made? Or did the court decide that the parties had made a contract, but that the term was too indefinite to enforce?
2. Do the examples cited by the court differ in any significant way from the case at bar?
3. The trial court believed it could ascertain the needs and ability to pay of these ex-spouses. Did the court offer a reason to reject these determinations?
4. Is the plaintiff entitled to any support for the years in question? Did the parties' agreement contemplate that possibility?

[26]For sales of goods, the UCC specifies that default term. UCC §2-309(1).
[27]*See, e.g.*, UCC §§2-305-2-315.

Chavez v. McNeely

287 S.W.3d 840 (Tex. App. 2009)

Sherry Radack, Chief Justice.

. . .

Appellant, Brenda T. McNeely Chavez ("Brenda"), and appellee, Joe D. McNeely ("Joe"),[1] were first married in 1969, and they have three children together. Joe and Brenda had a rocky relationship and were divorced and remarried twice. After their second remarriage in 2000, Joe was involved in a horseback riding accident that left him completely paralyzed.[2]

In June 2001, Joe and Brenda divorced for a third time. . . . In the ["Agreed Final Decree of Divorce"], Joe and Brenda divided their properties. The divorce decree gave Joe a life estate in a 120-acre ranch in Waller County, with the remainder going to Brenda. Page 12 of the 14-page divorce decree contains the following paragraph:

> Responsibility for Care of Joe D. McNeely: The parties stipulate that Joe D. McNeely's sister, Patsy Brewer and her family will be responsible for the daily physical care of Joe D. McNeely. Brenda T. McNeely stipulates that she will provide *as much* toward the care and providing for *the needs* of Joe D. McNeely as possible, *limited only by her personal financial situation.* (Emphasis added).

. . .

[On April 10, 2007, Joe filed] suit. . . . The case was tried to the bench in Waller County. Brenda took the position that . . . (2) the provision of the divorce decree that served as the basis of Joe's claim was too indefinite to be enforced as a contract. Brenda testified that she continued to pay the mortgage, taxes, and insurance on the ranch where Joe lived. She also testified that she had paid what she could for Joe's care until her business began to fail in 2003. Joe, however, contended that Brenda's personal spending habits did not reflect a decline in her financial ability to contribute toward his care.

The trial court rendered judgment for Joe on his breach of contract claim and awarded him $950,000 in damages, plus interest and attorney's fees. The trial court made the following findings of fact and conclusions of law, which are relevant to the disposition of this appeal.

> A contract existed between the Plaintiff and the Defendant, as set forth in the Agreed Final Decree of Divorce (Contract/Decree).
>
> . . .
>
> Defendant failed to comply with her agreement to provide as much toward the care and providing for the needs of Joe D. McNeely as possible, limited only by her, Brenda McNeely's[,] personal financial situation. Such breach of her agreement

---

[1]This Court has received notice that appellee, Joe D. McNeely is deceased. Because Mr. McNeely died after the trial court rendered judgment but before the case was finally disposed of on appeal, we will proceed to adjudicate the appeal as if all parties were alive. [Citation omitted.]

[2]As a result of this accident, Joe filed a personal injury action against Brenda's company, Chavez Construction. Joe recovered a money judgment, which this Court affirmed. While pending at the Texas Supreme Court, the case settled, and Joe recovered $4 million gross or $1.9 million net.

mentioned above occurred continuously between April 10, 2003 and the date of trial, December 12, 2007.

The contract between the parties, especially the paragraph headed "Responsibility for Care of Joe D. McNeely" contained on Page 12 of the Agreed Final Decree of Divorce, was not vague but was clear and unambiguous.

Plaintiff Joe D. McNeely's needs have exceeded $500,000 per year since April 10, 2003.

Defendant's personal financial situation since the entry of the Agreed Final Decree of Divorce has been such that she could have provided substantial care and provisions for the needs of Joe D. McNeely, in excess of $300,000 per year for the years 2003 through 2007.

Plaintiff Joe D. McNeely's damages directly resulting from Defendant's breach of the contract/Decree and from Defendant's failure to comply with her obligations set forth in the contract/Decree are $950,000.

. . .

[B]renda contends that the clause requiring her to continue to pay "as much as possible" toward Joe's "needs," limited only by her "personal financial situation," is too indefinite to be enforced. We agree.

A contract is legally binding only if its terms are sufficiently definite to enable a court to understand the parties' obligations. *Fort Worth ISD v. City of Fort Worth*, 22 S.W.3d 831, 846 (Tex. 2000). "The rules regarding indefiniteness of material terms of a contract are based on the concept that a party cannot accept an offer so as to form a contract unless the terms of that contract are reasonably certain." *Id.*

A contract is sufficiently definite if a court is able to determine the respective legal obligations of the parties. Contract terms are reasonably certain "if they provide a basis for determining the existence of a breach and for giving an appropriate remedy." Restatement (Second) of Contracts §33(2) (1981). If an alleged agreement is so indefinite as to make it impossible for a court to fix the legal obligations and liabilities of the parties, it cannot constitute an enforceable contract. Whether an agreement fails for indefiniteness is a question of law for the court. [Citations omitted.]

In *Pine v. Gibraltar Sav. Ass'n*, 519 S.W.2d 238, 243 (Tex. Civ. App.—Houston [1st Dist.] 1974, writ ref'd n.r.e), the bank allegedly agreed to lend Pine whatever amount of money he needed to construct houses on 108 lots. The loans were to be made according to "prevailing market rates" and "industry standards." This Court held that the agreement was unenforceable because, among other things, there was no agreement as to the total amount to be loaned, when and how the interest was to be paid, when the principal was to be paid, or how to determine "prevailing market rate" or "industry standards."

In *T.O. Stanley Boot Co.*, the bank allegedly promised to lend the corporation $500,000. The supreme court held that the agreement was too indefinite to be enforced because, although it provided the amount of the loan, many terms, including the interest rate and repayment terms were missing. *T.O. Stanley Boot Co.*, 847 S.W.2d at 222.

. . .

In *Ski River Dev., Inc. v. McCalla*, 167 S.W.3d 121, 129 (Tex. App.—Waco 2005, pet. denied), lessees, the Bakers, sub-leased a two-acre tract of land to the McCallas. The sub-lease provided:

> That, in the event Lessees [Bakers] shall purchase or otherwise obtain legal ownership of *said Property* from Lessor [Glazier] and later *elect to sell*, Lessees [Bakers] hereby grant Sub-Lessees [McCallas] the First Option to Purchase all, or a portion of said Property from Lessees [Bakers] at market value.

Id. at 133. (Emphasis added). The court of appeals held that the agreement was too indefinite to enforce because it did not, among other things, (1) define "said property" or "portion of said property," (2) state whether "elect to sell" included merely listing the property for sale, (3) state when the market value was to be determined, or (4) provide a method for determining market value. *Id.* at 134.

Brenda argues that this case presents a situation of indefiniteness "cubed" because there are three indefinite terms. First, the clause provides that Brenda will pay "as much as possible," but it does not define that term, nor explain how the parties will reach an agreement as to what that term means. Second, the clause refers to paying for Joe's "needs," but again, it does not specify what those "needs" are. There is no way to determine whether "needs" refers to basic needs such as food, shelter, and clothing, or whether it includes medical or caregiving needs. Finally, the clause concludes that Brenda's obligation is limited by her "personal financial situation," but it does not explain how or when Brenda's "personal financial situation" would be impacted such that it would excuse or reduce any performance required by her.

Nevertheless, Joe argues that "Brenda's performance, and Joe's acceptance of it, provides a measuring stick by which the trial court could determine what the parties understood the provision in the Divorce Agreement to mean." *See* Restatement (Second) of Contracts §34(2) cmt. c. (explaining that partial performance may remove uncertainty and give meaning to otherwise indefinite term). However, Brenda's attempt to comply with the indefinite term for some time does nothing to clarify the clause in question. There is simply no guidance in the clause to tell Brenda or the court how much she is required to pay each month or how and when her personal financial situation would be such that it would reduce or excuse her performance. [Citation omitted.]

Because we hold that the clause relied upon by Joe is too indefinite to be enforced as a contract, we sustain Brenda's second issue on appeal.

CONCLUSION

We reverse the judgment of the trial court and render judgment that Joe take nothing on his breach of contract claim against Brenda.

Post-Case Follow-Up

The appellate court did not try very hard to ascertain whether McNeely's needs could be defined or whether the portion Chavez could possibly pay (given changing financial circumstances) could be calculated. If McNeely tried to hold Chavez to an oral promise made during negotiations, the vagueness of these terms suggests that the deal was not yet struck. The context here — a written agreement not only signed by the parties but also adopted by a judge as a court order — might deserve more attention.

Divorce decrees offer the parties a different way to build flexibility into the agreement. A decree (agreed or litigated) specifying the exact amount of monthly support usually can be modified at the request of either party if circumstances change (needs increase or ability to pay declines). Modifications to court orders do not require agreement by the parties, even if the original decree was agreed. Thus, the decree itself need not try to build flexibility into the initial terms.

When negotiating contracts that will not be embodied in a judicial order, parties seeking flexibility may need to negotiate the term from the outset. Judicial reluctance to enforce terms without some detailed guidance puts some strain on people drafting contracts.

Chavez v. McNeely: Real Life Applications

1. Should divorcing parties have agreed on a specified amount, relying on their ability to seek modifications from the court to provide any necessary flexibility? Are there reasons to try to build flexibility into the agreement itself? Could they have drafted language that would be sufficiently definite to allow the court to enforce it, but still flexible enough to satisfy their concerns? What details would that language need to include?

2. Consider a variation on *T.O. Stanley Boot Co.*, discussed in the case. Suppose the lender provided the $500,000 promised, but the borrower alleged the loan contract was too indefinite to enforce because "many terms, including the interest rate and repayment terms were missing." Should a court enforce the agreement anyway, ascertaining an appropriate interest rate and repayment schedule based on market conditions? Or should the court declare the contract unenforceable? If the contract is not enforceable, what, if anything, can the lender recover? Would it matter if the borrower had already used the money to improve the business? (Banks don't lend this way, but perhaps a wealthy relative would.)

3. Recall *Trademark Properties Inc. v. A & E Television Networks*, 422 Fed. Appx. 199 (4th Cir. 2011). In addition to arguing that the contract was not formed because the parties had not entered a written agreement, A & E urged that the contract was indefinite because the parties "did not discuss let alone agree on . . . the categories of revenue that would be included in 'net revenue,' the categories of expenses that would be deducted from 'net revenue,' the duration of the agreement, the grounds for termination, or the identities of the parties." Should the court have declared the contract unenforceable instead of trying to calculate net revenue without agreement of the parties? Is this deal more definite than the loan cases discussed in *Chavez*?

4. Employee has been asked to relocate to Washington, D.C. and open a new branch for employer — at a considerable raise in pay. Employee is content, but is willing to take the position if he can return if things don't work out in the new position. The letter offering the promotion concluded: "Regardless of your decision, you know you have a home here . . . and your career will not be impeded either way." Is the promise sufficiently definite to protect employee? What if employer also

said (in front of reliable witnesses) that she would "bring the employee back to [this state] with the same position he had when he left." If you need more, what language would you seek in order to make the commitment enforceable? (Remember, the employer will need to agree to the terms. And it is a lucrative promotion, if things go well.)

---

5. UCC: Auctions

Similar to advertisements, an auction might offer items for bidders to accept (provided that they make the highest bid); or it might invite bidders to make offers, which the auctioneer (on behalf of the seller) may accept or reject. The law uses both paradigms, depending on whether an item is offered **with reserve**—a right to remove items from the sale if bids are unsatisfactory—or **without reserve**. In an auction without reserve, once items are announced for sale, they cannot be withdrawn unless no bids are made within a reasonable time.[28]

At an auction with reserve, the seller invites offers. It reserves the right to reject those offers, removing the item from sale. Alternatively, it may accept one of the offers, usually the highest offer. Because bids are merely offers, the offerors may revoke the offers (withdraw bids) at any time prior to acceptance (by the auctioneer's gavel).

An auction without reserve, on the other hand, is an offer. The highest bidder accepts the offer. Participants understand the condition that limits acceptance to the highest bid. Each bid could be an acceptance, but will satisfy the condition only if no higher bid occurs. The highest bid is an acceptance. Any effort by the seller to withdraw the item from sale after a bid is made would breach the contract with the highest (even if only) bidder.

Try your hand at applying these rules to the following situation. At an auction without reserve, Sean and Cameron bid against one another. Cameron ultimately bid $1,000. The auctioneer asks, "Do I hear $1,100?" Sean considers bidding as the auctioneer announces, "Going once. Going twice." Just before the auctioneer's gavel falls, Sean signals with the paddle. Jean, Sean's spouse, grabs the paddle and pulls it down, saying "What are you doing?!" The auctioneer, however, recognizes Sean's bid of $1,100. Can Sean withdraw the bid?

D. REVOCATION

Revocation refers to withdrawing an offer. Until an offer is accepted, an offeror may revoke it. This protects an offeror's ability to change his mind and decide not to proceed with a deal. Having created the offeree's power of acceptance by making an offer, the offeror may destroy the offeree's power of acceptance by revoking an offer. Offerors may make irrevocable offers, either intentionally or unintentionally.

---

[28]UCC §2-328.

Subsections 2 and 3 below address circumstances in which offerors may not revoke offers. Aside from those situations, revocation can occur any time before acceptance becomes effective.

Revocation consists of the offeror's manifestation of an intention not to enter into the proposed contract.[29] It requires language or conduct that communicates the revocation to the offeree. A change of mind is ineffective until manifest. Revocation takes effect when received by the offeree.

An offeror may communicate the revocation personally, but need not do so. She may ask another (say, her attorney) to revoke the offer on her behalf. Acts and words of an **agent** (a person authorized to act on behalf of another) are treated as acts of the **principal** (the person employing the agent). Thus, whether the offeror speaks directly or through an agent, the communication comes from the offeror.

A revocation might be communicated indirectly, from someone other than an agent of the offeror. If the offeree knows the offeror no longer wishes to deal, the power to create a binding contract ends. When the message arrives from a third party, the reliability of the information becomes important. To qualify as a revocation, the message must involve

1. definite actions taken by the offeror
2. inconsistent with a continued intention to enter the contract; and
3. information about those actions from a reliable source.[30]

Rumor does not constitute a revocation. Mere words spoken by the offeror, even if repeated by a reliable source, do not revoke an offer. Action by the offeror — such as selling the item to another buyer — may negate an offer. Even then, information about the action must reach the offeree from a reliable source. Otherwise, the offeree may continue to rely on the offer. The offeree may trust the offeror's own communication (the offer) over that of the unreliable source (the revocation).

For example, consider the famous case of *Dickinson v. Dodds*,[31] which both illustrates this point and raises questions about how far it should apply. While considering an offer to sell land, an offeree was informed that the owner had either sold or offered the land to someone else. The court did not discuss what made the source reliable. In addition, news of a sale differs from news of an offer in significant ways. A sale is completely inconsistent with an intent to keep the offer open. An offer, however, may not be inconsistent with a willingness to sell to the offeree. The second offer may be a contingent offer (in case the offeree does not accept) or may reflect a willingness to sell to either party, whichever accepts first. Nonetheless, the case stands as a famous example of indirect revocation.

Revoking offers made to the public at large (or to a group where the offeror does not know the identity of all offerees) poses special problems. Offerors typically

---

[29] Restatement (Second) of Contracts §41.
[30] *Id.* §43.
[31] 2 Ch. D. 463 (C.A. 1876).

cannot communicate with each individual offeree. The law nonetheless permits revocation in these settings. Revocation of a general offer is effective

1. if (and when) the revocation receives publicity equal to that of the offer;
2. unless a better means of notification was reasonably available.[32]

Thus, to revoke an offer made in an advertisement, an ad of equal prominence in the same media that carried the original ad should suffice. The revocation becomes effective when it achieves publicity equal to the original ad. Acceptances before the revocation receives adequate publicity remain effective.

Where a better means of notice would be reasonable, revocation by publication may not suffice. If the offeror could identify some offerees and notify them directly, publication may not be sufficient to revoke the offer to those offerees. Publication still may revoke the offer to offerees for whom individual notice was not feasible. Similarly, a store might revoke an offer by posting prominent notices at the entrance to the store. Relying on an ad instead of signs might fail if signs offered a better means of notification.

Equal publicity does not require exactly the same medium. An offer in a magazine might be revoked by a newspaper, television, or radio ad that received equal exposure. Equal publicity probably requires that audience size for the revocation match that of the offer. Courts may require other similarities, such as geography or demographics, in determining whether better means of notification were available. For instance, an ad in the *New York Times* seems an odd way to revoke an offer made in the *Boston Globe*, regardless of relative circulation.

Equal publicity may require more than just similar audience size. If the offer was published for several days, that may require publishing the revocation for several days. Because situations vary significantly, any prediction lacks confidence. For instance, an advertising blitz for one day may reach the same audience as an offer made in a few TV ads over the course of a week. But viewers who saw the ad during *NCIS* may miss the revocation if the blitz occurs on Wednesday.

Once the revocation becomes effective, it will not matter that someone who saw the ad did not see the revocation. The revocation, like the offer, may not reach its entire intended audience. Rather than treat the offer as irrevocable, courts accept a reasonable substitute for individual notification.

1. Receipt

Revocation terminates an offer upon receipt by the offeree. Receipt of a writing occurs when "the writing comes into the possession of the person addressed, or of some person authorized by him to receive it for him, or when it is deposited in some place which he has authorized as the place for this or similar communications

[32]Restatement (Second) of Contracts §46.

to be deposited for him."[33] These rules apply equally to rejections and counteroffers, discussed in Chapter 3.

The definition of receipt in these rules has several significant implications. First, messages are received before they are opened. For mail, holding the envelope is enough to constitute receipt, even if the recipient never opens it. Second, delivery to an assistant or a company mail clerk may suffice. Businesses authorize these people to receive mail for them and to distribute the mail as appropriate. The message need not reach the hands of the individual addressee. Finally, receipt does not require that any person actually notice the message, let alone actually read it. Arrival at an authorized place will suffice. Thus, a letter placed in a person's mailbox has been received.

A letter placed in a person's mailbox has been received.
Hurst Photo/Shutterstock.com

Disputes about authorization to receive messages by particular people or at specific locations for a given message can arise. Even delivery to the wrong place takes effect when the message comes into a person's possession.

These rules contemplate physical writings delivered to physical places. The same analysis can apply to messages sent electronically. For some technologies, identifying a place designated for deposit of those messages may require a bit of imagination. But the generalizations seem likely to remain constant. Receipt does not require reading the message or even realizing it was delivered. Once the message has been placed at the recipient's disposal, courts seem likely to find receipt.

Receipt of E-mail

E-mail is received before you open and read it. When is it deposited at a place you authorized for this purpose? Reaching your e-mail provider — Google, Hotmail, NetZero, and so on — seems sufficient. You authorize them to receive messages for you. Even if you never open the mailbox or download the e-mail messages, they have been deposited in your account, and therefore are considered "received."

2. Option Contracts

Offerors may promise to keep offers open for a specified period to allow the offeree time to consider the offer. Despite a promise to keep an offer open, an offeror usually may revoke an offer at any time prior to acceptance. For example, recall the offer to sell real estate in *Dickinson v. Dodds.*[34] The offeror promised to keep the offer open until Friday, a deadline the offeree met. The court treated a revocation the offeree received on Thursday as effective despite the offeror's promise. A promise to keep an offer open, like any other promise, requires **consideration**, something given in exchange for that promise, before it becomes enforceable.

An enforceable promise to keep an offer open is called an **option contract**. The offeree has the option to accept (or not) because the offeror sold the right to revoke

[33] *Id.* §68.
[34] 2 Ch. D. 463 (C.A. 1876), discussed on page 65 above.

the offer. An option contract is a separate exchange, independent of the underlying deal. It always relates to an offer of some underlying deal. That offer must be sufficiently definite to be accepted and enforced. The option involves a promise to keep the offer open for a specified period of time, typically in exchange for a promise of good and valuable consideration — often a nominal sum, such as $1 or $5. Options are valuable promises, but often the value is hard to ascertain. Small amounts of consideration — and in some cases, consideration that was recited in the agreement but never really paid — will make option promises enforceable.

Typically, a promise to keep an offer open will be enforceable in one of three situations:

1. Paying for the promise would constitute consideration.
2. Relying on the promise might create an exception to consideration.
3. A statute might make an offer irrevocable despite the absence of consideration.[35]

Other exceptions that justify enforcing a promise without consideration may apply to enforcing promises to keep an offer open. The details of consideration and exceptions to that rule are discussed in Chapters 4 and 5.

Once an option has been obtained, the offer remains open for the promised period. Events that normally would terminate an offer (see Chapter 3) do not terminate an option. Any effort by the offeror to revoke the offer has no effect — unless it fools the offeree into missing the deadline to accept the offer. The option allows the offeree time to decide whether to accept, but does not replace the need to accept the offer in a timely and effective manner. Of course, the offeree may decide not to exercise the option (decide not to accept the offer) if it prefers.

Acceptance under an option contract takes effect when received by the offeror, not when dispatched by the offeree. Because revocation no longer looms, the need to advance the date of acceptance to the time of dispatch diminishes. Exhibit 2.1 compares offer versus option.

EXHIBIT 2.1 Offer versus Option Contract

	Offer	Option
Rejection	ends offer	no effect
Revocation	ends offer	no effect
Counteroffer	ends offer	no effect
Death or Incapacity of Offeror	ends offer	no effect, unless offeror's performance impossible
Acceptance	effective when sent, if properly dispatched	effective when received

Exceptions to consideration can produce enforceable options. In particular, reliance on a promise to keep an offer open may lead a court to enforce the promise

[35]Restatement (Second) of Contracts §87(1).

to keep the offer open. The requirements of Restatement (Second) of Contracts §90, if satisfied, would make a promise to keep an offer open enforceable. Some authorities go further, suggesting that an option might be created based on reliance even if the promisor did not promise to keep an offer open for a particular period.[36]

Case Preview

Case Preview: Drennan v. Star Paving Co.

A promise to keep an offer open becomes enforceable if the offeree gives consideration for that promise. As you will study in Chapter 5, promises may be enforceable without consideration in some exceptional circumstances. Those exceptions apply to any promise, including a promise to keep an offer open. As you will learn in Chapter 3, those exceptions long applied to offers that require an offeree to accept an offer by performing instead of by promising to perform. The court here addresses a case that appears to fall in the middle of these familiar rules.

As you read *Drennan v. Star Paving Co.*, look for the following:

1. Did the subcontractor expressly promise to keep the offer open for any period of time? Did the court infer that promise from the context?
2. Did the court require the offeror to keep the offer open even if it did not promise (even implicitly) to keep the offer open? Could the offeror have submitted a bid that would not have been subject to this rule?
3. Was the bid an offer that could be accepted only by performance? Does the court's discussion of this doctrine suggest that it thinks this was such an offer?
4. How long was the subcontractor required to keep the offer open?

Drennan v. Star Paving Company

51 Cal. 2d 409, 333 P.2d 757 (1958) (en banc)

TRAYNOR, Justice.

Defendant appeals from a judgment for plaintiff in an action to recover damages caused by defendant's refusal to perform certain paving work according to a bid it submitted to plaintiff.

On July 28, 1955, plaintiff, a licensed general contractor, was preparing a bid on the "Monte Vista School Job" in [Lancaster]. Bids had to be submitted before 8:00 p.m. [I]t was customary . . . for general contractors to receive the bids of subcontractors by telephone on the day set for bidding and to rely on them in computing their own bids. Thus on that day plaintiff's secretary, Mrs. Johnson, received by telephone

[36] *Id.* §87(2).

between fifty and seventy-five subcontractors' bids for various parts of the school job. . . .

Late in the afternoon, Mrs. Johnson had a telephone conversation with Kenneth R. Hoon, an estimator for defendant. He . . . stated that he was bidding for defendant for the paving work at the Monte Vista School according to plans and specifications and that his bid was $7,131.60. At Mrs. Johnson's request he repeated his bid. . . . Defendant's was the lowest bid for the paving. Plaintiff computed his own bid accordingly and submitted it with the name of defendant as the subcontractor for the paving. When the bids were opened on July 28th, plaintiff's proved to be the lowest, and he was awarded the contract.

[T]he next morning plaintiff stopped at defendant's office. The first person he met was defendant's construction engineer, Mr. Oppenheimer. Plaintiff testified: "I introduced myself and he immediately told me that they had made a mistake in their bid to me the night before, they couldn't do it for the price they had bid, and I told him I would expect him to carry through with their original bid because I had used it in compiling my bid and the job was being awarded them. And I would have to go and do the job according to my bid and I would expect them to do the same."

Defendant refused to do the paving work for less than $15,000. Plaintiff . . . "got figures from other people" and [eventually hired] a firm in Lancaster to do the work for $10,948.60.

The trial court found . . . that defendant made a definite offer to do the paving . . . for $7,131.60, and that plaintiff relied on defendant's bid in computing his own bid for the school job and naming defendant therein as the subcontractor for the paving work. Accordingly, it entered judgment for plaintiff in the amount of $3,817.00 (the difference between defendant's bid and the cost of the paving to plaintiff) plus costs.

Defendant contends that . . . it made a revocable offer and revoked it before plaintiff communicated his acceptance to defendant.

There is no evidence that defendant offered to make its bid irrevocable in exchange for plaintiff's use of its figures in computing his bid. Nor is there evidence that would warrant interpreting plaintiff's use of defendant's bid as the acceptance thereof, binding plaintiff, on condition he received the main contract, to award the subcontract to defendant. In sum, there was neither an option supported by consideration nor a bilateral contract binding on both parties.

Plaintiff contends, however, that he relied to his detriment on defendant's offer and that defendant must therefore answer in damages for its refusal to perform. Thus the question is squarely presented: Did plaintiff's reliance make defendant's offer irrevocable?

Section 90 of the Restatement of Contracts states: "A promise which the promisor should reasonably expect to induce action or forbearance of a definite and substantial character on the part of the promisee and which does induce such action or forbearance is binding if injustice can be avoided only by enforcement of the promise." This rule applies in this state.

Defendant's offer constituted a promise to perform on such conditions as were stated expressly or by implication therein or annexed thereto by operation of law. Defendant had reason to expect that if its bid proved the lowest it would be used by plaintiff. It induced "action . . . of a definite and substantial character on the part of the promisee."

Had defendant's bid expressly stated or clearly implied that it was revocable at any time before acceptance we would treat it accordingly. It was silent on revocation, however, and we must therefore determine whether there are conditions to the right of revocation. . . . In the analogous problem of an offer for a unilateral contract, the theory is now obsolete that the offer is revocable at any time before complete performance. Thus section 45 of the Restatement of Contracts provides: "If an offer for a unilateral contract is made, and part of the consideration requested in the offer is given or tendered by the offeree in response thereto, the offeror is bound by a contract, the duty of immediate performance of which is conditional on the full consideration being given or tendered within the time stated in the offer, or, if no time is stated therein, within a reasonable time." In explanation, comment b states that the "main offer includes as a subsidiary promise, necessarily implied, that if part of the requested performance is given, the offeror will not revoke his offer, and that if tender is made it will be accepted. Part performance or tender may thus furnish consideration for the subsidiary promise. Moreover, merely acting in justifiable reliance on an offer may in some cases serve as sufficient reason for making a promise binding (see s 90)."

Whether implied in fact or law, the subsidiary promise serves to preclude the injustice that would result if the offer could be revoked after the offeree had acted in detrimental reliance thereon. Reasonable reliance resulting in a foreseeable prejudicial change in position affords a compelling basis also for implying a subsidiary promise not to revoke an offer for a bilateral contract.

The absence of consideration is not fatal to the enforcement of such a promise. It is true that in the case of unilateral contracts the Restatement finds consideration for the implied subsidiary promise in the part performance of the bargained-for exchange, but its reference to section 90 makes clear that consideration for such a promise is not always necessary. The very purpose of section 90 is to make a promise binding even though there was no consideration "in the sense of something that is bargained for and given in exchange." Reasonable reliance serves to hold the offeror in lieu of the consideration ordinarily required to make the offer binding. In a case involving similar facts the Supreme Court of South Dakota stated that "we believe that reason and justice demand that the doctrine (of section 90) be applied to the present facts. . . . We are of the opinion, therefore, that the defendants in executing the agreement (which was not supported by consideration) made a promise which they should have reasonably expected would induce the plaintiff to submit a bid based thereon to the Government, that such promise did induce this action, and that injustice can be avoided only by enforcement of the promise."

When plaintiff used defendant's offer in computing his own bid, he bound himself to perform in reliance on defendant's terms. Though defendant did not bargain for this use of its bid neither did defendant make it idly, indifferent to whether it would be used or not. On the contrary it is reasonable to suppose that defendant submitted its bid to obtain the subcontract. It was bound to realize the substantial possibility that its bid would be the lowest, and that it would be included by plaintiff in his bid. . . . Defendant had reason not only to expect plaintiff to rely on its bid

but to want him to. Clearly defendant had a stake in plaintiff's reliance on its bid. Given this interest and the fact that plaintiff is bound by his own bid, it is only fair that plaintiff should have at least an opportunity to accept defendant's bid after the general contract has been awarded to him.

It bears noting that a general contractor is not free to delay acceptance after he has been awarded the general contract in the hope of getting a better price. Nor can he reopen bargaining with the subcontractor and at the same time claim a continuing right to accept the original offer. In the present case plaintiff promptly informed defendant that plaintiff was being awarded the job and that the subcontract was being awarded to defendant.

. . .

***Leo F. Piazza Paving Co. v. Bebek & Brkich*, 141 Cal. App. 2d 226, 296 P.2d 368, 371 [(1956), is] not to the contrary. In the *Piazza* case the court sustained a finding that defendants intended, not to make a firm bid, but only to give the plaintiff "some kind of an idea to use" in making its bid; there was evidence that the defendants had told plaintiff they were unsure of the significance of the specifications. There was thus no offer, promise, or representation on which the defendants should reasonably have expected the plaintiff to rely. . . .**

. . .

The judgment is affirmed.

Post-Case Follow-Up

On one interpretation, *Drennan* created a new rule applicable to any offer on which an offeree foreseeably might rely. Restatement (Second) of Contracts §87(2). That differs from section 90 by applying to any offer, even if there was no promise to keep it open (not even an implied promise). Section 87 also differs from section 90 by requiring reliance of a substantial character, language found in section 90 of the first Restatement, but deleted in the second Restatement. *Drennan* might instead be interpreted to apply section 90 to cases in which offers implicitly include a promise to keep the offer open, as seems to be true of bids for construction contracts. Perhaps both sections remain available, depending on which fits a party's needs or a jurisdiction's willingness to apply them.

Drennan v. Star Paving Co.: Real Life Applications

1. ConCon, a construction contractor preparing to bid on a government contract, sought bids from subcontractors on the work. Its request for bids specified that "bids must be held open for 60 days." PaCon, a paving subcontractor, submitted a price quote of $310,000 on the paving work. The quote included the following term: "This is provided for informational purposes only and no reliance should be placed thereon. PaCon will not be responsible or liable in any manner pending execution of a written agreement covering the work in question." PaCon's quote was lower than any other bid on paving work. ConCon immediately

called you to ask whether it can rely on this quote in preparing its bid on the government contract. You must respond immediately or ConCon will not be able to finish its bid in time to compete for the project. In one word, what is your answer? In one sentence, what is your reason?

2. Suppose ConCon had no time to seek legal advice and relied on the $310,000 quote from PaCon. After receiving the contract, ConCon accepted PaCon's offer, but PaCon refused to perform. ConCon paid $500,000 for paving work, the lowest it could find after PaCon breached. How would you urge a court to rule in favor of enforcing the contract against PaCon? How would you persuade a court to rule against ConCon?

3. ConCon also received a bid on the plumbing subcontract from FlushCo. ConCon used FlushCo's bid in preparing its bid and named FlushCo as its proposed plumbing subcontractor in the paperwork it submitted to the government. After receiving the contract, ConCon was approached by HydroCo, a plumbing subcontractor, with an offer to do the work for less than FlushCo's bid. After confirming that the government had no objection to the change. ConCon hired HydroCo to do the plumbing work on the job. Can FlushCo sue ConCon for breach of contract for failing to hire it to do the work?

   a. Would your answer be any different if ConCon had not included language requiring bids to remain open for 60 days in its initial solicitation of bids?

   b. Does it matter whether HydroCo bid on the work originally or was a new company that was not formed in time to bid on the contract?

   c. Would your answer be any different if HydroCo was a minority-owned enterprise that helps ConCon fulfill a social obligation to support minority businesses? What if the government required ConCon to award a percentage of the subcontracts to minority-owned businesses, but other subcontracts satisfied the minimum requirement? What if ConCon needed to hire HydroCo to meet the minimum requirements of the government contract?

---

3. UCC: Firm Offers

By statute, some offers are treated as firm offers, made irrevocable without regard to consideration or reliance. Consider UCC §2-205:

> An offer by a merchant to buy or sell goods in a signed writing which by its terms gives assurance that it will be held open is not revocable, for lack of consideration, during the time stated or if no time is stated for a reasonable time, but in no event may such period of irrevocability exceed three months; but any such term of assurance on a form supplied by the offeree must be separately signed by the offeror.[37]

[37] UCC § 2-205.

Cultural Differences

European legal systems treat any date mentioned for acceptance as a promise that the offer will not be revoked before that date — a promise that is enforceable without consideration in most European nations. Culturally, the technical linguistic distinction between deadlines and firm offers may not register with all listeners. Perhaps a clear disclaimer, expressly reserving the right to revoke before the deadline, would overcome this doctrinal preference for finding assurance in a date. Article 16 of the CISG, a treaty governing sales of goods between parties in different countries, is ambiguous, containing provisions that might support either the European or the U.S. approach to firm offers.

Note the limited circumstances in which a promise becomes enforceable without consideration. The provision applies only to offers by merchants. When individuals offer a used car, they can revoke the offer despite promising to keep it open. A used car dealer cannot. It applies only to offers made in writing and must explicitly assure the offeree that the offer will remain open. These limitations reduce the risk that someone inadvertently would make an offer firm. The statute, however, does not require that the offer specify how long it will remain open. If a firm offer does not specify its duration, it remains irrevocable for a reasonable time — but never more than three months, even if the offer specified a longer period.

What constitutes an assurance that an offer will be held open? Language specifying a time for acceptance may reflect two different purposes. It may specify a date the offer will lapse: the maximum time the offer will remain open, a deadline, the last possible date for acceptance. Alternatively, the language might promise to keep the offer open: a minimum time the offer will remain open, assurance that it will not expire any earlier.

Consider two examples:

1. "I must know your decision no later than June 20 in order to finish the work on time."
2. "Think it over, let me know any time before June 20."

The second example seems to offer assurance that the offer will remain open until June 20. After June 20, the offeror might be willing to consider the same deal, but this language does not commit her beyond that date. The first example, however, does not seem to contain any assurance at all. It sets a deadline, specifying that the offer will lapse on that date. It does not seem to promise that the offer will remain open that long. If things changed and the offeror needed to know by June 19, would anything in the first statement prevent him from moving the deadline a day (or a week) earlier? If not, then the offer seems revocable at will, containing no assurance that it will remain open that long.

Chapter Summary

- Assent generally requires an offer and an acceptance. The contract becomes binding at the point of acceptance.
- Assent is evaluated based on the objectively observable words and conduct of parties, not their secret intentions.
- The offeror is the master of the offer. She may specify the time, place, and manner of acceptance, as well as the terms of the deal.
- A proposal is not an offer if the other party has reason to know that the party making the proposal does not intend to be bound until after it makes some further expression of assent. Reason to know may exist if a proposal is vague or incomplete or where the other party indicated that it intends to make its final decision after reviewing a written agreement.
- Even if parties intend to enter a contract on vague terms, a court will refuse to enforce the deal unless the terms are sufficiently definite to allow the court to identify a breach and formulate an appropriate remedy.
- An offeror can determine how long an offer remains open. The offeror can end a power of acceptance by setting a deadline in the offer or by revoking the offer (even if the deadline has not yet passed).
- An offeror's power to revoke an offer can be limited by an enforceable promise to keep the offer open. A promise to keep an offer open may become enforceable because the offeree gave consideration for that promise or because an exception to the requirement of consideration made the promise enforceable.

Applying the Rules

1. At a beauty salon, the stylist offers a client $100 if she will allow the stylist to cut the client's very long hair and donate the locks to a charity that makes wigs for victims of cancer who lose their hair during chemotherapy. Assume the client intends to reject the offer. Would any of the following replies be interpreted as an acceptance?

   a. "Sure. NOT!"
   b. "Yeah. Right."
   c. Would the answer be different if, after the first word of each answer, the client had a brief fit of coughing, at which point the client added the second word?

2. While shopping online for shoes, Chris identified a pair of shoes offered at $300 (expensive, but much less than the list price of $1,500 for this pair). Chris followed the required steps to buy the shoes, providing credit card information, shipping and billing address, clicking the box confirming that Chris had read the site's terms and conditions (even though Chris merely scrolled to the bottom

without glancing at the terms), and making a final click confirming everything was correct and submitting the order. When the shoes arrived, they fit perfectly, but Chris decided they did not look as good as anticipated. When seeking to return the shoes, Chris learned that the terms and conditions for this site provided that all sales are final, allowing no returns (even for shoes that do not fit) unless the shoes are defective. What recourse does Chris have? Would the answer be different if the site allowed returns for a 20 percent restocking fee (here, $60) — a little higher than the 15 percent many sites charge?

3. Terry visited an online store offering clothing, and selected the item, size, and color. The site reported that this item was "In Stock." Terry placed the order, electing standard shipping ("arrives in 3-5 business days"). Instead of an e-mail confirmation, Terry received an e-mail explaining that the particular item was not in stock and had been discontinued by the manufacturer, making back orders impossible. Was a contract formed before the retailer's response, allowing Terry to seek damages from the seller? Would the answer be different if the e-mail reported that the item was out of stock, but would be shipped within two weeks?

4. Following a flood at its storage facility, Newspaper required an emergency shipment of newsprint to continue operations. Byer, Newspaper's procurement officer, called Sirius, Newspaper's usual supplier, which offered to deliver the newsprint the next day (Friday) for $50,000, but only if Newspaper accepted by 3:00 P.M. that day. Byer called several other suppliers, but failed to find a better price. At 2:55 Byer called Sirius, but was put on hold until 3:01. After Byer accepted the earlier offer, Sirius stated that Friday delivery was no longer possible and Saturday delivery would cost an additional $200. Is Sirius legally obligated to perform according to the original offer?

5. George offered to sell two tickets to a Rolling Stones concert to Cameron for $400 each. George later regreted the offer and sent a text revoking it at 9:00 A.M. Unknown to George, Cameron's phone had died, so the text was not available for Cameron to view. At 9:30 A.M., Cameron (using a friend's phone) left a voice message for George accepting the offered tickets. At 1:00 P.M., Cameron obtained a new phone and saw the text revoking the offer. At 1:30 P.M., George noticed a voice mail message and listened to Cameron's acceptance. Did Cameron receive George's revocation before George received Cameron's acceptance?

6. Coal Mine offered to supply all of Utility's requirements for coal for the next five years at a specified price per ton. Utility orally accepted the offer, stating that it would draw up a written agreement for them to sign. The meeting concluded with a handshake and expressions by both parties that they were happy with this deal. Utility prepared and signed a document on the terms agreed and sent it to Coal Mine. Coal Mine never signed the document. When pressed, Coal Mine stated it could not keep the price open for a full five years, but needed an annual adjustment in the contract. Utility would like to enforce the contract

as originally negotiated. How would you argue the oral contract formed during negotiations was binding? Do you anticipate prevailing over the best arguments Coal Mine can raise? (In Chapter 7, you can discuss whether the absence of a writing signed by Coal Mine prevents enforcement even if an offer was accepted.)

Contract Law in Practice

1. When sending a package via overnight delivery, a customer filled out a form prepared by the carrier, but crossed out two provisions: one limiting claims for loss to $100; another stating that personnel at the counter lacked authority to alter the terms of the form. The clerk apparently did not notice the alterations, accepting the package and the money. The package was lost and the customer sought to recover the value of the contents. Craft the best argument you can to persuade a court to rule in favor of your client (either client). Find a classmate who wrote for the opposing party, exchange papers, and prepare a rebuttal to the classmate's argument. Share your rebuttals with each other.

2. In the preceding problem, how would the following additional facts alter your analysis?
   a. The customer called the changes to the clerk's attention; the clerk responded, "Yeah, whatever."
   b. The customer called the changes to the clerk's attention; the clerk noted that he lacked authority to agree to the changes, but did not make the customer fill out a new form.
   c. The package contained a passport. Late arrival forced the recipient to postpone travel to Europe by one day, incurring a $6,000 charge to change the flight.
   d. The package contained irreplaceable family films from the 1960s, for which the customer seeks $100,000.
   e. The package contained a bid on a multimillion dollar contract, which the customer lost because the bid was late. Customer seeks $17 million in lost profits.

3. V, who operates a vineyard, received an offer to purchase all the cabernet franc grapes grown on a specifically identified hillside at a specified price per acre. V accepted the offer, but the e-mail inadvertently read "cabernet sauvignon" grapes grown on that specific hillside. Buyer had visited the property and knew that no cabernet sauvignon grapes were grown on that hillside. V corrected the error three days later, but heard nothing from buyer in response. Weather conditions produced a much smaller crop than expected. After harvest, buyer refused to accept delivery of the grapes, claiming no contract existed. V can resell the grapes, but the small quantity is likely to bring a much lower price

than buyer offered. The amounts in question will justify litigation. Offered the case on a contingency, should you accept? If not, draft a letter explaining to V why you will reject the case. Be specific so V does not waste time seeking out other lawyers for this hopeless cause. If you will take the case, map out the strategy you will use to avoid application of rulings like *Braunstein*. Be specific so V can evaluate whether to invest the time and energy the lawsuit might require. Exchange papers with a classmate. Comment on your classmate's paper, identifying strengths and weaknesses, including any objections you have to the approach taken or the reasoning employed. If you were the client, would you hire this attorney?

4. A senior partner at your firm has asked you to prepare a brief memorandum evaluating offer and acceptance as it applies to the negotiations recounted below. Produce the best argument possible on behalf of Mr. Townsend. If you find the best argument insufficient, explain to your partner why you anticipate Mr. Townsend's case will fail. If you find the best argument persuasive, be sure to explain how it will survive any challenges you anticipate from counsel for DMJM.

> Daniel Townsend [was a vice-president of] DMJM, an architectural and engineering firm. . . . In 1992, Townsend was diagnosed with a terminal illness [and felt some] pressure . . . to quit and apply for disability benefits. Dissatisfied with . . . standard DMJM disability policies, Townsend sought to negotiate an agreement that would allow him to go on disability, thereby reducing company overhead, while maintaining his insurance benefits until his death or age 65. . . . DMJM's president told him to work with William Cavanagh ("Cavanagh"), another vice-president and the company's chief financial officer. . . . Townsend proposed that he . . . (2) . . . go on long-term disability [but continue to] work eight hours per week at one-fifth of his previous salary; and (3) remain employed by DMJM until his death or age 65, whichever came first. This [involved] an exception to DMJM's usual policy [requiring] an employee to work a minimum of 30 hours per week to retain health and life insurance benefits.
>
> On August 8, 1994, Townsend had a conference call with Cavanagh [and others]. Townsend testif[ied] that an agreement was reached with respect to all aspects of his plan, including duration of employment, and others testif[ied] that duration was not specifically discussed.
>
> The next day, Townsend sent a memo to Cavanagh confirming his understanding of the agreement. . . . Cavanagh responded by memo that he . . . "conceptual[ly agreed]," but [deleted the section on employment until death or retirement] "because . . . it implies a guarantee of future employment and benefits, something DMJM is not authorized to do under any circumstances for any employee."
>
> Townsend . . . regarded the statement as Cavanagh's opinion, rather than company policy, so he called Gerald Seelman ("Seelman") . . . (the second highest [officer] in the company), and a personal friend. . . . Townsend . . . told Seelman of his concerns. . . . Seelman told Townsend to go on disability and not worry about the memo because "we have the agreement we talked about" and added "If you can't trust your friends, who can you trust?"

Townsend v. Daniel, Mann, Johnson & Mendenhall, 196 F.3d 1140 (10th Cir. 1999).

5. A developer buying 26 acres of land from seller agreed to pay $50,000 down, $150,000 over time, and a $250,000 mortgage on the property to be repaid by:

> (1) [developer's] construction and conveyance of a 3,100 square foot single-family residence for plaintiff on an undesignated and undefined portion of the property pursuant to plans and specifications to be thereafter agreed upon by the parties, with such property and residence to be conveyed to plaintiff within 48 months of the date of the mortgage, and (2) granting plaintiff the right to have possession of the first townhouse constructed by [developer] on the property no later than 30 months from the date of the mortgage and continuing until a certificate of occupancy is issued for the single family residence.

Wilson v. Ledger, 97 A.D. 3d 1028 (N.Y. App. Div. 2012). Do you anticipate any difficulty with enforcing this provision? Draft a provision that will avoid those difficulties. If sellers need time to find a suitable design for the residence, can that component be postponed without undermining enforceability?

3

Acceptance

It takes two to make a contract. An offer demonstrates one party's willingness to enter an agreement. Acceptance by the offeree remains vital to formation. This chapter covers the rules governing several different ways parties may accept an offer. In the process, it also covers several reasons parties fail to convey an effective acceptance. As with offers, much of the work requires careful interpretation of what the parties said. The rules allow parties room to make a deal in almost any way they desire. Careful attention to the message conveyed can achieve each party's objectives.

Key Concepts

- Requirements of an effective acceptance
- Distinguishing a counteroffer from an acceptance
- Ascertaining whether acceptance takes effect before an offer expires
- Circumstances in which beginning performance accepts an offer or precludes an offeror from revoking the offer
- Circumstances in which silence (or the failure to reject an offer) accepts an offer
- Circumstances in which new terms in an acceptance may become part of the parties' contract under the UCC (sometimes called the battle of the forms)

A. ACCEPTANCE

Acceptance is an expression of assent to the terms of an offer in a manner authorized by the offer.[1] The definition carries several implications, but it can be summarized easily: acceptance must conform to the requirements of the offer.

First, acceptance must be manifest. Deciding to accept does not create a contract until a party acts on that decision. Avoid the words "meeting of the minds"; acceptance requires a meeting of the words or actions. In rare cases—usually

[1] RESTATEMENT (SECOND) OF CONTRACTS §52.

Returning the dog accepts the offer.
Fer Gregory/Shutterstock.com

because the offer so specifies — a failure to object (silence) in the face of an offer may be considered an action, as discussed below. As a rule, however, acceptance requires affirmative steps to communicate the acceptance.

Second, only an offeree can accept. The offeror may direct the offer to individuals or groups, as few or as many people as she desires. Only someone to whom the offer is directed can accept the offer. Further, only an offeree who knows about the offer can accept the offer. One who performs what the offer requested without knowing the offer existed cannot be said to accept the offer. An offeree who learns of the offer before completing performance may accept the offer (and give consideration) by finishing performance. For example, someone might find a lost dog unaware of a reward, but learn of the reward before returning the dog. Returning the dog (finishing the performance) accepts the offer.

Third, the **mirror image rule** requires the substance of the acceptance, its terms, to match the terms of the offer exactly. The offer empowers the offeree to create a binding contract by accepting the offeror's terms — but only those terms. Efforts to alter the terms of the deal, even slightly, do not constitute acceptance — with one statutory exception addressed later.[2] Proposing changes may create a **counteroffer** — a new offer made by the original offeree that the other party (originally the offeror, but the offeree of the counteroffer) can accept or reject, as she sees fit. This rule protects each party's assent by refusing to find a contract until each party has agreed to all terms. Any new variation will not bind a party until she has had an opportunity to reject it. As discussed below, some states have loosened the rule in recent years. It remains the starting point for finding assent.

Fourth, the form of acceptance must comply with any requirements in the offer. If the offer limits the means of acceptance, the response must conform to those limits. An offer may not make specific requirements, in which case any reasonable means of signaling acceptance will suffice. When an offer mentions a particular means of indicating assent, the language may suggest (rather than require) that means. If so, other reasonable means of signaling assent remain available. If, however, an offer requires a specific means of manifesting assent, only that means will operate as an acceptance. For example, in *Fender & Latham, Inc. v. First Union National Bank of South Carolina*,[3] a borrower's oral acceptance did not create a contract where the lender's offer specifically required acceptance in writing.

[2]UCC §2-207.
[3]446 S.E.2d 448 (S.C. Ct. App. 1994).

The form requirement extends beyond the medium of communication (for example, accept by phone, or accept by signing and returning this document). Some specifications, such as a deadline on when acceptance must occur, also limit the offeree's power to accept. People who miss a deadline on a rebate coupon often discover that failure to accept on time precludes recovery.

Most offers seek acceptance in the form of a return promise. The offeror wants some assurance that the other party will perform. A landowner offering to pay a contractor to build a house (or a shopping mall) wants confirmation of the contractor's commitment to perform the work. The contractor could indicate assent by simply starting work, but the landowner usually wants something more definitive. The same applies to the employer offering a job to an employee, a borrower seeking money from a bank, a business seeking to rent space in a building, and so on through a vast array of contracts. As a result, the specifications in an offer usually involve the means by which an offeree can convey a return promise.

Tweeting "I Agree"

Can a tweet or other text message create a contract? Not if the offer specifically requires a different form of communication. But text or tweet might be a reasonable means of expressing acceptance in many circumstances. Texts are no more ephemeral than oral communications, which often suffice. Be careful what you tweet. For example, during an IM conversation discussing ways a web advertiser could increase sales for a seller, the seller sent the message "NO LIMIT," apparently offering to eliminate their contract's previous limit of 200 sales per day. The advertiser responded "awesome!," satisfying a federal court in Florida that the parties had modified their contract.[4]

In some cases, however, offerors prefer (or will tolerate) other means of acceptance. Acceptance by performance, though rarely preferred by offerors, can create a contract under some circumstances. In general, silence or inaction does not accept an offer. Silence by an offeree can signify assent in a few rare situations. Both silence and starting to perform raise special concerns addressed later in this chapter. For now, recognize that an offeror who specifically insists on acceptance by one of these means may make that method the only means of acceptance. While courts may prefer to interpret the offer as inviting rather than requiring these means of acceptance, they generally will give effect to an offer that makes this requirement clear.

1. Acceptance or Counteroffer?

Offerees frequently respond to an offer with more than a simple "Yes" or "I agree." Every additional word in the response creates a risk that the response differs in some way from the offer. Every difference creates a risk that the two communications do not really agree—that the response altered the terms of the deal in some way that the offeror might find objectionable. To meet the requirement of mutual assent, both parties must agree to the same terms—all of them. Until then, negotiations continue.

[4] *CX Digital Media, Inc. v. Smoking Everywhere, Inc.*, No. 09-62020-CIV, 2011 WL 1102782 (S.D. Fla. Mar. 23, 2011).

Sometimes the additional words in a response do not undermine the expression of assent. As a matter of interpretation, the response may constitute an acceptance even if it includes thoughts beyond "Yes." The law has ways to honor the expressed assent even if its communication was complicated by other words. This section addresses the ways in which courts try to honor the intent of the parties and the ways in which they identify that intent.

Rejection and Counteroffer: The Mirror Image Rule

Traditionally, acceptance must match the terms of the offer.[5] Even a slight difference between the terms of the offer and those of the reply prevent the reply from being an acceptance. Courts treated it as a rejection of the offer and the proposal of a counteroffer. Neither party could be held to the other's proposal because it had not agreed to those terms. The offeree has agreed to the changes, but not the original offer without the changes. The offeror has not (yet) agreed to the changes. No matter how minor the variation may seem to outside parties, the offeror may decide for itself whether to accept the change. Treating the reply as a counteroffer gives the (original) offeror a chance to accept the new proposal or to reject it.

This rule serves to protect each party's ability to assent or, more importantly, to reject terms of a proposed deal. That admirable goal, pursued too vigorously, can produce questionable results. In some cases, replies that clearly intended to accept the terms of an offer inadvertently varied a detail of the offer. For example, in *Nebraska Seed Co. v. Harsh*, 152 N.W. 310 (Neb. 1915), a farmer offered a buyer "1800 bu. or thereabouts." The buyer wired an acceptance of "1800 bushels," rather than "about 1800 bushels." The court called this a counteroffer. Seller might not have a full 1800 bushels or might be stuck with a few leftover bushels.

Even when the parties understand exactly what the other meant, a change in terms may preclude contract formation. Recall *United States v. Braunstein*,[6] discussed in Chapter 2: after receiving a bid of ten cents per pound, the government accepted at "ten cents per box," 96 percent less than the bid. The reply obviously meant 10 cents per pound. Yet the government lost its suit because the acceptance did not match the offer. Despite criticism of the result, the decision has not been overruled.

Acceptance: Proposal to Modify

In some cases, courts may interpret a reply as an acceptance even if it contains different or additional terms. Despite the proposed changes, a reply may unambiguously accept an offer. If so, the reply may constitute an acceptance of the terms

[5] Restatement (Second) of Contracts §58.
[6] 75 F. Supp. 137 (S.D.N.Y. 1947), *app. dismissed*, 168 F.2d 749 (2d Cir. 1948).

of the offer.[7] The additional terms are not part of the contract, but a proposal to modify the contract formed by the acceptance. If the original offeror agrees to the proposed modifications, the terms become part of the contract.

This interpretation applies only if the reply suggests changes, rather than insisting on the changes. Thus, if the reply expresses assent *if* the changes are made, no unequivocal assent exists. Conditional language creates a counteroffer.[8]

Try your hand at applying this rule to the following situation: Sellers e-mailed Bayer an offer to sell a farm. Bayer immediately replied with the following e-mail: "I accept. I suggest that we set up an escrow with First National to handle the transaction." A day later, Sellers e-mailed rejecting First National and calling off the deal. Did Bayer's reply accept the offer, creating a binding contract at that time?

Counteroffer Without Rejection: Equivocal Communications

A reply that indicates an intention to consider the offer further falls between acceptance and rejection. Standing alone, such a statement does not reject the offer, but neither does it accept. It simply postpones the time when one of those communications will occur. The reply might include a suggestion of different terms. The original offeror might treat that suggestion as a counteroffer and accept it. But in this context suggesting new terms does not reject the original offer; the expressed intention to think about the offer prevents the counteroffer from operating as a rejection.

For example, in response to an employment offer, the applicant responds: "I'll have to think about it. Of course, if you add a company car, that will seal the deal." The message is fairly clear. The applicant did not accept the offer, but also did not reject it. The proposal of different terms seeks to elicit a better deal. (It probably is a counteroffer, but it might be interpreted as asking the offeror to make a better offer.) If the offeror does not sweeten the pot, the original offer remains on the table.

The same result can occur without a proposed change in terms. Normally, any response that is not an acceptance is a rejection. But an offeree might express a desire to take an offer under advisement. A manifestation of intention to consider an offer further is not a rejection.[9]

Applying these rules to actual communications can pose some difficulty. Consider the following case.

[7] Restatement (Second) of Contracts §61.
[8] *Id.* §59.
[9] *Id.* §38(2).

Case Preview

McReynolds v. Krebs

In this case, a jury awarded Krebs more than a million dollars for injuries sustained in a traffic accident. One issue involved whether the trial ever should have occurred. The defendant tried to accept plaintiff's offer to settle the case for $25,000—the maximum amount available from defendant's liability insurer. The case illustrates how difficult it may be for the parties to know whether an agreement has been reached. Parties make important decisions based on their beliefs about formation, making mistakes potentially costly. To appreciate the court's discussion, you need to know something about liens against the recovery. Basically, those who provide care to a tort victim (usually health care providers who have not been paid or health insurers who paid the providers) are entitled to share in the award if plaintiff recovers amounts that they paid. Their claims to a share of the award represent liens on any payments the plaintiff receives from the defendant.

As you read *McReynolds v. Krebs*, look for the following:

1. Why did plaintiff offer to settle the case for $25,000 when her losses exceeded $1 million?
2. Did the response add a new term? Did the response insist on that term or merely ask plaintiff to consider that term?
3. Why didn't plaintiff accept the new term—or at least discuss it with defendant?
4. Does extrinsic evidence of intent help plaintiff know whether the response was an acceptance or a counteroffer? Does that matter?

McReynolds v. Krebs

290 Ga. 850, 725 S.E.2d 584 (2012)

NAHMIAS, Justice.

Lisa Krebs sued Carmen McReynolds and General Motors (GM) for serious injuries she received when McReynolds's car struck the GM vehicle in which Krebs was a passenger. McReynolds cross-claimed against GM for contribution and set-off. After Krebs settled with GM for an undisclosed amount, the trial court dismissed McReynolds's cross-claims. . . . The jury found McReynolds liable for Krebs's injuries and awarded $1,246,000.42 in damages. The trial court entered judgment against McReynolds for that full amount and denied her motion for new trial.

[T]he Court of Appeals affirmed. We granted certiorari to consider . . . [whether] the Court of Appeals correctly [ruled] that McReynolds's insurer made a counteroffer in response to Krebs's settlement demand. [W]e affirm.

. . .

McReynolds contends that the Court of Appeals erred in upholding the trial court's denial of her motion for summary judgment, in which she argued that she

and Krebs had entered into an enforceable settlement agreement. "'To constitute a contract, the offer must be accepted unequivocally and without variance of any sort. . . . A purported acceptance of a plaintiff's settlement offer which imposes conditions . . . will be construed as a counter-offer to the offer to settle for the [insurance] policy limits.'" *Frickey v. Jones*, 280 Ga. 573, 574, 630 S.E.2d 374 (2006) [citations omitted]. "'[T]he circumstances surrounding the making of the contract, such as correspondence and discussions, are relevant in deciding if there was a mutual assent to an agreement, and courts are free to consider such extrinsic evidence.'" Id. at 575, 630 S.E.2d 374 [citation omitted].

On August 24, 2005, Krebs offered to settle her claims against McReynolds for the bodily injury limit available under McReynolds's insurance policy, specifying that the offer would expire on September 6, 2005. On September 1, 2005, McReynolds's insurance carrier faxed this response:

> Our limits are $25,000/$50,000 and we agree to settle this matter for the $25,000 per person limit. Please call me in order to discuss how the lien(s) (Specifically, but not limited to the $273,435.35 lien from Grady Memorial Hospital) will be resolved as part of this settlement.

McReynolds argues that the sentence about liens was merely a request for information and not the introduction of a new condition of settlement. However, McReynolds's insurer did not merely inquire about the existence or amount of the liens against Krebs's causes of action, which it already knew far exceeded the bodily injury limit on McReynolds's policy. Instead, the insurer wrote that counsel needed to "discuss how the lien(s) . . . will be *resolved as part of this settlement*." (Emphasis added.) Krebs's offer had made no mention of liens, nor did it contemplate any particular resolution of the hospital lien . . . or any other liens as a condition of settlement. As we explained in *Frickey*, while a "mere request for confirmation that no liens exist" will not transform a purported acceptance into a counteroffer, an added condition involving the "*resolution* of . . . actual and potential liens of the health care providers" will. 280 Ga. at 575, 576, n. 2, 630 S.E.2d 374 (emphasis in original). Thus, like the trial court and the Court of Appeals, we construe the response by McReynolds's insurer to Krebs's settlement offer, proposing to resolve the hospital and other liens "as part of this settlement," as a counteroffer rather than an unconditional and unequivocal acceptance. Accordingly, no binding settlement agreement was formed.

Judgment affirmed.

MELTON, Justice, concurring in part and dissenting in part.

[B]ecause I believe that McReynolds' insurance carrier fully accepted Krebs' offer to settle her claims rather than making a counteroffer, I respectfully dissent. . . . In response to Krebs' offer to settle for the bodily injury limit of McReynolds' policy, McReynolds' insurance carrier responded [as quoted above]. McReynolds' insurer stated an unequivocal agreement to pay policy limits. Then, it merely requested a phone call to discuss outstanding liens. Nothing more. Ostensibly, McReynolds' insurance carrier was simply trying to determine to whom Krebs wished the check to be sent.

This is in sharp contrast to *Frickey,* a case in which extrinsic evidence proved that an insurer issued a counteroffer to an initial offer to settle a claim. In *Frickey,* State Farm was presented with an offer to settle a claim for $100,000, and State Farm responded by facsimile dated June 25, 2003 (with a copy sent by certified mail), stating its willingness to tender $100,000 as full settlement of all claims, "upon receipt of the fully executed release enclosed. Obviously, payment is complicated by what appears to be a Grady Hospital lien as well as potential liens by your client's health carrier. Please advise me of the status of these liens."

. . . [S]ubsequent correspondence from State Farm . . . explicitly indicated that " 'State Farm offered to tender the policy limits of $100,000 to [the plaintiff] in *June 2003 if [the plaintiff was] able to resolve the Grady Hospital lien as well as potential liens by [the plaintiff's] health carriers.'* " (Emphasis in original.) Id. at 575. We emphasized that we were relying on State Farm's own characterization of its settlement response which clearly indicated that State Farm considered resolution of outstanding liens a condition precedent to a binding settlement. We further emphasized that "[w]e do not suggest, however, that the mere request for confirmation that no liens exist renders an 'acceptance a counteroffer which rejects the plaintiff's offer.' " Id. at 576, n. 2.

. . . Unlike *Frickey,* there is no additional extrinsic evidence which alters the nature of McReynolds' insurance carrier's unequivocal statement that "we agree to settle this matter for the $25,000 per person limit." There is no requirement that other liens be resolved first in the settlement acceptance, and there is no subsequent correspondence which indicates that any such additional condition was required or expected. To the contrary, the letter here gives an unequivocal acceptance and then a simple request for a phone call to discuss outstanding liens. The call is neither a mandatory requirement (the request is prefaced by "please" rather than "you must") nor a condition precedent to payment. [I]t is merely a request for information, not a counteroffer. Accordingly, there was an offer and acceptance of a settlement in this case, and the resulting contract should be enforced.

Post-Case Follow-Up

A lot was riding on whether the offeree's response was interpreted as requiring settlement of the liens or just inquiring how the liens affect distribution of the proceeds. A strict application of the mirror image rule might have made it unreasonable for defendant to think the case had settled. But the court applies a rule that leaves room for parties to mention new topics without negating their acceptance, so the details of the communications become significant. Even after the fact, justices of the Georgia Supreme Court differed regarding whether defendant accepted. Perhaps defendant should have been more cautious in confirming the deal (or more alert to the plaintiff's failure to respond to efforts to finalize the transaction). Still, the relatively subtle distinctions drawn by the justices suggest parties may have difficulty knowing how their responses ultimately will be perceived by the courts.

McReynolds v. Krebs: Real Life Applications

1. A real estate company offered to buy a pool of 35 foreclosed properties from Fannie Mae. The offeror explicitly noted that its lender would take a mortgage on the properties to secure the loan. After the offeror had paid a nonrefundable $100,000 deposit, Fannie Mae noted that lenders could not take a mortgage on the property. The offeror tried but failed to find different financing. Fannie Mae accepted the offeror's bid and, when the offeror failed to pay, kept the deposit as damages for breach. Did the real estate company breach a contract with Fannie Mae? *See REO Acquisition Group v. Federal National Mortgage Assn.*, No. 13-CV-1953, 2015 WL 2346336 (D.D.C. May 15, 2015).
2. A bank offered to modify the mortgage terms for distressed borrowers. The borrowers signed the bank documents, but corrected the spelling of their first names on the documents. The bank later sought to enforce the terms of the original mortgage. Was the modification effective?
3. After owner's death, his daughter and his companion disputed ownership of several parcels of land. To settle the litigation, counsel for the daughter prepared a settlement agreement and submitted it to counsel for the companion. Counsel for the companion added some terms and sent the revised agreement to daughter's counsel. Counsel for daughter, by e-mail, responded, "The changes are fine." Daughter later refused to sign the agreement. Should the court enforce the agreement? Would your answer differ if daughter's counsel's response had been oral rather than by e-mail? *See Estate of Briggs*, 449 S.W.3d 421 (Mo. Ct. App. 2014).

---

2. Timing of Assent

Many problems of assent involve timing. Each party, at some point, was willing to enter the deal. But one changed its mind and tried to withdraw its assent. In somewhat rarer cases, a party that refused a deal tries to revive it before that refusal has become effective. Contract formation depends on whether the assent was complete before the withdrawal took effect. If an offer was accepted before the withdrawal of assent took effect, the contract was formed and remains binding. If, however, the contract was not yet formed at the time the withdrawal of assent took effect, no contract is formed.

Offers become effective when received by the offeree. Until the offeree knows of the offer, no acceptance can occur. Once the offer is effective, the offeree can accept at any time until the offer terminates.

An offer terminates when:

1. The offeror revokes the offer;
2. It expires due to lapse of time;
3. The offeree rejects the offer;

4. The offeree makes a counteroffer;
5. Either the offeree or the offeror dies or suffers an incapacity;
6. A condition of acceptance no longer can occur.[10]

If any of these takes effect before the acceptance takes effect, then the offer was not open at the time of acceptance and no contract was formed. But if acceptance takes effect before the offer terminated, a contract was formed.

The previous chapter introduced the topic of revocation by the offeror and the limits on the offeror's ability to revoke the offer. This chapter raises some of the same issues, focusing on the ways in which the offeree's conduct may affect the continued vitality of an offer and the ways in which acceptance occurs.

Time of Acceptance: The Mailbox Rule

Most written communications take effect when received, as discussed in Chapter 2.[11] That rule governs revocations, rejections (including counteroffers), and acceptances. In many circumstances, however, acceptances take effect before receipt; the moment it is "put out of the offeree's possession, without regard to whether it ever reaches the offeror."[12] This approach is sometimes called the **mailbox rule** because it originated in cases where an offeree put an acceptance out of its control by depositing it in a mailbox. The rule applies to any mode of assent authorized by the offer, not just mail. (A mode of assent not authorized by the offer is ineffective at any time.)[13] For instantaneous communications, dispatch and receipt occur simultaneously, making it unnecessary to discuss which occurred first. The rule might apply even to very fast communications—e-mail, for example—if a gap occurred between the time one party hit send and the time it arrived at the recipient's designated location.

Timing of an acceptance matters when an offer might terminate before acceptance. Making acceptance effective upon dispatch means an offeree must send the acceptance before the offer lapses or either party dies or becomes incapacitated. (It also gives effect to an acceptance sent before the offeree rejects the offer or makes a counteroffer, though these situations are rarer.) Perhaps most important, the acceptance is effective when it is sent before the offeree receives a revocation. See Exhibit 3.1.

That bears repeating: if acceptance is *sent* before a revocation is *received*, the acceptance is effective and a contract is formed. This is the primary function of the mailbox rule.

This general rule has three exceptions:

1. improperly dispatched messages;
2. offers that require receipt of an acceptance;
3. option contracts.

---

[10]Restatement (Second) of Contracts §36.
[11]*Id.* §68.
[12]*Id.* §63.
[13]*Id.* §60.

EXHIBIT 3.1 Mailbox Rule

	Revocation **sent**	Revocation **received**
Acceptance sent **before**	Contract	Contract
Acceptance sent **after**	Contract	**None**

Each exception deserves a brief discussion.

First, acceptance is not effective upon dispatch unless the offeree takes ordinary precautions to ensure its proper delivery.[14] For example, mail must be properly addressed and carry the correct postage. It must be deposited in an appropriate place: dropping regular postal mail in a FedEx box (or vice versa) won't count. E-mail must be properly addressed and (probably) must satisfy any limits the sender's e-mail service places on messages (for example, size limits on attachments). Ordinary precautions for senders may not include limits imposed by the addressee's e-mail service if unknown to the sender.

Second, the offeror can specify in the offer when an acceptance takes effect. An offeror may specify that acceptance will be effective only upon receipt by the offeror, avoiding the risk of being bound to a contract without receiving any notice of acceptance.

Third, under option contracts, acceptance occurs only upon receipt by the offeror.[15] (See discussion in Chapter 2.) An option prevents revocation from having any effect. As long as the offeree accepts before the option period expires, the acceptance is effective. Even a counteroffer or rejection will not prevent a timely acceptance from having effect. The option contract protects the offeree from revocation, making it less important to accelerate the time at which acceptance occurs. Requiring receipt of the acceptance poses less risk for the offeree in this setting.

An option contract allows the offeree time to decide whether to accept, but does not replace the need to accept the offer in a timely and effective manner. The offeree may decide not to exercise the option (not to accept the offer) if it prefers. An offeree who misses the deadline for acceptance, for whatever reason, has not created a contract. If a revocation fools the offeree into believing acceptance would be futile, the revocation may have its desired effect.

---

[14] *Id.* §66. An improperly dispatched acceptance may be effective upon dispatch if it actually reaches an offeror in the same time it would have taken a properly dispatched acceptance to arrive. *Id.* §67.

[15] *Id.* §63(b).

Lapse of Time

Offers expire from the passage of time if either

1. the offer specifies a time when it expires; or
2. a reasonable time elapses without an acceptance.

A reasonable time varies with the circumstances.

The mode of communication may affect how much time is reasonable. Offers made face to face, or using an instantaneous means of communication (such as a telephone), typically expire when the conversation ends. The offeror, of course, may specify that the offer remains open longer. Offers made by other means, such as by mail, typically allow offeree to accept on the day of receipt.

A reasonable time may vary with the volatility of the market involved. An offer to sell real estate may not expire quickly because real estate prices change relatively slowly. (Most offerors of real estate will specify when an offer expires instead of letting a court decide how much time was reasonable.) An offer to buy or sell a stock may expire more quickly, because stock prices change by the minute. Allowing the offeree to wait to see how the price would change before accepting the offer gives more power than the offeror probably intended to convey. Because the offeror controls how long an offer stays open, courts seem likely to consider how long the offeror probably intended the offer to remain open when deciding how much time is reasonable. In effect, the courts fill in for the offeror an amount of time that she seems likely to have chosen if asked at the time the offer was made.

Rejection and Counteroffer

A rejection or counteroffer terminates an offer. Once the offer is rejected, the offeree loses the power to accept the offer. Rejection, however, takes effect upon receipt by the offeror.

In some circumstances, an offer may remain open despite language that seems like a rejection or counteroffer. One example was discussed above: when an offeree states an intention to think about the offer before responding, a suggestion of different terms will not terminate the offer, even if it operates as a counteroffer. However, a rejection, rather than a suggestion for different terms, probably would end the offer, in effect indicating that the time for thinking about the offer was concluded. The response "Let me think about it. . . . No!" seems a clear rejection, not a desire to consider the matter further.

In addition, an offeror may reopen an offer after a rejection or counteroffer. The offeror may manifest an intention to keep the offer open longer. Technically, the rejection or counteroffer terminates the original offer, but the offeror makes a new offer on identical terms. In any event, the offer remains available for the offeree to accept until some other event terminates it.

Finally, rejection or counteroffer does not terminate an offer that is held open by an option contract. Having paid for the right to postpone decision, the offeree retains that power even if, while considering the offer, the offeree asks about different terms. Without the option contract, that might be a counteroffer that would terminate the offer. The option keeps the offer open despite those remarks.

Try your hand at applying this rule to the following situation: Leslie offered to sell a house to Terry for $700,000, agreeing (in exchange for $5) to keep the offer open for 30 days. After 10 days, Terry proposed changing the price to $680,000, but Leslie never responded. After 20 days, Terry delivered an acceptance to Leslie (along with the down payment and other required documents). Is Terry's acceptance timely?

Try your hand at applying this rule to the following situation: Leslie offered to sell a house to Terry for $700,000, agreeing (in exchange for $5) to keep the offer open for 30 days. After 10 days, Terry rejected the offer, telling Leslie to sell it to someone else. After 20 days, Terry delivered an acceptance to Leslie (along with the down payment and other required documents). Leslie, however, already had offered the house to Chris.

The same problem can arise without an option. A party who sent a rejection of an ordinary offer might later dispatch an acceptance — which would be effective immediately upon dispatch, perhaps before the rejection arrived. Conduct of this sort is rare, but has occurred.

Conflicting signals could pose problems for an offeror, especially if the rejection or counteroffer arrived before the acceptance arrived. The offeror might rely on the rejection and make a contract with someone else, only to discover that an effective acceptance had already been made. An offeror that can perform both contracts (such as a seller with an ample supply of the goods at issue) may face no problem. An employer with one job to fill — or an employee who can accept only one job — may face more serious difficulty if both contracts are binding.

If the acceptance is received before the rejection or counteroffer, the offeror faces no prejudice. The normal rule, that the acceptance was effective upon dispatch, works no hardship in these cases. The legally effective answer arrived first, so no reliance on the wrong answer would exist.

Problems arise if the rejection or counteroffer, sent before the acceptance was dispatched, is received before the acceptance was received. Courts treat the attempted acceptance as if it is a counteroffer, not an acceptance. As a counteroffer, the attempted acceptance allows the original offeror either to accept these terms (which he proposed originally) or to reject them. This power is not limited to situations where the offeror has already made another deal or relied on the rejection. The offeror may reject the acceptance/counteroffer if, for any reason, she has changed her mind. (For example, the offeree's original rejection of the offer may affect the offeror's enthusiasm for entering a contract with the offeree.)

A rejection dispatched after an acceptance poses practical problems, not conceptual ones. The rejection has no effect. The acceptance was effective when sent; nothing the offeree does afterward prevents the offeror from treating the acceptance as final. However, the offeror may treat the rejection or counteroffer as an offer to **rescind** (to cancel) the contract. The offeror can insist on the contract, but can release the offeree by accepting the offer to rescind. That alternative is important, especially if the rejection arrives before the acceptance. Knowing only about the rejection, an offeror may rely on it, making other commitments that interfere with the ability or willingness to perform the contract with the offeree. Treating the rejection as an offer to rescind protects the offeror.

Death or Incapacity

Death or incapacity of either the offeror or the offeree normally terminates the offer. The rule has been criticized but remains in effect with a few statutory exceptions (such as powers of attorney by servicemen). Occasional exceptions arise. For instance, the offeree's incapacity may permit her to enter voidable contracts. Because the offeree retains some power to contract, courts may recognize an acceptance as effective. It also seems likely that a temporary incapacity, such as intoxication, will not prevent acceptance by a sober person of an offer made by a sober person, even if intoxication occurred after the offer and before the acceptance. In short, good reasons for recognizing a contract can erode the rule that death or incapacity terminates an offer.

Conditions

Offers may contain **conditions**, events that must occur for the power of acceptance to arise. Conditions express limits on a party's willingness to deal with another; unless the condition occurs, the deal never comes into existence. For instance, a buyer might offer to buy all of its computers from one provider, if the provider (within a certain time) divests its holdings in a nation with a poor record on civil rights. Divestiture must occur before the seller's acceptance will create a contract. If timely divestiture becomes impossible, the condition cannot occur, and the offer terminates.

Conditions need not be in one party's control. For instance, the offer might be conditioned on one candidate winning the next presidential election. That offer could not be accepted before the election — and if the wrong candidate won, could not be accepted at all.

Some conditions may be implied from circumstances. For example, rewards for information concerning a crime might go to the first person to provide useful information. Being the first is a condition on the ability to accept. Once one person has provided an important piece of information, others providing the same information do not satisfy the condition. (Rewards might be split between parties providing different pieces of useful information, depending on the terms of the reward offer.)

Some conditions affect performance rather than assent. For instance, an offer of marriage might be conditioned on one party moving to the other's home town. Worded one way, this offer could be accepted immediately. The contract (engagement) occurs

Different Contexts for Conditions

Conditions arise in several contexts. Contract terms may specify conditions on a party's duty to perform. For instance, life insurance pays upon a party's death; death is a condition of payment. Chapter 11 addresses conditions within a contract. Here, the issue involves conditions on formation, not conditions on performance. One condition is acceptance; no contract exists until the offeree accepts. But the offer may express other conditions that limit the power of acceptance. The text here addresses those kinds of conditions.

immediately, but the performance (marriage) does not become due until and unless the offeree moves. Worded differently, the same condition could limit the power of acceptance, so that no engagement could occur until after the move. (Perhaps, "You may accept this proposal within 30 days after moving to Chicago" — although that language is one reason to reject the proposal on the spot.)

B. ACCEPTANCE BY PERFORMANCE

Acceptance often takes the form of written or oral communication. The offeree agrees to perform the obligations the offeror proposed in the offer. In some cases, however, the offeree begins to perform without making any verbal commitment. Conduct, like any other manifestation, can signal acceptance. The effect of conduct depends largely on whether the offer either allows or requires acceptance via conduct. The offeror, as master of the offer, may require a promise. But the offer may permit, or even require, other means of communicating assent.

The two basic situations can be summarized as follows:

- If an offer allows acceptance by either a promise or a performance, then beginning performance accepts the offer. The conduct serves as a promise to finish performance.[16]
- If an offer requires acceptance by performance (that is, not by promise), then completing performance accepts the offer. Beginning performance creates an option, making the offer irrevocable until the offeree has a reasonable opportunity to complete performance.[17]

You might wonder why an offeror would want a performance instead of a promise. In some contexts, promises have no value. The owner of a lost dog who offers a reward does not want phone calls from people promising to find the dog. She wants to hear from the one person who found the dog when she returns the dog. Other rewards — say, for information about a crime — follow the same pattern. In other situations, performance will be faster if the offeree starts immediately instead of sending a promise first and then beginning to perform. That might suit both the offeror and the offeree. While an offeror frequently will want the assurance that an express promise provides, there are occasions when an offeror might not exclude performance as a permissible mode of acceptance.

1. Offers Inviting Promise or Performance

If an offer invites acceptance by either a promise or a performance, then beginning to perform accepts the offer. Beginning to perform is treated as a promise to perform. Starting indicates an intent to accept the offer, communicating an acceptance as clearly as any words. Because beginning performance accepts an offer, the

[16] Restatement (Second) of Contracts §62.
[17] *Id.* §45.

offeree must complete performance. If she changes her mind and decides to stop performing, she breaches. Having accepted, the contract binds both the offeree and the offeror.

For sales of goods, the UCC permits a party who begins performance to negate the acceptance by promptly notifying the offeror that she does not intend to accept the offer.[18] This response permits an offeree to help the offeror by offering part of the performance requested without committing to perform the entire contract. The approach may extend beyond sales of goods.[19]

Offers may fail to specify clearly whether they require performance as the only means of acceptance or, alternatively, invite acceptance by either a promise or performance. When clear, the offeror's specification governs. When ambiguous, courts tend to treat either mode of acceptance as permissible. Thus, the offeree may choose whether to make a promise first or simply to start performance. This preference probably matches the intent of offerors, who can count on offerees to complete performance more often under this rule. When acceptance by performance is invited, either an express promise or starting performance binds the offeree. Treating the offer as requiring acceptance by performance means neither an express promise nor starting performance would bind the offeree, providing the offeror with considerably less comfort.

2. Offers Requiring Acceptance by Performance: Unilateral Contracts

If an offer requires acceptance by performance, the only way to accept is to perform. Acceptance occurs when performance is complete, not when the offeree begins. Because the contract becomes binding after one party has already completed performance, proposals of this type sometimes are called **unilateral contracts**. Only one party, the offeror, incurs duties under the contract. The offeree has already finished performing at the time the acceptance takes effect. Thus, the offeree's duties are discharged at the moment of contract formation.

The offeree can stop performing at any time, without incurring any liability to the offeror. No acceptance occurs before completion, so no contract yet exists for the offeree to breach. The offeree should be sure that the offer required acceptance by performance; if the offer merely invited either a promise or performance, then quitting is breach.

[18] UCC §2-206(1)(b).
[19] RESTATEMENT (SECOND) OF CONTRACTS §53.

Case Preview

Vanegas v. American Energy Services

In this case, the court addressed an employer's efforts to encourage employees to remain with a company despite concerns for their future. Concerns for the company's viability gave employees an incentive to look for other jobs immediately. Losing key employees might hasten the firm's demise, giving the employer a reason to want employees to remain as long as possible. The case introduces you to contracts at will: here, employment contracts that have no duration term. Either party could end the employment at will without breaching the contract because neither had promised that the employment would continue for any fixed period of time. The case also introduces employment manuals, a combination of rules and benefits an employer creates to address a variety of workplace issues. Employers need to revise these from time to time. The case introduces the way contract law might inhibit this revision.

As you read *Vanegas v. American Energy Services*, look for the following:

1. Could the employees accept this offer by promising to remain or was performance the only way to accept it?
2. Did the employer ever intend to pay the promised bonus? Is there any evidence of an initial intent not to pay? Should that intent matter?
3. How did the employees accept the offer? Did the offeror receive any notice of their acceptance? Does that matter?

Vanegas v. American Energy Services

302 S.W.3d 299 (Tex. 2009)

Justice Green delivered the opinion of the Court.

In this case, we are asked to decide the enforceability of an employer's alleged promise to pay five percent of the proceeds of a sale or merger of the company to employees who are still employed at the time of the sale or merger. The employer, American Energy Services (AES), argues that because these were at-will employees, any promise was illusory and therefore not enforceable — the company could have avoided the promise by firing the employees at any time. The employees respond that the promise represented a unilateral contract, and by staying on with the company until AES Acquisition, Inc. acquired AES several years later, they performed on the contract, making it enforceable. We agree with the employees; continuing their employment with the company until it was sold would constitute performance under such a unilateral contract, making the promise enforceable, regardless of whether that promise may have been considered illusory at the time it was made. We therefore reverse the court of appeals' judgment and remand the case to the trial court to consider the merits.

I

AES was formed in the summer of 1996. AES hired the petitioners in this case (collectively, the employees) that same year. The employees allege that in an operational meeting in June 1997, they voiced concerns to John Carnett, a vice president of AES, about the continued viability of the company. The employees complained that the company required them to work long hours with antiquated equipment. The employees allege that, in an effort to provide an incentive for them to stay with the company, Carnett promised the employees, who were at-will and therefore free to leave the company at any time, that "in the event of sale or merger of AES, the original [eight] employees remaining with AES at that time would get 5% of the value of any sale or merger of AES." AES Acquisition, Inc. acquired AES in 2001. Seven of the eight original employees were still with AES at the time of the acquisition. Those remaining employees demanded their proceeds, and when the company refused to pay, the employees sued, claiming AES breached the oral agreement.

. . .

II

. . .

The issue turns on the distinction between bilateral and unilateral contracts. "A bilateral contract is one in which there are mutual promises between two parties to the contract, each party being both a promisor and a promisee." [Citation omitted.] A unilateral contract, on the other hand, is "created by the promisor promising a benefit if the promisee performs. The contract becomes enforceable when the promisee performs." [Citations omitted.] [The court of appeals relied on cases that] concerned *bilateral* contracts in which employers made promises in exchange for employees' promises not to compete with their companies after termination [citation omitted]. The court of appeals' explanation of these cases — describing an exchange of promises where one party makes an illusory promise and the other a non-illusory promise — describes the attempted formation of a *bilateral* contract, not a unilateral contract. [Citation omitted.] Our discussion [in those cases] was confined to situations where a non-illusory promise could salvage an otherwise ineffective bilateral contract by transforming it into a unilateral contract, enforceable upon performance. This was not a blanket pronouncement about unilateral contracts in general.[2]

The court of appeals held that even if AES promised to pay the employees the five percent, that promise was illusory at the time it was made because the employees

---

[2]In fact, *Williston on Contracts* disapproves of the use of the term "unilateral contract" to describe an agreement in which one of the promises in a bilateral contract fails:

> [T]he term unilateral contract should be reserved for cases in which a legal obligation has been created, but only one party to the obligation has made a promise. When there is no obligation, the transaction may be a unilateral promise or a unilateral offer, but it cannot properly be called a unilateral contract. Thus, for example, when the promisor seeks a return promise and obtains an illusory promise, his or her own undertaking may properly be characterized as unilateral; but since no enforceable obligation exists, it is not properly called a unilateral contract.

1 Williston on Contracts §1.17.

were at-will, and AES could have fired all of them prior to the acquisition. 224 S.W.3d at 549. But whether the promise was illusory at the time it was made is irrelevant; what matters is whether the promise became enforceable by the time of the breach. [Citations omitted.] Almost all unilateral contracts begin as illusory promises. Take, for instance, the classic textbook example of a unilateral contract: "I will pay you $50 if you paint my house." The offer to pay the individual to paint the house can be withdrawn at any point prior to performance. But once the individual accepts the offer by performing, the promise to pay the $50 becomes binding. The employees allege that AES made an offer to split five percent of the proceeds of the sale or merger of the company among any remaining original employees. Assuming that allegation is true, the seven remaining employees accepted this offer by remaining employed for the requested period of time. [Citation omitted.] At that point, AES's promise became binding. AES then breached its agreement with the employees when it refused to pay the employees their five percent share.

Furthermore, the court of appeals' holding would potentially jeopardize all pension plans, vacation leave, and other forms of compensation made to at-will employees that are based on a particular term of service. *Corbin on Contracts* observed as much in discussing the court of appeals' opinion in this case:

> The court's analysis may attempt to prove too much. The argument that a promise to grant a raise to a terminable-at-will employee is necessarily illusory raises the question, why is an employer's original promise to pay a certain wage to an at-will employee enforceable when the employee performs? The court's analysis would suggest that the employer's promise was never enforceable. If an at-will employee is hired at a promised compensation and performs for some period, the court's analysis would suggest that the promised rate of compensation was never enforceable.

John E. Murray, Jr. & Timothy Murray, Corbin on Contracts §1.17 (Supp. Fall 2009). We agree that the court of appeals' opinion could have far-reaching adverse effects on well-established forms of compensation.

The fact that the employees were at-will and were already being compensated in the form of their salaries in exchange for remaining employed also does not make the promise to pay the bonus any less enforceable.

> It is now recognized that these are not pure gratuities but compensation for services rendered. The employer's promise is not enforceable when made, but the employee can accept the offer by continuing to serve as requested, even though the employee makes no promise. There is no mutuality of obligation, but there is consideration in the form of service rendered. The employee's one consideration, rendition of services, supports all of the employer's promises, to pay the salary and to pay the bonus.

2 Corbin on Contracts §6.2; [other citations omitted]. Therefore, any promise to pay sale or merger proceeds became an enforceable unilateral contract when the employees performed.

III

AES allegedly promised to pay any remaining original employees five percent of the proceeds when AES was sold. Assuming AES did make such an offer, the seven

remaining employees accepted the offer by staying with AES until the sale. Regardless of whether the promise was illusory at the time it was made, the promise became enforceable upon the employees' performance. The court of appeals erred in holding otherwise. Accordingly, we reverse the court of appeals' judgment and remand the case to the trial court for further proceedings consistent with this opinion. Tex. R. App. P. 60.2(d).

Post-Case Follow-Up

The court spends considerable time discussing whether the initial offer was illusory, a topic taken up in Chapter 5. If the employer could refuse to pay on a whim and yet not be held liable for breach, then it made no promise in the first place. The right to fire the employees left the employer room to avoid performance if the employees were fired. By not firing the employees before the sale, however, the ability to refuse to perform disappeared. In effect, the essential condition of the promise (employment until sale) could have been prevented from occurring by either the employees (who could quit) or the employer (who could fire them). But once the condition occurred, the illusory nature of the promise disappeared. The employees, having done what the employer asked them to do, accepted the offer in the manner the offeror anticipated.

Vanegas v. American Energy Services: Real Life Applications

1. You have been consulted by Jan, an at-will employee, who recently received notice that the company had been restructured and the office would be closed. To encourage employees to remain with the office (instead of seeking new jobs immediately), company officials said, "Whatever you do, don't quit," pointing out that the company's policy manual provided substantial severance pay to employees if they waited for the company to let them go when the office closed. Jan showed you the policy manual, which contains the following language: "[Employer] reserves the right to change or rescind, in whole or in part, at any time and without liability to anyone, the policies, principles and practices stated in this manual." Jan conveyed her fear that waiting will make it harder to find a new job, as some employees will leave early, taking the best openings that arise. Jan's years of service, however, make the severance promise in the manual substantial. Jan is concerned that the employer may try to avoid paying the promised severance despite the encouragement to stay. How would you advise Jan?
2. Sam publishes an online directory of service providers in the vicinity of Santiago, California. Persons interested in being listed submit order forms containing their information and any advertising material they wish included in the directory. The form specifies that the person submitting the form may withdraw

the order at any time before it is posted, but promises to pay the specified fee once the listing appears online. Recently, Sam was sued by Chris, who submitted an order form, but whose listing was never included in the directory. Sam seeks your advice on whether the failure to post the listing was a breach of contract. If so, advise Sam how to avoid liability for any future oversights of this sort. *See Papa v. New York Tel. Co.*, 72 N.Y.2d 879, 528 N.E.2d 512 (1988).

3. Lani owns an apartment building, but has had trouble making the payments on the mortgage. After discussions, Banco, the lender, agreed that it would not foreclose on the property if Lani could obtain a refinancing proposal (on specific terms) prior to December 1. On November 15, Lani presented Banco with a proposal from Insco, a reputable lender, that satisfied the requirements Banco specified. Banco decided to foreclose on the property despite the impending refinancing. Advise Banco whether it remains free to foreclose on the property despite its promise not to foreclose. *See Lick Creek Sewer Systems, Inc. v. Bank of Bourbon*, 747 S.W.2d 317 (Mo. Ct. App. 1988).

4. ConCo agreed to buy 20 electrical converters (for use in a weapons system ordered by NATO) from SubCo for $2,200 each. Later, ConCo offered to buy an additional 30 converters for $2,000 each—a discount the parties had discussed for future orders. SubCo ordered the materials for the additional 30 converters and began work on manufacturing them. E-mails from SubCo to ConCo include statements that work on the second order was progressing much faster than work on the original order. ConCo revoked the order for the additional 30 converters when NATO cancelled its order for the weapons system. Had a contract for the additional 30 units been formed or did ConCo remain free to cancel its order? *See SEC America v. Marine Electric Systems, Inc.*, 39 A.3d 1054 (Vt. 2011).

Revocation of Unilateral Offers

The normal rule—that an offeror may revoke an offer at any time before acceptance—creates special risks when only performance can accept an offer. Because acceptance takes effect upon completion of performance, the offeree would face a serious risk. Revocation might occur after she begins performance, perhaps only moments before she completes performance. In the *Vanegas* court's example about the offer to paint the house, the court implied the offeror could revoke the offer when the work was nearly completed, despite the losses (time and materials, not to mention profit) that would impose on the painter.

The law addresses this risk by limiting the power of an offeror to revoke offers once the offeree has relied on the promise. In effect, the law creates an option contract to protect the offeree. Several overlapping and sometimes inconsistent doctrines provide protection against revocation of unilateral offers.

If an offer can be accepted by a promise or performance, the offeree does not need an option to avoid the risk. An offeree can accept by promising to perform, thus binding both parties to a bilateral contract. In this situation, courts interpret beginning performance as promise, accepting the offer and creating a binding contract.[20] In addition, a **tender** of performance — an offer to perform with the "manifest present ability to do so"[21] — or a tender of a beginning of performance will have the same effect as beginning performance. For example, consider how a photographer might begin, tender a beginning, or tender performance of a promise to take a family portrait for buyer.

- Beginning: photographer snaps the first shot of the posed family.
- Tender a beginning: photographer, with camera in hand at a place suitable for the sitting, states that she is ready to begin taking photos.
- Tender: photographer extends the finished prints to the family.

In this example, tender of performance comes long after tendering a beginning. But if the duty involved paying money, a party might tender complete performance by holding the entire amount in hand (spread out to demonstrate that it is all there) and extending it to the recipient. (Even extending a credit card might suffice.) The payer might not let go until the seller tenders her performance, extending the goods for her to take. In that case, tendering a beginning might involve tendering the first installment.

Steps that precede tender may not suffice. Preparing to perform does not actually begin to perform or tender performance. The rules stated here give effect to performance or tender, not to all forms of reliance that precede performance or tender.

Try your hand at applying this rule to the following situation: To perform a duty to photograph a family portrait, a photographer goes to the family home, sets up appropriate lighting in the designated location, sets up the camera on a tripod, helps pose the family, and then snaps the first shot. At what point did the photographer's preparations to perform cross the line and become beginning to perform?

Where an offer cannot be accepted by a promise, these same acts create an option. Once the offeree begins performance, tenders performance, or tenders a beginning of performance, the offeror cannot revoke the offer — at least, not until the offeree has been allowed a reasonable amount of time to finish performance.[22] Preparations to perform do not create an option until the preparations begin or tender something to the offeror — at least not under the traditional rule.

The offeror retains some power to terminate the offer if the offeree abandons the transaction. Beginning does not constitute acceptance, so the offeree may back out at any time. The offeror must be free to obtain substitute performance if this occurs. But the offeror cannot frustrate the offeree's efforts to complete performance by purporting to revoke the offer in the middle of the offeree's performance.

---

[20] Restatement (Second) of Contracts §62.
[21] *Id.* §238.
[22] *Id.* §45.

Case Preview

Sylvestre v. Minnesota

In this case, an employer who had promised a pension to employees, who were state court judges, tried to adjust the terms of the pension in order to reduce costs. Rather than negotiate a contract modification, the state passed an amendment to the statute that provided the pensions. The court had to evaluate whether that statute impaired the contract rights of the employees.

As you read *Sylvestre v. Minnesota*, look for the following:

1. How did the court determine that the statute was an offer? How did it decide whether the offer called for acceptance by promise or acceptance by performance?
2. When did the employees' acceptance take effect? How would that apply to the judge who elected to retire before the statute changed, but did not complete his duties on the bench until after the statute changed?
3. If the statute was an offer, why couldn't the offeror revoke it prior to acceptance?
4. Have the judges here suffered any detrimental reliance? Is it unjust to limit their pensions to amounts calculated at the time of retirement, without any future increases?

Sylvestre v. Minnesota

298 Minn. 142, 214 N.W.2d 658 (1973)

KNUTSON, Chief Justice.

[Six Minnesota judges sought a declaratory judgment that changes to the amounts Minnesota paid to retired judges did not apply to them. Each began service under a statute promising retired judges half the salary paid to sitting judges, an amount that would increase as the salary paid to sitting judges increased. Changes in 1967 and 1969 limited judges to half the salary paid to sitting judges at the time of their retirement. Thus, subsequent increases in pay to sitting judges would not affect the pensions received by retired judges. The trial court ruled that the changes did not apply to judges who elected retirement before the changes took effect, but did apply to judges that elected retirement after the statutes took effect. The court discussed whether these changes were an unconstitutional impairment of contract rights, which in turn required it to decide whether the judges had a contract right to the pensions originally promised.]

While cases involving private employment are not controlling, we think the rationale of the case of *Hartung v. Billmeier*, 243 Minn. 148, 66 N.W.2d 784 (1954), is persuasive. That case involved a promise by an employer to give his employees a stated bonus if they stayed with him 5 years. The employee stayed with the employer for 6 years and 9 months. When the employer thereafter sued him for the price of goods sold to him, the employee counterclaimed to collect the bonus which had been promised to him. In upholding his right to recover, we said (243 Minn. 153, 66 N.W.2d 789):

> . . . Inasmuch as plaintiff's offer or promise to pay a bonus was not accepted by a promise of the defendant to work continuously for him for five years, no bilateral contract resulted when the offer was made.
>
> . . .
>
> A promisee may, however, accept an offer or promise to pay a bonus by performing the act or forbearance specified in the offer, but such act or forbearance must differ from what the promisee is already obligated to do either by law or by existing contract. When a promise is thus accepted by performance of the designated act or forbearance, the promisor's offer is converted into a unilateral contract which comes into being the moment the act or forbearance has been fully performed.
>
> Here the defendant accepted plaintiff's offer by forbearing to leave plaintiff's employment for five years. The moment plaintiff's offer was thus converted into a contract, the bonus became due and payable.

The same is true of the cases now before us. When these judges entered upon their judicial position, the state in effect said to them, "If you will stay on the job for at least 15 years and then retire after having reached the specified retirement age, we will pay you a part of your salary for the remainder of your life." Up to 1967, the law provided that they would be paid, upon retirement, one-half of the salary allotted to the office. By Ex. Sess. L. 1967, c. 38, §5, this provision was altered to read that a judge should be paid one-half the compensation allotted to the office at the time of his retirement, and by L. 1969, c. 987, to provide that he should be paid one-half the compensation allotted to the office at the time of his retirement or on July 1, 1967, whichever is greater.

In *Hickey v. Pittsburgh Pension Board*, 378 Pa. 300, 310, 106 A.2d 233, 238, 52 A.L.R.2d 430, 436 (1954), the Pennsylvania Supreme Court said:

> . . . Whether it be in the field of sports or in the halls of the legislature it is not consonant with American traditions of fairness and justice to change the ground rules in the middle of the game.

. . .

[As to judges who had fully performed their duties and retired before the changes in the law took effect, the court concluded that their completed performance accepted the offered pension, creating a contract right to the pension promised at the time they retired—which included any increases that might result if the pay of sitting judges was increased. The remaining discussion involved Judge Flynn, who retired after the statutes took effect, and Judge Underhill, who elected retirement before the changes took effect, but did not leave the bench until after the changes became effective.]

While *Hartung v. Billmeier*, Supra, presented only the issue of acceptance by full performance, the court in *Hartung* explicitly left open the question of the effect of part performance with this reservation (243 Minn. 153, note 7, 66 N.W.2d 789, note 6):

> Query: What remedy has offeree when offeror revokes offer for unilateral contract after partial performance by the offeree? [Citations omitted.]

Mooney v. Daily News Co., 116 Minn. 212, 133 N.W. 573 . . . has been cited . . . for the proposition that partial performance of the act requested by an offer for unilateral contract may render the offer binding to a certain extent. Judges Flynn and Underhill are essentially in the position of offerees who, after partial performance, found that the offer made to them was revoked and a new offer attempted to be substituted. While the problem of the revocability of offers for unilateral contracts after part performance has not been decisively treated by this court before and is not without theoretical difficulties, see 1 Williston, Contracts (3 ed.) §§60 and 60A, we believe the better view is that adopted by the Restatement. Under the Restatement view, part performance by the offeree prevents the revocation of the offer (Restatement, Contracts, §45):

> If an offer for a unilateral contract is made, and part of the consideration requested in the offer is given or tendered by the offeree in response thereto, the offeror is bound by a contract, the duty of immediate performance of which is conditional on the full consideration being given or tendered within the time stated in the offer.[4]

A change in the terms of the offer which reduces the terms of the original offer is, of course, tantamount to a revocation of the offer and the substitution of a new offer.

Thus, following the analogy to private employment cases, once Judges Flynn and Underhill began their service as judges, the state was bound by a contract to pay "one-half the compensation allotted to the office" in retirement benefits, although of course the state's duty of immediate performance did not arise until the judge's completion of the requisite years of service. Since under the principle advanced by the Restatement the state was irrevocably bound by this contract from the time Judges Flynn and Underhill took office, there is no reason for treating their situation differently from that of the other judges.

---

[4]Under Restatement, Contracts 2d, Tentative Draft, §45, the same principle is retained although beginning performance is said to create an option contract:

> (1) Where an offer invites an offeree to accept by rendering a performance and does not invite a promissory acceptance, an option contract is created when the offeree tenders or begins the invited performance or tenders a beginning of it.

An option contract is of course irrevocable. The following illustration given by the Restatement seems particularly appropriate to the present case:

> "In January A, an employer, publishes a notice to his employees, promising a stated Christmas bonus to any employee who is continuously in A's employ from January to Christmas. B, an employee hired by the week, reads the notice and continues at work beyond the expiration of the current week. A is bound by an option contract, and if B is continuously in A's employ until Christmas a notice of revocation of the bonus is ineffective." Restatement, Contracts 2d, Tentative Draft, §45, illustration 8.

Post-Case Follow-Up

If the statute promising a pension is treated as an offer, the rest of the case seems fairly straightforward. The state did not expect judges to accept the offer as they began their service (say, by promising to stay on the bench long enough to qualify for the pension). Acceptance by performing their duties until they qualified seems more realistic. As a matter of principle, allowing an offeror to revoke an offer while the offerees are in the process of performing their duties (that is, in the process of accepting the offer in the only way they can) offends fundamental notions of fairness.

In some ways, the case is harder than it seems. The state did not really revoke the offer of a pension, but altered the amount by limiting future increases in pensions — perhaps a sound budget decision faced by many public employers today. Similarly, the government normally has the power to amend or repeal statutes without asking those affected by the statute. Giving the pension statute a special status, precluding amendment as to existing employees, limits the ability of elected representatives to deploy taxpayer dollars in the manner that best serves the interest of the state.

Sylvestre v. Minnesota: Real Life Applications

1. Junior became a judge in Minnesota one week before the legislature enacted the changes to the pension structure discussed in *Sylvestre*. If Junior retires 30 years later, is Junior entitled to the pension under the original statute or subject to the revisions? Would your answer be any different if Junior became a judge one week before the amendment was introduced to the legislature rather than one week before it was passed?

2. A cigarette company included coupons in every package of cigarettes, offering various merchandise in exchange for a certain number of coupons. After the program has been in place for 15 years, the company announced that it would stop including coupons in its cigarettes immediately, but would continue to accept coupons for redemption for another five months. The company advised program participants to redeem their coupons early, because supplies of merchandise available for redemption would be limited and might run out. In fact, supplies were extremely limited, leaving many customers with hundreds (in some cases, thousands) of coupons they could not redeem. Advise the company whether it bears any liability for breach of contract to the frustrated coupon-holders. What could it do to perform its duties under the contract (at the least possible expense)? If it considers implementing a new coupon program — say, for another of its products — could it structure the program in a way that would avoid similar contract claims in the future?

3. Banco holds the mortgage on an apartment building owned by Lani. Lani failed to make the last two monthly payments on the loan. Lani asked Banco if it would

abstain from foreclosing on the property for three months (until December 1) while Lani sought refinancing that would pay off Banco. Banco agreed. After two months (during which Lani made no additional payments on the loan), Banco has run out of patience and prefers to foreclose on the property. Before beginning foreclosure proceedings, Banco seeks your advice on whether it has a legal obligation to wait until December 1. How do you advise Banco? If you conclude that it cannot foreclose now, is there anything it can do now to regain the right to foreclose before December 1?

4. You have been consulted by Rapper, who lost a laptop computer on which several new songs were recorded (prior to their release to the public). Online, Rapper announced a $1 million reward for the return of the computer with the data intact. Later, reconsidering the size of the offer, Rapper tried to remove the $1 million post and replace it with a $10,000 reward. Tourist found the computer and e-mailed the person designated in the posting containing the reward. Arrangements were made to meet the next day to make the exchange. Tourist returned the computer with the data intact, but was surprised to be offered only $10,000. Tourist claimed to have seen only the $1 million posting. Tourist said that if Rapper would not pay the $1 million, Tourist would keep the machine — a threat that proved impractical because Rapper's powerful bodyguard already had possession of it. Tourist told Rapper that he never would have changed his plans (incurring $1,000 in change fees for an international flight home) if he had been aware that the reward had been reduced. Rapper seeks your advice regarding the amount of reward owed to Tourist. Assume that Tourist would sue in American courts, rather than suing in Tourist's home country. (Aside: Did Tourist have a right to leave with the machine if that had been possible?)

Exhibit 3.2 illustrates the second Restatement's approach to unilateral offers and acceptance by performance.

C. ACCEPTANCE BY SILENCE

Normally, acceptance requires some manifestation of assent, typically words or conduct. Courts rarely find the offeree's silence or failure to object sufficient to signal acceptance. The offeree's silence or inaction is at best an ambiguous response to an offer. It may indicate satisfaction with the offer and agreement to the terms. Alternatively, it might mean the offeree refuses

Evolving Rules

The rule limiting revocation of offers that can be accepted by performance predates options based on reliance. These older rules are narrower: they apply to fewer offers (those permitting acceptance by performance) and recognize fewer kinds of reliance (preparations to perform will not qualify). Newer decisions recognize options based on reliance when an offeror reasonably should expect such reliance before acceptance, a potentially broader class of cases. If cases following the approach described in Restatement (Second) of Contracts §45 do not produce the result you need, consider whether your jurisdiction might recognize the approach in Restatement (Second) of Contracts §§87 and 90. Consider how you would respond to the Real Life Applications above — or the *Sylvestre* case itself — if you had to argue the problems under §87.

EXHIBIT 3.2 Unilateral Offers and Acceptance

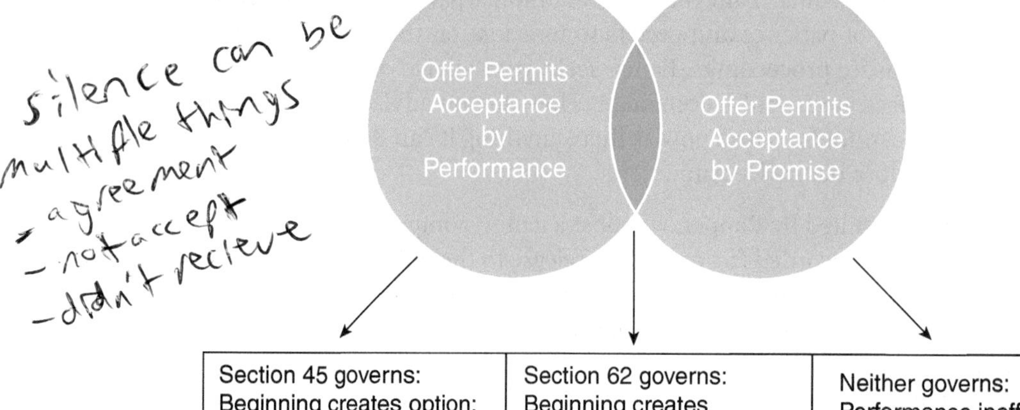

Section 45 governs: Beginning creates option; completion creates acceptance.	Section 62 governs: Beginning creates acceptance.	Neither governs: Performance ineffective as acceptance.
In any situation, section 87 or 90 might create an option based on foreseeable reliance.		

to dignify such a ridiculous proposal with a response. Equally important, silence might result because the offeree did not receive the offer or had not read it. It requires a leap of faith to infer from silence that an offeree intended to accept the offer. Objectively, a reasonable person probably would not understand silence to signal assent in most settings.

Silence, without more, is not acceptance. But additional facts may give some reason to treat silence as acceptance. As discussed above, silence accompanied by beginning performance might be acceptance. The conduct adds reassurance that the offeree intended to accept. Other exceptional cases occasionally lead courts to infer assent from an offeree's silence. In three limited situations, silence may be acceptance:

1. The offeree intends its silence to signify assent (to an offer that invites silent acceptance).
2. Prior dealings make silence a reasonable means of signaling assent.
3. The offeree accepts the benefits of the offeror's performance without objection.[23]

In addition, the Uniform Commercial Code provides that silence may accept a proposed modification of contract in limited circumstances, as will be discussed below.

Offeree Intends Silence as Acceptance

If both the offeror and the offeree intend the offeree's silence to create assent, courts honor those wishes. This situation generally arises when an offer specifies that, in

[23]Restatement (Second) of Contracts §69(1).

the absence of objection, the offeror will assume the offeree accepts the proposal. An offeree who intended to accept might say nothing, an understandable choice by one invited to accept by silence. An offeror who later refuses to perform can hardly complain that the offeree did not communicate assent; the offer specified silence as a means of acceptance.

More troublesome cases arise if the offeror begins to perform and the offeree objects that its silence was not intended as assent. For example, suppose a merchant receives a request for discontinued merchandise and responds by offering to supply the newest version, specifying that "I will ship the new model on Thursday unless I hear from you by then." Shipping on Thursday is risky; seller cannot *know* whether the buyer intends its silence as assent.

Try your hand at applying this rule to the following situation: In the example above, buyer did not reply to merchant's offer to ship by Thursday. Buyer began looking for a better deal, planning to accept the Thursday shipment if it found none, but to reject the shipment if it could find a better deal. Merchant shipped on Thursday. Buyer found a better deal on Friday and placed an order for identical goods at a lower price. Buyer received merchant's goods on Saturday and promptly rejected them, stating it did not intend its silence to accept the offer. If merchant can prove buyer's state of mind, should a court enforce the deal? How could merchant prove buyer's state of mind if buyer testifies that it never intended its silence to accept the offer?

Offerors rarely can have any confidence that silence accepts an offer. For this reason, a prudent offeror will not specify silence as a means of indicating assent, requiring instead some form of actual notice.

Lack of Assent: Reason or Excuse?

Arguments about assent often seem like an afterthought. A party who wanted to enter a contract looks for a loophole when it turns out to be a bad deal. *Massasoit Whip* looks that way: Massasoit didn't want to pay for the snake skins because a fire had destroyed them. Rather than pay for nothing, it alleged that it did not accept the skins. Why did they reject this shipment but not others? Massasoit said these snake skins were too small to use; they planned to reject them as soon as they could contact Hobbs. Hobbs said the skins were the right size. The fire made it impossible to measure them again. We can't tell whether this was an honest dispute over the quality or a pretense to avoid paying for goods one cannot enjoy. In practice, skepticism on assent claims may help you sniff out such pretexts.

Prior Dealings

Prior dealings may establish the meaning of silence between parties. Where an offeror and offeree deal repeatedly and often treat silence as assent in their transactions, neither one has much room to complain that silence should not be treated as assent in this transaction. *Hobbs v. Massasoit Whip Co.*[24] offers a popular example. Hobbs frequently sent snake skins to Massasoit, which used them to make whip handles. Massasoit, without otherwise indicating assent, paid Hobbs for each shipment. When Massasoit failed to pay for a shipment, Hobbs sued. The court's decision could be taken two ways. The Restatement (Second) of Contracts §69 interpreted the decision as holding that Massasoit's silence accepted Hobbs' offer because prior dealings between them showed they each treated Massasoit's

[24] 33 N.E. 495 (Mass. 1893).

failure to object as assent to the purchase of the goods. Arguably, the prior dealings involved acceptance by performance when Massasoit paid for the skins.

The court offered another way to view the case: Massasoit's dealings with Hobbs might establish a standing offer to buy skins of suitable size and quality. Hobbs, by delivering skins, could accept that offer by performance. Massasoit's silence, then, would be irrelevant. Hobbs accepted its offer by delivering the goods, completing the contact at that point. The case is not cited for this holding. The alternative illustrates that assent cases can be viewed from several angles. When one view of the case does not produce a favorable result, consider whether identifying a different (usually earlier) communication as the offer would lead to a better conclusion.

Accepting Benefits Without Objection

In limited cases, where an offeree accepts the benefits of an offer without objection, that silence may be treated as assent to a contract. This type of ratification can occur where the offeror provides property or where the offeror provides services. The rule has one foot in assent to contract and one foot in unjust enrichment.

Case Preview

Nirvana International v. ADT Security Services

In this case, Nirvana (a jewelry store) received an offer of services from ADT (a security company). Nirvana contends it never agreed to the terms proposed by the offer, even though it allowed ADT to install the alarm system and to provide service for six months. After the security system failed to function during a robbery, Nirvana sued ADT for the losses it suffered. ADT defended based on one of the terms in the offer, requiring the court to consider whether that offer was accepted.

ADT Security Services was hired to install an alarm system in the plaintiff's jewelry store. *360b/Shutterstock.com*

As you read *Nirvana International v. ADT Security Services*, look for the following:

1. Why is ADT permitted to rely on Nirvana's silence as assent in the face of uncontradicted allegations that Nirvana did not intend to agree to the limited remedy?
2. Does Nirvana allege there was no contract? According to Nirvana, what offer was accepted to create a contract?
3. What benefit did Nirvana receive by having the alarm system installed? Was Nirvana unjustly enriched?

Nirvana International, Inc. v. ADT Security Services, Inc.

881 F. Supp. 2d 556 (S.D.N.Y. 2012), *aff'd,* 525 Fed. Appx. 12 (2d Cir. 2013)

McMahon, District Judge.

Plaintiff Nirvana International, Inc. ("Plaintiff") . . . hired Defendant ADT Security Services, Inc. ("Defendant") . . . to install an alarm system in Plaintiff's jewelry store. Defendant did, but the alarm didn't go off when burglars came, and Plaintiff was relieved of $2.4 million in merchandise.

Plaintiff sued for Defendant [sic] breach of contract and gross negligence, seeking the full value of its loss — and for forgery and fraud, seeking more limited damages.

Defendant moves to dismiss the complaint, on the ground that it owes Plaintiff at most $1000, relying on a contractual limitation of liability provision that it says was part of the contract between the parties. For the reasons discussed below, Defendant's motion is GRANTED.

BACKGROUND

The relationship between Plaintiff and Defendant is governed by a contract. [Citation omitted.]

The contract consists of three double-sided pages. Each sheet is numbered in the bottom left corner . . . To avoid confusion, I will refer to each page as [1 of 6], [2 of 6], and so on.

. . .

[1 of 6] sets forth the service and price terms and the signatures of Plaintiff's owner (Amit Sharma) and Defendant's sales representative. Above the signature line, the contract warns that "SECOND AND THIRD PAGES ACCOMPANY THIS PAGE WITH ADDITIONAL TERMS AND CONDITIONS."

[2 of 6] itemizes the service and equipment that Defendant agreed to provide.

[3 of 6] contains a bank authorization for billing signed by Sharma.

[4 of 6] (the back side of [3 of 6]) is titled "IMPORTANT TERMS AND CONDITIONS" [continued on] [5 of 6] (the back side of [2 of 6]) and [6 of 6] (the back side of [1 of 6]).

Term "E," which appears on [6 of 6], is titled "LIMITATIONS ON LIABILITY." It provides, in relevant part, that:

> [DEFENDANT] IS NOT AN INSURER. THE AMOUNTS [DEFENDANT] CHARGES CUSTOMERS ARE NOT INSURANCE PREMIUMS. SUCH CHARGES ARE BASED ON THE VALUE OF THE SERVICES, SYSTEM AND EQUIPMENT ADT PROVIDES AND ARE UNRELATED TO THE VALUE OF CUSTOMER'S PROPERTY.

Term E goes to explain the possibility that Defendant's system will sometimes fail to detect the occurrences it is designed to guard against, but says that Defendant does not undertake any of that risk. Rather, the customer is required to obtain insurance to cover the value of its property, and required to waive any right it might otherwise have against Defendant. It then says that:

> IF NOTWITHSTANDING THE PROVISIONS OF THIS SECTION E, [DEFENDANT] IS FOUND LIABLE FOR LOSS, DAMAGE OR LIABILITY UNDER ANY LEGAL THEORY DUE TO THE FAILURE OF ITS SERVICES, SYSTEM OR EQUIPMENT IN ANY RESPECT, ITS LIABILITY SHALL BE LIMITED TO A SUM EQUAL TO 10% OF THE ANNUAL SERVICE CHARGE OR $1000, WHICHEVER IS GREATER. . . .

The parties agree that, if term E is part of their contract, it limits Defendant's liability — under any and all theories — to $1000. . . .

At the bottom of [6 of 6] there is a signature and date line, under the words "Customer Acceptance." Beneath that, in a boxed off area, the following language appears:

> BY CUSTOMER INITIALING IN THE SPACE PROVIDED BELOW, CUSTOMER ACKNOWLEDGES AND ADMITS THAT CUSTOMER HAS READ THE IMPORTANT TERMS AND CONDITIONS SET FORTH ON PAGES 4 THROUGH 6, INCLUSIVE, OF THIS AGREEMENT AND UNDERSTANDS AND AGREES TO ALL SUCH TERMS AND CONDITIONS.

Beneath this language, space is provided for the initials of the customer, Defendant's sales representative, and Defendant's manager. (Contract.)

On May 17, 2010, Sharma sat down with Defendant's sales representative to execute the contract. Sharma read, understood, and agreed to pages [1 of 6], [2 of 6] and [3 of 6] by signing and initialing each of them. However, Sharma told Defendant's representative he could not agree to the terms and conditions on [4 of 6] through [6 of 6] until he reviewed them more carefully. Defendant's representative left without obtaining initial or a signature on pages [4 of 6], [5 of 6] or [6 of 6].

Sharma later decided that the terms and conditions on [4 of 6] through [6 of 6] were not acceptable to him. However, Sharma did not communicate his point of view to Defendant. [Citation omitted.]

On June 8, 2010, Defendant installed its alarm system, even though Sharma had not initialed the terms and conditions or signed page [6 of 6]. Sharma permitted Defendant to install the alarm, without alerting Defendant that he objected to any of the terms and conditions. Thereafter, Plaintiff paid the monthly monitoring fee of $44. [Citation omitted.]

On December 4, 2010, [a] burglary resulted in the theft of 150 pieces of jewelry and loose stones, valued at approximately $2.4 million.

When Sharma notified Defendant of the burglary, Defendant disclaimed liability for losses of more than $1000, relying on the limitation of liability contained on sheet [6 of 6] of the contract. Defendant produced a "central storage" copy of the contract that showed Sharma's signature on page [6 of 6]. Plaintiff alleges that Sharma never signed [6 of 6], and that the signature on Defendant's copy was a forgery [citation omitted], and I assume the truth of this allegation.

. . .

A. Breach of Contract (Count I)

[Even though] Sharma's signature on [6 of 6] was forged . . . Plaintiff is bound by the limitation of liability provision.

Plaintiff was given the entire six-page contract, consisting of three-page double-sided pages. The document states, above the signature line on the first page, that it includes "SECOND AND THIRD PAGES WITH ADDITIONAL TERMS AND CONDITIONS." [T]his language clearly incorporates the "IMPORTANT TERMS AND CONDITIONS" included on . . . [4 of 6] through [6 of 6]. . . . Plaintiff does not deny that he read all six sheets and understood their terms.

"It is standard contract doctrine that when a benefit is offered subject to stated conditions, and the offeree makes a decision to take the benefit with knowledge of the terms of the offer, the taking constitutes an acceptance of the terms, which accordingly become binding on the offeree." *Register.com, Inc. v. Verio, Inc.*, 356 F.3d 393, 403 (2d Cir. 2004). The rule is given in the Second Restatement of Contracts as follows: "(1) Where an offeree fails to reply to an offer, his silence and inaction operate as an acceptance . . . (a) Where an offeree takes the benefit of offered services with reasonable opportunity to reject them and reason to know that they were offered with the expectation of compensation." Restatement (Second) of Contracts §69 (1981). A comment explains that "The resulting duty is not merely a duty to pay fair value, but a duty to . . . perform according to the terms of the offer." *Id.* cmt. b.

Applying this "standard contract doctrine" here, Plaintiff admits that: (1) Sharma knew about all of the terms and conditions of the contract, including the limitation on liability; (2) he never expressly communicated to Defendant his rejection of any of the terms, despite having an opportunity to do so; and (3) he accepted the benefits of Defendant's performance by allowing Defendant to install the alarm system. Sharma told Defendant's representative that he needed to read the provisions before he could agree to them; however, he never told any representative of Defendant that he would not agree to any of the terms. Instead, he allowed Defendant to install the system, accepted its benefits (such as they were) and paid the agreed upon-price. Thus, he is bound by all of the conditions of Defendant's offer, including the terms and conditions set forth on page [6 of 6].

Plaintiff argues that Sharma's failure to sign and initial sheet [6 of 6] in the marked spaces somehow makes sheets [4 of 6] through [6 of 6] not part of the parties' agreement. But Plaintiff is wrong as a matter of law. Defendant's offer was conditioned on Plaintiff's accepting the terms and conditions contained on pages [4 of 6] through [6 of 6]. Sharma neither expressly *accepted* nor expressly *rejected* the terms and conditions contained on those pages; rather, he said he needed to consider them more carefully. [Citation omitted.] But Sharma knew of their existence, and the law construes his silence, combined with his acceptance of the benefits of Defendant's performance, as an implicit acceptance. Thus, the failure to sign page six does not assist Plaintiff.

The case of *National City Golf Finance v. Higher Ground Country Club Management Co., LLC*, 641 F. Supp. 2d 196 (S.D.N.Y. 2009), is analogous. There, the issue was whether the parties agreed to arbitrate disputes arising out of a series of contracts. The contested arbitration provision was in a document termed the "Service Agreement," the fourth of four separate documents submitted to Higher Ground to be signed. Higher Ground alleged that it never signed the Service Agreement, and argued that it was therefore not bound by its terms, including the arbitration provision.

Then-District Judge Lynch rejected this argument, relying on the doctrine discussed above. Higher Ground had accepted the benefits of the Service Agreement by requesting and receiving service, without communicating its rejection of any of the Service Agreement's terms; it was therefore bound by the entire Agreement. . . .

In another arbitration case, *Deloitte Noraudit A/S v. Deloitte Haskins & Sells, U.S.*, 9 F.3d 1060 (2d Cir. 1993) . . . the Second Circuit held that Noraudit — a party seeking to avoid an arbitration provision in an agreement it did not sign — was bound by the provision, because, as here, Noraudit [without objection] "knowingly accepted the benefits of the Agreement." Thus, it was bound by all the terms of the Agreement of which it had notice, and to which it failed to object, when it silently accepted the benefits of performance.

Likewise here: Sharma knowingly accepted the installation of the alarm system and the ongoing provision of services from June through December 2010. Under the rule stated in Restatement (Second) §69, and the cases cited above, Sharma is bound by all of the provisions of the contract, including the limitation on liability on page [6 of 6].

The Court recognizes that this result may appear strange in light of Defendant's behavior, particularly its effort to forge what turned out to be a legally superfluous signature. However, Defendant's ignorance of the law (and its alleged chicanery) does not alter the operation of the fundamental contract doctrine implicated in this case. The presence of an unnecessary signature line on page [6 of 6] is no more controlling than the (effectively) superfluous signature lines in *National City Golf, Deloitte*, or any other case that arises under Restatement §69, where acceptance is implied by silence rather than express. Sharma communicated an implicit acceptance of the whole contract when he failed to notify Defendant that he was unwilling to agree to the limitation of liability, while at the same time allowing Defendant to install the alarm system. Among the terms he thereby accepted was that in no event would Defendant's liability exceed $1000.

. . .

CONCLUSION

Defendant's motion is granted and the complaint is dismissed. Plaintiff is free to seek its $1000 from Defendant in State court, where the jurisdictional deficiencies herein identified are no barrier to recovery.

Post-Case Follow-Up

Like many assent cases, this one allows for several different explanations. The court focused on Nirvana's silence in the face of ADT's performance in accord with the offer it proposed and Nirvana apparently accepted. This might reflect that Nirvana subjectively did agree to the terms (explaining why it did not object) or that ADT reasonably believed Nirvana agreed to the terms. Keeping the services for six months suggests Nirvana really did intend to make some contract. Relying on silence as assent makes it unnecessary to decide whether a signature on page one of the proposed contract accepted the terms on pages four through six. It also makes it unnecessary to resolve whether ADT forged Nirvana's signature on page six or whether Nirvana signed and later recanted the signature. (An expert's affidavit makes the latter seems unlikely, but the former remains unproven. In other cases, courts have relied on silence when it seems likely the offeree actually signed, but proving that is difficult.)

Nirvana International v. ADT Security Services: Real Life Applications

1. After reaching a settlement agreement in a divorce action, Sandy proposed modifying the agreement by releasing a claim to have Leslie provide her a rental home if Leslie would pay some money immediately to allow Sandy to purchase a home individually. Leslie signed the agreement and obtained a cashier's check in the specified amount, to be delivered to Sandy only after Sandy signed the modification. Without signing, Sandy obtained the check, cashed it, and used the money to satisfy a lender's concerns for Sandy's ability to pay closing costs. Later, Sandy refused to agree to the modification and refunded Leslie's payment via a personal check. Leslie prefers the modification and seeks your advice on whether (and how) to establish that the modification was accepted by Sandy.

2. Hunter, an executive placement firm, offered its services to Biz, a company in need of a new vice president. Biz agreed to look at resumes submitted by Hunter. Hunter submitted to Biz its terms of service along with the first resume. Biz did not respond to Hunter's terms, but recognized the first resume as someone interviewed for the same position several years earlier. Biz contacted and hired that candidate, contending that Hunter did not call that candidate to its attention. The terms of service submitted by Hunter provided that the fee is owed unless, before Hunter submitted the resume, Biz knew the person was currently available for the position — a test Biz probably cannot satisfy. Hunter seeks your advice concerning whether the terms were accepted by Biz. If not, could Hunter recover on any other theory?

3. Jock offered to sell his friend, Fan, four tickets to game seven of the World Series for $10,000. Fan, unsure if he could go, asked to hold on to the tickets just in case. Jock agreed, asking that Fan return them that night if he could not go. Fan used the tickets.

   a. Scalpers at the game were selling similar seats for $4,000. Fan paid Jock $4,000. Jock would like to recover the rest of the asking price. Will Jock succeed?

   b. Scalpers at the game were selling similar seats for $15,000, but Fan paid Jock face value for the tickets ($600). Jock would like to recover the full value of the tickets ($15,000) instead of the discount offered to a one-time friend. Will Jock succeed?

D. UCC §2-207 AND THE BATTLE OF THE FORMS

For sales of goods within the United States, the UCC dramatically reduced the role of the mirror image rule. An acceptance that includes new or different terms is less likely to be treated as a counteroffer and more likely to be treated as an acceptance that proposes modification.

1. Assent Under §2-207

Section 2-207 of the UCC provides:

> (1) A definite and seasonable expression of acceptance or a written confirmation operates as an acceptance even though it states terms additional to or different from those offered or agreed upon, unless acceptance is expressly made conditional on assent to the additional or different terms.
>
> (2) The additional terms are to be construed as proposals for addition to the contract. Between merchants such terms become part of the contract unless:
>
> (a) the offer expressly limits acceptance to the terms of the offer;
>
> (b) they materially alter it; or
>
> (c) notification of objection to them has already been given or is given within a reasonable time after notice of them is received
>
> (3) Conduct by both parties which recognizes the existence of a contract is sufficient to establish a contract for sale although the writings of the parties do not otherwise establish a contract. In such case the terms of the particular contract consist of those terms on which the writings of the parties agree, together with any supplementary terms incorporated under any other provisions of this Act.[25]

Subsection (1) treats some communications as acceptances despite their request for different or additional terms. Parties can make counteroffers if they do so carefully. By expressly stating that their willingness to deal is limited to the terms of their proposal, offerees may reject the offer and make a counteroffer. But the mere existence of changes will not automatically create a counteroffer, at least not when that would involve overriding clear language of acceptance. Warned by the code of how language will be interpreted, offerees bear the onus to express their intentions appropriately. Exhibit 3.3 offers an example of a contract term, drawn from a Seller's "Customer Acknowledgment Form," sent in response to purchase orders received for the company's goods. In *PCS Nitrogen Fertilizer, L.P. v. Christy Refractories, L.L.C.*,[26] the court held this language created a counteroffer rather than accepted the purchaser's offer.

---

[25] UCC § 2-207(1).

[26] 225 F.3d 974, 976 (8th Cir. 2000).

EXHIBIT 3.3 Contract Term Expressly Conditioning Assent

1. Offer and Acceptance . . . Seller's acceptance of any offer by Purchaser to purchase the Products is expressly conditional upon the Purchaser's assent to all the terms and conditions herein, including any terms additional to or different from those contained in the offer to purchase. Seller hereby objects to any different or additional terms or conditions contained in any acceptance by Purchaser of any offer made by Seller or in any other document submitted by Purchaser. No modification, addition, deletion, rescission or waiver by Seller of any term or condition set forth herein or of any of Seller's rights or remedies hereunder shall be binding upon Seller unless agreed to in a writing signed by Seller. Purchaser shall be deemed to have assented to these terms and conditions unless Seller receives written notice of any objection within 10 days after Purchaser's receipt of this form and in all events prior to delivery or other performance by Seller.

While §2-207 starts by recognizing assent, it must resolve a second question: to which terms did the parties assent? Do the different or additional terms proposed in the acceptance become part of the contract? This is the primary difference between the UCC and the mirror image rule. Most of the discussion below relates to identifying which terms were accepted and, thus, become binding on the parties.

Try your hand at applying this rule to the following situation: By e-mail, Chris offered to buy Terry's used car for $11,000. Terry replied, "I accept. Let's meet Tuesday and make the exchange." Is this an acceptance? Is making the exchange (money for title and keys) on Tuesday a term of the contract?

The Problem: The Last Shot Rule

Section 2-207 responds to a serious problem in contract formation that can arise when parties pay too little attention to each other's communications—as commonly happens when using form contracts. A buyer may request goods, using a purchase order form that specifies not only price, quantity, and delivery terms, but a host of other **boilerplate** terms (terms governing details, typically ones that don't vary from deal to deal and, thus, don't justify time to renegotiate or redraft with each deal). A seller may respond with an invoice, identical in terms of price, quantity, and delivery, but with different boilerplate terms. Under the mirror image rule, no contract is formed despite agreement on the key terms. Still, the seller may ship the goods and the buyer may pay. If a dispute arises falling within the boilerplate terms, a court must decide which set of terms, if either, constituted the contract.

Under the mirror image rule, the order of communication took on controlling significance. The court could interpret a party's performance as acquiescence to the terms in the other's form. The terms of the contract were those in the last form sent before the other performed. That form would serve as a rejection of any previous different communications (because of the mirror image rule), but usually would not be rejected by the other party's performance. Delivery of goods or payment, unless accompanied by a rejection (such as a form reiterating different terms), would accept rather than reject the most recent proposal. Giving effect to the most recent communication was called the **last shot rule** — not really a rule, but a result reached by rigid application of the mirror image rule.

The UCC Approach: The First Shot Rule

Section 2-207 replaced this with the **first shot rule** — again, not a rule but a description of the effect of applying §2-207. An acceptance, even one with different or additional terms, accepts all the terms of the offer. Thus, whoever makes the offer provides the governing terms.

For example, suppose a buyer offered to pay $1 apiece for 10,000 ball bearings to be shipped by October 1. A prompt response from seller unequivocally accepted the offer and requested payment within 30 days of delivery with 9 percent interest on past due amounts, but nothing in the response suggested that seller was unwilling to proceed unless buyer agreed to these terms. The response accepted the buyer's offer, on the buyer's terms. The terms suggested in seller's e-mail might become part of the contract, but not until buyer has a chance to respond. Until then, the contract has been formed on seller's terms.

New terms in the acceptance propose modifications to the deal, which the offeror can accept or reject. The text of the code (subsection (2)) specifies this for additional terms — terms that do not change a term in the offer — but does not mention different terms. The official comments to the code and the prevailing interpretation by courts treat different and additional terms identically.

Global Concerns

For international sales of goods, the CISG rejects the first shot rule. Article 19 prefers to treat any response with new terms as a counteroffer. It carves out an exception if none of the changes materially alter the terms of the offer. In that case, the response is an acceptance proposing the changes, which will become part of the contract unless the offeror objects without undue delay. In cases where the initial response was a counteroffer (and probably where the offeror objects to the changes), the last shot rule appears to apply. No assent has yet been reached based on the communications. But after each proposal, a performance could be construed as assent to those terms. This is not the rule within Europe or under the UCC. But it appears to govern international sales.

Including New or Different Terms

Try your hand at applying this rule to the following situation: Gail offered to sell a coin collection to Shelly for $3,000. Shelly accepted, requesting that Gail ship the coins in time to arrive by December 1, Shelly's spouse's birthday. Without comment, Gail shipped the coins via the U.S. Postal Service, which could have arrived by December 1 but in fact did not arrive until December 3. Was arrival by December 1 a term of the contract? Variation: What if Shelly suggested insuring the coins in transit and adding the price of insurance to the price, but Gail shipped the coins without insuring them?

When an acceptance includes an offer to modify the contract, that offer can be expressly accepted by words. In some circumstances, silence may accept the proposed modifications. Section 2-207(2) provides that if both parties to the transaction are merchants, the proposed changes will become part of the contract unless some objection to the terms is or has been made or the changes materially alter the transaction. The offeror retains considerable control of the situation. Any objection by the offeror can expressly reject proposals to modify. The objection might be found in the original offer, if it expressly provided that only the offer's terms could be accepted. Similarly, terms the offeror sends after the offer may reject proposals to modify the deal, even if they are sent before the proposal to modify is received — as when buyer's form and seller's form cross in the mail. Often, however, businesses pay very little attention to each other's forms. Objections to terms will not be made — unless their lawyers drafted objections into the forms themselves. Even without objection, however, any significant change to the deal will not be deemed accepted by silence. Material changes require express assent.

No bright line determines whether new terms materially change the transaction. Comments to the UCC offer some examples of terms that materially alter the deal and some that don't.[27] Changes that result in surprise or hardship are material, including warranty disclaimers, clauses requiring stricter compliance than usage of trade allows, and clauses severely limiting the time in which to complain about breaches. Terms that do not involve unreasonable surprise include **force majeure** clauses (excusing performance for extreme events, such as tornadoes or fires), clauses reasonably limiting the time to complain of breaches, clauses providing for interest on overdue payments, or clauses reasonably limiting available remedies. For example, recall the ball bearing sale in the previous section. A request for interest on the overdue payments seems unlikely to be a material change. Thus, if both parties were merchants, that term would become part of the contract unless the buyer objected. The significance of any given proposed change may depend on the context and each party's needs under the circumstances. The rule identifies the focus of the arguments (the materiality of the changes), but cannot resolve the arguments.

Contract by Conduct

Despite efforts to find assent in communications that differ, sometimes the communications make this impossible. The offer may expressly limit assent to its terms, the reply may be expressly conditioned on assent to the changes, and subsequent communications may contain similar express language that makes it impossible to interpret any communication as assent to the previous one. Yet performance by the parties might establish that they did intend a contract for sale. In these circumstances, as a last resort, UCC §2-207(3) provides the terms of the contract: any terms on which the communications agree plus the default terms provided in the UCC, used to fill any gap in the contract. Neither party can insist on a term to which the other did not agree. Instead, the agreed-upon terms remain and any conflicts between the proposals knock out both disputed terms, leaving the UCC to fill any gaps as it would in any other incomplete contract. Chapter 10 discusses some examples of UCC gap fillers or default terms.

[27] *See* UCC §2-207 cmts. 4-5.

Starting with §2-207(3) If the Parties Have Performed

If the parties have performed, should you just start with §2-207(3)? If you do, you risk missing the real terms of the agreement. Sometimes the writings (or phone calls) really do establish a contract that includes the terms one party requested plus some of the terms (the nonmaterial changes) the other party sought. If you start with §2-207(3), you won't recognize assent to those terms. Start at the beginning. You might get down to §2-207(3), but it is your last resort. Consider again the ball bearing sale discussed above. If seller shipped and buyer paid, that conduct would indicate assent. But starting there overlooks the original acceptance and the modification accepted by silence. Thus, a court might knock out the terms on payment 30 days after delivery and 9 percent interest on past due amounts, which appear only in seller's response. The result might be bad for both parties: payment due on delivery disfavors buyer; a lower market interest rate disfavors seller. The parties' agreement might be better than the one a court makes up for them.

Confirming Memoranda

UCC §2-207 also applies to "a written confirmation that is sent within a reasonable time." The language covers parties who enter an oral contract, then confirm their agreement in writing. The drafting of the section is a little odd; technically, it states that a confirming memorandum "operates as an acceptance," even though the memorandum confirms an agreement already accepted. On one reading, "operates as an acceptance . . . unless" might suggest that the memorandum negates or replaces the earlier acceptance. The drafters probably did not intend that result. Even a memorandum that expressly provides that the party is willing to deal only on the terms it contains should not supersede an earlier acceptance that failed to include that qualification. It might announce an intent to breach or it might propose a modification, but cannot realistically turn the clock back to the time before the contract was formed.

Including confirming memoranda in §2-207(1) specifies how to deal with any new terms in the memoranda. They are proposals to modify the agreement already reached, just as they would be if included in an acceptance.

When memoranda follow a contract already reached, neither party's additional terms have an advantage over the other's terms. The original agreement, however rudimentary, can be interpreted and enforced without any of the terms in either party's confirming memorandum. Each party's memorandum serves as an objection to inconsistent terms in the other's writing, regardless of which memorandum was sent first. This effectively knocks out all terms on which the writings disagree (sometimes called the **complete knockout** rule): terms do not become part of the contract if "notification of objection to them has already been given."[28]

When either party's memorandum is silent on a term that the other party's memorandum proposes, that term is not knocked out. It may become part of the contract, as discussed in the preceding subsection. Terms need not be mentioned specifically to be knocked out. A memorandum may include a blanket objection to any terms other than those it specifies.

[28] *See* UCC §2-207(2)(c).

Applying §2-207

Even if the rules of §2-207 seem fairly clear, their application can be tricky. Because the terms of the offer have considerable weight, a lot turns on which communication you start with as the offer. Other points of difference include whether a proposed modification materially alters an agreement and whether the response was sufficiently explicit about being conditional on assent to its terms and no others.

Case Preview

Wachter Management Co. v. Dexter & Chaney, Inc.

In this case, a software supplier sought to enforce the terms of its software license agreement against the licensee. But the terms of the license agreement were not part of the negotiations between the parties. The licensee argued that these terms proposed modifications to the original contract, to which the licensee never agreed. The court applied UCC §2-207 to sort out whether the terms were part of the agreement between the parties. In so doing, the court reviewed several prominent cases applying the same rule in different ways.

As you read *Wachter Management Co. v. Dexter & Chaney, Inc.*, look for the following:

1. Did the supplier provide the recipient with fair notice that license terms would be part of the transaction? Should the recipient have realized those terms would be an important part of the deal?
2. Did the recipient expressly accept the terms of the license by making use of the software (without objection) despite knowing that the provider expected the terms of the license agreement to apply?
3. How did the court distinguish cases in which courts held the first offer occurs when the supplier delivers the product with the proposed additional terms? Do these cases provide a better account of the negotiations?

Wachter Management Co. v. Dexter & Chaney, Inc.

282 Kan. 365, 144 P.3d 747 (2006)

Rosen, J.

Wachter Management Company (Wachter) filed an action for breach of contract, breach of warranty, and fraudulent inducement against Dexter & Chaney, Inc. (DCI). DCI filed a motion to dismiss the action based on improper venue. The district court denied DCI's motion, holding that a choice of venue provision contained in a "shrinkwrap" software licensing agreement was not enforceable. DCI brings this interlocutory appeal pursuant to K.S.A. 60-2102(b).

FACTS

Wachter is a construction management company. . . . DCI is a software services company that develops, markets, and supports construction software, project management software, service management software, and document imaging software for construction companies like Wachter. . . .

. . . After detailed negotiations, DCI issued a written proposal to Wachter on October 15, 2003, for the purchase of an accounting and project management software system. The proposal included installation of the software, a full year of maintenance, and a training and consulting package. The proposal did not contain an integration clause or any provision indicating that it was the final and complete agreement of the parties, nor did the proposal contain any provision indicating that additional terms might be required. An agent for Wachter signed DCI's proposal at Wachter's Lenexa [Kansas] office on October 17, 2003.

Thereafter, DCI shipped the software and assisted Wachter in installing it on Wachter's computer system. Enclosed with the software, DCI included a software licensing agreement, also known as a "shrinkwrap" agreement, which provided:

> This is a legal agreement between you (the "CUSTOMER") and Dexter & Chaney, Inc. ("DCI"). By opening this sealed disk package, you agree to be bound by this agreement with respect to the enclosed software as well as any updates and/or applicable custom programming related thereto which you may have purchased or to which you may be entitled. If you do not accept the terms of this agreement, promptly return the unopened disk package and all accompanying documentation to DCI.
>
> . . .
>
> CUSTOMER ACKNOWLEDGES HAVING READ THIS AGREEMENT, UNDERSTANDS IT, AND AGREES TO BE BOUND BY ITS TERMS AND CONDITIONS. CUSTOMER ALSO AGREES THAT THIS AGREEMENT AND THE DCI INVOICE ENUMERATING THE NUMBER OF CONCURRENT LICENSED USERS TOGETHER COMPRISE THE COMPLETE AND EXCLUSIVE AGREEMENT BETWEEN THE PARTIES AND SUPERSEDE ALL PROPOSALS OR PRIOR AGREEMENTS, VERBAL OR WRITTEN, AND ANY OTHER COMMUNICATIONS BETWEEN THE PARTIES RELATING TO THE SUBJECT MATTER OF THIS AGREEMENT.

The software license agreement also contained a choice of law/venue provision providing that the agreement would be governed by the laws of [DCI's home state] Washington and that any disputes would be resolved by the state courts in King County, Washington.

In February 2005, after encountering problems with the software, Wachter sued DCI in Johnson County, Kansas . . . seeking damages in excess of $350,000. DCI moved to dismiss Wachter's petition, alleging improper venue based on the provision of the software licensing agreement. . . . In response, Wachter argued that the software licensing agreement was an unenforceable addition to the parties' original contract.

The district court denied DCI's motion, finding that the parties entered into a contract when Wachter signed DCI's proposal and concluding that the software license agreement contained additional terms that Wachter had not bargained for or accepted. . . .

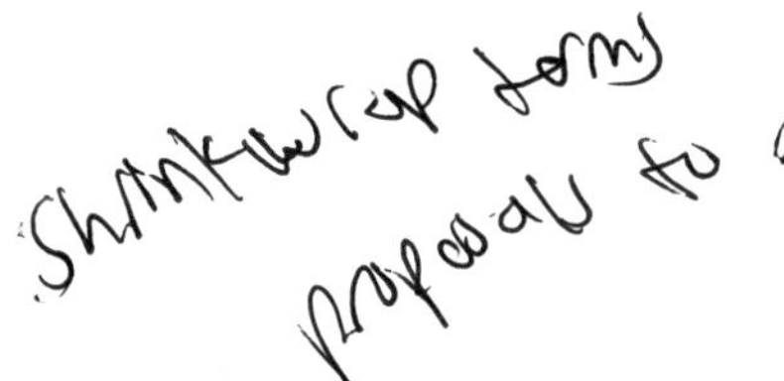

ANALYSIS

. . .

Computer software is considered to be goods subject to the UCC even though incidental services are provided along with the sale of the software. . . . Although DCI's proposal included maintenance, training, and consulting services . . . [b]ecause the services were incidental to Wachter's purchase of computer software, we conclude that the software at issue in this case qualifies under the definition of goods, and the UCC applies.

Pursuant to K.S.A. 84-2-204, a contract for the sale of goods is formed "in any manner sufficient to show agreement, including conduct by both parties which recognizes the existence of such a contract." . . .

In this case, DCI issued a written proposal to Wachter containing an itemized list of the software to be purchased, the quantity to be purchased, the price of the software, the time period for execution, and the cost for the incidental maintenance, training, and consulting services. DCI's proposal requested Wachter to accept its offer to sell Wachter software by signing the proposal above the words "[p]lease ship the software listed above." Accordingly, Wachter accepted DCI's offer to sell the software to it by signing the proposal at Wachter's office in Lenexa. Thus, a contract was formed when Wachter accepted DCI's offer to sell it the software, indicating agreement between the parties. [Citation omitted.]

K.S.A. 84-2-201 requires contracts for the sale of goods over $500 to be in writing and signed by the parties. The signed proposal constitutes a written contract in this case. The cover letter with DCI's proposal stated that it included "modules and licenses." However, DCI did not attach a copy of its Software Licensing Agreement to the proposal or incorporate it by reference in the proposal to indicate that there would be additional contract language regarding the licenses. Consequently, the parties' contract did not contain the terms of the Software Licensing Agreement. Wachter was advised of the terms of the Software Licensing Agreement after DCI shipped the software in partial performance of its duties under the contract. Because the Software Licensing Agreement was attached to the software rather than the original contract, it must be considered as an attempt to amend the contract.

The UCC addresses the modification of a contract. K.S.A. 84-2-207 provides in pertinent part:

> (1) A definite and seasonable expression of acceptance or a written confirmation which is sent within a reasonable time operates as an acceptance even though it states terms additional to or different from those offered or agreed upon, unless acceptance is expressly made conditional on assent to the additional or different terms.
>
> (2) The additional terms are to be construed as proposals for addition to the contract. . . .
>
> (3) Conduct by both parties which recognizes the existence of a contract is sufficient to establish a contract for sale although the writings of the parties do not otherwise establish a contract. In such case the terms of the particular contract consist of those terms on which the writings of the parties agree, together with any supplementary terms incorporated under any other provisions of this act.

[The court also quoted K.S.A. 84-2-209.]

Proposed amendments that materially alter the original agreement are not considered part of the contract unless both parties agree to the amendments. [Citation omitted.] . . .

DCI argues that Wachter expressly consented to the shrinkwrap agreement when it installed and used the software rather than returning it. However, continuing [to exercise rights granted under the original] contract after receiving a writing with additional or different terms is not sufficient to establish express consent to the additional or different terms. . . .

. . .

The *Klocek* case addressed the validity of an arbitration clause contained in a shrinkwrap-type agreement. In *Klocek*, a consumer purchased a Gateway computer. Gateway included its Standard Terms and Conditions Agreement (Agreement) inside the box with the computer. When the consumer sued for breach of contract and breach of warranty, Gateway filed a motion to dismiss, claiming that the consumer was bound by the arbitration clause in its Agreement. Assuming that the consumer offered to purchase the computer and Gateway accepted the offer by agreeing to ship or shipping the computer, the *Klocek* court treated Gateway's Agreement as an expression of acceptance or written confirmation of the consumer's offer to purchase and applied K.S.A. 84-2-207. [Citation omitted.] According to Gateway's Agreement, retaining the computer for more than 5 days constituted an acceptance of its Agreement. [T]he *Klocek* court rejected Gateway's argument, finding that the consumer was unaware that the transaction depended on his acceptance of the Agreement and concluding that the consumer had not expressly agreed to Gateway's terms. . . .

. . .

DCI does not address the application of the UCC or the analysis of *Step-Saver, Arizona Retail Systems, Klocek,* or *Orris.* Instead, DCI relies on Hill v. Gateway 2000, Inc., 105 F.3d 1147 (7th Cir. 1997); *ProCD v. Zeidenberg,* 86 F.3d 1447 (7th Cir. 1996); and *Mortenson Co. v. Timberline Software,* 140 Wash. 2d 568, 998 P.2d 305 (2000), for the proposition that shrinkwrap agreements are valid, and the terms contained within them are enforceable, because the purchaser accepts the terms when it uses the product.

In *ProCD,* a consumer purchased a software database program at a retail store. A license enclosed in the package with the software limited its use to non-commercial applications. The software also required a user to accept the license agreement by clicking an on-screen button before activating the software. Contrary to the license, the consumer made the database available on the internet at a reduced price. ProCD sued, seeking an injunction against further dissemination of its database.

The *ProCD* court determined that the *vendor* is the master of the offer under the UCC and may invite acceptance by conduct or limit the kind of conduct that constitutes acceptance. 86 F.3d at 1452. The court found that ProCD proposed a contract that invited acceptance by using the software after having an opportunity to review the license. If the buyer disagreed with the terms of the contract, he or she could return the software. Holding that the consumer was bound by the terms of the license agreement, the *ProCD* court stated that "[n]otice on the outside, terms on the inside, and a right to return the software for a refund if the terms are unacceptable (a right the license expressly extends), may be a means of doing business valuable to buyers and sellers alike." 86 F.3d at 1451.

In *Hill*, a consumer ordered a Gateway computer over the telephone. When the computer arrived, the box contained Gateway's standard terms governing the sale. According to Gateway's standard terms, the consumer accepted the terms by retaining the computer for 30 days. When the consumer was not satisfied with the operation of the computer, he sued Gateway on behalf of a class of similarly situated consumers. Relying on the *ProCD* court's analysis that the *vendor* is the master of the offer, the *Hill* court enforced the arbitration clause found in Gateway's standard terms even though the consumer was not aware of the terms until he received the computer. 105 F.3d at 1150. The *Hill* court noted that there are many commercial transactions in which money is exchanged for products with disclosure of certain terms of the sale following the execution of the sale. [Citations omitted.] The *Hill* court announced its policy that "[p]ractical considerations support allowing vendors to enclose the full legal terms with their products. . . . Customers as a group are better off when vendors skip costly and ineffectual steps such as telephonic recitation [of standard terms], and use a simple approve-or-return device." 105 F.3d at 1149.

Both *ProCD* and *Hill* can be distinguished from this case. The buyers in *ProCD* and *Hill* were both consumers who did not enter into negotiations with the vendors prior to their purchases. Wachter, on the other hand, participated in detailed negotiations with DCI before accepting DCI's proposal to sell Wachter the software. The *ProCD* and *Hill* courts concluded that the offer to sell software to the consumers was not accepted until the consumers opened the packaging with the terms of the sale enclosed and retained the product after having an opportunity to read the terms of the sale. Accordingly, the contract was not formed until the last act indicating acceptance occurred. Here, however, the last act indicating acceptance of DCI's offer to sell software to Wachter occurred when Wachter signed DCI's proposal. Thus, the contract was formed before DCI shipped the software and Wachter had an opportunity to consider the licensing agreement.

. . . In *Mortenson*, a construction contractor purchased software to assist with its bid preparation. The contractor issued a purchase order and the developer shipped the software accompanied by a shrinkwrap license, which included a limitation of remedies clause. Applying UCC 2-204, the *Mortenson* court held that the initial purchase order and the shrinkwrap license were part of a "layered contract" where the initial purchase order was not an integrated contract because it did not contain an integration clause and required additional terms to be determined later. . . . The *Mortenson* court adopted the contract formation analysis from *ProCD* and *Hill* and concluded that Mortenson's use of the software constituted its assent to the terms of the shrinkwrap license. . . .

Two of the Washington Supreme Court justices dissented from the *Mortenson* opinion, stating that "the majority abandons traditional contract principles governing offer and acceptance and relies on distinguishable cases with blind deference to software manufacturers' preferred method of conducting business." [Citation omitted.] The dissent [noted] that under traditional contract law principles the *offeror*, not just the *vendor*, is the master of the offer. [Citation omitted.] Observing that the construction contractor made an offer to purchase when it sent a purchase order to the software developer, the dissenting justices concluded that the parties formed a contract when the software developer accepted the terms of the purchase order by signing it. Because the contract was formed before the software developer delivered the product with the shrinkwrap license agreement, the dissenting justices treated the shrinkwrap agreement as a proposal to modify the terms of the contract pursuant to UCC 2-209. . . .

Although the facts in *Mortenson* are similar to the facts in this case, we disagree with the *Mortenson* court's analysis of when the contract was formed. We adhere to the traditional contract principles outlined by the dissenting justices in *Mortenson* and the decisions in *Step-Saver, Arizona Retail Systems, Klocek,* and *Orris.* The offeror, whether the seller or the buyer, is the master of the offer. See 84-2-206, Kansas Comment 2, 1996.

In this case, DCI and Wachter negotiated prior to entering into a contract for the sale of software. DCI's written proposal following the parties' negotiations constituted an offer to sell. Wachter accepted that offer when it signed the proposal, requesting shipment of the software. The contract was formed when Wachter accepted DCI's proposal. See K.S.A. 84-2-204. Because the contract was formed before DCI shipped the software with the enclosed license agreement, the Software Licensing Agreement must be treated as a proposal to modify the terms of the contract. See K.S.A. 84-2-209. There is no evidence that Wachter expressly agreed to the modified terms, and Wachter's actions in continuing the preexisting contract do not constitute express assent to the terms in the Software Licensing Agreement. Thus, the forum selection clause in the Software Licensing Agreement is not enforceable against Wachter. We affirm the district court's denial of DCI's motion to dismiss and remand the matter for further proceedings.

[Three justices dissented, primarily on the ground that DCI's proposal included a reference to "modules and licenses." This should have alerted Wachter that additional license terms would be required, in the same way that the outside of the box should have alerted Zeidenberg that additional license terms would be included in the software. Aware that the offer included additional terms, Wachter could not accept an offer that did not include those terms.]

Post-Case Follow-Up

The majority opinion represents a good interpretation of the UCC, but not one that is uniformly accepted. The approach starts by asking whether there was an agreement already in place before new terms were proposed. (That differs from *Hill v. Gateway*, where the court held shipment of the computer as the offer, treating the phone order and payment as preliminary discussions.) DCI's order might have been preliminary negotiations if Wachter had reason to know that DCI did not intend to be bound until Wachter agreed to the license terms that would be submitted later. The dissent believed the DCI's cover letter, by mentioning forthcoming "modules and licenses," alerted Wachter to the additional terms. On that view, the case would resemble *ProCD v. Zeidenberg*, where the software box warned the buyer that the license terms were inside, making it unrealistic to believe that the sale at the cash register formed a contract unlimited by the license terms.

The conclusion that the signed proposal was an enforceable contract forced discussion of whether a modification occurred. The court almost certainly is correct that if Wachter already had a right to use the software without the license terms, then using it does not expressly assent to the new terms. Opening the packages is consistent with exercising the contract rights already granted (though, of course, Wachter might have intended to accept the modification).

Wachter Management Co. v. Dexter & Chaney, Inc.: Real Life Applications

1. The Wachter court did not discuss whether the forum selection clause materially altered the deal DCI entered with Wachter—and even omitted that portion of §2-207 when quoting the statute. Should DCI seek rehearing, arguing that the forum selection clause became part of the deal by silence?
2. Portal Computers, a manufacturer of personal computers, seeks your advice. After decisions like *Klocek* and *Wachter*, it seeks a reliable way to ensure that the boilerplate terms it includes when it ships computers become part of any contract it enters with consumers over the phone. But it does not want to subject telephone buyers to lengthy recitation of terms, for fear they will hang up instead of completing the order. How would you advise them to proceed? If Portal asks about sales online, what advice would you give?
3. Val sells agricultural supplies to retailers, including goods bearing the retailer's logo. For five years, Kelly ordered supplies from Val, all bearing Kelly's logo. Kelly would place orders by phone; Val would ship the goods and send an invoice, which Kelly would pay. This year, Val shipped goods that did not bear Kelly's logo, thus failing to conform to the contract. In protest, Kelly refused to pay any of Val's invoices until Val corrected the problem. Val sued Kelly for payment on 30 invoices totaling $250,000, including interest at 1.5 percent per month, a term specified on the invoices but never discussed by the parties. Kelly seeks your advice concerning whether the interest term in the invoices is part of their contract. Apparently, the term has been in every invoice for the last five years, though Kelly never saw it before.

Chapter Summary

- Acceptance must conform to all the requirements of an offer, including both the substantive terms of the offer and any requirements relating to the time, place, and manner for conveying acceptance.
- An offer terminates when it is rejected, a counteroffer is made, it is revoked by the offeror, the time specified in the offer expires (or a reasonable time passes), either the offeror or offeree dies or becomes incapacitated, or a condition of acceptance no longer can occur.

- Revocations, counteroffers, rejections, and some acceptances take effect when received (meaning delivered, not necessarily noticed or read). If the mailbox rule applies, acceptance takes effect when dispatched.
- If the offer permits (but does not require) acceptance by performance, an offeree can accept the offer by beginning to perform (or tendering performance or a beginning of performance). Beginning to perform operates as a promise to finish performance, creating a binding contract immediately.
- If an offer requires acceptance by performance, an offeree can accept the offer by completing the required performance. Once the offeree begins to perform (or tenders performance or a beginning of performance), the offeror may not revoke the offer until the offeree has a fair opportunity to complete performance or the offeree abandons performance.
- Silence generally is a rejection rather than assent. In some unusual circumstances, a failure to object to an offer will accept the offer.
- For sales of goods, a definite acceptance may propose new terms without being a counteroffer, unless the response expressly limits acceptance to the new terms. The contract arises on the terms of the original offer unless the new terms are accepted by the offeror.
- For sales of goods between merchants, failure to object to new terms proposed in an acceptance or confirming memorandum may accept those terms, unless the new terms materially alter the transaction. If either party is not a merchant, a new term proposed in an acceptance or confirming memorandum will not become part of the contract unless expressly accepted by the other party.
- When parties' performance of a sale of goods demonstrates the existence of a contract despite the lack of any assent in the communications exchanged, courts will enforce a contract on any terms to which the parties did agree in their communications, filling in any gaps with the default provisions in the Uniform Commercial Code.

Applying the Rules

1. Cameron owned a small collection of baseball memorabilia collected over decades as a fan. Knowing that Val, Cameron's adult child, cherished the memorabilia as much as Cameron did, Cameron offered to sell the collection to Val for $5,000 (much less than its market value). While Cameron was considering the offer, Lynn, Val's sibling, visited Cameron, said, "I accept your offer to sell the collection for $5,000," and tendered $5,000 cash to Cameron on the spot.

    a. Does Lynn's acceptance of the offer create a contract with Cameron?
    b. If Cameron took the $5,000 from Lynn, but Val accepted the offer the next day, is Cameron now bound to sell the collection to Val? Does it matter whether Val knew that Lynn already had paid $5,000 for it?
    c. Suppose Cameron delivered the memorabilia to Val and offered to return Lynn's money. Can Lynn enforce the contract against Cameron?

2. Alex owned a classic 1955 MGA sports car. Alex needed to sell the car to generate cash for a divorce settlement. Alex first offered the car to Lou, an acquaintance, for $75,000. Lou responded via e-mail, "I'll take it as long as you include any spare parts you have obtained over the years." Alex held relatively few spare parts worth no more than $1,000 to someone with a 1955 MGA and worthless to anyone else. Before Alex could respond, Alex received word that a reconciliation might be possible. Alex decided not to sell the car right now. If Lou asserts a contract right to buy the car, will Lou prevail?

3. Sam offered to sell Bobby a used boat for $15,000, asking Bobby to accept by e-mail before noon on Thursday. Wednesday morning, Sam sent an e-mail to Bobby accepting the offer and asking when Sam would like to meet to make the exchange. Wednesday night, Sam e-mailed Bobby saying Sam had just received a better offer for the boat and, since Bobby had not yet responded, Sam had decided to take that offer. Bobby replied by forwarding the acceptance sent that morning (with a clear time stamp on it). In trying to figure out why Sam had not received the acceptance, Sam noticed that the e-mail address was mistyped, using a comma instead of a dot. Bobby immediately (still Wednesday night) sent Sam a new e-mail accepting the offer and explaining how the error had occurred. Has Bobby accepted Sam's offer in a timely manner?

4. On August 1, Owen offered to sell Barrett an undeveloped parcel of real estate for $80,000. In exchange for $5, Owen agreed to keep the offer open until August 10, allowing Barrett time to evaluate the development potential of the property. On August 3, Owen informed Barrett that the land was no longer for sale because Owen's children wanted Owen to keep the land for them to use. Barrett urged Owen to reconsider but Owen remained firm, even when Barrett threatened to sue. On August 9, Owen sent Barrett a certified letter accepting the offer, along with a cashier's check for the down payment required upon acceptance. Owen signed for the letter on August 11. Was a contract for the sale of the real estate formed?

5. Shelly, knowing Jean admired a painting Shelly owned, offered to sell it to Jean for $10,000. Initially confused about which painting Shelly meant, Jean said, "No way. I would never pay that much for that ugly thing. Oh, wait, do you mean the one in your office? I love that painting. Yes, please. How soon do you want your money?" Shelly did mean the one in the office, but was insulted by Jean's comment about the other painting and no longer wanted to sell. Has a contract already been formed for the sale of the painting? Or does Shelly remain free to keep the painting?

6. Jan and Chris wanted to sell the furniture in their apartment in preparation for a move across the country. They offered their dining room set (table, chairs, buffet, and hutch) to Sascha for $8,000. Sascha wanted to confer with Gene (Sascha's spouse) before paying so much and asked how long they would keep the offer open. Jan said they needed to know by 5:00 P.M. that day.

a. At 5:30 P.M., Sascha called Jan and accepted the offer of the furniture. Was a contract formed by that phone call?
b. The reason Jan needed to know by 5:00 was to provide accurate information to the estimator for a moving company about how much furniture would be moved. The estimator arrived late, so Jan received Sascha's call before the estimator arrived. On these facts, did Sascha's response create a contract? (Assume Jan was piqued by the late acceptance without so much as a polite "Is it still available?" and, therefore, prefers not to sell to Sascha at that price anymore.)

7. FUZZ!, a cable television reality show, offered a $25,000 reward for anyone who provided information leading to the arrest and indictment of an individual who committed a series of assaults in a beachfront neighborhood. The offer included a hotline number for the show and pledged to protect the caller's anonymity. Gail became a victim of the assailant and managed to provide police with a description that allowed them to identify and indict a suspect. Gail never called the FUZZ! hotline. Gail later demanded that FUZZ! pay the reward. Has Gail accepted the reward offer?

8. City hired Optix to install fiber-optic cable in specified neighborhoods in the city. The contract required Optix to start on August 1 and finish within 90 days. Both parties expected the actual work to require only 45 days, but included extra days for weather or other unavoidable delays. A backlog in orders for the required poles forced Optix to request a change in the start date to October 20, the earliest the poles would be available. City agreed, provided that Optix agree to complete the work within 45 days. Optix did not respond. Optix began work on October 20. Optix encountered delays due to inclement weather. Nonetheless, Optix completed the work on January 17, the 90th day after October 20. City paid for the work, minus the liquidated damages for 45 days, alleging Optix breached by failing to complete the work by December 4. Did the contract require completion within 45 days or 90 days?

Contract Law in Practice

1. Casey's house suffered flood damage. Desperate to make the house presentable before a family reunion that weekend, Casey sent an e-mail to Recovery, a local company specializing in restoring homes damaged by floods. The e-mail gave the address and described the extent of the damage, then stated, "If you will complete the restoration of my home by noon on Friday, I will pay you $4,000." The offer made no other provisions regarding when or how Recovery should reply. That offer was about $1,000 more than the usual price for work of this magnitude. Upon reading the e-mail, Recovery dispatched a team to the address, arriving within two hours of the time the e-mail was sent. The team began unloading its equipment while Jesse, the foreman, knocked on the

door and asked to see the damaged area. Casey showed Jesse the damage and Jesse began planning where to locate fans, what carpet to remove, and other details of the work. Before work began, a representative of DryFast, a competitor of Recovery, arrived to do the work. Casey explained that when Recovery did not respond, Casey hired DryFast to do the work for $3,700. He sent Recovery an e-mail revoking the offer 30 minutes ago (while Jesse was already en route and the dispatcher was at lunch). Casey let Jesse into the house believing Jesse was from DryFast. (Casey did not look at the van outside with Recovery's name prominently displayed.) Casey honors the deal struck with DryFast and refused to allow Jesse to proceed with the work. After returning to the office, Jesse learned that the dispatcher refused two other jobs because Recovery had no remaining personnel to do the work. Recovery seeks compensation for its losses. Prepare a demand letter for Recovery explaining to Casey why Recovery is entitled to damages for breach of contract. (If you believe Recovery is not entitled to damages, prepare a memorandum for Jesse explaining why Recovery should not send the demand letter.)

2. You have been consulted by AlphaCo, a company with 3,000 at-will employees. AlphaCo wants to change its policy and procedure manual to add a provision requiring that all employment disputes be submitted to binding arbitration. Its current employment manual provides that "[Employer] reserves the right to change or rescind, in whole or in part, at any time and without liability to anyone, the policies, principles and practices stated in this manual." What steps must it take in order to make the change effective and binding on the employees? If AlphaCo also wanted the change to apply to its 400 employees who have one-year contracts, would that require different steps? The one-year contracts renew automatically unless either party gives 30 days' notice of an intent not to renew the contract.

3. Rules governing the receipt of written communications have a long history. Rules governing the receipt of oral communications do not. Until recently, oral communications were spoken and heard simultaneously. The advent of answering machines and later voice mail now make it possible that a spoken communication can be put out of the speaker's control and yet the recipient may not hear it until much later, if at all. Research your jurisdiction to determine whether it treats oral communications that are not heard immediately the same way it treats written communications. If your jurisdiction does not have case law governing the point, draft a statute to clarify when an oral communication takes effect for purposes of contract formation. Exchange draft statutes with a classmate. Comment on your classmate's draft, offering any advice that would make it stronger. Discuss whether to propose a statute to the legislature.

4. Review the facts of the *Wachter* case. If these facts arose in your state, would the courts there hold that the forum selection clause materially altered the contract or that the forum selection clause became part of the contract when Wachter failed to object to it? If the cases in your jurisdiction are split (or if there are

none), prepare a memorandum explaining how the split should be resolved on the facts of *Wachter*.

5. Donald Khan, owner of a large wine and gourmet food store, recently decided to begin selling wine storage units—large wooden cabinets containing wine racks and climate control units designed to keep wine at the optimal temperature and humidity conditions for prolonged storage and aging. Khan called Cellar Sellers, a manufacturer of these units, and discussed the sizes, woods, and design, as well as the prices available to retailers. Cellar Sellers mentioned that, in addition to paying a lower price, retailers who ordered five or more units received an additional discount of 1 percent per unit ordered, up to a maximum of 20 percent. On January 15, Khan sent Cellar Sellers the following e-mail:

> Per our conversation, please send me 20 Vinophile 2000 model 1440 DeLuxe wine storage units. Please ship the units in 4 lots, 5 units each, to arrive on or immediately before March 1, July 1, October 1, and December 1. In the shipment for March 1, please send 2 units of oak, 2 of teak, and 1 of mahogany. Please call to confirm price and availability of mahogany [a wood not discussed on the phone]. I will specify woods for July shipment by May 1.

Khan immediately alerted customers to the new line of merchandise, promising a debut March 1.

On January 16, Cellar Sellers' sales department replied as follows:

> Received your order for 5 model 1440 DeLuxe. Will ship March 1 via BatVan Lines, insured, at your expense. Invoice to accompany goods. Deposit of $1,000 per unit required before shipment. Payment in full due 30 days after delivery. Interest at 6% charged on overdue accounts. Not responsible for any commercial consequential damages. Our liability exclusively limited to repair or replacement of any nonconforming merchandise.

Mr. Khan sent Cellar Sellers a check for $5,000. He did not reply to the letter in any other way.

The goods were shipped March 1 and arrived March 7—six days late according to Khan, a delay that cost Khan at least one potential sale. The invoice allowed a discount of 5 percent rather than 20 percent.

a. Did the parties ever make a contract? What was the offer, and what was the acceptance? Would either party argue that there never was a contract?
b. What quantity of goods did the contract require?
c. Did the contract require shipment or delivery on March 1? Or is a different delivery term appropriate?
d. Did the limitation of remedy in Cellar Sellers' e-mail become part of the contract?
e. Did Khan's $5,000 payment agree to all of the terms in Cellar Sellers' e-mail or just to the deposit requirement? Did Khan do anything else that would

accept those terms? Can Khan do anything now to avoid the inference that he accepted those terms?

f. Cellar Sellers asks for help preventing disputes like this from recurring. What language should it include in future communications to avoid this kind of difficulty? Which communications should include that language?
g. Khan seeks to avoid similar disputes from occurring in the future. What steps would you recommend to Khan in order to avoid problems of this sort?

6. Compare §2-207 of the Uniform Commercial Code with Article 19 of the Convention on International Sale of Goods. How do they differ? Analyze the preceding problem under the CISG (which would apply if Cellar Sellers were located in France).

7. Parties engaged in international sales of goods may opt out of the CISG and specify a different rule of law (for example, the Uniform Commercial Code) to govern their disputes. Prepare a memorandum advising Khan whether (and if so, how) to include a provision specifying that the UCC governs any disputes arising under a contract.

4

Consideration

In our daily lives, we may make many promises to other people. We may feel bound to comply with our promises out of respect for our social obligations or our sense of ethics to stand by our promises. Yet not every promise we make is legally enforceable under contract law. A promise to pay rent under an apartment lease is quite different than a promise to give a law school friend a ride home after classes. Under the terms of a lease, your promise to pay your rent in exchange for the right to inhabit an owner's apartment, along with other lease terms, is likely a sufficient exchange to establish consideration. However, your social promise to give a friend a ride home is not likely to be viewed as a legally enforceable exchange. But why?

Finding consideration is the primary way in which courts separate out enforceable legal duties from other social relationships or ethical obligations. A valid offer and acceptance become a contract if there is consideration. If a court determines that there is no consideration, then there is no contract unless an exception to consideration applies. Enforcement without consideration will be discussed in Chapter 5. Courts have utilized different approaches in determining if consideration is present, and we will explore the classical and modern judicial views on consideration in this chapter.

In and outside of court, lawyers and their clients may spend a great deal of time and effort trying to determine whether or not a promise is legally enforceable under the doctrine of consideration. When dealing with contract matters for your clients, you will need a clear understanding of the intricacies of consideration and any applicable

Key Concepts

- The classical "benefit-detriment" approach to consideration
- The Holmesian modern "bargain" theory of consideration
- Exchanges that do not establish consideration, such as gratuitous promises, conditional gifts, sham consideration, and illusory promises
- Court deference to the parties on the adequacy or value of consideration

exceptions. In this chapter, we will also distinguish instances of exchanges that do not fit into the formal requirements of consideration.

A. INTRODUCTION TO CONSIDERATION

Chapter 1 offered an explanation for why the law limits enforcement to bargained-for exchanges. This chapter examines **consideration**, the doctrine requiring a legally recognized exchange in order to justify enforcement of a promise. Historically, contracts were only enforceable if parties delivered paper documents to each other bearing their personalized wax seals to show their agreement. Ultimately, this traditional method gave way to the legal development of the concept of consideration. It may not be as easy to spot consideration when there is no visual cue, such as an embossed seal upon which to rely. Courts have delved into a number of difficult situations when consideration is being questioned.

In many instances, it may be quite straightforward to find consideration. Promises to pay or the payment of money in exchange for delivering goods or performing services is a typical example of consideration. But in other cases, it may not be money, but an exchange of promises, a promise for an action, or a barter arrangement for goods or services. The cases in this chapter on consideration will look at a variety of challenging examples, probing the boundaries of the doctrine.

In certain cases, it may seem unfair to reject the enforcement of promises that do not meet the technical requirements of consideration. As a result, U.S. courts have permitted limited exceptions, allowing enforcement even when the technicalities of consideration are not satisfied. Some efforts to expand enforcement have been unsuccessful, as the effort to apply consideration to an exchange of gifts (a promise made out of gratitude for a gift already promised or received). Alternative approaches have been more successful, such as enforcing promises after the promisee relies on the promise under **reliance** (also known as **promissory estoppel**). Chapter 5 addresses reliance and other grounds for enforcement, which justify enforcement of some promises that lack consideration.

Expanding contract rights to promises for which no consideration exists could undermine the doctrine itself, allowing almost any promise to be enforced. But consideration is a legal doctrine, not an immutable commandment. This concept may evolve or be dispensed with over time. It is important to note that consideration is not broadly embraced outside of nations based in English common law. Generally, civil law nations do not employ the doctrine of consideration

CISG: Harmonizing Global Commerce in Goods

In 1980, the United Nations sponsored the CISG for goods transactions between commercial parties from different countries who are CISG signatories. The United States became a signatory on August 31, 1981. About 85 countries have either signed or agreed to abide by the provisions of the CISG and a current list of nations can be found on the UN's CISG site. This convention strives to harmonize key business and legal commercial norms on a global basis. In that vein, some major contract principles found in the United States under the UCC may not be recognized or may be viewed quite differently under the CISG. Exhibit 4.1 shows a summary chart of key contract principles comparing the UCC and CISG.

in contracts. The **Convention on Contracts for the International Sale of Goods (CISG)**, the treaty governing sales of **goods** (things that are moveable) between parties from different nations, does not require a showing of consideration. Since the CISG applies to sales of goods, there will be an exchange in most instances, consistent with consideration.

EXHIBIT 4.1 **Summary of Contract Principles Comparing the UCC and CISG**

Contract Concept	UCC Section	CISG	Relevant CISG Article(s)
Offer and Acceptance	2-204, 2-206	Yes	Arts. 14 & 18
Consideration	1-204(4)	No	Arts. 11 & 23
Firm Offer	2-205	Yes, but few formalities	Art. 16(2)
Battle of the Forms	2-207	No	Art. 19
Statute of Frauds	2-201	No	Art. 11
Parol Evidence Rule	2-202	No	Arts. 8 & 11
Perfect Tender Rule	2-601	No	Arts. 25 & 49

B. THE BASIC RULE OF CONSIDERATION

Consideration requires two key features: **legal sufficiency** and **bargained-for exchange**. Legal sufficiency indicates that something of legally recognized value must be the foundation of the agreement between the contracting parties. The Restatement (Second) of Contracts §71 offers several examples of things of value, including, but not limited to, a return promise; performing an act; not performing a particular act (forbearance); or creating, altering, or giving up legal rights and legal relationships.

In addition, this legally sufficient value must be given as part of a bargained-for exchange between the parties. A bargained-for exchange exists if a party making a promise seeks a performance or a return promise to be given by another in exchange for that promise. The rule limits enforcement to exchanges; once performed, each party will obtain something that it seeks (and presumably wants) in exchange for what it gives up.

For example, you may pay a company to put a fence around your property, in essence exchanging a promise to pay the company for its promise to install a fence. Conversely, you might promise to pay a neighbor $1,000 not to put up a fence that might block your access to a park or your view of a lake; promising to pay money in exchange for her promise not to act. Alternatively, offering to drive a friend home after classes may be socially rewarding, but it is not likely to be an exchange of legally recognized value. You are providing a ride to help out a friend, but your friend is not required to give anything of legal value, such as gas money, to you in return.

Under a **bilateral contract**, the parties are exchanging a promise for a promise. Most contracts are bilateral because each party is promising to do something for the other at the time the contract is signed or in the future. Consideration in a **unilateral contract** involves the exchange of a promise for an action. A party makes a promise seeking the performance of a particular act or course of conduct in return.

Clearly, money in exchange for property, goods, or services is a common form of consideration for many contracts, but money is not always required. Bartering for goods and/or services between contracting parties without money passing hands may also involve an exchange of legally recognized value. These examples may seem clear to you, but we will examine cases in which identifying consideration may be more difficult.

1. Classical View—"Benefit-Detriment" Analysis

In determining the existence of consideration, courts have used different approaches to address this doctrine. The traditional view examines consideration under the **"benefit-detriment"** analysis. This approach asks whether or not the promisor receives a benefit or the promisee suffers a detriment, loss, or forbearance. The "promisor" is the party resisting enforcement of the contract, the one arguing that consideration is not satisfied. The promisee is the party trying to enforce the claimed promise. The rule asks whether the promisor received something of legal value in exchange for the promise that she made to the other party, the promisee. Alternatively, the promisee may show a loss or detriment in carrying out obligations based on the promise to support consideration.

For example, Rodrigo agrees with his neighbor, Nina, to pay half of the costs of putting up a privacy fence between their backyards. Nina spends $5,000 to put up the fence and then Rodrigo refuses to pay his half. In trying to enforce their deal, Rodrigo is the promisor who is resisting enforcement and Nina is the promisee seeking to enforce his promise. Under the benefit-detriment approach, Rodrigo may argue that Nina suffered no detriment because the fence gives her privacy and marks their property boundaries regardless of whether or not he pays his 50 percent share. Nina could argue that she suffered a detriment of $2,500 by having to pay all the costs of the fence. In addition, she may claim that Rodrigo benefitted by improving his privacy and delineating their property boundaries with the fence. Although this example may offer a clear example of a benefit to a promisor or a detriment to a promisee, in other cases it may be more difficult to determine promisor benefit or promisee detriment. The case of *Hamer v. Sidway* is a good example of a case where it can be much more difficult to sort out promisor benefit or promisee detriment.

Case Preview

Hamer v. Sidway

The well-known case of *Hamer v. Sidway* provides a good example of the application of the classical "benefit-detriment" approach. The court must wrestle with whether or not the promisor (the uncle) received a benefit or the promisee (the nephew) suffered a detriment in order to find consideration for their agreement.

As you read *Hamer v. Sidway*, look for the following:

1. Who was the promisor in this dispute? Who was the promisee?
2. Did the promisor receive a benefit of legal value?
3. Did the promisee suffer any detriment in this case?
4. Was the uncle's promise merely a social commitment, but not a legal contract?

Hamer v. Sidway

124 N.Y. 538 (1891)

PARKER J.

[At the celebration of a wedding anniversary, an uncle, William E. Story, promises to pay $5,000 to his teenaged nephew, William E. Story, II, if he does not drink, use tobacco, swear, or play cards or billiards for money until age 21. There is no dispute that the nephew lives up to his uncle's high standards. In a series of letters, they agree that the uncle will keep the funds in trust for the nephew until he gets older, and help him grow his investment. Unfortunately, the uncle dies before distributing the funds to his nephew, who has assigned his rights to the money to his wife, with his uncle's knowledge and approval, and then on to Louisa Hamer, to whom a debt was owed. The executor for the uncle's estate, Franklin Sidway, refuses to pay the accumulated funds to Hamer, claiming that no contract ever existed.]

The question which provoked the most discussion by counsel on this appeal, and which lies at the foundation of plaintiff's asserted right of recovery, is whether by virtue of a contract defendant's testator William E. Story became indebted to his nephew William E. Story, 2d, on his twenty-first birthday in the sum of five thousand dollars. . . .

. . .

The defendant [executor Sidway] contends that the contract was without consideration to support it, and, therefore, invalid. He asserts that the promisee by refraining from the use of liquor and tobacco was not harmed but benefited; that that which he did was best for him to do independently of his uncle's promise, and insists that it follows that unless the promisor was benefited, the contract was without consideration. A contention, which if well founded, would seem to leave open for controversy in many cases whether that which the promise[e] did or omitted to do was, in fact, of such benefit to him as to leave no consideration to support the enforcement of the promisor's agreement. Such a rule could not be tolerated, and is without foundation in the law. The Exchequer Chamber, in 1875, defined consideration as follows: "A valuable consideration in the sense of the law may consist either in some right, interest, profit or benefit accruing to the one party, or some forbearance, detriment, loss or responsibility given, suffered or undertaken by the other." Courts "will not ask whether the thing which forms the consideration does in fact benefit the promisee or a third party, or is of any substantial value to anyone. It is enough that something is promised, done, forborne or suffered by the party to whom the promise is made as consideration for the promise made to him." [Citation omitted.]

"In general a waiver of any legal right at the request of another party is a sufficient consideration for a promise." [Citation omitted.]

"Any damage, or suspension, or forbearance of a right will be sufficient to sustain a promise." . . . "Consideration means not so much that one party is profiting as that the other abandons some legal right in the present or limits his legal freedom of action in the future as an inducement for the promise of the first."

Now, applying this rule to the facts before us, the promisee used tobacco, occasionally drank liquor, and he had a legal right to do so. That right he abandoned for a period of years upon the strength of the promise of the testator that for such forbearance he would give him $5,000. We need not speculate on the effort which may have been required to give up the use of those stimulants. It is sufficient that he restricted his lawful freedom of action within certain prescribed limits upon the faith of his uncle's agreement, and now having fully performed the conditions imposed, it is of no moment whether such performance actually proved a benefit to the promisor, and the court will not inquire into it, but were it a proper subject of inquiry, we see nothing in this record that would permit a determination that the uncle was not benefited in a legal sense. Few cases have been found which may be said to be precisely in point, but such as have been support the position we have taken.

In *Shadwell v. Shadwell* (9 C. B. [N. S.] 159), an uncle wrote to his nephew as follows:

> "My Dear Lancey—I am so glad to hear of your intended marriage with Ellen Nicholl, and as I promised to assist you at starting, I am happy to tell you that I will pay to you 150 pounds yearly during my life and until your annual income derived from your profession of a chancery barrister shall amount to 600 guineas, of which your own admission will be the only evidence that I shall require.
>
> "Your affectionate uncle,
>
> "CHARLES SHADWELL."

It was held that the promise was binding and made upon good consideration.

In *Lakota v. Newton*, an unreported case in the Superior Court of Worcester, Mass., the complaint averred defendant's promise that "if you (meaning plaintiff) will leave off drinking for a year I will give you $100," plaintiff's assent thereto, performance of the condition by him, and demanded judment [sic] therefor. Defendant demurred on the ground, among others, that the plaintiff's declaration did not allege a valid and sufficient consideration for the agreement of the defendant. The demurrer was overruled.

In *Talbott v. Stemmons* (a Kentucky case not yet reported), the stepgrandmother of the plaintiff made with him the following agreement: "I do promise and bind myself to give my grandson, Albert R. Talbott, $500 at my death, if he will never take another chew of tobacco or smoke another cigar during my life from this date up to my death, and if he breaks his pledge he is to refund double the amount to his mother." The executor of Mrs. Stemmons demurred to the complaint on the ground that the agreement was not based on a sufficient consideration. The demurrer was sustained and an appeal taken therefrom to the Court of Appeals, where the decision of the court below was reversed. In the opinion of the court it is said that "the right to use and enjoy the use of tobacco was a right that belonged to the plaintiff and not forbidden by law. The abandonment of its use may have saved him money or contributed to his health, nevertheless, the surrender of that right caused the promise, and having the right to contract with reference to the subject-matter, the abandonment of the use was a sufficient consideration to uphold the promise." Abstinence from the use of intoxicating liquors was held to furnish a good consideration for a promissory note in *Lindell v. Rokes* (60 Mo. 249).

. . .

In further consideration of the questions presented, then, it must be deemed established for the purposes of this appeal, that on the 31st day of January, 1875, defendant's testator was indebted to William E. Story, 2d, in the sum of $5,000, and if this action were founded on that contract it would be barred by the Statute of Limitations which has been pleaded, but on that date the nephew wrote to his uncle as follows:

> "Dear Uncle—I am now 21 years old to-day, and I am now my own boss, and I believe, according to agreement, that there is due me $5,000. I have lived up to the contract to the letter in every sense of the word."

A few days later, and on February sixth, the uncle replied, and, so far as it is material to this controversy, the reply is as follows:

> "Dear Nephew—Your letter of the 31st ult. came to hand all right saying that you had lived up to the promise made to me several years ago. I have no doubt but you have, for which you shall have $5,000 as I promised you. I had the money in the bank the day you was 21 years old that I intended for you, and you shall have the money certain. Now, Willie, I don't intend to interfere with this money in any way until I think you are capable of taking care of it, and the sooner that time comes the better it will please me. I would hate very much to have you start out in some adventure that you thought all right and lose this money in one year. . . . This money you have earned much easier than I did, besides acquiring good habits at the same time, and you are quite welcome to the money. Hope you will make good use of it. . . .
>
> "W. E. STORY.
> "P. S.—You can consider this money on interest."

The trial court found as a fact that "said letter was received by said William E. Story, 2d, who thereafter consented that said money should remain with the said William E. Story in accordance with the terms and conditions of said letter." And further, "That afterwards, on the first day of March, 1877, with the knowledge and consent of his said uncle, he duly sold, transferred and assigned all his right, title and interest in and to said sum of $5,000 to his wife Libbie H. Story, who thereafter duly sold, transferred and assigned the same to the plaintiff in this action."

. . .

It is essential that the letter interpreted in the light of surrounding circumstances must show an intention on the part of the uncle to become a trustee before he will be held to have become such; but in an effort to ascertain the construction which should be given to it, we are also to observe the rule that the language of the promisor is to be interpreted in the sense in which he had reason to suppose it was understood by the promisee. (*White v. Hoyt*, 73 N.Y. 505, 511.) At the time the uncle wrote the letter he was indebted to his nephew in the sum of $5,000, and payment had been requested. The uncle recognizing the indebtedness, wrote the nephew that he would keep the money until he deemed him capable of taking care of it. He did not say "I will pay you at some other time," or use language that would indicate that the relation of debtor and creditor would continue. On the contrary, his language indicated that he had set apart the money the nephew had "earned" for him so that when he should be capable of taking care of it he should receive it with interest. He said: "I had the money in the bank the day you were 21 years old that I intended for you and you shall have the money certain." That he had set apart the money is further evidenced by the next sentence: "Now, Willie, I don't intend to interfere with this money in any way until I think you are capable of taking care of it." Certainly, the uncle must have intended that his nephew should understand that the promise not "to interfere with this money" referred to the money in the bank which he declared was not only there when the nephew became 21 years old, but was intended for him. True, he did not use the word "trust," or state that the money was deposited in the name of William E. Story, 2d, or in his own name in trust for him, but the language used must have been intended to assure the nephew that his money had been set apart for him, to be kept without interference until he should be capable of taking care of it, for the uncle said in substance and in effect: "This money you have earned much easier than I did . . . you are quite welcome to. I had it in the bank the day you were 21 years old and don't intend to interfere with it in any way until I think you are capable of taking care of it and the sooner that time comes the better it will please me." In this declaration there is not lacking a single element necessary for the creation of a valid trust, and to that declaration the nephew assented.

The learned judge who wrote the opinion of the General Term, seems to have taken the view that the trust was executed during the life-time of defendant's testator by payment to the nephew, but as it does not appear from the order that the judgment was reversed on the facts, we must assume the facts to be as found by the trial court, and those facts support its judgment.

The order appealed from should be reversed and the judgment of the Special Term affirmed, with costs payable out of the estate. All concur.

Post-Case Follow-Up

Applying the classical approach, the *Hamer* court determined that a promisee's restriction on a legal right is sufficient consideration. The nephew may have also benefitted from refraining from smoking, drinking, or gambling. But this benefit did not undermine his detriment — giving up his legal right to do something, even if his forbearance benefitted his health or reputation. The court did not judge how much effort it took for the nephew to avoid these temptations, but only that he restrained his legal rights, which was sufficient to establish consideration.

Hamer v. Sidway: Real Life Applications

1. Your law firm is advising an executor of a will that bequeaths different amounts to three children of a deceased mother. Two daughters are each bequeathed $50,000 and the son, Doug, is bequeathed $30,000. The son contests his distribution, claiming that he complained to his mother about these unequal inheritances numerous times. Eventually, his mother offered to equalize his share if Doug stopped griping about his inheritance during her lifetime. Doug promised not to raise the issue and complied with their agreement. He now wants an equal share under his contract with his mother. The executor refuses to pay him any additional funds claiming no consideration. Is there consideration under the classical benefit-detriment theory?
2. Did Doug's mother benefit from his silence about her will distributions?
3. Did Doug restrict any legal right in exchange for an equal inheritance share?
4. Review the case of *White v. Bluett*, 23 LJ Ex 36 (1853), to determine how an English court decided a very similar dispute under the benefit-detriment theory.

---

2. Modern View—Bargain Theory

Over time, the benefit-detriment approach became less effective when applied to more complex contractual relationships. In most modern contracts, each party is willing to trade off benefits and risks in order to come to an agreement. Supreme Court Justice Oliver Wendell Holmes, Jr. (1841-1935) championed an emphasis on the bargain theory of consideration, later supported in the Restatement (Second) of Contracts §71. The **bargain theory** looks to the notion of reciprocal conventional inducement; each party's promise induces the other to respond with a return promise, action, or forbearance. Consideration does not turn on the motivations of either the promisor or the promisee, but whether a party is seeking something in an exchange. Despite its name, this approach to consideration does not mandate that parties expressly negotiate each and every detail in their contract. For example, a consumer may wish to buy perfume from a merchant's online website. The consumer agrees to buy the perfume for the stated price from the merchant under the site's terms and conditions by clicking on "I Agree." The promise to pay the purchase price induces the merchant to send the ordered perfume and the merchant's promise to send the requested perfume induces the consumer to promise to pay the price. The merchant receives the payment in exchange for the consumer receiving the perfume. Each party is promising to give something in return for getting something under the deal.

In contemporary contracts, we are often entering into **contracts of adhesion**, standardized contracts offered on a "take it or leave it" basis with little or no negotiation. These types of agreements provide efficiencies of time, expense, and effort in an era of mass-produced goods and services. Statutory law and judicial decisions on public policy and unconscionability may help to avoid excesses in these kinds of contracts and will be discussed in greater detail in Chapter 8. The bargain theory focuses on whether or not there was a valid exchange between the contracting parties, not mutual negotiations. The *Meadors* case illustrates the changing analysis of consideration in modern contract law.

Case Preview

United States v. Meadors

The *Meadors* case provides an interesting discussion of the evolution of consideration from the classical benefit-detriment approach to the modern Holmesian view with its focus on the exchange or bargain. The Restatement view also focuses on the exchange, rather than promisor benefit or promisee detriment.

As you read *United States v. Meadors*, look for the following:

1. If we apply the classical benefit-detriment approach, was there consideration for Betty Meadors's personal guaranty?
2. What was meant by the term "reciprocal conventional inducement"?
3. Under the modern bargain theory, was Betty Meadors's signature enough to establish consideration for a personal guaranty?

United States v. Meadors

753 F.2d 590 (7th Cir. 1985)

CUDAHY, J.

[Melton Meadors and others applied for and received approval for a Small Business Administration (SBA) loan to start a new business. Before the final signing of the loan agreement, Meadors got married and his new wife joined him at the signing. Although her name was not on any of the documentation, she was asked to sign a personal guaranty for the loan, which had already been approved for Mr. Meadors and his business associates. She signed the paperwork, and when the business failed the SBA sought to recover the loan from her under the guaranty. She argued a number of grounds, including a claim of no consideration to support the guaranty. Subsequently, the SBA admitted that the loan funds would have been provided without her signature. The trial court granted summary judgment to the government allowing it to collect on the loan guaranty. Meadors appealed.]

. . .

Betty Meadors argues, finally, that she received no consideration for her signature on the guaranty form. She reasons that the signature of a volunteer, who happens upon an agreement after the negotiations have been concluded and the terms set, and who signs as a guarantor although neither side has required her to sign, has not received consideration and therefore is not bound by the agreement.

Consideration has long and consistently been treated as an essential element of every contract. Yet there is little agreement about just what consideration is, and that fact makes it difficult to assess a defense of want of consideration in a novel setting. We venture that the setting in which it is raised here is very nearly unique, and the validity of the defense would seem to depend on which interpretation of the doctrine we adopt.

Every interpretation has serious faults. It used to be said that consideration was either a benefit to the promisor, or a detriment to the promisee. In other words, the one who made the promise receives consideration if he gets something, or if the one to whom he makes the promise gives something up. Either alternative will do. If I promise you a thousand dollars if you quit smoking, and you do quit, then even though there may be no benefit to me, I have received consideration: you have given something up. Similarly, I can promise you a thousand dollars if you teach my daughter to sing. If you do teach her — or if you promise to — then I have received consideration even if all the practice sessions and even the final result are of no real benefit to me.

But reflection shows that benefit-detriment is neither necessary nor sufficient for consideration. I may promise to give you a thousand dollars if you quit smoking — I may even do it in writing — and you may give up smoking, and yet my promise may be unenforceable and may be the sort of thing that everyone would agree was without consideration. For you may have given up smoking without ever having learned of my promise. So the detriment in isolation is not sufficient for consideration. On the other hand, I might agree to pay you for something that was neither a benefit to me nor a detriment to you. I might promise to pay you for bringing a benefit on yourself. The reasoning in the classic case of *Hamer v. Sidway,* 124 N.Y. 538, 27 N.E. 256 (N.Y. App. 1891), suggests that the courts will find consideration in such a case. An uncle had promised his nephew $5000 on his twenty-first birthday if the nephew would refrain from drinking, smoking, swearing and playing cards until that time. The nephew evidently fulfilled his part of the deal, but the uncle's executor resisted his claim against the estate. The court found the promise enforceable. . . .

. . .

Perhaps because of such difficulties, the benefit-detriment account of consideration was replaced by a "bargain" theory: there is consideration when each promise or performance has been bargained for, when each has been offered as inducement for the other:

> It is the essence of a consideration, that, by the terms of the agreement, it is given and accepted as the motive or inducement of the promise. Conversely, the promise must be made and accepted as the conventional motive or inducement for furnishing the consideration. The root of the whole matter is the relation of reciprocal conventional inducement, each for the other, between consideration and promise.

O. W. Holmes, The Common Law 293-94 (1881) [footnote omitted].

The bargain-exchange account fits rather neatly into an economic analysis of common law, which sees in this version of the doctrine of consideration an attempt to select out for enforcement those contracts — namely bargained-for exchanges — that promote the increase of value in society.

> The state has an independent interest in the enforcement of [bargain] promises. Exchange creates surplus, because each party presumably values what he gets more

> highly than what he gives. A modern free-enterprise system depends heavily on private planning and on credit transactions that involve exchanges over time. The extent to which private actors will be ready to engage in exchange, and are able to make reliable plans, rests partly on the probability that bargain promises will be kept. Legal enforcement of such promises increases that probability.

. . .

Since the just solution does not leap out at us, therefore, let us begin by pressing the doctrine of consideration as far as it will go. Where there is no consideration, it has been the general rule that the contract is not enforceable. In this case, under the versions of the doctrine we are acquainted with, there has been no consideration. The government suffered no detriment: its undertaking would have been precisely the same (on the account we have before us) whether or not Mrs. Meadors had signed the guaranty. She gained no benefit, either; whatever benefit passed to her and her husband because of the loan would have passed without her signature. And no bargain was involved. The SBA gave up nothing to induce Mrs. Meadors to sign; her signature induced no act or promise on the part of the SBA. Since there has been no consideration, the general rule would deny the government enforcement of the contract.

The general rule applies to guaranties. If there has been no consideration for a guaranty, the guaranty is not enforceable. . . .

. . .

. . . Whether or not there has been benefit to one party or detriment to the other, there has been no bargain here, and the SBA made the loan apparently in ignorance of Mrs. Meadors' signature. If those are the facts, then we believe that not only has there been no *independent* consideration, there has been no consideration at all.

. . .

For Corbin, the lack of consideration is clear from the fact that the signature was not originally contemplated as part of the deal. Where the creditor does not even know of the signature — as we are assured by both parties is the case here — the lack of a bargain and consequent lack of consideration is even clearer:

> Even if the promisee takes some action subsequent to the promise (so that there is no problem of past consideration), and even if the promisor sought that action in exchange for his promise, . . . that action is not bargained for unless it is given by the promisee in exchange for the promise. In other words, just as the promisor's purpose must be to induce an exchange, so the promisee's purpose must be to take advantage of the proposed exchange. *In practice, the principal effect of this requirement is to deny enforcement of the promise if the promisee takes the action sought by the promisor without knowledge of the promise.* As might be supposed, examples are infrequent.

E. Farnsworth, Contracts 64 (1982). [Footnote omitted.]

. . .

We hold, therefore, that summary judgment for plaintiff was not appropriate on this point. Although the parties have apparently agreed on the relevant facts, we feel that it would also be inappropriate for us to decide as a matter of law that the

guaranty is unenforceable. The district court, relying on a different construction of the law, did not take evidence on the question. Construing the law as we have construed it, it must be resolved whether in fact Betty Meadors' signature was in any respect whatsoever required, anticipated, requested or relied upon (or, in fact, known of); because if it was not, it was wholly irrelevant to the transaction and does not create an enforceable obligation.

REVERSED AND REMANDED.

Post-Case Follow-Up

The *Meadors* court discussed and indicated no consideration under its analysis of the classical and modern views on consideration. The court determined that the promisor, Meadors, likely received no benefit from her signing the loan given to her new spouse. The promisee, SBA, likely suffered no detriment as it planned to make the loan regardless of her signature. Similarly, under the modern approach, there was no reciprocal inducement as the SBA gave up nothing in exchange for her signature on the personal guaranty. Despite its evaluation, the court remanded the case for further fact-finding. Although in this instance both approaches yielded the same result, that outcome is not true in all cases.

United States v. Meadors: Real Life Applications

1. All-Star Paving (All-Star) is bidding on a county contract to resurface school parking lots. ABC Manufacturers (ABC) is discontinuing its sales of an alternative paving product, Asphalt XX. The company offers to give Asphalt XX to bidders for free, if they pick up the paving product at their own expense. When All-Star Paving wins the bid, it collects five tons of Asphalt XX and uses it on the parking lots. A few months later, extensive cracking appears and the county requires that the paving be removed and replaced. All-Star Paving notifies ABC of the problem and seeks its reimbursement of thousands of dollars to dispose of Asphalt XX, which is hazardous waste under statutory law. ABC refuses to pay for the costs to dispose of these materials, claiming no consideration. Under the modern view, is there consideration under the bargain theory?
2. Were All-Star and ABC required to expressly negotiate the issue of hazardous waste disposal under the bargain approach?
3. What might be the outcome in this case under the classical view of consideration?
4. Look up the case of *Pennsy Supply, Inc. v. American Ash Recycling Corp.*, 895 A.2d 595 (Pa. Super. Ct. 2006), to see how a court addressed the modern bargain theory in a similar contract case.

C. EXCHANGES THAT DO NOT ESTABLISH CONSIDERATION

1. Reward Situations

Occasionally, consideration fails even though the promisor sought something in exchange for the promise and the promisee gave that thing to the promisor. For example, if a promisee did not know of the promise at the time she performed a particular act, then she cannot have performed in exchange for the promise. These circumstances may be found in reward situations. Let's say that a person, unaware of a reward, takes actions that would qualify for the reward. For example, a neighbor finds a lost dog and returns it to the owner without knowing there was a $500 reward for the pet's return. The individual's performance was not given in exchange for the reward, so it does not satisfy the requirement of consideration. The neighbor did nothing different from what she would have done to help the lost pet, and she did not act in exchange for the reward. However, the outcome is different if the neighbor saw fliers offering a $500 reward for the dog's return and then started to scour the neighborhood to find the lost pet. If she locates the animal and returns it to its owner, then she has knowingly taken action in exchange for the reward, which meets the requirements of consideration.

2. Gratuitous Promises: Executory Gifts

Consideration focuses on whether or not the promisor sought something in exchange for a promise. **Gratuitous** or **gift** promises are common bases for challenging claims of consideration. Gifts are excluded from the doctrine of consideration because promises are being made without requiring anything in return. Seeking nothing in exchange typifies gifts; seeking something in exchange suggests a contract. Until the gift has been delivered, the promisor may change her mind and decide to break her promise without becoming liable for breach of contract. There may be ethical or social concerns about reneging on a promise, but there may not be legal grounds in contract law to demand the gift. A promised gift that is not yet delivered is known as an **executory gift**. Claims of executory gifts raise issues about whether or not there was consideration, as we will see in the upcoming case of *Dougherty v. Salt.*

Some promisees may show their gratitude with a thank-you card. Others might show gratitude by giving something in return. A second (return) gift will not convert the first gift (or promise of a gift) into a contract. For example, let's say a parent promises to give a law student a new car at the end of the academic year. This lavish gift is being offered to the law student as a gift without any conditions attached. A law student might respond by promising to improve his GPA to make the parent proud. If the parent did not demand that return promise in exchange for the car, there is no consideration. The promised car remains an offering of a gift and is not converted into consideration for a contract.

In some cases, even a request from the promisor might not constitute consideration. Even if the parent said, "I hope this gift encourages you to improve your

GPA at the end of the year," this promise does not propose a bargained-for exchange. While the parent might be pleased if the student studied harder, the initial promise of a car was unconditional. The parent did not make the promise of a car depend upon the student's academic performance.

Promissory notes are typically used in debtor-creditor situations.
alexskopje/Shutterstock.com

An exchange might be established if the promise was conditioned on the return promise or action. What if the parent says, "If you improve your GPA this semester, then I will give you a car as a graduation gift"? Improved grades is an action being sought and it must be achieved if the student wants to receive the car. On this language, the parent's use of the word "give" may suggest that he or she does not see this transaction as an exchange. But courts may take a different view. A proposal for an exchange may satisfy consideration even if the promisor did not originally intend to create an enforceable bargain. The *Dougherty* case is a good example of a gratuitous or gift promise in which no conditions are attached and nothing is expected in exchange.

Case Preview

Dougherty v. Salt

The *Dougherty* case provides a good example of a gratuitous promise. An aunt shows an interest in her eight-year-old nephew, who is being cared for by a guardian. With some coaxing from his guardian, the aunt drafts a $3,000 **promissory note** — typically used in debtor-creditor situations — to her eight-year-old nephew. The aunt uses a form document in making out this note, which will be payable upon her death to her nephew. As in *Hamer*, the estate refused to pay on the note after the aunt's death. On behalf of the child, the guardian brought an action to recover the funds under the signed note. Once again, the court must decide whether or not there was consideration.

As you read the *Dougherty v. Salt*, look for the following:

1. Under the classical benefit-detriment approach, was there consideration for the aunt's note to her nephew?
2. Applying the modern bargain theory, was there an effective exchange between the aunt and her young nephew?
3. What are the key similarities and distinctions between the facts and outcomes in *Hamer* and *Dougherty*?

Dougherty v. Salt

227 N.Y. 200 (1919)

CARDOZO, J.

The plaintiff, a boy of eight years, received from his aunt, the defendant's testatrix, a promissory note for $3,000 payable at her death or before. Use was made of a printed form, which contains the words "value received." How the note came to be given, was explained by the boy's guardian, who was a witness for his ward. The aunt was visiting her nephew. "When she saw Charley coming in, she said 'Isn't he a nice boy?' I answered her, yes, that he is getting along very nice, and getting along nice in school, and I showed where he had progressed in school, having good reports, and so forth, and she told me that she was going to take care of that child, that she loved him very much. I said, 'I know you do, Tillie, but your taking care of the child will be done probably like your brother and sister done, take it out in talk.' She said: 'I don't intend to take it out in talk, I would like to take care of him now.' I said, 'Well, that is up to you.' She said, 'Why can't I make out a note to him?' I said, 'You can, if you wish to.' . . . And she said, 'Well, will you make out a note for me?' I said, 'Yes, if you wish me to,' and she said, 'Well, I wish you would.'" A blank was then produced, filled out, and signed. The aunt handed the note to her nephew with these words, "You have always done for me, and I have signed this note for you. Now, do not lose it. Some day it will be valuable."

The trial judge submitted to the jury the question whether there was any consideration for the promised payment. Afterwards, he set aside the verdict in favor of the plaintiff, and dismissed the complaint. The Appellate Division, by a divided court, reversed the judgment of dismissal, and reinstated the verdict on the ground that the note was sufficient evidence of consideration.

We reach a different conclusion. The inference of consideration to be drawn from the form of the note has been so overcome and rebutted as to leave no question for a jury. . . . The transaction thus revealed admits of one interpretation, and one only. The note was the voluntary and unenforcible promise of an executory gift [citations omitted]. This child of eight was not a creditor, nor dealt with as one. The aunt was not paying a debt. She was conferring a bounty [citation omitted]. The promise was neither offered nor accepted with any other purpose. "Nothing is consideration that is not regarded as such by both parties" [citations omitted]. A note so given is not made for "value received," however its maker may have labeled it. The formula of the printed blank becomes, in the light of the conceded facts, a mere erroneous conclusion, which cannot overcome the inconsistent conclusion of the law [citations omitted]. The plaintiff, through his own witness, has explained the genesis of the promise, and consideration has been disproved [citations omitted].

We hold, therefore, that the verdict of the jury was contrary to law, and that the trial judge was right in setting it aside.

Post-Case Follow-Up

The *Dougherty* court illustrates that there must be an exchange for consideration to be present. In this case, the nephew provided nothing in exchange for his aunt's promissory note. Even though the language on the form stated "value received," the aunt neither requested nor received anything back from her nephew for the $3,000. The language on the form promissory note did not convert an unfulfilled gift into consideration.

Dougherty v. Salt: Real Life Applications

1. A widow, Jenny, and her children lived on leased public land in hopes of purchasing it in the future. By letter, her brother-in-law, Max, invited her to travel about 60 to 70 miles to settle on some land he occupied under a government lease. Max also offered to provide them with a comfortable home and land to cultivate as she raised her children. She and her family left their home and moved to his property. For two years, Jenny and her children lived in a home near Max and cultivated crops on his land. Max then moved Jenny and her family off the land and into a remote cabin in the woods. Max later required Jenny and her family to leave even that house in the woods. She later sued Max for failing to live up to his promise. Under the classical view, was there consideration for his promise to provide her with a home and farm land to raise her children?
2. What arguments might be made to support a finding of a gratuitous or gift promise?
3. How might you counter a finding of a gift to show that consideration exists?
4. Research *Kirksey v. Kirksey*, 8 Ala. 131 (1845), and decide whether or not you agree with the court's decision in this seminal case.

Kirskey v. Kirksey: Solving the Historical Mystery

The *Kirksey* case is often found in many contracts texts on the issue of consideration. Alabama Supreme Court Justice Ormond, who drafted the decision, is in disagreement with the court's majority. Where the majority sees only a gratuitous promise between family members, Justice Ormond finds sufficient detriment in the widow's packing up and moving based on her brother-in-law's offer of a comfortable home and land. For over 150 years, the case was shrouded in mystery about how this apparent offer of kindness turned into a story of family dysfunction and litigation. Law professors and students have enjoyed speculating about what happened between widowed Angelico Kirksey and her brother-in-law, Isaac Kirksey. In 2006, Professors William R. Casto and Val D. Ricks uncovered the true story behind this case, in their law review article, *"Dear Sister Antillico . . .": The Story of* Kirksey v. Kirksey, 94 Geo. L.J. 321 (2006). Research and review this article and you will find out that both parties were shrewd individuals, each trying to elbow the other out of valuable land with a hefty government discount and each retaining star attorneys, both of whom later became Alabama Supreme Court justices.

3. Conditional Gifts: Questioning Exchange

In some cases, gifts come with **conditions**: things that must occur before the promise must be performed. A promisor may attach conditions to a gift without seeking any promise or action in return. A condition of the gift merely specifies the manner in which the gift will be delivered or collected, but is not a request for return promise or performance. Consideration would lose any substance if the requirement could be met by a transaction such as "I promise to give you $5,000 if you promise to spend it." Spending the money is a condition of a gift, not consideration, as the giver is receiving nothing of legal value in return for her promise. This example is clearly a conditional gift that lacks the required exchange to meet the requirement of consideration. Distinguishing conditional gifts from bargained-for exchanges of consideration can be difficult. You can start by addressing whether the requested act is the way the recipient earns the promise from the giver (consideration) or if the act merely benefits the party already receiving the gift (conditional gift). The *Plowman* case offers a challenging instance when a court must decide if a conditional gift or consideration is at the heart of an arrangement between an employer and laid off older employees.

Case Preview

Plowman v. Indian Refining Co.

The *Plowman* case brings together many threads of legal issues raised in disputes over consideration. In this case, a court must determine whether payroll payments and health insurance participation for laid off older employees amounted to consideration or merely conditional gifts. The employees argued that the local manager promised them that these payments would continue for the rest of their lives, similar to some modern day pensions. The company sent a confirming letter, but it was silent on whether the payments and opportunity to retain health insurance options would continue for a lifetime. The employer argues that the manager had no authority to grant any lifetime payments and that the laid off workers gave nothing in exchange for these payments so there was no consideration.

In reading *Plowman v. Indian Refining Co.*, look the following:

1. Was there a bargained-for exchange for the payments at the time the workers were laid off?
2. If the laid off workers were required to pick up their checks at the company's office, is that consideration for the claimed promise of lifetime payments?
3. Why does the court determine that the refining company is not liable for the promises made by its manager, Mr. Anglin?

Plowman v. Indian Refining Co.

20 F. Supp. 1 (E.D. Ill. 1937)

LINDLEY, District Judge.

. . . **The theory of plaintiffs is that on July 28, 1930 (with two exceptions), the vice-president and general manager of the refinery plant called the employees,** who had rendered long years of service separately into his office and made with each a contract, to pay him, for the rest of his natural life, a sum equal to one-half of the wages he was then being paid. The consideration for the contracts, it is said, arose out of the relationship then existing, the desire to provide for the future welfare of these comparatively aged employees and the provision in the alleged contracts that the employees would call at the office for their several checks each pay-day.

Most of the employees were participants in group insurance, the premiums for which had been paid approximately one-half by the employee and one-half by the company, and, according to plaintiffs, their parts of the premiums were to be deducted from their payments as formerly. This procedure was followed. The employees were retained on the pay roll, but, according to their testimony, they were not to render any further services, their only obligation being to call at the office for their remittances. Most of them testified that it was agreed that the payments were to continue throughout the remainder of their lives. But two testified that nothing was said as to the time during which the payments were to continue. As to still others the record is silent as to direct testimony in this respect.

The payments were made regularly until June 1, 1931, when they were cut off and each of the employees previously receiving the same was advised by defendant's personnel officer that the arrangement was terminated.

Defendant does not controvert many of these facts, but insists that the whole arrangement was included in a letter sent to each of the employees as follows:

> "Confirming our conversation of today, it is necessary with conditions as they are throughout the petroleum industry, to effect substantial economies throughout the plant operation. This necessitates the reducing of the working force to a minimum necessary to maintain operation. In view of your many years of faithful service, the management is desirous of shielding you as far as possible from the effect of reduced plant operation and has, therefore, placed you upon a retirement list which has just been established for this purpose.
>
> "Effective August 1, 1930, you will be carried on our payroll at a rate of $___ per month. You will be relieved of all duties except that of reporting to Mr. T. E. Sullivan at the main office for the purpose of picking up your semi-monthly checks. Your group insurance will be maintained on the same basis as at present, unless you desire to have it cancelled." (Signed by the vice-president.)

It contends and offered evidence that nothing was said to any employee about continuing the payments for his natural life; that the payments were gratuitous, continuing at the pleasure and will of defendant; that the original arrangement was not authorized, approved, or ratified by the board of directors, the executive committee thereof, or any officer endowed with corporate authority to bind the company; that there was no consideration for the promise to make the payments; and that it was beyond the power of any of the persons alleged to have contracted to create by agreement or by estoppel any liability of the company to pay wages to employees during the remainders of their lives, if they did not render actual services. Defendant admits the payments as charged and the termination of the arrangement on June 1, 1931.

The employees assert that there was ample authority in the vice-president and general manager to make a binding contract of the kind alleged to have existed; that, irrespective of the existence or nonexistence of such authority, the conduct of the company in making payment was ratification of the original agreement and that defendant is now estopped to deny validity of the same.

. . .

In behalf of defendant, the assistant secretary testified that there were no minutes showing any corporate action with regard to the arrangement and that there was nothing in the records of the corporation, in bylaws, resolution or minutes authorizing, directing, or ratifying the payments or giving anybody authority to make the same. Anglin, vice-president and general manager in charge of manufacturing at the Lawrenceville Refinery where these men were employed, testified that he said to Kogan that, due to depressed conditions the company found it necessary to reduce expenses and lay off certain men; that it had no pension plan; that in an effort to be perfectly fair the company would keep him on the pay roll but relieve him of all duties except to pick up his check; that he said that the arrangement was voluntary with the company, and terminable at its pleasure, and that he hoped it would last during Kogan's lifetime, but that there might be a change in the policy of the company. His testimony as to the other employees was the same. He denied promising any of them that the payments would persist so long as they lived. . . .

. . .

Thus it is undisputed that a separate arrangement was made by the local office with each of the claimants, most of them on July 28, 1930, to continue them upon the pay roll, deliver to them semimonthly a check, upon their calling for same, for one-half of the former wages; that this was done until June 1, 1931. It is also undisputed that the letters sent out said nothing about how long the payments should continue but were wholly silent in that respect. It is also undisputed that insurance payments were deducted from the checks that were delivered; that the employees were retained on the pay roll; that they did no active work after August 1, 1931; that they received their checks as mentioned; that the payments terminated on June 1, 1931; that most of them called at the office for their checks and received same; and that in at least two instances the checks were mailed. The controverted question of fact arises upon the testimony of most of the plaintiffs that each of them was told that the payments would continue until their death. This is denied.

Let us assume, without so deciding, for the purpose of disposition of this case, that each of the employees was told that the payments would continue for his lifetime. Then the questions remaining are legal in character. The arrangement was made by no corporate officer having authority to make such a contract. Under the bylaws, corporation transactions as recorded in the minutes, there was no authorization or ratification of any such contract. It is urged, however, that by continuing to pay the checks the corporation ratified the previously unauthorized action. The facts render such conclusion dubious.

I am unable to see how knowledge of the mere fact that men's names were on the pay roll and checks paid to them could create any estoppel to deny authority, in the absence of proof of knowledge upon the part of the duly authorized officers of the company that the men were not working but were receiving in effect pensions or that they had been promised payments for life. Consequently, there was no ratification express or implied and no estoppel.

Presented also is the further question of whether, admitting the facts as alleged by plaintiffs, there was any consideration for a contract to pay a pension for life. However strongly a man may be bound in conscience to fulfill his engagements, the law does not recognize their sanctity or supply any means to compel their performance, except when founded upon a sufficient consideration. [Citation omitted.]

The long and faithful services of the employees are relied upon as consideration; but past or executed consideration is a self-contradictory term. Consideration is something given in exchange for a promise or in a reliance upon the promise. Something which has been delivered before the promise is executed, and, therefore, made without reference to it, cannot properly be legal consideration. [Citations omitted.]

It is further contended that there was a moral consideration for the alleged contracts. The doctrine of validity of moral consideration has received approval in some courts, but quite generally it is condemned because it is contrary in character to actual consideration. . . .

. . .

Plaintiffs have proved that they were ready, willing, and able to travel to and report semimonthly to the main office. But this does not furnish a legal consideration. The act was simply a condition imposed upon them in obtaining gratuitous pensions and not a consideration. The employees went to the office to obtain their checks. Such acts were benefits to them [promisees] and not detriments. They were detriments to defendant [promisor] and not benefits. This is not consideration. [Citations omitted.]

In the absence of valid agreement to make payments for the rest of their natural lives, clearly the arrangement was one revocable at the pleasure of defendant. If defendant agreed to make the payments for life, then, fatal to plaintiffs' cases is the lack of consideration. We have merely a gratuitous arrangement without consideration, and therefore, void as a contract.

In this enlightened day, I am sure, no one controverts the wisdom, justice, and desirability of a policy, whether promoted and fostered by industry voluntarily or by state or federal government, looking to the promotion and assurance of financial protection of deserving employees in their old age. We have come to realize that the industry wherein the diligent worker labors for many years should bear the cost of his living in some degree of comfort through his declining years until the end of his life. To impose this expense upon the industry, to the creation of whose product he has contributed, is not unfair or unreasonable, for, eventually, obviously, under wise budgeting and cost accounting systems, this element of cost is passed on to the consumer of the product. The public bears the burden — as, indeed, it does eventually of all governmental expenditures and corporate costs, either in taxes or price of products purchased. Surely no one would have the temerity to urge that such a policy is not more fair and reasonable, more humane and beneficent, than the poorhouse system of our earlier days. The recognition of the soundness of this proposition is justified by the resulting contribution to the advance of standards of living, hygienic and sanitary environment, and, in some degree at least, of culture and civilization. But, in the absence of statute creating it, such a policy does not enter into the relationship of employer or employee, except when so provided by contract of the parties. The

court is endowed with no power of legislation; nor may it read into contracts provisions upon which the parties' minds have not met.

Viewing the testimony most favorably for the plaintiffs, despite the desirability of the practice of liberality between employer and employee, the court must decide a purely legal question — whether under plaintiffs' theory there were valid contracts. The obvious answer is in the negative. Consequently, there will be a decree in favor of defendant dismissing plaintiffs' bill for want of equity. The foregoing includes my findings of fact and conclusions of law.

Post-Case Follow-Up

The *Plowman* court had to distinguish among gratuitous promises, conditional gifts, and consideration. The court determined that the payments to the workers were gifts in which no services nor anything else was expected in return. The case also determined that the employees' collection of their checks was not an exchange, but a conditional gift. The employer gained nothing from the condition that the former workers pick up their checks. The arrangement between the manager and the employees failed to meet the requirements of consideration under contract law. *Plowman* pre-dated the enactment of Social Security and other New Deal social legislation, and the court interestingly points to the need for future private pension plans and appropriate government programs to protect retiring and laid off workers, found in our contemporary employment law.

Plowman v. Indian Refining Co.: Real Life Applications

1. Deanna and Marco have been involved in a stormy relationship for several years. Marco proposes marriage to Deanna with his favorite grandmother's diamond ring. To Marco, the ring had both substantial monetary and sentimental value. Deanna accepts his proposal and the ring and then breaks it off, returning the ring. Several months later, they get back together and Marco makes a second proposal. Deanna accepts again and takes the ring. Eventually, Marco decides to break it off and wants Deanna to give back the ring. She refuses, contending that she accepted his offer and that the exchange is his grandmother's ring for her acceptance of his marriage proposal. Marco counters that there is no contract, just a conditional gift, and Deanna has not fulfilled the required condition of marriage. Is this situation a contract or a conditional gift?
2. Is there a bargained-for exchange between Deanna and Marco?
3. Courts differ on how to deal with engagement ring disputes. If it is viewed as a conditional gift, which condition do you think needs to be met to finalize the gift?
4. Retrieve and review *Lindh v. Surman*, 560 Pa. 1 (1999), which provides the basis for this fact pattern, and see what that court determined about the fate of the disputed engagement ring.

4. Charitable Pledges as Conditional Gifts

Conditional gifts often arise in instances of charitable pledges. Most courts require that a charitable pledge be supported by either consideration or reliance. If a donor offers a large gift to a university (donee) if it will name a building in honor of a loved one, giving what was sought (naming the building) is an exchange. However, if the donor's gift is unconditional and the university, in gratitude, subsequently names a building for the donor, then no exchange occurs. Some other conditions placed on pledges may not establish a bargained-for exchange. For instance, limits on how money is to be spent often create conditions on the gift, not consideration. The donee does not earn the money by spending it in a particular way. Rather, the limitations express the boundaries of the donor's generosity. Charitable pledges involving instances of reliance are discussed in greater detail in Chapter 5.

5. Adequacy of Consideration

In general, courts do not examine the **adequacy of consideration**, deferring to the parties to determine their own best interests. In recognizing that parties may appraise their exchanges differently from a court, consideration does not have to be of equal value in the exchange. The promisor and promisee decide for themselves whether what they will receive exceeds the value of what they will give up in exchange. Consideration asks whether a bargain exists, not whether the bargain is of equal, good, or sufficient worth. An unequal exchange is still an exchange, provided that it was founded upon good faith and fair dealing.

Nothing in the definition of bargain requires that the performance or return promise have any specific value or worth. Consideration exists if a person agrees to sell a valuable antique for $5, as occasionally happens at garage or estate sales, because she may want to get rid of it for a host of reasons. Perhaps the antique is crowding storage space in a garage or she wants to make room for other new items in her home. The court will not delve into her reasons for selling or the buyer's reasons for purchasing the antique, but will consider whether or not there was an exchange made in good faith.

The court's main focus will be whether or not there was an exchange made in good faith, not the adequacy of consideration.
Anthony Rosenberg/iStockphoto

Similarly, consideration exists if a person agrees to pay thousands of dollars for worthless junk, as occasionally happens when an item has sentimental value to an individual. As long as the party bargains for something in exchange, the law does not examine the relative values of the items exchanged. Rather, the law assumes that if someone was willing to pay more (or accept less) than an item's objective worth (on the market), this must reflect a difference in subjective value of the items to the parties. One person's trash is another person's treasure. Every voluntary exchange reflects some difference in subjective value. A seller prefers to receive the price rather than keep the item sold; the buyer prefers to receive the item sold rather than keep the price. The money and the item are identical before and after they change hands. The parties' willingness to exchange must reflect different values attached to at least one of the components of the exchange.

Severe inequality in an exchange may serve as a red flag signaling a need to examine the transaction for other problems. For instance, a one-sided exchange may result from fraud, duress, incapacity, or other problems that give rise to an affirmative defense that might preclude enforcement even if consideration exists, reviewed in Chapters 6 and 7. In some circumstances, a court may invalidate a contract when the differences in the exchange are so extreme that the exchange is unconscionable, which will be discussed further in Chapter 8.

Case Preview

Batsakis v. Demotsis

The *Batsakis* case is a good example of how courts will defer to the parties' freedom of contract in examining the relative worth of promises in an exchange. This dispute arose out of the extreme circumstances of World War II when Greece was under Axis occupation and then subjected to an Allied forces blockade to try to stop further military advances. Many lives were lost from famine, lack of medical supplies, and other deprivations. Prices for even basic items spiraled out of control. In this dire situation, Demotsis sought money to survive, but was unable to obtain funds, property, and credit that she owned in the United States. Batsakis was able to loan her 500,000 drachmae (Greek currency at that time), which the defendant claimed were worth about $25 US. But he demanded that she draft a letter promising $2,000 plus 8 percent interest to repay him. The court was faced with the issue of adequacy of consideration in this unsettling case.

As you read *Batsakis v. Demotsis*, look for the following:

1. What is the court's view on the issue of adequacy of consideration?
2. Did Demotsis receive what she bargained for under her letter to Batsakis?
3. Did the drachmae paid to Demotsis have any financial value?

Batsakis v. Demotsis

226 S.W.2d 673 (1949)

MCBILL, Justice.

. . . . Plaintiff [appellant Batsakis] sued defendant [respondent Demotsis] to recover $2,000 with interest at the rate of 8% per annum from April 2, 1942, alleged to be due on the following instrument, being a translation from the original, which is written in the Greek language:

> Peiraeus
> April 2, 1942
> Mr. George Batsakis
> Konstantinou Diadohou #7
> Peiraeus
> Mr. Batsakis:
>
> I state by my present (letter) that I received today from you the amount of two thousand dollars ($2,000.00) of United States of America money, which I borrowed from you for the support of my family during these difficult days and because it is impossible for me to transfer dollars of my own from America.
>
> The above amount I accept with the expressed promise that I will return to you again in American dollars either at the end of the present war or even before in the event that you might be able to find a way to collect them (dollars) from my representative in America to whom I shall write and give him an order relative to this.
>
> You understand until the final execution (payment) to the above amount an eight per cent interest will be added and paid together with the principal.
>
> I thank you and I remain yours with respects.
>
> The recipient,
> (Signed) *Eugenia The Demotsis.*

Trial to the court without the intervention of a jury resulted in a judgment in favor of plaintiff for $750.00 principal, and interest at the rate of 8% per annum from April 2, 1942 to the date of judgment, totaling $1163.83, with interest thereon at the rate of 8% per annum until paid. Plaintiff has perfected his appeal.

. . .

[The issue before the appeals court is whether] consideration upon which said written instrument sued upon by plaintiff herein is founded, is wanting and has failed to the extent of $1975.00, and defendant pleads specially under the verification hereinafter made the want and failure of consideration stated, and now tenders, as defendant has heretofore tendered to plaintiff, $25.00 as the value of the loan of money received by defendant from plaintiff, together with interest thereon.

The allegations in paragraph II . . . were that the instrument sued on was signed and delivered in the Kingdom of Greece on or about April 2, 1942, at which time both plaintiff and defendant were residents of and residing in the Kingdom of Greece and [Demotsis] avers that on or about April 2, 1942 she owned money and property and had credit in the United States of America, but was then and there in the Kingdom of Greece in straitened financial circumstances due to the conditions produced by World War II and could not make use of her money and property and credit existing in the United States of America. That in the circumstances the plaintiff agreed to and did lend to defendant the sum of 500,000 drachmae, which at that time, on or about April 2, 1942, had the value of $25.00 in money of the United States of America. That the said plaintiff, knowing defendant's financial distress and desire to return to the United States of America, exacted of her the written instrument plaintiff sues upon, which was a promise by her to pay to him the sum of $2,000.00 of United States of America money.

Plaintiff specially excepted to paragraph IV because the allegations thereof were insufficient to allege either want of consideration or failure of consideration, in that it affirmatively appears therefrom that defendant received what was agreed to be delivered to her, and that plaintiff breached no agreement. . . .

Defendant testified that she did receive 500,000 drachmas from plaintiff. It is not clear whether she received all the 500,000 drachmas or only a portion of them before she signed the instrument in question. Her testimony clearly shows that the understanding of the parties was that plaintiff would give her the 500,000 drachmas if she would sign the instrument. She testified:

> *Q.* . . . who suggested the figure of $2,000.00?
> *A.* That was how he asked me from the beginning. He said he will give me five hundred thousand drachmas provided I signed that I would pay him $2,000.00 American money.

The transaction amounted to a sale by plaintiff of the 500,000 drachmas in consideration of the execution of the instrument sued on, by defendant. It is not contended that the drachmas had no value. Indeed, the judgment indicates that the trial court placed a value of $750.00 on them. . . . Therefore the plea of want of consideration was unavailing. A plea of want of consideration amounts to a contention that the instrument never became a valid obligation in the first place. [Citation omitted.]

Mere inadequacy of consideration will not void a contract. 10 Tex. Jur., Contracts, Sec. 89, p. 150; *Chastain v. Texas* Christian Missionary Society, Tex. Civ. App., 78 S.W.2d 728, loc. cit. 731(3), Wr. Ref.

Nor was the plea of failure of consideration availing. Defendant got exactly what she contracted for according to her own testimony. The court should have rendered judgment in favor of plaintiff against defendant for the principal sum of $2,000.00 evidenced by the instrument sued on, with interest as therein provided. . . .

Post-Case Follow-Up

The *Batsakis* court followed the general rule that courts will not examine the adequacy of consideration, but will look only for a bargained-for exchange. Despite the World War II circumstances, the court found that Demotsis received precisely what she bargained for — 500,000 drachmae from Batsakis in exchange for a payment of $2,000 US at 8 percent interest. Although we may be sympathetic to Demotsis's situation, the court echoed established precedent that consideration asks whether a bargain exists, not whether the bargain is equal or good value for both of the parties.

Batsakis v. Demotsis: Real Life Applications

1. Dr. Melendez agreed to sell his practice and equipment to Dr. Ronan. Melendez regretted his decision and tried to undo his agreement. Ronan agreed to cancel the deal if Melendez paid him $40,000. Melendez agreed, but then decided against this new bargain and sought to be released from this second bargain claiming a lack of adequate consideration. The court confronted the issue by looking at whether or not there was sufficient consideration.

1. How might a court distinguish between the term "sufficient consideration" as opposed to "adequate consideration"?
2. What arguments might be made to support a finding of a gratuitous or gift promise?
3. How might you counter a finding of a gift to show that consideration exists?
4. Research *Browning v. Johnson*, 70 Wis. 2d 145 (1967), and decide whether or not you agree with the court's decision in this seminal case.

6. Sham Consideration — Not Consideration

A lopsided deal may cast doubt upon whether the party receiving less really sought that particular thing in exchange for the promise. If parties add things not really sought to give the transaction an appearance of a bargain, a court may treat this as an instance of **sham consideration** and not a valid exchange. This problem may arise if a party receiving a gift seeks to create consideration by offering something minuscule in return not really sought by the promisor. When a promisor seeks very little in exchange for a promise, the line between a gift and a contract blurs. If someone promises to sell a brand new car worth $25,000 for $1 to a friend, this situation may be a gift disguised as an exchange. Conversely, a person might bid $1,500 for a photo valued at only $50 because that item holds tremendous personal value to that person. The law is clear: if one seeks something of value in exchange for a promise, the promise is enforceable. But if the exchange is a mere sham, the promise is not enforceable. The trick is to tell the difference.

A subjective approach may never find a sham deal, negating too few invalid exchanges. Each party is likely to contend that they really want the deal and contradictory evidence will be hard to find. If the promisor has now changed her mind, perhaps she will admit that the transaction was a sham. She might assert this point even if it wasn't a sham to get out of a bad deal. Alternatively, an objective approach may invalidate too many bargains. No reasonable person would accept so little for a new car or pay so much for a photo, so it must be a gift disguised as an exchange. This approach endangers each individual's freedom of contract and the ability to pursue one's own values, even if they seem outrageous to others.

Analyzing sham consideration is more useful in cases that do not involve efforts to make gifts enforceable. Occasionally, courts find a sham when a bargain seems to have been imposed upon a promisor. A person making a gift or other unenforceable promise may sign an agreement drafted by the recipient, which recites a purported consideration. The promisor has not tried to make the promise enforceable by seeking the thing that the promisee offers in exchange. The promisee has maneuvered the gift into a form that looks like an exchange, undermining the donor's right to change his mind and back out of the gift promise. Despite clever drafting that makes it seem as though the promisor sought something in exchange, courts may find a sham.

For example, in *Newman & Snell's State Bank v. Hunter*, 220 N.W. 665 (Mich. 1928), a widow promised to repay a debt her deceased husband owed to the bank, even though the debt was uncollectable. She did not owe the money and her husband's estate could not afford to pay it. The bank sold her the husband's **promissory note** in exchange for her promise to repay his debt. The widow could bargain for the note, even though it had absolutely no monetary value. However, it seemed unlikely that she sought an uncollectable note in exchange for her promise to pay. The court refused to enforce the contract.

In some cases, negligible consideration may also be a telltale sign of fraud, mistake, or other legal excuses or justifications. Courts may look to other legal doctrines to resolve these issues, which are further addressed in Chapters 6, 7, and 8.

7. Illusory Promises—Not Consideration

Another challenge to consideration is the claim of illusory promise in which one party preserves the full discretion over whether or not to carry out its contract duties. If one party retains the choice to perform or not, there is not a mutual exchange of promises or duties that is required to establish consideration. In addition, this discretion may make a promise too indefinite to meet the requirements of consideration.

The issues of illusory promises often arise in instances in which a party's performance of its duties is based solely on unfettered discretion. For example, a homeowner might engage a painter to paint his home, indicating that payment will be subject to his unrestricted approval of the job. In this instance, the painter is promising to do the work, but the homeowner is not promising anything definite in return. The homeowner can simply reject the work when completed without having promised to pay the painter for his labor and materials.

Further, this issue may be raised in exclusive dealings or distributorship agreements. In these exclusive arrangements, one party has discretion in handling another's business affairs or product distributions. An athlete might have an exclusive agent whose role is to find marketing prospects for that athlete and who takes a percentage of any new deals. The athlete is relying on the agent to promote her brand. But the agreement might not spell out the specific duties that the agent must carry out, leaving a great deal of discretion in the agent to determine whether or not to aggressively pursue promotional opportunities. If there is party disagreement over branding direction, this type of contract may give rise to a claim of illusory promise.

It is important to note that actual instances of illusory promises are not common. To avoid invalidating an agreement, courts will often imply terms into a contract based on standards of reasonableness and good faith and fair dealing. The issue of implied terms is discussed in greater detail in Chapter 10.

Chapter Summary

- The doctrine of consideration requires a legally recognized exchange to warrant enforcement of a promise.
- Consideration consists of both legal sufficiency and bargained-for exchange.
- The classical "benefit-detriment" approach examines whether the promisor receives a benefit or the promisee suffers a detriment, loss, or forbearance necessary to establish consideration.
- The modern bargain theory of consideration focuses on reciprocal conventional inducement; an exchange in which each party's promise induces the other to respond with a return promise, action, or forbearance.
- Gratuitous promises, conditional gifts, and sham consideration do not meet the mandates of consideration.
- In general, courts do not examine the adequacy of consideration, leaving it to the parties to assess their own best interests under freedom of contract.
- The Convention on Contracts for the International Sale of Goods (CISG) does not require a showing of consideration for goods transactions between parties in different nations.

Applying the Rules

In September 2015, David Moore and his mother, Wanda, spent $4,000 to fly from their Florida home to Alaska International University for an informal visit. David had been accepted to the school and planned to study marine biology. He also wanted to play on the university's football team, the Grizzlies. Mrs. Moore had sent video of her son's playing activities and playing statistics to the school's head coach, Don Watson. During their visit, Moore and his mother met with an assistant coach of the team at that time, Jeff Johnson. They allege that on September 7 Coach Johnson verbally offered David a $25,000 sports scholarship for his first academic year at the school, starting August 1, 2016. Moore claims that Coach Johnson promised him the scholarship as long as Moore did not seek or accept sports scholarship offers from any other schools. Happy about his scholarship offer, Moore replied that he would not pursue or agree to any other football scholarship opportunities and sent a confirming e-mail to Coach Johnson. Moore did not seek out any other scholarships and actually turned down $20,000 football scholarship offers from two other colleges.

Before National Signing Day, Moore's mother received a telephone call from Coach Watson, telling her that Coach Johnson was no longer with the university or its football program. "How will this affect David's sports scholarship?" she asked. Coach Watson told Mrs. Moore that her son did not receive an official offer to play or attend the university on a sports scholarship. When she tried to dispute this claim, Coach Watson replied that Coach Johnson lacked the authority to even make the oral offer and only written offers would be honored by the school on National Signing Day. By the time the Moore family received the call, it was too late for David to pursue a sports scholarship with another school. The Moore family has come to your law firm for advice. Respond to the following in essay form:

1. Under the classical view, discuss whether or not there is consideration.

2. Applying the modern view, is there valid consideration for the alleged scholarship contract?

3. What cases in this chapter might you argue to support a finding of consideration?

4. What cases in this chapter might be used to dispute a finding of consideration?

5. If you were a judge assigned to this case, what would your ruling be on the issue of consideration and why?

Contract Law in Practice

1. The concept of consideration is included in the preamble of most written contracts. Typically, the contract language indicates that the parties agree that their exchange of promises in the agreement constitutes consideration. You have been asked to develop a form contract for a commercial client who deals extensively with consumers. Research whether or not your home state requires consumer form contracts to be in plain English. Review a wide range of contract forms and draft three options to address consideration in that standardized contract's preamble.

2. In general, contract law is determined on a state-by-state basis. You are a law clerk for a judge in your home state. A contract dispute has been assigned to your judge focusing on how consideration is defined and whether the classical or modern view is utilized to analyze consideration. Research your state statutory law and case precedent on consideration. Draft a brief memo on your home state's definition and analytical approach to this concept.

3. You are an attorney for a major U.S. manufacturer of children's clothing and are negotiating a $15 million (US) goods contract with a commercial distributor in China. The parties have agreed to a Florida choice of law clause. In drafting the contract, you need to determine whether or not the CISG applies to your client's contract. If that convention does apply, you may want to incorporate language disclaiming its application to this contract. Research and decide if the CISG applies to this contract, and if it does, draft language to disclaim its application to this contract.

4. You are participating in a law school debate about whether or not consideration should be abolished as a contract requirement. Research and draft arguments on both sides of this issue. Be prepared to present your key arguments orally in class.

5. Research online for a recent news article about a contract dispute dealing with consideration. Provide a hyperlink to the article to your professor for review and class distribution, if appropriate. Briefly summarize the selected article for three to five minutes and pose a relevant question to your peers during a Contracts class for discussion.

5

Exceptions to Consideration

As you learned in Chapter 4, the basic rule and definition of consideration are relatively straightforward. Applying the rule to a complex or subtle set of facts will require careful analysis. However, there are numerous situations that will arise where a lack of consideration suggests that a promise should not be enforced. In certain instances, courts find reasons to enforce these promises, especially if issues of good faith and fair dealing are at stake. The exceptions — or, in some cases, the artful avoidance of established doctrine — offer interesting examples of how lawyers and courts have shaped the common law. This chapter addresses the most significant ways in which promises have been enforced without consideration.

A. PAST CONSIDERATION AND MORAL OBLIGATION

Past consideration is an oxymoron; it implies treating a performance received in the past as if it is the consideration for a subsequent promise. It is logically impossible for the promisee to have given the performance in exchange for the promise because the promise had not yet been made at the time of the performance. A promise may reflect gratitude for a past performance, but that does not satisfy the requirement of a bargained-for exchange. As we discussed earlier in the *Plowman* case, the refining company's gratitude for the employees' long years of service did not furnish consideration for the later promise to pay them half of their salary for the rest of their lives. Similarly, it is odd to say the refining company sought the performance when making the promise since the employer had already received

Key Concepts

- Past consideration is no consideration
- Moral obligation is unenforceable
- Promissory restitution and the material benefit rule
- The preexisting duty rule and modifications made in good faith
- Reliance or promissory estoppel as a substitute for consideration

the employees' performance of their duties. So the employer had no reason to seek it, let alone promise to pay for it. Courts traditionally reject claims that a prior act constitutes consideration for a promise made after the fact.

However, a promise to pay out of a feeling of moral duty or gratitude for another's past performance raises both legal and ethical issues. In the famous case of *Mills v. Wyman*, we see the court struggle with the boundaries of legal duty and moral obligation when a promise is made after performance is rendered.

Case Preview

Mills v. Wyman

In *Mills v. Wyman*, an adult son, Levi Wyman, fell ill after a journey. Daniel Mills, a Hartford, Connecticut innkeeper and farmer, provided him with food, housing, and medical care before his supposed death. Levi's father, Seth Wyman, learned of Mills' aid and allegedly promised to pay for his son's expenses, but then later reneged on that promise. Mills later sued Seth Wyman seeking to enforce his promise and to recover his expenses in caring for Levi.

As you read *Mills v. Wyman*, look for the following:

1. Did the court enforce Seth Wyman's promise to Mills?
2. How did Levi's age factor into the court's decision? Would the outcome be different if Levi was a minor?
3. What kinds of moral obligations did the court decide may be converted into legal duties?

Mills v. Wyman

20 Mass. 207 (1825)

PARKER, C. J.

. . . General rules of law established for the protection and security of honest and fair-minded men, who may inconsiderately make promises without any equivalent, will sometimes screen men of a different character from engagements which they are bound in *foro conscientioe* [in Latin, before the tribunal of conscience] to perform. This is a defect inherent in all human systems of legislation. The rule that a mere verbal promise, without any consideration, cannot be enforced by action, is universal in its application, and cannot be departed from to suit particular cases in which a refusal to perform such a promise may be disgraceful.

The promise declared on in this case appears to have been made without any legal consideration. The kindness and services towards the sick son of the defendant were not bestowed at his request. The son was in no respect under the care of the defendant. He was twenty-five years old, and had long left his father's family. On his return from a foreign country, he fell sick among strangers, and the plaintiff

acted the part of the good Samaritan, giving him shelter and comfort until he died. The defendant, his father, on being informed of this event, influenced by a transient feeling of gratitude, promises in writing to pay the plaintiff for the expenses he had incurred. But he has determined to break this promise, and is willing to have his case appear on record as a strong example of particular injustice sometimes necessarily resulting from the operation of general rules.

It is said a moral obligation is a sufficient consideration to support an express promise; and some authorities lay down the rule thus broadly; but upon examination of the cases we are satisfied that the universality of the rule cannot be supported, and that there must have been some preexisting obligation, which has become inoperative by positive law, to form a basis for an effective promise. The cases of debts barred by the statute of limitations, of debts incurred by infants, of debts of bankrupts, are generally put for illustration of the rule. Express promises founded on such preexisting equitable obligations may be enforced; there is a good consideration for them; they merely remove an impediment created by law to the recovery of debts honestly due, but which public policy protects the debtors from being compelled to pay. In all these cases there was originally a *quid pro quo*; and according to the principles of natural justice the party receiving ought to pay; but the legislature has said he shall not be coerced; then comes the promise to pay the debt that is barred, the promise of the man to pay the debt of the infant, of the discharged bankrupt to restore to his creditor what by the law he had lost. In all these cases there is a moral obligation founded upon an antecedent valuable consideration. These promises therefore have a sound legal basis. They are not promises to pay something for nothing; not naked pacts; but the voluntary revival or creation of obligation which before existed in natural law, but which had been dispensed with, not for the benefit of the party obliged solely, but principally for the public convenience. If moral obligation, in its fullest sense, is a good substratum for an express promise, it is not easy to perceive why it is not equally good to support an implied promise. What a man ought to do, generally he ought to be made to do, whether he promise or refuse. But the law of society has left most of such obligations to the *interior* forum, as the tribunal of conscience has been aptly called. Is there not a moral obligation upon every son who has become affluent by means of the education and advantages bestowed upon him by his father, to relieve that father from pecuniary embarrassment, to promote his comfort and happiness, and even to share with him his riches, if thereby he will be made happy? And yet such a son may, with impunity, leave such a father in any degree of penury above that which will expose the community in which he dwells, to the danger of being obliged to preserve him from absolute want. Is not a wealthy father under strong moral obligation to advance the interest of an obedient, well disposed son, to furnish him with the means of acquiring and maintaining a becoming rank in life, to rescue him from the horrors of debt incurred by misfortune? Yet the law will uphold him in any degree of parsimony, short of that which would reduce his son to the necessity of seeking public charity.

Without doubt there are great interests of society which justify withholding the coercive arm of the law from these duties of imperfect obligation, as they are called; imperfect, not because they are less binding upon the conscience than those which are called perfect, but because the wisdom of the social law does not impose sanctions upon them.

A deliberate promise, in writing, made freely and without any mistake, one which may lead the party to whom it is made into contracts and expenses, cannot be broken without a violation of moral duty. But if there was nothing paid or promised for it, the law, perhaps wisely, leaves the execution of it to the conscience of him who makes it. It is only when the party making the promise gains something, or he to whom it is made loses something, that the law gives the promise validity. And in the case of the promise of the adult to pay the debt of the infant, of the debtor discharged by the statute of limitations or bankruptcy, the principle is preserved by looking back to the origin of the transaction, where an equivalent is to be found. An exact equivalent is not required by the law; for there being a consideration, the parties are left to estimate its value: though here the courts of equity will step in to relieve from gross inadequacy between the consideration and the promise.

These principles are deduced from the general current of decided cases upon the subject, as well as from the known maxims of the common law. The general position, that moral obligation is a sufficient consideration for an express promise, is to be limited in its application, to cases where at some time or other a good or valuable consideration has existed. [Footnote omitted.]

A legal obligation is always a sufficient consideration to support either an express or an implied promise; such as an infant's debt for necessaries, or a father's promise to pay for the support and education of his minor children. But when the child shall have attained to manhood, and shall have become his own agent in the world's business, the debts he incurs, whatever may be their nature, create no obligation upon the father; and it seems to follow, that his promise founded upon such a debt has no legally binding force.

The cases of instruments under seal and certain mercantile contracts, in which considerations need not be proved, do not contradict the principles above suggested. The first import a consideration in themselves, and the second belong to a branch of the mercantile law, which has found it necessary to disregard the point of consideration in respect to instruments negotiable in their nature and essential to the interests of commerce.

Instead of citing a multiplicity of cases to support the positions I have taken, I will only refer to a very able review of all the cases in the note in 3 Bos. & Pul. 249. The opinions of the judges had been variant for a long course of years upon this subject, but there seems to be no case in which it was nakedly decided, that a promise to pay the debt of a son of full age, not living with his father, though the debt were incurred by sickness which ended in the death of the son, without a previous request by the father proved or presumed, could be enforced by action. . . .

For the foregoing reasons we are all of opinion that the nonsuit directed by the Court of Common Pleas was right, and that judgment be entered thereon for costs for the defendant.

Post-Case Follow-Up

The *Mills* court determined that Seth Wyman's promise to repay Mills for aiding his ill son was unenforceable as past consideration. After his son's death, Seth Wyman's moral obligation to compensate Mills for the debts of his adult son could not be converted into a legal duty as there was no consideration underlying his initial promise. New promises to pay may reestablish consideration and legal duty in cases of debts barred by the statute of limitations, debts owed by minors or bankrupt parties, or merchant contracts under seal. However, none of these exceptions were present in this situation, so Wyman was not legally obligated to pay Mills under contract law.

Mills v. Wyman: Real Life Applications

1. Irv's son, Monte, is a troubled youth who ran away from home at age 15 to see the world. A year later, he becomes gravely ill and is admitted to an emergency room at a local hospital. The hospital takes care of him for a week while it tries to locate his family. When the hospital reaches Irv, he expresses gratitude for its care of his son and promises to pay for his medical care. Monte recovers and the hospital sends a bill to Irv for payment. Having recently lost his job, Irv does not pay the hospital bill and is being sued by the hospital for nonpayment. Irv comes to you seeking advice on his legal obligations, if any, to pay his son's bill. What do you advise him based on *Mills*?

2. A widow's husband dies owing a loan to a bank. His business and estate are insolvent and cannot afford to pay for his funeral costs. After his death, his widow promises in writing to pay his loan if the bank turns over his note to her. Later the bank sues her to collect the money owed by her deceased husband due to her promise. She argues that her promise is not supported by consideration since her husband's note is worthless after his death. Will her promise to pay her husband's loan be enforced? *Newman and Snell's State Bank v. Hunter*, 243 Mich. 331 (1928).

Mills v. Wyman: What Really Happened to Levi Wyman?

Seth Wyman's integrity was impugned after he refused to pay Mills for his son's debt. Professor Geoffrey R. Watson casts this dispute in a different light in his article, *In the Tribunal of Conscience:* Mills v. Wyman *Reconsidered*, 71 Tul. L. Rev. 1749 (1997). His historical research offers alternative interpretations of Wyman's promise through actual correspondence between the two men. He also discovers that Levi did not die as the court stated in its decision. In fact, testimony and documents show that Levi married about seven months after his illness and lived for many more decades back home in Massachusetts. Watson's research indicates that Levi led a troubled life with spendthrift ways and bouts of "excessive drinking and idleness" resulting in the appointment of a legal guardian to manage his affairs. Although Levi's parents lived a relatively comfortable life, perhaps they grew weary of paying their wastrel son's bills. Access and read Watson's article for more surprises about the *Mills* case.

B. RENEWING PAST PROMISES—SUPPORTED BY CONSIDERATION

Despite the legal analysis in *Mills*, courts often find reasons to enforce promises made after the fact. Courts have created several exceptions that permit enforcement of such promises. Traditional exceptions usually arise when one party made a promise in the past that was supported by consideration, but which is no longer enforceable. For example, Margaret borrows money from David and her promise to repay the debt is consideration. If Margaret does not pay David, then other legal defenses may make the promise unenforceable. For example, the statute of limitations might lapse, preventing David's lawsuit, or a bankruptcy court might discharge her debt. If Margaret renews the promise to pay David after her original debt becomes unenforceable, courts sometimes enforce the new promise. There is no consideration for the new promise. The original loan was made in the past, not in exchange for the new promise. Margaret's willingness to pay despite the defense reflects a sense of moral duty to repay the debt, even though her legal duty to pay no longer exists. The existence of a bargain supported by consideration in the past leads some courts to make that leap from past consideration and moral duty to recognition of prior consideration and a renewed legal duty.

In the wake of our review of the *Mills* case, we turn to four key situations in which courts have recognized that a new promise will be enforceable even if the consideration lies in a past performance:

1. Statutory law (typically, **statute of limitations**) precludes enforcement of a contractual duty (RESTATEMENT (SECOND) OF CONTRACTS §§82, 110);
2. Discharge in bankruptcy prevents collection of a debt that once was valid (RESTATEMENT (SECOND) OF CONTRACTS §83);
3. The nonoccurrence of a **condition** (an event that must occur before performance is due) would excuse performance of a contractual duty (RESTATEMENT (SECOND) OF CONTRACTS §84); and
4. The original duty was **voidable** (could be declared void by the promisor, usually based on a defense to contract formation) but not yet avoided or declared invalid by a court (RESTATEMENT (SECOND) OF CONTRACTS §85).

In each situation, an original contractual duty was created, complete with consideration or other grounds for enforcing the promise. The promisee cannot sue on the original promise, but the promisor makes a new promise, in effect renewing the original obligation. The new promise lacks consideration, but it is treated as enforceable. The key issue that courts address involves whether to enforce the new promise, not whether to reinstate the original promise. The terms of the new promise govern if they differ from the original promise. For instance, a new promise to repay a debt might specify a lower monthly payment or a longer payment period.

Similarly, the collection of a debt may be barred under the statute of limitations, which precludes bringing a breach of contract lawsuit after a certain time period. Revisiting our earlier example, let's say David must bring an action to enforce Margaret's promise to pay her debt within four years of her breach. If David seeks to collect his debt from Margaret five years after her breach, his contract action is barred under the statute of limitations. Now David cannot enforce her promise, but Margaret subsequently achieves financial security and promises once again to pay her earlier debt. The time period begins to run from Margaret's new promise, not the original one. Time for performance is measured from the date of the new promise, in effect starting a new limitations period if her new promise is breached. The exception permits enforcement of the new promise, rather than simply reviving the old one.

In another statutory example, *Homefinders v. Lawrence*, 335 P.2d 893 (Idaho 1959), a real estate broker was unable to collect commissions under the **statute of frauds**, which bars enforcement of certain oral promises if not contained in a proper signed writing. The court allowed recovery of these commissions when the promisor, after the sale, agreed to pay them despite the statutory bar on enforcement of that oral promise.

These exceptions should not simply be viewed as a **waiver**, an intentional relinquishment of a known right, of the original defense. All the goals of consideration are satisfied by the original promises supported by consideration. The promises were important enough to justify enforcement without requiring a second inquiry into consideration. In addition, some of the details of these provisions resemble waiver. For instance, a promise not to invoke the statute of limitations, a clear example of waiver of a legal defense, is treated as if it renews the promise. Similarly, a party that promised to perform despite nonoccurrence of a condition may reinstate the condition if there has been no reliance on the waiver—just as other waivers can be revoked prior to reliance. Conditions will be discussed in greater detail in Chapter 11, while voidable duties will be considered further in Chapters 6-8 and 13 of this text.

C. PROMISSORY RESTITUTION—SUBSEQUENT PROMISE AND MORAL DUTY

In contrast with *Mills*, modern courts have enforced promises even without a prior bargained-for exchange under the concept of **promissory restitution**. Courts apply promissory restitution in situations in which a promise to pay or compensate is made *after* a benefit is received. Under the traditional view, this subsequent promise would not be enforced since it is based upon past consideration as in *Mills*.

Under promissory restitution, a court may enforce a subsequent promise under the **material benefit rule** (Restatement (Second) of Contracts §84). This rule examines whether or not (1) a promisor received a benefit from the promisee; (2) the promisor made a promise to the promisee in recognition of the benefit received; and (3) an injustice would result unless the promise is enforced. These elements closely resemble the elements of a cause of action for unjust enrichment, which may require compensation for benefits even if the party did not make such a promise. Unjust enrichment was introduced in Chapter 1 and will be discussed further in Chapter 16.

Under this rule, the subsequent promise must be made by a person who actually benefited to the person who conferred that benefit. This rule does not apply to instances in which a party has received a gift or in cases of unjust enrichment. Enforcement of this kind of promise is normally limited to reasonable value of benefit conferred on the promisor. Courts are careful to avoid enforcing a later promise whose value is disproportionate to the reasonable value of benefit bestowed. At times, it may be difficult for a court to determine the value of a benefit received, especially if the benefit involved saving another person from serious injury or death. In the following case, the court must reconcile the morality of risking one's life to save another person from the legal duty to compensate one's rescuer.

Case Preview

Webb v. McGowin

A lumber company employee, Webb, heroically sacrificed his own well-being to protect a co-worker, McGowin, from serious injury or death. McGowin made a subsequent promise to compensate Webb for the rest of Webb's life after his physical and mental injuries prevented him from future labors. When McGowin died, his estate stopped paying Webb, who then brought an action to enforce McGowin's promise. The court needed to decide whether or not to enforce McGowin's promise made *after* a benefit was bestowed upon him.

As you read *Webb v. McGowin*, look for the following:

1. What material benefit did McGowin, the promisor, receive from Webb, the promisee?
2. How did the court distinguish the enforcement of McGowin's subsequent promise from unenforceable past consideration?
3. Was McGowin's promise merely an unenforceable moral obligation rather than a legal duty to pay Webb for life?

Webb v. McGowin

168 So. 196 (Ala. App. 1935), cert. denied, 168 So. 199 (Ala. 1936)

BRICKEN, Presiding Judge.

. . .

A fair statement of the case presenting the questions for decision is set out in appellant's brief, which we adopt.

"On the 3d day of August, 1925, appellant while in the employ of the W. T. Smith Lumber Company, a corporation, and acting within the scope of his employment, was engaged in clearing the upper floor of mill No. 2 of the company. While so engaged he was in the act of dropping a pine block from the upper floor of the mill to the ground below; this being the usual and ordinary way of clearing the floor, and it being the duty of the plaintiff in the course of his employment to so drop it. The block weighed about 75 pounds.

"As appellant was in the act of dropping the block to the ground below, he was on the edge of the upper floor of the mill. As he started to turn the block loose so that it would drop to the ground, he saw J. Greeley McGowin, testator of the defendants, on the ground below and directly under where the block would have fallen had appellant turned it loose. Had he turned it loose it would have struck McGowin with such force as to have caused him serious bodily harm or death. Appellant could have remained safely on the upper floor of the mill by turning the block loose and allowing it to drop, but had he done this the block would have fallen on McGowin and caused him serious injuries or death. The only safe and reasonable way to prevent this was for appellant to hold to the block and divert its direction in falling from the place where McGowin was standing and the only safe way to divert it so as to prevent its coming into contact with McGowin was for appellant to fall with it to the ground below. Appellant did this, and by holding to the block and falling with it to the ground below, he diverted the course of its fall in such way that McGowin was not injured. In thus preventing the injuries to McGowin appellant himself received serious bodily injuries, resulting in his right leg being broken, the heel of his right foot torn off and his right arm broken. He was badly crippled for life and rendered unable to do physical or mental labor.

"On September 1, 1925, in consideration of appellant having prevented him from sustaining death or serious bodily harm and in consideration of the injuries appellant had received, McGowin agreed with him to care for and maintain him for the remainder of appellant's life at the rate of $15 every two weeks from the time he sustained his injuries to and during the remainder of appellant's life; it being agreed that McGowin would pay this sum to appellant for his maintenance. Under the agreement McGowin paid or caused to be paid to appellant the sum so agreed on up until McGowin's death on January 1, 1934. After his death the payments were continued to and including January 27, 1934, at which time they were discontinued. Thereupon plaintiff brought suit to recover the unpaid installments accruing up to the time of the bringing of the suit."

. . .

The action was for the unpaid installments accruing after January 27, 1934, to the time of the suit.

The principal grounds of demurrer to the original and amended complaint are: (1) It states no cause of action; (2) its averments show the contract was without consideration; (3) it fails to allege that McGowin had, at or before the services were rendered, agreed to pay appellant for them. . . .

1. The averments of the complaint show that appellant saved McGowin from death or grievous bodily harm. This was a material benefit to him of infinitely more value than any financial aid he could have received. Receiving this benefit, McGowin became morally bound to compensate appellant for the services rendered. Recognizing his moral obligation, he expressly agreed to pay appellant as alleged in the complaint and complied with this agreement up to the time of his death; a period of more than 8 years.

Had McGowin been accidentally poisoned and a physician, without his knowledge or request, had administered an antidote, thus saving his life, a subsequent promise by McGowin to pay the physician would have been valid. Likewise, McGowin's agreement as disclosed by the complaint to compensate appellant for saving him from death or grievous bodily injury is valid and enforceable.

Where the promisee cares for, improves, and preserves the property of the promisor, though done without his request, it is sufficient consideration for the promisor's subsequent agreement to pay for the service, because of the material benefit received. [Citation omitted.]

In *Boothe v. Fitzpatrick*, 36 Vt. 681, the court held that a promise by defendant to pay for the past keeping of a bull which had escaped from defendant's premises and been cared for by plaintiff was valid, although there was no previous request, because the subsequent promise obviated that objection; it being equivalent to a previous request. On the same principle, had the promisee saved the promisor's life or his body from grievous harm, his subsequent promise to pay for the services rendered would have been valid. Such service would have been far more material than caring for his bull. Any holding that saving a man from death or grievous bodily harm is not a material benefit sufficient to uphold a subsequent promise to pay for the service, necessarily rests on the assumption that saving life and preservation of the body from harm have only a sentimental value. The converse of this is true. Life and preservation of the body have material, pecuniary values, measurable in dollars and cents. Because of this, physicians practice their profession charging for services rendered in saving life and curing the body of its ills, and surgeons perform operations. The same is true as to the law of negligence, authorizing the assessment of damages in personal injury cases based upon the extent of the injuries, earnings, and life expectancies of those injured.

In the business of life insurance, the value of a man's life is measured in dollars and cents according to his expectancy, the soundness of his body, and his ability to pay premiums. The same is true as to health and accident insurance.

It follows that if, as alleged in the complaint, appellant saved J. Greeley McGowin from death or grievous bodily harm, and McGowin subsequently agreed to pay him for the service rendered, it became a valid and enforceable contract.

2. It is well settled that a moral obligation is a sufficient consideration to support a subsequent promise to pay where the promisor has received a material benefit, although there was no original duty or liability resting on the promisor. [Citation omitted.] In the case of *State ex rel. Bayer v. Funk, supra*, the court held that a moral obligation is a sufficient consideration to support an executory promise where the promisor has received an actual pecuniary or material benefit for which he subsequently expressly promised to pay.

The case at bar is clearly distinguishable from that class of cases where the consideration is a mere moral obligation or conscientious duty unconnected with receipt by promisor of benefits of a material or pecuniary nature. *Park Falls State Bank v. Fordyce, supra*. Here the promisor received a material benefit constituting a valid consideration for his promise.

3. Some authorities hold that, for a moral obligation to support a subsequent promise to pay, there must have existed a prior legal or equitable obligation, which

for some reason had become unenforceable, but for which the promisor was still morally bound. This rule, however, is subject to qualification in those cases where the promisor, having received a material benefit from the promisee, is morally bound to compensate him for the services rendered and in consideration of this obligation promises to pay. In such cases the subsequent promise to pay is an affirmance or ratification of the services rendered carrying with it the presumption that a previous request for the service was made. [Citation omitted.]

Under the decisions above cited, McGowin's express promise to pay appellant for the services rendered was an affirmance or ratification of what appellant had done raising the presumption that the services had been rendered at McGowin's request.

4. The averments of the complaint show that in saving McGowin from death or grievous bodily harm, appellant was crippled for life. This was part of the consideration of the contract declared on. McGowin was benefited. Appellant was injured. Benefit to the promisor or injury to the promisee is a sufficient legal consideration for the promisor's agreement to pay. [Citation omitted.]

5. Under the averments of the complaint the services rendered by appellant were not gratuitous. The agreement of McGowin to pay and the acceptance of payment by appellant conclusively shows the contrary.

. . .

From what has been said, we are of the opinion that the court below erred in the ruling complained of; that is to say, in sustaining the demurrer, and for this error the case is reversed and remanded.

. . .

Samford, Judge (concurring).

The questions involved in this case are not free from doubt, and perhaps the strict letter of the rule, as stated by judges, though not always in accord, would bar a recovery by plaintiff, but following the principle announced by Chief Justice Marshall in *Hoffman v. Porter*, Fed. Cas. No. 6,577, 2 Brock. 156, 159, where he says, "I do not think that law ought to be separated from justice, where it is at most doubtful," I concur in the conclusions reached by the court.

Post-Case Follow-Up

Generally, a moral obligation does not make an agreement enforceable. Yet where a material benefit is conferred upon a promisor, the material benefit serves as sufficient consideration for the subsequent promise. McGowin's subsequent promise to pay for services rendered is an affirmance or ratification of what Webb did for McGowin, raising a presumption that a previous request for services was made (or would have been made if time had allowed for it). When Webb saved McGowin's life, McGowin received a material benefit from him, which provided the necessary consideration to make his subsequent promise enforceable.

Webb v. McGowin: Real Life Applications

1. A real estate agent enters into a listing agreement with a homeowner. After the initial agreement expires, the agent brings a potential purchaser to the home who subsequently makes a written offer to the homeowner. The homeowner and real estate agent subsequently sign a renewal of the listing agreement so that the real estate agent could receive a commission. Will a court enforce this promise to pay a real estate commission after the expiration of the listing agreement? Research and review *Realty Assocs. v. Valley Nat'l Bank*, 153 Ariz. 514 (1986), to see if the real estate agent will recover her commission.

2. Celia and her husband are injured in a serious car accident during a honeymoon trip in Fiji. Her parents travel to Fiji and decide in collaboration with her doctors that the couple should be flown home for further medical treatments, costing $350,000. During their recuperation, the couple promises to repay Celia's parents for these medical expenses once they receive reimbursement from their travel insurance. The insurance company refuses to pay, claiming that her parents have paid the expenses so the couple suffered no travel losses. Celia consults your firm for your assistance. Look up *Braka v. Travel Assistance Intl.*, 7 Misc. 3d 1019(A) (N.Y. Sup. Ct. 2005), to see what a New York court decided on this issue of moral obligation.

3. An uncle becomes the guardian of a nephew and niece after their father's accidental death. Death benefits paid under a worker's compensation program are deposited in an account for the children. The uncle withdraws the funds to help support his business. Over a dozen years later, the nephew learns about the death benefits and demands that the uncle pay interest on the funds taken from the account. The uncle repays the funds and initially agrees to pay the outstanding interest, but then later backs out, claiming a six-year statute of limitations on the debt. The nephew seeks your help in recovering the interest on the benefits. Guide your client after examining the case of *Slayton v. Slayton*, 55 Ala. App. 351 (Ala. Civ. App. 1975).

D. PREEXISTING DUTY—INVALID CONTRACT MODIFICATIONS

Preexisting duty refers to conduct or actions that a person already has a legal obligation to do. Promising to do something that one is already legally obligated to perform is not consideration. It amounts to selling something to the person who already owns it. One who borrows a car cannot sell it back to the owner or even charge a modest return fee. Doing something you already have an undisputed legal duty to do is not consideration.

Preexisting duty cases often involve questions about a contract **modification**, a change or revision to the terms of an existing contract. One party requests an adjustment in the terms, often a higher price than originally agreed to in the contract. A party demanding more money for the same performance already promised does not provide consideration for the revised contract terms. A contract modification that changes only one party's obligations raises concerns about coercive tactics, unfair threats of breach, and **economic duress**, a wrongful or improper threat that will be discussed in greater detail in Chapter 6. These kinds of conduct contradict notions of good faith and fair dealing. The classic case of *Alaska Packers' Assn. v. Domenico*, 117 F. 99 (9th Cir. 1902), illustrates concerns about coercion and the lack of consideration to support changing duties already agreed upon by the parties.

Salmon packed by the Alaska Packers' Association
Alaska State Library/ASL-MS108-7-04

Case Preview

Alaska Packers' Assn. v. Domenico

A fish packing collaborative hired fishermen in San Francisco to work the salmon season in Alaska. After they arrived in Alaska, the fishermen refused to work unless defendant agreed to raise their pay. Since the cannery asserted that it was too late to bring in replacements, the association's agent in Alaska eventually gave in and agreed to pay the fisherman more for the same contracted services. The court needed to determine whether or not the fishermen were entitled to the increased compensation.

As you read *Alaska Packers' Assn. v. Domenico*, look for the following:

1. When the cannery agent agreed to the modified contract, was it enforceable as supported by consideration? Was there an effective waiver of the original contract terms?
2. How did the court define the preexisting duty rule?
3. How did the court apply earlier precedent on preexisting duty to support its decision in this case?

Alaska Packers' Assn. v. Domenico

117 F. 99 (9th Cir. 1902)

Ross, Circuit Judge.

. . .

The evidence shows without conflict that on March 26, 1900, at the city and county of San Francisco, the libelants entered into a written contract with the appellant, whereby they agreed to go from San Francisco to Pyramid Harbor, Alaska, and return, on board such vessel as might be designated by the appellant, and to work for

the appellant during the fishing season of 1900, at Pyramid Harbor, as sailors and fishermen, agreeing to do "regular ship's duty, both up and down, discharging and loading; and to do any other work whatsoever when requested to do so by the captain or agent of the Alaska Packers' Association." By the terms of this agreement, the appellant was to pay each of the libelants $50 for the season, and two cents for each red salmon in the catching of which he took part.

On the 15th day of April, 1900, 21 of the libelants signed shipping articles by which they shipped as seamen on the Two Brothers, a vessel chartered by the appellant for the voyage between San Francisco and Pyramid Harbor, and also bound themselves to perform the same work for the appellant provided for by the previous contract of March 26th; the appellant agreeing to pay them therefor the sum of $60 for the season, and two cents each for each red salmon in the catching of which they should respectively take part. Under these contracts, the libelants sailed on board the Two Brothers for Pyramid Harbor, where the appellant had about $150,000 invested in a salmon cannery. The libelants arrived there early in April of the year mentioned, and began to unload the vessel and fit up the cannery. A few days thereafter, to wit, May 19th, they stopped work in a body, and demanded of the company's superintendent there in charge $100 for services in operating the vessel to and from Pyramid Harbor, instead of the sums stipulated for in and by the contracts; stating that unless they were paid this additional wage they would stop work entirely, and return to San Francisco. The evidence showed, and the court below found, that it was impossible for the appellant to get other men to take the places of the libelants, the place being remote, the season short and just opening; so that, after endeavoring for several days without success to induce the libelants to proceed with their work in accordance with their contracts, the company's superintendent, on the 22d day of May, so far yielded to their demands as to instruct his clerk to copy the contracts executed in San Francisco, including the words "Alaska Packers' Association" at the end, substituting, for the $50 and $60 payments, respectively, of those contracts, the sum of $100, which document, so prepared, was signed by the libelants before a shipping commissioner whom they had requested to be brought from Northeast Point; the superintendent, however, testifying that he at the time told the libelants that he was without authority to enter into any such contract, or to in any way alter the contracts made between them and the company in San Francisco. Upon the return of the libelants to San Francisco at the close of the fishing season, they demanded pay in accordance with the terms of the alleged contract of May 22d, when the company denied its validity, and refused to pay other than as provided for by the contracts of March 26th and April 5th, respectively. Some of the libelants, at least, consulted counsel, and, after receiving his advice, those of them who had signed the shipping articles before the shipping commissioner at San Francisco went before that officer, and received the amount due them thereunder, executing in consideration thereof a release in full, and the others being paid at the office of the company, also receipting in full for their demands.

On the trial in the court below, the libelants undertook to show that the fishing nets provided by the respondent were defective, and that it was on that account that they demanded increased wages. On that point, the evidence was substantially conflicting, and the finding of the court was against the libelants, the court saying:

> The contention of libelants that the nets provided them were rotten and unserviceable is not sustained by the evidence. The defendant's interest required that libelants should be provided with every facility necessary to their success as fishermen, for on such success depended the profits defendant would be able to realize that season from its packing plant, and the large capital invested therein. In view of this self-evident fact, it is highly improbable that the defendant gave libelants rotten and unserviceable nets with which to fish. It follows from this finding that libelants were not justified in refusing performance of their original contract. 112 Fed. 554.

The evidence being sharply conflicting in respect to these facts, the conclusions of the court, who heard and saw the witnesses, will not be disturbed. [Citation omitted.]

The real questions in the case as brought here are questions of law, and, in the view that we take of the case, it will be necessary to consider but one of those. Assuming that the appellant's superintendent at Pyramid Harbor was authorized to make the alleged contract of May 22d, and that he executed it on behalf of the appellant, was it supported by a sufficient consideration? From the foregoing statement of the case, it will have been seen that the libelants agreed in writing, for certain stated compensation, to render their services to the appellant in remote waters where the season for conducting fishing operations is extremely short, and in which enterprise the appellant had a large amount of money invested; and, after having entered upon the discharge of their contract, and at a time when it was impossible for the appellant to secure other men in their places, the libelants, without any valid cause, absolutely refused to continue the services they were under contract to perform unless the appellant would consent to pay them more money. Consent to such a demand, under such circumstances, if given, was, in our opinion, without consideration, for the reason that it was based solely upon the libelants' agreement to render the exact services, and none other, that they were already under contract to render. The case shows that they willfully and arbitrarily broke that obligation. . . .

Certainly, it cannot be justly held, upon the record in this case, that there was any voluntary waiver on the part of the appellant of the breach of the original contract. The company itself knew nothing of such breach until the expedition returned to San Francisco, and the testimony is uncontradicted that its superintendent at Pyramid Harbor, who, it is claimed, made on its behalf the contract sued on, distinctly informed the libelants that he had no power to alter the original or to make a new contract; and it would, of course, follow that, if he had no power to change the original, he would have no authority to waive any rights thereunder. The circumstances of the present case bring it, we think, directly within the sound and just observations of the supreme court of Minnesota in the case of *King v. Railway Co.*, 61 Minn. 482, 63 N.W. 1105:

> "No astute reasoning can change the plain fact that the party who refuses to perform, and thereby coerces a promise from the other party to the contract to pay him an increased compensation for doing that which he is legally bound to do, takes

an unjustifiable advantage of the necessities of the other party. Surely it would be a travesty on justice to hold that the party so making the promise for extra pay was estopped from asserting that the promise was without consideration. A party cannot lay the foundation of an estoppel by his own wrong, where the promise is simply a repetition of a subsisting legal promise. There can be no consideration for the promise of the other party, and there is no warrant for inferring that the parties have voluntarily rescinded or modified their contract. The promise cannot be legally enforced, although the other party has completed his contract in reliance upon it."

In *Lingenfelder v. Brewing Co.*, 103 Mo. 578, 15 S.W. 844, the court, in holding void a contract by which the owner of a building agreed to pay its architect an additional sum because of his refusal to otherwise proceed with the contract, said:

"It is urged upon us by respondents that this was a new contract. New in what? Jungenfeld was bound by his contract to design and supervise this building. Under the new promise, he was not to do anything more or anything different. What benefit was to accrue to Wainwright? He was to receive the same service from Jungenfeld under the new, that Jungenfeld was bound to tender under the original contract. What loss, trouble, or inconvenience could result to Jungenfeld that he had not already assumed? No amount of metaphysical reasoning can change the plain fact that Jungenfeld took advantage of Wainwright's necessities, and extorted the promise of five per cent, on the refrigerator plant as the condition of his complying with his contract already entered into. Nor had he even the flimsy pretext that Wainwright had violated any of the conditions of the contract on his part. Jungenfeld himself put it upon the simple proposition that "if he, as an architect, put up the brewery, and another company put up the refrigerating machinery, it would be a detriment to the Empire Refrigerating Company," of which Jungenfeld was president. To permit plaintiff to recover under such circumstances would be to offer a premium upon bad faith, and invite men to violate their most sacred contracts that they may profit by their own wrong. That a promise to pay a man for doing that which he is already under contract to do is without consideration is conceded by respondents. The rule has been so long imbedded in the common law and decisions of the highest courts of the various states that nothing but the most cogent reasons ought to shake it. [Citing a long list of authorities.] But it is "carrying coals to Newcastle" to add authorities on a proposition so universally accepted, and so inherently just and right in itself.

...

What we hold is that, when a party merely does what he has already obligated himself to do, he cannot demand an additional compensation therefor; and although, by taking advantage of the necessities of his adversary, he obtains a promise for more, the law will regard it as nudum pactum, and will not lend its process to aid in the wrong."

...

... [T]he subsequent case of *Cobb v. Cowdery*, 40 Vt. 25, 94 Am. Dec. 370 ... held that:

"A promise by a party to do what he is bound in law to do is not an illegal consideration, but is the same as no consideration at all, and is merely void; in other words, it is insufficient, but not illegal. Thus, if the master of a ship promise his crew an addition to their fixed wages in consideration of, and as an incitement to, their extraordinary exertions during a storm, or in any other emergency of the voyage, this promise is nudum pactum; the voluntary performance of an act which it was before legally incumbent on the party to perform being in law an insufficient consideration; and so it would be in any other case where the only consideration for the promise of one party was the promise of the other party to do, or his actual doing, something which he was previously bound in law to do. Chit. Cont. [10th Am. Ed.] 51; Smith, Cont. 87; 3 Kent, Comm. 185."

. . .

It results from the views above expressed that the judgment must be reversed, and the cause remanded, with directions to the court below to enter judgment for the respondent, with costs. It is so ordered.

Post-Case Follow-Up

The court found that the fishermen were already obligated by contract to perform their duties. No consideration existed to support their demand for increased wages because the new deal was for the exact same services they previously contracted to perform at lower rates of pay. The court also reasoned that allowing such a modification would encourage people to abandon their contractual obligations in bad faith. In addition, there was no valid waiver of the terms of the original contract and the superintendent informed the men that he lacked the authority to enter into a new contract.

Alaska Packers' Assn. v. Domenico: Real Life Applications

1. A consulting company, Lopez & Taylor, enters into a contract for project management services to supervise a hotel development to deal with flooding and construction delays. Subsequently, Lopez & Taylor seeks additional compensation for consulting services that they claim exceed the scope of work under the original contract. The consultants turn to you for help on recovering additional pay for their services. How will the preexisting duty rule impact this effort to receive higher compensation? Check out *Plante & Moran Cresa, L.L.C. v. Kappa Enters., L.L.C.*, 251 Fed. Appx. 974 (6th Cir. 2007), to determine the likely outcome.

2. Stu is involved in an accident that totals his car. As a salesperson, he needs a vehicle quickly to visit his customers. He contracts to buy a car for $10,000 and put down a $1,000 deposit until delivery a week later. The dealership contacts Stu the next day to tell him that the car in his contract is not available, but he could take delivery of the same model of the car with two additional features, worth $200 more. Desperate for a car, Stu decides to pay the extra $200 to obtain the car. When he arrives at the dealership a week later, the sales associate tacks on another $150 because of cost increases on the features between the time of

Another Perspective on *Alaska Packers*

A number of legal scholars have interpreted this classic case as a warning against coercive conduct or self-interested behavior to renegotiate unfavorable contracts. However, Professor Debora L. Threedy discusses alternative legal and factual interpretations of this famous case. Although the cannery claimed an inability to find substitute workers during the limited fishing season, it appears that local indigenous Alaskan fishermen could have provided salmon catches to the cannery. In addition, the fishermen claimed the defendant breached by providing them with defective nets, which would negatively impact their seasonal wages. The court discredited the fishermen's claim, but there may have been legitimate confusion over the quality of the nets, which may have been exacerbated by language barriers. An honest dispute over the quality of the nets might justify court enforcement of the modification. The cannery may also have wanted to avoid catching too many fish, potentially overwhelming the cannery's production capacity. For more on reconsidering this case, review Professor Threedy's article, *A Fish Story:* Alaska Packers' Association v. Domenico, 2000 UTAH L. REV. 185.

Stu's order and the car's delivery date, with applicable sales tax. Stu pays to get the car and comes to you complaining that he has been overcharged by the dealership. Under the UCC, advise Stu about whether or not a court is likely to enforce the extra charges. Review *Palmer v. Safe Auto Sales, Inc.*, 114 Misc. 2d 964 (N.Y. Civ. Ct. 1982) for support.

3. Your client, CompuDeal, Inc., enters into a requirements contract for the purchase of laptops from Hardware Depot (HD) for a three-year term under fixed price terms. Recently, HD contacts CompuDeal informing it of its decision to shut down its laptop manufacturing plant. Recognizing the risks to its customers by an immediate shutdown, HD makes an offer to CompuDeal and other customers to keep making laptops for a price increase of 30 percent. CompuDeal protests this offer as amounting to a breach of contract, but pays the extra costs in order to retain its laptop supplies, until it can find a comparable vendor. If CompuDeal wants to later recover its damages from HD, has it waived its right to seek compensation? Look at *Kelsey-Hayes Co. v. Galtaco Redlaw Castings Corp.*, 749 F. Supp. 794 (E.D. Mich. 1990), on issues of compensation and waiver.

E. VALID CONTRACT MODIFICATIONS — FINDING NEW CONSIDERATION

The most effective way to combat arguments of preexisting duty involves finding additional consideration for the modified promise. New consideration can indicate that the parties are voluntarily amending or waiving their duties in response to changed circumstances or new objectives. Consider three ways that the new promise might include new consideration:

1. the modification altered both parties' performance;
2. the modification included the settlement of a claim or defense; and
3. the original duty was rescinded or waived.

Even if there is no new consideration, modification might reflect the parties' understandable willingness to adjust the deal due to unanticipated circumstances.

When parties act in good faith to produce a fairer exchange, refusing to enforce the modification on technical grounds does not appeal to all courts. These types of modified promises are discussed below.

1. Modifications Altering Both Parties' Performance

If the parties change their duties on both sides, a bargain may exist. Each sought a change in the other's performance in exchange for the change to its own performance. For example, many consulting contracts are modified in progress, with the client specifying the changes it needs and the consultant specifying the cost of those changes. A client may decide to expand the statement of work in the original consulting contract. The consultant may be willing to make these changes and may increase its prices on the order to comply with the client's request. Both parties may agree to make these changes in good faith furnishing fresh consideration to reach their revised bargain.

However, a pretense of a bargain will not suffice. If one party extracts better terms from the other, throwing in something the promisor did not seek, the addition may not rescue the modification. Be alert for sham exchanges designed to disguise the lack of a real bargain. Sham consideration is reviewed in Chapter 4.

2. Modifications Settling Disputes

Under a contract, disputed duties may give rise to consideration without changing the substance of the deal. Sometimes the higher price serves to settle a legitimate claim or valid defense. For instance, unexpected subsurface conditions in a construction contract might make the agreement voidable for **mutual mistake**, a defense allowing rescission when both parties were mistaken about basic assumptions on which they agreed to the contract. If the contractor honestly believes that the defense exists, it has a right to raise and litigate that defense. It can refuse to perform and, if sued for breach, raise the defense. A modification may buy the right to avoid costly litigation. The project owner agrees to pay more to the contractor provided that the contractor waives its defense of mutual mistake under the first agreement. Each party gains something of value from this exchange. The contractor gets paid more—while the project owner avoids any construction delays necessary to find a substitute and the costs of litigation for suing for breach of contract. Although the performance itself did not change, the modification added something to that bargain: the waiver of a valid defense in litigation. The modification was made after the parties became aware of the unanticipated subsurface conditions. Neither party could pretend that it was mistaken about the reasons for the modified contract. Even without any mention of waiving the defense, the defense effectively disappears because any assertion of mutual mistake has been dealt with through the increased payment for the newly discovered subsurface conditions.

This refinement negates the preexisting duty rule not only where no duty exists, but also where the duty is questionable. Even if a reasonable person would not find the duty doubtful, an honest belief that the duty might be excused will suffice for consideration under the Restatement (Second) of Contracts §73. But if a party has no honest belief in his own mutual mistake defense, then pleading it may be a wrong in itself. A defense you know you do not legitimately have a right to raise in litigation is not consideration.

In rare situations, parties can settle claims that neither of them believes are valid, despite the preexisting duty rule. These involve efforts to eliminate even a remote risk of a claim. A party with a strong aversion to risk might want to buy another's potential claim even if neither one of them thinks the claim has any validity. Courts will honor some contracts to buy claims that no one believes are valid under the Restatement (Second) of Contracts §74(2). As long as the buyer truly bargains for the release in exchange for payment, courts will find consideration. The issue arises occasionally in large real estate transactions when a title search reveals a remotely plausible claim of ownership. The lender refuses to proceed with the financing unless the owner extinguishes the claim. The owner agrees to pay the remote claimant—who often had no idea that any claim might exist—to release the claim. The deal is enforceable as the money is given in exchange for avoiding a future ownership claim and to allow for the completion of the planned real estate purchase.

The danger here arises if people with no honest claim nonetheless assert a claim in bad faith, threatening to hold up a project unless they are paid off. Yet these bad faith cases may cross the line into economic duress. While consideration may not provide a means of denying enforcement, an assertion of economic duress should help prevent such contract abuses.

3. Modifications After Rescission or Waiver

The preexisting duty rule has no bite unless a prior legal obligation exists. If for any reason the promisor is not entitled to performance of the original duty, a different promise to perform may be consideration for the promisor's promise. Courts confronted with a revised transaction that seems reasonable sometimes stretch to find that the original duty ceased to bind the parties. Judges may find that the parties rescinded the original contract, and then made a new contract. Once the original is rescinded, no duty to perform it remains, leaving the parties free to enter a new deal—or to walk away and deal with others instead. Their decision to deal with each other is a new contract, not really a modification of the defunct original. For example, in *Schwartzreich v. Bauman-Basch, Inc.*, 131 N.E. 887 (N.Y. 1921), an employee received a better offer from another employer with about a month remaining on his contract with Bauman-Basch. The employer, in the middle of the busy season, negotiated with the employee for a raise in pay. The parties entered into a new contract with the higher salary. The employer later discharged the employee before the term of the new contract expired and the employee sued for breach of the second contract. The court interpreted tearing up the old contract as a rescission, leaving the parties free to enter the new contract. Technically, the original contract was not modified, but rescinded, and a new contract was voluntarily created.

In other cases, courts may find that the promisor waived its right to receive performance. The waiver effectively removed any duty the promisee had to perform, leaving the parties able to make a new deal. This situation occurred in *Watkins & Son v. Carrig*, 21 A.2d 591 (N.H. 1941). A contractor agreed to excavate an owner's land. Unexpected subsurface conditions made the job 11 times as expensive as planned. The owner promised to pay more, but later urged that the agreement lacked consideration because the contractor had a preexisting duty to do the work for less. The court found a waiver of rights under the original agreement, allowing the new negotiations to create an enforceable contract.

The rationale in these cases may not withstand careful attention to detail. The acts constituting the rescission or waiver may not be as clear as one would hope—and they may not strictly occur before the modification. Courts inclined to enforce the new deal may be more concerned with attaining a just result or upholding good faith and fair dealing, than a focus on doctrinal details.

4. Modifications Made in Good Faith

The preexisting duty rule may preclude the enforcement of agreements, even if they do not smack of coercive conduct or economic duress. In some instances, two parties may agree to a reasonable adjustment in their contract in the face of unexpected changes in conditions. When one party later changes its mind and tries to enforce the original contract, the preexisting duty rule looks more like a loophole or technicality that allows one party to back out of the modified deal.

Over time, courts recognized that adjusting contracts during performance often produced fairer contracts. Even without coercion, some parties are willing to adjust their dealings in light of changed circumstances. Rather than impede voluntary adjustments, courts now facilitate them, relying on the rules governing duress to prevent claimed abuses. Preexisting duty remains a component of the common law. But it has become riddled with exceptions.

Today, modifications frequently are enforceable, with or without additional consideration, occurring before either party completes performance. The Restatement (Second) of Contracts §89 supports contract modifications that are fair and equitable based upon unanticipated circumstances that crop up after a contract has been executed or has been only partially performed. Similarly, in goods transactions, UCC §2-209 does not require new consideration to support a modification provided that a contract modification is made in good faith under the circumstances. Good faith may require a victim to protest modification as part of showing the existence of coercive tactics. Failure to object at the time risks deceiving the other party about one's intent to resist enforcement or seek redress.

In addition, the CISG does not require a showing of consideration to modify a contract under Article 29(1). Parties only need to show that there is an agreed-upon modification in order to enforce the revised agreement. This more flexible approach is consistent with the CISG overall approach to international commercial dealings and its rejection of the requirement of consideration in entering into binding contracts.

Case Preview

Angel v. Murray

A contractor agreed to collect all of the refuse within a particular city under a government contract. Yet growth within the city limits added hundreds of more dwellings, and the contractor sought an increase to compensate for its increased services and associated costs. When the city council approved increased compensation, that decision was challenged in court. The court needed to consider whether modifications to the contract were warranted or were precluded under the preexisting duty rule.

As you read *Angel v. Murray*, look for the following:

1. What arguments were made that the contractor should not have been paid additional funds to collect the refuse within the city's boundaries?
2. What arguments supported compensating the contractor for collecting additional refuse from the expanding number of dwellings within the city's boundaries?
3. What was the court's view on the modern approach to preexisting duty under the Restatement (Second) of Contracts and the UCC? How did this modern perspective impact the outcome of this case?

Angel v. Murray

113 R.I. 482 (1974)

Roberts, C. J.

This is a civil action brought by Alfred L. Angel and others against John E. Murray, Jr., Director of Finance of the City of Newport, the city of Newport, and James L. Maher, alleging that Maher had illegally been paid the sum of $20,000 by the Director of Finance and praying that the defendant Maher be ordered to repay the city such sum. The case was heard by a justice of the Superior Court, sitting without a jury, who entered a judgment ordering Maher to repay the sum of $20,000 to the city of Newport. Maher is now before this court prosecuting an appeal.

The record discloses that Maher has provided the city of Newport with a refuse-collection service under a series of five-year contracts beginning in 1946. On March 12, 1964, Maher and the city entered into another such contract for a period of five years commencing on July 1, 1964, and terminating on June 30, 1969. The contract provided, among other things, that Maher would receive $137,000 per year in return for collecting and removing all combustible and noncombustible waste materials generated within the city.

In June of 1967 Maher requested an additional $10,000 per year from the city council because there had been a substantial increase in the cost of collection due to an unexpected and unanticipated increase of 400 new dwelling units. Maher's testimony, which is uncontradicted, indicates the 1964 contract had been predicated on the fact that since 1946 there had been an average increase of 20 to 25 new dwelling

units per year. After a public meeting of the city council where Maher explained in detail the reasons for his request and was questioned by members of the city council, the city council agreed to pay him an additional $10,000 for the year ending on June 30, 1968. Maher made a similar request again in June of 1968 for the same reasons, and the city council again agreed to pay an additional $10,000 for the year ending on June 30, 1969.

The trial justice found that each such $10,000 payment was made in violation of law. His decision, as we understand it, is premised on two independent grounds. First, he found that the additional payments were unlawful because they had not been recommended in writing to the city council by the city manager. Second, he found that Maher was not entitled to extra compensation because the original contract already required him to collect all refuse generated within the city and, therefore, included the 400 additional units. The trial justice further found that these 400 additional units were within the contemplation of the parties when they entered into the contract. It appears that he based this portion of the decision upon the rule that Maher had a preexisting duty to collect the refuse generated by the 400 additional units, and thus there was no consideration for the two additional payments.

. . .

Having found that the city council had the power to modify the 1964 contract without the written recommendation of the city manager, we are still confronted with the question of whether the additional payments were illegal because they were not supported by consideration.

As previously stated, the city council made two $10,000 payments. The first was made in June of 1967 for the year beginning on July 1, 1967, and ending on June 30, 1968. Thus, by the time this action was commenced in October of 1968, the modification was completely executed. That is, the money had been paid by the city council, and Maher had collected all of the refuse. Since consideration is only a test of the enforceability of executory promises, the presence or absence of consideration for the first payment is unimportant because the city council's agreement to make the first payment was fully executed at the time of the commencement of this action. See *Salvas v. Jussaume,* 50 R.I. 75, 145 A. 97 (1929); *Young Foundation Corp. v. A. E. Ottaviano, Inc.,* 29 Misc. 2d 302, 216 N.Y.S.2d 448, aff'd 15 A.D.2d 517, 222 N.Y.S.2d 685 (1961); *Sloan v. Sloan,* 66 A.2d 799 (D.C. Mun. Ct. App. 1949); *Hines v. Ward Baking Co.,* 155 F.2d 257 (7th Cir. 1946); *Julian v. Gold,* 214 Cal. 74, 3 P.2d 1009 (1931); 1 Williston, Contracts §130A at 543 (Jaeger 3d ed. 1957); Simpson, Contracts §58 at 102 (2d ed. 1965). However, since both payments were made under similar circumstances, our decision regarding the second payment (Part B, infra) is fully applicable to the first payment.

It is generally held that a modification of a contract is itself a contract, which is unenforceable unless supported by consideration. See Simpson, supra, §93. In *Rose v. Daniels,* 8 R.I. 381 (1866), this court held that an agreement by a debtor with a creditor to discharge a debt for a sum of money less than the amount due is unenforceable because it was not supported by consideration.

Rose is a perfect example of the preexisting duty rule. Under this rule an agreement modifying a contract is not supported by consideration if one of the parties to the agreement does or promises to do something that he is legally obligated to do or refrains or promises to refrain from doing something he is not legally privileged to do[.] *See* Calamari & Perillo, Contracts §60 (1970); 1A Corbin, Contracts §§171-72 (1963); 1 Williston, supra, §130; Annot., 12 A.L.R.2d 78 (1950). In *Rose* there was no consideration for the new agreement because the debtor was already legally obligated to repay the full amount of the debt.

. . .

The primary purpose of the preexisting duty rule is to prevent what has been referred to as the "hold-up game." *See* 1A Corbin, *supra*, §171. A classic example of the "hold-up game" is found in *Alaska Packers' Ass'n v. Domenico, 117 F. 99 (9th Cir. 1902)*. . . . The court found that the subsequent agreement to pay the men an additional $50 was not supported by consideration because the men had a preexisting duty to work on the ship under the original contract, and thus the subsequent agreement was unenforceable.

Another example of the "hold-up game" is found in the area of construction contracts. Frequently, a contractor will refuse to complete work under an unprofitable contract unless he is awarded additional compensation. The courts have generally held that a subsequent agreement to award additional compensation is unenforceable if the contractor is only performing work which would have been required of him under the original contract. *See, e.g., Lingenfelder v. Wainwright Brewing Co., 103 Mo. 578, 15* S.W. 844 (1891), which is a leading case in this area. *See also* cases collected in Annot., 25 A.L.R. 1450 (1923), supplemented by Annot., 55 A.L.R. 1333 (1928), and Annot., 138 A.L.R. 136 (1942); *cf. Ford & Denning v. Shepard Co.*, 36 R.I. 497, 90 A. 805 (1914).

These examples clearly illustrate that the courts will not enforce an agreement that has been procured by coercion or duress and will hold the parties to their original contract regardless of whether it is profitable or unprofitable. However, the courts have been reluctant to apply the pre-existing duty rule when a party to a contract encounters unanticipated difficulties and the other party, not influenced by coercion or duress, voluntarily agrees to pay additional compensation for work already required to be performed under the contract. For example, the courts have found that the original contract was rescinded, *Linz v. Schuck*, 106 Md. 220, 67 A. 286 (1907); abandoned, *Connelly v. Devoe,* 37 Conn. 570 (1871), or waived, *Michaud v. MacGregor,* 61 Minn. 198, 63 N.W. 479 (1895).

Although the preexisting duty rule has served a useful purpose insofar as it deters parties from using coercion and duress to obtain additional compensation, it has been widely criticized as a general rule of law. With regard to the preexisting duty rule, one legal scholar has stated: "There has been a growing doubt as to the soundness of this doctrine as a matter of social policy. . . . In certain classes of cases, this doubt has influenced courts to refuse to apply the rule, or to ignore it, in their actual decisions. Like other legal rules, this rule is in process of growth and change, the process being more active here than in most instances. The result of this is that a court should no longer accept this rule as fully established. It should never use it as the major premise of a decision, at least without giving careful thought to the circumstances of the particular case, to the moral deserts of the parties, and to the social feelings and interests that are involved. It is certain that the rule, stated in general and all-inclusive terms, is no longer so well-settled that a court must apply it though the heavens fall." 1A Corbin, *supra*, §171; *see also* Calamari & Perillo, *supra*, §61.

The modern trend appears to recognize the necessity that courts should enforce agreements modifying contracts when unexpected or unanticipated difficulties arise during the course of the performance of a contract, even though there is no consideration for the modification, as long as the parties agree voluntarily.

Under the Uniform Commercial Code, §2-209(1), which has been adopted by 49 states, "[an] agreement modifying a contract [for the sale of goods] needs no consideration to be binding." *See* G. L. 1956 (1969 Reenactment) §6A-2-209(1). Although at first blush this section appears to validate modifications obtained by coercion and duress, the comments to this section indicate that a modification under this section must meet the test of good faith imposed by the Code, and a modification obtained by extortion without a legitimate commercial reason is unenforceable.

The modern trend away from a rigid application of the preexisting duty rule is reflected by §89D(a) of the American Law Institute's Restatement Second of the Law of Contracts, [footnote omitted] which provides: "A promise modifying a duty under a contract not fully performed on either side is binding (a) if the modification is fair and equitable in view of circumstances not anticipated by the parties when the contract was made. . . ."

We believe that §89D(a) is the proper rule of law and find it applicable to the facts of this case. [Footnote omitted.] It not only prohibits modifications obtained by coercion, duress, or extortion but also fulfills society's expectation that agreements entered into voluntarily will be enforced by the courts. [Footnote omitted.] *See generally* Horwitz, *The Historical Foundations of Modern Contract Law*, 87 Harv. L. Rev. 917 (1974). Section 89D(a), of course, does not compel a modification of an unprofitable or unfair contract; it only enforces a modification if the parties voluntarily agree and if (1) the promise modifying the original contract was made before the contract was fully performed on either side, (2) the underlying circumstances which prompted the modification were unanticipated by the parties, and (3) the modification is fair and equitable.

The evidence, which is uncontradicted, reveals that in June of 1968 Maher requested the city council to pay him an additional $10,000 for the year beginning on July 1, 1968, and ending on June 30, 1969. This request was made at a public meeting of the city council, where Maher explained in detail his reasons for making the request. Thereafter, the city council voted to authorize the Mayor to sign an amendment to the 1954 contract which provided that Maher would receive an additional $10,000 per year for the duration of the contract. Under such circumstances we have no doubt that the city voluntarily agreed to modify the 1964 contract.

Having determined the voluntariness of this agreement, we turn our attention to the three criteria delineated above. First, the modification was made in June of 1968 at a time when the five-year contract which was made in 1964 had not been fully performed by either party. Second, although the 1964 contract provided that Maher collect all refuse generated within the city, it appears this contract was premised on Maher's past experience that the number of refuse-generating units would increase at a rate of 20 to 25 per year. Furthermore, the evidence is uncontradicted that the 1967-1968 increase of 400 units "went beyond any previous expectation." Clearly, the circumstances which prompted the city council to modify the 1964 contract were unanticipated. [Footnote omitted.] Third, although the evidence does not

indicate what proportion of the total this increase comprised, the evidence does indicate that it was a "substantial" increase. In light of this, we cannot say that the council's agreement to pay Maher the $10,000 increase was not fair and equitable in the circumstances.

The judgment appealed from is reversed, and the cause is remanded to the Superior Court for entry of judgment for the defendants.

Post-Case Follow-Up

The court reinforced the notion that contract modifications procured by coercion or duress will not be enforced. However, the modern trend moved away from a rigid application of the preexisting duty rule. If the parties voluntarily agreed to a modification, it will be enforced if (1) the promise modifying the original contract was made before the contract was fully performed on either side, (2) the underlying circumstances that prompted the modification were unanticipated by the parties, and (3) the modification was fair and equitable. The contractor's request for additional compensation met these requirements and the additional payments were valid.

Angel v. Murray: Real Life Applications

1. Your client, Secaton Inc., enters into a five-year installment contract of $1,000 per month to purchase a pre-owned corporate jet for business travels from a plane dealer, JetSec. Soon after entering into the contract, Secaton discovers that the engine needs to be replaced. Secaton offers to return the plane to JetSec rather than take on the additional expense of fixing the plane so soon after the purchase. To avoid adding the used jet back into its inventory, JetSec orally agrees to reduce Secaton's monthly payments to $500 a month for the next two years if it retains the plane. Secaton makes the reduced payments for about one year, then JetSec demands it now pay the $1,000 monthly amount or the plane will be repossessed. What will be likely outcome of this oral modification under the UCC? Consider *Skinner v. Tober Foreign Motors, Inc.*, 345 Mass. 429 (1963), in developing your response and drafting a client memo.

2. A subcontractor enters into a contract with a general contractor to purchase and install all electrical wiring in a new hotel. During the project, the subcontractor determines that special wiring may be needed for planned lighting and electrical work in a pool and spa area. The subcontractor agrees to provide this more expensive wiring if the general contractor promises to reimburse its costs. The general contractor approves and tells the subcontractor to install the special wiring. Later on the general contractor refuses to pay more for the wiring, claiming no consideration for its promise. The subcontractor argues that no consideration under the UCC is needed to pay the extra costs. Is a court likely to enforce this oral modification under the UCC? Read and brief *J & R Electric*

Div. of J. O. Mory Stores, Inc. v. Skoog Constr. Co., 38 Ill. App. 3d 747 (1976), to determine the likely outcome.

F. RELIANCE—PROMISSORY ESTOPPEL

Reliance plays an important role in contract law. In fact, the law enforces promises in large part to protect people who justifiably rely on those promises. By offering assurance that a party will in fact perform in the future, the law allows people to plan ahead and make other commitments secure in the assumption that the promise will be performed. When promises are breached, other arrangements made in reliance on a promise may be wasted or less valuable than expected. The prominence of reliance in the rationale for contract enforcement leads courts to use reliance as an exception in several areas of contract law. This section focuses on reliance as an exception to the requirement of consideration, often referred to as **promissory estoppel**.

People may rely on promises even if the promises were not part of a valid bargain. A person's reliance on the promise may leave the person in a worse position than if the promise had never been made. When reliance seems justified, courts may enforce the promise without consideration. Originally, courts referred to this exception as promissory estoppel: having induced another to rely on the promise, the promisor was **estopped** (legally barred or precluded) from denying the existence of consideration. In effect, the court ignored the defendant's denial that consideration existed, effectively making the promise enforceable. A number of states have enacted statutory law that directly addresses the concept of promissory estoppel. The Restatement (Second) of Contracts uses the term "reliance" and seeks to avoid the language of promissory estoppel. Yet many courts and lawyers still refer to promissory estoppel to describe this exception as established in case law or defined under state statutes.

1. Establishing the Exception for Reliance

As it has evolved today, the exception of reliance (promissory estoppel) requires four elements; two of which focus on the promisor's conduct and two of which look at the promisee's situation. First, the promisor makes a promise to another party. Second, the promisor must reasonably foresee that the other party will rely upon the promise (**foreseeable reliance**). Third, the promisee must actually rely upon this promise (**actual reliance**). Fourth, the promisee will suffer a substantial detriment if the promise is not enforced, resulting in an injustice (**detrimental reliance**). All four elements must be shown to establish the exception.

Reliance applies to a wide range of commercial and noncommercial contexts, including charitable pledges and gift promises. It also can apply to failed bargains, such as attempts to negotiate a contract that floundered because the parties' exchange did not meet one or more of the technicalities of consideration.

Promise—Promisor

The existence of a promise may seem too simple to explain. Contract law is about enforcing promises. A promise is the essential first step, whether enforceable based on consideration or on reliance. Occasionally, parties argue that they relied on another to perform in a particular way, without focusing on whether a promise was made. That omission is fatal to meeting the requirements of the reliance exception.

For example, in one case, a county enacted incentives to encourage taxi companies serving the airport to use cabs with less environmental impact. The county changed the incentives after one company had already purchased cabs that complied with the requirements. The cab company relied on the regulations, but the court found no promise by the county to maintain those incentives. *Cotta v. City of San Francisco*, 69 Cal. Rptr. 3d 612 (Cal. Ct. App. 2007). The taxi company's reliance does not require the county to continue these incentives.

Foreseeable Reliance—Promisor

Foreseeable reliance applies when the promisor reasonably should have expected the promisee's reliance on the promise. If a promisor has no reason to anticipate that the promisee will rely on the promise, holding the promisor responsible for losses that reliance causes seems unjust. But when the promisor should realize the promisee will change her position because of the promise, the promisor's ability to prevent the losses (by not making the promise) provides a rationale for holding the promisor responsible for those losses. Sometimes the promisor even expressly suggests reliance. Even without suggestions of this sort, a promisor may have reason to know that the promisee will rely on the promise.

The focus is on the reasonable promisor, not the reasonableness of the promisee. Did the promisor have reason to believe this promise would induce the other to rely in this way? The use of the word "reasonably" makes this an objective test, limiting a promisor's ability to plead ignorance or subjective misunderstanding. If a reasonable promisor should have expected reliance of this type, the exception will apply even if this promisor (subjectively) did not anticipate such reliance. Arguably, it might never be reasonable to rely on a promise without consideration. Rather than undermine the entire exception, the rule focuses on what a reasonable promisor should have anticipated in the circumstances, which might include anticipating unreasonable reliance by the promisee.

Some states treat action in reliance as if it is something divorced from contract formation. California, for example, treats promissory estoppel as a separate cause of action. A complaint must raise promissory estoppel separately from breach of contract. The substance of the rule, however, remains identical. It provides an exception to the requirement of consideration; changing the name does not change the role the exception serves.

Actual Reliance—Promisee

Actual reliance may take the form of action or forbearance, though action is easier to prove. Where reliance involves not acting, it is harder to prove just what a person would have done but for the promise, and thus harder to know if the person is worse off than if no promise had been made. Let's say, in reliance on a promised raise, an employee might forgo looking for a different job. Proving the effect of that inaction — how much the employee might have made if she had looked for a new job at that time — may not be easy. A concrete action, like rejecting an existing job offer, provides clearer reliance.

In some cases, courts may excuse the requirement of actual reliance. Under Restatement (Second) of Contracts §90(2), a pledge made to a charity may be enforceable under this exception even if the charity cannot prove that it relied on the pledge. The other elements — a promise, reason for the promisor to expect reliance, and injustice — remain necessary. But, in a few states, the charity need not prove reliance by arguing that it would not have incurred certain expenditures but for the promisor's pledge. Reliance would be particularly difficult to establish when charities spend first in emergency situations and then seek contributions later. As long as the reliance claimed falls within the scope of reliance a promisor should expect, the exception here applies. This aspect of the exception is not universally accepted.

In other cases, courts sometimes seek ways to limit the exception for reliance, especially in commercial contexts. One approach differentiates reliance on the party to keep the promise from reliance on the courts to enforce the promise, called enforcement reliance. Some courts limit the exception to cases involving enforcement reliance. This doctrine may not become widely accepted. It requires courts to ascertain why a party relied, a much more difficult task than determining whether a party relied. This factual issue decreases the predictability of the outcome.

Detrimental Reliance — Promisee

The finding of an injustice requires **detrimental reliance** — reliance that leaves the promisee worse off than if the promise had not been made. For example, after being promised a computer, a promisee might buy a printer. If the promisor breaches, the promisee may suffer some loss on the costs of the printer. The loss might be the costs of the printer if it cannot be returned or resold to recoup the expenses. The rule here does not set a minimum level of detriment necessary to justify enforcement. Even a small detriment might suffice, but could impact the remedies for the claimed loss.

The Multi-Faceted Uses of Promissory Estoppel

In this chapter, you are being introduced to promissory estoppel or reliance as a substitute for consideration or to enforce promises in cases of pre-acceptance reliance. As you read this text, you will see promissory estoppel serving as an equitable doctrine in a variety of other contract settings. In this chapter, you will read the *Pop's Cones* case in which protected a party's pre-acceptance reliance when an offeror sought to revoke an offer. In some instances, promissory estoppel has been utilized as an exception to the statute of frauds, which requires that certain types of contracts must be evinced by a writing in order to be enforced. Promissory estoppel is also being applied by some courts as an exception to the parol evidence rule, which excludes the admission of oral and written evidence prior to or contemporaneous to the execution of a written contract. As you continue to read this text, think about the many ways in which courts are applying promissory estoppel to avoid injustices in contract disputes.

2. Reliance in Family Situations

The exception for reliance is often appropriate in noncommercial settings. Noncommercial transactions may involve parties unfamiliar with the requirement of consideration. For instance, people may rely on promises by family members, not stopping to think about whether these promises are enforceable. It may be difficult for a court to distinguish between unenforceable promises made between family members as distinguished from enforceable promises under reliance. At times, courts may be reluctant to become entangled in promises between family members as part of their social, rather than contractual, relationships. In cases involving promises between family members, courts must scrutinize the factual circumstances to determine whether these family promises meet the requirements of promissory estoppel.

Case Preview

Wright v. Newman

The difficulties of addressing promises within the family arena is brought into sharp focus when an ex-wife seeks to enforce a promise of child support from her ex-husband. In this case, the defendant, Wright, is not the biological father of her son, but held himself out to be the child's father for ten years.

As you read *Wright v. Newman*, look for the following:

1. Under Georgia statutes, how did the majority opinion define the concept of promissory estoppel?
2. How did the majority and concurring opinions apply the concept of promissory estoppel to this promise of child support, in both its emotional and financial aspects?
3. What concerns did the dissenting opinion raise about applying promissory estoppel to this situation?

Wright v. Newman

266 Ga. 519, 467 S.E.2d 533 (1996)

CARLEY, Justice.

Seeking to recover child support for her daughter and her son, Kim Newman filed suit against Bruce Wright. Wright's answer admitted his paternity only as to Newman's daughter and DNA testing subsequently showed that he is not the father of her son. The trial court nevertheless ordered Wright to pay child support for both children. As to Newman's son, the trial court based its order upon Wright's "actions in having himself listed on the child's birth certificate, giving the child his surname and establishing a parent-child relationship. . . ." According to the trial court, Wright had thereby

> allowed the child to consider him his father and in so doing deterr[ed Newman] from seeking to establish the paternity of the child's natural father[,] thus denying

the child an opportunity to establish a parent-child relationship with the natural father.

We granted Wright's application for a discretionary appeal so as to review the trial court's order requiring that he pay child support for Newman's son.

Wright does not contest the trial court's factual findings. He asserts only that the trial court erred in its legal conclusion that the facts authorized the imposition of an obligation to provide support for Newman's son. If Wright were the natural father of Newman's son, he would be legally obligated to provide support. O.C.G.A. §19-7-2. Likewise, if Wright had formally adopted Newman's son, he would be legally obligated to provide support. O.C.G.A. §19-8-19(a)(2). However, Wright is neither the natural nor the formally adoptive father of the child and "the theory of 'virtual adoption' is not applicable to a dispute as to who is legally responsible for the support of minor children." *Ellison v. Thompson*, 240 Ga. 594, 596 (242 S.E.2d 95) (1978).

. . . A number of jurisdictions have recognized that a legally enforceable obligation to provide child support can be "based upon parentage *or* contract. . . ." (Emphasis supplied.) *Albert v. Albert,* 415 S2d 818, 819 (Fla. App. 1982). *See also* Anno., 90 ALR2d 583 (1963). Georgia is included among those jurisdictions. *Foltz v. Foltz,* 238 Ga. 193, 194 (232 S.E.2d 66) (1977). Accordingly, the issue for resolution is whether Wright can be held liable for child support for Newman's son under this state's contract law.

There was no formal written contract whereby Wright agreed to support Newman's son. Compare *Foltz v. Foltz,* supra. Nevertheless, under this state's contract law,

> [a] promise which the promisor should reasonably expect to induce action or forbearance on the part of the promisee or a third person and which does induce such action or forbearance is binding if injustice can be avoided only by enforcement of the promise. The remedy granted for breach may be limited as justice requires.

O.C.G.A. §13-3-44(a). This statute codifies the principle of promissory estoppel. [Citation omitted.] In accordance with that principle,

> "[a] party may enter into a contract invalid and unenforceable, and by reason of the covenants therein contained and promises made in connection with the same, wrongfully cause the opposite party to forego a valuable legal right to his detriment, and in this manner by his conduct waive the right to repudiate the contract and become estopped to deny the opposite party any benefits that may accrue to him under the terms of the agreement." [Cits.]

Pepsi Cola Bottling Co. of Dothan, Ala., Inc. v. First Nat. Bank of Columbus, 248 Ga. 114, 116-117 (2) (282 S.E.2d 579) (1981).

The evidence authorizes the finding that Wright promised both Newman and her son that he would assume all of the obligations and responsibilities of fatherhood, including that of providing support. As the trial court found, this promise was evidenced by Wright's listing of himself as the father on the child's birth certificate and giving the child his last name. Wright is presumed to know "the legal consequences of his actions. Since parents are legally obligated to support their minor children, [he] accepted this support obligation by acknowledging paternity." *Marshall v. Marshall,* 386 S2d 11, 12 (Fla. App. 1980). There is no dispute that, at the time he made his commitment, Wright knew that he was not the natural father of the child. Compare *NPA v. WBA,* 8 Va. App. 246, 380 S.E.2d 178 (Va. App. 1989). Thus, he undertook his commitment knowingly and voluntarily. Moreover, he continued to do so for some 10 years, holding himself out to others as the father of the child and allowing the child to consider him to be the natural father.

The evidence further authorizes the finding that Newman and her son relied upon Wright's promise to their detriment. As the trial court found, Newman refrained from identifying and seeking support from the child's natural father. Had Newman not refrained from doing so, she might now have a source of financial support for the child and the child might now have a natural father who provided emotional, as well as financial, support. If, after 10 years of honoring his voluntary commitment, Wright were now allowed to evade the consequences of his promise, an injustice to Newman and her son would result. Under the evidence, the duty to support which Wright voluntarily assumed 10 years ago remains enforceable under the contractual doctrine of promissory estoppel and the trial court's order which compels Wright to discharge that obligation must be affirmed. See *Nygard v. Nygard,* 156 Mich. App. 94, 401 NW2d 323 (Mich. App. 1986); *Marshall v. Marshall*, supra; *Re Marriage of Johnson,* 88 Cal. App. 3d 848, 152 Cal Rptr 121 (Cal. App. 1979); *Hartford v. Hartford,* 53 Ohio App. 2d 79, 371 NE2d 591 (Ohio App. 1977).

Judgment affirmed. All the Justices concur, except Benham, C.J., who dissents.

SEARS, Justice, concurring.

I concur fully with the majority opinion. I write separately only to address the dissenting opinion's misperception that Newman has not relied upon Wright's promise to her detriment.

It is an established principle in Georgia that a promise which the promisor should reasonably expect to induce action or forbearance on the part of the promisee or a third person and which does induce such action or forbearance is binding if injustice can be avoided only by enforcement of the promise. [Footnote omitted.] This doctrine, known as "promissory estoppel," prevents a promisor from reneging on a promise, when the promisor should have expected that the promisee would rely upon the promise, and the promisee does in fact rely upon the promise to her detriment. [Footnote omitted.] Sufficient consideration to enforce a contractual promise pursuant to promissory estoppel may be found in any benefit accruing to the promisor, or any reliance, loss, trouble, disadvantage, or charge imposed upon the promisee. [Footnote omitted.]

Bearing these principles in mind, and as explained very well in the majority opinion, it is clear that Wright's commitment to Newman to assume the obligations of fatherhood as regards her son are enforceable. Specifically, it is abundantly clear that Wright should have known that Newman would rely upon his promise, especially after he undertook for ten years to fulfill the obligations of fatherhood. In this regard, it could hardly have escaped Wright's notice that Newman refrained from seeking to identify and obtain support from the child's biological father while Wright was fulfilling his commitment to her. Moreover, Newman did in fact rely upon Wright's promise, to her detriment when, ten years after he undertook the obligations of fatherhood, Wright reneged on his promise.

Promissory estoppel requires only that the reliance by the injured party [promisee] be reasonable. [Footnote omitted.] In this case, it cannot seriously be argued that Newman's reliance was anything other than reasonable, as she had absolutely no indication that Wright would ever renege, especially after he fulfilled his promise for such a long time. Moreover, contrary to the dissent's implicit assertion, promissory estoppel does not require that the injured party exhaust all other possible means of obtaining the benefit of the promise from any and all sources before being able to enforce the promise against the promisor. In this regard, it is illogical to argue that Newman, after reasonably relying upon Wright's promise for ten years, can now simply seek to determine the identity of the biological father and collect support from him. First, there is nothing in the case law that requires Newman to do so before being entitled to have Wright's promise enforced. Second, this requirement would be an imposing, if not an impossible, burden, and would require Newman not only to identify the father (if possible), but also to locate him, bring a costly legal action against him, and to succeed in that action. Imposing this requirement would effectively penalize Newman for no reasons other than (1) her reasonable reliance upon a promise that was not kept, and (2) for allowing herself to be dissuaded by Wright from seeking the identity of the biological father. As noted, nowhere does the case law support imposing such a requirement, and none of the facts in this case support doing so now.

Finally, there can be no doubt that, unless Wright's promise to Newman is enforced, injustice will result. Given the approximately ten years that have passed since the child's birth, during which time Wright, for all purposes, was the child's father, it likely will be impossible for Newman to establish the identity of the child's biological father, bring a successful paternity action, and obtain support from that individual. Consequently, if Wright is allowed to renege on his obligation, Newman likely will not receive any support to assist in the cost of raising her son, despite having been promised the receipt of such by Wright. Furthermore, an even greater injustice will be inflicted upon the boy himself. A child who has been told by any adult, regardless of the existence of a biological relationship, that he will always be able to depend upon the adult for parenting and sustenance, will suffer a great deal when that commitment is broken. And when a child suffers under those circumstances, society-at-large suffers as well. [Footnote omitted.]

Because Wright's promise is capable of being enforced under the law, and because I believe that Wright's promise must be enforced in order to prevent a grave miscarriage of justice, I concur fully in the majority opinion.

BENHAM, Chief Justice, dissenting.

I respectfully dissent. While I agree with the majority opinion's statement that liability for child support may be based on promissory estoppel in a case where there is no statutory obligation or express contract, I first note that this issue was not brought by either of the parties. Further, there is a critical element that must be shown for promissory estoppel to apply. In addition to making a showing of expectation and reasonable reliance, a person asserting liability on the theory of promissory estoppel must show that she relied on the promise to her detriment. *Nickell v. IAG Federal Credit Union,* 213 Ga. App. 516 (445 S.E.2d 335) (1994); *Lake Tightsqueeze, Inc. v. Chrysler First Financial Services Corp.,* 210 Ga. App. 178 (435 S.E.2d 486) (1993). The majority states that Newman and her son incurred detriment by refraining from identifying and seeking support from the child's natural father. However, the record is completely bereft of any evidence that Newman met her burden of proof as to promissory estoppel, and the majority fails to state how she is prevented from now instituting a child support action against the natural father. Newman has not alleged, nor does the record reveal, that she does not know the identity of the natural father, nor does she show that the natural father is dead or unable to be found. Consequently, Newman has not shown that she is now unable to do what she would have had to do ten years ago — seek support from the natural father.

In fact, Wright contends, and Newman does not refute, that Newman severed the relationship and all ties with Wright when the child was approximately three years old. For approximately the next five years, until the child was eight, Newman and Wright did not communicate. Only for the past two years has Wright visited with the child. Importantly, Wright contends that during the past seven years he did not support the child. Thus, taking Wright's undisputed contentions as true, any prejudice incurred by Newman because of the passage of ten years in time is not due to Wright's actions, since, at least for the past seven years, Newman has been in the same situation — receiving no support payments from Wright. Thus, although Wright may be morally obligated to support the ten-year-old child, he is not legally obligated to do so because Newman has failed to show that she or the child incurred any detriment by Wright's failure to fulfill his promise made ten years ago.

For the foregoing reasons, I dissent.

The majority court determined that Wright, a non-biological parent, by words and conduct promised both emotional and financial support to his ex-wife's son. Wright could reasonably foresee that his ex-wife would rely upon this promise, and she did actually rely by not seeking support from her son's biological father. The son would suffer an injustice or detriment if the promise was not enforced. Under these circumstances, the court decided that promissory estoppel permitted enforcement of this promise between family members.

Wright v. Newman: Real Life Applications

1. A grandfather is concerned that his granddaughter is required to work, while his other grandchildren do not have to work to sustain themselves.

He promises his granddaughter $30,000 plus 6 percent interest per year if she quits her job, allowing her not to work. Elated with this news, the granddaughter accepts her grandfather's promise and quits her job. Upon her grandfather's death, the granddaughter seeks to recover from his estate the amount owed on his promise. The estate argues this promise is an undelivered gift, not a contract, because there is no consideration. Will the court enforce this gratuitous promise between family members? Read *Ricketts v. Scothorn*, 77 N.W. 365 (Neb. 1898), and apply the court's decision in this case on promissory estoppel.

2. In Chapter 4, there was an excerpt from *Dougherty v. Salt* regarding the gift of a signed promissory note to a nephew from his aunt, payable upon her death. In that instance, the court refuses to enforce the note as an unfulfilled gift that lacked consideration. Consider the concept of promissory estoppel and determine if the nephew could recover under this equitable approach. How does the *Dougherty* case compare with the outcome in the *Ricketts* case? What are the key factual and legal distinctions between the two cases? Develop a brief class presentation on the distinctions between these two cases.
3. An employee, Katz, the brother-in-law of the company's president, suffers a head injury trying to protect the company's property. Katz is subsequently convinced to retire and work part time after being offered a pension for the rest of his life. After retiring, Katz works for the company on a part-time basis. After two and a half years, the company cuts and then eliminates Katz's pension. Is Katz entitled to hold the company to its promised pension? Analyze *Katz v. Danny Dare, Inc.*, 610 S.W.2d 121 (Mo. Ct. App. 1980), on the application of promissory estoppel to these circumstances.

---

3. Reliance in Charitable Situations

In other noncommercial transactions, consideration may be harder to satisfy. Consideration or a quid pro quo can be difficult to find in cases of charitable pledges. Organized charities may find it difficult to include consideration in their quest for donations, yet may need to rely on pledges in pursuing their goals. Case law supports the enforcement of charitable pledges when such promises are supported either by consideration or reliance. However, the Restatement (Second) of Contracts §90(2) takes a more flexible view in addressing charitable pledges, keeping its focus on the question of donative intent. The Restatement does not require proof of reliance or forbearance, moving away from a showing of consideration. Many courts have not accepted the Restatement view and continue to look for either consideration or reliance to support promises in charitable situations.

Case Preview

King v. Trustees of Boston University

The widow of the late Martin Luther King, Jr., Coretta Scott King, initiated an action to recover Dr. King's papers from defendant Boston University, a nonprofit institution. In this case, the court considered statements made in a letter from Dr. King to Boston University (BU) about his historic papers. On appeal, the court addressed the issue of donative intent for a charitable pledge and questions of enforcement of such pledges.

As you read *King v. Trustees of Boston University*, look for the following:

1. Was there donative intent to support Dr. King's charitable pledge?
2. Did BU establish either consideration or reliance to support Dr. King's charitable pledge?
3. Did the court accept or reject the Restatement's view on the enforcement of charitable pledges?

Coretta Scott King, Martin Luther King's widow and plaintiff in the case

Photographs in the Carol M. Highsmith Archive, Library of Congress, Prints and Photographs Division

King v. Trustees of Boston University

420 Mass. 52 (1995)

Abrams, J.

A jury determined that Dr. Martin Luther King, Jr., made a charitable pledge to Boston University (BU) of certain papers he had deposited with BU. The plaintiff, Coretta Scott King, in her capacity as administratrix of the estate of her late husband, and in her individual capacity, appeals from that judgment. The plaintiff sued BU for conversion, alleging that the estate and not BU held title to Dr. King's papers, which have been housed in BU's library's special collection since they were delivered to BU at Dr. King's request in July, 1964.

. . . In response to special questions the jury determined that Dr. King made a promise to give absolute title to his papers to BU in a letter signed by him and dated July 16, 1964, and that the promise to give the papers was enforceable as a charitable pledge supported by consideration or reliance. The jury also determined that the letter promising the papers was not a contract. . . . The trial judge denied the plaintiff's motion for judgment notwithstanding the verdict or for a new trial. The plaintiff appealed. . . . We affirm.

I. *Facts*. . . . In 1963, BU commenced plans to expand its library's special collections. Once plans for construction of a library to house new holdings were firm, the newly appointed director of special collections, Dr. Howard Gotlieb, began his efforts to obtain Dr. King's papers. Dr. King, an alumnus of BU's graduate school program, was one of the first individuals BU officials sought to induce to deposit documents in the archives. Around the same time, Dr. King was approached regarding his papers by other universities, including his undergraduate alma mater, Morehouse College. Mrs. King testified that, although her late husband thought "Boston seemed to be the only place, the best place, for safety," he was concerned that depositing his papers with BU would evoke criticism that he was "taking them away from a black institution in the South." However, the volatile circumstances during the 1960s in the South led Dr. King to deposit some of his papers with BU pursuant to a letter, which is the centerpiece of this litigation and is set forth herewith:

> "563 Johnson Ave. NE
> Atlanta, Georgia
> July 16, 1964
> "Boston University Library
> 725 Commonwealth Ave.
> Boston 15, Massachusetts
> "Dear Sirs:
>
> "On this 16th day of July, 1964, I name the Boston University Library the Repository of my correspondence, manuscripts and other papers, along with a few of my awards and other materials which may come to be of interest in historical or other research.
>
> "In accordance with this action I have authorized the removal of most of the above-mentioned papers and other objects to Boston University, including most correspondence through 1961, at once. It is my intention that after the end of each calendar year, similar files of materials for an additional year should be sent to Boston University.
>
> "All papers and other objects which thus pass into the custody of Boston University remain my legal property until otherwise indicated, according to the statements below. However, if, despite scrupulous care, any such materials are damaged or lost while in custody of Boston University, I absolve Boston University of responsibility to me for such damage or loss.
>
> "I intend each year to indicate a portion of the materials deposited with Boston University to become the absolute property of Boston University as an outright gift from me, until all shall have been thus given to the University. In the event of my death, all such materials deposited with the University shall become from that date the absolute property of Boston University."
>
> "Sincerely yours,
> "Martin Luther King, Jr. /s/"

At issue is whether the evidence at trial was sufficient to submit the question of charitable pledge to the jury. BU asserts that the evidence was sufficient to raise a question of fact for the jury as to whether there was a promise by Dr. King to transfer title to his papers to BU and whether any such promise was supported by consideration or reliance by BU. We agree.

II. *Evidence of an enforceable charitable pledge.* [Footnote omitted.] Because the jury found that BU had acquired rightful ownership of the papers via a charitable pledge, but not a contract, we review the case on that basis. We note at the outset that there is scant Massachusetts case law in the area of charitable pledges and subscriptions. . . .

A charitable subscription is "an oral or written promise to do certain acts or to give real or personal property to a charity or for a charitable purpose." *See generally* E.L. Fisch, D.J. Freed, & E.R. Schacter, Charities and Charitable Foundations §63, at 77 (1974). To enforce a charitable subscription or a charitable pledge in Massachusetts, a party must establish that there was a promise to give some property to a charitable institution and that the promise was supported by consideration or reliance. [Citations omitted.]

The jurors were asked two special questions regarding BU's affirmative defense of rightful ownership by way of a charitable pledge: (1) "Does the letter, dated July 16, 1964, from Martin Luther King, Jr., to [BU], set forth a promise by Dr. King to transfer ownership of his papers to [BU]?"; and (2) "Did [BU] take action in reliance on that promise or was that promise supported by consideration?" In determining whether the case properly was submitted to the jury, we consider first, whether the evidence was sufficient to sustain a conclusion that the letter contained a promise to make a gift and second, whether the evidence was sufficient to support a determination that any promise found was supported by consideration or reliance.

[The court discussed a relevant case in a footnote as follows:

In *Congregation Kadimah Toras-Moshe v. DeLeo*, 405 Mass. 365, 540 N.E.2d 691 (1989), the Congregation sued the estate of a decedent who had made an oral gratuitous promise to give $25,000 to the synagogue. The Congregation planned to spend the $25,000 on renovation of a storage room in the synagogue into a library. The oral promise was never memorialized in a writing or consummated by delivery before the decedent died intestate. Noting that "[a] hope or expectation, even though well founded, is not equivalent to either legal detriment or reliance," id. at 366-367, 540 N.E.2d 691, we affirmed the judgment of the trial court that the oral charitable subscription was not enforceable because it was oral, not supported by consideration, and without evidence of reliance.

By requiring that a promise to make a charitable subscription be supported by consideration or reliance, we declined to adopt the standard for enforceable charitable subscriptions set forth in the Restatement (Second) of Contracts §90 (1981). See id. at 368, 540 N.E.2d 691. Section 90(1), as modified for charitable subscriptions by subsection (2), provides that, "[a] promise which the promisor should reasonably expect to induce action or forbearance on the part of the promisee or a third person . . . is binding if injustice can be avoided only by enforcement of the promise. . . . "We noted that, although §90 thus dispenses with a strict requirement of consideration or reasonable reliance for a charitable subscription to be enforceable, the official comments to the Restatement make clear that consideration and reliance remain relevant to whether the promise must be enforced to avoid injustice. [Citations omitted.]]

III(A). *Evidence of a promise to make a gift.* The plaintiff argues that the terms of the letter promising "to indicate a portion of the materials deposited with [BU] to become the absolute property of [BU] as an outright gift . . . until all shall have been thus given to [BU]," could not as a matter of basic contract law constitute a promise sufficient to establish an inter vivos charitable pledge because there is no indication of a bargained for exchange which would have bound Dr. King to his promise. The plaintiff asserts that the above-quoted excerpt (hereinafter "first statement") from the letter merely described an unenforceable "unilateral and gratuitous mechanism by which he might" make a gift of the papers in the future but by which he was not bound. In support of her position that Dr. King did not intend to bind himself to his statement of intent to make a gift of the papers he deposited with BU, the plaintiff points to the language which appears above the promise to make gifts of the deposited papers that "[a]ll papers and other objects which thus pass into the custody of [BU] remain my legal property until otherwise indicated, according to the statements below." According to the plaintiff, because of Dr. King's initial retention of legal ownership, BU could not reasonably rely on the letter's statements of intent to make a gift of the papers. We do not agree.

The letter contains two sentences which might reasonably be construed as a promise to give personal property to a charity or for a charitable purpose. The first statement, quoted above, is that Dr. King intended in subsequent installments to transfer title to portions of the papers in BU's custody until all the papers in its custody became its property. The second statement immediately follows the first, expressing an intent that "in the event of [Dr. King's] death, all . . . materials deposited with [BU] shall become from that date the absolute property of [BU]" (hereinafter "second statement"). BU claims that these two sentences should be read together as a promise to make a gift of all of the papers deposited with it at some point between the first day of deposit and at the very latest, on Dr. King's death.

Before analyzing the first and second statements, we note the considerations governing our review. A primary concern in enforcing charitable subscriptions, as with enforcement of other gratuitous transfers such as gifts and trusts, is ascertaining the intention of the donor [citations omitted]. . . . If donative intent is sufficiently clear, we shall give effect to that intent to the extent possible without abandoning basic contractual principles, such as specificity of the donor's promise, consideration, and reasonableness of the charity's reliance. *DeLeo,* supra 405 Mass. at 368 n.5, 540 N.E.2d 691. In determining the intention of Dr. King as expressed in the letter and the understanding BU had of that letter, we look first to the language of the letter, in its entirety, but also consider the circumstances and relationship of the parties with respect to the papers.

III(A)(1). *First statement.* Regarding the first statement, the plaintiff contends that it is not a promise but a mere statement of intent to do something in the future. [Citation omitted.] . . . We might agree that the first statement could induce nothing more than a "hope or mere expectation" on BU's part, if the statement were considered in a vacuum. [Citation omitted.] However, our interpretation of that first statement is strongly influenced by the bailor-bailee relationship the letter unequivocally establishes between Dr. King and BU.

A bailment is established by "delivery of personalty for some particular purpose, or on mere deposit, upon a contract, express or implied, that after the purpose has been fulfilled it shall be redelivered to the person who delivered it, or otherwise dealt with according to his directions, or kept until he reclaims it, as the case may be." 9 S. Williston, Contracts §1030 (3d ed. 1967), quoting *State v. Warwick,* 48 Del. 568, 576, 108 A.2d 85 (1954) [citation omitted]. . . . The terms of the letter establish a bailment in which certain "correspondence, manuscripts and other papers, along with a few of [Dr. King's] awards" were placed in "the custody of [BU]." The bailed papers were to "remain [Dr. King's] legal property until otherwise indicated." By accepting delivery of the papers, BU assumed the duty of care as bailee set forth in the letter, that of "scrupulous care." [Citations omitted.] . . .

Generally there will be a case for the jury as to donative intent if property allegedly promised to a charity or other eleemosynary institution is placed by the donor in the custody of the donee. [Footnote omitted.] . . . Furthermore, while we have been unwilling to abandon fundamental principles of contract law in determining the enforceability of charitable subscriptions, see *DeLeo, supra* [405 Mass. at 368 n.4] second par. (declining to adopt Restatement [Second] of Contracts rule that charitable subscriptions enforceable without consideration or reliance where justice so requires), we do recognize that the "meeting of minds" between a donor and a charitable institution differs from the understanding we require in the context of enforceable arm's-length commercial agreements. Charities depend on donations for their existence, whereas their donors may give personal property on conditions they choose, with or without imposing conditions or demanding consideration. [Citation omitted.] . . . In combination with the letter and in the context of a disputed pledge to a charity, the bailment of Dr. King's letters provided sufficient evidence of donative intent to submit to the jury the questions whether there was a promise to transfer ownership of the bailed property and whether there was consideration or reliance on that promise. [Footnote omitted.]

. . .

III(B). *Evidence of consideration or reliance.* The judge did not err in submitting the second question on charitable pledge, regarding whether there was consideration for or reliance on the promise, to the jury. "It may be found somewhat difficult to reconcile all the views which have been taken, in the various cases that have arisen upon the validity of promises, where the ground of defence has been that they were gratuitous and without consideration." *Ives v. Sterling*, 6 Met. 310, 315 (1843). There was evidence that BU undertook indexing of the papers, made the papers available to researchers, and provided trained staff to care for the papers and assist researchers. BU held a convocation to commemorate receipt of the papers. Dr. King spoke at the convocation. In a speech at that time, he explained why he chose BU as the repository for his papers. As we explained above, the letter established that so long as BU, as bailee, attended the papers with "scrupulous care," Dr. King, as bailor, would release them from liability for "any such materials . . . damaged or lost while in [its] custody." The jury could conclude that certain actions of BU, including indexing of the papers, went beyond the obligations BU assumed as a bailee to attend the papers with "scrupulous care" and constituted reliance or consideration for the promises Dr. King included in the letter to transfer ownership of all bailed papers to BU at some future date or at his death. [Citations omitted.]

The issue before us is not whether we agree with the jury's verdict but whether the case was properly submitted to the jury. We conclude that the letter could have been read to contain a promise supported by consideration or reliance; . . . "was, therefore, properly submitted to the jury, and their verdicts, unless otherwise untenable, must stand." [Citation omitted.]

Post-Case Follow-Up

The court determined that statements in Dr. King's letter to BU and his transfer of custody of certain papers to the non-profit university showed donative intent for his charitable pledge. BU's efforts to index, appraise for tax purposes, and undertake "scrupulous care" of Dr. King's papers support a finding of a promise supported by either consideration or reliance. The court rejected the Restatement view that charitable pledges need not be supported by reliance or forbearance.

King v. Trustees of Boston University: Real Life Applications

1. At a weekly gathering, Sam makes a pledge to a religious institution in the amount of $2,000. Later on, he refuses to fulfill his pledge. Sam argues that there was no consideration nor reliance on his promise so he is not bound to follow through on his pledge. The religious organization is seeking your assistance. Will Sam's pledge be enforceable? Review *Jewish Federation of Cent. New Jersey v. Barondess*, 234 N.J. Super. 526 (Law Div. 1989), on the issue of enforcing written versus oral charitable subscriptions.

2. A nonprofit hospital undertakes a campaign to raise funds to construct a new neuroscience wing. Donna agrees to donate $50,000. She pays $20,000 before the wing is completed and then files for bankruptcy after construction is completed. The hospital wants to recover the remaining $30,000 from Donna's pledge. The director of the hospital seeks your advice on whether or not the hospital will likely succeed in bringing a breach of contract action against Donna. Examine *In re Bashas' Inc.*, 2011 Bankr. LEXIS 5510 (Bankr. D. Ariz. Sept. 29, 2011), on this legal matter.

3. Abed is working with community and business leaders to establish a new city college. As part of the effort, Abed has developed pledge cards for donors to fill out. Healthdom International (Healthdom), a major employer, has offered to donate $100,000 to help construct and operate the school in a letter, rather than a pledge form. Healthdom never ends up fulfilling its charitable subscription. The school is completed and runs for about six months before closing due to a lack of operational funds. The college is now bringing a breach of contract action against Healthdom. You are a law clerk for a local judge handling the case. Review *Salsbury v. Northwestern Bell Tel. Co.*, 221 N.W.2d 609 (Iowa 1974), on the enforceability of the letter's pledge.

4. Reliance in Commercial Situations

Commercial parties normally understand that contracts require consideration. They should recognize the risks they run by relying on promises that are not part of an exchange. Nonetheless, reliance also extends to some commercial dealings.

When the promisee is not sophisticated in contract law, such as an employee, she may rely on a promise that technically lacks consideration. For example, in *Feinberg v. Pfeiffer Co.*, 322 S.W.2d 163 (Mo. Ct. App. 1959), an employer promised a long-term employee a pension in gratitude for her loyal service over the years. She retired 18 months later. The employer made pension payments for seven years before a new president refused to perform on the ground that there was no consideration for the promise. The employee did not give the past service in exchange for the promise, which had not been made yet. The employer did not seek future service or future retirement in exchange for the promise. Nonetheless, the court enforced this promise. The employer should have expected that the employee might retire earlier than necessary in reliance on the promise. Unless enforced, the promise would harm the employee. The court determined that she might have worked longer and saved more if no promise had been made, but could not return to work following the breach due to illness. Again, the court enforced the promise made, without regard to how much savings the employee actually would have managed but for the promise.

Outside of the employment context, courts will consider claims of promissory estoppel between commercial parties in arm's-length dealings. At times, the parties may enter into negotiations that result in a party making preparations to perform before the contract terms are finalized. If the contract is not executed, a party may suffer a loss and be unable to bring a contract action because there is no final agreement. Indefiniteness in the contract terms or a lack of consideration may become obstacles to compensating the damaged party. Some courts take reliance well beyond its role as an exception to the requirement of consideration. In some instances, promissory estoppel may provide an equitable option to protect commercial parties in instances of pre-acceptance reliance.

The growth of promissory estoppel in commercial situations threatens to expand reliance in ways that make contract law unpredictable. Consistent and predictable outcomes are essential to contract law. Individuals and businesses need to know whether they have a duty to perform promises without litigating every dispute. Especially when deciding whether to enter a deal, parties need to know where the point of no return lies: when they are still permitted to reconsider the project being negotiated and when it is too late to back out. Predictable rules give them the ability to resolve many disputes on their own, without wasting time and money in costly litigation or placing unnecessarily high demands on the judicial system funded by taxpayers.

Case Preview

Pop's Cones, Inc. v. Resorts International Hotel, Inc.

A small business owner claimed to suffer losses when a deal to move her franchise to a prime location on the Atlantic City Boardwalk failed to materialize. A court needed to examine whether a promise made during extended business negotiations would be enforced when a final agreement was not consummated. Lacking traditional consideration, an examination of the equitable notion of promissory estoppel was undertaken to determine if a party may recover some losses suffered in pre-acceptance reliance upon another's promise.

As you read *Pop's Cones, Inc. v. Resorts International Hotel, Inc.*, look for the following:

1. What promise by Resorts was being evaluated under the court's application of Restatement (Second) of Contracts §90?
2. How did the court examine the issues of foreseeable and actual reliance in this dispute?
3. What was Pop's Cones' detrimental reliance in these circumstances?

Pop's Cones, Inc. v. Resorts International Hotel, Inc.

307 N.J. Super. 46 (1998)

KLEINER, J. A. D.

Plaintiff, Pop's Cones, Inc., t/a TCBY Yogurt, ("Pop's"), appeals from an order of the Law Division granting defendant, Resorts International, Inc. ("Resorts"), summary judgment and dismissing its complaint seeking damages predicated on a theory of promissory estoppel. . . . In reversing summary judgment, we rely upon principles of promissory estoppel enunciated in Section 90 of the Restatement (Second) of Contracts, and recent cases which, in order to avoid injustice, seemingly relax the strict requirement of "a clear and definite promise" in making a prima facie case of promissory estoppel.

Pop's is an authorized franchisee of TCBY Systems, Inc. ("TCBY"), a national franchisor of frozen yogurt products. Resorts is a casino hotel in Atlantic City that leases retail space along "prime Boardwalk frontage," among other business ventures.

From June of 1991 to September 1994, Pop's operated a TCBY franchise in Margate, New Jersey. Sometime during the months of May or June 1994, Brenda Taube ("Taube"), President of Pop's, had "a number of discussions" with Marlon Phoenix ("Phoenix"), the Executive Director of Business Development and Sales for Resorts, about the possible relocation of Pop's business to space owned by Resorts. [Footnote omitted.] During these discussions, Phoenix showed Taube one location for a TCBY vending cart within Resorts Hotel and "three specific locations for the operation of a full service TCBY store."

According to Taube, she and Phoenix specifically discussed the boardwalk property occupied at that time by a business trading as "The Players Club." These discussions included Taube's concerns with the then-current rental fees and Phoenix's indication that Resorts management and Merv Griffin personally [footnote omitted] [Former talk show host Griffin was Resorts' Chief Executive Officer and a major shareholder.] were "very anxious to have Pop's as a tenant" and that "financial issues . . . could easily be resolved, such as through a percentage of gross revenue." In order to allay both Taube's and Phoenix's concerns about whether a TCBY franchise at The Players Club location would be successful, Phoenix offered to permit Pop's to operate a vending cart within Resorts free of charge during the summer of 1994 so as to "test the traffic flow." This offer was considered and approved by Paul Ryan, Vice President for Hotel Operations at Resorts.

These discussions led to further meetings with Phoenix about the Players Club location, and Taube contacted TCBY's corporate headquarters about a possible franchise site change. During the weekend of July 4, 1994, Pop's opened the TCBY cart for business at Resorts pursuant to the above stated offer. On July 6, 1994, TCBY gave Taube initial approval for Pop's change in franchise site. In late July or early August of 1994, representatives of TCBY personally visited the Players Club location, with Taube and Phoenix present.

Based on Pop's marketing assessment of the Resorts location, Taube drafted a written proposal dated August 18, 1994, addressing the leasing of Resorts' Players Club location and hand-delivered it to Phoenix. . . .

In mid-September 1994, Taube spoke with Phoenix about the status of Pop's lease proposal and "pressed [him] to advise [her] of Resorts' position. [Taube] specifically advised [Phoenix] that Pop's had an option to renew the lease for its Margate location and then needed to give notice to its landlord of whether it would be staying at that location no later than October 1, 1994." Another conversation about this topic occurred in late September when Taube "asked Phoenix if [Pop's] proposal was in the ballpark of what Resorts was looking for." He responded that it was and that "we are 95% there, we just need Belisle's [footnote omitted] [then-Chief Operating Officer of Resorts] signature on the deal." Taube admits to having been advised that Belisle had "ultimate responsibility for signing off on the deal" but that Phoenix "assured [her] that Mr. Belisle would follow his recommendation, which was to approve the deal, and that [Phoenix] did not anticipate any difficulties." During this conversation, Taube again mentioned to Phoenix that she had to inform her landlord by October 1, 1994, about whether or not Pop's would renew its lease with them. Taube stated: "Mr. Phoenix assured me that we would have little difficulty in concluding an agreement and advised [Taube] to give notice that [Pop's] would not be extending [its] Margate lease and 'to pack up the Margate store and plan on moving.'"

Relying upon Phoenix's "advice and assurances," Taube notified Pop's landlord in late-September 1994 that it would not be renewing the lease for the Margate location.

In early October, Pop's moved its equipment out of the Margate location and placed it in temporary storage. Taube then commenced a number of new site preparations including: (1) sending designs for the new store to TCBY in October 1994; and (2) retaining an attorney to represent Pop's in finalizing the terms of the lease with Resorts.

By letter dated November 1, 1994, General Counsel for Resorts forwarded a proposed form of lease for The Players Club location to Pop's attorney. . . .

By letter dated December 1, 1994, General Counsel for Resorts forwarded to Pop's attorney a written offer of the terms upon which Resorts was proposing to lease the Players Club space to Pop's. The terms provided:

> [Resorts is] willing to offer the space for an initial three (3) year term with a rent calculated at the greater of 7% of gross revenues or: $50,000 in year one; $60,000 in year two; and $70,000 in year three . . . [with] a three (3) year option to renew after the initial term. . . .

The letter also addressed a "boilerplate lease agreement" provision and a proposed addition to the form lease. The letter concluded by stating:

> ***This letter is not intended to be binding upon Resorts.*** It is intended to set forth the basic terms and conditions upon which Resorts would be willing to negotiate a lease and is subject to those negotiations and the execution of a definitive agreement.
>
> ... [W]e think TCBY will be successful at the Boardwalk location based upon the terms we propose. We look forward to having your client as part of ... Resorts family of customer service providers and believe TCBY will benefit greatly from some of the dynamic changes we plan.
>
> ... [W]e would be pleased ... to discuss this proposal in greater detail. (emphasis added)

In early-December 1994, Taube and her attorney met with William Murtha, General Counsel of Resorts, and Paul Ryan to finalize the proposed lease. After a number of discussions about the lease, Murtha and Ryan informed Taube that they desired to reschedule the meeting to finalize the lease until after the first of the year because of a public announcement they intended to make about another unrelated business venture that Resorts was about to commence. Ryan again assured Taube that rent for the Players Club space was not an issue and that the lease terms would be worked out. "He also assured [Taube] that Resorts wanted TCBY ... on the boardwalk for the following season."

Several attempts were made in January 1995 to contact Resorts' representatives and confirm that matters were proceeding. On January 30, 1995, Taube's attorney received a letter stating: "This letter is to confirm our conversation of this date wherein I advised that Resorts is withdrawing its December 1, 1994 offer to lease space to your client, TCBY." [Footnote omitted.] [The court noted that in late January 1995, Resorts began discussions with another TCBY franchise, Host Marriott, regarding the Players Club's space, which resulted in a lease with Host Marriott to operate a TCBY franchise at the Players Club location in late May 1995. Host Marriot's TCBY franchise opened shortly thereafter.]

According to Taube's certification, "As soon as [Pop's] heard that Resorts was withdrawing its offer, we undertook extensive efforts to reopen [the] franchise at a different location. Because the Margate location had been re-let, it was not available." Ultimately, Pop's found a suitable location but did not reopen for business until July 5, 1996.

On July 17, 1995, Pop's filed a complaint against Resorts seeking damages. The complaint alleged that Pop's "reasonably relied to its detriment on the promises and assurances of Resorts that it would be permitted to relocate its operation to [Resorts'] Boardwalk location...."

After substantial pre-trial discovery, defendant moved for summary judgment [which was granted. Plaintiff appealed.]

...

The doctrine of promissory estoppel is well-established in New Jersey. *Malaker*, supra, 163 N.J. Super. at 479, 395 A.2d 222. ... A promissory estoppel claim will be justified if the plaintiff satisfies its burden of demonstrating the existence of, or for purposes of summary judgment, a dispute as to a material fact with regard to, four separate elements which include:

> (1) a clear and definite promise by the promisor; (2) the promise must be made with the expectation that the promisee will rely thereon; (3) the promisee must in fact reasonably rely on the promise, and (4) detriment of a definite and substantial nature must be incurred in reliance on the promise.

The essential justification for the promissory estoppel doctrine is to avoid the substantial hardship or injustice which would result if such a promise were not enforced. Id. at 484, 395 A.2d 222.

...

Although earlier New Jersey decisions discussing promissory estoppel seem to greatly scrutinize a party's proofs regarding an alleged "clear and definite promise by the promisor," see, e.g., id. at 479, 484, 395 A.2d 222, as a prelude to considering the remaining three elements of a promissory estoppel claim, more recent decisions have tended to relax the strict adherence to the *Malaker* formula for determining whether a prima facie case of promissory estoppel exists. This is particularly true where, as here, a plaintiff does not seek to enforce a contract not fully negotiated, but instead seeks damages resulting from its detrimental reliance upon promises made during contract negotiations despite the ultimate failure of those negotiations.

...

Further, the Restatement (Second) of Contracts §90 (1979), "Promise Reasonably Inducing Action or Forbearance," provides, in pertinent part:

> (1) A promise which the promisor should reasonably expect to induce action or forbearance on the part of the promisee or a third person and which does induce such action or forbearance is binding if injustice can be avoided only by enforcement of the promise. The remedy granted for breach may be limited as justice requires.

...

As we read the Restatement, the strict adherence to proof of a "clear and definite promise" as discussed in *Malaker* is being eroded by a more equitable analysis designed to avoid injustice....

...

The facts as presented by plaintiff by way of its pleadings and certifications filed by Taube, which were not refuted or contradicted by defendant before the motion judge or on appeal, clearly show that when Taube informed Phoenix that Pop's option to renew its lease at its Margate location had to be exercised by October 1, 1994, Phoenix instructed Taube to give notice that it would not be extending the lease. According to Phoenix, virtually nothing remained to be resolved between the parties. Phoenix indicated that the parties were "95% there" and that all that was required for completion of the deal was the signature of John Belisle. Phoenix assured Taube that he had recommended the deal to Belisle, and that Belisle would follow the recommendation. Phoenix also advised Pop's to "pack up the Margate store and plan on moving."

It is also uncontradicted that based upon those representations that Pop's, in fact, did not renew its lease. It vacated its Margate location, placed its equipment and personalty into temporary storage, retained the services of an attorney to finalize the lease with defendant, and engaged in planning the relocation to defendant's property. Ultimately, it incurred the expense of relocating to its present location. That plaintiff . . . relied to its detriment on defendant's assurances seems unquestionable; the facts clearly at least raise a jury question. Additionally, whether plaintiff's reliance upon defendant's assurances was reasonable is also a question for the jury.

Conversely, following the Section 90 approach, a jury could conclude that Phoenix, as promisor, should reasonably have expected to induce action or forbearance on the part of plaintiff to his precise instruction "not to renew the lease" and to "pack up the Margate store and plan on moving." . . .

. . .

Plaintiff's complaint neither seeks enforcement of the lease nor speculative lost profits which it might have earned had the lease been fully and successfully negotiated. Plaintiff merely seeks to recoup damages it incurred, including the loss of its Margate leasehold, in reasonably relying to its detriment upon defendant's promise. . . . Plaintiff's complaint, therefore, should not have been summarily dismissed.

Reversed and remanded for further appropriate proceedings.

Post-Case Follow-Up

In this case, the court applied promissory estoppel to a case of pre-acceptance reliance. Although there was no final contract between the parties, Pop's Cones might be able to recover the damages suffered from its reliance on Resort's words and conduct in losing its leasehold and packing up its store in Margate. A promissory estoppel claim will be justified if the plaintiff satisfies its burden regarding the following: (1) a promise was made by the promisor; (2) the promise must be made with the reasonable expectation that the promisee will rely thereon; (3) the promisee must in fact rely on the promise, and (4) detriment of a definite and substantial nature must be incurred in reliance on the promise. Promissory estoppel doctrine seeks to avoid substantial hardship or injustice if a promise is not enforced.

Pop's Cones, Inc. v. Resorts International Hotel, Inc.: Real Life Applications

1. Nina owns and operates a bakery and wants to become part of a franchise for a baking school. The franchisor, Bakers Institute, tells Nina that for $20,000 she will be allowed to establish a franchise school in her community if she receives written approval of her application from the Institute's director of business development. The director calls Nina and tells her that her application looks great and that she should sell her bakery so she can devote her efforts to developing her new franchise. Nina sells her bakery and suffers a capital loss. Subsequently, the Institute advises Nina that she will need to invest $30,000 more to obtain a

new school franchise. Ultimately, the franchise deal between the Institute and Nina falls through. Nina has come to your law office to determine her potential legal actions and remedies. In preparation for your consultation meeting with Nina, review *Hoffman v. Red Owl Stores, Inc.*, 133 N.W.2d 267 (Wis. 1965), and consider what issues you want to explore with her in the meeting.

2. The DeMarcos obtain a mortgage on their home from defendant bank. Under the mortgage agreement, the plaintiffs are required to carry insurance on the property. Plaintiffs allege that they received a letter from the bank stating that their homeowner's insurance had been cancelled and, if a new policy was not purchased, the bank "might be forced" to purchase a policy and add the premium to their loan balance. The bank insures the home to protect the asset, but then lets the policy expire. The DeMarcos claim they did not realize the house was not insured until after it was destroyed by fire. The bank asks you to advise it on the issue of reliance. Analyze and apply *Shoemaker v. Commonwealth Bank*, 700 A. 2d 1003 (Pa. Super. Ct. 1997).

3. Sally Seller and Bailey Broker agree to a 90-day exclusive listing agreement, allowing Bailey to market Sally's home in exchange for a 6 percent commission. After 90 days, Bailey has not been able to find a buyer for Sally's home. Hoping to keep her business, Bailey asks Sally to renew their agreement, promising that if he does not sell her home within 90 days that he will purchase the home at its asking price. Sally finds another home to buy through another real estate agent. Her local bank approves a loan on the second home because of Bailey Broker's guarantee. When her home does not sell, she tries to set a closing date with Bailey. Bailey refuses to honor the guarantee, asserting that his promise is conditioned upon her using his services to find her new home. Sally is now juggling mortgages for two homes and has to come to you for help. Examine the issue of promissory estoppel in *Nott v. Bunning*, 1982 WL 5622 (Ohio Ct. App. 1982), to guide your client.

---

5. Remedies Following Reliance

Technically, the exception for reliance makes the promise enforceable in the same manner that any bargained-for promise is enforceable. Once enforcement is justified, the normal remedies for enforcement apply, as noted in the *Feinberg* and *King* cases.

In a controversial addendum, the drafters of the Restatement (Second) of Contracts invited courts to limit the remedy "as justice requires." The comments suggest that compensating the promisee for the amount of the detriment suffered may satisfy the needs of justice. Awarding the reliance interest (the amount of money necessary to restore the plaintiff to the position she would have occupied if the promise had not been made) compensates for the harm done by the promise. Especially if the amount of detriment is quite small, enforcing the **expectation interest**—an amount that will put the plaintiff in the position that she would have occupied if the promise had been performed — might appear excessive.

While some courts, like the *Pop's Cones* court, have accepted this invitation, most seem to enforce the promise as made, awarding the expectation interest. Reliance is the reason for enforcement, but that does not dictate that the remedy should be based on reliance. In a proper case, for example, breach of a computer purchase, the court could grant specific performance, such as the delivery of the computer. A court awarding reliance would limit recovery to any loss incurred in returning or reselling a printer bought in anticipation of delivery of the computer. A more detailed discussion of reliance damages is found in Chapter 16.

Chapter Summary

- Courts have found exceptions where promises will be enforced without a showing of consideration.
- New promises to pay may recreate a legal duty in cases of debts barred by the statute of limitations, debts owed by minors or bankrupt parties, or merchant contracts under seal, even if the new promise lacks fresh consideration.
- Generally, a moral obligation will not make an agreement enforceable.
- Under the concept of promissory restitution, some moral obligations may justify enforcing a promise made after benefits have been received under the material benefit rule.
- Under the preexisting duty rule, a party demanding more money for the same performance already promised does not provide consideration for the revised contract terms.
- A contract modification that changes only one party's obligations raises concerns about coercive tactics, unfair threats of breach, and economic duress. Contract modifications procured by coercion or duress will not be enforced.
- If the parties voluntarily agree to a modification, it will be enforced if (1) the promise modifying the original contract was made before the contract was fully performed on either side, (2) the underlying circumstances that prompted the modification were unanticipated by the parties, and (3) the modification is fair and equitable.
- Promises lacking consideration may be enforceable under promissory estoppel if there is also foreseeable reliance, actual reliance, and detrimental reliance, and enforcement will avoid an injustice.
- Under case law, a charitable pledge, supported by consideration or reliance, is enforceable. The Restatement view does not require reliance or forbearance to enforce charitable pledges.

Applying the Rules

Two fitness trainers, Sophia and Gordon Vasquez, own and operate a fitness training company, Strengthmakers. They approach Melba Megastar, CEO of a fast-growing television production and social media company, offering to create a customized physical fitness program for her 500 employees. The trainers hope that a successful program might lead to lots of positive buzz about their services on TV and social media. Megastar likes the idea of improving employee wellness and even suggests that the attractive couple might be featured in an upcoming fitness program that her company is producing for a major TV network. There was no written agreement for the fitness program. But Strengthmakers asserts that the parties agreed that Strengthmakers would offer its training services at a flat rate of $130,000, a 30 percent discount off its normal rates. Strengthmakers asserts that the discount was agreed to by Megastar, and that she was also required to give them ten corporate referrals and audition them for a planned fitness show.

Megastar is also associated with a nonprofit organization, Healthy Kids USA, that focuses on fighting childhood obesity. She promises to donate $500,000 to Healthy Kids USA to improve its gym facilities, and to provide a customized exercise program. The organization spends about $100,000 in architect fees to create a plan for updating and renovating its local gym in anticipation of Megastar's promised funds and exercise program and the expansion of its services. Megastar then asks Strengthmakers to adapt the employee program it is creating for children. Strengthmakers agrees to modify its proposed program for Megastar to support the efforts of Healthy Kids USA.

Over several months, the trainers spent many hours interviewing Megastar's employees at Megastar's headquarters to aid their development of the custom fitness program. A week before the formal roll out of the customized program, Megastar advises Sophia and Gordon that her company has decided to develop its own wellness program and will feature a pair of famous Olympic stars in the new fitness show. Disappointed, Strengthmakers sends an invoice charging the full amount for its services at $130,000 for development of the employee program and $30,000 for adapting the program to the needs of children for Healthy Kids USA.

Megastar refuses to pay the invoice and contends that her company never entered into a formal agreement with the couple and that they never delivered the customized program to her employees or to Healthy Kids USA. Due to budgetary concerns, she also informs Healthy Kids USA that she will not be making her donation and will no longer be providing the customized exercise program. Respond to the following in essay form:

1. What arguments might Strengthmakers make to support its claim for payment on each of the customized exercise programs?

2. How might Megastar defend against Strengthmakers' demand to be compensated on each of the exercise programs?

3. What legal action might Healthy Kids USA take against Megastar regarding her refusal to make her donation?

4. What are Megastar's best arguments to refute the claimed obligation to make the donation to Healthy Kids USA?

5. What kind of remedies might Strengthmakers seek if it succeeds in an action against Megastar? What kind of remedies might Healthy Kids USA seek?

Contract Law in Practice

1. A number of states have passed statutory law that expressly addresses the definition and application of promissory estoppel in contract situations. Research two state statutes on promissory estoppel. Draft a summary of each law and compare the similarities and contrast the differences in their approaches to promissory estoppel. Post that summary on your class discussion board.

2. Research online for a recent news article about a contract dispute in which promissory estoppel plays a key role. Create a blog post summarizing the case and reviewing the parties' assertions on this issue. Use hyperlinks in your blog article to direct your audience to the article, any accessible court rulings and documents on the dispute, and any recent updates on the matter.

3. In many contracts, there may be language that either prevents any oral contract modifications or requires all contract modifications to be writings signed by both parties to the original contract. Search through online and print sources for three examples of contract clauses that seek to limit contract modifications. Consider the key similarities and differences between these clauses and determine which of the three you think is the best drafted clause. Explain your choice in a class discussion or online discussion board.

4. Read about recent quantitative and qualitative research on how courts have been using promissory estoppel in contract actions in the law review article by Professor Marco J. Jimenez, *The Many Faces of Promissory Estoppel: An Empirical Analysis Under the Restatement (Second) of Contracts*, 57 UCLA L. Rev. 669 (2010). In this article, Professor Jimenez examines over 300 promissory estoppel cases decided from January 1, 1981 through January 1, 2008 to show how courts are defining, applying, and broadening the reach of promissory estoppel in contract disputes. Summarize the key ways courts have applied promissory estoppel and the areas in which the concept has continued to expand in contract law.

5. Nonprofit organizations are growing at a rapid pace, focusing on a wide range of social, economic, religious, and political interests. Charitable pledges are often at the heart of many contract disputes. Sometimes the charitable donation has

been made orally and sometimes in writing. Select a state and determine how that state defines "nonprofit organization" and "charitable pledge." What are that state's statutory and/or case law requirements for enforcing a charitable pledge? Create a brief slide presentation on your findings.

6. Today, many states have enacted statutes that allow a debtor to revive a debt after the expiration of the statute of limitations. Under most of these laws, the debtor must promise in writing to pay a debt barred by the statute of limitations. With the proper writing, these kinds of promises are enforceable. Research your state laws to determine if debts may be revived and what requirements must be met to permit enforcement.

7. Parties may modify their contracts in writing or orally. A number of state laws may require that only contract modifications in writing are enforceable. Research the laws in your state to determine if contract modifications must be in writing, what kinds of contract modifications must be in writing, and what are the requirements for a sufficient written modification. Provide a brief summary of your findings in a class blog or discussion board.

PART III

Defenses

When contracts do not turn out as well as expected, people sometimes look for ways to avoid their obligations. Many sources of regret offer no reason to reject the contract itself. It remains a fair deal, just one that didn't work out as well as a party hoped. For instance, when a stock goes down in value, the buyer may regret the purchase. When it goes up, the seller may regret the sale. Those are among the risks people take in entering contracts, not reasons to avoid the contract. Some regrets, however, go beyond the risks naturally assumed in contracts. In these situations, the law may recognize that a party should not be bound by the promises. Part II of this book reviews relevant contract defenses to avoid enforcement.

Mutual assent plays a crucial role in deciding which promises society will use its courts to enforce. Practices that undermine assent may destroy the confidence that the agreement really is mutually beneficial and raise concerns about good faith and fair dealing. When a contract does not reflect careful judgment of a party, the transaction may not deserve court enforcement. However, individual carelessness alone will not excuse enforcement.

The ability to draw the balance between negating inappropriate contracts and enforcing sound transactions depends on a sophisticated understanding of the defenses and the ability to use them. The defenses discussed in the next three chapters identify situations in which contracts should not be enforced despite the presence of the required elements of a contract. We will examine defenses grounded in party vulnerability, poor or insufficient information, and public policy constraints that prevent enforcement.

The choice of defenses reveals a great deal about the important roles assent and consideration play in contract law. Knowing each defense and how it relates to similar defenses will help you select an appropriate means of protecting a client trapped in a contract that should not have been made. Equally important, a thorough appreciation of the defenses is essential to prevent people who simply change their minds from escaping their voluntarily assumed obligations.

6

Contract Defenses—Vulnerable Parties

Defenses (or **affirmative defenses**) are arguments raised by a party accused of breaching a contract that, if established, negate the enforceability of the contract. The law generally treats a defense as defeating a contract, despite the existence of assent and consideration. The party raising the defenses has the burden of proof. In this chapter, we will examine defenses that are based in party vulnerability. These defenses challenge issues of whether parties truly voluntarily assented to an agreement and the notion of a mutually beneficial exchange under consideration. Chapters 7 and 8 address those defenses that are attributable to poor information (misconceptions and mistakes) and those contravening public policy considerations.

A. THE BASICS OF CONTRACT DEFENSES

Typically, defenses are viewed as shields against legal actions. When sued for breach of contract, a person raises a defense to explain why nonperformance was acceptable. The shield is protection from the attack brought by the plaintiff. For example, suppose a merchant takes advantage of a mentally ill person who makes a down payment on an overpriced, luxury item under an installment contract. When the person's family members discover the deal, they try to return the item, but the merchant refuses to take it back. The individual's family blocks any further payments. If the merchant sues for breach

Key Concepts

- The role of and burden of proof for contract defenses
- Defenses based upon incapacity or lack of legal ability to enter into contracts
- Defense of physical and economic duress
- Defense of undue influence and issues of overpersuasion

of the contract, the mentally ill person may argue incapacity as a defense—a shield against liability under the installment contract.

With rare exceptions, defenses can also be used as swords. A person who has already performed a contract may not need a defense; she needs a way to get back what she has already paid. For example, suppose the mentally ill person seeks to return the luxury item after only one week. She might want a refund of any down payment. A shield against having to make further payments to the merchant is not enough. Rather, she needs a sword she can use to attack the installment contract and obtain the relief she deserves from the merchant.

Most defenses can be raised as a sword in a complaint for **rescission** requesting that a contract be canceled or torn up, as if it never had been made. An action for rescission seeks to avoid or nullify the contract from the start. If the contract is rescinded, each party is entitled to **restitution**, a remedy seeking to recover from the other party any benefit it received under the invalid contract. The tenant would return the apartment to the landlord, and the landlord would return the security deposit and rental payment to the tenant.

Defenses may make a contract either **void** or **voidable**. Defenses rendering a contract void make it unenforceable because no valid contract ever existed due to the claimed defense. Courts will refuse to enforce a void contract, even if both parties want the contract enforced. Most defenses make contracts **voidable**, which means that a contract is enforceable unless one party exercises its right to claim a defense that will avoid or discharge its contract duties. A party may choose whether to raise or waive the defense for voidable contracts. A party seeking to exercise the defense may **disaffirm** or repudiate a voidable contract. A party satisfied with the contract despite the conditions under which it was made may **ratify** it by electing to treat the voidable contract as enforceable. Ratification of a voidable contract may be shown by party words or conduct. Issues of disaffirmance and ratification are quite common in cases involving party capacity or legal ability to enter into a contract, such as with **minors** (those under the age of 18).

A person need not disaffirm until he regains a capacity to contract (i.e., comes of age, sobers up, recovers from a mental illness). Once a party is out from under the power of the defense, a party must disaffirm the contract within a reasonable time. For example, a minor may have entered into an installment contract to buy a car. Under contract law, a minor may disaffirm a contract while he is still a minor or within a reasonable time thereafter. The time allowed for notice of the intent to disaffirm varies with the context. One need not disaffirm the contract until one is out from under the effects of the defense.

In some cases, ratification may be accidental. **Implied ratification** applies to people who have discovered the defense, but do not invoke it promptly. Failure to disaffirm within a reasonable time or to plead the defense in an answer to a complaint usually waives the defense. In effect, the contract has been ratified by the failure to raise the defense. Similarly, an action for rescission usually requires prompt notice to the other party of one's intent to avoid the contract. Failure to notify the other party promptly of the intent to disaffirm the contract may lead a court to find an implied ratification.

B. INCAPACITY

As you know, mutual assent presumes that the parties are able to evaluate and value the duties and benefits of the contract and to formulate and express their legal interests and preferences. Most of the defenses involve constraints on a person's ability to effectively examine and fully understand the relative costs and benefits and to act on that analysis. An individual's limitations may deprive assent of its usual significance, removing the justification for the law to enforce the promises. **Incapacity** applies to people who lack the ability to exercise the necessary legal judgment to assent to and carry out the terms of a contract. At times, incapacity is treated as a component of assent rather than as a separate defense.

Anyone who regretted a decision to enter a contract might plead that he did not understand the situation and thus should not be held to his prior assent. However, the law has limited incapacity to a relatively narrow range of issues. The defense protects people who *cannot* make good decisions, not people who *did not* make good decisions. Thus, incapacity will not help people who cannot read or who lack education that allows them to understand the contract. These people could ask someone, such as an attorney, to read or explain the contract to them. These parties can protect themselves. Incapacity protects those who cannot effectively protect themselves and their own self-interest.

The incapacity defense announces the public's judgment that people should not enter contracts with certain individuals. By making the contract unenforceable, the law warns those considering entering a contract with a minor, an intoxicated person, or a mentally ill person not to do it—or, at least, that they do so at their own risk. Contract law will not protect them from breaches by people suffering an incapacity.

By discouraging contracts, incapacity disempowers people. Contracts are a means by which people improve their situation, exchanging things they want less for things they want more. Telling people not to deal with the incapacitated effectively deprives the incapacitated of this ability. Disempowerment may not be limited to those who actually suffer an incapacity. Some vendors might exercise too much caution, refusing to deal with people who might have an incapacity rather than just those who do. Just as liquor and tobacco stores ask for identification from anyone who looks as though they

Historically Incapacity Disempowered Women and Minorities

Myra Bradwell attempted to become the first woman to be admitted to the Illinois bar, but was denied admission by the Illinois Supreme Court and the U.S. Supreme Court.
Library of Congress, Washington, D.C.; neg. no. LC USZ 62 21202

Although incapacity can be used to protect parties, it was also applied in the past to economically disempower and to deny freedom of contract to certain individuals and groups in society. Regarding incapacity, legal scholars have written extensively on our nation's history of discriminatory treatment based on race, involuntary servitude, national origin, and gender in contract law. During the slavery era in the United States, slaves were prohibited by law from being able to enter into contracts. Both before and after the Civil War, statutes limited free African Americans in making contracts. Historically, Native Americans and Asian Americans also faced restrictions on their ability to enter into contracts. In addition, married women were not permitted to enter into contracts without their husband's consent; the presumption being that marriage created a union in which only the husband was capable of executing contracts. In *Bradwell v. State*, 83 U.S. 130 (1873), the U.S. Supreme Court affirmed a denial of a woman's application to the Illinois bar, in part because married woman lacked the capacity to enter into contracts. The following law review articles explore more about this history: Anthony R. Chase, *Race, Culture, and Contract Law: From the Cottonfield to the Courtroom*, 28 CONN. L. REV. 1 (1995); Andrew L. Gates III, Thomas J. McDonald, Jr., J. Michael Veron & Cynthia Shoss Wall, *Contractual Incapacity in the Louisiana Civil Code*, 47 TUL. L. REV. 1093 (1973); David P. Weber, *Restricting the Freedom of Contract: A Fundamental Prohibition*, 16 YALE HUM. RTS. & DEV. L.J. 51 (2013).

might be under 30, just to be sure they do not accidentally break the law against selling to minors, other vendors might refuse to deal with people who may only appear to be intoxicated or mentally ill, but actually are not. Infancy is easy to verify by checking ID cards, making it easier for those who look young to enter contracts than those who appear to be, but are not, intoxicated or mentally ill. The prevalence of false IDs could undercut this right if there were no rules protecting merchants from fraudulent statements of age by minors.

To a large extent, efforts to limit the scope of incapacities protect incapacitated people from losing their power to make contracts. The law balances this important power (to make contracts) with an important concern (for contracts that should not be made). The exact demarcation might be improved, but moving too far in one direction, such as more defenses, threatens to exacerbate disempowerment and vice versa.

Incapacity applies to four specific types of situations: guardianship (where another person has been appointed to manage a person's affairs); mental illness or defect (medical or psychological difficulties, not illiteracy); intoxication (not just alcohol); and infancy (people under the age of 18).

The rules for each area differ slightly, reflecting differences in the degree of protection needed for each type of incapacity. These different forms of incapacity are discussed in further detail below.

Situations Where Incapacity Applies

Guardianship — a court-appointed third party manages another person's affairs
Mental incompetence — a person who suffers from a mental defect or illness
Intoxication — a party acting under the influence of alcohol or drugs
Infancy — people under the age of 18

1. Guardianship — Void

When people lack the ability to handle their own affairs, courts often appoint a **guardian**, someone to manage their affairs for them. People of any age may have a guardian appointed, depending on their mental state. Guardians may be appointed to protect older people afflicted by dementia or Alzheimer's. A young adult who suffered a traumatic brain injury, or children whose parents cannot protect them, may require a guardian. In these situations, the power to enter a contract shifts from the person who suffers an incapacity (the **ward**) to the guardian. A guardianship decree completely disempowers the ward. The ward's contracts have no legal effect and are considered void. He cannot make any contracts on his own. The ward must rely on the guardian to look after his interests. A contract made by the guardian on behalf of the ward is enforceable against the ward as if that ward had signed it himself.

The guardian is a **fiduciary** of the ward, one who must put the interests of the ward ahead of the guardian's own interests when making decisions for the ward. The guardian cannot deal with the ward at arm's length, expecting the ward to look out for herself. Misconduct by the guardian is a breach of **trust**, a special relationship between the **trustee** (who manages another's affairs) and the **beneficiary** (the person whose interests the trustee protects). A guardian is a true fiduciary. In other settings, you may encounter the term **quasi-fiduciary**, which describes situations where a person may need to compromise his or her own self-interest in order to protect the interests of another. This relationship resembles the duties of a fiduciary, even if there is no true fiduciary relationship.

2. Mental Illness or Defect—Voidable

Mental illness or defect covers an array of conditions that impair a person's decision-making ability. It refers to conditions recognized and diagnosable by mental health professionals. Mental illness or defect may afflict people who are not under court-ordered guardianship. Not all conduct associated with a mental illness or defect rises to the level of an incapacity defense. For example, a person may be unhappy without suffering from the mental illness of depression. In addition, the effects of the illness may not be sufficiently severe to require entirely removing any ability of a person to make her own decisions. Alternatively, the need for guardianship may not have been recognized or resolved at the time the person entered a contract. The defense of incapacity applies, making a contract voidable at the election of a person suffering from a mental illness or defect (or someone empowered to act on her behalf), provided the illness was sufficiently severe.

Under the Restatement (Second) of Contracts § 15(1), there are three key questions regarding the availability of the defense:

1. Did the person raising the defense suffer from a mental illness or defect?
2. Was the person either
   a. unable to understand the nature or consequences of the transaction; or
   b. unable to act reasonably (perform) in relation to the transaction and the other party knew or had reason to know of the condition?
3. Did the mental illness or defect cause the inability to understand or to act reasonably?

These three questions are essential to establish the defense and make a contract voidable (see Exhibit 6.1). A person incapable of understanding certain transactions because of a mental illness may be perfectly capable of making other decisions. A person may have the capacity to rent an apartment, but not the capacity to buy a time share. A person may have the capacity to take out a loan, but not to buy a complex financial derivative investment. Mental illness or defect, unlike guardianship, need not be all or nothing. Showing that a person *did not* act reasonably is not the same as showing that he *could not* act reasonably. Similarly, someone who did not understand the transaction has no defense unless he was unable to understand the transaction.

However, Restatement (Second) of Contracts §15(2) provides a catch-all provision that allows courts to view the circumstances as a whole to determine the fairness in contract terms and the notice that the other party has regarding the mental health of a contracting party. That provision is discussed below in greater depth.

Mental Illness or Defect Under Contract Law

Under contract law, mental illness or defect is limited to recognized disorders. Although psychological disorders are the most obvious source of mental incapacity, mental defects may also result from genetic disorders (such as Down's syndrome), diseases (such as strokes), substance abuse (such as overdoses that produce permanent mental effects), or accidents (such as traumatic brain injuries). In each case, however, the condition is recognized and diagnosable by appropriate health care professionals. Mental illness or defect does not extend to all causes for misunderstanding a proposed transaction. Rather than treat every mental impairment as incapacitating, the defense applies to those circumstances that meet the requirements of this contract defense.

In contract disputes, **cognitive disorders** may affect a person's ability to understand the nature and consequences of a proposed transaction. For example, certain persons with mental impairment from a serious head trauma may be unable to understand the transactions proposed sufficiently to determine their own best interests. **Volitional disorders** may impact a person's ability to act reasonably in relation to a contract—even though the person might understand the transaction and reasonable performance of her contract obligations. In these instances, a party's mental illness may create an uncontrollable compulsion to act unreasonably despite her understanding of the contract terms. For instance, if a person's mental illness manifests itself through compulsive gambling, then she may be unable to control herself, thereby making any gambling contracts voidable. It is important to note that some states may not recognize volitional disorders as grounds for incapacity in contracts. However, when an appropriate case arises, the court might or might not be persuaded to join the states that have expanded the incapacity to cover volitional disorders.

EXHIBIT 6.1 Proving Mental Illness or Defect Defense

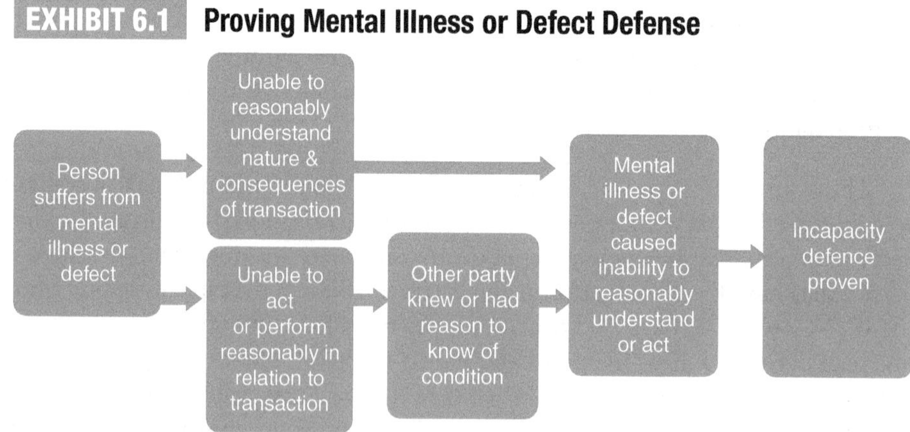

Severity of the Mental Illness or Defect

Mental health professionals treat many different conditions. But not every condition precludes contractual capacity, as mental illness may not make one incapable of handling some or all of one's contractual transactions. Traditionally, courts employed the **cognitive test** to determine incapacity, focusing on whether the metal illness or defect is so serious that the party is unable to reasonably comprehend the nature and consequences of the contract. Today, courts may also apply an additional test, the **motivational test**, which determines the severity of the mental illness or defect by examining whether it creates a compulsion that the party is unable to control and whether the party cannot act or perform the contract in a reasonable manner. Thus, many mental disorders may not prevent a person from making fully binding contracts. For example, a person may suffer from depression, but it may not be so severe that it prevents him from making appropriate decisions or adequately performing his contract duties. In light of the broad range of mental health issues, the severity of the illness plays an important role in determining whether or not a contract may become voidable under incapacity.

Case Preview

Ortelere v. Teachers' Retirement Board of New York

Ortelere v. Teachers' Retirement Board of New York offers a famous example of a volitional disorder. This case is the first to recognize the limitations of using only the cognitive test and argues for the additional application of a broader motivational test. In this case, a teacher undergoing treatment for mental illness decided to retire and elected to take larger monthly payments over her lifetime with nothing payable on or after her death. She died two months later, leaving no pension benefits for her husband and two children. Her family sought to invalidate her selection under incapacity due to mental illness.

As you read *Ortelere v. Teachers' Retirement Board of New York*, look for the following:

1. What evidence supported a finding that Mrs. Ortelere suffered from a mental illness impacting her ability to understand the nature and consequences of her retirement election?
2. What evidence indicated that Mrs. Ortelere possessed the ability to understand the nature and consequences of her retirement election?
3. How did the court address issues of knowledge and fairness in assessing whether the retirement election was voidable?

Ortelere v. Teachers' Retirement Board of New York

250 N.E.2d 460 (N.Y. 1969)

BREITEL, J.

This appeal involves the revocability of an election of benefits under a public employees' retirement system and suggests the need for a renewed examination of

the kinds of mental incompetency which may render voidable the exercise of contractual rights. The particular issue arises on the evidently unwise and foolhardy selection of benefits by a 60-year-old teacher, on leave for mental illness and suffering from cerebral arteriosclerosis, after service as a public schoolteacher and participation in a public retirement system for over 40 years. The teacher died a little less than two months after making her election of maximum benefits, payable to her during her life, thus causing the entire reserve to fall in. She left surviving her husband of 38 years of marriage and two grown children. There is no doubt that any retirement system depends for its soundness on an actuarial experience based on the purely prospective selections of benefits and mortality rates among the covered group, and that retrospective or adverse selection after the fact would be destructive of a sound system. It is also true that members of retirement systems are free to make choices which to others may seem unwise or foolhardy. The issue here is narrower than any suggested by these basic principles. It is whether an otherwise irrevocable election may be avoided for incapacity because of known mental illness which resulted in the election when, except in the barest actuarial sense, the system would sustain no unfavorable consequences.

The husband and executor of Grace W. Ortelere, the deceased New York City schoolteacher, sues to set aside her application for retirement without option, in the event of her death. It is alleged that Mrs. Ortelere, on February 11, 1965, two months before her death from natural causes, was not mentally competent to execute a retirement application. By this application, effective the next day, she elected the maximum retirement allowance (Administrative Code of City of New York, § B20-46.0). She thus revoked her earlier election of benefits under which she named her husband a beneficiary of the unexhausted reserve upon her death. Selection of the maximum allowance extinguished all interests upon her death.

Following a nonjury trial in Supreme Court, it was held that Grace Ortelere had been mentally incompetent at the time of her February 11 application, thus rendering it "null and void and of no legal effect." The Appellate Division, by a divided court, reversed the judgment of the Supreme Court and held that, as a matter of law, there was insufficient proof of mental incompetency as to this transaction (31 A D 2d 139).

Mrs. Ortelere's mental illness, indeed, psychosis, is undisputed. It is not seriously disputable, however, that she had complete cognitive judgment or awareness when she made her selection. A modern understanding of mental illness, however, suggests that incapacity to contract or exercise contractual rights may exist, because of volitional and affective impediments or disruptions in the personality, despite the intellectual or cognitive ability to understand. It will be recognized as the civil law parallel to the question of criminal responsibility which has been the recent concern of so many and has resulted in statutory and decisional changes in the criminal law (e.g., A. L. I. Model Penal Code, §4.01; Penal Law, § 30.05; *Durham v.* United States, 214 F. 2d 862).

Mrs. Ortelere, an elementary schoolteacher since 1924, suffered a "nervous breakdown" in March, 1964 and went on a leave of absence expiring February 5, 1965. She was then 60 years old and had been happily married for 38 years. On July 1, 1964 she came under the care of Dr. D'Angelo, a psychiatrist, who diagnosed her breakdown as involutional psychosis, melancholia type. Dr. D'Angelo prescribed, and for about six weeks decedent underwent, tranquilizer and shock therapy. Although moderately successful, the therapy was not continued since it was suspected that she also suffered from cerebral arteriosclerosis, an ailment later confirmed. However, the psychiatrist continued to see her at monthly intervals until March, 1965. On March 28, 1965 she was hospitalized after collapsing at home from an aneurysm. She died 10 days later; the cause of death was "Cerebral thrombosis due to [Hypertensive] [Heart] [Disease]."

As a teacher she had been a member of the Teachers' Retirement System of the City of New York (Administrative Code, §B20-30). This entitled her to certain annuity and pension rights, preretirement death benefits, and empowered her to exercise various options concerning the payment of her retirement allowance.

Some years before, on June 28, 1958, she had executed a "Selection of Benefits under Option One" naming her husband as beneficiary of the unexhausted reserve. Under this option upon retirement her allowance would be less by way of periodic retirement allowances, but if she died before receipt of her full reserve the balance of the reserve would be payable to her husband. On June 16, 1960, two years later, she had designated her husband as beneficiary of her service death benefits in the event of her death prior to retirement.

Then on February 11, 1965, when her leave of absence had just expired and she was still under treatment, she executed a retirement application, the one here involved, selecting the maximum retirement allowance payable during her lifetime with nothing payable on or after death. She also, at this time, borrowed from the system the maximum cash withdrawal permitted, namely, $8,760. Three days earlier she had written the board, stating that she intended to retire on February 12 or 15 or as soon as she received "the information I need in order to decide whether to take an option or maximum allowance." She then listed eight specific questions, reflecting great understanding of the retirement system, concerning the various alternatives available. An extremely detailed reply was sent, by letter of February 15, 1965, although by that date it was technically impossible for her to change her selection. However, the board's chief clerk, before whom Mrs. Ortelere executed the application, testified that the questions were "answered verbally by me on February 11th." Her retirement reserve totalled $62,165 (after deducting the $8,760 withdrawal). . . .

. . .

The Orteleres were in quite modest circumstances. They owned their own home, valued at $20,000, and had $8,000 in a savings account. They also owned some farm land worth about $5,000. Under these circumstances, as revealed in this record, retirement for both of the Orteleres or the survivor of them had to be provided, as a practical matter, largely out of Mrs. Ortelere's retirement benefits.

According to Dr. D'Angelo, the psychiatrist who treated her, Mrs. Ortelere never improved enough to "warrant my sending her back [to teaching]." A physician for the Board of Education examined her on February 2, 1965 to determine her fitness to return to teaching. Although not a psychiatrist but rather a specialist in internal medicine, this physician "judged that she had apparently recovered from the depression" and that she appeared rational. However, before allowing her to return to teaching, a report was requested from Dr. D'Angelo concerning her condition. It is notable that the Medical Division of the Board of Education on February 24, 1965 requested that Mrs. Ortelere report to the board's "panel psychiatrist" on March 11, 1965.

Dr. D'Angelo stated "[at] no time since she was under my care was she ever mentally competent"; that "[mentally] she couldn't make a decision of any kind, actually, of any kind, small or large." He also described how involutional melancholia affects the judgment process: "They can't think rationally, no matter what the situation is. They will even tell you, 'I used to be able to think of anything and make any decision. Now,' they say, 'even getting up, I don't know whether I should get up or whether I should stay in bed.' Or, 'I don't even know how to make a slice of toast any more.' Everything is impossible to decide, and everything is too great an effort to even think of doing. They just don't have the effort, actually, because their nervous breakdown drains them of all their physical energies."

. . .

The well-established rule is that contracts of a mentally incompetent person who has not been adjudicated insane are voidable. Even where the contract has been partly or fully performed it will still be avoided upon restoration of the *status quo*. (*Verstandig v. Schlaffer, 296 N. Y. 62, 64*; *Blinn v. Schwarz, 177 N. Y. 252, 262*; see, also, Ann., Contracts with Incompetent, 95 A. L. R. 1442; Ann., Incompetent — Contract Before Adjudication, 46 A. L. R. 416.)

Traditionally, in this State and elsewhere, contractual mental capacity has been measured by what is largely a cognitive test (*Aldrich v. Bailey, 132 N. Y. 85*; 2 Williston, Contracts [3d ed.], §256; see 17 C.J.S., Contracts, §133 [1], subd. e, pp. 860-862). Under this standard the "inquiry" is whether the mind was "so affected as to render him wholly and absolutely incompetent to comprehend and understand the nature of the transaction" (*Aldrich v. Bailey,* supra, at p. 89). A requirement that the party also be able to make a rational judgment concerning the particular transaction qualified the cognitive test (*Paine v. Aldrich,* 133 N. Y. 544, 546; Note, "Civil Insanity": The New York Treatment of the Issue of Mental Incompetency in Non-Criminal Cases, 44 Cornell L. Q. 76). Conversely, it is also well recognized that contractual ability would be affected by insane delusions intimately related to the particular transaction (*Moritz v. Moritz, 153 App. Div. 147,* affd. 211 N. Y. 580; see Green, Judicial Tests of Mental Incompetency, 6 Mo. L. Rev. 141, 151).

These traditional standards governing competency to contract were formulated when psychiatric knowledge was quite primitive. They fail to account for one who by reason of mental illness is unable to control his conduct even though his cognitive ability seems unimpaired. When these standards were evolving it was thought that all the mental faculties were simultaneously affected by mental illness. (Green, Mental Incompetency, 38 Mich. L. Rev. 1189, 1197-1202.) This is no longer the prevailing view (Note, Mental Illness and the Law of Contracts, 57 Mich. L. Rev. 1020, 1033-1036).

Of course, the greatest movement in revamping legal notions of mental responsibility has occurred in the criminal law. The nineteenth century cognitive test embraced in the *M'Naghten* rules has long been criticized and changed by statute and decision in many jurisdictions [citations omitted]. . . .

While the policy considerations for the criminal law and the civil law are different, both share in common the premise that policy considerations must be based on a sound understanding of the human mind and, therefore, its illnesses. Hence, because the cognitive rules are, for the most part, too restrictive and rest on a false factual basis they must be re-examined. Once it is understood that, accepting plaintiff's proof, Mrs. Ortelere was psychotic and because of that psychosis could have been incapable of making a voluntary selection of her retirement system benefits, there is an issue that a modern jurisprudence should not exclude, merely because her mind could pass a "cognition" test based on nineteenth century psychology.

There has also been some movement on the civil law side to achieve a modern posture. For the most part, the movement has been glacial and has been disguised under traditional formulations. Various devices have been used to avoid unacceptable results under the old rules by finding unfairness or overreaching in order to avoid transactions (see, e.g., Green, Proof of Mental Incompetency and the Unexpressed Major Premise, 53 Yale L. J. 271, 298-305).

In this State there has been at least one candid approach. In *Faber v. Sweet Style Mfg. Corp.* (40 Misc 2d 212) Mr. Justice Meyer wrote: "[incompetence] to contract also exists when a contract is entered into under the compulsion of a mental disease or disorder but for which the contract would not have been made" (at p. 216; noted in 39 N.Y.U. L. Rev. 356). This is the first known time a court has recognized that the traditional standards of incompetency for contractual capacity are inadequate in light of contemporary psychiatric learning and applied modern standards. Prior to this, courts applied the cognitive standard giving great weight to objective evidence of rationality (e.g., *Beisman v. New York City Employees' Retirement System, 81 N. Y. S. 2d 373*, revd. 275 App. Div. 836, affd. 300 N. Y. 580; *Schwartzberg v. Teachers' Retirement Bd.*, 273 App. Div. 240, affd. 298 N. Y. 741; *Martin v. Teachers' Retirement Bd.*, 70 N. Y. S. 2d 593).

It is quite significant that Restatement, 2d, Contracts, states the modern rule on competency to contract. This is in evident recognition, and the Reporter's Notes support this inference, that, regardless of how the cases formulated their reasoning, the old cognitive test no longer explains the results. Thus, the new Restatement section reads: "(1) A person incurs only voidable contractual duties by entering into a transaction if by reason of mental illness or defect . . . (b) he is unable to act in a reasonable manner in relation to the transaction and the other party has reason to know of his condition." (Restatement, 2d, Contracts [T.D. No. 1, April 13, 1964], §18C.) [citation omitted]. . . .

The avoidance of duties under an agreement entered into by those who have done so by reason of mental illness, but who have understanding, depends on balancing competing policy considerations. There must be stability in contractual relations and protection of the expectations of parties who bargain in good faith. On the other hand, it is also desirable to protect persons who may understand the nature of the transaction but who, due to mental illness, cannot control their conduct. Hence, there should be relief only if the other party knew or was put on notice as to the contractor's mental illness. Thus, the Restatement provision for avoidance contemplates that "the other party has reason to know" of the mental illness (*id.*).

When, however, the other party is without knowledge of the contractor's mental illness and the agreement is made on fair terms, the proposed Restatement rule is: "The power of avoidance under subsection (1) terminates to the extent that the contract has been so performed in whole or in part or the circumstances have so changed that avoidance would be inequitable. In such a case a court may grant relief on such equitable terms as the situation requires." (Restatement, 2d, Contracts, *supra*, §18C, subd. [2].)

The system was, or should have been, fully aware of Mrs. Ortelere's condition. They, or the Board of Education, knew of her leave of absence for medical reasons and the resort to staff psychiatrists by the Board of Education. Hence, the other of the conditions for avoidance is satisfied.

Lastly, there are no significant changes of position by the system other than those that flow from the barest actuarial consequences of benefit selection.

Nor should one ignore that in the relationship between retirement system and member, and especially in a public system, there is not involved a commercial, let alone an ordinary commercial, transaction. Instead the nature of the system and its announced goal is the protection of its members and those in whom its members have an interest.

It is not a sound scheme which would permit 40 years of contribution and participation in the system to be nullified by a one-instant act committed by one known to be mentally ill. This is especially true if there would be no substantial harm to the system if the act were avoided. On the record none may gainsay that her selection of a "no option" retirement while under psychiatric care, ill with cerebral arteriosclerosis, aged 60, and with a family in which she had always manifested concern, was so unwise and foolhardy that a factfinder might conclude that it was explainable only as a product of psychosis.

On this analysis it is not difficult to see that plaintiff's evidence was sufficient to sustain a finding that, when she acted as she did on February 11, 1965, she did so solely as a result of serious mental illness, namely, psychosis. Of course, nothing less serious than medically classified psychosis should suffice or else few contracts would be invulnerable to some kind of psychological attack. Mrs. Ortelere's psychiatrist testified quite flatly that as an involutional melancholiac in depression she was incapable of making a voluntary "rational" decision. Of course, as noted earlier, the trial court's finding and perhaps some of the testimony attempted to fit into the rubrics of the traditional rules. For that reason rather than reinstatement of the judgment at Trial Term there should be a new trial under the proper standards frankly considered and applied.

Accordingly, the order of the Appellate Division should be reversed, without costs, and the action remanded to Trial Term for a new trial.

JASEN, J. (dissenting). Where there has been no previous adjudication of incompetency, the burden of proving mental incompetence is upon the party alleging it. I agree with the majority at the Appellate Division that the plaintiff, the husband of the decedent, failed to sustain the burden incumbent upon him of proving deceased's incompetence.

The evidence conclusively establishes that the decedent, at the time she made her application to retire, understood not only that she was retiring, but also that she had selected the maximum payment during her lifetime.

Indeed, the letter written by the deceased to the Teachers' Retirement System prior to her retirement demonstrates her full mental capacity to understand and to decide whether to take an option or the maximum allowance. The full text of the letter reads as follows:

> February 8, 1965
>
> . . .
>
> Gentlemen:
>
> I would like to retire on Feb. 12 or Feb. 15. In other words, just as soon as possible after I receive the information I need in order to decide whether to take an option or maximum allowance. Following are the questions I would like to have answered:
>
> 1. What is my "average" five-year salary?
> 2. What is my maximum allowance?
> 3. I am 60 years old. If I select option four-a with a beneficiary (female) 27 years younger, what is my allowance?
> 4. If I select four-a on the pension part only, and take the maximum annuity, what is my allowance?
> 5. If I take a loan of 89% of my year's salary before retirement, what would my maximum allowance be?
> 6. If I take a loan of $5,000 before retiring, and select option four-a on both the pension and annuity, what would my allowance be?
> 7. What is my total service credit? I have been on a leave without pay since Oct. 26, 1964.
> 8. What is the "factor" used for calculating option four-a with the above beneficiary?
>
> Thank you for your promptness in making the necessary calculations. I will come to your office on Thursday afternoon of this week.

It seems clear that this detailed, explicit and extremely pertinent list of queries reveals a mind fully in command of the salient features of the Teachers' Retirement System. Certainly, it cannot be said that the decedent could possess sufficient capacity to compose a letter indicating such a comprehensive understanding of the retirement system, and yet lack the capacity to understand the answers.

As I read the record, the evidence establishes that the decedent's election to receive maximum payments was predicated on the need for a higher income to support two retired persons—her husband and herself. Since the only source of income available to decedent and her husband was decedent's retirement pay, the additional payment of $75 per month which she would receive by electing the maximal payment was a necessity. Indeed, the additional payments represented an increase of 20% over the benefits payable under option 1. Under these circumstances, an election of maximal income during decedent's lifetime was not only a rational, but a necessary decision.

Further indication of decedent's knowledge of the financial needs of her family is evidenced by the fact that she took a loan for the maximum amount ($8,760) permitted by the retirement system, at the time she made application for retirement.

Moreover, there is nothing in the record to indicate that the decedent had any warning, premonition, knowledge or indication at the time of retirement that her life expectancy was, in any way, reduced by her condition. Decedent's election of the maximum retirement benefits, therefore, was not so contrary to her best interests so as to create an inference of her mental incompetence. . . .

Post-Case Follow-Up

The court addressed the established rule that contracts entered into by a mentally incompetent person are voidable. Applying the Restatement view, Mrs. Ortelere's mental illness was well documented and her doctor testified that she lacked the ability to make rational decisions. The school district also knew that she took a medical leave due to her illness. The court also determined that it is unfair to permit 40 years of retirement contributions to be nullified by one known to be mentally ill.

Ortelere v. Teachers' Retirement Board of New York: Real Life Applications

1. Fred, an unmarried city employee with no children, decides to retire, electing the maximum monthly allowance for the rest of his life with no provision for his survivors. Six months later, he dies of cirrhosis of the liver, coronary arteriosclerosis, and anemia. His physician indicates that these illnesses may result in periods of mental confusion and disorientation. Fred's heirs want to invalidate his election under mental incapacity and consult with your law firm. Examine *In re Will of Whalen*, 51 A.D.2d 296 (N.Y. App. Div. 1st Dep't 1976) to provide them with your advice in a client letter.
2. Beverly and Howard are divorced and Beverly has primary custody of their daughter. Under a separation agreement, Howard must pay spousal and child support as well as provide the proceeds from the sale of certain property. Beverly suffers from bouts of alcoholism and Howard is concerned that his support checks are enabling her dependency. Subsequently, Howard has an attorney modify the terms of the separation agreement and has Beverly sign it, revising the custody and spousal support to his benefit. After a period in a rehab facility, Beverly seeks to rescind the revised agreement, claiming mental incapacity due to her chronic alcoholism. She has come to you for advice on this issue. Consider *D.M. v. K.M.*, 14 Misc. 3d 1206(A) (N.Y. Sup. Ct. 2006) in advising her on this matter.
3. Morgan is hospitalized in the final stages of Parkinson's disease. His wife, Nellie, comes to the hospital to obtain his signature on a power of attorney in order to obtain a loan to keep Morgan's farm financially afloat. She guides his hand on a power of attorney form to create his signature, but because he is heavily medicated he does not comprehend what is happening. Nellie signs loan documents in Morgan's name under the power of attorney using his farm as collateral for the loan. Morgan then dies from his illness. Subsequently, the bank forecloses on Morgan's farm and seeks to recover the funds from the loan from his estate. As Morgan's executor, can you prevent the bank from recovering the loan from his estate under incapacity? Review *Production Credit Assn. v. Kehl*, 148 Wis. 2d 225 (Wis. Ct. App. 1988) to determine the likely outcome.

Notice of the Mental Illness or Defect

In dealing with issues of mental incompetence, a court also addresses issues of good faith and fair dealing. The issue of the other party's knowledge or reason to know of the mental defect and the fairness of the contract terms may impact the ability to avoid one's contract obligations due to the mental illness. Unlike infancy, where vendors can ask to see proof of age, vendors cannot check for mental illness or defect by demanding identification proving mental capacity. At times, mentally ill persons may appear lucid and able to grasp their contract interactions. As a result, people unwittingly may enter contracts with the mentally ill. They cannot protect themselves from the possibility that the person on the other side of the contract suffers a mental illness or defect — and the substantial hardship that can result if that person disaffirms the contract.

A requirement that the other party knows or simply has reason to know of a mental illness allows some room for that party to protect itself by refusing to enter into the contract. The rule does not require actual notice of the condition; reason to know suffices. Some debate centers on whether the person must have reason to know of the mental illness or defect, or whether she also must have reason to know that the defect prevents the person from understanding or acting reasonably. The court in *Ortelere* concludes that reason to know of the mental illness or defect is all that is required. This approach prevents disingenuous claims of lack of notice by one who should have recognized the signs of the mental illness or defect. Unlike a person with notice, the person who lacks notice or a reason to know may be able to enforce the agreement under certain circumstances due to reliance.

Reliance Without Notice of the Mental Illness or Defect

A defense for the mentally ill may disadvantage people who enter contracts with them. Once they begin to perform, they may be unable to recover either their performance or the promised price. That detrimental reliance justifies limiting the mentally ill person's right to avoid the contract in some circumstances. Restatement (Second) of Contracts §15(2) limits the defense if three conditions are met:

1. The other party is without knowledge of the mental illness or defect;
2. The contract terms are fair; and
3. The party's reliance makes it unjust to allow the mentally ill person to refuse to perform.

A more narrow reading of the first provision suggests that only one with actual knowledge of the illness is disqualified from obtaining relief under this provision. However, the clause could also be given a more expansive interpretation to include actual knowledge or a reason to know of the mental illness. The second condition protects fair contracts and those people acting in good faith and fair dealing and excludes relief in situations where contract terms are unfair and parties are behaving unfairly. This approach seeks to avoid exploitation of the mentally ill when it may be unclear about the other party's knowledge of that illness. Objective fairness applies with the court reviewing a transaction to see if its terms are within the range of reasonable party expectations for these types of transactions.

Under this provision, the court may exercise its discretion in granting relief that best meets the interests of justice. The incapacity defense is ineffective only to the extent that reliance harmed the other party. This approach might mean enforcing the entire contract when performance was complete or losses could not be avoided on the remaining portions.

This section also implies that any unperformed portion of the contract can be rescinded. Often part of the contract can be rescinded: the other party has not performed yet or part of the performance can be returned. If so, a court is likely to negate the contract for incapacity as to the parts that can be undone, enforcing only the part that cannot be rescinded. This approach may require the incapacitated person to cover reliance losses in preparing for the contract by the other party, in addition to returning the benefit received.

Consider an example of how the exception might work when a contract has been partially performed. A homeowner, with a severe mental illness, hires a painter to paint her house. The painter, without knowledge of the illness, quotes a fair price for the work. After one side is painted, the homeowner disaffirms the contract, pleading her incapacity. It seems unjust for the homeowner to avoid the contract without paying for the work done so far. Similarly, any paint already mixed, but not yet applied, might require compensation. The homeowner probably can cancel the unperformed portion of the contract, owing no compensation for the profit lost by not finishing the job. If the painter lost out on other jobs, it may be difficult for him to seek compensation for lost business opportunities, which may be seen as too speculative and not foreseeable by the homeowner at the time they entered into the contract.

If the performance is complete and the original value or consideration cannot be returned at all, the contract is likely enforceable, provided that the other requirements of fairness and lack of knowledge are established. Where the contract allocated a risk of subsequent events, changes in the risk also may make rescission unjust. For example, allowing a person to rescind a stock purchase after the price went down may be unjust. The seller might have sold it to another person sooner had the mentally ill person not bought it. Forcing the seller to bear the entire loss might be unjust in this case. Yet it is up to the court to exercise its discretion in determining the interests of justice.

Case Preview

Hauer v. Union State Bank of Wautoma

In *Hauer v. Union State Bank of Wautoma,* a court addressed issues of mental capacity, knowledge, and fairness in a loan agreement with a woman who suffered a traumatic head injury in a motorcycle accident. No longer under guardianship, she subsequently entered into a loan agreement that used her entire settlement fund as collateral. With the money spent on another's failing business, she then sought to rescind the agreement and a return of her collateral from the bank, arguing mental incapacity.

As you read *Hauer v. Union State Bank of Wautoma*, look for the following:

1. Did the end of guardianship mean that Hauer no longer suffered from a mental defect and could handle her own business affairs?
2. What comparisons did the court make between incapacity of minors and those claiming a mental illness or defect?
3. Did the bank have knowledge of Hauer's mental defect at the time of the contract?

Were the loan agreement terms fair and did the bank act in good faith toward Hauer?

Hauer v. Union State Bank of Wautoma

192 Wis. 2d 576 (1995)

SNYDER, J.

The issues in this case arise out of a loan made by Union State Bank of Wautoma to Kathy Hauer. The Bank appeals from a judgment which (1) voided the loan on the grounds that Hauer lacked the mental capacity to enter into the loan, (2) required the Bank to return Hauer's collateral and (3) dismissed the Bank's counterclaim which sought to recover the proceeds of the loan from Hauer. Because we conclude that there is evidence in the record to support the jury's findings that Hauer was mentally incompetent at the time of the loan and that the Bank failed to act in good faith in granting the loan, we affirm.

I. FACTS

In order to place the loan in context, we must first set forth the relevant events giving rise to the loan. The following facts are taken from court documents and undisputed testimony at trial.

In 1987, Hauer suffered a brain injury in a motorcycle accident. She was subsequently adjudicated to be incompetent, resulting in a guardian being appointed by the court. On September 20, 1988, Hauer's guardianship was terminated based upon a letter from her treating physician, Kenneth Viste. Viste opined that Hauer had recovered to the point where she had ongoing memory, showed good judgment, was reasonable in her goals and plans and could manage her own affairs. Her monthly income after the accident was $900, which consisted of social security disability and interest income from a mutual fund worth approximately $80,000.

On October 18, 1988, the Bank loaned Ben Eilbes $7600 to start a small business. In December, Eilbes requested but was denied an additional $2000 loan from the Bank. By June of 1989, Eilbes was in default on the loan. Around this time, Eilbes met Hauer through her daughter, who told Eilbes about the existence of Hauer's mutual fund. Eilbes subsequently discussed his business with Hauer on several occasions and Hauer expressed an interest in becoming an investor in the business. Because Hauer could only sell her stocks at certain times, Eilbes suggested that she

take out a short-term loan using the stocks as collateral. Eilbes told Hauer that if she loaned him money, he would give her a job, pay her interest on the loan and pay the loan when it came due. Hauer agreed.

Eilbes then contacted Richard Schroeder, assistant vice president of the Bank, and told Schroeder that Hauer wanted to invest in his business but that she needed short-term financing and could provide adequate collateral. Eilbes told Schroeder that he would use the money invested by Hauer in part to in full. Schroeder then called Hauer's stockbroker and financial consultant, Stephen Landolt, in an effort to verify the existence of Hauer's fund. Landolt told Schroeder that Hauer needed the interest income to live on and that he wished the Bank would not use it as collateral for a loan. Schroeder also conceded that it was possible that Landolt told him that Hauer was suffering from brain damage, but did not specifically recall that part of their conversation.

At some later date Eilbes met personally with Schroeder in order to further discuss the potential loan to Hauer, after which Schroeder indicated that the Bank would be willing to loan Hauer $30,000. Schroeder gave Eilbes a loan application to give to Hauer to fill out. On October 26, 1989, Hauer and Eilbes went to the Bank to meet with Schroeder and sign the necessary paperwork. Prior to this date, Schroeder had not spoken to or met with Hauer. During this meeting Schroeder explained the terms of the loan to Hauer—that she would sign a consumer single-payment note due in six months and give the Bank a security interest in her mutual fund as collateral. Schroeder did not notice anything that would cause him to believe that Hauer did not understand the loan transaction.

On April 26, 1990, the date the loan matured, Hauer filed suit against the Bank and Eilbes. . . . In Hauer's third amended complaint, she alleged the following specific causes of action: (1) the Bank knew or should have known that she lacked the mental capacity to understand the loan, (2) the Bank intentionally misrepresented, negligently misrepresented, or misrepresented the circumstances surrounding the loan on which she relied, and (3) the Bank breached a fiduciary duty owed to her.

On January 7, 1992, the Bank moved for summary judgment on the grounds that Hauer failed to state any claim for which relief could be granted. The trial court granted summary judgment in part by dismissing Hauer's misrepresentation claims. However, the court held that the pleadings stated the following causes of action which required factual determinations: (1) Hauer lacked the mental capacity to enter into the loan agreement and the Bank knew or should have known about her condition, (2) the Bank breached its duty of good faith and fair dealing under §401.203, Stats., and (3) the Bank had a fiduciary duty to Hauer and breached that duty.

Prior to trial and over the Bank's objection, Hauer dismissed Eilbes because he appeared to be judgment proof and was filing bankruptcy. A twelve-person jury subsequently found that Hauer lacked the mental capacity to enter into the loan and that the Bank failed to act in good faith toward Hauer in the loan transaction. The trial court denied the Bank's motions after verdict and entered judgment voiding the loan contract, dismissing the Bank's counterclaim and ordering the Bank to return Hauer's collateral. The Bank appeals.

. . .

II. MENTAL CAPACITY TO CONTRACT

Over the Bank's objection, the jury was presented with the following special verdict question: Did the plaintiff, Kathy Hauer, lack the mental capacity to enter into the loan transaction at the time of that transaction? The jury answered this question, "Yes." In denying the Bank's motions after verdict, the trial court held that based on this finding, the note and security agreement were "void or voidable." Further, the court ruled that Hauer was not liable for repayment of the $30,000 loan because she no longer possessed the funds.

The Bank in its motions after verdict and on appeal argues that the jury's verdict as to mental incompetency is invalid. The Bank contends that Hauer failed to state a claim upon which relief can be granted or, in the alternative, that the evidence does not support the jury's verdict.

A. Mental Incompetence — Cause of Action

We first address the Bank's argument that Hauer's claim of mental incompetence fails to state a claim for which relief can be granted. This presents a question of law which we review independently. *Peterman v. Midwestern Nat'l Ins. Co.*, 177 Wis. 2d 682, 697, 503 N.W.2d 312, 318 (Ct. App. 1993). The Bank contends that a claim of mental incompetence is an affirmative defense to an action to enforce a contract only and that Hauer cannot avail herself of such a defense because she failed to plead any affirmative defenses. We disagree.

We have previously recognized that the vast majority of courts have held that an incompetent person's transactions are voidable — the incompetent has the power to void the contract entirely. [Citations omitted.] Further, Wisconsin has long recognized a cause of action to rescind a contract or conveyance based upon the lack of mental competency at the time of the transaction. *See, e.g., First Nat'l Bank v. Nennig*, 92 Wis. 2d 518, 521, 285 N.W.2d 614, 616 (1979). [Footnote omitted.] Accordingly, we conclude that Hauer properly stated a cause of action to void the loan contract.

B. Sufficiency of the Evidence

The Bank argues that even if Hauer has a cause of action to void the contract based upon the lack of mental capacity, the record is devoid of credible evidence to sustain the jury's verdict. In reviewing a jury's verdict, we will sustain the verdict if there is any credible evidence to support it. *Fehring v. Republic Ins. Co.*, 118 Wis. 2d 299, 305, 347 N.W.2d 595, 598 (1984). The weight and credibility of the evidence are left to the province of the jury. *Id.* When the evidence permits more than one inference, this court must accept the inference that favors the jury's verdict. *Id.* at 305-306, 347 N.W.2d at 598.

The law presumes that every adult person is fully competent until satisfactory proof to the contrary is presented. *First Nat'l Bank*, 92 Wis. 2d at 529-30, 285 N.W.2d at 620. The burden of proof is on the person seeking to void the act. *Nyka v. State*, 268 Wis. 644, 646, 68 N.W.2d 458, 460 (1955). The test for determining competency is whether the person involved had sufficient mental ability to know what he or she was doing and the nature and consequences of the transaction. *First Nat'l Bank*, 92 Wis.

2d at 530, 285 N.W.2d at 620; see also Restatement (Second) of Contracts §15(1)(a) (1979). Almost any conduct may be relevant, as may lay opinions, expert opinions and prior and subsequent adjudications of incompetency. Restatement, *supra*, at §15 cmt. *c*.

Our review of the record reveals that there is credible evidence which the jury could have relied on in reaching its verdict. First, it is undisputed that Hauer was under court-appointed guardianship approximately one year before the loan transaction. Second, Hauer's testimony indicates a complete lack of understanding of the nature and consequences of the transaction. [Footnote omitted.] Third, Hauer's psychological expert, Charles Barnes, testified that when he treated her in 1987, Hauer was "very deficient in her cognitive abilities, her abilities to remember and to read, write and spell . . . she was very malleable, gullible, people could convince her of almost anything." Barnes further testified that because Hauer's condition had not changed in any significant way by 1990 when he next evaluated her, she was "incompetent and . . . unable to make reasoned decisions" on the date she made the loan.

The Bank argues that Barnes's testimony was irrelevant and erroneously admitted because Viste, Hauer's treating neurologist, informed the court that in his opinion Hauer was no longer in need of a guardian and could manage her own affairs a year prior to the loan. [Footnote omitted.] [Over the bank's objection, a portion of Viste's deposition was read at trial. Viste concluded that he made a mistake in finding that Hauer was competent and no longer in need of a guardian in 1988.] The Bank contends that Hauer should be judicially estopped from asserting incompetence at the time of the loan after convincing the court the previous year that she was competent. However, competency must be determined on the date the instrument was executed. *Production Credit*, 148 Wis. 2d at 230, 434 N.W.2d at 818.

The Bank further points out that both Eilbes and Schroeder testified that Hauer was much different at trial than she was on the day the loan was executed. Nevertheless, the weight and credibility of the evidence are for the jury to decide, not this court. The jury apparently gave more credence to Hauer's and Barnes's testimony than Schroeder's testimony and Viste's 1988 opinion. In sum, while we agree that there is evidence which the jury could have relied on to find that Hauer was competent, we must accept the inference that favors the jury's verdict when the evidence permits more than one inference. *Fehring*, 118 Wis. 2d at 305-306, 347 N.W.2d at 598.

III. EFFECT OF INCOMPETENCE

Having concluded that Hauer stated a claim for relief and that sufficient credible evidence was presented to sustain the jury's verdict, we now turn to the unresolved problem regarding the rights and responsibilities of the parties relative to the disposition of the consideration exchanged in the loan transaction. We must decide the legal question of whether Hauer may recover her collateral without liability for the loan proceeds. . . .

Postverdict, the trial court ruled that Hauer's action to void the contract required the Bank to return her collateral and Hauer to return any loan proceeds in her possession. However, it is undisputed that Hauer loaned the entire $30,000 to Eilbes and that the money had long since disappeared. On appeal, the Bank contends that equity dictates that the proper remedy upon voiding the loan transaction is to return the parties to their preloan status—the Bank must return Hauer's stocks and Hauer must be held liable to the Bank for $30,000.

The trial court offered two explanations for voiding the contract but not holding Hauer liable for repayment of the loan: (1) the law and policy of the "infancy doctrine" set forth in *Halbman v. Lemke*, 99 Wis. 2d 241, 298 N.W.2d 562 (1980), and (2) the jury's finding that the Bank failed to act in good faith. We will address each in turn.

A. Infancy Doctrine

In *Halbman*, our supreme court held that a minor who disaffirms a contract may recover the purchase price without liability for use, depreciation or other diminution in value. *Id.* at 251, 298 N.W.2d at 567. As a general rule, a minor who disaffirms a contract is expected to return as much of the consideration as remains in the minor's possession. However, the minor's right to disaffirm is permitted even where the minor cannot return the property. *Id.* at 245-246, 298 N.W.2d at 565. The trial court ruled that the infancy doctrine was analogous and applies when the voidness arises from mental incapacity to contract. We disagree.

The purpose of the infancy doctrine is to protect "minors from foolishly squandering their wealth through improvident contracts with crafty adults who would take advantage of them in the marketplace." *Id.* at 245, 298 N.W.2d at 564. The common law has long recognized this policy to protect minors. *Id.* However, "[a] contract made by a person who is mentally incompetent requires the reconciliation of two conflicting policies: the protection of justifiable expectations and of the security of transactions, and the protection of persons unable to protect themselves against imposition." Restatement, *supra*, §15 cmt. *a.*

The trial court's analogy fails given the fact that the two types of incapacity are essentially dissimilar. Williston, *supra*, §10:3. "An infant is often mentally competent in fact to understand the force of his bargain, but it is the policy of the law to protect the minor. By contrast, the adult mental incompetent may be subject to varying degrees of infirmity or mental illness, not all equally incapacitating." *Id.* This difference in part accounts for the majority of jurisdictions holding that absent fraud or knowledge of the incapacity by the other contracting party, the contractual act of an incompetent is voidable by the incompetent only if avoidance accords with equitable principles. *Id.* Accordingly, we conclude that the infancy doctrine does not apply to cases of mental incompetence.

B. Good Faith

The jury was presented with the following special verdict question: "Did the defendant, Union State Bank of Wautoma, fail to act in good faith toward [Hauer] in the loan transaction?" The jury answered that question, "Yes." In denying the Bank's motions after verdict, the court concluded that even if the infancy doctrine did not apply, the jury's finding that the Bank failed to act in good faith in the loan transaction distinguished this case from the "general rule" providing that the person seeking relief from a contract must return the consideration paid. We agree. Before we address this issue, however, we must first deal with the Bank's preliminary arguments concerning the applicability of "good faith."

. . .

. . . Section 401.203, Stats., is a general provision of Wisconsin's Uniform Commercial Code. According to § 401.203, "[e]very contract or duty within [the Uniform Commercial Code] imposes an obligation of good faith in its *performance or enforcement.*" (Emphasis added.) However, at issue in this case is the Bank's good faith in the *formation* of the contract with Hauer. Because the general requirement of good faith under this section applies only to the performance or enforcement of a contract, it does not impose a duty of good faith in the negotiation and formation of contracts. See Robert S. Summers, *"Good Faith" in General Contract Law and the Sales Provisions of the Uniform Commercial Code,* 54 Va. L. Rev. 195, 220 (1968).

The trial court, therefore, erroneously created a cause of action under §401.203, Stats. . . .

. . .

3. Mental Incompetency and Common Law Duty of Good Faith

Based on the above discussion, we agree with the Bank that Hauer did not have a *separate* cause of action for lack of good faith in tort or in contract under §401.203, Stats. However, we disagree with the Bank that this ends the analysis. Rather, the concept of good faith is relevant to the effect of Hauer's successful claim to void the contract based on mental incompetence.

Wisconsin common law, like other states, reads the duty of good faith into every contract. *See Market Street Assocs. Ltd. Partnership v. Frey,* 941 F.2d 588, 592 (7th Cir. 1991) (citing Wisconsin law). The great weight of authority from other jurisdictions provides that the unadjudicated mental incompetence of one of the parties is not a sufficient reason for setting aside an executed contract if the parties cannot be restored to their original positions, provided that the contract was made in good faith, for a fair consideration and without knowledge of the incompetence. Williston, *supra,* §10:3.

Stated differently, if the contract is made on fair terms and the other party has no reason to know of the incompetency, the contract ceases to be voidable where performance in whole or in part changes the situation such that the parties cannot be restored to their previous positions. Restatement, *supra,* §15 cmt. *f.* [Footnote omitted.] If, on the other hand, the other party knew of the incompetency or took unfair advantage of the incompetent, consideration dissipated without benefit to the incompetent need not be restored. *Id.* at cmt. *e.*

The Bank asserts that "[i]f a contract is entered into between two adults, each of whom has no actual knowledge of incompetence about the other, it would produce profound, unfair and inequitable results if that contract . . . becomes void and leaves one party with absolutely no remedy or recourse to be returned to their precontract condition." We agree with this statement on its face. However, the Bank's argument assumes a material fact at issue—whether the Bank knew that Hauer was mentally incompetent at the time of the loan. Further, the question of knowledge is not limited to "actual knowledge," but also includes whether the Bank had reason to know of the incompetence. *See* Restatement, *supra*, §15(1)(b); *see also Casson,* 166 Wis. at 406, 166 N.W. at 24 (cause of action existed where mental incompetence was "known or ought to have been known by the defendants").

Whether the Bank knew or had reason to know that Hauer was incompetent is a question of fact for the jury to decide. . . .

. . .

The Bank argues that it does not have an affirmative duty to inquire into the mental capacity of a loan applicant to evaluate his or her capacity to understand a proposed transaction. We agree. However, a contracting party exposes itself to a voidable contract where it is put on notice or given a reason to suspect the other party's incompetence such as would indicate to a reasonably prudent person that inquiry should be made of the party's mental condition. *See Hedgepeth v. Home Savs. and Loan Ass'n,* 87 N.C. App. 610, 361 S.E.2d 888, 889-890 (1987). As the trial court aptly stated: "I did not say there's any duty to make an investigation, but the bank takes a risk the contract will be . . . voidable if they know of facts which support the claim of inability to contract."

We agree that ideally the knowledge question should have been given to the jury as suggested in Hauer's proposed special verdict. However, we are bound by the record as it comes to us. *Fiumefreddo v. McLean*, 174 Wis. 2d 10, 26, 496 N.W.2d 226, 232 (Ct. App. 1993). We conclude that the finding that the Bank knew or had reason to know that Hauer was mentally incompetent to understand the nature of the loan at the time it was entered into is inherent and intertwined in the jury's finding that the Bank failed to act in good faith. This is necessarily true because the Bank could not have been found to have lacked good faith as a matter of law absent knowledge of the incompetency. The two findings are inseparable. [Foonote omitted.]

4. Sufficiency of the Evidence

The last question we must address is whether there was any credible evidence to sustain the jury's verdict that the Bank failed to act in good faith. If there is, we are bound to sustain the jury's verdict. *Fehring*, 118 Wis. 2d at 305, 347 N.W.2d at 598.

The Bank contends that "[t]he record is devoid of any evidence that the Bank had knowledge of any facts which created a suspicion that it should not enter the loan." We agree with the trial court's summary that there is evidence in the record "that there were flags up that would prompt a reasonable banker to move more slowly and more carefully in the transaction."

For example, the Bank knew that Eilbes was in default of his loan at the Bank. Eilbes approached the Bank and laid all the groundwork for a loan to be given to a third-party investor, Hauer, whom the Bank did not know. Eilbes told Schroeder that he would make his defaulted loan current or pay it off entirely with Hauer's investment. Schroeder testified that upon investigating the matter initially, Hauer's stockbroker told him not to use Hauer's fund as collateral because she needed the fund to live on and Hauer could not afford to lose the fund. He further testified that it was possible that the stockbroker told him that Hauer suffered a brain injury. In addition, Hauer's banking expert opined that the Bank should not have made the loan. Accordingly, we conclude that the evidence and reasonable inferences that can

be drawn from the evidence support the jury's conclusion that the Bank failed to act in good faith.

. . .

. . . Judgment affirmed.

Post-Case Follow-Up

The court determined that Hauer's release from guardianship did not ensure that she was competent to enter into a loan contract a year later. She provided substantial expert testimony along with her own testimony to show that she lacked mental capacity. If a party had knowledge, either actual or constructive, that the other party lacked the mental capacity to enter into a contract, that contract was voidable by the party who lacked capacity. Based on expert testimony and the circumstances of the case, the court determined that the bank failed to show good faith in making the loan to Hauer. Therefore, the bank was required to return her mutual fund used as collateral for the loan. Her inability to return any of the loan funds was not unjust to the bank under the circumstances.

Hauer v. Union State Bank of Wautoma: Real Life Applications

1. Barton frequents a casino where he applied for and received a line of credit. Under the credit arrangement, he agreed to repay any gambling losses within a specified period of time. After a bad losing streak, he does not pay the loans on time and checks he deposited with the casino are returned due to insufficient funds. He claims he is not responsible for the debts because he lacked capacity due to the mental illness of "pathological gambling" and that medication he took for back pain altered his mental capacity to enter into the credit agreement. Examine *Mashantucket Pequot Gaming Enter. v. Freund*, 2005 Mashantucket Trib. LEXIS 6 (2005) and determine whether Barton has met his burden of proof as to mental incapacity.

2. Delia accumulates credit card debt and fails to pay her outstanding balance under the terms of her credit card agreement. She files for bankruptcy and seeks to discharge her credit card debt. Delia claims that she suffers from an obsessive-compulsive disorder and is unable to control her spending habits. As the law clerk for the bankruptcy court judge in this case, review *In re Borste*, 117 B.R. 995 (Bankr. W.D. Wash. 1990) and draft a brief memo discussing whether Delia is liable for her debt under the credit card agreement.

3. Pat suffers from bouts of epilepsy and chronic paranoid schizophrenia. She lives on a remote property and her illnesses have resulted in her no longer being able to drive. Although she is handling her own business and personal affairs, her doctor recommends that she move closer to family members for their longer-term assistance. Her brother, Joe, is concerned about her condition and applies to the court

to become her guardian. Before the court rules on Joe's application, Pat decides to sell her property to a neighbor, who has helped her out through the years, at below market value. Joe now wants to rescind the purchase agreement, claiming his sister's mental incapacity. What evidence will a court consider in determining Pat's mental state? Read and brief *First Nat'l Bank v. Nennig*, 92 Wis. 2d 518 (1979) and summarize the court's review of a similar case.

---

3. Intoxication—Voidable

Intoxication applies to people under the influence of substances that impair a person's ability to make good decisions. If one party has reason to know that intoxication prevents the other from being able to understand the nature and consequences of a transaction or from being able to act reasonably in relation to the transaction, the contract is voidable at the election of the intoxicated person. This rule resembles the rule for mental illness, but with some interesting differences. The analysis follows a nearly identical set of questions.

1. Was the person raising the defense intoxicated?
2. Was the person either
   a. unable to understand the nature or consequences of the transaction; or
   b. unable to act reasonably (perform) in relation to the transaction and the other party knew or had reason to know of the condition?
3. Did the intoxication cause the inability to understand or to act reasonably?

The existence of the intoxication, the severity of the intoxication, and the causal relationship between the two forms of incapacity are identical. See Exhibit 6.2.

But the notice requirement for intoxication is harder to satisfy than the notice provision for mental illness or defect. First, the notice provision applies to both cognitive and volitional problems. No matter how the intoxication affected the person, the defense applies only if the other party knew or had reason to know of the effects

EXHIBIT 6.2 Intoxication Defense

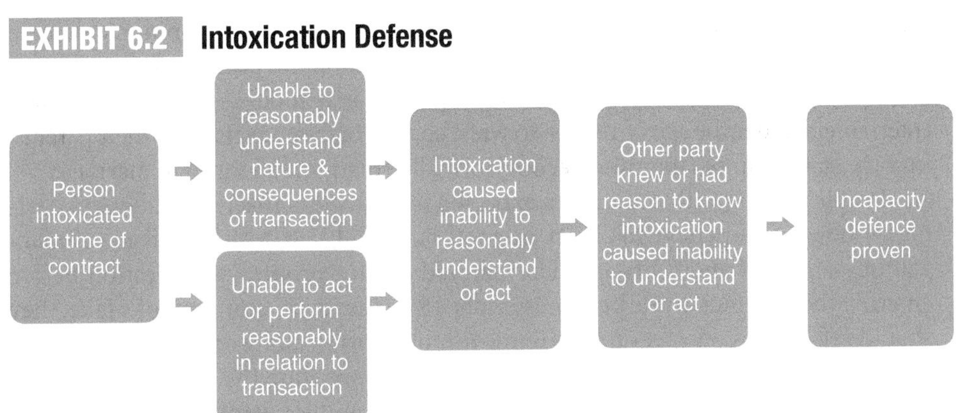

of intoxication on that person. Just knowing someone is intoxicated is not sufficient. Unless the other party knew or had reason to know that the intoxication caused an inability to understand or to act reasonably in relationship to the transaction, the defense fails. The reliance provision of the rule on mental illness also does not apply to intoxication, so there is no review of good faith or the interests of justice.

4. Infancy Doctrine—Voidable

Under the classical view, minors were not permitted to enter into contracts under the **infancy doctrine**, which viewed children as lacking capacity. This approach sought to protect minors from adults who might take advantage of their lack of maturity in contract situations and determined that such agreements were void.

Over time, classical contract law evolved to allow minors to enter into some contracts. The **doctrine of necessaries** allowed children to make contracts for the essentials of life—food, clothing, and shelter, and potentially more, such as emergency medical care or legal services. These contracts required a showing that the child needed the benefits of the contract, not just that she wanted them. Thus, if a child was welcome in her parents' house, an apartment lease might be voidable by her even though it provided shelter. The shelter may be viewed as unnecessary. If a contract for necessaries is challenged by a minor, a court may scrutinize the terms for fairness, particularly that the minor is not being overcharged, but is paying the fair market value under the contract for necessaries. Any other needs were considered nonnecessaries, and these contracts with minors remained void under the traditional view.

The modern view now recognizes that minors may be capable of entering into a broad range of contracts. The doctrine of necessaries remains, but minors may now enter into agreements for nonnecessaries. On the day before a person turns age 18, she attains the capacity to enter into contracts. Any contract entered by the minor before that day is voidable at the minor's election. Voidability applies to even the most intelligent and mature minors. No showing of inability to understand or to act reasonably is required. Age at the time the contract was made determines the defense. Presumably, parents (or a legal guardian) will make any contracts that a minor needs until that date.

A minor's incapacity may be stripped away if the minor seeks **formal emancipation**, which are legal proceedings allowing a court to decree that the minor should be treated as an adult, despite not having reached age 18. These proceedings were more common when the age of majority was 21, but can arise today—for example, when entertainers under the age of 18 seek to wrest control of their assets from their parents. In some states, minors may also become formally emancipated through marriage.

People dealing with minors are expected to protect themselves. The party dealing with a young person must act in good faith and fair dealing and not remain willfully ignorant about his age. They should ask for proper identification before entering the contract. If the person is under 18 or the identification looks fake, they should refuse the contract or require the minor to bring along an appropriate adult co-signer. If a minor lies about his age, fraud may preclude the incapacity defense in some states. In effect, the minor's inequitable conduct **estops** or prevents him from taking advantage of the incapacity defense. One who seeks equity must come before the court with **clean hands**, not having acted inequitably himself regarding this transaction. However, many courts will find that misrepresenting one's age is a sign of immaturity and still allow the minor to claim the incapacity defense.

If parties decide to enter into a contract with a minor, they do so at their own risk. The minor may disaffirm a contract any time until the age of 18 or a reasonable time thereafter. Reasonableness of the time period will depend upon the circumstances of the case. Traditionally, the minor who has received nonnecessary goods or services under a contract is only mandated to return in whole or part what she still possesses from the deal, such as the item or any proceeds from the contract, in return for a full refund. Similarly, a minor may continue to perform her contract duties after reaching age 18, providing she ratifies the contract entered into as a minor.

Problems can also arise when parents make a contract for a minor that involves rights or duties extending past the age of majority. For instance, if parents agree that photographs of their child may be used in an advertising campaign, there is a question as to whether the child (after reaching 18) may rescind the contract and prevent any future use of her image. These cases are rare and inconsistent. On one hand, competent parties on each side made a mutually beneficial bargain. This situation is not a case when the child's incapacity deprives the court of confidence that the transaction was mutually beneficial since assent came from adults. Barring a claim that the parents breached a fiduciary duty owed to the child, no reason for rescission appears. On the other hand, once the child is 18, she is entitled to make her own decisions, which might differ from those her parents made. As to any future performance, that autonomy may deserve respect. While the first argument seems more persuasive, the second has prevailed in some cases.

5. Restitution for Incapacity

When a party avoids a contract under an incapacity defense, she is entitled to restitution. That is, she returns whatever she received under the contract and receives whatever she gave up under the contract. For example, if a teenager buys a bunny at a pet store, she (or her parents) can return the bunny and get her money back. This basic remedy works well when a thing is bought and is still in the same condition as when purchased. It works less well when the thing has been consumed or damaged (say, the teen bought a motorcycle rather than a bunny). It may be more difficult, if not impossible, when the contract involves services that have already been performed, such as dance lessons or home remodeling.

In incapacity situations, restitution can break down into two steps. First, the party avoiding a contract recovers what it provided under the agreement. The contract has become invalid, so the other party has no right to keep that performance. Keeping it would unjustly enrich the recipient. If the other party cannot return exactly what the avoiding party provided, then the value of that performance will be calculated to accomplish restitution.

Second, the other party recovers what it provided to the avoiding (incapacitated) party. Restitution to the avoiding party means she has not paid for the performance.

Keeping the performance would unjustly enrich her. Where the specific thing provided cannot be returned, however, courts are reluctant to award the value of the performance. Doing so might enforce the contract itself, or something very close to it. For example, suppose an incapacity makes a contract to paint a house unenforceable. Returning the price to the homeowner is easy. But if the painter has a claim for the services provided at the fair market value, the owner still pays for something she arguably did not need or want, in an amount that might equal the contract price.

A minority of modern courts will balance protecting the party who performed under the contract with the protection the incapacitated person deserves under the **benefit rule**, which permits restitution against a person, despite the incapacity defense. It starts by recognizing the right of parties to recover restitution, in part or in whole, from an incapacitated person who received a benefit. The court will then consider whether that person, often a merchant, dealt in good faith and on reasonable terms with the incapacitated person. This rule provides that restitution to the performing party may be limited or denied if restitution would be inconsistent with the protection that the incapacity defense provides to individuals, as found in *Hauer*.

Case Preview

Dodson v. Shrader

Courts have struggled with the issue of protecting minors from adults while being fair to adults who dealt with minors in good faith. In *Dodson v. Shrader*, a court must determine whether a minor can return a vehicle that is practically worthless in exchange for a full refund of the purchase price. In this decision, the court charts the evolution of the infancy doctrine and points to a further change in the common law that balances party interests under the benefit rule.

As you read *Dodson v. Shrader*, look for the following:

1. How did the court define two different approaches to the benefit rule regarding refunds for minors claiming incapacity?
2. What obligations were placed on the merchant before a court will consider the application of the benefit rule?
3. What key facts were reviewed before the court decided what refund, if any, the minor should receive in exchange for his return of the damaged vehicle?

Dodson v. Shrader

824 S.W.2d 545 (Tenn. 1992)

O'Brien, J.

This is an action to disaffirm the contract of a minor for the purchase of a pick-up truck and for a refund of the purchase price. The issue is whether the minor is entitled to a full refund of the money he paid or whether the seller is entitled to a setoff for the decrease in value of the pick-up truck while it was in the possession of the minor.

In early April of 1987, Joseph Eugene Dodson, then 16 years of age, purchased a used 1984 pick-up truck from Burns and Mary Shrader. The Shraders owned and operated Shrader's Auto Sales in Columbia, Tennessee. Dodson paid $4,900 in cash for the truck, using money he borrowed from his girlfriend's grandmother. At the time of the purchase there was no inquiry by the Shraders, and no misrepresentation by Mr. Dodson, concerning his minority. However, Mr. Shrader did testify that at the time he believed Mr. Dodson to be 18 or 19 years of age.

In December 1987, nine (9) months after the date of purchase, the truck began to develop mechanical problems. A mechanic diagnosed the problem as a burnt valve, but could not be certain without inspecting the valves inside the engine. Mr. Dodson did not want, or did not have the money, to effect these repairs. He continued to drive the truck despite the mechanical problems. One month later, in January, the truck's engine "blew up" and the truck became inoperable.

Mr. Dodson parked the vehicle in the front yard at his parents' home where he lived. He contacted the Shraders to rescind the purchase of the truck and requested a full refund. The Shraders refused to accept the tender of the truck or to give Mr. Dodson the refund requested.

Mr. Dodson then filed an action in general sessions court seeking to rescind the contract and recover the amount paid for the truck. The general sessions court dismissed the warrant and Mr. Dodson perfected a *de novo* appeal to the circuit court. At the time the appeal was filed in the circuit court Mr. Shrader, through counsel, declined to accept the tender of the truck without compensation for its depreciation. Before the circuit court could hear the case, the truck, while parked in Dodson's front yard, was struck on the left front fender by a hit-and-run driver. At the time of the circuit court trial, according to Shrader, the truck was worth only $500 due to the damage to the engine and the left front fender.

The case was heard in the circuit court in November 1988. The trial judge, based on previous common-law decisions and, under the doctrine of stare decisis reluctantly granted the rescission. The Shraders were ordered, upon tender and delivery of the truck, to reimburse the $4,900 purchase price to Mr. Dodson. The Shraders appealed.

. . .

The earliest recorded case in this State, on the issue involved, appears to be in *Wheaton v. East,* 13 Tenn. 35 (5 Yeager 41) (1833). In pronouncing the rule to apply governing infant's contracts, the court said:

> We do not perceive that any general rule, as to contracts which are void and voidable, can be stated with more precision that is done by Lord Ch. J. Eyre in *Keane v. Boycott,* . . . that when the court can pronounce the contract to be to the infant's prejudice, it is void, and when to his benefit, as for necessaries, it is good; and when the contract is of any uncertain nature, as to benefit or prejudice, it is voidable only, at the election of the infant." . . .

The law on the subject of the protection of infant's rights has been slow to evolve. However, in *Human v. Hartsell,* 24 Tenn. App. 678, 148 S.W.2d 634, 636 (1940) the Court of Appeals noted:

> . . . In *Tuck v. Payne*, 159 Tenn. 192, 17 S.W.2d 8, in an opinion by Mr. Justice McKinney, the modern rule that contracts of infants are not void but only voidable and subject to be disaffirmed by the minor either before or after attaining majority appears to have been favored.
>
> Under this rule the efforts of early authorities to classify contracts as beneficial or harmful and determine whether they are void or only voidable upon the basis of such classification are abandoned in favor of permitting the infant himself when he has become of age to determine what contracts are and what are not to his interest and liking. He is thus permitted to assume the burden of a contract, clearly disadvantageous to him, if he deems himself under a moral obligation to do so.
>
> The adoption of this rule does not lead to any retrenchment of the infant's rights but gives him the option of invoking contracts found to be advantageous but which, if held void, could not be enforced against the other party to the contract. Thus the minor can secure the advantage of contracts advantageous to himself and be relieved of the effect of an injudicious contract.

In *Tuck, supra*, p. 9, the court applied the rule based upon the maxims that he who seeks equity must do equity, that he who comes into equity must come with clean hands, that no one can take advantage of his own wrong, that he that has committed inequity shall not have equity, and that minors will not be permitted to use the shield of infancy as a cover, or turn it into a sword with which to injure others dealing with them in good faith.

As noted by the Court of Appeals, the rule in Tennessee, as modified, is in accord with the majority rule on the issue among our sister states. This rule is based upon the underlying purpose of the "infancy doctrine" which is to protect minors from their lack of judgment and "from squandering their wealth through improvident contracts with crafty adults who would take advantage of them in the marketplace." *Halbman v. Lemke*, 99 Wis. 2d 241, 245, 298 N.W.2d 562, 564 (1980).

There is, however, a modern trend among the states, either by judicial action or by statute, in the approach to the problem of balancing the rights of minors against those of innocent merchants. As a result, two (2) minority rules have developed which allow the other party to a contract with a minor to refund less than the full consideration paid in the event of rescission.

The first of these minority rules is called the "Benefit Rule." [Citations omitted.] The rule holds that, upon rescission, recovery of the full purchase price is subject to a deduction for the minor's use of the merchandise. This rule recognizes that the traditional rule in regard to necessaries has been extended so far as to hold an infant bound by his contracts, where he failed to restore what he has received under them to the extent of the benefit actually derived by him from what he has received from the other party to the transaction. [Citations omitted.] . . .

The other minority rule holds that the minor's recovery of the full purchase price is subject to a deduction for the minor's "use" of the consideration he or she received under the contract, or for the "depreciation" or "deterioration" of the consideration in his or her possession. [Citations omitted.] . . .

We are impressed by the statement made by the Arizona Appeals Court in *Valencia v. White, supra*, citing the Court of Appeals of Ohio in *Haydocy Pontiac Inc. v. Lee*, 19 Ohio App. 2d 217, 250 N.E.2d 898 (1969):

> At a time when we see young persons between 18 and 21 years of age demanding and assuming more responsibilities in their daily lives; when we see such persons emancipated, married, and raising families; when we see such persons charged with the responsibility for committing crimes; when we see such persons being sued in tort claims for acts of negligence; when we see such persons subject to military service; when we see such persons engaged in business and acting in almost all other respects as an adult, it seems timely to re-examine the case law pertaining to contractual rights and responsibilities of infants to see if the law as pronounced and applied by the courts should be redefined.

. . .

Upon serious reflection we are convinced that a modified form . . . should be adopted in this State concerning the rights and responsibilities of minors in their business dealings.

. . .

We state the rule to be followed hereafter, in reference to a contract of a minor, to be where the minor has not been overreached in any way, and there has been no undue influence, and the contract is a fair and reasonable one, and the minor has actually paid money on the purchase price, and taken and used the article purchased, that he ought not to be permitted to recover the amount actually paid, without allowing the vendor of the goods reasonable compensation for the use of, depreciation, and willful or negligent damage to the article purchased, while in his hands. If there has been any fraud or imposition on the part of the seller or if the contract is unfair, or any unfair advantage has been taken of the minor inducing him to make the purchase, then the rule does not apply. Whether there has been such an overreaching on the part of the seller, and the fair market value of the property returned, would always, in any case, be a question for the trier of fact. This rule will fully and fairly protect the minor against injustice or imposition, and at the same time it will be fair to a business person who has dealt with such minor in good faith.

This rule is best adapted to modern conditions under which minors are permitted to, and do in fact, transact a great deal of business for themselves, long before they have reached the age of legal majority. Many young people work and earn money and collect it and spend it oftentimes without any oversight or restriction. The law does not question their right to buy if they have the money to pay for their purchases. It seems intolerably burdensome for everyone concerned if merchants and business people cannot deal with them safely, in a fair and reasonable way. Further, it does not appear consistent with practice of proper moral influence upon young people, tend to encourage honesty and integrity, or lead them to a good and useful business future, if they are taught that they can make purchases with their own money, for their own benefit, and after paying for them, and using them until they are worn out and destroyed, go back and compel the vendor to return to them what they have paid

upon the purchase price. Such a doctrine can only lead to the corruption of principles and encourage young people in habits of trickery and dishonesty.

. . .

We note that in this case, some nine (9) months after the date of purchase, the truck purchased by the plaintiff began to develop mechanical problems. Plaintiff was informed of the probable nature of the difficulty which apparently involved internal problems in the engine. He continued to drive the vehicle until the engine "blew up" and the truck became inoperable. Whether or not this involved gross negligence or intentional conduct on his part is a matter for determination at the trial level. It is not possible to determine from this record whether a counterclaim for tortious damage to the vehicle was asserted. After the first tender of the vehicle was made by plaintiff, and refused by the defendant, the truck was damaged by a hit-and-run driver while parked on plaintiff's property. The amount of that damage and the liability for that amount between the purchaser and the vendor, as well as the fair market value of the vehicle at the time of tender, is also an issue for the trier of fact.

The case is remanded to the trial court for further proceedings in accordance with this judgment. . . .

Post-Case Follow-Up

The *Dodson* court balanced the interests of the merchant acting in good faith with those of the minor claiming incapacity. The court found that absent any overreaching, fraud, or unfair advantage on the part of the adult, a seller was entitled to reasonable compensation for the use of, depreciation, or willful or negligent damage done to goods sold, while these goods were in the minor's possession. Embracing the minority point of view on the benefit rule, the court remanded the case for a factual determination of what amounts were due to the minor under the circumstances of this case.

Dodson v. Shrader: Real Life Applications

1. A 16-year-old, Johnny, goes to a car dealership to buy a vehicle. He is turned away as too young, but returns with an adult, Harry, he met that morning to finalize the deal. Johnny gives a cashier's check to the dealer who arranges the paperwork to make it appear that the car is being sold to Harry, not Johnny. The dealer drives the two to a local notary public so title can be transferred to Johnny. When Johnny's parents see the vehicle, they contact the dealer to try to return it, but the dealer refuses to take the car back. It is later badly damaged in two accidents. If Johnny's parents again try to disaffirm the purchase, will the court likely apply the benefit rule to the damaged car? Review *Quality Motors, Inc. v. Hays*, 216 Ark. 264 (1949) and summarize the case and its likely outcome.

2. A company agrees to make a loan to a minor who promised to repay it with funds from a guardianship account. She buys furniture and a new house with the loan money. When she turns 18, she disaffirms her agreement and tries to

turn over the house and furniture to the company. The company refuses and sues for payment from her guardianship account. She comes to you for advice on what to do. Read *In re Ferguson's Guardianship*, 41 N.Y.S.2d 862, 863 (N.Y. Sur. Ct. 1943) and draft a client letter with your advice.

3. A husband borrows $3,000 from a bank using his property as collateral. He does not pay his debt and the bank seeks to foreclose on his property to repay the debt. His wife brings an action on his behalf, claiming that he was insane at the time of the loan agreement. The husband has $3,000 or its equivalent to pay off the debt. If the husband is insane, will he have to pay restitution to rescind the agreement? Consider *Fields v. Union Cent. Life Ins. Co.*, 170 Ga. 239 (1930) in determining the likely outcome.

C. DURESS

The defense of duress considers situations in which a party lacks meaningful choice in entering into a contract. This lack of voluntary decision making taints claims of mutual assent by the parties—an integral element in contract formation. In addition, a party placing another under duress in order to gain a contractual commitment is not exercising good faith and fair dealing in its conduct.

Case law and the Restatement (Second) of Contracts identify two types of duress: **physical compulsion**, focusing on threats to life, limb, or liberty (§174); and **economic duress**, examining wrongful or improper financial or commercial threats, typically in a business context (§175). Physical compulsion or duress is considered void. Economic duress is viewed as voidable. We will discuss each concept in turn.

1. Physical Compulsion—Void

Until the nineteenth century, duress was a relatively simple defense. Only physical duress or compulsion counted as actionable duress involving fear of loss of life or limb, mayhem, or imprisonment. This fear must induce the party to agree to contract terms. Under the traditional view, one's fear was judged on an objective standard. The courts examined whether the circumstances would overpower the determination or will of a person of ordinary or reasonable courage. This measuring stick meant that victims had to risk their lives and justify their fear based on a mythical reasonable person to support this defense. Over time, this approach gave way to a subjective approach that examined the actual trepidation of the person being induced to enter into the contract by the physical threat.

The doctrine also broadened to cover inducement based on threats to third parties, such as family members or friends, as well as to violent threats against property. In *Central Bank of Frederick v. Copeland*, 18 Md. 305 (1862), a court found physical duress when a party threatened violent acts against property, burning down the family home, in order to force a wife to sign a mortgage for her husband's debt, at the urging of his creditors. Although instances of physical duress are not common in modern contract law, this form of duress is distinct from economic duress.

2. Economic Duress—Voidable

Unlike threats of physical harm, threats to one's finances often seem possible to resist. Instead of succumbing to the threat, one might "just say no!" The consequences are only money, which can be recovered in a later lawsuit. As parties found they could coerce assent by use of lesser threats, the law expanded duress to include a larger range of conduct, such as financial pressure under economic duress. The party claiming duress must show

1. a wrongful or improper threat;
2. actual inducement into the contract due to the threat; and
3. a lack of reasonable alternatives to avoid the threatened harm.

All three elements are necessary to establish duress. Failure to establish even one element makes this defense unsuccessful. See Exhibit 6.3.

EXHIBIT 6.3 Venn Diagram for Economic Duress

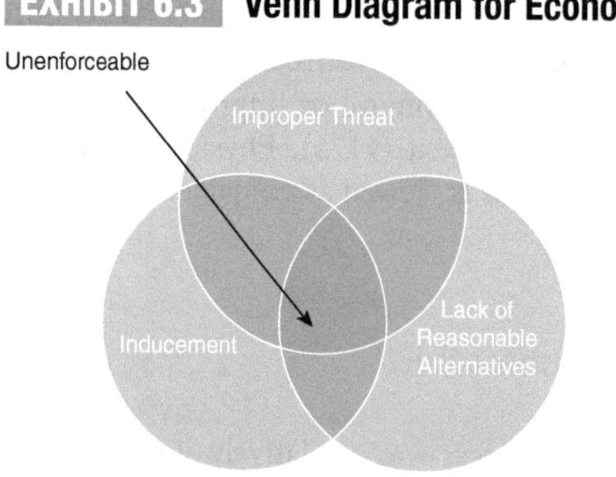

Wrongful or Improper Threat

In raising this defense, one must be able to identify a wrongful or improper threat. Such threats do not need to be illegal in character, but must be unfairly coercive in contravention of good faith and fair dealing. Implied threats or conduct that a reasonable person would understand as a threat may coerce assent along with more direct or express threats. Restatement (Second) of Contracts §176 attempts to identify improper threats, and courts commonly use this list to guide them as to coercive tactics. Some main examples are threatened crime or tort; threats of criminal prosecution; withholding payment of admitted debt; threatened civil process made in bad faith; and breach of duty of good faith and fair dealing (bad faith).

The general nature of these kinds of threats may end up applying this defense to too many contracts, including some that should be enforced. In addition, it may be difficult to draw a distinction between hard bargaining and improper threats. In general, courts are reluctant to apply this form of duress when the contract terms appear to be fair under the circumstances.

Crime or Tort

When the threatened act is a crime or a tort, the threat obviously is improper. No one has a right to commit a crime or a tort. Thus, forbearing from a crime or tort is not something a person has a right to demand. There is also a preexisting duty to refrain from the threatened conduct, so the promise cannot be consideration for that forbearance.

In some cases, the threatened act is not a crime or a tort, but the threat itself is a crime or a tort (or would be if it succeeded in obtaining property). Consider a person in possession of accurate but embarrassing information or photographs. The person has a right to send them to the press or to any other person who might be interested (say, a spouse). But a threat to reveal the information unless the other agrees to pay money constitutes extortion. The act is acceptable, but the threat is criminal if it results in the demanded payment.

Criminal Prosecution

Threatening a criminal prosecution is improper. One with information about a crime has a right (perhaps a duty) to report that information to the authorities. Threatening to report the information unless another agrees to a contract is improper. The state's power to prosecute crimes is intended to serve public purposes. People cannot harness that power for private gain by threatening to institute criminal proceedings.

This situation is particularly difficult for some lawyers. Suppose your client has a civil suit against another person. In the course of discovery, you learn that the opposing party may also have violated the criminal law. The temptation to ask them to settle your case in order to reduce exposure to criminal sanctions might be great. However, that threat is improper. There is no bright line to delineate how much one can say before the comments become an implicit threat to report the crime unless the other party settles. Steering well clear of this line and focusing on the matter in dispute seems to be the better course of action.

Abuse of Civil Process

Use of civil process in bad faith often is a tort. **Abuse of process** and **malicious prosecution** are two torts that allow remedies against people who file civil pleadings (claims or defenses) when they know they have no chance to succeed. This provision, then, may be superfluous. At a minimum, it clarifies the application of duress to **strike suits** (suits brought in the hope of obtaining a settlement, with no real expectation that the suit ever could prevail). People who threaten to bring suits that they know are invalid cannot enforce the settlements that they coerce. In addition, the language here may extend to some use of process that falls outside the tort law.

Breach of Good Faith Under a Contract

In some ways, breach of an obligation of good faith and fair dealing under a contract is the most important of the provisions. The rule must preserve parties' ability to bargain for changes to a contract without permitting one party to force changes on the other. Thus, when the cost of performance increases dramatically, a supplier might ask for a price increase — perhaps using words that imply a threat to breach unless the contract is modified (say, "I can't perform at this price"). Similarly, a financially strapped person might ask a creditor to accept less than full payment, perhaps saying that it will not pay at all unless the creditor accepts the proposed change in terms. Courts often find these threats to be legal efforts at renegotiation. Adjusting contracts in the face of new conditions is ordinary business behavior, not some improper conduct society should always squelch.

Other threats pose more difficulty, especially when the threat seems to take advantage of the other party's vulnerability rather than to seek adjustment for changed circumstances. A party entering a contract often gives up the ability to deal with others. Once dependent on the other party, that party's threat to breach gains power. It can extract terms that it never could have negotiated while the first party had others with whom it could deal instead. For example, in our earlier discussion of *Alaska Packers' Assn. v. Domenico*, 117 F. 99 (9th Cir. 1902), the fishermen's threat not to work took on added power because the employer claimed difficulty in obtaining substitute workers in time for that year's salmon run. Similarly, in the key case of *Totem Marine Tug & Barge, Inc. v. Alyeska Pipeline Service Co.*, 584 P.2d 15 (Alaska 1978), a court found economic duress when a company that owed a debt and knowing of the other party's immediate financial need, refused to pay unless the other party agreed to substantially less compensation than the debt amount in a release.

The best dividing line — albeit imprecise — may focus on the reason for threatening to breach. If the party threatening to breach a contract has a reasonable justification, then the threat may not be viewed as improper. Where a party faces unexpected hardship performing the contract, an honest reason seems present. But if a party has no honest reason for threatening to breach, the threat may be held improper. If the party seeks to take advantage of the other's vulnerability, without more extenuating circumstances, then the threat seems improper. This rule will run up against concerns for pretext. A party making a threat may find some reasons to justify the threat (such as the bad nets in *Alaska Packers*). In evaluating the legitimacy of the proposed justification, the test is not reasonableness, but good faith: did the person making the threat honestly believe the reasons for the threat required assent to the contract (or changes) it requested?

Threat Induces Party Assent

Duress requires that the threat induced a party's manifestation of assent with the threat being a substantial factor in the decision. The threatened party need not prove that she would not have agreed, but for the threat. However, there must be a clear causal link between the wrongful or improper threat and the party's inducement. Applying a subjective approach, the court considers if the wrongful or improper threat induced this person to agree to the contract, rather than whether it would induce a reasonable person.

On the other hand, the threatening party may undermine another's claim of inducement if it can be shown that the party claiming the defense would have agreed on other grounds, even if no threat had been made. A court will analyze the factual circumstances to determine whether or not the threat was a key factor in the decision. Allowing someone to avoid a contract that he would have made anyway, even if not threatened, does not support the purposes behind the defense.

It is important that the party claiming duress promptly raise the issue to avoid the other party's believing that the assent is voluntary. Protesting or otherwise communicating that the other party's conduct is coercive will strengthen a claim of economic duress. In addition, if a party benefits from the allegedly coerced agreement, courts may view delays in challenging the contract as ratifying the validity of the agreement and undermining a later claim of duress.

Lack of Reasonable Alternatives

Under duress, a person's free will may not be overcome if there are other reasonable ways to avoid the threatened harm without assenting to the contract. The existence of reasonable alternatives defeats the defense of duress, particularly if a party has an opportunity to explore options before entering into the contract. Some common options may be to seek protection from the courts or to find substitute goods if a party threatens nondelivery. In some instances, the risk of financial losses may be delayed by borrowing money to cover a temporary loss. Alternatives should help avoid the harm.

Often, legal action offers an effective alternative. Faced with a threat to breach a contract, the party claiming duress might avoid the threatened harm by suing. One might seek equitable relief, such as a court **injunction**, which may compel or stop certain conduct, to avoid succumbing to duress. Alternatively, a party may seek legal remedies that are money **damages** to compensate for any harm caused if one does not give in to a wrongful or improper threat. If legal action will fully protect the person's interests, rejecting the threatening behavior would be reasonable and illustrates that the party has not lost meaningful choice. However, legal action will not provide a reasonable option to turn back a wrongful or improper threat if it cannot be resolved in a timely manner.

Case Preview

Austin Instrument v. Loral Corp.

In *Austin Instrument v. Loral Corp.*, Austin Instrument, a subcontractor on a federal government contract, threatened not to supply parts promised unless paid a higher price. The threat was not motivated by any changed circumstances. The contractor, Loral Corp., could face serious penalties under its government contract if it did not make timely deliveries. The court must consider whether business wrangling over higher prices could be a form of economic duress.

As you read *Austin Instrument v. Loral Corp.*, look for the following:

1. What was the wrongful or improper threat in this instance?
2. Did Loral have other reasonable alternatives in light of Austin's plan to cease its deliveries?
3. Did Austin's threat induce Loral to revise the contract price? Did Loral act promptly or did it ratify its modifications in its contract with Austin?

Austin Instrument v. Loral Corp.

272 N.E.2d 533 (N.Y. 1971)

FULD, J.

The defendant, Loral Corporation, seeks to recover payment for goods delivered under a contract which it had with plaintiff Austin Instrument, Inc., on the ground that the evidence establishes, as a matter of law, that it was forced to agree to an increase in price on the items in question under circumstances amounting to economic duress.

In July of 1965, Loral was awarded a $6,000,000 contract by the Navy for the production of radar sets. The contract contained a schedule of deliveries, a liquidated damages clause applying to late deliveries and a cancellation clause in case of default by Loral. The latter thereupon solicited bids for some 40 precision gear components needed to produce the radar sets, and awarded Austin a subcontract to supply 23 such parts. That party commenced delivery in early 1966.

In May, 1966, Loral was awarded a second Navy contract for the production of more radar sets and again went about soliciting bids. Austin bid on all 40 gear components but, on July 15, a representative from Loral informed Austin's president, Mr. Krauss, that his company would be awarded the subcontract only for those items on which it was low bidder. The Austin officer refused to accept an order for less than all 40 of the gear parts and on the next day he told Loral that Austin would cease deliveries of the parts due under the existing subcontract unless Loral consented to substantial increases in the prices provided for by that agreement—both retroactively for parts already delivered and prospectively on those not yet shipped—and placed with Austin the order for all 40 parts needed under Loral's second Navy contract. Shortly thereafter, Austin did, indeed, stop delivery. After contacting 10 manufacturers of precision gears and finding none who could produce the parts in time to meet its commitments to the Navy, [footnote omitted] Loral acceded to Austin's demands; in a letter dated July 22, Loral wrote to Austin that "We have feverishly surveyed other sources of supply and find that because of the prevailing military exigencies, were they to start from scratch as would have to be the case, they could not even remotely begin to deliver on time to meet the delivery requirements established by the Government. . . . Accordingly, we are left with no choice or alternative but to meet your conditions."

Loral thereupon consented to the price increases insisted upon by Austin under the first subcontract and the latter was awarded a second subcontract making it the supplier of all 40 gear parts for Loral's second contract with the Navy. [Footnote omitted.] Although Austin was granted until September to resume deliveries, Loral did, in fact, receive parts in August and was able to produce the radar sets in time to meet its commitments to the Navy on both contracts. After Austin's last delivery under the second subcontract in July, 1967, Loral notified it of its intention to seek recovery of the price increases.

On September 15, 1967, Austin instituted this action against Loral to recover an amount in excess of $17,750 which was still due on the second subcontract. On the same day, Loral commenced an action against Austin claiming damages of some $22,250—the aggregate of the price increases under the first subcontract—on the ground of economic duress. The two actions were consolidated and, following a trial, Austin was awarded the sum it requested and Loral's complaint against Austin was dismissed on the ground that it was not shown that "it could not have obtained the items in question from other sources in time to meet its commitment to the Navy under the first contract." A closely divided Appellate Division affirmed (35 A D 2d 387). There was no material disagreement concerning the facts. . . .

The applicable law is clear and, indeed, is not disputed by the parties. A contract is voidable on the ground of duress when it is established that the party making the claim was forced to agree to it by means of a wrongful threat precluding the exercise of his free will. [Citations omitted.] The existence of economic duress or business compulsion is demonstrated by proof that "immediate possession of needful goods is threatened" (*Mercury Mach. Importing Corp. v. City of New York, 3 N. Y.* 2d 418, 425) or, more particularly, in cases such as the one before us, by proof that one party to a contract has threatened to breach the agreement by withholding goods unless the other party agrees to some further demand. (*See, e.g., du Pont de Nemours & Co. v. Hass Co., 303 N. Y. 785*; *Gallagher Switchboard Corp. v. Heckler Elec. Co.*, 36 Misc. 2d 225; *see, also*, 13 Williston, Contracts [3d ed., 1970], §1617, p. 705.) However, a mere threat by one party to breach the contract by not delivering the required items, though wrongful, does not in itself constitute economic duress. It must also appear that the threatened party could not obtain the goods from another source of supply [footnote omitted] and that the ordinary remedy of an action for breach of contract would not be adequate. [Footnote omitted.]

We find without any support in the record the conclusion reached by the courts below that Loral failed to establish that it was the victim of economic duress. On the contrary, the evidence makes out a classic case, as a matter of law, of such duress. [Footnote omitted.]

It is manifest that Austin's threat—to stop deliveries unless the prices were increased—deprived Loral of its free will. As bearing on this, Loral's relationship with the Government is most significant. As mentioned above, its contract called for staggered monthly deliveries of the radar sets, with clauses calling for liquidated damages and possible cancellation on default. Because of its production schedule, Loral was, in July, 1966, concerned with meeting its delivery requirements in September, October and November, and it was for the sets to be delivered in those months that the withheld gears were needed. Loral had to plan ahead, and the substantial liquidated damages for which it would be liable, plus the threat of default, were genuine possibilities. Moreover, Loral did a substantial portion of its business with the Government, and it feared that a failure to deliver as agreed upon would jeopardize its chances for future contracts. These genuine concerns do not merit the label "'self-imposed, undisclosed and subjective'" which the Appellate Division majority placed upon them. It was perfectly reasonable for Loral, or any other party similarly placed, to consider itself in an emergency, duress situation.

Austin, however, claims that the fact that Loral extended its time to resume deliveries until September negates its alleged dire need for the parts. A Loral official testified on this point that Austin's president told him he could deliver some parts in August and that the extension of deliveries was a formality. In any event, the parts necessary for production of the radar sets to be delivered in September were delivered to Loral on September 1, and the parts needed for the October schedule were delivered in late August and early September. Even so, Loral had to "work . . . around the clock" to meet its commitments.

Considering that the best offer Loral received from the other vendors it contacted was commencement of delivery sometime in October, which, as the record shows, would have made it late in its deliveries to the Navy in both September and October, Loral's claim that it had no choice but to accede to Austin's demands is conclusively demonstrated.

We find unconvincing Austin's contention that Loral, in order to meet its burden, should have contacted the Government and asked for an extension of its delivery dates so as to enable it to purchase the parts from another vendor. Aside from the consideration that Loral was anxious to perform well in the Government's eyes, it could not be sure when it would obtain enough parts from a substitute vendor to meet its commitments. The only promise which it received from the companies it contacted was for *commencement* of deliveries, not full supply, and, with vendor delay common in this field, it would have been nearly impossible to know the length of the extension it should request. It must be remembered that Loral was producing a needed item of military hardware. Moreover, there is authority for Loral's position that nonperformance by a subcontractor is not an excuse for default in the main contract. (See, e.g., McBride & Wachtel, Government Contracts, §35.10, [11].) In light of all this, Loral's claim should not be held insufficiently supported because it did not request an extension from the Government.

Loral, as indicated above, also had the burden of demonstrating that it could not obtain the parts elsewhere within a reasonable time, and there can be no doubt that it met this burden. The 10 manufacturers whom Loral contacted comprised its entire list of "approved vendors" for precision gears, and none was able to commence delivery soon enough. [Footnote omitted.] As Loral was producing a highly sophisticated item of military machinery requiring parts made to the strictest engineering standards, it would be unreasonable to hold that Loral should have gone to other vendors, with whom it was either unfamiliar or dissatisfied, to procure the needed parts. As Justice Steuer noted in his dissent, Loral "contacted all the manufacturers whom it believed capable of making these parts" (35 A D 2d, at p. 393), and this was all the law requires.

It is hardly necessary to add that Loral's normal legal remedy of accepting Austin's breach of the contract and then suing for damages would have been inadequate under the circumstances, as Loral would still have had to obtain the gears elsewhere with all the concomitant consequences mentioned above. In other words, Loral actually had no choice, when the prices were raised by Austin, except to take the gears at the "coerced" prices and then sue to get the excess back.

Austin's final argument is that Loral, even if it did enter into the contract under duress, lost any rights it had to a refund of money by waiting until July, 1967, long after the termination date of the contract, to disaffirm it. It is true that one who would recover moneys allegedly paid under duress must act promptly to make his claim known. (*See Oregon Pacific R. R. Co. v. Forrest, 128 N. Y. 83, 93*; *Port Chester Elec. Constr. Corp. v. Hastings Terraces*, 284 App. Div. 966, 967.) In this case, Loral delayed making its demand for a refund until three days after Austin's last delivery on the second subcontract. Loral's reason—for waiting until that time—is that it feared another stoppage of deliveries which would again put it in an untenable situation. Considering Austin's conduct in the past, this was perfectly reasonable, as the possibility of an application by Austin of further business compulsion still existed until all of the parts were delivered.

In sum, the record before us demonstrates that Loral agreed to the price increases in consequence of the economic duress employed by Austin. Accordingly, the matter should be remanded to the trial court for a computation of its damages. . . .

Post-Case Follow-Up

A contract is voidable on the ground of economic duress when a party makes a wrongful or improper threat that prevents another party from exercising its free will and there is a lack of reasonable alternatives. In *Austin Instrument*, a subcontractor, Austin, on a federal government contract threatened not to deliver gear parts promised under its contract unless the contractor, Loral, provided it with a price increase. The court determined that Austin exploited the contractor's vulnerability under the contract, when Loral could not find a substitute supplier in time to meet the government's deadline for performance. Loral actually had no choice, when the prices were raised by Austin, except to take the gears at the "coerced" prices and then sue later to get the excess back. Loral reasonably delayed making its demand for a refund because of legitimate concerns raised by Austin's past delivery stoppages.

Austin Instrument v. Loral Corp.: Real Life Applications

1. A contractor with a history of bankruptcy proceedings contracts with an oil company to modify three offshore drilling platforms. The oil company is aware of the contractor's previous financial issues. A number of disputed cost overruns occur during the project. The contractor claims that the oil company exploited

its shaky financial situation by offering only half of what it owed, knowing that the contractor could not afford any further delay in payment. The contractor signs the release, but later seeks to rescind it under economic duress. Were there any wrongful or improper threats by the oil company? Review *Northern Fabrication Co. v. UNOCAL*, 980 P.2d 958 (Alaska 1999), to determine if the contractor has met its burden of proof.

2. A cable television company promotes, sponsors, and sells a broadcast of a country music concert to cable subscribers. The concert only runs for two hours instead of the advertised three-hour program. Cable customer Howdy is billed for the concert and pays after viewing the shortened concert. He then files suit, claiming a host of statutory violations, and contends that he paid for the concert after its broadcast because of concerns that nonpayment to the cable company would harm his credit history. Has Howdy established a valid claim in economic duress? Brief *Smith v. Prime Cable*, 276 Ill. App. 3d 843 (Ill. App. Ct. 1st Dist. 1995), and post your review and response on your class discussion board.

3. Two major corporations enter into a letter of intent for the sale of tantalum, a rare elemental metal. Before finalizing their agreement, a global shortage of the metal causes prices to dramatically increase. The seller threatens to withhold the delivery of this metal without a substantial price increase. The buyer agrees to the price increase, requiring the seller to deliver the tantalum in the specified quantities and time frames. Eighteen months later, the buyer seeks damages for the price increases in excess of the amounts discussed in the letter of intent. You are the attorney for the seller. Review *Cabot Corp. v. AVX Corp.*, 448 Mass. 629 (2007), and advise your client on the likely outcome.

D. UNDUE INFLUENCE—VOIDABLE

While duress focuses on physical or improper threats, **undue influence** addresses issues of unfair persuasion brought to bear against a party in a lessened capacity to exercise free will in making a contract. A dominant party or parties induces a person in a weakened or vulnerable position to agree to terms that may not serve that individual's best interests. Undue influence extends to improper pressure, even if it does not involve explicit threats. In general, the burden is on the person claiming undue influence to prove the defense.

1. Unfair Persuasion

Unfair persuasion or overpersuasion defies precise definition. Many pressure tactics are easy to identify, but others may be legitimate conduct on their own. In *Odorizzi v. Bloomfield School District*, 54 Cal. Rptr. 533 (Cal. Ct. App. 1966), the court enumerated seven types of persuasion indicative of undue pressure:

(1) discussion of the transaction at an unusual or inappropriate time;
(2) consummation of the transaction in an unusual place;
(3) insistent demand that the business be finished at once;
(4) extreme emphasis on untoward consequences of delay;
(5) the use of multiple persuaders by the dominant side against a single servient party;
(6) absence of third-party advisers to the servient party; and,
(7) statements that there is no time to consult third party experts, such as financial advisers or attorneys.

A party claiming undue influence need not show all of these factors. But courts will consider the presence of these factors in reviewing the surrounding circumstances of a contract alleged to have been made under undue influence.

Yet making business deals on a golf course or at a restaurant (an unusual place) on a Sunday (an unusual time) before the markets open the next day (insistence on finishing the business at once) where only one member of the foursome is from the persuaded company (multiple persuaders against one individual) may not be either unusual or objectionable. These factors are not problematic in themselves.

We all may have felt under some kind of pressure in contract transactions. In most settings, people can and do resist high pressure tactics when that resistance is in their best interests. A person uncomfortable with the pressure usually can respond, "I'll think about it" or "See me in my office," perfectly polite ways to fend off pressure. High pressure tactics become problematic when used to create or exploit another's vulnerability.

2. Vulnerability

Vulnerability involves a party in a weakened position at the time of the undue influence. Parties may be in a compromised state due to physical condition, advanced age, or emotional anguish. In this weakened state, the party acting under another's undue influence may be more susceptible to unfair persuasion due to the nature of the overpersuasive tactics and the character of the parties' relationship. More specifically, the persuaded party may feel overwhelmed under these pressure tactics and may justifiably assume that the other person would not propose a deal that would be contrary to the persuaded party's interests. Although a party may be in a diminished condition, this situation alone does not give rise to the defense of incapacity.

Relationship of Trust

Undue influence requires some showing that the persuading party held some power over the persuaded party. This power may arise from relationships of trust or with authority figures or domineering persons. Under the classical view, undue influence could only apply to formal fiduciaries, such as accountants, financial advisors, or lawyers, who hold a place of trust with their clients. For example, a financial advisor may overpersuade a client to move retirement funds into certain investments that provide a lucrative commission, but put the client's financial or retirement goals at risk. Some courts will shift the burden to the fiduciary to show that undue influence was not exercised over the other party.

Today, undue influence has been expanded to a wider range of relationships of trust, often involving family members. In a family dynamic, one person takes advantage of this close relationship to obtain a favorable contract. A trusted son may persuade her elderly mother to move her funds to a joint bank account, so that the son could get the funds for the mother, if that ever became necessary. While exceptions exist, mothers often are justified in believing that their children would not act contrary to their mothers' interests. Long-time, close friends, like family members, may be expected not to propose contracts that exalt their own interests above those of the person being persuaded. Where these relations of trust exist, a person who abuses that trust may face an allegation of undue influence.

Domination over Subservient Party

Outside of relationships of trust, domination may arise when the persuaded party is subservient to an authority figure or a domineering personality. The dominant party or parties may exercise physical or emotional dominance or both in some combination. For example, a former linebacker handling in-home sales of insurance may seem physically intimidating (intentionally or not). If he continues his sales pitch despite several hints from the potential customer to move on, his physical dominance may induce a person to sign a contract just to get him out of the house.

In cases of emotional domination, a party in authority, such as a supervisor or established community figure, may be able to exercise undue influence over an employee or member of the general public, respectively. Or an elderly person may become dependent on her nurses or other in-home caregivers. If presented with an offer, it may be difficult for her to refuse, in part out of fear of losing the important support the caregiver provides. Understandably, persuaded parties might succumb to the pressure rather than resist it — even if the deal is not in their best interests. In these settings, overpersuasion coupled with physical or emotional domination may create or exploit a party's vulnerability. In either example, despite the dominance, normal negotiations may still result that do not amount to undue influence.

Emotional domination may occur when elderly people become dependent on nurses or other in-home caregivers.
Kzenon/Shutterstock.com

3. Inducement

Inducement exists when the unfair persuasion is a substantial factor in a party's assent to the contract. As in other settings, this inducement does not require the party claiming the defense to prove that the decision would have been different, but for the unfair persuasion. It does mandate that the party show the overpersuasion contributed in some significant way to the decision to enter the deal. Proof that the person would have assented anyway might defeat the defense.

When a relationship of trust is abused, it is less likely that the decision would have been made regardless of the overpersuasion. For instance, proof that the persuaded party would have signed anything that the family member asked her to sign might show that the overpersuasive tactics did not contribute to the assent. But a relationship of trust surely contributes to a party's assent, which may be enough to show that undue influence induced assent.

Case Preview

Odorizzi v. Bloomfield School District

In *Odorizzi v. Bloomfield School District*, a court had to determine whether a teacher, after an arrest, succumbed to undue influence in resigning from his position. In his effort to rescind his resignation, the teacher was required to show that the district superintendent and the school's principal exercised undue influence in the wake of his arrest. The court had to chart the boundaries of the school officials' efforts to secure the resignation to determine if their conduct could reasonably be viewed as undue influence.

As you read *Odorizzi v. Bloomfield School District*, look for the following:

1. Who was the dominant party and who was the servient party in this case?
2. What factors did the court identify as potential signs of undue influence?
3. Applying those factors, how was overpersuasion shown in this instance between the school officials and Odorizzi?

Odorizzi v. Bloomfield School District

246 Cal. App. 2d 123 (Cal. 1966)

FLEMING, J.

Appeal from a judgment dismissing plaintiff's amended complaint on demurrer.

Plaintiff Donald Odorizzi was employed during 1964 as an elementary school teacher by defendant Bloomfield School District and was under contract with the District to continue to teach school the following year as a permanent employee. On June 10 he was arrested on criminal charges of homosexual activity, and on June 11 he signed and delivered to his superiors his written resignation as a teacher, a resignation which the District accepted on June 13. In July the criminal charges against Odorizzi were dismissed under Penal Code, section 995, and in September he sought to resume his employment with the District. On the District's refusal to reinstate him he filed suit for declaratory and other relief.

Odorizzi's amended complaint asserts his resignation was invalid because obtained through duress, fraud, mistake, and undue influence and given at a time

when he lacked capacity to make a valid contract. Specifically, Odorizzi declares he was under such severe mental and emotional strain at the time he signed his resignation, having just completed the process of arrest, questioning by the police, booking, and release on bail, and having gone for forty hours without sleep, that he was incapable of rational thought or action. While he was in this condition and unable to think clearly, the superintendent of the District and the principal of his school came to his apartment. They said they were trying to help him and had his best interests at heart, that he should take their advice and immediately resign his position with the District, that there was no time to consult an attorney, that if he did not resign immediately the District would suspend and dismiss him from his position and publicize the proceedings, his "aforedescribed arrest" and cause him "to suffer extreme embarrassment and humiliation"; but that if he resigned at once the incident would not be publicized and would not jeopardize his chances of securing employment as a teacher elsewhere. Odorizzi pleads that because of his faith and confidence in their representations they were able to substitute their will and judgment in place of his own and thus obtain his signature to his purported resignation. A demurrer to his amended complaint was sustained without leave to amend.

By his complaint plaintiff in effect seeks to rescind his resignation pursuant to Civil Code, section 1689, on the ground that his consent had not been real or free within the meaning of Civil Code, section 1567, but had been obtained through duress, menace, fraud, undue influence, or mistake. . . . [The court discussed these defenses, including duress below, but found no basis for them, except for undue influence.]

. . .

No duress or menace has been pleaded. Duress consists in unlawful confinement of another's person, or relatives, or property, which causes him to consent to a transaction through fear. (Civ. Code, §1569.) Duress is often used interchangeably with menace [citation omitted], but in California menace is technically a threat of duress or a threat of injury to the person, property, or character of another. (Civ. Code, §1570; Restatement, Contracts, §§492, 493.) We agree with respondent's contention that neither duress nor menace was involved in this case, because the action or threat in duress or menace must be unlawful, and a threat to take legal action is not unlawful unless the party making the threat knows the falsity of his claim. (*Leeper v. Beltrami*, 53 Cal. 2d 195, 204, 1 Cal. Rptr. 12, 347 P.2d 12, 77 A.L.R.2d 803.) The amended complaint shows in substance that the school representatives announced their intention to initiate suspension and dismissal proceedings under Education Code, sections 13403, 13408 et seq. at a time when the filing of such proceedings was not only their legal right but their positive duty as school officials. (Educ. Code, §13409; *Board of Education, etc. v. Weiland*, 179 Cal. App. 2d 808, 4 Cal. Rptr. 286.) Although the filing of such proceedings might be extremely damaging to plaintiff's reputation, the injury would remain incidental so long as the school officials acted in good faith in the performance of their duties. (*Schumm by Whymer v. Berg*, 37 Cal. 2d 174, 185-186, 231 P.2d 39, 21 A.L.R.2d 1051.) Neither duress nor menace was present as a ground for rescission.

. . .

However, the pleading does set out a claim that plaintiff's consent to the transaction had been obtained through the use of undue influence.

Undue influence, in the sense we are concerned with here, is a shorthand legal phrase used to describe persuasion which tends to be coercive in nature, persuasion which overcomes the will without convincing the judgment. (*Estate of Ricks*, 160 Cal. 467, 480-482, 117 P. 539.) The hallmark of such persuasion is high pressure, a pressure which works on mental, moral, or emotional weakness to such an extent that it approaches the boundaries of coercion. In this sense, undue influence has been called overpersuasion. (*Kelly v. McCarthy*, 6 Cal. 2d 347, 364, 57 P.2d 118.) Misrepresentations of law or fact are not essential to the charge, for a person's will may be overborne without misrepresentation. By statutory definition undue influence includes "taking an unfair advantage of another's weakness of mind; or . . . taking a grossly oppressive and unfair advantage of another's necessities or distress." (Civ. Code, §1575.) While most reported cases of undue influence involve persons who bear a confidential relationship to one another, a confidential or authoritative relationship between the parties need not be present when the undue influence involves unfair advantage taken of another's weakness or distress. . . .

We paraphrase the summary of undue influence given the jury by Sir James P. Wilde in *Hall v. Hall, L.R.* 1, P & D 481, 482 (1868): To make a good contract a man must be a free agent. Pressure of whatever sort which overpowers the will without convincing the judgment is a species of restraint under which no valid contract can be made. Importunity or threats, if carried to the degree in which the free play of a man's will is overborne, constitute undue influence, although no force is used or threatened. A party may be led but not driven, and his acts must be the offspring of his own volition and not the record of someone else's.

In essence undue influence involves the use of excessive pressure to persuade one vulnerable to such pressure, pressure applied by a dominant subject to a servient object. In combination, the elements of undue susceptibility in the servient person and excessive pressure by the dominating person make the latter's influence undue, for it results in the apparent will of the servient person being in fact the will of the dominant person.

Undue susceptibility may consist of total weakness of mind which leaves a person entirely without understanding (Civ. Code, §38); or, a lesser weakness which destroys the capacity of a person to make a contract even though he is not totally incapacitated (Civ. Code, §39; *Peterson v. Ellebrecht*, 205 Cal. App. 2d 718, 721-722, 23 Cal. Rptr. 349); or, the first element in our equation, a still lesser weakness which provides sufficient grounds to rescind a contract for undue influence (Civ. Code, §1575; . . .) Such lesser weakness need not be long lasting nor wholly incapacitating, but may be merely a lack of full vigor due to age, . . . physical condition, . . . emotional anguish, . . . or a combination of such factors. [Citations omitted.] The reported cases have usually involved elderly, sick, senile persons alleged to have executed wills or deeds under pressure. (*Malone v. Malone*, 155 Cal. App. 2d 161, 317 P.2d 65 [constant importuning of a senile husband]; Stewart v. Marvin, 139 Cal. App. 2d 769, 294 P.2d 114 [persistent nagging of elderly spouse].) In some of its aspects this lesser weakness could perhaps be called weakness of spirit. But whatever name we give it, this first element of undue influence resolves itself into a lessened capacity of the object to make a free contract.

In the present case plaintiff has pleaded that such weakness at the time he signed his resignation prevented him from freely and competently applying his judgment to the problem before him. Plaintiff declares he was under severe mental and emotional strain at the time because he had just completed the process of arrest, questioning, booking, and release on bail and had been without sleep for forty hours. It is possible that exhaustion and emotional turmoil may wholly incapacitate a person from exercising his judgment. As an abstract question of pleading, plaintiff has pleaded that possibility and sufficient allegations to state a case for rescission.

Undue influence in its second aspect involves an application of excessive strength by a dominant subject against a servient object. Judicial consideration of this second element in undue influence has been relatively rare, for there are few cases denying persons who persuade but do not misrepresent the benefit of their bargain. Yet logically, the same legal consequences should apply to the results of excessive strength as to the results of undue weakness. Whether from weakness on one side, or strength on the other, or a combination of the two, undue influence occurs whenever there results "that kind of influence or supremacy of one mind over another by which that other is prevented from acting according to his own wish or judgment, and whereby the will of the person is overborne and he is induced to do or forbear to do an act which he would not do, or would do, if left to act freely." (*Webb v. Saunders*, 79 Cal. App. 2d 863, 871, 181 P.2d 43, 47.) Undue influence involves a type of mismatch which our statute calls unfair advantage. (Civ. Code, §1575.) Whether a person of subnormal capacities has been subjected to ordinary force or a person of normal capacities subjected to extraordinary force, the match is equally out of balance. If will has been overcome against judgment, consent may be rescinded.

The difficulty, of course, lies in determining when the forces of persuasion have overflowed their normal banks and become oppressive flood waters. There are second thoughts to every bargain, and hindsight is still better than foresight. Undue influence cannot be used as a pretext to avoid bad bargains or escape from bargains which refuse to come up to expectations. . . . A man who buys a tract of desert land in the expectation that it is in the immediate path of the city's growth and will become another Palm Springs, an expectation cultivated in glowing terms by the seller, cannot rescind his bargain when things turn out differently. If we are temporarily persuaded against our better judgment to do something about which we later have second thoughts, we must abide the consequences of the risks inherent in managing our own affairs. (*Estate of Anderson*, 185 Cal. 700, 706-707, 198 P. 407.)

However, overpersuasion is generally accompanied by certain characteristics which tend to create a pattern. The pattern usually involves several of the following elements: (1) discussion of the transaction at an unusual or inappropriate time, (2) consummation of the transaction in an unusual place, (3) insistent demand that the business be finished at once, (4) extreme emphasis on untoward consequences of delay, (5) the use of multiple persuaders by the dominant side against a single servient party, (6) absence of third-party advisers to the servient party, (7) statements that there is no time to consult financial advisers or attorneys. If a number of these elements are simultaneously present, the persuasion may be characterized as excessive. The cases are illustrative:

Moore v. Moore, 56 Cal. 89, 93, and 81 Cal. 195, 22 P. 589, 874. The pregnant wife of a man who had been shot to death on October 30 and buried on November 1 was approached by four members of her husband's family on November 2 or 3 and persuaded to deed her entire interest in her husband's estate to his children by a prior marriage. In finding the use of undue influence on Mrs. Moore, the court commented: "It was the second day after her late husband's funeral. It was at a time when she would naturally feel averse to transacting any business, and she might reasonably presume that her late husband's brother would not apply to her at such a time to transact any important business, unless it was of a nature that would admit of no delay. And as it would admit of delay, the only reason which we can discover for their unseemly haste is, that they thought that she would be more likely to comply with their wishes then than at some future time, after she had recovered from the shock which she had then so recently experienced. If for that reason they selected that time for the accomplishment of their purpose, it seems to us that they not only took, but that they designed to take, an unfair advantage of her weakness of mind. If they did not, they probably can explain why they selected that inappropriate time for the transaction of business which might have been delayed for weeks without injury to anyone. In the absence of any explanation, it appears to us that the time was selected with reference to just that condition of mind which she alleges that she was then in.

"Taking an unfair advantage of another's weakness of mind is undue influence, and the law will not permit the retention of an advantage thus obtained." (Civ. Code, §1575.)

Weger v. Rocha, 138 Cal. App. 109, 32 P.2d 417. Plaintiff, while confined in a cast in a hospital, gave a release of claims for personal injuries for a relatively small sum to an agent who spent two hours persuading her to sign. At the time of signing plaintiff was in a highly nervous and hysterical condition and suffering much pain, and she signed the release in order to terminate the interview. The court held that the release had been secured by the use of undue influence.

. . .

The difference between legitimate persuasion and excessive pressure . . . rests to a considerable extent in the manner in which the parties go about their business. For example, if a day or two after Odorizzi's release on bail the superintendent of the school district had called him into his office during business hours and directed his attention to those provisions of the Education Code compelling his leave of absence and authorizing his suspension on the filing of written charges, had told him that the District contemplated filing written charges against him, had pointed out the alternative of resignation available to him, had informed him he was free to consult counsel or any adviser he wished and to consider the matter overnight and return with his decision the next day, it is extremely unlikely that any complaint about the use of excessive pressure could ever have been made against the school district.

But, according to the allegations of the complaint, this is not the way it happened, and if it had happened that way, plaintiff would never have resigned. Rather, the representatives of the school board undertook to achieve their objective by overpersuasion and imposition to secure plaintiff's signature but not his consent to his resignation

through a high-pressure carrot-and-stick technique — under which they assured plaintiff they were trying to assist him, he should rely on their advice, there wasn't time to consult an attorney, if he didn't resign at once the school district would suspend and dismiss him from his position and publicize the proceedings, but if he did resign the incident wouldn't jeopardize his chances of securing a teaching post elsewhere.

Plaintiff has thus pleaded both subjective and objective elements entering the undue influence equation and stated sufficient facts to put in issue the question whether his free will had been overborne by defendant's agents at a time when he was unable to function in a normal manner. It was sufficient to pose ". . . the ultimate question . . . whether a free and competent judgment was merely influenced, or whether a mind was so dominated as to prevent the exercise of an independent judgment." (Williston on Contracts, §1625 [rev. ed.]; Restatement, Contracts §497, Comment *c.*) The question cannot be resolved by an analysis of pleading but requires a finding of fact.

We express no opinion on the merits of plaintiff's case, or the propriety of his continuing to teach school (Educ. Code, §13403), or the timeliness of his rescission (Civ. Code, §1691). We do hold that his pleading, liberally construed, states a cause of action for rescission of a transaction to which his apparent consent had been obtained through the use of undue influence.

The judgment is reversed.

Post-Case Follow-Up

The court held that undue influence usually involves someone in a dominant position using overpersuasion to take advantage of someone in a servient or weakened position. The court indicated that Odorizzi was in a weakened state of exhaustion and anguish over his arrest. The school officials were authority figures and the presence of both of them using a carrot-and-stick approach overpersuaded Odorizzi to act against his own best interests. The court also listed seven factors that may be considered to determine if undue influence was present. In applying these various factors to the facts of this case, the court determined that Odorizzi had pleaded sufficient facts to support his claim of undue influence from both a subjective and objective perspective. However, the court cautioned that undue influence cannot be used as pretext to avoid bad bargains or situations of buyer's remorse.

Odorizzi v. Bloomfield School District: Real Life Applications

1. A banker contacts a local attorney to assist one of the bank's customers in drafting a power of attorney and will. The elderly bank customer resides in a nursing home and the will named the lawyer and bank representative as the only beneficiaries of her will. After her death, the family challenged the validity of the will as to the bequests to the attorney and the banker under undue influence. In this case, determine who has the burden of proof as to undue influence and whether the court will sustain a claim of undue influence. Review *Krischbaum v. Dillon,*

58 Ohio St.3d 58 (1991) to determine the issues of burden of proof and the outcome of this case.

2. A union mechanic receives a lay-off notice from his employer. He then sues for wrongful discharge against his employer, asserting age discrimination and whistle-blower harassment claims. His employer counters by showing a release he signed as to all claims under state and federal law in order to receive severance benefits. The employee states that he read and signed the release, but did not understand or intend to waive his discrimination and harassment claims. He asserts that neither his employer nor his union representative advised him that signing the release would impact his other claims. Review *Skrbina v. Fleming Cos.*, 45 Cal. App.4th 1353 (Cal. App.3d Dist. 1996) to determine if he has shown undue influence in his signing of this release.

3. A local businessman asks an attorney to draft a prenuptial agreement for his pending marriage. His fiancée is given the document a month before it is signed. When the couple meets at the attorney's office, the lawyer advises her that he is only representing her fiancée and suggests that she seek legal counsel before signing the document. She tells him she does not have a lawyer and signs the document anyway. Subsequently, the couple divorces and she challenges the prenuptial agreement on a number of grounds, including undue influence. Read and brief *Sailer v. Sailer*, 2009 N.D. 73 (N.D. 2009) to see if the court agrees with her undue influence claim.

---

4. Third-Party Undue Influence

Undue influence by third parties poses the familiar problem of reliance by a person who was not aware of the defense. Consider the earlier example of the son who persuades his mother to move funds to a joint bank account. After the son withdraws all the money, the mother might sue the bank to rescind the contract (opening the accounts or transferring money into them). The bank did not use undue influence, the son did. Under Restatement (Second) of Contracts §177(3), undue influence by a nonparty will justify avoiding the contract—assuming all the elements are shown—unless

1. the other party relies on the contract
2. in good faith and
3. without reason to know of the duress.

As applied to this example, the bank relied on the contract, which allowed the son to withdraw the funds, to honor his withdrawal. Unless the bank acted in bad faith by knowing or having a reason to know of the undue influence, the mother cannot obtain rescission and restitution against the bank. Her remedy will be against the son for **conversion** (a property tort) or unjust enrichment (for example, an action for money had and received).

Chapter Summary

- Defenses that render a contract void are grounded in the idea that a contract is unenforceable because no valid contract ever existed due to the claimed defense. Courts will refuse to enforce a void contract, even if both parties want the contract enforced.
- Most defenses make contracts voidable, which means that a contract is enforceable, unless one party exercises its right to claim a defense that will avoid or discharge its contract duties.
- A contract entered into under physical duress or with a party under court-ordered guardianship makes a contract void and unenforceable by either party.
- Under the modern view, incapacity, economic duress, and undue influence make a contract voidable at the option of the party pleading the defense.
- A party may disaffirm or repudiate a contract during the time of incapacity or a reasonable time thereafter. A party satisfied with the contract despite the conditions under which it was made may ratify the voidable contract by words or conduct.
- Incapacity involves infancy (under 18), severe intoxication, mental illness and defect, and guardianship, all of which question whether the party has sufficient mental ability to decide for herself whether the benefits of the bargain outweigh its costs.
- The minority benefit rule balances the interests of the merchant acting in good faith with those of the minor claiming incapacity. Absent any overreaching, fraud, or unfair advantage on the part of the adult, a seller is entitled to reasonable compensation for the use of, depreciation, or willful or negligent damage done to goods sold, while these goods are in the minor's possession.
- Physical duress involves entering into a contract out of fear of loss of life or limb, mayhem, or imprisonment.
- Economic duress requires wrongful or improper threats that induce assent when a person has no reasonable alternatives. Examples of improper threats are threatened crime or tort; threats of criminal prosecution; withholding payment of admitted debt; threatened civil process made in bad faith; and breach of duty of good faith and fair dealing (bad faith).
- Undue influence requires a party to be in a weakened state and subject to overpersuasion by a dominating party over the subservient party. This power may arise from relationships of trust or from authority figures.

Applying the Rules

1. Charlie Skyhigh, 17, a young NBA basketball star, enters into a three-year written contract with Sports Stars Unlimited, to be compensated for signing autographs at various sporting events. He carries out his duties for two and one-half years and then decides that he wants to back out of the contract that he entered into as a minor. Under the modern view, a court will likely find that

a. Skyhigh must continue to complete his contract obligations because there was equal bargaining power.
b. Skyhigh is allowed to disaffirm any contract he entered into as a minor any time after he reaches the age of 18.
c. Skyhigh will likely be bound because he ratified the earlier contract by failing to disaffirm within a reasonable period of time after he turned 18.
d. Skyhigh is allowed to rescind the agreement because he was a minor when he signed the deal.
e. a and c above.

2. Using the facts of Question 1, let's say that Skyhigh claims that Sports Stars Unlimited threatened his life and the lives of his family if he did not agree to sign autographs at sporting events. If all other facts remain the same, a court will likely find that

a. Skyhigh's contract is voidable under physical compulsion if he showed reasonable courage under the circumstances.
b. Skyhigh's contract is void under physical compulsion if he can show he subjectively feared for his safety and that of his family.
c. Skyhigh's contract is void under physical compulsion if he showed reasonable courage under the circumstances.
d. a and b above.
e. b and c above.

3. Ken receives Austin's bill for $50,000 of marketing and social media services under an existing consulting contract between them. Under their agreement, Ken must pay for Austin's services within 30 days of receipt of Austin's bill. Forty-five days after receiving Austin's bill, Ken has failed to pay despite Austin's calls to Ken requesting payment. Since Ken did not pay Austin's bill, Austin has had trouble making his mortgage payments. Recently, Austin asked Ken to pay the bill immediately or else Austin may lose his home to foreclosure. Knowing Austin is struggling financially, Ken proposes to pay $30,000 immediately if Austin wipes the rest of the bill off his books. Otherwise, Ken tells Austin he won't be able to pay for another six or seven months. Under financial strain, Austin agrees in writing to the reduced amount to save his home. A week later, Austin goes to court and seeks to rescind his deal with Ken and to recover the remaining unpaid $20,000. Under the modern view, a court will likely find that

a. Ken will have to pay Austin $20,000 under the principle of economic duress.
b. Ken will not have to pay $20,000 since Austin agreed to the reduced payment and courts respect notions of freedom of contract.
c. Ken will have to pay Austin $20,000 under the principle of undue influence.
d. Ken will not have to pay Austin $20,000 under the principle of incapacity.
e. b and d above.

4. Louisa is looking for apartments and finds one she likes on Colonial Drive. She signs a year-long lease with Winona, the building owner, to rent the apartment.

Subsequently, Louisa claims that she was drunk when she signed the written lease and is now trying to be excused from her obligations under the lease. Under the Restatement view, Louisa may be excused from performance if

a. Louisa was intoxicated even if Winona had no knowledge Louisa was drunk.
b. Louisa, due to intoxication, was unable to understand the nature and/or consequences of the agreement at the time she entered into it.
c. Winona knew or had reason to know that Louisa was intoxicated.
d. Louisa had any amount of alcohol in her system when entering into the contract.
e. b and c above.

5. Mel, a 20-year-old, buys and sells used dirt bikes out of his garage. He knows his 16-year-old neighbor, Chad, is looking to buy one of Mel's bikes to have some fun riding around local trails with his friends. On February 1, Mel and Chad sign a written agreement that states that Chad must pay a $100 deposit and then an additional $500 in cash on the pick-up date of February 16 for the dirt bike. Chad pays the deposit. On February 16, Chad pays Mel the remaining $500 and takes the bike home. Chad uses the bike for six months without any difficulties, but decides he is tired of it and wants a full refund. Applying the minority benefit rule, a court will likely find that

a. Chad receives a refund minus any depreciation or damage for his use of the bike.
b. Chad receives a full refund because Mel sought to overreach or defraud Chad in entering into the original sales agreement.
c. Chad receives a full refund minus his $100 deposit.
d. Chad receives a full refund because disaffirmance does not apply to the purchase of nonneccessaries.
e. Chad will receive a full refund because disaffirmance applies to the purchase of nonneccessaries.

Contract Law in Practice

1. As *Dodson* noted, many minors today have greater independence than in the past and often hold jobs where they earn their own money. The benefit rule has only been embraced in a minority of states. Review online sources and law review articles to determine which states will apply the benefit rule in contracts involving minors. Determine if your state is following this trend or remains with the traditional approach to minors when nonnecessaries are at issue.

2. A recent study suggests that only a small fraction of duress claims are ever successful in contracts disputes. Professor Grace M. Giesel examined the poor track record for claims of duress in her article, *A Realistic Proposal for the Contract Duress Doctrine*, 107 W. VA. L. REV. 443 (2005). In a memo, summarize her

three main reasons for the lack of success of duress claims and her proposal for reworking duress to become a more viable defense in contract cases.

3. Contracts made directly with parties who are under the supervision of court-appointed guardians are void. Each state has different standards and procedures for determining whether parties are in need of court-ordered guardianships. Research your state law to determine the key statutory steps and court procedures for placing an individual under guardianship. Identify if there are any limits on the types of contracts that a guardian can enter into on behalf of the protected party.

4. Undue influence may be exercised by parties who are in fiduciary relationships with an individual. In some instances, attorneys have been reprimanded or disbarred for exhibiting undue influence in a weakened party's financial or testate matters. Research and review your state's professional responsibility code. What provisions deal with protecting a client from undue influence? What are the attorney's obligations in order to avoid claims of undue influence? Are there any recent bar decisions in your state relating to issues of undue influence by attorneys? Create a short presentation on these professional responsibility issues for class presentation.

5. Your client is a cell phone retailer who regularly deals with minors who want to buy cell phones and enter into service agreements. At times, it is difficult to determine if a consumer is old enough to enter into contracts to purchase a cell phone and to receive cell phone services. The store is located in an urban center where many city dwellers do not need a car or have a driver's license, but use public transportation to get around. The retailer is hoping to put together a uniform process for determining the age of customers before entering into contracts with them. The retailer has asked your help in devising processes for quickly and effectively determining whether or not a customer is old enough to enter into contracts when a driver's license is not available. Brainstorm options for the retailer and post your ideas on a class discussion board about this topic.

7

Poor Information: Misrepresentation and Mistake

Mutual assent signals that both parties believe they will gain more from the contract than they give to perform it. They might be wrong, particularly if they have incomplete or inaccurate information when making their decisions. When that occurs, assent alone may not signal an exchange that benefits both parties. Enforcing contracts formed with inadequate information, then, may not serve the goals of contract law. Thus, in some cases society will refuse to enforce contracts formed by parties who lacked information. That said, the onus to gather accurate information should rest with the parties themselves. Society expects parties to make their own decisions, including gathering any information they need before committing to an exchange. Allowing all parties who act on bad information to escape from performing their promises poses real problems, especially for those who relied on those promises. Thus, society balances the need to encourage parties to use caution before entering contracts and the desire to excuse performance when the failure to gather sufficient information seems justifiable or unavoidable.

To that end, courts recognize several defenses based on poor information. The most obvious involves **misrepresentation**, which applies when one party has misled another into entering the contract. When a party, without being misled by others, enters an agreement under an erroneous belief about some key aspect of the exchange, the defense of **mistake** may permit some redress. Mistake also varies, usually depending on whether the mistake was **mutual** (both parties shared the same mistaken belief) or **unilateral** (only one party was mistaken). Mistake does not require that the other party caused the mistake, but not every mistake justifies a defense.

Key Concepts

- Defense of misrepresentation
- Misrepresentation destroying assent
- Defense of mutual mistake
- Defense of unilateral mistake

A. MISREPRESENTATION

Misrepresentation may make a contract void or voidable. In extreme cases, misrepresentation negates assent. Deception may prevent people from realizing that the documents they are signing are contracts at all. For example, a woman's friend gave her a check for $1,000, telling her it was traveling money, and asked her to sign a receipt. Instead of a receipt, the document actually was an option to buy land owned by the woman. The woman never intended to sign a contract at all, but was deceived as to the very nature of the document. This version of misrepresentation, sometimes called **fraud in the execution**, makes a contract void. This form of misrepresentation will be discussed in more detail later in this chapter.

More commonly, both parties understand the nature of the contract, but deception leads one to miscalculate the costs or benefits of the transaction. Misrepresentations concerning the underlying subject matter of the deal (the land, the goods, and so on) are sometimes called **fraud in the inducement**. For example, a seller might mislead prospective buyers concerning termites in a house. The deceived person intends to sign a contract buying the house, but the false information induced her to enter this deal (at this price). These misrepresentations make the agreement voidable. The deceived party may elect to disaffirm the contract based on misrepresentation or to ratify the contract and keep its benefits.

The defense of misrepresentation covers much more than fraud. **Fraud** refers to intentional deception — lies. The defense of misrepresentation, however, applies even to innocent misstatements or to silence (where the failure to make any statement fails to disclose important information). The details of the defense are discussed below. From the outset, however, beware of thinking about this defense as fraud.

1. Structure of Misrepresentation

Assent reveals that a party to a contract values what she thought she was getting more than what she thought she was giving up. Misinformation undermines any confidence that she values what she actually was getting more than what she actually was giving up. Some misinformation must be laid at the feet of the misinformed party. However, if the other party's words or conduct cause the misinformation, the law allows the deceived person to elect to rescind the contract. Rescission seeks to return each party to their position before the bargain was entered: seller gives back the price, buyer gives back the thing purchased. The parties can start over and negotiate a deal based on the actual state of affairs, if a mutually beneficial contract remains possible. If not, then the parties remain in their original position, unbound by the contract induced by deception.

The rule governing misrepresentation includes four elements:

1. a misrepresentation;
2. that was either **fraudulent** (dishonest) or **material** (significant);

3. that **induced** the deceived party's assent to the contract (reliance);
4. under circumstances that make the reliance **justifiable** (reasonable).[1]

All four elements must be satisfied to make out the defense. The other party may enforce the contract if even one element is not shown. See Exhibit 7.1.

EXHIBIT 7.1 Venn Diagram of Misrepresentation

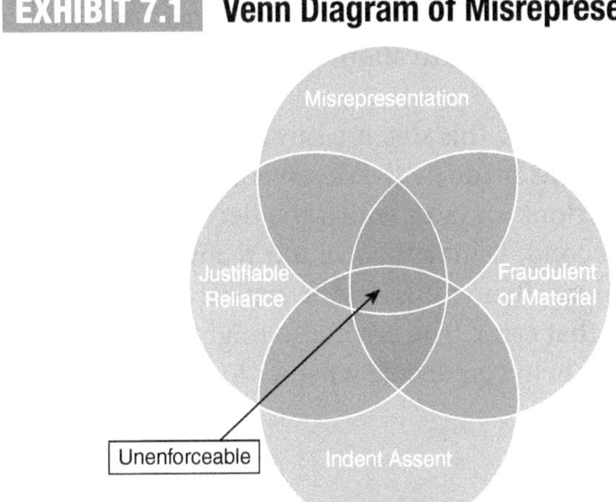

The rule is complicated by several factors. First, a misrepresentation may take any of three different forms: statements, actions, or silence. Those misrepresentations might involve facts or the state of mind of the speaker (what the speaker knows, believes, or intends). Second, the meaning of each element is fairly intricate in itself. Third, the concept of inducement appears in several different elements, playing a slightly different role each time. (Materiality depends on whether an assertion was *likely to induce* another; fraud on whether the assertion was *intended to induce* another.) Be careful to keep the various uses of "induce" straight. Finally, some courts require a different mix of elements, such as requiring materiality even if the statement is fraudulent. As you read the cases below, note ways in which courts state the elements a little differently.

Some of these complications are necessary for the rule to keep up with all the different ways people may be deceived during negotiations. The resulting rule is quite flexible and useful. Getting inside it, however, takes a little work.

Not all misrepresentations originate with a party to the contract. Misrepresentation by a third party—not a party to the contract, but some other person altogether—can support the defense. For example, a buyer may agree to buy a house based on misinformation provided by buyer's broker. No matter who causes the error, the miscalculation of costs and benefits undermines a party's assent. Where other parties to the contract did not contribute to the error, however, special

[1] Restatement (Second) of Contracts §164.

rules apply to protect their interest in what, to them, seemed a perfectly legitimate contract. This special situation will be discussed after the basic elements.

2. Initial Step: Identify the Error

Misrepresentation applies because one party erroneously believed something that was not in accord with the facts. Identifying that error is the essential first step. Before you can attribute the error to another person's misrepresentation, you must identify the error.

As obvious as this sounds, this step is easily overlooked. The temptation simply to start with the statements made by the deceiver is strong. That approach has two flaws. First, it may overlook ways in which the deceiver caused the error without express statements. Second, it may involve too many statements—at least, more than you need to analyze. By identifying the critical error first, you can focus on statements relating to that error. The error also might raise the defense of mistake. Identifying it early may help you decide whether to proceed with mistake, misrepresentation, or both.

3. Identifying an Assertion

A misrepresentation is an "assertion not in accord with the facts."[2] Note the two parts to this definition: (1) an assertion, and (2) the inaccuracy of the assertion. Assertions that are accurate do not mislead the other party and, thus, cannot form the basis of a misrepresentation defense. A true statement is not a misrepresentation, even if the person who makes the assertion believes it is false.

You will sometimes see this definition phrased differently: a false statement of facts. The first version is broader in two useful ways. First, it is not limited to express statements, but can find assertions in other conduct. Second, it is not limited to facts, but can apply to promises or opinions. The word "false" also would limit the defense to facts, since opinions and promises technically are not false. Where facts are involved, identifying the inaccuracy is relatively straightforward: was the assertion true or false? In identifying the error, your analysis already identified beliefs that are not in accord with the facts.

Assertions Inferred from Promises and Opinions

Promises and opinions, while not literally false, nonetheless may mislead. Their inaccuracy is easier to explain by thinking of them as assertions about a party's state of mind. If the promise or opinion inaccurately described the speaker's state of mind, it was a misrepresentation.

---

[2] *Id.* §159.

Promises imply a present intent to perform. Every statement "I promise to perform" can be interpreted as a second statement: "At this time, I intend to perform." This state of mind is a fact: either the person does or does not intend to perform. A person who does not intend to perform has lied: he said he did intend to perform when in fact he did not intend to perform. A person who intends to perform, but later changes her mind, has not made a misrepresentation. She may breach the promise, but did not misstate her intent.

Opinions imply a similar state of mind: an honest belief in the matter asserted as opinion. The state of mind — the belief — is a fact. Either the person does or does not believe the matter asserted. For example, if you say, "Those jeans do not make you look fat," you imply that you believe your words. If you don't, then you have lied: you said that you believed something when you in fact do not believe it. A person who honestly believes the matter asserted has not made a misrepresentation.

Some opinions may imply more than sincerity. Opinions may relate to facts or to subjective qualities. Listeners should instantly understand that some opinions state personal beliefs rather than expressing any objective reality. Thus, comments about value, quality, authenticity, beauty, and so on, are statements of pure opinion, where only the honesty of the opinion matters.[3] Beauty is in the eye of the beholder. Value will differ among people, depending on their tastes and their purposes. Opinions of this sort can be evaluated for good faith.

Opinions as to facts may imply a little more. When a person offers the statement "I believe there are no termites in the house," she might imply two things: (1) that she knows no facts that suggest that there are termites (that is, has seen no termite damage); or (2) she has some basis for this opinion (for example, a recent inspection report).[4] In some circumstances, it may be appropriate to treat a statement of opinion as including one or both of these two additional implications. Each converts the opinion into a statement of fact that will be true or false. A person either knows inconsistent facts or does not; she either has some basis for the opinion or does not.

The first seems like the least that an opinion regarding facts implies. A person who has seen termite damage seems unlikely to believe that there are no termites present. Inferring some basis for the facts will be less common, but may apply in some situations. When someone does not mention a termite report, it is harder to infer that the bald opinion implies its existence. In some cases, however, reassurances may imply that the speaker has some basis for the opinion. In those cases, the absence of that basis will make the opinion false.

Assertions Inferred from Silence

In some cases, a deceiver will not say anything false. She will simply allow the deceived party to continue to believe something false. Blaming a silent party for the error, while possible, is not inevitable. That person did not contribute to the creation of the error, only to its perpetuation. In some circumstances, however, the law will find an assertion without any express statement.

[3] *Id.* §168(1).
[4] *Id.* §168(2).

Concealment involves conduct intended to prevent another from learning a fact.[5] For example, the seller of a house might paint over cracks in the walls to hide evidence that the foundation is defective. This act seems likely to prevent a prospective buyer from investigating the foundation, thus qualifying as concealment. In effect, applying the paint to conceal the cracks would amount to a statement that "there are no cracks in the walls."

Nondisclosure involves silence when a person omits information that should have been shared. Normally, people have no duty to correct another person's errors or point out reasons that the contract might not benefit the other party. Parties negotiating at arm's length are entitled to look out for their own best interests and expect other parties to look out for theirs. Colloquially, the law does not make anyone the other party's keeper. But in some circumstances, silence crosses the line from a right to a wrong. In those settings, failure to speak will be treated as if the person had denied the existence of a fact.

Converting silence into an implied statement makes it easier to apply some of the other elements of misrepresentation. For example, proving reliance on the other party's failure to speak poses conundrums that disappear if the other party is treated as having spoken.

Concealment and nondisclosure offer ways to find an assertion. Additional steps remain: showing that the assertion was not in accord with the facts, then showing the other elements of the defense (fraudulent or material, inducement, justifiable reliance). Concealment and nondisclosure, then, are not separate defenses. They are tools you can use in the process of building a misrepresentation defense.

Case Preview

Barrer v. Women's National Bank

In this case, Barrer needed an emergency loan to save his house. A bank promised the loan, but later refused to pay based on inaccurate disclosures. The case offers an excellent discussion of the elements of the misrepresentation defense. It illustrates a critical point: that rescission does not depend on misconduct or intent to deceive. In addition, it discusses some of the nuances of nondisclosure, describing why Barrer's failure to reveal some details did not entitle the bank to avoid the transaction.

As you read *Barrer v. Women's National Bank*, look for the following:

1. How does the rule applied by the court differ from the Restatement rule above?
2. Under what circumstances will silence be treated as a misrepresentation?
3. Why wasn't the failure to reveal that his mortgage had not been paid in six months a material misrepresentation?
4. Why wasn't the failure to reveal that his mortgage was being foreclosed a material misrepresentation?

---

[5] *Id.* §160.

Barrer v. Women's National Bank

761 F.2d 752 (D.C. Cir. 1985)

HARRY T. EDWARDS, Circuit Judge.

The appellant, Lester A. Barrer, brought this action against Women's National Bank ("the Bank" or "WNB") for damages he allegedly sustained as the result of the Bank's eleventh hour decision to rescind a loan agreement. . . . The magistrate . . . granted WNB's motion for summary judgment. We find that the magistrate failed to apply the correct legal test for determining when an innocent material misrepresentation permits the rescission of a contract, and that there are material issues of fact that make summary judgment inappropriate. Accordingly, we reverse and remand. . . .

I. BACKGROUND

A. Factual Background

On June 24, 1981, Lester Barrer's personal home was sold at a tax sale by the Internal Revenue Service ("IRS") because of his inability to pay certain employment taxes. . . . At the tax sale, Barrer's home was purchased by Edward L. Curtis, Jr., for $16,326, subject to the underlying mortgage. . . . [Footnotes omitted throughout.] Barrer . . . could redeem his home by delivering $17,400, in cash or its equivalent, to the IRS or to Curtis on or before October 22, 1981.

On October 20, 1981, Barrer went to WNB to discuss a personal loan for the redemption amount. . . . [H]e waited until the last minute to seek a bank loan because he . . . had expected to close on the sale [of his business] before October 20, 1981, and . . . had intended to use the proceeds from that sale to redeem his house.

At WNB, Barrer spoke with Emily Womack, the President of the Bank, with whom he had a professional acquaintance. Barrer completed [a loan application form] and returned [it] to her the next day, . . . along with certain supporting documents, including those concerning the tax sale and his efforts to sell the business.

. . .

On October 21, Barrer and Womack reviewed his loan application line by line. [Barrer provided additional details explaining some of the liabilities listed, including a $65,000 mortgage on his home held by Columbia First Federal Savings and Loan Association ("Columbia").]

. . .

[At Womack's insistence] Barrer obtained [a] subordination agreement from the IRS and delivered it to the Bank. Barrer then executed a collateral note for $17,400, payable in 90 days at 15 percent interest, which gave the Bank the right to a security interest in his house. The Bank's Vice President, Emma Carrera, gave Barrer a cashier's check, payable to him, for the loan amount. Prior to granting the loan, neither Womack nor Carrera obtained a credit report on Barrer and neither officer phoned Columbia about the status of his mortgage.

That afternoon, Barrer delivered the endorsed check to the IRS in accordance with the required redemption procedure and returned home, believing that his home had been saved.

In the meantime, the tax sale purchaser, Curtis, phoned WNB and spoke with Carrera. [Curtis commented on Barrer's creditworthiness, leading Carrera to pull a credit report on Barrer.]

Based on the information furnished by Curtis . . . and the credit report, the Bank decided to stop payment on the cashier's check [and informed Barrer of that decision].

B. Procedural History

Barrer filed suit against the Bank in District Court to recover damages to compensate him for the loss of $94,000 equity in his home—the difference between the market value of the house and the balance due on the mortgage—that he allegedly suffered as a result of the Bank's rescission of the loan agreement. Barrer also claimed punitive damages for the embarrassment he endured and the rent he has been required to pay Curtis in order to remain in his home.

The case was referred to a magistrate for pretrial proceedings. On the Bank's motion for summary judgment, the magistrate found that Barrer did not disclose the following five material facts to the Bank: (1) that he was six months delinquent in mortgage payments, (2) that Columbia had begun foreclosure procedures, (3) that Barrer had at least an $11,000 contingent liability to the IRS in addition to his $38,000 actual liability, (4) that he had a contingent liability to IBM of approximately $5,000, and (5) that he had approximately $1,500 in unsatisfied judgments pending against him. The magistrate purported to rely on the law of innocent material misrepresentation to hold that these disclosure omissions justified WNB's rescission of the loan contract. On that basis, he granted summary judgment in favor of the Bank. This appeal followed.

II. ANALYSIS

. . .

B. Elements of Innocent Material Misrepresentation

[M]isrepresentation of material facts may be the basis for the rescission of a contract, even where the misrepresentations are made innocently, without knowledge of their falsity and without fraudulent intent. The rationale supporting this rule, which has its origins in equity, is that, as between two innocent parties, the party making the representation should bear the loss. "[O]ne who has made a false statement ought not to benefit at the expense of another who has been prejudiced by relying on the statement." This rule may be employed "actively," as in a suit at equity or law for rescission and restitution, or "passively," as a defense to a suit for breach of contract.

[F]our conditions must be met before a contract may be avoided for innocent misrepresentation. The recipient of the alleged misrepresentation must demonstrate that the maker made an assertion: (1) that was not in accord with the facts, (2) that was material, and (3) that was relied upon (4) justifiably by the recipient in manifesting his assent to the agreement. District of Columbia law adds a fifth condition, *i.e.,* that the recipient relied to his detriment.

Unfortunately, the applicable precedent does not elaborate on the meaning of these conditions. In trying to give them content, . . . the Restatement (Second) of Contracts ("Restatement (Second)") provides helpful guidance concerning the first four conditions.

1. *Misrepresentation*

Section 159 of the Restatement (Second) defines a misrepresentation as "an assertion that is not in accord with the facts." Comment c explains that an "assertion must relate to something that is a fact at the time the assertion is made in order to be a misrepresentation. Such facts include past events as well as present circumstances but do not include future events." Comment d observes that a person's state of mind is a fact and that an assertion of one's opinion constitutes a misrepresentation if the state of mind is other than as asserted.

According to section 161, the only non-disclosures that may be considered assertions of fact for purposes of misrepresentation analysis are non-disclosures of facts known to the maker where the maker knows that disclosure: (a) is necessary to prevent a previous assertion from being a misrepresentation or from being fraudulent or material, (b) would correct a mistake of the other party as to a basic assumption on which that party is making the contract, if non-disclosure amounts to a failure to act in good faith and in accordance with reasonable standards of fair dealing, or (c) would correct a mistake of the other party as to the contents or effect of a writing. The section also provides that where the other person is entitled to know the non-disclosed facts because a relation of trust and confidence exists between the parties, non-disclosure is equivalent to an assertion of facts.

2. *Materiality*

In section 162, comment c, the Restatement (Second) explains that a misrepresentation is material "if it would be likely to induce a reasonable person to manifest his assent." [I]t . . . asks whether the assertion is one to which a reasonable person might be expected to attach importance in making a choice of action. . . .

[T]he materiality requirement . . . encourage[s] stability in contract relations [by] prevent[ing] parties who become disappointed at the outcome of their bargain from seizing upon any insignificant discrepancy to void the contract.

3. *Reliance*

Section 167 requires that the misrepresentation be causally related to the recipient's decision to agree to the contract—that it have been an inducement to agree. [T]his reliance need not, however, be the sole or predominant factor influencing the recipient's decision. . . .

4. *Justifiability of Reliance*

Section 172 of the Restatement (Second) provides that a recipient's fault in not knowing or discovering the facts before making the contract does not make his reliance unjustified unless it amounts to a failure to act in good faith and in accordance with reasonable standards of fair dealing.

While section 169 suggests that reliance on an assertion of opinion often is not justified, section 168(2) and the accompanying comment d make clear that in some situations the recipient may reasonably understand a statement of opinion to be more than an assertion as to the maker's state of mind. Where circumstances justify it, a statement of opinion may also be reasonably understood as carrying with it an assertion that the maker knows facts sufficient to justify him in forming it.

5. *Detriment*

Because the Restatement (Second) does not require a showing of detriment for rescission, it does not define it. We think that, in the innocent material misrepresentation context, a recipient is appropriately considered to have relied to his detriment where he receives something that is less valuable or different in some significant respect from that which he reasonably expected.

C. Application of Legal Standards

Application of the foregoing principles to the facts of this case requires that the case be remanded for trial. The magistrate tested Barrer's alleged misrepresentations against only two of the five elements necessary for rescission — he asked only if the representations were in accord with the facts and if they were material. [T]he magistrate failed to consider the legal distinctions between assertions of fact and non-disclosure and between assertions of fact and statements of opinion. He neglected to investigate whether the Bank actually relied on the representations in deciding to make the loan; whether that reliance, if it existed, was justifiable; and whether the Bank relied to its detriment. Furthermore, the magistrate incorrectly concluded that there were no legally probative, material issues of fact in dispute.

1. *Elements the Magistrate Failed to Consider*

Initially, assuming for a moment that Barrer actually "misrepresented" certain facts, the materiality of the representations is hardly obvious. After deciding which representations meet the legal definition of misrepresentation, the trial court must determine with regard to each individual misrepresentation whether it was "likely to induce a reasonable [bank] to manifest [its] assent" to the loan agreement. If no single misrepresentation is found to be material, the court may consider, after ascertaining the assertions upon which WNB justifiably relied, whether those assertions are material when taken together.

All five alleged "misrepresentations" also raise serious factual questions as to whether the Bank actually and justifiably relied on them. Womack's expressed sympathy for Barrer combined with the fact that the loan was issued in a very short time, without either a credit check, which was obtainable in minutes, or an inquiry into the status of Barrer's mortgage, and the fact that the loan was withdrawn only when the Bank was placed in an embarrassing position by the tax sale purchaser — all these circumstances could suggest that the Bank was not very interested in the particulars of Barrer's financial condition. Indeed, it was clear from the loan application that Barrer did admit that he was experiencing financial difficulties, yet WNB chose to make no further inquiry into the details of these problems. These facts could be construed to show that Womack's sympathy for Barrer's predicament was the real inducement for the loan. If the trial court finds that the Bank actually relied on Barrer's alleged "misrepresentations," it nonetheless must proceed to decide whether that reliance was justified.

The trial court must also determine whether the Bank's reliance on Barrer's alleged "misrepresentations" caused it any detriment. Did WNB receive as its benefit of the bargain something less valuable or significantly different from what it reasonably expected? In addition, the trial court should consider whether the subordination agreement, in combination with the right to a security interest in Barrer's house granted by the collateral note, fully satisfied the Bank's expectations.

The magistrate also made individual errors with respect to the five representations. . . .

2. *Delinquency in Mortgage Payments*

Barrer and Womack disagree over whether he told her that he "thought" he was two months behind in his mortgage payments or whether he said that he was current. Because this case is before us on appeal from the magistrate's grant of summary judgment for the Bank, we must accept Barrer's statement of the facts. The Bank argues that even if Barrer's version is accepted, a misrepresentation still occurred because Barrer was actually six months behind. The Bank's position is not necessarily correct.

Barrer's statement that he "thought" he was in arrears by two months initially raises the factual question whether he made *any* misrepresentation. On the surface, the fact asserted by Barrer was his state of mind — what he thought. No finding was made below that Barrer's state of mind was other than what he declared. [Barrer explained that he thought his obligation to pay his mortgage ceased at the time of the tax sale and that he did not realize that he was responsible for more than the two months' mortgage payments that had been due before the sale.] On remand, before it may determine that this statement constituted a misrepresentation, the court must find either that Barrer misstated his thoughts, in accordance with the rule laid out in section 159, comment d of the Restatement (Second), or that Barrer's statement could reasonably have been understood as carrying with it an assertion that Barrer knew sufficient facts that justified him in forming his opinion, in accordance with section 168(2).

. . .

3. *Failure to Disclose Mortgage Foreclosure Proceedings*

Although the Bank evidently did not ask Barrer directly whether his mortgage was being foreclosed upon, it contends that he had an obligation to volunteer that information and that his failure to do so is tantamount to a misrepresentation. Barrer argues that he had no duty to reveal the existence of the foreclosure proceedings because he did not know about them. The Bank maintains that he must have known, because before Barrer applied for the loan his teenage daughter signed for a certified letter from Columbia notifying him of the foreclosure.

The magistrate erred in finding on summary judgment that this non-disclosure is equivalent to a misrepresentation. The Restatement (Second) provides that a non-disclosure may be considered an assertion of fact for purposes of misrepresentation analysis only if the non-disclosed fact is known to the maker and if certain other conditions are met. Because there exists a material issue of fact as to whether Barrer knew that Columbia had begun to foreclose, summary judgment was inappropriate.

4. *$11,000 Contingent Liability*

The magistrate also erred in finding on summary judgment that Barrer's alleged failure to list as a personal contingent liability an $11,000 tax debt owed to the IRS by his corporation constituted a misrepresentation. First, summary judgment is precluded by the existence of a factual dispute over whether this $11,000 was included in the $38,000 tax liability that Barrer did list. . . . Second, there is a mixed question of law and fact as to whether the IRS had, at the time of the loan application, taken any action to assert the $11,000 tax debt owed by Today News Service, Inc., against Barrer personally and, if not, whether the corporation's liability may be considered Barrer's contingent liability. If the $11,000 tax debt could not at that time have been considered Barrer's liability, his failure to list such a debt was not a misrepresentation.

5. *$5,300 Debt Owed to IBM*

The magistrate found that Barrer's failure to reveal as a personal liability a $5,300 debt owed to IBM for equipment purchased by his wife was a misrepresentation. We disagree as a matter of law. Although Barrer asked the probate court handling his wife's estate to charge him with the debt, the court refused, ruling that the debt was hers alone. Contrary to the Bank's protestations, it makes no difference to the determination whether a misrepresentation occurred that Barrer asked the probate court to charge him with the debt before, and the court refused after, Barrer submitted the loan application. A misrepresentation is "an assertion that is not in accord with the facts." The fact is that a court decided that this debt *never* legally belonged to Barrer. Barrer's thoughts or wishes on the matter are irrelevant. He made no legal misrepresentation to the Bank on this subject.

6. *$1,500 in Judgments*

Finally, the magistrate determined that Barrer's failure to list $1,500 in judgments that were outstanding against him constituted a misrepresentation. This issue should not have been resolved on summary judgment. Barrer disclosed on the loan application that he was a defendant in some lawsuits. Furthermore, in his deposition he stated that he had informed Womack that he owed some small judgments arising out of these suits and that he expected his health insurance to cover most of them. Accepting Barrer's version of the facts, . . . he revealed both his defendant status and the existence of judgments against him. It is true that he did not list them on the application form. Because, however, Barrer contends that he adequately disclosed these debts in connection with the question concerning lawsuits and in his discussion with Womack, there exists a dispute over whether he actually revealed these

debts; consequently the magistrate should not have resolved this issue on summary judgment. On remand, two factual questions must be decided. First, what information concerning these judgments did Barrer give to Womack? Second, was that information sufficient to give the Bank notice of them? If it was sufficient, then Barrer made no misrepresentation.

Post-Case Follow-Up

The court's cautious attitude toward nondisclosure reflects the rule's language confining the situations in which silence becomes an assertion to the most egregious situations. The court carefully explained that statements of opinion ("I think") become misrepresentations only if they do not reflect the speaker's actual thoughts. The court also limited nondisclosure to cases involving actual knowledge of the facts, rather than imputed knowledge. The court carefully distinguished Barrer's debts from debts owed by others associated with him (his wife, his company). Of course, none of this would save Barrer if, on remand, his explanations lack credibility. Ultimately, a finder of fact will need to evaluate the honesty of his assertions.

Barrer v. Women's National Bank: Real Life Applications

1. Sam sought to lease a semi-truck from Pat. In response to Pat's question, Sam assured Pat that Sam had insurance against any losses. Sam did not tell Pat that Sam's insurance had a $1 million deductible. After the lease had been in effect for three months, Pat discovered the truth and canceled the lease. If Sam sues for breach of contract, will Pat prevail by arguing that the nondisclosure amounts to a misrepresentation?

2. Gene owns a house in a quiet subdivision in a good school district. Gene's next-door neighbor is a registered sex offender who, from the limited contact Gene has had, seems a good neighbor. Gene plans to sell the house. Gene seeks your advice concerning how much information about the neighbor's criminal background Gene must disclose to prospective buyers. If Gene says nothing to prospective buyers, would that qualify as a nondisclosure? How little can Gene say to avoid a nondisclosure without jeopardizing the prospects for selling the home at a good price?

3. Leslie spotted a framed print at a yard sale with the price tag $10. Leslie recognized it as a valuable limited edition work and realized the owner must be mistaken about the work's authenticity. Without revealing that information to the seller, Leslie offered $8 for the print, which the seller accepted. A week later, the seller saw the print in Leslie's antique store with the price $10,000. If the seller seeks to rescind the transaction for misrepresentation, will Leslie's nondisclosure constitute a misrepresentation? (Would the case differ if Leslie paid the full $10 instead of offering only $8?)

4. BigCo recently announced that it would need to lay off about 1,000 employees. Leo's job was eliminated in this reduction in force. BigCo offered Leo a significant severance payment if Leo would sign a separation agreement in which, among other things, he agreed to waive any claim to sue for discharge. Leo carefully created a document almost identical to the original agreement, but deleted the waiver of the right to sue for age discrimination. Leo signed that document and accepted the severance check. Leo later sued for age discrimination. Can BigCo seek rescission for misrepresentation because Leo failed to disclose the changes to the document? Will rescission serve BigCo's interests?

Circumstances Requiring Disclosure

The *Barrer* court, relying on the Restatement (Second) of Contracts, identified four situations in which people should disclose information even if they are not asked. Specifically, a person should not remain silent if:

1. A relation of trust and confidence gives the other party a right to the information;
2. She knows that her prior statements contributed to the other party's error;
3. She knows that the other party is mistaken about the contents or effect of contract documents; or
4. She knows that the other party is mistaken concerning a basic assumption of the contract *and* "silence amounts to a failure to act in good faith."[6]

These categories try to summarize the explanations courts give for finding misrepresentations in a person's silence. They offer a good starting point for any discussion of nondisclosure. The discussion below explores the implications of this language, though courts may not apply it with the rigor suggested here, allowing some room for play at the edges.

Relation of Trust

Relation of trust and confidence lacks a precise definition. It includes **fiduciaries**, who have a legal obligation to put the interest of others ahead of their own interests. Examples include lawyers, who must put client interests ahead of their own, and trustees, who must act in the best interests of the beneficiaries of the trust, even if the trustee's own interests might differ. Relation of trust includes other relationships in which one party has a right to expect another to treat its interests equally or, in some cases, put the others' interests ahead of its own, such as family members and guardians. Most commercial relationships (e.g., employment and sales) are not relations of trust. You may trust the other party, but the relationship is strictly business. Parties are entitled to **bargain at arm's length**, each looking out for its own best interest and leaving the other to fend for itself.

[6] Restatement (Second) of Contracts §161.

Prior Assertions

Prior assertions, even if true when made, may mislead others. That prior assertion might become a misrepresentation — or may become fraudulent or material — in light of new information. If a person knows that disclosure would prevent a prior assertion from misleading the other party, then nondisclosure is the equivalent of saying the fact does not exist. This can apply to half-truths. For instance, in *Kannavos v. Annino*,[7] a real estate seller said the property contained multi-family rental units, but failed to disclose that the zoning laws prohibited that use, limiting the lots to single-family homes. The court allowed rescission; mentioning the multi-family use was enough to require disclosure of the zoning. The rule also can require updated information. Persons applying for insurance policies generally need to inform insurers if any information on their policy application has changed between the time they filled it out and the time the policy issued (say, a new diagnosis that affects the risk insured). Failure to do so is the equivalent of reiterating the statement at the time of formation, when it is no longer true or no longer believed.

Fighting Human Nature

The inclination not to share information (when silence is beneficial) is deeply embedded in human nature; the law is unlikely to change it. A rule that required counterintuitive disclosures is unlikely to encourage compliance. Rather, it will surprise people who find that their natural choices have been declared illegitimate — and perhaps deny them important contract benefits they expect. Finding valuable antiques at garage sales is a hobby (in some cases a business). Allowing rescission because good faith requires disclosure will sound odd to many people.

Contents of a Writing

Known mistakes about the contents or effect of contract documents require disclosure. One cannot legitimately rely on terms in a writing if one knows the other believes the writing does not contain such terms. For example, a used car seller accidentally uses a form contract that includes a warranty, thinking that she had pulled a form that disclaimed warranties. If buyer knows that seller is mistaken about the warranty term, silence about that mistake will be the equivalent of saying that the form does not include a warranty — a misrepresentation, under these facts.

When misrepresentations involve the terms of a writing, courts often **reform** (rewrite) the document to reflect the terms to which the parties originally agreed (or to which they intended to agree) instead of rescinding the contract. In the example above, if the court concludes that the parties agreed to a sale with no warranty, it might reform the writing to reflect the contract (the agreement actually made) — either by deleting the warranty term from the form the parties did use or by substituting the form the parties intended to use.

Good Faith

Good faith may require disclosing known mistakes regarding important assumptions. In arm's-length transactions, parties normally can bargain for their own benefit, without the need to protect the other party from any errors (of judgment or

[7] 247 N.E.2d 708 (Mass. 1969).

fact) that they may be making. Thus, in *Swinton v. Whitinsville Savings Bank*,[8] a seller knew a house was infested with termites but said nothing. The court denied rescission because the seller had no duty to reveal the termites to buyers.

Nonetheless, taking advantage of a known error of the other party may cross the line, especially where more than money is at stake. For instance, a landlord who knows that the pollen count from a nearby nursery makes an apartment unsuitable for a couple whose child has allergies probably should reveal the nearby nursery. Given risks to the child's health, good faith seems to require disclosure.

No clear test differentiates acceptable silence from breach of good faith. Revealing every known mistake seems wrong. But exactly when good faith requires disclosure will vary with the circumstances in ways that defy prediction.

EXHIBIT 7.2 Decision Tree for Assertions and Misrepresentations

4. Inducement

Misrepresentations do not justify rescission if they have no effect on a party's decision to enter the contract. The defense applies only if the misrepresentation

[8]42 N.E.2d 808 (Mass. 1942).

induced assent—that is, substantially contributed to a party's decision to enter the deal on these terms.[9] In effect, this requires actual reliance on the misrepresentation, but limits reliance specifically to the decision to enter the contract. This requirement rejects the defense unless the assertion was significant to the deceived party's decision-making process. The deceived party need not prove that she would have made a different decision. But if the evidence shows that the deceived party would have entered the contract anyway, the misrepresentation defense probably will fail. Where the matter was so minor that the same contract would have resulted even if the truth had been known, the defense serves no purpose.

Try your hand at applying this rule to the following common situation. Applicant seeks a life insurance policy from Insurer. On the application form, Applicant responds "no" to the question about smoking cigarettes, even though Applicant smokes a pack a day and has for many years. If it knew of Applicant's smoking, Insurer probably would have offered Applicant a policy at a higher premium. Instead, Insurer issues a policy to Applicant at the lower premium it offers to nonsmokers. Did the false statement induce the Insurer to manifest assent to the contract?

Inducement plays a role in finding materiality and fraudulent motives. In determining materiality, one considers whether the assertion was likely to induce assent. In determining fraud, one asks whether the other party intended to induce assent. Both of these elements look at inducement from the perspective of the deceiver. The definition of inducement (as substantially contributing to the decision) continues to apply.

5. Fraudulent or Material

To support the defense of misrepresentation, an assertion must be either fraudulent or material. In theory, it need not be both. In practice, cases rarely involve fraudulent misrepresentations that were not material. But cases often involve material misrepresentations that were not fraudulent. Thus, the *Barrer* case noted that an **innocent misrepresentation** (one that the speaker honestly and reasonably believes to be true) may justify rescission if it involves a matter of importance to the contract. A misrepresentation of a significant fact may cause the deceived party to miscalculate of the costs and benefits even if the speaker honestly believed the statement. Thus, a misled party may avoid the contract regardless of the speaker's innocence in making the statement.

Some jurisdictions require that misrepresentations be both fraudulent and material. Tort liability for deceit often requires both components before a court will award damages caused by the fraud. Even in tort, however, many jurisdictions allow recovery for negligent and sometimes innocent misrepresentations. In contract, misrepresentation does not produce a damage award, but only rescission of the contract and restitution of benefits bestowed on the other party. In these settings, states often allow the defense based on any material misrepresentation, without requiring fraud.

[9] Restatement (Second) of Contracts §167.

Material

An assertion is material in either of two situations:

1. the assertion is likely to induce the assent of a reasonable person; or
2. the maker of the assertion knows it is likely to induce the assent of this person.[10]

Both view materiality from the perspective of the speaker. In effect, they limit the defense to situations where the speaker should take pains to be accurate because he should realize the matter is of some importance.

If reasonable people are likely to attach significance to the matter asserted, then the maker should know not to make careless assertions — an objective test, without regard to what the speaker actually knew. For example, a person selling a home should realize that buyers will care about termites on the premises.[11]

In some settings, a person might learn that a particular buyer cares about something that others would not — say, whether the previous occupant had cats. Once aware that the fact is important to this person (subjectively), the speaker should exercise care not to make misleading assertions.

Fraudulent

To be fraudulent, the speaker must intend the assertion to induce the other party's assent. In addition to intent to induce, one of the following conditions must pertain to find fraud:

1. The maker knew the assertion was not in accord with the facts;
2. The maker believed the assertion was not in accord with the facts;
3. The maker stated or implied that she had a basis for the assertion, even though she lacked that basis; or
4. The maker did not have as much confidence in the truth of the assertion as she stated or implied that she had.[12]

The first two involve simple lies. If the maker knows or believes that the assertion is false, then saying it is a lie. The last two involve exaggeration, especially as to the maker's state of mind. Expressing confidence that one does not feel lies about one's state of mind. Confessing uncertainty might lead the other party to investigate further, avoiding the error. Similarly, exaggerating the basis for the assertion — especially an assertion of opinion — misleads the other party. Either may deter the other party from seeking to confirm the facts, believing the other has already confirmed them. This causes the error by preventing it from being discovered in advance. See Exhibit 7.3.

[10] *Id.* §162(2).
[11] *Halpert v. Rosenthal*, 267 A.2d 730 (R.I. 1970).
[12] Restatement (Second) of Contracts §162(1).

EXHIBIT 7.3 Diagram for Fraudulence

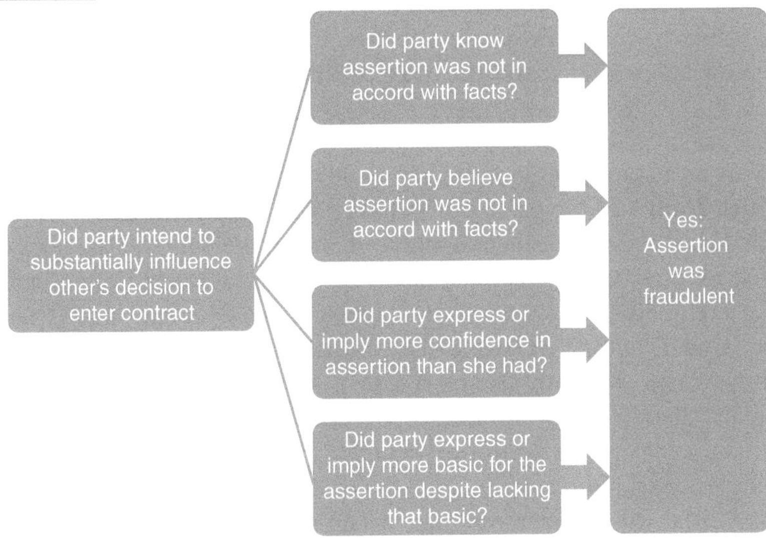

All of these situations apply only if the maker intends the assertion to induce the other party's assent. That is, the maker must intend for the assertion to contribute substantially to the decision to enter the contract. Most of the things a person says during contract negotiations seem likely to satisfy this requirement. But trivial lies during small talk may not justify rescission. For example, a seller who lies to prospective buyers about his age probably does not commit fraud.

6. Justifiable Reliance

The defense will not apply if the party's reliance on the assertion was not justifiable. (Reliance here refers to entering the contract.) In some cases, a party should not depend on assertions by the other party, but should make her own assessments of the situation. Yet liars generate little sympathy by arguing, "You never should have believed me!" Justifiable reliance tends to pose an issue in two categories: (1) a party's knowledge (or easy access to knowledge) makes reliance inappropriate; (2) or the nature of the representation (usually opinions) makes reliance inappropriate.

Reliance on Facts

Reliance on misrepresentations of fact usually is justifiable. There seems little reason to require the deceived party to verify independently all the facts the other party presents, especially when the other party is in a position to know the facts. For example, most sellers know their wares better than a buyer can, even after investigation.

Reliance on assertions of fact may be unjustified in two settings:

1. where the other party already knows the truth; or
2. where the failure to discover the truth constitutes a lack of good faith.

Relying on a known falsehood is unjustified. People who know the truth should rely on that truth, not the error others pass off as reality. For example, if a buyer knows that land is zoned residential only, relying on the seller's false statement that it is zoned commercial seems unjustifiable. Even if inducement is met (because the buyer does rely), it seems hard to justify allowing one who knows the true state of affairs to avoid a contract when she discovers that she was right all along.

In other cases, the truth may be staring the deceived party in the face. Failure to recognize the truth may amount to a lack of good faith.[13] When discovering the truth does not involve significant expense or effort, but simply involves opening one's eyes or asking reasonable questions, justifiable reliance may fail. In these cases, one often will wonder whether in fact the person really did discover the truth and is simply playing dumb. For example, consider the buyer of a used car who is told the car has air bags. A simple glance at the dashboard to see if the "SRS" symbol is there should alert the buyer to the true situation. Relying on the falsehood when verification is so easy may be unjustifiable. But in *Kannavos*, the court allowed rescission even though the buyer (who did not actually know how land was zoned) could have checked the zoning with relatively little effort. Even though the burden of confirmation was relatively small, the court did not find the failure to check displayed a lack of good faith.

In some business contexts, the requirements for justifiable reliance may be more substantial. For example, when one company buys another, it usually devotes a substantial amount of time to **due diligence**, verifying the other's accounts and objectively determining business value. In this setting, relying on the representations of the acquired company may seem less reasonable. Contracts of this sort often contain terms disclaiming reliance on representations by the other party—except representations and warranties expressly identified in the contracts.

Reliance on Opinions

Reliance on matters of opinion, no matter how sincere, usually is not justifiable. One normally should form one's own opinions, especially regarding inherently subjective matters, such as value or quality. This rule protects a whole range of sales talk often referred to as **puffing** (or **spin**): putting one's product in the best light, even if that involves exaggeration. When a used car salesman says the engine "purrs like a kitten," no one really expects to hear a cat-like sound from the car.

As noted earlier, opinions regarding facts may be treated as statements of fact. For example, an opinion may imply a basis that the maker does not in fact have.

---

[13] *Id.* §172.

Once converted to an assertion of fact, justifiable reliance would be analyzed under the preceding section.

In a few situations, however, courts have found reliance on opinions justifiable, even when the matter involves pure opinion (judgments of value, quality, and so on). Three circumstances may justify reliance on an opinion:

1. A relation of trust and confidence;
2. The misled party reasonably believes the other party has special skill, judgment, or objectivity with regard to this subject matter, at least in comparison to the misled party; or
3. The misled party is particularly susceptible to misrepresentations of the type involved.[14]

People are entitled to rely on the opinions of those who occupy a fiduciary relationship with them. Relying on opinions in arm's-length bargaining may be problematic. Realistically, however, people will rely on those they believe have expertise. Allowing these experts to profit from deceptive opinions holds little appeal. Stated broadly, however, expertise might justify reliance on opinions in an enormous number of transactions.

Special susceptibility has arisen in cases involving dance studios, where attractive instructors lured lonely, elderly people into paying thousands of dollars (in advance) for more hours of dance lessons than they were likely ever to use — perhaps by appearing to offer companionship rather than actual instruction.[15]

Case Preview

Jordan v. Knafel

Karla Knafel and her attorney Michael T. Hannafan
Getty Images

This case provides an interesting context in which to explore some of the issues surrounding misrepresentation, in addition to reviewing some aspects of consideration and duress. The case raises a number of interesting social issues, such as the extent to which rules governing misrepresentation and nondisclosure are realistic when applied to intimate relations. Primarily, the case probes whether the representations here were material, whether they induced assent, and whether reliance was justifiable.

As you read *Jordan v. Knafel*, look for the following:

1. How does the test for misrepresentation applied here differ from the one discussed above?

[14] *Id.* §169.

[15] *See, e.g.*, *Vokes v. Arthur Murray, Inc.*, 212 So. 2d 906 (Fla. App. 1968).

2. Did this case involve affirmative statements or nondisclosure? Does that difference matter?
3. How did the court determine whether the misrepresentations here were material?
4. How did the court determine whether reliance on these misrepresentations was justifiable?

Jordan v. Knafel

880 N.E.2d 1061 (Ill. App. 2007), app. denied, 888 N.E.2d 1184 (Ill. 2008)

Justice Theis.

. . .

BACKGROUND

[The dispute centers on allegations that Jordan promised to pay Knafel, the mother of a child allegedly sired by Jordan, $5 million when Jordan retired from basketball. Jordan sought declaratory judgment, denying that he made the promise and raising defenses including duress and lack of consideration.] Knafel filed a verified counterclaim [seeking damages of $5 million].

The following relevant facts were alleged in the verified counterclaim. . . .

In December 1989, three months after Jordan had married his wife, Knafel traveled to Chicago to meet Jordan, where they had unprotected sex. Thereafter, in November 1990, Knafel stayed with Jordan in Phoenix, Arizona, where they again had unprotected sex. In early 1991, Knafel learned that she was pregnant. She "was convinced that she was carrying Jordan's baby". . . .

. . . In the spring of 1991, Jordan offered . . . to pay her "$5 million when he retired from professional basket ball [*sic*] in return for her agreement not to file a paternity suit against him and for her agreement to keep their romantic involvement publicly confidential." Knafel accepted Jordan's offer. . . .

In July 1991, Knafel's child was born. Jordan paid certain hospital bills and medical costs and paid Knafel $250,000 for "her mental pain and anguish arising from her relationship with him." Knafel did not file a paternity suit against Jordan and she kept their relationship confidential.

[In 2000], after Jordan failed to pay the $5 million under the alleged agreement, Knafel's counsel contacted Jordan's counsel to resolve their contract dispute. Jordan denied that he had promised to pay Knafel $5 million and eventually [this litigation ensued.]

. . .

. . . Jordan filed . . . a motion for summary judgment on Knafel's counterclaims. For purposes of the motion . . . Jordan did not contest the existence of the alleged settlement agreement. Rather, he argued that the alleged agreement was unenforceable because it was either fraudulently induced or was based on a mutual mistake of fact as to the paternity of Knafel's child. In support, Jordan attached the affidavit of Dr.

Charles M. Strom . . . indicat[ing] that Jordan was excluded from being the father of Knafel's child by both DNA and serology testing.

In response, Knafel argued that Jordan's actual paternity was irrelevant to the enforceability of the alleged settlement agreement. [A]t the time of the alleged agreement she believed in good faith that she was pregnant with Jordan's child. Specifically, she stated that she informed Jordan throughout their relationship that she was having sex with another man and that he even teased her about it. . . . She and Jordan were together in Phoenix, Arizona, on November 19-20, 1990, when they had unprotected sex. On February 14, 1991, her obstetrician, Dr. Michael F. Grisanti, told her that her baby was conceived on November 19 or 20, 1990 . . . coincid[ing] with her stay with Jordan in Phoenix. . . .

. . .

After a hearing, the trial court granted Jordan's motion for summary judgment on the counterclaim [and his declaratory judgment action], finding that "as a result of Knafel's fraudulent misrepresentation to Jordan that he was the child's father or, alternatively, as a result of a mutual mistake of fact, the alleged settlement contract is voidable and is therefore unenforceable against Jordan."

ANALYSIS

. . .

In order for a representation to constitute fraud that would permit a court to set aside a contract, the party seeking such relief must establish that the representation was: (1) one of material fact; (2) made for the purpose of inducing the other party to act; (3) known to be false by the maker, or not actually believed by him on reasonable grounds to be true, but reasonably believed to be true by the other party; and (4) was relied upon by the other party to his detriment. [Citations omitted.]

Knafel asserts that there is a genuine issue of fact as to whether her affirmative representation to Jordan that "she was pregnant with his child" was material to the alleged settlement agreement and induced Jordan to act. Specifically, she argues that Jordan's actual paternity (1) was not a subject of discussion when they reached their settlement agreement; (2) it was not a term or contingent condition of their settlement agreement; and (3) Jordan has never actually stated that it was material to the agreement. Additionally, she maintains that she is entitled to an inference that Jordan's only motive was to preserve his image and protect his lucrative endorsements.

A misrepresentation is "material" if the party seeking rescission would have acted differently had he been aware of the fact or if it concerned the type of information upon which he would be expected to rely when making his decision to act. [Citations omitted.] To be material, the representation need not have been the "paramount or decisive inducement, so long as it was a substantial factor." [Citations omitted.]

Contrary to Knafel's assertions, her own allegations establish that paternity was material to the alleged settlement agreement and was made for the purposes of inducing Jordan to act. . . . In her verified statement, she asserted that it was not until "after [she] told Jordan of [her] pregnancy" that "Jordan said he was troubled at the prospect of destroying his public image" and he agreed to the alleged settlement. Thus, although a general fear of public exposure of their relationship may well have been a factor when Jordan proposed the alleged settlement, it was not Jordan's only inducement. Rather, by Knafel's own account, her statement to Jordan that he was the father of her child was indeed material and a substantial factor in inducing Jordan to act.

To hold otherwise would render her agreement not to file a paternity claim to have been a mere pretense to extort money. If Jordan's paternity was immaterial to the parties' settlement agreement, then her claim that she had a good-faith basis for a paternity action against Jordan would be unfounded. Without a good-faith basis, they would have lacked the necessary consideration for their bargain. [Citation omitted.] Since consideration is a material element of a contract Jordan's paternity must have been material to a good-faith settlement of her paternity claim. [Citation omitted.]

Next, we consider whether there is a genuine issue of fact as to whether Knafel's representation was known to be false or not reasonably believed by her to be true at the time of the alleged agreement. Jordan argues that because Knafel represented to him with certainty that "she was pregnant with his child," yet paternity testing ultimately revealed that someone else was the father, it necessarily follows that at the time she told Jordan he was the father, she must have lacked certainty about the paternity of the child. Therefore, Knafel's knowledge of her uncertainty regarding paternity satisfies the "knowledge" element of fraudulent misrepresentation. He relies upon *Lipscomb v. Wells*, 326 Ill. App. 3d 760, 260 Ill. Dec. 374, 761 N.E.2d 218 (2001), and section 162(1) of the Restatement (Second) of Contracts in support (Restatement (Second) of Contracts §162(1) (1981)).

In *Lipscomb*, the plaintiff brought a paternity action against the defendant to have him adjudicated the father of her child, alleging in a verified complaint that he was the natural father. [Citation omitted.] Thereafter, an agreed order of parentage was entered requiring the defendant to pay child support. Years later, after being told by the plaintiff that he was not the child's natural father and that she had been seeing another man at the time of conception, the defendant filed a petition seeking . . . to vacate the agreed order. . . . Therein, he asserted that he entered into the parentage agreement . . . based upon a representation . . . that he was the natural father of the child and . . . that she "had no other relations with men at the time of conception." [Citation omitted.] The trial court vacated the parentage judgment. . . .

[T]he appellate court affirmed, recognizing generally that concealing the paternity of a child from a man held liable for paternity of that child is fraud. [Citation omitted.] The court reasoned that when a party claims to know a material fact with certainty, yet knows that she does not have that certainty, the assertion constitutes a fraudulent misrepresentation. [A]s applied to this context, when a woman categorically represents to a man that he is the father of her child, it is implicit in her representation that during the period of conception she had only one sexual partner. If the man is actually not the father, that representation is categorically false, and constitutes a fraudulent misrepresentation. [Citation omitted.]

Although *Lipscomb* does not specifically rely on section 162(1) to support its reasoning, it is implicitly recognized therein. That provision is instructive and provides:

> (1) A misrepresentation is fraudulent if the maker intends his assertion to induce a party to manifest his assent and the maker
>
> (a) knows or believes that the assertion is not in accord with the facts, or
>
> (b) does not have the confidence that he states or implies in the truth of the assertion, or
>
> (c) knows that he does not have the basis that he states or implies for the assertion.

Restatement (Second) of Contracts §162(1) (1981).

Here, at the time of contract formation, Knafel represented with certainty that she knew Jordan was the father of her child. However, the paternity tests reveal that it was also the case that she was having sexual relations with someone other than Jordan around the time of conception. Therefore, the evidence presented establishes that she knew that she lacked the certainty about the paternity of the child or, at least, knew that she did not have the basis that she stated or implied for that categorical representation, thus making it fraudulent.

. . . Knafel asserts that she believed she had certainty about the paternity of her child, rel[ying] on Dr. Grisanti's office memo regarding the timing of conception. However, the memo is insufficient to defeat summary judgment. Knafel merely states that the doctor's information regarding the dates of conception coincided with the dates she was with Jordan in Phoenix. That assertion does not discount that she knew she was also with another partner around that same time period. Although one could contemplate a situation where a pregnant woman could be subjectively certain about paternity, Knafel has presented no such affirmative evidence to support an adequate basis for her certainty.

Additionally, Knafel argues that she indeed disclosed to Jordan throughout their relationship that she was having sex with another man. Nevertheless, the question is not whether she told him about her relationships with other men at some previous time, but whether she failed to disclose material information in the process of contract formation that would render the contract voidable. Section 161(b) is instructive here, providing that one makes a misrepresentation through nondisclosure:

> (b) Where he knows that disclosure of the fact would correct a mistake of the other party as to a basic assumption on which that party is making the contract and if non-disclosure of the fact amounts to a failure to act in good faith and in accordance with reasonable standards of fair dealing.

Restatement (Second) of Contracts §161(b) (1981).

Here, at the time of negotiating the settlement, Knafel was not forthcoming that she had sex with another partner at the time of conception. Instead, she made an affirmative representation with certainty that she was pregnant with Jordan's child. Her failure to disclose the information when she alone had access to that information amounts to a failure to act in good faith and in accordance with reasonable standards of fair dealing.

Finally, with respect to the element of reliance, Knafel initially argues that Jordan's failure to state that he relied upon Knafel's representation precludes summary judgment. However, "[w]here representations have been made in regard to a material matter and action has been taken, in the absence of evidence showing the contrary, it will be presumed that the representations were relied on." [Citations omitted.] Knafel argues that Jordan's statements to her in 1998, that he remembered their agreement and would still pay her, despite his knowledge that he was not the child's father, supports an inference that, at the time he entered into the contract, he never relied on her representation that he was the father of the child. However, as stated previously, if the alleged agreement had nothing to do with his paternity, then the agreement was merely an agreement to keep their romantic relationship confidential and could no longer be construed as a settlement of her paternity claim with a confidentiality provision. Accordingly, based upon Knafel's own allegations, Jordan must have relied on the representation or the alleged settlement agreement was otherwise untenable.

Furthermore, as the court in *Lipscomb* articulated, Jordan had a right to rely upon the categorical representation by Knafel that he was the father because "[i]t would make little sense to compel a putative father to conduct an independent investigation in the face of a clear and categorical representation of a mother (who is also his sexual partner) as to his parentage." [Citation omitted.] Additionally, we find no merit to Knafel's contention that Jordan should not have relied on the representation. """"[O]ne who has intentionally deceived the other to his prejudice is not to be heard to say, in defense of the charge of fraud, that the innocent party ought not to have trusted him or was guilty of negligence in so doing" [citations.]"" [Citations omitted.] Accordingly, for all of the foregoing reasons, the alleged settlement agreement was premised on a fraudulent misrepresentation and, therefore, was voidable by Jordan.

We further find Knafel's cited cases, primarily a Maryland case from 1956 and an Illinois case from 1880, to lack any persuasive or instructive value where contract law has evolved and societal notions regarding intimate relationships have changed. [The cases] merely stand for the unremarkable proposition . . . that forbearance to sue for a lawful claim or demand is sufficient consideration for a promise to pay for the forbearance "if the party forbearing had an honest intention to prosecute litigation which is not frivolous, vexatious, or unlawful, and which he believed to be well founded." [Citation omitted.]

. . .

Affirmed.

The court here follows an approach to misrepresentation that differs from the Restatement approach discussed in text. Illinois in effect requires the misrepresentation to be both fraudulent and material. It ruled that Jordan satisfied this test, even at the summary judgment stage. While the court begins by addressing the affirmative statement ("I'm pregnant with your child"), the case focuses on nondisclosure of the fact that Knafel had relations with another man at about the time of conception. That shift proves critical to the discussion of fraud, where Knafel may honestly have believed Jordan was the father, but, according to the court, could not honestly have believed that she had no relations with other men about the time of conception.

The discussion of materiality also varies from the Restatement (Second) approach. The court seems to address inducement here, discussing whether paternity was an important reason for Jordan's promise. Because an allegation of actual paternity would contribute substantially to a reasonable person's consideration of the deal, the court might have avoided discussing whether it was material to Jordan. The court's suggestion that fathers may rely on allegations of this sort rather than insist on paternity tests immediately seems a reasonable application of the usual rule, though one that may work less well in cases involving paternity than it does in commercial transactions.

Jordan v. Knafel: Real Life Applications

1. Connie, after serving time for bank fraud, applied for a position teaching business ethics at a community college. Connie's resume did not mention the conviction or time served, instead stating that in the immediate past she had been winding down the affairs of a company she owned and operated. The college could have conducted a reference check and learned the truth before hiring Connie, but failed to do so. After Connie started work, Connie's parole officer spoke with the college, which then learned of Connie's past. The college informed Connie that it elected to rescind the contract for fraud. Connie seeks your advice concerning whether to sue. Can Connie enforce the employment contract despite the deceit? *See Sarvis v. Vermont State Colleges*, 772 A.2d 494 (Vt. 2001).
2. Gallery operated art auctions on a cruise ship. Gallery's employees told potential bidders that the works of art offered were "good investments" and that they "would appraise at many times the price paid at the auction." Naif purchased several of the works offered aboard the ship. Upon seeking appraisals, Naif learned that the works were the product of a sweat shop where employees produce as many similar works as possible to meet their quota. The undistinguished works have no serious appraisal value and no likelihood of appreciating. Naif seeks your advice concerning whether to seek rescission against Gallery. What problems does Naif's action face? Can you overcome these obstacles? Would your case be stronger if Gallery also asserted that these works were authentic Caribbean folk art?
3. After the passing of Alex's spouse, Alex decided to pursue her dream of becoming a ballroom dancer. Alex signed up for Lessons at Danzen, taking all lessons from Barrett, an attractive younger instructor. Barrett frequently praised Alex's progress. In addition, Barrett encouraged Alex to sign up for additional lessons, trips to view and participate in local competitions, and other extras sold by Danzen. Based on Barrett's statements that Alex was becoming a beautiful dancer, was improving rapidly, and would soon be able to compete with the best dancers in the region, Alex signed (over the course of a year) four contracts to take a total of 2,500 hours of dance lessons at a total cost of $200,000. After receiving 750 hours of instruction, Alex became disenchanted with Barrett and Danzen. Alex now believes that their statements were not true, but just an effort to sell

more dance lessons. Alex wants to recover payments for lessons not already received. Evaluate the likelihood of rescission based on misrepresentation. *See Vokes v. Arthur Murray, Inc.*, 212 So. 2d 906 (Fla. App. 1968).

4. Sean wanted to buy a home in an area that will entitle Sean's children to attend a particularly good elementary school. Arti, a real estate broker helping Sean find a home, showed Sean a very appealing home, assuring Sean that the home was indeed within the boundaries for the school Sean prefers. After signing the contract, but before the sale closes, Sean discovered that the house was not in fact in the right school zone—that Arti had relied on an outdated map of the school boundaries. Sean wants to call off the deal with the sellers, seeking your advice on whether Arti's misrepresentation permits that result. (You will need to read the next section to address this question.)

---

7. Third-Party Misrepresentations

A misled party may miscalculate the costs and benefits of a contract regardless of who provides the misinformation. When the other party to a contract makes the assertion, allowing rescission based on that assertion poses no problems. When, however, people seek to rescind contracts because someone else misled them, rescission threatens to deprive parties who made no misrepresentations of the benefits of apparently legitimate bargains. The court must allocate the cost of the error, even though neither party caused the error. Miscalculation still erodes confidence that the exchange benefitted both parties, but concern for fairness to both innocent parties may lead a court to enforce the contract.

To avoid a contract for misrepresentation by a nonparty, the deceived person must satisfy all the elements of the defense: misrepresentation, inducement, fraud or materiality, and justifiable reliance. In addition, the defense will fail if the other party

a. relied on the contract;
b. in good faith; and
c. with no reason to know of the misrepresentation.[16]

Reliance often involves beginning performance, such as delivering goods, services, or payment to the deceived person. Preparing to perform, such as buying materials or rejecting other offers, also may qualify as reliance. Where the deceived party becomes aware of the truth and seeks rescission before the other party relies, allowing rescission will cause the other party minimal hardship. Even if the other party had no hint of the deception, the disaffirmation occurs early enough to allow rescission.

---

[16] Restatement (Second) of Contracts §164(2).

The twin requirements of good faith and no reason to know of the deceit allow this defense in situations where the other party either did realize or should have realized that deception had occurred. Good faith will be absent if the other party actually knows of the error; reason to know exists if the other party should have realized that the party had been misled. Even a party who has relied on the contract cannot object to rescission if she knew of the deception. Knowingly profiting from another's deceit is little better than profiting from one's own deceit. In some cases, the other party's silence despite knowing of the misrepresentation may amount to nondisclosure. Even if the innocent party can enforce the contract against the deceived party, a remedy may be available in tort against the person who committed the deception.

8. Misrepresentation Affecting Validity — Fraud in the Execution

Most misrepresentations involve parties who intend to enter a contract, even though misrepresentations make that contract less valuable than anticipated. Some misrepresentations involve matters that suggest the deceived party did not intend to enter a contract at all — or, at least, not the contract that was signed. For instance, a person who believes the document being signed is a Christmas card does not assent to any contract. He is not misled as to the benefits of the transaction, but as to its very existence.

In these most severe cases, a misrepresentation negates the existence of assent. To negate assent, the deceived party must show that

1. the misrepresentation involved the "character or essential terms of a contract"; and
2. the deceived party "neither knew nor had a reasonable opportunity to know the actual character or essential terms of the contract."[17]

The character or essential terms of a contract refers to deceptions that prevent a person from knowing what his assent involves. It certainly covers situations where the deceived party does not realize any contract is being offered. It also extends to situations where the deceiver misstates the nature of the contract. For instance, one spouse might ask the other to sign a contract selling their car to their oldest child, when in fact the document sells the house to some third party. Even if a person knows that the document sells the house, a misrepresentation of price (say, the deceived person believes the price is $800,000 when in fact it is $80,000) might alter the essential terms so greatly that the signature provides no meaningful indicia of assent. Modest differences — say, a loan at 7 percent instead of 6 percent — probably don't qualify.

[17] *Id.* §163.

In most cases, people can protect themselves from this kind of fraud by reading the document. (These cases almost always involve written contracts that differ from oral representations.) The defense aids only those who lack a reasonable opportunity to learn the true nature of the transaction. Even those who cannot read the document—the blind or illiterate—can have the document read to them. This defense covers situations where the reader participates in the fraud or where a different document is substituted surreptitiously after another document has been read.

In *Park 100 Investment Group II v. Ryan*,[18] a landlord persuaded officers of a corporation to sign a pledge making them personally liable to pay the company's rent by pretending the lease was the same document their attorney had already reviewed. By approaching the officers as they were late for their daughter's wedding on the night before they were scheduled to occupy the new premises, the opportunity to read the document was inadequate to avoid the effect of this fraud.

Because this form of fraud negates assent, no contract arises at all; it is void, not merely voidable. Thus, even if the person deceived wanted to enforce the deal (and the person who deceived them did not), no contract exists to enforce.

B. MISTAKE

A **mistake** is a belief not in accord with the facts. The defense differs from misrepresentation because the mistaken party need not attribute the mistake to anyone else. An individual's own mistake may justify avoiding the contract. Similar to misrepresentation, mistake addresses a party's miscalculation of the costs and benefits of a contract, even if no one else was responsible for providing the poor information.

Unchecked power to avoid contracts for mistake could eliminate contract liability altogether. Anyone who wants out of a deal can devise some mistake made at the time of formation. Mistake doctrine needs to differentiate those mistakes that justify rescinding the deal from mistakes that do not justify starting over. As with third-party misrepresentations, concern arises over protecting an innocent party's legitimate expectations. The doctrines below seek to balance these competing concerns, producing a fairly narrow defense.

The doctrine applies differently depending on whether both parties shared the same mistake (mutual mistake) or only one of them was mistaken (unilateral mistake). These two variations will be addressed separately.

1. Mutual Mistake

The ability to avoid a contract for mutual mistake involves several elements:

1. a mistake by the party claiming the defense;
2. that was shared by the other party;

[18] 180 Cal. App. 4th 795, 103 Cal. Rptr. 3d 218 (2009).

3. that concerned the situation at the time the contract was made;
4. that involved a basic assumption on which the contract was made;
5. the mistake materially affected the agreed exchange of performances; and
6. the risk of the mistake did not fall on the party claiming the defense.[19]

Each element must be shown to establish the defense. The absence of any one defeats the claim, leaving the contract enforceable.

Shared Mistake

Both parties must share the same mistake. If each party makes a different mistake, the mistake is not mutual. Sometimes carefully framing the mistake will make it mutual. For example, suppose the seller thinks a stone is a topaz, the buyer thinks it is an amethyst, but it really is a diamond. If you focus on what each party thinks the stone is, they made different mistakes. Shifting focus slightly, both parties think the stone is not a diamond, which is a shared mistake.

Time of Contract Formation

The mistake must concern facts that exist at the time the contract was made. Predictions about future events do not count. A mistake about whether property is zoned commercial at the time of contract formation would allow a defense, but a mistake about whether it would remain zoned commercial until buyer could complete a project would not qualify.

Basic Assumptions

The mistake must relate to a basic assumption on which the contract is made. This requirement has two prongs. First, a basic assumption must be central to the contract in some way. Peripheral or ancillary mistakes about minor details do not support the defense. To some extent, this prong may duplicate the requirement of a material effect on the exchange of performances.

Second, courts call something a basic assumption to express understanding for why a party did not question the assumption. Often the mistake affected something so fundamental that it did not occur to the parties to consider whether the belief was accurate. For instance, knowing that a building was being used as a four-unit rental property, it might not occur to the buyer that the zoning did not permit that use. In other cases, parties may have adverted to the possibility of error, but considered error so unlikely it was not worth discussing. Requiring a mistake of basic assumption seeks to limit the defense to issues that the parties should not be expected to allocate by contract.

For example, in the classic case *Sherwood v. Walker*,[20] a seller agreed to a modest price for a cow, believing it was barren. The parties could have inserted a **condition**

---

[19] RESTATEMENT (SECOND) OF CONTRACTS §152.
[20] 33 N.W. 919 (Mich. 1887).

(specifying circumstances under which performance will or will not become due), such as "unless the cow turns out to be fertile"—or could have specified "even if the cow is fertile." But unless the parties recognize a significant possibility that the cow is not barren, they will not consider adding language of this sort. Thus, the court found a mistake of basic assumption here despite a brief mention that the cow might be barren (probably seller's effort to avoid a claim of nondisclosure).

Material Effect on the Exchange

Courts will not rescind contracts over trivial mistakes. The mistake must have a material effect on the agreed exchange of performances. That is, the resulting contract must be sufficiently imbalanced that it seems unfair to require the adversely affected party to perform as promised. For example, art sold at a high price on the assumption that it was painted by a famous artist may prove to be nearly worthless if proven to be a forgery. Seller gives up very little value (a forged painting) in exchange for a great deal of value (the price). If the imbalance is significant, the effect is material. This requirement seems to serve the same function that inducement serves in other defenses: did this mistake substantially contribute to the decision to enter the contract? Evaluating whether something the parties did *not* consider contributed to a decision confuses the issue. Material effect replaces inducement, assuming the deal would not have been made where the error has a large effect, but assuming the parties might have agreed despite the error where the effects are modest.

The Risk of the Mistake

The adversely affected party must not bear the risk of the mistake. Contracts often allocate the risk of certain events. A party disappointed by the way events unfold should not be able to use mistake to reallocate those risks. As a result, in any case where the risk of the mistake falls upon the party claiming the defense, courts will deny avoidance.

A party may bear the risk of a mistake in three situations:

1. The contract may allocate the risk to a party;
2. A party, aware of its limited knowledge, may assume the risk of mistake by going forward with the deal in spite of the known limitations; or
3. The court may find other reasons to allocate the risk to the party claiming the defense under the factual circumstances.[21]

Conspicuously absent from this list is any consideration of whether the person claiming mistake bore the blame for its mistake. Some sources expressly reject fault in failing to discover or to avoid the mistake, holding it irrelevant unless it rises

[21] RESTATEMENT (SECOND) OF CONTRACTS §154.

to the level of bad faith.[22] Nonetheless, some courts assign the risk based on fault, holding a party failed to use adequate care to avoid a mistake.

Before discussing these means of allocating risk in more detail, consider the following case.

Case Preview

Lenawee County Board of Health v. Messerly

The Pickles bought a lot that contained a three-family rental building, only to discover that the lot was too small to hold even a single-family home (unless the county extended the sewer system in that direction). Like many mistake cases, the court must decide which of two innocent parties must bear the loss this discovery created. The Pickles prefer not to pay $25,000 for a worthless lot. The Messerlys, who sold it, do not want it either (and certainly prefer to keep the sale price). The court performs a masterful application of the rules governing mistake, touching on each element. In the process, the court recounts one of the most famous mistake cases, *Sherwood v. Walker*, which resolved the ownership of Rose II of Aberlone (a cow).

As you read *Lenawee County Board of Health v. Messerly*, look for the following:

1. What mistake did the court identify?
2. Were the parties mistaken on the date the contract was made?
3. Is a mistake about the value promised really collateral rather than fundamental? Isn't the lack of value central to the contract's lack of fairness?
4. If the Pickles established the existence of a mutual mistake, why did they lose?

Lenawee County Board of Health v. Messerly

417 Mich. 17, 331 N.W.2d 203 (Mich. 1982)

Ryan, Justice.

We are required to determine whether appellees should prevail in their attempt to avoid this land contract on the basis of mutual mistake and failure of consideration. We conclude that the parties did entertain a mutual misapprehension of fact, but that the circumstances of this case do not warrant rescission.

I

. . . In 1971, the Messerlys acquired approximately one acre plus 600 square feet of land. A three-unit apartment building was situated upon the 600-square-foot portion. [P]rior to this transfer, the Messerlys' predecessor in title, Mr. Bloom, had installed a septic tank on the property without a permit and in violation of the applicable health code. The Messerlys used the building as an income investment property

[22] *Id.* §157.

until 1973 when they sold it, upon land contract, to James Barnes who likewise used it primarily as an income-producing investment.

[The] Barnes, with the permission of the Messerlys, sold approximately one acre of the property in 1976, and the remaining 600 square feet and building were offered for sale soon thereafter when [the] Barnes defaulted on their land contract. Mr. and Mrs. Pickles evidenced an interest in the property, but prefer[red] to [deal] directly with the Messerlys[. The] Barnes . . . conveyed their interest in the property back to the Messerlys. After inspecting the property, [the] Pickles executed a new land contract with the Messerlys on March 21, 1977. It provided for a purchase price of $25,500. A clause was added to the end of the land contract form which provides:

> "17. Purchaser has examined this property and agrees to accept same in its present condition. There are no other or additional written or oral understandings."

Five or six days later, . . . the Pickleses . . . discovered raw sewage seeping out of the ground. Tests conducted by a sanitation expert indicated the inadequacy of the sewage system. The Lenawee County Board of Health subsequently condemned the property and . . . obtain[ed] a permanent injunction proscribing human habitation of the premises [until] brought into conformance with the Lenawee County sanitation code.

[The Pickles made no payments. The Messerlys sought foreclosure. The] Pickles then counterclaimed for rescission. . . .

After a bench trial, the court concluded that the Pickleses had no cause of action against either the Messerlys or the Barneses as there was no fraud or misrepresentation [in that] none of the parties knew of Mr. Bloom's earlier transgression or of the resultant problem with the septic system until it was discovered by the Pickleses. . . . Foreclosure was ordered against the Pickleses, together with a judgment . . . of $25,943.09.

. . . The Court of Appeals . . . in a two-to-one decision[4]. . . concluded that the mutual mistake between the Messerlys and the Pickleses went to a basic, as opposed to a collateral, element of the contract, and that the parties intended to transfer income-producing rental property but, in actuality, the vendees paid $25,500 for an asset without value.

We granted the Messerlys' application for leave to appeal.

II

We must decide initially whether there was a mistaken belief entertained by one or both parties to the contract in dispute and, if so, the resultant legal significance.

A contractual mistake "is a belief that is not in accord with the facts." [Citation omitted.] The erroneous belief of one or both of the parties must relate to a fact in existence at the time the contract is executed. [Citations omitted.] That is to say, the

---

[4]Judge MacKenzie dissented: "Mr. and Mrs. Pickles . . . received essentially the same property they bargained for and failed to prove that any mistake . . . existed at the time the parties entered into the contract."

[7]The . . . only way that the property could be put to residential use would be to pump and haul the sewage, . . . which [would] cost . . . double the income generated by the property. [B]oth [courts] found that the property was valueless, or had a negative value.

belief which is found to be in error may not be, in substance, a prediction as to a future occurrence or non-occurrence. [Citations omitted.]

The Court of Appeals concluded . . . that the parties were mistaken as to the income-producing capacity of the property in question. [Citation omitted.] We agree. The vendors and the vendees each believed that the property transferred could be utilized as income-generating rental property. All of the parties subsequently learned that, in fact, the property was unsuitable for any residential use.

Appellants assert that there was no mistake in the contractual sense because the defect in the sewage system did not arise until after the contract was executed. The . . . Messerlys are confusing the date of the inception of the defect with the date upon which the defect was discovered.

. . .

[T]he septic system was defective prior to the date on which the land contract was executed. The Messerlys' grantor installed a nonconforming septic system without a permit prior to the transfer of the property to the Messerlys in 1971. Moreover, virtually undisputed testimony indicates that, assuming ideal soil conditions, 2,500 square feet of property is necessary to support a sewage system adequate to serve a three-family dwelling. Likewise, 750 square feet is mandated for a one-family home. Thus, the division of the parcel and sale of one acre of the property by Mr. and Mrs. Barnes in 1976 made it impossible to remedy the already illegal septic system within the confines of the 600-square-foot parcel.[10]

. . .

. . . Appellants argue that the parties' mistake relates only to the quality or value of the real estate transferred, and that such mistakes are collateral to the agreement and do not justify rescission. . . .

In [*A & M Land Development Co. v. Miller*, 354 Mich. 681, 94 N.W.2d 197 (1959)] the . . . purchaser of 91 lots . . . was [unable] to develop 42 of the[m] because it could not obtain permits . . . to install septic tanks. . . . This Court refused to allow rescission because the mistake, whether mutual or unilateral, related only to the value of the property. . . .

Appellees contend, on the other hand, that in this case the parties were mistaken as to the very nature of the character of the consideration and claim that the pervasive and essential quality of this mistake renders rescission appropriate. They cite . . . *Sherwood v. Walker*, 66 Mich. 568, 33 N.W. 919 (1887), the famous "barren cow" case. In that case, the parties agreed to the sale and purchase of a cow which was thought to be barren, but which was, in reality, with calf. When the seller discovered the fertile condition of his cow, he refused to deliver her. In permitting rescission, the Court stated:

[10]It is crucial to distinguish between the date on which a belief relating to a particular fact or set of facts becomes erroneous due to a change in the fact, and the date on which the mistaken nature of the belief is discovered. By definition, a mistake cannot be discovered until after the contract is executed. If the parties were aware, prior to the execution of a contract, that they were in error concerning a particular fact, there would be no misapprehension in signing the contract. Thus stated, it becomes obvious that the date on which a mistaken fact manifests itself is irrelevant to the determination whether or not there was a mistake.

> the mistake or misapprehension of the parties went to the whole substance of the agreement. If the cow was a breeder, she was worth at least $750; if barren, she was worth not over $80. The parties would not have made the contract of sale except upon the understanding and belief that she was incapable of breeding, and of no use as a cow. It is true she is now the identical animal that they thought her to be when the contract was made; there is no mistake as to the identity of the creature. Yet the mistake was not of the mere quality of the animal, but went to the very nature of the thing. A barren cow is substantially a different creature than a breeding one. There is as much difference between them for all purposes of use as there is between an ox and a cow that is capable of breeding and giving milk. . . . She was not in fact the animal, or the kind of animal, the defendants intended to sell or the plaintiff to buy. . . .

As the parties suggest, the foregoing precedent arguably distinguishes mistakes affecting the essence of the consideration from those which go to its quality or value, affording relief on a per se basis for the former but not the latter. [Citation omitted.]

However, the distinctions which may be drawn from *Sherwood* and *A & M Land Development Co.* do not provide a satisfactory analysis of the nature of a mistake sufficient to invalidate a contract. Often, a mistake relates to an underlying factual assumption which, when discovered, directly affects value, but simultaneously and materially affects the essence of the contractual consideration. It is disingenuous to label such a mistake collateral. [Citation omitted.]

Appellant and appellee both mistakenly believed that the property which was the subject of their land contract would generate income as rental property. The fact that it could not be used for human habitation deprived the property of its income-earning potential and rendered it less valuable. However, this mistake, while directly and dramatically affecting the property's value, cannot accurately be characterized as collateral because it also affects the very essence of the consideration. "The thing sold and bought [income-generating rental property] had in fact no existence."

We find that the inexact and confusing distinction between contractual mistakes running to value and those touching the substance of the consideration serves only as an impediment to a clear and helpful analysis for the equitable resolution of cases in which mistake is alleged and proven. Accordingly, the holdings of *A & M Land Development Co.* and *Sherwood* with respect to the material or collateral nature of a mistake are limited to the facts of those cases.

Instead, we think the better-reasoned approach is a case-by-case analysis whereby rescission is indicated when the mistaken belief relates to a basic assumption of the parties upon which the contract is made, and which materially affects the agreed performances of the parties. [Citations omitted.] Rescission is not available, however, to relieve a party who has assumed the risk of loss in connection with the mistake.

All of the parties to this contract erroneously assumed that the property transferred by the vendors to the vendees was suitable for human habitation and could be utilized to generate rental income. The fundamental nature of these assumptions is indicated by the fact that their invalidity changed the character of the property transferred, thereby frustrating, indeed precluding, [the] Pickles' intended use of the real estate. Although the Pickleses are disadvantaged by enforcement of the contract, performance is advantageous to the Messerlys, as the property at issue is less valuable absent its income-earning potential. Nothing short of rescission can remedy the mistake. Thus, the parties' mistake as to a basic assumption materially affects the agreed performances of the parties.

Despite the significance of the mistake made by the parties, we reverse the Court of Appeals because we conclude that equity does not justify the remedy sought by [the] Pickles.

Rescission is an equitable remedy which is granted only in the sound discretion of the court. . . .

In cases of mistake by two equally innocent parties, we are required . . . to determine which blameless party should assume the loss resulting from the misapprehension they shared.[13] Normally that can only be done by drawing upon our "own notions of what is reasonable and just under all the surrounding circumstances."

Equity suggests that, in this case, the risk should be allocated to the purchasers. We are guided to that conclusion, in part, by the standards announced in §154 of the Restatement of Contracts 2d [which] suggests that the court should look first to whether the parties have agreed to the allocation of the risk between themselves. While there is no express assumption in the contract by either party of the risk of the property becoming uninhabitable, there was indeed some agreed allocation of the risk to the vendees by the incorporation of an "as is" clause into the contract which, we repeat, provided:

> "Purchaser has examined this property and agrees to accept same in its present condition. There are no other or additional written or oral understandings."

That is a persuasive indication that the parties considered that, as between them, such risk as related to the "present condition" of the property should lie with the purchaser. If the "as is" clause is to have any meaning at all, it must be interpreted to refer to those defects which were unknown at the time that the contract was executed. Thus, the parties themselves assigned the risk of loss to Mr. and Mrs. Pickles.

We conclude that Mr. and Mrs. Pickles are not entitled to the equitable remedy of rescission and, accordingly, reverse the decision of the Court of Appeals.

Post-Case Follow-Up

The court carefully analyzes each element of the defense. The mistake involved the nature of the property, its usefulness for rental purposes. Even if the septic system never broke, it was too small for rental use (even by one family), even though both parties assumed it was useful rental property and priced it accordingly. The court rejects old rules differentiating the nature of the thing from the quality or value of the thing. Unless a mistake affects value, a party is unlikely to seek rescission, and the court is unlikely to find that the mistake had a material effect on the exchange. The

[13]This risk-of-loss analysis is absent in both *A & M Land Development Co.* and *Sherwood*, and this omission helps to explain, in part, the disparate treatment in the two cases. Had such an inquiry been undertaken in *Sherwood*, we believe that the result might have been different. Moreover, a determination as to which party assumed the risk in *A & M Land Development Co.* would have alleviated the need to characterize the mistake as collateral so as to justify the result denying rescission. Despite the absence of any inquiry as to the assumption of risk in those two leading cases, we find that there exists sufficient precedent to warrant such an analysis in future cases of mistake.

court held that this mistake was central rather than collateral because it was a basic assumption and had a material effect. But the case ultimately turned on the allocation of risk. The parties here agreed that any problems with the property would be buyer's responsibility. They could have bargained for a warranty of habitability but instead entered a contract with a disclaimer of warranties. Both parties, or at least one of them, probably took that aspect into account when agreeing to the price. The court refuses to upset the parties' allocation of the risk of unknown conditions, such as the unsuitability for use as rental property.

Lenawee County Board of Health v. Messerly: Real Life Applications

1. Kellen sold a tract of undeveloped land on the edge of town to Evelyn, who intended to build a home on it. Both of them mistakenly believed the land was zoned for residential use, in part because all recent construction on adjacent tracts involved houses, not commercial buildings. After the sale closed, Evelyn's construction permits were denied because the land is zoned as green space, in which no permanent structures may be erected. Either party could have ascertained the correct zoning rule by checking public records. Evelyn consults you concerning the prospects for rescinding the transaction based on mutual mistake. What advice do you offer?

2. CornCo agreed to sell 1 million bushels of corn to Boeuf, a French feedlot that raises cattle. CornCo believed that its genetically modified corn met European regulations on corn fed to livestock. Boeuf believed the corn was not genetically modified. Both were mistaken. After delivery, local authorities prohibited Boeuf from selling (within the European Union) any livestock that ate the corn. Boeuf seeks to rescind the transaction on grounds of mutual mistake. If American common law applies, should CornCo resist Boeuf's request to return the goods for a refund? What arguments seem most likely to defeat the defense?

3. Terry and Chris divorced in 2005. Their settlement agreement divided the property and set support payments that would end in 2015. Terry alleges that the term ending support was based on a basic assumption that the property allocated to Terry under the agreement would generate sufficient dividends and interest by 2015 to support Terry without additional spousal support payments—an assumption that has proved inaccurate. Terry seeks to rescind the agreement and seeks a hearing to set the appropriate amount of spousal support. How should Chris respond? *See Ryan v. Ryan*, 640 S.E.2d 64 (W. Va. 2006).

Contractual Allocation of Risk

Parties aware that they lack full information may allocate the risk of uncertainty in the contract. Courts honor the allocation to which the parties agreed. The price presumably accounted for the risks each party assumed. Reversing the party's allocation of risk gives one party a benefit for which it did not bargain. For instance, a person who bought goods on the mistaken assumption that they were of a particular quality cannot avoid the contract if the contract contains a clause disclaiming any warranty on the quality of the goods. The parties agreed any losses resulting from shortcomings in the goods should fall upon the buyer — just as including a warranty would allocate the same risk to the seller. Thus, in *Lenawee County*, the buyer could not rescind the contract despite the uselessness of the land because the contract contained an "as is" clause, allocating the risk to the buyer.

To allocate the risk of mistake, a contract term may need to relate directly to the error. For instance, consider the sale of a used car, where buyer and seller both believe the odometer reads 66,000 miles, though in fact the car has traveled 166,000 miles. The contract may identify the car, but make no specific mention of the odometer, either by warranty or disclaimer. The duty to pay for the car seems absolute; no condition limits the buyer's promise. If that was enough to allocate the risk of mistake to the buyer, then mistake almost never would offer a defense. Reading allocations of risk into the general language of a sale gives too much force to this factor. Language may refer to the risk without specifically mentioning the odometer; a simple phrase like "as is" would suffice to allocate every flaw to the buyer (unless the clause proves unenforceable for other reasons).

Conscious Ignorance

A party that knows its knowledge is limited may bear the risk of error. Sometimes called **conscious ignorance** or **willful ignorance**, the rule applies only when a party realizes it lacks information, but treats that limited knowledge as sufficient. For instance, someone who buys a used car without even looking it over knows that he has no information upon which to base assumptions about its quality. Going forward in the face of that lack of information implies that the errors do not matter to the person — that is, he is willing to assume the risk that the car is not as good as he thinks.

The rule here requires *awareness* that one has limited knowledge. Every person making a mistake has limited knowledge, as she finds out when she discovers the mistake. If limited knowledge alone allocated the risk to the mistaken party, the defense would never apply. A party's awareness of her own limited knowledge makes a decision to go forward a decision to take the risk of error.

Courts may devise other reasons to allocate the risk to the disadvantaged party under certain circumstances. For instance, if the disadvantaged party could insure against the mistake more easily or more cheaply than the other party, assigning the risk to that person might make sense. Similarly, if a nonparty created the problem, placing the risk on the party with the best opportunity to seek redress against the person ultimately responsible for the mistake might offer advantages. This might offer a reason for the court to assign the risk to the adversely affected party. Finally, where a party's mistake results from her own lack of good faith, assigning the risk to that party seems fair. For example, if a party could have avoided the mistake at no inconvenience or expense, failure to take those simple steps might be deemed bad faith, leading a court to assign the risk to that party. As noted earlier, mere negligence usually does not justify assigning the risk, but some courts may assign the risk on this basis anyway.

EXHIBIT 7.4 **Decision Tree for Allocation of Risk**

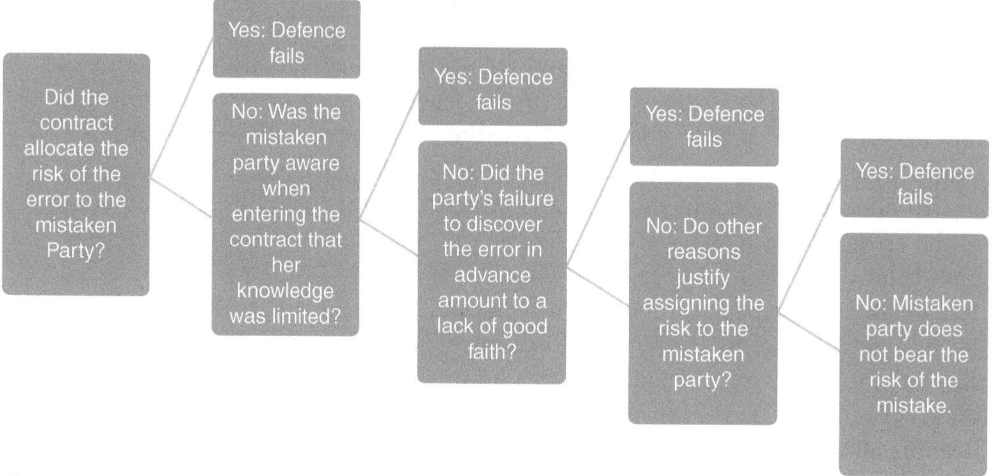

Case Preview

Wood v. Boynton

In *Wood v. Boynton*, a person of modest means sold a stone to a jeweler for \$1. The stone turned out to be an uncut diamond worth about \$700. At the time of the transaction, both parties believed it was not a diamond. The court rejects the seller's request to rescind the transaction under mutual mistake of fact.

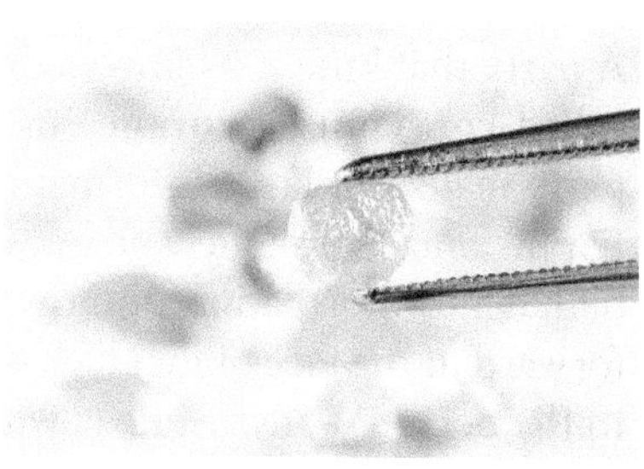

Would you realize this stone was an uncut diamond?
Imfoto/Shutterstock.com

As you read *Wood v. Boynton*, look for the following:

1. Did the court reject the mistake defense altogether or simply hold that Wood had failed to make out the necessary elements?
2. What elements did the court require to show a mistake? Are these consistent with the defense described in *Lenawee County*?
3. Did the court identify a reason to reject Wood's claim that would apply under the defense as outlined in the Restatement (Second) of Contracts?

Wood v. Boynton

25 N.W. 42 (Wis. 1885)

TAYLOR, J.

This action was brought . . . to recover the possession of an uncut diamond. . . . [A]fter hearing all the evidence in the case, the learned circuit judge directed the jury to find a verdict for the defendants. The plaintiff . . . appealed to this court.

The defendants are partners in the jewelry business. [B]efore the twenty-eighth of December, 1883, the plaintiff was the owner of and in the possession of a small stone of the nature and value of which she was ignorant; that on that day she sold it to one of the defendants for the sum of one dollar. Afterwards it was ascertained that the stone was a rough diamond, and of the value of about $700. After hearing this fact the plaintiff tendered the defendants the one dollar, and ten cents as interest, and demanded a return of the stone to her. The defendants refused to deliver it, and therefore she commenced this action.

The plaintiff testified to the circumstances attending the sale of the stone to Mr. Samuel B. Boynton, as follows: "The first time Boynton saw that stone he was talking about buying the topaz, or whatever it is, in September or October. I went into the store to get a little pin mended, and I had it in a small box, [along with] a small ear-ring . . . this stone, and a broken sleeve-button. . . . Mr. Boynton turned to give me a check for my pin. I thought I would ask him what the stone was, and I took it out of the box and asked him to please tell me what that was. He took it in his hand and seemed some time looking at it. I told him I had been told it was a topaz, and he said it might be. He says, 'I would buy this; would you sell it?' I told him I did not know but what I would. What would it be worth? And he said he did not know; he would give me a dollar and keep it as a specimen, and I told him I would not sell it; and it was certainly pretty to look at. He asked me where I found it, and I told him in Eagle. He asked about how far out, and I said right in the village, and I went out. Afterwards, and about the twenty-eighth of December, I needed money pretty badly, and thought every dollar would help, and I took it back to Mr. Boynton and told him I had brought back the topaz, and he says, 'Well, yes; what did I offer you for it?' and I says, 'One dollar'; and he stepped to the change drawer and gave me the dollar, and I went out." In another part of her testimony she says: "Before I sold the stone I had no knowledge whatever that it was a diamond. I told him that I had been advised that it was probably a topaz, and he said probably it was." . . .

. . . Mr. Samuel B. Boynton, the defendant to whom the stone was sold, testified that at the time he bought this stone, he had never seen an uncut diamond; had seen cut diamonds, but they are quite different from the uncut ones; "he had no idea this was a diamond, and it never entered his brain at the time." Considerable evidence was given as to what took place after the sale and purchase, but that evidence has very little if any bearing, upon the main point in the case.

. . . The only question in the case is whether there was anything in the sale which entitled the vendor (the appellant) to rescind the sale and so revest the title in her. The only reasons we know of for rescinding a sale and revesting the title in the vendor so that he may maintain an action at law for the recovery of the possession against his vendee are (1) that the vendee was guilty of some fraud in procuring a sale to be made to him; (2) that there was a mistake made by the vendor in delivering an article which was not the article sold — a mistake in fact as to the identity of the thing sold with the thing delivered upon the sale. This last is not in reality a rescission of the sale made, as the thing delivered was not the thing sold, and no title ever passed to the vendee by such delivery.

In this case, upon the plaintiff's own evidence, there can be no just ground for alleging that she was induced to make the sale she did by any fraud or unfair dealings on the part of Mr. Boynton. Both were entirely ignorant at the time of the character of the stone and of its intrinsic value. Mr. Boynton was not an expert in uncut diamonds, and had made no examination of the stone, except to take it in his hand and look at it before he made the offer of one dollar, which was refused at the time, and afterwards accepted without any comment or further examination made by Mr. Boynton. The appellant had the stone in her possession for a long time, and it appears from her own statement that she had made some inquiry as to its nature and qualities. If she chose to sell it without further investigation as to its intrinsic value to a person who was guilty of no fraud or unfairness which induced her to sell it for a small sum, she cannot repudiate the sale because it is afterwards ascertained that she made a bad bargain. [Citation omitted.] There is no pretense of any mistake as to the identity of the thing sold. It was produced by the plaintiff and exhibited to the vendee before the sale was made, and the thing sold was delivered to the vendee when the purchase price was paid. [Citations omitted.] Suppose the appellant had produced the stone, and said she had been told it was a diamond, and she believed it was, but had no knowledge herself as to its character or value, and Mr. Boynton had given her $500 for it, could he have rescinded the sale if it had turned out to be a topaz or any other stone of very small value? Could Mr. Boynton have rescinded the sale on the ground of mistake? Clearly not, nor could he rescind it on the ground that there had been a breach of warranty, because there was no warranty, nor could he rescind it on the ground of fraud, unless he could show that she falsely declared that she had been told it was a diamond, or, if she had been so told, still she knew it was not a diamond.

It is urged, with a good deal of earnestness, on the part of the counsel for the appellant that, because it has turned out that the stone was immensely more valuable than the parties at the time of the sale supposed it was, such fact alone is a ground for the rescission of the sale, and that fact was evidence of fraud on the part of the vendee. . . . When this sale was made the value of the thing sold was open to the investigation of both parties, neither knowing its intrinsic value, and, so far as the evidence in this case shows, both supposed that the price paid was adequate. How can fraud be predicated upon such a sale, even though after-investigation showed that the intrinsic value of the thing sold was hundreds of times greater than the price paid? . . .

We can find nothing in the evidence from which it could be justly inferred that Mr. Boynton, at the time he offered the plaintiff one dollar for the stone, had any knowledge of the real value of the stone, or that he entertained even a belief that the stone was a diamond. It cannot, therefore, be said that there was a suppression of knowledge on the part of the defendant as to the value of the stone which a court of equity might seize upon to avoid the sale. [I]n the absence of fraud or warranty, the

value of the property sold, as compared with the price paid, is no ground for a rescission of a sale. [Citations omitted.] However unfortunate the plaintiff may have been in selling this valuable stone for a mere nominal sum, she has failed entirely to make out a case either of fraud or mistake in the sale such as will entitle her to a rescission of such sale so as to recover the property sold in an action at law.

The judgment of the circuit court is affirmed.

Post-Case Follow-Up

The case describes an extremely narrow view of mistake: as long as the stone delivered was the stone they intended to buy/sell, mistake does not apply. That portion of the opinion probably does not describe the modern approach to mistake. The court's discussion of Wood's decision to sell the item in the face of acknowledged uncertainty offers a perfect illustration of conscious ignorance. Wood was aware that she did not know what the stone was, thinking perhaps it was a topaz. Rather than find out before selling, Wood elected to sell despite the uncertainty. She took the risk that the stone might be more valuable than she realized.

That conclusion may seem uncharitable. Wood did ask Boynton what the stone was. She tried to resolve the uncertainty and failed. Should he have told her? Professionals sell that service. He had no duty to give the information away, even if he already knew the stone was a diamond, much less if it would require some effort to make that determination. Should he have offered to tell her for a price? He can. But given a choice between selling the information and buying the rock, nothing compels one choice.

Wood v. Boynton: Real Life Applications

1. Gallery sold a painting by de Kooning to Collector. The work proved to be a very good forgery. Collector seeks to rescind the contract on the ground of mutual mistake. Which, if any, of the arguments below might lead a court to reject the mistake defense?

   a. Gallery described the painting as "attributed to de Kooning," but never said it was an authentic de Kooning.
   b. Gallery's brochure of works available, given to each person who entered, contained on page one several terms and conditions. Among them was a disclaimer: "Gallery makes no representations or warranties concerning the authenticity of any of the works offered for sale on the premises. Buyers are advised to make their own judgments concerning the authenticity of these works. Gallery will make works available for more extensive, noninvasive examination at the request of Buyers."
   c. Collector was aware of the risk that very good forgeries may be undetected and should have taken that risk into account when deciding whether and how much to offer for the painting.

d. Would it matter if Gallery maintained an insurance policy that covered its losses incurred as a result of buying bogus art?

2. At a garage sale, Jesse saw an old end table marked $10. Jesse bought it. After a little research, Jesse realized that the table was a valuable antique. If Jesse tells the seller about this discovery, can the seller seek rescission on the basis of mistake?

3. In a plea bargain, the defendant agreed to plead guilty to one count if the prosecution would dismiss all other counts. Both parties thought defendant was pleading guilty to a felony, but the amount involved in that count was too small, making it a misdemeanor. The prosecution sought to rescind the plea agreement on the basis of mutual mistake, allowing it to proceed on all of the charges (or, more likely, offer a plea deal on a different charge that really is a felony). As counsel for defendant, how would you rebut the defense of mutual mistake?

---

2. Unilateral Mistake

Unilateral mistake refers to situations where only one party was mistaken. The rule governing unilateral mistake closely resembles that for mutual mistake, with two significant differences. First, the mistake need not be shared, deleting the second element identified in the previous section. Second, some basis must be found for frustrating the expectations of the party who was not mistaken. An additional element offers three possible ways to justify that result.

Unilateral mistake requires:

(1) a mistake by the party claiming the defense;
(2) that concerned the situation at the time the contract was made;
(3) that involved a basic assumption on which the contract was made;
(4) which materially affected the agreed exchange of performances;
(5) the risk of the mistake did not fall on the party claiming the defense; and
(6) one of the following three things applies:
    (a) the other party had reason to know of the mistake; or
    (b) the other party's fault caused the mistake; or
    (c) enforcement would be **unconscionable** (creating an imbalance so great a judge, in good conscience, could not enforce the contract).[23]

Each element numbered must be shown to establish the defense, but any one lettered element will establish the sixth numbered element. If even one of the numbered elements fails, the contract is enforceable.

The analysis of the first five elements does not differ between mutual and unilateral mistake. The definition of mistake, basic assumption, material effect, and allocation of risk all remain the same. Only the last element requires separate attention.

[23]RESTATEMENT (SECOND) OF CONTRACTS §153.

Where a party had reason to know of the other's mistake, denying the benefit of the contract seems warranted. Recall that, in some circumstances, a party who made no misrepresentation may lose the benefit of a contract if she had reason to know that the other party had been misled by another. Similarly, sometimes a party with reason to know of another's mistake may not claim the benefit of the contract. In effect, when a unilateral mistake leads to a deal too good to be true, the person who leapt to accept may not keep the windfall. This situation often arises in contracts awarded by competitive bids. Where one bid is substantially lower than all the others, the party receiving the bid may be on notice that an error crept into the calculations at some point. Recognizing the likely error creates an opportunity to prevent the error. For instance, one might confirm the bid, asking the bidder to recalculate.

Where the other party is to blame for the mistaken party's error, the person at fault probably does not deserve the benefit of the other's mistake. Situations like this may border on concealment or nondisclosure. Impeding the other's efforts to discover the facts or failing to reveal important facts may cause the error. Similarly, negligent drafting of a request for bids (or request for proposals, known as an RFP) may lead a bidder to overlook some of its terms or requirements. A bid might omit elements of a job hidden in the RFP or contained in specifications the bidder never received. When the fault lies with the drafter, that party's expectations deserve less concern than those of the mistaken bidder.

If the resulting contract produces extreme hardship, courts may void the unconscionable exchange even though one party legitimately expected the benefits. As used here, unconscionable seems to mean extremely harsh or one-sided. A material effect on performance already requires a significant disadvantage to the party raising mistake. Unconscionable seems to require an even greater imbalance, one so severe that it cannot be tolerated, no matter how little notice of the mistake the other party had. Arguably, a contract this one-sided is so good that the

EXHIBIT 7.5 Decision Tree for Mistake

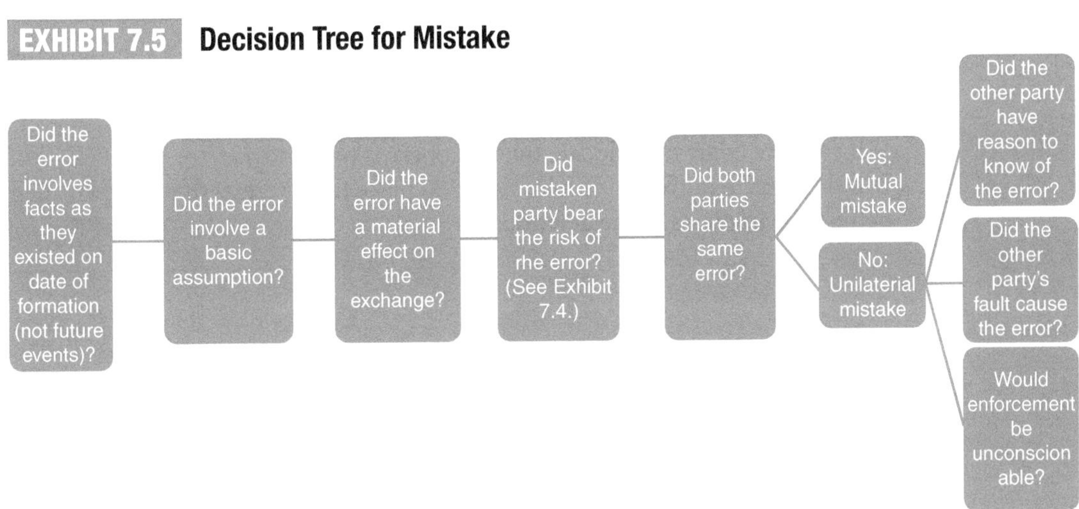

other party should have known that there must have been some mistake. Even if no reason to know can be demonstrated, unconscionability alone will satisfy this last aspect of unilateral mistake. (This meaning of unconscionable differs from what it means in the defense called unconscionability, discussed in Chapter 8. If it meant the same thing, a party could use that defense and forgo proving all the other elements of unilateral mistake.)

You might wonder if unilateral mistake seems worse than mutual mistake. You might also think it is harder to prove. Unilateral mistake seems worse where one party knows the other is mistaken and nonetheless keeps silent about it. That borders on misrepresentation via nondisclosure and seems deceptive or exploitative. Those cases are the ones where unilateral mistake will be easiest to prove: knowledge of the mistake works as well as reason to know of the mistake; and conduct approaching concealment or nondisclosure probably constitutes fault that causes the mistake. Unilateral mistake is harder to prove only when the other party was not exploiting the mistake, but did not have any reason to know the mistake existed at all. That party's legitimate expectations should not be discarded without some justification. Even without borderline misconduct, unilateral mistake may apply if the deal is so bad enforcement would be unconscionable. In short, the extra element in unilateral mistake may not make the defense much harder to prove in any case where it should be applied.

Case Preview

Sumerel v. Goodyear Tire & Rubber Company

Sumerel raises a very common problem: one party miscalculates the appropriate price, but does not discover the error until the other party has already attempted to accept the offer. The problem can happen when contractors or subcontractors submit bids. Courts could deny relief, putting the cost of the error on the party that made the miscalculation. The case discusses circumstances when courts may allow rescission despite carelessness by the mistaken party.

As you read *Sumerel v. Goodyear Tire & Rubber Company*, look for the following:

1. How did the court decide that the resulting deal was unconscionable?
2. Why did the court not allocate the risk of error to Goodyear?
3. Did the court require plaintiff's counsel to place the interests of their own client behind the interests of the defendant?

Sumerel v. Goodyear Tire & Rubber Company

232 P.3d 128 (Colo. Ct. App. 2009)

Opinion by Judge GABRIEL.

Defendant, Goodyear . . . appeals from the district court's order holding that Goodyear had entered into a valid and enforceable settlement agreement with Bob

and Sallie Sumerel, Steven and Ann Berzin, Dane and Kerry Dicke, and Bart Kaufman (collectively plaintiffs). [W]e reverse and remand to allow the parties to file a satisfaction of judgment for the amounts already paid by Goodyear.

In 2002, plaintiffs [won a jury verdict] against [another defendant] and Goodyear . . . [recovering] approximately $1.3 million against Goodyear. . . . [The] jury found that Goodyear was responsible for 36% of ["other costs and losses"] suffered by [two plaintiffs] and 48% of those incurred by [two others].

[After appeal, the case was] remanded [to determine] "the proper accrual dates for prejudgment interest on other costs and losses" and to calculate and award such interest.

. . . Goodyear's lead attorney, Roger Thomasch . . . discussed with plaintiffs' lead attorney, William Maywhort, a potential compromise on the applicable accrual dates. Thomasch proposed certain accrual dates and advised Maywhort of the amount of prejudgment interest that would result from using these proposed dates. Thomasch's calculation of these amounts took into account the jury's 36% and 48% allocations of fault, and Thomasch expressly conveyed that fact to Maywhort.

Following up on [those discussions], co-counsel for plaintiffs, Lee Gray . . . called Michael Brooks . . . co-counsel for Goodyear [and] agreed on the applicable accrual dates with little difficulty, [but] had trouble getting their calculations . . . to match. . . . Brooks [estimated] that . . . Goodyear [owed] approximately $2.7 million. . . . Gray responded that this amount appeared to be larger than his own estimates by "about six figures"[, but] did not elaborate or share . . . his calculations.

. . . Brooks called Gray and speculated that [plaintiffs had underestimated] the interest applicable to [one plaintiff] who had been awarded additional sums as a result of the prior appeal. Gray responded, "[T]hat could be it". . . . Brooks took from Gray's response that Gray either agreed or had no basis to disagree that Brooks had found the source of the discrepancy, although the parties had not yet exchanged their respective calculations. Without Gray's calculations, Brooks could not be sure whether he had, in fact, resolved the discrepancy.

Believing that he may have discovered the source of the discrepancy, however, on November 2, 2006, Brooks sent Gray an e-mail [and attachment], stating, "Here are our charts providing the numers [sic] that Goodyear believes are appropriate. . . . Please review these, then let's discuss."

After reviewing these charts, . . . plaintiffs' counsel recognized that Goodyear's calculations had failed to reduce the damages for "other costs and losses" according to the jury's finding that Goodyear was only liable for 36% [and] 48% of the[m]. [For] other categories of damages . . . Goodyear's charts . . . had correctly applied the jury's fault allocations. Goodyear's error resulted in an overstatement of the damages due by more than $550,000.

Plaintiffs' counsel did not call this obvious error to Brooks's attention or to the attention of any other representative of Goodyear. Instead, Maywhort later claimed that he . . . surmised that . . . Goodyear may have concluded that it was solely responsible for any such damages awarded. Maywhort took this position even though (1) the parties had tried the allocation of fault issue and the jury had allocated only 36% and 48% of such losses to Goodyear, and (2) Maywhort had previously discussed prejudgment interest calculations with Thomasch, Thomasch provided calculations that were based on the correct allocated fault percentages, and Thomasch called these allocations to Maywhort's attention.

. . .

Ultimately, neither Gray nor any of plaintiffs' co-counsel called Brooks to discuss his charts, as Brooks had requested. Rather, Maywhort, who had not been directly involved in the more recent discussions regarding the calculations, left a voicemail message for Thomasch, who also had not been directly involved, stating that plaintiffs accepted Goodyear's November 2, 2006 "offer." . . .

. . . Brooks prepared a form of satisfaction of judgment that he sent to Gray on November 16, 2006, with a notation that the document was a draft for discussion purposes only. That same day, before anyone had signed the satisfaction of judgment, Brooks realized the error in his earlier calculations. He immediately called the error to Gray's attention and sent Gray corrected versions of the charts and a revised satisfaction of judgment. . . .

Rather than acknowledging the error, signing the revised satisfaction, and concluding the action for the amounts actually awarded by the jury, [plaintiff's counsel] demanded that Goodyear adhere to the parties' alleged agreement, which would have resulted in plaintiffs' receiving over $550,000 more than what was due them. When Goodyear refused to do so, plaintiffs filed a motion to enforce the purported "settlement agreement." The district court granted plaintiffs' motion, and Goodyear now appeals, having paid, and plaintiffs having accepted, the amounts that the parties agreed were due and owing, without prejudice to plaintiffs' claims for the additional amounts.

[The court first held that Brooks' e-mail and attached charts were not an offer.]

III. UNILATERAL MISTAKE

Goodyear also contends that, even if its counsel's November 2, 2006 e-mail . . . constituted an offer, any agreement based on such an offer would be unenforceable. We again agree and thus hold, in the alternative, that any agreement reached by the parties here is unenforceable.

Regarding unilateral mistake, Professor Corbin states, "[T]here is practically universal agreement that, if the material mistake of one party was . . . known by the other or was of such character and accompanied by such circumstances that the other had reason to know of it, the mistaken party has the power to avoid the contract." 7 Joseph M. Perillo, *Corbin on Contracts* §28.41, at 255 (rev. ed. 2002). Corbin further states that relief due to unilateral mistake is available even if the offeree neither knew of nor had reason to know of the mistake, if enforcement of the contract would be "oppressive" to the mistaken party, and relief from the contract "would impose no substantial hardship" on the other party. *Id.* §28.39, at 224.

Pronouncements by our supreme court and the Restatement (Second) of Contracts are consistent with these principles. Thus, in *Powder Horn Constructors, Inc. v. City of Florence*, 754 P.2d 356, 363 (Colo. 1988), the supreme court held that a contractor was entitled to equitable relief from the consequences of a bid containing mathematical or clerical errors where the errors were made in good faith and related to a material part of the bid, and where the city that received the bid had not relied to its detriment on the mistaken bid. In such circumstances, the court held that equitable relief was appropriate because the bid that was apparently accepted was not the bid that was intended and, therefore, was not a valid bid. *Id.* The supreme court further stated that the contractor was entitled to equitable relief, because, where the contractor acted in good faith and where the city knew of the mistake before accepting the bid, it would "contravene fundamental principles of fairness" to allow the city to "take advantage of [the contractor's] mistake and gain a windfall profit." *Id.* at 364.

Similarly, Restatement (Second) of Contracts §§153-54 (1981), which have not yet been expressly adopted in Colorado (although §153 was cited with approval in *Powder Horn*), are fully consistent with these principles.

Restatement (Second) of Contracts §153 provides:

> Where a mistake of one party at the time a contract was made as to a basic assumption on which he made the contract has a material effect on the agreed exchange of performances that is adverse to him, the contract is voidable by him if he does not bear the risk of the mistake under the rule stated in §154, and
>
> (a) the effect of the mistake is such that enforcement of the contract would be unconscionable, or
>
> (b) the other party had reason to know of the mistake or his fault caused the mistake.

Restatement (Second) of Contracts §154 in turn provides:

> A party bears the risk of a mistake when
>
> (a) the risk is allocated to him by agreement of the parties, or
>
> (b) he is aware, at the time the contract is made, that he has only limited knowledge with respect to the facts to which the mistake relates but treats his limited knowledge as sufficient, or
>
> (c) the risk is allocated to him by the court on the ground that it is reasonable in the circumstances to do so.

Notably, comment f to §153 states, "It is, of course, unusual for a party to bear the risk of a mistake that the other party had reason to know of. . . ." Restatement (Second) of Contracts §153 cmt. f.

Applying these principles here, we conclude for the following reasons that even if an agreement had been formed, it was voidable under the circumstances.

First, it cannot reasonably be disputed that Goodyear's calculations were in error, and plaintiffs admit that they knew or had reason to know of the error.

Second, the purported agreement would clearly be oppressive and unconscionable, and relief from such an agreement would pose no substantial hardship on plaintiffs. Simply stated, plaintiffs are attempting to exploit Goodyear's mistake to gain a windfall of over $550,000 more than the jury in this case awarded to them. Such a windfall is most certainly oppressive to Goodyear and, in our view, would be unconscionable. Conversely, avoiding the purported agreement and awarding plaintiffs only what the jury awarded works no hardship on plaintiffs. They would receive the amount to which they are entitled.

Third, we reject plaintiffs' assertion that the risk of mistake here rested with Goodyear. As in *Powder Horn*, we perceive no basis for a determination that Goodyear did not act in good faith. Moreover, as noted above, it is unusual for a party to bear the risk of a mistake that the other party had reason to know of. Restatement (Second) of Contracts §153 cmt. f. Nor do we perceive any basis for concluding, as plaintiffs contend, that Brooks chose to charge ahead in conscious ignorance, believing that his limited knowledge was sufficient. The record reflects that someone had to share the first set of calculations here. Brooks did so, knowing that there was still a possible six-figure discrepancy. Hence, he asked Gray to review the calculations and to call him to discuss the numbers. Further, as was obvious from the November 2, 2006 e-mail, Brooks was continuing to try to identify the discrepancy and, thus, was seeking further discussion. In short, the record demonstrates that Brooks did not seek an agreement through conscious ignorance. Rather, the record shows that he sought further dialogue because he knew of the discrepancy in the parties' calculations.

. . .

For these reasons, we hold that even if Brooks's November 2, 2006 e-mail and charts could be characterized as an offer and that offer was accepted, Goodyear may properly avoid the resulting agreement on the facts presented here.

IV. CONCLUSION

The current phase of this litigation could, and should, have been avoided. When plaintiffs' counsel reviewed Brooks's charts, they immediately recognized the cause of the parties' six-figure discrepancy. At this point, the proper course was obvious to us: plaintiffs' counsel should have called Brooks, identified the discrepancy, and concluded the matter without further delay. Had plaintiffs' counsel done so, plaintiffs would have immediately received the considerable sums to which they were entitled, and all parties would have been spared the undoubtedly substantial expense of the current litigation over what can only be viewed as a quest by plaintiffs to obtain a substantial windfall. For the reasons set forth above, on the facts presented here, the law will not countenance the patently inequitable result that plaintiffs seek. [Citation omitted.]

The agreement in *Sumerel* presents a dilemma for the court: it can make Goodyear live with the results of its careless calculation or it can deny plaintiffs a windfall they obtained by subterfuge. The court favored the party that made a good faith mistake. That will not always be possible. In some cases, both parties are acting in good faith, forcing the court to deny one of them their honest expectations. The case illustrates the reasons some courts overlook negligence by the mistaken party, refusing to assign the risk of error on that basis alone. But other courts deny relief to a party whose own carelessness led to the agreement. Unilateral mistake is one area of law where jurisdictions differ on the extent to which they will award rescission.

Sumerel v. Goodyear Tire & Rubber Company: Real Life Applications

1. During settlement negotiations, plaintiff sent defendant an itemized calculation of the losses claimed along with an offer to settle for that total. The calculation contained an error in addition, making the total $300,000 lower than intended. Defendant, seeing a reasonable total, agreed to settle for that amount without examining the itemization to discover the error. The parties signed a settlement agreement for the total. Thereafter, plaintiff discovered the error and sought to continue the suit unless defendant pays $300,000 more than the agreement specified. Should the court rescind the agreement or enforce it (dismissing the suit if defendant pays the amount promised)? (Does it matter whether the total was $400,000, $1.4 million, or $14 million?)

2. On a cruise, Cameron saw a large (20 carat) diamond in the onboard jewelry shop. Cameron asked the price of the diamond. The proprietor, after consulting the home office in Miami, quoted the price as $235,000. After considering the purchase overnight, Cameron agreed to buy the diamond. The parties signed a written agreement and Cameron paid the full purchase price. After discovering that the price quoted should have been $235,000 per carat (about $4.8 million), the store refused to deliver the gem and refunded the payment to Cameron's credit card. Should a court permit the rescission or enforce the contract? Would the result be different if, while considering the purchase, a friend advised Cameron not to buy the diamond because, if it was real, it should cost at least $2 million (advice that Cameron ignored)? *See DePrince v. Starboard Cruise Services, Inc.*, 163 So. 3d 586 (Fla. App. 2015).

3. Kelly, a teacher eligible for retirement, applied for benefits from the state retirement fund. "Normal" retirement provided the largest monthly payments, but, unlike other options, did not provide benefits for a surviving spouse after the retiree's death. The election form, however, provided space to name a beneficiary on the line for each election, including normal retirement. Kelly elected normal retirement

Mistakes Regarding Contract Terms

People can make mistakes about a lot of different things. Most of the mistakes here involve mistakes of basic assumption, usually concerning the characteristics of the performances exchanged: was the stone a diamond, was the land useful as rental property. Sometimes mistakes of basic assumption concern qualities indirectly related to the performances: mistakes concerning health or ability to perform.

Mistakes concerning contract terms pose a different set of concerns. Often, there is no mistake concerning what term the parties used, but it was not the term they intended. This error can result from a mistake of integration: agreeing to one term but mistakenly writing a different term in the contract (e.g., ending in 2017 versus 2016, recording the price as $70,000 instead of $700,000 (or vice versa)). It can result from miscalculation that leads a party to agree to a term (say, a price) different from the one it meant to propose. Sometimes the parties intended the term, but were mistaken concerning what the term meant: believing that "normal" retirement included survivor benefits. Chapter 9 addresses mistakes concerning which terms were part of the contract or what those terms meant. These errors are not really mistakes of basic assumption, though courts sometimes try to apply the same rules to these errors.

Finally, some mistakes involve poor predictions or poor judgment: subsequent events do not quite match the parties' expectations. Mistake is not designed to help people who make a conscious choice, but come to regret their decision. No legal remedy exists for mistakes of judgment.

and named Jean, Kelly's spouse, as beneficiary, believing that allowed Jean survivor benefits. Kelly died of cancer three weeks after retiring. Jean received one month's pension payment, but no more. Should the court rescind Kelly's election on the ground of unilateral mistake? Does it matter when Kelly learned of the cancer?

a. Kelly was diagnosed with cancer before retiring, at a time when Kelly could have changed the election. Kelly left the election intact, believing it provided for Jean.
b. What if Kelly was unaware of the cancer or any other serious health issues until after retiring, when it was too late to change the election?

4. Chris, a contractor, prepared a bid on a job building a stretch of highway and a parking lot for the state. Chris obtained bids for concrete work from several subcontractors. Sean submitted the lowest bid—$550,000, 23 percent lower than the next lowest bid ($715,000). Sean prepared the bid based on the state's summary of specifications (provided by Chris) rather than examining the blueprints for the job. Chris used Sean's bid in preparing its bid for the work. After being awarded the contract by the state, Chris accepted Sean's bid to do the work. Upon starting work, Sean realized the blueprints differed from assumptions Sean made in preparing the bid. Most significantly, Sean assumed the job required slabs eight inches thick, but the blueprints required slabs three feet thick, requiring a lot more concrete than Sean included, raising the cost of the job by $100,000. If Sean seeks rescission of the contract, should a court grant that relief? Would the answer differ if Sean used the blueprints in preparing the bid, but made an error calculating the total cubic feet of concrete required, with the same net effect on costs? *See Riley Bros. Constr., Inc. v. Shuck*, 704 N.W.2d 197 (Minn. Ct. App. 2005).

Chapter Summary

- Rescission is available if a fraudulent or material misrepresentation induces assent and reliance was justifiable. The defense may arise from innocent misrepresentations, if material, not just from lies.
- Silence can be an assertion when circumstances make it necessary for a person to speak (nondisclosure) or when a party's conduct is intended to prevent another from discovering the truth (concealment).
- Misrepresentation (or duress or undue influence) by a third party may justify rescission unless the other party relies on the contract in good faith and without reason to know of the misrepresentation (or duress or undue influence).
- A party's mistake concerning a basic assumption on which the contract was made will justify rescission if it has a material effect on the agreed exchange, unless the mistaken party bears the risk of the error. If only one party was mistaken, that party also must show that the transaction is unconscionable, that the other had reason to know of the mistake, or that the other's fault caused the mistake.

Applying the Rules

1. Which, if any, of the following items need not be established in order to support the defense of misrepresentation? (Choose as many as apply.)

   a. A false statement of fact
   b. The misleading party's knowledge that an assertion is inaccurate
   c. That the misled party would not have entered the contract if aware of the truth
   d. That the assertion was made with the intent that the misled party rely on it
   e. That the misled party was not negligent in failing to discover the truth

2. Sammy owned a house and rented it to Barrett for $2,000 a month. After two years as a tenant, Barrett asked whether Sammy would consider selling the house. During discussions to set a price, Barrett informed Sammy that the house had significant termite damage and required some serious electrical work to become marketable. Sammy offered to sell the house to Barrett for $400,000—about $50,000 less than fair market value of similar homes in the area—if Barrett would take the house "as is." The parties signed the contract and closed the sale. Afterward, Carmen, a mutual friend, revealed that Barrett had lied about the termites and the need for electrical work. Can Sammy seek to rescind the contract based on Barrett's misrepresentations? Which element(s) pose the greatest difficulty for Sammy's effort to rescind the sale? What is the best argument you can make for Sammy? Do you expect to prevail?

3. Alex was looking for a house. Alex has an idiosyncratic distaste for cats and refuses to consider any house in which cats once lived. Alex found a house that seemed perfect at an affordable price. Before making an offer, Alex asked Gail, the owner, if any cats lived there. Gail's cat had lived there for many years, but had recently died. Gail said "No," but nothing more. Alex expressed joy at finally finding a cat-free home of this quality. Later that day, Alex's broker provided Gail with Alex's written offer to buy the house, which Gail accepted by signing. Before closing, Alex learned that a cat had in fact lived in the house. Alex seeks your advice concerning whether the contract can be rescinded.

4. Charly, believing that city officials would soon announce an extension of the city's trolley system, paid Leslie $10 million for a tract of land just outside the city limits near the anticipated end of the line. Without trolley access, the land probably would sell for about $2 million. City officials made no such announcement and, in fact, announced that no extensions of the trolley system were contemplated for the next five years. Charly would like to rescind the purchase on the basis of mistake.

a. Charly thinks Leslie asked the inflated price because Leslie shared the belief that the trolley would extend in that direction. If so, would mutual mistake justify rescission?

b. If Leslie persuasively denies sharing this belief, can Charly prevail on basis of a unilateral mistake?

5. At an estate sale, Bobby noticed a shoebox full of old baseball cards. Bobby asked Sandy how much they cost. Sandy offered the box for $50. Bobby accepted, paid, and took the cards. Bobby later discovered that there was one card worth $11,000 in the box of otherwise ordinary cards. A newspaper story alerted Sandy to Bobby's find. Sandy seeks advice concerning whether the sale can be rescinded.

6. On the facts of Question 5, suppose that Sandy was aware of this card's unique value and had removed the card from the box before putting the rest of the box for sale. Sandy does not know how the card got back in the box but suspects one of the friends helping to set up for the sale may have found the card and placed it in the box without consulting Sandy. How do these additional facts affect your advice on whether rescission is available?

Contract Law in Practice

1. Examine the statutes and cases in your state to determine the elements required to avoid a contract for misrepresentation. Compare the rule to the rule discussed in the text. Be careful to distinguish cases that establish the rule for tort liability from those discussing the rule for avoiding a contract. Does the rule require both a material and a fraudulent misrepresentation? Is it limited to express statements of fact or will it also apply to nondisclosure, to statements of opinion, and to statements of intention? (Hint: You may find it helpful to look at approved jury instructions for your jurisdiction.)

2. Examine the statutes and cases in your state to determine the elements required to avoid a contract for mistake. Compare the rule to the rule discussed in the text. Does the rule apply to mistake of law as well as to mistake of fact? Does unilateral mistake require different elements from mutual mistake? (Hint: You may find it helpful to look at approved jury instructions for your jurisdiction.)

3. Review the *Barrer* case. On remand, each party will need to decide whether to settle. Is it likely that the bank can produce evidence at trial that will solve the shortcomings in its defense? Is it likely that Barrer, without the benefit of the doubt he received at summary judgment, can overcome claims that he withheld important information? Pair up with a classmate, each representing one party, and see if you can reach an agreement. Compare your settlement to those reached by other members of the class.

4. Big Co. has agreed to sell its business to Huge Co. After a preliminary agreement, Huge Co. sent its inspectors in to examine Big Co.'s records to determine if there were any undisclosed liabilities or other issues concerning the financial statements of Big Co. (a process called due diligence). The parties are now preparing the final agreement. Big Co. wants a clause in the contract that eliminates any risk that Huge Co. later can seek to rescind the sale based on any problems that the due diligence failed to detect. Prepare a provision that would protect Big Co. from any such claims.

5. Depositor presented a check to Bank. The check was made out in euros. Bank accepted the check for deposit without telling Depositor (1) that Depositor's account would be credited in dollars, not euros; (2) that no money would be available until Bank collected the funds (unlike domestic checks, which by law require some provisional credit while collection proceeds); and (3) that Bank might receive an exchange rate better than the one it would apply in calculating the amount deposited. The trial court, without ruling on whether these omissions were nondisclosures, ruled that "there is no evidence of any detrimental reliance on Depositor's part. The record is devoid of evidence that a different bank would have collected payment in euros, or would have provided provisional credit, or would have applied the interbank rate of exchange." Prepare a memorandum advising Depositor whether to appeal the ruling on reliance. Consider whether, after remand, you would be able to establish that the omissions qualify as nondisclosures. (Assume the state will follow the Restatement (Second) of Contracts on both issues.)

6. What rule governs the misrepresentation defense for sales of goods? Examine the Uniform Commercial Code. Identify the section that addresses misrepresentation. Does it apply a different rule than the one your state applies to other contracts?

8

Contract Defenses — Policy Constraints

Society usually lets parties make their own choices regarding promises to make. Assent usually signifies that both parties would benefit from a contract. But situations arise where the interests of the parties may not coincide with the interests of society as a whole. Policy defenses may seek to protect the parties themselves, third parties not represented in the negotiations, or even the judicial system from agreements that present unacceptable societal risks. Society expects its courts to intercept these deals rather than enforcing them. As with defenses that undermine assent, these defenses identify situations in which contracts should not be enforced, despite the presence of both mutual assent and consideration. Policy issues here are designed to protect society's interests rather than solely the interests of individuals; understanding them thoroughly helps avoid their abuse.

The choice of defenses reveals a great deal about the balance between liberty and regulation and about society's power to foreclose some individual choices, even if citizens vigorously pursue them. More pragmatically, the defenses offer ways that parties can escape from agreements they regret based on larger societal concerns. Familiarity with the defenses also allows you to find ways to protect a client from hardships the other party may have built into the transaction. Equally important, knowing the parameters of these defenses helps you preserve legitimate bargains from attack by people who simply changed their minds.

Key Concepts

- Doctrine of unconscionability
- Public policy defenses related to illegal conduct or behavior that violates public morals
- Statute of frauds requirements for a sufficient writing
- Exceptions to the statute of frauds

A. INTRODUCTION TO DEFENSES BASED ON POLICY

The preceding chapters in Part II of this text discussed defenses that arise in situations where assent has been challenged under a variety of void and voidable defenses. This chapter addresses three additional defenses that inject public policy into contract cases.

1. **Unconscionability** addresses issues of flaws in the negotiation stage of the contract as well as contract terms considered harsh and one-sided. At its core, it covers situations where oppressive contract terms pose serious and unexpected hardships for a party. Disagreement concerning the scope and elements of the unconscionability defense leaves considerable room for parties to argue and for the court to interpret this defense as extending beyond these core cases.
2. **Public policy** applies primarily to contracts that require conduct that is illegal or violates well-established policies embodied in constitutional law, statutory law and case precedent. Yet the doctrine can be interpreted broadly to apply to unacceptable behavior based on notions of public morals, even when that conduct has not previously been declared illegal.
3. **Statutes of frauds** requires some contracts to be evidenced by a signed writing, even if they meet all of the requirements of contract formation. This defense promotes the use of written agreements, rather than oral ones, and helps to prevent frivolous or false claims of oral contracts in order to persuade a jury to award contract remedies.

Each defense raises issues that extend beyond the interests of the parties themselves, allowing societal concerns to override assent by the parties, even if they prefer the contract as negotiated.

B. UNCONSCIONABILITY—VOIDABLE

The concept of unconscionability is not a new theory. This doctrine allowing lopsided bargains to be rescinded dates back to Roman times. In the modern era, the defense looks at issues of gross inequality, oppression, or unfair surprise in contracts. Unconscionability is a question of law for the courts to decide. The famous quote regarding an unconscionable bargain is an agreement "such as no man in his senses and not under delusion would make on the one hand, and as no honest and fair man would accept on the other. . . ." *Hume v. United States*, 132 U.S. 406 (1889), language drawn from *Earl of Chesterfield v. Janssen*, 2 Ves. Sen. 125, 155, 28 Eng. Rep. 82, 100 (Ch. 1750).

Both Restatement (Second) of Contracts §208 and UCC §2-302 recognize the concept of unconscionability, but do not provide substantive guidance on how to define and analyze this defense. Through case law, two components of unconscionability have been identified: **procedural unconscionability**, looking at defects in the negotiation process, and **substantive unconscionability**, analyzing whether the contract terms themselves are too harsh or one-sided to be legally enforceable. Courts have applied different approaches to determine whether a contract is unconscionable. A majority of courts look for both procedural and substantive unconscionability. Other courts are willing to invalidate unconscionable terms on a showing of either procedural or substantive unconscionability. Further, some courts will applying a sliding scale, demanding more procedural unconscionability if a contract exhibits substantive unconscionability, and vice versa. Depending upon the circumstances, a court may rescind the entire contract, strike out offending clauses, or interpret the disputed term in a limiting way that avoids an unconscionable outcome, leaving the rest of the contract in force.

1. Procedural Unconscionability

Procedural unconscionability addresses unfair surprise and the absence of meaningful choice in the contract formation process. Courts will analyze the factual circumstances to determine the sophistication of the parties to the contract, inequalities in bargaining power, a lack of clear, conspicuous notice of contract terms, little or no meaningful chance to review of the terms in advance of agreeing, and whether major provisions are hidden in fine print or a blizzard of legalese that is difficult to comprehend. If reading the contract would not have put a party on notice of the surprising term, the blame falls on the drafter. Terms concealed in confusing language or hidden in obscure places may be unfairly surprising, even though set forth in the contract. In examining these types of issues, a court can decide whether or not a party may effectively claim unfair surprise and a lack of meaningful choice.

In the online context, unfair surprises in contracts can be created through website design, such as the font size of online text, temporary and disappearing pop-up windows, scrolling options to read text, and lack of print options to allow parties to review contracts offline before agreeing to online terms. Web pages laden with colorful graphics or dynamic animation may easily detract from consumer recognition of important contract terms and conditions. These concerns may be further exacerbated by the accessibility of consumer transactions on ever smaller handheld devices, such as cell phones and tablets.

In an era of form contracts, procedural unconscionability is often raised about disputes involving consumer **contracts of adhesion**: form contracts offered on a take it or leave it basis. These adhesion contracts do not allow parties to freely negotiate contract terms and sophisticated merchants may take advantage of a consumer's lack of business acumen to effectively assess the risks and benefits of the agreement. Unequal or superior bargaining power is an important part of the analysis, but standing alone it will not result in an agreement being found unconscionable. In addition, courts will not automatically invalidate standardized contracts under unconscionability, but will consider this circumstance, along with any others, that suggest a procedural flaw in the contract negotiation and formation process.

Case Preview

Williams v. Walker-Thomas Furniture Co.

The well-known case of *Williams v. Walker-Thomas Furniture Co.* considered both procedural and substantive unconscionability when a furniture store repossessed all furniture that a customer bought, even though her prior payments exceeded the cost of all but the most recent purchases. The case provided insight into the concerns about unsophisticated consumers having difficulty understanding and appreciating the long-term impact of complex contract clauses.

As you read *Williams v. Walker-Thomas Furniture Co.*, look for the following:

1. Why did the lower courts refuse to apply the unconscionability defense to Williams's case?
2. What judicial approach did the appeals court take in considering the application of the defense of unconscionability?
3. What facts supported a finding of procedural unconscionability? Substantive unconscionability?

Williams v. Walker-Thomas Furniture Co.

350 F.2d 445 (D.C. Cir. 1965)

SKELLY WRIGHT, Circuit Judge.

Appellee, Walker-Thomas Furniture Company, operates a retail furniture store in the District of Columbia. During the period from 1957 to 1962 each appellant in these cases purchased a number of household items from Walker-Thomas, for which payment was to be made in installments. The terms of each purchase were contained in a printed form contract which set forth the value of the purchased item and purported to lease the item to appellant for a stipulated monthly rent payment. The contract then provided, in substance, that title would remain in Walker-Thomas until the total of all the monthly payments made equaled the stated value of the item, at which time appellants could take title. In the event of a default in the payment of any monthly installment, Walker-Thomas could repossess the item. The contract further provided that "the amount of each periodical installment payment to be made by [purchaser] to the Company under this present lease shall be inclusive of and not in addition to the amount of each installment payment to be made by [purchaser] under such prior leases, bills or accounts; *and all payments now and hereafter made by [purchaser] shall be credited pro rata on all outstanding leases, bills and accounts* due the Company by [purchaser] at the time each such payment is made."

(Emphasis added.) The effect of this rather obscure provision was to keep a balance due on every item purchased until the balance due on all items, whenever purchased, was liquidated. As a result, the debt incurred at the time of purchase of each item was secured by the right to repossess all the items previously purchased by the same purchaser, and each new item purchased automatically became subject to a security interest arising out of the previous dealings.

. . . [O]n April 17, 1962, appellant Williams bought a stereo set of stated value of $514.95. [Footnote omitted.] She too defaulted shortly thereafter, and appellee sought to replevy all the items purchased since December, 1957. [At the time of this purchase her account showed a balance of $164 still owing from her prior purchases. The total of all the purchases made over the years in question came to $1,800. The total payments amounted to $1,400.] The Court of General Sessions granted judgment for appellee. The District of Columbia Court of Appeals affirmed, and we granted appellants' motion for leave to appeal to this court.

Appellants' principal contention, rejected by both the trial and the appellate courts below, is that these contracts, or at least some of them, are unconscionable and, hence, not enforceable. In its opinion in *Williams v. Walker-Thomas Furniture Company*, 198 A.2d 914, 916 (1964), the District of Columbia Court of Appeals explained its rejection of this contention as follows:

> Appellant's second argument presents a more serious question. The record reveals that prior to the last purchase appellant had reduced the balance in her account to $164. The last purchase, a stereo set, raised the balance due to $678. Significantly, at the time of this and the preceding purchases, appellee was aware of appellant's financial position. The reverse side of the stereo contract listed the name of appellant's social worker and her $218 monthly stipend from the government. Nevertheless, with full knowledge that appellant had to feed, clothe and support both herself and seven children on this amount, appellee sold her a $514 stereo set.
>
> We cannot condemn too strongly appellee's conduct. It raises serious questions of sharp practice and irresponsible business dealings. A review of the legislation in the District of Columbia affecting retail sales and the pertinent decisions of the highest court in this jurisdiction disclose, however, no ground upon which this court can declare the contracts in question contrary to public policy. . . . We think Congress should consider corrective legislation to protect the public from such exploitive contracts as were utilized in the case at bar.

We do not agree that the court lacked the power to refuse enforcement to contracts found to be unconscionable. In other jurisdictions, it has been held as a matter of common law that unconscionable contracts are not enforceable. [Footnote omitted.] While no decision of this court so holding has been found, the notion that an unconscionable bargain should not be given full enforcement is by no means novel. . . . Since we have never adopted or rejected such a rule, [footnote omitted] the question here presented is actually one of first impression.

Congress has recently enacted the Uniform Commercial Code, which specifically provides that the court may refuse to enforce a contract which it finds to be unconscionable at the time it was made. . . . In fact, in view of the absence of prior authority on the point, we consider the congressional adoption of §2-302 persuasive authority for following the rationale of the cases from which the section is explicitly derived. [Footnote omitted.] Accordingly, we hold that where the element of unconscionability is present at the time a contract is made, the contract should not be enforced.

Unconscionability has generally been recognized to include an absence of meaningful choice on the part of one of the parties together with contract terms which are unreasonably favorable to the other party. [Footnote omitted.] Whether a meaningful choice is present in a particular case can only be determined by consideration of all the circumstances surrounding the transaction. In many cases the meaningfulness of the choice is negated by a gross inequality of bargaining power. [Footnote omitted.] The manner in which the contract was entered is also relevant to this consideration. Did each party to the contract, considering his obvious education or lack of it, have a reasonable opportunity to understand the terms of the contract, or were the important terms hidden in a maze of fine print and minimized by deceptive sales practices? Ordinarily, one who signs an agreement without full knowledge of its terms might be held to assume the risk that he has entered a one-sided bargain. [Footnote omitted.] But when a party of little bargaining power, and hence little real choice, signs a commercially unreasonable contract with little or no knowledge of its terms, it is hardly likely that his consent, or even an objective manifestation of his consent, was ever given to all the terms. In such a case the usual rule that the terms of the agreement are not to be questioned [footnote omitted] should be abandoned and the court should consider whether the terms of the contract are so unfair that enforcement should be withheld. [Footnote omitted.]

In determining reasonableness or fairness, the primary concern must be with the terms of the contract considered in light of the circumstances existing when the contract was made. The test is not simple, nor can it be mechanically applied. The terms are to be considered "in the light of the general commercial background and the commercial needs of the particular trade or case." [Footnote omitted.] Corbin suggests the test as being whether the terms are "so extreme as to appear unconscionable according to the mores and business practices of the time and place." 1 Corbin, op. cit. supra note 2. [Footnote omitted.] We think this formulation correctly states the test to be applied in those cases where no meaningful choice was exercised upon entering the contract.

Because the trial court and the appellate court did not feel that enforcement could be refused, no findings were made on the possible unconscionability of the contracts in these cases. Since the record is not sufficient for our deciding the issue as a matter of law, the cases must be remanded to the trial court for further proceedings.

So ordered.

DANAHER, Circuit Judge (dissenting):

The District of Columbia Court of Appeals obviously was as unhappy about the situation here presented as any of us can possibly be. Its opinion in the *Williams* case, quoted in the majority text, concludes: "We think Congress should consider corrective legislation to protect the public from such exploitive contracts as were utilized in the case at bar."

My view is thus summed up by an able court which made no finding that there had actually been sharp practice. Rather the appellant seems to have known precisely where she stood.

There are many aspects of public policy here involved. What is a luxury to some may seem an outright necessity to others. Is public oversight to be required of the expenditures of relief funds? A washing machine, e.g., in the hands of a relief client might become a fruitful source of income. Many relief clients may well need credit, and certain business establishments will take long chances on the sale of items, expecting their pricing policies will afford a degree of protection commensurate with the risk. Perhaps a remedy when necessary will be found within the provisions of the "Loan Shark" law, D.C. Code §§26-601 et seq. (1961).

I mention such matters only to emphasize the desirability of a cautious approach to any such problem, particularly since the law for so long has allowed parties such great latitude in making their own contracts. I dare say there must annually be thousands upon thousands of installment credit transactions in this jurisdiction, and one can only speculate as to the effect the decision in these cases will have.

I join the District of Columbia Court of Appeals in its disposition of the issues.

Post-Case Follow-Up

The *Williams* court stated that the unconscionability defense requires an examination of both procedural and substantive unconscionability to determine if a contract is enforceable. Under procedural unconscionability, the court reviewed the facts to see if there was a lack of meaningful choice and unfair surprise in the contract terms. Procedural unconscionability can be supported, in part, when unequal bargaining power existed, especially when one of the parties was commercially unsophisticated. As to substantive unconscionability, the courts can analyze contract terms to see if they are extreme or unduly harsh in light of the case facts and business context; the pro rata clause in this instance. The appeals court remanded the case for further fact-finding on unconscionability.

Williams v. Walker-Thomas Furniture Co.: Real Life Applications

1. An office supply store negotiates with a copy machine manufacturer to lease copying equipment. The lease contains three clear disclaimers of any express warranties. The store claims that the equipment did not perform properly, and the manufacturer is unwilling to fix the claimed problems. The store stops making lease payments and seeks to rescind the contract as unconscionable. The manufacturer consults with your law firm on the likelihood of success of the store's defense. Review *Dillman & Associates, Inc. v. Capitol Leasing Co.*, 110 Ill. App. 3d 335 (Ill. App. Ct. 4th Dist. 1982), to help advise your client.
2. A retailer contracts with a security company for a burglar alarm system. The contract contains a waiver of liability of any of the retailer's losses due to a failure of

its systems or services. If the system fails, the security firm only needs to refund the costs of its annual services, about $1,000. A break-in results in $125,000 in losses, which are paid by the retailer's insurance company. The retailer's insurer tries to recover these losses from the security company, claiming that the limitation of liability clause is unconscionable. Under these circumstances, will the insurance company be able to invalidate the liability limit? Consider *E.H. Ashley & Co. v. Wells Fargo Alarm Services*, 907 F.2d 1274 (1st Cir. 1990), in developing your response.

3. Consumers enter into contracts of adhesion with a company offering long distance telephone services. In the service provider's contract, the dispute resolution clause waives the consumers' rights to class actions, mandates confidentiality, truncates the statute of limitations, and awards attorneys' fees only for the service provider. In a class action suit, the customers allege that the telephone service provider improperly levied illegal tax surcharges and exploitative late fees. The service provider moves to dismiss the class action under the dispute resolution clause. Will the defense of unconscionability aid the consumers' efforts to invalidate that clause? Examine *McKee v. AT&T Corp.*, 191 P.3d 845 (Wash. 2008), and discuss arguments for and against the use of the unconscionability defense.

---

2. Substantive Unconscionability

While procedural unconscionability addresses flaws in the contract formation stage, substantive unconscionability focuses on the specific contract terms in dispute. The contract provisions are reviewed to determine if they appear to be oppressively harsh or one-sided. Excessive price terms or clauses unfairly limiting the liability of the contract drafter, such as unusual warranty disclaimers, stringent damage limits, or onerous refund and dispute resolution clauses may be too one-sided. The unfairness or oppressive nature of the terms is considered in light of the factual circumstances and business standards of these types of transactions.

Often courts determine that a contract is unenforceable as unconscionable if the terms are oppressively harsh or one-sided in situations where there is also unequal bargaining power between the parties. Courts may find a contract unconscionable even if a sophisticated party is involved, but was unable to negotiate contract terms with the drafter that are later deemed to be harsh or oppressive.

However, if the terms seem out of balance, the drafter may be able to assert that there was a valid **business reality** that shows a justified commercial need for the questioned term(s). The burden is on the drafter to show a business reality.

Case Preview

Bragg v. Linden Research Inc.

Screen shot of Second Life virtual world
© *STR/Reuters/Corbis*

In *Bragg v. Linden Research Inc.*, a court examined both procedural and substantive unconscionability in a contract between an attorney and Linden, the operator of the virtual world, Second Life. Bragg, a licensed attorney, acquired a parcel of virtual land that Linden claimed violated its site's purchase terms. Linden seized the virtual land and froze Bragg's account, which was made up of virtual property and Second Life currency. The parties wrangled over whether Bragg may bring his action, challenging Second Life's confiscation of his virtual property, in the courts or in arbitration under a clause in the site's Terms of Service (TOS).

As you read *Bragg v. Linden Research Inc.*, look for the following:

1. How did the court apply the sliding scale approach to unconscionability in its decision?
2. Can a contracting party, who was a lawyer, successfully support a claim of a lack of meaningful choice under procedural unconscionability?
3. Was the arbitration clause oppressive or one-sided under substantive unconscionability?

Bragg v. Linden Research Inc.

487 F. Supp. 2d 593 (E.D. Pa. 2007)

Robreno, J.

This case is about virtual property maintained on a virtual world on the Internet. Plaintiff, March Bragg, Esq., claims an ownership interest in such virtual property. Bragg contends that Defendants, the operators of the virtual world, unlawfully confiscated his virtual property and denied him access to their virtual world. Ultimately at issue in this case are the novel questions of what rights and obligations grow out of the relationship between the owner and creator of a virtual world and its resident-customers. While the property and the world where it is found are "virtual," the dispute is real.

Presently before the Court are Defendants' Motion to . . . Compel Arbitration. . . . For the reasons set forth below, the motions will be denied.

I. BACKGROUND

A. Second Life

The defendants in this case, Linden Research Inc. ("Linden") and its Chief Executive Officer, Philip Rosedale, operate a multiplayer role-playing game set in the virtual world known as "Second Life." Participants create avatars [footnote omitted] to represent themselves, and Second Life is populated by hundreds of thousands of avatars, whose interactions with one another are limited only by the human imagination. [Footnote omitted.] According to Plaintiff, many people "are now living large portions of their lives, forming friendships with others, building and acquiring virtual property, forming contracts, substantial business relationships and forming social organizations" in virtual worlds such as Second Life. [Citation omitted.] Owning property in and having access to this virtual world is, moreover, apparently important to the plaintiff in this case. [Footnotes omitted.]

B. Recognition of Property Rights

In November 2003, Linden announced that it would recognize participants' full intellectual property protection for the digital content they created or otherwise owned in Second Life. As a result, Second Life avatars may now buy, own, and sell virtual goods ranging "from cars to homes to slot machines." [Footnote and citation omitted.] Most significantly for this case, avatars may purchase "virtual land," make improvements to that land, exclude other avatars from entering onto the land, rent the land, or sell the land to other avatars for a profit. Assertedly, by recognizing virtual property rights, Linden would distinguish itself from other virtual worlds available on the Internet and thus increase participation in Second Life. . . .

In 2005, Plaintiff Marc Bragg, Esq., signed up and paid Linden to participate in Second Life. Bragg claims that he was induced into "investing" in virtual land by representations made by Linden and Rosedale in press releases, interviews, and through the Second Life website. [Citation omitted.] Bragg also paid Linden real money as "tax" on his land. [Footnote omitted.] By April 2006, Bragg had not only purchased numerous parcels of land in his Second Life, he had also digitally crafted "fireworks" that he was able to sell to other avatars for a profit. Bragg also acquired other virtual items from other avatars.

The dispute ultimately at issue in this case arose on April 30, 2006, when Bragg acquired a parcel of virtual land named "Taessot" for $300. Linden sent Bragg an email advising him that Taessot had been improperly purchased through an "exploit." Linden took Taessot away. It then froze Bragg's account, effectively confiscating all of the virtual property and currency that he maintained on his account with Second Life.

Bragg brought suit against Linden and Rosedale in the Court of Common Pleas of Chester County, Pennsylvania, on October 3, 2006. Linden and Rosedale removed the case to this Court (doc. no. 1) and then, within a week, moved to compel arbitration. . . . [The parties did not challenge the California choice of law clause]. . . .

. . .

III. MOTION TO COMPEL ARBITRATION

Defendants have also filed a motion to compel arbitration that seeks to dismiss this action and compel Bragg to submit his claims to arbitration according to the Rules of the International Chamber of Commerce ("ICC") in San Francisco.

A. Relevant Facts

Before a person is permitted to participate in Second Life, she must accept the Terms of Service of Second Life (the "TOS") by clicking a button indicating acceptance of the TOS. Bragg concedes that he clicked the "accept" button before accessing Second Life. Compl. P 126. Included in the TOS are a California choice of law provision, an arbitration provision, and forum selection clause. Specifically, located in the fourteenth line of the thirteenth paragraph under the heading "GENERAL PROVISIONS," and following provisions regarding the applicability of export and import laws to Second Life, the following language appears:

> Any dispute or claim arising out of or in connection with this Agreement or the performance, reach or termination thereof, shall be finally settled by binding arbitration in San Francisco, California under the Rules of Arbitration of the International Chamber of Commerce by three arbitrators appointed in accordance with said rules.... Notwithstanding the foregoing, either party may apply to any court of competent jurisdiction for injunctive relief or enforcement of this arbitration provision without breach of this arbitration provision.

TOS P 13....

1. Unconscionability of the Arbitration Agreement

Bragg resists enforcement of the TOS's arbitration provision on the basis that it is "both procedurally and substantively unconscionable and is itself evidence of defendants' scheme to deprive Plaintiff (and others) of both their money and their day in court." Pl.'s Resp. at 16. [Footnote omitted.]

Section 2 of the FAA provides that written arbitration agreements "shall be valid, irrevocable, and enforceable, save upon such grounds as exist at law or in equity for the revocation of any contract." 9 U.S.C. §2. Thus, "generally applicable contract defenses, such as fraud, duress, or unconscionability, may be applied to invalidate arbitration agreements without contravening §2." *Doctor's Assocs. v. Casarotto*, 517 U.S. 681, 687, 116 S. Ct. 1652, 134 L. Ed. 2d 902 (1996); [citations omitted]....

Under California law, unconscionability has both procedural and substantive components. [Citation omitted]; *Comb v. Paypal, Inc.*, 218 F. Supp. 2d 1165, 1172 (N.D. Cal. 2002). The procedural component can be satisfied by showing (1) oppression through the existence of unequal bargaining positions or (2) surprise through hidden terms common in the context of adhesion contracts. *Comb*, 218 F. Supp. 2d at 1172. The substantive component can be satisfied by showing overly harsh or one-sided results that "shock the conscience." *Id.* The two elements operate on a sliding scale such that the more significant one is, the less significant the other need be. [Citations omitted.] However, a claim of unconscionability cannot be determined merely by examining the face of the contract; there must be an inquiry into the circumstances under which the contract was executed, and the contract's purpose, and effect. *Comb*, 218 F. Supp. 2d at 1172.

(a) Procedural Unconscionability

A contract or clause is procedurally unconscionable if it is a contract of adhesion. *Comb*, 218 F. Supp. 2d at 1172; *Flores v. Transamerica HomeFirst, Inc.*, 93 Cal.

App. 4th 846, 113 Cal. Rptr. 2d 376, 381-82 ([Cal. App.] 2001). A contract of adhesion, in turn, is a "standardized contract, which, imposed and drafted by the party of superior bargaining strength, relegates to the subscribing party only the opportunity to adhere to the contract or reject it." *Comb*, 218 F. Supp. 2d at 1172; *Armendariz*, 6 P.3d at 690. Under California law, "the critical factor in procedural unconscionability analysis is the manner in which the contract or the disputed clause was presented and negotiated." *Nagrampa v. MailCoups, Inc.*, 469 F.3d 1257, 1282 (9th Cir. 2006). "When the weaker party is presented the clause and told to 'take it or leave it' without the opportunity for meaningful negotiation, oppression, and therefore procedural unconscionability, are present." *Id.* [Citations omitted.]

The TOS are a contract of adhesion. Linden presents the TOS on a take-it-or-leave-it basis. A potential participant can either click "assent" to the TOS, and then gain entrance to Second Life's virtual world, or refuse assent and be denied access. Linden also clearly has superior bargaining strength over Bragg. Although Bragg is an experienced attorney, who believes he is expert enough to comment on numerous industry standards and the "rights" or [*sic*] participants in virtual worlds, [citation omitted], he was never presented with an opportunity to use his experience and lawyering skills to negotiate terms different from the TOS that Linden offered.

Moreover, there was no "reasonably available market alternatives [to defeat] a claim of adhesiveness." *Cf. Dean Witter Reynolds, Inc. v. Superior Court*, 211 Cal. App. 3d 758, 259 Cal. Rptr. 789, 795 (Ct. App. 1989) (finding no procedural unconscionability because there were other financial institutions that offered competing IRA's which lacked the challenged provision). Although it is not the only virtual world on the Internet, Second Life was the first and only virtual world to specifically grant its participants property rights in virtual land.

The procedural element of unconscionability also "focuses on . . . surprise." *Gutierrez v. Autowest, Inc.*, 114 Cal. App. 4th 77, 7 Cal. Rptr. 3d 267, 275 ([Cal. App.] 2003); [citations omitted]. In determining whether surprise exists, California courts focus not on the plaintiff's subjective reading of the contract, but rather, more objectively, on "the extent to which the supposedly agreed-upon terms of the bargain are hidden in the prolix printed form drafted by the party seeking to enforce the disputed terms." *Id.* In *Gutierrez*, the court found such surprise where an arbitration clause was "particularly inconspicuous, printed in eight-point typeface on the opposite side of the signature page of the lease." *Id.*

Here, although the TOS are ubiquitous throughout Second Life, Linden buried the TOS's arbitration provision in a lengthy paragraph under the benign heading "GENERAL PROVISIONS." *See* TOS P 13. *Compare Net Global Mktg. v. Dialtone, Inc.*, No. 04-56685, 217 Fed. Appx. 598, 2007 U.S. App. LEXIS 674 at *7 (9th Cir. Jan. 9, 2007) (finding procedural unconscionability where "[t]here was no 'clear heading' in the Terms of Service that could refute a claim of surprise; to the contrary, the arbitration clause is listed in the midst of a long section without line breaks under the unhelpful heading of 'Miscellaneous'") and *Higgins v. Superior Court*, 140 Cal. App. 4th 1238, 45 Cal. Rptr. 3d 293, 297 (2006) (holding arbitration agreement unconscionable where "[t]here is nothing in the Agreement that brings the reader's attention to the arbitration provision") *with Boghos v. Certain Underwriters at Lloyd's of London*, 36 Cal. 4th 495, 30 Cal. Rptr. 3d 787, 115 P.3d 68, 70 (Cal. 2005) (finding arbitration clause was enforceable where it was in bolded font and contained the heading "BINDING ARBITRATION"). Linden also failed to make available the costs and rules of arbitration in the ICC by either setting them forth in the TOS or by providing a hyperlink to another page or website where they are available. Bragg Decl. P 20.

Comb is most instructive. In that case, the plaintiffs challenged an arbitration provision that was part of an agreement to which they had assented, in circumstances similar to this case, by clicking their assent on an online application page. 218 F. Supp. 2d at 1169. The defendant, PayPal, was a large company with millions of individual online customers. *Id.* at 1165. The plaintiffs, with one exception, were all individual customers of PayPal. *Id.* Given the small amount of the average transaction with PayPal, the fact that most PayPal customers were private individuals, and that there was a "dispute as to whether PayPal's competitors offer their services without requiring customers to enter into arbitration agreements," the court concluded that the user agreement at issue "satisfie[d] the criteria for procedural unconscionability under California law." *Id.* at 1172-73. Here, as in *Comb*, procedural unconscionability is satisfied.

(b) Substantive Unconscionability

Even if an agreement is procedurally unconscionable, "it may nonetheless be enforceable if the substantive terms are reasonable." *Id.* at 1173 (citing *Craig v. Brown & Root, Inc.*, 84 Cal. App. 4th 416, 100 Cal. Rptr. 2d 818 (Ct. App. 2000) (finding contract of adhesion to arbitrate disputes enforceable)). Substantive unconscionability focuses on the one-sidedness of the contract terms. *Armendariz*, 6 P.3d at 690; *Flores*, 113 Cal. Rptr. 2d at 381-82. Here, a number of the TOS's elements lead the Court to conclude that Bragg has demonstrated that the TOS are substantively unconscionable.

(i) *Mutuality*

Under California law, substantive unconscionability has been found where an arbitration provision forces the weaker party to arbitrate claims but permits a choice of forums for the stronger party. *See, e.g., Ticknor v. Choice Hotels Int'l, Inc.*, 265 F.3d 931, 940-41 (9th Cir. 2001); *Mercuro v. Superior Court*, 96 Cal. App. 4th 167, 116 Cal. Rptr. 2d 671, 675 (Ct. App. 2002). In other words, the arbitration remedy must contain a "modicum of bilaterality." *Armendariz*, 6 P.3d at 692. This principle has been extended to arbitration provisions that allow the stronger party a range of remedies before arbitrating a dispute, such as self-help, while relegating to the weaker party the sole remedy of arbitration. [Footnote omitted.]

. . .

In *Comb*, for example, the court found a lack of mutuality where the user agreement allowed PayPal "at its sole discretion" to restrict accounts, withhold funds, undertake its own investigation of a customer's financial records, close accounts, and procure ownership of all funds in dispute unless and until the customer is "later determined to be entitled to the funds in dispute." 218 F. Supp. 2d at 1173-74. Also significant was the fact that the user agreement was "subject to change by PayPal without prior notice (unless prior notice is required by law), by posting of the revised Agreement on the PayPal website." *Id.*

Here, the TOS contain many of the same elements that made the PayPal user agreement substantively unconscionable for lack of mutuality. The TOS proclaim that "Linden has the right at any time for any reason or no reason to suspend or terminate your Account, terminate this Agreement, and/or refuse any and all current or future use of the Service without notice or liability to you." TOS P 7.1. Whether or not a customer has breached the Agreement is "determined in Linden's sole discretion." *Id.* Linden also reserves the right to return no money at all based on mere "suspicions of fraud" or other violations of law. *Id.* Finally, the TOS state that "Linden may amend this Agreement . . . at any time in its sole discretion by posting the amended Agreement [on its website]." TOS P 1.2.

In effect, the TOS provide Linden with a variety of one-sided remedies to resolve disputes, while forcing its customers to arbitrate any disputes with Linden. This is precisely what occurred here. When a dispute arose, Linden exercised its option to use self-help by freezing Bragg's account, retaining funds that Linden alone determined were subject to dispute, and then telling Bragg that he could resolve the dispute by initiating a costly arbitration process. The TOS expressly authorized Linden to engage in such unilateral conduct. As in *Comb*, "[f]or all practical purposes, a customer may resolve disputes only after [Linden] has had control of the disputed funds for an indefinite period of time," and may only resolve those disputes by initiating arbitration. 218 F. Supp. 2d at 1175.

Linden's right to modify the arbitration clause is also significant. "The effect of [Linden's] unilateral right to modify the arbitration clause is that it could . . . craft precisely the sort of asymmetrical arbitration agreement that is prohibited under California law as unconscionable. *Net Global Mktg.*, 217 Fed. Appx. 598, 2007 U.S. App. LEXIS 674, at *9. This lack of mutuality supports a finding of substantive unconscionability.

(ii) *Costs of Arbitration and Fee-Sharing*

Bragg claims that the cost of an individual arbitration under the TOS is likely to exceed $13,540, with an estimated initiation cost of at least $10,000. Pl.'s Reply at 5-6. He has also submitted a Declaration of Personal Financial Information stating that such arbitration would be cost-prohibitive for him (doc. no. 41). Linden disputes Bragg's calculations, estimating that the costs associated with arbitration would total $7,500, with Bragg advancing $3,750 at the outset of arbitration. *See* Dfts.' Reply at 11.

At oral argument, the parties were unable to resolve this dispute, even after referencing numerous provisions and charts contained within the ICC Rules. . . . Thus, the Court estimates the costs of arbitration with the ICC to be $17,250 ($2,625 + (3 × $4,875)), although they could reach as high as $27,375 ($2,625 + (3 × $8,250)). [Footnote omitted.]

These costs might not, on their own, support a finding of substantive unconscionability. However, the ICC Rules also provide that the costs and fees must be shared among the parties, and an estimate of those costs and fees must be advanced at the initiation of arbitration. *See* ICC Rules of Arbitration, Ex. D to Dfts.' Reply at 28-30. California law has often been applied to declare arbitration fee-sharing schemes unenforceable. *See Ting v. AT&T*, 319 F.3d 1126, 1151 (9th Cir. 2003). Such schemes are unconscionable where they "impose[] on some consumers costs greater than those a complainant would bear if he or she would file the same complaint in court." *Id.* In *Ting*, for example, the Ninth Circuit held that a scheme requiring AT&T customers to split arbitration costs with AT&T rendered an arbitration provision unconscionable. *Id.* [Citations omitted.]

Here, even taking Defendant's characterization of the fees to be accurate, the total estimate of costs and fees would be $7,500, which would result in Bragg having to advance $3,750 at the outset of arbitration. . . . The court's own estimates place the amount that Bragg would likely have to advance at $8,625, but they could reach as high as $13,687.50. Any of these figures are significantly greater than the costs that Bragg bears by filing his action in a state or federal court. Accordingly, the arbitration costs and fee-splitting scheme together also support a finding of unconscionability.

(iii) *Venue*

The TOS also require that any arbitration take place in San Francisco, California. TOS P 13. In *Comb*, the Court found that a similar forum selection clause supported a finding of substantive unconscionability, because the place in which arbitration was to occur was unreasonable, taking into account "the respective circumstances of the parties." 218 F. Supp. 2d at 1177. As in *Comb*, the record in this case shows that Linden serves millions of customers across the United States and that the average transaction through or with Second Life involves a relatively small amount. *See id.* In such circumstances, California law dictates that it is not "reasonable for individual consumers from throughout the country to travel to one locale to arbitrate claims involving such minimal sums." *Id.* Indeed, "[l]imiting venue to [Linden's] backyard appears to be yet one more means by which the arbitration clause serves to shield [Linden] from liability instead of providing a neutral forum in which to arbitrate disputes." *Id.*

(iv) *Confidentiality Provision*

Arbitration before the ICC, pursuant to the TOS, must be kept confidential pursuant to the ICC rules. *See* ICC Rules at 33. Applying California law to an arbitration provision, the Ninth Circuit held that such confidentiality supports a finding that an arbitration clause was substantively unconscionable. *Ting*, 319 F.3d at 1152. The Ninth Circuit reasoned that if the company succeeds in imposing a gag order on arbitration proceedings, it places itself in a far superior legal posture by ensuring that none of its potential opponents have access to precedent while, at the same time, the company accumulates a wealth of knowledge on how to negotiate the terms of its own unilaterally crafted contract. *Id.* The unavailability of arbitral decisions could also prevent potential plaintiffs from obtaining the information needed to build a case of intentional misconduct against a company. *See id.*

This does not mean that confidentiality provisions in an arbitration scheme or agreement are, in every instance, per se unconscionable under California law. *See Mercuro v. Superior Court*, 96 Cal. App. 4th 167, 116 Cal. Rptr. 2d 671, 679 (Ct. App. 2002) ("While [the California] Supreme Court has taken notice of the 'repeat player effect,' the court has never declared this factor renders the arbitration agreement unconscionable per se.") [citations omitted]. Here, however, taken together with other provisions of the TOS, the confidentiality provision gives rise for concern of the conscionability of the arbitration clause. [Citation omitted.]

Thus, the confidentiality of the arbitration scheme that Linden imposed also supports a finding that the arbitration clause is unconscionable.

(v) *Legitimate Business Realities*

Under California law, a contract may provide a "margin of safety" that provides the party with superior bargaining strength protection for which it has a legitimate commercial need. "However, unless the 'business realities' that create the special need for such an advantage are explained in the contract itself, . . . it must be factually established." *Stirlen v. Supercuts, Inc.*, 51 Cal. App. 4th 1519, 60 Cal. Rptr. 2d 138, 148 (Ct. App. 1997). When a contract is alleged to be unconscionable, "the parties shall be afforded a reasonable opportunity to present evidence as to its commercial setting, purpose, and effect to aid the court in making the determination." Cal. Civ. Code §1670.5. The statutory scheme reflects "legislative recognition that a claim of unconscionability often cannot be determined merely by examining the face of the contract, but will require inquiry into its setting, purpose, and effect." *Stirlen*, 60 Cal. Rptr. 2d at 148 (citations and internal quotations omitted).

Here, neither in its briefing nor at oral argument did Linden even attempt to offer evidence that "business realities" justify the one-sidedness of the dispute resolution scheme that the TOS constructs in Linden's favor.

(c) Conclusion

When a dispute arises in Second Life, Linden is not obligated to initiate arbitration. Rather, the TOS expressly allow Linden, at its "sole discretion" and based on mere "suspicion," to unilaterally freeze a participant's account, refuse access to the virtual and real currency contained within that account, and then confiscate the participant's virtual property and real estate. A participant wishing to resolve any dispute, on the other hand, after having forfeited its interest in Second Life, must then initiate arbitration in Linden's place of business. To initiate arbitration involves advancing fees to pay for no less than three arbitrators at a cost far greater than would be involved in litigating in the state or federal court system. Moreover, under these circumstances, the confidentiality of the proceedings helps ensure that arbitration itself is fought on an uneven field by ensuring that, through the accumulation of experience, Linden becomes an expert in litigating the terms of the TOS, while plaintiffs remain novices without the benefit of learning from past precedent.

Taken together, the lack of mutuality, the costs of arbitration, the forum selection clause, and the confidentiality provision that Linden unilaterally imposes through the TOS demonstrate that the arbitration clause is not designed to provide Second Life participants an effective means of resolving disputes with Linden. Rather, it is a one-sided means which tilts unfairly, in almost all situations, in Linden's favor. As in *Comb*, through the use of an arbitration clause, Linden "appears to be attempting to insulate itself contractually from any meaningful challenge to its alleged practices." 218 F. Supp. 2d at 1176.

The Court notes that the concerns with procedural unconscionability are somewhat mitigated by Bragg's being an experienced attorney. However, "because the unilateral modification clause renders the arbitration provision severely one-sided in the substantive dimension, even moderate procedural unconscionability renders the arbitration agreement unenforceable." ***Net Global Mktg.*****, 217 Fed. Appx. 598, 2007 U.S. App. LEXIS 674, at *9 (internal citations omitted).**

Finding that the arbitration clause is procedurally and substantively unconscionable, the Court will refuse to enforce it. . . .

Post-Case Follow-Up

The court determined that the clause was procedurally unconscionable because the disputed arbitration clause was hidden in fine print in a contract of adhesion. Bragg lacked meaningful choice because no other site offered virtual property ownership and he was not permitted to use his negotiation skills to change contract terms. The lack of mutuality, the costs of arbitration, the venue, and the confidentiality provision that Linden unilaterally imposed through the TOS demonstrated that the arbitration clause was not designed to provide Second Life participants with an effective means for resolving disputes. Rather, the clause was one-sided in Linden's favor with no business reality to justify its use. Applying a sliding scale approach, the court refused to enforce the arbitration clause as both procedurally and substantively unconscionable.

Bragg v. Linden Research, Inc.: Real Life Applications

1. A group of school teachers enters into a contract to invest in precious metals. The contract contains an arbitration clause that requires any disputes to be handled before a panel of three arbitrators and prohibits consolidation or joinder of any claims. The investment contract is a contract of adhesion, and the school teachers lack bargaining power to negotiate its terms. The clause is not hidden, and the school teachers have some prior experience with other firms offering better investment terms. When the teachers lose substantial amounts of money, they seek to have the matter heard in court because the arbitration process will be prohibitively expensive. Review *Parada v. Superior Court*, 176 Cal. App. 4th 1554 (Cal. Ct. App. 2009), and determine whether or not the arbitration clause will be viewed as unconscionable.

2. Abdul purchases a cell phone as a gift for his spouse. At the time of purchase, Abdul does not have access to a print copy of the cell phone activation agreement or notice that the terms are available online. He discovers that the online version of the terms is outdated. When the phone is activated, the consumer must agree to the lengthy terms on a small window. The terms include an arbitration clause that forbids class arbitrations. Later Abdul claims the

manufacturer hid information about the limited life of the phone's battery and costly battery replacement. The cell phone company wants the consumer to bring a case in arbitration on an individual basis. Abdul asks for your help on whether the clause is unconscionable. Read *Trujillo v. Apple Computer, Inc.*, 578 F. Supp. 2d 979 (N.D. Ill. 2008), and advise Abdul on the likely outcome.

3. An Oregon ice cream franchisor, Chill Out, leases retail space at Palm Tree Mall in Florida for a future shop. The Morgans, first-time business owners, sign a nonnegotiable franchise agreement with Chill Out. As part of the franchise relationship, the Morgans and Chill Out enter into a sublease agreement for the retail space at the mall to operate the new franchise. Chill Out withdraws monthly rental amounts from the Morgans' business account, but fails to pay the mall. The Morgans are evicted for nonpayment. When the Morgans sue in Florida, Chill Out points to a forum selection clause requiring any legal action to be brought in Oregon courts. The Morgans claim the clause is unconscionable because of the added expense of litigating Chill Out's wrongful conduct across the country. How will the decision in *Fowler v. Cold Stone Creamery, Inc.*, 2013 U.S. Dist. LEXIS 167241 (D.R.I. 2013), impact their unconscionability defense?

A European Perspective on Unfair Terms

MATULEE/Shutterstock.com

The European Union (EU) recognizes a form of unconscionability that emphasizes consumer protection from "unfair" terms under contracts of adhesion. Under Council Directive 93/13/EEC of 5 April 1993 on Unfair Terms in Consumer Contracts, EU regulators seek to promote good faith and fair dealing in consumer contracts through a host of consumer protection laws and policies. These regulations require transparency in consumer contracts, including full disclosures of contract terms before parties enter into a consumer contract and no ability to add terms in goods packaging subsequently delivered to consumers. Contracts of adhesion are also supposed to be written in easily understood language and any contract ambiguities are interpreted to favor consumers. Boilerplate forum selection and pre-dispute arbitration clauses are viewed automatically as unfair terms in consumer contracts of adhesion. Any unfair terms are stricken from the agreement between consumers and merchants. Unlike the case law approach to unconscionability in the United States, the EU approach emphasizes appropriate regulatory compliance to guard against abuses in merchant-consumer contracts.

C. PUBLIC POLICY—VOID

When a public policy defense is raised, courts will examine whether the contract violates a well-established public policy at the time the parties entered into the contract. Typically, if a contract violates constitutional law, statutory law, or judicial precedent on conduct that is illegal or harms public welfare, courts may refuse enforcement. As with unconscionability, a court may void the entire contract, or limit or strike out any offending clause while retaining the rest of the contract, based on the nature of the public policy violation.

Public policies prohibit a range of terms, from licensing laws to **usury** (excessive interest rates on loans) to the illegal sales of controlled substances and sexual services.

Clearly, contracts to commit crimes or to undertake tortious activities are illegal contracts. The close connection to criminal laws leads some to call this the **illegality defense**. Others refer to it as ***in pari delicto***—literally, in equal wrong. While it bans agreements among criminal wrongdoers, such as an agreement among thieves regarding how to divide their loot, public policy extends beyond illegal contracts to any term objectionable under state and/or federal laws or judicial rulings.

Statutes prohibiting enforcement may be less common than they seem. For instance, if murder is a crime, state legislatures may not think it necessary to also provide that a contract to pay for a murder is unenforceable. Statutes expressly making contracts unenforceable tend to be regulatory in nature. For example, a statute may provide that people who practice law (or other occupations) without a license cannot collect fees for their services. This statutory approach provides a disincentive to evade the licensing process and gives customers an incentive to help identify violators. Similarly, usury laws make a contract term charging excessive interest unenforceable—although perhaps not the entire loan agreement. In any event, a statute that prohibits enforcement of a particular term or agreement leaves little room for discussion. If the agreement falls within the statute's prohibitions, it is unenforceable.

Proving the public policy defense makes a contract void, not merely voidable. Even if all parties ask a court to apply a term, the court will refuse. The parties cannot waive the public interest in preventing a particular contract term. To some extent, this stance reflects one purpose of public policy; to negate terms that harm outsiders to the contract. The parties can be expected to look out for their own interests. But a contract might harm others or threaten the general public. Public policy is one way courts limit a contract's externalities.

Similar to unconscionability, a public policy defense may apply to specific terms in an agreement. A court may refuse to enforce an offending term, but leave the rest of the contract intact and enforceable. In some cases, public policy serves an interpretive role. If a term is open to interpretation, courts prefer to interpret contract terms in a manner that does not violate

The Highwayman's Case—Contract Between Accomplices

The famous 1725 case of *Everet v. Williams*, subsequently reported in 9 L.Q. Rev. 197 (1893), is better known as *The Highwayman's Case.* A robber promised to split the loot with a tavern worker, who identified suitably wealthy victims for the robber. The robber claimed that his accomplice had taken more than his agreed-upon share and hired an attorney to bring his civil case for an accounting of the illegal profits of their criminal activity. The court dismissed the lawsuit as "scandalous and impertinent" and fined the attorney for even bringing the action. After the court reported the men to the sheriff, both robbers were eventually hung for their crimes. Recently, *Thomas v. UBS AG*, 706 F.3d 846, 851 (7th Cir. Ill. 2013), discussed the case in addressing disputes between banks and account holders who colluded to hide assets to illicitly avoid taxes. The taxpayers contended that the bank should have stopped them from violating the law and wanted the bank to share the costs of their wrongdoing. The *Thomas* court stated, "Minus the hanging . . . *The Highwayman's Case* applies to accomplices in civil wrongdoing. . . . In *The Highwayman's Case* one accomplice was seeking a bigger share of the profit from the crime from the other one; here one accomplice is seeking a smaller share of the costs of the crime from the other one. The principle is the same; the law leaves the quarreling accomplices where it finds them." The story may be different, but the basic theory behind *The Highwayman's Case* still retains its vitality today.

public policy. If the terms cannot fairly be read as consistent with public policy, the court is likely to render the term, and perhaps the entire contract, unenforceable. Not only would the court reject the contract claim, it also would refuse to award recovery for benefits bestowed under an unenforceable contract or term under restitution. A party involved in an illegal contract would be unjustly enriched if damages were awarded, and the court does not want to support or participate in compensating illegal conduct.

Other cases involve moral divides, where public policy may be less clear or may be undergoing change. The issue of public morals may be a thorny one because it may differ between different states or communities. If an express law is in place, the decision may be easier for a court. However, in some circumstances the court must examine implied policies aimed at safeguarding public health and safety. In addition, some cases may be murkier when various public policies seem to compete with each other in a given situation.

1. The Restatement's Balancing Approach

The Restatement (Second) of Contracts §178 takes a more nuanced view on the public policy defense. Whether an express law or an implied issue of public morals, the Restatement approach moves away from an absolutist approach and calls upon courts to weigh the public policy concerns against any interests in enforcing a contract that violates the law or good morals. Under this balancing test, courts will consider the parties' justified expectations under the contract, any public interest in enforcing the agreement, and the potential for forfeiture for one party if the contract is not enforced. These party interests are weighed against the substance of the express or implied public policy, the seriousness and deliberateness of the misconduct, and the connection between the policy violation and the disputed contract or specific term. Balancing costs and benefits leaves courts more room to exercise their discretion, especially when there are competing public interests, legal actions that may be intertwined with illegal actions or conduct that harms public safety and/or morals. However, an express legislative declaration that the terms are not enforceable is not subject to a balancing test since the legislature has done the balancing already.

Case Preview

Bovard v. American Horse Enterprises

In *Bovard v. American Horse Enterprises*, the seller of a business that manufactured drug paraphernalia and jewelry sued the buyer for nonpayment under a promissory note. The business predominantly produced drug paraphernalia for marijuana, an illegal drug at that time under state and federal laws.

However, the manufacture of drug paraphernalia was not illegal at the time the parties entered into the contract of sale. Applying the Restatement view, the court sifted through a tangle of legal issues associated with the sale of a business, nonpayment on a promissory note, changing laws on the manufacture of drug paraphernalia, and the questionable nature of the business being sold.

As you read *Bovard v. American Horse Enterprises*, look for the following:

1. What factors did the court review to determine the public interest in this dispute over a business sale?
2. What circumstances supported the contract for the sale of the business and the obligation to pay under the promissory note?
3. Would Bovard suffer a forfeiture if the contract for the business sale was not enforced?

Bovard v. American Horse Enterprises

247 Cal. Rptr. 340 (Cal. Ct. App. 1988)

PUGLIA, P. J.

Robert Bovard appeals from the judgment dismissing his supplemental complaint against defendants, American Horse Enterprises, Inc., and James T. Ralph. Bovard contends the trial court erroneously concluded the contract upon which his action was founded was illegal and void as contrary to public policy; alternatively, he contends it is the law of the case that the contract does not violate public policy. . . .

This is the second appeal in this case. Our unpublished opinion disposing of the first appeal sets out much of the relevant procedural history of this dispute: "In two actions later consolidated, plaintiff Bovard separately sued defendants Ralph and American Horse Enterprises, Inc.[,] a corporation, . . . to recover on promissory notes executed by defendants in connection with Ralph's purchase of the corporation in 1978."

. . . [During the trial], Bovard testified as to the nature of the business conducted by American Horse Enterprises, Inc., at the time the corporation was sold to Ralph. Bovard explained the corporation made jewelry and drug paraphernalia, which consisted of "roach clips" and "bongs" used to smoke marijuana and tobacco. At that point the trial court excused the jury and asked counsel to prepare arguments on the question whether the contract for sale of the corporation was illegal and void.

The following day, after considering the arguments of counsel, the trial court dismissed the supplemental complaint. The court found that the corporation predominantly produced paraphernalia used to smoke marijuana and was not engaged significantly in jewelry production, and that Bovard had recovered the corporate machinery through self-help. The parties do not challenge these findings. The court acknowledged that the manufacture of drug paraphernalia was not itself illegal in 1978 when Bovard and Ralph contracted for the sale of American Horse Enterprises, Inc. However, the court concluded a public policy against the manufacture of drug paraphernalia was implicit in the statute making the possession, use and transfer

of marijuana unlawful. (*See* Health & Saf. Code, §§11357, 11358, 11359, 11360.) [Footnote omitted.] [The court indicated that a later-enacted county ordinance and state statute subsequently made the manufacture of marijuana paraphernalia illegal under criminal law. However, the court recognized that the public policy defense applies to laws in place at the time the parties entered into the contract.]

The trial court held the consideration for the contract was contrary to the policy of express law, and the contract was therefore illegal and void. Finally, the court found the parties were *in pari delicto* and thus with respect to their contractual dispute should be left as the court found them.

II. "The consideration of a contract must be lawful within the meaning of section sixteen hundred and sixty-seven." (Civ. Code, §1607.) "That is not lawful which is: [para.] 1. Contrary to an express provision of law; [para.] 2. Contrary to the policy of express law, though not expressly prohibited; or, [para.] 3. Otherwise contrary to good morals." (Civ. Code, §1667.) "If any part of a single consideration for one or more objects, or of several considerations for a single object, is unlawful, the entire contract is void." (Civ. Code, §1608.)

The trial court concluded the consideration for the contract was contrary to the policy of the law as expressed in the statute prohibiting the possession, use and transfer of marijuana. Whether a contract is contrary to public policy is a question of law to be determined from the circumstances of the particular case. (*Kallen v. Delug* (1984) 157 Cal. App. 3d 940, 951 [203 Cal. Rptr. 879]; *Russell v. Soldinger* (1976) 59 Cal. App. 3d 633, 642.) Here, the critical facts are not in dispute. Whenever a court becomes aware that a contract is illegal, it has a duty to refrain from entertaining an action to enforce the contract. (*Russell v. Soldinger*, *supra*; *Santoro v. Carbone* (1972) 22 Cal. App. 3d 721, 732, disapproved on another ground in *Liodas v. Sahadi* (1977) 19 Cal. 3d 278, 287 [137 Cal. Rptr. 635, 562 P.2d 316].) Furthermore the court will not permit the parties to maintain an action to settle or compromise a claim based on an illegal contract. (*Union Collection Co. v. Buckman* (1907) 150 Cal. 159, 165 [88 P. 708]; *see also First Nat. Bk. v. Thompson* (1931) 212 Cal. 388, 405 [298 P. 808].)

The question whether a contract violates public policy necessarily involves a degree of subjectivity. Therefore, ". . . courts have been cautious in blithely applying public policy reasons to nullify otherwise enforceable contracts. This concern has been graphically articulated by the California Supreme Court as follows: 'It has been well said that public policy is an unruly horse, astride of which you are carried into unknown and uncertain paths, . . . While contracts opposed to morality or law should not be allowed to show themselves in courts of justice, yet public policy requires and encourages the making of contracts by competent parties upon all valid and lawful considerations, and courts so recognizing have allowed parties the widest latitude in this regard; and, unless it is entirely plain that a contract is violative of sound public policy, a court will never so declare." The power of the courts to declare a contract void for being in contravention of sound public policy is a very delicate and undefined power, and, like the power to declare a statute unconstitutional, should be exercised only in cases free from doubt." . . . "No court ought to refuse its aid to enforce a contract on doubtful and uncertain grounds. The burden is on the defendant to show that its enforcement would be in violation of the settled public policy of this state, or injurious to the morals of its people." (*Moran v. Harris* (1982) 131 Cal. App. 3d 913,

919-920, 182 Cal. Rptr. 519, 28 A.L.R.4th 655], *quoting Stephens v. Southern Pacific Co.* (1895) 109 Cal. 86, 89-90.)

Bovard places great reliance on *Moran v. Harris, supra*, 131 Cal. App. 3d 913, to support his argument the trial court erred in finding the contract violative of public policy. In *Moran*, two lawyers entered into a fee splitting agreement relative to a case referred by one to the other. The agreement was made in 1972, 10 months before the adoption of a rule of professional conduct prohibiting such agreements. In 1975, the attorney to whom the case had been referred settled the case, but then refused to split the attorney's fees with the referring attorney. (*Id.*, at pp. 916-917.) The trial court held the fee splitting contract violated public policy. The appellate court reversed, noting the rule of professional conduct had been amended effective January 1, 1979, to permit fee splitting agreements; thus there was no statute or rule prohibiting fee splitting agreements either at the time the attorneys' contract was formed or after January 1, 1979, during the pendency of the action to enforce the fee splitting contract. Therefore, the court held there was no basis for a finding that the contract violated public policy. (*Id.*, at pp. 920-921.)

Here, in contrast to *Moran*, there is positive law on which to premise a finding of public policy, although the trial court did not find the manufacture of marijuana paraphernalia against public policy on the basis of the later enacted ordinance or statute prohibiting such manufacture. Rather, the court's finding was based on a statute prohibiting the possession, use and transfer of marijuana which long antedated the parties' contract. [Footnote omitted.]

Moran suggests factors to consider in analyzing whether a contract violates public policy: "Before labeling a contract as being contrary to public policy, courts must carefully inquire into the nature of the conduct, the extent of public harm which may be involved, and the moral quality of the conduct of the parties in light of the prevailing standards of the community." (*Id.*, at p. 920.)

These factors are more comprehensively set out in the Restatement Second of Contracts section 178: "(1) A promise or other term of an agreement is unenforceable on grounds of public policy if legislation provides that it is unenforceable or the interest in its enforcement is clearly outweighed in the circumstances by a public policy against the enforcement of such terms.

"(2) In weighing the interest in the enforcement of a term, account is taken of
"(a) the parties' justified expectations,
"(b) any forfeiture that would result if enforcement were denied, and
"(c) any special public interest in the enforcement of the particular term.
"(3) In weighing a public policy against enforcement of a term, account is taken of
"(a) the strength of that policy as manifested by legislation or judicial decisions,
"(b) the likelihood that a refusal to enforce the term will further that policy,
"(c) the seriousness of any misconduct involved and the extent to which it was deliberate, and
"(d) the directness of the connection between that misconduct and the term."

Applying the Restatement test to the present circumstances, we conclude the interest in enforcing this contract is very tenuous. Neither party was reasonably justified in expecting the government would not eventually act to geld American Horse Enterprises, a business harnessed to the production of paraphernalia used to facilitate the use of an illegal drug. Moreover, although voidance of the contract imposed a forfeiture on Bovard, he did recover the corporate machinery, the only assets of the business which could be used for lawful purposes, i.e., to manufacture jewelry. Thus, the forfeiture was significantly mitigated if not negligible. Finally, there is no special public interest in the enforcement of this contract, only the general interest in preventing a party to a contract from avoiding a debt.

On the other hand, the Restatement factors favoring a public policy against enforcement of this contract are very strong. As we have explained, the public policy against manufacturing paraphernalia to facilitate the use of marijuana is strongly implied in the statutory prohibition against the possession, use, etc., of marijuana, a prohibition which dates back at least to 1929. (*See* Stats. 1929, ch. 216, §1, p. 380.) Obviously, refusal to enforce the instant contract will further that public policy not only in the present circumstances but by serving notice on manufacturers of drug paraphernalia that they may not resort to the judicial system to protect or advance their business interests. Moreover, it is immaterial that the business conducted by American Horse Enterprises was not expressly prohibited by law when Bovard and Ralph made their agreement since both parties knew that the corporation's products would be used primarily for purposes which were expressly illegal. We conclude the trial court correctly declared the contract contrary to the policy of express law and therefore illegal and void. . . .

Post-Case Follow-Up

The court determined that the sale of the business that supported the use of illegal drugs violates public policy because of existing criminal laws against the sale and use of marijuana. Subsequent laws criminalizing the manufacture of drug paraphernalia shored up the contention that the sale contravened the public good. The parties could not reasonably expect enforcement based on the nature of the business. Bovard also did not suffer a forfeiture because he received his machinery back for the legal jewelry-making part of the business. The court's refusal to enforce the contract furthered public policy goals and put drug paraphernalia makers on notice that they may not resort to the judicial system to protect their business interests.

Bovard v. American Horse Enterprises: Real Life Applications

1. Ryan loses $5,000 playing poker at Faro's unlicensed gambling spot. Ryan writes two checks to pay his debt, but later stops payment on them. Faro sues on the debt that Ryan owes him. Ryan admits the debt, but claims the public policy defense. Will Ryan be able to avoid his admitted debt? Consider *Bryant v. Mead*, 1 Cal. 441 (Cal. 1851), in determining the likely outcome.

2. Ernie, Monica, and Will are licensed securities brokers who become involved in a scheme to defraud investors. Ernie, the mastermind behind the plot, helps

them to make connections with wealthy seniors in order to defraud them of millions. The trio decides to divide up their gains equally. Ultimately, they make $50 million from the plot. Ernie flees the country, taking all of the funds with him. Aside from criminal charges, the investors are seeking restitution from Monica and Will. Monica and Will assert that they are also victims of Ernie, who breached their contract, and that the investors need to seek compensation from him. Review *SEC v. Lyttle*, 538 F.3d 601 (7th Cir. 2008), to see how the court will address this situation.

3. Dante, a liquor store owner, was the holder of a valid state liquor license. He entered into a lease agreement with Zoe, who is running a small restaurant on an adjoining property with a three-year renewable lease. As a key part of their lease, Dante shares his liquor license with her so she can offer alcohol to her patrons. In the second year of her lease, Dante notifies Zoe that he plans to terminate her lease and expand his store into her restaurant space. She tries to prevent his termination, and he argues the lease is unenforceable under public policy. Zoe seeks your assistance. Review *DiGesu v. Weingardt*, 575 P.2d 950 (N.M. 1978), and offer her your legal guidance.

---

2. Policies in Restraint of Trade

In a free market economy, contracts that restrain trade not only impact the parties to the agreement, but can also impact other consumers and businesses. In the United States, **antitrust laws** governing monopolies and other anticompetitive practices expressly ban contracts that unfairly restrict trade and marketplace competition. The Restatement (Second) of Contracts §187 recognizes that contracts whose primary purpose is to restrain competition are not enforceable. For example, an agreement between competing businesses to fix prices or allocate sales territories would be unenforceable, as the primary goals of the agreement are to prevent competition and limit customer choice.

However, there are a number of situations in which parties may contract not to compete with another that are grounded in other valid interests, such as protecting a company's intellectual property and **business goodwill** (the value of its existing reputation and customer satisfaction). Contracts preventing competition often arise in the sale of a business, a perfectly legitimate thing to do. A noncompetition clause may benefit both parties. The buyer hopes to keep the existing customers. The seller relies on that prospect to ask for a higher price, covering the business's goodwill. If the seller could reopen a competing business the next day and woo all those customers to the new venture, the goodwill would have little value to the buyer. Buyers will not pay nearly as much for a business that lacks a strong reputation and robust customer base or that can be diluted through competition from the seller. Including a noncompetition clause in the contract for the sale of the business reassures the buyer that the goodwill is hers to keep—or lose, if the business is not properly managed.

The Restatement (Second) of Contracts §188 states that a reasonably limited promise not to compete will not violate public policy if the agreement has legitimate purposes, other than illegally stopping competition. If the purposes are ancillary to preventing competition, the contract or relevant clause still should not impose a restraint greater than is needed to protect the promisee's interests. Courts will typically examine the contract to make certain that the terms place reasonable limits on the time period, geographic area, and the promisor's use of her skills and specialties. The court will also address whether either the hardship on the party promising not to compete (promisor) or injury to the public interests may outweigh the promisee's interests.

Clauses that seek only to restrain competition are void, as the antitrust laws will come into play. If the contract terms apply a restraint greater than is needed to protect the promisee's interests, then a court may void it or, at a minimum, interpret it more narrowly to give the clause a legitimate scope. Weighing the issue of public interests allows the courts room to excuse performance of otherwise valid clauses if their effects prove unacceptable to the public good.

Restraints must not last too long. The buyer needs time to establish her own goodwill in the business. Once she has a fair period to establish relationships with customers, showing that the new management is good and trustworthy, the seller's reentry into the market poses less risk. Now the seller needs to win the customers back, after not serving them for a period of time. Similarly, after a time information held by an employee may become less useful to competitors. Allowing the employee to work for competitors after that time poses less risk for the former employer.

Covenants not to compete must not cover too broad a geographic area. The buyer has an interest in preventing the seller from reopening in competition with her. If a distant location would not compete with the buyer or interfere with her efforts to establish a reputation with the customers, then perhaps the clause should not preclude that distant competition. Similarly, an employer's information, known to the employee, may cause little harm in the hands of remote competitors. Global markets and the Internet may make broad geographic limits reasonable, at least for some businesses. But some businesses are inherently local — say, plumbers and veterinarians — such that the seller reopening in the next state may not interfere with the buyer.

Noncompetition clauses must not cover too broadly a promisor's set of skills or specialties. The buyer's interest in preventing a seller from stealing the customers back would not extend to local jobs or businesses that do not compete with the former employer. The seller of a business may fall on hard times and need to resume employment. Working for a company that offered different products or services, even to the same customers, is unlikely to interfere with the buyer's ability to realize the value of the business. Thus, a clause that encompasses too many forbidden occupations might be unreasonable.

In some cases, there may also be a public interest to consider in determining the validity of the covenant not to compete. The public's need for services may excuse the clause. For example, a noncompetition clause that prevents nurses from practicing in the face of a nursing shortage in a given community may present an unacceptable hardship on the public's health and welfare. Even if the nurses faced no hardship personally in remaining idle or finding a job in another state, the local community might suffer.

While covenants not to compete in the legitimate sale of a business are less likely to be controversial, there are numerous disputes about the use of noncompetition clauses in employment contracts. Before employers share private information with (i.e., technology, training, customer lists, and so on) or provide expensive training to employees, they may want some assurance that the employees will not take the information to a competitor. A noncompetition clause offers that assurance. Without that assurance, the job might not be awarded at all or duties might be structured in an inefficient way to protect private information. The employment contract is a legitimate concern and the noncompetition clause is ancillary to that purpose.

But courts are vigilant that these noncompetition clauses be narrowly tailored. Noncompetition clauses can severely limit an employee's ability to pursue a living. It is particularly troubling if the employer fires the employee since discharge usually does not relieve the employee of her obligations under the noncompetition clause. Courts exercise some flexibility to relieve employees from the hardships of such a clause. The employee cannot remain unemployed very long if she wishes to support herself. Preventing the employee from pursuing the career she knows best might be problematic. Thus, a restraint must not unreasonably limit the employee and cause added public expense through unemployment and other social welfare benefits.

However, some states, like California, have invalidated noncompetition clauses in employment by statute as putting too much hardship on employees who must work to support themselves and threatening the public interest in a robust employment marketplace. In addition, some states will not enforce noncompetition clauses in an effort to promote employee mobility and to attract a workforce centered on collaboration, creativity, and technological innovation. Many states allow such clauses provided that they meet the Restatement's policy requirements and standards of reasonableness.

Case Preview

Valley Medical Specialists v. Farber

In *Valley Medical Specialists v. Farber*, a court considered a covenant not to compete agreed to by a doctor who started as an employee and then later became a shareholder-owner of a medical practice. Using the Restatement approach, the court weighed the interests of the medical practice, the reasonableness of the clause, and the public interest concerns.

As you read *Valley Medical Specialists v. Farber*, look for the following:

1. Was this noncompetition clause more analogous to an employer-employee agreement or a sale of a business? What were Valley Medical's protectable interests here?

2. What hardships would be suffered by Dr. Farber, his patients, and the general public if the clause was enforced?
3. Was the noncompetition clause reasonable as to its limits on time, geography, and use of Dr. Farber's skills or specialties?

Valley Medical Specialists v. Farber

194 Ariz. 363 (1999)

FELDMAN, Justice

We granted review to determine whether the restrictive covenant between Dr. Steven Farber and Valley Medical Specialists is enforceable. We hold that it is not. Public policy concerns in this case outweigh Valley Medical's protectable interests in enforcing the agreement. We thus vacate the court of appeals' opinion, affirm the trial court's judgment, and remand to the court of appeals to resolve any remaining issues. . . .

FACTS AND PROCEDURAL HISTORY

In 1985, Valley Medical Specialists ("VMS"), a professional corporation, hired Steven S. Farber, D.O., an internist and pulmonologist who, among other things, treated AIDS and HIV-positive patients and performed brachytherapy—a procedure that radiates the inside of the lung in lung cancer patients. Brachytherapy can only be performed at certain hospitals that have the necessary equipment. A few years after joining VMS, Dr. Farber became a shareholder and subsequently a minority officer and director. In 1991, the three directors, including Dr. Farber, entered into new stock and employment agreements. The employment agreement contained a restrictive covenant, the scope of which was amended over time.

In 1994, Dr. Farber left VMS and began practicing within the area defined by the restrictive covenant. . . .

> . . . The Employee, in consideration of the compensation to be paid to him pursuant to the terms of this Agreement, expressly agrees to the following restrictive covenants:
>
> (a) The Employee shall not, directly or indirectly:
>
> (i) Request any present or future patients of the Employer to curtail or cancel their professional affiliation with the Employer;
>
> (ii) Either separately, jointly, or in association with others, establish, engage in, or become interested in, as an employee, owner, partner, shareholder or otherwise, or furnish any information to, work for, or assist in any manner, anyone competing with, or who may compete with the Employer in the practice of medicine.
>
> . . .
>
> (iv) Either separately, jointly or in association with others provide medical care or medical assistance for any person or persons who were patients [of] Employer during the period that Employee was in the hire of Employer.
>
> . . .

(d) *The restrictive covenants set forth herein shall continue during the term of this Agreement and for a period of three (3) years after the date of termination, for any reason, of this Agreement. The restrictive covenants set forth herein shall be binding upon the Employee in that geographical area encompassed within the boundaries measured by a five (5) mile radius of any office maintained or utilized by Employer at the time of execution of the Agreement or at any time thereafter.*

(e) The Employee agrees that a violation on his part of any covenant set forth in this Paragraph 17 will cause such damage to the Employer as will be irreparable and for that reason, that Employee further agrees that the Employer shall be entitled, as a matter of right, and upon notice as provided in Paragraph 20 hereof, to an injunction from any court of competent jurisdiction, restraining any further violation of said covenants by Employee, his corporation, employees, partners or agents. Such right to injunctive remedies shall be in addition to and cumulative with any other rights and remedies the Employer may have pursuant to this Agreement or law, including, . . . the recovery of liquidated damages equal to forty percent (40%) of the gross receipts received for medical services provided by the Employee, or any employee, associate, partner, or corporation of the Employee during the term of this Agreement and for a period of three (3) years after the date of termination, for any reason, of this Agreement. The Employee expressly acknowledges and agrees that the covenants and agreement contained in this Paragraph 17 are minimum and reasonable in scope and are necessary to protect the legitimate interest of the Employer and its goodwill.

(Emphasis added.)

VMS filed a complaint against Dr. Farber seeking (1) preliminary and permanent injunctions enjoining Dr. Farber from violating the restrictive covenant, (2) liquidated damages for breach of the employment agreement, and (3) damages for breach of fiduciary duty, conversion of patient files and confidential information, and intentional interference with contractual and/or business relations.

Following six days of testimony and argument, the trial court denied VMS's request for a preliminary injunction, finding that the restrictive covenant violated public policy or, alternatively, was unenforceable because it was too broad. Specifically, the court found that: any covenant over six months would be unreasonable; the five-mile radius from each of the three VMS offices was unreasonable because it covered a total of 235 square miles; and the restriction was unreasonable because it did not provide an exception for emergency medical aid and was not limited to pulmonology.

The court of appeals reversed, concluding that a modified covenant was reasonable. *Valley Med. Specialists v. Farber*, 190 Ariz. 563, 950 P.2d 1184 (App. 1997). The court noted that there were eight hospitals outside the restricted area where Dr. Farber could practice. Id. at 567, 950 P.2d at 1188. Although the covenant made no exceptions for emergency medicine, the court held that the severability clause permitted the trial court to modify the covenant so Dr. Farber could provide emergency services within the restricted area. Id. (citing *Phoenix Orthopaedic Surgeons, Ltd. v. Peairs* ("*Peairs*"), 164 Ariz. 54, 61, 790 P.2d 752, 759 (App. 1989)). Moreover, VMS was allowed to stipulate that Dr. Farber could perform brachytherapy and treat AIDS and HIV patients within the restricted area, again even though the covenant contained no such exceptions. *Valley Med. Specialists,* 190 Ariz. At 567, 950 P.2d at 1188.

. . .

B. History of Restrictive Covenants

A brief reference to basic principles is appropriate. Historically, covenants not to compete were viewed as restraints of trade and were invalid at common law. *Ohio Urology, Inc. v. Poll,* 72 Ohio App. 3d 446, 594 N.E.2d 1027, 1031 (Ohio App. 1991). . . . [Citations omitted.] Eventually, ancillary restraints, such as those incident to employment or partnership agreements, were enforced under the rule of reason. *See* Restatement (Second) of Contracts §188 (hereinafter "Restatement"). Given the public interest in doctor-patient relationships, the validity of restrictive covenants between physicians was carefully examined long ago in *Mandeville v. Harman*:

> The rule is not that a limited restraint is good, but that it may be good. It is valid when the restraint is reasonable; and the restraint is reasonable when it imposes no shackle upon the one party which is not beneficial to the other. The authorities are uniform that such contracts are valid when the restraint they impose is reasonable, and the test to be applied, . . . is this: To consider whether the restraint is such only as to afford a fair protection to the interest of the party in favor of whom it is given, and not so large as to interfere with the interest of the public. Whatever restraint is larger than the necessary protection of the party can be of no benefit to either; it can only be oppressive, and, if oppressive, it is, in the eye of the law, unreasonable and void, on the ground of public policy, as being injurious to the interests of the public.

42 N.J. Eq. 185, 7 A. 37, 38-39 (N.J. 1886) [citations omitted].

To be enforced, the restriction must do more than simply prohibit fair competition by the employee. [Citation omitted.] In other words, a covenant not to compete is invalid unless it protects some legitimate interest beyond the employer's desire to protect itself from competition. *Amex Distrib. Co. v. Mascari,* 150 Ariz. 510, 518, 724 P.2d 596, 604 (App. 1986). The legitimate purpose of post-employment restraints is "to prevent competitive use, for a time, of information or relationships which pertain peculiarly to the employer and which the employee acquired in the course of the employment." [Citation omitted.] Despite the freedom to contract, the law does not favor restrictive covenants. *Ohio Urology, Inc.,* 594 N.E.2d at 1031. This disfavor is particularly strong concerning such covenants among physicians because the practice of medicine affects the public to a much greater extent. *Id.*

In fact, "for the past 60 years, the American Medical Association (AMA) has consistently taken the position that noncompetition agreements between physicians impact negatively on patient care." Paula Berg, *Judicial Enforcement of Covenants not to Compete Between Physicians: Protecting Doctors' Interests at Patients' Expense*, 45 RUTGERS L. REV. 1, 6 (1992).

C. Level of Scrutiny—Public Policy Considerations

We first address the level of scrutiny that should be afforded to this restrictive covenant. Dr. Farber argues that this contract is simply an employer-employee agreement and thus the restrictive covenant should be strictly construed against the employer. *See Amex Distrib. Co.*, 150 Ariz. at 514, 724 P.2d at 600 (noting employer-employee restrictive covenants are disfavored and strictly construed against the employer). This was the approach taken by the trial court. VMS contends that this is more akin to the sale of a business; thus, the noncompete provision should not be strictly construed against it. *See id.* (courts more lenient in enforcing restrictive covenants connected to sale of business because of need to effectively transfer goodwill). Finding the agreement here not on all fours with either approach, the court of appeals applied a standard "somewhere between" the two. *Valley Med. Specialists*, 190 Ariz. at 566, 950 P.2d at 1187.

Although this agreement is between partners, it is more analogous to an employer-employee agreement than a sale of a business. *See* Restatement §188 cmt. h ("A rule similar to that applicable to an employee or agent applies to a partner who makes a promise not to compete that is ancillary to the partnership agreement or to an agreement by which he disposes of his partnership interest."). Many of the concerns present in the sale of a business are not present or are reduced where, as here, a physician leaves a medical group, even when that physician is a partner. When a business is sold, the value of that business's goodwill usually figures significantly into the purchase price. The buyer therefore deserves some protection from competition from the former owner. [Citations omitted.] A restraint accompanying the sale of a business is necessary for the buyer to get the full goodwill value for which it has paid. [Citations omitted.]

It is true that in this case, unlike typical employer-employee agreements, Dr. Farber may not have been at a bargaining disadvantage, which is one of the reasons such restrictive covenants are strictly construed. *See, e.g., Rash v. Toccoa Clinic Med. Assocs.*, 253 Ga. 322, 320 S.E.2d 170, 172-173 (Ga. 1984). Unequal bargaining power may be a factor to consider when examining the hardship on the departing employee. But in cases involving the professions, public policy concerns may outweigh any protectable interest the remaining firm members may have. Thus, this case does not turn on the hardship to Dr. Farber.

By restricting a physician's practice of medicine, this covenant involves strong public policy implications and must be closely scrutinized. *See Peairs*, 164 Ariz. at 60, 790 P.2d at 758; *Ohio Urology, Inc.*, 594 N.E.2d at 1032 (restrictive covenant in medical context "strictly construed in favor of professional mobility and access to medical care and facilities"). Although stopping short of banning restrictive covenants between physicians, the American Medical Association ("AMA") "discourages" such covenants, finding they are not in the public interest. [Citation omitted.]

... In addition, the AMA recognizes that free choice of doctors is the right of every patient, and free competition among physicians is a prerequisite of optimal care and ethical practice. *See* AMA Opinions, Section 9.06; *Ohio Urology, Inc.*, 594 N.E.2d at 1030.

For similar reasons, restrictive covenants are prohibited between attorneys. [Citations omitted.] In 1969, the American Bar Association adopted a code of professional conduct that contained a disciplinary rule prohibiting restrictive covenants between attorneys. [Citation omitted.] The ethical rules adopted by this court provide:

> A lawyer shall not participate in offering or making:
>
> (a) a partnership or employment agreement that restricts the rights of a lawyer to practice after termination of the relationship except an agreement concerning benefits upon retirement; or
>
> (b) an agreement in which a restriction on the lawyer's right to practice is part of the settlement of a controversy between private parties.

Ethical Rule ("ER") 5.6, Arizona Rules of Professional Conduct, Rule 42, Ariz. R. Sup. Ct.

Restrictive covenants between lawyers limit not only their professional autonomy but also the client's freedom to choose a lawyer. *See* ER 5.6 cmt. Ethical Rule ("ER") 5.6, Arizona Rules of Professional Conduct, Rule 42, Ariz. We do not, of course, enact ethical rules for the medical profession, but given the view of the AMA to which we have previously alluded, we believe the principle behind prohibiting restrictive covenants in the legal profession is relevant.

> Commercial standards may not be used to evaluate the reasonableness of lawyer restrictive covenants. Strong public policy considerations preclude their applicability. In that sense lawyer restrictions are injurious to the public interest. A client is always entitled to be represented by counsel of his own choosing. The attorney-client relationship is consensual, highly fiduciary on the part of counsel, and he may do nothing which restricts the right of the client to repose confidence in any counsel of his choice. No concept of the practice of law is more deeply rooted.

Dwyer, 336 A.2d at 500.

We therefore conclude that the doctor-patient relationship is special and entitled to unique protection. It cannot be easily or accurately compared to relationships in the commercial context. In light of the great public policy interest involved in covenants not to compete between physicians, each agreement will be strictly construed for reasonableness. [Footnote omitted.]

D. Reasonableness of covenant

Reasonableness is a fact-intensive inquiry that depends on the totality of the circumstances. [Citations omitted.] A restriction is unreasonable and thus will not be enforced: (1) if the restraint is greater than necessary to protect the employer's

legitimate interest; or (2) if that interest is outweighed by the hardship to the employee and the likely injury to the public. *See* Restatement §188 cmt. *a.*; . . . [citations omitted]. Thus, in the present case, the reasonableness inquiry requires us to examine the interests of the employer, employee, patients, and public in general. *See* 62 A.L.R.3d at 976; *see also Peairs*, 164 Ariz. at 57, 790 P.2d at 755; *Amex Distrib. Co.*, 150 Ariz. at 514, 724 P.2d at 600 (accommodating right to work, right to contract, and public's right to competition) [citations omitted]. . . . Balancing these competing interests is no easy task and no exact formula can be used. *See* Restatement §188 cmt. *a.*

. . . Here, however, the covenant prohibited Dr. Farber from providing any and all forms of "medical care," including not only pulmonology, but emergency medicine, brachytherapy treatment, and HIV-positive and AIDS patient care. . . .

E. VMS's Protectable Interest

VMS contends, and the court of appeals agreed, that it has a protectable interest in its patients and referral sources. In the commercial context, it is clear that employers have a legitimate interest in retaining their customer base. *See, e.g., Bryceland*, 160 Ariz. at 217, 772 P.2d at 40. "The employer's point of view is that the company's clientele is an asset of value which has been acquired by virtue of effort and expenditures over a period of time, and which should be protected as a form of property." [Citation omitted.] In the medical context, however, the personal relationship between doctor and patient as well as the patient's freedom to see a particular doctor, affects the extent of the employer's interest. *See Ohio Urology Inc.*, 594 N.E.2d at 1031-1032. "The practice of a physician is a thing so purely personal, depending so absolutely on the confidence reposed in his personal skill and ability, that when he ceases to exist it necessarily ceases also. . . ." *Mandeville*, 7 A. at 40-41 (holding medical practice's patient base is not protectable interest) [citation omitted].

Even in the commercial context, the employer's interest in its customer base is balanced with the employee's right to the customers. Where the employee took an active role and brought customers with him or her to the job, courts are more reluctant to enforce restrictive covenants. [Citation omitted.] Dr. Farber was a pulmonologist. He did not learn his skills from VMS. Restrictive covenants are designed to protect an employer's customer base by preventing "a skilled employee from leaving an employer and, based on his skill acquired from that employment, luring away the employer's clients or business while the employer is vulnerable—that is—before the employer has had a chance to replace the employee with someone qualified to do the job." *Bryceland*, 160 Ariz. at 217, 772 P.2d at 40. These facts support the trial judge's conclusion that VMS's interest in protecting its patient base was outweighed by other factors.

We agree with VMS, however, that it has a protectable interest in its referral sources. *See Medical Specialists, Inc. v. Sleweon*, 652 N.E.2d 517, 523 (Ind. App. 1995) ("Clearly, the continued success of [a specialty] practice, which is dependent upon patient referrals, is a legitimate interest worthy of protection.") [Citations omitted.]

F. Scope of the Restrictive Covenant

The restriction cannot be greater than necessary to protect VMS's legitimate interests. A restraint's scope is defined by its duration and geographic area. The frequency of contact between doctors and their patients affects the permissible length of the restraint. [Citation omitted.] The idea is to give the employer a reasonable amount of time to overcome the former employee's loss, usually by hiring a replacement and giving that replacement time to establish a working relationship. [Citation omitted.]

Even in the commercial context, "[w]hen the restraint is for the purpose of protecting customer relationships, its duration is reasonable only if it is no longer than necessary for the employer to put a new man on the job and for the new employee to have a reasonable opportunity to demonstrate his effectiveness to the customers." *Amex Distrib. Co.*, 150 Ariz. at 518, 724 P.2d at 604 (quoting Blake, *supra*, 73 Harv. L. Rev. at 677).

In this case, the trial judge found that the three-year period was an unreasonable duration because all of the experts agree that the practice of pulmonology entails treating patients with chronic conditions which require more hospital care than office care and which requires regular contact with the treating physician at least once within each six-month period so that any provision over six months is onerous and unnecessary to protect VMS's economic interests where virtually all of Dr. Farber's VMS patients had an opportunity by late 1994 or early 1995 (Farber left September 12, 1994) to decide which pulmonologist . . . they would consult for their ongoing treatment[.]

On this record, we cannot say this factual finding was clearly erroneous. The three-year duration is unreasonable.

The activity prohibited by the restraint also defines the covenant's scope. The restraint must be limited to the particular specialty of the present employment. *See* Blake, *supra*, 73 Harv. L. Rev. at 676. On its face, the restriction here is not limited to internal medicine or even pulmonology. It precludes any type of practice, even in fields that do not compete with VMS. Thus, we agree with the trial judge that this restriction is too broad. . . .

G. Public Policy

The court of appeals held that the restrictive covenant does not violate public policy, pointing out that the record contains nothing to suggest there will be a lack of pulmonologists in the restricted area if Dr. Farber is precluded from practicing there. Even if we assume other pulmonologists will be available to cover Dr. Farber's patients, we disagree with this view. It ignores the significant interests of individual patients within the restricted area. [Citation omitted.] A court must evaluate the extent to which enforcing the covenant would foreclose patients from seeing the departing physician if they desire to do so. See *Karlin,* 390 A.2d at 1170; see also AMA Opinions, Section 9.06.

Concluding that patients' right to see the doctor of their choice is entitled to substantial protection, VMS's protectable interests here are comparatively minimal.

[Citation omitted.] The geographic scope of this covenant encompasses approximately 235 square miles, making it very difficult for Dr. Farber's existing patients to continue treatment with him if they so desire. After six days of testimony, the trial judge concluded that this restrictive covenant was unreasonably broad and against public policy. Specifically, the judge found:

> (1) the three year duration was unreasonable because pulmonology patients typically require contact with the treating physician once every six months. Thus, a restriction over six months is unnecessary to protect VMS's economic interests. Patients would have had opportunity within approximately six months to decide which doctor to see for continuing treatment;
>
> (2) the five mile radius was unreasonable because with the three offices, the restriction covered more than 235 square miles;
>
> (3) the restriction was unreasonable because it did not expressly provide for an exception for emergency medical treatment;
>
> (4) the restriction was overly broad because it is not limited to pulmonology;
>
> (5) the covenant violates public policy because of the sensitive and personal nature of the doctor-patient relationship.

Given the facts and the principles discussed, that finding is well supported factually and legally. . . .

. . .

CONCLUSION

We hold that the restrictive covenant between Dr. Farber and VMS cannot be enforced. Valley Medical Specialists' interest in enforcing the restriction is outweighed by the likely injury to patients and the public in general. *See* Restatement §188. In so holding, we need not reach the question of the hardship imposed on Dr. Farber. The public policy implications here are enough to invalidate this particular agreement. We stop short of holding that restrictive covenants between physicians will never be enforced, but caution that such restrictions will be strictly construed. The burden is on the party wishing to enforce the covenant to demonstrate that the restraint is no greater than necessary to protect the employer's legitimate interest, and that such interest is not outweighed by the hardship to the employee and the likely injury to the public. Here VMS has not met that burden. The restriction fails because its public policy' implications outweigh the legitimate interests of VMS. . . .

Post-Case Follow-Up

Applying the Restatement approach, VMS had only protectable interests in its referral sources as VMS did not train Dr. Farber, who developed his own patient base. The clause was unreasonable in that its time period of three years was onerous for patients on six-month treatment schedules. It also covered too much geographic territory (235 square miles) and prevented Dr. Farber from applying any of his medical skills, including emergency medical care. As to public interest, the clause limited patient freedom of choice and reduced optimal care that results from competition among doctors. The AMA ethics rules (as well as ABA ethics for lawyers) disfavored these types of clauses due to the harm to professional autonomy and the impact on public choice in selecting physicians.

Valley Medical Specialists v. Farber: Real Life Applications

1. Lulu enters into a franchise agreement with Dipsy Donuts, a national franchise chain. As part of the franchise deal, Lulu must promise not to compete within ten miles of her franchise for two years after the end of her franchise contract. Lulu is very successful and operates several Dipsy franchises. Five years later, she sells her franchises to a third party and decides to go to Dipsy's main competitor to buy a new franchise. Dipsy brings an injunctive action to stop her under the noncompetition clause. Lulu claims that the clause unfairly restrains trade. Advise Dipsy in this matter under *Boulanger v. Dunkin' Donuts, Inc.*, 815 N.E.2d 572 (Mass. 2004).

2. Franco runs a successful restaurant at a ski resort in Vermont. He sells his business to Charlene and agrees to stay out of the restaurant business for 5 years within 25 miles of the ski resort. Three months later, he begins to work as a host at a local restaurant, but is not the business owner. Charlene brings an action under the covenant not to compete in the restaurant sales contract. Will the clause be viewed as unreasonable under *Fine Foods, Inc. v. Dahlin*, 523 A.2d 1228 (Vt. 1987)?

3. Partners in a law firm agree to dissolve their partnership, which primarily handles negligence cases for insurance companies. They decide to divide up their insurance company clients and to not poach business from each other's insurance clients. Later, a former partner is accused of pirating the other partners' insurance clients and they sue for breach of contract. How will a court view this covenant when only business clients are involved? Apply *Dwyer v. Jung*, 133 N.J. Super. 343 (1975), to resolve this dispute.

3. Policies Involving Licensing Laws

In limited cases, a court may enforce a contract that technically violates a licensing law, but does not put the public at risk. Typically, a wide range of professional services require a party to be licensed to protect the public, such as lawyers, doctors, contractors, and restaurants. For example, a contractor sues on a construction contract and the customer defends on the ground that the contractor did not have a license from the state. While technically a violation of the law, the contractor's conduct may seem far removed from that of the thieves dividing their ill-gotten gains in *The Highwayman's Case*. Having performed, some recovery may seem just. Yet other courts may be unwilling to compensate the unlicensed contractor because such laws are intended to protect the public from dangerous or shoddy work. Unenforceability becomes a reason the contractor should obtain a license, rather than continuing to operate outside the rules.

The Restatement (Second) of Contracts §181 directly addresses licensing situations and provides another balancing test. Failure to obtain a required license may make a contract unenforceable if there is a regulatory purpose behind the licensing requirements and the public policy for the regulation clearly outweighs the enforcement of the contract. The courts must review the purpose and objectives behind the licensing regulation and analyze the public interest at issue compared to the enforcement of the party promises. The court will decide if the regulatory objectives and the public interest outweigh the enforcement of the contract in making its determination. Conversely, if a licensing law's primary purpose is to generate government revenues, rather than to safeguard the public, a court may allow a contract to be enforced to avoid unfairness to the party who delivered goods or services to another party.

For example, in *McNairy v. Sugar Creek Resort, Inc.*, 576 So. 2d 185 (Ala. 1991), a contractor whose license was pending at the time of the contract sought to recover remaining payment for clearing and grading property for a golf course that eventually went bankrupt. His license was delayed due to an oversight at a bank in releasing his cashier's check to the licensing authority. Not formally licensed at the time of contract, his license became effective during the project and some payments were made, ratifying the obligation to pay him for the project. The court enforced the agreement between the parties because McNairy had substantially complied with the licensing requirements and forfeiture of the remaining monies owed would be unfair under these circumstances. In addition, his initial lack of a license was due to third-party error and did not undermine the purpose of the licensing statute.

4. Policies Involving Family Situations

When couples decide to live together instead of marrying, public policy may preclude enforcement of their agreements. Some cases note that the policy against **meretricious relationships** — where sexual relations are rewarded with money, property, or other valuable consideration — may make these agreements unenforceable. While few today compare living together outside wedlock with prostitution, courts tend to focus on the public policy favoring stability in relationships through marriage. Recognition of cohabitation contracts might undermine that policy preference.

Courts reach different conclusions on these issues. In *Marvin v. Marvin*, 557 P.2d 106 (Cal. 1976), the California Supreme Court held that as long as sex was not an explicit part of the consideration, the agreement did not violate public policy. That ruling held that either contract law or unjust enrichment would support recovery. In *Morone v. Morone*, 413 N.E.2d 1154 (N.Y. 1980), the New York Court of Appeals held that express contracts of this sort were enforceable, but that unjust enrichment was not available. In *Hewitt v. Hewitt*, 394 N.E.2d 1204 (Ill. 1979), the Supreme Court of Illinois focused on the policy favoring marriage, holding that neither contract nor unjust enrichment would justify recovery, while *Watts v. Watts*, 405 N.W.2d 303 (Wis. 1987), held the opposite and permitted restitution.

On occasion, contracts between married people raise public policy arguments if the contract terms may encourage divorce. For example, a prenuptial agreement may increase the percentage of property to be shared and the amount of spousal support after a certain number of years of marriage. This approach may encourage divorce by making it more profitable for one of the spouses to terminate the marriage sooner rather than try to work issues out.

Surrogacy contracts also raise public policy issues. Statutes often specify that no consideration may be given or received in connection with an adoption. Surrogacy contracts generally specify that payments are for the services of gestation, not for the adoption. But other terms often reveal that a biological surrogate's relinquishment of all parental rights is central to the contract, allowing courts to see past the facade to the reality. Thus, in *Matter of Baby M*, 537 A.2d 1227 (N.J. 1988), and *R.R. v. M.H.*, 689 N.E.2d 790 (Mass. 1998), each court found a surrogate's promise to relinquish parental rights unenforceable under the terms of the state's adoption statute. A biological surrogate may have bonded during the pregnancy with the child and should receive the same deliberation period as others in the adoption process before surrendering parental rights. Aside from compliance with the adoption statutes, these courts raised a number of other policy issues, including concerns that surrogacy contracts will produce exploitation of the poor, who need money, by the rich, who can afford to pay for surrogacy. Today, many states have statutes to address surrogacy contracts and most courts (along with the Restatement (Second) of Contracts §191) determine the enforceability of such contracts depending upon what serves the best interest of the child involved, not the contracting parties. A family law class will examine these issues in greater depth. But be aware of the contract issues embedded in these discussions.

5. Restitution Under Public Policy

Generally, restitution is unavailable when a contract is void as against public policy. As in *The Highwayman's Case*, between two quarreling wrongdoers, the court leaves them in the position it finds them. The courts' refusal to enforce illegal deals has not had much effect on crime. But for less serious wrongs, the refusal to grant restitution might be excessive.

A party who performs (in whole or in part) only to find that the other party's duty is excused under public policy faces forfeiture and perhaps hardship. Explaining that the person should not have entered a contract that was void for public policy reasons offers no consolation. A wrongdoer may deserve no consolation. But in some cases, unjust enrichment remains an injustice that should be addressed, as in the *McNairy* case.

Restitution in this setting may be in flux. The recently approved Restatement (Third) of Restitution and Unjust Enrichment permits, but does not require restitution when contracts violate public policy. Courts may relent and allow restitution in public policy cases in special situations, primarily in favor of those with relatively minor culpability or those participants who help undermine a dishonest scheme.

Relatively minor culpability can be established in either of two ways. First, a party seeking restitution may show that the other party was more in the wrong. This view reflects the older doctrine of *in pari delicto*. While the court will not resolve disputes between parties equally in the wrong, the greater wrongdoer might be required to make restitution to the lesser wrongdoer. Second, a party who was excusably ignorant of the wrong may recover in restitution. This provision may protect one who was the greater wrongdoer. However, it is likely to cover only minor wrongs. A party's ignorance of important laws is unlikely to be excusable. Only ignorance of minor laws may justify restitution.

Parties who undermine a dishonest scheme may be entitled to restitution, as long as their participation did not involve serious misconduct. Thus, a person who withdraws from a transaction (before it achieved its improper goals, not after it already succeeded) may recover restitution. Withdrawing from the scheme may deal it a blow, especially once the restitution claim reveals the scheme to authorities for appropriate action. In addition, restitution may be permitted if allowing the claim would end a continuing harm to the public interest. Yet a person guilty of serious misconduct may find the court less willing to forgive the earlier wrong, even if the current action is laudable.

D. STATUTES OF FRAUDS

In contract formation, one is able to establish the existence of a contract by showing the elements of offer, acceptance, and consideration. Yet even if a contract is formed, a court may not enforce certain contracts unless there is a signed writing. Each state enacts its own version of the statute of frauds. If a party seeks to enforce a contract, the other contracting party may raise a statute of frauds defense. Primarily, it is a defense against the enforcement of an oral contract. The statute makes it harder for a party to fabricate an agreement that never existed by requiring a writing signed by the other party.

The statute of frauds serves a channeling function, guiding people to practices the law prefers. It warns people not to rely on some promises until they "get it in writing." Even the uninitiated intuitively understand the need for a writing. People may overestimate the need for a writing, believing that oral agreements are not enforceable, even in circumstances where the statute of frauds does not apply.

These statutes reacted to the common law, which routinely enforced oral contracts as long as the evidence showed the existence of an enforceable promise. Concerned that some allegations of oral promises were fraudulent, Parliament (and later the legislatures of the states) enacted statutes requiring a signed writing for the most important contracts or, in some cases, contracts whose nature might easily be misunderstood in conversation.

These concerns were exacerbated by procedural rules that precluded parties from testifying in contract disputes. In earlier times, only the **complaint** (a pleading beginning a lawsuit by alleging defendant's wrongs) or **answer** (defendant's pleading, denying, or admitting the allegations in a complaint) were permitted as testimony, making credibility harder to assess. That concern disappeared with the increased use of **interrogatories** (written responses to questions under oath), **depositions** (oral responses to questions transcribed under oath), and oral testimony at trial, but these statutes remained in place.

Today, without a statute requiring a signed writing, a persuasive liar may convince a jury that a promise was made, despite truthful denials from the other party. Fraud can pose a problem with or without statutes requiring a writing. Yet the application of the statute of frauds may help to reduce fraudulent claims of contract obligations by encouraging that promises be put into writing. In addition, these statutes promote the use of written contracts that may help parties to fully recognize the parameters of their bargains from the outset, reducing future meritless contract claims.

However, the use of these statutes may also allow a party to avoid performing an oral agreement because there is no signed writing. It makes it easier for a party to avoid performing an oral agreement that really existed, even if the other party relied on it. The statute, then, avoids some frauds but may enable others. In light of this concern, numerous exceptions to the statute of frauds have been adopted. In some cases, an exception may provide a partial remedy rather than full enforcement of the contract.

In undertaking statute of frauds analysis, a court usually examines these three questions:

1. Does the statute apply to this type of contract?
2. Does a sufficient writing exist?
3. Does an exception apply that allows enforcement?

The party asserting the statute of frauds needs to prevail on all three questions: the statute must apply to the contract at issue, no adequate signed writing may exist, and no exception may apply. See Exhibit 8.1.

EXHIBIT 8.1 Statute of Frauds Analysis

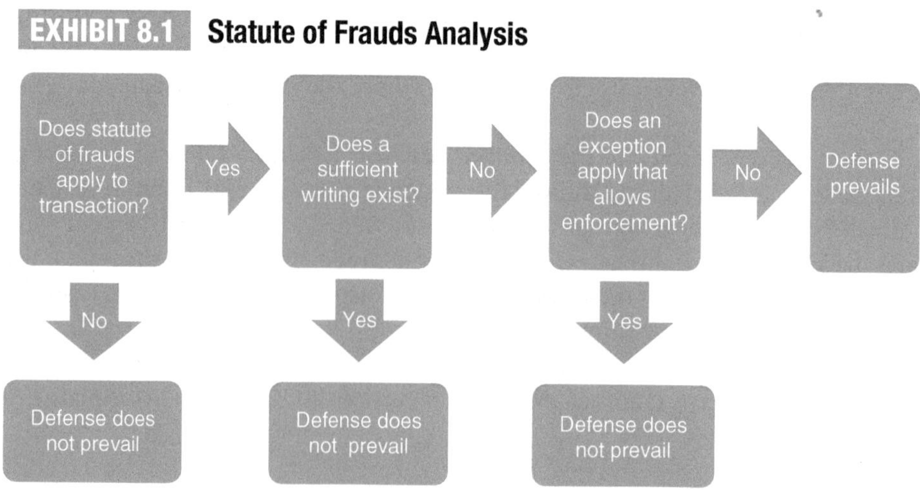

1. What Types of Agreements

The first step in the analysis is to determine what types of contracts come within the coverage of the statute of frauds. If a contract comes within the coverage of the statute, then it must be in writing. If it does not, then it does not need to be in writing to be enforceable. Each state will have its own statute of frauds, which may cover different types of agreements. Special statutes may extend the requirement of a writing to additional types of agreements. For example, some states will require that credit card agreements, magazine subscriptions, and prenuptial agreements need to be in writing. In practice, research may be required to determine what contracts fall within the coverage of a statute of frauds in your state. For our purposes, we will focus on the Restatement (Second) of Contracts §110 and UCC §2-201. It is important to note that CISG Article 11 does not require contracts to be in writing to be enforceable.

The statute of frauds covered six main classes of contracts:

1. a conveyance of an interest in real property;
2. a promise in consideration of marriage;
3. a promise that cannot be performed within a year of the time it was made;
4. a promise to pay the debt of another person (suretyship);
5. a promise by the executor of an estate to pay the estate's debts from the executor's assets;
6. a sale of goods for a price of $500 or more.

Other contracts may be enforceable without evidence of a writing. For example, employment contracts and construction contracts may fall outside the statute of frauds—unless they cannot be performed within a year.

Conveyances of real property include any transfer of an interest in land, such as sales, leases, and easements. The promise to pay for land falls within the statute, not just the promise to sell the land. Thus, where no signed writing evinces the buyer's promise, the buyer can raise the statute of frauds as a defense. Regarding leases, many states apply the writing requirement only to longer leases, typically those for one year or longer. Shorter terms may not need to be in writing, but it varies by state law.

Promises in consideration of marriage usually relate to wedding gifts, not the mutual promises to marry between the affianced couple. Thus, a promise to bestow a gift if the couple weds is within the statute. Mutual promises of wedding gifts may not fall within the statute. If the groom's parents promise a wedding gift of $10,000 if the bride's parents make an equal gift, the marriage is not the consideration for either gift. Rather, each parental gift serves as consideration for the other parents' gift.

A promise that, by its terms, cannot be performed within a year falls within the statute. The question is not whether completion within a year is likely or expected, only whether it is possible. The one-year period begins on the day the contract is formed. Thus, an athlete's five-year contract falls within the statute since it cannot be performed within a year. But a promise to build a skyscraper, if no definite time period is specified, does not come within the statute, even if construction almost certainly would take more than a year. Nor does employment for life come within the statute since performance might be completed the next day (if the employee's death comes that quickly).

The statute of frauds does apply to promises to pay the debt of another creating a **suretyship** or **guaranty**. If the borrower defaults, the lender may seek repayment from the surety or guarantor. If someone co-signed for your student loans, then that co-signer has created a suretyship or guaranty to pay the loans if you default. There must be a sufficient writing for these obligations to be enforced.

Promises by an executor of an estate to pay the estate's debts are a special kind of surety. In effect, the executor is alleged to have promised to pay from her personal assets a debt owed by the estate — promising to pay the debt of another. Like suretyship, the statute of frauds requires a writing in order to enforce a promise by an executor to pay the estate's debts.

Sales of goods for a price of $500 or more fall within the UCC's statute of frauds. A proposal to increase the threshold amount to $5,000 has not yet been adopted. The provision may apply to barter transactions, if the exchange of goods has a value of $500 or more. An exchange of goods is a sale of goods, even if no money passes between the parties. If one party receives a price in goods, valued at $500 or more, the statute applies.

Remembering Which Contracts Require a Writing

It may be difficult to remember all of the kinds of contracts that come within the coverage of the statute of frauds. A simple mnemonic device may help you remember the key categories of contracts where the statute of frauds governs: **MY LEGS**.

Marriage, promises in consideration of
Year, contracts that cannot be completed within one year
Land, sale or transfer of any interest in
Executor, promising to pay the estate's debts from the executor's own assets
Goods, for a price of $500 or more
Suretyship, promises to pay the debts of another

Despite this list of contracts, it is important to note that most statute of frauds disputes focus on three main areas: transfers of interests in land, sales of goods of $500 or more, and promises for services that cannot be performed within one year.

2. Sufficiency of Signed Writing

Under the statute of frauds, a writing does not need to be signed by both parties. Both Restatement (Second) of Contracts §131 and UCC §2-201 require a writing signed by the **party to be charged** (the person resisting enforcement of the contract) or his **agent** (someone authorized to sign on his behalf). The party trying to enforce a contract must provide a signed writing by the party who is raising the statute of frauds defense. The statute of frauds does not require that the full contract be signed by both parties.

A signed writing does not mandate a full signature of the party trying to avoid the contract. Neither the Restatement nor UCC provisions require a formal signature. A writing may be signed by using any mark intended to authenticate the writing. Initials, a company logo, or an "X" may signal the intent to authenticate a document. (*See* Restatement (Second) of Contracts §134.) The requirement may also be met by the use of letterhead or standard forms, if intended to authenticate the document. This inclusive definition of signature accommodates those who cannot write or who choose alternative methods to satisfy the requirement of a signed writing.

The statute of frauds requires that a signed writing was made, not necessarily that it is produced in court. The statute is satisfied even if the writing is lost or destroyed before it is admitted into evidence. The statute requires a party to "get it in writing." Once a writing exists, a party has done what the statute requires. Subsequent mishaps will not preclude enforcement. Of course, the credibility of assertions that a writing existed may be attacked by a party who denies that it ever signed anything. Failure to produce the writing may not help.

The easiest way to show a signed writing is to provide the written contract signed by the party against whom enforcement is sought. By getting all the contract's promises in a signed writing, a statute of frauds defense can be quickly defeated. However, in many instances, contract obligations may not appear in one document. A court may examine other written documents to determine the existence and enforceability of a contract. More than one written document may be linked together, either expressly or impliedly by the subject matter and occasion, to supply a writing that satisfies the statute of frauds. (*See* RESTATEMENT (SECOND) OF CONTRACTS §132.)

Typically, statutes recognize that a signed note or memorandum clearly referencing the parties' agreement may be sufficient to satisfy the requirement of a writing. One purpose of the statute—providing some assurance that an agreement actually was made—does not require the entire contract to be reduced to writing. But statutes vary, both among states and among different types of contracts within a state. Some statutes of frauds have been interpreted to require evidence of the terms of the deal, not merely evidence that a deal was made. In practice, it is important to verify the exact nature of the writing required in your jurisdiction.

The statute of frauds requires that the writing contain some indication of assent. Writings that signify ongoing preliminary negotiations will not suffice. The writing must reflect some commitment by the party signing it. The details of the content of the signed writing for the Restatement and the UCC are discussed below and summarized in Exhibit 8.2.

Restatement: Content of a Writing

Aside from the signed writing by the party to be charged, the Restatement requires that the contents of the writing or linked writings reasonably identify the subject matter of the contract, such as a contract for computer consulting services or the purchase and sale of a residential property. The writing must be adequate enough to show that a contract existed between the parties or that the party against whom enforcement is sought had signed an offer to the other party. By definition, an offer manifests commitment to a proposal, such that the other party can seal the deal by accepting it. The existence of a contract or a signed offer by the party to be charged indicates that assent to the contract. It would be difficult for a party to deny the presence of an agreement under these circumstances.

But the existence of an agreement does not mean there is sufficient detail about the contract duties. The writing must also provide reasonable certainty about the essential terms of the unperformed promises under the deal. Without reasonable certainty about what has not yet been performed, courts will not have adequate guidance on what needs to be enforced under the claimed contract.

Case Preview

Crabtree v. Elizabeth Arden Sales Corp.

In *Crabtree v. Elizabeth Arden Sales Corp.*, a former employee, Nate Crabtree, sought to enforce an alleged employment contract not contained in a single unified document. In addition, the company president, Elizabeth Arden, did not sign any of the writings being considered. She contended that there was no contract to enforce due to the statute of frauds. Applying the Restatement approach, the court must decide whether or not to enforce the contract and the remaining salary payments to Crabtree.

As you read *Crabtree v. Elizabeth Arden Sales Corp.*, look for the following:

1. Did the contract come within the coverage of the statute of frauds?
2. Was the claimed agreement signed by the party to be charged in this case?
3. Did the writings set out the essential terms of unperformed promises with reasonable certainty?

Crabtree v. Elizabeth Arden Sales Corp.

110 N.E.2d 551 (N.Y. 1953)

Fuld, J.

In September of 1947, Nate Crabtree entered into preliminary negotiations with Elizabeth Arden Sales Corporation, manufacturers and sellers of cosmetics, looking toward his employment as sales manager. Interviewed on September 26th, by Robert P. Johns, executive vice-president and general manager of the corporation, who had apprised him of the possible opening, Crabtree requested a three-year contract at $25,000 a year. Explaining that he would be giving up a secure well-paying job to take a position in an entirely new field of endeavor — which he believed would take him some years to master — he insisted upon an agreement for a definite term. And he repeated his desire for a contract for three years to Miss Elizabeth Arden, the corporation's president. When Miss Arden finally indicated that she was prepared to offer a two-year contract, based on an annual salary of $20,000 for the first six months, $25,000 for the second six months and $30,000 for the second year, plus expenses of $5,000 a year for each of those years, Crabtree replied that that offer was "interesting." Miss Arden thereupon had her personal secretary make this memorandum on a telephone order blank that happened to be at hand:

"EMPLOYMENT AGREEMENT WITH
NATE CRABTREE Date Sept 26-1947
At 681 - 5th Ave 6: PM
. . . Begin 20000.
6 months 25000.
6 months 30000.
5000. - per year
Expense money
[2 years to make good]
Arrangement with
Mr. Crabtree
By Miss Arden
Present
Miss Arden
Mr. John
Mr. Crabtree
Miss OLeary"

A few days later, Crabtree phoned Mr. Johns and telegraphed Miss Arden; he accepted the "invitation to join the Arden organization," and Miss Arden wired back her "welcome." When he reported for work, a "pay-roll change" card was made up and initialed by Mr. Johns, and then forwarded to the payroll department. Reciting that it was prepared on September 30, 1947, and was to be effective as of October 22d, it specified the names of the parties, Crabtree's "Job Classification" and, in addition, contained the notation that "This employee is to be paid as follows:

"First six months of employment $20,000. per annum
Next six months of employment 25,000. per annum
After one year of employment 30,000. per annum
Approved by RPJ [initialed]"

After six months of employment, Crabtree received the scheduled increase from $20,000 to $25,000, but the further specified increase at the end of the year was not paid. Both Mr. Johns and the comptroller of the corporation, Mr. Carstens, told Crabtree that they would attempt to straighten out the matter with Miss Arden, and, with that in mind, the comptroller prepared another "pay-roll change" card, to which his signature is appended, noting that there was to be a "Salary increase" from $25,000 to $30,000 a year, "per contractual arrangements with Miss Arden." The latter, however, refused to approve the increase and, after further fruitless discussion, plaintiff left defendant's employ and commenced this action for breach of contract.

At the ensuing trial, defendant denied the existence of any agreement to employ plaintiff for two years, and further contended that, even if one had been made, the statute of frauds barred its enforcement. The trial court found against defendant on both issues and awarded plaintiff damages of about $14,000, and the Appellate Division, two justices dissenting, affirmed. Since the contract relied upon was not to be performed within a year, the primary question for decision is whether there was a memorandum of its terms, subscribed by defendant, to satisfy the statute of frauds (Personal Property Law, §31) [Footnote omitted.].

Each of the two payroll cards — the one initialed by defendant's general manager, the other signed by its comptroller — unquestionably constitutes a memorandum under the statute. That they were not prepared or signed with the intention of evidencing the contract, or that they came into existence subsequent to its execution, is of no consequence [citations omitted]; it is enough, to meet the statute's demands, that they were signed with intent to authenticate the information contained therein and that such information does evidence the terms of the contract. [Citations omitted.] Those two writings contain all of the essential terms of the contract — the parties to it, the position that plaintiff was to assume, the salary that he was to receive — except that relating to the duration of plaintiff's employment. Accordingly, we must consider whether that item, the length of the contract, may be supplied by reference to the earlier unsigned office memorandum, and, if so, whether its notation, "2 years to make good," sufficiently designates a period of employment.

The statute of frauds does not require the "memorandum . . . to be in one document. It may be pieced together out of separate writings, connected with one another either expressly or by the internal evidence of subject matter and occasion." [Citations omitted.] Where each of the separate writings has been subscribed by the party to be charged, little if any difficulty is encountered. [Citation omitted.] Where, however, some writings have been signed, and others have not — as in the case before us — there is basic disagreement as to what constitutes a sufficient connection permitting the unsigned papers to be considered as part of the statutory memorandum. The courts of some jurisdictions insist that there be a reference, of varying degrees of specificity, in the signed writing to that unsigned, and, if there is no such reference, they refuse to permit consideration of the latter in determining whether the memorandum satisfies the statute. [Citations omitted.] That conclusion is based upon a construction of the statute which requires that the connection between the writings and defendant's acknowledgment of the one not subscribed, appear from examination of the papers alone, without the aid of parol evidence. The other position — which has gained increasing support over the years — is that a sufficient connection between the papers is established simply by a reference in them to the same subject matter or transaction. [Citations omitted.] The statute is not pressed "to the extreme of a literal and rigid logic" [citation omitted] and oral testimony is admitted to show the connection between the documents and to establish the acquiescence, of the party to be charged, to the contents of the one unsigned. [Citations omitted.]

The view last expressed impresses us as the more sound, and, indeed — although several of our cases appear to have gone the other way (see, e.g., *Newbery v. Wall*, 65 N.Y. 484; *Wilson v. Lewiston Mill Co.*, 150 N.Y. 314) — this court has on a number of occasions approved the rule, and we now definitively adopt it, permitting the signed and unsigned writings to be read together, provided that they clearly refer to the same subject matter or transaction. [Citations omitted.]

The language of the statute — "Every agreement . . . is void, unless . . . some note or memorandum thereof be in writing, and subscribed by the party to be charged" (Personal Property Law, §31) — does not impose the requirement that the signed acknowledgment of the contract must appear from the writings alone, unaided by oral testimony. The danger of fraud and perjury, generally attendant upon the admission of parol evidence, is at a minimum in a case such as this. None of the terms of the contract are supplied by parol. All of them must be set out in the various writings presented to the court, and at least one writing, the one establishing a contractual relationship between the parties, must bear the signature of the party to be charged, while the unsigned document must on its face refer to the same transaction as that set forth in the one that was signed. Parol evidence — to portray the circumstances surrounding the making of the memorandum — serves only to connect the separate documents and to show that there was assent, by the party to be charged, to the contents of the one unsigned. If that testimony does not convincingly connect the papers, or does not show assent to the unsigned paper, it is within the province of the judge to conclude, as a matter of law, that the statute has not been satisfied. True, the possibility still remains that, by fraud or perjury, an agreement never in fact made may occasionally be enforced under the subject matter or transaction test. It is better to run that risk, though, than to deny enforcement to all agreements, merely because the signed document made no specific mention of the unsigned writing. . . .

Turning to the writings in the case before us — the unsigned office memo, the payroll change form initialed by the general manager Johns, and the paper signed by the comptroller Carstens — it is apparent, and most patently, that all three refer on their face to the same transaction. The parties, the position to be filled by plaintiff, the salary to be paid him, are all identically set forth; it is hardly possible that such detailed information could refer to another or a different agreement. Even more, the card signed by Carstens notes that it was prepared for the purpose of a "Salary increase per contractual arrangements with Miss Arden." That certainly constitutes a reference of sorts to a more comprehensive "arrangement," and parol is permissible to furnish the explanation.

The corroborative evidence of defendant's assent to the contents of the unsigned office memorandum is also convincing. Prepared by defendant's agent, Miss Arden's personal secretary, there is little likelihood that that paper was fraudulently manufactured or that defendant had not assented to its contents. Furthermore, the evidence as to the conduct of the parties at the time it was prepared persuasively demonstrates defendant's assent to its terms. Under such circumstances, the courts below were fully justified in finding that the three papers constituted the "memorandum" of their agreement within the meaning of the statute.

Nor can there be any doubt that the memorandum contains all of the essential terms of the contract. (See *N.E.D. Holding Co. v. McKinley*, 246 N.Y. 40; *Friedman & Co. v. Newman*, 255 N.Y. 340.) Only one term, the length of the employment, is in dispute. The September 26th office memorandum contains the notation, "2 years to make good." What purpose, other than to denote the length of the contract term, such a notation could have, is hard to imagine. . . . Quite obviously, as the courts below decided, the phrase signifies that the parties agreed to a term, a certain and definite term, of two years, after which, if plaintiff did not "make good," he would be subject to discharge. And examination of other parts of the memorandum supports that construction. Throughout the writings, a scale of wages, increasing plaintiff's salary periodically, is set out; that type of arrangement is hardly consistent with

the hypothesis that the employment was meant to be at will. The most that may be argued from defendant's standpoint is that "2 years to make good," is a cryptic and ambiguous statement. But, in such a case, parol evidence is admissible to explain its meaning. [Citations omitted.] Having in mind the relations of the parties, the course of the negotiations and plaintiff's insistence upon security of employment, the purpose of the phrase — or so the trier of the facts was warranted in finding — was to grant plaintiff the tenure he desired.

Post-Case Follow-Up

The *Crabtree* court found that the statute of frauds applied to a two-year contract for services under the one-year provision. The court adopted the prevailing view that a combination of signed and unsigned writings may be viewed together if they deal with the same subject matter or transaction. The court found that the memo written on the telephone order and the payroll change forms initialed by defendant's general manager and signed by defendant's comptroller, all referred to the same transaction on their face. Under the case facts, there was little likelihood that the unsigned memo was fraudulently manufactured or that the defendant had not assented to its contents.

Crabtree v. Elizabeth Arden Sales Corp.: Real Life Applications

1. Branco Associates wants to recruit Nora, a top salesperson at another technology company. Branco tells Nora that she will have a lifetime employment contract with the firm if she leaves her current employer to work for Branco. The parties enter into an oral employment agreement. A year later, Branco wrongfully discharges Nora. She sues Branco for her lost wages, and the company raises a statute of frauds defense, claiming that her contract had to be in writing. Will Branco's defense succeed against Nora? Review *Hodge v. Evans Financial Corp.*, 823 F.2d 559 (D.C. Cir. 1985), to determine the likely result.

2. Gyro Motors (Gyro) writes a letter to Samuel offering him a two-year employment contract to be its new sales manager and to supervise all of its sales staff at three dealerships. After serving in the role for two years, the parties orally renew the contract for three more years at a higher compensation rate. Later, Gyro gives Samuel a typed memo confirming his renewal. A year later, Gyro hires a new sales manager and tells Samuel to report to him and takes away his supervisory responsibilities and reduces his pay. Samuel sues and Gyro claims statute of frauds. What is the likely analysis and outcome under the statute of frauds as discussed in *Marks v. Cowdin*, 226 N.Y. 138 (1919)?

3. A paralegal suggests that his employer, an attorney, should get involved in a class action against a pharmaceutical company. The attorney takes the case and the

paralegal works with her for five years on the case and other legal matters. Right before settling the class action, the attorney orally promises to pay $1 million over a ten-year period to her employee to reward him for his paralegal work on the case. The attorney makes several payments and then stops. The paralegal sues for the rest of the money, and the attorney claims statute of frauds. Who will likely prevail in this employment situation? Review *Sawyer v. Mills*, 295 S.W.3d 79 (Ky. 2009), and see if you agree with this decision.

EXHIBIT 8.2 Sufficient Writings Checklist

Source	Signed Writing by Party to Be Charged	Signed Contract	Signed Offer	Identify Subject Matter	Quantity	Essential Unperformed Promises
UCC	✔	✔		✔	✔	
Restatement	✔	✔	✔	✔		✔

UCC: Content of a Writing

The UCC and the common law differ in the amount of detail that the writing must contain to satisfy the statute of frauds. The UCC takes a fairly minimalist approach, requiring only that the writing indicate that it is a contract for the sale of goods (subject matter) and the quantity of goods involved. It seems likely that the writing must identify the goods, although the code does not expressly require this. It might be difficult to establish that the writing relates to a sale of goods if it does not describe the goods in some way.

The UCC will recognize a writing even if it incorrectly states the quantity. However, the court will not enforce the contract beyond the quantity stated in the writing. The writing sets the maximum amount that the court may enforce. Other missing terms can be filled in by various UCC **gap filler** provisions, which will add in terms such as price, delivery, and warranties if not specified in the contract.

3. General Exceptions Under Statute of Frauds

In some cases, courts have decided to enforce contracts, at least to some extent, despite the absence of a signed writing. Some exceptions are provided by the legislature while others are created by courts. It seems fair to ask people to refrain from relying on agreements without a written promise. Nonetheless, occasions arise when people start to perform when there is no writing or before the writing is signed. The hardship they face if the agreement is held unenforceable produces several exceptions under both the common law and the UCC.

Full Performance

Once both parties have fully performed, the statute of frauds ceases to apply. (*See* RESTATEMENT (SECOND) OF CONTRACTS §130.) The statute precludes a court from enforcing a contract without a signed writing. Once performance is complete, no enforcement is required. No action for breach is necessary. This exception is particularly useful in contracts for services where one party may have fully performed its contract duties, but the other party is now trying to deny its obligations, often payment, under the statute of frauds.

The statute of frauds can be used as a shield, but not as a sword. The defense protects a party who seeks to avoid a contract before it is performed. The statute does not justify rescission of a contract that has already been **fully executed** (completely performed).

Partial Performance

Partial or part performance of contract duties is another exception to the statute of frauds requirement of a sufficient writing. (*See* RESTATEMENT (SECOND) OF CONTRACTS §130; UCC §2-201(3)(c).) Partial performance is often applied in situations that involve the land provision or the goods provision of the statute of frauds. As to land, judicial interpretations have indicated that paying money alone is not sufficient to show part performance. Taking possession of the land or making valuable improvements will indicate part performance. In land situations, the court may order specific performance, requiring a party to hand over a deed or otherwise relinquish control of the property, since land is considered to be unique.

In the goods context, a contract is enforceable for goods under part performance where the goods have been received and accepted or payments for goods have been made and accepted. The provision is not satisfied by mere reliance: sending the payment or shipping the goods, by itself, has no effect on the statute of frauds. The exception applies once the buyer receives and accepts the goods or the seller receives the payment for such goods. By not rejecting the goods or returning the payment, the party demonstrates that it felt entitled to keep the goods or payment—which suggests it indeed entered a contract entitling it to the shipment or payment. This exception applies only to goods and payments actually received and accepted. If a contract called for several shipments, the statute of frauds may preclude enforcement of the contract regarding subsequent shipments. The amount actually received and accepted reflects assent as to those quantities, but does not necessarily evince a larger commitment.

Promissory Estoppel—Reliance

The doctrine of promissory estoppel is discussed at length in Chapter 5. This doctrine may also be utilized in instances where there is a lack of a sufficient writing under the statute of frauds. Reliance may justify enforcement in two ways. First, reliance may show assent. Conduct by the parties may establish their agreement so clearly that a writing seems unnecessary. Second, reliance may prevent a party from being left worse off than if the promise had never been made. This exception makes the agreement enforceable, in whole or in part.

Some (but not all) states use this exception in statute of frauds cases, but may require a heightened standard of review. When a party raises a statute of frauds defense, the other may be required to show promissory estoppel with clear and convincing evidence, a higher requirement than a preponderance of the evidence (more likely than not) found in most civil lawsuits. In addition, courts may require that promissory estoppel may be used as a last resort when no other adequate remedies, such as cancellation or restitution, are available to the party claiming detrimental reliance.

Promissory estoppel allows courts to redress harms in cases where restitution will not suffice to avoid injustice when the lack of a writing precludes enforcement of a contract. Sometimes the party invoking the statute has received no benefit, even though the other party has incurred considerable expense in reliance on the transaction.

Consider this example of reliance on a lease. A landowner agrees to lease office space to a business for five years. The oral agreement requires the landowner to remodel the space to suit the business's needs. The landlord begins making the changes, but the business never signs the lease and ultimately chooses a different location. Expectation damages—the promised rent for five years—is not recoverable since the statute of frauds prevents enforcement of the contract. Restitution would not help because the tenant never occupied the improved space and, thus, received no benefit from the changes. But promissory estoppel, however, might allow the landowner to recover expenses incurred building the space to suit the business's needs. The costs of remodeling the space, if wasted (that is, unwanted by the next tenant), is recoverable as reliance costs.

Not every court limits recovery to the reliance interest. In *Alaska Democratic Party v. Rice*, 934 P.2d 1313 (Alaska 1997), the court awarded the expectation interest, enforcing the contract rather than compensating for reliance. Plaintiff, in reliance on a two-year job offer, quit her job in Maryland and moved back to Alaska. When defendant breached, the court awarded her lost income under the contract. The court held that the exception for reliance defeated the statute, leaving the promise enforceable.

4. Special UCC Exceptions Under the Statute of Frauds

UCC §2-201 outlines some additional exceptions when a party is unable to evidence a sufficient writing under the statute of frauds. The three UCC exceptions are (1) a merchant's confirmation without objection; (2) goods specially manufactured for a buyer; and (3) voluntary admissions made in pleadings, testimony, and other court documents.

UCC: Merchant Confirmation Without Objection

In limited circumstances, a writing signed by one party may be treated as if it was signed by the other party, too. In effect, my writing becomes your writing. Between merchants, when one of them signs and sends a sufficient writing and the other does not object within ten days, the failure to object satisfies the statute of frauds. The rule contains several limitations:

1. The writing must be sent *within a reasonable time* of contract formation. Waiting to confirm the deal after it is already falling apart typically does not work;
2. The writing must be *sufficient against the sender*. That is, it must satisfy all the UCC's requirements for a signed writing (assent, quantity, signed by the sender);
3. It must be *received* by the other party. Failure to object to a writing one never received proves nothing;
4. The recipient must have *reason to know of the contents* of the writing.

The last limitation protects a party who has no reason to know that the writing identifies alleged contract terms and, thus, has no reason to know that an objection is appropriate. Confirmations in unexpected places — perhaps including the back of checks, which sometimes are mailed directly to the bank without even going to the offices of the seller — will not satisfy this requirement.

The provision assumes that merchants typically object when another party asserts in writing that a contract has been made, unless the writing accurately states the agreement. Merchants, who undertake repeated transactions in goods, probably can be expected to know the requirements of the UCC and can protect themselves from any fraudulent efforts to create contracts to which they never agreed.

UCC: Goods Specially Manufactured

The UCC also recognizes an exception for custom goods that are specially made for a buyer and may not be suitable for resale to other third parties. In these cases, any expense incurred in the production of the goods may be wasted. Trying to sell custom goods to another may be impossible. For example, business cards, once printed, are unlikely to be bought by any other buyer. Even if resale is possible, reselling custom goods may involve either substantial discounts in the price or substantial expense to find an interested buyer. In this limited setting, a contract is enforceable without a writing, once the seller has substantially commenced its production of the custom goods or made commitments in an effort to procure the custom materials. The exception also requires that circumstances indicate that the goods manufactured or procured were intended for the buyer. If the efforts might be attributed to other contracts, reliance may not satisfy the exception.

The exception will not apply where a seller reasonably can abandon the project without much detriment. Nor will it apply if the seller begins performance or makes commitments after it receives notice of the buyer's **repudiation** (notice that buyer will not perform contract duties). Once substantial steps to manufacture the goods have been undertaken, the oral contract becomes enforceable. Similarly, if the seller has made commitments for procurement of the goods, seller does not want to have to breach those third-party commitments. That reliance also will make the agreement enforceable despite the statute of frauds.

UCC: Admissions Exception

The UCC also provides a statute of frauds exception based on admissions of the party who is raising the defense. These admissions may be found in pleadings, such as written answers to interrogatories and oral responses to questions in a deposition, party stipulations about the agreed-upon facts of a case, or court testimony.

This exception relies upon the notion that the statute of frauds defense is intended to protect parties from oral contracts they did not make. The statute of frauds is not intended to allow parties to shirk contract duties for an oral agreement that they admit existed between them. The court will enforce an oral contract that the party raising the defense admits to in court documents or proceedings.

Case Preview

Cohn v. Fisher

In *Cohn v. Fisher*, a dispute arose over the purchase of a sailboat where the buyer, Fisher, stopped payment after his initial deposit. The seller, Cohn, eventually resold the boat for less than his agreed-upon price with Fisher. Cohn sought compensation for his losses by trying to enforce their oral agreement for the purchase of the boat. Fisher raised a statute of frauds defense and Cohn responded with exceptions to the statute.

As you read *Cohn v. Fisher*, look for the following:

1. Did the contract come within the coverage of the statute of frauds?
2. Did the deposit check, on which Fisher later stopped payment, meet the UCC's writing requirements under the statute of frauds?
3. Did any exceptions to the statute of frauds writing requirement apply here?

Cohn v. Fisher

287 A.2d 222 (N.J. Super. 1972)

ROSENBERG, J.C.C.

Plaintiff Albert L. Cohn (hereinafter Cohn) moves for summary judgment against defendant Donal L. Fisher (hereinafter Fisher). The controversy concerns an alleged breach of contract for the sale of Cohn's boat by Fisher.

On Sunday, May 19, 1968, Fisher inquired of Cohn's advertisement in the *New York Times* for the sale of his 30-foot auxiliary sloop. Upon learning the location of the sailboat, Fisher proceeded to the boatyard and inspected the sloop. Fisher then

phoned Cohn and submitted an offer of $4,650, which Cohn accepted. Both agreed to meet the next day at Cohn's office in Paterson. At the meeting on Monday, May 20, Fisher gave Cohn a check for $2,325 and affixed on same: "deposit on aux. sloop, D'Arc Wind, full amount $4,650." Both parties agreed to meet on Saturday, May 25, when Fisher would pay the remaining half of the purchase price and Cohn would presumably transfer title.

A few days later Fisher informed Cohn that he would not close the deal on the weekend because a survey of the boat could not be conducted that soon. Cohn notified Fisher that he would hold him to his agreement to pay the full purchase price by Saturday. At this point relations between the parties broke down. Fisher stopped payment on the check he had given as a deposit and failed to close the deal on Saturday.

Cohn then re-advertised the boat and sold it for the highest offer of $3,000. In his suit for breach of contract Cohn is seeking damages of $1,679.50 representing the difference between the contract price with Fisher and the final sales price together with the costs incurred in reselling the boat.

. . .

Defendant contends in his answer that there was no breach of contract since the agreement of sale was conditional upon a survey inspection of the boat. However, in his depositions defendant candidly admits that neither at the time the offer to purchase was verbally conveyed and accepted nor on the following day when he placed a deposit on the boat did he make the sale contingent upon a survey. This court holds that it may render a decision on the applicable law involved since the movant has clearly excluded any reasonable doubt as to the existence of any genuine issue of material fact. . . .

The essentials of a valid contract are: mutual assent, consideration, legality of object, capacity of the parties and formality of memorialization. In the present litigation dispute arises only to the elements of mutual assent and formality of memorialization.

N.J.S.A. 12A:2-204(1) states that "A contract for sale of goods may be made in any manner sufficient to show agreement, including conduct by both parties which recognizes the existence of such a contract." Although defendant has admitted to the court that at no time did he condition his offer to purchase the boat upon a survey inspection, he still asserts that the survey was a condition precedent to the performance of the contract. Thus, the issue arises as to the nature of the bargain agreed upon by the parties. N.J.S.A. 12A:1-201(3) defines "agreement" as meaning:

> the bargain of the parties in fact as found in their language or by implication from other circumstances including course of dealing or usage of trade or course of performance as provided in this Act (12A:1-205 and 2-208). Whether an agreement has legal consequences is determined by the provisions of this Act, if applicable; otherwise by the law of contracts (12A:1-103).

Under the objective theory of mutual assent followed in all jurisdictions, a contracting party is bound by the apparent intention he outwardly manifests to the other contracting party. To the extent that his real, secret intention differs therefrom, it is entirely immaterial. See *Looman Realty Corp. v. Broad St. Nat. Bank of Trenton,* 74 N.J. Super. 71 (App. Div. 1962); *Leitner v. Braen*, 51 N.J. Super. 31 (App. Div. 1958).

The express language of the contract, failing to manifest an intention to make the sale of the boat conditioned on a survey, and defendant failing to present evidence that the condition of a survey was implied under any section of the Uniform Commercial Code or in the general law of contracts, this court concludes that the agreement between the parties was exclusive of a condition precedent for a survey of the boat.

As to the element of formality of memorialization, N.J.S.A. 12A:2-201 requires that a contract for the sale of goods for the price of $500 or more, to be enforceable, must comply with the statute of frauds.

. . .

Thus in the present case, there are three alternatives by which the contract could be held enforceable:

> (1) under N.J.S.A. 12A:2-201(1) the check may constitute a sufficient written memorandum;
>
> (2) under N.J.S.A. 12A:2-201(3)(b) defendant's testimony in depositions and his answers to demands for admission may constitute an admission of the contract, or
>
> (3) under N.J.S.A. 12A:2-201(3)(c) payment and acceptance of the check may constitute partial performance.

The above issues, arising under the Uniform Commercial Code adopted by this State on January 1, 1963, are novel to the courts of New Jersey. For such reason this court will determine the enforceability of the contract under each of the alternatives. Ample authority for resolving the issues is found in the notes provided by the framers of the Code and in the decisions of our sister states.

With regard to the question of whether the check satisfies the statute of frauds as a written memorandum, N.J.S.A. 12*A*:2-201(1) requires (1) a writing indicating a contract for sale, (2) signed by the party to be charged, and (3) the quantity term must be expressly stated. The back of the check in question bore the legend "deposit on aux. sloop, D'Arc Wind, full amount $4,650." Thus the check seems to *prima facie* satisfy the requirements in that: it is a writing which indicates a contract for sale by stating the subject matter of the sale (aux. sloop, D'Arc Wind), the price ($4,650), part of the purchase terms—50% down (deposit of $2,325), and by inferentially identifying the seller (Albert Cohn, payee) and the purchaser (Donal Fisher, drawer); it is signed by the party against whom enforcement is sought (Donal Fisher); and it expressly states the quantity term (the D'Arc Wind). Thus the check, although not a sales contract, would comply with the requirements of the statute of frauds under N.J.S.A. 12*A*:2-201(1).

. . .

Had the check not satisfied the requirements of N.J.S.A. 12A:2-201(1), the check, together with defendant's admission of a contract in his depositions and demands for admission, may satisfy N.J.S.A. 12A:2-201(3)(b). This subsection states, in effect, that where the requirements of 12A:2-201(1) have not been satisfied, an otherwise valid contract will be held enforceable if the party charged admits that a contract was made. Such a contract would be enforceable only with respect to the quantity of goods admitted.

. . .

This court is of the opinion that if a party admits an oral contract, he should be held bound to his bargain. The statute of frauds was not designed to protect a party who made an oral contract, but rather to aid a party who did not make a contract, though one is claimed to have been made orally with him. This court would therefore hold that the check, together with defendant's admission of an oral contract, would constitute an enforceable contract under N.J.S.A. 12A:2-201(3)(b).

Finally, under N.J.S.A. 12A:201(3)(c) the check may constitute partial performance of the contract in that payment for goods was made and accepted, and, as such, the contract would be held enforceable under the statute of frauds. N.J.S.A. 12A:2-201(3)(c) provides that although the requirements of N.J.S.A. 12A:2-201(1) have not been met, an otherwise valid contract will be held enforceable with respect to goods (1) for which payment has been made and accepted, or (2) which have been received and accepted.

. . . Under the Code, oral contracts would be held enforceable only to the extent that goods have been paid for or received. Thus, part payment or receipt and acceptance of part of the goods would satisfy the statute of frauds, not for the entire contract, but only for the *quantity* of goods which have been received and accepted or for which payment has been made and accepted.

In the present case, since the quantity term has been clearly indicated by the check itself, namely "aux. sloop, D'Arc Wind," the check, by representing that payment had been made and accepted, would constitute partial performance and the contract would be held enforceable under N.J.S.A. 12A:2-201(3)(c). That such a decision results in upholding the entire contract is due solely to the fact that the entire contract concerned only the sale of one boat.

The fact that defendant had stopped payment on the check is of no legal significance. As stated by Professor Corbin, "The requirements of the statute [of frauds] are satisfied even though the drawer of the check causes its dishonor by stopping payment; the oral contract is still enforceable and the holder can maintain suit against the drawer for the amount of the check." Corbin on Contracts, §495 (1950). The Uniform Commercial Code takes the same view in N.J.S.A. 12A:3-802(1)(b): "If the instrument is dishonored action may be maintained on either the instrument or the obligation." Thus, a subsequent stop-payment order has no bearing on whether or not an enforceable contract came into being upon the delivery and acceptance of the check.

In sum, the case at bar has fully complied with the statute of frauds in that under each of the alternative subsections — N.J.S.A. 12A:2-201(1), (3)(b), and (3)(c) — the enforceability of the contract is upheld.

The time and place for performance of the contract is not in dispute: both parties agree that final payment was to be made on May 25, 1968 at the boat yard where plaintiff's sloop was stored. N.J.S.A. 12A:2-507(1) requires tender of delivery as a condition to seller's right to payment according to the contract. It appears from the facts that plaintiff seller complied with N.J.S.A. 12A:2-507(1) in tendering delivery, since he was ready, willing and able to close the deal. Defendant buyer's failure to rightfully reject under N.J.S.A. 12A:2-601 and 2-602 or to accept under N.J.S.A. 12A:2-606 constituted a breach of the contract.

Under N.J.S.A. 12A:2-706 the seller may resell the goods and recover from the defaulting buyer the difference between the contract price and the resale price, together with incidental damages allowed by N.J.S.A. 12A:2-710, but less any expense saved in consequence of the buyer's breach. The resale must be made in good faith and in a commercially reasonable manner with reasonable notification of the resale to the defaulting buyer. "Incidental damages are additional expenses reasonably incurred by the aggrieved party by reason of the breach. They would include resale charges, storage charges, notice charges and the like." New Jersey Study Comment to §12A:2-710.

By letter of May 27, 1968 plaintiff notified defendant of his intention to resell the boat. Plaintiff then re-advertised the boat in the *New York Times* and accepted the highest offer of $3,000 in early June. This court holds such a sale to have been conducted in good faith and in a commercially reasonable manner which, together with the fact of notice to the defendant, satisfies the requirements of N.J.S.A. 12A:2-706.

By reason of the foregoing, this court hereby grants plaintiff's motion for summary judgment against defendant for breach of contract and awards damages in the amount of $1,679.50 representing resale damages under N.J.S.A. 12A:2-706 of $1,650 and incidental damages under N.J.S.A. 12A:2-710 of $29.50.

Grant SJ

Post-Case Follow-Up

Under the UCC, the statute of frauds applied to an oral contract for the sale of a boat at $4,650 (goods of $500 or more). The check deposit met the requirements for a sufficient writing as it was signed by the party to be charged and referenced the purchase of the sailboat. Even if the writing was not sufficient, the UCC exceptions of court admissions and partial performance justified awarding resale damages to the seller.

Cohn v. Fisher: Real Life Applications

1. Plaintiff Juno rents tobacco barns from Defendant Farmer. Tobacco barns are moveable structures for curing tobacco crops and are considered goods under the UCC. The parties orally agree to the sale of the five barns for $20,000. Juno gives a $5,000 check to Farmer who accepts this initial payment. Juno takes physical possession of the barns and pays for repairs. Farmer returns Juno's check four days later and sells the barns to others. Juno sues for the barns, but Farmer claims a statute of frauds defense. Juno seeks your input. Apply the statute of frauds to this dispute and determine if any exceptions may be used to aid Juno under *Buffaloe v. Hart*, 114 N.C. App. 52 (1994).

2. The Warrens agree to sell land for a home site to the Spencers for $100,000. Mr. Spencer works for Mr. Warren at a horse farm. The Spencers take possession of land with the Warrens' consent, building a small home and making other property improvements, totaling $70,000. The sellers later renege on their agreement

when Spencer took a new job with a competitor. The Warrens claim no obligation to sell the land under the statute of frauds. You are a law clerk for a judge handling this case. Draft a short memo with your analysis of this defense under *Beaver v. Brumlow*, 148 N.M. 172 (Ct. App. 2010), for the judge's consideration.

3. Jenn and Tom entered into an oral partnership agreement and invested money to lease and run a restaurant for five years. After Tom dies from injuries from a car accident, his widow agrees orally to operate the restaurant with Jenn. Six months later, Jenn decides to run the restaurant on her own and refuses to share any partnership profits with Tom's widow. His widow sues and Jenn claims statute of frauds regarding the oral partnership arrangement. Will Jenn prevail using the statute of frauds defense? Consider *Sheela v. Mathew*, 2008 Tex. App. LEXIS 4331 (Tex. App. Houston 14th Dist. 2008), in drafting a memo on this dispute.

Chapter Summary

- Unconscionability usually requires both unfair surprise (procedural unconscionability) and oppression (substantive unconscionability), making a contract voidable. Under a finding of unconscionability, a court may refuse to enforce the entire contract, strike out offending clauses or interpret the disputed term in a limiting way, leaving the rest of the contract in force.
- Procedural unconscionability addresses unfair surprise and the absence of meaningful choice in the contract formation process. Courts will analyze the sophistication of the parties to the contract, inequalities in bargaining power, a lack of clear, conspicuous notice of contract terms, little or no meaningful chance to review of the terms in advance of agreeing, and if major provisions are hidden in fine print or a blizzard of legalese.
- Substantive unconscionability focuses on the specific contract terms in dispute to see if they are oppressively harsh or one-sided. Excessive price terms or clauses unfairly limiting the liability of the contract drafter, such as unusual warranty disclaimers, stringent damage limits, or onerous refund and dispute resolution clauses, are examples.
- Well-established policies may be found in constitutional law, statutory law, or case precedent. Public policy precludes enforcement if the recognized policy makes certain contracts or terms unenforceable; typically making a contract void. Public policy precludes enforcement when a public policy against enforcement significantly outweighs the interests in enforcing a contract.
- Under the statute of frauds, some contracts must be shown by a signed writing in order for a court to enforce them. The mnemonic device of **MY LEGS** identifies the main contracts to which the statute applies: in consideration of **M**arriage, contracts that cannot be performed within a **Y**ear from the date they are made, contracts conveying an interest in **L**and, promises by an **E**xecutor to pay personally the debts of an estate, **G**oods priced at $500 or more, and promises of **S**uretyship.

- A writing must be signed by the party to be charged, the one who is resisting enforcement of the contract. Informal signatures (initials, logos, letterhead, and so on) may suffice, if intended to authenticate the document. The signed writing must indicate that an agreement was made (or at least offered).
- Under the Restatement view, a sufficient writing must also identify the subject matter of the contract and state the essential terms of the unperformed promises with reasonable certainty. Under the UCC, the signed writing must also indicate a contract for the sale of goods and specify the quantity.
- There are several general exceptions to the writing requirement under the statute of frauds, including completed performance (services), partial performance (land and goods), and promissory estoppel, if recognized in that state.
- There are three special UCC exceptions to the requirement of a signed writing under the statute of frauds: a merchant's confirmation without objection within ten days; goods specially manufactured for a buyer; and admissions made in pleadings, testimony, and other court documents.

Applying the Rules

Al is a promising amateur boxer. Two boxing coaches decide to work with him and pay for his training expenses, living expenses, and his first dozen fights under a two-year management agreement. Al agrees orally to the deal and to pay them a 20 percent commission on his fights in management fees as well as pay back their investment at the end of the two years. Al quickly moves up in the rankings and is soon signing lucrative deals for his upcoming boxing matches. Al's father, Roger, then decides to take over the management of his son's career.

Roger cuts off all communications between Al and his former coaches. Al's father refuses to pay any commission to Al's coaches or to compensate them for his son's expenses. The coaches seek compensation in court; $140,000 for their investment in Al and $200,000 in commissions. Al contends that the agreement is illegal because the coaches are not licensed boxing managers as required under state statute to receive commissions. There is no state law requiring boxing coaches to be licensed. Consult *Halpern v. Greene*, 24 Misc. 3d 1251(A) (S. Ct. N.Y. 2009), in responding to the following:

1. What public policy interest would be served by only allowing licensed boxing managers to receive managerial commissions?

2. Will Al have to pay $200,000 in commissions to the two coaches?

3. Can the coaches seek restitution for their $140,000 investment?

4. How would you analyze the enforceability of the management agreement under the statute of frauds?

5. Will any exceptions to the statute of frauds apply to this dispute?

Contract Law in Practice

1. Emmett, a licensed attorney in your state, renders legal services to residents of a condo development in another state who agree to pay him $50,000. He successfully negotiates a settlement on their behalf against a contractor for poor workmanship on community renovations. The residents never pay for his legal services. Is Emmett allowed to recover legal fees from the residents? Review your state's code of professional responsibility and draft a presentation about whether or not the fee agreement is enforceable under your state's public policy.

2. The UCC and Restatement provide general categories of contracts that must be in writing to be enforced under the statute of frauds. States may expand upon the categories of writings that fall within the mandates of the statute of frauds. Research your state law to determine what additional types of contracts come within the coverage of the statute of frauds.

3. Disputes over oral contracts are common situations. Search online for recent news articles about statute of frauds cases. Draft a blog post with hyperlinks to the relevant articles and any supplementary materials. Post your information to a class discussion board or blog for student comments on the sufficiency of the writing in the case and any exceptions that might apply.

4. A state's statute of frauds may be amended by legislation. Research any recent legislative proposals that seek to amend your state's statute of frauds. Will they expand or limit coverage under the statute of frauds? Do you agree with the proposed changes? If not, prepare a letter to the sponsoring representative explaining why the proposal should be rejected. Alternatively, draft legislation to address any changes you would make to your state's current statute and work with your class on finalizing your proposal for presentation to your class or local legislator for consideration.

5. A majority of state courts require a showing of both procedural and substantive unconscionability. Other courts expect only a showing of either procedural or substantive unconscionability. A third approach applies a sliding scale to determine unconscionability. Research how states in your region or nationally approach the issue of unconscionability. Create a chart that identifies which of these three approaches are used by the states in the selected region or nationally.

6. There is a lively debate about whether or not states that enforce noncompetition clauses in employment agreements are harming technological innovation and economic vitality in that state. Read Matt Marx, Jasjit Singh & Lee Fleming, *Regional Disadvantage? Non-Compete Agreements and Brain Drain* (2011), http://siepr.stanford.edu/system/files/shared/pubs/papers/braindrain110707%5B1%5D.pdf. What are the key conclusions they reach based upon their research? Are there opposing views on this issue? How might you advise a state legislative committee considering the issue of enforcement of covenants not to compete under state statute?

9 Interpretation

Performance involves doing what the contract requires. Whether advising a client how to proceed or litigating a dispute, lawyers need the ability to assess whether a client's (or opponent's) conduct performs the promises made or fails to measure up to the contract's requirements. To a large extent, that involves determining what a contract means. Even if parties agree that they entered an enforceable contract, they may disagree about what the terms of that contract require. Careful interpretation includes determining the meaning of words the parties used. Not all contractual requirements derive from the parties' words. The law imposes some duties, the parties may assume duties without expressing them in words, and courts may infer other duties to fill gaps in an agreement. Determining whether the parties' conduct meets the requirements involves evaluating all these sources of obligation.

The skills of interpretation are critical to a lawyer, not only when interpreting contracts, but when interpreting statutes, court decisions, witness statements, and any other use of language that plays a role in legal proceedings or documents. Some of the techniques described in this chapter apply uniquely to contract interpretation, but you may find some of them useful in other settings.

A. INTERPRETATION IN CONTEXT

Interpretation refers to determining the meaning and effect of people's communications, expressed by words or by conduct. Interpreting contracts usually requires comparing the conduct of one party to the terms of the agreement to determine whether the conduct satisfies the requirements of the contract.

Key Concepts

- The goal of interpretation (shared meaning)
- The sources of contract meaning and how to use them
- Restricting sources outside of a writing under the parol evidence rule
- Correcting a flawed writing (reformation)

Interpretation is not a discrete issue to be dealt with before moving on to other issues. Interpretation is ubiquitous; it lies within other issues. Interpretation often arises in discussing whether certain conduct performed the contract or breached it. For example, in *Shrum v. Zeltwanger*,[1] the contract called for the sale of "134 head of Cows." Seller tendered 134 female bovines, some of which had not yet borne a calf. Buyer refused to accept any animal that had not been bred already (what buyer called heifers). To determine whether the shipment performed the contract or breached it, the court needed to interpret the word "Cows," deciding whether it excluded heifers. In other cases, whether performance is due will depend on interpreting the contract language as either a promise (a commitment to perform) or as a condition (an event that must occur before performance is due, reviewed in Chapter 11). Interpretation may be required to determine whether assent occurred — evaluating whether a response agreed to the terms of the offer and proposed a modification, or rejected the offer and proposed a counteroffer. Interpretation is one step in resolving the larger issues of breach, condition, and assent.

Interpretation has one primary goal: to determine what the speaker (or writer) meant when she used that language. You have been doing that in your everyday life for years. Perhaps you have persuaded a professor to change a grade because your answer reflected what she said, even if she meant something different. Perhaps you were the student who correctly interpreted the presentation — who understood what the professor meant — and did not have to make that argument, having received credit in the first place. Either way, you used your skill in interpretation.

The interpretation of rules, whether stated in a statute or a common law decision, involves many of the same skills and techniques of interpretation.

Several factors complicate contract interpretation. First, contracts involve two or more coequal speakers. Each party's meaning when assenting to the contract deserves equal weight. In a contract, the parties may have intended different meanings. Second, what each party stated may differ from what was written down, which may in turn differ from what each meant. Parties often ask courts to sort out the objective manifestations in the contract from the parties' subjective intent. As discussed in Chapter 2, objective manifestations must be given considerable weight — but subjective intent still works its way into the analysis from time to time. Third, contract interpretation arises from terms agreed upon in a specific factual context. That context may influence the interpretation as much as the words themselves do.

The immense variety of settings makes interpretation very difficult to explain. Generalizations about how to interpret language take you only so far. They present the tools for interpretation; the challenge comes in applying those tools to specific words or deeds in a particular context — and perhaps with a certain inflection. The expression "Yeah, right" can mean opposite things, depending on how it is said.

This chapter will focus on guides courts have laid down for interpretation and some of the things they consider when interpreting language. Armed with these tools, you will need to use your judgment to pick out which one applies in any given problem and to present it in a way that produces a favorable argument.

---

[1] 559 P.2d 1384 (Wyo. 1977).

You may find the following steps a useful way to approach interpretation issues.

1. Identify the outcome your client intended.
2. Identify a meaning that would support that intended outcome (and competing meanings your opponent may propose).
3. Find sources that support the intended meaning.
4. Address competing interpretations, explaining why they are less appropriate.

The rules and techniques of interpretation tend to be comparative. Your interpretation need not be perfect, just better than the alternatives proposed by other parties. Once you identify the competing interpretations, you can discuss how the various tools of interpretation favor one approach over the other. One party might be favored by a natural reading of the terms. If so, the other party may need some creativity to explain how the words might be understood differently. That creativity must come from the lawyer, not the court. The court will compare competing interpretations, but rarely invents a new one that neither party proposed, unless each party offers an unrealistic interpretation.

1. The Goals of Interpretation

Interpretation primarily seeks the parties' shared intent. This primary goal stems in large part from the fundamental tenets and purposes of contract law. Contract law enforces obligations because the parties agreed to undertake those commitments. Without their assent, the law would have no particular reason to impose these duties. The parties assented to the agreement as they understood it at the time the agreement was formed. That understanding, then, is the one a court is justified in enforcing. That original understanding represents the mutually beneficial exchange to which the parties agreed. Their assent says nothing about whether an agreement they did not contemplate would be mutually beneficial. To the extent possible, interpretation seeks to identify the duties the parties intended to assume. Therefore, if the parties attached the same meaning to a term, that meaning prevails.[2]

Finding the parties' original understanding often poses problems. Lawyers get involved in interpretation issues because the parties no longer agree on what the contract means. Even when they agree that they committed to the same words, the parties now disagree about what the terms mean. Thus, one contends it agreed to one deal while the other claims it agreed to a slightly different deal. Recall *Shrum*, in which the seller claimed it promised to deliver female bovines, but buyer claimed it agreed to pay for bovines that already had been bred. Whether this represents the original understanding or an understanding the parties developed in light of subsequent events may be difficult to discern.

The goal of finding shared assent works best if a shared understanding once existed. Some parties raise disingenuous arguments; the parties originally shared

[2]Restatement (Second) of Contracts §201(1).

an understanding of what the contract required, but one party now regrets that deal and argues for a different interpretation. This situation involves a real agreement between the parties, if the finder of fact can determine what it is.

Too often, the parties may not have reached a real agreement. The parties agreed to the same words, but not to any particular meaning. Whether they intended different things or did not form an intention at all as to that term, no shared understanding existed that a court now can identify and enforce. In extreme cases, enforcing any agreement at all will lack justification. In *Shrum*, the court might have said their disagreement about what "cow" meant prevented assent to the sale, leaving no agreement in the first place.

In some cases, however, one party may be held to perform terms she never intended to accept because the court decides that interpretation reflects the deal the parties made or appeared to make. The **objective** approach (focused on words and actions, as opposed to thoughts) finds assent even when the parties intended different things. Where the parties did intend to agree, the objective manifestations continue to urge the court to enforce the deal as it appears, even if that is not the deal one of them imagined. The court in *Shrum* preferred an objective interpretation of the word cow, which might require the buyer to pay for heifers, even if that is not what buyer intended to purchase.

In other cases, the agreement may be incomplete. The parties' shared agreement on the terms they specified poses no problems. Yet some detail, perhaps an important detail, may not be addressed by the agreement. In these cases, the contract might fail for lack of definiteness (discussed in Chapter 2), the requirement that contracts be sufficiently clear to allow a court to identify breaches and formulate remedies. Negating the contract, however, frustrates the parties' legitimate expectations under the agreement they made, depriving at least one party of the benefits it procured under a contract that seemed binding. Courts often prefer to salvage the agreement the parties did make by filling in gaps the parties left in the agreement. While not exactly interpretation (if by that we mean discovering what the parties intended), the process resembles the quest for an enforceable meaning despite the absence of a shared intent.

2. Misunderstanding and Interpretation

Misunderstanding arises when parties use the same words, but mean significantly different things. A party claiming misunderstanding argues that it never assented to the agreement as interpreted by the other party. It understood the agreement differently at the time the contract was formed and assented to that understanding, but no other. For example, in *Raffles v. Wichelhaus*,[3] a famous example of misunderstanding, a buyer agreed to buy cotton to arrive from Bombay on a specific ship, the *Peerless*. There were many ships of that name, two of which left Bombay at about that time. The seller tendered cotton that arrived on the ship that left Bombay in December, but the buyer refused it, claiming that it intended to buy cotton to

[3] 2 Hurl. & C. 906 (Exch. 1864).

arrive on the *Peerless* that left Bombay in October. The court held that even though the parties had signed the same paper, the different meanings they attached to the word *Peerless* meant they never really assented to the same deal. Their words differed as much as if one said *Peerless* and the other said *Unequalled.*

Parties rarely plead misunderstanding as a defense. More commonly, parties argue that the other party misunderstands the agreement: our interpretation is the true meaning of the contract; their interpretation is incorrect. Misunderstanding is a second line of defense, to which parties resort only if they lose on interpretation.

Negating the Contract for Misunderstanding

Misunderstanding requires three components:

1. the parties attached different meanings to a term of their agreement;
2. the differences between the meanings are material; and
3. at the time of contract formation, one of the following was true:
   a. neither party knew or had reason to know the other party's intended meaning; or
   b. each party knew the meaning the other party intended; or
   c. each party had reason to know the meaning the other party intended.[4]

Each aspect offers the court a way to enforce the contract. Rejecting the existence of a contract based on misunderstanding becomes a last resort. Courts prefer to preserve the parties' deal if they can find a suitable interpretation.

If the parties actually shared an understanding of the agreement at the time of formation, no problem with assent exists. The court rejects misunderstanding and enforces the parties' shared understanding.[5] Attorneys may struggle to demonstrate that the parties shared an understanding when one party now contends that it did not share the other's understanding. A party might raise misunderstanding in an effort to avoid an unfavorable deal, even if the agreement was fully understood at formation. For example, the buyer in *Raffles* wanted out of the contract because the price of cotton had fallen; it could buy cotton cheaper from other sources and preferred not to pay this seller the contract price. Thus, even if the seller intended the December *Peerless*, it might pretend it meant the October *Peerless* to avoid the contract. Such a pretext offers no justification for refusing to enforce the deal. If the evidence establishes that the parties originally shared an understanding, then that ends the issue.

Similarly, if the differences between the parties' understandings are not material, the deal will be enforced. The parties' objective manifestations of assent will dominate unless the differences in meaning are significant. Different meanings involving a material term may suffice. It seems more likely, however, that the differences in meaning must produce a significantly different outcome in the case. Different meanings attached to a relatively minor term might qualify, if they would

[4] Restatement (Second) of Contracts §20(1).
[5] *Id.* §201(1).

produce a large difference in the outcome. On the other hand, a modest difference concerning a material term might not sustain misunderstanding, if the difference in meaning produced little difference in the outcome. Modest differences suggest a pretext—an effort to avoid the contract for reasons unrelated to the difference in meaning. Parties seem unlikely to litigate cases involving immaterial differences. Rather than risk a finding that the contract was invalid, the party seeking an enforceable contract may concede the interpretation point (establishing a shared meaning, although one mildly disadvantageous to the conceding party).

Finally, a court will enforce the agreement despite alleged misunderstanding if it can assign responsibility for the misunderstanding to one party, as discussed in the next section. Misunderstanding negates assent when the parties are equally responsible for the failure to agree on a single, shared meaning. That occurs if

1. both parties knew the other's meaning (but neither clarified the term); or
2. both parties had reason to know (but neither actually knew) of the other's meaning; or
3. neither party knew and neither party had reason to know of the other's meaning.

In the last situation, both parties are blameless. Neither could have been expected to avoid the misunderstanding because neither had notice of the other's meaning—neither **actual notice** (subjective knowledge of what the other party intended) nor **constructive notice** (notice imputed to a party with no actual knowledge because that party had reason to know of the other's meaning). If either party had knowledge or reason to know, then that party should have avoided the problem by clarifying the meaning during negotiations. However, if both parties were equally able to avoid the problem, then it makes no sense to favor the interpretation urged by either one. If both knew of the other's meaning, but neither spoke up, the court will nullify the contract based on misunderstanding. Similarly, if each had reason to know (but neither actually knew) of the other's meaning, neither has a better claim to have its interpretation imposed on the other party.

Interpretation of Different Meanings

Most misunderstanding arguments begin as efforts to interpret the contract. Each urges the court to impose its interpretation on the other party. To some extent, the reasons to reject misunderstanding also offer reasons to impose one party's interpretation on the other party, even though that party did not intend to agree to those terms. A court will interpret a contract in accordance with one party's meaning if

(a) that party did not know of the different meaning the other party intended, but the other knew the meaning the first party intended; or
(b) that party had no reason to know of the different meaning the other intended, but the other had reason to know the meaning the first party intended.[6]

[6] *Id.* §201(2).

This result will apply even if the court believes that the parties intended materially different things when they entered the contract. This reluctance to find misunderstanding counterbalances the difficulty of determining whether a party really intended a different meaning at formation or whether it now pretends to have a different meaning because its original meaning has become disadvantageous. As an illustration, consider how *Raffles* might be decided in two slightly different situations.

First, if the buyer knew that the seller intended the December *Peerless*, but the seller did not know the buyer meant the October *Peerless*, the buyer would be in breach for refusing the cotton. This outcome would apply even if the seller had reason to know the buyer intended the October *Peerless*. The buyer, aware of both meanings, could have clarified which ship was meant at the time of formation. Having failed to raise the issue during negotiations, he cannot use the ambiguity to escape the obligation later. The seller's mere reason to know, without actual knowledge, does not put the same responsibility on the seller.

Second, even if buyer did not know seller meant the December *Peerless*, it might have reason to know seller's intent. Perhaps some comments by seller were inapt if the October *Peerless* was intended, raising some reason to believe that seller did not intend that ship. Reason to know again gives buyer a chance to speak up and clarify the situation during negotiations. This second case is objective, not subjective. Even though the buyer did not know that seller meant the December ship, it had reason to know. Buyer's subjective ignorance of seller's intent does not prevent a court from enforcing the contract on seller's interpretation.

When a word has an objective meaning, the case is much more likely to be resolved by interpretation than by misunderstanding. One party's interpretation is likely to conform to the objective meaning. The other may find it difficult to persuade a court that it did not have reason to know of that objective meaning or that the one party intended that objective meaning. The more obvious and reasonable the one party's interpretation, the harder it is for the other party to explain that it did not consider it.

Try your hand at applying this rule to the following situation. Buyer and seller agreed to the sale of imported pima cotton (a particular type of cotton plant). Buyer mistakenly believed that pima cotton meant the same thing as Egyptian cotton. In fact, Egyptian cotton comes from a different plant that shares many of the qualities of pima cotton. Those who know the difference generally consider Egyptian cotton slightly better than pima cotton. When seller tendered pima cotton from Peru (as seller always intended), buyer refused the delivery on the ground that it was not Egyptian cotton. Will a court enforce the contract? Which party breached?

Case Preview

Perez v. State of Maine

Perez v. State of Maine illustrates how parties can use the same word and yet mean different things. The words chosen were not clear, making it entirely plausible that each party had a different idea of what the language meant. Rather than treat the agreement as a nullity—something neither party intended—Justice Breyer (then a judge on the First Circuit) sought out an interpretation that the court fairly could impose on the parties even though one of the parties did not intend to agree to that term.

As you read *Perez v. State of Maine*, look for the following:

1. How does the court address the possibility that the parties never really agreed at all?
2. How does the court justify imposing a meaning on one party that the party never intended to accept?
3. Is this result based on a suspicion that both parties intended this meaning in the first place?

Perez v. State of Maine

760 F.2d 11 (1st Cir. 1985)

BREYER, Circuit Judge.

In 1976, the Maine Department of Manpower Affairs (DMA) decided not to hire Nazario Perez. Perez, believing DMA's decision reflected discrimination against Hispanics, complained to the appropriate state and federal administrative agencies. He also sued DMA in state court, alleging a violation of state antidiscrimination law, 5 M.R.S.A. §§4612(4)(A), 4613(1). In 1979, Perez and DMA entered into a settlement agreement. The Agreement referred explicitly to Perez's claims under *state* antidiscrimination law: Perez agreed to waive all claims against DMA "with respect to any alleged violations of the Maine Human Rights Act." The Agreement did not explicitly refer to any claims under *federal* antidiscrimination law. But, it used language that could be taken as settling the entire discrimination dispute, regardless of which particular statute granted Perez a legal right. It said:

> As evidence of its good faith in settling *this matter*, the Respondent [DMA] agrees to pay the Complainant [Perez] a sum of money in the amount of $20,000 as full and final settlement of *this matter.*

(Emphasis added.)

After signing the Agreement and receiving the money, Perez sued DMA again; but this time he sued in federal court alleging that the same facts made out a violation of federal antidiscrimination law, Title VII, 42 U.S.C. §2000e et seq. The district court, in an initial opinion, wrote that the key issue in the case concerned the meaning of the quoted language in the settlement agreement. What was the Agreement supposed to settle—*all* antidiscrimination claims or just the *state* law claims? The court found the language ambiguous and set the matter for trial. At the trial a different district judge presided. He eventually found for DMA. 585 F. Supp. 1535. Victorina Perez (daughter of Nazario Perez, who had died in the interval) now appeals. We affirm the district court's decision.

At the outset appellant argues that the district court, seeing great similarity between state and federal laws, concluded from that fact alone that a settlement of a claim under the first must *necessarily* be a settlement of the second. She argues that such a holding would be wrong. And, we agree with her about that conclusion. We are aware of nothing in the statutes, in case law, or in logic that requires parties seeking to settle claims under two similar laws to settle both at the same time. Whether or not the laws in question are antidiscrimination statutes, the parties would seem free to agree to settle the one, or the other, or both. They would seem free to settle, or not, as they choose. . . . Thus, the issue in this case is not whether Perez and the DMA were legally free to settle the federal claim; they were. Nor is it whether they *had* to settle the federal claim; they did not have to do so. The issue, as the first district judge pointed out, is what the parties agreed upon. What is the meaning of their agreement?

We, like both district judges, believe that the Agreement's language is ambiguous. The words "this matter," quoted above, might refer to the specific state law claim, or they might refer, more generally, to the underlying discrimination dispute between the parties. We therefore have reviewed the trial record to determine what these words meant in the context of the bargain made by the parties. [Citations omitted.]

The district court found that DMA thought these words referred to the entire dispute. And that finding has more than adequate support. For one thing, DMA paid $20,000 for the settlement; and it is difficult to see why it would have paid the money — 80 percent of the monetary relief Perez sought in the complaint — unless it thought it was buying freedom from a second law suit. Appellant argues that DMA paid this amount because Perez's case was so strong that DMA virtually conceded 80 percent of it; but this logical possibility is not supported in any way in the record. For another thing, DMA's lawyer testified, without contradiction, that DMA intended to settle both state and federal claims. Finally, the absence of specific language in the Agreement about a federal suit, while arguably showing an intent to allow such a suit, is more plausibly explained by DMA's belief that the federal administrative agency would not typically issue a "right to sue" letter (a precondition for federal court action) once a discrimination claim had been settled.

The district court also found, however, that Perez did not want to settle the federal claim and did not intend the settlement agreement to do so. Unbeknownst to his lawyer or DMA, Perez had received a "right to sue" letter from the federal agency only nine days before signing the settlement. He then asked a second lawyer — not the lawyer representing him in negotiations — whether he could still bring the federal suit. And, the second lawyer told him he thought Perez still could do so. These facts, appellant argues, demonstrate that there was no "meeting of the minds," hence no contract barring suit.

Appellant is wrong, however, about the legal conclusion that follows from these facts. The law is clearly set forth in §20(2)(b) of the Restatement (Second) of Contracts (1981), entitled "Effect of Misunderstanding." That section says

> The manifestations of the parties are operative in accordance with the meaning attached to them by one of the parties if . . .
>
> (b) that party has no reason to know of any different meaning attached by

> the other, and the other has reason to know the meaning attached by the first party.

This case fits squarely within the Restatement's rule.

The previous discussion makes clear—as the district court found—that DMA attached to the words "this matter" the meaning "this entire discrimination controversy." Our examination of the record also makes clear to us that Perez had "reason to know the meaning attached" to those words by DMA. The size of the settlement and the lack of any good reason for DMA's settling only the state claim, at the least, put Perez on notice of what DMA intended the settlement to do. Perez's own attorney testified that her belief about what the words meant was the same as DMA's. Perez's refusal to tell even his own attorney about his receipt of a letter authorizing him to bring a federal suit—indeed his seeking legal advice about the federal claim elsewhere—makes clear that DMA had no reason to know about Perez's interpretation, and it also suggests that Perez knew in fact what DMA was likely thinking. Perez's subjective intent, under these circumstances, is beside the point. In the absence of any evidence that Perez had good reason to believe DMA intended something else, the district court, in our view, had to conclude as a matter of law that the quoted Restatement rule fits this case. And, the settlement contract must then be interpreted as DMA meant it.

There is considerable discussion, in these briefs, of various cases concerning "waiver" of rights under federal antidiscrimination statutes. Those cases do not forbid settlement of claims like this one. *See, e.g., Alexander v. Gardner-Denver Co.*, 415 U.S. 36, 52, 94 S. Ct. 1011, 1021, 39 L.Ed.2d 147 (1974) (an employee may waive Title VII claims in voluntary settlement). . . . Indeed, they speak favorably of settlements. This is a case in which plaintiff was represented by counsel. He received significant monetary compensation. As the district court repeatedly said, he entered the settlement contract voluntarily. We see no reason, under these circumstances, why, in this federal context, ordinary principles of contract law ought not to govern its interpretation.

The judgment of the district court is

Affirmed.

Post-Case Follow-Up

Having found that each party attached a different plausible meaning to the term "this matter," the court could find the parties never assented. Instead, it chose to interpret the agreement and enforce it against a party who did not intend to agree to a contract on those terms. The rule applied seeks to limit that approach to circumstances where it seems fair to insist that a party perform a contract it did not intend to make. The court suspects that Perez knew the DMA intended to settle the entire matter, which gave Perez an opportunity to clarify the ambiguity during negotiations instead of hoping a court would resolve the ambiguity more favorably. In any event, the court finds DMA's intent sufficiently apparent that Perez should have recognized it and resolved the difference during negotiations. The court refused to give Perez a contract better than the one he could have negotiated for himself if the issue had been discussed.

Perez v. State of Maine: Real Life Applications

1. In a plea bargain agreement, Mickey (a youthful offender) pled guilty to armed robbery in exchange for probation. The terms of probation included a sentence of ten years if Mickey was rearrested within one year. Mickey understood this to mean rearrested for actual misconduct, based on the court's comment that "if you get rearrested, that's a *voluntary choice* you made by *going out and doing something which you should not have been doing.* It rests *solely with you.*" Mickey was rearrested one month later, but according to five credible alibi witnesses was at home at the time of the crime. The state argues the rearrest requires sentencing on the armed robbery charge. Should Mickey's understanding of the agreement prevail?
2. Char is a member of Price Co., which operates warehouse stores at which members obtain goods at a discount. Char's membership expired in January 2015. In March 2015, Char renewed the membership for one year. In January 2016, Char received a notice from Price Co. stating that the membership had expired and needed to be renewed. Char objected that the membership should not expire until March, but was informed that any renewal within 90 days of expiration operates as a renewal from the date of expiration, not the date of the actual renewal. Should Char's understanding of the renewal term prevail? For a fuller context, consider the facts presented in *Cappalli v. BJ's Wholesale Club*, 904 F. Supp. 2d 1084 (D.R.I. 2012).
3. Desi leased land from Ohner in order to subdivide and develop the property. The lease provided that additional rent would be due on the entire parcel unless Desi completed development of the subdivided lots within five years. Desi understood that completed development required grading each subdivided lot and installing water and sewer connections, allowing building to begin. That meaning was commonly used in the local real estate market. Ohner thought completed development required a finished building on each subdivided lot. One early letter between the parties mentioned "completed construction," but later communications used the term "completed development." Within five years, all lots were developed (by Desi's understanding) and construction was completed on all but one of the lots. Construction on the last lot began after the five-year period and was completed within 18 months. After the last building was finished, Ohner sought the additional rent provided in the contract. Is Ohner entitled to the additional rent?

Private Meanings

In theory, the rules permit parties to write their contracts using a term to which they give a special meaning, different from the common understanding of this word. Their shared understanding would settle the meaning of the contract, even though any other reader would believe it referred to something entirely different. For example, parties could agree to a sale of cotton, but use the word "wool" in the contract to conceal its subject matter from others. In one sense, that should not be surprising. Parties are free to use any language they choose: French, German, Arabic, Hindi, Swahili, Chinese, Esperanto, and so on. Similarly, parties may (and often do) define terms in the contract itself. The parties' freedom to use words as they choose suggests they may assign meanings that differ from those others would understand. Problems arise only if the parties do not understand each other (or later claim they did not) or if the code is used to deceive others who read the contract. Efforts to protect a deceived third party may be useful. Yet the need to ban deception does not require banning more benign uses of codes. The risk that a party will change its mind and pretend the contract means what it says seems likely to limit the use of codes in business transactions.

The rules more commonly apply to slips of the tongue. People may misspeak when making an oral offer. For example, a person who owns both a Honda and a Nissan might offer to sell his Honda meaning to sell his Nissan. As long as the other party understands which car is offered (for example, they both point to the Nissan, even as they say Honda), it makes little sense to reject the sale of the Nissan and even less to enforce the sale of the Honda, a contract neither party intended. In circumstances such as these, subjective intent, if known, will govern interpretation.

EXHIBIT 9.1 Decision Tree for Misunderstanding

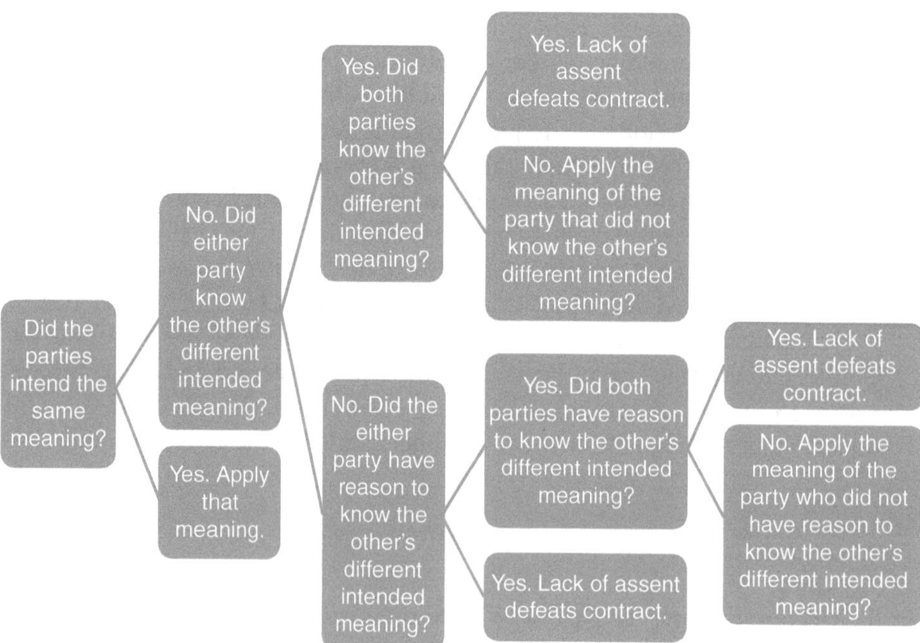

3. Sources of Meaning (Dictionaries and Beyond)

In determining what a contract means, courts resort to a number of different kinds of information. The sources remain the same regardless of whether the court sees the task as objective or subjective. This section identifies the sources most commonly used to resolve disputes. Later sections, especially on the parol evidence rule, identify limitations on some of them.

Written Contracts

The contract itself offers the most obvious and most basic source of meaning. The words the parties used are the best evidence of what they said or intended to say. At least for written contracts, courts can see the language used with relative ease.

Contracts, especially more formal business contracts, often contain definitions. The parties can define terms to inform the court and each other of exactly what those terms mean when used in the contract. Definitions may occupy a separate section of the contract or may be interspersed as important terms are used, such as using parentheticals. Either way, when parties expressly define terms, those meanings usually govern over any other possible meanings the terms might have if undefined.

Even without definitions, contract language often helps a court determine meaning. The syntax the parties use may reveal how they intended a term to be understood and applied. The way the parties used terms in context provides clues to their understanding. The next section identifies several **canons of interpretation**: rules of thumb courts sometimes use to find the meaning of contract language.

Negotiations

Sometimes the parties' negotiations will reveal what they intended the words to mean. Having discussed the meaning of the term, the parties may sign an agreement without including the meaning they discussed. Testimony about those negotiations may help a court discern what the parties intended. Even if the negotiations did not define the term, negotiations may reflect what the parties expected the contract to achieve. Armed with that knowledge, the court may find one interpretation more consistent with the parties' expressed purposes.

Negotiations are objective manifestations of intent, not subjective intent. Negotiations involve words expressed between the parties, not thoughts one of them had but kept secret from the other. Nonetheless, negotiations pose special problems for courts. Parties may say many things during negotiations, without intending all of them to be part of the agreement. Statements made in connection with one offer may not apply to later offers. Parties may remember the negotiations differently. Courts may struggle to distinguish negotiations that help understand the final agreement from negotiations that change the final agreement. Thus, courts are wary of according undue weight to negotiations, sometimes going so far as to exclude evidence of negotiations.

Dictionaries

Dictionaries offer a second-best source of definitions. They do not tell us what the parties intended, but they do tell us how most other people understand certain words. It seems likely that the parties meant terms the same way, especially where they did not offer any contrary indications in the contract. This is a presumption: the parties *probably* intended the words to mean what they usually mean.[7] Contrary evidence may overcome the presumption. Ordinarily, courts will assume the parties intended the plain meaning of the terms.

Reliance on dictionary meanings requires some caution. General dictionaries catalogue all possible meanings rather than selecting one true meaning. They might help rule out meanings so odd the dictionary omits them entirely, but even that can be hazardous. Languages change, sometimes rapidly. Dictionaries react to those changes, always falling a little behind the times. Where old words take on new meaning, the dictionary may not include them yet—but the contract might. In addition, words often have special meanings in some contexts. Technical terms, especially scientific terms, may not appear in the dictionary or may be defined in ways that differ from the way specialists use them.[8] In some businesses, terms may have special meanings understood within the trade even if not generally known. Specialized dictionaries may offer insight into the way terms are used in a particular trade or field. General dictionaries, however, rarely offer the final word on the meaning of contract terms.

Usage of Trade

Usage of trade refers to terms that, within a particular type of business, have taken on a meaning that everyone (or nearly everyone) in the trade knows.[9] The definition may not appear in the contract because everyone already knows what it means. Thus, enforcing some other meaning of the term would change the deal the parties made, perhaps in ways to which they never would have agreed if discussed during negotiations. If parties in the trade want to use a term in its usual sense outside the trade, they need to specify that particular meaning in the contract. Express contract terms, such as definitions, receive greater weight than usage of trade.[10]

Some trade usages enter the common language. Traditionally, a baker who is asked for a dozen bagels or donuts supplies 13 (a baker's dozen), not 12. Everyone in that trade knows a dozen means 13 and sets the price accordingly. If you request a dozen and get only 12, the baker may be in breach. But you will not get 13 eggs when you buy a dozen. Other trade terms are not as widely understood outside the trade. Yet within the trade, one who relies on the common definition of the term rather than the usage of trade may breach the contract. Courts will interpret contracts in accord with usage of trade once evidence establishes that usage.

[7] Restatement (Second) of Contracts §202(3).
[8] *Id.* §202(3)(b).
[9] UCC §1-303(c).
[10] UCC §1-303(e); Restatement (Second) of Contracts §203(b).

Usage of trade is difficult to establish. It requires near unanimity in the way parties in the trade use the term. If a substantial portion of members of the trade use the term differently, parties should clarify which usage they intend in negotiations, rather than assume the other means what the majority means.

Enforcing usage of trade against newcomers to the trade raises controversy. The newcomer may not understand the usage, intending the term's ordinary meaning. Occasionally, courts suggest using the ordinary meaning unless the newcomer had actual knowledge of the usage of trade or the usage was so common even outside the trade that the new entrant should have known of the usage. That approach, however, negates the intent of others in the trade when they deal with newcomers. The established members of the trade understand the usage and never intended to agree to the ordinary meaning of the term. Protecting the newcomer frustrates the other's legitimate expectations. Even if they know (or have reason to know) they are dealing with a newcomer, they may assume the newcomer prepared itself before entering the trade, learning the pertinent lingo.

Consider the problem in context. Imagine a city slicker who retires from Wall Street and buys a cattle ranch. He may not know the difference between a cow and a heifer. (Assume, for this illustration, that in the trade everyone understands cow to mean a female bovine that has produced at least one calf.) Applying usage of trade even to newcomers in effect asks the city slicker to learn the trade before donning the boots and Stetson — or at least before entering a contract to sell cows. He will need to deliver what people in the trade expected. An exception limiting usage of trade against newcomers, on the other hand, might allow him to deliver heifers to people who paid for cows. The others, who did know the usage, would need to define the term in the contract to ensure that it applied. Otherwise, a newcomer (who may or may not seem like a newcomer) might hornswoggle them.

Course of Dealing

Course of dealing refers to the way these parties' prior contracts have been interpreted by the parties themselves. When parties have used the same contract language in past dealings, courts assume that the language means the same thing in the new contract that it meant in the prior dealings. A failure to object to the performance tendered under those prior contracts suggests that the parties believed that performance satisfied the requirements of the contract.[11] If disputes develop about what the new contract requires, the uncontested performance under the earlier contract may allow the court to invoke course of dealing to hold that performance acceptable under the current contract.

Consider an example. A company frequently orders assorted sandwiches from a local deli. The deli decides what assortment to make, delivers them, and the company pays at the end of each month. The assortment usually includes a variety of lunchmeats, but the deli has delivered just turkey sandwiches in the past without objection from the company. One week, the deli delivered all roast beef. The

[11] UCC §1-303(b).

company refused the delivery, arguing that "assorted" means at least two varieties of sandwich in the assortment. While that argument makes sense on the language of the contract, the company's failure to object in the past when the assortment included only one choice suggests that "assorted," as used by these parties, does not require a variety each day.

Watch out for differences between the current contract and the prior dealings. If the parties used different contract language this time, it may reflect an effort to change the way they had been conducting their affairs. Experience on prior contracts may have less relevance, especially if it pertains to the language changed.

Course of Performance

Course of performance refers to the way parties have interpreted this contract, as inferred from their acceptance of prior conduct under the contract. Course of performance resembles course of dealing. It uses the same logic—actions help reveal what parties intended by their words—extending it to situations involving repeated performance under a single contract. Thus, a failure to object to the performance offered on the first few occasions suggests that the parties believe that performance satisfies the requirements of the contract.[12]

For example, if a contract covering a one-year period calls for monthly deliveries, the failure to object to the deliveries made in the first three months suggests that they complied with the contract requirements, as the parties understood them at the time. If subsequent shipments live up to the same standards, but are rejected, it appears that the buyer has changed its mind about what the contract requires. Course of performance suggests the contract requires no more than was accepted without objection in the earlier deliveries. Demanding more seems like an effort to change the contract rather than to enforce it.

Course of performance differs from course of dealing in significant ways. First, parties know their course of dealing (in past contracts) at the time they negotiate later contracts. Course of performance, on the other hand, will occur only after contract formation. Thus, the parties probably entered the current contract with course of dealing in their minds, but not course of performance. Course of performance, if relevant to what the parties intended, draws its relevance from the assumption that their intentions at the time of the early performances coincide with their intentions at the time of formation. That seems valid when early performance occurs shortly after formation. If circumstances change between formation and

A Trap for the Tolerant

Suppose a party lets small defects in the other's performance slide the first time or two, objecting only after the defects continue. This forgiveness may not indicate that the party believes the contract language permits that performance—yet it resembles course of performance closely enough that a court may treat it as such. Attorneys should be wary of efforts to invoke course of dealing or course of performance when a party's conduct reflects patience rather than acquiescence.

[12] *Id.* §1-303(a).

beginning performance, the intentions at performance may not coincide with the intentions at formation.

Course of performance differs from modification by conduct. Tendering performance that differs from what the contract required could constitute an offer to modify the contract to include this kind of performance. Accepting the performance without objection might accept the offer to modify. Yet in many cases efforts to find a modification will go nowhere. Performance without comment makes a rather vague proposal, perhaps too vague to expect the other party to recognize it as an offer. A stealth offer makes it harder to infer that accepting the performance included assent to modifying the contract. Even then, statutes or contract terms requiring written modifications would impede modification by performance.

Course of performance distinctly rests on the assumption that the performance reflects the meaning of the original contract, not a replacement contract. It seeks to interpret the parties' original intent under an existing contract.

4. Guidelines for Interpretation

Given so many sources of relevant evidence concerning the parties' intent, conflicting inferences can arise. The contract language may not coincide with usage of trade, which may differ from course of dealing, and so on. Deciding how to use these various sources to persuade a court to balance them in favor of your position requires skill and logic. While the arguments depend on the specifics of each case, some general guidelines can be derived from past efforts to use these sources. These guidelines sometimes are presented as rules, sometimes as rules of thumb. That is, courts may feel bound to apply some preferences, especially those established by statute, while others remain guidelines from which a judge may deviate if the context so requires.

The Entire Contract

The parties agreed to the entire contract. Courts prefer interpretations that give effect to the entire contract.[13] Presumably, parties had a reason for including each term. A court that overlooks or fails to give due significance to one term deprives a party of a benefit it negotiated to obtain. The court, by interpretation, creates a deal to which the parties did not agree (though one party may be perfectly happy with the new deal, having gotten better terms that it negotiated for itself.) Giving effect to the entire contract has several implications.

First, courts will consider all of the contract terms or contract documents. While one clause may seem to answer the interpretation issue clearly, arguments based on other components of the contract are permissible. Courts read terms in context, not in a vacuum.

---

[13]Restatement (Second) of Contracts §202(2)(b).

Courts prefer interpretations that do not create conflicts among different contract terms. If one interpretation creates a conflict between two parts of the contract, but an alternative interpretation does not create a conflict, a court is likely to adopt the second interpretation. In part, this preference seeks to comply with the parties' intent. Having negotiated both terms, they probably intended for both terms to have effect. An interpretation that forces the court to choose which of two conflicting terms will apply does not seem to honor the parties' intent. Of course, if the parties really have negotiated terms that conflict — if no plausible interpretation explains how both terms could be read in harmony — then the court cannot avoid applying one to the case at the expense of the other.

Case Preview

Random House v. Rosetta Books LLC

In this case, the court must determine how a term applies to circumstances the parties could not possibly have anticipated: a new technology (e-books) that may or may not be included within the license agreement's exclusive right to publish the works "in book form." The parties clearly had no direct intention regarding e-books decades before they were invented. But the contract does offer some clues to the scope of rights the agreement included and those reserved to the authors. The opinion exhibits several ways courts use other terms of a contract to shed light on the meaning of a critical term.

As you read *Random House v. Rosetta Books LLC*, look for the following:

1. Which terms of the contract does the court consider in ascertaining the meaning of "book form"? How do those terms help discern the right to publish e-books?
2. E-books compete with sales of physical books. How does the court address the authors' duty not to compete with the publisher's sales of the book?
3. What clues from outside the contract help the court determine which party has the right to publish e-books?

Random House v. Rosetta Books LLC

150 F. Supp. 2d 613 (S.D.N.Y. 2001), aff'd, 283 F.3d 490 (2d Cir. 2002)

STEIN, District Judge.

In this copyright infringement action, Random House, Inc. seeks to enjoin Rosetta Books LLC . . . from selling in digital format eight specific works on the grounds that the authors of the works had previously granted Random House — not Rosetta Books — the right to "print, publish and sell the work[s] in book form." Rosetta Books, on the other hand, claims . . . the licensing agreements . . . do not include a grant of digital or electronic rights. Relying on the language of the contracts and basic principles of contract interpretation, this Court finds that the right to "print, publish and sell the work[s] in book form" in the contracts at issue does not include the right to publish the works in the format that has come to be known as the "ebook." Accordingly, Random House's motion for a preliminary injunction is denied.

BACKGROUND

In the year 2000 and the beginning of 2001, Rosetta Books contracted with several authors to publish certain of their works — including *The Confessions of Nat Turner* and *Sophie's Choice* by William Styron; *Slaughterhouse-Five, Breakfast of Champions, The Sirens of Titan, Cat's Cradle,* and *Player Piano* by Kurt Vonnegut; and *Promised Land* by Robert B. Parker — in digital format over the internet. . . . Random House filed this complaint [and] moved for a preliminary injunction prohibiting Rosetta from infringing plaintiff's copyrights.

[The court described e-book technology at some length and offered details of the various agreements. The details vital to the decision are repeated in the discussion section below.]

DISCUSSION

. . .

1. Contract Interpretation of Licensing Agreements — Legal Standards

Random House claims to own the rights in question through its licensing agreements with the authors. Interpretation of an agreement purporting to grant a copyright license is a matter of state contract law. [Citations omitted.] All of the agreements state that they "shall be interpreted according to the law of the State of New York."

In New York, a written contract is to be interpreted so as to give effect to the intention of the parties as expressed in the contract's language. [Citations omitted.] The court must consider the entire contract and reconcile all parts, if possible, to avoid an inconsistency. [Citations omitted.]

. . .

[T]he U.S. Court of Appeals for the Second Circuit [has analyzed] contractual language in disputes, such as this one, "about whether licensees may exploit licensed works through new marketing channels made possible by technologies developed after the licensing contract — often called 'new use' problems." *Boosey & Hawkes Music Publishers, Ltd. v. Walt Disney Co.*, 145 F.3d 481, 486 (2d Cir. 1998). The two leading cases in this Circuit on how to determine whether "new uses" come within prior grants of rights are *Boosey* and *Bartsch v. Metro-Goldwyn-Mayer, Inc.*, 391 F.2d 150 (2d Cir. 1968), decided three decades apart.

In *Bartsch*, [a 1930 license] granted [MGM] "the motion picture rights throughout the world," including the right to "copyright, vend, license and exhibit such motion picture photoplays throughout the world; together with the further sole and exclusive rights by mechanical and/or electrical means to record, reproduce and transmit sound, including spoken words. . . ." [MGM licensed its motion picture for viewing on television in 1958.] Bartsch [claimed] television [rights] had not been given to MGM.

[T]he Second Circuit [concluded] that the words of the grant . . . "were well designed to give [MGM] the broadest rights with respect to its copyrighted property[, including] the new use — i.e. viewing on television. . . .

In *Boosey* . . . Stravinsky [in 1939] licensed Disney's use of "The Rite of Spring" in the motion picture "Fantasia." [I]n 1991, Disney released "Fantasia" in video format and Boosey [asserted] that [exceeded Disney's] rights. . . . In *Boosey*, just as in *Bartsch*, the language of the grant was broad, enabling the licensee "to record in any manner, medium or form, and to license the performance of, the musical composition [for use] in a motion picture." 145 F.3d at 484. [Again, the broad language was interpreted to include the new use.]

. . .

The Second Circuit's neutral approach was specifically influenced by policy considerations on both sides. On the one hand, the approach seeks to encourage licensees — here, the publishers — to develop new technologies that will enable all to enjoy the creative work in a new way. On the other hand, it seeks to fulfill the purpose underlying federal copyright law — to encourage authors to create literary works. [Citation omitted.]

2. Application of Legal Standards

[T]his Court finds that the most reasonable interpretation of the grant in the contracts at issue to "print, publish and sell the work in book form" does not include the right to publish the work as an ebook. At the outset, the phrase itself distinguishes between the pure content — i.e. "the work" — and the format of display — "in book form." The *Random House Webster's Unabridged Dictionary* defines a "book" as "a written or printed work of fiction or nonfiction, usually on sheets of paper fastened or bound together within covers" and defines "form" as "external appearance of a clearly defined area, as distinguished from color or material; the shape of a thing or person." *Random House Webster's Unabridged Dictionary* (2001), available in searchable form at http://www.allwords.com.

Manifestly, paragraph #1 of each contract — entitled either "grant of rights" or "exclusive publication right" — conveys certain rights from the author to the publisher. In that paragraph, separate grant language is used to convey the rights to publish book club editions, reprint editions, abridged forms, and editions in Braille. This language would not be necessary if the phrase "in book form" encompassed all types of books. That paragraph specifies exactly which rights were being granted by the author to the publisher. Indeed, many of the rights set forth in the publisher's form contracts were in fact not granted to the publisher, but rather were reserved by the authors to themselves. For example, each of the authors specifically reserved certain rights for themselves by striking out phrases, sentences, and paragraphs of the publisher's form contract. This evidences an intent by these authors not to grant the publisher the broadest rights in their works.

Random House contends that the phrase "in book form" means to faithfully reproduce the author's text in its complete form as a reading experience and that, since ebooks concededly contain the complete text of the work, Rosetta cannot also possess those rights. While Random House's definition distinguishes "book form" from other formats that require separate contractual language — such as audio books and serialization rights — it does not distinguish other formats specifically mentioned in paragraph #1 of the contracts, such as book club editions and reprint editions. Because the Court must, if possible, give effect to all contractual language in order to "safeguard against adopting an interpretation that would render any individual provision superfluous," *Sayers*, 7 F.3d at 1095, Random House's definition cannot be adopted.

Random House points specifically to the clause requiring it to "publish the work at its own expense and in such a style and manner and at such a price as [Random House] deems suitable" as support for its position. However, plaintiff takes this clause out of context. It appears in paragraph #2, captioned "Style, Price and Date of Publication," not paragraph #1, which includes all the grants of rights. In context, the phrase simply means that Random House has control over the appearance of the formats granted to Random House in the first paragraph; i.e., control over the style of the book.

Random House also cites the non-compete clauses as evidence that the authors granted it broad, exclusive rights in their work. Random House reasons that because the authors could not permit any material that would injure the sale of the work to be published without Random House's consent, the authors must have granted the right to publish ebooks to Random House. This reasoning turns the analysis on its head. First, the grant of rights follows from the grant language alone. [Citation omitted.] Second, non-compete clauses must be limited in scope in order to be enforceable in New York. [Citations omitted.] Third, even if the authors did violate this provision of their Random House agreements by contracting with Rosetta Books — a point on which this Court does not opine — the remedy is a breach of contract action against the authors, not a copyright infringement action against Rosetta Books. [Citation omitted.]

The photocopy clause — giving Random House the right to "Xerox and other forms of copying, either now in use or hereafter developed" — similarly does not bolster Random House's position. Although the clause does appear in the grant language paragraph, taken in context, it clearly refers only to new developments in xerography and other forms of photocopying. Stretching it to include new forms of publishing, such as ebooks, would make the rest of the contract superfluous because there would be no reason for authors to reserve rights to forms of publishing "now in use." This interpretation also comports with the publishing industry's trade usage of the phrase. *See, e.g.* (Fowler Decl. ¶¶12, 20, Congdon Decl. ¶27, Borchardt Decl. ¶23).[6]

---

[6]Similarly, Rosetta's argument that the contractual clause in which the authors reserve motion picture and broadcasting rights for themselves in certain contracts also means that the authors reserved the ebook rights is without merit. Such reservation clauses, unless they expressly cover the new use in question, "contribute[] nothing to the definition of the boundaries of the license." *See Boosey*, 145 F.3d at 488.

Not only does the language of the contract itself lead almost ineluctably to the conclusion that Random House does not own the right to publish the works as ebooks, but also a reasonable person "cognizant of the customs, practices, usages and terminology as generally understood in the particular trade or business," *Sayers*, 7 F.3d at 1095, would conclude that the grant language does not include ebooks. "To print, publish and sell the work in book form" is understood in the publishing industry to be a "limited" grant. *See Field v. True Comics*, 89 F. Supp. 611, 613-14 (S.D.N.Y. 1950); *see also* Melville B. Nimmer & David Nimmer, *Nimmer on Copyright*, §10.14[C] (2001) (citing *Field*).

In *Field v. True Comics*, the court held that "the sole and exclusive right to publish, print and market *in book form*"—especially when the author had specifically reserved rights for himself—was "much more limited" than "the sole and exclusive right to publish, print and market *the book*." 89 F. Supp. at 612 (emphasis added). In fact, the publishing industry generally interprets the phrase "in book form" as granting the publisher "the exclusive right to publish a hardcover trade book in English for distribution in North America." 1 *Lindey on Entertainment, Publishing and the Arts* Form 1.01-1 (2d ed. 2000) (using the Random House form contract to explain the meaning of each clause); [citations to nine witnesses omitted]. *But see* Klebanoff Dep. at 153-54 (acknowledging that the phrase, on its own, outside the context of a specific contract may include other forms of books such as book club editions, large print editions, leather bound editions, trade and mass market paperbacks); [citations to two witnesses omitted].

3. Comparison to Prior "New Use" Caselaw

The finding that the five licensing agreements at issue do not convey the right to publish the works as ebooks accords with Second Circuit and New York case law. Indeed, the two leading cases limned above that found that a particular new use was included within the grant language . . . can be distinguished from this case on four grounds.

First, the language conveying the rights in *Boosey* and *Bartsch* was far broader than here. Second, the "new use" in those cases—i.e. display of a motion picture on television or videocassette—fell squarely within the same medium as the original grant. [Language in each case suggested that television and video tapes simply show the movie the licensee was permitted to make and distribute.]

In this case, the "new use"—electronic digital signals sent over the internet—is a separate medium from the original use—printed words on paper. Random House's own expert concludes that the media are distinct because information stored digitally can be manipulated in ways that analog information cannot. Ebooks take advantage of the digital medium's ability to manipulate data by allowing ebook users to electronically search the text for specific words and phrases, change the font size and style, type notes into the text and electronically organize them, highlight and bookmark, hyperlink to specific parts of the text, and, in the future, to other sites on related topics as well, and access a dictionary that pronounces words in the ebook aloud. The need for a software program to interact with the data in order to make it usable, as well as the need for a piece of hardware to enable the reader to view the text, also distinguishes analog formats from digital formats. [Citation omitted.]

. . .

The third significant difference between the licensee in the motion picture cases cited above and the book publisher in this action is that the licensees in the motion picture cases have actually created a new work based on the material from the licensor. Therefore, the right to display that new work — whether on television or video — is derivative of the right to create that work. In the book publishing context, the publishers, although they participate in the editorial process, display the words written by the author, not themselves.

Fourth, the courts in *Boosey* and *Bartsch* were concerned that any approach to new use problems that "tilts against licensees [here, Random House] gives rise to antiprogressive incentives" insofar as licensees "would be reluctant to explore and utilize innovative technologies." [Citations omitted.] However, in this action, the policy rationale of encouraging development in new technology is at least as well served by finding that the licensors — i.e., the authors — retain these rights to their works. In the 21st century, it cannot be said that licensees such as book publishers and movie producers are ipso facto more likely to make advances in digital technology than start-up companies.

[The court distinguished two other cases, *Dolch v. Garrard Pub. Co.*, 289 F. Supp. 687 (S.D.N.Y. 1968), and *Dresser v. William Morrow & Co.*, 278 A.D. 931, 105 N.Y.S.2d 706 (1951), *aff'd*, 304 N.Y. 603, 107 N.E.2d 89 (1952).]

CONCLUSION

Employing the most important tool in the armamentarium of contract interpretation — the language of the contract itself — this Court has concluded that Random House is not the beneficial owner of the right to publish the eight works at issue as ebooks. . . .

Post-Case Follow-Up

The court found other terms of the contract that suggested the words "in book form" had a fairly narrow meaning. Most important may be the decision to list other kinds of books (book club editions, Braille books) that might fall within the meaning of "in book form" if the parties intended that phrase to have a broad meaning. Other terms raised by Random House did not avoid this central conflict. The court was able to give those terms meaning that did not contradict the narrow meaning of "in book form," while Random House never found a way to give that phrase a broad meaning without making the terms covering other kinds of books meaningless. The court also considered usage of trade and whether the incentives each reading might create comported with the goals of copyright law. In the end, the court was convinced that the grant of rights did not include e-books. Different language can produce different results. *See HarperCollins Publishers LLC v. Open Rd. Integrated Media, LLP*, 7 F. Supp. 3d 363 (S.D.N.Y. 2014).

Procedurally, this was a very limited decision. The case arose on a motion for preliminary injunction, heard near the beginning of a case before very much discovery occurs. To decide that motion, the court must predict whether the plaintiff is likely to prevail on the merits. It denied relief because Random House was unlikely to prevail. But if the case proceeds to full trial on the merits after discovery, the finder of fact at that trial could reach a different conclusion. Based on what you know so far, would you advise Random House drop the case or proceed to trial?

Random House v. Rosetta Books LLC: Real Life Applications

1. After the case, Random House seeks advice concerning how it can draft its form license agreements in a way that would avoid the court's narrow interpretation of "in book form." Obviously, it can add e-books to its form, but that will not address the next technology. Without knowing what the next invention might be, advise Random House how it might amend its forms to reduce the risk that the new technology will fall outside the license agreement. Remember, established authors often will want to retain movie rights, so your language should provide a way to omit these. (The current form includes an assignment of movie rights to Random House, which can be crossed out when the parties agree the author retains those rights.) Test your suggestions by asking whether they would have produced a different result in this case if they had been adopted before e-books were invented.

2. Manufacturer agreed to supply all of Distributor's requirements of various Products (chemicals specified in an appendix to the document) to specific Customers (listed in another appendix), sharing profits for the sales of Products to Customers under a specified formula. Distributor could cancel the agreement if its sales of Products to Customers fell below 10 percent of its total sales. Over time, the parties' course of performance included additional Products and Customers, sharing profits on those sales under the contract formula. The parties never amended the appendices in writing, as required by the contract terms. In 2016, Distributor's sales of Products to Customers fell below 10 percent of total sales, if only the listed Products and Customers are considered. If all Products and Customers added by course of performance are considered, sales remained above that threshold. Distributor wishes to cancel the contract in order to take advantage of better prices it can obtain from other sources. It seeks your advice concerning whether Products and Customers as used in the termination clause is limited to those listed in the appendices. What advice would you offer? *See Honeywell Intl. Inc. v. Air Products & Chemicals, Inc.*, 872 A.2d 944 (Del. 2005).

3. Lou, age 53, is a full professor with tenure. University policies permit disciplining a tenured professor for good cause and specify procedures for that determination. University procedures also require annual renewal of all professors, specifying that a professor's failure to accept a renewal offer from University ends the employment relationship. Tenured professors must be offered a renewal

until age 70. In 2015, University, without following any of its disciplinary procedures, determined that a book Lou published in 2005 contained substantial amounts of material plagiarized from others' work. University offered to renew Lou's contract for 2016 as an Associate Professor at a salary substantially lower than what Lou earned in 2015. Lou reluctantly accepted the offer to avoid ending the employment relationship. Lou would like to sue for breach of contract. Did University breach its contract by disciplining Lou without using appropriate procedures to determine good cause?

Resolving Internal Conflicts

Sometimes parties produce contracts that contain conflicts a court cannot avoid. In these situations, the court must decide how to handle the conflicts. Two guidelines help courts handle these situations. These guidelines share a common thread: they seek out what the parties intended at the time they entered the contract. Later, parties who know what outcome they want might say they intended something different (and may be telling the truth). The approaches below all are explained by how well they help a court discern what the parties originally intended.

Specific Terms Outweigh General Terms

Parties frame some contract terms generally, others more specifically. A specific provision may seem to deviate from the general standard created elsewhere in the contract. Nonetheless, courts usually prefer to enforce the specific provision.[14] Its inclusion suggests the parties considered how to handle the specific problem and selected this means to resolve it. The general terms reflect the parties' general attitudes, but offer less insight into how they would want the specific issue resolved. The specific term becomes a limited exception to the general term.

For example, consider a contract requirement that seller "use best efforts" to supply a retailer's requirements for tomatoes. Normally, this suggests that failure to meet those needs would not breach the contract, as long as the seller tried hard enough to make the deliveries. Suppose the contract also contained a more specific clause, such as "Failure to deliver at least 80 percent of the tomatoes requested during any given week constitutes a breach of contract that justifies retailer in canceling this contract, at its option." The specific term clarifies that best efforts are not enough, that the supplier must achieve results (at least 80 percent of the order) to satisfy the contract. Given these two inconsistent standards, the court is likely to enforce the more specific one.

The 80 percent provision does not make the best efforts clause superfluous. Delivering 80 percent will breach the contract if the seller could have delivered more by using best efforts. Seller committed to both terms and must live up to both terms.

---

[14] Restatement (Second) of Contracts §203(c).

Negotiated Terms Outweigh Standardized Terms

Many contracts start on preprinted forms. These terms, usually drafted by one party and offered to the other, represent one party's preferences, to which the other may acquiesce. Parties may make the effort to add or to change the terms of the printed form, inserting additional provisions or altering a printed term by hand. They may overlook, however, other terms of the standard form that specify a different, inconsistent approach. If courts cannot reconcile the provisions, they tend to enforce the separately negotiated terms.[15] The new terms more closely reflect the intent of the parties to this contract in this situation. The parties specifically considered them before inserting them into the contract.

Every realtor has a standard form on which it prepares offers to buy homes.
vustock/Shutterstock.com

For example, every realtor has a standard form on which it prepares offers to buy homes. The terms include one allowing the seller to keep the buyer's deposit if the buyer breaches the contract. Suppose the standard terms limit the seller to the amount of the deposit as liquidated damages. In a falling market, the seller might want to alter that term, allowing it to keep the deposit "in addition to any other remedies allowed by law." In effect, this insertion makes the deposit the minimum amount the seller can collect, not the maximum amount. Seller's counteroffer might add that term without striking or amending the original term, and buyer might accept the counteroffer. If buyer later breaches, the court may need to resolve the apparent conflict between these two provisions. If the court cannot reconcile the differences between these terms, it probably will enforce the added term. The parties appear to have preferred it over the original term in the standardized agreement.

Primacy of Express Terms

When conflicts arise among the various sources of interpretation, courts must decide which arguments are most persuasive. In this context, the express terms of a contract reign supreme. Parties are free to agree to provisions that differ from the way others in the trade handle things or the way these parties handled things in the past. If the contract clearly specifies a different approach, that interpretation supersedes usage of trade, course of dealing, and course of performance—just as a definition in the contract supersedes dictionary definitions and statements

[15]*Id.* §203(d).

during negotiations. The contract itself deserves primacy in the effort to interpret its requirements.[16]

When the contract itself does not decide the issue, courts may need to resolve conflicts among usage of trade, course of dealing, and course of performance. Two principles seem to resolve these conflicts:

1. actions speak louder than words; and
2. actions today speak louder than past actions.

In other words, usage of trade yields in the face of course of dealing or course of performance. Actions (accepting similar performance without objection) speak louder than words (what everyone in the trade means when they use the term). Perhaps as important here, the conduct of these parties speaks louder than the words of other people. These parties tendered and accepted this performance. What everyone *else* in the trade intends by the terms carries less weight than evidence of what these two parties intended.[17]

Similarly, course of performance outweighs course of dealing. What these parties did under their last contract may help a court to infer what they intended in their current contract. But what they did in their current contract offers a better reflection of their current intent. Thus, course of performance carries more weight than course of dealing, while both carry more weight than usage of trade.

Remember, however, the primary point: the contract language governs over all. What the parties agreed dominates other clues to their intent.

Usage of trade, course of dealing, and course of performance help courts infer what the parties intended, particularly when interpreting unclear contracts, those that leave doubt concerning what the parties intended. Usage of trade and course of dealing, however, do not limit the parties' ability to make other arrangements. The contract they made, not the deal others would have made in their situation, governs their obligations to one another. Course of performance poses a somewhat more difficult question. The contract itself does not preclude them from accepting performance that differs from the contract's express terms. A contract term, however, might specify that accepting nonconforming performance does not constitute a waiver of the right to insist that subsequent performances comply with the express terms of the contract — effectively rejecting course of performance as an interpretive tool. Similarly, a contract clause may be so clear in what it requires that a court lacks any justification for inferring that accepting less than was promised satisfied the contract. The nonconformity may remain a breach under the express terms, which override course of performance.

Interpretation Against a Party

Courts sometimes say that they will interpret a contract against the party responsible for drafting a term. That approach bears little relation to the purpose of

[16]UCC §1-303(e); Restatement (Second) of Contracts §203(b).
[17]UCC §1-303(e); Restatement (Second) of Contracts §203(b).

interpretation: to find the parties' shared meaning. Rather, it purports to prefer one of the parties' meaning to another without asking which interpretation might make more sense under the circumstances. In some cases, the tool serves as a useful form of consumer protection.

In one form, the rule merely breaks ties. If every other effort to interpret a clause fails, a court needing to resolve the case might employ this rule. In that role, it seems less an interpretation and more a sanction. Having failed to identify a better justification for determining the meaning of a term, the court places the responsibility for the ambiguity on the drafting party. Assigning the risk of ambiguity to the drafter, the court decides the issue in favor of the other party. In some ways, this resembles interpretation against a party that knew or should have known the other party intended a different meaning. In effect, the drafter is treated as better able to foresee the possible ambiguity and to eliminate it.

Blaming the drafter, while apt in some cases, may apply even if the drafter had no way to anticipate that the term would be unclear. Parties may not be able to foresee all the problems that they will encounter or the ways that the language might not apply as clearly as they believe. Even if foreseeable, drafting terms that specifically resolve every potential problem may be wasteful, especially as the likelihood of the problems discussed diminishes. In addition, aside from adhesion contracts, either party could have suggested clearer language. Blaming the drafter has the effect of resolving the case, but does not really interpret the contract and may not reflect fault.

In some cases courts invoke the rule against a powerful party (say, an insurer) that drafted terms disadvantageous to a much weaker party (say, an insured individual). One-sided terms might justify invocation of unconscionability or public policy. Before these doctrines matured, courts used interpretation against the drafter to avoid the harsh results a term might have created. Using interpretation as a tool for substantive review of contract terms remains with us, despite the advent of state insurance regulators that have the power to approve or to disapprove policy terms that take unfair advantage of the public. In this context, insurers face thousands of claims a year, giving them a better sense of a term's lack of clarity. Their ability to improve the language clearly surpasses that of an individual insured. Courts invoke the rule as a first resort in insurance cases. Courts use it occasionally in other cases involving form contracts.

Interpretation against the drafter should not displace efforts to determine the meaning the parties intended. When possible, use other tools of interpretation to offer a court reasons to interpret the term in favor of your client. Relying on this maxim instead of careful interpretation will prove risky if the court feels it can resolve the ambiguity by other means.

Presumption of Legality

Courts prefer an interpretation under which the contract does not require either party to violate the law or other public policies. Unless the contract language clearly requires illegal conduct, the court will reject that interpretation in favor of an alternative that does not require illegal conduct.[18]

[18] Restatement (Second) of Contracts §203(a).

A legal interpretation probably reflects the parties' intentions. Ordinarily, people do not intentionally agree to things that the law prohibits. If parties were aware of the law at the time they negotiated the contract, they probably intended the benign interpretation, not the illegal one.

Parties unaware of a legal prohibition might intend a meaning that violates the law. If so, the presumption of legality will not honor their actual intent. The presumption might honor their constructive intent: what they would have intended if they had known about the law. That is, they might have entered the same deal, without the offending clause (or with the offending clause rewritten in order to comply with the law). That is not inevitable. If aware of the law, the parties might have preferred to cancel the entire deal rather than to enter it without the illegal clause. If so, the illegal interpretation may be preferable. First, it will match the parties' intent. Second, it will avoid enforcement of a contract that the parties would not have made. (When the court interprets the clause to be illegal, it may void the entire contract on the ground that it violates public policy.) On the whole, courts prefer not to go down this path. They simply enforce the contract, interpreting the offending clause in a manner consistent with the law.

Some cases refer to government regulations that do not make a contract illegal. Similar to usage of trade, the way government agencies use a term may help a court decide how the parties used the term. This inference is perilous. It seems to assume that the parties knew how the government used a term and approved of that usage. Parties are free to incorporate government regulations into the contract by reference. Sometimes courts find such an incorporation, either express or implied. For example, in the *Frigaliment* case below, notice how the court considers treating a contract reference to Department of Agriculture (DOA) health regulations on chickens as incorporating the DOA definition of chicken into the contract.

Case Preview

Frigaliment Importing Co. v. B.N.S. International Sales Corp.

The parties here disagreed fundamentally about the meaning of a fairly simple word: chicken. Buyer needed young chickens to fulfill its commitments to customers in Europe. But seller believed buyer wanted older chickens and agreed to a price on that basis. The court works through several of the techniques discussed above to resolve the issue. The case is justly famous as an example of judicial interpretation of contracts.

As you read *Frigaliment Importing Co. v. B.N.S. International Sales Corp.*, look for the following:

1. Which of the techniques discussed above did the court address? Which did it omit?
2. On which arguments did the court rely most heavily in resolving the meaning of the contract?
3. What role did government regulations play in interpreting the contract?

Frigaliment Importing Co. v. B.N.S. International Sales Corp.

190 F. Supp. 116 (S.D.N.Y. 1960)

FRIENDLY, Circuit Judge.

The issue is, what is chicken? Plaintiff says "chicken" means a young chicken, suitable for broiling and frying. Defendant says "chicken" means any bird of that genus that meets contract specifications on weight and quality, including what it calls "stewing chicken" and plaintiff pejoratively terms "fowl." Dictionaries give both meanings, as well as some others not relevant here. To support its, plaintiff sends a number of volleys over the net; defendant essays to return them and adds a few serves of its own. Assuming that both parties were acting in good faith, the case nicely illustrates Holmes' remark "that the making of a contract depends not on the agreement of two minds in one intention, but on the agreement of two sets of external signs — not on the parties' having meant the same thing but on their having said the same thing." The Path of the Law, in Collected Legal Papers, p. 178. I have concluded that plaintiff has not sustained its burden of persuasion that the contract used "chicken" in the narrower sense.

The action is for breach of the warranty that goods sold shall correspond to the description [citation omitted]. Two contracts are in suit. In the first, dated May 2, 1957, defendant, a New York sales corporation, confirmed the sale to plaintiff, a Swiss corporation, of

> "US Fresh Frozen Chicken, Grade A, Government Inspected, Eviscerated 2 1/2-3 lbs. and 1 1/2-2 lbs. each all chicken individually wrapped in cryovac, packed in secured fiber cartons or wooden boxes, suitable for export
>
> 75,000 lbs. 2 1/2-3 lbs........ @$33.00
>
> 25,000 lbs. 1 1/2-2 lbs........@$36.50
>
> per 100 lbs. FAS New York
>
> scheduled May 10, 1957 pursuant to instructions from Penson & Co., New York." [Footnote omitted.]

The second contract, also dated May 2, 1957, was identical save that only 50,000 lbs. of the heavier "chicken" were called for, the price of the smaller birds was $37 per 100 lbs., and shipment was scheduled for May 30. The initial shipment under the first contract was short but the balance was shipped on May 17. When the initial shipment arrived in Switzerland, plaintiff found, on May 28, that the 2 1/2-3 lbs. birds were not young chicken suitable for broiling and frying but stewing chicken or "fowl"; indeed, many of the cartons and bags plainly so indicated. Protests ensued. Nevertheless, shipment under the second contract was made on May 29, the 2 1/2-3 lbs. birds again being stewing chicken. Defendant stopped the transportation of these at Rotterdam.

This action followed. . . .

Since the word "chicken" standing alone is ambiguous, I turn first to see whether the contract itself offers any aid to its interpretation. Plaintiff says the 1 1/2-2 lbs. birds necessarily had to be young chicken since the older birds do not come in that size, hence the 2 1/2-3 lbs. birds must likewise be young. This is unpersuasive — a

what does the word chicken mean?

contract for "apples" of two different sizes could be filled with different kinds of apples even though only one species came in both sizes. Defendant notes that the contract called not simply for chicken but for "US Fresh Frozen Chicken, Grade A, Government Inspected." It says the contract thereby incorporated by reference the Department of Agriculture's regulations, which favor its interpretation; I shall return to this after reviewing plaintiff's other contentions.

The first hinges on an exchange of cablegrams which preceded execution of the formal contracts. The negotiations leading up to the contracts were conducted in New York between defendant's secretary, Ernest R. Bauer, and a Mr. Stovicek, who was in New York for the Czechoslovak government at the World Trade Fair. A few days after meeting Bauer at the fair, Stovicek telephoned and inquired whether defendant would be interested in exporting poultry to Switzerland. Bauer then met with Stovicek, who showed him a cable from plaintiff dated April 26, 1957, announcing that they "are buyer" of 25,000 lbs. of chicken 2 1/2-3 lbs. weight, Cryovac packed, grade A Government inspected, at a price up to 33¢ per pound, for shipment on May 10, to be confirmed by the following morning, and were interested in further offerings. After testing the market for price, Bauer accepted, and Stovicek sent a confirmation that evening. Plaintiff stresses that, although these and subsequent cables between plaintiff and defendant, which laid the basis for the additional quantities under the first and for all of the second contract, were predominantly in German, they used the English word "chicken"; it claims this was done because it understood "chicken" meant young chicken whereas the German word, "Huhn," included both "Brathuhn" (broilers) and "Suppenhuhn" (stewing chicken), and that defendant, whose officers were thoroughly conversant with German, should have realized this. Whatever force this argument might otherwise have is largely drained away by Bauer's testimony that he asked Stovicek what kind of chickens were wanted, received the answer "any kind of chickens," and then, in German, asked whether the cable meant "Huhn" and received an affirmative response. Plaintiff attacks this as contrary to what Bauer testified on his deposition in March, 1959, and also on the ground that Stovicek had no authority to interpret the meaning of the cable. The first contention would be persuasive if sustained by the record, since Bauer was free at the trial from the threat of contradiction by Stovicek as he was not at the time of the deposition; however, review of the deposition does not convince me of the claimed inconsistency. As to the second contention, it may well be that Stovicek lacked authority to commit plaintiff for prices or delivery dates other than those specified in the cable; but plaintiff cannot at the same time rely on its cable to Stovicek as its dictionary to the meaning of the contract and repudiate the interpretation given the dictionary by the man in whose hands it was put. [Citations omitted.] Plaintiff's reliance on the fact that the contract forms contain the words "through the intermediary of: _____," with the blank not filled, as negating agency, is wholly unpersuasive; the purpose of this clause was to permit filling in the name of an intermediary to whom a commission would be payable, not to blot out what had been the fact.

Plaintiff's next contention is that there was a definite trade usage that "chicken" meant "young chicken." Defendant showed that it was only beginning in the poultry trade in 1957, thereby bringing itself within the principle that "when one of the parties is not a member of the trade or other circle, his acceptance of the standard must be made to appear" by proving either that he had actual knowledge of the usage or that the usage is "so generally known in the community that his actual individual knowledge of it may be inferred." 9 Wigmore, Evidence (3d ed. §1940) 2464. Here there was no proof of actual knowledge of the alleged usage; indeed, it is quite plain that defendant's belief was to the contrary. In order to meet the alternative requirement, the law of New York demands a showing that "the usage is of so long continuance, so well established, so notorious, so universal and so reasonable in itself, as that the presumption is violent that the parties contracted with reference to it, and made it a part of their agreement." *Walls v. Bailey*, 1872, 49 N.Y. 464, 472-473.

Plaintiff endeavored to establish such a usage by the testimony of three witnesses and certain other evidence. Strasser, resident buyer in New York for a large chain of Swiss cooperatives, testified that "on chicken I would definitely understand a broiler." However, the force of this testimony was considerably weakened by the fact that in his own transactions the witness, a careful businessman, protected himself by using "broiler" when that was what he wanted and "fowl" when he wished older birds. . . . [A] witness' consistent failure to rely on the alleged usage deprives his opinion testimony of much of its effect. Niesielowski, an officer of one of the companies that had furnished the stewing chicken to defendant, testified that "chicken" meant "the male species of the poultry industry. That could be a broiler, a fryer or a roaster," but not a stewing chicken; however, he also testified that upon receiving defendant's inquiry for "chickens," he asked whether the desire was for "fowl or frying chickens" and, in fact, supplied fowl, although taking the precaution of asking defendant, a day or two after plaintiff's acceptance of the contracts in suit, to change its confirmation of its order from "chickens," as defendant had originally prepared it, to "stewing chickens." Dates, an employee of Urner-Barry Company, which publishes a daily market report on the poultry trade, gave it as his view that the trade meaning of "chicken" was "broilers and fryers." In addition to this opinion testimony, plaintiff relied on the fact that the Urner-Barry service, the Journal of Commerce, and Weinberg Bros. & Co. of Chicago, a large supplier of poultry, published quotations in a manner which, in one way or another, distinguish between "chicken," comprising broilers, fryers and certain other categories, and "fowl," which, Bauer acknowledged, included stewing chickens. This material would be impressive if there were nothing to the contrary. However, there was, as will now be seen.

Defendant's witness Weininger, who operates a chicken eviscerating plant in New Jersey, testified "Chicken is everything except a goose, a duck, and a turkey. Everything is a chicken, but then you have to say, you have to specify which category you want or that you are talking about." Its witness Fox said that in the trade "chicken" would encompass all the various classifications. Sadina, who conducts a food inspection service, testified that he would consider any bird coming within the classes of "chicken" in the Department of Agriculture's regulations to be a chicken. The specifications approved by the General Services Administration include fowl as well as broilers and fryers under the classification "chickens." Statistics of the Institute of American Poultry Industries use the phrases "Young chickens" and "Mature chickens," under the general heading "Total chickens." and the Department of Agriculture's daily and weekly price reports avoid use of the word "chicken" without specification.

Defendant advances several other points which it claims affirmatively support its construction. Primary among these is the regulation of the Department of

Agriculture, 7 C.F.R. §70.300-70.370, entitled, "Grading and Inspection of Poultry and Edible Products Thereof." and in particular 70.301 which recited:

"Chickens. The following are the various classes of chickens:
(a) Broiler or fryer . . .
(b) Roaster . . .
(c) Capon . . .
(d) Stag . . .
(e) Hen or stewing chicken or fowl . . .
(f) Cock or old rooster . . .

Defendant argues, as previously noted, that the contract incorporated these regulations by reference. Plaintiff answers that the contract provision related simply to grade and Government inspection and did not incorporate the Government definition of "chicken," and also that the definition in the Regulations is ignored in the trade. However, the latter contention was contradicted by Weininger and Sadina; and there is force in defendant's argument that the contract made the regulations a dictionary, particularly since the reference to Government grading was already in plaintiff's initial cable to Stovicek.

Defendant makes a further argument based on the impossibility of its obtaining broilers and fryers at the 33¢ price offered by plaintiff for the 2 1/2-3 lbs. birds. There is no substantial dispute that, in late April, 1957, the price for 2 1/2-3 lbs. broilers was between 35 and 37¢ per pound, and that when defendant entered into the contracts, it was well aware of this and intended to fill them by supplying fowl in these weights. It claims that plaintiff must likewise have known the market since plaintiff had reserved shipping space on April 23, three days before plaintiff's cable to Stovicek, or, at least, that Stovicek was chargeable with such knowledge. It is scarcely an answer to say, as plaintiff does in its brief, that the 33¢ price offered by the 2 1/2-3 lbs. "chickens" was closer to the prevailing 35¢ price for broilers than to the 30¢ at which defendant procured fowl. Plaintiff must have expected defendant to make some profit—certainly it could not have expected defendant deliberately to incur a loss.

Finally, defendant relies on conduct by the plaintiff after the first shipment had been received. On May 28 plaintiff sent two cables complaining that the larger birds in the first shipment constituted "fowl." Defendant answered with a cable refusing to recognize plaintiff's objection and announcing "We have today ready for shipment 50,000 lbs. chicken 2 1/2-3 lbs. 25,000 lbs. broilers 1 1/2-2 lbs.," these being the goods procured for shipment under the second contract, and asked immediate answer "whether we are to ship this merchandise to you and whether you will accept the merchandise." After several other cable exchanges, plaintiff replied on May 29 "Confirm again that merchandise is to be shipped since resold by us if not enough pursuant to contract chickens are shipped the missing quantity is to be shipped within ten days stop we resold to our customers pursuant to your contract chickens grade A you have to deliver us said merchandise we again state that we shall make you fully responsible for all resulting costs."[2] Defendant argues that if plaintiff was sincere in thinking it was entitled to young chickens, plaintiff would not have allowed the shipment under

[2]These cables were in German; "chicken," "broilers" and, on some occasions, "fowl," were in English.

the second contract to go forward, since the distinction between broilers and chickens drawn in defendant's cablegram must have made it clear that the larger birds would not be broilers. However, plaintiff answers that the cables show plaintiff was insisting on delivery of young chickens and that defendant shipped old ones at its peril. Defendant's point would be highly relevant on another disputed issue — whether if liability were established, the measure of damages should be the difference in market value of broilers and stewing chicken in New York or the larger difference in Europe, but I cannot give it weight on the issue of interpretation. Defendant points out also that plaintiff proceeded to deliver some of the larger birds in Europe, describing them as "poulets"; defendant argues that it was only when plaintiff's customers complained about this that plaintiff developed the idea that "chicken" meant "young chicken." There is little force in this in view of plaintiff's immediate and consistent protests.

When all the evidence is reviewed, it is clear that defendant believed it could comply with the contracts by delivering stewing chicken in the 2 1/2-3 lbs. size. Defendant's subjective intent would not be significant if this did not coincide with an objective meaning of "chicken." Here it did coincide with one of the dictionary meanings, with the definition in the Department of Agriculture Regulations to which the contract made at least oblique reference, with at least some usage in the trade, with the realities of the market, and with what plaintiff's spokesman had said. Plaintiff asserts it to be equally plain that plaintiff's own subjective intent was to obtain broilers and fryers; the only evidence against this is the material as to market prices and this may not have been sufficiently brought home. In any event it is unnecessary to determine that issue. For plaintiff has the burden of showing that "chicken" was used in the narrower rather than in the broader sense, and this it has not sustained.

This opinion constitutes the Court's findings of fact and conclusions of law. Judgment shall be entered dismissing the complaint with costs.

Post-Case Follow-Up

The court here never really resolved the meaning of the term. Instead, it merely held that plaintiff had failed to prove that the word had a narrow meaning, which the plaintiff needed to do in order to show a breach. This result may have been a tactful way to describe the shortcomings in plaintiff's evidence. The court arguably could have held that the parties never agreed at all, due to misunderstanding, but neither party sought this result. Buyer wanted damages and seller wanted the price; neither wanted the contract rescinded.

Frigaliment Importing Co. v. B.N.S. International Sales Corp.: Real Life Applications

1. Consider several variations on *Frigaliment*. Would the outcome be different?
   a. Should buyer have argued that the two meanings were so different that the parties never agreed at all? How would seller respond to that argument? Would rescission be preferable to this result?

b. If seller had been in the poultry trade for a longer period of time, would the court have resolved the usage of trade argument differently?
c. What if the court considered the possibility that a new seller might have priced the contract as a loss leader: a bid low enough to get business so that it could establish a track record that would encourage others to provide it business and generate repeat business from this buyer?

2. From 1996 to 1998, Plaintiff purchased small trout from Defendant (a hatchery) and sold them back to the hatchery when they were "market size." In 1998, the parties entered a formal six-year contract. From 1996 until 2001, Defendant accepted fish that were about one pound because that is what the market demanded. In 2001, market demand shifted, requiring larger fish. Raising larger fish took longer, slowing purchases and overcrowding plaintiff's facilities. Plaintiff sued, arguing that market size meant about one pound. Defendant argued that market size varied depending on what its customers demanded. What arguments would you raise for Plaintiff? How would you support them? For additional details, see *Griffith v. Clear Lakes Trout Co., Inc.*, 143 Idaho 733, 152 P.3d 604 (Idaho 2007).

3. Plaintiff, a sandwich shop, leased space in the food court of a mall. The lease granted Plaintiff the exclusive right to sell "sandwiches" in the mall; the mall promised not to lease space to any other provider of sandwiches. After two years, the mall leased space to a taco shop. Plaintiff sued the mall owners, arguing that tacos, burritos, and quesadillas are sandwiches: a filling wrapped in bread. How should a court resolve the issue? What arguments will be most persuasive? Would the arguments differ if the new lessee sold wraps instead of tacos? What about gyros, falafels, and other Greek or Lebanese foods in a pita?

EXHIBIT 9.2 Guidelines in Interpretation

- Consider the entire contract and all the facts and circumstances
- When possible, consider the parties' principal purpose
- Prefer the generally prevailing meaning of a term
- But within a technical field, prefer the technical meaning of a term
- Prefer an interpretation in which the parties' manifestations are consistent with one another
- Prefer an interpretation in which performance is lawful
- Prefer an interpretation in which performance is reasonable
- Prefer an interpretation in which each term has some effect
- Prefer specific terms over general language
- Prefer negotiated terms over form terms
- Prefer express terms over inferences from conduct or usage of trade
- Prefer inferences from conduct over usage of trade
- Prefer inferences from conduct under this contract over inferences from prior contracts
- When in equipoise between two reasonable interpretations, prefer the meaning attached by the party that did not draft the contract

B. PAROL EVIDENCE

Parol evidence literally means oral evidence, but may include any **extrinsic evidence**: that is, any evidence, written or oral, other than the contract documents themselves. Where the contract is oral, the only evidence of its terms comes from testimony, primarily from those present at contract formation. A written contract, however, can speak for itself, without supplementation by oral testimony. The rules discussed above establish that the terms expressed in the parties' writing provide the best evidence of the bargain the parties made. In some cases, parties may prefer that the court treat the writing as the only evidence of that bargain or, more realistically, limit severely recourse to materials outside the contract itself.

The **parol evidence rule** makes evidence of prior or contemporaneous agreements or negotiations inadmissible to vary or to contradict (or, in some cases, to supplement) the promises recorded in **integrated agreements**: those that the parties adopt as the final expression of their agreement (or part of their agreement). The rule embodies several limitations on efforts to exclude extrinsic evidence.

1. The parol evidence rule applies only to integrated writings. It will not apply to more casual or unintegrated writings.
2. The rule precludes admission of prior or contemporaneous agreements or negotiations, but not of subsequent communications or events.
3. The rule precludes admission for some, but not all, purposes. Extrinsic evidence cannot be introduced to contradict the terms of a written agreement. The rule does not preclude admitting extrinsic evidence for other purposes, such as to establish a defense to enforcement of the agreement.
4. Some things outside the written contract documents are not treated as extrinsic evidence (for example, dictionaries).

The parol evidence rule primarily limits the promises a court will enforce to those recorded in a writing. Parties take time to create detailed writings in large part to protect against claims that the agreement included other or different promises. A party who complies with all the requirements of a written agreement expects that performance to satisfy the contract obligations. If, however, the other party could introduce extrinsic evidence of promises different from or additional to those recorded in the writing, a court could find a breach despite complete compliance with the written terms. The parol evidence rule limits the ability to introduce that evidence, helping to preserve the value and integrity of written agreements. The limitations on its scope seek to avoid the mischief a party could do by making commitments during negotiations, but keeping them out of the final writing. As

Parol Evidence and Statutes of Frauds

The parol evidence rule exists independently of statutes of frauds. The statute of frauds requires evidence of certain contracts by a signed writing. It does not require the agreement itself to be in writing, let alone that the writing be made the parties' final expression of the agreement. A writing that is not integrated may satisfy the statute of frauds. On the flip side, parties may create an integrated writing even if the statute of frauds would not require any writing at all.

limited, the rule strikes an uneasy balance between protecting people from those who invent promises that never were made and those who make promises but do not record and later try to deny them.

1. Integration

The parol evidence rule applies if and only if the parties created an integrated writing. Not every writing is integrated. For instance, a letter offering you a job with a law firm may be a contract (once you accept it, perhaps by signing and returning a copy). It mentions some terms, such as start date, salary, maybe a job description (assignment to a department), maybe an end date (for a summer job). The parties, however, probably do not expect the letter to be the final expression of their agreement. The firm may expect you to sign a written contract when you show up for work. It probably has an employment manual full of additional terms it expects to govern your employment relationship. The letter is a contract, but it may not be an integrated writing.

Often a writing will contain an integration clause or **merger clause** (merging all prior discussions into the writing), stating that the parties intend the writing to be integrated. Courts may ignore integration clauses in contracts of adhesion, where the clause may not reflect the intent of both parties. But even in form contracts, courts often treat an integration clause as conclusive evidence that the parties intended their writing to express their final agreement. Without an integration clause, the completeness and specificity of the writing may imply that the parties intended it as their final expression. Writings that lack these qualities typically are not treated as integrated agreements. Courts may not treat writings as integrated even if they seem complete and specific, if other evidence demonstrates that the parties did not intend integration.

Parties may integrate an agreement with relatively few terms, but probably need to do so expressly. Parties also may integrate several writings into a single agreement. For instance, that letter from a law firm might incorporate by reference the employment manual, stating that the letter and the manual, together, are the complete agreement between you. The letter remains skeletal, but the two writings together form an integrated writing.

In essence, the requirement of an integration allows parties to opt into the parol evidence rule. Courts do not impose it upon unwilling parties. Parties elect it for themselves by creating an integrated writing. Having decided to create a document that embodies their final agreement, the parties empower the courts to give that decision its natural effect, limiting the parties' promises to those expressed in the writing.

Courts recognize two degrees of integration. A writing is **partially integrated** if it states the parties' final expression as to the terms that it contains, even if it is not necessarily the parties' exclusive agreement concerning their relationship. Partial integration allows parties to enter side agreements separate from the main agreement. A writing is **completely integrated** if it provides the parties' final and exclusive agreement. An integration clause may indicate whether the agreement is the parties' exclusive agreement. In addition, the completeness and specificity of the agreement may reflect complete integration of their agreement. When one party claims that a second agreement included additional terms, courts may examine whether the parties credibly intended to enter two agreements rather than recording the entire agreement in a single document.

The degree of integration affects the purposes for which courts will admit evidence. The rule excludes evidence that would contradict the terms of any integrated writing, whether completely or partially integrated. For completely integrated writings, courts also exclude evidence of additional promises, even if the additional terms do not contradict the writing, but merely supplement it. That differs from partially integrated writings, where the rule does not preclude evidence to supplement the terms, as long as the additional terms do not contradict terms in the writing. For example, in *Brown v. Oliver*,[19] the parties entered a written agreement that mentioned the sale of land and a hotel, but made no mention of the furniture or other **chattels** (personal property, things not attached to the land) inside the hotel. Evidence that the sale included the furniture might not contradict any term of the writing. Finding a partially integrated writing, the court admitted evidence to show that the parties intended to include the furniture in the deal. If the writing had been completely integrated, the rule would have forbidden admitting that evidence. A completely integrated agreement excludes the possibility of additional terms not included in the writing.

Consider the integration clause from the American League Standard Baseball Player's contract shown in Exhibit 9.3. Notice the following:

1. It is not labeled "merger clause" or "integration clause." Scanning the titles of each section of the contract will not reveal the integration clause.
2. The integration includes several writings, all of which are part of the integrated agreement.
3. The clause creates a complete integration; it includes "all understandings between them."
4. The provision also limits modifications. That isn't necessary for integration, but the two often go together. Parties concerned about prior oral promises also worry about allegations of subsequent changes, especially if agreed orally. A rule of recognition limits their ability to modify the terms. Agreements often require a writing signed by both parties to modify a written contract. Specifying exactly who has authority to sign them is less common; requiring the authority to be recorded with another body (the Commissioner) still less common.

[19] 256 P. 1008 (Kan. 1927).

EXHIBIT 9.3 American League Standard Baseball Player's Contract Clause

Supplemental Agreements

The Club and the Player covenant that this contract, the Basic Agreement and the Agreement Re Major League Baseball Players Benefit Plan effective April 1, 1996 and applicable supplements thereto fully set forth all understandings and agreements between them, and agree that no other understanding or agreements, whether heretofore or hereafter made, shall be valid, recognizable, or of any effect whatsoever, unless expressly set forth in a new or supplemental contract executed by the Player and the Club (acting by its President or such other officer as shall have been thereunto duly authorized by the President or Board of Directors as evidenced by a certificate filed of record with the League President and Commissioner) and complying with the Major League Rules.

The court determines integration as a matter of law, usually outside the hearing of the jury. In deciding whether a writing is or is not integrated — and whether it is completely or partially integrated — many courts consider extrinsic evidence, such as the parties' testimony concerning their intent to create an integrated writing. Some courts, however, refuse to consider extrinsic evidence introduced to show that the agreement was not integrated, especially if the writing contains a clear integration clause. If the court concludes that the writing is integrated, it will exclude some evidence or limit the purposes for which it may be introduced to the jury. If, however, the writing is not integrated, the parol evidence rule will not limit parties' efforts to introduce extrinsic evidence. Concluding that the parol evidence rule will not preclude admission does not necessarily mean that the evidence is admissible. Many other rules might limit its admissibility, such as relevance, hearsay, and so on, that you will learn about in your upper level Evidence classes.

2. Prior and Contemporaneous Communications

The parol evidence rule precludes admission of prior or contemporaneous communications. Usually, this refers to negotiations or agreements made leading up to the creation of the integrated writing or at the time of contract signing. The parol evidence rule starts from a simple inference: if the parties intended to include a promise in their agreement, then they would have included it in their writing. That inference applies only when the writing is the parties' final expression — and even then only if it is reasonably complete. In addition, it applies to those promises made at or before the time the contract was formed. The parties cannot include in their writing promises that they will make later, after signing the writing. Thus, extrinsic evidence of modifications to the contract or other subsequent negotiations or agreements never violates the parol evidence rule. For this reason, the rule does not exclude evidence of course of performance, which occurs after contract formation.

Testimony about prior negotiations is more susceptible to distortion than most kinds of evidence. Negotiations may have occurred without anyone present except the parties, reducing the evidence to a classic "he said, she said" dispute.

Exaggeration and outright falsification are only one concern. Psychological forces, such as selective perception, selective retention, and cognitive dissonance, may distort memories, producing testimony that is inaccurate, but completely sincere. Credibility judgments by the jury may be unreliable in that setting. Parties may choose to face these difficulties by not integrating the agreement. Integrating the agreement reflects a choice to reduce these problems by excluding negotiations from the mix of evidence admitted, if the party seeks to contradict or, if completely integrated, to supplement the written agreement.

3. Permissible Purposes

The parol evidence rule excludes extrinsic evidence offered to contradict (and sometimes to supplement) an integrated writing. The same evidence might be admitted if offered for other purposes. Permissible purposes include:

1. to prove whether the writing is integrated;
2. to prove whether a writing is partially or completely integrated;
3. to prove the meaning of a term in the writing, at least if the term is ambiguous;
4. to establish a contract defense, such as illegality, fraud, duress, mistake, or lack of consideration; or
5. to establish or rebut entitlement to a remedy such as rescission, reformation, or specific performance.[20]

While some items on the list seem too obvious to require discussion, the debate surrounding the parol evidence rule sometimes produces unexpected results.

Parol evidence can help establish whether the parties intended the agreement to be integrated. That is particularly true if the agreement does not include an express integration clause. When a writing does include an express integration clause, introducing parol evidence to rebut integration is, in effect, using extrinsic evidence to vary or contradict the writing—the very thing the integration clause is intended to prevent. And it may be the first step in a larger effort: first, negate the written integration clause; then, introduce extrinsic evidence of other promises not included in the writing. Permitting this deprives parties of the benefit of the integration clause, even though they sincerely wanted integration and may have bargained away other benefits to obtain an integration clause. Some courts refuse to take that first step. They take an integration clause as conclusive evidence of integration, without allowing recourse to extrinsic evidence that would contradict it.

Despite this reasoning, many courts consider extrinsic evidence in evaluating whether a writing is integrated and the degree of integration. The parol evidence rule applies to integrated agreements. Logically, courts must determine integration before they can exclude extrinsic evidence. Excluding extrinsic evidence while evaluating integration extends the rule, effectively presuming that the writing is

[20]Restatement (Second) of Contracts §214.

integrated unless a party can prove it is not—and at the same time impairing any effort to prove it is not integrated. The Restatement (Second) of Contracts finds more support for the admissibility of extrinsic evidence in evaluating integration.

Three other permitted uses require additional discussion. Allegations of fraud may completely negate the effect of an integration clause. Yet courts prefer not to let fraudfeasors use an integration clause to conceal their fraud. The next subsection addresses the interrelationship between misrepresentations and parol evidence.

Introducing extrinsic evidence to show the meaning of a term in the writing might allow a party to contradict a term in the guise of interpreting that term. That end run around the parol evidence rule could undermine the protection it seeks to provide. Subsection 5 below addresses the parol evidence rule in the context of interpretation.

In addition, parties sometimes realize that their writings inaccurately recorded the agreement—a **mistake of integration**. Once a party recognizes the mistake, she may seek **reformation**, an action that requests the court to correct the writing to reflect the parties' actual agreement. The entire point is to change the terms recorded in the writing, by definition contradicting the terms originally included there. The very existence of reformation diverges from the purposes of the parol evidence rule, as discussed in section C below.

Case Preview

Myskina v. Condé Nast Publications, Inc.

This case involves a classic example of how the parol evidence rule arises. Condé Nast obtained permission to take photos allegedly based on oral reassurance that it would publish only a few of them. The release signed by the plaintiff, however, allowed much broader publication rights. When additional photographs were published, the court needed to decide whether to allow evidence of the prior assurances or to take the release on its face. The case illustrates the difficulties that the parol evidence rule can create and solve.

Tennis player Anastasia Myskina, plaintiff in the case
Robyn Wilson/Shutterstock.com

As you read *Myskina v. Condé Nast Publications*, look for the following:

1. What steps did the court take in considering whether the parol evidence rule precluded evidence of the prior agreement?
2. How did the court conclude that the release was an integrated writing? Were you persuaded?

Myskina v. Condé Nast Publications, Inc.

386 F. Supp. 2d 409 (S.D.N.Y. 2005)

MUKASEY, District Judge.

In this diversity action, plaintiff Anastasia Myskina sues defendants Condé Nast Publications, Inc. ("Condé Nast") and its magazine Gentleman's Quarterly ("GQ"), Mark Seliger, and Mark Seliger Studio for violations of Sections 50 and 51 of New York Civil Rights Law, misappropriation, unjust enrichment, negligence, and breach of contract. [Footnotes omitted.] The claims arise out of the alleged unauthorized dissemination of photographs taken of Myskina by defendants in connection with the October 2002 "Sports" issue of GQ, and publication of these photographs in the July/August 2004 issue of the Russian magazine Medved. Defendants move . . . for summary judgment. . . . For the reasons set forth below, defendants' motion is granted.

I.

Myskina, a Russian citizen, is the 2004 French Open champion. . . . She was 20 years old at the time that the photographs at issue were taken. Condé Nast [publishes] GQ. . . . Seliger . . . is a professional photographer. . . .

In July 2002, Condé Nast editor Beth Altschull contacted International Sports Advisors [which] represented Myskina [to] inquire whether Myskina would be interested in being photographed in the nude [for] GQ's 2002 "Sports" issue. . . . Myskina expressed interest. . . .

Myskina arrived at the photoshoot with Gantman [a 23-year-old administrative assistant at International Sports] and Jens Gerpach, who was her coach and then-boyfriend. Gantman claims that it was only at the photoshoot—and not during previous conversations with Altschull—that Altschull explained that the cover photograph of Myskina would depict her as "Lady Godiva"—lying nude on the back of a horse. . . . Myskina expressed concern about being photographed in the nude. According to Myskina and Gantman, Altschull explained that Myskina would wear nude-colored underpants . . . and that, except for the Lady Godiva photographs to be published in the GQ issue, the photographs taken during the photoshoot would not be published anywhere. Myskina claims that only after this assurance did she agree to be photographed.

Before shooting began, Altschull presented Gantman with Condé Nast's standard release form ("Release") for models. . . . The Release . . . provides that the signatory model "hereby irrevocably consent[s] to the use of [her] name and the pictures taken of [her] . . . by [Condé Nast], . . . and others it may authorize, for editorial purposes." The Release does not contain a merger clause. Myskina's signature appears on the Release.

[The circumstances surrounding the signature were disputed.] [G]antman . . . [denied] that he was ever presented with the Release. . . . Myskina does not recall signing or discussing a Release with Condé Nast. Moreover, Myskina claims that she could not have understood the terms of the Release because at the time she was not fluent in English and "would not have signed [the Release] had it been explained to her that [it] would or might authorize GQ and Mark Seliger to publish, sell or disseminate her photographs . . . beyond publication of the Lady Godiva photograph for the 2002 'Sports Issue' of GQ."

Myskina claims that she was photographed topless in blue jeans after Seliger finished with the Lady Godiva photographs and that these had "nothing to do with the 'Lady Godiva' concept." She recalls that Seliger asked her whether he could take these topless photographs "for himself" so long as they were already in the studio. She "told him he could only take these photographs if these photographs would not be published anywhere," to which he "understood and agreed."

Condé Nast eventually published Myskina's profile and a "Lady Godiva" photograph from the photoshoot. . . . Myskina was not paid [for] her photograph in GQ.

[By contract,] Condé Nast [authorized Seliger] to exploit all photographs taken on assignment by Condé Nast . . . subject to certain restrictions. . . .

[Operating within these restrictions] five of the . . . photoshoot images [were licensed] to Medved.

[T]hese photographs appeared in the July/August 2004 issue of Medved and soon after on Medved's website. . . . Three . . . depict frontal nudity. . . .

. . .

Myskina claims that the publication of the photographs in Medved "are highly embarrassing and have caused [her] great emotional distress and economic harm and injury to her reputation." She also claims that Seliger has sold the same photographs to other parties.

Myskina filed the instant complaint on August 5, 2004. She sues for compensatory and exemplary damages as well as injunctive relief restraining the sale and dissemination of the photographs at issue.

The Photos

You can see the photos online. The authorized shot for GQ appears at https://perma.cc/2FMT-97G9. The cover of Medved appears at https://perma.cc/UD2S-LWB2.

II.

Section[s] 50 [and 51] of New York Civil Rights Law [prohibits publishing photographs without the written consent of the individual.] The statutes apply to "cases where the plaintiff generally seeks publicity . . . but has not given written consent for a particular use" or where "the defendant has otherwise exceeded the limitations of the consent." [Citation omitted.] Although plaintiffs suing under Sections 50 and 51 often couch their claims in a right to privacy, "[t]he right which the statute permits the plaintiff to vindicate [in such circumstances] may, perhaps, more accurately be described as a right of publicity." [Citation omitted.]

In any event, defendants argue with respect to Myskina's claims under Sections 50 and 51(i) that Myskina consented in writing to the unrestricted editorial use of the photographs taken during the July 16, 2002 photoshoot, including the ones that appeared in Medved. . . .

Myskina contends that the Release was not "knowingly or intelligently signed, that she could not in any event understand its meaning," and that regardless, "defendants agreed with [ ] Myskina to limit publication to [the] 'Lady Godiva' photograph" in the October 2002 issue of GQ.

. . .

According to Myskina, Altschull assured her and Gantman "that the only photographs of [her] that would ever be published would be the Lady Godiva photographs in the October 2002 sports issue of GQ." Gantman states the same. Myskina claims also that the other photographs that appeared in Medved were taken after the Lady Godiva photographs, and only upon Seliger's request to "take [them] for himself since [they] were already in the photo studio." "He indicated that he understood and agreed" with Myskina's condition that these photographs could not be published anywhere. None of these understanding and agreements were put in writing.

Absent allegations of fraud, duress, or some other wrongdoing, Myskina's claimed misunderstanding of the Release's terms does not excuse her from being bound on the contract. *See Feinblum v. Liberty Mut. Ins. Co.*, No. 02-5085, 2003 WL 21673620, at*2 (S.D.N.Y. July 16, 2003) ("[W]hen a party to a written contract accepts it as a contract he is bound by the stipulations and conditions expressed in it whether he reads them or not. Ignorance through negligence or inexcusable trustfulness will not relieve a party from his contract obligations.") [citations omitted]. Nor can she avoid her obligations under the Release because of her purported failure to read its contents, [citation omitted], or because of a language barrier. [Citations omitted.]

As for the oral agreement that Myskina claims limited her consent to publication only of the GQ photographs, the parol evidence rule bars the admission of any prior or contemporaneous negotiations or agreements offered to contradict or modify the terms of a written agreement. [Citations omitted.] Even where an agreement is not completely integrated—meaning that the writing was intended by the parties to be a final and complete expression of all the terms agreed upon—parol evidence may be admitted only to complete the agreement or to resolve some ambiguity therein, and not to vary or contradict its contents. *See* Restatement (Second) of Contracts §215 (1981); [citations omitted].

Application of the parol evidence rule involves a three-step inquiry: (i) determine whether the written contract is an integrated agreement; if it is, (ii) determine whether the language of the written contract is clear or is ambiguous; and, (iii) if the language is clear, apply that clear language. *See Morgan Stanley High Yield Sec., Inc. v. Seven Circle Gaming Corp.*, 269 F. Supp. 2d 206, 213 (citing *Investors Ins. Co. v. Dorinco Reinsurance Co.*, 917 F.2d 100, 103-05 (2d Cir. 1990)).

Absent a merger clause or language that explicitly states that the written agreement is integrated, the issue of whether the writing is an integrated agreement is determined "by reading the writing in the light of surrounding circumstances, and by determining whether or not the agreement was one which the parties would ordinarily be expected to embody in the writing." [Citations omitted.]

Several factors indicate that the Release is an integrated agreement as to which photographs Myskina authorized the defendants to use for editorial purposes. The Release does not mention the alleged oral agreement—or any other agreement outside the Release, for that matter—that would limit Myskina's consent to the GQ photographs. Further, it addresses a straightforward transaction and plainly sets forth that Myskina consented to defendants' use of all photographs taken on July 16, 2002. Although the Release does not contain an explicit merger or integration clause, its language ("I, the undersigned, hereby irrevocably consent. . . .") indicates an intention to treat the issue of consent comprehensively and to be bound only by the terms of the Release. [Citation omitted.]

Moreover, the purported oral agreement contemplates a condition fundamental to Myskina's consent, such that it hardly would have been omitted by the parties. [Citation omitted.] Also, however unwise it may have been to bring only an administrative assistant from the publicity firm to the photoshoot, there appears to be no dispute that Myskina was still represented by the firm throughout the process. Under these circumstances, the Release constitutes a fully integrated contract as to Myskina's consent. [Citations omitted.]

The purported oral agreement contradicts the plain language of the Release. Under the alleged oral agreement, Myskina consented only to the publication of the photographs in the October 2002 issue of GQ. By contrast, under the Release, Myskina expressly consented to the "use . . . for editorial purposes" by defendants of all photographs taken of her on July 16, 2002. Hence, the Release and the oral agreement are inconsistent in that the Release does not single out or otherwise limit which photographs taken during the July 16, 2002 photoshoot could be used for editorial purposes. Hence, the oral agreement is not admissible.

Although the Release is plainly integrated, evidence of an extrinsic oral agreement to limit Myskina's consent nevertheless could be considered if it satisfies three conditions: "(1) the agreement must in form be a collateral one; (2) it must not contradict express or implied provisions of the written contract; (3) it must be one that parties would not ordinarily be expected to embody in the writing. . . . It must not be so clearly connected with the principal transaction as to be part and parcel of it." *Namad v. Salomon,* 147 A.D.2d 385, 387, 537 N.Y.S.2d 807. . . . However, the alleged oral agreement in this case fails to satisfy any of the three conditions. It is not "collateral," but central to the parties' agreement as to Myskina's consent. It contradicts directly the plain language of the Release. Finally, its central provision — restriction of publication — was Myskina's main, if not only condition of participating in the photoshoot, and is a matter that the parties would have been expected to memorialize in writing. [Citations omitted.]

[The court rejected claims that the use of the photographs fell outside the scope of the release as written.]

For the reasons set forth above, defendants' motion for summary judgment is granted.

D wins SJ

Post-Case Follow-Up

The court's refusal to consider parol evidence applies the rule mechanically without attention to the purpose of the rule. It gives conclusive weight to the document the parties signed, negating earlier oral promises. The case shows the dilemma courts face under the parol evidence rule. Myskina may have intended a full release, changing her mind only after seeing the subsequent use of the photos at a time when her popularity had risen. That possibility could be raised at trial, but would not matter at summary judgment. But if Condé Nast really gave these assurances, omitting them from the subsequent writing lets the publisher escape from its obligations. It can promise anything without fear of having to comply. By failing include the limitations in the release itself, Myskina lost any benefit of obtaining the oral promise.

Myskina v. Condé Nast Publications: Real Life Applications

1. A union agreed to hold a conference at a resort hotel. The union's experienced negotiator had included union-only terms in the past, but in this case the integrated writing omitted the resort's promise that the hotel employees be union workers. After signing, the hotel was sold and the new owner replaced union workers with nonunion workers. The union canceled the conference and sought a refund of its deposit. The resort counterclaimed for breach. The resort employee who negotiated the deal admitted she had agreed to provide a union hotel. That employee was one of the discharged union workers. Should the court exclude evidence of the promise based on the parol evidence rule?

2. In 1985, Chaz sold Francis (one of Chaz's five children) an option to buy a parcel of real estate from Chaz for $250,000. Francis orally agreed not to exercise the option until after Chaz died. The option was recorded properly, but the oral stipulation to await Chaz's death was not part of the option document. Upon Chaz's death in 2015, Francis exercised the option and tendered the price to the estate. Gene (Francis's sibling), as executor of the estate, refused to honor the option on the ground that it had expired. The option contained no term specifying when it could be exercised and did not include an integration clause. Francis offered a handwritten note signed by Chaz on the day the option was sold to Francis. The note indicated the option was to be exercised after Chaz's death. Should the court consider the note and other testimony concerning whether the exercise of the option was timely? Would your answer be different if the dates were closer together — say, an option issued in 2012 and exercised in 2015?

3. In negotiating a gaming compact with several tribes of Native Americans, the state intended to preclude the Tohono O'odham Nation from building a new casino in the vicinity of Phoenix, but did not express that restriction in the compact, apparently because the Nation did not own tribal land in that vicinity. The compact was approved by voters in a referendum. The Nation later acquired eligible tribal land near Phoenix and sought to build a casino on it. Can the state submit extrinsic evidence of the prior communications suggesting a Phoenix site was forbidden by the compact? Nothing in the compact permits a Phoenix site. Would this be a consistent additional term suitable for inclusion based on parol evidence? The full story can be found in *Arizona v. Tohono O'odham Nation*, 944 F. Supp. 2d 748, 765 (D. Ariz. 2013).

4. Lee and Cal each owned half of a liquor distributorship. Cal wanted to retire but Lee wanted to operate a smaller distributorship with Lee's adult children. Lee agreed to sell the distributorship to Seagram if Seagram would help Lee find and purchase a suitable, smaller distributorship. Seagram agreed. Seagram bought the distributorship from Lee and Cal in a contract that was recorded in an integrated writing. That writing did not mention the promise to find a smaller distributorship for Lee and family. Will the parol evidence rule prevent Lee from proving the agreement to obtain a new distributorship?

Extrinsic Evidence and Misrepresentation

The admissibility of extrinsic evidence to prove defenses, such as fraud and duress, seems uncontroversial. These defenses could undermine the validity of the entire agreement, including the integration clause. If the agreement is unenforceable, the integration clause in it also is unenforceable. Before a court can decide to enforce the integration clause, it must first resolve any defenses to enforcement of the contract.

That analysis can open up a loophole for parties seeking to avoid the integration clause. They allege that the failure to include an omitted promise (or the inaccurate recording of an included promise) constitutes misrepresentation or fraud. Thus, the very promises the integration clause seeks to exclude become the evidence of fraud intended to show that the agreement (as integrated) is unenforceable. The net effect could deprive the integration clause of any force.

Some allegations of misrepresentation require the admission of extrinsic evidence. Courts generally allow extrinsic evidence to establish fraud relating to the integration clause itself (say, an allegation that the other party lied about the existence of an integration clause in the writing). Similarly, fraud that relates to the subject matter of the contract (the thing sold, such as a lie about the mileage on a used car) justifies the use of extrinsic evidence. However, when the only fraud alleged relates to promises that the integration clause excludes, some courts exclude extrinsic evidence of the additional promises. On one hand, this seems like an enormous loophole. Promise anything to get assent, but omit it from the writing and include an integration clause. The clause will preclude evidence of the fraud. That concern led California recently to reverse longstanding precedent that the parol evidence rule precluded evidence of promissory fraud.[21]

Promissory Estoppel and Parol Evidence

A party might claim promissory estoppel in an effort to avoid the parol evidence rule. This might involve little more than alleging the very promise that the integrated agreement was intended to prevent. For instance, suppose Myskina urged that she relied on Condé Nast's promise not to publish the photographs anywhere but the 2002 Sports issue of GQ. Condé Nast might have reason to know that she would rely (by signing the Release). If a court enforces the promise on the ground that injustice can be avoided only by enforcement, the integrated agreement loses its preclusive effect. Any integration may disappear once a party alleges estoppel—arguably relief under a different cause of action from breach of contract.

Most courts reject this circumvention. An integrated agreement precludes admission of prior or contemporaneous promises regardless of whether the claim is based on consideration or an exception to consideration, such as reliance. Some states create exceptions. The most common exception involves an explicit promise not to raise the parol evidence rule. Any defense of this sort can be waived. Reliance

[21] *Riverisland Cold Storage, Inc. v. Fresno-Madera Prod. Credit Assn.*, 55 Cal. 4th 1169, 1182, 291 P.3d 316, 324 (2013) (overruling *Bank of America Etc. Assn. v. Pendergrass*, 4 Cal. 2d 258, 48 P.2d 659 (1935)).

EXHIBIT 9.4 Decision Tree for the Parol Evidence Rule (PER)

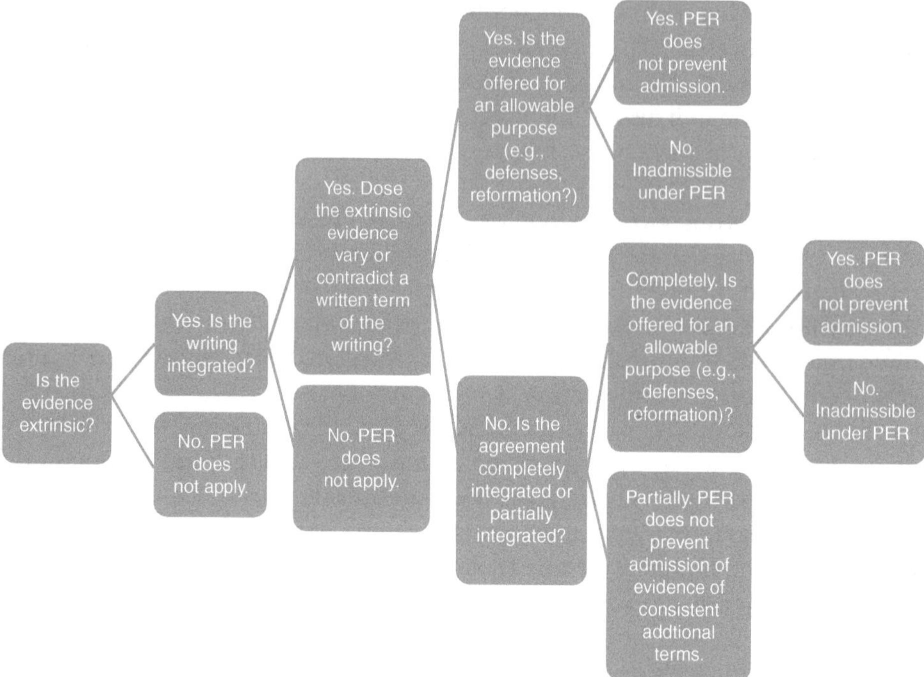

on that waiver normally makes the waiver irrevocable. Rarely, a court goes further and recognizes estoppel based on the underlying promise. A jurisdiction that treats promissory estoppel as a separate cause of action, distinct from contract, has less reason to apply the parol evidence rule, a substantive rule of contract law, to the estoppel claim.

Extrinsic Evidence and Interpretation

The parol evidence rule seeks to exclude promises the parties did not intend to include in their final agreement. The rule excludes testimony seeking to add them to an integrated writing. Extrinsic evidence could be used more subtly, to ask the court to interpret the promises of an integrated agreement. That could produce the same effect: interpreting words of a contract may alter or add a promise that the parties did not intend to include in their writing.

Even the strictest (or classical) version of the parol evidence rule permits extrinsic evidence to help determine the meaning of an **ambiguous** term, one that, in context, could mean at least two different things. Yet when the plain meaning of a contract is apparent from the document itself, courts refuse to admit extrinsic evidence to contradict or to vary that meaning. In this way, the rule precludes parties from using interpretation as a means of contradicting the promises recorded in an integrated writing.

This classic approach to interpretation rests heavily on judges' understanding of the words of the writing. Words the particular judges find clear require no explanation by the parties, so the court excludes extrinsic evidence. The meaning the judge finds clear may not coincide with the meaning the parties shared at the time of formation. The rule prevents any attempt to prove that shared understanding.

For example, in *Eskimo Pie Corporation v. Whitelawn Dairies, Inc.*,[22] Eskimo Pie granted Supermarket Advisory Sales (SAS) a "non-exclusive" license to sell products bearing the Eskimo logo within the New York City metropolitan area. SAS objected when Eskimo issued new licenses to competitors. SAS offered parol evidence that the parties intended "non-exclusive" to permit Eskimo to continue existing licenses and to issue new licenses to national chains, but that Eskimo would not issue new licenses to independent dairies. Eskimo objected on the ground that "non-exclusive" was clear on its face, allowing it to issue any licenses it desired. Neither interpretation is exclusive; SAS did not claim a right to be the only licensee. They differed in *how* "non-exclusive" the license was: zero exclusivity or limited exclusivity. The court, though skeptical that the term was ambiguous, reserved judgment on the issue of ambiguity pending an evidentiary hearing, the results of which are not reported. But SAS was not permitted to introduce evidence of the parties' private, subjective meaning at that hearing. SAS needed to show that strangers to the negotiations would find the word ambiguous.

Efforts to rescue the parties' interpretation from a judge's misunderstanding can take two forms. First, courts may confine the definition of extrinsic evidence. If fewer and fewer types of evidence are defined as extrinsic, then courts may consider more sources of interpretation despite the parol evidence rule. Second, courts may expand the notion of ambiguity. As more terms are considered ambiguous, extrinsic evidence becomes available in more cases, despite the parol evidence rule.

Confining Extrinsic Evidence

If extrinsic meant everything outside the four corners of the integrated writing, the parol evidence rule would exclude much more than just prior agreements and negotiations. Many kinds of evidence, such as dictionaries, fall outside the four corners of the contract.

Courts frequently consider several kinds of evidence that technically fall outside the contract, including dictionary definitions, usage of trade, course of dealing, course of performance,[23] and government regulations. The parties need not copy these sources into the contract documents, although they could become intrinsic if incorporated by reference in the contract documents.

While not intrinsic, dictionaries, usage of trade, and course of dealing often are verifiable from relatively objective sources. A party cannot easily distort these to suit its current purpose, at least not as easily as it can spin testimony about prior negotiations. Thus, the parol evidence rule may exclude negotiations when interpreting a contract, even though other arguably extrinsic guides are used freely.

[22] 284 F. Supp. 987 (S.D.N.Y. 1968).
[23] UCC §2-202 (explicitly permitting usage of trade, course of dealing, and course of performance).

Expanding Ambiguity

Recently, some courts have relaxed the classical approach by considering extrinsic evidence when deciding whether a term is ambiguous or, stated another way, fairly susceptible to either party's asserted meaning. If the evidence establishes that the term is ambiguous, then the court admits the evidence and weighs it (or lets the jury weigh it) in deciding upon the better interpretation. If, however, the term does not seem ambiguous even after hearing the extrinsic evidence, the court strikes the extrinsic evidence and treats the term as clear. This differs slightly from the *Eskimo Pie* example above, which excluded some extrinsic evidence when considering ambiguity.

The modern approach makes some sense. A court must determine what a term in the writing means before it can know whether extrinsic evidence would contradict that meaning. But the approach undermines the certainty that parties seek when recording their agreement in an integrated writing. A party seeking to contradict the terms of the writing has an avenue to present the extrinsic evidence to the court. This creates a risk that the court might give weight to that evidence rather than to the writing—the very risk that the parol evidence rule seeks to prevent.

For example, in *Pacific Gas & Electric v. G. W. Thomas Drayage & Rigging*,[24] a contractor agreed to **indemnify** a landowner (pay any losses the landowner suffered because of the contractor's conduct). Indemnity clauses ordinarily cover harm the contractor does to third persons; if they sue the landowner, the contractor pays instead. But the language of this clause was not limited to third parties; read literally, it covered losses the landowner suffered. When the landowner sued for damage to a building that resulted from a construction accident, the contractor argued that the clause should be interpreted to include only third-party claims, not the landowner's claim. That directly contradicted the language of the contract, which plainly had no such limitation. By interpretation, the contractor was trying to alter the contract, changing one of the promises. The court decided to hear extrinsic evidence before deciding whether the clause was ambiguous. After former executives of the landowner testified that they really intended a third-party indemnity clause, not the blanket clause they actually wrote, the court decided the term was ambiguous. It then used the extrinsic evidence to resolve the ambiguity, interpreting the term as limited to third-party claims. That interpretation unquestionably

Living Without the Parol Evidence Rule

The Convention on International Sales of Goods includes neither a parol evidence rule nor any requirement that contracts ever be in writing (or any other special form). This frees tribunals to consider any evidence of contract meaning that seems suitable, including negotiations. The parties, by contract, can specify how they want their contract applied. Thus, the parties can include a merger clause in their agreement. A tribunal will interpret that clause to determine whether the parties intended to preclude recourse to extrinsic evidence. But in making that interpretation, the tribunal may include consideration of extrinsic evidence. For more details, you may want to examine CISG Advisory Council Opinion No. 3, *Parol Evidence Rule, Plain Meaning Rule, Contractual Merger Clause and the CISG*, https://perma.cc/6K6Q-PZNQ.

[24] 442 P.2d 641 (Cal. 1968).

varied the plain meaning of the written term in an integrated agreement. It probably reflected what the parties intended to write. It certainly reflects what the contractor wished had been written.

The modern approach makes it nearly impossible to resolve cases short of a trial. The classical approach permits a court to interpret the writing on its face. If it is plain, the court may grant a **motion to dismiss** (throw the case out before discovery) or grant **summary judgment** (granting judgment before trial to one party because the other party lacked even minimal evidence to show a genuine issue as to a material fact). The modern approach requires the court to consider the extrinsic evidence before interpreting the contract. At a minimum, this requires the court to allow discovery to proceed so the parties can gather extrinsic evidence. By allowing a party to prolong the litigation, the costs increase, making it easier for the party seeking to contradict the writing to negotiate a settlement, no matter how weak the claim is.

C. MISTAKE OF INTEGRATION AND REFORMATION

Sometimes a writing will not accurately record the agreement the parties reached. Parties may make inadvertent mistakes, such as typing too many zeroes in the price or accidentally omitting a line or paragraph. Some parties intentionally alter the writing, deleting or adding critical language, but disguise the revised document to make it look like the original. In either event, the court may correct the mistake, reforming (or rewriting) the document to match the agreement the parties originally reached.

At first blush, reformation seems inconsistent with the parol evidence rule. Rewriting the agreement seems the opposite of enforcing it as written. Reformation does not preclude a court from enforcing the agreement as written. It simply allows the court to correct the writing before enforcing it as written. Once corrected, the parol evidence rule applies with full force (assuming the other requirements are met). However, as noted above, the parol evidence rule does not preclude the admission of extrinsic evidence for the purpose of seeking reformation. In addition, correcting the writing does not necessarily prevent interpretation. The term agreed upon may be clear or ambiguous. Reformation inserts the right words, but does not necessarily answer the question of what the words mean.

Consider a simple case. Buyer agrees to pay $1 million for seller's home. In preparing the writing

Words or Numerals?

Careful parties may type both words and numerals, in an effort to avoid mistakes. That might help, but sometimes it just creates a conflict within the writing. The contract might read "$10,000,000 (one million dollars)." The conflict between numerals and words requires the court to decide which of two inconsistent terms it should enforce. By rule, courts often resolve conflicts between words and numerals in favor of the words. That might be right.

But suppose the words were inserted by the typist, who misread the numerals. The price might read "$1,000,000 (one hundred thousand dollars)" — the equivalent of having too few zeroes, this time in the words rather than the numerals. If the agreed price was $1 million, should numerals govern? Ideally, the court should consider a claim for reformation and get the agreed price right.

both parties will sign, a typist's tic produces one too many zeroes in the price ($10,000,000, not $1,000,000), an error neither party notices before signing. Unless the writing can be corrected, seller could collect the extra $9 million. If a zero were omitted, seller might be limited to $100,000. A sale for $1 million seems likely to be mutually beneficial. Neither of the mistyped deals offers any confidence of mutual benefit. Few would argue that either party should suffer the error—even if the disadvantaged party did the typing and thus caused the error. Whatever cost that erring party might deserve, a price ten times (or one-tenth) that promised seems disproportionate.

While reformation sometimes seems apt, courts must take care not to add mistakes in their effort to correct mistakes. Three limitations on reformation reduce that risk. First, reformation usually requires a higher standard of proof. Instead of a **preponderance of the evidence** (more likely than not or 50 percent plus an iota), reformation may require clear and convincing evidence or even proof beyond a reasonable doubt. (Your Civil Procedure class may address the details of each standard of proof.) Second, courts limit reformation to recording the agreement the parties actually did make, not creating the agreement they wish they had made. Thus, where the parties really did agree on $1 million, that price will be written into the contract. Where the parties did not reach agreement on a term, neither can use reformation to persuade a court to insert the term it prefers. Third, reformation may be denied if third parties have relied on the contract as written in **good faith** (honestly, without notice of the error). In this case, the third party may enforce the contract as written; the disadvantaged party will need to seek relief from the other party to the original contract, not from the third party. For example, the owner of a condominium sold it to buyer but neglected to exclude the two parking spaces assigned to the unit, which seller intended to keep and lease to others. If buyer resold the unit to another, a court might deny reformation (of the first sale) to protect the interests of the subsequent buyer, who would receive less than its contract officially allowed.

Mutual mistake of integration occurs when both parties believed, when signing the document, that it accurately reflected their agreement. If the writing was inaccurate, both parties were mistaken in this belief. This offers the clearest case for reformation, which can eliminate the mistake. Once the court corrects the writing, restoring the original terms both parties expected it to embody, the mistake disappears. The remedy is perfectly suited to the problem.

Unilateral mistake of integration occurs if one party believes that the written agreement includes a term, but the other believes that it does not. Sometimes the party recognizes an error made by others

Reformation and Misunderstanding

When one party really intended the language in the writing to govern, reformation looks a lot like misunderstanding (where each party intended its meaning to be *the* meaning of a term). A court is unlikely to frustrate a party's reliance on the written words (or intended meaning) unless she knew of the error: in reformation, she knew the other intended the writing to include different language than it in fact includes. The mistaken party, on the other hand, typically does not know that the one party intends the written terms to be any different from their discussions. As a result, a court legitimately may impose the meaning (under misunderstanding) or the term (under reformation) the party ignorant of the error intended.

(the other party or a scrivener); sometimes the party intentionally alters the writing. In either event, the mistake ceases to be mutual.

Unilateral mistake of integration, standing alone, does not justify reformation. One party, when signing the document, knew exactly what it said and (apparently) preferred the agreement as written to the original agreement. Thus, one party honestly can state that she intended the document as written. And the other party could have known (and arguably should have known) if it had read the agreement carefully. To justify reformation for unilateral mistake of integration, courts require some dishonesty by the party that was not mistaken. Dishonesty may consist of misrepresentation, such as false statements ("sign here, it is exactly what we discussed"), active concealment (saying "you don't need to read this" or perhaps inserting the error in a way designed to conceal it from the other party), or simple nondisclosure of an error she knows is present (if a duty to speak exists). When dishonest conduct prevents the error from coming to the other party's attention, courts feel justified in reforming the contract to the term originally agreed upon.

Chapter Summary

- Interpretation seeks to identify the parties' shared intention concerning what their agreement required of each of them.
- When intentions differed even at the start, courts seek a meaning that fairly can be imposed on a party who may not have intended that meaning. A court may select a meaning one party knew the other intended, that it should have known the other intended, or that it should have known a court might find the language objectively provided.
- A court may conclude the parties never assented if they did not share a meaning and neither's meaning can fairly be attributed to the other. Courts prefer not to frustrate parties' expectations unless absolutely unavoidable, making negating assent a last resort.
- The array of sources courts consider in an effort to interpret language include the contract itself, negotiations between the parties, dictionaries, usage of trade, course of dealing, course of performance, government regulations, and canons of construction designed to help infer parties' intent based on the way they used language.
- The parol evidence rule precludes the use of prior or contemporaneous agreements and negotiations to vary, contradict, or supplement completely integrated agreements. For partially integrated agreements, the rule precludes the use of extrinsic evidence to vary or contradict the writing, but permits its use to explain or supplement the contract documents.
- The parol evidence rule does not preclude introducing extrinsic evidence for some purposes, such as to establish the integration of an agreement, defenses to contract formation, or entitlement to equitable relief such as rescission or reformation.

- The parol evidence rule does not preclude introducing extrinsic evidence to resolve the meaning of an ambiguous term, even if the agreement is integrated. In some jurisdictions, extrinsic evidence may be introduced to determine whether the agreement is ambiguous.
- Where a writing erroneously records the parties' agreement, a court may reform the writing to correct the error. Reformation requires either mutual mistake concerning the contents of the writing or a unilateral mistake by one party and knowledge or dishonesty by the other.

Applying the Rules

1. Tavern leased space in a shopping mall from Malloner. Both Tavern and Malloner intended the word "premises" in the lease to include 16 parking spaces adjacent to the leased building, though their written agreement referred only to the building. Malloner sold the mall to Badger. Badger decided to build on some of the parking spaces reserved for Tavern. Does Tavern have a contract right to those spaces based on its lease with Malloner?

2. Les placed an order online for "bath salts," believing that the product would contain a synthetic cathinone (a stimulant similar to amphetamine). The seller delivered bath salts meant to be dissolved in bath water. The confusion was immediately apparent from the quantity and packaging, neither of which was typical of the bath salts Les sought.

   a. Can Les sue for breach, demanding damages for failure to deliver bath salts? Which interpretation rule poses the greatest difficulty?
   b. Can Les seek rescission and a refund? Which interpretation rule poses the greatest difficulty?
   c. Would your answer be different if the "bath salts" Les sought were not illegal under the strictest reading of the statutes then in effect?

3. Gay owns a home with a basement apartment. Gay leased the basement apartment to Terry. The lease requires rent to be paid on or before the first day of each month, specifies that time is of the essence, and provides for a late payment fee of $50 per week. Terry paid the first month's rent before moving in. Terry paid the next month's rent on July 3, but Gay did not complain. Terry paid the August rent on August 4, but again Gay let it slide. When Terry had not yet paid the rent on September 3, Gay spoke with Terry and insisted that rent be paid by the first of each month or the late payment fee would be collected.

   a. Does Terry have a legal basis to argue that the contract should be interpreted to allow rent payment on or before the fourth day of each month?
   b. Would it matter that the lease has an integration clause making the lease the parties' final and complete agreement?

c. Would it matter that the integration clause also specifies that modifications to the lease must be in writing and signed by both parties?

4. Sandy owns 90 percent of Su Casa, a restaurant. Cameron, Sandy's relative, received 10 percent in exchange for financial support starting the business. Sandy sought a loan in order to open a second location. Bank agreed to make the loan if both Sandy and Cameron would provide personal guaranties (promises to repay the loan if the business defaulted). Sandy, who had no assets except the business, agreed. Cameron hesitated. Syd, Bank's loan officer, assured Cameron that Bank would not ask Cameron to repay the loan, but would merely foreclose on the collateral (the restaurant's assets, such as equipment, furniture, decorations, etc.). Cameron then signed the guaranty, which clearly stated that Cameron promised to pay the loan if Su Casa defaulted and contained an integration clause making it the parties' final agreement (along with other loan documents not pertinent here). The second location failed. Su Casa defaulted on the loan. After foreclosing on the business assets, Bank still is owed $100,000. Bank sues Cameron to recover on the guaranty. Can Cameron successfully defend on the ground that Bank promised not to seek recovery from Cameron?

5. Bank issued a commitment letter to Borrower, promising to loan $4.5 million at an interest rate based on an index plus 2.5 percent. The promissory note the parties signed differed from the commitment letter by adding the words "but in no event less than 10 percent" to the indexed interest rate. The note contains an integration clause, stating that it is the final and complete agreement of the parties. After three years, the indexed rate fell below 10 percent, but Bank continued to bill and Borrower continued to pay 10 percent. Borrower discovered the discrepancy and calculates that Bank now has collected $1 million more interest than it would have received if the interest rate in the note conformed to that agreed in the commitment letter. Can Borrower recover the excess interest received by Bank?

Contract Law in Practice

1. Sam sells poultry. Bobby is a broker who obtains food for hospitals and other large-scale cafeteria operations, most of which operate under very tight budgets. Bobby negotiates a favorable price on 10,000 pounds of chicken from Sam, expecting to receive young chickens suitable for frying. Sam believes the word chicken encompasses older chickens and quotes a price appropriate for those less expensive birds. Upon discovering that Sam delivered older chickens, Bobby rejects the birds. Can Bobby prevail on the theory that the parties understood the word chicken differently, producing no agreement in the first place? After considering the case on these skeletal facts, consider whether the additional facts in *Frigaliment* would alter your basic conclusion.

2. Arti wrote a novel that has generated considerable interest. In 2015, Arti sold the television rights to the novel to ABC, but retained the movie rights (and any other rights not within the definition of television rights). ABC produced a miniseries based on the novel. ABC now has produced CDs of the miniseries, has made the miniseries available for streaming on its website, and is considering licensing others to stream the miniseries. Arti believes that television rights include only the right to produce and air the miniseries on broadcast TV (though she understands that cable companies that carry a broadcast station also have a right to display the miniseries when it appears on that station). Arti seeks your advice concerning whether her interpretation of the contract is sustainable.

3. ABC is considering purchasing the right to make a miniseries from a popular novel. The author wishes to retain the right to license another to produce a motion picture based on the novel. Draft a clause that will protect ABC's rights to distribute its miniseries in the various forms now available for television shows, without jeopardizing the author's right to license the novel to a motion picture studio.

4. Several aspects of the parol evidence rule vary by jurisdiction. Explore the decisions in your jurisdiction to determine whether:

   a. Courts consider extrinsic evidence when deciding whether a term of the contract is ambiguous or only after determining the term is facially ambiguous.
   b. Courts consider extrinsic evidence to support a claim of promissory fraud (that the party pleading the parol evidence rule never intended to perform the promise that the parol evidence would prove existed).
   c. Courts allow promissory estoppel to prevent invocation of the parol evidence rule and, if so, whether courts limit the doctrine to promises not to invoke the parol evidence rule or will apply it based on other promises prior to signing the integrated writing.

5. Ascertain whether your jurisdiction permits reformation based on unilateral mistake and, if so, the degree of awareness or dishonesty required on the part of the party who was not mistaken in order to justify reformation.

6. A friend is selling her used car. Knowing you are studying contracts, she asks you to look at the simple bill of sale that she has drafted. You notice that she has not included an integration clause. Should you advise her to include one? If so, draft a clause suitable for the document—not so long or scary that the buyer runs from the sale, but sufficient to protect your friend from any claims that additional promises were made but not recorded in the document. Now try drafting a provision for a used car dealer, whose contracts are long enough to allow a fuller clause. Include language that will minimize the ability of buyers to avoid the integration clause by claiming fraud, without violating the public

policy against clauses that waive liability for fraud. If necessary, make it a separate clause.

7. You represent Chris in a divorce action. During settlement negotiations, Sean, Chris's spouse, insists the plumbing business Chris owns and operates is worth \$700,000, while Chris contends it is worth only \$500,000. Both parties insist on these valuations consistently. After months of discussions, Sean's attorney sent you a settlement offer for dividing the marital property evenly. The total offer is very close to the amounts Chris had proposed. In examining the calculation, you notice that Sean's attorney has made a mathematical or typographical error: the calculation shows the total value of the business as \$700,000, but in dividing it by 2 Sean's share became \$250,000. That is exactly the correct share based on Chris's evaluation of the business (\$500,000 ÷ 2). How should you proceed? What risks do you anticipate? How can you minimize them?

10

Implied Terms

Crafting a contract requires parties to think about the nature and details of their contract relationship. In theory, parties could produce their own agreement with no gaps. In practice, that outcome would be rare. The time spent anticipating and providing for remote possibilities will often be wasted — costing much more, in the long run, than will be saved in the few cases where those terms become pertinent. Where terms are understood, parties often assume them rather than wasting time expressing what they both understand.

Most of the time, parties complete their contract obligations without any serious difficulties. However, in some cases, conflicts may arise about party rights and duties that are not expressly addressed in their contracts. In these instances, parties may look to the courts to help them sort out the murky boundaries of their agreements. Over time, the courts have developed a number of implied terms to fill in gaps in order to preserve the agreement. These gap fillers save time and money, freeing parties to devote their resources to tasks more productive than restating the obvious or anticipating the unlikely.

In this chapter, we will examine contract terms that have been implied by the courts. Implied terms are drawn from judicial interpretations of good faith and fair dealing, recognized business practices, and the provisions of the UCC in goods cases. In the absence of express provisions, these default terms play an important role in the flexibility and efficiency of contract law.

Key Concepts

- Implied terms grounded in good faith and fair dealing
- Standard of reasonableness in contract dealings
- UCC default terms on price, delivery, and time of payment and performance
- Express and implied warranties
- Output and requirements contracts

A. OVERVIEW OF IMPLIED TERMS

At times, courts deal with cases in which the contract terms do not expressly address the issues in dispute. For instance, the contract may not express a specific deadline for performance of contract obligations. A party might refuse to perform indefinitely without ever being held liable for breach because the contract lacks a deadline. The nonperforming party can always state that it plans to perform, sometime in the future, but just not yet. Taken literally, nonperformance might never become a breach because the parties' contract sets no deadline for the completion of contract duties. However, it would be illogical or unfair to state that the parties did not intend for their contract obligations to be fulfilled at some point in time.

Courts facing gaps in a contract have a limited number of options. A court may rule that an agreement lacks definiteness, making it unenforceable. Alternatively, a court might stretch to find words in the contract that would allow it to impose some limit on a party's ability to avoid performance. Finally, the court could simply add a term of its own choosing to fill the gap left by the parties. But each of these options has significant drawbacks.

Refusing to enforce the contract may frustrate the parties' shared intention. Both of them intended to reach an enforceable contract. Allowing one party to back out by identifying some technicality not covered by the terms of the agreement destroys the contract's value as a planning device. A mutually beneficial exchange is frustrated. In effect, one party gets an option to perform or to withdraw, depending on how future events unfold. Stretching to find hidden meaning in a contract might work, but there may not be any term that can be broadly interpreted to meet this objective. Finding it in that situation seems little different from making it up. Moreover, the outcome of this quest may be hard for the parties to predict, lending uncertainty to their contract dealings.

Instead, courts have developed a series of implied or default terms. Where parties intended to enter a binding contract, but omitted some term, courts will fill the gap in order to preserve the agreement. Many of the default terms are known in advance through case precedent; statutory law, such as the UCC; and even the CISG in cases of international commercial dealings for goods. Thus, parties will know what term the court will likely add to their contract. They can perform accordingly—and even negotiate appropriately. If the parties like the term courts employ for time of performance, they can save time and ink by making no mention of delivery dates. If a lawsuit for breach becomes necessary, the court will fill in the term for them. If the parties want a different term, they know they must specify it in the agreement. They can avoid the court's term, but only by express terms. Although it makes sense to be specific in contracts to avoid future disputes or confusion, gap fillers can later help preserve the parties' intent to enter into an agreement.

Ideally, default terms are those that the fewest number of parties would want to change. This approach will help keep the cost of negotiation at a minimum and maximize flexibility, since more people can omit the term and rely on the default subsequently, if needed. When a court chooses a term that more people would want to change, the cost of negotiations increases. No matter how fair the court thinks its term is, it simply will cost parties more to avoid it because the term parties prefer will need to be expressly included in their contracts.

B. IMPLYING GOOD FAITH

All contracts are based upon an implied promise of good faith and fair dealing. For some contracts, this requirement is imposed by common law decision. (*See* Restatement (Second) of Contracts §205.) For contracts for the sales of goods, the promise is stated in UCC §1-203 or CISG Art. 7(1). The duty of good faith cannot be waived or disclaimed by agreement of the parties. It is a foundational requirement of a contract, not a default term.

At a minimum, good faith requires honesty in fact and often looks to reasonableness in conduct, such as reasonable notice or reasonable efforts. In addition, at least for merchants, good faith requires conduct in accord with reasonable commercial standards of fair dealing in the trade. Article 1 of the UCC originally applied this standard only to merchants, and proposed changes to the UCC expand this duty to all contracting parties.

Good faith is an intentionally vague requirement, applied in different ways depending on the setting. Most of the applications can be described by a few rules of thumb:

- Show honesty in fact in your contract dealings.
- Perform in line with reasonable commercial standards.
- Don't pretend that another's acceptable performance is unacceptable.
- Don't reject another's performance that meets reasonable commercial standards.
- Don't interfere with the other party's ability to perform.
- Don't try to unilaterally recapture rights bargained away when entering the contract, even if the contract doesn't seem to prohibit your efforts.

This list oversimplifies matters, but the discussion below further fleshes out these ideas.

Occasionally, the requirement of honesty in fact will apply directly to a case. For instance, when a party promises to buy land provided that he obtains satisfactory leases for the shopping mall he intends to build on the land, good faith limits the right to avoid the contract based on those leases. If the leases are in fact satisfactory, it would be a breach of good faith to pretend that they are not in order to back out of (or renegotiate) the deal. At a minimum, good faith requires honesty in fact. Stating that the leases are not satisfactory when in fact they are satisfactory fails even that minimal test. Similarly, a party that requires consent for any assignments must do so in good faith. Pretending to object to an assignment that a party finds perfectly acceptable would not comport with the requirement of honesty in fact. Today, many contracts include a clause stating that a party may not unreasonably withhold consent.

More commonly, however, courts use the obligation of good faith as a means to expound upon party duties under a contract. Some duties may be omitted from a contract because the parties never considered the possibility that one of them would act in such a way. In these situations, a court may decide that the conduct violates the obligation of good faith and fair dealing. In effect, the court finds that good faith requires a party to do something (or refrain from doing something) that the express terms of the contract do not require (or do not preclude). The court adds terms to the contract in support of good faith.

1. Satisfaction Clauses

It is not uncommon that a contract may include a satisfaction clause that may not clearly explain how satisfaction will be measured. Courts may imply an objective standard of the reasonable person to measure party satisfaction. Typically, the objective standard is utilized when a contract involves commercial quality, operative fitness, or mechanical utility that other reasonable persons can determine. For example, a contract may include a satisfaction clause about the quality of certain raw materials to manufacture certain goods. Typically, these materials may be objectively measured or assessed under a reasonableness standard.

However, in cases involving personal tastes or aesthetics, a subjective standard of good faith is applied. Implying a subjective standard allows a party to decide what satisfies its needs, allowing for an unreasonable decision provided that it is made in good faith, and is not a bad faith desire to avoid contract duties. For example, in *Gibson v. Cranage*, 39 Mich. 49 (1878), Cranage entered into an agreement with an artist, Gibson, to paint a portrait of his deceased daughter, subject to his satisfaction in the final work. When he received the painting, he disliked it and refused to accept or pay for it, and the painter sued for payment. The court found that under the subjective approach acceptance of the portrait was subject to Cranage's personal decision if that decision was not tainted by fraud or mistake, but reflected his honestly held belief.

2. Interference with Performance

Most courts agree that the obligation of good faith prohibits a party from interfering with the other's ability to perform the contract. For instance, suppose a homeowner hired painters to paint the interior of a house, but locked the doors and would not admit them on the specified day of performance. The contract might not mention this situation—although painters are likely to include a new term once this happens to them. The homeowner has not breached any express provision of the contract. The painters, on the other hand, failed to perform on the day specified. Can the homeowner sue the painter for breach? Surely not, as the court is likely to conclude that the painter's duty to perform was conditioned on reasonable access to the premises. Having defeated access to the premises, the painter's duty to perform did not mature. Further, the court is likely to find that the homeowner's conduct breached the obligation of good faith and fair dealing. Even if the express terms of the contract did not specify allowing access on the day for performance, the homeowner had an implied obligation to make access available. Breach of that obligation is breach of the contract, allowing the painter to sue the homeowner, not the other way around.

Beyond holding that good faith precludes actions that interfere with the other's ability to perform, little consensus emerges concerning what good faith does or does not require in a given contract. It becomes a useful argument in many situations. But it is argued far more often than it is applied. Good faith does not require that every party to a contract take charity into their hearts for the well-being of their contract partners. Contract remains a system of mutual self-interest. Yet, in some cases, courts do find that good faith augments the express terms of the contract. The occasions tend to be fact-specific.

For example, some courts have held that good faith precludes an employer from firing a long-term employee without some reason. Even if the employee technically serves at will, courts sometimes hold that discharge without a good reason breaches an obligation of good faith and fair dealing. The duty of good faith, then, adds a protection that the express terms of the contract did not include. Similarly, in franchise relationships, courts often imply reasonable notice of termination of a franchise in order to allow a franchisee a reasonable amount of time to recoup some of its investment and to wind up its franchise activities.

Another example arises in some leases, which contain provisions allowing the landlord to receive a percentage of the tenant's profits or revenues, once they exceed a certain level. If the tenant shuts down the operation, effectively preventing the income from reaching the level where percentage rent would be owed, the court may examine the decision to determine whether it was made in good faith. Normally, a business can make its own decisions regarding how and where to operate. A landlord, even one entitled to a percentage of the rent, does not become a partner in the tenant's business, with a veto over how the business operates. Nonetheless, some business conduct may violate standards of fair dealing.

Taken to extremes, the duty of good faith could permit courts to find that any conduct it found questionable or ethically suspect violated the contract. In fact, courts tend to show more restraint. They understand that commercial contracts involve parties that are each looking out for their own self-interest. A party has no particular obligation to protect the other party's interest. But parties should not take undue advantage of gaps in the contract to recapture advantages they bargained away during contract negotiations. Yet their freedom to extract for themselves the greatest advantage they can under the contract should not be unduly constrained. It is a delicate balancing act that courts must consider when implying terms into an agreement.

Case Preview

Wood v. Lucy, Lady Duff-Gordon

Lady Lucy Duff-Gordon was a fashion designer and a well-known survivor of the Titanic. She sought to lend her name to a wide range of fashion designs through lucrative marketing deals. She entered into an exclusive contract with Wood to help promote her brand for a 50-50 split in the profits. When she made her own side deals without splitting the profits with Wood, he sued under the terms of their exclusive marketing contract.

As you read *Wood v. Lucy, Lady Duff-Gordon*, look for the following:

1. What arguments did Lady Duff-Gordon make to try to avoid splitting the profits with Wood?
2. What contentions did Wood assert to counter her grounds for failing to share the profits?
3. How did the court apply the concept of implied terms to determine the outcome of this case?

Wood v. Lucy, Lady Duff-Gordon

222 N.Y. 88 (Ct. App. N.Y. 1917)

CARDOZO, J.

The defendant styles herself "a creator of fashions." Her favor helps a sale. Manufacturers of dresses, millinery and like articles are glad to pay for a certificate of her approval. The things which she designs, fabrics, parasols and what not, have a new value in the public mind when issued in her name. She employed the plaintiff to help her to turn this vogue into money. He was to have the exclusive right, subject always to her approval, to place her indorsements on the designs of others. He was also to have the exclusive right to place her own designs on sale, or to license others to market them. In return, she was to have one-half of "all profits and revenues" derived from any contracts he might make. The exclusive right was to last at least one year from April 1, 1915, and thereafter from year to year unless terminated by notice of ninety days. The plaintiff says that he kept the contract on his part, and that the defendant broke it. She placed her indorsement on fabrics, dresses and millinery without his knowledge, and withheld the profits. He sues her for the damages, and the case comes here on demurrer.

The agreement of employment is signed by both parties. It has a wealth of recitals. The defendant insists, however, that it lacks the elements of a contract. She says that the plaintiff does not bind himself to anything. It is true that he does not promise in so many words that he will use reasonable efforts to place the defendant's indorsements and market her designs. We think, however, that such a promise is fairly to be implied. The law has outgrown its primitive stage of formalism when the precise word was the sovereign talisman, and every slip was fatal. It takes a broader view today. A promise may be lacking, and yet the whole writing may be "instinct with an obligation," imperfectly expressed (Scott, J., in *McCall Co. v. Wright*, 133 App. Div. 62; *Moran v. Standard Oil Co.*, 211 N. Y. 187, 198). If that is so, there is a contract.

The implication of a promise here finds support in many circumstances. The defendant gave an *exclusive* privilege. She was to have no right for at least a year to place her own indorsements or market her own designs except through the agency of the plaintiff. The acceptance of the exclusive agency was an assumption of its duties.

[Citations omitted.] We are not to suppose that one party was to be placed at the mercy of the other. [Citation omitted.] Many other terms of the agreement point the same way. We are told at the outset by way of recital that "the said Otis F. Wood possesses a business organization adapted to the placing of such indorsements as the said Lucy, *Lady Duff-Gordon* has approved." The implication is that the plaintiff's business organization will be used for the purpose for which it is adapted. But the terms of the defendant's compensation are even more significant. Her sole compensation for the grant of an exclusive agency is to be one-half of all the profits resulting from the plaintiff's efforts. Unless he gave his efforts, she could never get anything. Without an implied promise, the transaction cannot have such business "efficacy as both parties must have intended that at all events it should have" (Bowen, L. J., in *The Moorcock*, 14 P. D. 64, 68). But the contract does not stop there. The plaintiff goes on to promise that he will account monthly for all moneys received by him, and that he will take out all such patents and copyrights and trademarks as may in his judgment be necessary to protect the rights and articles affected by the agreement. It is true, of course, as the Appellate Division has said, that if he was under no duty to try to market designs or to place certificates of indorsement, his promise to account for profits or take out copyrights would be valueless. But in determining the intention of the parties, the promise *has* a value. It helps to enforce the conclusion that the plaintiff *had* some duties. His promise to pay the defendant one-half of the profits and revenues resulting from the exclusive agency and to render accounts monthly, was a promise to use reasonable efforts to bring profits and revenues into existence. For this conclusion, the authorities are ample. [Citations omitted.]

The judgment of the Appellate Division should be reversed, and the order of the Special Term affirmed, with costs in the Appellate Division and in this court.

Post-Case Follow-Up

The court implied an obligation to make reasonable efforts to give value to the contract. Without an implication to make reasonable efforts, the contract would be worthless to both parties whose sole compensation was one-half of the proceeds. Wood also had obligations to provide monthly accounting of the profits and to secure patents, copyrights, and trademarks necessary to protect the rights and articles of fashion under the agreement. These contract duties would be worthless if he did not have an implied obligation to make reasonable efforts to secure endorsements.

Wood v. Lucy, Lady Duff-Gordon: Real Life Applications

1. Suzie rents a store space from Margo for a monthly rental amount plus an additional percentage of Suzie's retail sales. Under the agreement, the lease can be terminated if Suzie's monthly sales fall below a certain dollar amount. Suzie's shop is so successful that she opens up a second location that she owns. Tired of paying her monthly sales percentage to Margo, Suzie sends her customers to her

other location to help invoke the termination of her lease with Margo. Consider whether or not Suzie's conduct violates good faith and fair dealing under *Goldberg 168-05 Corp. v. Levy*, 9 N.Y.S.2d 304 (Sup. Ct. 1918).

2. Carlos leases a small lot from Winnie for a ten-year term at $1,500 per month. The lease agreement between the parties provides an option to renew for an additional ten years, but does not set an amount for rent. The lease option states that the rent would be set by the parties' mutual agreement reflecting "the comparative business conditions." Carlos sought to renew his lease, but Winnie and Carlos are unable to reach an agreement on the rent amount. Will a court imply a reasonable rent into the lease renewal? Review *Walker v. Keith*, 382 S.W.2d 198 (Ky. 1964), for the likely outcome.

3. Mega Motors, Inc. (MMI) hires Gray Construction (Gray) to install aluminum siding on a factory addition. The installation work is subject to the final approval of MMI's architect, with her decision final on its artistic effect. After the completion of the siding, MMI's agent rejects the work as lacking a uniform finish and refuses to pay Gray. Another contractor removes and replaces the siding, which MMI's agent approves. The siding appearance looks virtually the same as Gray's efforts. Gray sues for payment. What reasonable satisfaction standard will be applied and who will likely prevail under *Morin Bldg. Prods. Co. v. Baystone Constr., Inc.*, 717 F.2d 413 (7th Cir. 1983)?

3. Modern Use of Best Efforts Clauses

In the *Wood* case, we considered exclusive dealings in a marketing services agreement. In that context, the court implied an obligation of reasonable efforts to defeat a claim of an illusory contract. Previously, best efforts clauses were not often found written into such exclusive dealing contracts because it was assumed that both parties would work to make the agreement profitable. Today, a wide range of exclusive dealing contracts, where one party agrees to allow another the exclusive right to handle some aspect of the first party's business, expressly call for best efforts. The implied duty of reasonable efforts is giving way to contracts specifically requiring the use of best efforts.

Similarly, in sales of goods, exclusive dealings can arise where one party has the exclusive right to distribute the goods of another. UCC §2-306(2) requires best efforts in exclusive dealing contracts: best efforts by the seller to supply the goods and best efforts by the buyer to promote their sale. Failure to get those

Lady Duff-Gordon's Name Still Making Sales Today

Today, it is quite standard for celebrities to lend their names to a broad range of products and services, from designer perfumes and fashions to grills and life insurance.

Lady Duff-Gordon
Library of Congress Prints and Photographs Division Washington, D.C. neg. no. LC-USZ62-135822

goods into stores or to give them a prominent placement where buyers can see them may leave the other party with reduced income—and no way to improve the income, because the distributor has the exclusive right to handle these matters. Any effort by the maker to improve distribution would interfere with the distributor's exclusive right. Conversely, a distributor that has promised to distribute the goods of only one provider may be unable to do much business unless the provider actually supplies enough goods to make this possible. Imagine a cell phone company that agreed to carry only one product line. If the phone manufacturer did not supply phones as needed, the cell phone company would not be able to do much business.

Although a best efforts provision may seem like a good idea, it may be difficult in practice to define what is required to achieve best efforts. One recent court referred to the requirement of best efforts as "murky." By some definitions, "best efforts" sounds a lot like "reasonable efforts." Best efforts cannot be taken literally; it does not require a person to do everything humanly possible to promote sales. The argument that the exclusive distributor could have done more if it dropped other clients, hired more workers, invested more in advertising, or gave up leisure and sleep makes little headway, as long as the efforts made seem reasonable. Once the reasonableness of other uses of time enters the picture, best and reasonable seem to merge. Indeed, cases that invoke best efforts sometimes involve efforts so minimal that they easily could be described as unreasonable or even bad faith.

But "best efforts" appears to require something beyond reasonable efforts; unless some reasonable conduct falls short of best efforts, the language might as well read "reasonable efforts," avoiding any confusion. Best efforts may prohibit conduct that seems reasonable to the exclusive distributor, even though it sacrifices the other party's interests.

For instance, if an exclusive agent cut back work to ten hours per week, using the rest of the time to write a book (or focus on any other unrelated project), that may not satisfy the best efforts the other party has a right to expect, even if it is perfectly reasonable from the standpoint of the agent. Best efforts requires some consideration of the needs of the other party; focusing entirely on one's own interests seems insufficient. Therefore, establishing good faith and reasonableness may not suffice to establish best efforts. Best efforts demands more than the minimum effort necessary to satisfy reasonableness, even if courts have not yet been able to say just how much more is needed.

But it may surprise us that Lady Duff-Gordon, a member of the British aristocracy, contracted with Wood's firm to help promote her own designs and to seek her endorsement on others' designs to help sell them in retail shops back in the early 1900s. Her celebrity status also made her a target for the tabloids when she and her husband, Sir Cosmo Duff-Gordon, survived the sinking of the Titanic. Scandalous allegations were made of bribery and a refusal to rescue others when they escaped the doomed ship on Lifeboat 1. The couple survived on a boat, dubbed the "Money Boat," that was intended for 40 people, but which carried only 12 survivors. Both Duff-Gordons were the only passengers called to testify in a formal inquiry into the circumstances of that tragic event. In 2015, a letter written by Lady Duff-Gordon sold for $12,000 at auction, in which she laments her poor treatment in the press over the "Money Boat" charges. So her name and her association with the tragedy of the Titanic are still keeping her celebrity alive over 100 years later. For more on this story and video about the auctioned item, visit Stephanie Gallman, *Titanic Survivor's Indignant Letter Sells for Nearly $12,000*, CNN.com (19:53 GMT, Jan. 23, 2015), http://edition.cnn.com/2015/01/23/us/titanic-letter-auction/.

C. COMMON UCC DEFAULT TERMS

The discussion so far suggests courts will supply implied or default terms. That is true. For sales of goods, however, legislatures have provided default terms in the UCC, sometimes referred to as "gap fillers," which are applied unless the parties specify a different term. This section will introduce you to key UCC default terms, which you may explore in greater depth in upper level UCC courses. Exhibit 10.1 summarizes commonly implied UCC default terms.

1. Open Price Term — UCC §2-305

Parties may make a contract without specifying the price. The old saying, "If you have to ask, you can't afford it," really does describe some transactions. A person places an order, without ever asking the price. On one hand, one might assume that the price to which the buyer agrees is the seller's list price. The parties can agree that the price is to be fixed by one of them. But that requires actual language — not specifying the price, but specifying who has the power to fix the price. A seller might say, "I'll ship them to you. You look them over and pay me what they're worth to you." Or a buyer might say, "I'll pay your usual price." In either case, the party with the power to fix the price must do so in good faith.

Where the parties say nothing about the price, the price is a reasonable price at the time for delivery. A reasonable price also applies if the parties intend to agree on the price later, but fail to agree, or if the price is to be fixed by some agreed standard, but the standard fails to set a price. For instance, the parties might agree to sell stock at the price at which it closes on the New York Stock Exchange on April 15. If on April 15 trading in the stock is suspended (or if April 15 turns out to be a Sunday), there may be no closing price that day. A reasonable price will govern under those circumstances.

2. Place for Delivery — UCC §2-308(a)

Normally, delivery occurs at the seller's place of business (or, if he has none, at his residence). Thus, if buyer wants delivery to occur at some other place, she must specify that in the contract. The issue is important primarily because of the risk of loss in transit. Suppose seller puts the goods into the hands of a carrier, but the goods are not delivered to buyer. If seller performed by delivering to the carrier, buyer owes the price. Under UCC §2-509(1), the risk of loss during transit was born by buyer, so buyer had the obligation to insure the goods during transit. If the contract calls for the seller to deliver the goods at a particular place (say, buyer's home or business), then the risk passes when the goods are tendered at that place. Under UCC §2-509(2), the seller bears the risk of loss (and burden to insure) until the goods reach that destination.

3. Time for Performance — UCC §2-309

Any action promised under a contract must be performed within a reasonable time. Failure to perform within a reasonable time is breach. A contract that is open-ended — that is, that does not specify when it expires — is binding for a reasonable time, after which either party may withdraw at any time. In addition, parties may decide that their goods agreement will continue for an indefinite period of time, but may be terminated at will; either party may terminate the contract at any time for any reason or for no reason at all, provided it does not violate the law. However, an at-will termination requires reasonable notice to the other party. An agreement that waives notification may not be enforceable if it is seen as creating an unconscionable result.

Case Preview

Leibel v. Raynor Mfg. Co.

In this case, a garage door manufacturer, Raynor, entered into an oral distributorship contract with Leibel, who would sell, install, and service Raynor products in an exclusive territory. Under their agreement, either party could terminate at will. After two years, Raynor decided to terminate their relationship, effective immediately. Leibel, burdened with inventory and other costs, sued Raynor over the abrupt end of their business relationship.

As you read *Leibel v. Raynor Mfg.*, look for the following:

1. Did Raynor provide written notice to Leibel under its at-will relationship?
2. What arguments did Leibel make against his termination becoming effective immediately?
3. How did the court apply UCC §2-309 to the issue of reasonable notice of termination in this case?

Leibel v. Raynor Mfg. Co.

571 S.W.2d 640 (Ky. Ct. App. 1978)

Howerton, J.

. . .

The essential facts are that the parties entered into an oral agreement whereby appellant was to have an exclusive dealer-distributorship for appellee's garage doors in a territory extending for a 50-mile radius from Lexington, Kentucky. The agreement was entered into on or about March 1, 1974. The appellee agreed to sell and deliver to the appellant its garage doors, operators and parts at the factory distributor price, and the appellant agreed to sell, install and service Raynor products exclusively, thereby establishing a relationship of dealer-distributor and manufacturer-supplier. There is no real dispute concerning the nature of the relationship.

As a result of the agreement, the appellant borrowed substantial sums of money in order to make certain capital expenditures, purchase an inventory, and to provide working capital for starting the business, including the rental of storage and office space, employment of personnel, and the purchase of a service truck, tools and equipment.

After two years of what appears to have been decreasing sales of Raynor products in the Lexington area, appellee notified the appellant on or about June 30, 1976, that as of that date the relationship was terminated. Appellant was also notified that Helton Overhead Door Sales had been established by the appellee as the new dealer-distributor for the area, and that the appellant would be required to order all future doors, operators and parts from the new dealer-distributor.

Appellee's motion for a summary judgment was based on the ground that the agreement was for an indefinite duration, and that it could be terminated at will by either party. The appellant resisted the motion on the theory that he was entitled to reasonable notice of appellee's intention to terminate the agreement.

On April 20, 1977, the circuit court granted the summary judgment and entered its memorandum opinion, setting forth its four reasons for the judgment. Appellant had relied in part upon the provisions regarding sales in the Uniform Commercial Code, and specifically subsections (2) and (3) of KRS 355.2-309. The trial court concluded that the Code, as it applies to the sale of goods, was not intended to apply to the situation in this case. Secondly, the court concluded that even if the Uniform Commercial Code did apply, KRS 355.2-309(2), (3) means merely that actual notice of the termination must be given. Written notice had been given. The court concluded that the additional requirement of "reasonable notification" was not necessary. The opinion next concluded that although there are no Kentucky cases directly on point, *Peters Branch of International Shoe Company v. Jones*, 247 Ky. 193, 56 S.W.2d 994 (1933), holds that in an exclusive franchise agreement where there was no agreement as to the duration of the contract, either party could terminate the agreement at will, and there was no mention of notice. Finally, the court concluded that if it required reasonable notification for termination of the agreement, it would be making a contract for the parties by stating a time for the duration of the contract.

We disagree with the conclusions of the trial court and hold that reasonable notification is required in order to terminate an on-going oral agreement for the sale of goods in a relationship of manufacturer-supplier and dealer-distributor or franchisee. The summary judgment must therefore be set aside and a determination must be made on the factual issue of whether or not the notification of termination given in this case was reasonable under the circumstances.

Appellant argues that this contract is now controlled by Article II of the Uniform Commercial Code. The opinion of the trial court provided only that, "It is the opinion of the court that the Uniform Commercial Code applies to the sale of goods and is not intended to apply to the type of situation we have in this case." The rule for application of Article II in Kentucky was stated in *Buttorff v. United Electronic Laboratories, Inc., Ky.*, 459 S.W.2d 581 (1970). According to the opinion in *Buttorff, supra*, we are to look to the real nature of the agreement, the real purpose, and what the parties really intended. It appears that the case sub judice can be distinguished from *Buttorff, supra*, on its facts. The relationship in *Buttorff, supra*, was found to be a contract for personal services, not for the sale of goods or merchandise. *Buttorff* was actually a commissioned salesman for United Electronics Laboratories' cameras and related equipment.

We must now consider the provisions of the Uniform Commercial Code in order to determine whether or not the article on sales is applicable to the situation at bar. This question has not yet been decided by a Kentucky court.

...

In the case at bar, we have a clear situation where the dealer-distributor was to sell the "goods" of the manufacturer-supplier. Appellant was not a commissioned salesman, and the agreement appears to be for the sale of goods.

We conclude that the time has come to recognize that a distributorship agreement must be recognized as an agreement for the sale of goods and subject to the provisions of Article II of the Uniform Commercial Code, which has been adopted by Kentucky in Chapter 355 of the Kentucky Revised Statutes. The amount of money being invested pursuant to distributorship agreements is ever increasing. Often there are no formal written agreements, and it may be that the manufacturer's policy is to have no written agreements. By not establishing a length of time for the contract to exist, either party may terminate the relationship at will, but without a requirement for good faith and fair play, either party may be severely damaged. When sales are the primary essence of the distributorship agreement, the dealer is compelled to keep a large inventory on hand. If the distributorship is terminated without allowing the dealer sufficient time to sell his remaining inventory, substantial damages may result, even if the manufacturer agrees to repurchase the inventory. Reasonable notification should be the minimum amount of protection afforded to either party upon the termination of an ongoing sales agreement. When such reasonable notice is not given, a cause of action for damages may exist.

Having concluded that the Code is applicable to the relationship between the appellant and appellee, we must look at the specific requirements of KRS 355.2-309, "Absence of Specific Time Provisions — Notice of Termination." Subsection (2) reads, "Where the contract provides for successive performances, but is indefinite in duration, it is valid for a reasonable time but unless otherwise agreed may be terminated at any time by either party." Subsection (3) goes on to provide, "Termination of a contract by one (1) party except on the happening of an agreed event requires that reasonable notification be received by the other party and an agreement dispensing with notification is invalid if its operation would be unconscionable." There can be no doubt that reasonable notice is now required, whether or not prior Kentucky decisions, such as *Peters Branch of International Shoe Company v. Jones, supra*, which was relied upon by the trial court, held that notification was not required in an agreement which could be terminated at will. There is a real question of whether *Jones*, supra, actually reached a decision on the reasonable notice question, but we need not determine that point here. Today, in Kentucky, if the provisions of Article II of the Uniform Commercial Code apply to the relationship, reasonable notice of the intention to terminate the agreement must be given. In some cases, it would be required even if a written agreement provided for dispensing with notification. We therefore find additional error in the trial court's opinion when it concluded that even if the provisions of the Code were applicable, only actual notice of termination would be required.

Comment 8 to §2-309 in 1 Anderson, *supra*, at p. 445 reads:

> Subsection (3) recognizes that the application of principles of good faith and sound commercial practice normally call for such notification of the termination of a going contract relationship as will give the other party reasonable time to seek a substitute arrangement. An agreement dispensing with notification, or limiting the time for the seeking of a substitute arrangement, is of course valid under this subsection unless the results of putting it into operation would be the creation of an unconscionable state of affairs.

It is also quite clear that the requirement of a reasonable notification does not relate to the method of giving notice, but to the circumstances under which the notice is given and the extent of advanced warning of termination that the notification gives.

Anderson, *supra*, in the cumulative supplement volume at p. 282, cites two Minnesota cases relating to the time which might be needed for recoupment of investment. *McGinnis Piano and Organ Co. v. Yamaha International Corporation*, 480 F.2d 474 (8th Cir. 1973) is cited for the proposition that "in some states, it is implied that a dealership contract which may be terminated upon notice must be allowed to continue for a sufficient period to enable the franchisee to recoup his investment." The case of *O. M. Droney Beverage Co. v. Miller Brewing Co.*, 365 F. Supp. 1067 (D. Minn. 1973), is cited for the proposition that "under Minnesota law 'a reasonable duration will be implied in franchise agreements where a dealer has made substantial investments in reliance on the agreement.'"

The distributorship agreement existing between appellant and appellee is one in which the essence was the sale of goods. Appellant was certainly not an employee or commissioned salesman of appellee. Appellant purchased the products of the appellee at wholesale prices, and marketed them in the Lexington area. The appellant does not dispute the fact that the agreement was terminable at will, but he contends, and the law so holds, that the appellee was required to give reasonable notification of intent to terminate the contract. What length of time constitutes reasonable notice is a question of material fact which remains to be decided. We cannot say that the written notice given in this case was "reasonable" as a matter of law.

The summary judgment granted by the trial court must therefore be vacated, and the case remanded for further proceedings.

All concur.

Post-Case Follow-Up

The court determined that good faith in at will contracts was needed to avoid terminations that may severely damage either party. Here the distributor had made substantial investments in the business and could be seriously harmed if the termination was effective immediately. The court held that UCC §2-309 required that reasonable notice, not just actual notice, be given if the agreement was for an indefinite duration. The court noted that some judicial decisions looked to a sufficient time period for recoupment of one's investment in determining reasonableness. Since reasonable notice was a question of fact, the court could not conclude that notice was "reasonable" as a matter of law and remanded the case for additional fact-finding by the trial court.

Leibel v. Raynor Mfg. Co.: Real Life Applications

1. A vineyard enters into an exclusive distribution agreement with a wine wholesaler to sell its red and white wines to retailers. The wholesaler is permitted to sell other wine brands under the agreement. Under the agreement, the wholesaler may terminate the agreement under a 60-day termination clause. The vineyard's red wines sell very well, but its white wines do not. The wholesaler stops selling the vineyard's white wines and sells only the more popular white wines of the vineyard's main competitor. The vineyard sues for breach of contract, and the wholesaler claims that it is simply responding to market demand in good faith. What is the likely result in this case based on *California Wine Assn. v. Wisconsin Liquor Co.*, 20 Wis. 2d 110 (1963)?
2. Several farmers agree to sell wheat to a large scale grain operator for later distribution nationally. Under the contract, the farmers may deliver their grain within specified time periods. There is a clause stating that the buyer could extend the time of delivery or declare the farmers in default for any unfulfilled deliveries at the expiration of the contract. After making initial deliveries, the grain operator tells the farmers that he will let them know when to make the remaining deliveries. Due to transportation and oversupply issues, the grain operator delays in advising them for three months after the specified delivery time periods. The farmers cancel the contract due to their claim of unreasonable delay and seek damages. Is the operator's delay unreasonable under *Farmers Union Grain Terminal Assn. v. Hermanson*, 549 F.2d 1177 (8th Cir. 1977)?
3. An organic tomato farmer enters into a contract with a produce supplier before the start of the tomato growing season. The price is $20 for each carton weighing 25 pounds. It is not unusual for tomatoes to become bruised and damaged during harvesting and transporting to the buyer. The contract mandates that the parties must renegotiate a price for any substandard shipments. The parties agree that 35 percent of the tomatoes shipped were substandard, but they cannot agree on the renegotiated price for the damaged produce. Consider *Licklyey v. Max Herbold*, 133 Idaho 209 (1999), in addressing how to determine a reasonable price for the substandard tomatoes.

4. Time for Payment—UCC §2-310(a)

Unless otherwise specified, payment is due at the time and place of delivery—in other words, "Cash On Delivery" (COD). Because delivery occurs when the seller ships the goods at its place of business, payment is due before shipment. Many commercial contracts provide terms like "net 30 days," which requires payment within 30 days after delivery. In effect, the seller extends credit to the buyer for 30 days.

Nothing in these default terms truly requires the parties to make any particular promise. Rather, they identify the promises the law will assume the parties made unless they expressly provide otherwise. Therefore, the parties know which of them has the onus of negotiating for a contrary term in the agreement. In most cases, the final terms probably are the same as they would be with no implied promises—especially in a world where businesses draft form contracts that consumers accept without even reading. But the business drafting the contract must pay some attention to the default terms, if only to determine how to disclaim them.

EXHIBIT 10.1 Common UCC Default Terms

Contract Term Not Specified	Common UCC Default Term	Relevant UCC Section
Price	*Reasonable Price* at the time and place for delivery	2-305
Payment Details	Payment due at the *Time and Place of Delivery*	2-310(a)
Place for Delivery	Delivery at *Seller's Place of Business*	2-308(a)
Time for Performance/Delivery	Performance/Delivery due within *Reasonable Time*	2-309(1)
Termination of Contract	Must provide *Reasonable Notice*	2-309(3)

D. EXPRESS AND IMPLIED WARRANTIES

A **warranty** is a promise relating to the quality of the performance of contract duties. Warranties can attach to any contract. Land sales are made by warranty deed, which includes a promise that the seller holds good title to the land. Residential leases include an implied warranty of habitability. Home remodeling may include warranties, perhaps even promising that satisfaction is guaranteed and that the remodeling complies with all pertinent construction codes.

Classical contract law applied the doctrine ***caveat emptor***: let the buyer beware. No promises relating to quality existed unless the parties expressly made such promises. **Express warranties**—promises that arise from statements or conduct of the seller that suggest a promise relating to the quality of performance—remain an important part of contract law. Most cars or electronics come with an explicit warranty that they will be free from defects in material or labor for a period of time. A seller is not required to make an express warranty, but if a seller does so, then the seller is bound by that contract obligation.

But modern law also recognizes **implied warranties**—those that arise by operation of law unless the parties agree otherwise. Unlike express warranties, which are created by a seller, the law creates the implied warranty as part of the bargain.

Today, the law assumes that parties expect at least some minimal level of quality in every transaction. Parties may **disclaim** these warranties — agree to terms that exclude these implied promises. Yet without a disclaimer — and in some cases with one, unless the disclaimer is sufficiently prominent and clear — implied warranties are automatically part of the contract.

1. Express Warranties — UCC §2-313

Parties may include an express warranty in their contract. In some contracts, such as for the sale of a business, warranties are fully negotiated and drafted for the specific transaction. In sales of goods, warranties may arise more casually. Even an offhand remark by a salesperson may turn out to be a promise to provide goods of a certain quality.

UCC §2-313(1) recognizes three ways that express warranties may be created and become part of the underlying exchange:

1. a promise or an affirmation of fact about the quality of the goods;
2. a description of the goods; or
3. a sample or model.

By offering any of these, the seller creates in the buyer an expectation that the goods delivered will conform to the quality implied: they will be as good as the model or sample, they will match the description, and they will conform to the promises or statements concerning their quality.

By offering any of these, the seller probably makes them part of the basis of the bargain. Buyer's reliance upon the assertions of quality (by buying the goods) would establish that they became the basis of the bargain. However, buyers may not need to prove they attached significance to the warranty. Unless facts indicate that the seller negated any implication that the delivered goods would conform to the expectations it created, these descriptions became part of the basis of the bargain. Seller can make such disclaimers: recall the ever popular "EPA mileage estimates are for comparison only; your mileage may vary."

Not every statement by a salesperson will necessarily become a warranty. Two types of statements do not take on that significance:

1. statements concerning the value of the goods; and
2. statements purporting to be the seller's opinion or commendation of the goods.

Statements of this sort are considered **sales puffery** — self-promoting sales talk and statements of opinion about intangible qualities of products — and are not warranties. They are not misrepresentations because it is not justifiable to rely on pure opinions about product value or quality. Courts have consistently found that claims that one's products are the "best" or "greatest" are not statements of fact, but sales puffery that does not provide grounds for legal actions. Conversely, objectively

Statements of this sort are considered sales puffery, not warranties.
mmac72/iStockphoto

measurable claims about products may be viewed as warranties, especially when safety concerns are involved.

You may be able to distinguish puffery from warranties by keeping the basis of the rule in mind: what did the seller promise to deliver? Statements of fact—"This printer puts out 45 pages per minute"—sound like a promise to deliver a printer that meets that speed. Statements of opinion—"This is a top-notch printer"—are harder to convert into a description of what the seller promised to deliver. After all, you wouldn't really want to let a buyer return a used car because it didn't "purr like a kitten," would you? Some statements really aren't part of the basis of the bargain.

Differentiating statements of fact concerning the goods from statements of opinion concerning the quality or value of the goods may not be easy in any given case, especially if the statements were oral. Proving they were made may be hard enough, without trying to prove what form they took. Nonetheless, some room for marketing or promotional talk is preserved, without turning everything into a warranty.

2. Implied Warranties—UCC §§2-312, 2-314, 2-315

The UCC recognizes three key implied warranties that arise by operation of law, even if the parties do not expressly include them in their agreement:

1. a warranty of title and against infringement (UCC §2-312);
2. a warranty of merchantability (UCC §2-314); and
3. a warranty of fitness for a specific purpose (UCC §2-315).

In each case, the parties may exclude the warranties by express terms in their agreement.

Warranty of Title—UCC §2-312

The warranty of title and against infringement promises that it is legal for the seller to sell these goods, and that the sale will not violate another person's claim to own the goods or any undisclosed **security interest** in the goods (right to foreclose on or to repossess the goods). Whether or not seller has clean title, he promises to convey clean title to the goods. Similarly, a **merchant** (one who regularly deals in goods of this type) implicitly promises that goods will be free of any rightful claim of infringement, such as infringement of a **patent** (an inventor's exclusive right to her invention), a **copyright** (an exclusive right to creative works, such as books, music, photographs, computer programs, and so on), or a **trademark** (an exclusive right to use identifying packaging or symbols, such as corporate logos). There is an exception when the buyer provides the specifications — say, blueprints seller must follow to produce the goods. In that case, the buyer must warrant to the seller that the specifications do not infringe.

Merchantability — UCC §2-314

The warranty of **merchantability** promises that the goods satisfy a minimal level of quality. It seeks to describe the assumptions that a buyer is likely to make when dealing in goods. Just calling a good by name (car) frequently suggests that it has certain qualities (four wheels, engine, windshield, and so on). According to UCC §2-314, the goods must meet the following basic requirements:

1. be of fair, average quality within reasonable variations in quality;
2. be fit for their ordinary purposes or typical uses;
3. pass without objection in the trade; and
4. be adequately contained, packaged, and labeled, with the product conforming to the promises on that packaging or container.

Some of these standards reflect commercial practices — what people in the trade would expect when dealing in goods of this description. All are subject to variation by express contract terms. That is particularly true of those related to variations where the contract may define the tolerable limits or packaging requirements. If the goods fall short on even one of these provisions, the buyer may seek redress against the seller.

Fitness for a Particular Purpose — UCC §2-315

Under UCC §2-315, the warranty of fitness for a particular purpose arises in a specific kind of transaction. A buyer may rely on the seller's expertise to select goods appropriate to the buyer's purpose. In those situations, seller implicitly promises that the goods it selects are fit for that purpose. The warranty arises if seller has reason to know two things at the time of contract formation:

1. the buyer has communicated a particular (not ordinary) purpose for the required goods; and
2. the buyer is relying on the seller's skill or judgment in choosing appropriate goods for that particular purpose.

The warranty does not apply to ordinary uses of a product or when buyers make their own decisions about which goods will satisfy their specific needs. It applies to those who rely on sellers' judgment — and then only when the sellers have reason to know of the reliance. When the warranty arises, if the goods supplied prove unsuitable for the buyer's purpose, buyer may sue for their failure to live up to the quality implicitly promised.

3. Disclaiming Warranties—UCC §2-316

Some sellers prefer the good old days of *caveat emptor*; they often seek to disclaim the warranties described here. Like most terms of the UCC, the warranty terms apply unless the parties make their own express agreement regarding those terms. Thus, excluding these warranties is acceptable. But because the warranties reflect buyers' natural assumptions, efforts to negate these warranties may surprise and frustrate buyers. As a result, the UCC contains rules about how warranties may be disclaimed.

Typically, an express warranty cannot be disclaimed. The express warranty is created by the contract or sometimes the negotiations leading up to the contract. To promise a particular quality in one paragraph and then disclaim it in another is surprising and objectionable. Where the disclaimer can be interpreted as consistent with the express warranty, that interpretation is preferred. However, if a consistent interpretation is impossible, the warranty is enforced and the disclaimer is not given effect.

Implied warranties can be disclaimed, but the disclaimer must be conspicuous. A writing is required to exclude a warranty of fitness; it cannot be done orally. To disclaim the warranty of merchantability, the exclusion must mention merchantability (and, if in writing, must be conspicuous). Simply excluding all implied warranties will exclude the others, but not merchantability. Alternatively, all warranties can be excluded by language that in the common understanding excludes implied warranties, including words such as "as is" or "with all faults"—even if the disclaimer does not mention merchantability. However, it is important to note that state consumer protection laws and the federal Magnuson-Moss Warranty Act may prevent the disclaimer of implied warranties to protect the public from efforts to evade responsibilities for poor product quality that cause personal injury.

Case Preview

Bayliner Marine Corp. v. Crow

In *Bayliner Marine Corp. v. Crow*, a customer was unhappy with the performance of a boat he purchased for offshore fishing and sued a boat manufacturer. He raised issues of express and implied warranties of merchantability and fitness for a particular purpose to support his claim for damages. In reviewing his claims, the appeals court also considered issues of disclaimers and sales puffery in rendering its decision.

As you read *Bayliner Marine Corp. v. Crow*, look for the following:

1. What were Crow's arguments in support of his express warranty claims regarding the boat?
2. What were Crow's contentions regarding implied warranties and the boat's performance?
3. How did warranty disclaimers and sales puffery play into the court's decision in this case?

Bayliner Marine Corp. v. Crow

257 Va. 121 (1999)

MILANO KEENAN, JUSTICE

In this appeal, the dispositive issue is whether there was sufficient evidence to support the trial court's ruling that the manufacturer of a sport fishing boat breached an express warranty and implied warranties of merchantability and fitness for a particular purpose.

In the summer of 1989, John R. Crow was invited by John Atherton, then a sales representative for Tidewater Yacht Agency, Inc. (Tidewater), to ride on a new model sport fishing boat known as a 3486 Trophy Convertible, manufactured by Bayliner Marine Corporation (Bayliner). At that time, Tidewater was the exclusive authorized dealer in southeastern Virginia for this model Bayliner boat. During an excursion lasting about 20 minutes, Crow piloted the boat for a short period of time but was not able to determine its speed because there was no equipment on board for such testing.

When Crow asked Atherton about the maximum speed of the boat, Atherton explained that he had no personal experience with the boat or information from other customers concerning the boat's performance. Therefore, Atherton consulted two documents described as "prop matrixes," which were included by Bayliner in its dealer's manual.

Atherton gave Crow copies of the "prop matrixes," which listed the boat models offered by Bayliner and stated the recommended propeller sizes, gear ratios, and engine sizes for each model. The "prop matrixes" also listed the maximum speed for each model. The 3486 Trophy Convertible was listed as having a maximum speed of 30 miles per hour when equipped with a size "20x20" or "2019" propeller. The boat Crow purchased did not have either size propeller but, instead, had a size "20x17" propeller.

At the bottom of one of the "prop matrixes" was the following disclaimer: "This data is intended for comparative purposes only, and is available without reference to weather conditions or other variables. All testing was done at or near sea level, with full fuel and water tanks, and approximately 600 lb. passenger and gear weight."

Atherton also showed Crow a Bayliner brochure describing the 1989 boat models, including the 3486 Trophy Convertible. The brochure included a picture of that model fully rigged for offshore fishing, accompanied by the statement that this model "delivers the kind of performance you need to get to the prime offshore fishing grounds."

In August 1989, Crow entered into a written contract for the purchase of the 3486 Trophy Convertible in which he had ridden. The purchase price was $120,000, exclusive of taxes. The purchase price included various equipment to be installed by Tidewater. . . . The total weight of the added equipment was about 2,000 pounds. Crow did not test drive the boat after the additional equipment was installed or at any other time prior to taking delivery.

When Crow took delivery of the boat in September 1989, he piloted it onto the Elizabeth River. He noticed that the boat's speed measuring equipment, which was installed in accordance with the contract terms, indicated that the boat's maximum speed was 13 miles per hour. Crow immediately returned to Tidewater and reported the problem.

During the next 12 to 14 months, while Crow retained ownership and possession of the boat, Tidewater made numerous repairs and adjustments to the boat in an attempt to increase its speed capability. Despite these efforts, the boat consistently achieved a maximum speed of only 17 miles per hour, except for one period following an engine modification when it temporarily reached a speed of about 24 miles per hour. In July 1990, a representative from Bayliner wrote Crow a letter stating that the performance representations made at the time of purchase were incorrect, and that 23 to 25 miles per hour was the maximum speed the boat could achieve.

In 1992, Crow filed a motion for judgment against Tidewater, Bayliner, and Brunswick Corporation, the manufacturer of the boat's diesel engines. [Footnote omitted.] Crow alleged, among other things, that Bayliner breached express warranties, and implied warranties of merchantability and fitness for a particular purpose.

At a bench trial in 1994, Crow, Atherton, and Gordon W. Shelton, III, Tidewater's owner, testified that speed is a critical quality in boats used for offshore sport fishing in the Tidewater area of Virginia because of the distance between the coast and the offshore fishing grounds. According to these witnesses, a typical offshore fishing site in that area is 90 miles from the coast. Therefore, the speed at which the boat can travel to and from fishing sites has a major impact on the amount of time left in a day for fishing.

Crow testified that because of the boat's slow speed, he could not use the boat for offshore fishing, that he had no other use for it, and that he would not have purchased the boat if he had known that its maximum speed was 23 to 25 miles per hour. Crow testified that he had not used the boat for fishing since 1991 or 1992. He admitted, however, that between September 1989, and September 1994, the boat's engines had registered about 850 hours of use. Bob Schey, Bayliner's manager of yacht testing, testified that a pleasure boat in a climate such as Virginia's typically would register 150 engine hours per year.

The trial court entered judgment in favor of Crow against Bayliner on the counts of breach of express warranty and breach of implied warranties of merchantability and fitness for a particular purpose. The court awarded Crow damages of $135,000, plus prejudgment interest from June 1993. The court explained that the $135,000 award represented the purchase price of the boat, and about $15,000 in "damages" for a portion of the expenses Crow claimed in storing, maintaining, insuring, and financing the boat.

On appeal, we review the evidence in the light most favorable to Crow, the prevailing party at trial. [Citations omitted.] We will uphold the trial court's judgment unless it is plainly wrong or without evidence to support it. [Citations omitted.]

Crow argues that the "prop matrixes" he received created an express warranty by Bayliner that the boat he purchased was capable of a maximum speed of 30 miles per hour. We disagree.

. . .

The issue whether a particular affirmation of fact made by the seller constitutes an express warranty is generally a question of fact. . . . *Daughtrey v. Ashe*, 243 Va. 73, 78, 413 S.E.2d 336, 339 (1992). In *Daughtrey*, we examined whether a jeweler's statement on an appraisal form constituted an express warranty. We held that the jeweler's description of the particular diamonds being purchased as "v.v.s. quality" constituted an express warranty that the diamonds were, in fact, of that grade. *Id.* at 77, 413 S.E.2d at 338.

Unlike the representation in *Daughtrey*, however, the statements in the "prop matrixes" provided by Bayliner did not relate to the particular boat purchased by Crow, or to one having substantially similar characteristics. By their plain terms, the figures stated in the "prop matrixes" referred to a boat with different sized propellers that carried equipment weighing substantially less than the equipment on Crow's boat. Therefore, we conclude that the statements contained in the "prop matrixes" did not constitute an express warranty by Bayliner about the performance capabilities of the particular boat purchased by Crow.

Crow also contends that Bayliner made an express warranty regarding the boat's maximum speed in the statement in Bayliner's sales brochure that this model boat "delivers the kind of performance you need to get to the prime offshore fishing grounds." While the general rule is that a description of the goods that forms a basis of the bargain constitutes an express warranty, Code §8.2-313(2) directs that "a statement purporting to be merely the seller's opinion or commendation of the goods does not create a warranty."

The statement made by Bayliner in its sales brochure is merely a commendation of the boat's performance and does not describe a specific characteristic or feature of the boat. The statement simply expressed the manufacturer's opinion concerning the quality of the boat's performance and did not create an express warranty that the boat was capable of attaining a speed of 30 miles per hour. Therefore, we conclude that the evidence does not support the trial court's finding that Bayliner breached an express warranty made to Crow.

We next consider whether the evidence supports the trial court's conclusion that Bayliner breached an implied warranty of merchantability. Crow asserts that because his boat was not capable of achieving a maximum speed of 30 miles per hour, it was not fit for its ordinary purpose as an offshore sport fishing boat. Bayliner contends in response that, although the boat did not meet the needs of this particular sport fisherman, there was no evidence from which the trial court could conclude that the boat generally was not merchantable as an offshore fishing boat. We agree with Bayliner's argument.

Code §8.2-314 provides that, in all contracts for the sale of goods by a merchant, a warranty is implied that the goods will be merchantable. To be merchantable, the goods must be such as would "pass without objection in the trade" and as "are fit for the ordinary purposes for which such goods are used." Code §8.2-314(2)(a), (c). The first phrase concerns whether a "significant segment of the buying public" would object to buying the goods, while the second phrase concerns whether the goods are "reasonably capable of performing their ordinary functions." *Federal Signal Corp. v. Safety Factors, Inc.*, 125 Wash. 2d 413, 886 P.2d 172, 180 (Wash. 1994). In order to prove that a product is not merchantable, the complaining party must first establish the standard of merchantability in the trade. *Laird v. Scribner Coop, Inc.*, 237 Neb. 532, 466 N.W.2d 798, 804 (Neb. 1991). Bayliner correctly notes that the record contains no evidence of the standard of merchantability in the offshore fishing boat trade. Nor does the record contain any evidence supporting a conclusion that a significant portion of the boat-buying public would object to purchasing an offshore fishing boat with the speed capability of the 3486 Trophy Convertible.

Crow, nevertheless, relies on his own testimony that the boat's speed was inadequate for his intended use, and Atherton's opinion testimony that the boat took "a long time" to reach certain fishing grounds in the Gulf Stream off the coast of Virginia. However, this evidence did not address the standard of merchantability in the trade or whether Crow's boat failed to meet that standard. Thus, we hold that Crow failed to prove that the boat would not "pass without objection in the trade" as required by Code §8.2-314(2)(a).

We next consider whether the record supports a conclusion that Crow's boat was not fit for its ordinary purpose as an offshore sport fishing boat. Generally, the issue whether goods are fit for the ordinary purposes for which they are used is a factual question. *See Federal Ins. Co. v. Village of Westmont*, 271 Ill. App. 3d 892, 649 N.E.2d 986, 990, 208 Ill. Dec. 626 (App. Ct. Ill. 1995); *Tallmadge v. Aurora Chrysler Plymouth, Inc.*, 25 Wash. App. 90, 605 P.2d 1275, 1278 (Wash. Ct. App. 1979). Here, the evidence is uncontroverted that Crow used the boat for offshore fishing, at least during the first few years after purchasing it, and that the boat's engines were used for 850 hours. While Crow stated that many of those hours were incurred during various repair or modification attempts and that the boat was of little value to him, this testimony does not support a conclusion that a boat with this speed capability is generally unacceptable as an offshore fishing boat. Thus, considered in the light most favorable to Crow, the evidence fails to establish that the boat was not fit for the ordinary purpose for which it was intended.

We next address Crow's claim that Bayliner breached an implied warranty of fitness for a particular purpose. Code §8.2-315 provides that when a seller "has reason to know any particular purpose for which the goods are required and that the buyer is relying on the seller's skill or judgment to select or furnish suitable goods, there is . . . an implied warranty that the goods shall be fit for such purpose." *See also Medcom, Inc. v. C. Arthur Weaver Co., Inc.*, 232 Va. 80, 84-85, 348 S.E.2d 243, 246 (1986). This statute embodies a long-standing common law rule in Virginia. *Layne-Atlantic Co. v. Koppers Co.*, 214 Va. 467, 471, 201 S.E.2d 609, 613 (1974). The question whether there was an implied warranty of fitness for a particular purpose in a sale of goods is ordinarily a question of fact based on the circumstances surrounding the transaction. *Stones v. Sears, Roebuck & Co.*, 251 Neb. 560, 558 N.W.2d 540, 547 (Neb. 1997).

Crow contends that the "particular purpose" for which the boat was intended was use as an offshore fishing boat capable of traveling at a maximum speed of 30 miles per hour. However, to establish an implied warranty of fitness for a particular purpose, the buyer must prove as a threshold matter that he made known to the seller the particular purpose for which the goods were required. *See Medcom*, 232 Va. at 84, 348 S.E.2d at 246. The record before us does not support a conclusion that Crow informed Atherton of this precise requirement. Although Crow informed Atherton that he intended to use the boat for offshore fishing and discussed the boat's speed in this context, these facts did not establish that Atherton knew on the date of sale that a boat incapable of travelling at 30 miles per hour was unacceptable to Crow. Thus, we conclude that the evidence fails to support the trial court's ruling that Bayliner breached an implied warranty of fitness for a particular purpose.

For these reasons, we will reverse the trial court's judgment and enter final judgment in favor of Bayliner. . . .

Post-Case Follow-Up

The *Bayliner* court ruled that statements contained in the prop matrixes were not express warranties about the boat's performance because those documents explicitly referred to a boat that carried less weight and had different propeller sizes than the one that Crow purchased. The brochure statements describing the boat as one that "delivers the kind of performance you need to get to the prime offshore fishing grounds" was a simply a statement of opinion or sales puffery, not an express warranty. The court found no evidence that the boat generally was not merchantable as an offshore fishing boat and found that Crow used the boat for many more hours than typical boaters. Crow failed to introduce evidence that he made his 30 mph requirement known to the seller as a particular purpose. In addition, the seller told Crow that he had no personal experience with boat so Crow was not relying on the seller's skill or judgment.

Bayliner Marine Corp. v. Crow: Real Life Applications

1. Norton legally purchased a firearm. There are a number of warnings about the gun on the product box and in an owner's manual that comes with the gun. After finishing a firearm safety program. Norton accidentally suffers a gunshot wound to his leg after depressing the gun's trigger while putting it away in its case. He later sues the gun manufacturer claiming a breach of warranty, contending that the warnings were inadequate and the gun did not perform in compliance with the packaging and owner's manual. Is there a breach of express or implied warranties according to *Wasylow v. Glock, Inc.*, 975 F. Supp. 370 (D. Mass. 1996)?

2. Tonya enters into a contract to purchase a new car from her local car dealership. The car manufacturer knows of a defect in that model's taillight assemblies that

causes early rusting and a need for replacement after 15,000 miles. The manufacturer only warrants the entire vehicle for the first 12,000 miles, as stated in its brochure and owner's manual. Tonya notifies the car manufacturer of this rust problem, but it does nothing since the warranty is expired. Tonya then seeks a full refund, claiming a breach of the implied warranty of merchantability. Will Tonya succeed under this implied warranty? Review *Taterka v. Ford Motor Co.*, 86 Wis. 2d 140 (1978) to see the likely judicial response.

3. Christi starts a new a gym with a broad range of expensive equipment. She asks the company installing her equipment, Gymtastic Renovators, Inc., about the best ways to maintain this equipment. The company sells her $5,000 in oil, which is supposed to be used to extend the life of the equipment. Over a short period of time, Christi finds that the equipment is breaking down and another repair company advises her that Gymtastic supplied her with the wrong kind of oil for her type of equipment, which has damaged it and limited its long-term life. Will any implied warranty support Christi's claim for breach for warranty? Read *Lewis v. Mobil Oil Corp.*, 438 F.2d 500 (8th Cir. 1971), and determine what implied warranty, if any, will support her claim.

Magnuson-Moss Warranty Act—Federal Consumer Product Safety

In general, contract law is a state matter. But there are also federal laws that impact government contracting as well as consumer protection on a nationwide basis. Enacted in 1975, the Magnuson-Moss Warranty Act addresses written warranties on consumer goods valued at more than ten dollars. The Act requires that warranties be properly labelled as either a full warranty (free repair or replacement of defective goods) or limited warranty (restricts scope and remedies of product guarantees). No implied warranties are created under the Act. Yet if a seller creates an express warranty, the federal law does not allow a seller to disclaim the implied warranties of merchantability or fitness for a particular purpose. Any time period that a seller sets for its express warranty must also be applied to these implied warranties. The Federal Trade Commission administers the Act to help ensure seller compliance. Visit the FTC's website to review its guide on this law and its application at https://www.ftc.gov/tips-advice/business-center/guidance/businesspersons-guide-federal-warranty-law.

E. REQUIREMENTS AND OUTPUT CONTRACTS

Some contracts allow one party flexibility to determine quantity as its business situation dictates. In a **requirements contract**, the buyer agrees to buy all of some good that it needs from the seller. This gives the buyer the flexibility to determine its needs as they develop, rather than trying to predict them up front. Predictions are risky. Guessing too low may leave the buyer looking for another source of supply and perhaps paying a higher price at the end of a year. Guessing too high may leave the buyer with more of a good than it needs (for which it had to pay). If seller agrees to meet all of the buyer's requirements, buyer can order what it wants, when it wants, without facing either problem.

Conversely, in an **output contract**, a seller agrees to sell all of some performance to a single buyer, who agrees to take the entire output. Seller need not predict how much will be produced and specify that amount in the contract; buyer agrees to take it all, without a more precise figure. (A contract is either an output contract or a requirements contract. If seller agrees to meet all of buyer's requirements, it lacks discretion to set its own output any lower; if buyer agrees to take all of seller's output, it lacks discretion to purchase any less, no matter how little it requires.)

1. Illusoriness and Definiteness

The doctrines governing requirements and output contracts are important. Requirements and output contracts are real commitments to perform. They are not **illusory**: neither party has unbridled discretion to back out of the deal without consequences, even if the discretion to order none or to produce none is retained by one party. Under some circumstances, an effort to back out by claiming zero requirements or zero output will be breach, constraining the discretion of a party that has changed its mind. A buyer might not promise to require any at all, but it has promised that if it has requirements, it will buy them from seller. Thus, buyer cannot back out of the deal and purchase its needs elsewhere. That would breach the requirements contract. Buyer's discretion is constrained: either buy from seller or buy none at all (or pay damages for breach). A seller might not promise to produce any output at all, but it has promised that if it has output, it will sell it to buyer. Thus, seller cannot back out of the deal and sell to another. Its discretion is constrained: either sell to this buyer or produce none at all (or pay damages for breach). In practice, contracts may specify a minimum that removes any question of illusoriness. The doctrines discussed below may preclude a party from ordering none or producing none.

Requirements or output contracts are **definite**, providing courts with a sufficient basis for determining whether one party has breached the contract and for determining an appropriate remedy. The quantity may not be **liquidated** (reduced to a specific number or formula in the agreement), but it is ascertainable. In a requirements contract, if the buyer makes any purchases of the good from a different seller, it has breached the requirements contract. Breach can be ascertained. But as long as a buyer makes no purchases of the good from any other seller, it has performed its promise to buy all of its requirements from this seller no matter how much or how little it actually buys from the seller (with some constraints). Similarly, in an output contract, if the seller keeps some of its production for itself or sells some to another buyer, it has breached. If it delivers all of its output to the buyer, it has performed.

2. Limiting the Quantity

There are limits on the amount a buyer may demand (in a requirements contract) or a seller may tender (in an output contract). The limits are most important when the amounts involved are unexpectedly large. But the rules have been applied when unexpectedly low amounts are at stake.

In agreeing to supply all of buyer's requirements, seller probably considered whether its capacity to produce could keep pace with buyer's needs. An unexpectedly large demand may outstrip seller's ability to produce enough, forcing the seller to breach. Similarly, an unexpectedly large output may outstrip a buyer's ability to pay for or to use the goods supplied. Unexpectedly small quantities, while not as taxing, may disappoint the other party, who believed that the amounts involved would be larger. Smaller quantities may require efforts to replace the amount that was expected but that did not appear.

UCC §2-306(1) reads key limitations into the words requirements or output:

1. actual output or requirements must be determined in good faith, and
2. are not "unreasonably disproportionate" to the anticipated output or requirements.

Anticipated output or requirements refers to any estimate stated by the parties in the agreement. If there was no estimate stated, a party's normal output or requirements for a comparable prior period will provide a baseline from which to determine whether the amount demanded or tendered was unreasonably disproportionate.

The rule seeks to identify limits the parties probably intended at the time they entered the contract. Seller's output refers to its production, not to any amount it can get its hands on from other manufacturers. Buyer's requirements refer to the amount buyer uses in its business, not any amount buyer decides to request.

Good Faith

Good faith requires each party to be honest in fact and to comply with reasonable commercial standards of fair dealing. A demand that exceeds the amount a buyer really desires (that is, pretending to want more than it really wants) would not be honest in fact. For example, a buyer who wanted out of a contract might demand an excessive amount, hoping the seller would breach, providing an excuse for cancellation. But that is a risky strategy as the seller might meet the demand.

Honest requests for large quantities might not conform to commercial standards of fair dealing. For instance, most requirements contracts specify a time period, such as all the requirements for 2014. Excessive orders at the end of the year, in order to stockpile at the more favorable current price, might not comport with reasonable commercial standards of fair dealing. The requirements for 2015 were not promised. Similarly, a buyer with a really good price on material might decide to resell it to others who need it. Good faith might preclude the buyer from going into competition with the seller. The seller promised to supply the buyer's requirements, but not the requirements of everyone that the buyer knows. The exact content of reasonable commercial standards is hard to specify. Fair dealing means different things to different people in different contexts. It may be useful to relate the issue back to interpretation of the contract: if the parties had discussed these reasons for purchasing more up front, would they have agreed that the seller would need to meet these kinds of demands?

In output contracts, the issue is whether seller can increase production dramatically. Like buyer, seller may have actual increases in production that do not arise from good faith decisions. Putting on an extra shift to take advantage of an advantageous price locked in by the contract might not comport with reasonable commercial standards of fair dealing. Within limits, variations in production were expected and included in the agreement. Dramatic shifts without any business justification beyond extracting maximum benefit from this contract may not qualify as good faith.

Unreasonably Disproportionate

Amounts that greatly exceed the amount anticipated need not be accepted or tendered, even if the requests reflect actual and good faith output or requirements. The parties, in entering the contract, probably had in mind a range within which the quantity would fall. The contract expresses their agreement to a quantity within that range, not to quantities dramatically different from it. The parties may express the range for themselves, including minimum and maximum quantities in the contract. Without an express term, the court will compute an appropriate range based on an estimate in the contract. If no estimate is in the contract, quantities from comparable periods in other years or normal quantities for the enterprise offer the court a baseline that the parties probably had in mind during negotiations.

While differences are permissible, unreasonably disproportionate amounts are not. Without context, it is difficult to say when an amount becomes unreasonably disproportionate. A 100 percent increase describes an increase from 2 to 4, or from 8 million to 16 million. Either might be reasonable or unreasonable, depending on context. Four oil tankers might be unreasonably disproportionate to two; 16 million paper clips might not be unreasonably disproportionate to 8 million. (Of course, no one should promise to sell all the oil tankers another requires.)

Unexpectedly Small Quantities

Excessive demands can pose serious problems. The need to limit unexpectedly small quantities is less clear. For one thing, a small quantity is disappointing, but usually not a hardship. The other party is free to deal with others for unmet needs. For another, small quantities are harder to fake. A buyer who really does not buy from anyone apparently does not need (or even want) more than she orders. A seller who shuts down a product line (as opposed to pretending to shut it down while selling the production to another) really does have low output. These decisions undoubtedly were made in the best interest of the business cutting back; cutting back on profitable business is a pretty unusual move.

It seems difficult to argue that a seller under a requirements contract (or a buyer under an output contract) obtained the right to demand that the other increase its operations. These terms retain discretion for the seller (output) or buyer (requirements) to make adjustments as their circumstances change. Turning that into the other party's right to demand increased efforts stands the term on its head. But there may be situations when those adjustments may raise issues of good faith and fair dealing as discussed in the *Feld* case below.

Case Preview

Feld v. Henry S. Levy & Sons

In *Feld v. Henry S. Levy & Sons*, a bakery stopped producing bread crumbs before an output contract expired with Feld, a wholesale bread maker. Feld challenged the bakery's decision to stop providing its products under an output contract. There is a question as to whether or not the bakery may simply cease production of certain goods under an output contract and repurpose the raw materials for sales to another party. The court must weigh the baking company's concerns about losses with the buyer's demands for the goods under their output contract.

As you read *Feld v. Henry S. Levy & Sons*, look for the following:

1. What were the bakery's arguments for ceasing the making of bread crumbs?
2. How did good faith apply to the obligation to continue to produce goods under an output contract?
3. What good faith grounds did the court indicate might permit the cessation of the production of the bread crumbs?

Feld v. Henry S. Levy & Sons

335 N.E.2d 320 (N.Y. 1975)

Cooke, J.

Plaintiff operates a business known as the Crushed Toast Company and defendant is engaged in the wholesale bread baking business. They entered into a written contract, as of June 19, 1968, in which defendant agreed to sell and plaintiff to purchase "all bread crumbs produced by the Seller in its factory at 115 Thames Street, Brooklyn, New York, during the period commencing June 19, 1968, and terminating June 18, 1969," the agreement to "be deemed automatically renewed thereafter for successive renewal periods of one year" with the right to either party to cancel by giving not less than six months' notice to the other by certified mail. No notice of cancellation was served. Additionally, pursuant to a contract stipulation, a faithful performance bond was delivered by plaintiff at the inception of the contractual relationship, and a bond continuation certificate was later submitted for the yearly term commencing June 19, 1969.

Interestingly, the term "bread crumbs" does not refer to crumbs that may flake off bread; rather, they are a manufactured item, starting with stale or imperfectly appearing loaves and followed by removal of labels, processing through two grinders, the second of which effects a finer granulation, insertion into a drum in an oven for toasting and, finally, bagging of the finished product.

Subsequent to the making of the agreement, a substantial quantity of bread crumbs, said to be over 250 tons, were sold by defendant to plaintiff but defendant stopped crumb production on about May 15, 1969. There was proof by defendant's comptroller that the oven was too large to accommodate the drum, that it was stated

that the operation was "very uneconomical," but after said date of cessation no steps were taken to obtain more economical equipment. The toasting oven was intentionally broken down, then partially rebuilt, then completely dismantled in the summer of 1969 and, thereafter, defendant used the space for a computer room. It appears, without dispute, that defendant indicated to plaintiff at different times that the former would resume bread crumb production if the contract price of 6 cents per pound be changed to 7 cents, and also that, after the crumb making machinery was dismantled, defendant sold the raw materials used in making crumbs to animal food manufacturers.

Special Term denied plaintiff's motion for summary judgment on the issue of liability and turned down defendant's counter-request for a summary judgment of dismissal. From the Appellate Division's order of affirmance, by a divided court, both parties appeal.

Defendant contends that the contract did not require defendant to manufacture bread crumbs, but merely to sell those it did, and, since none were produced after the demise of the oven, there was no duty to then deliver and, consequently from then on, no liability on its part. Agreements to sell all the goods or services a party may produce or perform to another party are commonly referred to as "output" contracts, and they usually serve a useful commercial purpose in minimizing the burdens of product marketing (see 1 Williston, Contracts [3d ed.], §104A). The Uniform Commercial Code rejects the ideas that an output contract is lacking in mutuality or that it is unenforceable because of indefiniteness in that a quantity for the term is not specified (6 Encyclopedia New York Law, Contracts, §442, 1974-1975 Supp by Professor Schwartz, p 43). Official Comment 2 to section 2-306 (McKinney's Cons Laws of NY, Book 62 1/2, Uniform Commercial Code, pp 206-207) states in part: "Under this Article, a contract for output . . . is not too indefinite since it is held to mean the actual good faith output . . . of the particular party. Nor does such a contract lack mutuality of obligation since, under this section, the party who will determine quantity is required to operate his plant or conduct his business in good faith and according to commercial standards of fair dealing in the trade so that his output . . . will approximate a reasonably foreseeable figure." (*See, also, Matter of United Cigar Stores Co. of Amer.*, 8 F Supp 243, 244, *affd* 72 F2d 673, *cert den sub nom. Consolidated Dairy Prods. Co. v Irving Trust Co.*, 293 U.S. 617; 9 NY Jur, Contracts, §10, p 531.)

The real issue in this case is whether the agreement carries with it an implication that defendant was obligated to continue to manufacture bread crumbs for the full term. Section 2-306 of the Uniform Commercial Code, entitled "Output, Requirements and Exclusive Dealings" provides:

> "(1) A term which measures the quantity by the output of the seller or the requirements of the buyer means such actual output or requirements as may occur in good faith, except that no quantity unreasonably disproportionate to any stated estimate or in the absence of a stated estimate to any normal or otherwise comparable prior output or requirements may be tendered or demanded.
>
> "(2) A lawful agreement by either the seller or the buyer for exclusive dealing in the kind of goods concerned imposes unless otherwise agreed an obligation by the seller to use best efforts to supply the goods and by the buyer to use best efforts to promote their sale." (Emphasis supplied.)

The Official Comment thereunder reads in part: "Subsection (2), on exclusive dealing, makes explicit the commercial rule embodied in this Act under which the parties to such contracts are held to have impliedly, even when not expressly, bound themselves to use reasonable diligence as well as good faith in their performance of the contract. . . . An exclusive dealing agreement brings into play all of the good faith aspects of the output and requirement problems of subsection (1). It also raises questions of insecurity and right to adequate assurance under this Article."

Section 2-306 is consistent with prior New York case law. [Citations omitted.] Under the Uniform Commercial Code, the commercial background and intent must be read into the language of any agreement and good faith is demanded in the performance of that agreement (Official Comment 1, McKinney's Cons Laws of NY, Book 62 1/2, Uniform Commercial Code, §2-306), and, under the decisions relating to output contracts, it is clearly the general rule that good faith cessation of production terminates any further obligations thereunder and excuses further performance by the party discontinuing production. (*Du Boff v Matam Corp.*, 272 App Div 502; *HML Corp. v General Foods Corp.*, 365 F2d 77, 83 [applying New York law]; *Matter of United Cigar Stores Co. of Amer., supra; see Neofotistos v Harvard Brewing Co.*, 341 Mass 684; 6 Encyclopedia New York Law, Contracts, §442, 1974-1975 Supp by Professor Schwartz, p 44).

This is not a situation where defendant ceased its main operation of bread baking (*see Neofotistos v Harvard Brewing Co., supra*). Rather, defendant contends in a conclusory fashion that it was "uneconomical" or "economically not feasible" for it to continue to make bread crumbs. Although plaintiff observed in his motion papers that defendant claimed it was not economically feasible to make the crumbs, plaintiff did not admit that as a fact. In any event, "economic feasibility," an expression subject to many interpretations, would not be a precise or reliable test.

There are present here intertwined questions of fact, whether defendant performed in good faith and whether it stopped its manufacture of bread crumbs in good faith, neither of which can be resolved properly on this record. The seller's duty to remain in crumb production is a matter calling for a close scrutiny of its motives (1 Hawkland, A Transactional Guide to the Uniform Commercial Code, p 52, see, also, p 48), confined here by the papers to financial reasons. It is undisputed that defendant leveled its crumb making machinery only after plaintiff refused to agree to a price higher than that specified in the agreement and that it then sold the raw materials to manufacturers of animal food. There are before us no componential figures indicating the actual cost of the finished bread crumbs to defendant, statements as to the profits derived or the losses sustained, or data specifying the net or gross return realized from the animal food transactions.

The parties by their contract gave the right of cancellation to either by providing for a six months' notice to the other. The apparent purpose of such a stipulation was to provide an opportunity to either the seller or buyer to conclude their dealings in the event that the transactions were not as profitable or advantageous as desired or expected, or for any other reason. Correspondingly, such a notice would also furnish the receiver of it a chance to secure another outlet or source of supply, as the case might be. Short of such a cancellation, defendant was expected to continue to perform in good faith and could cease production of the bread crumbs, a

single facet of its operation, only in good faith. Obviously, a bankruptcy or genuine imperiling of the very existence of its entire business caused by the production of the crumbs would warrant cessation of production of that item; the yield of less profit from its sale than expected would not. Since bread crumbs were but a part of defendant's enterprise and since there was a contractual right of cancellation, good faith required continued production until cancellation, even if there be no profit. In circumstances such as these and without more, defendant would be justified, in good faith, in ceasing production of the single item prior to cancellation only if its losses from continuance would be more than trivial, which, overall, is a question of fact.

The order of the Appellate Division should be affirmed, without costs.

Post-Case Follow-Up

In *Feld*, the court considered the bakery's good faith obligations to continue to produce goods under an output contract. The court determined that issues of fact needed to be resolved to determine if the cessation of bread crumb production was warranted. The bakery's claim that the production process was uneconomical needed to be supported by facts. If the continued production of the crumbs would result in bankruptcy or genuine risk to the company's future, stopping production might be warranted as commercially reasonable and not bad faith. Yet merely receiving less profits from its sale than expected would not comply with the bakery's good faith obligations. There was a six-month termination provision that also must be factored into the court's decision on good faith.

Feld v. Henry S. Levy & Sons: Real Life Applications

1. Blue Sky, a regional airline, agrees to a two-year requirements contract with an aviation fuel company. In the final six months of its contract term, the airline becomes aware that prices are climbing due to business uncertainties about global oil production. Blue Sky begins to double its monthly purchases to stockpile its lower-priced jet fuel for the future and decides to sell some of the excess fuel as an added revenue source. The fuel company realizes what the airline is doing and refuses to supply more than the airline's average monthly fuel supply. Blue Sky sues and claims that the fuel company is not complying with its requirements. Has Blue Sky acted in good faith under its requirements contract? Consider *Eastern Air Lines, Inc. v. Gulf Oil Corp.*, 415 F. Supp. 429 (S.D. Fla. 1975), in determining the likely court decision.

2. Benny's Bagels (Benny's) sells a variety of bagels under its own brand name. Benny's enters into a two-year contract for refrigerated dough with Doughboys Company (Doughboys). Under the contract, Benny's provides Doughboys with a three-month forecast of its likely needs, but Benny's may change its forecasts at any time. A year into the contract, Benny's decides to purchase a dough-making

company to supply its needs. Under a 90-day termination clause, Benny's terminates its contract with Doughboys. Later Doughboys sues Benny's, contending that this termination breaches their requirements contract and violates Benny's duty of good faith and fair dealing. Is there a requirements contract that Benny's must follow through on until the end of the two-year period? Review *Brooklyn Bagel Boys v. Earthgrains Refrigerated Dough Prods.*, 212 F.3d 373 (7th Cir. Ill. 2000), and determine Benny's obligations to Doughboys.

3. A retail distributor enters into a multi-year requirements contract with a camera manufacturer for professional photographers. The contract may be renewed (or not) every year by mutual agreement on the anniversary of the agreement. Typically, the retailer orders 50 units per month. The week before the anniversary date, the camera manufacturer informs the retailer that it does not plan to renew their agreement as professional camera prices are dramatically increasing above their negotiated pricing. The retailer orders 600 cameras for immediate delivery. The manufacturer refuses to send this final order and the retailer sues. Has the manufacturer violated the terms of this contract when it failed to fulfill this order? Check out *Massachusetts Gas & Electric Light Supply Corp. v. V-M Corp.*, 387 F.2d 605 (1st Cir. Mass. 1967) to see the result in this dispute.

In some instances, a best efforts mandate has been applied to requirements and output contracts. That probably is a mistake. Parties to a requirements or output contract do not need best efforts. They already have a promise for the appropriate quantity of goods; failure to provide that amount is breach, regardless of whether the other party made best efforts, reasonable efforts, good faith efforts, or no efforts. If buyer places an order that seller refuses, that is breach of a requirements contract, without any mention of seller's efforts. If seller tenders goods produced and buyer refuses to take them and pay for them, then that is breach of an output contract, without any mention of buyer's efforts. Some courts have concluded that best efforts should not apply when the party is entitled to compensation that is not contingent on the other party's efforts. Output and requirement contracts promise performance, even though the exact amount of performance remains within one party's discretion that must be exercised in good faith.

Chapter Summary

- When parties intend a binding contract but omit some terms, courts can fill the gap with an implied or default term. Implied terms avoid negating an exchange that the parties clearly intended to make simply because a detail was omitted from their communications.
- Good faith is required in every contract—as a mandatory term, not a default term. Good faith requires honesty in fact and may require conformance to reasonable commercial standards of fair dealing.

- Good faith precludes interfering with another's ability to perform the contract. It also may lead a court to infer additional terms not expressed in the contract.
- An exclusive dealing contract includes a requirement that one party diligently promote the other's performance. For sales of goods, diligence requires best efforts, although reasonable efforts or good faith efforts may be required in other settings.
- Created by the seller, express warranties concerning the quality of goods can arise from promises, statements of fact about the goods, descriptions of the goods, or samples or models of the goods, if those comments become a basis of the bargain. Once made, express warranties cannot be disclaimed.
- Failure to deliver goods that conform to the promises, statements, descriptions, samples, or models is a breach of warranty.
- Imposed by law, implied warranties indicate that goods are free from claims of ownership or infringement, are merchantable, and are fit for the buyer's particular purpose.
- A disclaimer of an implied warranty must be conspicuous and, in the case of merchantability, must mention merchantability.
- A contract that specifies the quantity by reference to one party's requirements or output is definite and is not illusory.
- A party may not demand a quantity as its requirements or output unless that quantity represents its actual requirements or output, is set in good faith, and is not unreasonably disproportionate to the quantity the parties anticipated at the outset of the contract.

Applying the Rules

Jane Pinski, the president of Solar Pool Systems, is holding discussions with Don Winton, owner of Splashdown Pools, about becoming a distributor of her firm's solar heating systems for pools. Winton currently provides electric pool heating systems for residential pools. During their negotiations, Winton tells Pinski that he doesn't know anything about solar systems, but would be interested in learning more about them for potential sales to his energy-conscious residential customers. Pinski, a solar energy expert, shows Winton samples of her solar products and provides him with brochure materials about her company's "first rate energy-saving and effective pool solar heating systems." As indicated in the company brochures and consumer owner's manuals, she points out that her firm's solar systems can heat most 10' × 20' or smaller residential pools up to 85 degrees, if customers use pool covers every night and whenever their pools are not in use.

In April 2015, Pinski and Winton agree orally that Winton will be the exclusive distributor of her firm's solar pool heating systems in central Florida for the next two years. Winton may not represent any other solar pool heating systems company. They do not discuss specific pricing, but agree that Winton is permitted to buy the company's goods at a 10 percent discount below standard wholesale prices.

The parties also decide that either party may terminate the contract at will. In their oral discussions, there are no agreed-upon guarantees or refunds.

Winton invests money in hiring and training new employees, rents a larger showroom and warehouse, and routinely maintains a six-month inventory of the solar systems for quick installation. Winton does a brisk business for about eight months, but as winter sets in he begins to receive complaints from many of his customers that the solar pool heating systems are not operating effectively. In January 2016, many customers complain that the solar devices are only warming the pools to about 72 degrees, not reaching the promised 85 degrees. He reminds them to follow the instructions in the owner's manual, but the complaints continue to flood in. Winton contacts Pinski about the solar systems, looking for refunds. Pinski advises Winton that the solar systems are not defective, but that his customers are failing to cover their pools at night and/or when the pool is not in use. In the next three months, Winton's sales of Pinski's solar pool heating systems severely decline. Winton refuses to sell any more of Pinski's solar systems, and goes back to selling electric heating systems. Pinski then sends a letter dated April 5, 2016, to Winton terminating his distributorship effective immediately. Winton brings a breach of contract lawsuit against Pinski for breach of warranty on the solar pool systems and she counterclaims against Winton.

1. Discuss any issues of express warranty in this hypothetical situation.

2. Review any implied warranty issues raised in this hypothetical.

3. Discuss any issues of implied terms under this fact pattern.

4. Are there any disclaimers of warranties in this transaction?

5. What issues of good faith and fair dealing may be present in this dispute?

Contract Law in Practice

1. Many states have specific warranty laws that address consumer purchases of automobiles, sometimes referred to as "lemon laws." These laws may imply warranty protections not found under the provisions of the UCC. Research the lemon law in your state (or a neighboring state, if your state does not have one) and summarize its key similarities and distinctions from the implied warranty provisions of the UCC.

2. The ABA Model Rules of Professional Conduct address issues of honesty in fact and fair dealing. Review the ABA rules and identify ethical rules that require that lawyers act in good faith and fair dealing in contract negotiation and drafting situations. How do these provisions relate to the attorney's role as an officer

of the legal system? Draft a memo outlining these key rules and their impact on contracts attorneys.

3. You are an attorney for a company that makes desk lamps for consumer purchase. The company offers an express warranty that provides that their products will be free from any defects in workmanship or materials for six months from the date of consumer purchase. You have been asked to draft the express warranty clause and a disclaimer of all implied warranties. Review a range of standard form warranty and disclaimers clauses. Draft a clause that meets the needs of your client and the requirements of existing law.

4. Beyond goods and distributorship agreements, best efforts clauses are found in a growing number of contracts situations. Search online and in legal research databases for examples of best efforts clauses in three different types of contract situations, outside of transactions in goods. Summarize these diverse situations and post them on a class discussion board or class blog.

5. Satisfaction clauses are common in the purchase of residential real estate agreements. The clauses seek to protect buyers who may discover new issues with a home after an inspection. Research recent cases involving disputes over satisfaction clauses in residential real estate contracts. Draft a memo that briefly outlines the key judicial perspectives on interpreting satisfaction clauses in these types of contract situations.

Conditions and Material Breach

Breach consists of unexcused nonperformance when performance is due. This chapter addresses two parts of that statement: (1) was performance due?, and (2) did performance occur? Chapter 13 discusses situations in which performance might be excused. Conditions limit promises, specifying the circumstances under which a party commits to perform. Performance is due when any conditions have occurred. Material breach also plays a role in deciding whether performance is due. A performance is not due if the other party has committed an uncured material breach. But performance will be due, despite the other party's breach, if that breach was not material. That poses some risk for a party deciding whether or not to perform. A party may commit a material breach if it refuses to perform based on a mistaken belief that its performance was not due (a condition did not occur or the other party's breach was material).

These issues will be fact-specific, comparing the actual conduct to the conduct specified in the contract. The factual issues — whether the seller ever shipped the goods or the buyer ever mailed the check — require investigation and evidence. Little can be said here to help resolve them. Yet knowing the law and the terms of the contract can help resolve issues once the facts are known.

Key Concepts

- Identifying express conditions
- Excusing conditions
- Determining the order of performance
- Identifying material breach
- Identifying when uncured breach justifies cancellation of a contract
- Consequences of cancellation for breach

A. CONDITIONS ON PERFORMANCE

A **condition** (sometimes called a **condition precedent**) is an event that must occur (or be excused) before a party's duty to perform a contract becomes due.[1]

Conditions arise when a party promises to perform *if* something occurs or *unless* something occurs. They allow parties to provide for doubt, to specify how the contract should work if the future unfolds differently than they expect or hope.

Conditions limit promises; promisors commit to perform in some circumstances, but not others. Parents may promise to take their children to the zoo if the weather is good. The parents make a real commitment, but not an absolute commitment; they do not promise the trip regardless of what happens. Commercial promises offer similar examples. An insurer may promise to pay the insured's losses if a fire damages the residence and if the insured submits proof of loss in writing within 45 days of the event. Conditions limit each promise based on events that might or might not occur. If that event does not occur, the words of promise simply do not apply. In good weather, the promise comes due. But the parents did not promise to visit the zoo in the rain. The insurer made no promise to pay unless fire damages the property.

You will encounter the term **condition subsequent**, used to describe events that discharge a duty after performance has already come due. For example, an insurance policy may provide that the insurer's duty to pay the loss is extinguished unless the insured brings suit on the claim within two years of the fire. The insurer's duty to pay comes due upon the occurrence of the fire (or perhaps the filing of a claim), satisfying the conditions precedent. That duty might disappear if the insured delays suing on the claim. The time limit specifies an event (failure to sue within two years) that discharges (ends) the duty to pay. Today, events after a duty arises are called discharging events, or, more formally, events that terminate a duty.[2] The language is in flux, some preferring the older term, conditions subsequent.

The definition of condition at the start of this section states or implies several provisions, each having some importance.

A condition is an event—good weather, fire, submitting proof of loss. The event either occurs or does not occur. Some refer to the contract terms as conditions, an imprecise usage. The contract terms describe the conditions (the events), but are not themselves conditions.

Conditions relate to uncertain events. An event certain to occur is not a condition. Rather, it simply specifies the time for performance. Sometimes they sound like conditions: "I will give you your allowance if the sun comes up tomorrow." Sunrise, being certain to occur, is not a condition. On the other hand, an event certain not to occur (such as, "if the sun rises in the West tomorrow") undermines the existence of a promise. It negates commitment, making the words illusory. The ways to identify a condition are discussed in subsections 1 and 2 below.

A condition must occur before performance is due. This language specifies the effect of including a condition in the contract. It also helps identify whether

[1] Restatement (Second) of Contracts §224.
[2] *Id.* §230.

a term in a contract creates a condition. If the term does not make performance depend on occurrence of the event, then the term does not create a condition. The parties can specify the effect that nonoccurrence of an event will have upon their duties. For example, a contract between a little league and a group of umpires might include the following term: "League will owe no payment to Umpires in connection with any game League cancels prior to its scheduled start time based on inclement weather or poor field conditions." By making the effect clear (League owes nothing), the language states a condition. Less explicit language may require careful interpretation to determine whether it prevents performance from becoming due. The effects of conditions are discussed in subsection 3 below.

Nonoccurrence of an event might be excused; that is, performance might become due even though the event did not occur. The party who benefits from a condition may waive it, moving forward with performance even though the condition did not occur. For example, the parents may relent and take the children to the zoo even in bad weather. Alternatively, estoppel might preclude one party from invoking a condition in order to protect the other party's reliance. For example, suppose an insurer implied that it would not insist on receiving a written proof of loss within 45 days. If the victims rely by postponing preparation of the document, estoppel might prevent the insurer from later insisting on a timely filing. Finally, in rare circumstances, a court might forgive the nonoccurrence of a condition to avoid disproportionate forfeiture. The ways conditions might be excused are discussed in subsections 4 and 5 below.

Conditions help parties allocate risks. Where risks are anticipated, the parties can decide how those risks affect their duties. Conditions allow them to make promises today that they can avoid if events prove disadvantageous. Consider the condition of a home inspection in Exhibit 11.1. Any house might have problems buyers cannot detect. Agreeing to buy the home without an inspection would risk being stuck with a faulty home. Inspecting the home before making an offer also is risky; the cost will be wasted if seller rejects the offer. A condition avoids the risks. Seller commits to the sale before buyer pays for the inspection. But buyer need not proceed if the inspection reveals concerns. The condition allocates these risks between buyer and seller.

Consider how conditions allocate several risks involved in the purchase of a home.

- Buyers condition purchase on finding an affordable mortgage (for example, no more than 6.35 percent with 1 point). If no lender agrees, buyers need not perform. An unconditional offer might leave buyers with impossibly high monthly payments.
- Buyers condition purchase on the sale of their own home. They may need that money to pay for the new house — or perhaps simply cannot pay two mortgages at once.
- Buyers condition purchase on inspections for termites, structural defects, and so on. If defects are found, buyer can refuse to perform — or seller might offer a discount if buyer will waive the defects.

- Sellers condition sale on availability of their next home, preferring to move once, not twice.
- Sellers condition sale on buyer clearing the conditions within two weeks of acceptance. If buyer cannot find a mortgage and make inspections in that time, sellers need not perform. Buyer can waive any conditions not yet fulfilled if it wants the house despite the risk.

EXHIBIT 11.1 Contract Language Creating Conditions

The language used to identify conditions varies. The following language illustrates one way a contract might address some of the risks identified in the text regarding the sale of a home.

If buyer fails to obtain loans at the interest rate and points stated below, buyer shall have no obligation to proceed with the purchase and is entitled to the return of any partial payments already made.

Buyer's obligation to proceed with the purchase is dependent upon receipt of satisfactory inspection reports as specified below, including inspections for (a) pests or other organisms that might destroy of damage wood, (b) any defects in condition of the property, including mechanical, electrical, or plumbing defects, and (c) any environmental hazards present on the property. If buyer is dissatisfied with the state of the property as described in any required report, buyer shall notify seller of any corrective action necessary to correct the problems. If seller fails to correct any problems specified by buyer, buyer shall have no obligation to proceed with the purchase and is entitled to the return of any partial payments already made.

No later than fifteen (15) days before the closing date specified in this agreement, buyer must either (a) inform seller in writing that all inspections or other conditions have been completed to buyer's satisfaction or (b) inform seller that buyer elects not to proceed with the purchase.

Conditions can be central to a contract. For instance, insurers agree to pay if you suffer a covered loss—a fire, a traffic accident, an illness, and so on. You pay for their conditional promise. If you suffer no covered loss, the insurer's failure to pay you is not breach. Nor are you entitled to a refund of the premiums. If you were, the insurer would have no money to pay people who did suffer insured losses. You got what you paid for: a conditional promise.

Conditions can create risks. When an insurance policy demands written proof of loss within 45 days of the fire, it sets a potential trap. A claimant who gives the insurer an oral list of damaged property on the 30th day and written list on the 50th day gets no payment—despite paying premiums, perhaps for several years. Insurers have perfectly sound reasons for wanting the submission in writing, especially as a check against fraud by the claimant. But a careless claimant can find itself in a difficult position when it does not meet an express condition.

Conditions differ from promises. A party may refuse to perform when a condition does not occur, but might have to perform anyway if the other merely breaches a promise. That difference can be huge. If the duty to submit a written claim were a promise, not a condition, then the insurer could recover damages it suffered because the insured did perform. But unless the insured's breach was material (as discussed in section C, below), the insurer would need to pay the insured's claim, minus the amount it could offset as damages for the breach. As a condition, however, failure to file a timely written claim means the insurer's performance never comes due. It need not pay the claim at all, even if the claim was just a little late. "Almost" does not count for conditions.

*Conditions can produce **forfeiture**.* Forfeiture occurs if a party does not receive the benefit of a contract and cannot recover what she invested in the contract. The insured may pay for coverage, but never receive its promised benefits. She loses the cost of the policy without getting the benefit of the policy. Forfeiture is measured by the costs; to be entitled to the benefits, the condition must be satisfied.

Courts try to limit forfeiture in several ways. First, they try to interpret language in a way that reduces the number of conditions. Second, they acknowledge several ways to defeat a condition even if one exists. Finally, they sometimes excuse conditions to avoid forfeiture.

Abuse of Conditions

In the nineteenth century, some insurers drafted policies that included conditions that surprised their insureds. Unaware that the policy contained these conditions, insureds failed to satisfy them, justifying insurers in refusing to pay claims that otherwise might have been covered. Although some conditions served legitimate ends, others appeared to be abuses intended to allow the insurer to keep the premiums without paying claims. State agencies now regulate insurance policies to prevent insurers from inserting conditions that serve no legitimate business purpose.

Case Preview

Solar Applications Engineering v. T.A. Operating Corp.

This case involves a common situation: a contractor completed a project and sought final payment, but the owner refused to pay. Here, the owner was concerned about the cost of delays that it blamed on the contractor and inadequacies in the work. The contractor's failure to comply with one requirement of the process for requesting final payment gave the owner a reason for refusing payment. The case turns on whether or not that requirement was a condition of final payment.

As you read *Solar Applications Engineering v. T.A. Operating Corp.*, look for the following:

1. How much did the contractor recover for the unfinished work? How did that compare to the amount the contractor initially claimed? How did it compare to the amount the owner withheld?
2. How did the court determine whether the term was a condition or a promise?
3. Did the court's decision deprive the contractor of an important benefit it obtained as part of the contract?

Solar Applications Engineering, Inc. v. T.A. Operating Corporation

327 S.W.3d 104 (Tex. 2010)

Justice WAINWRIGHT delivered the opinion of the Court.

In this case, a general contractor and an owner dispute performance and final payment under a construction contract. Solar Applications Engineering, Inc.[,] the general contractor, and T.A. Operating Corporation[,] the owner, entered a contract to build a truck stop in San Antonio, Texas. After Solar substantially completed the project, disputes arose regarding the completion of certain remaining work and the attachment of liens on the property by subcontractors and Solar. TA eventually terminated the contract and refused to make final payment to Solar. Solar sued TA for breach of contract to recover the contract balance, and TA counterclaimed for delay and defective work. At trial, the court's jury charge focused primarily on damages. The verdict substantially favored Solar, with the jury awarding actual damages of $400,000 offset by $8,000 in defects and omissions.

[T]he court of appeals reversed . . . holding that [a] lien release provision was a condition precedent [that] Solar failed to [satisfy].

The issue before this Court is whether the lien-release provision is a condition precedent to Solar's recovery. . . . Under normal circumstances, Solar might have provided a conditional lien-release affidavit . . . [b]ut the standard operating procedure broke down here. . . .

We hold that the lien-release provision is a covenant, not a condition precedent to Solar's recovery on the contract. . . .

I. BACKGROUND

lien

. . .

The contractual sequence for the truck stop project is as follows: The parties agree on a construction schedule and then Solar begins work according to the schedule. On application for payment by Solar, TA is required to provide monthly progress payments. When Solar believes the construction project ready for its intended use, that it is "substantially complete," it so notifies TA. After an inspection, if TA agrees that the project is substantially complete, TA issues a "certificate of Substantial Completion" and attaches a list of items, referred to as the "punch list," to be completed or corrected before final payment. Next, upon written notice from Solar that the punch list is done and the project is complete, TA conducts a final inspection with Solar to identify any deficiencies, and Solar remedies those deficiencies. After Solar corrects the identified deficiencies, it may submit a "final Application for Payment" that is accompanied by complete and legally effective releases or waivers of all lien rights ("lien-release affidavit").

[T]he parties agree that the project was substantially complete in August 2000. A few weeks later, TA presented Solar with a punch list, but disputes arose over the remaining items that needed to be completed before final payment. Solar then filed a lien against the project for $472,393, and subcontractors also filed liens against the property. TA terminated Solar pursuant to the contract's "for cause" termination provision contending that, among other things, Solar had failed to keep the project lien-free and failed to complete the punch list. The termination letter also notified Solar that TA was asserting claims for $736,800.15 against Solar for its failure to complete the construction project on time. The day after TA terminated the contract, Solar provided TA with an "Application and Certificate for Payment" for $472,149, the amount Solar believed to be the remaining contract balance. TA refused to make payment, contending Solar had not complied with the lien-release provision by failing to submit a lien-release affidavit. . . .

By the time of trial, subcontractors filed $246,627 in liens against the project. The trial court severed the subcontractors' claims and ordered that any sums recovered by Solar, other than attorney's fees, would be held in trust for the benefit of the subcontractors' claims. The jury found in favor of Solar, and the trial court entered a judgment on the verdict in favor of Solar, awarding $392,000 in damages, which represented the balance due under the contract less an $8,000 offset to remedy all remaining "punch list" defects and omissions found by the jury.

. . .

II. LAW AND ANALYSIS

Whether Solar is barred from receiving the contract balance depends on whether the lien-release provision is a condition precedent to Solar's recovery for breach of contract. "A condition precedent is an event that must happen or be performed before a right can accrue to enforce an obligation." *Centex Corp. v. Dalton*, 840 S.W.2d 952, 956 (Tex. 1992) (citations omitted); *see also* Restatement (Second) of Contracts §224 (1981). . . . A covenant, as distinguished from a condition precedent, is an agreement to act or refrain from acting in a certain way. *Reinert v. Lawson*, 113 S.W.2d 293, 294 (Tex. Civ. App.-Waco 1938, no writ). Breach of a covenant may give rise to a cause of action for damages, but does not affect the enforceability of the remaining provisions of the contract unless the breach is a material or total breach. *E.g., Hernandez v. Gulf Group Lloyds*, 875 S.W.2d 691, 692-94 (Tex. 1994); Restatement (Second) of Contracts §§236 cmt. a, 241, 242 cmt. a. Conversely, if an express condition is not satisfied, then the party whose performance is conditioned is excused from any obligation to perform. *See Dalton*, 840 S.W.2d at 956; Restatement (Second) of Contracts §225.

. . .

"In order to determine whether a condition precedent exists, the intention of the parties must be ascertained; and that can be done only by looking at the entire contract." *Criswell* [*v. European Crossroads Shopping Ctr., Ltd.*], 792 S.W.2d [945,] 948 [(Tex. 1990)] (citing references omitted); *see also* Restatement (Second) of Contracts §226. "In order to make performance specifically conditional, a term such as 'if,' 'provided that,' 'on condition that,' or some similar phrase of conditional language must normally be included." [Citations omitted.] "While there is no requirement that such phrases be utilized, their absence is probative of the parties [*sic*] intention that a promise be made, rather than a condition imposed." [Citations omitted.] When no conditional language is used and another reasonable interpretation of the contract is possible, "the terms will be construed as a covenant in order to prevent a forfeiture." *Id.*

Section 14.07(A) of the contract states:

> 1. After [Solar] has, satisfactorily completed all corrections identified during the final inspection and has delivered . . . [pertinent] documents, [Solar] may make application for final payment following the procedure for progress payments.
>
> . . .
>
> 2. The final Application for Payment shall be accompanied (except as previously delivered) by: (i) all documentation called for in the Contract Documents, including but not limited to the evidence of insurance; (ii) consent of the surety, if any, to final payment; and (iii) complete and legally effective releases or waivers (satisfactory to [TA]) of all Lien rights arising out of or Liens filed in connection with the Work.

The operative language, that Solar will provide "complete and legally effective releases or waivers . . . of all Lien rights" does not contain language that is traditionally associated with a condition precedent. The language preceding the lien-release provision does not make performance conditional. In the absence of any conditional language, a reasonable reading of the lien-release provision is that it is a promise or covenant by Solar to provide a lien-release affidavit in exchange for receiving final payment. This interpretation avoids forfeiture and completes the contract: Solar is paid for the work it completed, and TA receives an unencumbered building. . . . Solar's breach results in "a delay in payment to Solar until the liens are released." The court of appeals' contrary interpretation results in a forfeiture to Solar and a windfall to TA. [Citations omitted.]

TA alleges that key language in section 14.07(B) creates the condition precedent. That section states:

> If, on the basis of [TA's] observation of the Work during construction and final inspection, and [TA's] review of the final Application for Payment and accompanying documentation as required by the Contract Documents, [TA] is satisfied that the Work has been completed and [SOLAR's] other obligations under the Contract Documents have been fulfilled, [TA] will, within ten days after receipt of the final Application for Payment, indicate in writing [TA's] recommendation of payment and present the Application for Payment for payment. At the same time [TA] will also given [*sic*] written notice to [SOLAR] that the Work is acceptable. . . . Otherwise [TA] will return the Application for Payment to [SOLAR], indicating in writing the reasons for refusing to recommend final payment, in which case [SOLAR] shall make the necessary corrections and resubmit the Application for Payment.

While TA is correct that section 14.07(B) contains the conditional language "if," the section does not create a condition of payment to the lien-release affidavit. Rather, the condition is *if* TA is satisfied with the Work and the Contractual Documents, *then* it will recommend that Solar be paid the retainage. If TA is not satisfied with the work, then Solar "shall make the necessary corrections and resubmit the Application for Payment." Solar's obligation to provide a lien-release affidavit, and TA's obligation to pay, lie separate and apart from TA's approval of the project. If this condition were allowed to prevent Solar from suing on the contract when a building was substantially complete, then Solar would be beholden to TA to be "satisfied." In other words, if either Solar or TA disagreed with the other party's performance under the document, TA could likely sue Solar, but Solar could not sue to be paid, because TA was not satisfied under the contract.

[T]he overall scheme of the Property Code suggests interpreting the provision to avoid a forfeiture. The process for final payment common to construction contracts is complemented by statutes that protect contractors and owners in case the contractual process breaks down. First, the Texas Constitution and the Texas Property Code grant a lien in favor of contractors and builders extending to the building on which they have labored. Tex. Const. art. XVI, §37; Tex. Prop. Code §§53.001-.260. Thus, if the owner becomes insolvent or refuses to pay, the contractor has recourse to recover the sums owed by foreclosing on the liens on the property. However, the contractor's lien gives contractors unequal leverage over owners and leaves owners vulnerable to insolvent contractors. For instance . . . , if the owner pays the general contractor the full contractual sum, but the general contractor does not pay a subcontractor, the subcontractor can place a lien on the property. The owner, after already paying the general contractor in full, is forced to pay the subcontractor in order to receive the property lien-free and must again resort to litigation to recover the money already paid to the general contractor, who at this point may be insolvent.

The unequal bargaining positions created by the contractor's lien rights is addressed through the mechanism of "retainage." The Property Code requires that, during the progress of work under a contract for which a contractor's lien may be claimed, the owner shall retain ten percent of the contract price. Tex. Prop. Code §53.101. This retainage secures the payment of any contractor or subcontractor who may assert a lien on the property in the event that the general fails to pay them. *Id.* §53.102. In turn, retainage gives the owner offsetting leverage against the general contractor, whose receipt of the final ten percent of the contract balance is subject to its payment of the subcontractors in full. Thus, the contractor [and] the owner [b]oth . . . have the incentive to complete the terms of the deal and the enforcement mechanisms to help ensure payment.

Finally, the Property Code allows the parties to contract for payment of the retainage to the contractor upon the owner's receipt of a lien-release affidavit. *Id.* §53.085. This contractual mechanism preserves the rights of the parties but avoids the more cumbersome statutory process for retainage release. *See, e.g., id.* §53.106. Essentially, the owner trades the retainage for the contractor's sworn assurance that property is lien-free. . . . However, the parties may agree that, as part of the affidavit, the contractor swears that lien rights are released "conditioned on the receipt of actual payment or collection of funds. . . ." Tex. Prop. Code §53.085(c)(1). Under peaceful circumstances, the . . . affidavit accomplishes the statutory goals of the contractor's lien and retainage in a voluntary and efficient manner. The general contractor provides an affidavit and conditional release of lien, stating that when the contractor receives payment, all liens on the property will be released. [Citations omitted.] The standoff is resolved; the contractor gets paid (to be distributed to the subcontractors, with whom they have a conditional lien release), and the owner gets its building free of encumbrances.

Nonetheless, TA argues we should hold that the lien release is not only a condition to receive the retainage, but also a condition to fulfillment of Solar's contractual duties and thus entitlement to the contractual balance. Under this reading, Solar effectively waived its statutory and constitutional contractor's lien rights in the contract because it would not be entitled to the contractual balance until it released those rights. That view would have a contractor bargain away any leverage it had under the default rules, as an owner could simply accept the lien release and then refuse to pay, forcing the contractor to sue for the retainage. Holding that these lien-release provisions, common to construction contracts for the reasons outlined above, are conditions precedent to suit on the contract without express conditional language contravenes the lien statutes' goal of allowing the contractor . . . to avoid litigation by foreclosing on their lien. . . . Parties are free, of course, to contract out of statutory default rules. . . . [Citation omitted.] But there would be little need for TA to bargain *ex ante* for a forfeiture clause in the contract in case Solar refused to provide a lien release. [T]he default rules already give TA the ability to withhold the retainage. A forfeiture clause would be overkill and expensive.

[U]nder our interpretation of section 14.07 of the contract, TA will not be saddled with concerns about double-payment. The trial court will determine whether any subcontractor liens are still pending and, if so, TA may seek to discharge the liens, sue Solar for breach of the lien-release provision, or seek indemnification (either through common law or express terms of the parties contracts) from Solar for Solar's failure to pay the subcontractors.

For all of these reasons, absent clear language that a lien release is a condition precedent to a general contractor performing under the contract and receiving the contract balanced owed to it, we interpret the lien-release provision to be a covenant. We recognize that parties are free to contract as they choose, and TA should not be denied the benefit it specifically bargained for in the lien-release provision. [Citations omitted.] The lien-release provision here gives TA the right to sworn assurances that it will receive a lien-free property prior to making final payment. . . . Accordingly, on remand the trial court must determine whether the subcontractors' liens have been satisfied and TA is adequately assured of a lien-free property before reinstating the judgment in favor of Solar for the balance owed under the contract.[10]

III. CONCLUSION

For the foregoing reasons, we reverse the court of appeals' judgment and remand to the trial court for proceedings consistent with this opinion.

Post-Case Follow-Up

The court suggested at least three reasons to prefer treating this language as a promise: the term did not use the typical language of a condition; the preference for finding promises when the language is unclear; and concern for the way conditional language might be used to produce injustice through a forfeiture. The court pays serious attention to the business

[10]Evidently, the trial court attempted to protect TA from double liability by severing the subcontractors' liens and ordering that any recovery Solar obtained would be held in trust for the benefit of the subcontractors. However [t]he judgment did not bind the subcontractors and did not necessarily guarantee that TA would receive a lien-free property prior to making final payment. At oral argument, TA conceded that the liens have all been satisfied, but this fact is not in the record.

needs of each party, trying not to put either one in an untenable position. The court also suggests the parties can negotiate for a condition, if their language more clearly specifies that result. If the business risks are worse than the court believes, the parties can reallocate those risks using different contract language in future transactions.

Solar Applications Engineering v. T.A. Operating Corp.: Real Life Applications

1. Lessor owns a shopping mall. In order to induce Pharmacy to lease space in the mall, Lessor included the following term in Pharmacy's lease:

   > B. Lessor represents it has entered into a lease with Grocery for a minimum of 45,000 square feet for a minimum period of 20 years, and said lease obligates Grocery to initially open for business and to lease and pay rent for its store. The continued leasing and payment of rent for its store in the Shopping Center by Grocery is part of the consideration to induce Lessee to lease and pay rent for its store. Accordingly, should Grocery fail or cease to lease and pay rent for its store in the Shopping Center during the Lease Term, Lessee shall have the right and privilege of: (a) canceling this Lease and of terminating all of its obligations hereunder at any time thereafter upon written notice by Lessee to Lessor. . . .

   Does this language create a condition (that Grocery continue to lease and pay rent for the store), a promise, or something else? Does that depend on how the issue arises? Consider the circumstances in *Jenkins v. Eckerd Corp.*, 913 So. 2d 43 (Fla. App. 2005) (after operating store for years, Grocery went bankrupt; different Grocer operated store without interruption under assignment, but Pharmacy invoked clause to cancel lease a year later).

2. Solutions, an executive search firm, referred Exec to Employer, which hired Exec. After the hire, Employer asked Solutions to defer payment of the commission due until Employer received payment from Government for the project Exec was hired to implement. Solutions and Employer agreed to the following addendum to the contract:

   > In consideration of Employer's delayed receipt of federal funds, and services rendered by Solutions for the recruitment and identification of Exec, Solutions will extend our initially agreed upon payment terms to be payable upon Employer's receipt of said funds. Services have been rendered and payment is due at the time funding is received regardless of Exec's start date.

   Does this language make receipt of federal funds a condition of Employer's duty to pay Solutions or is it a promise to pay at a particular time? What happens if federal funds never are paid? Consider *Lokan & Assocs. v. American Beef Processing, LLC*, 311 P.3d 1285 (Wash. Ct. App. 2013).

3. A federal crop insurance policy promised to pay tobacco farmers for losses if weather damaged their crops. To ensure that the loss resulted from weather rather than other causes, the policy specified: "The tobacco stalks on any acreage

. . . shall not be destroyed until [inspected]." Did this language create a condition or a promise? Does it matter how other provisions of the policy were drafted? For example, suppose another term began: "It shall be a condition precedent to the payment of any loss that the insured. . . ." *Howard v. Federal Crop Insurance Corporation*, 540 F.2d 695 (4th Cir. 1976).

---

1. Identifying Conditions

As noted in *Solar Applications*, conditions usually reveal themselves by the language used to create them. Words such as "if," "unless," "provided," "when," "after," and "subject to" usually signal the existence of a condition. They limit the circumstances under which a promise applies. The promisor has committed to perform if/provided/when/after an event occurs (or subject to an event occurring), but made no commitment if the event does not occur. Alternatively, the promise could specify performance unless an event occurs, making no commitment to perform if the event occurs. Conditions define the scope of a party's commitment and may affect the value of that commitment.

Clauses creating a condition sometimes specify the substantive effect on a promise if an event occurs (or does not occur). The effect can be specified without the telltale words listed here. For instance, a provision that payment is due within 30 days of delivery seems to make delivery a condition of payment. If delivery does not occur, payment will never be due. In some circumstances, common sense will reveal a condition. A term may make no sense as a promise, allowing recovery of damages. The only sensible role the term could play is as a condition, limiting when performance is due.

2. Effect of Conditions

Nonoccurrence of a condition means a party's performance is not due. Thus, when a condition has not yet occurred, a party's duty to perform a contract is **suspended** (on hold until the condition occurs). For example, if the lien release in *Solar Applications* were a condition, Solar's failure to provide it would allow TA to suspend its performance, refusing to make the final payment yet. When a condition cannot occur, a party's duty is **discharged**: no obligation to perform remains, just as if the party had already fully performed.[3] In *Solar Applications*, discharge seems unlikely unless the contract put some time limit on submission of the lien release. A schedule for completing work would not necessarily equate to a deadline on submitting the final paperwork.

Nonoccurrence of a condition is not breach—unless the language creates both a promise and a condition. An insurer does not promise that you will have an

---

[3]Restatement (Second) of Contracts §225.

insured claim; it promises to pay you if you do have an insured claim. Absence of a fire is not breach by either party; in fact, both parties prefer that (usually). Similarly, parents do not promise that it will not rain. They limit the promise to visit the zoo to allow for the possibility of rain.

A party can promise to cause a condition to occur — or at least to try to cause a condition to occur. For instance, the homebuyer probably has an obligation to make good faith efforts to find a loan that would satisfy the conditions she included in her offer (recall Exhibit 11.1). She does not promise to find such a loan. The condition is designed to protect her against failure; the opposite would occur if failure to find a loan was breach of a promise, allowing seller to seek damages. Nonetheless, including a condition that falls within one person's power may require at least some effort on her part; otherwise, liability for breach of good faith might arise.

In some cases, language can create both an obligation and a condition. For example, recall the language promising payment within 30 days of delivery. Delivery here is a condition of the promise to pay. If delivery never occurs, then payment will never fall due, because the 30 days will never start to run. But delivery is also the seller's promise. It promises to deliver the goods — perhaps by a specified date. The seller has a duty to cause the condition to occur. Nonoccurrence gives the buyer both a reason not to pay and grounds to sue for damages.

3. Interpretation: Condition or Promise

Where language unmistakably creates a condition — or when treating a term as a promise simply makes no sense — a court will treat a provision as creating a condition. When in doubt, however, courts prefer to interpret provisions as promises, creating duties rather than negating duties.[4] Therefore, if the insurer drafted its policy badly, a court might hold that the term requiring written notice within 45 days created a promise by the insured to submit a written claim in that time, but not a condition that limited the insurer's duty to pay. (Insurers usually draft their policies very clearly, to avoid just this kind of interpretation.)

In other situations, courts may need to determine whether language created a condition or created both a promise and a condition. Faced with that choice, courts prefer to treat the language as a condition. That reduces the risk to the party by removing a duty that a party cause the condition to occur. Nonoccurrence, then, will not be breach, even if it excuses the other party's performance. See Exhibit 11.2.

[4] *Id.* §227.

EXHIBIT 11.2 Conditions versus Promises

	Condition	Promise
Description	Does (or does not) occur	Is (or is not) performed
Effect of nonoccurrence or nonperformance	Other's performance is not due	Allows damages for breach
Any leeway?	Occurrence strictly required	Substantial performance OK
Excuses?	Waiver Estoppel Judicial excuse to avoid disproportionate forfeiture	Waiver Estoppel Impracticability Frustration

4. Waiver and Estoppel

A party benefited by a condition can **waive** it — intentionally relinquish a known right, here the right to refuse to perform on the ground that the condition did not occur. After a waiver, the condition has no effect; performance becomes due regardless of whether the event occurs or does not occur.

Waiver often occurs when the terms of the contract are so good that a party wants to go forward even if the condition did not occur. Suppose, for instance, buyer offered to buy a home if she obtained a 30-year fixed rate mortgage at 6.375 percent or better with zero points. After diligent search the best mortgage she obtained was 6.5 percent at zero points. If the buyer decides that she can afford the house anyway and wants to proceed with the sale, she can waive the condition. The seller could not use the condition as grounds for refusing to go forward. The condition almost certainly was written as a limitation on buyer's promise, not on seller's. In any event, the purpose involved protecting buyer from paying more than that house was worth to her. The price protects seller, who collects the same amount regardless of how much interest buyer pays. (Seller has no reason to agree to the price if buyer pays less interest but to reject it if buyer pays more interest.) Insurers, too, may waive conditions. An insurer may tell the insured that it will accept a written claim within 60 days, effectively waiving any shorter period the policy specified.

Sometimes a party may revoke a waiver. By timely notice, a party may insist upon the occurrence of the condition in the future. For example, a party who has waived the right to receive timely notices or payments in the past may insist upon timely notices or payments going forward. Estoppel, however, may make a waiver irrevocable.

Estoppel arises if a party relies on the other's indication (whether words or conduct) that it will not invoke a condition to justify a refusal to perform. For example, suppose an insured stopped preparing a written claim for several weeks based on the insurer's statement that it would accept a claim within 60 days. Allowing the insurer to insist on a written claim within 45 days may impose hardship on the insured. Reliance on the waiver creates an estoppel, which makes the waiver irrevocable.

Estoppel need not be permanent or complete. Reliance may preclude revocation of part of a waiver, but not the rest. A party may insist on strict compliance with a condition by appropriate notice, provided the revocation does not leave the other party worse off than if the waiver had never been made. Thus, a party cannot revoke the waiver for a completed transaction (past deliveries or payments). Revocation cannot retroactively convert excused nonoccurrence into unexcused nonoccurrence. A party may revoke a waiver for future occasions (the next delivery or payment), unless reliance has made it harder to satisfy the future conditions than it would have been if no waiver had occurred.

Try your hand at applying the rule to the following situation. By contract, Creditor may repossess a car if Borrower fails to make timely payments on the first of each month. Borrower consistently paid on the fifth of the month, with no objection from Creditor. After one year, Borrower received notice from Creditor that, after the next payment, it would insist on strict compliance with the requirement of payment by the first of the month. If Borrower continues to make payments on the fifth rather than the first, may Creditor repossess the car, as permitted by the contract terms?

Try your hand at applying the rule to this variation of the situation. After six months without any objection from Creditor to payments on the fifth, Borrower took a new job with a different payday, making payment on the first much harder than if she had kept her original job. Six months later, Borrower received the Creditor's notice that it would require payment on the first. If Borrower continues to make payments on the fifth rather than the first, may Creditor repossess the car, as permitted by the contract terms?

5. Judicial Forgiveness

In rare cases, a court may forgive (or excuse) nonoccurrence of a condition. Excuse depends on two components:

1. enforcing the condition would produce disproportionate forfeiture; and
2. the condition was not a material part of the agreed exchange.[5]

Again, forfeiture usually refers to the lost investment, not the inability to receive the gains of a contract. Disproportionate forfeiture does not necessarily require substantial losses. Rather, forfeiture is compared to the risk faced by the party the condition protected.

Fundamental aspects of the bargain lie beyond the court's power to excuse a condition. For example, a court would never excuse the nonoccurrence of a fire and order a fire insurer to pay the insured even though no covered loss occurred. Nor would a court excuse the insured's failure to pay the insurance premiums, if that was a condition. A court's ability to excuse a condition for forfeiture does not extend to material aspects of the agreed exchange.

[5] *Id.* §229.

Excuse by a court is discretionary. Even if a court has the power to excuse a condition, it may not decide to do so. Thus, a party should never count on a court to rescue it by excusing a condition. For instance, in *Indian Harbor Insurance Company v. City of San Diego*,[6] insurance would have covered the city on three environmental claims. But the city did not give notice "as soon as practicable," waiting two months to give notice of one claim (and 12 months and 30 months on two others). The court did not calculate the insurer's loss to determine whether the city's loss was disproportionate. Acknowledging the reasons for the condition, it found disproportionate forfeiture "inapposite."

Case Preview

135 East 57th Street LLC v. Daffy's Inc.

Daffy's discount clothing store, the defendant in this case
Anthony Behar/Sipa USA (Sipa via AP Images)

An option to renew a lease often tells tenants when and how to exercise the option. Notice requirements give landlords time to find new tenants and to prepare for renovations the new tenant may seek. Here, a tenant that intended to renew a lease failed to satisfy the conditions for renewal, leading the landlord to terminate the lease. The tenant asked the court to excuse the condition (effectively, to forgive the failure to comply with it) based on the relative hardship involved.

As you read *135 East 57th Street LLC v. Daffy's*, look for the following:

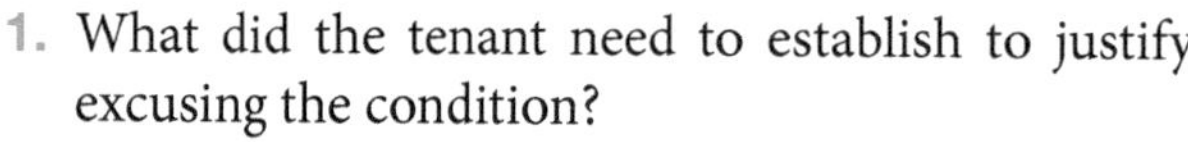

1. What did the tenant need to establish to justify excusing the condition?

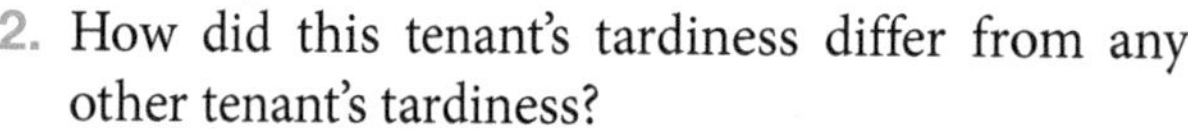

2. How did this tenant's tardiness differ from any other tenant's tardiness?

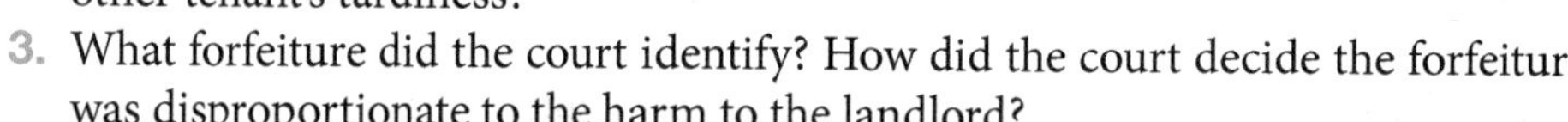

3. What forfeiture did the court identify? How did the court decide the forfeiture was disproportionate to the harm to the landlord?

135 East 57th Street LLC v. Daffy's Inc.

91 A.D.3d 1, 934 N.Y.S.2d 112 (2011)

SAXE, J.P.

The law generally exacts a high price for failure to comply with the precise language of a contract (*see e.g. Vermont Teddy Bear Co. v. 538 Madison Realty Co.*, 1

[6]972 F. Supp. 2d 634 (S.D.N.Y. 2013).

N.Y.3d 470, 775 N.Y.S.2d 765, 807 N.E.2d 876 [2004]). But, in some situations, principles of equity have softened the often harsh results of common-law rules of strict contract construction. These equitable principles, such as the doctrine of substantial performance, import the concept of fundamental fairness to the context of contract-dispute litigation. One equitable construct that has been used to protect parties from the harsh results of strict contract construction is the principle underlying this appeal, that equity will intervene to avoid a forfeiture.

The trial court exercised its equitable power in this case to excuse the lateness of a commercial tenant's notice to the landlord of its intent to renew a lease. The main issue presented is whether this exercise of equitable authority was proper, given that the tenant did not prove that it made substantial improvements in anticipation of continued occupancy.

Daffy's Inc., a popular discount clothing retailer [with 18 locations], has operated its store at 135 East 57th Street in Manhattan since the lease term began on November 7, 1994. While the term of the lease expired on January 31, 2011, the lease gave Daffy's the option of two five-year renewal terms, the first of which was to be exercised no later than January 31, 2010. However, due to the failure of its controller to calendar this particular option date, Daffy's did not give written notice of its intention to renew until February 4, 2010. . . . The landlord rejected this late attempt to exercise the renewal option [on] February 5, 2010 [noting that the renewal notice was late and] was not delivered in the manner prescribed by the lease. Daffy's responded by sending its renewal letter in the manner prescribed by the lease on February 9, 2010.

Two days later . . . the landlord commenced this action, seeking a declaration that Daffy's [failure] to timely renew the lease [meant] that the lease would expire on January 31, 2011. . . . After a nonjury trial, the court found that Daffy's was entitled to equitable relief under *J.N.A. Realty Corp. v. Cross Bay Chelsea*, 42 N.Y.2d 392, 397 N.Y.S.2d 958, 366 N.E.2d 1313 (1977), and issued a declaration excusing the lateness of Daffy's exercise of its renewal option. The landlord now appeals. . . .

As . . . a rule, when a contract requires written notice to be given within a specified time, the notice is ineffective unless it is received within that time (*see Oppenheimer & Co. v. Oppenheim, Appel, Dixon & Co.*, 86 N.Y.2d 685, 693, 636 N.Y.S.2d 734, 660 N.E.2d 415 [1995]; . . .). However, an exception to the rule may be applied on equitable grounds where a forfeiture would result from the tenant's neglect or inadvertence (*J.N.A. Realty*, [*supra*]).

The requirements for granting such equitable relief have been articulated as follows:

> "Equity will relieve a tenant from a failure to timely exercise an option in a lease to renew or purchase if (1) the tenant in good faith made substantial improvements to the premises and would otherwise suffer a forfeiture, (2) the tenant's delay was the result of an excusable default, and (3) the landlord was not prejudiced by the delay" (*Vitarelli v. Excel Automotive Tech. Ctr., Inc.*, 25 A.D.3d 691, 811 N.Y.S.2d 689 [2006]).

We note initially that the four-day delay in providing the one-year's notice required by the lease did not prejudice the landlord. On the question of whether

Daffy's delay should be treated as excusable . . . the corporate controller who prepared the letter provided a credible explanation for the error. We accept the trial court's conclusion that the misdating was not prompted by either bad faith or an intent to defraud, and that the four-day delay was an honest mistake.

The more difficult issue is whether Daffy's evidence established the type of forfeiture for which equitable relief is appropriate under the rule articulated in *J.N.A. Realty.*

As *J.N.A. Realty* explains, equity does not generally intervene when a party fails to timely exercise a contractual option, because "the loss of the option does not ordinarily result in the forfeiture of any vested rights" (42 N.Y.2d at 397, 397 N.Y.S.2d 958, 366 N.E.2d 1313). "The reason is that the option itself does not create any interest in the property, and no rights accrue until the condition precedent has been met by giving notice within the time specified" (*id.*). However, while options such as stock options or options to buy goods do not create a vested interest in the property so that the loss of the property may be treated as a forfeiture, lease renewal options are different. Equity may intervene where a tenant in possession of premises under an existing lease neglects to timely exercise a renewal option, because "he might suffer a forfeiture if he has made valuable improvements on the property" (*id.*).

Although the trial court concluded that Daffy's made alterations to the space, including tearing down walls that had divided the space into separate antique stores, and customizing the space to its needs, we find no support for these findings in the record. Rather, Daffy's CEO testified only to the painting of the 57th Street store, and to Daffy's inability to undertake flooring work due to leaking at the premises. In fact, there was testimony that the premises were "highly improved when Daffy's took it."

Even if . . . Daffy's removed walls at the start of the lease term in 1994, that improvement was made too long ago to justify equitable relief under *J.N.A. Realty.* In a case where the improvements relied on by the tenant had been made during the first two years of the lease, this Court observed that they had already been amortized and depreciated by the time of the attempted renewal, so that the tenant had "reaped the benefit of any initial expenditure," and concluded that there was insufficient evidence that the tenant would suffer a forfeiture (*see Soho Dev. Corp. v. Dean & DeLuca*, 131 A.D.2d 385, 386, 517 N.Y.S.2d 498 [1987], quoting *Wayside Homes v. Purcelli*, 104 A.D.2d 650, 651, 480 N.Y.S.2d 29 [1984], *lv. denied* 64 N.Y.2d 602, 485 N.Y.S.2d 1027, 475 N.E.2d 126 [1984]; . . .).

Nevertheless, the Court of Appeals has authorized equitable relief against untimely renewal where there was no indication that substantial improvements had been made. Indeed, in *J.N.A. Realty* the Court cited *Sy Jack Realty Co. v. Pergament Syosset Corp.*, 27 N.Y.2d 449, 318 N.Y.S.2d 720, 267 N.E.2d 462 (1971), in which it had affirmed the grant of equitable relief to the commercial tenant, not because substantial improvements to the premises would otherwise be forfeited, but "to preserve the tenant's interest in a 'long-standing location for a retail business' because this is 'an important part of the good will of that enterprise, [and thus] the tenant stands to lose a substantial and valuable asset'" (*J.N.A. Realty* at 398, 397 N.Y.S.2d 958, 366 N.E.2d 1313, quoting *Sy Jack Realty* at 453, 318 N.Y.S.2d 720, 267 N.E.2d 462). The equivalent circumstance is presented here.

Daffy's introduced evidence that the 57th Street store in particular had become highly successful and popular, that the company had searched for alternative space into which to relocate that store and had not identified any prospects, and that even if it found a viable site, it would require the better part of a year to open the new store. So, although there was evidence that Daffy's, like Dean & DeLuca in *Soho Dev. Corp.* . . . , had widespread name recognition unrelated to any particular store location, the evidence was sufficient to support a finding that Daffy's 57th Street store in particular had garnered substantial goodwill in its approximately 15 years at the location, which goodwill was a valuable asset that would be damaged by its ouster from the premises.

. . .

Thus, given the loss of goodwill that would accompany the loss of the store, enforcing the lease's time restraint for renewal would result in a forfeiture that warranted the court's consideration of whether equity ought to intervene. In this context, the court properly considered the testimony that most of the store's 114 employees would lose their jobs and benefits if the store were to close and no alternate location was available, as well as the evidence of the mistake made by the corporation's controller in failing to calendar the renewal deadline. . . . Finally, the location was shown to be "one of [Daffy's] top producing retail locations, and [the landlord] failed to establish that any prejudice resulted from the breach" [citation omitted].

"By its nature, equitable relief must always depend on the facts of the particular case and not on hypotheticals" [citation omitted]. The facts here justify the relief awarded to Daffy's.

Accordingly, the judgment of the [trial court] should be affirmed, with costs.

Post-Case Follow-Up

Having concluded that the landlord suffered no loss from the late renewal, perhaps any loss to the tenant would be disproportionate. Had the landlord relied on the lack of notice to lease the premises to a new tenant or even to advertise seeking one, a comparison might be required. The tenant's investment in advertising this location and developing a reputation would be wasted, at least to the extent that recent investments would not generate a return before the tenant had to move. Rather than cause the tenant to forfeit that investment, the court excused the condition. Of course, holding for the landlord would not necessarily require the tenant to move.

The three dissenters in *JNA Realty* expressed concern that the result ignored commercial realities and added instability to business transactions. Excuse requires a judicial proceeding, which is unnecessary if the only question is whether the condition occurred. The dissenters preferred not to inject that uncertainty into the negotiations to rescue a party from its own carelessness in failing to pay sufficient attention to deadlines.

135 East 57th Street LLC v. Daffy's Inc.: Real Life Applications

1. Guy built a marina on land leased from Ramey for 25 years, with two 25-year renewal options. Guy missed the deadline to exercise the first renewal on July 1, apparently having forgotten it. On July 21, Ramey notified Guy that the lease would expire on December 31. On July 22, Guy gave oral notice exercising the option to renew. On July 25, Guy exercised the option in the manner specified in the lease. The lease gives Ramey title to all improvements once the lease expires. In addition, Guy has built up considerable goodwill for the business at this location, the only location Guy operates. Guy asks whether a Nebraska court will allow it to renew the lease despite the failure. *See Guy Dean's Lake Shore Marina, Inc. v. Ramey*, 518 N.W.2d 129 (Neb. 1994).

2. While riding on (not in) a car driven by Sasha, Alex was thrown from the vehicle and suffered head injuries that required a two-day hospitalization. Later, Alex was diagnosed with permanent brain damage apparently related to the injury. Alex's parents' uninsured motorist coverage would cover this injury if the insured gave notice to the insurer "as soon as possible after the accident." Alex sued Sasha about one year after the accident and joined the insurer, which was the first time the insurer received notice of the accident. Alex's parents assert that they did not give notice earlier because they did not realize uninsured motorist coverage under their automobile insurance policy applied to accidents when they were not operating the vehicle. They also assert that they did not realize the damage was sufficiently severe to require coverage or a lawsuit until long after the accident. Should a court excuse the failure to comply with the notice provision on the ground of disproportionate forfeiture? *See Alcazar v. Hayes*, 982 S.W.2d 845 (Tenn. 1998).

3. Armcar transports bags full of cash for businesses, including Taverna. Armcar's standard contract provides that it will reimburse businesses for bags lost after they have been delivered to an Armcar employee and that employee has provided a receipt to the business for the bag. On December 1, a bag containing $130,000 was stolen after Taverna had delivered it to Armcar's employee, but before that employee provided Taverna a receipt for the bag. Can Taverna recover under the contract even though it never received a receipt for the bag? *See Acme Markets, Inc. v. Fed. Armored Exp., Inc.*, 648 A.2d 1218 (Pa. Super. Ct. 1994).

6. Subsequent Events Altering Duties

If the parties agree that the occurrence of an event will excuse a party's obligation to perform, then the duty will be discharged by the occurrence of that event.[7] Recall the example at the beginning of the chapter of an insurance claim that disappeared unless the insured sued on the claim within two years of the fire. The fire occurred and the proof of loss was filed on time, making the insurer's duty to pay due. But

[7] RESTATEMENT (SECOND) OF CONTRACTS §230.

that duty vanishes if the insured does not comply with the additional condition to sue in a timely manner (a condition applicable only to unpaid claims). Sometimes called conditions subsequent, they do not fit the definition of condition because performance already was due. Modern usage prefers to call events after a duty arises "events that terminate a duty."

Subsequent events can protect some important interests. For example, a person willing to sell land to a city for a park may prefer to keep it if the city elects a different use (say, a parking lot). The conveyance may specify that if the city stops using the land as a party specified, title reverts to the seller. In *Girl Scouts of Southern Illinois v. Vincennes Indiana Girls*,[8] a donor specified that unless land was used as a Girl Scout camp for 50 years, it would revert to the donor. Similar provisions have appeared in commercial transactions, requiring return of land if the buyer does not begin building by a certain date or uses the land for purposes other than those specified in the contract.

Discharging a duty that already has come due often produces forfeiture. Performance often becomes due because the other party has performed. In real estate transactions, buyer may need to return land despite having paid for it already. If the land was donated, as in the *Girl Scouts* case, the recipient will not forfeit the price, but may forfeit any investments made improving the land.

Courts and legislatures seek to limit forfeiture. In real estate, statutes may limit how quickly a claimant must invoke the provision. Some limit how long the provision may limit the recipient's use of the property. Contracts can work around these provisions by reducing forfeiture. For example, in *Bruggeman v. Jerry's Enterprises*,[9] the seller retained an option to repurchase land if buyer failed to begin construction within two years. Buyer would not forfeit the payment, but recover the agreed price for returning the land.

Courts dislike events that take away contract rights after they initially accrue. Thus, courts employ a range of devices to prevent forfeiture, including waiver and estoppel. In addition, breach of good faith may preclude invocation of the discharging event, especially if one party's breach of good faith and fair dealing caused the event to occur. In addition, where the event is caused or prevented by extreme circumstances (for example, fire or tornado), the event may not excuse performance. For instance, if the insured is in another country where a war precludes it from bringing suit within two years, the event may not excuse the insurer's performance.

B. ORDER OF PERFORMANCE

The party that performs first faces some risk; the other party might keep the performance and not provide the promised return. Insisting that the other party perform first minimizes that party's risk—but really just puts the risk on the other party, without changing the risk at all. The possible impasse requires some resolution. The problems are not insurmountable. Without any recourse to courts, drug

[8] 988 N.E.2d 250 (Ind. 2013).
[9] 583 N.W.2d 299 (Minn. Ct. App. 1998).

dealers manage to find a way to decide whether the buyer should pay first or the seller should deliver the drugs first.

Where parties do not specify the order of performance, the court may need to infer which of them should perform first or, more often, whether a party's refusal to perform first was justified or was breach. Courts sometimes evaluate whether the contract included an implied condition. The party that refused to go first would be justified in withholding performance if the other party's performance was an implied condition. Until the condition occurred (that is, the other party performed), this party's performance was not due. Courts also discuss whether a promise was dependent or independent. An **independent promise** must be performed regardless of whether the other party performs first. This duty exists independent of what the other party does or does not do. A **dependent promise** need not be performed unless the other party has performed first; the duty to perform depends on prior performance by the other party.

The terminology threatens to obscure three relatively straightforward rules about the order of performance.

1. The parties, in their agreement, can specify who must perform first.
2. Simultaneous performance is preferred over sequential performance.
3. When one party's performance requires time, that party probably must perform first.[10]

Knowing who must perform first is critical when addressing the issues discussed in Section C, below. Breach by the other party might excuse a party's performance — if the other party was required to perform first. The buyer's nonperformance cannot excuse the seller's duty to perform if the buyer was not yet required to perform because the seller's performance was due first or at the same time. Section C discusses when a party might be required to perform even if the other party has already failed to perform.

Simultaneous performance leaves neither party at risk. Each receives performance as they give performance. If you agree to buy an individual's used car, typically you hand over the money and the other hands over the keys and the signed title. Even that, however, can become complicated. The seller might insist that you hand over the money first. That might be breach; you have no obligation to pay unless he simultaneously hands over the title and keys. As neither must go first, impasse can result.

To avoid impasse in simultaneous transactions, the law relies on the requirement of **tender**: an offer to perform immediately with the demonstrated ability to do so. Buyer's tender of payment is a condition on seller's duty to deliver the car. Seller's tender of the car is a condition on buyer's duty to pay.[11] Neither needs to perform until the other tenders performance. Once each tenders — one shows the money, the other the keys (and title and the car) — a simultaneous exchange is a little easier to require. You grab the keys, he grabs the money, and you each let go.

[10] Restatement (Second) of Contracts §234.
[11] *Id.* §238.

With a little common sense (or courtesy), this does not become a legal problem. But cases do arise. Sometimes a party wants out of the deal, refusing to tender as a way to induce the other to breach.

Simultaneity is not always possible. An employer cannot easily pay the employee by the day, the minute, or the hour. Either the employee works (a day, a week, a month) and then gets paid, or the employee gets paid in advance. Either way, one is at risk. The same is true of construction. Even with progress payments (which most contractors request in their contracts), some period of construction occurs, then a duty to pay arises — or then payment for the next phase is required.

The rule noted above suggests payment after work. The employee and the contractor require time to perform, while the employer or landowner can pay in an instant. Performance should precede payment.

Agreement by the parties or customs in the trade (which the parties presumably adopt voluntarily as an unspoken part of their agreement) can alter any of these presumptions. When you order a pizza, they deliver, then you pay (as the rule implies). But if you use a credit card, you may need to pay first (giving them the card number over the phone). At a coffee shop, you pay first, then they make your coffee. Agreements can create more complex terms regarding the order of performance. Construction contracts have elaborate terms for progress payments, including a retention of certain percentages on each payment so the owner still has something withheld until it approves the work after completion. Lawyers often take a retainer up front, subtracting their fees from it as they work. When exhausted, the client must replenish the retainer. Others work on contingency, getting paid out of the proceeds of a judgment when the case concludes.

C. MATERIAL BREACH AND SUBSTANTIAL PERFORMANCE

Every promise to perform a contract includes an implied condition: the absence of a **material** (significant — but see the full discussion below) failure to perform by the other party that remains **uncured** (not yet corrected by subsequent performance). Commonly called **material breach**, the rule applies to any nonperformance, not just to breaches. As Chapter 13 discusses, sometimes courts excuse nonperformance rather than treating it as breach. By negating breach, excuse protects the party from owing damages, but nonperformance may still justify the other party in refusing to perform. For example, if fire burns down a building rented for a wedding reception, the couple may not be entitled to damages for breach; but the lessor's nonperformance excuses their duty to pay rent for the premises.

If one party has failed to perform in material ways, the other party need not perform any additional duties until that nonperformance is cured (at least to the point of no longer being material). Until cure occurs, the party is entitled to suspend its performance. If cure cannot occur, the party is entitled to **cancel** the contract: refuse to perform any more of its duties, replace the party that failed to perform with another provider, and resort to other remedies for breach of contract (if the nonperformance was breach).

Substantial performance is the opposite of material breach. If a party's performance was close enough to the promise, a court may decide the breach is not material and therefore call it substantial performance. In that case, the other party has no right to cancel the contract. It may resort to other remedies, such as damages, but must continue to perform its part of the deal. There is no middle ground between substantial performance and material breach: either the breach is material (and performance excused) or the performance is substantial. You may see an occasional reference to immaterial breach, but you are unlikely to see a discussion of insubstantial performance. Another (but more confusing) way to say the same things: a party's duty to perform is independent where the other substantially performed. But the promise is dependent where there has been a material breach. See Exhibit 11.3.

Damages are available for any breach, no matter how minor. Material breach is important only if a party wants to escape from a contract: to stop performing the duties the contract otherwise requires. The doctrine determines when a party can cancel the agreement and seek a different contract.

EXHIBIT 11.3 Degrees of Breach

As performance gets closer to full performance a court is less likely to treat a breach as material.

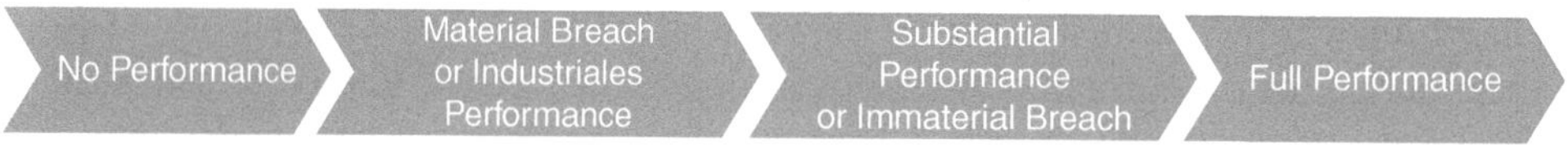

No Performance → Material Breach or Industriales Performance → Substantial Performance or Immaterial Breach → Full Performance

Canceling a contract based on the other's material breach involves a serious risk: if unjustified, the canceling party's nonperformance is a breach that entitles the other party to seek remedies. For example, a homeowner may refuse to pay a contractor for poor work. If, however, the contractor substantially performed the contract (the flaws were not material), nonpayment becomes breach by the homeowner. Parties need confidence that the other's breach justifies cancellation. This setting requires careful analysis of the rules governing material breach. The risk, however, makes it safer to continue to work out problems with the other party rather than try to cancel the contract.

In one sense, these rules are intuitive. If one party stops performing, it seems fair to allow the other party to stop performing, too. If the contractor stops building, the owner may stop making progress payments—or vice versa. Some may wonder why the rule limits the right to stop performing to cases of material breach. Why must a party tolerate any breach, even small ones? Indeed, under the UCC's perfect tender rule (discussed in Chapter 12), even a small defect in the tender of goods may justify a buyer's cancellation of the contract.[12] In most circles, however, the real puzzle is why the UCC allows rejection for minor problems.

Consider the following situation. A contractor owes the subcontractor a progress payment of $12,344. The contractor sends a check for $12,334—maybe a

[12] UCC §2-601.

typographical error, maybe someone just misheard or misread the amount. If any breach, no matter how minor, justifies the subcontractor to refuse to perform under the contract, then the subcontractor could walk off the job. The contractor could not sue for breach because the subcontractor's refusal to perform was justified. This result would hold true no matter how sincerely the contractor apologized or how quickly (after the deadline for payment) the contractor made amends.

The subcontractor's cancellation might be entirely rational. Suppose the subcontractor had underbid the job: instead of making a profit, it will lose money on the work. Walking off the job will save money, not lose money. Any excuse, no matter how flimsy, might lead it to cancel the entire contract. Even if the deal is profitable, the subcontractor may sense an opportunity to get a better deal. The contractor faces more than the inconvenience of replacing the sub. In the time it would take the contractor to hire a new sub, enormous disruptions in a project might result (especially if one subcontractor's absence sets other subcontractors back on their timetables). The delay might constitute a breach, allowing other subs to cancel their contracts. The contractor may need to pay more than budgeted to get a substitute for the subcontractor. Knowing that, the subcontractor may threaten to walk off the job unless the contractor agrees to increase the price of the subcontract. In effect, a small error becomes an excuse for renegotiating any contract.

In some cases, canceling the contract may be more advantageous than renegotiating it. If the subcontractor's expenses significantly exceed the contract price, termination may allow it to seek recovery for unjust enrichment (a claim that defendant received a benefit that it would be unjust for her to retain without compensating the plaintiff for providing it, as introduced in Chapter 1). If the breach justifies cancellation, the contractor no longer has a contract right to keep the sub's performance. It would be unjustly enriched unless it compensated the sub for the fair market value of the services — arguably, the amount that it would have cost the contractor to get these services from another provider. Recovery might be based on restitution (the benefit the contractor received), not necessarily the contract price. Thus, instead of getting the extra $10 the contractor should have paid, the subcontractor might get the fair market value of the services, even if that significantly exceeds the contract price it was promised. A new provision in the Restatement

Termination or Cancellation

The UCC draws a distinction between cancellation and termination of a contract. Cancellation refers to ending a contract following another party's breach. UCC §2-106(4). Termination puts an end to the contract for reasons other than breach. UCC §2-106(3). Termination includes ending a contract based on defenses (such as misrepresentation), excuses (such as impracticability), or defects in formation (such as lack of assent). Following termination, neither party has a duty to continue performance and either may have a claim for unjust enrichment. Termination may not erase a prior breach, but the grounds for termination do not justify a claim for damages. Following a material breach, a party may cancel the contract. Cancellation, too, ends any further duty to perform either party may have had under the contract, but also includes the right to seek damages for breach of contract (or any other appropriate remedy). The distinction is not always strictly observed outside the UCC. Nonetheless, paying attention to the distinction in other contexts will help avoid using the wrong term when dealing with the UCC. A little care in choosing the right word may pay off.

A Classic

Jacob & Youngs v. Kent is a classic case, for decades one that almost every law student has read. Benjamin Cardozo, the author of the opinion, was one of the most renowned judges in American history. He served on the U.S. Supreme Court near the end of his career, but his work on the New York Court of Appeals receives more attention today. This decision helped change the course of the law. Instead of asking whether performance was excused because the promise was dependent, Cardozo asked whether performance was excused because the breach was material. The nature of the breach, not the nature of the promise, determined the outcome — a controversial position in its day that has become standard doctrine today. The opinion, though nearly a century old, continues to deserve study.

(Third) of Restitution and Unjust Enrichment might change this analysis by limiting recovery to a pro rata share of the contract price.[13] Whether courts will follow this course remains to be seen.

Limiting cancellation to material breaches reduces the ability of parties to engage in strategic behavior of this sort. Courts may find a breach too minor to justify a party in refusing to perform. The breach, however minor, will permit the injured party to recover damages. In the example above, the subcontractor could collect the unpaid $10, plus interest. However, if the subcontractor tried to cancel the contract, the court might find this refusal to perform unjustified. If so, the contractor can sue for damages caused by the subcontractor's unexcused nonperformance.

The rule makes it very risky for a party to refuse to perform. A premature cancellation of the contract can transform a nonbreaching party, justifiably complaining about the other's breach, into the breaching party, whose refusal to perform was unjustified. Thus, parties have good reason to continue performing unless they have a very good reason to cancel the contract.

Case Preview

Jacob & Youngs v. Kent

In this case, a landowner's dissatisfaction with the construction of his new custom home led him to refuse to make the final payment for the work. The primary dispute involved the contractor's failure to ensure that all of the pipe used in the plumbing was "of Reading manufacture." The court needed to determine whether the deviation would excuse the owner's duty to make the payment.

As you read *Jacob & Youngs v. Kent*, look for the following:

1. What did the court consider in deciding whether the breach excused the buyer's performance?
2. Do the buyer's reasons for wanting Reading pipe matter? Should they?
3. Even if buyer must make the last payment, should damages compensate for the cost to have the nonconforming pipe replaced with Reading pipe?

[13] Restatement (Third) of Restitution and Unjust Enrichment §38 (2011).

Jacob & Youngs, Inc. v. Kent

129 N.E. 889 (N.Y. 1921)

Apes

CARDOZO, J.

The plaintiff built a country residence for the defendant at a cost of upwards of $77,000, and now sues to recover a balance of $3,483.46, remaining unpaid. The work of construction ceased in June, 1914, and the defendant then began to occupy the dwelling. There was no complaint of defective performance until March, 1915. One of the specifications for the plumbing work provides that—

> all wrought-iron pipe must be well galvanized, lap welded pipe of the grade known as 'standard pipe' of Reading manufacture.

The defendant learned in March, 1915, that some of the pipe, instead of being made in Reading, was the product of other factories. The plaintiff was accordingly directed by the architect to do the work anew. The plumbing was then encased within the walls except in a few places where it had to be exposed. Obedience to the order meant more than the substitution of other pipe. It meant the demolition at great expense of substantial parts of the completed structure. The plaintiff left the work untouched, and asked for a certificate that the final payment was due. Refusal of the certificate was followed by this suit.

The evidence sustains a finding that the omission of the prescribed brand of pipe was neither fraudulent nor willful. It was the result of the oversight and inattention of the plaintiff's subcontractor. Reading pipe is distinguished from Cohoes pipe and other brands only by the name of the manufacturer stamped upon it. . . . Even the defendant's architect, though he inspected the pipe upon arrival, failed to notice the discrepancy. The plaintiff tried to show that the brands installed, though made by other manufacturers, were the same in quality, in appearance, in market value, and in cost as the brand stated in the contract—that they were, indeed, the same thing, though manufactured in another place. The evidence was excluded, and a verdict directed for the defendant. The Appellate Division reversed, and granted a new trial.

We think the evidence, if admitted, would have supplied some basis for the inference that the defect was insignificant in its relation to the project. The courts never say that one who makes a contract fills the measure of his duty by less than full performance. They do say, however, that an omission, both trivial and innocent, will sometimes be atoned for by allowance of the resulting damage, and will not always be the breach of a condition to be followed by a forfeiture. *Spence v. Ham*, 163 N.Y. 220, 57 N.E. 412 [1900]; *Woodward v. Fuller*, 80 N.Y. 312 [1880]; [citations omitted]. The distinction is akin to that between dependent and independent promises, or between promises and conditions. [Citations omitted.] Some promises are so plainly independent that they can never by fair construction be conditions of one another. [Citations omitted.] Others are so plainly dependent that they must always be conditions. Others, though dependent and thus conditions when there is departure in point of substance, will be viewed as independent and collateral when the departure is insignificant. 2 Williston on Contracts, §§841, 842; *Eastern Forge Co. v. Corbin*, 182 Mass. 590, 592, 66 N. E. 419 [1903]; [citations omitted]. Considerations partly of justice and partly of presumable intention are to tell us whether this or that promise shall be placed in one class or in another. . . . The margin of departure within the range of normal expectation upon a sale of common chattels will vary from the margin to be expected upon a contract for the construction of a mansion or a "skyscraper." There will be harshness sometimes and oppression in the implication of a condition when the thing upon which labor has been expended is incapable of surrender because united to the land, and equity and reason in the implication of a like condition when the subject-matter, if defective, is in shape to be returned. [Where an implied condition would be unjust, the parties may not have intended a condition. If they want a harsh result, they must be explicit. The court will not assume] a purpose to visit venial faults with oppressive retribution.

Those who think more of symmetry and logic in the development of legal rules than of practical adaptation to the attainment of a just result will be troubled by a classification where the lines of division are so wavering and blurred. [An inflexible rule might be more consistent and predictable, but fairness outweighs these concerns.] Where the line is to be drawn between the important and the trivial cannot be settled by a formula. "In the nature of the case precise boundaries are impossible." 2 Williston on Contracts, §841. The same omission may take on one aspect or another according to its setting. Substitution of equivalents may not have the same significance in fields of art on the one side and in those of mere utility on the other. Nowhere will change be tolerated, however, if it is so dominant or pervasive as in any real or substantial measure to frustrate the purpose of the contract. *Crouch v. Gutmann*, 134 N.Y. 45, 51, 31 N.E. 271 [1892]. There is no general license to install whatever, in the builder's judgment, may be regarded as "just as good." *Easthampton L. & C. Co., Ltd. v. Worthington*, 186 N.Y. 407, 412, 79 N.E. 323 [1906]. The question is one of degree, to be answered, if there is doubt, by the triers of the facts [citations omitted] and, if the inferences are certain, by the judges of the law [citations omitted]. We must weigh the purpose to be served, the desire to be gratified, the excuse for deviation from the letter, the cruelty of enforced adherence. Then only can we tell whether literal fulfillment is to be implied by law as a condition.

[¶] This is not to say that the parties are not free by apt and certain words to effectuate a purpose that performance of every term shall be a condition of recovery. That question is not here. This is merely to say that the law will be slow to impute the purpose, in the silence of the parties, where the significance of the default is grievously out of proportion to the oppression of the forfeiture. The willful transgressor must accept the penalty of his transgression. *Schultze v. Goodstein*, 180 N.Y. 248, 251, 73 N.E. 21 [1905]; *Desmond-Dunne Co. v. Friedman-Doscher Co.*, 162 N.Y. 486, 490, 56 N.E. 995 [1900]. For him there is no occasion to mitigate the rigor of implied conditions. The transgressor whose default is unintentional and trivial may hope for mercy if he will offer atonement for his wrong. [Citation omitted.]

In the circumstances of this case, we think the measure of the allowance is not the cost of replacement, which would be great, but the difference in value, which would be either nominal or nothing. Some of the exposed sections might perhaps have been replaced at moderate expense. The defendant did not limit his demand to them, but treated the plumbing as a unit to be corrected from cellar to roof. . . . It is true that in most cases the cost of replacement is the measure. [Citation omitted.] The owner is entitled to the money which will permit him to complete, unless the cost of completion is grossly and unfairly out of proportion to the good to be attained. When that is true, the measure is the difference in value. Specifications call, let us say, for a foundation built of granite quarried in Vermont. On the completion of the building, the owner learns that through the blunder of a subcontractor part of the foundation has been built of granite of the same quality quarried in New Hampshire. The measure of allowance is not the cost of reconstruction. "There may be omissions of that which could not afterwards be supplied exactly as called for by the contract without taking down the building to its foundations, and at the same time the omission may not affect the value of the building for use or otherwise, except so slightly as to be hardly appreciable." *Handy v. Bliss*, 204 Mass. 513, 519, 90 N.E. 864 [1910; citations omitted]. The rule that gives a remedy in cases of substantial performance with compensation for defects of trivial or inappreciable importance has been developed by the courts as an instrument of justice. The measure of the allowance must be shaped to the same end.

The order should be affirmed, and judgment absolute directed in favor of the plaintiff upon the stipulation, with costs in all courts.

McLaughlin, J.

I dissent. The plaintiff did not perform its contract. Its failure to do so was either intentional or due to gross neglect which, under the uncontradicted facts, amounted to the same thing. . . .

Under its contract it obligated itself to use in the plumbing only pipe (between 2,000 and 2,500 feet) made by the Reading Manufacturing Company. The first [1,000 feet of] pipe delivered [was examined and verified, but subsequent deliveries were] delivered and installed in the building, without any examination whatever . . . by the plaintiff, the subcontractor, defendant's architect, or any one else. . . . Plaintiff's [sic] architect then refused to give the certificate of completion, upon which the final payment depended. . . . [The subcontractor's inspection revealed that, of the 900 feet that could be examined without demolishing part of the building, only 70 feet were from Reading.]

I am of the opinion the trial court was right in directing a verdict for the defendant. The plaintiff agreed that all the pipe used should be of the Reading Manufacturing Company. Only about two-fifths of it, so far as appears, was of that kind. . . . The question of substantial performance of a contract . . . depends in no small degree upon the good faith of the contractor. If the plaintiff had intended to, and had, complied with the terms of the contract except as to minor omissions, due to inadvertence, then he might be allowed to recover the contract price, less the amount necessary to fully compensate the defendant for damages caused by such omissions. [Citations omitted.] But that is not this case. . . . No explanation was given why pipe called for by the contract was not used. . . . The defendant had a right to contract for what he wanted. He had a right before making payment to get what the contract called for. It is no answer to this suggestion to say that the pipe put in was just as good as that made by the Reading Manufacturing Company, or that the difference in value between such pipe and the pipe made by the Reading Manufacturing Company would be either "nominal or nothing." Defendant contracted for pipe made by the Reading Manufacturing Company. What his reason was for requiring this kind of pipe is of no importance. He wanted that and was entitled to it. It may have been a mere whim on his part, but even so, he had a right to this kind of pipe. . . . The rule, therefore, of substantial performance, with damages for unsubstantial omissions, has no application. *Crouch v. Gutmann*, 134 N.Y. 45, 31 N.E. 271 [1892; citations omitted].

. . .

For the foregoing reasons I think the judgment of the Appellate Division should be reversed and the judgment of the Trial Term affirmed.

HISCOCK, C.J., and HOGAN and CRANE, JJ., concur with CARDOZO, J.

POUND and ANDREWS, JJ., concur with MCLAUGHLIN, J.

[In denying reargument, the court noted:] The court did not overlook the specification which provides that defective work shall be replaced. The promise to replace, like the promise to install, is to be viewed, not as a condition, but as independent and collateral, when the defect is trivial and innocent. The law does not nullify the covenant, but restricts the remedy to damages.

Post-Case Follow-Up

By a 4-3 vote, the court decided that the contractor had substantially performed despite the inadvertent breach, thus entitling the contractor to receive the final payment. The court mentioned several factors, but started by noting that the difference in pipe seemed insignificant in relation to the project. The court emphasized the contractor's good faith, suggesting a contractor could not expect this treatment for an intentional breach. The dissent thought carelessness should suffice to deprive the contractor of relief for its default. The inability to fix the problem without destroying (and then rebuilding) significant portions of the walls played a role in the court's evaluation. The final payment might be less than damages if defendant could install Reading pipe and seek damages for the cost of repair. Perhaps the most significant ruling was the first: that it would consider the degree of breach in deciding whether the promise was dependent or independent—that the importance of the promise depended in part on the degree of the breach.

Jacob & Youngs v. Kent: Real Life Applications

1. Desi hired Clem to build a custom house. Clem unilaterally decided to alter the pitch of the roof to make it stronger, more attractive (to Clem), and less expensive to frame. Desi found the change aesthetically objectionable, but did not dispute testimony that it might be more functional. It would cost $20,000 to remove the roof and replace it with a roof that conforms to the original plans. Desi has not made the final payment of $28,000. May Desi withhold this payment? Does

the answer depend on whether Desi actually uses the money to alter the roof to the original specifications?

2. Alex owned a business that distributed tortilla chips. Casey agreed to buy the business for $500,000, payable over three years, if Alex promised to remain with the business (on salary) for five years. Alex agreed, but later left the business after only 18 months, intending to open a bagel shop. Casey had paid $235,000 of the price. Casey asked to rescind the contract and offered to return the business to Alex, but Alex elected not to reenter the business. Is Alex's breach material, allowing Casey to stop making payments? *See Famiglietta v. Ivie-Miller Enterprises, Inc.*, 966 P.2d 777 (N.M. Ct. App.), *cert. denied*, 972 P.2d 351 (N.M. 1988).

3. Buyers agreed to pay Sellers $320,000 for their home, making payments over time. Until payments were complete, Sellers would live in the basement apartment while Buyers occupied the house upstairs. The contract allowed Sellers to inspect the upstairs with reasonable notice, a term made necessary by Sellers' prior unannounced intrusions into Buyers' upstairs residence, which Sellers promised to stop. Seventeen days after signing the contract, Sellers (a) made another unannounced intrusion into Buyers' residence, (b) objected that the locks had been changed, (c) damaged some of the locks, (d) threatened to poison Buyers' cattle, and (e) cut power to the residence for a few hours in retaliation for Buyers' summoning the sheriff to investigate the break-in. Was Sellers' conduct a material breach that would justify Buyers in canceling the contract and recovering their down payment? *See Greenstreet v. Fairchild*, 313 S.W.3d 163 (Mo. Ct. App. 2010).

4. Jean operated a coffee shop in space leased from a mall for a five-year term. During the first two years, Jean occasionally was late with rent payments and also engaged in some conduct offensive to patrons of the mall. The mall owner notified Jean that it demanded strict compliance with the lease, including prompt payment of rent on or before the first day of each month. Jean complied with these terms for three months, but paid the January rent on Monday, January 3, instead of by Saturday, January 1. The owner refused the payment, elected to cancel the lease, and sought to evict Jean. Did Jean commit a material breach? Does it matter what the other conduct involved? Consider the conduct in *Rubloff CB Machesney, LLC v. World Novelties, Inc.*, 844 N.E.2d 462 (Ill. App. 2006).

1. Identifying Material Breach

Decisions building on *Jacob & Youngs* have considered five factors in deciding whether a breach is material:

1. the extent of the benefit the injured party will lose as a result of the nonperformance;
2. the extent to which damages or other remedies might compensate the injured party for the lost benefit;

3. the extent of any forfeiture suffered by the breaching party;
4. the likelihood that the breaching party will cure that failure to perform; and
5. the extent to which the breaching party acted in good faith.[14]

In applying this test, keep several critical aspects clearly in mind.

These are factors a court will consider and weigh. They differ from the elements of a claim or defense, where a party needs to establish each element to prevail. Instead, courts balance all five factors, as appropriate in each situation. The failure to establish any one of them will prevent a finding of materiality. At least in theory, any one factor may be so important that it outweighs the other four.

The rule addresses the extent, not merely the existence, of each factor. Each factor includes language of degree. Thus, one cannot simply show that forfeiture exists; the extent (or amount) of forfeiture counts. Similarly, merely showing loss of a benefit may not carry the day; the extent (or amount) of that loss counts. Recall the discussion in *Jacob & Youngs* about the relatively small difference between Reading pipe and pipe actually used. In balancing these factors, the weight will vary with the magnitude of the problem.

The first factor favors materiality, followed by four mitigating factors. The amount of benefit the nonbreaching party will lose supports treating a breach as material. The other four factors offer countervailing reasons, reducing the likelihood that a court will find the breach material. Even if the loss would be great, the ability of damages to compensate for it may persuade a court to treat the breach as immaterial. In the same way, the breaching party's good faith, the likelihood of cure, and the extent of harm the breaching party will suffer following cancellation all suggest reasons to limit the power of cancellation — perhaps even if the breach caused significant losses. As stated above, however, the rule leaves some room to argue that the breaching party's bad faith justifies cancellation even if the other factors outweigh the significance of the loss.

Courts consider the nonbreaching party's loss relative to the entire performance. In *Jacob & Youngs*, the builder delivered a house; the pipe was a modest portion of the performance. But even small defects may be material. For example, a subcontractor provided steel for a bridge, but defects in the coating on the steel led the party buying the bridge to refuse to allow the contractor to use that steel in the bridge. Although minor relative to the steel itself, breach relating to the coating seems material, making the steel itself useless for the buyer's purposes.[15]

Adequacy of Compensation

Where damages can offset the benefit lost, the victim may not need to cancel the contract. Instead, she can continue to perform and seek compensation from the other party in some other way. A damage suit offers one way to recover if the

[14]Restatement (Second) of Contracts §241.
[15]*See Lane Enterprises, Inc. v. L.B. Foster Co.*, 700 A.2d 465 (Pa. Super. Ct. 1997), *rev'd on other grounds*, 710 A.2d 54, 55 (Pa. 1998).

contract goes forward. Alternatively, the victim might reduce amounts she pays under the contract by the amount of loss caused by the breach, eliminating any net loss.

In some cases, however, compensation may not cover the loss. If damages are hard to calculate or to prove, a jury might award too little. If the other party is **insolvent** (broke), the plaintiff may not collect damages even if a court awards them, making it dangerous to continue performing. Sometimes damages will not replace the value lost while waiting for the other party to decide whether to cure the breach. For instance, where an insured refuses to pay the premiums, damages (in the amount of the unpaid premiums) may not make up for the insurer's loss. Unless able to cancel the contract, the insurer might need to pay large sums, even if it never was paid to assume the risk. Likewise, where breach threatens to cause the loss of unique property, damages may not suffice. For instance, a kennel's breach of a promise to provide a pet with appropriate shelter may harm a loved pet. Money offers a poor substitute. Finding the breach material allows the family to cancel the contract and find a better kennel.

Extent of Breaching Party's Forfeiture

The extent of forfeiture looks to the loss suffered by the breaching party if the other party may cancel the contract. Forfeiture does not refer to the breaching party's expectation of receiving the other's performance. As a breaching party, her right to expect the other to perform carries little weight. (Even if breach is not material, a damage award to the nonbreaching party will leave the breaching party short of her expected gain.) Rather, forfeiture refers to costs already incurred that the breaching party may not recoup if the other party can cancel the agreement. For instance, consider a contractor that has built an asphalt driveway where the contract called for concrete. If the owner can cancel and refuse payment, the contractor loses the cost of the materials and labor for the driveway. Courts measure that forfeiture by the performance already rendered, not by the price the breaching contractor would have received. Restitution may reduce the amount of forfeiture. If the contractor can recover in unjust enrichment for the driveway installed, the amount of forfeiture would be reduced by the recovery (which may or may not equal the cost of the work done).

Whose Forfeiture Matters?

Forfeiture refers to loss by the *breaching* party. The loss to the nonbreaching party also matters, but under the first factor: the extent to which the nonbreaching party loses the benefit of the bargain. Forfeiture adds the loss that the *breaching* party will suffer in order to compare the relative losses of the two parties. You should consider each party's losses, but be careful to relate them to the appropriate factor.

Also beware of treating the breaching party's loss of contract benefits as the forfeiture. True, cancellation will deprive the breaching party of any return performance. But cancellation will not cause forfeiture if the breaching party retains its performance, and is able to resell it to another. Forfeiture refers to sunk costs that cannot be recouped following cancellation. A party that cannot keep (or avoid the cost of) its performance suffers forfeiture.

Likelihood of Cure

If the breaching party is likely to correct any nonconformity within a relatively short time, allowing the nonbreaching party to cancel the contract seems unnecessary. The party does not lose the performance, but receives it a little later. Consider a breaching builder that fixes most of the problems the owner identified, but cannot correct one. Late performance was breach; the owner did not receive the complete house when promised. But prompt cure may avoid material breach. Especially if arranging for a substitute would take longer than cure by the breaching party, the breach may not be material. At that point, one begins to suspect strategic reasons for seeking cancellation.

A breaching party's assurance that it will cure the defects affects the likelihood of cure. How much weight the assurance deserves may depend on the credibility of the promise to cure. A party already in breach — and who may have a history of not meeting deadlines — may fail to show that cure was likely, despite promises to cure promptly.

Extent of Good Faith

The extent of good faith by the breaching party offers reason to tolerate breaches. A party may have believed, honestly, that the performance tendered satisfied the contract. Under these circumstances, requiring the other party to continue dealing with the breaching party poses little risk of hardship. On the other hand, a party that intentionally breached a known duty poses some risk for the other party. Requiring it to continue to deal with the offender involves some risk of additional breaches. A party caught cutting corners to save costs might start looking for other corners to cut (or a way to collect more than promised to make up for the inability to cut corners).

Breach in bad faith could be treated as an aggravating factor, perhaps allowing cancellation for material breach even if the loss caused was relatively small and could be compensated by damages. That reasoning converts this rule into a penalty for breach, which is alien to most theories of contract law. Contract law prefers to honor bargains, which requires keeping them in place unless good reasons justify cancellation. Where the breach caused only minor loss, courts may reject cancellation, even for a calculated breach.

Try your hand at applying the rule to the following situation. Suppose that in *Jacob & Youngs*, the foreman on the job intentionally ordered the wrong pipe, which, though just as good, was available for a slight discount. The loss to the homeowner remains quite small, the forfeiture to the builder quite large. Should the court nonetheless treat the breach as material based on the builder's bad faith?

2. Suspension and Discharge of Performance

When a material breach occurs, the other party may suspend performance: it may stop performing its part of the contract temporarily, while awaiting cure by the other party. Suspending performance would breach the contract unless justified by the other party's material breach, suggesting parties should reserve this course for cases where the materiality of the breach is clear or the risk of continuing to perform is significant.

The right to suspend performance falls short of the right to cancel the contract. Cancellation is permitted when cure cannot occur. At that point, the nonbreaching party's duties under the contract are discharged.

Late performance differs from an uncured material breach. Subsequent performance curing a breach is not as good as timely performance. However, cure does convert nonperformance (which may deprive the nonbreaching party of a substantial benefit) into a late performance (which may have much less serious effects on the nonbreaching party). Thus, a contract term specifying time for performance sets the point at which breach occurs, but does not necessarily set the time at which cure becomes impossible.

For example, recall the example of a contractor who paid $10 too little. It breached by failing to pay the entire amount on time. Delivering the unpaid portion the next day would not be performance, but it would cure the breach, reducing or eliminating the harm caused by the failure to perfume as promised. Even if the underpayment were deemed material (say, the contractor paid $1,234.40 instead of $12,344), it probably would justify suspension rather than immediate cancellation. While significant, the partial breach suggests some possibility that cure will follow. If the contractor promptly pays the balance due, no uncured material breach would exist to justify continued nonperformance by the subcontractor. Late performance can be a material breach in itself, perhaps because performance was very late or because timely performance was very important. Thus, a wedding photographer who shows up a week later cannot cure the failure to photograph the wedding. Even where cure remains theoretically possible for a very long time, at some point failure to cure (and the diminishing likelihood that cure will occur) will justify cancellation.

Case Preview

Mart v. Mart

The case involves breach of a lease of farm land. The tenant farmer paid the rent, but violated federal law by planting corn on wetlands, which jeopardized serious benefits for the landlords. The tenant cured the violation the following year, returning the wetlands to a permissible use. But the landlords sought to cancel the lease anyway, forcing the court to determine whether the breach justified cancellation.

As you read *Mart v. Mart*, look for the following:

1. How did the court determine whether the breach was material?
2. Why did the court decide that the tenant's actions did not justify cancellation of the lease?

Farming wetlands

Mart v. Mart

824 N.W.2d 535 (Iowa Ct. App. 2012)

Danilson, J.

[In] 1998, [Mike Mart leased farmland for 20 years from his father] George for "$85.00 per acre for tillable acres . . . as determined by Government survey." [Previously, 8.7 acres of the land had been determined to be wetlands, where planting a commodity crop would violate federal law, making the owners ineligible to receive federal agricultural benefits.]

George died in 1999, and the property at issue passed to his four children as joint tenants in common. Mike continued to farm the property. Mike was aware of the wetland designation since 1987 and the 8.7 acres of wetland were left in alfalfa and not farmed until the 2008 crop year when Mike tilled it and planted corn.

Mike informed the USDA office that he had planted corn on the wetland[, appealing the ruling that he had] violated the Swampbuster provisions of the Food Security Act of 1985 (16 U.S.C. §§3801, 3821-3824).

[After losing the appeal,] Mike restored the wetlands for the 2009 crop year. [His siblings initially faced sanctions totaling more than $152,000, but appealed as innocent landlords unaware of the breach and prevailed. Nonetheless, the siblings sought to cancel Mike's lease in August 2009.]

[In May 2010, landlords] Dennis, Thomas, and Cheryl filed a petition for forcible entry and detainer (FED) against Mike. [After a trial in 2011,] the district court . . . rejected the contention . . . that the undisputed Swampbuster violation also constituted a violation of the farm lease. The landlords appeal.

[Four pages later, the court concluded that Mike did breach the lease.]

C. DO THE BREACHES OF LEASE TERMS SUPPORT TERMINATION?

Section twelve of the lease provides that a tenant who violates the terms of the lease is subject to legal and equitable remedies to which the landlord is entitled. Here, the landlords have sought termination of the leasehold rather than damages. Our supreme court has long determined that substantial compliance with the terms of the lease will avoid a forfeiture. *Beck*, 150 N.W.2d at 659. This action was brought in equity, and "it is the general rule that equity abhors a forfeiture." *Jamison v. Knosby*, 423 N.W.2d 2, 4 (Iowa 1988).

Mike testified he was not aware he had jeopardized the petitioners' benefits in tilling and planting the acres. Mike also restored the wetlands the next crop year. Pursuant to 16 U.S.C. §3821,

> any person who in any crop year produces an agricultural commodity on converted wetland, as determined by the Secretary, shall be (1) in violation of this section; and (2) ineligible for loans or payments in an amount determined by the Secretary to be *proportionate to the severity of the violation.*

(Emphasis added.) Here, Mike and the landlords were initially denied all federal farm program benefits. At the time this action was initiated, the land had been damaged by the conversion of the wetlands by Mike's tilling and planting corn, and the wetlands had not yet been restored. In light of the severity of the benefits that were initially denied, and the loss of the wetlands, at least before their restoration, we conclude the breach was a material breach by Mike's failure to substantially comply with the terms of the lease. *See Beck*, 150 N.W.2d at 659.

Mike urges that if his actions constituted a breach of the lease, termination of the lease and forfeiture are not equitable because the wetlands were restored and no financial cost was ultimately incurred by the landlords. We agree.

Even where a material breach exists, ordinarily a party may cure the failure. Restatement (Second) Contracts §§237(b) ("Even if the failure is material, it may still be possible to cure it by subsequent performance without a material failure."), 242 cmt a. ("Ordinarily there is some period of time between suspension and discharge, and during this period a party may cure his failure."), *available at* Westlaw (database current through April 2012). Our supreme court has similarly determined that although the commission of waste on leased properties "will work a forfeiture," where the acts complained of could be removed easily without damage to the building and the landlord incurred no expense, forfeiture was not justified. *See Bentler v. Poulson*, 258 Iowa 1008, 141 N.W.2d 551, 553 (1966) (concluding that tenant's installation of a dishwasher and a new furnace, which both required holes be cut into the roof for ventilation, may be repaired easily). Here, the landlords have not incurred any significant damages and have only sought a forfeiture of the lease. Although we appreciate their desire to terminate this lease due to its length and minimal cash rent, the facts reflect that the tenant has cured his material breach of the farm lease and equity does not support enforcing a forfeiture.

Our decision here is also consistent with cases in other jurisdictions where landlords have sought termination of a lease for a violation of law where the tenant cured or corrected the violation in a reasonable amount of time, and the courts held that the termination was not warranted. *McNeece v. Wood*, 204 Cal. 280, 267 P. 877, 879 (1928) (noting tenant took prompt action in removing bookmakers from leased property); *Sherwood Med. Indus., Inc. v. Building Leasing Corp.*, 527 S.W.2d 407, 411 (Mo. Ct. App. 1975) (finding lack of continuous or customary illegal use and prompt correction of violation); *Lewis v. Clothes Shack, Inc.*, 67 Misc. 2d 621, 322 N.Y.S.2d 738, 739 (N.Y. Sup. Ct. 1971) (noting removal of illegal storefront in three days). Here, the restoration of the wetlands has sufficiently cured the violation of the law and breaches to the extent that termination is not an equitable remedy under these facts.

In conclusion, upon our de novo review of the circumstances, and in light of the principle that "equity abhors a forfeiture," *Jamison*, 423 N.W.2d at 4, we find no error in the district court's dismissal of this FED petition.

AFFIRMED.

Post-Case Follow-Up

The court seems convinced that the breach did not threaten the landlords' likelihood of realizing the benefits to which the lease entitled them. They received the rent regularly. Cure, which occurred before the landlord gave notice canceling the lease, avoided any sanctions the landlord might suffer from the tenant's misuse of the land. Cure also suggested that the tenant would not misuse the property again. The court seemed to sense an ulterior motive. The landlords might have sought cancellation in order to enter a new lease at a higher rent: not the bargain Mike's father charged ten years ago, but something closer to current market values for the land. Because cancellation was unnecessary to preserve the benefits of this contract, the court refused to allow the rather drastic remedy of cancellation.

Mart v. Mart: Real Life Applications

1. Sandy agreed to buy Terry's condominium, paying 5 percent upon signing and promising an additional 5 percent deposit by June 1. The contract recited that time was of the essence. Sandy failed to make the additional deposit by June 1. Terry canceled the contract. On June 3, Sandy tendered the deposit plus interest for two days, but Terry refused to accept it because the contract already had been canceled. If Terry suffered no loss from late payment, can Sandy successfully bring an action for breach against Terry?

2. The sidewalk in front of Leslie's house was buckled and uneven, creating dangerous conditions for pedestrians. Following complaints, a city inspector issued a citation requiring Leslie to repair the sidewalk and remove a tree (that was causing the problem) by August 1 or pay a significant fine. On July 7, Leslie hired Chris to repair the sidewalk by July 21, a job that typically would require one week. Work was to begin on July 14, but Chris failed to appear. Leslie's efforts to contact Chris between July 15 and 17 received no response. On July 18, Leslie hired Sam to do the work (starting on July 23) and sent Chris a notice canceling the contract. On July 19, Chris appeared at Leslie's house, ready to perform the work. Leslie asks you whether refusing to allow Chris to complete the work would breach that contract. Does it matter why Chris was out of communication?

3. Loehmann's leases space in a mall. In addition to monthly rent, Loehmann's owes annual assessments for maintenance of common areas, calculated based on the percent of the mall Loehmann's occupies. The lease provides that if Loehmann's fails "to pay any installment of minimum annual rental or additional rental or other charges [and did not cure] within ten (10) days after receipt . . . of notice of such neglect or failure," the lessor could "prior to the removal of such Condition of Default," elect to terminate the lease. The lease also provides that

time is of the essence for any payment or act by lessee. Loehmann's questioned the amount of the most recent assessment, but lessor satisfactorily justified the assessment. On Good Friday (April 17), Loehmann's received notice of failure to pay the assessment. The notice received attention on April 20, when it was sent to the accounting department. After approval, a check was sent on April 24. Lessor brought suit seeking to cancel the lease on April 28. The check arrived on April 29. Was lessor entitled to cancel the lease for the uncured material breach by Loehmann's? Does it matter what the parties' practice has been regarding the timeliness of monthly rent payments? *Foundation Development Corp. v. Loehmann's, Inc.*, 788 P.2d 1189, 1191 (Ariz. 1990) (en banc).

Factors Justifying Cancellation

In determining whether a material nonperformance has lasted long enough to justify cancellation, courts consider the following factors:

1. all of the factors considered in determining whether the breach was material;
2. the extent to which delay may jeopardize efforts to make substitute arrangements; and
3. the extent to which the agreement requires timely performance.[16]

Again, the rule states factors, not elements. Each factor's weight varies with the extent of the problem it identifies. The balancing may be hard to predict.

The preceding section discussed the factors governing materiality. The more significant the loss, the more likely it is to justify cancellation, not just suspension. But again, the mitigating factors may outweigh the significance of the loss—or may add to the need for cancellation. For instance, where a party declares that it has no intention of curing the breach, immediate cancellation seems more appropriate.

The two additional factors add reasons to allow a party to cancel the contract sooner rather than later. They apply only if the breach was material.

Effect on Substitute Arrangements

Delay may jeopardize substitute arrangements. Canceling a contract for breach allows the victim to replace the breaching party. For instance, when a caterer breaches its promise to cater a wedding (or other celebration), the couple may need to make prompt arrangements to find a substitute. Insisting that they wait a few days to see if the first caterer will cure simply slows down the process—and risks making it impossible to find a suitable substitute, as other caterers fill their calendars. Where the nonbreaching party reasonably needs to make substitute arrangements promptly, courts are likely to find its duties under the first contract discharged soon after breach.

---

[16] *See* RESTATEMENT (SECOND) OF CONTRACTS §242.

Timeliness as a Contract Requirement

Generally, a contractual deadline or time for performance, without more, will not justify immediate cancellation. The deadline determines the existence of a breach; failure to perform by that date is nonperformance. But that will be true of contracts where the parties expect time to cure as well as of contracts where parties expect immediate discharge. The indication that time is critical to the parties requires more than just a stated time for performance to occur.

Contractual provisions may require timely performance, even making timely performance a condition. Alternatively, many contracts provide that "time is of the essence." That language may not create a condition, but does tell the courts that the parties believed timely performance was important. In effect, the parties agree that courts should allow cancellation immediately upon a material breach, without having to await cure. Courts generally give these terms their desired effect.

Even without an express provision, such as "time is of the essence," a court may find indications in the contract that timely performance was critical to the parties. If so, discharge may follow promptly upon a material breach, without a waiting period for cure.

A court could decide that late performance does not justify cancellation even though the contract says time is of the essence. Courts risk frustrating legitimate expectations by disregarding the parties' agreement. Parties include the clause to reduce the risk that the court may not fully appreciate the importance of timely performance for their needs. Allowing a court to decide that time is not really of the essence defeats the point.

In some circumstances, deference to the parties' term has less appeal. A form contract might include a boilerplate provision requiring timeliness even though it has little relevance to the transaction involved. The Restatement (Second) of Contracts §242 suggests a court could refuse to honor a clause unless other circumstances indicate the importance of timeliness. Few cases override real assent by the parties unless a state statute justifies ignoring the provision.

D. EFFECT OF DISCHARGE

If material breach discharges a party's obligation to perform, her duties under the contract end. In some cases, a party needs nothing more. If she has already received compensation for any performance already delivered, eliminating her obligation to perform in the future may end the matter. For instance, suppose an employee on a one-year contract quits after eight months. The employer may have suffered no loss. As long as the employee cannot sue the employer for the four months' salary not paid (because not worked), the employer requires no additional remedy.

Often one party or the other will have a claim for compensation. For example, the employee may have a claim if she has not been paid for all of the time she worked. Similarly, the employer may have a claim for losses in arranging for a substitute to fill the remaining term of the employee's contract. In some cases, the employer might seek to treat the entire contract as unenforceable, seeking a partial refund of payments made during the first six months.

1. Claims by the Breaching Party

The breaching party's claim for the value of performance already delivered usually arises under unjust enrichment. The breaching party generally cannot sue the non-breaching party for breach of contract. Discharge means the nonbreaching party had no further duty to perform under the contract. Thus, the breaching party must find a noncontractual ground for relief.

If the services already rendered enriched the nonbreaching party, it may be unjust for her to keep those services without compensating the breaching party. In that case, the breaching party may recover the fair market value of the services rendered. Specifically, she may recover the amount it would have cost the nonbreaching party to obtain the services from another similar provider at the time they were performed.[17] However, the breaching party cannot recover more than a pro rata share of the contract price. Having agreed to perform the services for a particular rate, he cannot recover more under unjust enrichment than he would recover under the contract. If the breaching party could recover more than the contract price for the services rendered, it would create an incentive for any party in a losing contract to breach, thereby increasing his compensation for the services. The law rejects that perverse incentive.

In one situation, a breaching party may have a contract claim. Where a contract is **divisible** — can fairly be divided into two parts, one performed and one not performed[18] — performance completed before the breach might be compensable at the contract rate. For example, suppose an employee works three days in a pay period, then walks off the job (or commits another material breach). If the contract specifies pay at a daily or hourly rate, contract law would permit enforcing the contract for the three days preceding the breach (and cancellation). Discharge excuses the employer from owing any amounts after the employee's material breach, but the contract is enforceable for performance rendered before the breach. Subsection 4 below discusses divisibility in greater detail.

2. Damage Claims by the Discharged Party

The breach often causes the discharged party a significant loss. To qualify as material, the breach must deprive the other party of a significant portion of the expected benefit. In some cases, the discharged party may obtain substitute performance for the same cost (or even less) than the original contract. But where breach forces the discharged party to incur additional costs to find and pay for substitute

[17] Restatement (Second) of Contracts §371. *See also* Restatement (Third) of Restitution and Unjust Enrichment §49(3) (offering additional ways to measure the value received by the nonbreaching party).
[18] *See* Restatement (Second) of Contracts §240.

performance, the discharged party may claim damages for the breach. Damages are addressed in Chapter 14.

3. Restitution Claims by the Discharged Party

A party whose performance was discharged by the other's uncured material breach may seek restitution instead of damages for breach of contract. The discharged party may claim the benefit its performance bestowed on the breaching party, calculated at the fair market value of the services rendered. Because material breach deprives the breaching party of a contract right to the performance, keeping it without compensating the discharged party would unjustly enrich the breaching party. Unlike restitution claims by the breaching party, however, courts may not limit the discharged party to a pro rata share of the contract price. If the benefit bestowed exceeds the contract price, recovery for unjust enrichment may provide a larger recovery than the party would have received without the other party's material breach.

For an extreme example, consider *Boomer v. Muir*,[19] in which a subcontractor agreed to build a dam for about $300,000. After nearly completing the project and receiving about $280,000 in progress payments, the subcontractor left the project because of the contractor's material breach. At that point, the subcontractor's costs greatly exceeded the contract price, at least in part as a result of the contractor's breaches. The court affirmed a jury award of about $258,000 to the subcontractor as the fair market value of the work performed so far — instead of the $20,000 it could have recovered if the contract price limited the recovery. Instead of $300,000 for a finished dam, the subcontractor received $538,000 for a not-quite-finished dam.

The Restatement (Third) of Restitution and Unjust Enrichment takes a slightly different approach to restitution following material breach. It rejects rescission for material breach unless both parties can be restored to their initial position. Thus, if goods can be returned in their original condition (or were never delivered), a refund of the price seems apt. But when construction has been attached to the other party's land, the materials and labor cannot be returned to the contractor and empty land cannot easily be given to the landowner, making rescission a less appealing alternative. The contract can be canceled for material breach, but its terms continue to specify the parties' rights going forward, allowing for damages but not restitution.

Warning Label Concerning the Restatement (Third)

The Restatement (Third) of Restitution and Unjust Enrichment was completed in 2011. It remains to be seen how the courts will receive this Restatement. Courts may not seek guidance on contract damages in a work that, from its title, appears to be addressed to restitution. The impact of this work may depend on whether you quote and rely on it in your briefs. You will help shape the law.

[19] 24 P.2d 570 (Cal. App. 1933).

4. Divisibility

In some cases, a contract may involve several pieces of a deal. If so, a party that performs one piece of the deal might deserve compensation for that piece, even if it breaches the other parts of the deal. Instead of treating the contract as one big deal (where the breaches might justify cancellation of the entire contract), courts may divide the contract into its pieces and enforce (or discharge) each one separately. By enforcing the performed piece of the contract, the court avoids restitution claims on that part of the deal. Claims for restitution arise for the unperformed portion of the contract.

Divisibility applies only if the contract involves "corresponding pairs of part performances" that can fairly be "regarded as agreed equivalents."[20] This often occurs in sales of goods, where an order might include many different items, with a price quoted separately for each. Divisibility can apply to a single item, such as an employee's services or leased premises, where the price is quoted for a period of time. Performance for a period may deserve a return performance for that period, even if a subsequent breach left room for a restitution claim regarding later periods.

Some contracts may divide the performances in a manner that cannot realistically be treated as agreed equivalents. For example, a contract may call for equal periodic payments even though the work involved is not distributed equally throughout the year. For example, suppose a farm worker agrees to a one-year contract at a fixed amount per month. Duties during the winter may not deserve as much pay as the work at planting and harvest. Treating each month's pay as the equivalent of each month's work might produce unfair results to either party, depending on when the breach occurred. Construction contracts often include progress payments, but the payments often involve a withholding of 10 percent, pending completion of the project. Treating the progress payment as an agreed equivalent of the work so far would undercompensate the contractor by 10 percent. In both situations, the contract specifies the timing of payments, not necessarily the value of the work so far.

Another problem can arise when several separately priced items have value as a set. For instance, a company may seek to rent three buildings in an office park in a lease that quotes the rent for each building separately. If the landlord breached regarding one of the buildings, but tendered the other two, the company might want to cancel the entire transaction. It wanted three buildings together, not two, plus a third it could find somewhere else. Treating this contract as divisible would compel the tenant to accept the two buildings. Because the landlord tendered its performance of those agreed equivalents, it would be entitled to the tenant's performance of its part of the agreed equivalents. Only the one building withheld would be subject to an action for breach or restitution. Carefully evaluate whether parts of a performance really have value independently or as a unit. Watch for situations where divisibility works one way but not the other. For example, if the tenant company breached regarding one of the three buildings, the landlord might rent

---

[23]Restatement (Second) of Contracts §240.

it to another without difficulty. Treating the contract as divisible in that situation might not deprive either party of the benefit of the bargain. Of course, if the rent was discounted because the tenant took all three buildings, agreed equivalents still may not exist.

Try your hand at applying these rules to the following situation. Survivors make funeral arrangements for the deceased, including arranging for the funeral home to keep someone on watch over the body at all times, as required by the deceased's faith. The funeral home performs all parts of the agreement (casket, services, burial plot, etc.), but fails to provide watch over the body for three of the six shifts involved. The contract itemized the price for each service, including each shift, as required by state laws governing funeral homes. The survivors allege material breach of contract, but the funeral home seeks to recover the price of all provided services, including the three shifts actually provided. Are the other services divisible from the watch? Are the three shifts provided divisible from the three shifts missed?

In some cases, division will not work out evenly; some portion of performance may be included in the breached portion of the contract. Consider a construction contract that required the contractor to build ten houses for $100,000 per house. The contractor quit the project after completing seven houses and part of an eighth. As to seven houses, the contractor might claim the contract price ($700,000), because the contract seems divisible. Yet the portion of the eighth house falls into the part of the contract breached. Any recovery for that partial performance would require an action in unjust enrichment. The contract does not appear to be divisible into parts of a house. No equivalent for part of house is agreed.

Divisibility can make it easier to assess whether a breach was material. By segregating out the performance that was completed, the remaining nonperformance becomes a more significant part of the whole. For example, once the contract is treated as enforceable for seven houses, the failure to complete any of the remaining three houses seems material. Left as a single contract, one might argue that finishing seven of ten houses was substantial performance (although the argument seems unlikely to prevail). But when the seven finished houses are divided out, the remaining performance (part of one house) almost certainly is not substantial performance of a contract requiring three houses. Division of the contract may simplify the discussion of material breach.

Example of Divisibility

Suppose an employee earning $100,000 per year materially breaches a one-year contract by quitting after six months. The employer may cancel the contract. If the employee's services already rendered had a value of only $40,000, the employer might seek restitution for $10,000 (the amount paid minus the value received).

A court may treat the contract as divisible. The employee performed for the first six months. Taking that separately, she was entitled to the pay for those months. (Unless the work was uneven, dividing the salary per month poses no problems.) The breach affected the second half of the contract, during which no services were rendered or salary paid, making restitution unnecessary. The employer can seek damages, if any.

The same would work with a lease or a construction contract — or even a sale of goods. The same approach would work whether the breach occurred near the beginning (say, after three months) or near the end (after ten months). The amount due on the part of the contract performed would change, as would any damages the employee might owe on the portion of the contract breached.

Chapter Summary

- Breach is unexcused nonperformance when performance is due. Performance is due when all conditions upon performance have occurred.
- Conditions limit promises, often using words such as "if," "unless," provided," or "after." Unless the language is clear, courts prefer to interpret language as a promise rather than a condition. Although language can be both a promise and a condition, that interpretation is disfavored unless the language is very clear.
- Conditions may be excused by waiver, estoppel, or judicial excuse to avoid disproportionate forfeiture. If a condition is excused, performance comes due even though the condition did not occur.
- Agreements requiring one party to perform first are enforced. If ambiguous, courts require simultaneous performance. When simultaneous performance is impossible, a party that requires time to perform must perform first.
- The absence of any uncured material nonperformance by the other party is a condition of a party's duty to perform. A material nonperformance by the other party allows a party to suspend performance and, if not cured, will allow a party to cancel the contract.
- Whether nonperformance is material depends on a balance of five factors: (i) the extent to which the nonbreaching party will lose the benefit of the contract; (ii) the extent to which damages will compensate for the lost benefit; (iii) the extent of forfeiture by the breaching party (if cancellation of the contract is permitted); (iv) the likelihood of cure; and (v) the extent to which the breaching party acted in good faith.
- Even after material nonperformance, a party may need to allow the other party an opportunity to cure the nonperformance before canceling the contract. How soon a party may cancel depends on the factors listed above and two others: (i) the extent to which delay will jeopardize the nonbreaching party's efforts to make substitute arrangements; and (ii) the extent to which the contract makes timely performance critical.

Applying the Rules

1. Sandy offered to buy Terry's house for $450,000, "contingent on a civil engineer's inspection report," among other things. On August 1, Terry accepted the offer, provided Sandy would clear the contingencies (either waive them or invoke them to avoid the sale) by August 15. The civil engineer's report identified several problems that would require about $5,000 in repairs (to fix some wiring, replace corroded plumbing, repair a rotted porch column, etc.). On August 12, Sandy asked Terry to fix these problems. On August 13, Terry refused and did not offer Sandy a rebate on the price to cover the repairs.

   a. If Sandy refuses to proceed with the sale, is Sandy in breach?
   b. If Sandy agrees to go forward with the sale, can Terry refuse to close?

2. While leaving a dinner party at Chris's house, Bobby slipped on the walk and fell, suffering a serious hip injury. Bobby informed Chris that the fall was caused by the unsafe condition of the walk. Alarmna, Chris's homeowner's insurer, would defend Chris against claims of this nature and cover liability if Chris is liable, provided Chris gives Alarmna "written notice as soon as possible after the occurrence of an event that may reasonably be expected to be the basis of a claim against you." The Alarmna agent who sold Chris the policy advised Chris not to notify Alarmna unless Bobby filed suit, in order to preserve Chris's discount based on number of years without a claim being made. Chris followed this advice. When Bobby filed suit, Chris immediately notified Alarmna of the claim. Upon learning that Chris was aware of Bobby's allegations months earlier, the adjuster sent a letter denying a claim for failure to give timely notice. Should Chris challenge the rejection in court? Outline Chris's strongest argument in favor of requiring coverage despite the late notice.

3. Shelly's car required repairs. Shelly took the car to Motorworks, which estimated that the repairs would cost $400. Shelly authorized Motorworks to repair the car and signed the estimate. Motorworks then asked for Shelly's credit card to pay the $400. Shelly promised to pay when the work was completed, but refused to pay in advance. Motorworks refused to do the repairs unless Shelly paid the $400 in advance. If their words and the estimate created a contract, did Motorworks breach by refusing to perform the promised work? Did Shelly breach by refusing to pay as requested?

4. Carmen bought a home in which the landscape had been neglected for some time. Carmen hired Zen to repair and improve the landscaping. Zen prepared plans that Carmen approved, agreeing to the price of $25,000 for the work. Carmen paid for materials (soil, stone, plants, etc.) as they were brought to the property. Payment of the balance was due upon completion. When work was completed, Carmen inspected the results but refused to pay Zen the balance due of $17,000. Carmen identified two objections: three large trees had been trimmed so severely that they no longer provided the shade Carmen expected; and four small fruit trees Zen had planted were too immature to produce a crop in the first year.

   a. If these concerns breach the contract, is Carmen justified in refusing to pay the balance for the work done?
   b. Would your answer differ if, in addition to these breaches, the retaining walls for a terraced portion of the back yard seemed unlikely to prevent a serious rainstorm from washing earth from the higher levels down onto the rest of the yard? Replacement will cost $6,000, though doing it right the first time would have increased the original cost by only $2,000.

5. Jesse ordered a laptop bag from ModernManBags.com. Upon delivery, the bag was not quite the color Jesse expected based on the online photo, but in other

respects the bag seemed perfectly acceptable. Does Jesse have the right to reject the bag and insist upon a refund?

6. Chaz provides billing services for Doc. Based on Doc's computerized records, Chaz produces billing statements and submits them to insurers, government agencies, businesses, and individuals who are liable to pay the bills. The contract calls for Doc to pay Chaz $5,000 a month for two years. For six months (July to December), Chaz's performance was exemplary. In January, a change in law took effect, requiring additional information on bills for patients covered by Medicaid or Medicare. Chaz overlooked this change, submitting bills sufficient under the old rules but not under the new. Chaz became aware of the problem in June and was able to submit amended billing statements for services rendered in April, May, and June, and has made the necessary software adjustments to produce appropriate bills going forward. Amendments for services rendered in the first three months of the year were rejected by the government as untimely. As a result, Doc will not receive any of the $200,000 that the government should have paid for that period. Because the contract contains a clause limiting recovery of damages, Doc seeks to cancel the contract.

   a. Was Chaz's breach material?
   b. Did Chaz cure in a way that prevents Doc from canceling the contract?
   c. If Doc may cancel the contract, may Doc recover all amounts paid under the contract from its inception?

Contract Law in Practice

1. You represent a Church that is about to build a place of worship. Church wishes to ensure that none of the materials purchased for the construction come from companies that profit from alcohol, tobacco, firearms, or sexually explicit publications or are affiliated with such a company (say, because the company that owns the supplier also owns a brewery). Church wants the construction contract to be completely clear that builder must remove and replace material from any unclean source as a condition of receiving final payment. Draft a term that clearly makes this requirement a condition, not a promise that might allow the court to hold that the breach was not material.

2. Does your jurisdiction strictly enforce conditions on options to renew leases? Or does it allow room for courts to recognize renewal even when a tenant does not exercise an option on time in exactly the manner required by the lease? Does your jurisdiction treat leases differently from other contracts (say, insurance contracts)?

3. Does your jurisdiction employ the five-factor test for material breach? If not, how does your jurisdiction state the definition of material breach? Does it leave

the definition general or does it also provide guidance concerning what to consider in applying the definition?

4. Company occasionally requires employees to participate in online training. Failure to complete required training affects periodic performance reviews and can lead to discharge or other sanctions. Leslie hired Sean for an entry-level position in Leslie's department. With the deadline approaching, Sean experienced difficulty in logging on to receive required training concerning sexual harassment. Leslie reported the difficulty to Company and sought ways to expedite Sean's ability to obtain the required training. Problems persisted. When it became apparent that Sean would be unable to complete training in time, Leslie signed on and, pretending to be Sean, completed the required training. Company discovered the subterfuge and fired Leslie. Aside from this event, Leslie's job performance has been excellent for ten years, earning praise and promotions. If Leslie sues, can Company establish that discharge was justified by Leslie's material breach?

   a. Prepare a memo producing the strongest case Company can make that the five factors of the Restatement (Second) of Contracts justify the discharge.
   b. Exchange memos with a classmate. Respond to your classmate's memo, making the strongest rebuttal you can on behalf of Leslie. Show your classmate your response.

5. Contractor agreed to build a highway for State, promising to finish each section by a particular date and to finish the entire project by December 1 (before cold weather made additional work impractical for several months). Contractor failed to complete the first two sections by the specified dates. If all future work takes as long as originally projected, Contractor will miss the December 1 deadline by two weeks, probably forcing work to stop until March or April. If so, the highway will open approximately May 1 instead of December 15. State seeks your advice regarding whether it can discharge Contractor for material breach and hire a new contractor to finish the work on an expedited basis. (State hopes to collect any excess costs from Contractor as damages for the breach, an issue you may need to address after reading Chapter 15.) Advise State how to proceed.

12

UCC Perfect Tender, Repudiation, and Insecurity Issues

In Chapter 11, we learned about issues of material breach in contract and issues of promises and conditions. In most instances, only substantial compliance with contract terms is required to avoid material breach, unless promises are viewed as conditions. If another party has committed a total material breach, the aggrieved party is allowed to suspend unperformed contract duties and sue for breach of contract. But issues of repudiation are not limited to these circumstances. In certain goods transactions, a buyer may lawfully repudiate a contract, even if the seller has substantially complied with its contract duties.

In other cases, parties may make it clear that they will not perform their contract duties before performance is due. Alternatively, party conduct may raise insecurities about whether or not party will perform when performance becomes due. Questions of good faith and fair dealing arise, and aggrieved parties must determine if they will perform their contract duties, suspecting or even knowing that the other party will not provide the return performance. This chapter will address special issues of repudiation and issues of insecurity that occur before performance is due.

A. UCC §2-601: PERFECT TENDER

Prior to the development of the UCC, sellers were required to provide exactly what had been agreed to under goods contracts. This approach arose out of the

Key Concepts

- UCC perfect tender rule
- Cure in goods transactions
- Anticipatory repudiation
- Retraction of repudiation
- Adequate assurances of due performance

typical face-to-face dealings of contracting parties in the nineteenth century, before the emergence of mass-produced goods. Over time, this rule for goods transactions seemed out of sync with developing case law that only allowed rescission of contracts for material breaches where a party had not substantially complied with contract duties. It raised concerns about some buyers unfairly using minor defects or nonconformance to avoid contract duties.

Under the UCC, this rule still survives, but in a more limited form.[1] The UCC provides buyers with considerable discretion to reject seller's performance for even slight shortcomings, but only in instances of **single delivery contracts**; a one-time, voluntary transfer of the possession of goods.[2] The UCC's **perfect tender rule** allows buyers the right to reject, accept, or accept part and reject the rest of a delivery of goods. Thus, tender even a little bit late or a delivery even a little bit short appears to permit the buyer to reject the whole without being found to have breached the agreement. The rule applies to both merchant and consumer transactions, but only in single delivery contracts. On its face, the rule seems to eliminate arguments about whether a breach was material enough to justify cancellation of a contract. A buyer may decide for itself whether or not to waive an imperfection, without being second-guessed by a court. So the notion of substantial compliance discussed in Chapter 11 will not apply to these single delivery goods contracts.

For example, a buyer may contract for 1,000 green umbrellas and may receive a shipment of 900 green and yellow umbrellas. Under the perfect tender rule, the buyer may reject the delivery as nonconforming without requiring the error to be a material breach. To meet its needs, the buyer could seek **cover**, buying substitute goods from another source, if desired. Cover is the preferred method under the UCC to keep the wheels of commerce moving and to avoid unnecessary delays in commercial activity. Conversely, the buyer could decide to accept the shipment in total or accept some of the umbrellas, but reject others in that shipment. In this example, the buyer might accept all of the green umbrellas, but reject all the yellow ones. In the buyer's discretion, the recipient may decide to keep all of the umbrellas, despite the nonconformity to its order. This rule may seem harsh on a seller who has made an error. But it is intended to require sellers to be careful in handling their obligations to buyers.

Yet in practice, there are limits on a buyer's ability to reject goods under this rule. Most important, a party must act in good faith and fair dealing in all of its contracts. Thus, a buyer's rejection must be honest in fact and, at least for merchants who regularly deal in these types of goods, in accord with reasonable commercial standards of fair dealing. If the buyer does not honestly object to the imperfection or if the objection would be commercially unreasonable, a party may not use the nonconformity as an excuse to reject the shipment. For example, where a seller delivers too many goods, it is hard to see how rejecting the entire shipment would be in good faith. Rejecting the excess would eliminate any problem the buyer might face. Rejection seems to reflect a desire to buy from another (probably cheaper)

[1]UCC §2-601.

[2]*See id.* §1-201(15).

seller, rather than a serious concern with the variation in quantity. Where the shipment is short, rejecting the portion delivered may not be good faith, especially if the seller offers to **cure**—promptly correct any problems with performance by adjusting the price or supplying the missing goods in a timely manner. Thus, a minor breach may not justify rejecting delivery, despite the perfect tender rule.

UCC provisions governing cure may also limit the ability to avoid a contract. The buyer's ability to reject the nonconforming goods may not be affected. But if the seller can correct the problem, the buyer will need to accept the corrected performance. Rejection, then, will not necessarily allow the buyer to seek cover from another supplier. Cure is permitted if, at the time buyer rejects the goods, the time for delivery has not yet expired and the seller notifies the buyer of its plan to cure the nonconforming delivery.

Under the UCC, the seller can deliver conforming goods up until the time for performance expires.[3] However, the seller must promptly inform the seller of its intention to cure the problem before the delivery date. For example, suppose a contract required seller to send 1,500 gallons of "mason blue" paint to buyer by August 15. On August 10, seller delivered paint that was the wrong shade of blue. When buyer rejects the goods, seller still has until August 15 to deliver the right color. The seller must notify the buyer of its intention to cure the defective delivery before the time for performance has expired. Once notified, the buyer cannot cancel the contract and seek paint elsewhere unless seller fails to cure by August 15.

Cure may be permitted even if no time remains before performance is due.[4] If a seller had a reasonable belief that the nonconforming shipment, with or without a price reduction, would still be acceptable to the buyer, then the buyer may be required to give a seller a reasonable time to cure. This approach may also consider the parties' prior course of dealing to determine the reasonableness of the seller's belief that nonconforming goods would be acceptable. For example, suppose the shade of blue delivered was so close to mason blue that the seller believed buyer would agree to take it instead—either because the seller thought the buyer would not care about the difference based on past transactions or because the seller thought that offering a discount for the slightly different shade would persuade the buyer to agree to the substitution. Unless the seller's belief was unreasonable—say, because buyer had repeatedly and adamantly insisted that mason blue and only mason blue would serve its needs—the seller is entitled to a reasonable time to correct the problem, even if the original delivery occurred on August 15, leaving no additional time under the contract.

---

[3] *Id.* §2-508(1).
[4] *Id.* §2-508(2).

Case Preview

Ramirez v. Autosport

In this case, the Ramirez family entered into a contract with Autosport to purchase a new camper and traded in a van as part of the purchase. After a series of problems and delays on delivery of the camper, the Ramirezes sued to cancel the deal and get back their van. However, the van had already been sold to an innocent third party. In deciding the case, the court reviewed the policies and limits on the perfect tender rule in deciding this case.

As you read *Ramirez v. Autosport*, look for the following:

1. What were the claimed nonconformities in Autosport's one-time delivery of the camper to the Ramirezes?
2. Did Autosport try to cure these claimed deficiencies in its delivery of the camper?
3. Did the Ramirez family act in good faith and fair dealing in trying to cancel their contract with Autosport?

Ramirez v. Autosport

88 N.J. 277 (1982)

POLLOCK, J.

This case raises several issues under the Uniform Commercial Code ("the Code" and "UCC") concerning whether a buyer may reject a tender of goods with minor defects and whether a seller may cure the defects. We consider also the remedies available to the buyer, including cancellation of the contract. The main issue is whether plaintiffs, Mr. and Mrs. Ramirez, could reject the tender by defendant, Autosport, of a camper van with minor defects and cancel the contract for the purchase of the van.

The trial court ruled that Mr. and Mrs. Ramirez rightfully rejected the van and awarded them the fair market value of their trade-in van. The Appellate Division affirmed in a brief *per curiam* decision which, like the trial court opinion, was unreported. We affirm the judgment of the Appellate Division.

I

Following a mobile home show at the Meadowlands Sports Complex, Mr. and Mrs. Ramirez visited Autosport's showroom in Somerville. On July 20, 1978 the Ramirezes and Donald Graff, a salesman for Autosport, agreed on the sale of a new camper and the trade-in of the van owned by Mr. and Mrs. Ramirez. Autosport and the Ramirezes signed a simple contract reflecting a $14,100 purchase price for the new van with a $4,700 trade-in allowance for the Ramirez van, which Mr. and Mrs. Ramirez left with Autosport. After further allowance for taxes, title and documentary fees, the net price was $9,902. Because Autosport needed two weeks to prepare the new van, the contract provided for delivery on or about August 3, 1978.

On that date, Mr. and Mrs. Ramirez returned with their checks to Autosport to pick up the new van. Graff was not there so Mr. White, another salesman, met them. Inspection disclosed several defects in the van. The paint was scratched, both the electric and sewer hookups were missing, and the hubcaps were not installed. White advised the Ramirezes not to accept the camper because it was not ready.

Mr. and Mrs. Ramirez wanted the van for a summer vacation and called Graff several times. Each time Graff told them it was not ready for delivery. Finally, Graff called to notify them that the camper was ready. On August 14 Mr. and Mrs. Ramirez went to Autosport to accept delivery, but workers were still touching up the outside paint. Also, the camper windows were open, and the dining area cushions were soaking wet. Mr. and Mrs. Ramirez could not use the camper in that condition, but Mr. Leis, Autosport's manager, suggested that they take the van and that Autosport would replace the cushions later. Mrs. Ramirez counteroffered to accept the van if they could withhold $2,000, but Leis agreed to no more than $250, which she refused. Leis then agreed to replace the cushions and to call them when the van was ready.

On August 15, 1978 Autosport transferred title to the van to Mr. and Mrs. Ramirez, a fact unknown to them until the summer of 1979. Between August 15 and September 1, 1978 Mrs. Ramirez called Graff several times urging him to complete the preparation of the van, but Graff constantly advised her that the van was not ready. He finally informed her that they could pick it up on September 1.

When Mr. and Mrs. Ramirez went to the showroom on September 1, Graff asked them to wait. And wait they did—for one and a half hours. No one from Autosport came forward to talk with them, and the Ramirezes left in disgust.

On October 5, 1978 Mr. and Mrs. Ramirez went to Autosport with an attorney friend. Although the parties disagreed on what occurred, the general topic was whether they should proceed with the deal or Autosport should return to the Ramirezes their trade-in van. Mrs. Ramirez claimed they rejected the new van and requested the return of their trade-in. Mr. Lustig, the owner of Autosport, thought, however, that the deal could be salvaged if the parties could agree on the dollar amount of a credit for the Ramirezes. Mr. and Mrs. Ramirez never took possession of the new van and repeated their request for the return of their trade-in. Later in October, however, Autosport sold the trade-in to an innocent third party for $4,995. Autosport claimed that the Ramirez' van had a book value of $3,200 and claimed further that it spent $1,159.62 to repair their van. By subtracting the total of those two figures, $4,159.62, from the $4,995.00 sale price, Autosport claimed a $600-700 profit on the sale.

On November 20, 1978 the Ramirezes sued Autosport seeking, among other things, rescission of the contract. Autosport counterclaimed for breach of contract.

II

Our initial inquiry is whether a consumer may reject defective goods that do not conform to the contract of sale. The basic issue is whether under the UCC, adopted in New Jersey as N.J.S.A. 12A:1-101 *et seq.*, a seller has the duty to deliver goods that conform precisely to the contract. We conclude that the seller is under such a duty to make a "perfect tender" and that a buyer has the right to reject goods that do not conform to the contract. That conclusion, however, does not resolve the entire dispute between buyer and seller. A more complete answer requires a brief statement of the history of the mutual obligations of buyers and sellers of commercial goods.

In the nineteenth century, sellers were required to deliver goods that complied exactly with the sales agreement. *See Filley v. Pope*, 115 U.S. 213, 220, 6 S. Ct. 19, 21, 29 L. Ed. 372, 373 (1885) (buyer not obliged to accept otherwise conforming scrap iron shipped to New Orleans from Leith, rather than Glasgow, Scotland, as required by contract); *Columbian Iron Works & Dry-Dock Co. v. Douglas*, 84 Md. 44, 47, 34 A. 1118, 1120-1121 (1896) (buyer who agreed to purchase steel scrap from United States cruisers not obliged to take any other kind of scrap). That rule, known as the "perfect tender" rule, remained part of the law of sales well into the twentieth century. By the 1920's the doctrine was so entrenched in the law that Judge Learned Hand declared "[t]here is no room in commercial contracts for the doctrine of substantial performance." *Mitsubishi Goshi Kaisha v. J. Aron & Co., Inc.*, 16 F.2d 185, 186 (2 Cir. 1926).

The harshness of the rule led courts to seek to ameliorate its effect and to bring the law of sales in closer harmony with the law of contracts, which allows rescission only for material breaches. *LeRoy Dyal Co. v. Allen*, 161 F.2d 152, 155 (4 Cir. 1947). *See* 5 Corbin, *Contracts* §1104 at 464 (1951); 12 Williston, *Contracts* §1455 at 14 (3 ed. 1970). Nevertheless, a variation of the perfect tender rule appeared in the Uniform Sales Act. N.J.S.A. 46:30-75 (purchasers permitted to reject goods or rescind contracts for any breach of warranty); N.J.S.A. 46:30-18 to -21 (warranties extended to include all the seller's obligations to the goods). *See* Honnold, "*Buyer's Right of Rejection, A Study in the Impact of Codification Upon a Commercial Problem,*" 97 U. Pa. L. Rev. 457, 460 (1949). The chief objection to the continuation of the perfect tender rule was that buyers in a declining market would reject goods for minor nonconformities and force the loss on surprised sellers. *See* Hawkland, *Sales and Bulk Sales Under the Uniform Commercial Code*, 120-122 (1958), cited in N.J.S.A. 12A:2-508, New Jersey Study Comment 3.

To the extent that a buyer can reject goods for any nonconformity, the UCC retains the perfect tender rule. Section 2-106 states that goods conform to a contract "when they are in accordance with the obligations under the contract." N.J.S.A. 12A:2-106. Section 2-601 authorizes a buyer to reject goods if they "or the tender of delivery fail in any respect to conform to the contract." N.J.S.A. 12A:2-601. The Code, however, mitigates the harshness of the perfect tender rule and balances the interests of buyer and seller. *See* Restatement (Second), Contracts, §241 comment (*b*) (1981). The Code achieves that result through its provisions for revocation of acceptance and cure. N.J.S.A. 12A:2-608, 2-508.

Initially, the rights of the parties vary depending on whether the rejection occurs before or after acceptance of the goods. Before acceptance, the buyer may reject goods for any nonconformity. N.J.S.A. 12A:2-601. Because of the seller's right to cure, however, the buyer's rejection does not necessarily discharge the contract. N.J.S.A. 12A:2-508. Within the time set for performance in the contract, the seller's right to cure is unconditional. *Id.*, subsec. (1); *see id.*, Official Comment 1. Some authorities recommend granting a breaching party a right to cure in all contracts, not merely those for the sale of goods. Restatement (Second), Contracts, ch. 10, especially §§237 and 241. Underlying the right to cure in both kinds of contracts is the recognition that parties should be encouraged to communicate with each other and to resolve their own problems. *Id.*, Introduction p. 193.

The rights of the parties also vary if rejection occurs after the time set for performance. After expiration of that time, the seller has a further reasonable time to cure if he believed reasonably that the goods would be acceptable with or without a money allowance. N.J.S.A. 12A:2-508(2). The determination of what constitutes a further reasonable time depends on the surrounding circumstances, which include the change of position by and the amount of inconvenience to the buyer. N.J.S.A. 12A:2-508, Official Comment 3. Those circumstances also include the length of time needed by the seller to correct the nonconformity and his ability to salvage the goods by resale to others. *See* Restatement (Second), Contracts, §241 comment (*d*). Thus, the Code balances the buyer's right to reject nonconforming goods with a "second chance" for the seller to conform the goods to the contract under certain limited circumstances. N.J.S.A. 12A:2-508, New Jersey Study Comment 1.

After acceptance, the Code strikes a different balance: the buyer may revoke acceptance only if the nonconformity substantially impairs the value of the goods to him. N.J.S.A. 12A:2-608. *See Herbstman v. Eastman Kodak Co.*, 68 N.J. 1, 9 (1975). [Citation omitted.] This provision protects the seller from revocation for trivial defects. *Herbstman, supra,* 68 N.J. at 9. It also prevents the buyer from taking undue advantage of the seller by allowing goods to depreciate and then returning them because of asserted minor defects. *See* White & Summers, *Uniform Commercial Code*, §8-3 at 391 (2 ed. 1980). Because this case involves rejection of goods, we need not decide whether a seller has a right to cure substantial defects that justify revocation of acceptance. *See Pavesi v. Ford Motor Co.*, 155 N.J. Super. 373, 378 (App. Div. 1978) (right to cure after acceptance limited to trivial defects) and White & Summers, *supra*, §8-4 at 319 n.76 (open question as to the relationship between §§2-608 and 2-508).

Other courts agree that the buyer has a right of rejection for any nonconformity, but that the seller has a countervailing right to cure within a reasonable time. [Citations omitted.]

One New Jersey case, *Gindy Mfg. Corp. v. Cardinale Trucking Corp.*, suggests that, because some defects can be cured, they do not justify rejection. 111 N.J. Super. 383, 387 n.1 (Law Div. 1970). *Accord, Adams v. Tremontin,* 42 N.J. Super. 313, 325 (App. Div. 1956) (Uniform Sales Act). *But see Sudol v. Rudy Papa Motors,* 175 N.J. Super. 238, 240-241 (D. Ct. 1980) (§2-601 contains perfect tender rule). Nonetheless, we conclude that the perfect tender rule is preserved to the extent of permitting a buyer to reject goods for any defects. Because of the seller's right to cure, rejection does not terminate the contract. Accordingly, we disapprove the suggestion in *Gindy* that curable defects do not justify rejection.

A further problem, however, is identifying the remedy available to a buyer who rejects goods with insubstantial defects that the seller fails to cure within a reasonable time. The Code provides expressly that when "the buyer rightfully rejects, then with respect to the goods involved, the buyer may cancel." N.J.S.A. 12A:2-711. "Cancellation" occurs when either party puts an end to the contract for breach by the other. N.J.S.A. 12A:2-106(4). Nonetheless, some confusion exists whether the equitable remedy of rescission survives under the Code. [Citations omitted.]

The Code eschews the word "rescission" and substitutes the terms "cancellation," "revocation of acceptance," and "rightful rejection." N.J.S.A. 12A:2-106(4); 2-608; and 2-711 & Official Comment 1. Although neither "rejection" nor "revocation of acceptance" is defined in the Code, rejection includes both the buyer's refusal to accept or keep delivered goods and his notification to the seller that he will not keep them. White & Summers, *supra*, §8-1 at 293. Revocation of acceptance is like rejection, but occurs after the buyer has accepted the goods. Nonetheless, revocation of acceptance is intended to provide the same relief as rescission of a contract of sale of goods. N.J.S.A. 12A:2-608 Official Comment 1; N.J. Study Comment 2. In brief, revocation is tantamount to rescission. . . . Accordingly, we . . . suggest the UCC expressly recognizes rescission as a remedy.

Although the complaint requested rescission of the contract, plaintiffs actually sought not only the end of their contractual obligations, but also restoration to their pre-contractual position. That request incorporated the equitable doctrine of restitution, the purpose of which is to restore plaintiff to as good a position as he occupied before the contract. Corbin, *supra*, §1102 at 455. In UCC parlance, plaintiffs' request was for the cancellation of the contract and recovery of the price paid. N.J.S.A. 12A:2-106(4), 2-711.

General contract law permits rescission only for material breaches, and the Code restates "materiality" in terms of "substantial impairment." *See Herbstman v. Eastman Kodak Co., supra*, 68 N.J. at 9; *id.* at 15 (Conford, J., concurring). The Code permits a buyer who rightfully rejects goods to cancel a contract of sale. N.J.S.A. 12A:2-711. Because a buyer may reject goods with insubstantial defects, he also may cancel the contract if those defects remain uncured. Otherwise, a seller's failure to cure minor defects would compel a buyer to accept imperfect goods and collect for any loss caused by the nonconformity. N.J.S.A. 12A:2-714.

Although the Code permits cancellation by rejection for minor defects, it permits revocation of acceptance only for substantial impairments. That distinction is consistent with other Code provisions that depend on whether the buyer has accepted the goods. Acceptance creates liability in the buyer for the price, N.J.S.A. 12A:2-709(1), and precludes rejection. N.J.S.A. 12A:2-607(2); N.J.S.A. 12A:2-606, New Jersey Study Comment 1. Also, once a buyer accepts goods, he has the burden to prove any defect. N.J.S.A. 12A:2-607(4); White & Summers, *supra*, §8-2 at 297. By contrast, where goods are rejected for not conforming to the contract, the burden is on the seller to prove that the nonconformity was corrected. *Miron v. Yonkers Raceway, Inc.*, 400 F.2d 112, 119 (2 Cir. 1968).

Underlying the Code provisions is the recognition of the revolutionary change in business practices in this century. The purchase of goods is no longer a simple transaction in which a buyer purchases individually-made goods from a seller in a face-to-face transaction. Our economy depends on a complex system for the manufacture, distribution, and sale of goods, a system in which manufacturers and consumers rarely meet. Faceless manufacturers mass-produce goods for unknown consumers who purchase those goods from merchants exercising little or no control over the quality of their production. In an age of assembly lines, we are accustomed to cars with scratches, television sets without knobs and other products with all kinds of defects. Buyers no longer expect a "perfect tender." If a merchant sells defective goods, the reasonable expectation of the parties is that the buyer will return those goods and that the seller will repair or replace them.

Recognizing this commercial reality, the Code permits a seller to cure imperfect tenders. Should the seller fail to cure the defects, whether substantial or not, the balance shifts again in favor of the buyer, who has the right to cancel or seek damages. N.J.S.A. 12A:2-711. In general, economic considerations would induce sellers to cure minor defects. [Citation omitted.] Assuming the seller does not cure, however, the buyer should be permitted to exercise his remedies under N.J.S.A. 12A:2-711. The Code remedies for consumers are to be liberally construed, and the buyer should have the option of cancelling if the seller does not provide conforming goods. See N.J.S.A. 12A:1-106.

To summarize, the UCC preserves the perfect tender rule to the extent of permitting a buyer to reject goods for any nonconformity. Nonetheless, that rejection does not automatically terminate the contract. A seller may still effect a cure and preclude unfair rejection and cancellation by the buyer. N.J.S.A. 12A:2-508, Official Comment 2; N.J.S.A. 12A:2-711, Official Comment 1.

III

The trial court found that Mr. and Mrs. Ramirez had rejected the van within a reasonable time under N.J.S.A. 12A:2-602. The court found that on August 3, 1978 Autosport's salesman advised the Ramirezes not to accept the van and that on August 14, they rejected delivery and Autosport agreed to replace the cushions. Those findings are supported by substantial credible evidence, and we sustain them. *See Rova Farms Resort v. Investors Ins. Co.*, 65 N.J. 474, 483-484 (1974). Although the trial court did not find whether Autosport cured the defects within a reasonable time, we find that Autosport did not effect a cure. Clearly the van was not ready for delivery during August, 1978 when Mr. and Mrs. Ramirez rejected it, and Autosport had the burden of proving that it had corrected the defects. Although the Ramirezes gave Autosport ample time to correct the defects, Autosport did not demonstrate that the van conformed to the contract on September 1. In fact, on that date, when Mr. and Mrs. Ramirez returned at Autosport's invitation, all they received was discourtesy. On the assumption that substantial impairment is necessary only when a purchaser seeks to revoke acceptance under N.J.S.A. 12A:2-608, the trial court correctly refrained from deciding whether the defects substantially impaired the van. The court properly concluded that plaintiffs were entitled to "rescind"—i.e., to "cancel"—the contract.

Because Autosport had sold the trade-in to an innocent third party, the trial court determined that the Ramirezes were entitled not to the return of the trade-in, but to its fair market value, which the court set at the contract price of $4,700. A buyer who rightfully rejects goods and cancels the contract may, among other possible remedies, recover so much of the purchase price as has been paid. N.J.S.A. 12A:2-711. The Code, however, does not define "pay" and does not require payment to be made in cash.

A common method of partial payment for vans, cars, boats and other items of personal property is by a "trade-in." When concerned with used vans and the like, the trade-in market is an acceptable, and perhaps the most appropriate, market in which to measure damages. It is the market in which the parties dealt; by their voluntary act they have established the value of the traded-in article. *See Frantz Equipment Co. v. Anderson*,

37 N.J. 420, 431-432 (1962) (in computing purchaser's damages for alleged breach of uniform conditional sales law, trade-in value of tractor was appropriate measure); *accord, California Airmotive Corp. v. Jones*, 415 F.2d 554, 556 (6 Cir. 1969). In other circumstances, a measure of damages other than the trade-in value might be appropriate. *See Chemical Bank v. Miller Yacht Sales*, 173 N.J. Super. 90, 103 (App. Div. 1980) (in determining value of security interest in boat, court rejected both book value and contract trade-in value and adopted resale value as appropriate measure of damages).

The ultimate issue is determining the fair market value of the trade-in. This Court has defined fair market value as "the price at which the property would change hands between a willing buyer and a willing seller when the former is not under any compulsion to buy and the latter is not under any compulsion to sell, both parties having reasonable knowledge of relevant facts." *In re Estate of Romnes*, 79 N.J. 139, 144 (1978). Although the value of the trade-in van as set forth in the sales contract was not the only possible standard, it is an appropriate measure of fair market value.

For the preceding reasons, we affirm the judgment of the Appellate Division.

Post-Case Follow-Up

The court determined that the UCC's perfect tender rule allows a buyer to reject goods for any nonconformity in single delivery contracts. However, the buyer's rejection did not automatically terminate the contract. The seller was permitted to provide a timely cure to prevent unfair rejection and cancellation by the buyer. The Ramirezes were entitled to reject the van, which had several minor defects that Autosport did not cure in a timely fashion. With the termination of the contract, the Ramirez family was entitled to the fair market value of $4,700 for their trade-in van, which had been sold to an innocent third party.

Ramirez v. Autosport: Real Life Applications

1. Surf Town enters into a contract with a surf board manufacturer for 1,000 surf boards. The manufacturer is supposed to deliver the goods to the surf shop's warehouse in Cocoa Beach, Florida on August 1. On August 1, the manufacturer makes the delivery of the correct amount and type of boards at Surf Town's Virginia Beach, Virginia warehouse. May Surf Town reject the delivery and terminate the contract? Consider *Filley v. Pope*, 115 U.S. 213 (1885) in drafting your response.

2. A printer and publisher agrees to the printing of 10,000 copies of a famous chef's cookbook for $50,000. Under the contract, the printer is required to provide a sample of the planned print version of book for approval. Publisher reviews and approves the sample and puts down a $5,000 deposit for the final print run. But the final print version of the books does not conform to the sample, including

misaligned text and cover art, gray rather than white pages, and wrinkled pages. Publisher sues for the return of its deposit and to cancel the contract. Under the perfect tender rule, will the publisher prevail? Analyze *Printing Center of Texas, Inc. v. Supermind Publg. Co.*, 669 S.W.2d 779 (Tex. App. 1984) to determine the likely result in this case.

3. Retailer, Home Renovators (HR), agrees with a lumber company based in Oregon to purchase 10,000 feet of sustainable white ash hardwood from the eastern United States. Delivery is scheduled for September 15 at HR's fulfillment center in North Carolina. The contract states that time is of the essence as to the delivery date. On September 15, there is no lumber delivery. HR contacts the lumber company, which later delivers the lumber that HR ordered two weeks late. Can HR cancel the contract because of the late delivery under *Alaska Pac. Trading Co. v. Eagon Forest Prods.*, 85 Wash. App. 354 (1997)?

The parties may also limit the application of the perfect tender rule by the terms of their contract. The contracting parties can agree to limit the impact of the perfect tender rule for a nonconforming delivery. The contract itself may limit a buyer's right to reject the goods. For example, some contracts specify that a buyer's remedy is limited to repair or replacement, at the seller's option.[5] This provision negates a buyer's right to reject the goods, in favor of seller's right to repair them. Alternatively, the parties may provide that any nonconforming delivery be subject to a liquidated damages clause, which specifies a certain amount in damages for late or nonconforming deliveries.[6]

The perfect tender rule does not apply to **installment contracts**, those permitting or requiring a seller to deliver in more than one lot (for example, monthly deliveries).[7] A single lot may be rejected only if the nonconformity cannot be cured and "substantially impairs the value of that installment."[8] Even if one lot is rejected, the party cannot reject future (or past) installments unless the defective delivery "substantially impairs the value of the whole contract."[9] Substantial impairment of the value of performance sets a standard similar to material breach. A minor breach will not justify rejection. Thus, the breach must affect the value to the buyer in some significant way.

You might wonder, with all of these exceptions, does perfect tender ever allow cancellation for a breach that would not be material? Perhaps all the cases would come out the same way if the court discussed the factors of material breach. If so, the rule just reduces the evidence a plaintiff needs to submit and the issues discussed in the opinion. But the perfect tender rule reaches a number of cases where a court would not call the breach material. For example, the usefulness of damages and the breaching party's forfeiture do not seem to limit a plaintiff's ability

---

[5]UCC §2-719(1).
[6]*Id.* §2-718(1).
[7]UCC §2-612(1).
[8]*Id.* §2-612(2).
[9]*Id.* §2-612(3).

CISG Rejects the Perfect Tender Rule

Throughout this text, we have seen differences between the CISG and the UCC in a number of instances, including consideration, option contracts, the statute of frauds, and the parol evidence rule. The CISG also takes a different approach than the UCC's perfect tender rule. The CISG does not recognize the perfect tender rule. Article 49 of the CISG requires that a seller's failure to perform must constitute a "fundamental breach." This type of breach is addressed in Article 25 of the CISG. This article requires a showing that the breach has substantially deprived the other party of its expected benefits under the contract. The seller or a reasonable person must also be able to foresee this harm from its breach of a contract duty. In some ways, the CISG approach hews more closely to notions of material breach and substantial compliance discussed in Chapter 11.

to reject imperfect performance—and may not limit the ability to reject performance under installment contracts. Substantial impairment resembles the first factor of material breach in which good faith and cure come into play. The other two factors may not have the same weight.

Despite these exceptions, the basic rule requires perfect tender with any nonconformity entitling the buyer to reject the goods. This rule can simplify the buyer's decision regarding whether to reject the goods. Worry that rejection itself will be deemed a breach diminishes. A court need not agree that the breach is significant since any breach will justify rejection. Buyer still faces some uncertainty regarding how long she must await the seller's cure.

The perfect tender rule may be justified, especially for fungible (easily replaceable) goods. Forfeiture rarely will be a problem in these cases. If buyer rejects the goods, seller will have them and can sell them to someone else. Seller may not get as good a price as buyer promised, but seller rarely forfeits the goods themselves. Similarly, with fungible goods, buyer's cover is easy and may avoid problems with **consequential damages** — damages that arise from the way the buyer intended to use the goods (such as lost profits on reselling them) — which will be discussed in greater detail in Chapter 16. Asking the buyer to postpone cover while awaiting cure can increase consequential damages. Because consequential damages are harder to prove, avoiding them by immediate cover may be a preferable approach, at least where goods are fungible. Custom goods — for example, stationery printed with a company logo — pose a problem for the perfect tender rule. Forfeiture is possible; the goods are worthless to any other buyer, so seller may not be able to resell them to another. Similarly, cover is not immediate when another supplier must make goods to order. The original seller may be able to cure before cover is possible. The perfect tender rule seems designed for fungible goods, although the text is not limited to fungible goods.

B. IDENTIFYING ANTICIPATORY REPUDIATION

Primarily, parties enter contracts to assure that a performance will be made as agreed. They may pay more today than they would by waiting because they prefer the assurance provided by an enforceable contract. Indications that the other party may not perform undermine key contract objectives. Once a party cannot rely on performance of a promise, it may be prudent to prepare for the possibility that breach will occur. Unless the other party's conduct amounts to a material breach, the concerned party cannot cancel the contract and deal with a more reliable contracting party. Material breach is the unexcused nonperformance when performance is due. But disconcerting conduct before performance is due does not meet the ordinary requirements of material breach, no matter how severely it impairs the reliability of the contract.

Recognizing the need to protect the reliability of contracts, the law sometimes allows a party to treat the prospective material breach as a current material breach under the concept of anticipatory repudiation.[10] Under anticipatory repudiation, the nonbreaching party may protect its rights as if the breach had already occurred. The aggrieved party may immediately terminate the contract, making substitute arrangements in an effort to minimize the loss and bringing suit for breach. For example, in the famous case of *Hochster v. De La Tour*, 2 E. & B. 678 (1853), Hochster entered into an employment contract to serve as a courier to De La Tour during his summer travels throughout Europe, beginning on June 1. However, on May 11, De La Tour changed his mind and notified Hochster that he no longer required his services. The letter put Hochster in a difficult position since summer courier jobs were filling up, but De La Tour had not yet breached since the contract did not begin until June 1. The court determined that De La Tour's renunciation was clear and should be treated as a breach. Further, it would be unfair for Hochster to have to wait around until June 1 to seek his remedy or to pursue alternative employment options.

You might wonder if it would be simpler to just wait until performance is due to see whether breach occurs. But for parties wondering whether they should enter into a substitute transaction — and worried about receiving (or having to deliver) duplicative performances if they do — repudiation simplifies the matter.

1. Identifying Anticipatory Repudiation

Express repudiation occurs when a party communicates an unequivocal intention not to perform when performance is due. For example, a statement like "I'll never pay you another dime" would be a repudiation if money is still owed under the contract. Two features are critical:

1. only a material breach; and
2. only a clear and unequivocal expression give rise to a repudiation.

Express repudiation must involve a material breach. An announced intent to commit a minor breach will not constitute a repudiation of the contract. Thus, an employee who announces that he may arrive a little late on Thursday has not repudiated the employment contract because the breach is likely too minor to be called material. Express repudiation must be clear and unequivocal. Expressions of doubt about a party's ability to perform or requests for a **rescission** (agreement to

[10]UCC §2-610; Restatement (Second) of Contracts §250.

rescind or call off the deal) or **modification** (agreement to change the deal) are not repudiations in themselves.

Implied repudiation occurs when a party's voluntary acts make it seem impossible for that party to perform when performance is due. For example, a contract for the sale of land might be repudiated if the seller conveyed the land to another. This conduct makes it seem impossible for the seller to perform the promise to convey the land to this buyer. It is still possible if the seller could reacquire the land from the other party in time to convey it to this buyer. However, the appearance of impossibility is sufficient to establish an implied repudiation. The apparent impossibility must involve a material breach. Where the entire tract under contract was sold to another, the breach will be material. If only a tiny portion of it was conveyed, perhaps substantial performance remains possible.

Implied repudiation requires voluntary conduct. Events the other party did not cause or could not avoid are not repudiation. For example, suppose an actor is severely injured in an automobile accident, making it seem impossible that he will begin movie production on the promised date. The apparent impossibility does not arise from voluntary acts, so no implied repudiation exists. A party's words or actions may raise **reasonable grounds for insecurity**, which are justifiable concerns or fear that the other party may not perform, but do not establish a repudiation.

2. Effect of Anticipatory Repudiation

Once the other party makes it clear that he will not be performing his obligations before they are due, the aggrieved party has options to consider. If the repudiation is a material breach, she is justified in suspending performance immediately. Material breach by repudiation is no different from any other material breach. She may treat the contract as canceled. Essentially, the breaching party is electing to terminate the contract by refusing to perform it any further. In this situation, no purpose is served by asking the aggrieved party to postpone cancellation pending cure. The nonbreaching party may immediately treat the contract as canceled. Recourse to other remedies, such as making substitute arrangements, may proceed without delay. She may seek immediate relief from the courts. She may notify the repudiating party that she considers the breach final and may bring a breach of contract action.[11]

But if the party really wants the other to continue to perform, she need not immediately cancel the deal. The aggrieved party may decide to wait a commercially reasonable time to see if the other party will pull back the repudiation, called a **retraction**—perhaps even urging the other party to do so.[12] She can urge retraction and, up to a point, wait to see if the party will reconsider. Even if the aggrieved party has urged the other party to retract the repudiation, she need not await that retraction.[13] At some point, continued silence from the other party signals an intent

[11]UCC §2-610 (a, b); Restatement (Second) of Contracts §253.
[12]*Id.*
[13]UCC §2-610(b); Restatement (Second) of Contracts §257.

to persist in the repudiation. Beyond that point, waiting becomes unreasonable and the nonbreaching party may be viewed as failing to properly mitigate her damages, which could limit her recovery of damages for breach.

3. Retraction

However, the breaching party could decide to perform and communicate a retraction of a repudiation to the other party; in essence, pulling back on its anticipatory repudiation of its contract duties. However, this retraction is only effective when received by the aggrieved party, provided that the nonbreaching party has not already acted in reliance upon the repudiation or has not already informed the repudiating party that she considers the repudiation final. Even if the repudiation is withdrawn promptly, in response to the aggrieved party's encouragement, the retraction may arrive too late. Retraction, if timely, reinstates the contract obligations as they existed before the repudiation. The repudiation virtually disappears, as if it never happened. Continued suspension of performance would be unjustified, breaching the contract. Each must continue to perform, until some other problem arises.[14]

After repudiation, it probably is prudent to find out quickly what substitute arrangements are possible. If a good opportunity opens up, the party can take it immediately, without having to first call the repudiator to make the repudiation final. It won't matter who sent what communication first (shades of the mailbox rule). The reliance ends the ability to reinstate the original duty without the assent of the victim. Yet a party willing to receive both performances can agree to the retraction even if she already has a substitute lined up.

The Danger of Jumping Too Soon

A party fearing the other party will not make a timely performance must act prudently and not overstate the other party's deficiencies. Hasty action in response to the other party's provocative behavior poses serious risks. It is a short step from complaining about the other party's breach to committing a material breach yourself. Consider three possible missteps:

1. a party suspends (or cancels) performance based on the other's breach, only to find the breach was not material (or the time for cure had not expired);
2. a party suspends (or cancels) performance because the other's words constitute repudiation, only to find that they were equivocal (or perhaps immaterial);
3. a party suspends (or cancels) performance because the assurance requested was not provided in a reasonable time, only to find that defects in the demand for assurance justify the refusal to comply with the request.

In each case, the party may have legitimate objections to the other's performance or other conduct. But overreacting, even a little, as we will see in the *Flatt* case, can turn the once aggrieved party into the breaching party.

[14] UCC §2-611; Restatement (Second) of Contracts §256.

Case Preview

Truman L. Flatt & Sons Co. v. Schupf

In *Truman L. Flatt & Sons Co. v. Schupf*, two parties agreed to the purchase of a parcel of land for $160,000, conditioned upon a zoning change to permit the land's use for an asphalt plant. Public outcry regarding the plant squashed Flatt's plan for the plant. Flatt decided to abandon the rezoning effort and sought a purchase price reduction because of the failed rezoning effort. The sellers refused this request for a price reduction, leading to seller's assertions of anticipatory repudiation and buyer's claims of retraction.

As you read *Truman L. Flatt & Sons Co. v. Schupf*, look for the following:

1. Did Flatt anticipatorily repudiate its contract with the sellers by abandoning the zoning process and requesting a purchase price reduction?
2. What are the requirements to show an anticipatory repudiation?
3. Had Flatt made a timely retraction of any claimed anticipatory repudiation?

Truman L. Flatt & Sons Co. v. Schupf

271 Ill. App. 3d 983 (1995)

KNECHT, PRESIDING JUSTICE

Plaintiff Truman L. Flatt & Sons Co., Inc., filed a complaint seeking specific performance of a real estate contract made with defendants Sara Lee Schupf, Ray H. Neiswander, Jr., and American National Bank and Trust Company of Chicago (American), as trustee under trust No. 23257. Defendants filed a motion for summary judgment, which the trial court granted. Plaintiff now appeals from the trial court's grant of the motion for summary judgment. We reverse and remand.

In March 1993, plaintiff and defendants entered a contract in which defendants agreed to sell plaintiff a parcel of land located in Springfield, Illinois. The contract stated the purchase price was to be $160,000. The contract also contained the following provisions:

> **"1. This transaction shall be closed on or before June 30, 1993, or upon approval of the relief requested from the Zoning Code of the City of Springfield, Illinois, whichever first occurs ('Closing Date'). The closing is subject to contingency set forth in paragraph 14.**
>
> **. . .**
>
> **14. This Contract to Purchase Real Estate is contingent upon the Buyer obtaining, within one hundred twenty (120) days after the date hereof, amendment of, or other sufficient relief of, the Zoning Code of the City of Springfield to permit the construction and operation of an asphalt plant. In the event the City Council of the City of Springfield denies the request for such use of the property, then this contract shall be voidable at Buyer's option and if Buyer elects to void this contract Buyer shall receive a refund of the earnest money paid."**

On May 21, plaintiff's attorney sent a letter to defendants' attorney informing him of substantial public opposition plaintiff encountered at a public meeting concerning its request for rezoning. The letter concluded:

> "The day after the meeting all of the same representatives of the buyer assembled and discussed our chances for successfully pursuing the re-zoning request. Everyone who was there was in agreement that our chances were zero to none for success. As a result, we decided to withdraw the request for rezoning, rather than face almost certain defeat.
>
> The bottom line is that we are still interested in the property, but the property is not worth as much to us a 35-acre parcel zoned I-1, as it would be if it were zoned I-2. At this juncture, I think it is virtually impossible for anyone to get that property re-zoned I-2, especially to accommodate the operation of an asphalt plant. In an effort to keep this thing moving, my clients have authorized me to offer your clients the sum of $142,500.00 for the property, which they believe fairly represents its value with its present zoning classification. Please check with your clients and advise whether or not that revision in the contract is acceptable. If it is, I believe we can accelerate the closing and bring this matter to a speedy conclusion. Your prompt attention will be appreciated. Thanks."

Defendants' attorney responded in a letter dated June 9, the body of which stated, in its entirety:

> "In reply to your May 21 letter, be advised that the owners of the property in question are not interested in selling the property for $142,500 and, accordingly, the offer is not accepted.
>
> I regret that the zoning reclassification was not approved."

Plaintiff's attorney replied back in a letter dated June 14, the body of which stated, in its entirety:

> "My clients received your letter of June 9, 1993[,] with some regret, however upon some consideration they have elected to proceed with the purchase of the property as provided in the contract. At your convenience please give me a call so that we can set up a closing date."

After this correspondence, plaintiff's attorney sent two more brief letters to defendants' attorney, dated June 23 and July 6, each requesting information concerning the status of defendants' preparation for fulfillment of the contract. Defendants' attorney replied in a letter dated July 8. The letter declared it was the defendants' position plaintiff's failure to waive the rezoning requirement and elect to proceed under the contract at the time the rezoning was denied, coupled with the new offer to buy the property at less than the contract price, effectively voided the contract. Plaintiff apparently sent one more letter in an attempt to convince defendants to honor the contract, but defendants declined. Defendants then arranged to have plaintiff's earnest money returned.

Plaintiff filed a complaint for specific performance and other relief against defendants and American, asking the court to direct defendants to comply with the terms of the contract. Defendants responded by filing a "motion to strike, motion to dismiss or, in the alternative, motion for summary judgment." The motion for summary judgment sought summary judgment on the basis plaintiff repudiated the contract.

Prior to the hearing on the motions, plaintiff filed interrogatories requesting, among other things, information concerning the current status of the property. Defendants' answers to the interrogatories stated defendants had no knowledge of any third party's involvement in a potential sale of the property, defendants had not made any offer to sell the property to anyone, no one had made an offer to purchase the property or discussed the possibility of purchasing the property, and defendants had not sold the property to, received any offer from, or discussed a sale of the property with, any other trust member.

After a hearing on the motions, the trial court granted the defendants' motion for summary judgment without explaining the basis for its ruling. Plaintiff filed a post-trial motion to vacate the judgment. The trial court denied the post-trial motion, declaring defendants' motion for summary judgment was granted because plaintiff had repudiated the contract. Plaintiff now appeals the trial court's grant of summary judgment, arguing the trial court erred because (1) it did not repudiate the contract, and (2) even if it did repudiate the contract, it timely retracted that repudiation.

Plaintiff contends the trial court erred in granting summary judgment. Summary judgment is proper when the resolution of a case hinges on a question of law and the moving party's right to judgment is clear and free from doubt. In considering a motion for summary judgment, the court must consider the affidavits, depositions, admissions, exhibits, and pleadings on file and has a duty to construe the evidence strictly against the movant and liberally in favor of the nonmoving party. (*In re Estate of Hoover* (1993), 155 Ill. 2d 402, 410-11, 615 N.E.2d 736, 739-40, 185 Ill. Dec. 866.) The motion will be granted if the court finds there is no genuine issue as to any material fact and the moving party is entitled to judgment as a matter of law. (735 ILCS 5/2-1005 (West 1992).) A triable issue of fact exists where there is a dispute as to material facts or where the material facts are undisputed but reasonable persons might draw different inferences from those facts. In a case involving summary judgment, a reviewing court reviews the evidence in the record *de novo*. (*Hoover*, 155 Ill. 2d at 411, 615 N.E.2d at 740.) Here, there are no facts in dispute. Thus, the question is whether the trial court erred in declaring defendant was entitled to judgment as a matter of law based on those facts.

Plaintiff first argues summary judgment was improper because the trial court erred in finding plaintiff had repudiated the contract.

> "The doctrine of anticipatory repudiation requires a clear manifestation of an intent not to perform the contract on the date of performance.... That intention must be a definite and unequivocal manifestation that he will not render the promised performance when the time fixed for it in the contract arrives.... Doubtful and indefinite statements that performance may or may not take place are not enough to constitute anticipatory repudiation." (*In re Marriage of Olsen* (1988), 124 Ill. 2d 19, 24, 528 N.E.2d 684, 686, 123 Ill. Dec. 980.)

These requirements exist because "anticipatory breach is not a remedy to be taken lightly." (*Olsen*, 124 Ill. 2d at 25, 528 N.E.2d at 687.) The Restatement (Second) of Contracts adopts the view of the Uniform Commercial Code (UCC) and states "language that under a fair reading 'amounts to a statement of intention not to perform except on conditions which go beyond the contract' constitutes a repudiation. Comment 2 to Uniform Commercial Code §2-610." (Restatement (Second) of Contracts §250 Comment, *b*, at 273 (1981).) Whether an anticipatory repudiation occurred is a question of fact and the judgment of the trial court thereon will not be disturbed unless it is against the manifest weight of evidence. *Leazzo v. Dunham* (1981), 95 Ill. App. 3d 847, 850, 420 N.E.2d 851, 854, 51 Ill. Dec. 437.

As can be seen, whether a repudiation occurred is determined on a case-by-case basis, depending on the particular language used. Both plaintiff and defendants, although they cite Illinois cases discussing repudiation, admit the cited Illinois cases are all factually distinguishable from the case at hand because none of those cases involved a request to change a term in the contract. According to the commentators, a suggestion for modification of the contract does not amount to a repudiation. (J. Calamari & J. Perillo, Contracts §12-4, at 524 n.74 (3d ed. 1987) (hereinafter Calamari), *citing Unique Systems Inc. v. Zotos International, Inc.* (8th Cir. 1980), 622 F.2d 373.) Plaintiff also cites cases in other jurisdictions holding a request for a change in the price term of a contract does not constitute a repudiation. (*Wooten v. DeMean* (Mo. Ct. App. 1990), 788 S.W.2d 522; *Stolper Steel Products Corp. v. Behrens Manufacturing Co.* (1960), 10 Wis. 2d 478, 103 N.W.2d 683.) Defendants attempt to distinguish these cases by arguing here, under the totality of the language in the letter and the circumstances surrounding the letter, the request by plaintiff for a decrease in price clearly implied a threat of nonperformance if the price term was not modified. We disagree.

The language in the May 21 letter did not constitute a clearly implied threat of nonperformance. First, although the language in the May 21 letter perhaps could be read as implying plaintiff would refuse to perform under the contract unless the price was modified, given the totality of the language in the letter, such an inference is weak. More important, even if such an inference were possible, Illinois law requires a repudiation be manifested clearly and unequivocally. Plaintiff's May 21 letter at most created an *ambiguous implication* whether performance would occur. Indeed, during oral argument defense counsel conceded the May 21 letter was "ambiguous" on whether a repudiation had occurred. This is insufficient to constitute a repudiation under well-settled Illinois law. Therefore, the trial court erred in declaring the May 21 letter anticipatorily repudiated the real estate contract as a matter of law.

Moreover, even if plaintiff had repudiated the contract, the trial court erred in granting summary judgment on this basis because plaintiff timely retracted its repudiation. . . . Only one published decision has discussed and applied Illinois law regarding retraction of an anticipatory repudiation, *Refrigeradora Del Noroeste, S.A. v. Appelbaum* (1956), 138 F. Supp. 354 (holding the repudiating party has the power of retraction unless the injured party has brought suit or otherwise materially changed position), *aff'd in part & rev'd in part on other grounds* (1957), 248 F.2d 858. The Restatement (Second) of Contracts states:

> "The effect of a statement as constituting a repudiation under *§250* or the basis for a repudiation under §251 is nullified by a retraction of the statement if notification of the retraction comes to the attention of the injured party before he materially changes his position in reliance on the repudiation or *indicates* to the other party

> that he considers the repudiation to be final." (Emphasis added.) (Restatement (Second) of Contracts §256(1), at 293 (1981).)

The UCC adopts the same position:

> "Retraction of Anticipatory Repudiation. (1) Until the repudiating party's next performance is due he can retract his repudiation unless the aggrieved party has since the repudiation cancelled or materially changed his position or otherwise *indicated* that he considers the repudiation final." (Emphasis added.) (810 ILCS 5/2-611(1) (West 1992).)

Professors Calamari and Perillo declare section 2-611 of the UCC:

> ". . . is in general accord with the common law rule that an anticipatory repudiation may be retracted until the other party has commenced an action thereon or has otherwise changed his position. The Code is explicit that no other act of reliance is necessary where the aggrieved party *indicates* 'that he considers the repudiation final.'" (Emphasis added.) (Calamari §12.7, at 528.)

"The majority of the common law cases appear to be in accord with this position." (Calamari §12.7, at 528 n.93.) Other commentators are universally in accord. Professor Farnsworth states: "The repudiating party can prevent the injured party from treating the contract as terminated by retracting before the injured party has *acted* in response to it." (Emphasis added.) (2 E. Farnsworth, Contracts §8.22, at 482 (1990).) Professor Corbin declares one who has anticipatorily repudiated his contract has the power of retraction until the aggrieved party has materially changed his position in reliance on the repudiation. (4 A. Corbin, Corbin on Contracts §980, at 930-31 (1951) (hereinafter Corbin).) Corbin goes on to say the assent of the aggrieved party is necessary for retraction only when the repudiation is no longer merely anticipatory, but has become an actual breach at the time performance is due. (4 Corbin §980, at 935.) Williston states an anticipatory repudiation can be retracted by the repudiating party "unless the other party has, before the withdrawal, *manifested* an election to rescind the contract, or changed his position in reliance on the repudiation." (Emphasis added.) 11 W. Jaeger, Williston on Contracts §1335, at 180 (3d ed. 1968) (hereinafter Williston).

Defendants completely avoid discussion of the common-law right to retract a repudiation other than to say Illinois is silent on the issue. Defendants then cite *Stonecipher v. Pillatsch* (1975), 30 Ill. App. 3d 140, 332 N.E.2d 151, *Builder's Concrete Co. v. Fred Faubel & Sons, Inc.* (1978), 58 Ill. App. 3d 100, 373 N.E.2d 863, 15 Ill. Dec. 517, and Leazzo v. Dunham (1981), 95 Ill. App. 3d 847, 420 N.E.2d 851, 51 Ill. Dec. 437, as well as Williston §1337, at 185-86. These authorities stand for the proposition that after an anticipatory repudiation, the aggrieved party is entitled to choose to treat the contract as rescinded or terminated, to treat the anticipatory repudiation as a breach by bringing suit or otherwise changing its position, or to await the time for performance. The UCC adopts substantially the same position. (810 ILCS 5/2-610 (West 1992).) Defendants here assert they chose to treat the contract as rescinded, as they had a right to do under well-settled principles of law.

Plaintiff admits the law stated by defendants is well settled, and admits if the May 21 letter was an anticipatory breach, then defendants had the right to treat the contract as being terminated or rescinded. However, plaintiff points out defendants' assertions ignore the great weight of authority, discussed earlier, which provides a right of the repudiating party to retract the repudiation *before* the aggrieved party has chosen one of its options allowed under the common law and listed in *Stonecipher, Builder's Concrete,* and *Leazzo.* Plaintiff argues defendants' letter of June 9 failed to treat the contract as rescinded, and absent *notice* or *other manifestation* defendants were pursuing one of their options, plaintiff was free to retract its repudiation. Plaintiff is correct.

Defendants' precise theory that plaintiff should not be allowed to retract any repudiation in this instance is ambiguous and may be given two interpretations. The first is Illinois should not follow the common-law rule allowing retraction of an anticipatory repudiation before the aggrieved party elects a response to the repudiation. This theory warrants little discussion, because the rule is well settled. Further, defendants have offered no public policy reason to disallow retraction of repudiation other than the public interest in upholding the "sanctity of the contract."

The second possible interpretation of defendants' precise theory is an aggrieved party may treat the contract as terminated or rescinded *without* notice or other indication being given to the repudiating party, and once such a decision is made by the aggrieved party, the repudiating party no longer has the right of retraction. It is true no notice is required to be given to the repudiating party if the aggrieved party materially changes its position as a result of the repudiation. [Citations omitted.] Here, however, the defendants admitted in their answers to plaintiff's interrogatories they had not entered another agreement to sell the property, nor even discussed or considered the matter with another party. Defendants had not changed their position at all, nor do defendants make any attempt to so argue. As can be seen from the language of the Restatement, the UCC, and the commentators, shown earlier, they are in accord that where the aggrieved party has not otherwise undergone a material change in position, the aggrieved party must *indicate to the other party* it is electing to treat the contract as rescinded. This can be accomplished either by bringing suit, by notifying the repudiating party, or by in some other way manifesting an election to treat the contract as rescinded. Prior to such indication, the repudiating party is free to retract its repudiation. . . .

. . .

This rule makes sense as well. If an aggrieved party could treat the contract as rescinded or terminated without notice or other indication to the repudiating party, the rule allowing retraction of an anticipatory repudiation would be eviscerated. No repudiating party ever would be able to retract a repudiation, because after receiving a retraction, the aggrieved party could, if it wished, simply declare it had already decided to treat the repudiation as a rescission or termination of the contract. Defendants' theory would effectively rewrite the common-law rule regarding retraction of anticipatory repudiation so that the repudiating party may retract an anticipatory repudiation only upon assent from the aggrieved party. This is not the common-law rule, and we decline to adopt defendants' proposed revision of it.

Applying the actual common-law rule to the facts here, plaintiff sent defendants a letter dated June 14, which clearly and unambiguously indicated plaintiff intended to perform under the contract. However, defendants did not notify plaintiff, either

expressly or impliedly, of an intent to treat the contract as rescinded until July 8. Nor is there anything in the record demonstrating any indication to plaintiff, prior to July 8, of an intent by defendants to treat the contract as rescinded or terminated. Thus, assuming plaintiff's May 21 request for a lower purchase price constituted an anticipatory repudiation of the contract, plaintiff successfully retracted that repudiation in the letter dated June 14 because defendants had not yet materially changed their position or indicated to plaintiff an intent to treat the contract as rescinded. Therefore, because plaintiff had timely retracted any alleged repudiation of the contract, the trial court erred in granting summary judgment for defendants on the basis plaintiff repudiated the contract. Defendants were not entitled to judgment as a matter of law. . . .

Post-Case Follow-Up

The *Flatt* court determined that anticipatory repudiation required a clear and unequivocal manifestation of intent not to perform the contract when performance was due. Doubtful or indefinite statements were not sufficient. Flatt's request for a price modification did not show a clear and unequivocal intention not to perform its contract duties. Even if the price reduction sought were viewed as an anticipatory repudiation, Flatt timely retracted any repudiation by having promised on several occasions to complete the sale under the original price terms before the agreed-upon closing date. The sellers did not change their position in reliance as they did not sell the land and did not entertain offers from other third parties. In addition, the sellers gave no notice to Flatt that they viewed the claimed repudiation as final. Thus, the sellers, not Flatt, breached their contract for the sale of the land.

Truman L. Flatt & Sons Co. v. Schupf: Real Life Applications

1. In February, Hamilton enters into a contract to work as a bodyguard for 1980s rock star Rebel Rowley during his summer comeback tour, starting June 1. On April 2, Rowley cancels his concert tour due to poor ticket sales. He informs Hamilton that he will not need his services. Hamilton scrambles to find a replacement job, but most of the major concert tours already have their security teams. Can he bring an action for breach immediately or must he wait until Rowley's performance is due in June? Review *Hochster v. De La Tour*, 2 E. & B. 678 (1853) to determine if Hamilton can sue immediately.

2. In a 7-2 vote, a city council approves a 10-year lease with a developer who would renovate and pay monthly rents on a downtown historic building. In September, the lease is signed with conditions that the developer obtain financing and proper approvals for the remodeling project by November 30. In a hotly contested local election, the development project becomes an issue for many voters. On October 1, the city council then votes 5-4 not to reaffirm the lease with

the developer. After the vote, the developer makes no further efforts to seek financing or to gain approvals for the remodeling project under the lease. On November 15, the developer sues the city seeking damages, claiming anticipatory repudiation of its lease and development deal by its second council vote. Has the city committed an anticipatory repudiation by its second vote? Consider *STC, Inc. v. Billings*, 168 Mont. 364 (1975) in deciding the likely result.

3. Polly obtains and pays premiums on a disability insurance policy with LifeCare Insurance. If Polly is ever totally disabled, the policy will pay her medical expenses, pay 50 percent of her salary, and discontinue her premiums during this period of disability. Polly suffers a stroke and collects disability benefits from LifeCare for two years. In reassessing its claims reports, LifeCare sends Polly a notice that it plans top terminate her benefits as she should now be able to return to some light work duties. Polly objects and LifeCare advises her that its doctor will reexamine her for fitness to return to work. After her examination and tests, it turns out that LifeCare's physician finds that Polly has a serious heart defect and determines she is unable to continue any form of work. LifeCare reviews its report and decides to continue her benefits when it is served with a breach of contract complaint by Polly. Polly demands immediate payment of damages measured by the total sum of her expected lifetime disability benefits under her claim of anticipatory repudiation. Did LifeCare commit anticipatory breach of its insurance agreement with Polly? Address these issues in *Mobley v. New York Life Ins. Co.*, 74 F.2d 588 (5th Cir. 1935) to find out the likely result of this breach of contract action.

---

4. Adequate Assurances of Due Performance

Any uncertainty concerning the other's performance undermines reliability, but repudiation requires near certainty that breach will occur. Yet treating uncertainty as a breach overreacts. Instead, the law has framed a way to resolve the uncertainty. A party who has commercially reasonable grounds for insecurity that the other party may not perform may demand adequate assurances of due performance in both nongoods[15] and goods transactions.[16] For sales of goods, the request must be in writing. For nongoods contracts, no specific form is required. Some examples of reasonable grounds for insecurity may involve repeated late payments, or growing debt, or the failure to address delivery delays or product defects.

Once an appropriate demand for assurance has been made, the party seeking assurance may suspend its performance, pending a response. If appropriate assurances are provided, the insecure party must resume performance. If an adequate assurance is not provided within a reasonable time under the Restatement, the insecure party may treat the failure as if it were a repudiation of the contract. For

[15] Restatement (Second) of Contracts §251.

[16] UCC §2-609.

sales of goods, the UCC specifies that a reasonable time expires no more than 30 days after receipt of the demand for assurance. Circumstances, such as perishable goods, may shorten that time period and require a response in fewer than 30 days. The provisions of the Restatement and the UCC both envision that a party may have to make multiple demands for assurances of due performance as different issues may crop up throughout the life of a contract.

Similar to the UCC, the CISG does recognize the concept of anticipatory repudiation and the aggrieved party's ability to suspend performance and terminate the contract for a "fundamental breach."[17] In addition, the aggrieved party must continue to perform if the other party provides adequate assurances of due performance.[18] Unlike the UCC, there is no requirement of written notice and no specific time period for assurances under the CISG.

The reasonableness of grounds for insecurity will vary with context. For sales of goods, commercial standards govern the reasonableness of a party's concerns, at least between merchants. Commercial standards may differ among different trades. Outside sales of goods, a party must have reasonable grounds to believe that the other party may commit a material breach. Equivocal communications from the other party probably suffice: statements such as "I don't think I can deliver on schedule" certainly create grounds to suspect a breach. Words or conduct of the other party are not essential, but mere rumors or doubts may not suffice.

Under the UCC, a demand for assurance must be made in writing. Oral demands do not justify a suspension of performance. Cases exist where a party that received an oral request for reassurance treated it as an appropriate request, in effect waiving the requirement of a writing. While a party may waive that rule, a court probably cannot waive the statutory requirement if the opposing party asserts lack of a writing as a basis for not providing reassurance as requested. A writing also helps determine when the request was made, whether the demands in it were appropriate, and whether it actually was a request for reassurance.

However, where a party demands more onerous assurances, the other party may reject those demands but, at the same time, offer some lesser form of reassurance. This might occur if a party demanded reassurance that essentially modified the contract. For example, a seller that is insecure might demand payment in advance (perhaps into escrow), even though the contract allowed payment within 30 days after delivery. A request for modification is appropriate; a refusal to perform unless the party agrees to a modification borders on **duress** (an improper threat that induces assent to a contract). Refusing to agree to the modification generally is permissible. The insecure party is entitled to as much security as the original contract provided, not more.

Merely demanding too much reassurance is not a problem in itself. Problems arise if a party treats the failure to comply with the demand as a failure to provide adequate assurance. If a court determines that the other party gave adequate assurance, the response is not a repudiation. The response need not satisfy the demanding party's subjective preference for a particular form of assurance. A reasonable

[17]CISG arts. 71(1), 72(1) & 73.
[18]CISG arts. 71(3) & 72(2-3).

assurance under the circumstances will suffice. While theoretically possible, few cases exist in which courts find assurances adequate even though they provide less assurance than the insecure party sought.

Suspension of Performance

The ability of a party to suspend performance is a powerful tool. It allows a party to refuse to perform contract duties as they come due. If suspension of performance is permitted too easily, suspensions might reduce the reliability of contract performance. Any party that wanted to stop performing temporarily could simply pretend to be insecure, demand reassurance, and suspend its performance. To avoid allowing the unscrupulous to manipulate this doctrine, limits on the ability to suspend must be observed with some strictness. The rights here arise only if a commercially reasonable demand for assurances has been made in an appropriate way.

Suspending performance may itself breach a contract unless the suspension is justified. Parties seeking assurance under this section may overreact in four different ways, any of which may convert their effort to suspend performance into a breach.

1. A party may demand reassurance without reasonable grounds for insecurity.
2. A party may demand reassurance in an inappropriate manner.
3. A party may suspend performance too soon, before demanding reassurance.
4. A party may demand more reassurance than it is entitled to receive.

Each situation poses some risk that the party demanding reassurance will not be entitled to suspend performance and, thus, will itself be in breach of the contract.

A party may suspend performance after demanding adequate assurances of performance. No justification for suspending performance exists until an appropriate demand for reassurance has been made. Parties are entitled to receive adequate assurance of performance. They may not be entitled to the specific reassurance that they request. Where demands are reasonably limited — say, a demand that the other party confirm in writing that it will perform the contract — no difficulty arises. Refusal or silence may properly be treated as repudiation; satisfying the demand will end the ground for suspension of performance.

Case Preview

Starchem Labs., LLC v. Kabco Pharms., Inc.

In *Starchem Labs., LLC v. Kabco Pharms.*, a court must consider the issues of breach and demands for adequate assurances of due performance under the UCC. A buyer, Starchem Labs., LLC, falls behind on payments for dietary and nutritional supplements from defendant seller, Kabco Pharmaceuticals. When Starchem puts in another order that exceeds its credit limit, Kabco refuses to ship product until payment has been made in cash. Starchem then sues for breach of contract.

As you read *Starchem Labs., LLC v. Kabco Pharms., Inc.*, look for the following:

1. Did Kabco have commercially reasonable grounds for insecurity in this case?
2. Was Kabco able to show that it had made adequate demands for assurance of due performance by Starchem?
3. Did Starchem provide adequate assurances that would support its claim of breach against Kabco?

Starchem Labs., LLC v. Kabco Pharms., Inc.

43 Misc. 3d 1213(A) (N.Y. Sup. Ct. 2014)

EMERSON, J.

The plaintiff is in the business of developing, marketing, and selling dietary and nutritional supplements. The defendants are in the business of manufacturing vitamins as well as dietary and nutritional supplements. On or about February 6, 2008, the plaintiff sent a purchase order to the defendant Kabco Pharmaceuticals, Inc. ("Kabco") for the manufacture and packaging of various nutritional supplements ("Purchase Order 64" or "PO 64"). Purchase Order 64 was revised several times between February 6 and June 4, 2008, when it was finalized. The final version provided that Kabco was to manufacture 13,000 bottles of *Armageddon* and 4,000 bottles of *Evolution*, two of the plaintiff's products, for $190,120.00. The payment terms were "30 days." Kabco ordered the raw materials and bottles from third-party vendors, but did not commence manufacturing or deliver any products to the plaintiff. On August 28, 2008, Kabco sent the following letter to the plaintiff regarding PO 64:

> The above stated Purchase Order valued at $190,120.00 was received by us more than 2 months back. As you know the bottles that are to be used for filling out your PO are customized bottles and had to be special ordered for Starchem. Apart from ordering the bottles, we also had to order the raw material for filling out your order. The bottles and the raw material are not returnable to the vendors as such Kabco has already invested a huge amount of money for this transaction.
>
> The payment term set by Kabco for Starchem is net 30 days, while your credit limit is for $25,000. This order far exceeds your credit limit.
>
> Your payment history for the previous orders was also not satisfactory as they were delayed. We have also been informed that Starchem has failed to live up to its payment obligations by not paying our sister Company (Futurebiotics) in spite of several written and verbal promises made to several Managers of Futurebiotics including a promise to Saiful Kibra who visited your facility in the not too distant past.
>
> In view of the above, please be informed that your orders will be processed as soon as we receive a payment (bank certified check) for $165,120 towards the above referenced PO. The balance amount of $25,000 will be net 30 as per our agreed payment terms. We also would like you to pay the outstanding balance due to Futurebiotics.

Both Kabco and Futurebiotics are owned by Abu Kabir and Saiful Kibra. The record reveals that the plaintiff owed Kabco $3,192.60 for another purchase order (PO 63), which remained unpaid. The record also reveals that the plaintiff ordered products from Futurebiotics valued at $25,140.00 and $22,800.00, respectively, $27,880.00 of which remained unpaid.

On September 4, 2008, Kabco e-mailed the plaintiff that it would begin manufacturing if the plaintiff agreed to accept Kabco's $25,000 credit limit. On September 5, 2008, Kabco e-mailed the plaintiff that it would begin producing the plaintiff's products on Monday, September 8, 2008, and asked if the plaintiff wanted to be present when production began or if it wanted Kabco to send it a sample for tasting. The plaintiff responded by asking Kabco to extend it credit in the amount of $60,000 to $90,000. In its final e-mail to the plaintiff on September 5, 2008, Kabco stated, "We understand that you have not paid Futurebiotics for the outstanding invoice as of today. We also understand that Futurebiotics has been in touch with you asking for payment. Please confirm that you will be present at our facility at 8:30AM Monday morning for sampling the first blend of Armageddon." The plaintiff did not respond and subsequently commenced this action against Kabco and Futurebiotics.

The complaint contains three causes of action against Kabco for breach of contract, fraudulent inducement, and estoppel. The plaintiff alleges that Kabco breached their agreement by unilaterally changing the terms of PO 64, by creating a credit limit in the amount of $25,000, and by demanding that the plaintiff make payments to Futurebiotics. . . . The defendants move for summary judgment dismissing the complaint and for summary judgment in their favor on the counterclaims.

The court finds that the conduct of the plaintiff and Kabco is sufficient to establish that Purchase Order 64 was an enforceable contract for the sale of goods under the Uniform Commercial Code (*see*, UCC 2-204[1]; UCC 2-207[3]; *Hornell Brewing Co. v Spry*, 174 Misc 2d 451, 455, 664 N.Y.S.2d 698). UCC 2-609(1) imposes on each party an obligation that the other's expectation of receiving due performance will not be impaired. If either the willingness or the ability of one party to perform declines materially between the time of contracting and the time of performance, the other party is threatened with the loss of a substantial part of what he has bargained for. A seller needs protection not merely against having to deliver on credit to a shaky buyer, but also against having to procure and manufacture the goods, perhaps turning down other customers. Once the seller has been given reason believe that the buyer's performance has become uncertain, it is an undue hardship to force the seller to continue his own performance (UCC 2-609, Official Comment 1, McKinney's Cons Laws of NY, Book 62 1/2, at 122). Thus, UCC 2-609(1) authorizes a party, upon reasonable grounds for insecurity, to demand adequate assurances of due performance and, if commercially reasonable, to suspend any performance for which he has not already received the agreed return until he receives such assurances (*Hornell Brewing Co. v Spry, supra* at 456). Whether a seller has reasonable grounds for insecurity depends on various factors, including the buyer's exact words or actions, the course of dealing or performance between the parties, and the nature of the sales contract and the industry (*Id.* at 457). Reasonable grounds for insecurity can arise from the sole fact that the buyer has fallen behind in his account with the seller, even when the items involved have to do with separate and legally distinct contracts, because it impairs the seller's expectation of due performance (*Id.*).

The court finds that the plaintiff's poor payment history with both Kabco and Futurebiotics constituted reasonable grounds for insecurity (*Id.* at 458). Thus, Kabco had the right demand adequate assurances, which it did by letter dated August 28, 2008 (*see*, UCC 2-609, Official Comment 1, McKinney's Cons Laws of NY, Book 62 1/2, at 123, *citing Corn Products Refining Co. v Fasola*, 94 NYLJ 181[seller demanded cash before shipment]). If a party demands and receives specific assurances then, absent a further change of circumstances, the assurances demanded and received are adequate, and the party who has demanded the assurances is bound to proceed (*Hornell Brewing Co. v Spry, supra* at 458). On the other hand, a failure to respond constitutes a repudiation of the parties' agreement, which entitles the party who demanded the assurances to suspend performance and terminate the agreement (Id.). Here, the plaintiff failed to offer any assurances to Kabco and responded merely by making a request for more credit. Accordingly, the court finds that Kabco properly suspended its performance under PO 64.

UCC 2-702(1) is also applicable to the facts of this case. It provides, "Where the seller discovers the buyer to be insolvent, he may refuse delivery except for cash including payment for all goods theretofore delivered under the contract. . . ." A person is insolvent when he has either ceased to pay his debts in the ordinary course of business or cannot pay his debts as they come due (*see*, UCC 1-201 [23]). The court finds that the plaintiff was insolvent within the meaning of the Uniform Commercial Code and that Kabco could have properly demanded that the full amount due under PO 64 be paid in cash. Instead, it extended credit to the plaintiff in the amount of $25,000 and demanded payment of only the remaining balance by certified bank check, which is a cash equivalent. When payment was not forthcoming, Kabco properly declined to deliver any products to the plaintiff under PO 64.

In view of the foregoing, the court finds that, contrary to the plaintiff's contentions, Kabco did not breach the agreement evinced by Purchase Order 64, but properly exercised its rights under the Uniform Commercial Code. Accordingly, Kabco is entitled to summary judgment dismissing the first cause of action for breach of contract.

Whether a seller has reasonable grounds for insecurity depends on various factors, including the buyer's exact words or actions, the course of dealing or performance between the parties, and the nature of the sales contract and the industry (*Id.* at 457). Reasonable grounds for insecurity can arise from the sole fact that the buyer has fallen behind in his account with the seller, even when the items involved have to do with separate and legally distinct contracts, because it impairs the seller's expectation of due performance (*Id.*).

The court finds that the plaintiff's poor payment history with both Kabco and Futurebiotics constituted reasonable grounds for insecurity (*Id.* at 458). Thus, Kabco had the right [to] demand adequate assurances, which it did by letter dated August 28, 2008 (*see*, UCC 2-609, Official Comment 1, McKinney's Cons Laws of NY, Book 62 1/2, at 123, *citing Corn Products Refining Co. v Fasola*, 94 NYLJ 181 [seller demanded cash before shipment]). If a party demands and receives specific assurances then, absent a further change of circumstances, the assurances demanded and received are

adequate, and the party who has demanded the assurances is bound to proceed (*Hornell Brewing Co. v Spry, supra* at 458). On the other hand, a failure to respond constitutes a repudiation of the parties' agreement, which entitles the party who demanded the assurances to suspend performance and terminate the agreement (*Id.*). Here, the plaintiff failed to offer any assurances to Kabco and responded merely by making a request for more credit. Accordingly, the court finds that Kabco properly suspended its performance under PO 64. . . .

Post-Case Follow-Up

The *Starchem* court determined that the test of reasonable grounds for insecurity depended upon a number of different factors, including the buyer's words and conduct, the nature of the conduct, the parties' prior dealings, and industry practices. In this case, the court found that the sole fact that the buyer Starchem failed to make timely payments on the goods provided reasonable grounds for insecurity. Kabco did demand adequate assurances of due performance and Starchem's failure to respond, except to seek more credit, constituted a repudiation. Kabco was entitled to suspend its performance under the circumstances and did not breach its contract with Starchem.

Starchem Labs., LLC v. Kabco Pharms., Inc.: Real Life Applications

1. A beverage company, Healthy Drinks LLC, (Healthy) enters into a distributorship agreement with Refresh, Inc. to distribute its healthy smoothie drinks in California. Early in the relationship, Refresh often pays for its goods late and sells only a fraction of its agreed-upon quarterly quota. Healthy sends several letters about these problems, seeking proof that Refresh has obtained a verifiable line of credit for future shipments and created a marketing plan for distributing Healthy's product to meet its quota. Refresh does not respond, but submits an order $100,000 over its product limit. When Healthy refuses to ship any more products, Refresh sues for breach of contract. Healthy seeks your advice on this matter. Read and apply *Hornell Brewing Co. v. Spry*, 174 Misc. 2d 451 (N.Y. Sup. Ct. 1997) to this dispute.

2. Joe Publisher runs a regional newspaper and agrees to sell the majority of his shares of stock to Marty Moneybags for $80,000 in three payments. Publisher plans to use much of this capital to invest further in the newspaper. Moneybags makes the first two smaller payments, and then sends a third payment of $50,000 by check that bounces. Publisher makes repeated requests for the funds and Moneybags claimed he was "ready, willing, and able" to make the final payment. Without the additional capital, Publisher mortgages his home to help keep the paper running and then cuts back from a daily to a weekly paper

to save costs. Publisher grants several extensions to Moneybags, who continues to claim a willingness to perform his duties, but fails to meet these deadlines. Publisher eventually sells the shares at a lower rate and sues Moneybags for damages. Was Publisher's sale of the stocks to another party permissible under the circumstances? Review *Sackett v. Spindler*, 248 Cal. App. 2d 220 (1967) for the court's decision on this dispute.

3. Tech Square, Inc. (TSI) agrees to manufacture and sell 100 of its new cash registers to Craft Stores USA (CSU) by May 2016. In April 2016, TSI delivers its new registers to three CSU stores in Texas for trial runs. The registers show immediate problems processing customer payments and frequently break down, leading to losses in store revenues. After several calls between CSU and TSI about these problems, CSU and TSI agree to a face-to-face meeting. They are unable to agree on required performance standards for these registers. At that meeting, TSI also informs CSU that it may not meet its May 2016 delivery deadline as the new registers are taking longer to manufacture than the prior model. CSU tells TSI that it is canceling its order and expects a refund on the defective registers. TSI objects and then brings a breach of contract lawsuit against CSU. Who will likely prevail? Consider *AMF v. McDonald's Corp.*, 536 F.2d 1167 (7th Cir. 1976) in developing your response.

---

5. Remedies After Repudiation

Repudiation raises one potential complication in calculating remedies. Events that occur after repudiation, but before performance would have become due, might excuse the nonperformance. For example, events might occur that would justify excuse for **impracticability**—an excuse that protects a party against unusual events, such as fire at the factory. If the repudiator's factory burned down before the date for delivery, performance probably would have been excused as a result of the fire. Similarly, a condition on performance may not occur, so that the duty to deliver never would have matured. In rare cases, a repudiator may discover that the other party would have committed a material breach, if the repudiation had not made that unnecessary. In each case, the repudiating party would not have been liable for breach if the repudiation had not occurred. By the time performance was due, performance would have been excused for other reasons.

Subsequent excusing events will have the same effect on recovery for repudiation that they would have had if no repudiation had occurred. If impracticability would have excused part of the repudiator's performance, damages for breach will be denied for any portion of the performance that would have been excused.[19] For example, suppose a landlord leased business premises for ten years, but repudiated the lease before the tenant took possession. The tenant could bring suit immediately, seeking to recover any extra rent it paid as a result of the breach. Before

---

[19]Restatement (Second) of Contracts §§254-255.

trial, the building might be destroyed by a disaster that would excuse the landlord's duty. If so, tenant may recover damages for the period before the destruction, but the excuse would relieve the landlord of liability following the disaster. Issues of changed circumstances are discussed in greater detail in Chapter 13.

Chapter Summary

- In sales of goods, any defect in a one-time delivery contract allows the buyer to reject all or part of the goods in good faith under the UCC's perfect tender rule.
- Installment contracts and seller's right to cure the nonconformity are limitations on the application of the perfect tender rule.
- Anticipatory repudiation is a clear and unequivocal indication that a party intends to commit a total material breach before performance is actually due. This type of repudiation is treated as total material breach.
- After an anticipatory repudiation, a party must begin to minimize damages after a commercially reasonable time, even if it hopes for retraction before the time for performance has arrived.
- A party may retract its repudiation until the other party either relies on it or notifies the repudiating party that it considers the repudiation to be final.
- A party who has commercially reasonable grounds for insecurity that the other party may not perform may demand adequate assurances of due performance in both nongoods and goods transactions. For sales of goods, the request must be in writing.
- Once an appropriate demand for assurance has been made, the party seeking assurance may suspend its performance, pending a response.
- An adequate assurance must be provided within a reasonable time under the Restatement and no more than 30 days after receipt of the demand under the UCC, unless circumstances require a shorter time period. A failure to make adequate assurances allows the insecure party to treat the failure as a repudiation of the contract.

Applying the Rules

1. BH Textiles (BH) is a Chicago distributor of women's clothing to a network of national retailers. Madison International (Madison), the owner and operator of an exclusive New York designer clothing business, is excited that BH wants to distribute her clothing line throughout the country. Madison and BH enter into a written agreement in which Madison agrees to sell 100,000 long-sleeve blouses to BH. Each blouse costs $125 with a one-time delivery of all the blouses due on December 7 in time for BH's major holiday sale on December 15. On December 4, Madison makes its delivery to BH. BH inspects Madison's blouses

and discovers that about 30 percent of the blouses are short-sleeved, rather than long-sleeved for the winter sale. Which of the following best indicates the position that BH may legally take in this situation?

a. BH must accept the blouses because Madison has substantially performed her promises and the defects can be easily cured.
b. BH may reject all of the blouses as in *Ramirez.*
c. BH may reject 30 percent of the blouses that are short-sleeved and accept the 70 percent of the blouses with long sleeves.
d. BH must accept the blouses because there is only a partial material breach.
e. Both b and c above.

2. Let's add a few facts to Question 1. BH determines that it needs the blouses to meet consumer demand and notifies Madison that it must provide 70,000 blouses with long sleeves by December 7 so these items can be included in BH's holiday sale. Madison replies that it can send 70,000 long-sleeved blouses on January 3. Under these facts:

a. BH may treat Madison's response as an anticipatory repudiation and seek commercially reasonable substitutes for its sale as in *Flatt.*
b. Madison's response properly cures its defect, so BH may not claim any breach of contract.
c. BH must wait 30 days for Madison's adequate assurance under the UCC.
d. BH must wait a reasonable time to see if Madison will retract.
e. B and C above.
f. Both c and d above.

3. In January, FunCo Amusement Park (FunCo) enters into a contract with Benches Unlimited (BU) for the provision of custom benches that relate to different theme rides throughout the park. There are seven scheduled delivery dates for different customized benches. All shipments must be completed on or before May 25. The new park benches are part of the park's renovation project and its grand summer opening celebration over the Memorial Day weekend in May. Payment of $50,000 for each delivery is made within 30 days of receipt of a confirming delivery. The first two February deliveries are made on time, but the third one arrives a day late on March 2, but it does not impact FunCo's construction schedule. The fourth delivery on March 15 arrives a week late and several of the benches are missing wood slats and have chipped paint. FunCo rejects that delivery. BU delivers the benches properly painted two days later, and FunCo accepts them. So far the late deliveries have not negatively impacted the project. Fearing future delays, FunCo notifies BU that it is immediately terminating its contract with BU. If BU brings a breach of contract action, the likely outcome will be that

a. FunCo will prevail because its cancellation is proper under the perfect tender rule as in *Ramirez.*
b. FunCo will not prevail because its generalized concerns are not commercially reasonable grounds for insecurity as in *Flatt.*

c. FunCo will prevail because BU's late deliveries and poor quality benches in the March 15 delivery are an anticipatory repudiation.
d. FunCo will not prevail because BU has adequately cured its product defects.
e. Both b and d above.

4. Changing the facts of Question 3, instead of canceling the contract, FunCo sends BU a letter demanding that BU restate its willingness to meet the delivery demands of the contract. BU sends back a written response indicating that it has worked out its manufacturing issues and will make sure that its next delivery is on time and in compliance with their contract. On March 20, BU's fifth delivery is made on time and in compliance with the contract requirements. The sixth delivery is not made on the contract delivery date of March 25. FunCo e-mails and telephones BU seeking assurances about its performance, with no response from BU for three days. Under the UCC, FunCo should

   a. suspend its own performance and terminate the agreement immediately with BU since it previously sought assurances as in *Starchem*.
   b. demand that BU respond by March 27 to avoid a claim of a total material breach.
   c. allow BU an opportunity to provide adequate assurances within a reasonable time period, not to exceed 30 days.
   d. refuse to pay for the next shipment of goods received from BU.
   e. Both a and b above.

5. Adding to the facts of Question 4, let's say that BU does respond and indicates that it will make delivery of its sixth shipment on April 10. FunCo is satisfied with this response since the delivery will occur before the contract deadline of May 25. While completing its work, BU then learns from other suppliers that FunCo has stopped paying its vendor bills and may go bankrupt because it spent too much money on its renovation project. A BU manager goes to the park and finds that renovation efforts are stopped and signs announcing the Memorial Day event have been removed from the park's billboards. What may BU do in light of this new information?

   a. BU may demand that FunCo provide evidence of a line of credit sufficient to pay for BU's final delivery as in *Starchem*.
   b. BU may refuse to make the next shipment of goods and terminate the agreement immediately with FunCo as in *Starchem*.
   c. BU must make its delivery and wait the required 30 days for its $50,000 payment as a showing of good faith under the UCC.
   d. BU may make a written demand for adequate assurances of due performance from FunCo and suspend its own performance until FunCo makes such assurances within a reasonable time.
   e. A and D above.

Contract Law in Practice

1. In this chapter, we have learned about more differences between the CISG and the UCC. Create a chart of key contract principles and specify key distinctions between these two approaches to goods transactions. Share this information with your study group or on a class blog to aid your peers in recognizing these major differences.

2. To avoid the perfect tender rule, parties may agree to eliminate or restrict the application of this rule under the terms of their contract. Review examples of contract clauses online and in form books that (1) eliminate the rule's application; or (2) limit the application of the rule through a liquidated damages clause. Provide an example of each of these types of clauses for a class presentation or as part of a class discussion board on drafting contract terms.

3. As noted above, parties must be mindful to properly assess whether or not a party is committing an anticipatory repudiation to avoid committing breach. The issue of requests to modify a contract price has received mixed decisions from courts as to whether or not such requests will support a claim of anticipatory repudiation. Research case law in your state or federal circuit to see what is the prevailing view in your jurisdiction. What other examples did you find of conduct that supports an assertion of anticipatory repudiation?

4. The perfect tender rule has been viewed as harsh by some legal scholars because it may allow a party to terminate a contract for minor issues. However, the rule may be appropriate in consumer transactions where savvy sellers may try to take advantage of inexperienced consumers. Examine your state's consumer protection laws and court decisions interpreting such laws in the context of consumer contracts for goods. Identify and summarize key examples in which consumers received protection and the main judicial policy reasons for safeguarding consumers under the application of the perfect tender rule.

5. Professor Keith Rowley provides a detailed review of the historical development of anticipatory repudiation in *A Brief History of Anticipatory Repudiation in American Contract Law*, 69 U. CIN. L. REV. 565 (2001). Read this law review article and summarize some of the main arguments both in support and opposition to the concept of anticipatory repudiation. What are the key U.S. Supreme Court decisions on this concept? Discuss the main reasons that the Supreme Court embraced this doctrine. Draft a memo with your findings.

13

Excusing Performance

Some legal systems require fault as an element of contract liability. If the plaintiff cannot show that the defendant's nonperformance resulted from some fault on its part — or perhaps if the defendant can show that its nonperformance was not a result of any fault on its part — liability for breach of contract does not attach.

United States contract law takes the opposite approach. Strict liability applies to any nonperformance. Failure to perform when performance is due results in liability for breach without regard to fault. Yet, in a limited number of instances, the law recognizes that the failure to perform due to changed circumstances after the contract was entered into may allow parties to be excused from their contract duties. In those settings, the law excuses nonperformance. Excuse means that the nonperformance is not a breach. Therefore, the nonbreaching party is not entitled to damages for breach of contract resulting from such nonperformance. But a party seeking to claim the excuse has the burden of proof in supporting its excuse.

In Chapters 6, 7, and 8, we discussed contract defenses that exist at the time the parties entered into the contract, such as fraud or mistake, for which a party seeks to avoid contract enforcement. However, the excuses in this chapter arise or occur unexpectedly after the parties have entered into a contract. Instead of seeking to prevent contract enforcement, these excuses are aimed at relieving a party from performing remaining contract duties.

Traditionally, courts recognized the excuse of **impossibility** of performance indicating that changed circumstances have made it literally impossible for a party to perform its contract duties. Although courts may still examine impossibility today, the modern trend tends to focus on two key excuses; impracticability and frustration of purpose. **Impracticability** applies to situations where performance has become so difficult a party should not be expected to perform any further. **Frustration of purpose** deals with

Key Concepts

- Impossibility of performance
- Impracticability of performance
- Frustration of purpose
- Force majeure clauses in contracts

circumstances that make the contract pointless, destroying a party's reason for entering into the contract in the first place.

Defining the circumstances in which excuse should apply is largely a matter of factual interpretation. In some instances, the parties may try to draft contract terms to try to capture unexpected circumstances, sometimes called force majeure clauses. In this chapter, we will explore excuses that arise from changed circumstances after the parties have entered into a contract.

A. IMPOSSIBILITY

Under the classical view, courts were quite strict about party compliance with contract duties. Impossibility was the only excuse that was recognized. Impossibility is the predecessor to the doctrine of impracticability. Today, impossibility is considered to be subsumed into the doctrine of impracticability under the provisions of the Restatement.[1] Although the Restatement tends to speak in terms of impracticability, modern courts will still often address the doctrine of impossibility under its classical iteration.

Traditionally, impossibility covered the following three situations:

1. the death or incapacity of a person in a personal services contract;
2. the nonexistence (the destruction) of a specific thing required for performance; and
3. government regulations precluding performance.

1. Death or Incapacity

The death or incapacity of a party who is critical to the performance of contract duties can give rise to the excuse of impossibility. When parties enter into a personal services contract, a specific person's skills and abilities may be needed to carry out contract duties. For example, actors, athletes, architects, and fiduciaries, such as lawyers, doctors, or accountants, may have been selected for their special talents or expertise. Death or disability, making it impossible for parties to perform their obligations, will excuse them from their contract duties. These unexpected events that arise after the parties entered into a contract are sometime referred to as **supervening causes**. The *Phoenix* case provides a good example of court application of the traditional view of impossibility of performance in a modern context.

[1] RESTATEMENT (SECOND) OF CONTRACTS §§261-264.

Case Preview

CNA International Reinsurance Co., Ltd. v. Phoenix

The unfortunate death of River Phoenix led to the dispute in this case.
Copyright © Universal. Courtesy Everett Collection

In *CNA International Reinsurance Co., Ltd. v. Phoenix*, insurance companies seek to recover the costs of claims recovery from the estate of River Phoenix. The young actor had signed to participate in two films, but his death led to coverage claims due to losses experienced by the film production companies. The insurance companies contested excusing Phoenix for liability under his failure to perform his duties under impossibility of performance.

As you read *CNA International Reinsurance Co., Ltd. v. Phoenix*, look for the following:

1. What argument did the insurance companies make in their effort to challenge the application of the excuse of impossibility?
2. Was the court willing to address issues of fault in one's own death when determining the applicability of the excuse of impossibility?
3. Did the court think that the parties could address their concerns in the clauses contained in their agreement?

CNA Int'l Reinsurance Co., Ltd. v. Phoenix

678 So. 2d 378 (Fla. Ct. App. 1996)

JOANOS, J.

In these consolidated appeals from final orders granting appellee's motions to dismiss, appellants raise two issues: (1) whether the defense of impossibility of performance due to death applies when the impossibility is, allegedly, the fault of the person obligated to perform the personal services contract, and (2) whether the trial court erred in ruling that the effective dates of the policies of insurance involved here were in November, 1993, after the widely publicized death in question. We affirm in part and reverse in part.

The case arises from the unfortunate death of the young actor, River Phoenix, originally of Gainesville, Florida, apparently due to an overdose of illegal drugs, before completion of two films, "Dark Blood" and "Interview With the Vampire," in which he had contracted to appear. As a result of the death, the "Dark Blood" project was totally abandoned. "Interview With the Vampire" was completed with another actor replacing Phoenix. CNA and American Casualty, which are both members of

the CNA group of insurance companies, had written entertainment package insurance policies covering various aspects of the two productions. After paying the policy holders, CNA and American Casualty became subrogated to the claims the insureds had against the estate.[1]

CNA attempted to state a cause of action for breach of contract against Phoenix's estate, based on an "actor loanout agreement," between Jude Nile, a corporation owned and run by Phoenix and his mother, Arlyn Phoenix, and Scala Productions.[2] The agreement, signed by Phoenix, allegedly included a general obligation not to do anything which would deprive the parties to the agreement of its benefits. CNA further alleged that by deliberately taking illegal drugs in quantities in excess of those necessary to kill a human being, Phoenix deprived the parties of his services and breached his obligation. American Casualty also couched its complaint for declaratory judgment in terms of breach of contract based on an actor loanout agreement between Jude Nile and Geffen Pictures, which gave Geffen the right to loan Phoenix to Time Warner. In addition to the count for breach of contract, the CNA complaint contained a second count, for fraud and misrepresentation, based on an allegedly false representation in a medical certificate, allegedly signed by Phoenix, denying that Phoenix had ever used "LSD, heroin, cocaine, alcohol in excess, or any other narcotics, depressants, stimulants or psychedelics whether prescribed or not prescribed by a physician."

The estate moved to dismiss both complaints, contending there could be no cause of action for breach of contract because the personal services contracts were rendered impossible to perform due to the death. The estate further alleged that reliance on any representation in the medical certificate was unreasonable as a matter of law as of the effective dates of the policies, which it contended were in November, 1993, after the widely publicized death on October 31, 1993. After hearings, the trial court granted the motions to dismiss with prejudice.

On appeal, CNA and American Casualty contend that the defense of impossibility of performance does not apply in this case because that doctrine requires that the impossibility be fortuitous and unavoidable, and that it occur through no fault of either party. They contend that because the death occurred from an intentional, massive overdose of illegal drugs, that this is not a situation in which neither party was at fault. The trial court very clearly ruled that even if the death was a suicide (there is no indication in the record that it was) or the result of an intentional, self-inflicted act, the doctrine of impossibility of performance applied.

Appellants have candidly conceded that no case authorities exist in support of their position concerning fault in a case of impossibility due to death. Appellants ask this court to find support for their theory in the following language of the Restatement of Contracts 2d §§261 and 262:

---

[1]CNA paid out over $5.7 million under its policy. American Casualty had not yet paid all claims, and sought a declaratory judgment on the coverage issue. It had paid out $15,000 of approximately $400,000 in claims.

[2]Scala Productions, Ltd., the production company for "Dark Blood," later assigned its rights to Shapray Ltd. The additional appellants in case no. 95-401 provided financing or other services for that production.

§261 Where, after a contract is made, a party's performance is made impracticable without his fault by the occurrence of an event the non-occurrence of which was a basic assumption on which the contract was made, his duty to render that performance is discharged, unless the language or the circumstances indicate the contrary.

§262 If the existence of a particular person is necessary for the performance of a duty, his death or such incapacity as makes performance impracticable is an event the non-occurrence of which was a basic assumption on which the contract was made.

Appellants contend the Restatement dictates that impossibility of performance due to the destruction of one's own health is not the sort of conduct that will excuse performance, citing *Handicapped Children's Education Board v. Lukaszewski*, 112 Wis. 2d 197, 332 N.W.2d 774 (Wis. 1983), and that the same reasoning should apply in a case of self-induced death. Appellants also suggest a policy basis for the ruling they advocate, arguing that in a society dealing with increasing problems created by illegal drug abuse, such conduct should not excuse the performance of the contract.

At oral argument of this case, it became apparent that any attempt to discern fault in a death case such as this one, or in a similar case, perhaps involving the use of tobacco or alcohol would create another case by case and hard to interpret rule of law. Being mindful that there are already too many of these in existence, we are not persuaded by the facts or the arguments presented to depart from the clear and unambiguous rule that death renders a personal services contract impossible to perform. *See* 17A Am. Jur. 2d "Contracts" §688 (1991). In such contracts, "there is an implied condition that death shall dissolve the contract." *Id.* With this implied condition in mind, we believe the parties to the agreements could have provided specifically for the contingency of loss due to the use of illegal drugs, as they provided for other hazardous or life threatening contingencies.[3] We affirm the trial court's ruling that the doctrine of impossibility of performance applies in this case.

We reverse the trial court's ruling that, as a matter of law, the policies were not effective until the issuance date, November 12, 1993, after Phoenix's death on October 31, 1993. The policies, as well as pertinent endorsements, clearly reflect earlier effective dates of July 23, 1993, and August 15, 1993 on their faces. Generally, the parties to a contract are competent to fix the effective date. [Citation omitted.] At the very least, further development of the record is in order on this issue. [Footnotes omitted.]

AFFIRMED in part, REVERSED in part, and REMANDED for further proceedings consistent with this opinion.

---

[3]For example, the actor loanout agreement pertaining to "Interview With the Vampire" provided:

> From the date two (2) weeks before the scheduled start date of principal photography until the completion of all services required of Employee hereunder, Employee will not ride in any aircraft other than as a passenger on a scheduled flight of a United States or other major international air carrier maintaining regularly published schedules, or engage in any ultrahazardous activity without Producer's written consent in each case.

The entertainment package policies contained exclusions based on similar activities.

Post-Case Follow-Up

The *Phoenix* court upheld the classical view that death renders a personal services contract impossible to perform. The court refused to try to determine if Phoenix's death was due to his own fault. This approach would be difficult to determine in many cases and would unnecessarily depart from the clear and unambiguous rule of the classical approach. The decision indicated that the parties could have provided contract language to specifically address a contingency of loss due to the use of illegal drugs, as they had provided for other hazardous or life-threatening contingencies in their contracts.

CNA Int'l Reinsurance Co., Ltd. v. Phoenix: Real Life Applications

1. Webb agrees to purchase 50 acres of Knott's land with a closing date two months later on September 1. Knott's attorney was tasked with handling title examination and appraisal of the property's value. The attorney believes it will only take a couple of weeks to handle these duties, so she waits until August 12 to undertake these matters. Both the appraisal process and title review are unexpectedly complicated, and she requests an extension until September 17. Before Webb responds to this request, Knotts tells his attorney that he is going to keep the land and not sell it to Webb. Webb sues and Knotts claims impossibility of performance since the attorney would be unable to complete the required tasks before the agreed-upon September 1 closing date. Will Knotts prevail with this excuse under *Waddy v. Riggleman*, 216 W. Va. 250 (2004)?

2. A contractor wins a bid to construct a new school annex for $10 million. Under the contract with the county, the contractor will receive a series of progress payments based on the completion of project milestones. Construction delays slow progress and the contractor is running two weeks behind the scheduled completion date. As the project nears the end, the contractor is required to finish painting a few classrooms in order to receive its final 20 percent payment. An electrical fire in the original school spreads to the new annex, destroying both buildings. Claiming impossibility, the contractor tries to recover its final payment for the new annex. The county refuses to pay the final amount to the contractor, asserting that the contractor's performance would not have become impossible if it had remained on schedule. Will the county be successful in fending off the contractor's excuse? Consider *Krause v. Board of Trustees*, 162 Ind. 278 (1904) in drafting a response.

3. A donor agrees to a pledge of $1 million toward the creation of a sculpture garden to help revitalize a park through an urban nonprofit community foundation. In the donor agreement, the donor explicitly requires that his name be put on a plaque in a particular place in the new sculpture garden. That specific

location holds a special significance to him as it was where his parents met. The donor makes good on his pledge. But when the park is complete, the nonprofit organization decides to move his plaque to another location so as not to detract from the aesthetic beauty of the sculpture garden. He sues and the foundation claims that their aesthetic vision makes it impossible to put his plaque in the sculpture garden. Review *Matter of Reed Found., Inc. v. Franklin D. Roosevelt Four Freedoms Park, LLC*, 964 N.Y.S.2d 152 (2013) for the probable outcome in this dispute.

---

2. Destruction of a Necessary Thing

The destruction of a thing necessary to performance made performance impossible. For example, if parties sign a lease for office space and a fire destroys or prevents the habitability of the building, the parties are excused from the lease due to impossibility. Similarly, unique goods, such as a famous work of art or piece of sports memorabilia, which are destroyed or badly damaged will excuse the parties from their contract duties. So failure to produce a thing necessary for performance or severe deterioration of that thing without a party's fault will make the thing nonexistent for purposes of performing the contract.

3. Preclusion by Government Regulations

A change in government regulations may prevent certain contract duties from being performed. For example, a company enters into a development contract with a construction company to build a manufacturing facility on a particular plot of land. Under the contract, the construction company must obtain the necessary commercial building permits. Before construction begins, the city changes zoning for that area to solely residential purposes. The contractor is likely to argue impossibility of performance since it will be unable to receive building permits for the commercial development. Arguably, changing laws do not make performance impossible, but simply impose legal consequences on a party who performs despite the regulations. Historically, government regulations were recognized by the impossibility defense, the predecessor of impracticability and frustration of purpose.

B. IMPRACTICABILITY

In entering into a contract, parties try to balance risks and benefits and may not be able to anticipate unexpected or supervening events that will affect their agreement under impracticability (or the related concept of frustration of purpose). Impracticability recognizes that drastic changes may occur after the parties enter into a contract that make one party's performance substantially more difficult or burdensome than anticipated during contract negotiations. The court will consider whether contract performance has become impracticable due to a supervening event that causes extreme loss, injury, cost, or difficulty. If a court concludes that the parties would not have insisted on continued performance if the changes had been anticipated, it may excuse further performance by the disadvantaged party. The inquiry is partly interpretive, partly imaginative. Trying to discover the parties' intent, the court's goal is to find the term that the parties would have agreed upon if they had anticipated these events. Because the parties did not anticipate the circumstances, that intent is hypothetical and the court must imagine what it would have been. In effect, the court is filling a gap in the contract left by the parties' failure to specify how or if the contract should be adjusted in case certain extreme events occur.

By doctrine, courts assume that parties would have intended to excuse performance when unexpected, extreme events occur. The parties need not draft their own term creating an excuse, saving them some time in negotiating such terms. But if the parties want to limit the excuse or to expand upon it, they must take the time to draft terms that specify the scope they prefer. A **force majeure** clause spells out that parties may be excused from their contract duties due to superior forces outside of party control, such as earthquakes, tsunamis, civil unrest, wars, and other extreme events. In other instances, the parties may have included a liquidated damages clause to address the relevant damages for a party's failure to perform in a timely manner.

The impracticability excuse is applied one contract at a time, even if events affect more than one contract. The issue arises when one party sues the other for breach and the other raises impracticability as an excuse. The effect on this contract, not on the business as a whole, determines whether it was impracticable. Either the parties would or would not have insisted on performance of this contract under these circumstances.

Impracticability can also be either partial or total. A reduction in supply may preclude a seller delivering part of the promised performance or from delivering any of it. Impracticability can be temporary or permanent. A supplier may be able to resume full performance before the end of a contract period or the contract may end before the impracticability subsides.

Arguably, the excuse of impracticability is not essential. Even if a party cannot possibly perform its duties, it can pay damages caused by its nonperformance. The effect nonperformance has on the other party will be just as severe whether the nonperformance results from an intentional breach or from an unavoidable catastrophe. An airline without jet fuel faces the same hardship whether a foreign embargo cuts off supply or the refinery fails to get its trucks loaded on time.

Nonetheless, courts are unlikely to apply impracticability to nonpayment of money. For sales of goods, the UCC limits impracticability to sellers, excusing their failure to deliver goods. A buyer's duty to pay cannot be excused for impracticability. As a matter of interpretation, it seems unlikely that the parties, negotiating in advance, would agree to excuse payment if difficulties arise. The creditor should be able to collect whatever she can — and almost certainly would have insisted on that right if she asked up front. Loan documents often provide that missing a payment allows the creditor to **accelerate** the loan, allowing a demand for repayment of the entire outstanding balance immediately.

Yet extreme circumstances may make excuse more credible. For instance, a flood or earthquake might destroy a party's bank, so that records verifying the account balance or line of credit are not available, even online. Or the government might freeze a person's bank accounts believing (mistakenly or not) that he is a terrorist or a drug lord. Creditors might be understanding, but it is not clear that the law should prevent them from insisting on performance, even if these represent delayed payment rather than excused payment.

Case Preview

Sassower v. Blumenfeld

In the *Sassower* case, Blumenfeld, a victim of Bernard Madoff's fraud scheme, tried to plead impossibility of performance to excuse his contract obligation to purchase real estate. He wanted to recover his deposit on the contract, which the seller retained as liquidated damages for the breach. The court examined the melding of contract excuses under the Restatement's modern elements of impracticability to determine who should prevail when payment was not made in a timely manner.

As you read *Sassower v. Blumenfeld*, look for the following:

1. When did the court indicate that the impossibility defense may be applied?
2. Was Blumenfeld able to show that his financial hardship amounted to impracticability as an excusable difficulty in paying for the real estate?
3. Did the court require Sassower to return Blumenfeld's deposit in this matter?

Sassower v. Blumenfeld

878 N.Y.S.2d 602 (2009)

DESTEFANO, J.

In this action for a declaratory judgment, etc., the plaintiffs move, inter alia, for summary judgment pursuant to CPLR 3212, seeking a declaration that they are entitled to retain a deposit paid by the defendant for the purchase of real property based upon the defendant's failure to close on the "time of the essence" closing date. The plaintiffs also seek an award of attorneys' fees, to be determined at inquest, based upon the breach of contract, and dismissal of the defendant's answer and counterclaims.

The plaintiffs assert that on November 18, 2008, they entered into an agreement with the defendant whereby the defendant was to purchase real property, consisting of a residence and other improvements, located at 108 Stonebridge Court, New Hartford, New York for $1.8 million, with a deposit of $180,000 to be paid on the signing of the contract, the balance to be paid at closing [citation omitted]. It is undisputed that the deposit was paid and held in escrow by the plaintiffs' attorney [citation omitted].

The contract contains the following relevant provisions:

> "15. Closing Date and Place. Closing shall take place at the office of Seller's attorney at 10:00 A.M. on or about December 12, 2008 or upon reasonable notice (by telephone or otherwise) by Purchaser, at the office of lender's attorney, if any, in Nassau or New York County . . .
>
> "23. Defaults and Remedies.
>
> > "(a) If Purchaser willfully defaults hereunder, Seller's sole remedy shall be to receive and retain the Downpayment as liquidated damages, it being agreed that Seller's damages in case of Purchaser's default might be impossible to ascertain and the Downpayment constitutes a fair and reasonable amount of damages under the circumstances and is not a penalty. . . .
>
> "41. In the event that either party commences an action or proceeding to enforce their rights under this Agreement, then the prevailing party shall be entitled to recover its reasonable legal fees and expenses from the other party which are incurred in such action or proceeding. . . .
>
> "47. Supplementing Paragraph 15. Purchaser shall on five (5) business days notice to Seller be entitled to adjourn the closing on one or more occasion but in no event to a date beyond December 31, 2008 (the 'Adjourned Closing Date') and time Shall be Of the Essence with respect to Purchaser's obligations to close on the Adjourned Closing Date. If the closing is adjourned past December 12, 2008, then all adjustments to be made pursuant to Paragraph 18 of the Contract shall be made at the closing as of December 12, 2008, and in addition to any other amounts due Seller by Purchaser, Purchaser shall reimburse Seller the per diem costs of the Seller's existing mortgages (in the amount of $288.36 per day) and insurance premiums for the period December 12, 2008 through the Adjourned closing Date."

Prior to the scheduled closing date, the plaintiffs signed deed and transfer tax documents and arranged for the delivery of payoff letters from the first and second mortgages as well as the satisfaction of a third mortgage. [Footnote omitted.]

On December 10, 2008, the defendant requested an adjournment of the closing date until

December 19, 2008, asserting that "his lender was not ready to close" [citation omitted].

In a letter dated, December 24, 2008, the defendant terminated the contract and asked that the plaintiffs' counsel "release Purchaser's $180,000.00 downpayment [*sic*] from escrow, and return it to me in the enclosed FedEx envelope. . . . Be advised that as directed you are not to release the Purchaser's downpayment [*sic*] from escrow to anyone other than Purchaser" [citation omitted].

On this motion, plaintiffs argue that inasmuch as they were ready, willing and able to perform and that the closing did not take place on the scheduled date because of defendant's wrongful termination of the contract, they are entitled to a declaration that they may retain the down payment as liquidated damages.

In opposition to the motion, the defendant asserts that on December 11, 2008,

> "without advance warning of any kind — I became aware that I had lost nearly all of my personal assets as a result of the fraudulent scheme of Bernard Madoff. . . . One of the many, many hardships I suffered as a result of Mr. Madoff's crimes was that my performance and ability to close pursuant to the Contract terms was rendered

impossible. As a result, I terminated the Contract . . . and requested a return of my $180,000 down payment, which I desperately need to meet creditor and family obligations" [citation omitted].

In support of his contention regarding impossibility of performance, the defendant cites a number of cases, none of which are apposite. In this regard, the Court of Appeals, in *Kel Kim Corp. v Central Mkts.* (70 NY2d 900, 519 NE2d 295, 524 NYS2d 384 [1987]), held that

> "[w]hile . . . defenses [such as impossibility] have been recognized in the common law, they have been applied narrowly, due in part to judicial recognition that the purpose of contract law is to allocate the risks that might affect performance and that performance should be excused only in extreme circumstances (*see*, Wallach, *The Excuse Defense in the Law of Contracts: Judicial Frustration of the U.C.C. Attempt to Liberalize the Law of Commercial Impracticability,* 55 Notre Dame Law 203, 207 [1979]). Impossibility excuses a party's performance only when the destruction of the subject matter of the contract or the means of performance makes performance objectively impossible. Moreover, the impossibility must be produced by an unanticipated event that could not have been foreseen or guarded against in the contract (*see, 407 E. 61st Garage v Savoy Fifth Ave. Corp.,* 23 NY2d 275, 244 NE2d 37, 296 NYS2d 338; *Ogdensburg Urban Renewal Agency v Moroney,* 42 AD2d 639, 345 NYS2d 169)."

In addition, in *407 East 61st Garage, Inc. v Savoy Fifth Ave. Corp.* (23 NY2d 275, 244 NE2d 37, 296 NYS2d 338 [1968]) the Court of Appeals stated:

> "Generally, . . . the excuse of impossibility of performance is limited to the destruction of the means of performance by an act of God, *vis major*, or by law (*International Paper Co. v Rockefeller,* 161 App Div 180, 184, 146 NYS 371; 6 Williston, Contracts [Rev. ed.], §1935; 10 N. Y. Jur., Contracts, §357; Restatement, Contracts, §457). Thus, where impossibility or difficulty of performance is occasioned only by financial difficulty or economic hardship, even to the extent of insolvency or bankruptcy, performance of a contract is not excused [citations omitted]. Notably, in this case, Savoy does not even assert that bankruptcy or insolvency was a likely consequence of continuing operation of the hotel. Further, in view of its admittedly contemporaneous financial difficulties, Savoy could and should have insisted that the agreement provide for the anticipated contingency of economic hardship (cf. Restatement, Contracts, §457). In sum, performance by Savoy was at all times possible, although unprofitable, since the hotel could simply have remained in business, and the legal excuse of impossibility of performance would not be available to it."

Also relevant to the court's determination is *Di Scipio v Sullivan* (30 AD3d 660, 661, 816 NYS2d 576 [3d Dept *2006]),* in which the Third Department held that

> "'[i]t has long been the rule in New York that a purchaser who defaults on a real estate contract without lawful excuse cannot recover the down payment' (*Korabel v Natoli,* 210 AD2d 620, 621-622, 619 NYS2d 833 [1994] . . .). This is the result 'notwithstanding that a seller's actual damages may be less than a given down payment' (*Barton v Lerman,* 233 AD2d 555, 556, 649 NYS2d 107 [1996]). Therefore, absent a legally cognizable excuse for defendant's failure to perform the contract, plaintiff

may retain the down payment. . . . Defendant's asserted excuse—the illiquidity of the estate and its inability to obtain financing—is unavailing" (citations omitted).

At bar, therefore, that the defendant may have been the victim of an unfortunate fraud which impacted on his assets and finances would not excuse his performance under the contract of sale. Furthermore, even assuming that the defendant could raise impossibility as a defense to nonperformance based on a change in financial condition occasioned by the actions of Bernard Madoff, he has utterly failed to provide any details as to the amounts lost, the nature of his lost investments, or the actual state of his current finances and assets. In short, the opposing papers are wholly insufficient to raise any issue regarding impossibility, assuming it were otherwise a viable defense. . . .

Post-Case Follow-Up

The *Sassower* court determined that financial difficulty or economic hardship, even to the extent of insolvency or bankruptcy, does not excuse a breach of contract under impossibility or impracticability. In addition, Blumenfeld had provided no evidence of the amounts lost, the nature of his lost investments, or the actual state of his current finances and assets. Since the contract indicated that time was of the essence, Sassower was permitted to retain Blumenfeld's deposit and to be awarded attorneys' fees due to the defendant's breach.

Sassower v. Blumenfeld: Real Life Applications

1. A farm equipment dealer enters into a franchise agreement with a manufacturer of a wide range of construction and farming equipment. The franchisee receives an exclusive territory in northern California to sell only manufacturer's farm equipment. The agreement specifies the terms and process under which the contract may be terminated. A year later, the farm equipment market suffers a serious recession and the manufacturer suffers substantial losses of $2 million per day and a serious loss of stock value. The manufacturer unilaterally sells its farm equipment division to a third party to boost its bottom line. The franchisee does not receive a territory from the new buyer and its business is left in shambles. The franchisee sues for breach and the manufacturer claims impracticability due to severe financial hardship. Will the manufacturer be excused under impracticability according to *Karl Wendt Farm Equip. Co. v. International Harvester Co.*, 931 F.2d 1112 (6th Cir. 1991)?

2. In the above-cited *Wendt* case, there was a vigorous dissent on the issue of impracticability. Review and summarize the arguments in the dissenting opinion. Do you agree with the dissent's view on economic loss as grounds for excuse of performance under impracticability in these circumstances?

3. Several timber companies enter into five-year contracts to harvest required amounts of timber from large tracts of government land at fixed prices. The timber companies then sell the harvested wood on the open market, gaining a hefty profit. During the third year of the agreement, government economic policy changes, allowing interest rates to rise to combat price inflation, which leads to a serious decrease in housing construction. Lumber prices fall dramatically and the lumber companies stop harvesting timber. The government terminates the timber companies' contracts and sues for the failure to harvest the mandated amounts of timber. The timber companies claim impracticability of performance due to the serious slump in lumber prices. Under *Seaboard Lumber Co. v. United States*, 308 F.3d 1283 (Fed. Cir. 2002), will the timber firms be able to support a claim of impracticability resulting from the government's economic policies?

---

1. Establishing the Excuse of Impracticability

Performance may be deemed impracticable if performance would require altering the essential nature of a party's performance. This applies to situations where a party's role changes dramatically. In general, it may not apply to parties performing the same duties in the same way, even if that performance has become significantly more expensive. Under the Restatement view, a party seeking to claim the excuse of impracticability must show the following elements:

1. an event made performance impracticable;
2. nonoccurrence of that event was a basic assumption on which the contract was made;
3. a lack of party fault for the claimed event; and
4. the party claiming the excuse does not bear the risk of loss by the terms of the contract or the surrounding circumstances.[2]

The first two elements are intertwined and examine the nature of the event in light of the parties' intentions. The final two elements consider the issues of party fault and agreed-upon allocation of risks.

The elements differ slightly in the UCC. First, the UCC defense applies only to sellers. Buyers, whose obligation is to pay money, cannot seek excuse because payment has become difficult. Second, the UCC does not refer to a party's fault. However, the UCC does require good faith in the performance and enforcement of a contract. A party at fault seems unlikely to establish good faith. The seller must timely notify buyers of any delay or nondelivery of goods due to impracticability. Due to the impracticability, the seller must advise a buyer of any estimated amount

[2]Restatement (Second) of Contracts §261; *see also* UCC §2-615(a).

of goods that it can deliver and allocate any goods produced among its buyers in a fair, reasonable manner.

The CISG imposes somewhat different limits on the excuse. To justify excuse, the impediment to performance must be one that:

1. was beyond a party's control;
2. the party could not reasonably have been expected to anticipate at contract formation; and
3. the party could not reasonably be expected to avoid or overcome the consequences of the impediment.[5]

The CISG does not directly address issue of party fault or allocation of risk. Its focus is on issues of party control and reasonable expectations at time of contract formation. The CISG also requires the party who cannot perform to promptly notify the other party within a reasonable time or else face liability for damages.[6]

2. Determining Nature of Events

To show impracticability, the event that yields the excuse must be unexpected. The unexpected event must cause the impracticability. Although the Restatement speaks in terms of an unexpected event, courts often examine whether an event was foreseeable. In an uncertain world, one can always foresee a long list of terrible disasters, but those events may be unlikely to occur in most situations so parties may not address them in their contracts. So you may notice that some courts may discuss impracticability (and frustration of purpose) in terms of foreseeability while the Restatement approach looks more narrowly to unexpected events.

To show impracticability, the event that yields the excuse must be unexpected or unanticipated. The unexpected event must cause the impracticability. Drawing the line between serious hardships and mere challenges may not be easy. A performance that is impossible clearly satisfies this test. Similarly, a party may be able to perform, but to do so might now become extremely expensive or difficult to complete due to a government regulation or order. In these instances, a seller who fails to perform contract duties to avoid government sanctions or fines may be excused from claims of breach as impracticable. In *Swift Canadian Co. v. Banet*, 224 F.2d 36 (3d Cir. 1955), an importer bought lamb pelts, to be delivered in Canada, en route to Philadelphia. U.S. law changed, making the importation illegal. The court rejected impracticability since delivery was legal in Canada. However, changes in law are more likely to lead to the application of the excuse of frustration of purpose discussed later in this chapter.

The most difficult cases involve performance that remains possible but has become more expensive. Changes in cost are a risk parties undertake when they quote prices. Up to a point, a party must perform despite changes in cost—even

[5]CISG Art. 79(1).
[6]*Id* 79(4).

if the changes make performance unprofitable. In some cases, however, significant increases in cost may satisfy the requirement of impracticability. The obvious cases involve significant increases caused by extreme events, such as earthquakes, hurricanes, crop failures, or wars. But if the event should have been anticipated and addressed in the contract, the excuse is unavailable even though the expense makes performance impracticable.

The nonoccurrence of this event is a basic assumption on which the contract was made. If the nonoccurrence was a basic assumption, then the parties did not assume that the event would happen. In some instances, the parties did not consider the possibility that the event would occur. Alternatively, the parties may have considered it so unlikely that it did not deserve the time necessary to negotiate how to adjust obligations if it did occur.

It is not merely a matter of foreseeability, because parties can foresee a broad range of both actual and imagined disasters. The court will apply an objective standard to determine whether or not a reasonable party should have expected the event. The goal of impracticability is to recognize circumstances in which the parties would not have required performance if they had considered the possibility at the time the contract was made. Naturally, if the parties did consider the possibility and did not provide for an excuse, it seems likely that these parties intended to require performance despite the occurrence of the event. An express provision requiring performance despite the event would resolve this issue — a possibility discussed below. But even without an express provision, the excuse is warranted only for events the parties did not consider likely to occur and therefore did not address in their contract.

On the other hand, changes in market conditions unrelated to extreme events seem unlikely to qualify as events the parties assumed would not occur. Market fluctuations are common and expected and within the range of causes endless and interrelated. Unless changes in the market result from unusual circumstances, the risk of changed prices seems unlikely to justify excuse. For example, a surge in oil prices during 2008 led to an increased demand for biodiesel fuel. Because sugar cane makes a good biodiesel fuel, the demand for cane increased. The price of sugar, therefore, jumped significantly. The market forces at work here — increased demand producing increased prices — are ordinary. The fact that the source of the demand (biodiesel companies) was not foreseen at the time a contract was formed probably does not make this an event the nonoccurrence of which was a basic assumption.

Case Preview

Clark v. Wallace County Cooperative Equity Exchange

In *Clark v. Wallace County Cooperative Equity Exchange,* a court considered the impracticability defense after a freeze damaged a crop harvest. Unable to deliver the agreed-upon grain order, a farmer claims impracticability of performance when he cannot harvest the required amount under the contract. In examining the situation, the court explored whether the freeze is objectively an unanticipated or unexpected event and whether the nonoccurrence of this event was a basic assumption upon which the contract was made.

As you read *Clark v. Wallace County Cooperative Equity Exchange*, look for the following:

In this case, a court considered the impracticability defense after a freeze damaged a crop harvest.
ProdavacSlika/iStockphoto

1. Did the court determine that the freeze was an unexpected event?
2. Did the parties expect Clark to deliver the required grain even if a freeze reduced his crop harvest?
3. Was it objectively impracticable for Clark to provide grain under the contract when his crops were damaged by the freeze?

Clark v. Wallace County Cooperative Equity Exchange

26 Kan. App. 2d 463 (1999)

LEWIS, J.

Ray C. Clark is a farmer. The Wallace County Cooperative Equity Exchange (Coop) operates, among other things, a grain elevator through which it buys and sells grain. In January 1995, Clark and Coop entered into a written agreement in which Clark agreed to sell Coop 4,000 bushels of corn to be delivered after the crop was harvested. At the time the contract was made, there may have been corn planted somewhere in Kansas, but it would have been far short of maturity. In September 1995, there was a freeze in the area, which severely damaged the corn crop. As a result of this freeze, Clark raised only 2,207.41 bushels of corn, which he delivered to Coop. Clark then maintained he was excused from delivering the remaining 1,392.59 bushels (after an allowed 10% reduction) because of the freeze. Coop insisted he was not excused and held the cost of the shortage out of the grain sale by Clark to Coop. This action was brought by Clark to recover the $1,622.97 that Coop withheld from his grain sale.

First, we note that these are rather common agreements used in the grain business. Anyone involved in this sort of an agreement realizes that one of the big risks is that the farmer may not be able to grow sufficient grain to deliver the required number of bushels. Clark seeks to be excused from his obligation to deliver because his crop was damaged by the weather. We suspect that if we adopted his reasoning, we would put an end to trading grain in this manner throughout the entire state of Kansas. It would have the effect of taking all the risk away from the farmer and placing the entire risk of loss on the grain elevators and, in fact, creating a potential situation where grain elevators could be bankrupted in the event of a large area crop loss.

Clark first argues that K.S.A. 84-2-613 excuses his performance. That particular provision of the Uniform Commercial Code (UCC) provides that "where the contract requires for its performance *goods identified when the contract is made*, and the goods suffer casualty without fault of either party before the risk of loss passes to the buyer . . . (b) if the loss is partial . . . the buyer may . . . accept the goods with due allowance from the contract price for the deterioration or the deficiency in quantity but without further right against the seller." (Emphasis added.)

We conclude this particular statute does not relieve defendant from his obligation under the agreement in question because the goods were not identified at the time the contract was made. In *Milling Co. v. Edwards*, 108 Kan. 616, 618, 197 P. 1113 (1921), the Kansas Supreme Court stated that in order to constitute a contract for the sale of a certain commodity under which the performance of delivery is excused by the destruction of the commodity, the contract must specify the land on which the commodity is to be grown.

Since the *Edwards* decision, the UCC was adopted in Kansas. There are, to the best of our knowledge, no post-UCC cases from Kansas which address this issue. However, we focus on a decision from the state of Washington. In *Colley v. Bi-State, Inc.*, 21 Wash. App. 769, 586 P.2d 908 (1978), Colley failed to deliver the remaining bushels of wheat due under certain contracts with Bi-State, Inc. Colley was short on wheat and did not raise enough wheat to make delivery due to a hot, dry summer. He argued that because of the hot, dry summer, that Washington UCC §2-613 excused delivery of the remaining wheat. The Washington court held that the contract did not expressly require Colley to grow the wheat himself or to grow it in any particular location, only to deliver 25,000 bushels to the elevator. Under those circumstances, the Washington court concluded that UCC §2-613 did not excuse the delivery performance of the farmer. The court also indicated that the parties to this type of agreement intend to be bound to it regardless of the success of the seller's crop. 21 Wash. App. at 773-74.

We believe that the Washington decision is soundly reasoned and should be adopted as the law of this state.

Clark argues the trial court should have looked at the parties' intent when the agreement was made. However, at the same time, Clark stipulates that the agreement was complete, unambiguous, and free of uncertainty. Whether a contract's terms are ambiguous is a question of law to be decided by the court. If the contract is found to be unambiguous, the court must interpret the contract solely within its four corners, and extrinsic evidence is inadmissible. *U.S. v. Mintz*, 935 F. Supp. 1178, 1179 (D. Kan. 1996). Insofar as Clark's specific complaint is concerned, there is no evidence in the record on appeal to indicate that Clark ever attempted to submit evidence of trade usage for the parties' intent or that the trial court ever denied the admission of such evidence. Under these circumstances, an appellant cannot raise a point for the first time on appeal. . . . We hold that a seller of grain is not excused by K.S.A. 84-2-613 from the delivery performance specified in an agreement of this nature when the grain is not identified by a specific tract of land on which it is to be grown.

Clark next argues that K.S.A. 84-2-615 provides some relief. Again, we do not agree.

K.S.A. 84-2-615 reads as follows:

> "Except so far as a seller may have assumed a greater obligation and subject to the preceding section on substituted performance:

(a) Delay in delivery or nondelivery in whole or in part by a seller who complies with paragraphs (b) and (c) is not a breach of his duty under a contract for sale *if performance as agreed has been made impracticable by the occurrence of a contingency the nonoccurrence of which was a basic assumption on which the contract was made.*" (Emphasis added.)

The first element which must be established to apply the statute quoted above is that performance must be impracticable. We addressed the issue of impracticability in *Sunflower Electric Coop., Inc. v. Tomlinson Oil Co.*, 7 Kan. App. 2d 131, 638 P.2d 963 (1981), rev. denied 231 Kan. 802 (1982). In that case, we indicated there was a difference between subjective and objective impracticability. This difference can be illustrated by an individual who says "I cannot do it" versus a statement to the effect that "the thing cannot be done." Only objective impracticability may relieve a party of his or her contractual obligation. 7 Kan. App. 2d at 139. In this case, there was no objective impracticability since the corn was not identified to be from specific land. The thing Clark had to do in this case was deliver 4,000 bushels of corn to the elevator. He could have done this. This is shown by the fact that Coop was able to cover the shortage on the instant contract by acquiring corn from another source. The fact is, Clark did not want to deliver the grain, but he had the ability to do so by purchasing grain to replace the grain he did not raise.

The Kansas comments to K.S.A. 84-2-615 state: "A seller . . . will not be excused under this section if (1) the non-occurrence of the contingency was the seller's fault; (2) the seller had reason to know of the impracticability (i.e., the contingency was foreseeable); or (3) the seller assumed the risk of the contingency." We do not deem it difficult to conclude that farmers in Kansas can foresee late September freezes which will reduce their corn yields. It has happened a number of times. If we were to excuse Clark from his obligation to deliver on the agreement, we would allow a farmer to enter into a forward grain contract on unspecified land, gamble on the extent of his supply, being aware of the fact that he may not raise sufficient grain, and then escape with impunity when his grain crop proves inadequate.

In addition, official UCC comments (5) and (9) to K.S.A. 84-2-615 refer to the concept of identifying the source of supply of the crop to be sold. As we pointed out above, the contract before this court did not identify a particular source of supply or a particular area where the corn was to be grown.

We hold that Clark's performance on the grain sales agreement in question was not excused by the provisions of K.S.A. 84-2-615.

Affirmed.

Post-Case Follow-Up

The *Clark* court decided that the grain contract did not require or assume that the grain would be provided from Clark's farm or from a particular tract of land on his farm. Objectively, Clark could provide the agreed-upon amount of grain from his crops and by purchasing available grain from other farms. The court found that a late freeze reducing crop yields was certainly foreseeable among Kansas farmers. Clark was not excused from providing the grain amounts under his contract with the grain wholesaler.

Clark v. Wallace County Cooperative Equity Exchange: Real Life Applications

1. A contractor agrees to excavate all the gravel required to build a bridge from a particular site and to pay the costs of the gravel. As the project progresses, it becomes apparent that the remaining gravel is now well below the water table. The contractor needs to dredge the gravel and dry it out before it can be used to construct the bridge. Yet this process is different from the initial excavation efforts and will require completely different equipment that costs at least ten times as much as the earlier gravel excavation efforts. Will the contractor be excused under impracticability? Examine *Mineral Park Land Co. v. Howard*, 172 Cal. 289 (1916) for the result in this case.

2. The U.S. government enters into a contract with a manufacturer of military supplies to deliver 100,000 pairs of combat boots by November 5. The contract specifies that time is of the essence in the delivery of these goods. The manufacturer provides these rugged boots to governments and wholesalers all over the globe. However, the company does not make a timely delivery of the boots under the government contract. The government sues for breach. The company claims that it is excused from its duties due to an unexpected train derailment that delayed its delivery. There is no force majeure clause, and the risk of loss for the goods had not yet passed to the government. Will the court view the derailment in this case as an unanticipated event under *Bende & Sons, Inc. v. Crown Recreation, Inc.*, 548 F. Supp. 1018 (E.D.N.Y. 1982), *aff'd*, 722 F.2d 727 (2d Cir. 1983)?

3. An electric power utility contracts to buy gas from certain leased gas fields of an oil company. The contract calls for minimum levels of gas availability for the utility company and contains no force majeure clause. From the start, the oil company breaches the contract by not providing the required minimum amounts of gas required under the contract. The power company sues for breach and the oil company claims impossibility of performance because the contracted gas reservoirs are exhausted. Is this occurrence an act of nature excusing the oil company from its contract duties? Review *Sunflower Electric Cooperative, Inc. v. Tomlinson Oil Co.*, 7 Kan. App. 2d 131 (1981) to determine the outcome.

If the parties expected an event may occur, then they expected performance of the contract to occur despite the event. When they assumed an event would not occur, the contract itself does not establish that they expected performance to occur despite the eventual occurrence of this event. Thus, if the threat is known or readily foreseeable to the parties, they will have difficulty claiming impracticability due to an unanticipated event. For example, a manufacturing company located in

> **Impracticability and Issues of Profitability**
>
> Courts are reluctant to apply impracticability based solely on economic difficulties. In one sense, any event that makes a contract unprofitable makes performance impractical. Impracticable means more than just unprofitable. Businesses often take a loss on contracts — sometimes intentionally as loss leaders to entice future business. In other instances, a party may unintentionally underbid a project for any number of reasons, such as unanticipated increases in fuel or equipment costs. No matter how big the loss, impracticability does not apply to ordinary business risks. The doctrine is not about saving people from their own judgment calls. Impracticability is intended for situations outside the normal range of business risks. When significant losses result from causes beyond the parties' usual expectations, impracticability comes into play. But it is a case-by-case determination as to whether or not parties claiming the excuse have properly proven their cases.

an earthquake-prone area can foresee that earthquakes may disrupt its production facilities and would be wise to address such potential delays in its contract. During contract negotiations and drafting, parties should carefully consider realistic risks that could impact their contract duties and spell out their expectations accordingly.

3. Party Fault and Risk Allocation

The final two elements of impracticability consider party fault and party allocation of risk under the contract terms or the factual circumstances of the case. If a party wrongfully causes an event that leads to impracticability, then that party is not entitled to be excused. For example, a person who burns down his own factory cannot then seek excuse on the ground that the fire made performance of contracts impracticable. Extreme cases (such as arson) are unusual. But negligently causing a fire also may qualify as wrongful in some contexts. Negligence is considered fault in many situations. Indeed, comments to the Restatement (Second) of Contracts suggest that no-fault conduct, such as breach of contract, may be sufficiently wrongful to justify denying excuse for impracticability. The UCC takes a narrower view of fault, allowing excuse unless the conduct approaches willfulness. In fact, the UCC does not mention a party's fault as a reason to deny excuse. Unless a party's conduct breaches the omnipresent duty of good faith, the excuse may be available.

The parties may determine the allocation of their risks in express terms or to specify their own acceptable excuses, often in a force majeure clause. Many force majeure clauses echo concern that the events fall outside a party's control. A typical clause would specify events like drought, earthquake, fire, flood, pestilence, strike, tornado, terrorist acts, civil unrest, and war. Alternatively, the parties could provide that performance (or damages for nonperformance) is expected despite any of these events. Where the parties' agreement is silent, a court may attempt to infer how the parties would have wanted to handle unusual circumstances. Where it seems likely that the parties would not have expected each other to perform (or to pay damages) when events of this sort occur, then it may interpret the contract to include an excuse for these extreme events. Given the frequency with which force majeure clauses appear in contracts, courts reasonably infer that parties often are willing to excuse nonperformance when it results from extreme circumstances.

At one time, parties routinely drafted force majeure clauses. These clauses were essential when courts refused to allow excuses unless the parties provided for them.

Courts created the impracticability defense largely because force majeure clauses became so prevalent. Rather than compel parties to draft their own clauses, courts inferred excuses in all contracts unless parties specified otherwise. In theory, this approach reduced the need to draft such clauses in contracts.

The continued use of force majeure clauses allows parties to alter the parameters of excuse. Instead of letting the court decide which events are sufficiently unexpected to justify an excuse, the parties can specify the events they consider worthy of excuse. This approach allows them to expand excuse to additional situations or to narrow the excuse to a more limited set of circumstances.

Impracticability is an effort to determine what the parties would have done if they anticipated an event occurring. Parties drafting a contract may agree what should be done if unusual events occur. When the parties so provide, an imaginative reconstruction of what the parties would have provided is unnecessary. A court can focus on interpreting the clause the parties drafted. Contracts may require performance despite an event in either of three ways:

1. a clause allowing excuse under some circumstances, implicitly excluding others;
2. a clause specifically excluding excuse for some circumstances; or
3. an unconditional clause that excludes any claims of excuse, often found in commercial contracts ("hell or high water" clauses).

A contract's silence regarding excuses is not grounds for concluding the contract requires performance despite an event. Impracticability (and frustration of purpose) rest on the assumption that the parties did not address whether to provide an excuse. If silence justifies the conclusion that they agreed to perform despite the event, these excuses never apply. Historically, courts took exactly that approach, with results that bordered on the absurd. For example, in *Whitman v. Anglum*, 103 A. 114 (Conn. 1918), a dairy farmer whose cows were destroyed after contracting hoof and mouth disease was required to pay damages under a contract to sell milk. If he wanted an excuse, the court reasoned, he should have drafted one into the contract. The modern rules put the shoe on the other foot. Unless the contract provides for a greater obligation, the excuse of impracticability will apply.

That last point requires one caveat. Sometimes courts may look beyond the contract when looking for indications that the parties intended the obligations to continue despite the event. The "language or the circumstances" may indicate that the parties did not intend for an excuse to apply.[3]

With no force majeure clause or a poorly written one, a court may consider the factual context to determine the allocation of risks. The facts may indicate who is liable if certain problems arise based on party conduct and intentions. A court may also consider the parties' course of performance, prior course of dealing, or trade usage. Exactly what circumstances beyond the contract language might support the inference that the parties intended to exclude an excuse is not generally agreed.

[3]Restatement (Second) of Contracts §261; *see also* UCC §2-615 ("Except so far as a seller may have assumed a greater obligation," without specifying where that greater obligation might be found).

The contract itself remains the primary place to look for indications that the parties meant to require performance despite an unusual event.

Parties may specify a narrower range of excuses than impracticability would allow. Under such clauses, the parties implicitly agree to perform unless the excuses specified in the contract arise — even if events make performance impracticable in the eyes of the court. Like many provisions of the law, the impracticability defense is a default provision and it governs unless the parties agree upon a different term. A force majeure clause, if different from impracticability, controls the parties' obligations to each other.

Less commonly, parties may specify that performance will be required regardless of events that might occur. For example, an oil buyer might negotiate for a clause requiring performance "despite any political or military turmoil in the Middle East, including any embargo relating to oil." Such a clause suggests that nonoccurrence of turmoil was not a basic assumption on which the contract was made. Further, it clearly specifies that the parties agree to perform — or, at least, to pay damages for nonperformance — regardless of events that might make performance more difficult, more expensive, or even impossible. In effect, one party is warned to buy insurance against this event as the other party is unwilling to take that risk.

A clause need not be that specific to qualify. Consider a general clause, requiring performance "regardless of any unusual event, such as" those typically mentioned in force majeure clauses. The parties have spoken and this term would make performance due unconditionally, without regard to the excuses courts otherwise might employ. These types of unconditional clauses are referred to as "hell or high water" clauses and are commonly found in commercial contracts. Parties who intend unconditional duties should draft something on this order, rather than simply expect silence in the contract to make performance inexcusable.

To avoid court intervention, it makes sense for the parties to draft a clear and comprehensive force majeure clause that meets their needs. In drafting the clause, the parties must be careful to express their acceptable excuses in a manner that reflects their agreed-upon concerns. In the next case, we will see how a court dealt with a force majeure clause that did not clearly address a problem that arose later in the life of the contract.

Case Preview

Kel Kim Corp. v. Central Markets, Inc.

In this case, a lessee, Kel Kim Corp. (Kel Kim), entered into a ten-year lease with lessor, Central Markets, Inc. for a vacant space to develop a roller skating rink. Under the lease, Kel Kim was required to obtain liability insurance from a reputable insurance company. In the seventh year of the lease, Kel Kim's insurance policy was not renewed due to the financial instability of the insurance company. The lessor notified Kel Kim that it had breached the insurance requirement of the lease and threatened eviction. The court examined the lessee's claim of impossibility of performance and the contract's force majeure clause to determine if Kel Kim was properly excused.

As you read *Kel Kim Corp. v. Central Markets, Inc.*, look for the following:

1. Had Kel Kim supported its assertion of impossibility of performance to justify its failure to obtain liability insurance under the terms of the lease?
2. Was the inability to find another insurer an unexpected event excusing Kel Kim's performance of its contract duties?
3. What role did the force majeure clause play in the court's decision in this dispute?

Kel Kim Corp. v. Central Markets, Inc.

70 N.Y.2d 900 (1987)

WACHTLER, C.J.

. . .

In early 1980, plaintiff Kel Kim Corporation leased a vacant supermarket in Clifton Park, New York, from defendants. The lease was for an initial term of 10 years with two 5-year renewal options. The understanding of both parties was that plaintiff would use the property as a roller skating rink open to the general public, although the lease did not limit use of the premises to a roller rink.

The lease required Kel Kim to "procure and maintain in full force and effect a public liability insurance policy or policies in a solvent and responsible company or companies . . . of not less than Five Hundred Thousand Dollars . . . to any single person and in the aggregate of not less than One Million Dollars . . . on account of any single accident." Kel Kim obtained the required insurance coverage and for six years operated the facility without incident. In November 1985 its insurance carrier gave notice that the policy would expire on January 6, 1986 and would not be renewed due to uncertainty about the financial condition of the reinsurer, which was then under the management of a court-appointed administrator. Kel Kim transmitted this information to defendants and, it asserts, thereafter made every effort to procure the requisite insurance elsewhere but was unable to do so on account of the liability insurance crisis. Plaintiff ultimately succeeded in obtaining a policy in the aggregate amount of $500,000 effective March 1, 1986 and contends that no insurer would write a policy in excess of that amount on any roller skating rink. As of August 1987, plaintiff procured the requisite coverage.

On January 7, 1986, when plaintiff's initial policy expired and it remained uninsured, defendants sent a notice of default, directing that it cure within 30 days or vacate the premises. Kel Kim and the individual guarantors of the lease then began this declaratory judgment action, urging that they should be excused from compliance with the insurance provision either because performance was impossible or because the inability to procure insurance was within the lease's force majeure clause.* Special Term granted defendants' motion for summary judgment, nullified the lease, and directed Kel Kim to vacate the premises. A divided Appellate Division affirmed.

---

*The clause reads: "If either party to this Lease shall be delayed or prevented from the performance of any obligation through no fault of their own by reason of labor disputes, inability to procure materials, failure of utility service, restrictive governmental laws or regulations, riots, insurrection, war, adverse weather, Acts of God, or other similar causes beyond the control of such party, the performance of such obligation shall be excused for the period of the delay."

Generally, once a party to a contract has made a promise, that party must perform or respond in damages for its failure, even when unforeseen circumstances make performance burdensome; until the late nineteenth century even impossibility of performance ordinarily did not provide a defense (Calamari and Perillo, Contracts §13-1, at 477 [2d ed. 1977]). While such defenses have been recognized in the common law, they have been applied narrowly, due in part to judicial recognition that the purpose of contract law is to allocate the risks that might affect performance and that performance should be excused only in extreme circumstances (see, Wallach, The Excuse Defense in the Law of Contracts: Judicial Frustration of the U.C.C. Attempt to Liberalize the Law of Commercial Impracticability, 55 Notre Dame Law 203, 207 [1979]). Impossibility excuses a party's performance only when the destruction of the subject matter of the contract or the means of performance makes performance objectively impossible. Moreover, the impossibility must be produced by an unanticipated event that could not have been foreseen or guarded against in the contract (*see, 407 E. 61st Garage v Savoy Fifth Ave. Corp.*, 23 NY2d 275; *Ogdensburg Urban Renewal Agency v Moroney*, 42 AD2d 639).

Applying these principles, we conclude that plaintiff's predicament is not within the embrace of the doctrine of impossibility. Kel Kim's inability to procure and maintain requisite coverage could have been foreseen and guarded against when it specifically undertook that obligation in the lease, and therefore the obligation cannot be excused on this basis.

For much the same underlying reason, contractual force majeure clauses — or clauses excusing nonperformance due to circumstances beyond the control of the parties — under the common law provide a similarly narrow defense. Ordinarily, only if the force majeure clause specifically includes the event that actually prevents a party's performance will that party be excused. (*See, e.g., United Equities Co. v First Natl. City Bank*, 41 NY2d 1032; Squillante & Congalton, Force Majeure, 80 Com LJ 4 [1975].) Here, of course, the contractual provision does not specifically include plaintiff's inability to procure and maintain insurance. Nor does this inability fall within the catchall "or other similar causes beyond the control of such party." The principle of interpretation applicable to such clauses is that the general words are not to be given expansive meaning; they are confined to things of the same kind or nature as the particular matters mentioned (see, 18 Williston, Contracts §1968, at 209 [3d ed. 1978]).

We agree with the conclusion reached by the majority below that the events listed in the force majeure clause here are different in kind and nature from Kel Kim's inability to procure and maintain public liability insurance. The recited events pertain to a party's ability to conduct day-to-day commercial operations on the premises. While Kel Kim urges that the same may be said of a failure to procure and maintain insurance, such an event is materially different. The requirement that specified amounts of public liability insurance at all times be maintained goes not to frustrated expectations in day-to-day commercial operations on the premises — such as interruptions in the availability of labor, materials and utility services — but to the bargained-for protection of the landlord's unrelated economic interests where the tenant chooses to continue operating a public roller skating rink on the premises.

Post-Case Follow-Up

The *Kel Kim* court stated that impossibility did not apply because Kel Kim's inability to procure and maintain requisite coverage. The court decided that this situation could have been foreseen and guarded against when the parties negotiated and entered into the lease. The force majeure clause did not specifically include lessee's inability to procure and maintain insurance. In addition, Kel Kim's inability to procure insurance was not covered under the catch-all provision of "or other similar causes beyond the control of such party."

Kel Kim Corp. v. Central Markets, Inc.: Real Life Applications

1. A California manufacturer enters into a contract to sell 50 communication radios to a foreign country. A civil war breaks out in that country and the U.S. government applies sanctions on the foreign nation and seizes the radios under its sanctions program. The company negotiates the release of 20 radios intended for nonmilitary purposes with the U.S. government. The foreign nation lobbies the manufacturer to find other subsidiaries or suppliers who can lawfully provide the contracted radios. The manufacturer balks, concerned about violating the sanctions program, and points to contract language excusing performance due to government actions. The foreign nation argues that the clause does not apply since suppliers in other nations can lawfully provide the equipment and the manufacturer voluntarily negotiated with the government over the earlier radio shipments. Will the contract language excuse the manufacturer's duties? Consider *Harriscom Svenska v. Harris Corp.*, 3 F.3d 576 (2d Cir. 1993) in your response.

2. Print Central Inc. (PCI) leases five industrial copiers from Copy Corp. for three years. In year two of the contract, an unexpected hurricane hits the Northeast. Flooding severely damages the copiers, which are very expensive to repair or replace. PCI does not have flood insurance so it does not repair or replace the copiers and stops its monthly payments. Copy Corp. sues for breach of contract while PCI claims the excuse of impracticability. The commercial lease contained a "hell or high water" clause. Will PCI prevail on its excuse? Read and brief *Gen. Capital Corp. v. FPL Serv. Corp.*, 986 F. Supp. 2d 1029 (N.D. Iowa 2013) to determine the likely outcome.

3. A paint manufacturer agrees to provide 10,000 buckets of industrial paint to a commercial boat builder. State regulations change, banning the use of a particular chemical in the paint for environmental protection purposes. The manufacturer could use a substitute legal chemical, making it more expensive to produce the paint, but the manufacturer could still turn a small profit. The

parties' contract contained a force majeure clause that excused performance for any circumstances beyond a party's reasonable control. Will the manufacturer be excused from its contract obligation applying this clause under *Sherwin Alumina L.P. v. AluChem, Inc.*, 512 F. Supp. 2d 957 (S.D. Tex. 2007)?

What Does a Force Majeure Clause Look Like?

There are a wide range of force majeure clauses that are tailored to meet the parties' needs and expectations. Some clauses provide a detailed laundry list of excused events while others may generally excuse severe events outside of party control. Here is one example of a force majeure clause used in licensing digital information:

> Force Majeure. Neither party shall be liable in damages or have the right to terminate this Agreement for any delay or default in performing hereunder if such delay or default is caused by conditions beyond its control, including Acts of God, Government restrictions (including the denial or cancellation of any export or other necessary license), wars, insurrections, labor strikes, and/or any other cause beyond the reasonable control of the party whose performance is affected.

Liblicense Model License Agreement with Commentary (Version 5.0), http://liblicense.crl.edu/licensing-information/model-license/.

This clause specifies some events that justify being excused, but does not exclude others. It provides a catch-all provision that applies broadly to any cause beyond the reasonable control of the affected party. The clause applies to an event that either delays or prevents performance and excludes the right to seek damages or terminate the contract. The language appears to make excuse easier to invoke in the stated circumstances as long as the delayed or breaching party has not caused the unexpected event.

C. FRUSTRATION OF PURPOSE

Sometimes performance is possible, but will hold no value for party due to changed circumstances. A buyer may have the funds, but if the performance has become worthless, paying the price achieves no useful end. Frustration of purpose recognizes an excuse when, as a result of changed circumstances, the performance no longer has value to the party who will receive it. Because payment of money rarely is impracticable, buyers cannot resort to that doctrine. Frustration of purpose provides a potential excuse in appropriate cases.

As with impracticability, frustration is intended to excuse performance when circumstances change so drastically that the parties probably would not have required performance if they had considered the possibility. Where the events seem to be part of the normal business risk that parties are expected to bear, frustration will be rejected. Frustration, however, can be a little harder to confine than impracticability. Impracticability applies when performance becomes so difficult that this difficulty can be assessed. Frustration applies when performance becomes pointless or undesirable. Relating as it does to a party's attitude toward the performance, the excuse of frustration might be more easily manipulated, unless defined rather narrowly.

1. Establishing Frustration of Purpose

The party claiming the excuse must prove the following elements to establish frustration, which are nearly identical to those required to prove impracticability:

1. an event substantially frustrated a party's principal purpose for entering the contract;
2. nonoccurrence of that event was a basic assumption on which the contract was made;
3. the party was not at fault for the event; and
4. the party claiming the excuse does not bear the risk of loss by the terms of the contract or the surrounding circumstances.[4]

Impracticability focuses on extreme costs, loss, or difficulty in performing contract duties. But frustration of purpose considers whether receiving the other party's performance will provide little or no value to the party claiming frustration. So establishing that a party's principal purpose was substantially frustrated raises different issues than impracticability, despite the similarities in the elements of each doctrine.

2. Substantially Frustrates Principal Purpose

When entering into contracts, parties are bargaining for performances to meet their own objectives. If these reasons cease to apply, then the basis for contract duties becomes pointless. When changed circumstances make a performance pointless, the principal purpose has been substantially frustrated. For example, in the classic case of *Krell v. Henry*, 2 K.B. 740 (1903), a person rented a flat in London at a higher rate for one day because it overlooked the route of the royal coronation parade. When the coronation was postponed, renting the flat became pointless. The principal purpose (to see the coronation parade) was substantially (perhaps entirely) frustrated. As a result, the lessee's duty to pay the unpaid portion of the rental price was excused.

Only one party's purpose is pertinent here since each party will seek different self-interests under a contract. The lessor hardly cared that the coronation was that day as his purpose was to obtain money by leasing the flat. Of course, knowing the flat overlooked the coronation route affected the price charged for the flat that day. The occurrence of the coronation parade (or the nonoccurrence of its postponement) was a shared assumption or understanding. The purpose of the party seeking the excuse is the one that must be substantially frustrated, with both contracting parties having knowledge or understanding of this principal purpose of the agreement.

Allowing the buyer broad discretion to describe the purpose would expand frustration dramatically. A buyer often can frame a purpose that was substantially frustrated. For instance, suppose the buyer states that the purpose was to resell the goods at a profit. Any event that makes resale unprofitable would substantially frustrate that purpose. Similar to impracticability, frustration is not intended to allow parties to escape from every deal that turns out to be unfavorable. Without

[4] Restatement (Second) of Contracts §265.

some constraint on the buyer's ability to frame the purpose, the defense would be available in far too many cases.

The preamble of a contract may contain a brief discussion or recitation of the parties' main purposes for entering into a contract. In drafting this language, be aware that a court may later consider these provisions in assessing a claim for frustration of purpose. Other parol evidence, such as e-mails, meeting notes, witness testimony, and other documents, may help to identify the main purposes of a contract.

Case Preview

Mel Frank Tool & Supply v. Di-Chem Co.

In this case, Di-Chem leased a facility from Mel Frank to store chemicals. A subsequent city ordinance and fire department inspection prohibited Di-Chem from storing hazardous materials at the site without substantial renovations to the building. The lessor, Mel Frank, was unwilling to make these costly changes to the facility. Di-Chem notified the lessor that it would terminate the lease and vacated the premises, claiming the excuse of frustration of purpose.

As you read *Mel Frank Tool & Supply v. Di-Chem Co.*, look for the following:

1. What arguments did Di-Chem make to support its excuse of frustration of purpose?
2. Did the court find that Di-Chem met its burden of proof as to its claimed excuse?
3. According to the court, how might the parties have drafted their contract to avoid this dispute over frustration of purpose?

Mel Frank Tool & Supply v. Di-Chem Co.

580 N.W.2d 802 (Iowa 1998)

LAVORATO, J.

City authorities informed a lessee, a chemical distributor, that it could no longer use its leased premises to store its hazardous chemicals because of a recently enacted ordinance. The lessee vacated the premises, and the lessor sued for breach of the lease and for damages to the premises. The district court awarded the lessor judgment for unpaid rent and for damages to the premises. The lessee appeals. . . . We affirm.

I. FACTS

Di-Chem Company is a chemical distributor. In May 1994, Di-Chem began negotiating with Mel Frank Tool & Supply, Inc. to lease a storage and distribution facility in Council Bluffs, Iowa. Mel Frank's real estate agent handled the negotiations so there were no actual face-to-face negotiations between the parties. However, a day before the lease was executed, Mel Frank's owner, Dennis Frank, talked with Di-Chem representatives who were touring the premises. Frank asked them what Di-Chem was going to be selling and was told chemicals. The agent brought the lease to Frank for his signature.

The lease appears to be an Iowa State Bar Association form. [Citation omitted.] The lease was to start June 1, 1994 and end May 31, 1997. The lease limited Di-Chem's use of the premises to "storage and distribution."

Some of the chemicals Di-Chem distributes are considered "hazardous material." There was no testimony that Dennis Frank was aware of this at the time the lease was executed. A Di-Chem representative, who was present during the earlier-mentioned conversation with Dennis Frank, testified that hazardous materials did not come up in the conversation.

The lease contained several provisions that bear on the issues in this appeal. One requires Di-Chem to "make no unlawful use of the premises and . . . to comply with all . . . City Ordinances." . . .

On July 21, 1995, the city's fire chief and several other city authorities inspected the premises. Following the inspection, the city's fire marshal wrote Di-Chem, stating:

> At the time of the inspection the building was occupied as Hazardous Materials Storage. I have given you a copy of 1994 Uniform Fire Code, which the City has adopted, covering Hazardous Material Storage. As you can see the building does not comply with the Code requirements which creates Health and Life Safety Hazards. The Hazardous Materials must be removed within seven (7) days to eliminate the hazard.

The letter also informed Di-Chem of the following code deficiencies: complete fire sprinkler system, mechanical exhaust system, spill control, and drainage control. Both Frank and Di-Chem representatives testified they understood the letter to mean that if these deficiencies were eliminated, Di-Chem could continue to store hazardous material. There was testimony that the changes in the code occurred after Di-Chem took occupancy of the premises.

On August 2 Di-Chem informed Mel Frank by letter of the city's action and enclosed a copy of the city's July 25 letter to Di-Chem. In its August 2 letter Di-Chem informed Mel Frank of its intention to re-locate "as soon as possible to avoid civil and criminal proceedings at the hands of the city." Di-Chem also stated

> we believe the city has overreacted and probably has no authority to order us to remove our materials from the property. . . . Nevertheless, we are not willing to contest the city's position, and we feel compelled to remove our operation beyond the city limits.

Di-Chem also stated it intended to pay the rental for the month of August and vacate the premises by September 1.

Thereafter Dennis Frank and Di-Chem representatives met with city officials about what it would take to correct the various code deficiencies to allow Di-Chem to continue storing hazardous materials. Di-Chem representatives and Dennis Frank briefly considered bringing the building up to code. There was talk about the possibility of Di-Chem splitting the costs with Mel Frank, but Dennis Frank felt the cost was prohibitive.

On October 23 Di-Chem notified Mel Frank by letter of its intention to vacate the premises by the end of October. The letter in part stated: "The city's position that we cannot legally store *all of our inventory* at this site prior to extensive alteration of the building makes the structure useless to us as a chemical warehouse." [Emphasis added.] True to its word, Di-Chem vacated the premises.

. . .

IV. IMPOSSIBILITY OF PERFORMANCE

A. The law. The introduction to the Restatement (Second) of Contracts covers impossibility of performance but with a different title: impracticability of performance and frustration of purpose. *See* Restatement (Second) of Contracts ch. 11, at 309 (1981) [hereinafter Restatement]. According to the Restatement,

> Contract liability is strict liability. . . . The obligor is therefore liable in damages for breach of contract even if he is without fault and even if circumstances have made the contract more burdensome or less desirable than he had anticipated. . . . The obligor who does not wish to undertake so extensive an obligation may contract for a lesser one by using one of a variety of common clauses: . . . he may reserve a right to cancel the contract. . . . The extent of his obligation then depends on the application of the rules of interpretation. . . .

Id.

Even though the obligor has not restricted his or her obligation by agreement, a court may still grant relief: "An extraordinary circumstance may make performance so vitally different from what was reasonably to be expected as to alter the essential nature of that performance." *Id.* In these circumstances, "the court must determine whether justice requires a departure from the general rule that the obligor bear the risk that the contract may become more burdensome or less desirable." Restatement (Second) of Contracts ch. 11, at 310 (1981). Whether extraordinary circumstances exist justifying discharge is a question of law for the court. *Id.*

The Restatement recognizes three distinct grounds for the discharge of the obligor's contractual duty:

> First, the obligor may claim that some circumstance has made his own performance impracticable. . . . Second, the obligor may claim that some circumstance has so destroyed the value to him of the other party's performance as to frustrate his own purpose in making the contract. . . . Third, the obligor may claim that he will not receive the agreed exchange for the obligee's duty to render that agreed exchange, on the ground of either impracticability or frustration.

Id.

The rationale behind the doctrines of impracticability and frustration is whether the nonoccurrence of the circumstance was a basic assumption on which the contract was made. Restatement (Second) of Contracts ch. 11, at 310-311 (1981). The parties need not have been conscious of alternatives for them to have had a "basic assumption." Restatement (Second) of Contracts ch. 11, at 311 (1981). The Restatement gives an example: Where an artist contracts to paint a painting and dies, the artist's death is an "event the nonoccurrence of which was a basic assumption on which the contract was made, even though the parties never consciously addressed themselves to that possibility." *Id.*

. . .

B. Discharge by supervening frustration. For reasons that follow, we think the facts of this case fall within the parameters of section 265 of the Restatement. . . .

The rule deals with the problem that arises when a change in circumstances makes one party's performance virtually worthless to the other, frustrating the purpose in making the contract. *Id.* §265 cmt. a, at 335. The obligor's contractual obligation is discharged only if three conditions are met:

> First, the purpose that is frustrated must have been a principal purpose of that party in making the contract. It is not enough that he had in mind some specific object without which he would not have made the contract. The object must be so completely the basis of the contract that, as both parties understand, without it the transaction would make little sense. *Second, the frustration must be substantial. It is not enough that the transaction has become less profitable for the affected party or even that he will sustain a loss. The frustration must be so severe that it is not fairly to be regarded as within the risks that he assumed under the contract.* Third, the non-occurrence of the frustrating event must have been a basic assumption on which the contract was made. . . . The foreseeability of the event is . . . a factor in that determination, but the mere fact that the event was foreseeable does not compel the conclusion that its non-occurrence was not such a basic assumption.

Id.

Under this Restatement section, the following pertinent illustration appears:

> A leases a gasoline station to B. A change in traffic regulations so reduces B's business that he is unable to operate the station except at a substantial loss. B refuses to make further payments of rent. If B can still operate the station, even though at such a loss, his principal purpose of operating a gasoline station is not substantially frustrated. B's duty to pay rent is not discharged, and B is liable to A for breach of contract. The result would be the same if substantial loss were caused instead by a government regulation rationing gasoline or a termination of the franchise under which B obtained gasoline.

Id. §265 cmt. a, illus. 6, at 336.

Iowa case law is in accord with Restatement section 265. *See Conklin v. Silver*, 187 Iowa 819, 822-23, 174 N.W. 573, 574 (1919). The facts in *Conklin* parallel those in illustration 6 set out above.

In *Conklin*, the lease provided that the lessees were "to only use the premises for iron, metal, and rag business." *Id.* at 820, 174 N.W. at 573. The lease also prohibited the lessees from "engaging in or permitting any unlawful business on the premises, nor to permit the premises to be occupied for any business deemed extra hazardous on account of fire." *Id.*

About a month into the lease, the Iowa legislature passed a statute declaring as a nuisance the storage of rags "within the fire limits of any city, unless it be in a building of fireproof construction." *Id.* at 821, 174 N.W. at 573. The statute applied to the lessees because the premises were within the fire limits of the city and were not of fireproof construction. *Id.* For this reason, the lessees claimed the statute made its business unlawful, exposed them to criminal prosecution, and deprived them of any substantial or beneficial use of the property thereby releasing them from further obligation to pay rent. *Id.*

This court rejected the lessees' contention and affirmed a directed verdict in favor of the plaintiff-lessor for the unpaid rent. There was evidence that the lessee also dealt in junk metal. For this reason the court concluded:

> Altogether, we are satisfied that, while the operation of the statute mentioned served to narrow or restrict, to some extent, the scope of the business of the lessees, we think the evidence is insufficient to sustain a finding that it deprives them of the beneficial use of the leased property; and, as the defense is an affirmative one, the burden of establishing which is upon the party pleading it, the trial court did not err in refusing to submit it to the verdict of the jury.

Id. at 822, 174 N.W. at 574. The court continued:

> The right to buy, sell, store, and ship junk metals of all kinds, not only in the building but upon the entire lot, is not, in any sense, a mere incident of the rag business, and that a loss of the privilege of using the building for the handling of rags does not deprive the lessees of the beneficial enjoyment of the property for the other specified uses. It may possibly render the use less valuable or less profitable, but there is no rule or principle of law which makes that fact a matter of defense or of counterclaim in an action upon the lease.

187 Iowa at 822-23, 174 N.W. at 574.

The Restatement and *Conklin* represent the prevailing view:

> The parties to a lease may lawfully agree or stipulate that if by reason of a subsequent prohibitory or restrictive statute, ordinance, or administrative ruling, the tenant is prevented from legally using the premises for the purpose for which it was contemplated, the tenant may surrender or terminate the lease for which it was contemplated and be relieved from further liability for rent. In the absence of such a provision for termination, however, there is some uncertainty as to the effect of subsequent legal prohibition or restriction on the use of the premises. *It may generally be said that in the absence of any such stipulation, a valid police regulation which forbids the use of rented property for certain purposes, but leaves the tenant free to devote the property to other legal uses not forbidden or restricted by the terms of the lease, does not invalidate the lease or affect the rights and liabilities of the parties to the lease. And, even though the lease by its terms restricts the tenant's use of the premises to certain specified purposes, but not to a single purpose, the prevailing view is that the subsequent enactment of the legislation prohibiting the use of the premises for one, or less than all, of the several purposes specified does not invalidate the lease or justify the tenant in abandoning the property, even though the legislation may render its use less valuable. If there is a serviceable use for which the property is still available consistent with the limitations of the demise, the tenant is not in a position to assert that it is totally deprived of the benefit of the tenancy.*

49 Am. Jur. 2d *Landlord & Tenant* §531, at 442-43 (1995) (emphasis added).

Based on the foregoing authorities, we reach the following conclusions. A subsequent governmental regulation like a statute or ordinance may prohibit a tenant from legally using the premises for its originally intended purpose. In these circumstances, the tenant's purpose is substantially frustrated thereby relieving the tenant from any further obligation to pay rent. The tenant is not relieved from the obligation to pay rent if there is a serviceable use still available consistent with the use provision in the lease. The fact that the use is less valuable or less profitable or even unprofitable does not mean the tenant's use has been substantially frustrated.

C. The merits. It is clear from the pleadings and testimony that Di-Chem was asserting a defense of frustration of purpose. Di-Chem had the burden of persuasion to prove that defense. *See Conklin*, 187 Iowa at 822, 174 N.W. at 574. The district court's decision in favor of Mel Frank is a determination that Di-Chem did not carry its burden on this defense.

Di-Chem produced no evidence that *all* of its inventory of chemicals consisted of hazardous material. In fact, its own correspondence to Mel Frank indicates otherwise. For example, Di-Chem's October 23 letter to Mel Frank stated: "The city's position that we cannot legally store *all* of our inventory at this site prior to extensive alteration of the building makes the structure useless to us as a chemical warehouse." (Emphasis added.) A reasonable inference from this statement is that not all of Di-Chem's inventory consisted of hazardous material.

Testimony from one of Di-Chem's representatives corroborates this inference:

> Q. Were you involved at all in the discussions with the City of Council Bluffs relative to the various code deficiencies that existed at the building? A. My involvement was that the city had pointed out that there was some deficiencies with the building and asked us to remove *what* chemicals they found objective.

(Emphasis added.) Another Di-Chem representative testified that Di-Chem's product line included industrial chemicals and *food additives*. Presumably, food additives are not hazardous materials.

Given the posture of this appeal, Di-Chem has to establish as a matter of law that its principal purpose for leasing the facility—storing and distributing chemicals—was substantially frustrated by the city's actions. Di-Chem presented no evidence as to the nature of its inventory and what percentage of the inventory consisted of hazardous chemicals. The company also failed to show what its lost profits, if any, would be without the hazardous chemicals. Thus, there is no evidence from which the district court could have found the city's actions substantially frustrated Di-Chem's principal purpose of storing and distributing chemicals. Put another way, there is insufficient evidence that the city's action deprived Di-Chem of the beneficial enjoyment of the property for other uses, i.e., storing and distributing nonhazardous chemicals.

Simply put, Di-Chem failed to establish its affirmative defense. . . . We must therefore affirm the district court's decision as to this issue.

The *Mel Frank* court determined that frustration of purpose requires a showing that changed circumstances makes one party's performance virtually worthless to the other party, and that particular purpose was encompassed in the making of the agreement. In this case, despite subsequent governmental regulation, Di-Chem was not relieved from its obligation to pay rent since there was still a serviceable use of the property consistent with allowed uses under the lease. The fact that Di-Chem's use was less valuable or less profitable (or even unprofitable) did not mean its use had been substantially frustrated. Di-Chem's non-hazardous chemicals could still be legally stored on the premises. Thus, Di-Chem failed to provide sufficient evidence of substantial frustration.

Mel Frank Tool & Supply v. Di-Chem Co.: Real Life Applications

1. DronePro Inc. enters into a two-year lease for a lot to sell new personal drones to consumers at a time when regulations on these devices are still being formulated. The company stocks up on personal drones hoping to sell as many as possible before the regulations are finalized. After entering into the lease and selling drones for a month, new government regulations are enacted that severely limit consumer use of drones and require special licensing for consumer purchasers. The following month, DronePro's sales drop 90 percent. DronePro tries to avoid its lease based on frustration of purpose. The lease prohibits other uses and subletting of the property, but the lessor is willing to waive these provisions. Will DronePro prevail on frustration of purpose? Research and summarize *Lloyd v. Murphy*, 25 Cal. 2d 48 (1944) for a likely outcome.

2. Madison Reynolds agrees to a job reassignment in a new city. Her employer agrees to pay her rent for the first year as a company moving benefit. She rents a townhome and decides to buy it, with a closing date at the end of the one-year lease from Homebuilder Company. Eleven months later, she loses her job and seeks to renew the lease for three months in hopes of finding another job. Homebuilder agrees to the lease and closing date extension. Still unemployed, but hoping to stay put, Madison offers to buy the home if Homebuilder will finance her purchase. Homebuilder declines and the sale never takes place. Madison moves out and Homebuilder sues for breach. Madison claims frustration of purpose due to her unexpected unemployment. Review *Hubbell Homes, L.C. v. Key*, 2010 Iowa App. LEXIS 480 (2010), to see if Madison will prevail.

3. A father agrees to pay the annual tuition to a private elementary school to hold a seat for his child in the next academic year. The child is currently attending the school which is now on summer break. Before school restarts in the fall, the parents divorce and the mother is granted primary custody. She refuses to allow

the child to attend the school. The father seeks to be excused from his obligation to pay the tuition due to frustration of purpose. Will he succeed in raising this excuse? Access the decision in *Brenner v. Little Red School House, Ltd.*, 47 N.C. App. 19 (1980) to determine the result.

EXHIBIT 13.1 Case Comparison Chart

Issues Addressed	Impossibility	Impracticability	Frustration	Force Majeure	Other Exclusions
Clark		✔			
Kel Kim	✔			✔	
Mel Frank	✔	✔	✔		
Phoenix	✔				✔
Sassower		✔			

D. UNTANGLING CLAIMS OF EXCUSE

The occurrence of an event that excuses performance does not automatically produce an excuse. Rather, parties must invoke the excuse by notice to the others that they will no longer perform. Prior performance—and prior breaches—are unaffected by the excuse. But some performance—for example, a payment for a performance that has been excused—may require restitution. In addition, impracticability and frustration can be partial or temporary, excusing some but not all of a party's duties under a contract. These issues are nearly identical whether the excuse is impracticability or frustration so they are discussed together in this section.

1. Procedure for Claiming Excuse

A party claiming impracticability or frustration must seasonably notify its affected contract partners that performance will not be forthcoming as expected. The remaining consequences of the excuse vary with the degree to which the excuse may be temporary or partial, rather than total and permanent. Notice should estimate the amount of performance a contract partner may expect, if any, and the degree of delay it should expect. Under the UCC, this notice must be in writing.[5] But, in general, it is a good practice to put all notices in writing.

Prompt notice is critical. It allows the other party to make substitute arrangements. Good faith probably would require prompt notice even if the rules on excuse did not expressly include the requirement. Notice also may police borderline uses of excuse. Failure to give notice promptly once the problem arises suggests

[5] UCC §2-615(c).

the excuse is an afterthought, not a real reason for the failure to perform. The UCC does not specify the effect of failure to give notice; without notice, the excuse may be unavailable. Under the CISG, failure to give prompt notice does not defeat the excuse, but will justify the other party's recovery of any damages caused by delay in providing notice.[6]

Excuse does not alter any performance or nonperformance that preceded it. Any performance already provided must be compensated according to the terms of the contract. If a party already had breached, damages owed for that breach remain collectible. Impracticability and frustration prevent subsequent nonperformance or some portion of it from constituting a breach.

Once notified of prospective nonperformance, the remaining remedies will vary depending on the amount of performance excused. Three possibilities emerge:

1. the excuse may affect the entire remaining performance;
2. the excuse may affect a material portion of the remaining performance; or
3. the excuse may affect an immaterial or minor portion of the remaining performance.

When excuse affects the entire remaining performance, the other party's right to terminate the agreement is clear — and nearly inevitable. No additional performance will be forthcoming, so little reason exists to keep the contract in force. If a reason does exist, such as continuing duties of confidentiality or a noncompetition clause, the party need not elect to terminate the agreement. But no future performance will be provided and no future payment will be due.

When excuse affects a material portion of the performance,[7] the party notified of the excuse must elect whether to keep the contract in force or to terminate it. She may reject the partial performance proffered by the excused party and make substitute arrangements. Or she may accept the proffered partial performance, in effect modifying the contract to delete any obligation to provide the excused portion of the performance and any obligation to pay for it. In effect, this terminates the contract as to the excused performance, but keeps the contract in place for any performance due despite the excuse. In either event, the party must notify the excused party of its election. Under the UCC, notice must be made in writing.[8] It may be difficult for the party to predict whether the portion of the performance excused will be deemed material. Thus, some parties may attempt to terminate the contract when they have no justification for that election.

When excuse affects an immaterial or minor portion of the agreement, the right to terminate the contract is limited to the excused performance; it will not be provided and need not be paid for by the other party. But no right to terminate exists concerning the remaining portion of the performance under the contract. Naturally, the other party may make substitute arrangements for any amounts the

---

[6]CISG art. 79(4).
[7]*See, e.g.*, Restatement (Second) of Contracts §241; UCC §2-611.
[8]UCC §2-616(1).

excused party will not provide—even if the contract ordinarily would require it to deal exclusively with the excused party.

2. Partial Excuse

Impracticability or frustration may totally and permanently excuse performance. The postponement of the coronation parade may make the entire lease period useless to the tenant. The destruction of a building makes it impossible to lease it for a performance—at least until rebuilt, which may require more time than the lease would have covered. Once notified of the excuse, the other party may need to make substitute arrangements. These substitute arrangements will be at the injured party's expense. Excuse means that the nonperformance is not breach, so the injured party has no claim to damages to cover the losses caused by nonperformance.

When impracticability precludes a party from satisfying some, but not all, of its contract obligations, it must allocate the performance available among the parties to whom it owes performance.[9] When notifying its contract partners about the impracticability, it should include an estimate of the performance each can expect to receive. That estimate will be critical to each, as they consider whether to terminate the contract or to accept the proffered amount as a modification.

In determining how much each contract partner may receive, the excused party may consider both its contract commitments and any regular customers who, without firm commitments, rely on the supplier. In addition, if the excused party needs some of the goods for its own purposes, it may include those needs in the allocation. Allocation may be calculated using methods that are fair and reasonable under the circumstances.[10]

While the excused party must offer partial performance to its contract partners, the partners may not be required to accept it. Nonperformance, while not breach, may still justify the other parties in terminating the contract, at least if the nonperformance is material.

UCC §2-615(b)—A Hypothetical Example of Allocation

CC, a chemical company, produces ammonia. It uses some ammonia to produce fertilizer; the rest it sells to other customers. Some of those customers have long-term requirements contracts. Others place spot orders as they need ammonia.

If a fire reduced production at one of CC's production facilities by half, impracticability might apply. CC would need to notify its customers that it would be unable to provide their full needs. In allocating its available ammonia, CC may allocate some ammonia to its own needs, some ammonia to its regular customers, and some ammonia to its customers making spot orders. It could choose to prefer its contractual commitments by allocating less or even none to customers who have no binding right to receive it. It could decide to waive its right to retain some ammonia for its own uses. It could and probably must reject orders from new customers while the needs of existing customers go unsatisfied.

It is not required that each customer receive half the amount of ammonia it requests. But a pro rata allocation giving each customer the same proportion as related to its needs would likely satisfy the requirement of a fair and reasonable allocation.

[9] *Id.* §2-615(b).
[10] *Id.*

3. Temporary Excuse

Impracticability or frustration may involve a delay in performance rather than an inability to perform. The excuse may be temporary. For example, an actor who contracts an autoimmune syndrome may be unable to perform a role on schedule. But in a matter of weeks (or months or years), he will recover to the point that he can perform the contract. Damage to a factory or interruptions in the supply of raw materials may prevent timely performance, but performance may eventually be feasible when (or perhaps if) conditions return to normal. A nightclub may not need the entertainers it hired for the period it is under water following a hurricane and flood, but may need them for later dates included in the same contract.

The other party may prefer not to wait. With the rest of the cast and crew ready to shoot on schedule, the production company may decide not to await the actor's availability. A customer needing supplies immediately may prefer to find a substitute supplier rather than await the original provider's ability to resume deliveries. Entertainers denied the employment promised for one period may want to make different plans for other periods covered by the contact as well as the period covered by the excuse.

If the delay is material, the other party may treat the nonperformance as a justification for terminating the contract. It does not matter that the nonperformance is excused. Nonetheless, material nonperformance justifies termination of the contract. Thus, the disappointed party may find another actor, another supplier, or another gig. It must bear any costs it incurs as a result of the termination since impracticability or frustration excuses the party from any obligation to pay damages. As with any termination, materiality may present a closer issue than the examples here. For instance, suppose a contractor who promised to renovate a kitchen must delay performance for reasons that qualify for impracticability. A one-week delay might not justify termination, but a one-year delay probably would be material. Somewhere in the middle, a very close case would arise as to the proper course to follow.

If the other party is willing to accept the delay, the excused party generally must perform when she is able to do so. Thus, if the production company was willing to wait for the actor to recover, the duty to perform the role might remain once the disability receded. Unless performance after recovery would be "materially more burdensome than had there been no impracticability or frustration," the duty remains in effect after recovery.[11] Because the role seems likely to be equally burdensome no matter when the filming occurs, the actor may have no justification for refusing to perform the role. However, if the role required stunts that have become more difficult as a result of the intervening disability, perhaps the burden has increased materially.

---

[11] Restatement (Second) of Contracts §269.

4. Restitution Following Excuse

Impracticability or frustration may excuse performance after one or more parties have partially performed. Where a contract is divisible, partial performance by one party may be earned in exchange for partial performance by the other. In some cases, no performance has been received in exchange for the performance already provided. Untangling partial performance typically involves restitution for unjust enrichment.

Having not performed, the excused party would be unjustly enriched by retaining any compensation already received under the contract. The party that provided that performance was neither a donee nor a volunteer, but someone acting under what was a legitimate contract. Performance of the return duty would entitle the recipient to keep the performance received, but the return duty has been excused. The excuse precludes a judgment of damages for breach, but does not preclude an action for unjust enrichment.

Consider a familiar scenario. Owner leases business premises to a tenant. The premises are destroyed. If the tenant had occupied the premises for a period, the contract would be divisible: until the premises were destroyed, rent would be due. After the premises were destroyed, the landlord's failure to provide the premises is excused. Any rent already paid for that period would unjustly enrich the landlord. It must be refunded. The same would be true for goods a seller no longer needed to deliver following impracticability. Any payment for those goods would need to be refunded to the buyer; retaining it without providing the goods would unjustly enrich the seller.

Frustration poses a similar issue as to partial performance by the excused party, for which it has not received the promised exchange. By pleading frustration, the party indicates that it does not want to receive the promised exchange; that performance has lost its value to the excused party. But the other party may remain willing to provide it — and unwilling to refund any performance the excused party has rendered prior to the excuse. The issue remains one of unjust enrichment: is the excused party entitled to recover benefits bestowed on the other party because retaining them would unjustly enrich the other party?

Courts analyzing this issue have not been entirely consistent. For example, those renting flats along the coronation route were excused from any subsequent payments of rent on the leases once frustration had occurred. The amount already paid was not refunded — even in cases where the entire rent was paid in advance.

The other party's right to retain partial performance is problematic. Applying unjust enrichment principles, the excused party usually can identify a benefit it provided to the other party. The benefit was not a gift nor was the excused party a volunteer. The benefit was bestowed under what seemed to be a valid and enforceable contract. Excuse seems to undermine any claim that the contract entitles the other party to retain the performance. It was not unjust to receive the money, but it is unjust to retain it. An excused party certainly could not keep the other party's performance and refuse to pay for it, regardless of whether an excuse applies or not.

Chapter Summary

- Impossibility of performance indicates that changed circumstances have made it literally impossible for party to perform its contract duties, including death or disability for personal services or the destruction of goods or other things required for performance.
- Impracticability applies to situations where performance has become so difficult that a party should not be expected to perform any further. These difficulties could include extreme loss, injury, or costs outside of the parties' reasonable expectations.
- Frustration of purpose deals with circumstances that make the contract pointless, destroying a party's reason for entering into the contract in the first place.
- Excuses may apply unless expressly excluded by contract terms. Parties may include a force majeure clause to excuse nonperformance based on unusual events, such as drought, earthquake, embargo, war, and other occurrences, outside of the parties' control.
- The application of excuse may be precluded due to a party's fault or bad faith in causing an event, or if a party bears the risk of loss by contract terms or surrounding circumstances.
- Impracticability and frustration may permit partial or temporary excuse, requiring some performance even though the rest is excused—subject to the other party's ability to terminate the contract for material nonperformance.
- Following excuse, unjust enrichment permits recovery of any benefit provided to the other party before the event permitting excuse.

Applying the Rules

Argon Enterprises, a U.S. cellphone manufacturer, enters into a contract with Veriocast, a cellphone service provider, to provide one million of its new smart phones at $200 US per phone in five separate deliveries. Veriocast agrees to pay this higher price for Argon's phones because they are popular consumer items and because the parties are aware that the rare earth minerals needed for Argon's phones are in high demand and are mined in war-torn areas of the world, including the country of Zendayan. Payment for the phones is 50 percent in advance of each shipment and the remainder 30 days after the date of actual delivery. Veriocast would be Argon's third largest customer, buying 20 percent of its cellphone production. Veriocast carries the risk of loss once Argon provides the goods to the shipper.

Argon makes its first delivery of 100,000 phones on time on November 1. The second shipment, scheduled for November 10, is placed on a cargo jet that crashes in bad weather, destroying all of the phones. Veriocast does not pay the balance on the phones in the second delivery.

On November 12, the U.S. government bans all imports from Zedayan, which has been declared a terrorist state. Argon imports 70 percent of its rare earth minerals from Zedayan. In light of this development, Veriocast withholds the outstanding balance on the November 1 delivery until Argon promises to put its upcoming deliveries ahead of its other customers' orders. Argon scrambles for other suppliers of these minerals and finds that because of the U.S. government ban. These resources will now cost 20 times more than usual, meaning that Argon will suffer severe losses under existing contracts. There is no force majeure clause in the agreement.

1. Identify and apply any excuses that are relevant under this fact pattern to Argon.

2. Identify and apply any excuses that are relevant under this fact pattern to Veriocast.

3. What obligations do the parties owe to each other regarding any claimed excuses?

4. Does the absence of a force majeure clause impact the claimed excuses in this fact pattern?

5. What remedies may the parties seek under this hypothetical?

Contract Law in Practice

1. Consider the Argon-Veriocast hypothetical above. You are the attorney for Argon. Review a wide range of force majeure clauses in online resources and form books. Draft a force majeure clause that would have proved useful for your client when it negotiated its contract with Veriocast.

2. Revisit the *Clark* case excerpted above (p. 588). In that dispute, the court determined that the grain farmer could not use the excuse of impracticability. Examine the facts and determine how you might have rewritten the contract to better protect Clark. Create mock law firms and draft your clauses. Exchange them with another class law firm to see how each group handled these issues. Now consider whether, as counsel for the Cooperative, you would have agreed to the term. What changes might you demand? Send the clause back to the drafting firm with your comments.

3. Government actions may impact private and government contract obligations. Everything from changes in laws to new government sanctions can impact party duties, costs, and risk under a contract. Review recent news articles about government actions that have impacted private or government contracts. Summarize that article with links to the article and other supporting resources and post your materials to a class blog for discussion.

4. In times of high demand and short supply, costs can skyrocket for parties under their contracts. During the gas shortages of the 1970s, oil companies were faced with allocating supplies among their gas station dealers across the nation. Aware of uncertainty in the oil markets, Atlantic Richfield included contract language to deal with allocations during unexpected shortages. A number of dealers questioned the fairness of the contract allocations under UCC §2-615(b). Review the case of *Terry v. Atlantic Richfield Co.*, 72 Cal. App. 3d 962 (Cal. App. 3d Dist. 1977). Do you agree with the court's determination about frustration of purpose and the fairness of the allocation methods spelled out in these contracts for long-term dealers? For new dealers? Draft a memo summarizing the court's decision and your views on this case.

5. Visit one of your favorite online news, shopping, or entertainment websites. Review its terms of use to locate clauses that specifically deal with possible excuses to performance. List those excuses and cite to the specific contract provisions. Further, identify if there is a force majeure clause in its terms of use. What contingencies are spelled out to protect the website from interruptions in its services and other contract obligations? Create a brief slide presentation on this website's terms of use and compare it to others presented in class.

14

Third-Party Rights and Duties

Typically, we think about contract as an agreement between two parties exchanging promises or performances. But some agreements may create rights and duties for others who were not parties to the original contract. In certain instances, parties enter into a contract that establishes rights for third parties at the time of contract formation. These third parties can later enforce these rights as if they were a signatory to the original contract. In other cases, a party to a contract may transfer its rights or duties to another party after the contract has been made. A party may give his rights to payment to another person or seek to substitute that person to perform his duties. Whether third parties possess these rights and duties and the limits on their exercise can be the subject of conflict between third parties and the original parties to the contract. In this chapter, we will explore the main contract doctrines relating to third parties. Knowing these basic rules is essential to unraveling more complex contractual relationships involving multiple parties.

A. INTRODUCTION TO THIRD-PARTY RIGHTS

This chapter addresses three ways that third parties may enter a transaction. First, a contract may specify that some or all of the consideration one party gives will be provided to another person or entity, not a party to the contract, called a **third-party beneficiary**. If the promisor fails to perform, questions arise concerning who

Key Concepts

- Intended and incidental third-party beneficiaries
- Assignment of rights
- Delegation of duties
- Novation

may seek to enforce the contract. The promisee can sue the promisor to enforce the contract. But if the promisee does not take action, a third party might be permitted to step into its shoes to enforce the promises independently against the promisor. A court must determine whether or not the promisee intended to give the third party the right to enforce the contract independently.

Second, one party may make an **assignment** of rights under the contract, voluntarily transferring any benefits under the contract to another party. After two parties enter a contract, one of them may decide that, instead of receiving the other person's performance directly, she would like to give or to sell that performance to a third party. For example, a law student might assign her right to live in an apartment to another person, a vacationer, over summer break, if this action is permitted under the terms of the lease. Like a third-party contract beneficiary, that third party has no contract with the property owner who promised to provide a habitable apartment and other benefits under the original lease. The law student is the **assignor** who gives rights to the subletting party who receives rights as the **assignee.**

The assignee's rights may arise without the consent of the **obligor**, the person with an obligation to perform; the property owner in the apartment lease example. The obligor (property owner) owes duties to the law student who is the **obligee**, the party who is entitled to receive the obligor's performance of duties under the original lease. Under the assignment, the assignor (law student) is agreeing that the obligor (property owner) should perform for the assignee (vacationer) instead of the assignor. If the assignment is valid, the assignee is entitled to sue to collect the performance promised under the contract.

The assignor may notify the obligor about the assignment, rather than asking him to agree to the change, depending upon the terms of the lease. For example, the property owner may undertake a criminal background check on all prospective tenants to ensure they do not pose a security risk to other tenants. The assignor might transfer her rights to live in the apartment to an assignee who might pose a safety risk to the other tenants. As a result, some rules are necessary to protect the obligor from assignments that may prove disadvantageous to the obligor's interests.

Third, one party to a contract may designate someone else to perform some or all of her contract duties, called a **delegation**. As to the duty to pay rent, the law student is the obligor who is required to carry out her duties, the payment of the rent, for the benefit of the obligee, the property owner, under the terms of the lease. If she delegates her lease to another person, she is delegating her obligation to pay the rent to the **delegated party** or sublessor. Again, rules limit delegation to protect the obligee from inappropriate delegations.

It is important to note that although an assignment and a delegation are two separate legal concepts, courts sometimes collectively refer to them as an assignment. So in reviewing court cases, be mindful that a court may use the term "assignment" when it is collectively referring to the assignment of rights and the delegation of duties. But there are key distinctions between these concepts and the cases in this chapter will further explore the parameters of these doctrines.

B. THIRD-PARTY BENEFICIARIES

Any number of contracts include benefits delivered to someone other than the party negotiating (and paying) for the benefit. Parties to a contract need not negotiate for benefits they will receive. Sometimes they bargain for a performance that will be delivered to or, at least, benefit another. For example, you may have an online retailer send a $50 gift e-card to a friend by e-mail. When you make the purchase, the retailer includes terms and conditions about when and where the gift e-card can be used. At the time of purchase, you are entering into this agreement to benefit a third party. If the retailer wrongly refuses to honor the gift e-card later, your friend or you may seek to enforce its terms. See Exhibit 14.1.

EXHIBIT 14.1 Third-Party Beneficiaries Gift—Cards

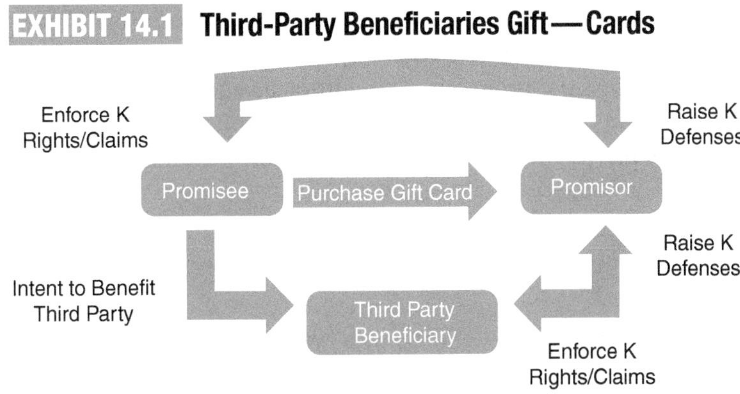

In these situations, questions arise concerning who may seek to enforce the promise. The party who negotiated and paid for the benefit (the promisee) may sue the other party (the promisor) for breach. Sometimes, however, the promisee does not sue on the contract (or does not do so as quickly as the beneficiary would like). She may even rescind, waive, or modify the contract. In these situations, the beneficiary may want to enforce the contract in her own name. The beneficiary, however, was not a party to the contract. The promisor made its promise to the promisee, not the beneficiary. The promisee, not the beneficiary, gave consideration for the promise. The beneficiary's right to sue requires some further justification.

1. Development of Third-Party Beneficiary Doctrine

Traditionally, courts only recognized the rights and duties of the parties who entered into a contract, known as **privity**. Unless parties were in privity of contract, others possessed no rights or duties under these agreements. In part, this approach recognized that unless there had been an exchange of consideration between the parties, there was no contract. As in the gift e-card example, the friend who receives it has neither paid nor promised anything in return. It is merely a gift without any contract rights or duties attaching to it.

But over time, this approach became too restrictive on the parties' freedom of contract and on the growing complexity of contractual relationships. Through case law, courts began to move beyond strict privity requirements and recognized two categories of third-party beneficiaries: creditor beneficiaries and donee beneficiaries. **Creditor beneficiaries** are parties to whom a promisee owes money and who want the promisor's performance or payment to satisfy that debt in whole or in part. In the famous case of *Lawrence v. Fox*, 20 N.Y. 268 (1859), Fox borrowed $300 from Holly and promised to repay the loan to Lawrence, to whom Holly already owed that same amount. When Fox did not pay Lawrence, the court recognized Lawrence's right to sue Fox to collect. The promisee, Holly, had intended that the promisor, Fox, repay the loan to benefit Lawrence, creating a right for him to enforce the deal.

The second category involved **donee beneficiaries**, or those whom a promisee intended to receive a gift under an agreement with a promisor. If the promisee intends to bestow a gift on a third party as part of that bargain, the beneficiary may bring an action against the promisor if the gift or its equivalent is not provided. In *Seaver v. Ransom*, we see the evolution of the recognition of donee beneficiaries, despite the lack of privity or consideration between the promisor and the third party.

Case Preview

Seaver v. Ransom

In *Seaver v. Ransom*, a wife was near death as her will was being drawn up. The will did not contain a gift of her home or its equivalent to a favorite niece. But her husband, a judge, promised to rectify that oversight in his will if she agreed to sign the will that had already been prepared, giving him a life estate in the property. When the judge died, it turned out that he had failed to provide for the niece, and she sought to recover as a donee beneficiary.

As you read *Seaver v. Ransom*, look for the following:

1. Did the Bemans agreement create a trust for the benefit of Mrs. Beman's niece?
2. Did the familial relationship impact the court's view of the applicability of third-party beneficiaries?
3. According to the court, what reasons supported the development and application of the third-party beneficiary doctrine?

Seaver v. Ransom

224 N.Y. 233 (1918)

POUND, J.

Judge Beman and his wife were advanced in years. Mrs. Beman was about to die. She had a small estate consisting of a house and lot in Malone and little else. Judge

Beman drew his wife's will according to her instructions. It gave $1,000 to plaintiff, $500 to one sister, plaintiff's mother, and $100 each to another sister and her son, the use of the house to her husband for life, remainder to the American Society for the Prevention of Cruelty to Animals. She named her husband as residuary legatee and executor. Plaintiff was her niece, thirty-four years old, in ill health, sometimes a member of the Beman household. When the will was read to Mrs. Beman she said that it was not as she wanted it; she wanted to leave the house to plaintiff. She had no other objection to the will, but her strength was waning and although the judge offered to write another will for her, she said she was afraid she would not hold out long enough to enable her to sign it. So the judge said if she would sign the will he would leave plaintiff enough in his will to make up the difference. He avouched the promise by his uplifted hand with all solemnity and his wife then executed the will. When he came to die it was found that his will made no provision for the plaintiff.

This action was brought and plaintiff recovered judgment in the trial court on the theory that Beman had obtained property from his wife and induced her to execute the will in the form prepared by him by his promise to give plaintiff $6,000, the value of the house, and that thereby equity impressed his property with a trust in favor of plaintiff. Where a legatee promises the testator that he will use property given him by the will for a particular purpose, a trust arises. (*O'Hara v. Dudley*, 95 N.Y. 403; *Trustees of Amherst College v. Ritch*, 151 N.Y. 282; *Ahrens v. Jones*, 169 N.Y. 555.) Beman received nothing under his wife's will but the use of the house in Malone for life. Equity compels the application of property thus obtained to the purpose of the testator, but equity cannot so impress a trust except on property obtained by the promise. Beman was bound by his promise, but no property was bound by it; no trust in plaintiff's favor can be spelled out.

An action on the contract for damages or to make the executors trustees for performance stands on different ground. (*Farmers Loan & Trust Co. v. Mortimer*, 219 N.Y. 290, 294, 295.) The Appellate Division properly passed to the consideration of the question whether the judgment could stand upon the promise made to the wife, upon a valid consideration, for the sole benefit of plaintiff. The judgment of the trial court was affirmed by a return to the general doctrine laid down in the great case of *Lawrence v. Fox* (20 N.Y. 268) which has since been limited as herein indicated.

Contracts for the benefit of third persons have been the prolific source of judicial and academic discussion. (Williston, Contracts for the Benefit of a Third Person, 15 Harvard Law Review, 767; Corbin, Contracts for the Benefit of Third Persons, 27 Yale Law Review, 1008.) The general rule, both in law and equity (*Phalen v. U.S. Trust Co.*, 186 N.Y. 178, 186), was that privity between a plaintiff and a defendant is necessary to the maintenance of an action on the contract. The consideration must be furnished by the party to whom the promise was made. The contract cannot be enforced against the third party and, therefore, it cannot be enforced by him. On the other hand, the right of the beneficiary to sue on a contract made expressly for his benefit has been fully recognized in many American jurisdictions, either by judicial decision or by legislation, and is said to be "the prevailing rule in this country." (*Hendrick v. Lindsay*, 93 U.S. 143; *Lehow v. Simonton*, 3 Col. 346.) It has been said that "the establishment of this doctrine has been gradual, and is a victory of practical utility over theory, of equity over technical subtlety." (Brantly on Contracts [2d ed.], p. 253.) The reasons for this view are that it is just and practical to permit the person for whose benefit the contract is made to enforce it against one whose duty it is to pay. Other jurisdictions still adhere to the present English rule (7 Halsbury's Laws of England, 342, 343; Jenks' Digest of English Civil Law, §229) that a contract cannot be enforced by or against a person who is not a party. (*Exchange Bank v. Rice,* 107 Mass. 37; but see, also, *Forbes v. Thorpe,* 209 Mass. 570; *Gardner v. Denison,* 217 Mass. 492.) In New York the right of the beneficiary to sue on contracts made for his benefit is not clearly or simply defined. It is at present confined, *first,* to cases where there is a pecuniary obligation running from the promisee to the beneficiary; "a legal right founded upon some obligation of the promisee in the third party to adopt and claim the promise as made for his benefit." [Citations omitted.] *Secondly,* to cases where the contract is made for the benefit of the wife [citations omitted], affianced wife [citation omitted], or child [citations omitted] of a party to the contract. . . . The natural and moral duty of the husband or parent to provide for the future of wife or child sustains the action on the contract made for their benefit. "This is the farthest the cases in this state have gone," says Cullen, J., in the marriage settlement case of *Borland v. Welch* (162 N.Y. 104, 110).

The right of the third party is also upheld in, *thirdly,* the public contract cases [citations omitted] where the municipality seeks to protect its inhabitants by covenants for their benefit and, *fourthly,* the cases where, at the request of a party to the contract, the promise runs directly to the beneficiary although he does not furnish the consideration. [Citations omitted.] It may be safely said that a general rule sustaining recovery at the suit of the third party would include but few classes of cases not included in these groups, either categorically or in principle.

The desire of the childless aunt to make provision for a beloved and favorite niece differs imperceptibly in law or in equity from the moral duty of the parent to make testamentary provision for a child. The contract was made for the plaintiff's benefit. She alone is substantially damaged by its breach. The representatives of the wife's estate have no interest in enforcing it specifically. It is said in *Buchanan v. Tilden* that the common law imposes moral and legal obligations upon the husband and the parent not measured by the necessaries of life. It was, however, the love and affection or the moral sense of the husband and the parent that imposed such obligations in the cases cited rather than any common-law duty of husband and parent to wife and child. If plaintiff had been a child of Mrs. Beman, legal obligation would have required no testamentary provision for her, yet the child could have enforced a covenant in her favor identical with the covenant of Judge Beman in this case. [Citation omitted.] The constraining power of conscience is not regulated by the degree of relationship alone. The dependent or faithful niece may have a stronger claim than the affluent or unworthy son. No sensible theory of moral obligation denies arbitrarily to the former what would be conceded to the latter. . . .

Kellogg, P.J., writing for the court below well said: "The doctrine of *Lawrence v. Fox* is progressive, not retrograde. The course of the late decisions is to enlarge, not to limit the effect of that case." The court in that leading case attempted to adopt the general doctrine that any third person, for whose direct benefit a contract was intended, could sue on it. . . . "In every case in which an action has been sustained," says Allen, J., "there has been a debt or duty owing by the promisee to the party claiming to sue upon the promise." (69 N.Y. 285.) As late as *Townsend v. Rackham*

(143 N.Y. 516, 523) we find Peckham, J., saying that "to maintain the action by the third person there must be this liability to him on the part of the promisee." . . .

In *Wright v. Glen Telephone Co.* (48 Misc. Rep. 192, 195) the learned presiding justice who wrote the opinion in this case said, at Trial Term: "The right of a third person to recover upon a contract made by other parties for his benefit must rest upon the peculiar circumstances of each case rather than upon the law of some other case." "The case at bar is decided upon its peculiar facts." (Edward T. Bartlett, J., in *Buchanan v. Tilden.*) But, on principle, a sound conclusion may be reached. If Mrs. Beman had left her husband the house on condition that he pay the plaintiff $6,000 and he had accepted the devise, he would have become personally liable to pay the legacy and plaintiff could have recovered in an action at law against him, whatever the value of the house. (*Gridley v. Gridley,* 24 N.Y. 130; *Brown v. Knapp,* 79 N.Y. 136, 143; *Dinan v. Coneys,* 143 N.Y. 544, 547; *Blackmore v. White,* [1899] 1 Q.B. 293, 304.) That would be because the testatrix had in substance bequeathed the promise to plaintiff and not because close relationship or moral obligation sustained the contract. The distinction between an implied promise to a testator for the benefit of a third party to pay a legacy and an unqualified promise on a valuable consideration to make provision for the third party by will is discernible but not obvious. The tendency of American authority is to sustain the gift in all such cases and to permit the donee-beneficiary to recover on the contract. (*Matter of Edmundson's Estate,* [1918, Pa.] 103 Atl. Rep. 277.) The equities are with the plaintiff and they may be enforced in this action, whether it be regarded as an action for damages or an action for specific performance to convert the defendants into trustees for plaintiff's benefit under the agreement.

The judgment should be affirmed, with costs.

Post-Case Follow-Up

The *Seaver* court considered the agreement between the judge and his dying wife to sign the will before her imminent death if a legacy of a home, after the judge's life estate, was left to her favorite niece. The court did not have rely upon a close family relationship or moral obligation to uphold the contract in the niece's favor. The court considered earlier precedent, including the seminal case of *Lawrence v. Fox* on creditor beneficiaries. The court held that the right of a third person to recover on a contract made by other parties for his benefit is based upon a review of the peculiar circumstances of each case. Based upon the facts of this case and prior case law, the *Seaver* court followed most American case authority in sustaining the gift and permitting the donee beneficiary to recover under the contract.

Seaver v. Ransom: Real Life Applications

1. A landowner provides an easement to a county for underground power lines. Subsequently, the landowner wants to develop some of his property, including the easement area. The owner contracts with a construction company to raise

the grade of the property. The contract includes language that the contractor must carry out its grading work in a manner that does not harm the power lines nor infringe the landowner's easement to the county. During the project, the county claims that the construction company damages the power lines and brings an action as a third-party beneficiary of the agreement between the landowner and the contractor. Review *Greenburgh v. J.F. Shea Co.*, 48 N.Y.S.2d 69 (N.Y. Sup. Ct. 1944), for the likely outcome on this issue.

2. A couple enters into an prenuptial agreement in which the wife is given a life estate to her husband's farm upon his death. At the end of her life estate, the land is to be given to the husband's grandson. Later the couple divorces and the wife releases all interest in her husband's farm. The husband dies without a will and the grandson seeks specific performance as to the ownership of the farm. Is the grandson a third-party beneficiary of the prenuptial agreement? Under *Ball v. Cecil*, 285 Ky. 438 (1941), determine if the court grants ownership of the farm to the grandson.

3. An uncle owns a large estate and agrees to finance his nephew's purchase of a portion of the property. The purchase agreement states that the nephew must make monthly payments over a number of years and work on the land. The uncle agrees to pay his nephew's monthly expenses in improving the property. Later, the nephew makes various personal purchases on credit from local merchants. When the nephew fails to pay for his goods, the merchants bring an action against the uncle under the purchase agreement's monthly expense clause as third-party beneficiaries. Research *Burton v. Larkin*, 36 Kan. 246 (1887), to see if the merchants are third-party beneficiaries.

You might wonder, why not just make the beneficiary persuade the promisee to sue to enforce the original agreement? In some cases, the promisee is deceased, as in *Seaver*. If alive, the promisee may benefit by not enforcing the promise or may not have a stake in whether the promisor performs for the beneficiary—at least, not a stake that makes it worth hiring an attorney and taking time for discovery. Unless the beneficiary can sue, the promisor may be able to breach without any consequences.

The concepts of creditor and donee beneficiaries remained influential for many decades. Discussions of creditor and donee beneficiaries may still play a role in a court's legal analysis today. For example, in *Ehret v. Uber Techs., Inc.*, 68 F. Supp. 3d 1121 (N.D. Cal. 2014), the plaintiffs were consumers who claimed that Uber added a 20 percent fee to each metered fare, allegedly misrepresenting the fee as a gratuity for the driver. The plaintiffs complained that Uber actually retained part of the gratuity as an additional revenue source. In addressing a motion to dismiss, the court discussed issues of creditor and donee beneficiaries in rendering its decision to dismiss the plaintiffs' breach of contract claim while letting other statutory claims stand for further review.

Both debt and gift explain why the promisee might want to bestow a right to enforce the contract on the beneficiary directly. But other settings might produce an intent to allow the beneficiary to sue directly. When that intent is demonstrated, strict limitation to creditors and donees can frustrate the parties' intention.

2. Identifying Intended Beneficiaries

Modern third-party beneficiary doctrine no longer focuses on the categories of creditor or donee beneficiaries. The modern view examines whether one is an **intended beneficiary** with the legal right to enforce the contract.[1] A court will examine the surrounding circumstances of a contract to determine if the promisee intends to benefit a third party by bestowing a legal right or pecuniary benefit. Typically, when a third party brings a breach of contract claim, the promisor may challenge his **standing** or legal right to bring the lawsuit. If he is an intended beneficiary, then he can bring the action.

But if the party is classified as **incidental beneficiary**, a party not intended to receive a benefit under the contract, he has no right to sue.[2] In deciding whether a party has a right to sue to enforce the contract, courts reject claims by incidental beneficiaries, who may receive some marginal benefit from the contract, but not a benefit that justifies allowing them to sue to enforce contract rights. A beneficiary's right to enforce the contract depends on the intent of the parties who entered the contract that allegedly created those rights, specifically the promisee's intent.

If the parties included an express term either granting or denying a right to sue to enforce the agreement to specific persons, that term would be enforceable. Often, parties make no express provisions of this sort. In fact, sometimes the parties may not know who the intended beneficiaries will be. For example, a contract may provide that an airline will provide a free flight to a person who wins a contest. Uncertainty as to the identity of the beneficiaries does not preclude their status as intended beneficiaries—although in some cases this uncertainty may weigh against finding an intent to empower the beneficiaries to enforce the contract. If the intent is present, then a court must determine if the right to enforce is appropriate. The right to enforce is permissible if the promise to perform fulfills a promisee's obligation to pay money to a third-party beneficiary or the promisee intends to confer a right or economic benefit on a third-party beneficiary.

The court allowed a museum to sue to recover the Howdy Doody puppet as a third-party beneficiary in *Detroit Institute of Arts Founders Society v. Rose.*
© Everett Collection

To a large extent, the work is done by the first provision; that recognition of a right to performance is appropriate in order to effectuate the parties' intent.

[1] Restatement (Second) of Contracts §302(1).
[2] *Id.* §302(2).

That is not quite the same as asking whether the parties intended to allow the beneficiary to sue, although it seems to include any case in which the parties did have that intent. It also extends to cases in which the parties did not specifically contemplate suit, but where a right to enforce the contract seems consistent with their objective to benefit the third party. For example, in a case involving the famous television puppet Howdy Doody, NBC (promisee) and a repairman who had possession of the puppet (promisor) agreed that the Detroit Institute of Art should receive the puppet. The promisee (NBC) did not owe money to the museum and appeared to care very little whether the museum received the puppet (apparently the repairman's idea). Nonetheless, the court allowed the museum to sue to recover the puppet as a third-party beneficiary in *Detroit Institute of Arts Founders Society v. Rose*, 127 F. Supp. 2d 117 (D. Conn. 2001).

The issue of sorting out intended from incidental beneficiaries is a fact-intensive process. In the following case, a court must decide whether parties are intended or incidental beneficiaries based on the terms of the contract and the surrounding circumstances.

Tredrea v. Anesthesia & Analgesia, P.C.

In this case, Genesis, a medical center, signed an exclusive contract with A & A, an anesthesiology practice, for its services. However, the exclusive deal was subject to a contract clause that other anesthesiologists, who currently worked with the center, were also permitted to provide services as independent contractors if they responded by a specific date. Any deadline extensions were subject to A & A's consent within a short time window. When A & A refused a third extension to the independent anesthesiologists, the doctors brought an action claiming they were third-party beneficiaries of the Genesis-A & A agreement and that A & A had unreasonably withheld consent in violation of that agreement.

As you read *Tredrea v. Anesthesia & Analgesia, P.C.*, look for the following:

1. Who was the promisee and who was the promisor under the Genesis-A & A agreement?
2. Were the independent anesthesiologists intended or incidental beneficiaries of the Genesis-A & A agreement?
3. What aspects of the contract and the surrounding circumstances did the court rely upon in rendering its decision?

Tredrea v. Anesthesia & Analgesia, P.C.

584 N.W.2d 276 (Iowa 1998)

LARSON, JUSTICE

The Genesis Medical Center in Davenport, Iowa, signed a contract with Anesthesia and Analgesia, P.C. (A & A) under which A & A would provide anesthesiology services for Genesis. These plaintiffs, Colin R. Tredrea and Douglas G. Wells, had previously provided such services for the medical center. However, under this new contract, the services of A & A were to be exclusive, subject to a provision in the contract that other anesthesiologists, including these plaintiffs, could provide services under agreements with Genesis which were to be executed by a certain date. Any extensions in the deadline were subject to the consent of A & A. The Genesis-A & A agreement provided that A & A would not "unreasonably withhold" its consent to an extension of the deadline.

These plaintiffs, two independent anesthesiologists, attempted to enter into a contract with Genesis after the deadline. A & A consented to two extensions of the deadline but refused to consent to a third. The plaintiffs sued several defendants, claiming to be third party beneficiaries of the Genesis-A & A agreement. Their petition alleged that A & A had unreasonably refused the third extension and improperly interfered with the plaintiffs' right to contract with Genesis. A jury found for the plaintiffs, and A & A appealed. . . .

FACTS

The plaintiffs, Colin R. Tredrea and Douglas G. Wells, were two of fifteen anesthesiologists on staff at Genesis as of October 1994. Seven of the other doctors were employees of A & A, which was a professional corporation of anesthesiologists organized as a group practice.

The anesthesiology department at Genesis had been suffering from a number of problems, including critical evaluations by the Iowa Board of Medical Examiners. As a result, Genesis decided to reorganize its system of employing anesthesiologists. Genesis reached this decision after conducting an extensive review process of the various models for delivering anesthesiology services. It eventually adopted a model under which it would enter into an exclusive contract with a single group of anesthesiologists. Genesis contacted all fifteen anesthesiologists on its staff, explained the new model, and requested bids for contracts.

In January 1995 Genesis signed the contract under which A & A would be the exclusive provider of anesthesiology services. Although the contract was "exclusive," it provided that Genesis could offer contracts to independent anesthesiologists, including these plaintiffs, during a limited time period. In relevant part the contract provided:

> 2. *Exclusivity*. During the term of this Agreement and any subsequent renewal, Contractor shall have the exclusive right to provide all anesthesiology services to in-patients and out-patients of the Hospital, including patients of any out-patient facilities established, directly or indirectly, by the Hospital.
>
> Notwithstanding the foregoing, Contractor acknowledges that the Hospital intends to offer to enter into agreements with those anesthesia providers who are

> performing anesthesia services at the Hospital as of the date of this Agreement and who are identified on Schedule B hereto (the "Independent Contractors") under which Independent Contractors would continue to perform anesthesia services at the Hospital. Contractor agrees that the Hospital may contract with the Independent Contractors to provide anesthesia services in the Department, provided that such agreement shall, by no later than January 31, 1995, be in writing and shall provide that: (i) it shall expire no later than June 30, 1996, (ii) the Hospital shall not be obligated to renew the agreement upon the expiration of its initial term, and (iii) each Independent Contractor shall not be obligated to renew the agreement upon the expiration of its initial term, and (iv) each Independent Contractor shall abide by such rules, regulations and procedures with respect to the operation of the Department as may from time to time be established by the Medical Director.... *Contractor agrees that it shall not unreasonably withhold its consent to the Hospital's request for an extension of time to execute the agreement with Independent Contractors contemplated above*, provided that Hospital demonstrates that it has used good faith efforts to cause the execution of such agreements by the January 31, 1995 deadline and, provided further, that Contractor shall not, under any circumstances, be obligated to consent to an extension of time beyond March 1, 1995.

(Emphasis added.)

On January 10, 1995, Genesis sent a letter to Wells, Tredrea, and the other six on-staff independent anesthesiologists, advising them that A & A had been granted the exclusive contract and that any of them would be able to sign an "independent contractor" agreement under which they could provide anesthesiology services. The letter set a deadline of January 25, 1995, to execute these agreements. Initially, all eight doctors rejected the contract offer made to them. While the contract established a deadline of January 31, 1995, Genesis offered the plaintiffs three extensions. A & A consented to the first two extensions. The first extended deadline was February 2, then February 10, and then February 15 at 6 P.M. On February 17, the plaintiffs approached Genesis to sign the independent contractor agreements they had previously rejected. Genesis sought the approval from A & A for the extension, but A & A refused.

The plaintiffs sued Genesis, A & A, and Dr. Edwin A. Maxwell, the medical director of anesthesia services at the hospital, on theories of: (1) breach of medical staff bylaws, (2) third party beneficiary breach-of-contract claims based on the Genesis-A & A contract, (3) promissory estoppel, and (4) intentional interference with prospective business advantage....

The trial began in March 1996 against Dr. Maxwell and A & A. The court granted Maxwell a directed verdict and dismissed him from the case. The court allowed the plaintiffs to prove damages only prior to June 30, 1996, an issue the plaintiffs raise in their cross-appeal. The jury returned judgments in favor of Wells against A & A for $310,560 and in favor of Tredrea against A & A for $ 306,352....

...

IV. The Contract Suit

A & A contends that the court should not have submitted the plaintiffs' claim for breach of contract because (1) the plaintiffs were not third party beneficiaries under the contract and therefore lacked standing to sue on the contract, and (2) in any event there was insufficient evidence to find a breach of the agreement by A & A.

A. *The plaintiffs' standing.* The contract language at the heart of this claim is set out in the statement of the facts. The specific language claimed by the plaintiffs to give them a claim against A & A as third party beneficiaries is this:

> Contractor [A & A] agrees that the Hospital [Genesis] may contract with the Independent Contractors [identified by name including these plaintiffs] to provide anesthesia services in the [surgery] department, provided that such agreement shall [be executed] no later than January 31, 1995, [and] shall expire no later than June 30, 1996. Contractor [A & A] agrees that it shall not unreasonably withhold its consent to the Hospital's request for an extension of time to execute the agreement with the Independent Contractors, contemplated above....

The agreement was signed by A & A and Genesis. The plaintiffs were identified as "independent contractors" in an exhibit attached to the agreement, but the plaintiffs did not participate in the drafting of the agreement, and they did not sign it. Nevertheless, the plaintiffs claim the right to sue for the enforcement of the agreement because, they claim, they are third party beneficiaries.

We have adopted the following principles applicable in third party beneficiary cases as set out in the Restatement (Second) of Contracts:

> "(1) Unless otherwise agreed between promisor and promisee, a beneficiary of a promise is an intended beneficiary if recognition of a right to performance in the beneficiary is appropriate to effectuate the intention of the parties and either
>
> (a) the performance of the promise will satisfy an obligation of the promisee to pay money to the beneficiary; or
>
> (b) the circumstances indicate that the promisee intends to give the beneficiary the benefit of the promised performance.
>
> (2) An incidental beneficiary is a beneficiary who is not an intended beneficiary."

Midwest Dredging Co. v. McAninch Corp., 424 N.W.2d 216, 224 (Iowa 1988) (quoting Restatement (Second) of Contracts §302 (1979)). As we observed in *Midwest Dredging*, the primary question is whether the contract manifests an intent to benefit a third party. *Id.* at 224.

Using the terms of the Restatement of Contracts, A & A is the "promisor," the party sought by a third party to be bound by the agreement. Genesis is the "promisee" which, for reasons later discussed, stood to benefit from being able to sign a service agreement with the independent contractors.

A & A argues that there is no intent shown in the agreement to benefit these plaintiffs and that the agreement was solely for A & A to provide anesthesiology services in exchange for compensation by Genesis. "There simply is no promise to enter into contract with plaintiffs, nor does the language convey an intent that Plaintiffs have a contractual right to such an agreement," according to A & A.

We believe A & A misperceives the nature of the "intent" required for enforcement of a contract by a third party beneficiary. The intent need not be to benefit a third party directly....

In third party cases, the right of such party does not depend upon the purpose, motive, or intent of the promisor. The motivating cause of his making the promise is usually his desire for the consideration given by the promisee. In few cases will he be moved by a desire to benefit a third person. If A buys Blackacre of B and promises B to pay the price to C, he makes this promise in order to get Blackacre, not to benefit C; and this is true whether C is a creditor of B's or is B's dearly beloved daughter. . . . 4 Arthur Linton Corbin, *A Comprehensive Treatise on the Working Rules of Contract Law* §776, at 15-16 (1951) [hereinafter Corbin]. In the present case, Genesis desired to retain its right to hire additional anesthesiologists because Genesis needed their services. Genesis therefore negotiated with A & A for the right to hire independent contractors, and that agreement became a part of the Genesis-A & A contract. This authority continues:

> A third party who is not a promisee and who gave no consideration has an enforceable right by reason of a contract made by two others . . . if the promised performance will be of pecuniary benefit to [the third party] and the contract is so expressed as to give the promisor reason to know that such benefit is contemplated by the promisee as one of the motivating causes of his making the contract.

Corbin §776, at 18.

The bargaining by Genesis to preserve the rights of the independent contractors did not arise out of the kindness of its corporate heart. Evidence at trial established that Genesis' anesthesiology department had been criticized for several reasons. Genesis needed more anesthesiologists than A & A could furnish, so Genesis needed the right to contract with additional anesthesiologists. The agreement in question was clearly meant to apply to the plaintiffs; their names were included as independent contractors listed on a sheet attached to the agreement. The plaintiffs qualify as third party beneficiaries of the agreement and therefore have standing to enforce A & A's promise not to "unreasonably withhold its consent to the Hospital's request" for the extension.

In considering the reasonableness of A & A's refusal of the last requested extension, we note that from the original deadline of January 31, 1995, to the end of the last extension agreed to by A & A, February 15, 1995, it was only fifteen days. The reasons given by A & A for its refusal to further extend the deadline (that A & A had begun negotiations with other providers and thus "acted to protect itself under its contractual obligation to Genesis") apparently failed to persuade the jury. We believe that substantial evidence supports the jury's finding that A & A had acted unreasonably in denying the last extension.

Post-Case Follow-Up

The court stated that the intent of the promisee, Genesis, not the promisor, A & A, was key to determining third-party beneficiary rights. The Genesis-A & A agreement was clearly intended to apply to the doctors, as their names were included on a list of independent contractors attached to the agreement. Genesis also needed the services of these doctors due to recent criticisms about inadequate staffing and based on concerns voiced by fellow medical staff at the center that these doctors be allowed to negotiate further with A & A for their services. The court found that the independent doctors qualified as third-party beneficiaries under the terms of the agreement and the surrounding circumstances of the center's medical needs.

Tredrea v. Anesthesia & Analgesia, P.C.: Real Life Applications

1. The Garcias obtain a $170,000 construction loan from a local savings bank to build a new home. The bank enters into a services agreement with Dailey to monitor the construction and to make certain that payments from the loan are made based on the completion of different stages of the project. Over time, it becomes clear that Dailey approved payments before proper completion of each phase of the project. The Garcias are forced to sign an additional mortgage and pay more money from their personal funds to complete the home's construction. The Garcias sue both the bank and Dailey for allowing funds to be drained and for failing to hold back sufficient funds until project completion. Are the Garcias third-party beneficiaries of the contract between the bank and Dailey? Read and brief *Vogan v. Hayes Appraisal Associates, Inc.*, 588 N.W.2d 420 (Iowa 1999), for the result.
2. A general contractor enters into agreement with a roofing company to construct a roof on a new facility being built for a regional paper supplier. The contractor and roofer agree that the roofer is warranting the workmanship of its labor and the quality of its roofing materials. The construction project is completed, and the general contractor and the roofing subcontractor are paid. The paper manufacturer is purchased by another major U.S. company. When the roof shows defects, the new owner of the business brings an action as a third-party beneficiary against the roofer. Review and analyze *Weyerhaeuser Corp. v. D.C. Taylor Co.*, 2005 U.S. Dist. LEXIS 17283 (N.D. Iowa 2005) to determine if the new company qualifies as an intended beneficiary.
3. A processing bank agrees with a major retailer to handle the retailer's funds for all of its credit card transactions with customers. Under this agreement, the parties expressly exclude any third-party beneficiaries. The processing bank has an existing contract with Mega Credit Card Company to handle transactions with retailers and to ensure that its retailers comply with Mega's identity theft safeguards. The bank fails to properly enforce Mega's credit card safeguards with the retailer. The retailer is hacked and the identities of thousands of customers are compromised. The consumers' bank, a local credit union that issues Mega credit cards, suffers losses. Can the credit union support a third-party beneficiary claim under the retailer-processing bank agreement? Under the Mega-processing bank agreement? Consider *Pennsylvania State Employees Credit Union v. Fifth Third Bank*, 398 F. Supp. 2d 317 (M.D. Pa. 2005), in drafting your response.

Reversing the question may prove useful when applying the rule. Instead of asking whether a party was an intended beneficiary, ask whether she was an incidental beneficiary. Try to identify good reasons the parties would not have wanted the beneficiary to be able to sue. For instance, where one party might want to keep control over the enforcement of the contract, it is less likely that the beneficiaries were intended to have the right to enforce the contract directly. Allowing enforcement by the beneficiary is less likely to be appropriate to effectuate the parties' intent.

In *Bain v. Gillespie*, 357 N.W.2d 47 (Iowa Ct. App. 1984), a basketball fan sued the referee for breach, alleging he had blown a call at a critical point in the game. The fan claimed to be an intended beneficiary of the contract between the league and the referee. The league undoubtedly intended the referee's presence to benefit the fans — who came to see a basketball game, not a free-for-all. Nonetheless, the league probably intended to decide for itself how to address missed calls, whether by suing the referee or otherwise. The court had no trouble deciding the sports fan was an incidental beneficiary.

Contracts with the government present another situation.[3] Everything the government does should benefit the public (or part of the public). When and how to enforce its contracts is a matter the government usually intends to retain for itself. For example, in *Martinez v. Socoma Cos.*, 521 P.2d 841 (Cal. 1974), the Department of Labor paid several businesses to establish factories and employ residents in an underdeveloped area. When the companies breached, residents who would have been hired sued to enforce the contract. The court held they were not intended beneficiaries. The government intended for them to benefit from performance, but did not intend to allow them to sue to enforce the contract. Disputes were to be submitted to the government's contracting officer and damages were liquidated (a refund to the government). The government intended to keep control of the enforcement of this contract; the residents were incidental beneficiaries.

Some government contracts will create third-party beneficiaries. For example, in *Rathke v. Corrections Corporation of America*, 153 P.3d 303 (Alaska 2007), a court held that prisoners were beneficiaries of a contract between Alaska and the private company (CCA) the state had hired to operate the prison located in Arizona. Promises benefiting prisoners were not exactly gifts. Under the terms of an earlier settlement agreement, Alaska was obligated to satisfy certain commitments, which it included in the contract with CCA. Recognizing a right for prisoners to sue CCA directly seemed to effectuate the parties' intent. In the following case, the court considers when it may be appropriate for private individuals to enforce an action based upon a government contract.

Case Preview

Zigas v. Superior Court

In *Zigas v. Superior Court*, the tenants sued owners of an apartment building under the conditions of a financing agreement of a federally-insured mortgage. Under the conditions of the federally insured mortgage, the property owners are not permitted to charge rents higher than rates authorized by the Department of Housing and Urban Development (HUD). The tenants claimed that the property owners charged rents in excess of those permitted by the owners' financing agreement with HUD. The court had to determine

[3] Restatement (Second) of Contracts §313.

whether the tenants were third-party beneficiaries who were permitted to bring an enforcement action.

As you read *Zigas v. Superior Court*, look for the following:

1. What was the purpose behind the federally insured mortgage agreement between the property owners and HUD?
2. What contract terms and other circumstances did the court review to determine if the tenants were intended beneficiaries?
3. How did the court distinguish the *Martinez* case from its decision in this case?

Zigas v. Superior Court

174 Cal. Rptr. 806 (1981), cert. denied, 455 U.S. 943 (1982)

FEINBERG, J.

. . .

Petitioners are tenants of an apartment building at 2000 Broadway in San Francisco, which was financed with a federally insured mortgage in excess of $5 million, pursuant to the National Housing Act (12 U.S.C. §1701 et seq.) (the Act) and the regulations promulgated thereunder (24 C.F.R. §207 et seq.). They seek in a class action, inter alia, damages for the landlords' (real parties in interest) violation of a provision of the financing agreement which requires that the landlords charge no more than the Department of Housing and Urban Development (HUD) approved schedule of rents. The trial court has sustained demurrers without leave to amend to 5 causes of action of 15 alleged, apparently on the ground that there is no right in the tenants to enforce the provisions of an agreement between their landlords and the federal government.

Petitioners allege that their landlords were required under their contract with HUD to file a maximum rental schedule with HUD and to refrain from charging more than those rents without the prior approval of the Secretary of HUD. Petitioners further allege that real parties are, and have been, charging rent in excess of the maximums set out in the rental schedule; the complaint avers that real parties have collected excessive rents and fees in an amount exceeding $2 million.

In addition to sustaining demurrers as to the third party causes of action, the trial court granted real parties' motion to strike all references to the Act, the regulations promulgated thereunder, and the terms of the agreement between HUD and real parties. It is these orders sustaining the demurrers and granting the motion to strike that petitioners seek to have set aside.

. . .

STANDING TO SUE—THIRD PARTY BENEFICIARY

California law clearly allows third party suits for breaches of contract where no government agency is a party to the contract. (Civ. Code, §1559.) Whether such suits are allowed when the government contracts with a private party depends upon analysis of the decisions in *Shell v. Schmidt* (1954) 126 Cal. App. 2d 279 [272 P.2d 82] and *Martinez v. Socoma Companies, Inc.*, supra, 11 Cal. 3d 394.

In *Shell*, plaintiffs sued as third party beneficiaries to defendant's contract with the Federal Housing Authority (FHA). The contract entailed an agreement by the defendant to build homes for sale to veterans according to plans and specifications submitted by the defendant to FHA in return for which FHA gave priorities to the defendant to secure the materials necessary for the building.

In deciding that plaintiffs had standing to enforce the terms of the contract between the defendant and the FHA, the *Shell* court relied on common law principles as embodied in Civil Code section 1559, which states: "A contract, made expressly for the benefit of a third person, may be enforced by him at any time before the parties thereto rescind it." Applying this provision to the facts before it, the *Shell* court observed: "Once it is established that the relationship between the contractor and the government is contractual, it follows that veterans purchasing homes, that is, the class intended to be protected by that contract, are third party beneficiaries of that contract. As already pointed out, the statute and the regulations passed thereunder resulting in the contract were passed to aid and assist veterans and for their benefit. Purchasing veterans constitute the class intended to be benefitted, and the contract must therefore be for their benefit." (Id., at p. 290.)

It is evident that petitioners are entitled to maintain a third party cause of action under the *Shell* rationale. Real parties do not dispute the contractual nature of their relationship with HUD. And it is clear that a requirement of HUD approval of rent increases could only benefit the tenants.

Furthermore, even the most cursory review of the statutes and regulations which resulted in the contract in the present case leads to the conclusion that the tenants constitute the class which Congress intended to benefit. As stated in 12 United States Code section 1701t: "The Congress affirms the national goal, as set forth in section 1441 of Title 42, of 'a decent home under a suitable living environment for every American family.'" (Section 1713(b) of title 12, United States Code, also provides, in part: "The insurance of mortgages under this section is intended to facilitate particularly the production of rental accommodations, at reasonable rents, . . . The Secretary is, therefore, authorized . . . to take action, by regulation or otherwise, which will direct the benefits of mortgage insurance hereunder primarily to those projects which make adequate provision for families with children, and in which every effort has been made to achieve moderate rental charges." (Italics added, see also 24 C.F.R. §207.19(e).)

This national goal, along with the purposes enunciated throughout the Act and the regulations promulgated thereunder, can leave no doubt that petitioners are members of the class which this legislation was intended to benefit. Under *Shell*, this conclusion, coupled with the uncontested contractual relationship between real parties and HUD, is sufficient to support the tenants' standing to sue as third party beneficiaries to a government contract.

In the subsequent case of *Martinez v. Socoma Companies, Inc., supra*, 11 Cal. 3d 394, the court approved of the result in *Shell* but, at the same time, applied a different standard. [Footnote omitted.] Plaintiffs in *Martinez* sought to enforce the terms of a contract between Socoma Companies, Inc. and the Secretary of Labor. Under this agreement, defendants received government funds in exchange for a promise to hire and train "hard core unemployed" residents of a "Special Impact Area" in East Los Angeles. Defendants failed to perform, and plaintiffs, who were residents of East Los Angeles and members of the class which the government intended to benefit, sought to recover under the contract.

In holding that the plaintiffs had no standing to sue as third party beneficiaries, the *Martinez* court adopted a more restrictive standard than that embodied in Civil Code section 1559, choosing instead to be guided by the principles set forth in section 145 of the Restatement of Contracts: "'A promisor bound to the United States or to a State or municipality by contract to do an act or render a service to some or all of the members of the public, is subject to no duty under the contract to such members to give compensation for the injurious consequences of performing or attempting to perform it, or of failing to do so, unless, . . . an intention is manifested in the contract, as interpreted in the light of the circumstances surrounding its formation, that the promisor shall compensate members of the public for such injurious consequences. . . .'" (*Martinez v. Socoma Companies, Inc., supra,* at pp. 401-402; *City & County of San Francisco v. Western Air Lines, Inc.* (1962) 204 Cal. App. 2d 105, 121; Rest., Contracts, supra, §145. [Footnote omitted.]

Thus, under *Martinez,* standing to sue as a third party beneficiary to a government contract depends on the intent of the parties as manifested by the contract and the circumstances surrounding its formation. "Insofar as intent to benefit a third person is important in determining his right to bring an action under a contract, it is sufficient that the promisor must have understood that the promisee had such intent. [Citations omitted.] No specific manifestation by the promisor of an intent to benefit the third person is required." (*Lucas v. Hamm* (1961) 56 Cal. 2d 583, 591) We therefore must determine, from the terms of the contract between HUD and real parties and the attendant circumstances, whether there was manifested an intention that petitioners be compensated in the event of real parties' nonperformance. Mindful of the rule that "[when] a complaint is based on a written contract which it sets out in full, a general demurrer to the complaint admits not only the contents of the instrument but also any pleaded meaning to which the instrument is reasonably susceptible. . . ." (*Martinez v. Socoma Companies, Inc., supra,* 11 Cal. 3d at p. 400) and focusing upon the precepts of *Martinez* as to standing, we are of the view that the case falls within *Shell;* that is to say, appellants were direct beneficiaries of the contract and have standing, and not, as in *Martinez,* incidental beneficiaries without standing.

We explicate:

1. In *Martinez,* the contract between the government and Socoma provided that if Socoma breached the agreement, Socoma would refund to the government that which the government had paid Socoma pursuant to the contract between them. Thus, it is clear in *Martinez* that it was the government that was out of pocket as a consequence of the breach and should be reimbursed therefor, not the people to be trained and given jobs. In the case at bench, as in *Shell,* the government suffered no loss as a consequence of the breach, it was the renter here and the veteran purchaser in *Shell* that suffered the direct pecuniary loss.

2. Unlike *Martinez*, too, in the case at bench, no governmental administrative procedure was provided for the resolution of disputes arising under the agreement. Thus, to permit this litigation would in no way affect the "efficiency and uniformity of interpretation fostered by these administrative procedures." (*Martinez v. Socoma Companies, Inc.*, *supra*, 11 Cal. 3d at p. 402.) On the contrary, as we earlier noted, lawsuits such as this promote the federal interest by inducing compliance with HUD agreements.

3. In *Martinez*, the court held that "To allow plaintiffs' claim would nullify the limited liability for which defendants bargained and which the Government may well have held out as an inducement in negotiating the contracts." [Citation omitted.] Here, there is no "limited liability." As we shall point out, real parties are liable under the agreement, without limitation, for breach of the agreement.

4. Further, in *Martinez*, the contracts "were designed not to benefit individuals as such but to utilize the training and employment of disadvantaged persons as a means of improving the East Los Angeles neighborhood." [Citation omitted.] Moreover, the training and employment programs were but one aspect of a "broad, long-range objective" (ibid.) contemplated by the agreement and designed to benefit not only those to be trained and employed but also "other local enterprises and the government itself through reduction of law enforcement and welfare costs." (Ibid.)

   Here, on the other hand, as in *Shell*, the purpose of the Legislature and of the contract between real parties and HUD is narrow and specific: to provide moderate rental housing for families with children; in *Shell*, to provide moderate priced homes for veterans.

5. Finally, we believe the agreement itself manifests an intent to make tenants direct beneficiaries, not incidental beneficiaries, of real parties' promise to charge no more than the HUD approved rent schedule.

Section 4(a) and 4(c) of the agreement, providing that there can be no increase in rental fees, over the approved rent schedule, without the prior approval in writing of HUD, were obviously designed to protect the tenant against arbitrary increases in rents, precisely that which is alleged to have occurred here. Certainly, it was not intended to benefit the government as a guarantor of the mortgage.

Furthermore, the provision in section 11(d) of the agreement, authorizing the Secretary of HUD to "[apply] to any court . . . for specific performance . . . , for an injunction against any violation . . . or for such other relief as may be appropriate" (italics added) would entitle the secretary to seek restitution on behalf of the tenants overcharged, for such relief would surely be "appropriate." [Citation omitted.] Thus, there was an intent upon the part of the government in executing the agreement with real parties, to secure the return of any rents exacted in excess of the rent schedule.

. . .

By the allegations of the complaint, real parties have "retained" in excess of $2 million in violation of the Agreement. Therefore, they are liable for that sum. To whom should they be liable? To ask the question is to answer it. It is not the government from whom the money was exacted; it was taken from the tenants. Therefore, it should be returned to the tenants.

In the face of this evidence of intent to direct the benefits of mortgage insurance to the tenants of the facilities involved, real parties argue that petitioners have no standing to sue because enforcement of the agreement is vested solely in the Secretary. They point to 12 United States Code section 1731a, which empowers the Secretary to refuse the benefits of participation to any mortgagor who violates the terms of the agreement. However, section 1731a's authorization does not constitute the exclusive remedy for enforcement of the agreement by the Secretary or by third parties. As stated by the court in *Shell v. Schmidt*, supra, 126 Cal. App. 2d at p. 287: "This fundamental purpose would, in many cases, be defeated if the statute were interpreted so as to deprive the veterans of their normal remedies to the benefit of defaulting contractors — the very class it was the purpose of the statute to protect the veterans against. It must be held, therefore, that the enumeration of remedies in the statute merely created new enumerated remedies and was not intended to and did not deprive the veterans of any action for fraud or breach of contract that they might have under general common law principles."

Similarly, it would be anomalous if a congressional program, and the regulatory agreement formed thereunder, all of which was designed to assist in providing housing for low and moderate income families, were construed so as to provide cheap financing for the housing industry while at the same time denying tenants any means of protecting the benefits which they were intended to receive.

. . .

CONCLUSION

Surely it would be unconscionable if a builder could secure the benefits of a government guaranteed loan upon his promise to charge no more than a schedule of rents he had agreed to and then find there is no remedy by which the builder can be forced to disgorge rents he had collected in excess of his agreement simply because the government had failed to act. . . . The matter is remanded for such further proceedings as may be appropriate.

Post-Case Follow-Up

The *Zigas* court reasoned that the terms of the contract between property owners and HUD were done for the express benefit of the tenants. The purpose stated in the **National Housing Act** — providing affordable rentals — was the main purpose of the contract. The court reasoned that the instant case is more similar to the *Shell* case, allowing veterans purchasing homes based upon contracts between private parties building homes and the FHA to proceed with their lawsuit as third-party beneficiaries. The court distinguished *Martinez* from this dispute. In this case, the renters suffered the pecuniary loss in overcharged rents, and the contract was executed for the sole purpose of benefiting tenants. The court concluded that it would be inconsistent for the law to be interpreted to assist low and moderate income tenants while denying tenants any means to protect those benefits.

Zigas v. Superior Court: Real Life Applications

1. The U.S. government charges a meat processing company with having violated antitrust laws in the purchase of two meat packing plants. In a consent decree to avoid further government antitrust action, the meat processing company agrees to sell the two companies, to continue its normal business operations, and to take no action against the unionized employees that may prevent a successful sale of the companies. Subsequently, the meat processor shuts down the plants, lays off all the employees, and does not reopen these plants for a year. When the facilities reopen, the union sues the meat processor, claiming that the employees were third-party beneficiaries of the consent decree between the government and the meat processor. Are the unionized employees third-party beneficiaries under this decree? Consider *Bailey v. Iowa Beef Processors, Inc.*, 213 N.W.2d 642 (Iowa 1973), in drafting your response.
2. Property owners seek the demolition of train tracks no longer in use in a city. Other community members lobby for retaining historical train buildings and to turn train tracks into a bike trail. The property owners enter into an agreement with the city allowing the use of the train corridor as a bike path and releasing claims against the government in return for certain benefits. The U.S. government later approves of this new use of this train corridor. Six years later, the property owners seek the fair market value for their property, which they claim was illegally taken for the bike trail without fair compensation and sue the U.S. government. Is the federal government an intended beneficiary of the covenant not to sue in the agreement between the property owners and the city under *West Chelsea Bldgs. v. United States*, 109 Fed. Cl. 5 (2013)?
3. Aviators, Ltd. is a subcontractor of a government prime contractor, Filmore Associates, providing jet maintenance services to National Aeronautics and Space Administration (NASA). Ultimately, NASA terminates Filmore for failing to comply with its contract duties. Aviators Ltd. claims that Filmore failed to pay it for its services to NASA and that it continued to provide services to NASA after Filmore's default that were not compensated. Aviators, Ltd. sues NASA for payment of its services, claiming it is a third-party beneficiary of the contract between NASA and Filmore. Under *Threshold Techs., Inc. v. United States*, 117 Fed. Cl. 681 (2014), is Aviators, Ltd. an intended beneficiary of the prime contractor's agreement with NASA?

---

3. Beneficiaries and Contract Defenses

Even if allowed to sue, an intended beneficiary's rights depend on the enforceability of the contract that provided these rights. In essence, the intended beneficiary stands in the shoes of the promisee. Thus, the promisor may raise any claims or defenses it would have against the original promise as well as any it may have against the third-party beneficiary. The promisor may assert several types of defenses:

a. The contract is invalid or unenforceable,
b. Performance is not yet due or has been excused, or
c. Performance has been excused by the beneficiary's conduct.[4]

The invalidity or unenforceability of the contract between the promisor and promisee negates any duty to the promisee, and in turn, the third-party beneficiary. For instance, if the agreement between the promisor and promisee lacked consideration, no enforceable promise exists on which the beneficiary could base a suit. Similarly, if the promisor's assent was induced by misrepresentation, the underlying agreement is voidable. The promisor can raise the defense and, if successful, the contract becomes unenforceable and cannot confer rights on the beneficiary. Rather, the beneficiary's rights are no greater than the promisee's rights. If the promisee has no rights because the agreement was unenforceable, then the beneficiary also has no rights under the contract.

Likewise, excuses that apply to the contract between the promisor and promisee may be raised by the promisor against the beneficiary. If the agreement between the promisor and promisee would be excused for impracticability or because the promisee materially breached the contract, the excuse also would be applicable against the beneficiary. For example, let's say that a homeowner purchased a home with a loan from a bank that requires the homeowner to buy adequate insurance to protect the home from damage or loss. The homeowner then entered into an agreement for homeowner's insurance in exchange for the payment of monthly premiums with an insurance company. The bank that holds the mortgage on the home would be a third-party beneficiary of the insurance contract as it is intended not only to protect the owner, but also the bank's collateral under the loan. If the homeowner stops paying the insurance premiums, then the insurance company may cancel the policy in accordance with the terms of their agreement. Subsequently, if the uninsured home is destroyed by fire or a hurricane, the insurance company may raise the homeowner's breach to fend off a claim by the bank as a third-party beneficiary.

Defenses based on conduct by the beneficiary remain valid. For instance, if the beneficiary released the promisor, the promisor could raise that release as a defense. If the beneficiary agreed to defer delivery of the benefit to a time later than that specified in the contract, failure to deliver according to the contract terms would not be breach. The beneficiary's own conduct provided the basis for a defense. The concepts of release and novation are discussed later in section D.2 of this chapter.

At least two types of defenses are unavailable to the promisor. First, the promisor cannot assert defenses that the promisee could assert against the beneficiary. For instance, if the promisor was to repay a debt the promisee owed to the beneficiary, the promisor may not defend on the ground that the debt was invalid. For example, Delia borrows $500 from Reggie and agrees to repay her loan by paying Reggie's debt to Liam. If Delia later tries to back out of the loan repayment, she may not claim that the debt between Reggie and Liam was invalid. The promisee,

[4] RESTATEMENT (SECOND) OF CONTRACTS §309.

Reggie, in making arrangements to pay his debt to Liam, through the promisor, Delia, in effect waived those defenses.

The approach is also particularly important where the beneficiary is a donee. Donees give no consideration to the promisee in exchange for the gift the promisee contracted to provide. While the promisee could raise that defense against the beneficiary, the promisor has no right to raise it. The promisee, having paid the promisor for the gift, effectively waives the right to deny consideration. The promisor cannot rely on promisee's defenses.

Second, defenses the promisor may have against the promisee may not be raised against the beneficiary if they are unrelated to the contract at issue. For instance, suppose the promisee owes the promisor money on a transaction under a different contract. Failure to repay the debt might entitle the promisor to offset the amount owed under the other contract against amounts the promisor owes to the promisee on this one. Yet the promisor cannot offset the promisee's debt against amounts owed to a beneficiary. As long as the contract creating the benefit was valid and unexcused, unrelated defenses between the promisor and promisee do not alter the beneficiary's right to the benefit (and to sue to enforce the contract).

4. Modifications by the Promisee

The promisee and the promisor may alter their contract. They vested the beneficiary with these rights; they also can take them away. The beneficiary may still have rights against the promisee, especially if the beneficiary is a creditor. The promisee and promisor cannot change those rights by themselves. But they can eliminate the promisor's duty to pay the promisee's creditors or any other beneficiary. Thus, the promisee and promisor might rescind their contract or modify it in ways that alter the beneficiary's rights.

However, there are exceptions that limit the power of the parties to alter the beneficiary's rights under the contract. The promisor and promisee cannot alter the beneficiary's rights if:

a. the contract limits their power to alter the beneficiary's rights; or
b. justifiable reliance by the beneficiary makes modification by the parties unjust.[5]

First, a term in the original contract limiting the power to alter the beneficiary's rights is enforceable. Thus, if the contract makes the beneficiary's rights irrevocable, subsequent efforts to revoke or modify them may have no effect. For example, if you use your frequent flyer miles to have a ticket issued in your sister's name, your agreement with the airline may limit your ability to cancel the deal or to change the passenger.

Second, reliance by the beneficiary may negate subsequent efforts to **rescind** (cancel the contract) or alter her rights, at least to the extent of the reliance. The reliance must be justifiable and must occur before the beneficiary learns of the

[5] *Id.* §311.

purported rescission or modification. She cannot rely after she learns of the rescission and expect her subsequent reliance to lock in her original entitlement.

C. ASSIGNMENT OF RIGHTS

For many reasons, a party entitled to receive performance under a contract may wish to transfer the benefits to someone else. A tenant may wish to assign a lease. A lender may wish to sell a promissory note. The owner of a business may wish to assign the business's contract rights from employees or vendors to a buyer of the business, and so on. The other party to these contract(s) has not made promises to the assignee; the promises were made to the assignor. Requiring the obligor to perform for the assignee alters the contract, at least a little. If the obligor resists the change in the identity of the recipient (from the assignor to the assignee), courts may need to resolve whether to enforce the original contract despite the change in the recipient. With some exceptions, the law recognizes a party's ability to assign its rights under a contract.

Society prefers for parties to be able to give or sell their rights, including their contract rights. The owner of a business could never sell the business if she could not do the following: assign the lease of the business's location; delegate the duty to pay the employees and assign the right to receive their labor; delegate the duty to repay any debts the business owes; delegate responsibility to perform any contracts the business has made with customers; and assign the right to receive any performance the business is entitled to receive from its suppliers. Free alienability of property, including contract rights, serves our economy well. The rules here seek to balance that societal preference for alienability of property with the need to limit alienation when it creates problems for another person without that person's consent.

1. Assignment Defined

Assignment refers to one person's voluntary transfer of his rights under a contract to a third party. Assignment affects only the right to receive performance.

Assignment: The Roles of Obligor, Assignor, and Assignee

In discussing assignment, authorities refer to the obligor, assignor, and assignee. To understand the discussion, let alone to apply the rule, you must be able to identify which role a party plays. Sometimes just keeping the parties' roles straight is half the battle.

- The **obligor** is someone who owes a contract duty to another. The obligor is not a party to the assignment, but becomes obligated to perform for the assignee under the assigned contract.
- The **assignor** is the person to whom those duties are owed and who transfers rights to a third person: the assignee.
- The **assignee** receives the rights from the assignor. The assignee is not a party to the first contract, but becomes entitled to receive the obligor's performance of that contract.

For example, Pat owes Sandy $100. Sandy assigns her right to that $100 to Leslie. Pat is the obligor — has the duty to pay the debt to Sandy. Sandy is the assignor — has transferred the right to Leslie. Leslie is the assignee — entitled to now receive the payment from Pat.

It would be valid, but ambiguous, to call the obligor the promisor and the assignor the promisee. The assignment is a separate deal with its own promisor and promisee. Some confusion might result. Stick with obligor and assignor. Most authorities use obligor and assignor, so using that language communicates in terms others expect to see.

The duties remain unchanged. An attempt to transfer the duty to perform one's obligations under the contract is called a delegation, which will be discussed below. For example, when a tenant assigns a lease, the right to use the premises is transferred to the assignee, but the assignor still has a duty to pay rent.

The word "assignment" is not always used with precision. You must be careful to determine whether the word "assignment," when used by parties making an agreement, really refers to assignment of rights or to something else. Some use assignment to describe a transaction that both assigns rights and delegates duties. In one context — contract clauses prohibiting assignment — misuse is so common that the word "assignment" is presumed to mean a bar on one's delegation of duties.[6] This section addresses only assignment of rights, not delegation of duties.

An assignment transfers the performance assigned to the assignee, extinguishing any right in the assignor. Thus, when a lender assigns a note, the right to receive payments goes to the assignee. The original lender has no right to demand the performance or to sue for failure to perform. Assignment can be partial. For example, persons with health insurance often assign to the hospital or doctor their right to collect payment from the insurer. The assignment transfers the right to receive payment for the services that hospital provided. It extinguishes the insured's claim against the insurer to have those amounts paid to it. However, the assignment does not extinguish the health insurance policy. It remains in effect for any other claims not included in the assignment.

In some cases, parties do not assign rights, but simply empower others to collect on their behalf. In the health insurance example, the insured might authorize the provider to collect from the insurer, without giving up its right to seek payment on its own behalf. Interpreting the language of the purported assignment may be necessary to determine whether the assignor intended to relinquish the rights entirely. The difference is important. An assignee gains a right under the original contract, including the right to sue. The assignee resembles a beneficiary — one created by the assignment, not by the original contract. By contrast, an agent seeking to collect on behalf of the insured does not gain a right to sue. That right remains with the original contract party who never relinquished it.

Case Preview

Herzog v. Irace

In *Herzog*, a client, Gary Jones, was expecting a $20,000 settlement from a motorcycle accident. He instructed his attorneys, Irace and Lowry, to make several partial assignments of these funds to creditors as well as to Dr. Herzog for his surgical services. Later Jones changed his mind and told his attorneys to

[6] *Id.* §322(1).

pay his other creditors and he would pay Dr. Herzog directly. When Jones's check bounces, Dr. Herzog sought to recover the assigned funds from Jones's attorneys.

As you read *Herzog v. Irace*, look for the following:

1. Did the court determine that Jones's future rights to his settlement funds were assignable?
2. Had Jones effectively assigned part of his settlement to Dr. Herzog?
3. What did the court determine were Irace and Lowry's legal and ethical duties regarding Jones's assignment to Dr. Herzog?

Herzog v. Irace

594 A.2d 1106 (Me. 1991)

Brody, J.

Anthony Irace and Donald Lowry appeal from an order entered by the Superior Court (Cumberland County, Cole, J.) affirming a District Court (Portland, Goranites, J.) judgment in favor of Dr. John P. Herzog in an action for breach of an assignment to Dr. Herzog of personal injury settlement proceeds[1] collected by Irace and Lowry, both attorneys, on behalf of their client, Gary G. Jones. On appeal, Irace and Lowry contend that the District Court erred in finding that the assignment was valid and enforceable against them. They also argue that enforcement of the assignment interferes with their ethical obligations toward their client. Finding no error, we affirm.

The facts of this case are not disputed. Gary Jones was injured in a motorcycle accident and retained Irace and Lowry to represent him in a personal injury action. Soon thereafter, Jones dislocated his shoulder, twice, in incidents unrelated to the motorcycle accident. Dr. Herzog examined Jones's shoulder and concluded that he needed surgery. At the time, however, Jones was unable to pay for the surgery and in consideration for the performance of the surgery by the doctor, he signed a letter dated June 14, 1988, written on Dr. Herzog's letterhead stating:

> **I, Gary Jones, request that payment be made directly from settlement of a claim currently pending for an unrelated incident, to John Herzog, D.O., for treatment of a shoulder injury which occurred at a different time.**

Dr. Herzog notified Irace and Lowry that Jones had signed an "assignment of benefits" from the motorcycle personal injury action to cover the cost of surgery on his shoulder and was informed by an employee of Irace and Lowry that the assignment was sufficient to allow the firm to pay Dr. Herzog's bills at the conclusion of the case. Dr. Herzog performed the surgery and continued to treat Jones for approximately one year.

[1]This case involves the assignment of proceeds from a personal injury action, not an assignment of the cause of action itself.

In May, 1989, Jones received a $20,000 settlement in the motorcycle personal injury action. He instructed Irace and Lowry not to disburse any funds to Dr. Herzog indicating that he would make the payments himself. Irace and Lowry informed Dr. Herzog that Jones had revoked his permission to have the bill paid by them directly and indicated that they would follow Jones's directions. Irace and Lowry issued a check to Jones for $10,027 and disbursed the remaining funds to Jones's other creditors. Jones did send a check to Dr. Herzog but the check was returned by the bank for insufficient funds and Dr. Herzog was never paid.

Dr. Herzog filed a complaint in District Court against Irace and Lowry seeking to enforce the June 14, 1988 "assignment of benefits." The matter was tried before the court on the basis of a joint stipulation of facts. The court entered a judgment in favor of Dr. Herzog finding that the June 14, 1988 letter constituted a valid assignment of the settlement proceeds enforceable against Irace and Lowry. Following an unsuccessful appeal to the Superior Court, Irace and Lowry appealed to this court. . . .

. . .

VALIDITY OF ASSIGNMENT

An assignment is an act or manifestation by the owner of a right (the assignor) indicating his intent to transfer that right to another person (the assignee). *See Shiro v. Drew*, 174 F. Supp. 495, 497 (D. Me. 1969). For an assignment to be valid and enforceable against the assignor's creditor (the obligor), the assignor must make clear his intent to relinquish the right to the assignee and must not retain any control over the right assigned or any power of revocation. *Id.* The assignment takes effect through the actions of the assignor and assignee and the obligor need not accept the assignment to render it valid. *Palmer v. Palmer*, 112 Me. 149, 153, 91 A. 281, 282 (1914). Once the obligor has notice of the assignment, the fund is "from that time forward impressed with a trust; it is . . . impounded in the [obligor's] hands, and must be held by him not for the original creditor, the assignor, but for the substituted creditor, the assignee." *Id.* at 152. After receiving notice of the assignment, the obligor cannot lawfully pay the amount assigned either to the assignor or to his other creditors and if the obligor does make such a payment, he does so at his peril because the assignee may enforce his rights against the obligor directly. *Id.* at 153.

Ordinary rights, including future rights, are freely assignable unless the assignment would materially change the duty of the obligor, materially increase the burden or risk imposed upon the obligor by his contract, impair the obligor's chance of obtaining return performance, or materially reduce the value of the return performance to the obligor, and unless the law restricts the assignability of the specific right involved. *See* Restatement (Second) Contracts §317(2)(a) (1982). In Maine, the transfer of a future right to proceeds from pending litigation has been recognized as a valid and enforceable equitable assignment. *McLellan v. Walker*, 26 Me. 114, 117-18 (1896). An equitable assignment need not transfer the entire future right but rather may be a partial assignment of that right. *Palmer*, 112 Me. at 152. We reaffirm these well established principles.

Relying primarily upon the Federal District Court's decision in *Shiro*, 174 F. Supp. 495, a bankruptcy case involving the trustee's power to avoid a preferential transfer by assignment, Irace and Lowry contend that Jones's June 14, 1988 letter is invalid and unenforceable as an assignment because it fails to manifest Jones's intent to permanently relinquish all control over the assigned funds and does nothing more than request payment from a specific fund. We disagree. The June 14, 1988 letter gives no indication that Jones attempted to retain any control over the funds he assigned to Dr. Herzog. Taken in context, the use of the word "request" did not give the court reason to question Jones's intent to complete the assignment and, although no specific amount was stated, the parties do not dispute that the services provided by Dr. Herzog and the amounts that he charged for those services were reasonable and necessary to the treatment of the shoulder injury referred to in the June 14 letter. Irace and Lowry had adequate funds to satisfy all of Jones's creditors, including Dr. Herzog, with funds left over for disbursement to Jones himself. Thus, this case simply does not present a situation analogous to *Shiro* because Dr. Herzog was given preference over Jones's other creditors by operation of the assignment. Given that Irace and Lowry do not dispute that they had ample notice of the assignment, the court's finding on the validity of the assignment is fully supported by the evidence and will not be disturbed on appeal.

ETHICAL OBLIGATIONS

Next, Irace and Lowry contend that the assignment, if enforceable against them, would interfere with their ethical obligation to honor their client's instruction in disbursing funds.[2] Again, we disagree.

Under the Maine Bar Rules, an attorney generally may not place a lien on a client's file for a third party. M. Bar R. 3.7(c). The Bar Rules further require that an attorney "promptly pay or deliver to the client, as requested by the client, the funds, securities, or other properties in the possession of the lawyer which the client is entitled to receive." M. Bar R. 3.6(f)(2)(iv). The rules say nothing, however, about a client's power to assign his right to proceeds from a pending lawsuit to third parties. Because the client has the power to assign his right to funds held by his attorney, *McLellan v. Walker*, 26 Me. at 117-18, it follows that a valid assignment must be honored by the attorney in disbursing the funds on the client's behalf. The assignment does not create a conflict under Rule 3.6(f)(2)(iv) because the client is not entitled to receive funds once he has assigned them to a third party. Nor does the assignment violate Rule 3.7(c), because the client, not the attorney, is responsible for placing the incumbrance upon the funds. Irace and Lowry were under no ethical obligation, and the record gives no indication that they were under a contractual obligation, to honor their client's instruction to disregard a valid assignment. The District Court correctly concluded that the assignment is valid and enforceable against Irace and Lowry. . . .

---

[2]Lowry and Irace rely upon *Twin Valley Motors, Inc. v. John Morale et al.*, 136 Vt. 115, 385 A.2d 678 (Vt. 1978) to support their position on this issue. Whatever the merits of the Vermont court's decision in the context of that case and in the context of Vermont law regarding equitable assignments and professional ethics, the decision cuts against authority in Maine which clearly recognizes the validity and enforceability of equitable assignments by a client of all or part of his right to proceeds expected from pending litigation. *McLellan v. Walker*, 26 Me. at 117-18.

Post-Case Follow-Up

The *Herzog* court stated that for an assignment to be valid and enforceable, the assignor must make clear his intent to relinquish the right to the assignee and must not retain any control over the right assigned or any power of revocation. Jones's assignment gave effective notice of his assignment to Irace and Lowry (obligor). Jones's rights were extinguished upon his assignment and the obligor should have held the funds in trust for Herzog (assignee). The lawyers would not violate their ethical duties to their client by not honoring his instructions seeking to later revoke his assignment as he no longer possessed any legal rights to those funds.

Herzog v. Irace: Real Life Applications

1. Norton loans his friend, Ogden, $5,000 to buy a small fishing boat. Ogden promises to pay back the loan or else Norton may claim ownership to the boat. Norton assigns his rights to the loan to McGuinn. Ogden uses the boat for a time and then leaves it dry-docked at McGuinn's home for several months. When Ogden does not repay his loan to Norton, McGuinn retains the boat from Ogden. Ogden sells the boat to Pelly for $1,000, but McGuinn refuses to hand over the boat to Pelly. In this case, sort out the parties' roles and determine who owns the boat according to *Doughty v. Sullivan*, 661 A.2d 1112 (Me. 1995).

2. Bowman is the sole shareholder and owner of Excavation Services, Inc. (ESI). ESI enters into a contract with a town for snowplowing services for five years. The contract contains a clause that ESI must meet certain service and equipment standards or the town may cancel the deal. Bowman officially dissolves the corporation, transferring any of its remaining assets to himself. He does not inform the town about the dissolution of ESI. The town eventually terminates the contract for poor service and equipment problems. Bowman claims that the corporate dissolution assigns the rights of payment under the contract to him as an individual and sues the town for lost profits on the remaining years of the contract. Is there a valid assignment of the snowplowing contract from ESI to Bowman? Review and brief *Sturtevant v. Town of Winthrop*, 1999 Me. 84 (1999) to determine the likely outcome.

3. A family court enters a child support order requiring the father to make weekly payments to the mother. When the father falls behind on his child support payments, the mother brings a legal action. The court orders the father to pay $2,000 in arrearages to her and $500 to the state's welfare program for benefits the child previously received during the time of the father's nonpayment. The court's order states that any arrearage payments must be made in full to the mother first, before the state's welfare agency may be paid. Subsequently, the mother applies again for state assistance and signs an agreement assigning her rights to child support payment to the state welfare agency to repay any benefits received. When the father finally begins to pay on the court order, the state

EXHIBIT 14.2 Charting Assignment in *Herzog*

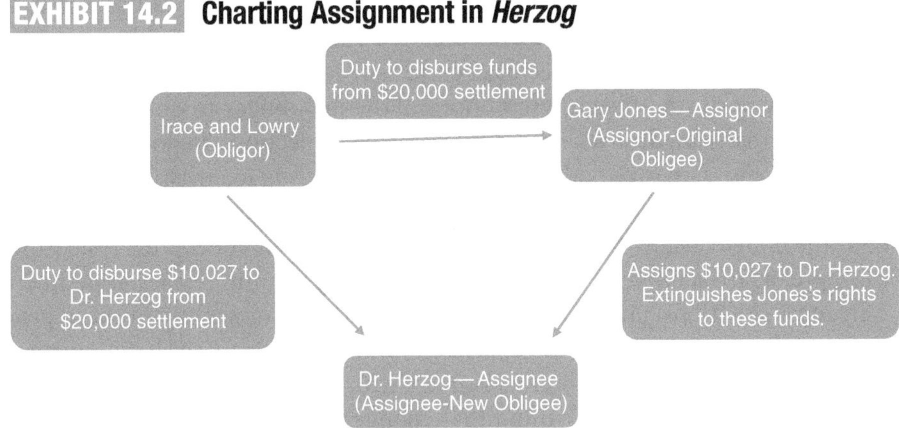

welfare agency seeks to collect those payments under the mother's assignment. The court must decide if the mother's assignment includes her rights under the court order. Review *Desrochers v. Desrochers*, 173 Vt. 312 (2002), to see how the court handles this assignment dispute.

The right to receive performance under a contract has come to be viewed as any other form of property right. As such, people generally are entitled to sell or to give away those rights. The law recognizes the right to assign contract rights, with only a limited number of exceptions:

a. if assignment materially alters the obligor's duties;
b. if assignment materially increases the burden on the obligor;
c. if assignment materially increases the risk to the obligor;
d. if assignment materially impairs the obligor's chance of obtaining return performance;
e. if assignment materially reduces the value of return performance to the obligor;
f. if a statute or public policy precludes assignment; or
g. if the contract limits the right to assignment.[7]

The word "material" is a critical component of most of these limitations. The value of assignment makes minor changes in the duty, the burden, or the risk insufficient to challenge the validity of the assignment. Unless the changes significantly affect the obligor, the obligor must tolerate the assignment. When the changes take on significance, objections by the obligor will be heard.

The assignment requires the assent of the obligor in order to be valid, if the contract between the obligor and assignor so provides. But if the obligor has not

[7]Restatement (Second) of Contracts §317(2); *see also* UCC §2-210(2) (omitting an explicit mention of the public policy and material change in the value of return performance exclusions).

reserved the right to approve or refuse assignments, the law does not automatically provide it. One concern involves obligors who might withhold assent in an effort to extract an assignment fee or even to renegotiate the terms of the contract with the new party. In effect, these options allow the obligor to obtain more than he originally bargained to receive. While limiting objections to good faith might reduce some abuse, many good faith reasons for objecting to an assignment can be found — and even more can be alleged in terms that make them sound reasonable, even if the obligor really does not care about them. Absent an express reservation, the law prefers to facilitate assignment by not creating an unnecessary impediment.

In most situations, an assignment is unlikely to transgress any of these provisions. Assignment is quite commonplace. Banks often assign your loan, mortgage, or credit card agreements to another bank. The party you pay may make little difference to you. When the only thing that changes is the identity of the recipient, objections to the change are hard to justify. The other limitations reflect situations where something more than just the identity of the recipient changes.

Material Change in Obligor's Duties

Normally, assigning rights does not change what the obligor must do, but merely to whom or for whom it must be done. A borrower makes the same payment, but a different person receives it. The performance does not change at all. But if the assignment changes the duties of the obligor, then the obligor has grounds to resist the assignment.

Most cases in which the duty appears to be different really reflect an increase in the obligor's burden or risk. For example, if seller promised to deliver goods to the buyer in Dallas, assigning the right to another buyer in Philadelphia might change the cost of shipping. The duty — to deliver — is the same. The same is true of assigning rights to an employee's services — such as trading a player from one team to another. The duty — to play ball — remains the same; but performing in Philadelphia may be more or less burdensome than performing in Dallas. In either example, defining the duty more narrowly — to deliver to Dallas, to play ball in Dallas — makes it appear that the duty itself changed when the assignment occurred. The ability to describe the duty at varying levels of specificity makes this provision hard to apply with any consistency. Reliance on the burden or risk may produce more predictable results.

Material Change in Obligor's Burden

Even if the nature of the obligation does not change, the burden might increase. Modest differences will be ignored. A borrower who complains that the assignee has a longer name, requiring more time and ink to make out the check, has no real complaint about the assignment. This complaint seems more like a pretext for some other purpose, rather than a serious concern for the conservation of effort and ink. But some assignments may increase the burden substantially.

For example, suppose a homeowner has a contract for cleaning services from an individual every Thursday. Can she assign the right to receive those services to another homeowner, even for one week? The houses might be significantly different in size or in cleanliness. Travel time to and from the assignee's house may differ significantly. One might say that the duty itself has changed: instead of cleaning one house, the duty is to clean another house. On that reasoning, which may be persuasive, this limitation may apply. But framed more generally, the duty is to clean a house, exactly what it was before. The extent to which the burden is changed could provide a stronger justification for rejecting or approving the assignment. If the burden is not much greater, a party resisting assignment may need to raise the esoteric issue of whether the duty itself differs materially. Where the burden changes significantly, that alone justifies resisting the assignment. Reported cases challenging assignments overwhelmingly involve contract clauses limiting or prohibiting assignment. Parties rarely rely on statutory or judicial limits on assignment.

Material Increase in the Obligor's Risk

Sometimes the obligor will not know whether the burden will change following the assignment. For example, the assignment of a car insurance policy might produce no different burden—either because the assignee has no claims or because the assignor's claims would have been just as large. At the time of the assignment, no one knows what claims might arise during the remaining term of the policy. The obligor, however, may face a materially greater risk, if the assignee has a worse driving record or is at a more dangerous age for accidents. A material change in the risk itself justifies the obligor's resistance to the assignment. In effect, this protects the obligor's ability to decide for itself which risks to take. The insurance contract with assignor did not cede that discretion to the assignor.

Material Impairment of the Chances of Return Performance

Assigning rights does not affect duties. The assignor remains liable to perform any duties the contract requires. Thus, assignment of a lease does not extinguish the assignor's duty to pay the rent. Typically, the assignee will agree to pay the rent as part of the assignment. But if the assignee fails to pay, the landlord may sue the assignor instead of the assignee. The assignment extinguished the assignor's right to occupy the premises, but had no effect on the assignor's duty to pay rent. Once the assignor no longer is entitled to receive the benefits of the contract, her incentive to perform her duties under the contract may diminish. If assignment significantly reduces the chance that the obligor will receive its consideration under the contract, the obligor may resist the assignment. That is why many landowners will not allow a tenant to assign an apartment without prior written approval.

To some extent, this provision is a special case of the preceding rule. The risk that the other parties (assignor and assignee) will not perform their duties is just one example of the risks that the obligor might face. For example, consider an employee who has assigned the right to receive a paycheck to a creditor. The employee may be less likely to work diligently if the pay is sent directly to creditors. The obligor's ability to sue the employee for breach (or fire her) is little consolation. Contracting parties usually expect and prefer performance without recourse to the courts. The increased likelihood of having to sue to recover the consideration is itself an increased risk.

Many assignments raise no issue of this sort. For instance, lenders have fully performed before borrowers begin to make payments. Assignment of the note to a different person will not have any effect on the borrower's receipt of the benefits expected under the contract.

Material Change in the Value of Return Performance

It is somewhat difficult to imagine cases in which the obligor will value the performance it receives less just because an assignee now receives the obligor's performance. This provision does not appear in the UCC approach to assignment. Problems seem most likely to arise where part of the benefit the obligor expects is personal satisfaction, perhaps arising from a working relationship. For instance, where a person agrees to work for a reduced price because of the relationship she enjoys with the assignor, assignment may not produce the same value.

The value need not involve a business relationship. Consider a gardener who takes pride in his work. If the right to receive those services is assigned to a different garden, the satisfaction derived from the work itself may diminish, even if the change does not materially affect any other aspect of the contract. Neither example involves the value of the return performance. Strictly speaking, the return performance is a paycheck, not the right to work with a specific individual or in a particular garden. Nonetheless, the price of the services under the contract might be lower when the obligor expects to receive some benefits under the contract other than the pay. Assignment may undermine those ancillary benefits. Perhaps a provision of this sort will allow an obligor to resist assignment.

Public Policy

The general rule allowing assignment reflects a public interest in allowing people to alienate their property, including their contract rights. Restrictions on assignment, not assignment itself, interfere with public policy. In most situations, it is difficult to imagine why the public would care whether a party assigned its rights under a contract or kept them. The other limitations identify reasons the parties might care, but reasons for the public to care are relatively rare. This provision is also not found in the UCC's view of assignment.

Statutes may preclude or limit the assignment of rights. For example, most states limit the amount of an employee's paycheck that an employee can assign (commonly, no more than 15-25 percent) since one will need a substantial part of her pay to survive. The statute protects employees even though they agreed to the assignment. It also protects employers. An employee who receives none of the income earned by her work, because it is paid to an assignee instead, might not perform diligently. Even without a statute, other limitations might preclude assignments of wages. The assignment might materially reduce the likelihood that the employer will receive the return performance or may materially reduce the value of the return performance to the employer. The law eliminates the need to litigate these issues.

Less commonly, a court may find an assignment violates public policy even though it does not violate a statute. For instance, some courts have determined that it violates public policy to assign certain tort actions, such as legal malpractice or tort claims, as noted in *Irace v. Herzog*. The assignment of claims, rather than the proceeds of settled or adjudicated claims, may generate frivolous lawsuits.

Contractual Limitations on Assignment

Parties to a contract can make their own decision regarding the acceptability of assignment. Courts will honor a clause limiting or forbidding assignment, up to a point. Because public policy favors assignment, courts limit the effect of clauses restricting assignment.

First, courts tend to interpret clauses prohibiting assignment narrowly, unless the text and circumstances indicate a broader intent. For example, when the contract precludes "assignment," without defining the term, courts often limit this clause to precluding the delegation of duties.[8] Thus, an assignment of rights that did not delegate duties would be enforceable, despite the clause.

Second, courts have held that clauses prohibiting assignment do not apply following a material breach.[9] A party entitled to cancel the contract or to sue for damages for breach of the whole contract may assign the right to sue to another, despite a nonassignment clause. Denying the breaching party a right to prevent assignment makes some sense. A total breach entitles the other party to cancel the entire contract, so enforcing the nonassignment provision would be inconsistent.

In both situations, courts will enforce the nonassignment clause if the circumstances — which usually means very clear contract language, but can include other factors — indicate that the parties intended the clause to apply to these situations. These principles express a preference for a narrower interpretation, but do not preclude parties from making agreements on different terms.

Instead of prohibiting assignments, some contracts require the assignor to obtain the obligor's approval of the assignment — which typically means the obligor's approval of the assignee. For example, a landlord wants to determine whether the assignee will be a good tenant before approving (or refusing) an assignment. Courts require the obligor to use good faith in evaluating the assignment. While any honest reason to reject the assignee may suffice, an unreasonable decision to reject the assignee may look like strategic behavior — an effort to persuade the assignor to pay a little extra in order to obtain the obligor's approval. Under the UCC, good faith may require a consideration of trade usage and reasonable industry standards. But if the obligor has not reserved the right to approve or refuse assignments, the law does not automatically provide it. Absent an express reservation, the law prefers to facilitate assignment by not creating an unnecessary impediment.

---

[8] RESTATEMENT (SECOND) OF CONTRACTS §322(1).
[9] *Id.* §322(2)(a).

2. Ineffective Assignment

If the obligor refuses to perform for the assignee, the assignee may sue seeking enforcement of the contract. If the assignment was effective—that is, if none of the grounds for objection apply—then the obligor's nonperformance is breach. If, however, the purported assignment was ineffective, then failing to perform for the assignee is not breach. The purported assignee gains no rights under an ineffective assignment. The obligor's duty to perform for the assignor probably remains enforceable. In addition, the assignee may have an action against the assignor for the ineffective assignment. Where the assignor received consideration for the assignment, the assignee may sue for breach of contract or for **unjust enrichment** (a cause of action allowing recovery of benefits from a recipient if retention by the recipient would be just).

Contractual limitations on assignment offer an additional option for the obligor: it can sue the assignor for breach of the promise not to assign the contract. That breach would allow the obligor to recover any damages caused by the assignment. Whether the provision also negates the effect of the assignment is less certain.

In some cases, courts may require the obligor to perform for the assignee and seek redress, if at all, against the assignor. The assignee, who may not have done anything wrong, need not be deprived of the performance under the assignment. Courts may interpret anti-assignment provisions as limiting the obligor to a suit against the assignor.[10] If so, the assignment would be effective, despite the contractual prohibition. The obligor would need to perform for the assignee, then sue the assignor for breach.

When a clause prohibiting assignment is sufficiently clear, the assignment itself may be treated as ineffective. Courts prefer to interpret a nonassignment clause in a more limited fashion, but do not prevent parties from agreeing to stricter limitations on assignment. The breaching assignor is liable in both instances; either the assignee sues because the obligor avoided the assignment, or the obligor sues because the assignment caused harm.

D. DELEGATION OF DUTIES

Delegation of duties may have a more serious effect on the other party. Where a party chose to enter a contract with one provider, receiving performance from a different person may deprive her of part of what she expected under the bargain. In those situations, delegation may be ineffective.

However, in many situations, a party is not concerned about who performs the contract as long as the performance is the same. Thus, when one buys something on Amazon.com, one does not care whether Amazon.com itself ships the goods or whether Amazon.com asks another person to supply the goods to you on its behalf. As long as the right goods arrive in good condition, the identity of the shipper does

[10] *Id.* §322(2)(b).

not matter. The same can be true of many services. If you take your car to a shop for repairs, you may not care whether they have another shop do the work, as long as the price is the same and the car is repaired properly.

1. Limitations on Delegation

Delegation generally is permitted. A party may perform through delegated parties unless

1. delegation violates a statute or public policy;
2. delegation violates a contract term limiting or prohibiting delegation; or
3. the obligee has a substantial interest in having the other party perform or control the performance.[11]

Again, statutes against delegation are rare. In general, the public has little reason to care whether a party receives performance from one person or another. However, a party with proper licensing, such as a contractor, may not be permitted to delegate duties to an unlicensed contractor, to protect the public from shoddy or dangerous construction practices.

The parties, if they care, are free to limit delegation by contract. Contract provisions prohibiting delegation typically are enforced. The reasons for limiting contract clauses concerning assignment are not as persuasive when applied to clauses prohibiting delegation. Sometimes, a court will infer a limit on the power to delegate from broad language in a clause prohibiting assignment.

A delegation may also be ineffective if the obligee has a substantial interest in having the delegating party perform or control the acts required under the contract. The last applies in the vast majority of contracts that call for personal services or expertise. In personal service contracts in which a particular individual promises to perform services, delegation usually is impermissible without the obligee's consent. Under personal services agreements, parties select an individual to provide those services, often paying a price

Delegation: The Roles of Obligee, Delegating Party, and Delegated Party

In discussing delegation, authorities refer to the obligee, the delegating party, and the delegated party. As with assignments, you must be able to determine which role a party plays and then apply the law to that role.

The **obligee** is a person entitled to receive a contract performance from another (the original obligor). The obligee is not a party to the delegation, but a third-party beneficiary of the second contract. The obligee obtains a right to performance from a third party under the delegation.

The obligor is the one bound to perform for the obligee. The obligor becomes a **delegating party** if it tries to arrange for another to perform contract duties.

The **delegated party** or new obligor is substituted for the original obligor/delegating party. The delegated party is not a party to the first contract, but becomes obligated to perform duties under the delegation.

For example, Kelly (obligor) agrees to provide computer consulting services to Alex (obligee). Kelly (delegating party) delegates her duties to perform to Gail (delegated party). Alex is entitled to receive performance from Gail under the delegation.

As we discussed earlier with assignments, the use of the terms "promisee" and "promisor" may create confusion so using the terms "obligee," "delegating party," and "delegated party" will help keep these roles more clear.

[11] *See id.* §318.

appropriate for that individual. When entering contracts for personal services, parties usually assume that they will receive the performance of the individual hired, especially if that person has special skills or relationship that makes their services individually beneficial to the obligee.

The obligee presumably would like to pick its own substitute provider if the original obligor (the delegating party) chooses not to perform personally. That will not always be the case. Persons hiring a law firm probably realize that the partner they hire will delegate much of the work to associates. Yet even there, the client may expect the partner to control the work. Delegating the duty to a different law firm probably falls outside the expectations of the parties. Similarly, employers probably expect the work to be done by the people they hire. If an employee sent in a substitute employee, the employer justifiably might object. It might prefer to pick its own substitute instead of accepting services from someone chosen by the employee. Thus, in these settings, delegation rarely is acceptable.

The reasons for preferring the original obligor (delegating party) over the delegated party need not be objectively reasonable. Subjective reasons to prefer one provider over another are permissible and, in most cases, deserve legal protection. A person who hires a nanny may have many subjective reasons for preferring the person chosen. Even if, objectively, the delegated party seems as good as the delegating party, the obligee's right to choose a substitute deserves protection. The parent has a substantial interest in having the original person perform or, at least, supervise the performance of the substitute.

Case Preview

Rossetti v. New Britain

In *Rossetti v. New Britain*, a city and an architectural partnership entered into an agreement for architectural services for the construction of a new police station. When the firm was dissolved and its assets sold to Rossetti and another partner, they continued the architectural work of the original partnership. Subsequently, the city refused payment on the services provided, claiming that the contract was not delegable without its permission as a personal services contract.

As you read *Rossetti v. New Britain*, look for the following:

1. Did the court determine that the architectural services agreement was a personal services contract?
2. How did the court consider the intention of the parties, the nature of the contract, and the surrounding circumstances in determining the limits on the delegation of personal services?
3. Was the delegation of personal services under the agreement effective or ineffective in this case?

Rossetti v. New Britain

163 Conn. 283 (1972)

RYAN, C. J.

In the first count of the complaint the plaintiff sought recovery from the defendant for breach of contract for architectural services rendered. In the second count, he alleged that the firm of which he was a partner was hired by the defendant city to perform architectural services in connection with a new police station and Circuit Court quarters; that after a great deal of work and service had been performed the defendant terminated the services of the firm by hiring new architects for the project; that the plaintiff now owns all the assets of the partnership and that he has not been paid for the work. He sought damages in quantum meruit for the work and services rendered to the defendant. . . . On the trial of the case to the jury, the trial court directed a verdict for the defendant on the first count. The jury returned a verdict for the plaintiff on the second count in the sum of $12,300. . . . From the judgment rendered on the second count the defendant has appealed to this court. . . .

. . .

The plaintiff made the following claims of proof: The police building committee held its organization meeting on June 10, 1957. The function of this committee was to construct a new police station and Circuit Court building. At the organizational meeting the mayor reported the passage by the legislature of a special act authorizing a bond issue in the sum of $750,000. The committee unanimously chose a site at Main and East Main Streets for the proposed building. This was agreed on by the mayor and the redevelopment commission. In 1954 the plaintiff, Andrew Rossetti, associated with Philip DiCorcia in a partnership, and, in January, 1956, William Mileto joined this partnership. DiCorcia remained as a partner until December 31, 1957, and Mileto remained as a partner until December, 1960.

Andrew Rossetti, either as a member of his firm or individually, had performed architectural services on numerous public buildings. The New Britain common council, by resolution approved August 23, 1957, by the mayor, authorized the committee to hire an architect to prepare plans and specifications for the new police station and courthouse. . . . The committee then hired the firm of the plaintiff, Rossetti, DiCorcia and Mileto, as the architects to draw sketches and plans for the new building and intended to pay for these services. Prior to July 25, 1957, Rossetti was notified by a telephone call from the mayor's office that his firm was awarded the architectural contract for the building. His firm was engaged as architect at standard rates established by the Blue Book to prepare plans and specifications and the firm expected to be paid for their services. . . . By December, 1957, the set of preliminary and basic working drawings for this project was completed. All architectural work and other work was done before December 31, 1957. . . . By December 31, 1957, Rossetti's firm had completed 30 percent of the project and the blueprints were turned over to the chairman of the committee. The plaintiff, Andrew Rossetti, was at all times in charge of this project to build a new courthouse and police station. Prior to the partnership dissolution on December 31, 1957, when the plaintiff Rossetti and Mileto took over from DiCorcia, Rossetti had given notice of this change during the latter part of November, 1957, to the chairman of the building committee and no objection was made. Neither Rossetti nor his firm ever received a letter from the building committee or from the city of New Britain informing them that the project was abandoned.

When DiCorcia left the partnership on December 31, 1957, all draftsmen, officers, secretaries' desks, books, supplies and records remained at the firm office in Bristol. On December 31, 1957, the firm of Rossetti, DiCorcia and Mileto was dissolved and a new partnership was formed in the name of Rossetti and Mileto. When DiCorcia left the partnership he agreed that the business should belong to and be carried on by Rossetti and Mileto as continuing partners and that all assets, good will and accounts receivable would be assigned to the continuing partners, Rossetti and Mileto. This was done. On April 12, 1963, Rossetti wrote to the chairman of the police board and advised him that a great deal of preliminary planning work had been completed and offered to complete the planning of the new facility for the city of New Britain. He also informed the mayor of the city and offered to complete the work. The services of the plaintiff's firm were accepted by the defendant. Expert testimony was offered that if the project cost was $700,000, $12,800 would be a fair fee based on 30 percent of the work. Testimony was also offered on the basis of 30 percent of the services being completed that the reasonable value of these services done by the plaintiff's firm based on a cost of $661,000 would amount to $12,300.

. . .

The gravamen of the defendant's appeal as expressed in its assignment of error, is that the court erred "[I]n failing to charge that the act of voluntary dissolution of the partnership, Rossetti, DiCorcia and Mileto without the prior knowledge or approval of the building committee made it impossible as a matter of law for the partnership to perform its agreement, and it was, therefore, entitled to no payment for any services claimed to have been performed prior to its dissolution." In its brief, the city urges that the "impossibility" resulted from the assignment of the contract by DiCorcia and Mileto to the plaintiff. The defendant argues that contracts for personal professional services cannot be transferred by assignment without the prior knowledge and consent of the other party, and since the defendant had no notice and gave no consent to the assignment, it cannot be held liable under the contract. This argument is not persuasive on the facts of this case. First, the plaintiff offered evidence to prove that there was notice given to the defendant and that no objection was made. Second, it is a principle of partnership law that, on dissolution, the partnership remains in existence for the purpose of performing existing executory contracts. *Burkle v. Superflow Mfg. Co.*, 137 Conn. 488, 494, 78 A.2d 698; 60 Am. Jur. 2d, Partnership, §198.

As to the defendant's claim concerning the non-assignability of personal service contracts, it is indeed the general rule that contracts for personal services cannot be assigned. To be technically accurate, it is not the benefits that are nonassignable; rather, it is the duties which are nondelegable. Performance, in other words, cannot be delegated to another. 4 Corbin, Contracts, p. 439; 6 Am. Jur. 2d, Assignments, §11. Thus if a specific artist is hired to paint a picture, the artist cannot delegate his duty of performing. *See LaRue v. Groezinger*, 84 Cal. 281, 24 P. 42; 6 Am. Jur. 2d, Assignments, §13. Personal performance is of the essence. Agreements to render

professional services as a physician or lawyer fall within this rule. *Deaton v. Lawson*, 40 Wash. 486, 82 P. 879; *Corson v. Lewis*, 77 Neb. 446, 109 N.W. 735. Whether a duty is personal such that it cannot be delegated, however, is a question of the intention of the parties to be ascertained from the contract, its nature, and the attending circumstances. Clearly, a contract to render architectural services could be one where personal performance is of the essence. *Smith v. Board of Education*, 115 Kan. 155, 22 P. 101. The claims of proof, by which the charge is to be tested, do not support such a conclusion in the case at bar. The defendant's contention is that the contract was personal to the Rossetti, DiCorcia and Mileto partnership. From the claims of proof, however, it is clear that all dealings were with the plaintiff. He was the person in charge of and responsible for the contract. There was nothing offered to show an intent that the plaintiff's partners could not delegate whatever duties they had to the plaintiff. We cannot say that the court erred in its charge in this respect.

Post-Case Follow-Up

The *Rossetti* court determined that the agreement was for personal services that could not be delegated without prior notice and consent from the city. However, Rossetti offered evidence to prove that there was notice given to the city, which made no objection to his continued services after the dissolution of the original partnership. Second, under partnership law, the partnership remains in existence for the purpose of performing existing executory contracts. As to the personal nature of the duties, it was clear that all of the city's dealings were with Rossetti. Rossetti was the person in charge of and responsible for the contract. There was nothing offered to show an intent that the original architectural partners could not delegate whatever duties they had under the original contract to their fellow partner.

Rossetti v. New Britain: Real Life Applications

1. Beauty Supply Company (BSC) agrees to become the exclusive distributor of products from Luxury Hair Care (Luxury) for hair stylists throughout Texas for three years. The agreement contains a provision stating that termination of the distribution relationship could only occur on the anniversary date of the appointment of distributor with 120 days' notice. A year later, Luxury's main competitor, Styles International, acquires BSC. Luxury terminates the distribution agreement. Styles argues that its acquisition results in an effective delegation of distribution duties under the distributorship agreement. It adds that Luxury may only cancel under the notice and anniversary clause of the original agreement. Under the UCC, may Luxury terminate now or does it have to follow the time limits in the termination clause? Review the majority decision in *Sally Beauty Co. v. Nexxus Prod. Co.*, 801 F.2d 1001 (7th Cir. 1986) for the likely outcome.

2. A vineyard owner enters into a contract to provide grapes to a wine maker under a ten-year contract. The vineyard owner provides grapes for five years and then sells his fields and assigns and delegates his contract with the wine maker to the new owner. Even though the grapes are of sound quality, the wine maker refuses to accept the grapes from the new owner of the fields. The new owner sues the wine maker for losses suffered after being forced to sell the grapes on the open market. Was the vineyard owner's assignment and delegation effective under *LaRue v. Groezinger*, 84 Cal. 281 (1890)?

3. Maxwell is ill and seeks help at a local medical institute. The institute's owner advises him that if he paid $5,000 that they could guarantee a cure in six weeks. Maxwell signs the agreement with the center and pays part of the fees. He finds out later that the treatments will not cure his illness, as promised, and he demands a refund. The center refuses to give him a refund. He asserts that the center's owner is dispensing medical care without a license. There is a doctor on staff, but he did not sign the agreement. The institute claims that the doctor delegated his medical skills to the institute so the treatments are legal under its contract with Maxwell. Is there an effective delegation or transfer of duties in this case from the doctor to the institute? Can Maxwell receive a refund? Read *Deaton v. Lawson*, 40 Wash. 486 (1905) to review the dispute and determine the probable result.

---

2. Release or Novation

Delegation creates duties for the delegated party. It does not extinguish duties owed by the original obligor or delegating party.[12] Therefore, if the delegated party does not perform as required under the contract, the obligee can seek redress from either the delegated party or the delegating party. The delegating party cannot escape the duties owed to the obligee without the obligee's consent. An agreement between the delegating party and the delegated party cannot change the rights of the obligee. For example, if a tenant persuades another to assume his lease and to pay the rent, the landlord's right to seek the rent from the tenant is unaffected. If the rent is not paid, the landlord can choose whether to sue the new tenant or the original tenant. The landlord can sue the original tenant under the lease, a contract. In addition, the landlord is a third-party beneficiary of the contract in which the delegated party agreed to pay the rent.

The obligee can agree to **release** or extinguish the obligation of the delegating party, agreeing to seek redress only against the delegated party. Often this will take the form of a **novation**, a new contract between the obligee and the delegated party, in which the obligee agrees to **discharge**, treating as if fully performed, any duties owed by the delegating party. A novation substitutes for the original contract, discharging that agreement in light of this new one. See Exhibit 14.3.

---

[12] Restatement (Second) of Contracts §318(3).

EXHIBIT 14.3 Novation

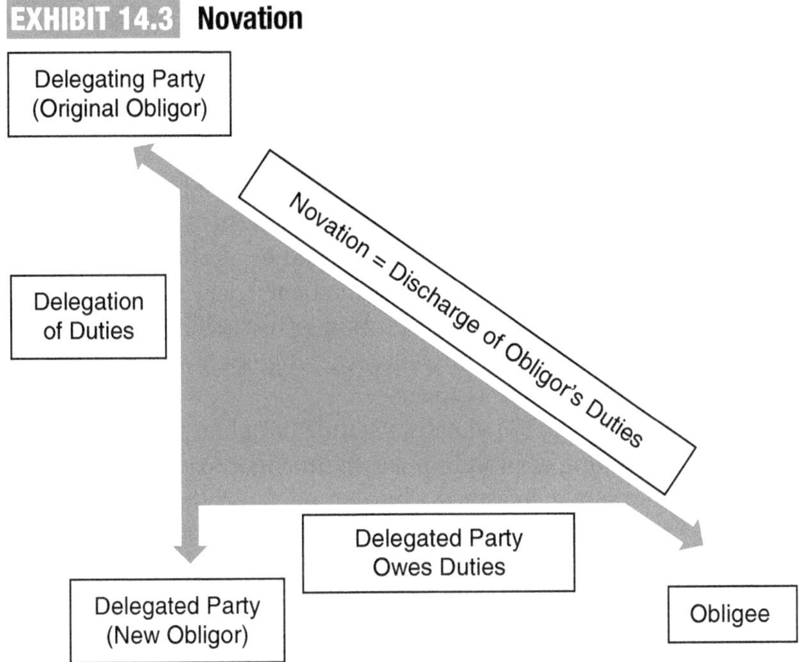

An obligee does not release the delegating party merely by accepting the delegation. Agreeing to look *primarily* to the delegated party is different from agreeing to look *exclusively* to the delegated party. Thus, a landlord may accept a new tenant, perhaps even getting the new tenant to sign a lease. But without an express release for the original tenant, the delegating party is still on the hook. If the new tenant stops paying the rent, the landlord still has recourse to either the new tenant or the original tenant.

Depending on the language used and other circumstances, one might interpret the agreement to look to the delegated party as an agreement to look exclusively to the delegated party, arguably releasing the delegating party from any further obligations under a novation. But that additional promise is required before the delegated party is off the hook. Courts do not assume the obligee intended to make such a release. The delegating party must prove the novation or release.

Chapter Summary

- A contract may specify that some or all of the consideration one party gives will be provided to a third party, not a party to the contract, called a third-party beneficiary. Intended beneficiaries may enforce the contract against the promisor.

- The rights of an intended beneficiary are no greater than the rights of the promisee.
- If the promisor has an excuse or defense against the promisee, it will apply equally to the intended beneficiary's action unless unrelated to the contract at issue.
- The party classified as an incidental beneficiary is a party not intended to receive a benefit under a third-party contract and has no right to sue.
- The promisor and promisee retain the right to rescind or modify their contract unless the contract itself precludes changes or the beneficiary justifiably relied on the contract before learning of the modification or rescission.
- Assignment of rights is generally permissible. An assignment extinguishes the rights of the assignor in favor of the assignee.
- An assignment is unenforceable if it violates a statute or public policy; it violates a term of the contract limiting or prohibiting assignment; it materially alters the obligor's duties; it materially increases the burden on the obligor; it materially increases the risk to the obligor; it materially impairs the obligor's chance of obtaining return performance; or it materially reduces the value of return performance to the obligor.
- Delegation is a transfer of duties to a third party. The delegating party under the original contract and the delegated party under the delegation are obligated to perform to the original obligee, unless there is a novation or release.
- Delegation of duties is permissible unless it violates a statute or public policy; it violates a term of the contract limiting or prohibiting delegation; or the obligee has a substantial interest in having the delegating party perform or control the acts required under the contract, which is common in personal service contracts.

Applying the Rules

Genome Therapy Services (GTS) is a company that is developing cutting edge gene treatments for a variety of illnesses. GTS receives $15 million in a government grant to research and develop a gene therapy for a form of skin cancer. Under the grant contract, GTS must be certain to safeguard its research subjects' personally identifiable information and to protect its proprietary lab research and results. GTS enters into a two-year agreement for secure cloud storage of its patient data, research findings, and test results from Cloud Nine Storage (Cloud Nine). GTS may cancel the contract with a three-month notice.

As part of the government grant agreement, GTS must recruit top scientific talent for its research team, and it hires Dr. Monteiro to head up one of its labs, funded under the government grant. Under the doctor's three-year contract, there is a $150,000 bonus after the first six months of service. There is a boilerplate "no assignment/delegation" clause in this agreement. Dr. Monteiro has debts from a new home renovation and medical school tuition. She transfers $50,000 of her future bonus to a home contractor and $75,000 of it to the bank holding the note for her medical school loan.

During the life of GTS's contract with Cloud Nine, a multinational corporation acquires the cloud storage company. The acquiring corporation owns a number of diverse companies, including GTS's main gene therapy competitor, Alternative Genomics. GTS becomes concerned about the protection of its trade secrets and proprietary data after the sale. GTS wants to terminate its cloud storage agreement immediately. Later, Cloud Nine's storage servers are hacked and GTS's patient and research results are compromised.

Meanwhile, the CEO of GTS is fired after it is determined that he stole millions of dollars in government grant funds, including about 80 percent of the funds intended for Dr. Monteiro's project. The day after her sixth month of service, Dr. Monteiro transfers her contract to her highly qualified research assistant. She notifies GTS of her actions, but receives no response because of the turmoil at GTS over its CEO's conduct. Dr. Monteiro is soon hired by another firm for nearly twice her salary at GTS. A number of cancer advocacy groups then bring an action against GTS for the loss of the government funds without any meaningful development of gene treatments for skin cancer.

Your law firm is selected to advise GTS on its various contract issues.

1. Discuss any third-party rights and duties that can be raised in this dispute.
2. What arguments might be asserted against any third-party claims?
3. Identify various forms of parol evidence that might be considered in assessing third-party claims.
4. Which third-party claims are likely to prevail in this situation?
5. What kind of remedies may be available in these various conflicts?

Contract Law in Practice

1. A sports team is negotiating a contract with a superstar player. The contract is for three years at $10 million per year. The contract duties involve undertaking training and playing for the team, participating in team marketing events, participating in certain community charities, and allowing use of the player's name and likeness in team programs and advertising. However, the team wants to be able to trade the player to undertake these activities for another team, if later desired. Your law firm has been asked to draft an assignment and delegation clause that limits the star's ability to delegate his duties, but leaves flexibility for the team in assignment and delegation. Examine a wide range of sample clauses both in form books and online resources and draft an appropriate clause.
2. Based on the modern Restatement approach, courts must now determine if parties are intended beneficiaries with the right to enforce contract terms.

Typically, a court will review the language of the contract and the surrounding circumstances to try to determine party intent as to intended third-party beneficiaries. Some courts will focus on the intent of the promisee, while others will look at both promisee and promisor intent. Research case law in your state or a neighboring state on intended beneficiaries. Identify whose intent courts focus on in making these determinations. Create a list of interview questions you may ask a client that will help provide support for a finding of party intent to create a third-party beneficiary.

3. In some instances, a party may release an original party from its contract duties under a novation. Review online resources to explore different standard form novations. Using a landowner-tenant example, draft a novation that will release the tenant from her contract obligations under a two-year apartment lease with rental payments of $1,200 per month. Provide both the original form and your revised draft of the novation for this lease situation.

4. A contractor is developing a condominium community in south Florida. In preparing the condo agreement for all of its future owners, the contractor wants to restrict the terms and benefits of this agreement solely to the condo owners, and not any other third parties who are not owners. Review sample condo agreements utilized by your state real estate attorneys. Locate two different examples of such clauses that expressly limit any third-party beneficiaries. Summarize the clauses and explain any key differences between them for a class discussion board.

5. In some states, there is still a continued resistance to finding intended third-party beneficiaries who may enforce contract terms. Under case law and/or statute, there may be a legal presumption against a finding of third-party beneficiaries that must be overcome by the party claiming intended beneficiary status. This presumption can be defeated if there is a clear and unequivocal showing of party intent to benefit a third party in the text of the contract and in the surrounding circumstances. Research your state case and statutory law to determine if there is a presumption against the finding of an intended third-party beneficiary. Review the types of parol evidence used in meeting this elevated burden of proof. Create a presentation on this issue for class discussion.

Remedies

Remedies covers the things a court can do for the winning party. Sometimes the winner will want the court to do nothing more than throw out the other party's claim. But a party who brings a case to court, perhaps even a breaching party, wants some remedy. In breach of contract cases, remedies usually take one of three basic forms: injunctions, damages, or restitution. Those seeking money want a court to award damages or restitution, which are two different ways to assess recovery. Damages are addressed in Chapter 15. Chapter 16 will discuss how to calculate restitution. Those seeking the other party's performance want a court order that compels the other party to perform some or all of the promises, also discussed in Chapter 16.

Knowing what you can get if you win (or what the other party might get if it wins) affects everything a lawyer does in pursuit of a case. Where the remedies are insufficient, even filing the case may waste everyone's time. Where the remedies are substantial, parties may devote extra efforts to pursue (or to defeat) the case.

Remedies also may dictate which claims you decide to bring, for example, when the preferred remedy is available for one claim but not another. In many cases, you need to evaluate the possible remedies from the outset in order to advise a client what, if any, claims to bring. Accurately evaluating which remedies are available and, in the case of damages, how much is at stake, is absolutely critical to being a good lawyer.

Even when drafting a contract, lawyers often pay attention to remedies. Where liability for damages may be enormous, a party may seek a contract term limiting the recovery. Where damages may be hard to prove, a party may seek a term specifying an amount or a formula for calculating damages. Concerns for remedies also may lead parties to seek an arbitration clause, preferring decision by experienced professionals to that of an unknown selection of jurors. Remedies play a role in almost every aspect of contract law, which is why many of the earlier chapters included some mention of remedial issues.

15

Damages

Most plaintiffs suing for breach of contract want money. Rather than ask a breaching party to perform, the plaintiff will make its own substitute arrangements. Money can compensate for the added cost of the substitute. A simple refund may suffice. But substitute arrangements can add a lot more to the cost of a project. Damages need to cover those added costs. This chapter addresses ways to calculate damages that result from the other party's breach.

A. INTRODUCTION: BASIC DAMAGE PRINCIPLES

In awarding damages, courts apply relatively few principles. The implications of these principles can be expressed in more detailed rules. But the principles themselves often resolve damage issues. Understanding the principles makes it easier to understand and apply the rules effectively.

1. Monetary Equivalent of Performance

Damages primarily seek to place the prevailing plaintiff in the position she would have occupied if the contract had been performed, commonly referred to as her **expectation interest**. An enforceable promise entitles the party to expect performance. If performance is incomplete, damages should make up the difference between the performance received (if any) and full, timely performance. Expectation includes gains the breach prevented a party from realizing, not just the losses suffered as a result of the breach.

Key Concepts

- Defining and identifying the expectation, reliance, and restitution interests
- Identifying the components of damages in context
- Applying the limitations on damage awards (avoidability, foreseeability, and uncertainty)
- Enforceability of contract terms that alter the damages available

The definition of expectation limits recovery to losses caused by the breach without ever using the word causation. Losses caused by things other than the breach would have been suffered even if the promise had been performed. Thus, the party's position if the promise had been performed will not include those losses. Only losses a party would not have suffered but for the breach — that is, losses caused by the breach — come within the definition of the expectation interest.

Consider a simple example. Grocer agrees to pay Broker \$15/case for 1,000 cases of a new soft drink, to be delivered July 1. Grocer plans to resell the goods at \$30 a case, earning a profit of \$10/case (after accounting for the cost of resale). Broker repudiates the deal on June 15. Before July 1, published research reveals a serious health risk associated with the new product, driving the retail price to \$15/case. Grocer's position if the contract had been performed would be negative: Grocer would pay \$15/case plus the expense of putting it on the shelves, etc., but would recover only the price of the drink. The bad publicity for the product caused the inability to profit, not the breach. Even if Broker performed, Grocer would not have earned a profit.

Damages will not always place a party in the exact position she deserves. Sometimes a party can use money damages to obtain the equivalent of performance — buy the goods somewhere else, hire someone else to do the work. Sometimes money will not provide what was promised. For example, if a party hired to restore a priceless painting damages it beyond repair, money may seem a little hollow compared to the work of art. But the value the painting would have had if restored as promised — the monetary equivalent of the restored painting — provides the best relief that a court can offer under the circumstances.

Alternative Remedies

Occasionally, courts employ alternative remedies, measures that do not seek the monetary equivalent of performance. The **reliance interest** allows a prevailing plaintiff recovery based on the position he would have occupied if the promise had never been made. If the contract had not been made, a party would not have received any benefits from the contract, but also probably would not have incurred any of the costs involved in performing it. (Reliance can encompass the possibility that the party would have made a different, similar contract, but the terms of the other contract often defy proof.) The **restitution interest** seeks to place the breaching party in the position he would have occupied if the promise had never been made — that is, to return any benefit the breaching party received as a result of the promise. This may be as simple as a refund, but can cover other things, as discussed in Chapter 16.

A plaintiff may request any of these remedies. With some exceptions, courts honor the plaintiff's election. Damage rules focus on the expectation interest because it tends to provide the largest recovery (because it includes the gains she would have realized from performance). Expectation, thus, becomes plaintiffs' first choice. Begin evaluating damages with expectation, resorting to other remedies only if problems arise with an expectation recovery.

Distinguishing Remedial Interests

To illustrate the differences among these remedial interests, consider an example based on *Hawkins v. McGee*.[1] Plaintiff, who had a scarred hand, hired a physician to repair the hand because the physician promised to make the hand perfect. The operation actually further harmed the hand. Restitution would allow the plaintiff to recover the fee paid to the physician, leaving the physician no better off than if the promise had not been made. Reliance would allow a refund plus recovery for any harm to the hand, leaving the plaintiff with a hand as good as it was before—at least, to the extent that money could do that. (Money might pay for another surgeon to repair the damage done by the first.) Expectation, however, would award the plaintiff the value of a perfect hand—better than it was before, as promised by the physician (but not a refund of the price). Again, the measure might include the cost to obtain surgery to achieve that result. If additional treatment cannot fix the hand, a court would award an amount of money to compensate for the shortcomings.

If the financial equivalent of a perfect hand seems hard to imagine, consider a repair shop promising a perfect car, but instead damaging the car. Restitution would require a refund. Reliance would require a refund plus the cost to repair the car to its original condition. If it could not be repaired, reliance would compensate for the reduction to the **value** or **fair market value** of the car (the amount a willing buyer would pay and a willing seller would accept if neither was under compulsion to deal and each was reasonably informed). More specifically, a court would award the value of the car in its original condition minus the value of the car in its current condition. The cost to make the car perfect (or the value if the shop had made the car perfect minus the value of the car as it is) would measure expectation.

Try your hand at identifying the three remedial interests in the following situation. Artist drew a picture of Neighbor's garden. Neighbor asked to buy it. Artist agreed to sell the drawing to Neighbor for $50 plus three pounds of Neighbor's home-grown heirloom tomatoes, the exchange to occur at harvest time. Neighbor spent about $10 per pound growing these tomatoes, though similar tomatoes could have been purchased at the local farmer's market for $5 per pound. At harvest, Neighbor delivered the tomatoes, but needed to pay the rest the next day after visiting an ATM. Artist served the tomatoes at a dinner party that night, at which Guest, delighted by the tomatoes, offered Artist $500 for the drawing. Artist accepted; Guest paid and took the drawing home. The next day, Artist told Neighbor not to bother getting cash because the drawing was already sold. How much would Artist need to pay Neighbor as compensation under each of the three remedial interests?

2. Damages Are Compensatory

The expectation interest implies two goals:

1. damages should not leave a party worse off than performance would have; and
2. damages should not leave a party better off than performance would have.

---

[1] 146 A. 641 (N.H. 1929).

Ideally, then, damages will compensate fully for all losses caused by the breach, but will do no more than compensate for those losses. This principle requires courts to consider any benefits or savings that ensued from a breach, in addition to the costs. For example, a seller who has not yet delivered the goods cannot collect the full price promised. Having the price *and* the goods would be a better position than if the contract had been performed.

Contract law rejects **punitive damages** (sometimes called **exemplary damages**) — recovery over and above the amount plaintiff lost, imposed to punish or to make an example of the breaching defendant. Unless a party's conduct involves a separate tort, punitive damages are unavailable. The presence of a contract does not affect the right to recover punitive damages for the tort. But courts generally do not award punitive damages in the contract action.

Several explanations are offered. Some suggest breach is not a moral issue, but a practical one. The harm to the other party deserves compensation, but society feels no outrage at the breach, even an intentional breach. A party may change its mind as long as it does not harm others — or compensates the others for any harm it does cause. On a practical level, some fear that punishing breach might discourage some contracts, reducing the number of beneficial exchanges actually entered into. Others urge that breach may actually benefit society in some cases. An **efficient breach** occurs if the breaching party can gain enough from the breach to compensate the other party's loss and still come out ahead. Expectation damages discourage inefficient breaches (where losses to others exceed the breaching party's gains), but do not discourage efficient breaches. Punitive damages, by increasing the payment to the other party, would discourage some efficient breaches. Regardless of which explanation appeals, almost every state rejects punitive damages for mere breach of contract.

Nominal damages — a modest amount (such as $1) awarded where a breach caused no measurable harm — are available for breach of contract. Unlike torts such as negligence or fraud, where injury is an essential element of liability, a plaintiff can establish contract liability even if she fails to prove she suffered any damages. Nominal damages are an exception to the rule that recovery will not leave a party better off than if the breach had not occurred. But enriching the plaintiff by $1 is a very modest deviation from the rule. Generally, people paying their own attorneys do not sue if nominal damages are all they expect to recover. Nominal damages usually result from cases where plaintiff thought it could recover substantial damages, but failed to prove them to a court's or jury's satisfaction.

3. Damage Calculations Compare Two Positions

To put the plaintiff in the position it would have occupied if the contract had been performed, you need to consider two things:

1. how much plaintiff would have received if the contract had been performed; and
2. how much the plaintiff did receive (or retain) despite the breach.

Subtracting the position plaintiff does occupy today from the position she should occupy gives the amount necessary to compensate for the breach.

The first aspect is easy to remember, but can be hard to prove. Plaintiff must identify what the defendant promised to provide in order to show that a breach occurred. But measuring the benefit can be tricky. Predictions about the benefit a plaintiff would have received if performance had occurred may vary. The breaching party has every reason to offer a low estimate; the recovering party's estimate will be higher.

The second aspect, the plaintiff's actual position, usually is easier to measure and to prove. Sometimes calculations overlook this component. Where buyer refused to pay the price, awarding the full price seems obvious. But if the plaintiff still has (some of) the goods or has already received a deposit, recovery needs to be adjusted to account for these benefits. If the contract had been performed, plaintiff would not have received the full price plus the deposit and would not have received the full price plus retaining (some of) the goods.

Remedies move a plaintiff from its current position to a new one. The amount depends on both the starting point and the desired ending point.

4. Damages Can Be Reduced

Courts often limit damage awards to advance other policy considerations. The **certainty requirement** rejects damages that exceed the amount proven with reasonable certainty. The **avoidable consequences doctrine** (sometimes called **mitigation of damages**) precludes recovery for losses the plaintiff could have avoided by reasonable conduct. The **foreseeability requirement** limits recovery to amounts the defendant had reason to anticipate at the time of contract formation. Any of these doctrines might reduce recovery to a point below what compensation seems to require. That is, plaintiff may recover less in damages than she would have received if the contract had been performed.

These limitations often support the compensatory goals. For example, a plaintiff convinced the contract would have been enormously lucrative may feel the certainty doctrine prevents full recovery by requiring more proof than normal. Requiring reasonable certainty, however, prevents juries from making speculative awards, perhaps seeking to punish defendants by awarding the highest plausible amount. In this way, certainty keeps the recovery closer to the loss defendant really caused, fulfilling the compensatory goal rather than undermining it.

Similarly, the avoidable consequences doctrine discourages parties from incurring unnecessarily large losses simply because the other party will need to pay for them. A party who acts reasonably will receive full recovery. An unreasonable party has only itself to blame for the inadequate damage award. For example, consider a discharged employee who could get another job immediately but decides not to seek work until the breached contract expires. The income lost in the interim results as much from the employee's decision not to seek new work as from the employer's decision to discharge the employee. Rejecting the employee's claim leaves the employee worse off than if the contract had been performed, but only because the employee caused the losses to grow by not seeking a new job.

Foreseeability serves different policy goals, largely aimed at pre-contract disclosure. Defendant may not anticipate some contract risks unless the plaintiff reveals them. Revealing risks before the contract is made allows the parties to negotiate over special concerns that might arise during the contract. For example, warned how large buyer's loss might be, a seller could take extra precautions to prevent breach, buy insurance against the consequences of breach, or perhaps reject the offer in light of the unacceptably large risk. By denying recovery for unforeseeable losses, the rules encourage disclosure and preserve the right to bargain in advance.

While applicable to all damages, these limitations most commonly arise when damage claims go beyond the value of the performance itself.

5. Damages May Affect a Project

Some contracts are self-contained. When you buy concert tickets or a restaurant meal, the expected benefit usually extends no further than receiving and enjoying the thing itself. Even in these simple cases, consequences might go further. Perhaps you would have been the envy of all your friends if the promoters had not breached by refusing to let you see the concert by the hottest new band. Normally, however, damages that address the value of the thing itself will completely compensate any loss.

Some contracts are part of a larger venture. Breach of the contract may affect an entire project, not just the thing promised. A manufacturer buys leather to make boots or furniture. A restaurateur rents a building to open a restaurant. Employers hire employees in order to earn profits on their labor. In each case, a breach of contract might affect the success of the underlying venture, not just the contract performance itself. Compensating for the value of the leather, the building, or the employee may not be enough. If the losses extend to the boots, the restaurant, or whatever the employees would have provided, compensation for those losses may be necessary to place the prevailing plaintiff in the position it would have occupied if the contract had been performed.

B. DAMAGES GENERALLY

Discussions of contract damages frequently identify three categories of damages: direct loss, incidental loss, and consequential loss.

Direct loss relates to the thing promised. But for the breach, a party would have received the performance of the other party. That performance has a value, the loss of which flows directly from the breach. If promised a car, the direct loss starts with the value of the car (or, in some cases, the cost to obtain a similar substitute car). These are sometimes called **market damages**, as courts frequently measure them by the market value of the performance.

Incidental loss involves costs involved in reacting to the breach. A buyer may need to seek out substitute goods; a seller may need to seek a substitute buyer. These efforts may involve costs, perhaps as little as a phone call, perhaps as much as advertising, storage, and insurance on goods while seeking a new buyer. A party may incur transportation costs to recover the goods. None of these expenses relate directly to the value of the goods, but each involves a cost that a party would not have incurred if the original contract had been performed.

Consequential loss involves the way the party would have used the performance promised. As noted in the preceding section, a buyer might have used a performance to earn profits, using leather to make boots or an actor to make a film. Consequential loss refers to the ways that a party might have used an item to create additional income (or avoid additional costs). Consequential losses frequently involve lost profits, but can affect nonpecuniary interests. For instance, a defective exercise machine may deprive a person of health benefits. Breach by an airline or hotel may deprive a person of the benefits of a vacation. While difficult to measure in dollars, full compensation may require awards to include the value of these uses.

A prevailing plaintiff can recover direct, incidental, and consequential losses. Thus, you may not need to know how to classify each item of damages. Thinking about each category helps you catch a loss that you might have overlooked. The distinctions become important in two ways. First, some legal doctrines apply differently depending on the type of damage at issue. Second, contract terms may limit one type of damage but not others. For instance, contracts often exclude the recovery of consequential losses. Under these clauses, to determine whether a client can recover for a particular loss, you need to differentiate direct losses from consequential losses.

Consider an example. During remodeling, Terry needed to put some furniture in storage. UCrates agreed to rent a 200 square foot locker for $150/month, a special discount off its usual price of $300/month. Terry loaded the furniture on a rented truck ($40/day, plus $25/day insurance, plus $0.80/mile) and took it to UCrates, but UCrates repudiated the contract and refused to let Terry unload. Terry frantically called other storage facilities, finally locating one from StorSure available the next day for $400/month. Terry agreed to lease the space and left the furniture in the rented truck overnight, parking it at home. Terry took an extra day off work the next day in order to drive to the new facility, losing eight hours of pay at $25/hour. StorSure was a little farther from Terry's home, so Terry ended up driving the truck about 15 miles more than if it had been returned after the trip to UCrates. Terry unloaded the furniture without incident.

Terry's direct loss consists of the additional $250/month needed to obtain substitute storage (for as many months as the contract with UCrates would have lasted). The $65 cost to rent the truck for an extra day could be direct loss (the truck was the substitute storage for one night) or incidental loss (the cost of moving the goods from UCrates to the new facility). Either

Damage Formulas

The UCC has many specific damage formulas. The Restatement (Second) of Contracts §346 offers a more general formula: the value of the lost performance, plus any including incidental and consequential loss caused by the breach, minus any savings, typically from saved by not having to perform. Each formula has one goal: to help you identify the various elements to include in a damage award. The details matter only to the extent they help you do that. The formulas seek the same bottom line: the position the injured party would have occupied if the contract had been performed.

way, Terry recovers the additional charges, including $12 for the additional miles driven because of the breach. Incidental loss also accounts for Terry's lost wages, totaling $200. Because Terry obtained a suitable substitute, no consequential losses seem to arise. If, however, the furniture had been stolen or damaged while in the truck overnight, that loss seems consequential, but raises an issue about whether UCrates could foresee the loss at the time of contract formation. Note also that Terry made reasonable choices here. If Terry had left the furniture in the truck for a month ($1,950) or left it on the front lawn unprotected (no direct loss, but consequential losses from weather damage and theft), a court might limit damages to the $250/month Terry would have lost if he had acted reasonably.

The discussion below uses the terms "seller" and "buyer" in their broadest sense. Those terms most commonly apply to sales of goods, governed by the UCC. Upon seeing those terms (especially if capitalized), many lawyers instantly think of transactions involving goods. The terms also apply quite naturally to sales of other things, such as real estate, shares of stock, insurance policies, and tickets to sporting or entertainment events. It may sound odd to refer to employees as sellers of services and employers as buyers. But the terms capture the underlying nature of the transactions. Similarly, contractors sell services (whether construction contractors, lawyers, accountants, or consultants) and others buy them. Seller and buyer sound even odder when applied to leases, but the terms still work: lessors sell the right to use a place or a thing for a limited time; lessees buy that right. The type of transaction will affect the things you take into account and the way you use them to compute damages. The text below addresses the most important variations. Each section starts, however, with a general approach that, in principle, applies across all of these contexts. In describing those fundamentals, the terms seller and buyer avoid unduly lengthening the text.

1. Direct Loss

To compensate for direct loss, courts award the value of the performance promised. Sellers usually need to recover the contract price, the amount the buyer promised to pay them. Buyers usually need to recover the value of the thing promised, whether a physical thing (such as goods or land), a service (such as labor or construction), or an intangible (such as insurance coverage or shares of stock). Each thing has a value, usually the cost to replace it with something just as good. Where nothing else will do, a party may seek an injunction compelling performance, as discussed in Chapter 16.

Damages include the value of the performance not delivered minus any savings that result from the breach. For instance, in a contract to sell land for $500,000, suppose buyer paid $50,000 before seller repudiated the contract. The buyer has lost the value of the land (which might exceed $500,000 — say $530,000 for purposes of this illustration), but she has saved $450,000 (the unpaid part of the price). To put her in the position she would have occupied if the promise had been performed, she must recover $80,000: the value of the undelivered performance ($530,000) minus the amount she saved by not paying for it ($450,000). The money she kept plus the money she recovers equal the value promised. She has no right to both the performance and the price; she may claim the performance, but must offset the unpaid price.

Two Uses of Offset

In damages, you will see offset used two ways, though both refer to a subtraction from the amount due. The text here uses offset to describe reductions to the plaintiff's claim for expenses the plaintiff avoided, often by not completing its performance. Offset also refers to cases where each party has a claim for breach. For example, suppose seller delivered goods that failed to live up to the warranties, and buyer kept the goods without paying for them. Seller has a claim for payment of the price, but buyer has a claim for damages for breach of warranty. Seller's claim for the price will be offset by any losses buyer suffered as a result of seller's breach — or vice versa, if the buyer's claim is larger.

Seller's Recovery of the Price

Whether $1,000 for a television, $10,000 for a month of work, $500,000 for a house, or $1.5 million to build a parking garage, the seller's remedies start with the price. Sellers may recover the promised price minus **offsets** (reductions) for any benefits they received, either under the contract or as a result of the breach. Benefits received under the contract often flow from a buyer's partial performance, for example, a down payment or deposit against the price. Sometimes a breach may save the seller some of the cost to perform the contract. For example, a seller who has not yet shipped goods to a buyer may keep the goods or resell them to another, a benefit that would not be possible if seller had fully performed by delivering the goods. A contractor who has not yet finished a construction project may save the cost of finishing the work. In these situations, the breaching buyer pays the price minus the value of any benefits to the seller.

In some cases, sellers may deserve to recover the entire price. The most obvious situation involves sellers who have fully performed, thus saving nothing that justifies reducing the amount awarded below the price. The UCC makes this explicit for sellers of goods,[2] but the same reasoning would apply where a seller delivered land or stock certificates instead of goods. The UCC also recognizes situations where a seller may save nothing as a result of the breach, even if she has not performed fully. If seller cannot realize any value from reselling the goods to another, keeping the goods may produce no benefit. For example, if goods specially manufactured for one buyer have no use to other buyers, seller may have no way to benefit by using or reselling the goods. In *Biedebach v. Charles*,[3] metal cabinets made for a highly specialized purpose had no resale value or even salvage value, allowing seller to recover the full price of the goods. In *Commonwealth Edison Co. v. Decker Coal Co.*,[4] buyer purchased coal in the ground. After repudiation, buyer had to pay the promised price of coal in the ground. No one else would buy the coal in the ground because the cost to remove it exceeded the value of the coal once removed. Thus, keeping the coal offered the seller no benefit to offset the price.

---

[2] UCC §2-709.
[3] 215 P.2d 114 (Cal. App. 1950).
[4] 653 F. Supp. 841 (N.D. Ill. 1987).

Several kinds of evidence may help establish the value of benefits retained by the seller. In sales of goods, an actual resale of the goods determines their value, provided the sale is made in good faith and a commercially reasonable manner (including, for sales of goods, compliance with several specific requirements that limit resales to bona fide arm's-length transactions).[5] Thus, seller ultimately obtains the entire price: part from the resale of the goods, the rest in damages from the buyer. (Seller recovers the cost to resell the goods and to store them pending resale as incidental damages.) If the seller keeps the goods instead of reselling them (or resells them in an unreasonable manner), the offset equals the fair market value of the goods — the amount the seller could have obtained in a reasonable resale.[6] Again, the seller obtains the equivalent of the entire price: part in the value of goods retained, the rest in damages from buyer.

Keeping the goods may not be the only benefit of a breach. For example, buyer's breach might save seller the cost of delivering the goods or of post-contract service (say, repairs to a car covered by a warranty). Breach might save seller the cost of making custom goods in the first place. Breach might also reduce the cost to seller of paying commissions. For example, suppose a seller will owe a broker 6 percent of the sale price of a house. If seller resells the house for $350,000 after buyer breaches a contract to pay $400,000 for the house, seller may save $3,000 in commissions. (Instead of paying the broker $24,000 on the first contract, seller pays only $21,000 on the second contract.) Subtracting that savings from the damages leaves buyer with the same $376,000 net she would have earned on the first contract.

If that seems puzzling, take it step by step. On the first contract, seller would have received $400,000, but would only net $376,000 after paying the broker 6 percent ($24,000). On the resale contract, buyer received only $350,000, but only paid $21,000 in commissions, netting $329,000. For breach of the first contract, contract price ($400,000) minus benefits (resale price plus saved commissions equals $353,000) produces a damage award of $47,000. That $47,000 plus the $329,000 seller netted on the resale ($350,000 minus commissions of $21,000) produces $376,000, the same net benefit expected on the first contract.

Tolar Construction v. Kean Electric Co.

In this case, the contractor breached the contract by dismissing a subcontractor before the subcontractor completed work. That choice illustrates the hazards of canceling a contract based on the other party's breach. Instead of collecting damages from the subcontractor for its failure to perform in a timely manner, the contractor was liable for damages to the subcontractor. The case shows how courts evaluate the appropriate damages for a seller — here, a seller of construction services.

[5]UCC §2-706.
[6]*Id.* §2-708(1).

As you read *Tolar Construction v. Kean Electric Co.*, look for the following:

1. Did the court consider awarding the full price to the contractor?
2. How did the court evaluate the amount to offset against the price?
3. Was the cost the contractor incurred to hire another to finish the job some evidence of how much the subcontractor saved by not completing work?

Tolar Construction v. Kean Electric Company

944 So. 2d 138 (Ala. 2006)

HARWOOD, Justice.

Tolar Construction, LLC ("Tolar"), appeals from an order of the DeKalb Circuit Court denying its motion for a new trial.... We affirm the trial court's judgment.

FACTS AND PROCEDURAL HISTORY

Tolar . . . secured a general contract . . . for an expansion of Wills Valley Elementary School. . . .

[Tolar hired Kean as] subcontractor for electrical services, [promising to] pay Kean [$230,331.82] upon completion and acceptance of the electrical work [by] January 18, 2001.

In June 2000, Tolar began work on the expansion project; Kean began work as scheduled in August. The project proceeded smoothly until November, when the Board of Education informed Tolar that the roof [already partially installed] was not the roof the Board of Education intended for the school. More than a month elapsed before the roof situation was resolved, during which much of the scheduled electrical work was delayed [making it impossible for Kean to complete work on time].

Although Tolar understandably did not find fault with Kean for not having completed its work by January 18, the project manager for Tolar eventually began to voice some frustration with Kean's allegedly slow completion time. [E]ach company began to complain about the deficient nature of the other's work. On April 27, 2001, [Tolar informed Kean that it needed] to complete its work by the afternoon of May 3. On May 14, [Tolar] ordered Kean "to get off [the] job and do not come back." After completing some minor remedial measures, Kean complied with this order. Other than $3,000 paid to Kean . . . Tolar never paid Kean for its work.

[In] 2003, Kean sued Tolar . . . alleging breach of contract. . . . Tolar [denied] the allegations and filed a counterclaim alleging that Kean had breached the subcontract. . . .

. . .

The . . . jury returned a verdict in favor of Kean on both its breach-of-contract claim and Tolar's breach-of-contract counterclaim, and awarded Kean $88,652.27 in compensatory damages. . . .

[T]he trial court entered its final judgment denying Tolar's motion for a new trial. . . .

Tolar appeals. . . .

. . .

ANALYSIS

I. Were the Damages Awarded Excessive?

On appeal, Tolar argues that the damages awarded by the jury were excessive. In *Ex parte Woodward Construction & Design, Inc.*, 627 So. 2d 393 (Ala. 1993), this Court . . . [explained]:

> When a plaintiff sues on a contract to recover the amount he would have received for the full performance prevented by the defendant's breach, he seeks in effect to recover as damages the profit from performance of the contract which profit defendant's breach prevented him from earning. *In such a case, plaintiff has the burden of alleging and proving not only (a) what he would have received from the performance so prevented, but also (b) what such performance would have cost him (or the value to him of relief therefrom).* Unless he proves both of those facts, he cannot recover as damages the profits he would have earned from full performance of the contract.

627 So. 2d at 394 (quoting Whiting v. Dodd, 39 Ala. App. 80, 83, 94 So. 2d 411, 414 (1957), quoting in turn *Allen, Heaton & McDonald, Inc. v. Castle Farm Amusement Co.*, 151 Ohio St. 522, 526, 86 N.E.2d 782, 784 (1949)).

Tolar's argument that the damages award was excessive, however, is limited in scope: "The jury verdict in favor of Kean against Tolar was excessive *because the jury failed to give Tolar proper credit for payments made by Tolar* which were necessary to complete the terms of the Subcontract Agreement." Tolar then cites the above-quoted rule of law from *Woodward Construction*, as well as what it says was "uncontroverted" evidence indicating that Tolar paid over $43,000 in "completion payments" to third parties, as support for its argument.

The rule set forth in *Woodward Construction*, however, does not necessarily support Tolar's argument. That rule requires the proffer of two types of evidence: (a) what the nonbreaching party (Kean) would have received had the contract been fully discharged, and (b) what it would have cost the nonbreaching party (Kean) to complete the contract had it been fully discharged. The first type of evidence was presented by Kean through the introduction of both the written subcontract as well as testimony corroborating the subsequent increase in the contract price. The second type of evidence was presented by Kean in the form of proof of the amounts that Kean would have owed its sub-subcontractors for completing their work. Tolar does not challenge any of this evidence on appeal.

Tolar's argument is that Kean did not fully perform its subcontract and that Tolar consequently was forced to find third parties to complete certain aspects of it. Although there is a dispute between the parties as to whether Tolar provided credible evidence indicating the amount it paid, resolution of that dispute is not required to resolve Tolar's argument. Even if Tolar had presented concrete evidence, agreed by both parties to be accurate, indicating the amount of money Tolar had spent to complete Kean's electrical subcontract, such evidence does not indicate the amount of money Kean would have had to spend to complete the subcontract. For instance, any third party completing "last minute" work at the behest of Tolar could, and probably would, have charged more than an original subcontractor or sub-subcontractor would have, because of "start up" transitioning costs, and may have charged a premium in recognition of the immediacy of Tolar's needs. Had Tolar not breached the contract, however, Kean's sub-subcontractors would have been obliged to perform their work at the agreed-upon price, without any "discontinuity" costs. In short, the rule of *Woodward Construction* does not envision that the completion-cost offset would be computed from the perspective of the breaching party, but rather that it would be computed from the perspective of the nonbreaching party.

Moreover, a review of the jury instructions indicates that the jury was never charged with respect to completion payments. Rather, the court simply stated:

> "Damages for breach of contract is that sum which would place the injured party in the same condition it would have occupied if the contract had not been breached. . . . The law defines substantial performance as performance of all the important parts of a contract, but the doctrine of substantial performance does not require a full or exact performance of every slight or unimportant detail. If a party to a contract substantially performs a contract as I have defined substantial performance to you, the party may recover the contract price *less the reasonable cost of remedying any trivial defects or omissions left to be performed.*"

(Emphasis added.)

The quoted language does not speak of deducting the cost of "completion payments," but rather the likely smaller sum necessary to remedy "trivial" defects or omissions caused by the failure to fully perform. Additionally, the instruction does not clarify whether the jury was to determine how much it would cost to remedy those "trivial defects or omissions" from the perspective of the breaching party or the substantially performing party. Because Tolar failed to object to the trial court's jury instructions, those instructions are the law of the case, and Tolar cannot now complain about the jury's obedience to them.

Because Tolar has not otherwise challenged Kean's presentation of evidence indicating the amount of damages to which it was entitled, but instead has presented evidence indicating only the amount of money Tolar spent in consequence of its own breach, we hold that the trial court did not err in denying Tolar's motion for a new trial, and we thus affirm the trial court's judgment as to this ground.

Post-Case Follow-Up

The cost that a substitute subcontractor charged might reflect how much of the work remained. It is possible that, if Kean had finished the job, its sub-subcontractors would have encountered cost overruns that Kean would need to pay. But that possibility did not overcome direct evidence of how much plaintiff would have paid those providers. Without more, the court decided not to infer additional cost overruns. Plaintiff recovered the full price, minus the amounts it saved by not having to pay its own subcontractors to finish the work.

Tolar Construction v. Kean Electric Co.: Real Life Applications

1. Buyer agreed to pay Collector $12 million for a painting by the famous artist Raphael. Buyer never paid for or took delivery of the painting, but tried unsuccessfully to resell it to others. Collector sued for $12 million, contending that despite diligent efforts, she failed to find a buyer willing to pay a reasonable price. Collector attributed the failure to Buyer's efforts to resell the painting, which allegedly made the painting seem less like a masterwork and more like a commodity. Is Collector entitled to recover the entire price? If so, can Collector keep the painting?

2. Buyer agreed to pay seller $400,000 for a condominium. Buyer paid a deposit of $20,000, but then repudiated the contract. Seller subsequently sold the condominium for $370,000, the best offer Seller received in the two months following Buyer's repudiation. How much should Seller recover from Buyer?
   a. Would the answer be different if the property were a private plane instead of a condominium? *See* UCC §2-706.
   b. Would your answer be different if Seller sold the plane or condominium to a relative for $300,000 without trying to find another buyer who might pay more? *See* UCC §2-708(1).

3. In exchange for $1,000 a month, Jesse agreed to work for Professor Parrish for one year, helping prepare an important book for submission to a publisher. After six months, Professor Parrish decided to scrap the project and informed Jesse that no further work would be needed. A law firm offered Jesse $800 a month for the same amount of time that Jesse worked for Professor Parrish. What damages, if any, can Jesse recover from Professor Parrish?

4. Buyer agreed to pay Seller, a boat dealer, $150,000 for a new boat ordered from the factory. Before the boat arrived, Buyer repudiated the deal for health reasons and asked for a return of the $15,000 deposit. When the boat arrived, Seller managed to sell it to another buyer for the same price $150,000 (a profit of $20,000).
   a. Is Buyer entitled to recover the $15,000 deposit? *See* UCC §2-718(2).
   b. Is Seller entitled to any damages for Buyer's breach? *See* UCC §2-708(2).

Lost Volume Sellers

In some circumstances, a resale may not offset the loss. A second contract may not be a substitute for the first (breached) contract. Rather, a seller might have been able to perform both contracts, earning profits on each. If so, subtracting the amount obtained in the second transaction will leave the seller worse off than if the first contract had been performed. Instead of earning profit on two transactions, seller obtains the benefit of only one. In these situations, special rules allow the seller to recover as damages the profit lost on the breached contract, including overhead.[7]

[7]UCC §2-708(2).

Consider an example. Seller makes potato chips—and can make as many potato chips as people will buy. Buyer orders 1,000 cartons of potato chips, but later repudiates the contract. The next day, other buyers order 1,000 cartons of potato chips at the same price buyer had agreed to pay. At first glance, it appears that seller suffered no loss. Instead of receiving the price from the breaching buyer, it gets the same price for the same chips from other buyers. But it could have filled both orders, getting the price of both orders (but having to make more chips to fill both orders). Seller has lost volume—lost the profits on 1,000 cartons it could have sold but did not. The savings, if any, comes in not having to produce another 1,000 cases. Seller should recover the contract price minus the cost saved in not having to make and deliver the extra 1,000 cartons. Essentially, this awards the profit lost on the transaction plus overhead.

EXHIBIT 15.1 UCC Remedies for Seller

The UCC remedies discussed above can be written as formulas.

UCC §2-706	UCC §2-708	UCC §2-709
Contract Price	Contract Price	Contract Price
– Resale Price*	– Market Price**	– 0***
+ Incidental Damages	+ Incidental Damages	+ Incidental Damages
– Savings	– Savings	
Damages	Damages	Damages

*if seller entered a reasonable and good faith resale transaction
**if no qualifying resale transaction occurred
***if goods were delivered or reasonably could not be sold

Contracts for Services

Employers buy services; employees sell services. If the employer breaches, the employee wants the price (paychecks). For services already delivered, the price ends the contract inquiry (but statutes may impose additional obligations on breaching employers). For services not yet performed, the employee arguably gains the benefit of devoting that time to other pursuits, a benefit that might require an offset. If the employee actually resells the time to another, courts usually subtract the earnings actually received from the recovery. If the employee did not resell the time to another employer, courts might offset the market value of the time. In some cases, no offset will be required, as where the employee cannot obtain a reasonable substitute transaction. Similarly, an employee who would have worked both jobs might be a lost volume seller.

While the outline resembles seller's recovery for goods, the rules for employment work just a little differently. Offsets are not addressed as the benefits of the breach, but under the avoidable consequences doctrine, discussed in section C.1. below. For most people, free time after discharge does not feel like a benefit. A job search feels like work, not leisure. Fewer opportunities take less search time, but feel worse, not better, than a successful search with a lot of interviews. Instead of holding that the employee received free time that had a market value, courts examine actual substitute transactions or unreasonable failures to enter (or to seek) a substitute transaction. In effect, an offset of zero is the normal result, unless the defendant proves an offset is appropriate as avoidable consequences.

Some service contracts involve more than the employment of an individual. Contractors sell services; others buy those services. That applies to construction contractors, consulting firms, accounting and law firms, and a host of other services sold by persons (including individuals) who are not employees. On the whole, the same equations apply when those selling services seek recovery from those buying services. Again, context can produce variations.

In construction, courts rarely treat projects that the contractor undertakes following a breach as substitute projects. In part, this reflects industry reality, where contractors can work multiple projects simultaneously, adding more workers as needed. The new project often does not substitute for the old, but adds volume. In addition, other work may differ substantially from the original contract—and may produce losses rather than profits. Assuming that other jobs are not substitutes avoids a host of complexities courts prefer not to address. Offsets for savings related to the original breached contract continue to apply.

The same principles may apply to other contractors. Advertising agencies, accounting firms, consulting firms, and others all may take on new projects in addition to existing work rather than as a substitute for the breached contract. In some situations, however, courts recognize that a contractor operating at capacity could not have taken on additional work while continuing with the original contract. In those settings, offsets for the benefit of the new work may apply.

Real Estate Leases

The discussion above applies reasonably well to sales of real estate. Leases require special attention. In some ways, lessors are sellers; lessees are buyers. If the contract had been performed, lessor would have received the price (rent) and would have delivered possession of the property to the lessee. Breach by the lessee usually involves nonpayment. The lessor recovers the unpaid portion of the rent, less any savings realized as a result of the breach—such as recovering possession of the property.

Leases unfold over time (typically, but not always, monthly), posing some additional complications. For any period in which the tenant retains possession, no benefit requires offset against the rental price for that period. But vacating the premises does not necessarily benefit the lessor. Moving out technically may not breach the lease, which often requires the tenant to pay rent but may not require occupancy. Nor does moving out necessarily entitle the lessor to resume possession. Thus, the common law originally did not offset the rent owed by the value of the premises, deeming them to remain in the tenant's possession unless the lessor reclaimed them. In effect, this required the tenant to pay the full rent for the entire lease term, even after the tenant stopped receiving any benefit from the lease. That rule remains common for commercial leases. Nonpayment may permit the owner to recover possession via eviction. Yet an owner might prefer to sue for the rent instead of evicting the tenant and seeking to use the premises (e.g., leasing to another).

Recent statutes have treated residential lessees who vacate with notice to the lessor as if they have returned the premises, even when early departure breaches the lease. The lessor's recovery of rent is then offset by the amount she can realize by reasonable efforts to relet the premises to another tenant. As with services, the offset often is determined under the avoidable consequences doctrine: the offset is measured by the amount the lessor did earn by reletting the premises or could have earned by reasonable efforts to relet the premises. Unless the lessor acts unreasonably, market value will not be offset for vacated premises.

Breaches may not involve the price. Apartment dwellers may violate restrictions, such as using a charcoal grill on the balcony or owning a forbidden pet. Business lessees may violate limitations on the uses of the property, for example, selling things that another tenant has an exclusive right to sell in this mall (thus putting the lessor in breach of that tenant's lease). In these cases, the discussion of damages starting with price does not work well. In reality, these breaches by lessees resemble those of a provider of services: the lessee has obligations to do (or not do) something, in effect a service that the lessee performs in exchange for the premises (the price the lessor pays for the promise to abide by the lease restrictions). Thinking of these cases as breach by the seller of services, depriving the lessor of the conduct promised, may provide a more useful way to think about this kind of breach.

Buyer's Damages

If the contract had been performed, buyer would have received the seller's performance and would have paid for it. The buyer is entitled to recover the value of any performance not delivered by the seller, with due offset for any amounts saved as a result of the breach. For example, if the breach occurred before the buyer had paid the full price, buyer saved the unpaid portion. Similarly, breach may relieve buyer of the need to incur other expenses (such as delivery costs, if the contract required buyer to pay for shipping).

The calculation of buyer's direct loss is the flip side of the seller's direct loss. To determine the loss, one must ascertain the value of the performance seller did not deliver; to determine the offset, one subtracts any savings buyer realized by not receiving the performance. The same techniques might determine the value of the performance:

1. an actual market transaction purchasing the performance from another (**cover**), provided buyer acted reasonably and in good faith;[8] or
2. the market price of the performance if no substitute transaction had been made.[9]

---

[8]UCC §2-712.
[9]*Id.* §2-713.

For sales of goods, buyers are entitled to a refund of the price paid so far.[10] This serves a restitutionary function. Even if the buyer can get the same goods at a better price, it still is entitled to a full refund. The breaching seller is not entitled to keep any part of the price simply because the market shifted in buyer's favor. In other contexts, courts sometimes treat the unpaid portion of the contract price as the offsetting benefit.

When the substitute differs in significant ways from the performance promised, a substitute transaction is less likely to provide an accurate measure. But where the performances are indistinguishable, a substitute transaction can set the value of the performance. Once buyer has what it was promised, damages consist of the difference in the price: subtract the original price from the price in the substitute transaction to determine how much more the buyer had to pay to receive the performance. Alternatively, subtracting the contract price from the market value of the performance — the amount it would have cost if a reasonable substitute transaction had been entered — offers another way to estimate the direct loss buyer suffered.

For example, if dealership fails to deliver a car, buyer can cover with the same model, similarly equipped, from a different dealership. If the same model was unavailable, a reasonable choice of a different make or model of similar quality might justify an award for cover. But a buyer who purchases an Audi as a substitute for a Kia probably cannot recover the difference in price.

For contracts other than sales of goods, differences in quality make cover a less useful remedy. In real estate, courts generally do not award damages based on substitute transactions, usually because location can make a huge difference despite similarity in other features (size, age, condition, amenities). Even small differences between two properties may produce large discrepancies in price. But in other contexts, an imprecise substitute performance may suffice. Covering steel screws with aluminum screws (or vice versa) might be reasonable, if the promised screws were unavailable in time and the substitute is the closest that would serve buyer's needs. Exigencies may make stepping up in quality reasonable.

Toto We're Home, LLC v. Beaverhome.com, Inc.

This case offers a straightforward illustration of how damages put buyers into the same position they would occupy if the contract had been performed. The court both lays out the rules and applies them well.

As you read *Toto We're Home, LLC v. Beaverhome.com, Inc.*, look for the following:

1. Did the trial court put the buyer in the position it would have occupied if the contract had been performed? What remedial interest did it award?

[10] *Id.* §2-711(1).

2. Did the appellate court put the buyer in the position it would have occupied if the contract had been performed?
3. Was it reasonable to pay more than the original contract price when buying substitute goods?

Toto We're Home, LLC v. Beaverhome.com, Inc.

754 N.Y.S.2d 334 (App. Div. 2003)

. . .

ORDERED that the judgment is modified, on the law, by adding thereto a provision awarding the plaintiffs "cover" damages of $4,041.56, plus prejudgment interest thereon from June 4, 2001; as so modified, the judgment is affirmed. . . .

. . .

In February 2001 the plaintiffs contracted with the defendant to purchase wood flooring for the total price of $15,124.69, which the plaintiffs paid in full. When the defendant was unable to deliver the flooring, the plaintiffs cancelled the order, and promptly contracted to purchase comparable flooring from a different supplier who had it in stock, at a cost of $19,166.25. The Supreme Court granted the plaintiffs' motion for summary judgment to the extent of recovering the purchase price of $15,124.69, but denied the plaintiffs' motion insofar as it sought to recover the additional costs of obtaining replacement goods.

This case is governed by Uniform Commercial Code article 2. Pursuant to UCC 2-711(1)(a): "(1) Where the seller fails to make delivery . . . the buyer may cancel [the contract] and . . . may in addition to recovering so much of the price as has been paid (a) 'cover' and have damages under [UCC 2-712]." UCC 2-712, in turn, provides:

> (1) After a breach within the preceding section the buyer may "cover" by making in good faith and without unreasonable delay any reasonable purchase of or contract to purchase goods in substitution for those due from the seller.
>
> (2) The buyer may recover from the seller as damages the difference between the cost of cover and the contract price together with any incidental or consequential damages as hereinafter defined (Section 2-715), but less expenses saved in consequence of the seller's breach."

The plaintiffs established the seller's breach, which necessitated the reasonable and prompt purchase of replacement goods from another seller at increased cost. The plaintiffs thus demonstrated their entitlement to recover their cover costs (*see Fertico Belgium v. Phosphate Chems. Export Assn.*, 70 N.Y.2d 76, 82, 517 N.Y.S.2d 465, 510 N.E.2d 334). While the plaintiffs also are eligible to recover consequential damages (UCC 2-712[2]; 2-715), they failed to establish that they sustained any such damages.

. . .

Post-Case Follow-Up

The court awarded cover price minus contract price without discussing whether the substitute transaction was reasonable. The trial court's refusal to grant summary judgment on cover might stem from concerns about the reasonableness of the cover transaction, concerns that could have been addressed at trial, if one had been held. The trial court, however, did not hold a trial, instead entering final judgment for plaintiffs — the equivalent of ruling that the cover was unreasonable, without any explanation for that conclusion. The appellate court's failure to discuss the reasonableness of the cover transaction suggests the record lacked much evidence on that point. Cover might cost more for several reasons. Buyers probably chose the least expensive source available, so that other sellers would have charged more even if nothing changed. The price may have risen after the initial contract was formed. Sellers may have charged for prompt delivery. Without facts to suggest an unreasonable cover, the court awarded plaintiff its full loss.

Toto We're Home, LLC v. Beaverhome.com, Inc.: Real Life Applications

1. Studio agreed to pay Mira Nukira, a famous actress, $6 million to star in its new movie. Three weeks before shooting began, Nukira repudiated the contract. Laurie Jenson, an even more famous actress, agreed to perform the role for $12 million. Studio agreed and shooting began on time. Can Studio recover the difference in salaries? What damages would be available?

2. Bobbi agreed to pay Sam $230,000 for a home. When Sam refused to close the deal, Bobbi found a similar home in a nearby neighborhood for $275,000. Can Bobbi recover the additional $45,000 required to obtain a suitable substitute home? What facts might you need to advise Bobbi regarding the likely recovery? Would your answer be different if the contract were a one-year lease at $2,300 a month and the substitute lease were $2,750 a month?

3. Rad owns a restaurant with a large wine list. Rad purchased ten cases of 2000 Chateau Leoville-Barton (rating 95) from Conn for $18,000. Rad inspected the wine upon delivery and discovered that its quality had degraded, probably as a result of improper storage. While not yet vinegar, the wine was not suitable for sale in the restaurant. Rad rejected the wine and looked for a substitute supply. Initially, Rad found no one willing to sell 2000 Chateau Leoville-Barton for less than $4,000 a case, a price Rad refused to pay. In the following three months, Rad purchased some similar wines: five cases of 2000 Chateau Lynch Bages (rating 97) for $18,000; two cases of 2000 Chateau Haut Brion (rating 99) for $16,000; and most recently, three cases of 2000 Chateau Leoville-Barton for $9,000. What damages should Rad request when suing Conn? What damages is the court most likely to award?

4. In a long-term supply contract, Mine promised to sell Utility all its requirements for coal, up to a maximum of two million tons per year, at $30/ton. The contract set a maximum sulfur content for the coal. Mine breached two years before the contract expired. In the first year after breach, Utility covered with one million tons of low sulfur coal ($50/ton) and one million tons of high sulfur coal ($30/ton), which when combined produced a fuel of the promised sulfur content. In later years, Utility bought two million tons of low sulfur coal ($52/ton), seeking to improve its environmental compliance without paying for permits to emit more sulfur. Should the court award Utility damages based on these cover transactions? How should the court calculate the damages? *See Coalsales Co. v. Gulf Power II*, 522 Fed. Appx. 699 (11th Cir. 2013).

Breaches can be partial rather than total. Seller's breach may not entitle buyer to reject all of the goods. For instance, if a contract involved monthly shipments, seller's breach one month may not permit buyer to cancel the contract for subsequent months. In these situations, the extent of the refund and damages are limited to the extent of the breach. No breach exists for earlier months and none exists yet for later months.

In some cases, a buyer may decide to keep the performance despite the breach. This commonly occurs when the goods delivered fall short of the promised quality, but not by so much that the buyer rejects them. Buyers who retain goods can recover the difference between the value the goods would have had if they had been as promised and the value the goods actually have as delivered.[11] The same measure applies to real estate or construction that falls short of that promised.

In these circumstances, buyers cannot receive a full refund; having kept the goods (or other performance), buyer must pay something for them. But having paid for performance of one quality, it is entitled to any difference between what it received and what it was promised.

In some cases, other measures may work, such as the cost to repair performance to satisfy the contract. For example, if seller delivers a car without a working air conditioner, the cost to repair the air conditioner may cure the breach by bringing the goods up to the promised quality. Repairs give the buyer exactly what was promised. When repairs are impossible or unreasonably expensive, the difference in value between the goods received and the goods promised can be awarded.

[11] UCC §2-714.

EXHIBIT 15.2 UCC Remedies for Buyers

The UCC remedies discussed above can be written as formulas.

UCC §2-712*	UCC §2-713**	UCC §2-714***
Refund	Refund	
+ Cover Price	+ Market Price	Value of Goods as Warranted
– Contract Price	– Contract Price	– Value of Goods as Received
+ Incidental Damages	+ Incidental Damages	+ Incidental Damages
+ Consequential Damages	+ Consequential Damages	+ Consequential Damages
– Savings	– Savings	
Damages	Damages	Damages

* if buyer purchased substitute goods in a reasonable and good faith cover transaction
** if no qualifying cover transaction occurred
*** for accepted goods that did not live up to promised quality

Consider an example. Buyer, a construction contractor, agrees to pay seller, a lumber yard, \$2.50 per linear foot (lft) for 10,000 lft of seasoned 2×4s. Seller delivers green 2×4s instead of seasoned 2×4s. Buyer, under time pressure, accepts the nonconforming goods under protest. In a suit, buyer would be entitled to the value of the lumber promised minus the value of the lumber received — plus any incidental or consequential damages. Direct damages would be measured by subtracting the market value of green 2×4s from the market value of seasoned 2×4s. Normally, the contract price might be the value of the goods as promised. But it is possible buyer got a good deal; the value as promised might be more than the contract price, say \$3/lft. Presumably, the value as delivered is less than that; that is, green 2×4s probably sell for less than seasoned 2×4s — say, \$2/lft. Buyer is entitled to the difference: \$1/lft × 10,000 linear feet = \$10,000.

Repair might work in this situation. Suppose the 2×4s could be seasoned, at some cost. The cost to season the lumber would leave the buyer where it would have been if the contract had been performed. Of course, the time required to season the lumber makes it available much later than promised, which might require compensation for consequential losses.

Services and Employment

Cover price minus contract price serves as a useful measure for many service contracts. It does not apply to employment contracts very often. While some employees (movie stars, professional athletes, and so on) may have the resources to pay damages for breaching an employment contract, many employees cannot pay a judgment, making it useless to sue them. Other service contracts, however, raise the issue. If a construction contractor walks off the job, hiring a new contractor seems prudent. Direct loss consists of the difference in cost between the original (promised) provider and the substitute provider. While courts usually do not call the substitute transaction cover, the substance remains identical. The same concerns for reasonableness and good faith also apply. Similarly, if a caterer backs out on your wedding, hiring a last minute substitute of equal quality may cost more than the original contract price. Compensation for the difference measures the direct loss.

Where services are provided, but are not of the promised quality, the same remedies may apply. If the services can be repaired — say, the plumbing redone to code — the cost of repair measures the loss. If the services cannot feasibly be repaired, the difference in value between the services promised and the services received offers an estimate of the direct loss.

Real Estate: Nondelivery of the Premises

When a seller (or lessor) of land breaches, buyers' remedies start with entitlement to the property. Chapter 16 addresses **injunctive relief** (court orders, such as an order of **specific performance**, compelling a party to perform the specific act promised), which may entitle buyer to obtain the property in question. If buyers seek damages instead, direct loss consists of the value of what was promised minus any savings attributable to the breach — typically, the price buyer would have paid for the property under the contract. Thus, if seller agreed to sell land to buyer for $500,000, upon seller's breach buyer may recover any amount paid so far, plus the difference between the value of the property and the contract price. If the property is worth less than $500,000, buyer suffers no direct loss. (But sellers usually don't breach when they are being overpaid.) If the property was worth $575,000, buyer may recover the $75,000 profit it would have realized by getting the land at a bargain price. If seller resells the land (in a reasonable, good faith transaction), that resale price might set the market value for buyer's claim. However, buyer may submit evidence that the market value at the time of breach was different. (Alternatively, buyer might claim restitution for unjust enrichment, seeking to recover the benefit the seller received on the resale, even if that exceeded the market value — another remedy discussed in Chapter 16.)

The same would be true of a lease, if the lessor deprives the lessee of the premises. The lessee may recover the value of the promised premises (for the promised term) minus the amount it saved by not paying rent to the lessor. The remedy will deal with the remaining term of the lease at the time the breach occurs. Any months during which the lessee enjoyed undisturbed occupancy of the premises will probably be severed. The contract for those periods was performed, not breached.

In real estate, buyer's or lessee's remedies focus on market value, not substitute transactions. Cover offers some evidence of the market value, but is not treated as dispositive. If the owner resells or relets the same property, that may establish the market value of that property. A buyer or lessee who enters a substitute transaction obtains different real estate. Buyer is entitled to the value of the real estate promised, not necessarily to the value of this different property. A higher price for cover may reveal what a good deal buyer had made with the original seller. Alternatively, it might reflect subtle ways in which the new property is better than the original: a Mercedes, or maybe an Audi, rather than a Kia. (Buyer probably didn't cover with a worse parcel if it expected to recover damages.) To the extent that the substitute land is similar to the promised land, the cover transaction offers some evidence of market value. But other recent comparable transactions also deserve consideration. The buyer's specific transaction is not necessarily the measure of direct loss.

In some states, sellers who lack good title to real estate are not required to compensate the buyer for the value of the property. Rather, they need only pay the reliance interest: any costs the buyer incurred in reliance on the contract. This requires a refund and may include other expenses, such as a title search, inspection costs, escrow fees, and other costs related to the property. The exception protects sellers who believed in good faith that they had good title, but who in fact did not own the property. The exception will not protect sellers who had good title, or who knew they lacked title, or who caused their own inability to convey good title (say, by selling to another). In these situations, seller must pay full expectation damages.

Try your hand at applying the rule to the following situations.

Example 1: Sean agrees to sell land to Terry for $350,000. After Terry makes a down payment of $35,000, Sean receives an offer from Leslie to buy the same land for $400,000. Sean conveys to Leslie, breaching the contract with Terry. How much can Terry recover?

Example 2: Sasha sells land to Chris $125,000, even though Sasha knows Pat owns the land. Chris pays Sasha and receives a deed, but Pat later recovers the land from Chris. Chris sues Sasha. The land is worth $200,000. How much can Chris recover from Sasha?

Example 3: Bank forecloses on land and sells it to Carmen for $70,000, including a down payment of $5,000. Carmen immediately finds a buyer willing to pay $100,000 for the land. Unknown to Bank, defects in the foreclosure process permit Gail, the former owner, to redeem the land. When Bank cannot deliver title, Carmen sues Bank for breach. How much can Carmen recover from Bank?

Real Estate: Defects in the Premises

Some breaches may involve the quality of delivered property. Seller may **warrant** (make a promise related to quality) that a home is free from termites, but deliver a home that is infested. If the difference is material and buyer cancels for breach, damages for nondelivery may apply. If buyer keeps the premises despite the nonconformity, direct loss may be measured by either (a) the cost of repair (exterminating the termites and fixing any damage they caused); or (b) diminution in value, the difference between the value of the house if it had been of the promised quality (no termites) and the value of the house as it was delivered (infested). Note the similarity to UCC §2-714 for sales of goods.

Defects in the premises are common in leases: the roof leaks, the heater doesn't work, the windows won't open, the lock sticks, and so on. When these problems make the premises uninhabitable, cancellation may be justified. Short of that, repair is the most realistic remedy here. Suing for damages is not always practical when damages are relatively small. Offsetting rent payments with the cost of repairs is dangerous, given special rules governing leases (and expedited procedures for eviction).

Repair or Diminution in Value

Whenever repairs might measure direct loss, the reasonableness of repair may pose an issue. Repairs might cost more than they add to the thing repaired. In construction cases (the most common setting), two principles govern recovery of repairs:

1. plaintiff generally may elect to recover the cost of repairs; but
2. courts deny repair costs if they are clearly disproportionate to the probable loss in value to the plaintiff.[12]

Alternatively, plaintiff may recover the diminution in the market value of the property. In sales of goods, repair of accepted goods is recoverable if reasonable.[13] This resembles the avoidable consequences doctrine, which denies recovery when an unreasonable decision increases the loss. As described in the Restatement (Second) of Contracts, the rule does not call for simple cost-benefit analysis. The fact that repairs cost more than the value to the plaintiff is not enough to reject repairs. The repairs are available unless they are *disproportionate* to the probable loss in value to the plaintiff. Thus, the rule favors repairs unless the difference is dramatic.

Comparing cost of repair to the value *to the plaintiff* appears to include elements of subjective value. The value to the plaintiff may exceed diminution in market value. Contract allows people to pursue their individual preferences (as long as others are willing to enter the contract on those term). Thus, if plaintiffs attach idiosyncratically large value to a particular performance, that value may justify repairs that produce a relatively small change in market value (the value to others).

You encountered one example of this rule in Chapter 11: *Jacob & Youngs v. Kent.*[14] The court refused to award the cost to tear down a house and rebuild it using the specific brand of pipe the contract required, instead awarding the diminution in value of the house (which may have been zero).

Extreme cases like *Jacob & Youngs* make diminution in value seem preferable. In other cases, however, repairs may seem more reasonable, even if they cost more than they add to the market value of the property. Consider the following example.

Landis v. William Fannin Builders, Inc.

This case involves another construction mistake that affected the appearance of the house but not its function. Owners insisted on exactly the finish prescribed by the contract, even though problems during construction made that very expensive to achieve. Repairs added almost 20 percent to the total

[12]Restatement (Second) of Contracts §348(2).
[13]UCC §2-714(1).
[14]129 N.E. 889 (N.Y. 1921).

cost to build the home, but increased its value only modestly. This time, the court awarded the owners the cost of repair.

As you read *Landis v. William Fannin Builders, Inc.*, look for the following:

1. What rule does the court apply to determine whether the cost of repairs exceeds the value by so much that it should be denied? Does that rule differ from the one identified in the Restatement (Second) of Contracts?
2. What economic waste will result here? How does the court determine whether that amount of waste is unreasonable?
3. How does the court distinguish this case from *Jacob & Youngs v. Kent*?

Landis v. William Fannin Builders, Inc.

951 N.E.2d 1078 (Ohio Ct. App. 2011)

KLATT, Judge.

[In 2004, Landis agreed to pay Fannin Builders $356,750 to build a custom home on land that Landis owned. The specifications called for T1-11 exterior siding covered with two coats of stain in a color of appellees' choice. Appellees chose T1-11 plywood siding because it provided a more natural, rustic look than other types of siding, which a semitransparent stain in a green color named "allagash" accentuated. By subcontract, 84 Lumber would procure and install the siding and Precision Applied Coating Enterprises (PACE) would stain it.

[84 Lumber underestimated the amount of siding needed to completely clad appellees' home. Thus, PACE stained 19 additional sheets separately from the majority of the siding. One batch turned out noticeably darker than the other. Fannin assured Landis that a second coat applied after installation would produce a uniform color. In that belief, 84 Lumber did not attempt to group same-colored siding together, giving the home a striped or patchwork appearance. A second coat required warmer weather, so application was postponed until spring. The second coat did not improve the patchwork appearance of the siding. 84 Lumber and PACE agreed to replace the siding. The replacement siding turned out yellow, even though PACE applied the correct stain. Efforts to correct the siding failed. PACE suggested a solid stain in allagash would cover the patchwork appearance. A test left Landis displeased with both the color and opacity of the solid stain, which masked rather than highlighted the grain and natural imperfections of the T1-11 siding, failing to achieve the natural, rustic look that appellees wanted. Eighteen months of discussions, including proceedings before the Professional Standards Committee of the Building Industry Association of Central Ohio (BIA), failed to resolve the problem. BIA opined that the color variance in the siding on appellees' home did not comply with professional standards in the residential construction industry. BIA also concluded that application of a solid stain would constitute a commercially reasonable repair of the siding.

[Appellees filed suit. After a bench trial, the court found in appellees' favor on their breach-of-contract claim and awarded them $62,997.26: the cost to replace

the siding minus the amount Landis still owed to Fannin Builders. Fannin Builders appealed.]

. . .

Fannin Builders argues that the trial court erred in awarding appellees damages based on the cost to replace the mismatched siding instead of the difference in the market value of the house as contracted for and as received. We disagree.

Generally, the appropriate measure of damages in an action for a breach of a construction contract is the cost to repair the deficient work, that is, the cost of placing the building in the condition contemplated by the parties at the time they entered into the contract. *Hansel v. Creative Concrete & Masonry Constr. Co.* (2002), 148 Ohio App. 3d 53, 59, 772 N.E.2d 138; [citation omitted]. . . . Some Ohio courts subscribe to an exception to this general measure of damages[,] appl[ying] the economic-waste rule to determine damages for the breach of a construction contract. *Angles v. West*, 4th Dist. No. 02CA16, 2003-Ohio-464, 2003 WL 203593, ¶9; [citations omitted]. Under the economic-waste rule, if repair of a construction defect "will involve unreasonable economic waste, damages are measured by the difference between the market value that the structure contracted for would have had and that of the imperfect structure received by the plaintiff." *Ohio Valley Bank v. Copley* (1997), 121 Ohio App. 3d 197, 210, 699 N.E.2d 540. Economic waste arises when the total cost to remedy a construction defect is grossly disproportionate to the good to be attained. *Short v. Greenfield Meadows Assoc.*, 4th Dist. No. 07CA14, 2008-Ohio-3311, 2008 WL 2589659, ¶15; [citation omitted].

The seminal case of *Jacob & Youngs, Inc. v. Kent* (1921), 230 N.Y. 239, 129 N.E. 889, best articulates the economic-waste rule. In that case, a contract for the construction of a house required the use of plumbing pipe manufactured in Reading. A subcontractor's oversight led to the installation of plumbing pipe manufactured in Cohoes, not Reading. Although Cohoes pipe equaled Reading pipe in quality, the homeowner demanded that the builder tear out the Cohoes pipe and replace it with Reading pipe. To tear out the pipe, the builder would have had to demolish substantial parts of the completed structure. When the builder refused to replace the Cohoes pipe with Reading pipe, the plaintiff sued. The court held that given the circumstances:

> [T]he measure of the allowance is not the cost of replacement, which would be great, but the difference in value, which would be either nominal or nothing. . . . The owner is entitled to the money which will permit him to complete, unless the cost of completion is grossly and unfairly out of proportion to the good to be attained. When that is true, the measure is the difference in value.

Id. at 244.

The economic-waste rule emanates from courts' disinclination to award windfalls. [Citation omitted.] Sometimes, the owner of a defective structure receives sufficient value from the builder's work that he or she will decide not to fix the defect, and instead, will pocket any damages awarded based on the cost of repairs. The likelihood of this outcome increases in situations such as those presented in *Kent*, where the wrong pipe was commensurate to the contracted-for pipe in both quality and functionality. In such situations, the injured party is unjustly enriched because he or she receives work of approximately equal value to the contracted-for work and, in addition, money damages based on the cost of repair. Restatement of the Law 2d, Contracts (1981), Section 348, Comment c (if "the cost to remedy the defects will be clearly disproportionate to the probable loss in value to the injured party," then "[d]amages based on the cost to remedy the defects would [ ] give the injured party a recovery greatly in excess of the loss in value to him and result in a substantial windfall"); [citation omitted].

Similar concerns about unjust enrichment underlie the rule establishing the measure of damages for temporary injury to real property. In *Ohio Collieries v. Cocke* (1923), 107 Ohio St. 238, 248-249, 140 N.E. 356, the Supreme Court of Ohio held that if wrongful injury to real property can be repaired, then:

> [T]he measure of damages is the reasonable cost of restoration, plus reasonable compensation for the loss of the use of the property between the time of the injury and the restoration, unless such cost of restoration exceeds the difference in the market value of the property before and after the injury, in which case the difference in market value becomes the measure.

Like the economic-waste rule, this rule seeks to preclude the injured party from receiving a monetary windfall. In the case of temporary injury to real property, the injured party achieves this windfall by choosing to sell the property rather than restore it, resulting in a profit to the extent that the restoration costs exceed the diminution in market value. *Duquesne Light Co. v. Woodland Hills School Dist.* (Pa. Commw. 1997), 700 A.2d 1038, 1053; [citation omitted].

Recently, in *Martin v. Design Constr. Servs., Inc.*, 121 Ohio St. 3d 66, 2009-Ohio-1, 902 N.E.2d 10, the Supreme Court of Ohio limited the rule enunciated in *Ohio Collieries.* The court recognized the relevance of evidence regarding the diminution in market value of injured property in setting a damage award. However, the court abjured *Ohio Collieries'* automatic limitation of damages to the loss of market value when the cost of restoration exceeded that loss. In the place of the *Ohio Collieries* rule, the court imposed a reasonableness test. While diminution in market value remains a consideration, "the essential inquiry is whether the damages sought are reasonable." Id. at ¶25.

The economic-waste rule and the rule expressed in *Ohio Collieries* developed in different contexts. The economic-waste rule restricts the damages recoverable for breach of contract. The rule governing imposition of damages for the temporary injury to real property originated from, and is generally applied to, tort cases. [Citations omitted.] Nevertheless, we conclude that the reasonableness test announced in *Martin* precludes a strict application of the economic-waste rule.

"The fundamental rule of the law of damages is that the injured party shall have compensation for all of the injuries sustained." *Fantozzi v. Sandusky Cement Prods. Co.* (1992), 64 Ohio St. 3d 601, 612, 597 N.E.2d 474. Thus, in both contract and tort actions, the appropriate measure of damages is that which will make the injured party whole. [Citations omitted.] Consequently, both the economic-waste rule and the rule governing temporary injury to real property share the same objective. . . . Given the rules' identical purpose and origin, we conclude that the economic-waste rule, like the *Ohio Collieries* rule, must cede in favor of the reasonableness test.

Therefore, in a case involving a breach of a construction contract where the breaching party seeks to limit damages to the diminution in value, a fact-finder must determine whether under the facts of that case, it is more reasonable to award damages based on the cost of the remedy or based on the diminution in value. Although a fact-finder may consider whether the cost of the remedy grossly exceeds the difference in the value of the structure with and without the defect, that consideration will not necessarily control the amount of the damage award. Since the goal of any damage award is to make a party whole, a fact-finder must determine which measure of damage best accomplishes that goal without exceeding the bounds of reasonableness.

Here, the trial court awarded appellees the cost to replace the siding because it determined that damages based on loss of market value could not fully compensate appellees. Because the purpose of the contract was the construction of a custom-built home with the aesthetics appellees desired, Fannin Builders' failure to achieve those aesthetics warranted an award of damages that would allow appellees to correct the defect. We find the trial court's decision to award appellees the cost of replacement, rather than the loss of market value, reasonable in this case.

[A]ppellees . . . contracted for the construction of a custom-built home [and] explained to Fannin Builders that they wanted their house to have a natural, rustic look. . . . [U]nder the contract, Fannin Builders was obligated to apply stain with the opacity that appellees chose[:] semitransparent stain.

Because appellees placed such importance on the natural appearance of their home, they repeatedly rebuffed Fannin Builders' suggestion that they accept a solid stain. Appellees hired Fannin Builders to construct their "dream home," in which they planned to live many years. Consequently, appellees vigorously opposed Fannin Builders' attempts to get them to compromise on [the stain].

According to 84 Lumber's expert witness, the market value of appellees' home is $8,500 less than it would be if it was stained a uniform color. The expert witness arrived at this valuation because the cost to apply two coats of solid stain to the siding is $8,500. Under the economic-waste rule, appellees' damages might have amounted to only $8,500, as opposed to the $66,906.24 necessary to replace the siding.[2] We, however, concur with the trial court that $8,500 could not fully compensate appellees. Given that appellees contracted for a custom home and that appellees place a high value on the rustic look, the cost to achieve the rustic look is the only reasonable measure of damages. Thus, the trial court did not err in awarding appellees damages based on the cost to replace the siding.

---

[2]We question the likelihood of this outcome. Courts outside of Ohio exempt cases from the economic-waste rule and award damages based on the cost of remedy when aesthetic values make correction of the defect particularly important to a homeowner. See, e.g., *Advanced, Inc. v. Wilks* (Alaska 1985), 711 P.2d 524, 527; *Carter v. Quick* (1978), 263 Ark. 202, 209-210, 563 S.W.2d 461; *Fox v. Webb* (1958), 268 Ala. 111, 119, 105 So. 2d 75; *Lyon v. Belosky Constr., Inc.* (N.Y. App. Div. 1998), 247 A.D.2d 730, 732, 669 N.Y.S.2d 400; *Kangas v. Trust* (1982), 110 Ill. App. 3d 876, 883, 65 Ill. Dec. 757, 441 N.E.2d 1271. As one court observed:

> If a proud householder, who plans to live out his days in the home of his dreams, orders a new roof of red barrel tile and the roofer instead installs a purple one, money damages for the reduced value of his house may not be enough to offset the strident offense to aesthetic sensibilities, continuing over the life of the roof.

Gory Assoc. Industries, Inc. v. Jupiter Roofing & Sheet Metal, Inc. (Fla. App. 1978), 358 So. 2d 93, 95.

Fannin Builders also attacks the damages award on the basis that it should not include the cost to remove and replace the lap siding, porch ceiling, and porch columns. Fannin Builders contends that it should not have to pay for the removal and replacement of these items because they did not evince an inconsistent stain color like the siding.

. . .

Damages for the repair of deficient of [sic] work may include the cost of additional activities necessitated by the deficient work. *Jarupan [v. Hanna,* 173 Ohio App. 3d 284, 2007-Ohio-5081, 878 N.E.2d 66] at ¶19. [T]estimony [by the company that bid on the repairs] indicates that replacement of the bevel siding is necessary to achieve a uniform stain color, and replacement of the existing yellow pine soffit and fascia with fir is necessary because fir accepts stain better than yellow pine. Consequently, competent, credible evidence establishes that the cost of the removal and replacement of the bevel siding, soffit, and fascia are recoverable damages.

Because the trial court's award of damages is both reasonable and supported by competent, credible evidence, we conclude that the trial court did not err in setting appellees' damages at $62,997.26. Accordingly, we overrule Fannin Builders' third assignment of error.

Judgment affirmed.

Post-Case Follow-Up

The court's reasonableness test differs from the disproportionality test in the Restatement (Second) of Contracts. The court focused on whether $8,500 was reasonable compensation to the plaintiffs — not quite the same as asking whether $63,000 is unreasonable or disproportionate. Because $8,500 was unreasonably low, the court awarded the cost to replace the siding. The focus may result from relying on tort cases (where repairs may compensate plaintiff for damage to property) to guide results in contract cases (where repairs may allow plaintiff to realize the promised benefit of the bargain). The same concerns for avoiding waste or overcompensating plaintiffs should apply in both contexts. The court offers less clarity in discussing what made the smaller award unreasonable, especially given testimony that a solid stain was commercially reasonable and would give the house the same value it would have after replacing the siding. A solid stain would not give plaintiffs the performance they wanted, but that applies whenever plaintiffs seek repairs, including extreme cases such as *Jacob & Youngs*. The result suggests the court approves the suggestion in footnote 2 that diminution in value should not apply to cases involving aesthetic choices. That approach would avoid the hard task of comparing the amount of waste to the aesthetic value plaintiffs would obtain.

Landis v. William Fannin Builders, Inc.: Real Life Applications

1. Barrett needed a root canal and several crowns. Barrett specified that the crowns be gold covered by porcelain, not entirely made of porcelain. Lynn offered a

better price than other dentists and Barrett accepted. In the months between the initial work and the creation of the crowns, Lynn forgot Barrett's preference for gold with porcelain and instead ordered crowns made entirely of porcelain. Crowns without gold cost and (once in place) look the same as the gold-porcelain combination, but are therapeutically superior. Barrett was satisfied with the crowns for a year, until x-rays revealed that the crowns were pure porcelain. Barrett sued Lynn for breach of contract. Should the court award the cost to replace the crowns with gold-based crowns, the diminished value, or some other measure of damages? *See Khiterer v. Bell*, No. 7247/04 (N.Y. Civ. Ct. Jan. 28, 2005) (2005 WL 192354).

2. Kelly hired Carmen to pour, stamp, color, and seal a concrete driveway, patio, and sidewalk at Kelly's home for $30,000. Within three days of completing work, the concrete already showed cracks. Within a month, some concrete had chipped off the edges. The cracking resulted from Carmen's failure to install contraction joints, a breach of Carmen's promise to perform in a workmanlike manner. The best bid Kelly obtained to repair the work was $120,000: $35,000 to remove the defective concrete and $85,000 to replace it in a workmanlike manner. The home, worth $600,000, may not have lost any value as a result of the cracks. In this neighborhood, every house had cracked concrete and buyers here were unlikely to care about cracks unless they created tripping hazards. What remedy should Kelly recover?

3. Jean hired Louis to build a custom home for $280,000. Because Jean lived in a different state, Jean hired Chris to supervise construction and ensure that the home was built according to the plans. The roofing subcontractor hired to frame the roof centered it over the library instead of the living room, which changed the roof proportions, enlarged the overhang over the entrance, and altered the ceiling height in some rooms. The misframed roof created problems in building the dormer, which had to be rebuilt and, when that proved unsatisfactory, removed. Although problems with the dormer should have alerted the contractors to the mistake in framing the roof, that error was not discovered until after construction was complete. At that point, rebuilding the roof as originally designed would require $73,000. The problem affects the aesthetics of the house, but does not seem to alter the market value of the home. Should the court award cost of repair?

A rule favoring repairs serves several interests that might justify tolerating some degree of waste. First, it encourages careful performance. The cost of repair may be great, but the cost of getting it right in the first place may be modest. The prospect of paying the cost of repair may encourage parties to take precautions to avoid mistakes. Of course, a defendant who cuts corners or intentionally fails to perform may need to pay the cost of repairs no matter how much waste that involves. For example, in *Roudis v. Hubbard*,[15] a court awarded damages for the cost of repair against a

[15] 574 N.Y.S.2d 95 (App. Div. 1991).

contractor who chose to omit Styrofoam insulation and footing drains because he thought they were not necessary. Second, cost of repair protects subjective value. Willingness to pay for a particular color, roofline, or brand of pipe suggests that choice has value to the party. Even if the market does not think the repairs are worth the cost, the plaintiffs may attach more value to those aspects of the performance. Both facts influenced the court in *Groves v. John Wunder Co.*,[16] where the court approved cost of repair ($60,000) rather than diminished value ($12,000) when a quarry breached a promise to restore land after taking gravel from it. The court noted the willfulness of the breach and the owner's right to improve the land (say, to build on it) even if the land had limited market value.

Some courts apply the rule more mechanically. In *Peevyhouse v. Garland Coal Mining Co.*,[17] the defendant breached a promise to reclaim land after strip mining the property. The cost of repair ($29,000) greatly exceeded the diminution in value ($300), leading a court to award the smaller amount. The court did not inquire into the idiosyncratic value of scarring the family farm.

2. Incidental Loss

Incidental loss refers to costs incurred to react to the breach. It does not involve the value of the performance itself—neither its intrinsic or market value (direct loss) nor the ways the performance would have been used (consequential loss). Rather, it refers to the little (or not-so-little) things that a party must undertake as a result of the breach.

Incidental losses are recoverable, unless

1. the cost would have been incurred even if the contract had been performed; or
2. the cost incurred was unreasonably large.

Losses that would have been incurred even if the contract had been performed were not caused by the breach. No recovery is available for those costs under the general rule of damages: placing the aggrieved party in the position it would have occupied if the contract had been performed. If the party caused the breach, reasonable incidental costs are recoverable. If a party incurs unreasonably large costs, the excess is attributed to its own failure to keep the costs in check. Plaintiff may recover reasonable incidental losses, but no more.

Incidental costs vary with context. Rules do not try to define it too tightly. The following examples illustrate incidental losses, but other types of incidental costs also might qualify.

Sellers incur incidental costs to resell the performance. They may need to advertise the property or the sale in order to meet the requirement of a commercially reasonable resale. They may need to hire or pay commissions to sales agents, such as auctioneers. Sellers may need to store, preserve, repair, and/or insure the

[16]286 N.W. 235 (Minn. 1939).
[17]382 P.2d 109 (Okla. 1962), *cert. denied*, 375 U.S. 906 (1963).

property pending resale. Sellers might incur some expenses reclaiming the property from buyer and transporting it to an appropriate place for resale.[18] See Exhibit 15.3.

Similar incidental losses may affect employees or consultants (sellers of services). After an employer's breach, an employee may need to print resumes, send out applications, travel to job interviews, and perhaps pay a headhunter or other adviser. Purchasing publications that advertise job openings also might be an incidental loss.

EXHIBIT 15.4 UCC: Incidental Losses

§2-710. **Seller's Incidental Damages.** Incidental damages to an aggrieved seller include any commercially reasonable charges, expenses or commissions incurred in stopping delivery, in the transportation, care and custody of goods after the buyer's breach, in connection with return or resale of the goods or otherwise resulting from the breach.

§2-715. **Buyer's Incidental . . . Damages.**

(1) Incidental damages resulting from a seller's breach include expenses reasonably incurred in inspection, receipt, transportation and care and custody of goods rightfully rejected, any commercially reasonable charges, expenses or commissions in connection with effecting cover and any other reasonable expense incident to the delay or other breach.

A buyer may incur similar costs finding cover. Cover may require no more than a phone call to another seller, but might involve a more significant search. Arrangements for delivery of substitute goods might create additional costs. Finding some defective goods may force buyer to conduct a full-scale inspection to ascertain the nature and extent of the defects. Buyer may need to store and insure goods until seller reclaims them. In some cases, expenses that could have been incurred once will need to be paid twice; because the breach forced a second transaction, a second inspection, delivery charge, or other costs would be recoverable as incidental expenses.[19]

Employers and others who pay for services also may face incidental costs. When an employee breaches, the employer incurs costs to screen resumes and interview applicants to replace the employee and training costs to help the new employee become as proficient as the breaching employee. Some searches may involve fees or commissions paid to an executive search firm (headhunter). After a contractor breaches, a landowner may incur significant costs to find someone to complete the work, perhaps requiring a new round of bidding to locate a suitable substitute.

Incidental losses often relate to the avoidable consequences doctrine. A plaintiff cannot recover for losses it reasonable could have avoided. Avoiding losses may involve some costs — seller's cost to store goods and advertise them for resale, buyer's cost to find a substitute supplier or store defective goods until seller reclaims

[18] UCC §2-710.
[19] UCC §2-715(1).

them. The cost of reasonable efforts to minimize the loss typically fall within the incidental costs plaintiffs may recover.

The definition of expectation offers a good key to all incidental losses. If the cost would not have been incurred if the original contract had been performed, then compensation is necessary to make the nonbreaching party whole.

3. Consequential Loss

Consequential losses typically refer to the way a party would have used the performance if it had been provided on time and without defects. Where the performance would have enabled the recipient to realize gains by using the performance in a productive way, courts must award compensation for any gains prevented in order to put the plaintiff in the position she would have occupied if the contract had been performed.

Consequential damages arise in a variety of ways. Consider a few:

1. A supplier fails to provide a retail store with goods it would resell.
2. A supplier fails to provide a manufacturer with materials it would use to produce goods.
3. An actor refuses to perform in a movie.
4. A lessor breaches a lease of retail (or office) space to a business.
5. A partner refuses to contribute funds promised to a business venture.

In each case, direct loss would involve replacing the promised performance: finding a new source of goods, a new actor, a new business space, a new partner (or lender). Success in that endeavor might permit the project to go forward, avoiding any consequential losses. However, if an acceptable substitute is not available in time or is not as good as the original, the project itself may suffer. Measuring the cost of a substitute will not necessarily measure the loss suffered when the venture itself is postponed or even fails.

Recovery of consequential loss is vital to effective compensation. Unless these losses are included in the recovery, the court cannot place the party in the position it would have occupied if the contract had been performed. Each contract involves using the performance for some profitable end. Breach may undermine those ends. To put the plaintiff in the position it would have occupied if the promise had been performed, compensation may need to include consequential damages.

Courts award consequential damages in appropriate cases. But courts find a number of reasons to refuse to award consequential damages. In fact, the UCC defines buyer's consequential damages without describing them, but by listing reasons to reject them: any loss, unless the seller lacked reason to know of the buyer's needs or the buyer reasonably could have avoided the losses.[20] This reflects a historical suspicion of consequential damages that remains evident today. For

[20]UCC §2-715.

example, the UCC calls for remedies to be "liberally administered to the end that the aggrieved party may be put in as good a position as if the other party had fully performed *but neither consequential [n]or special damages . . . may be had except as specifically provided. . . .*"[21]

EXHIBIT 15.3 UCC: Defining Consequential Damages

> **§2-715. Buyer's . . . Consequential Damages.**
>
> (2) Consequential damages resulting from the seller's breach include
>
> (a) any loss resulting from general or particular requirements or needs of which the seller at the time of contracting had reason to know and which could not reasonably be prevented by cover or otherwise; and
>
> (b) injury to person or property proximately resulting from any breach of warranty.

Concerns for consequential losses stem in part from their speculative nature. Although a party may have planned to use the performance in a productive way, profit from the performance is not guaranteed. Performance might have enabled the party to realize gains, but might have generated losses instead. If the actor had performed, the movie might have been a hit or a flop. If the lessor had performed, the retail store might have prospered or failed. The breach prevented the party from using the performance as expected, forcing recourse to projections of what might have happened if the performance had been provided as promised.

Concern for accurate projections leads courts to subject consequential damage claims to close scrutiny. Courts apply several doctrines that limit consequential damages, including:

1. denying damages that plaintiff could have avoided by reasonable conduct (for example, by obtaining a substitute performance);
2. denying damages that plaintiff cannot prove with reasonable certainty (for example, if the business has no history of profit in prior years);
3. denying damages that were unforeseeable by defendant at the time of contract formation (for example, because plaintiff failed to mention how losses might result from a breach).

The limitations — addressed in detail later in this chapter — apply to all damages. But they relate most strongly to consequential damages.

The ways consequential damages arise vary with context. Any gain a party would have realized from use of the performance (if it had been provided in a timely manner) is a consequential loss if the breach precludes that gain. Whether it is a recoverable consequential loss often depends on the limitations or exclusions provided by the law or by the contract.

---

[21]UCC §1-305 (italics added).

QVC, Inc. v. MJC America, Ltd.

QVC bought space heaters from MJC and resold them. When the heaters developed problems, QVC recalled them and compensated their buyers. That deprived QVC of the profit on resale and also imposed some incidental costs. This case offers a reasonable example of how consequential losses arise and how damages are calculated. It also raises some interesting questions of litigation strategy, such as defendant's decision not to submit any evidence on damages.

In this case, QVC sued to recover losses caused by a recall.
Associated Press

As you read *QVC, Inc. v. MJC America, Ltd.*, look for the following:

1. If the contract had not specifically provided for recall costs, should the court have awarded them anyway as incidental or consequential losses? Which are they? Does it matter?
2. Did QVC miscalculate its lost profit, as the court suggests?
3. Why did the court award lost profit damages for the goods QVC sold but not on the goods QVC still had in inventory?

QVC, Inc. v. MJC America, Ltd.

904 F. Supp. 2d 466 (E.D. Pa. 2012)

O'NEILL, District Judge.

[In 2007, QVC purchased 25,473 space heaters from MJC America, Ltd., d/b/a Soleus International, Inc. QVC sold 16,721 of them via their cable channel. QVC] "received over 70 reports of heaters smoking, overheating, sparking, melting and/or emitting odors of burning. Nine additional customers [had] reported observing flames or fire coming out of or inside the heaters." [After investigating, QVC concluded the heaters were defective. QVC recalled the heaters and compensated its customers. It then sued Soleus to recover its losses caused by the recall. After determining liability, the court discussed the amount QVC could recover.]

XI. QVC's Claimed Damages for the Heaters

At trial, Alan Kujawa, QVC's Vice President of Inventory Accounting[,] testified as to QVC's claimed damages. Exclusive of prejudgment interest and attorneys' fees, QVC seeks a total of $1,838,855.59 in damages related to the Heaters. QVC seeks damages for the cost price of the Heaters in addition to lost profits, refunded outbound customer shipping costs, shipping costs for the return of Heater Cords to QVC, refunded

customer shipping costs for Heaters returned to QVC, return-to-vendor shipping costs, returns center processing costs and other costs associated with the recall.

A. Cost Price Damages

Each Heater had a cost price to QVC of $41.07 — $36.00 to Soleus and $5.07 to third parties for landed costs. . . . QVC's claimed cost price damages for all of the Heaters at issue in this action is $1,046,176.11. [The court divided the costs among the 4,284 "Shipped Customer Return Heaters," 1,824 "Unshipped Customer Return Heaters," 8,572 "Unsold Heaters," and 10,613 "Heater Cords."]

B. Lost Profit

Upon receipt of a Customer Return Heater or a Heater Cord, QVC refunded to its customer the full value that the customer paid to QVC for the Heater. The Today's Special Value® price for the Heaters was $67.86, the lowest per unit price at which QVC offered the Heaters for sale. QVC claims that $26.49[11] constituted its profit on the sale of each Heater — profit that QVC would have realized had it not refunded the sales price to its customers. QVC's total claimed lost profit damages for the [16,721] Heaters or Heater Cords that were returned to QVC are $442,939.29.

C. Refunded Outbound Customer Shipping Costs

In addition to refunding customers with the full value that they paid for Heaters, all QVC customers who purchased Heaters from QVC were refunded the full value of the cost they paid to have the Heater shipped to them when they purchased it from QVC. QVC's customers paid $8.04 for delivery of Heaters purchased as a Today's Special Value®. As damages for refunded outbound customer shipping costs, QVC seeks $8.04 for each of the [16,721] Heaters it sold, . . . for a total of $134,436.84.

D. Costs for Heater Cord Returns

Pursuant to the recall, QVC instructed customers to cut the Heater Cords off of their Heaters and to send them back to QVC. QVC provided its customers with packaging and prepaid postage for the Heater Cords at a cost of $2.00 per Heater Cord. QVC seeks $21,226.00 in damages — $2.00 multiplied by 10,613 Heater Cords — for the shipping costs to return the Heater Cords to QVC.

E. Refunded Customer Shipping Costs for Heaters Returned to QVC

QVC customers who returned intact Heaters to QVC (as opposed to just Heater Cords), were refunded the full value of their cost to ship their Heater back to QVC. As damages for refunded customer shipping costs for Heaters returned to QVC,

---

[11]In fact the TSV price of $67.86 less the per-Heater cost price of $41.07 equals $26.79, not $26.49. QVC, however, calculated its lost profits at a rate of $26.49/Heater and I will award damages based on that calculation.

QVC seeks $8.04 for each of 4,284 Shipped Customer Return Heaters and 1,824 Unshipped Customer Return Heaters, for a total of $49,108.32.[12]

F. Return-to-Vendor Shipping Costs

Return-to-vendor shipping costs are the estimated shipping costs to return goods back to a vendor. QVC calculates this cost on a company-wide basis and expresses the costs as a percentage of the per-unit cost of merchandise to be shipped. The cost varies over time because it is an average and reflects the potential savings that QVC derives from having contracts with shipping carriers. In or around 2008, the return-to-vendor shipping cost to QVC was one percent or, as applied to the Heaters, $0.41 per Heater. . . . QVC's total claimed return-to-vendor shipping cost damages for [14,860] Heaters returned or to be returned to Soleus are $6,092.60.

G. Returns Center Processing Costs

QVC incurs returns center processing costs [footnote omitted] when its customers return products. QVC calculates this cost as a company-wide average by taking the total cost involved with QVC's returns process by the total number of returns processed by its returns center. The per unit price for the Heaters for the return center processing cost was $1.65. . . . QVC's total claimed damages for return center processing costs for the Heaters [including cords] are $27,589.65.

H. Other Recall Costs

QVC seeks $111,286.78 in other costs associated with the recall. Costs incurred in conjunction with recalling the Heaters included: (1) the initial customer notification letter (12,393 letters at $0.55 each); (2) customer service calls (26,423 calls at $1.78 per call); (3) testing by Intertek [an independent testing company]; (4) recall letters sent using Provide; (5) recorded telephone calls to customers; and (6) customer contact letters.

. . .

XIII. Offset to Soleus

QVC and Soleus have stipulated that [Soleus was entitled to an offset of] $315,321.34 for vendor credits [amounts QVC had not paid Soleus for the goods. Footnote omitted.]

[12]QVC derived the amount of $8.04 per Heater from the original shipping and handling fee paid by its customers. In many instances QVC refunded to its customers shipping costs in excess of $8.04 per Heater.

CONCLUSIONS OF LAW

. . .

II. Damages

A. Damages Related to the Heaters

[The court concluded that it was reasonable to recall all the heaters because no information from Soleus permitted isolating the defect to any portion of the order.]

2. Damages for Breach of the Heater Purchase Orders

QVC is entitled to recover the costs it incurred as a result of the sale by Soleus of defective Heaters — including the costs to conduct the recall — because Soleus breached the warranties set forth in the Purchase Orders and because QVC was entitled to conduct a voluntary recall of the Heaters.

Under Section 7 of the Purchase Orders, QVC was entitled to "receive a credit or refund equal to the average cost of amounts paid by [QVC] for each [Heater], including, without limitation, in-bound freight charges. . . ." Section 7 also provides that "[a]ll expense of unpacking, examining, repacking, storing, returning and reshipping any Merchandise rejected (or acceptance of which has been revoked) . . . shall be at [Soleus's] expense and risk."

Section 4 of the Purchase Orders provides, inter alia, that Soleus would

> protect, defend, hold harmless and indemnify [QVC] . . . from and against any and all claims, actions, suits, costs, liabilities, damages and expenses (including but not limited to, all direct, special, incidental, exemplary and consequential damages and losses of any kind [including, without limitation, present and prospective lost profits and lost business] and reasonable attorneys' fees) based upon or resulting from (b) any alleged or actual defect in any of the [Heaters] . . . [and] (d) breach by [Soleus] of any representations, warranties or covenants[.]

Further, under the UCC, as adopted in Pennsylvania, incidental damages "include (1) expenses reasonably incurred in inspection, receipt, transportation and care and custody of goods rightfully rejected; (2) any commercially reasonable charges, expenses or commissions in connection with effecting cover; and (3) any other reasonable expense incident to the delay or other breach." 13 Pa. Cons. Stat. Ann. §2715(a). Consequential damages include: "(1) any loss resulting from general or particular requirements and needs of which the seller at the time of contracting had reason to know and which could not reasonably be prevented by cover or otherwise; and (2) injury to person or property proximately resulting from any breach of warranty." *Id.* §2115(b).

I find that QVC has met its burden to pass the costs of the recall along to Soleus. Soleus was aware when it entered into the Purchase Orders that QVC was reselling the Heaters to its customers and that QVC retained the right to conduct a recall of the Heaters in the event of a breach of warranty. "[I]n an appropriate case, where the record supports the logic and reasonability of costs of same, this element of damages should be allowed." *In re Repco Products Corp.*, 100 B.R. 184, 200 (Bankr. E.D.

Pa. 1989); *see also United Cal. Bank v. Eastern Mountain Sports Inc.*, 546 F. Supp. 945, 970-71 (D. Mass. 1982) (finding costs of recall campaign necessitated by seller's breach of contract were recoverable as consequential damages where seller had reason to know of buyer's standards), *aff'd without op.*, 705 F.2d 439 (1st Cir. 1983).

Costs that QVC is entitled to recover include cost-price damages, lost profits, refunded outbound customer shipping costs, the cost of the Heater cord returns, refunded customer shipping costs for Heaters returned to QVC, return-to-vendor shipping costs, returns center processing costs and other recall costs. Accordingly, and because Soleus did not offer evidence at trial to rebut the damages evidence set forth by Kujawa, QVC's damages expert, I will award Heater related damages to Soleus in the [amount of $1,838,855.59, the entire amount QVC requested].

. . .

[The court offset the award by subtracting the $315,321.34 that QVC owed Soleus for merchandise. The court reserved judgment on the amount of attorneys' fees and prejudgment interest to add to the award.]

Post-Case Follow-Up

Refunding the price is the first step for compensating direct loss. Incidental loss explicitly covers the cost to return the goods from QVC to Soleus. Lost profit is the classic consequential loss. But to recover any profit, QVC first needs to recoup its expenses. The court carefully parses which ones to award and how to calculate them.

QVC, Inc. v. MJC America, Ltd.: Real Life Applications

1. Val bought a Soleus heater from QVC. Val received the refund, but still did not have what QVC promised: a safe and reliable heater for $67.86 plus $8.04 shipping. Can Val seek additional recovery against QVC? What elements should Val seek? Are they incidental or consequential? If the cost of bringing the claim were not prohibitive, how much should Val recover? (If necessary, imagine the sale involved $6,786 for outdoor heaters for use when Val entertained on a large patio.)

2. Connor Construction Co. (CCC) bid on large construction contracts, about half of them from government entities. State law requires general contractors working on public projects to post a bond for at least half the contract price of the project. CCC obtained a contract to build a new office building for Bigtown and posted a $1.5 million bond from Sureco. When the project was nearly complete, Bigtown declared CCC in default for failure to complete in a timely manner, hired a new contractor to finish the work, and made a claim on the bond from Sureco. Sureco cut CCC's bonding capacity in half and, later, refused to issue any bonds to CCC. Because CCC was unable to find another company

willing to issue it bonds, it was unable to bid on any government building projects for three years. CCC sued Bigtown for breach, alleging it wrongfully refused appropriate time extensions and wrongfully terminated the contract. CCC prevailed. In addition to collecting the amount owed on the office building contract, what other losses might CCC claim? What problems might CCC face in proving those claims? *See Denny Construction Inc. v. City of Denver, Colorado*, 199 P.3d 742 (Colo. 2009).

3. EngineCo sold ChemCo a machine used to produce ammonia. The machine broke less than a year later. EngineCo attempted repairs, but the machine broke again and again: three times over a seven-year period, each time going offline for ten working days while repairs were made. ChemCo presented evidence of how much more ammonia would have been produced if the machine had operated as promised (1,400 tons per day or tpd), the price for which it could have sold that ammonia at the times the machine broke ($600/ton), and how much ChemCo saved in operating costs during the months the machine was offline ($500/ton). Can ChemCo recover the losses from EngineCo? If so, how should you calculate the damages? *See Mississippi Chemical Corp. v. Dresser-Rand Co.*, 287 F.3d 359 (5th Cir. 2002).

4. BigBox agreed to buy all of Winery's output of chardonnay, provided that Winery label it as BigBox wine. Winery delivered its entire output of 2014 chardonnay on May 1, 2016. BigBox failed to pay when due on June 1, 2016. When BigBox still had not paid (or even answered Winery's inquiries about payment) by December 1, 2016, Bank foreclosed on Winery. Winery wishes to sue BigBox not only for the payment and interest, but also for future profits it would have earned if Bank had not foreclosed. Advise Winery what recovery it can expect.

Buyers' Consequential Losses

The calculation of buyers' consequential losses varies with the way buyer would have used the performance. For example, in sales of goods, a buyer might plan to

1. resell the goods as they are (for example, a wholesaler);
2. resell the goods in an altered state (for example, a manufacturer);
3. enjoy the goods as they are (for example, a consumer); or
4. enjoy the goods in an altered state (for example, a home-improver buying paint).

The type of breach also affects consequential damages. Breach may delay obtaining the goods (late delivery or nondelivery followed by cover) rather than deprive the buyer of the goods entirely. Or breach may affect the quality of the goods, making them less profitable or less enjoyable, but not precluding profit or satisfaction altogether.

While the language here refers to goods, the same categories apply to other contracts. A buyer might plan to resell the real estate as it is, build on it before reselling it, live in it as it is, or remodel it before living in it. An employer typically profits by combining the labor of many employees to make a product or service. But an employer might send out employees as they are (for example, an agency supplying temporary employees to other businesses). Similarly, the employer might hire others to produce satisfaction rather than profit, such as hiring someone to clean a house or paint it. Construction services, too, may produce profitable property (for sale or rent) or property the owner will enjoy (by living on the premises).

Consumer Gains

Consumers often enjoy property, rather than using it to generate profits. Breach, then, deprives a party of the enjoyment. The satisfaction expected probably exceeded the cost of the contract; **assent** (agreeing to the contract) suggests the buyer expected to receive something she would enjoy more than the price promised. The increment is known as **consumer surplus**: the additional satisfaction a consumer receives over and above the satisfaction of keeping the price.

Consumer surplus is difficult to measure. Knowing it exists does not help assess how much money would compensate for it. Measurement difficulty makes it rare to include consumer surplus as a component of monetary recovery. Rather, consumers can avoid lost satisfaction by replacing the performance as quickly as practicable. That approach avoids trying to put a monetary value on lost satisfaction. Satisfaction lost by delay (between the time defendant should have performed and the time plaintiff obtained a substitute) suffers the same uncertainty. Costs incurred to reduce the delay (obtain a substitute more quickly) probably are included in incidental damages.

In some cases, lost satisfaction has a financial component. For instance, homeowners seek remodeling because they will enjoy the results. But breaches may involve costs. For instance, a kitchen remodel that is not completed on time may force a family to incur the expense of eating out. Other remodeling delays might force the family to rent an apartment for longer than promised. While the cost to repair poor work is a direct loss, consequential losses include the inability to use of the premises while repairs are completed. Therefore, even when the primary loss of use involves the consumer's utility, that loss of utility might involve a cost capable of quantification.

Transmuting Consequential Damages

In some cases, attorneys can persuade courts to treat consequential losses as direct losses, with only a slight difference in measure. In deciding how much to pay for something, buyers generally consider the profit they can derive from using the performance. Thus, a profitable performance might increase the market price of property. For example, buyers base the price of an apartment building on the expected profit gained from the rents. Proving the lost income and avoided expenses would establish consequential losses. Proving the price someone would pay for the building establishes market value, a direct loss — but one that already includes buyers' estimates of the rents and expenses.

For example, consider a real estate transaction, where the buyer agrees to pay $1 million for land, but agrees to resell it to another almost immediately for $1.5 million. If $1 million is the market price of the land, breach by the seller causes the buyer no direct loss (market price - contract price = 0), but causes consequential loss of $500,000, the profit the buyer would have realized by reselling the land. However, if the resale contract is an **arm's-length transaction** — a contract negotiated between unrelated parties, each looking out for its own best interest — the resale contract suggests that $1.5 million is the true market value of the land. Buyer might recover market price ($1.5 million) minus contract price ($1 million), collecting $500,000. This approach, when available, may avoid some of the issues raised by limitations on damages, such as foreseeability. Even if the resale transaction has unique features that prevent it from representing the actual market value, it may still help establish that market value exceeds $1 million, allowing some recovery of direct damages even if the court denies consequential damages.

Sellers' Consequential Damages

Where the breach involves a failure to pay money, sellers may recover interest on the unpaid amount from the time it should have been paid to the time that it was paid. Some authorities say that interest replaces consequential damages: that is, sellers cannot recover consequential damages, but can recover interest on unpaid amounts. Realistically, this means that interest is the way courts measure consequential damages for unpaid amounts. Exceptions exist, but they are more common in tort cases than in contract. The UCC has no provision for seller's consequential damages. Seller's incidental damages cover most loss of use, including interest.[20]

C. LIMITATIONS ON DAMAGES

As noted above, several rules limit a plaintiff's ability to recover damages. The rules identify several ways that damage rules might overcompensate plaintiffs in practice. Some relate to ways the plaintiff may contribute to the losses, such as failing to take reasonable steps to keep the loss to a minimum. Foreseeability questions the fairness of asking defendant to pay surprisingly large damages, especially if plaintiff failed to share important information with the defendant during contract negotiations. Requiring reasonable certainty for contract damages ensures that defendant pays the losses it caused, rather than a speculative amount that a jury decided to award. In each case, the rules may leave a plaintiff worse off than if the contract had been performed. The limitations try to locate the right balance, avoiding both overcompensation and undercompensation.

1. Avoidable and Avoided Consequences

A plaintiff cannot recover for losses that

1. the plaintiff actually avoided; or
2. the plaintiff could have avoided by reasonable effort.

---

[20]UCC §2-710.

The expectation interest rejects awarding losses the plaintiff actually avoided. Otherwise, damages would put plaintiff in a better position than if the contract had been performed.

The avoidable consequences doctrine treats losses the plaintiff could have avoided by reasonable efforts the same way it treats losses the plaintiff actually avoided. That reduces the temptation on plaintiffs to increase their damage recovery by letting their losses pile up even if they could have been avoided. (Courts sometimes refer to the temptation to take fewer precautions when someone else will pay the cost of that decision as **moral hazard**.) Plaintiff need not make extraordinary efforts to minimize the loss—those that involve "undue risk, burden, or humiliation."[21] Nor must the efforts succeed; as long as the plaintiff made reasonable efforts to minimize the loss, courts will award the actual losses. If losses could have been reduced by reasonable efforts, however, courts limit recovery to the unavoidable losses—even if that leaves the plaintiff worse off than she would have been if the contract had been performed. Thus, if a tomato grower breaches a promise to supply tomatoes to a cannery, the cannery loses money because it sells fewer cans of tomato sauce. But if it could have bought substitute tomatoes and continued making sales, it cannot recover any losses that it could have avoided that way, even if it actually suffered lost sales.

Judges and lawyers often refer to the avoidable consequences doctrine by a different name: the **duty to mitigate damages**. Technically, the doctrine does not create a duty. The rule does not require any plaintiff to make any efforts, reasonable or otherwise, and gives no one any right of action for breach of the so-called duty. The avoidable consequences doctrine simply limits damages payable to those who do not make sufficient efforts. In the example above, no one will force the cannery to buy additional tomatoes. The cannery, however, cannot blame the grower for losses that the cannery could have avoided rather easily. As long as you keep the effect of the doctrine clear, calling it mitigation seems harmless, even if imprecise.

To reduce plaintiff's recovery, the defendant must prove two things:

1. that the plaintiff acted unreasonably;
2. that the losses would have been lower (and by how much) if the plaintiff had acted reasonably.

Failure to establish either aspect leaves the plaintiff able to recover its full actual loss.

Unreasonableness

Unreasonableness requires more than just identifying a better way to reduce the loss. Plaintiffs may choose any reasonable alternative, based on the information available to them at the time. They need not select what, in hindsight, defendant now argues would have been the best alternative. Only if plaintiff's choice was

---

[21] RESTATEMENT (SECOND) OF CONTRACTS §350.

unreasonable at the time it was made will defendant satisfy the first requirement. Even if plaintiff's efforts failed to reduce the loss at all, as long as the choice was reasonable, this doctrine will not justify reducing the damages.

While the details will vary with context, a few generalizations will help understand how plaintiffs can avoid having awards reduced.

First, plaintiffs should not increase the loss. Often the loss can be reduced by doing nothing—by stopping any further work on a contract. If buyer cancels an order for custom letterhead stationery, stop printing it. An architect should stop working on blueprints when a client decides not to build the building after all. One who incurs more expense by completing unwanted work may not recover the avoidable expenses.

Rockingham County v. Luten Bridge Co.[22] offers an amusing example. The county hired a contractor to build a bridge, then decided not to build a road there after all (after a change of administration). The county ordered the builder to stop work, but the builder finished the job anyway and sued for the full price. The normal rule—price minus savings—would entitle the builder to the full price; builder saved nothing as a result of the breach. The court, however, subtracted the savings the builder would have had if it had acted reasonably. Thus, the court treated as savings all expenses the builder would have avoided by stopping work when the county canceled the project.

Second, plaintiffs should salvage what they can. If materials can be resold or used in another project and billed to that contract, redeploy them in any reasonable manner. Perhaps some expenses can be avoided or reduced by terminating other contracts. A contractor fired from a construction job might reduce its loss by laying off any employees it hired specifically for that job and returning any equipment it leased to perform that job.

Third, substitute transactions might reduce additional harm. Cover with substitute goods, especially if that will avoid consequential losses. Resell the goods to somebody else rather than letting them sit and rot. Hire a new employee rather than suffering losses by leaving the job vacant. Go find a new job instead of remaining idle.

The suggestions here will not apply in all settings. The ultimate test is reasonableness. When a buyer of custom goods repudiates the order, it may make sense for the manufacturer to complete the goods. Salvaging completed goods may recoup more of the cost than salvaging the materials, even after accounting for the cost of completion. The UCC recognizes this option, provided the manufacturer exercises "reasonable commercial judgment for the purposes of avoiding loss."[23]

Amount of Avoidable Loss

Showing the amount of loss that plaintiff would have avoided may prove difficult. Defendant cannot merely show that damages *might* have been lower had plaintiff acted differently. Defendant must show that losses *would* have been lower. That

[22] 35 F.2d 301 (4th Cir. 1929).
[23] UCC §2-704(2).

doesn't require absolute certainty; proof by a **preponderance of the evidence** (more likely than not, 50 percent plus an iota) will suffice. Just showing other opportunities falls short, without some reason to believe plaintiff would have been able to take advantage of them.

Even if the plaintiff made no efforts at all to reduce the loss, if defendant cannot show that efforts would have reduced the loss, no reduction occurs. The rule does not require futile efforts. The plaintiff who, by foresight or by luck, refrains from efforts that, although reasonable, would have been pointless, recovers the full loss.

Parker v. Twentieth Century Fox Film Corp.

This case involved Shirley MacLaine, an influential movie actress who continues to make films. Faced with the cancellation of a film in which she was to star, Ms. MacLaine rejected the substitute role offered by the studio. The court needed to decide whether rejecting the role was an unreasonable failure to minimize the loss. The court discussed several differences between the roles that might make it reasonable to reject the substitute position.

Shirley MacLaine, plaintiff in this case
Courtesy Everett Collection

As you read *Parker v. Twentieth Century Fox Film Corp.*, look for the following:

1. What differences between the two jobs made it reasonable to reject the second role? Would the same differences apply to a substitute job offered a salesman, a teacher, or a lawyer?
2. Did the award leave the plaintiff better off than if the contract had been performed? Could the award have been adjusted to avoid overcompensation?
3. Did Parker make any efforts to find a substitute job after the film was canceled? What did the court say about that?

Parker v. Twentieth Century Fox Film Corp.

474 P.2d 689 (Cal. 1970) (en banc)

BURKE, Justice.

[Plaintiff, a well-known actress, agreed to play the female lead in defendant's musical *Bloomer Girl* for $750,000, which required 14 weeks of work. The contract promised to pay plaintiff, but did not promise to use her in the movie. Defendant decided not to produce the picture, but offered plaintiff the same salary to play the female lead in *Big Country, Big Man* during the same time period.] Unlike "Bloomer Girl," however, which was to have been a musical production, "Big Country" was a dramatic "western type" movie. "Bloomer Girl" was to have been filmed in

California; "Big Country" was to be produced in Australia. Also, certain terms in the proffered contract varied from those of the original.[2] [Plaintiff rejected the offer and sued for compensation under the original contract. Defendant admitted repudiating the contract, but denied owing plaintiff any money because she deliberately failed to mitigate damages by unreasonably refusing the role in *Big Country*.]

[S]ummary judgment for $750,000 plus interest was entered in plaintiff's favor. This appeal . . . followed.

. . . Summary judgment is proper only if the . . . opponent does not by affidavit show facts sufficient to present a triable issue of fact.

The general rule is that the measure of recovery by a wrongfully discharged employee is the amount of salary agreed upon for the period of service, less the amount which the employer affirmatively proves the employee has earned or with reasonable effort might have earned from other employment. (*W. F. Boardman Co. v. Petch* (1921) 186 Cal. 476, 484, 199 P. 1047; . . . *De La Falaise v. Gaumont-British P. Corp.* (1940) 39 Cal. App. 2d 461, 469, 103 P.2d 447 [citations and footnote omitted].) However, before projected earnings from other employment opportunities not sought or accepted by the discharged employee can be applied in mitigation, the employer must show that the other employment was comparable, or substantially similar, to that of which the employee has been deprived; the employee's rejection of or failure to seek other available employment of a different or inferior kind may not be resorted to in order to mitigate damages. (*Gonzales v. Internat. Assn. of Machinists* (1963) 213 Cal. App. 2d 817, 822-824, 29 Cal. Rptr. 190;. . . .)

In the present case defendant has raised no issue of *reasonableness of efforts* by plaintiff to obtain other employment; the sole issue is whether plaintiff's refusal of defendant's substitute offer of "Big Country" may be used in mitigation. Nor, if the "Big Country" offer was of employment different or inferior when compared with the original "Bloomer Girl" employment, is there an issue as to whether or not plaintiff acted reasonably in refusing the substitute offer. Despite defendant's arguments to the contrary, no case cited or which our research has discovered holds or suggests that reasonableness is an element of a wrongfully discharged employee's option to reject, or fail to seek, different or inferior employment lest the possible earnings therefrom be charged against him in mitigation of damages.[5]

---

[2][For *Bloomer Girl*, plaintiff had the right to approve the director, dance director, and script changes and had already approved both the script and the director. For *Big Country*, defendant offered to consult regarding the director or photography and the script, but retained final discretion in itself. There would be no dance director, so that provision was deleted. Defendant's offer relied on plaintiff's prior expression of interest in the project and the limited time before filming to explain the changes. — EDS.]

[5]Instead, in each case the reasonableness referred to was that of the *efforts* of the employee to obtain other employment that was not different or inferior; his right to reject the latter was declared as an unqualified rule of law. Thus, *Gonzales v. Internat. Assn. of Machinists, supra*, 213 Cal. App. 2d 817, 823-824, 29 Cal. Rptr. 190, 194, holds that the trial court correctly instructed the jury that plaintiff union member, a machinist, was required to make "such *efforts* as the average [member of his union] desiring employment would make at that particular time and place" (italics added); but, further, that the court *properly rejected* defendant's *offer of proof of* the *availability of other kinds of employment* at the same or higher pay than plaintiff usually received and all outside the jurisdiction of his union, as plaintiff could not be required to accept different employment or a nonunion job.

In *Harris v. Nat. Union, etc., Cooks and Stewards*, Supra, 116 Cal. App. 2d 759, 761, 254 P.2d 673, 676, the issues were stated to be, inter alia, whether comparable employment was open to each plaintiff employee, and if so whether each plaintiff made a *reasonable effort* to secure such employment. It was held that the trial court *properly*

Applying the foregoing rules to the record in the present case . . . the trial court correctly ruled that plaintiff's failure to accept defendant's tendered substitute employment could not be applied in mitigation of damages because the offer of the "Big Country" lead was of employment both different and inferior, and that no factual dispute was presented on that issue. The mere circumstance that "Bloomer Girl" was to be a musical review [*sic*] calling upon plaintiff's talents as a dancer as well as an actress, and was to be produced in the City of Los Angeles, whereas "Big Country" was a straight dramatic role in a "Western Type" story taking place in an opal mine in Australia, demonstrates the difference in kind between the two employments; the female lead as a dramatic actress in a western style motion picture can by no stretch of imagination be considered the equivalent of or substantially similar to the lead in a song-and-dance production.

Additionally, the substitute "Big Country" offer proposed to eliminate or impair the director and screenplay approvals accorded to plaintiff under the original "Bloomer Girl" contract (see fn. 2, *ante*), and thus constituted an offer of inferior employment. No expertise or judicial notice is required in order to hold that the deprivation or infringement of an employee's rights held under an original employment contract converts the available "other employment" relied upon by the employer to mitigate damages, into inferior employment which the employee need not seek or accept. [Citation omitted.]

Statements found in affidavits submitted by defendant . . . to the effect that the "Big Country" offer was not of employment different from or inferior to that under the "Bloomer Girl" contract . . . constitute only conclusionary assertions with respect to undisputed facts, and do not give rise to a triable factual issue. . . . [Citations omitted.]

The judgment is affirmed.

SULLIVAN, Acting Chief Justice (dissenting).

The basic question in this case is whether or not plaintiff acted reasonably in rejecting defendant's offer of alternate employment. The answer depends upon whether that offer (starring in "Big Country, Big Man") was an offer of work that was substantially similar to her former employment (starring in "Bloomer Girl") or of work that was of a different or inferior kind. To my mind this is a factual issue which the trial court should not have determined on a motion for summary judgment. The majority have not only repeated this error but have compounded it by applying the rules governing mitigation of damages in the employer-employee context in a misleading fashion. Accordingly, I respectfully dissent.

---

sustained an objection to an offer to prove a custom of accepting a job in a lower rank when work in the higher rank was not available, as "The duty of mitigation of damages . . . does not require the plaintiff 'to seek or to accept other employment of a different or inferior kind.'" [Citations omitted.]

. . .

Chisholm v. Preferred Bankers' Life Assur. Co. (1897) 112 Mich. 50, 70 N.W. 415 . . . *approved* a jury *instruction* that a *substitute offer* of the employer to work for a lesser compensation was *not to be considered in mitigation*, as the employee was not required to accept it.

Williams v. National Organization, Masters, etc. (1956) 384 Pa. 413, 120 A.2d 896, 901(13): "Even assuming that plaintiff . . . could have obtained employment in ports other than . . . where he resided, *legally* he was not compelled to do so in order to mitigate his damages." (Italics added.)

The familiar rule requiring a plaintiff in a tort or contract action to mitigate damages embodies notions of fairness and socially responsible behavior which are fundamental to our jurisprudence. Most broadly stated, it precludes the recovery of damages which, through the exercise of due diligence, could have been avoided. Thus, in essence, it is a rule requiring reasonable conduct in commercial affairs. This general principle governs the obligations of an employee after his employer has wrongfully repudiated or terminated the employment contract. Rather than permitting the employee simply to remain idle during the balance of the contract period, the law requires him to make a reasonable effort to secure other employment.[1] He is not obliged, however, to seek or accept any and all types of work which may be available. Only work which is in the same field and which is of the same quality need be accepted.[2]

Over the years the courts have employed various phrases to define the type of employment which the employee [must] accept. Thus in California alone it has been held that he must accept employment which is "substantially similar" (*Lewis v. Protective Security Life Ins. Co.* (1962) 208 Cal. App. 2d 582, 584, 25 Cal. Rptr. 213; . . .); "comparable employment" (*Erler v. Five Points Motors, Inc.* (1967) 249 Cal. App. 2d 560, 562, 57 Cal. Rptr. 516; . . .); employment "in the same general line of the first employment" (*Rotter v. Stationers Corporation* (1960) 186 Cal. App. 2d 170, 172, 8 Cal. Rptr. 690, 691); "equivalent to his prior position" (*De Angeles v. Roos Bros., Inc.* (1966) 244 Cal. App. 2d 434, 443, 52 Cal. Rptr. 783); "employment in a similar capacity" (*Silva v. McCoy* (1968) 259 Cal. App. 2d 256, 260, 66 Cal. Rptr. 364); employment which is "not . . . of a different or inferior kind. . . ." (*Gonzales v. Internat. Assn. of Machinists* (1963) 213 Cal. App. 2d 817, 822, 29 Cal. Rptr. 190, 193.) [Footnote omitted.]

For reasons which are unexplained, the majority cite several of these cases yet select . . . one particular phrase, "Not of a different or inferior kind," with which to analyze this case. I have discovered no historical or theoretical reason to adopt this phrase, which is simply a negative restatement of the affirmative standards set out in the above cases, as the exclusive standard. Indeed, its emergence is an example of the dubious phenomenon of the law responding not to rational judicial choice or changing social conditions, but to unrecognized changes in the language of opinions or legal treatises.[4] However, the phrase is a serviceable one and my concern is not with its use as the standard but rather with what I consider its distortion.

---

[1]The issue is generally discussed in terms of a duty on the part of the employee to minimize loss. The practice is long-established and there is little reason to change despite Judge Cardozo's observation of its subtle inaccuracy. "The servant is free to accept employment or reject it according to his uncensored pleasure. What is meant by the supposed duty is merely this: That if he unreasonably reject, he will not be heard to say that the loss of wages from then on shall be deemed the jural consequence of the earlier discharge. He has broken the chain of causation, and loss resulting to him thereafter is suffered through his own act." (*McClelland v. Climax Hosiery Mills* (1930) 252 N.Y. 347, 359, 169 N.E. 605, 609, concurring opinion.)

[2]This qualification of the rule seems to reflect the simple and humane attitude that it is too severe to demand of a person that he attempt to find and perform work for which he has no training or experience. Many of the older cases hold that one need not accept work in an inferior rank or position nor work which is more menial or arduous. This suggests that the rule may have had its origin in the bourgeois fear of resubmergence in lower economic classes.

[4][The court traced how the language "different or inferior kind" entered California case law, finding its origin in legal encyclopedias that used it as synonymous with "service of a *more menial kind*" or "employment of an *entirely different nature*." (Emphasis in original). — Eds.]

The relevant language excuses acceptance only of employment which is of a *different kind.* [Citations omitted.] It has never been the law that the mere existence of *differences between two jobs in the same field* is sufficient, as a matter of law, to excuse an employee wrongfully discharged from one from accepting the other in order to mitigate damages. Such an approach would effectively eliminate any obligation of an employee to attempt to minimize damage arising from a wrongful discharge. The only alternative job offer an employee would be required to accept would be an offer of his former job by his former employer.

Although the majority appear to hold that there was a difference "in kind" between the employment offered plaintiff in "Bloomer Girl" and that offered in "Big Country" . . . the majority merely point out differences between the two *films* (an obvious circumstance) and then apodically [*sic*] assert that these constitute a difference in the *kind* of *employment.* The entire rationale of the majority boils down to this: that the "mere circumstances" that "Bloomer Girl" was to be a musical review [*sic*] while "Big Country" was a straight drama "demonstrates the difference in kind" since a female lead in a western is not "the equivalent of or substantially similar to" a lead in a musical. This is merely attempting to prove the proposition by repeating it. It shows that the vehicles for the display of the star's talents are different but it does not prove that her employment as a star in such vehicles is of necessity different in kind and either inferior or superior.

I believe that the approach taken by the majority (a superficial listing of differences with no attempt to assess their significance) may subvert a valuable legal doctrine.[5] The inquiry in cases such as this should not be whether differences between the two jobs exist (there will always be differences) but whether the differences which are present are substantial enough to constitute differences in the *kind* of employment or, alternatively, whether they render the substitute work employment of an *inferior kind.*

[*T*]*his* inquiry involves . . . factual determinations which are improper on a motion for summary judgment. Resolving whether or not one job is substantially similar to another or whether, on the other hand, it is of a different or inferior kind, will often (as here) require a critical appraisal of the similarities and differences between them in light of the importance of these differences to the employee. This necessitates a weighing of the evidence, and it is precisely this undertaking which is forbidden on summary judgment. [Citation omitted.]

. . . No case has come to my attention . . . in which summary judgment has been granted on the issue of whether an employee was obliged to accept available alternate employment[, though] there may well be cases in which the substitute employment is so manifestly of a dissimilar or inferior sort, the declarations of the plaintiff so complete and those of the defendant so conclusionary and inadequate that no factual issues exist for which a trial is required. This, however, is not such a case.

---

[5]The values of the doctrine of mitigation of damages in this context are that it minimizes the unnecessary personal and social (e.g., nonproductive use of labor, litigation) costs of contractual failure. If a wrongfully discharged employee can, through his own action and without suffering financial or psychological loss in the process, reduce the damages accruing from the breach of contract, the most sensible policy is to require him to do so. I fear the majority opinion will encourage precisely opposite conduct.

It is not intuitively obvious, to me at least, that the leading female role in a dramatic motion picture is a radically different endeavor from the leading female role in a musical comedy film. Nor is it plain to me that the rather qualified rights of director and screenplay approval contained in the first contract are highly significant matters either in the entertainment industry in general or to this plaintiff in particular. Certainly, none of the declarations introduced by plaintiff in support of her motion shed any light on these issues. [Footnote omitted.]

[After identifying weaknesses in the evidence submitted to support summary judgment, Justice Sullivan reiterated concern that the plaintiff's reasonableness should be considered by a jury, not addressed as a matter of rule by the reviewing court.]

Post-Case Follow-Up

The studio tactics here almost look like bait and switch: lure her in with the promise of one film; once locked in, cancel that project but offer a way to mitigate damages with a film she might not have accepted if offered originally. By defining Shirley MacLaine's career as a leading lady in musical films, the court was able to say as a matter of law that it was reasonable to reject the western. The dissent's concern that such a narrow definition may not play well in other settings seems justified. While MacLaine's efforts to find a different film were minimal at best, defendant did not try to argue that she could have found any other film for this time period. That may reflect how far in advance casting decisions are made or overconfidence in the reasonableness of its own substitute offer.

Parker v. Twentieth Century Fox Film Corp.: Real Life Applications

1. Alex was superintendent of schools for a small rural city in Michigan, where no private schools exist within a 50-mile radius. In breach of contract, the School Board fired Alex two years before the contract expired. Is it reasonable for Alex to make no effort at all to find a new job until the two years expire? For what types of jobs should Alex send out resumes in order to conduct a reasonable job search? Suppose the School Board also breached the contract of Alex's spouse, Cameron, a math teacher. Would it be reasonable for Cameron to make no job search at all? What other jobs should Cameron seek? *See Salem Community School Corp. v. Richman*, 406 N.E.2d 269 (Ind. App. 1980); *Mason County Board of Education v. State Superintendent of Schools*, 295 S.E.2d 719 (W. Va. 1982).

2. Franchisee declared bankruptcy and breached a lease with Owner. Franchisor (a guarantor of Franchisee) offered to lease the premises from Owner on exactly the same terms as Franchisee. Owner refused unless Franchisor agreed to allow Owner to reclaim the property on 60 days' notice (a term not in the original

lease with Franchisee). Franchisor refused this term. Owner eventually relet the property without a 60-day cancellation provision at a rent lower than that offered by the Franchisor. Owner now sues Franchisor (as guarantor of Franchisee's lease) for its losses. May Owner recover rent lost during (a) the six-month period after Franchisor offered to lease the space during which Owner tried to negotiate a 60-day cancellation term; (b) the additional one year the premises were vacant before Owner relet the premises; and (c) the difference between the rent Franchisee promised to pay and the rent paid by the new tenant for the remainder of the period covered by Franchisee's lease?

3. Buyer agreed to pay $325,000 for Seller's condominium. Buyer demanded Seller fix a minor electrical issue in a short period. When Seller failed to comply, Buyer breached the contract by refusing to complete the sale. Seller tried to find a new buyer, but listed the condominium at a price higher than the market justified. When offered $250,000 for the condo, Seller counteroffered for $290,000, again higher than the market justified. The potential buyer refused. After four years, Seller eventually sold the condo for $200,000. What, if any, damages may Seller recover for Buyer's breach?

Discharged Employees

A discharged employee need not seek or accept any other work. Yet failure to seek or to accept reasonable substitute employment will lead to a reduction in recovery by the amount that would have been earned. An employee can decide to take a vacation instead of (or before) reentering the workforce. But defendant need not pay for that vacation, if other work was available.

The court in *Parker* identified several reasons an employee might limit a job search or refuse a job offer:

1. It is reasonable to confine a job search to one's current career.
2. It is reasonable to confine a job search to one's current location.
3. It is reasonable to confine a job search to employers other than the one that breached.

Some courts follow these guidelines strictly. Others consider circumstances in which narrowing the job search in this way becomes unreasonable. For example, after prolonged lack of success in finding new work in one career or location, it may be unreasonable not to expand the search.

Courts differ in how different employment must be before it becomes so different the employee may refuse the alternative job. The dissent in *Parker* thought leading actress in a movie was close enough; the majority preferred leading actress in a musical comedy movie. Careers can be described at different levels of specificity: teacher, math teacher, or algebra teacher; lawyer, intellectual property lawyer, or patent prosecution lawyer. Any substitute job a person would want to refuse will be different or inferior in some way. Lawyers need to explain what justified plaintiff's narrow search.

An offer from the employer that just breached the contract carries additional risks. Agreeing to new terms may look like a modification. For example, if an employer threatens to fire an employee unless he agrees to a pay cut, does the employee's assent modify the original contract? Or did the employer breach, after which the employee took the substitute job to minimize the loss? Refusing the offer is generally deemed reasonable. The situation might differ if, after discharge, the employer later offered a lower paying job. Even after leaving, however, an offer to return on inferior terms may insult the employee's dignity, making return on those terms an undue humiliation.

Refusing substitute work because it involves lower pay may not be reasonable. Damages can compensate for the difference between what was promised and what the new work pays. If the job is in the same career and the same locale, and with a different employer, refusing it may be unreasonable. Even here, however, reasons exist to keep looking for a job with better pay, reasons a court might find persuasive.

Any job actually taken avoids losses. Losses actually avoided are not recoverable. Thus, taking work that one reasonably could refuse will reduce damages, where refusing it would not. Some employers, however, have argued that plaintiff should have found a more lucrative job that would offset all the losses, instead of taking work at lower pay.

Discharged Contractors

Generally, construction contractors can take on more than one project at a time. The central office staff can handle multiple contracts by hiring more temporary laborers for each project. Thus, any new job does not really offset the loss caused by discharge from an old job. The contractor could have taken the new job anyway. In effect, this approach treats contractors as lost volume sellers. Factually, it may be inaccurate in some circumstances. Rather than misjudge particular cases, courts tend to apply this rule to all construction contractors. In one case, a contractor discharged from a job was hired to complete the work by someone who bought the building from the breaching party. The court held that the new job did not replace the old one, even though the contractor clearly could not have been paid twice to do the same job. Having a settled rule treating contractors as lost volume sellers was so useful the court did not want to create an exception even in the most obvious of cases.

2. Foreseeability

Foreseeability refers to a contract party's ability to anticipate, at the time a contract is made, the type (and perhaps the amount) of loss the other party might suffer if a breach occurs. Specifically, the rule rejects recovery of damages "for loss that the party in breach did not have reason to foresee as a probable result of the breach when the contract was made."[24]

---

[24]Restatement (Second) of Contracts §351(a); *see also* UCC §2-715(2)(a).

The foreseeability rule requires that losses be

1. foreseeable, not necessarily foreseen (an objective test);
2. at formation, not at breach;
3. a probable, not merely a possible, result.

Note that the losses, not the breach, must be foreseeable. At the time of formation, the defendant probably does not anticipate that it probably will breach. That does not matter. The issue involves whether the losses are foreseeable as a consequence of a breach. That is, if defendant had been asked (at the time of contract formation) how a later breach probably would affect the other party, what losses should it anticipate?

At a minimum, the type of loss must be foreseeable. Thus, if a manufacturer knows (or should know) that a wholesaler will resell the goods, lost profits are a foreseeable result of the failure to deliver goods. The manufacturer should anticipate that type of damage (lost profits), even if it cannot predict the amount. In extreme cases, where the amount of consequential damage greatly exceeds what the parties might have expected, courts may limit recovery to the amount of consequential loss the defendant had reason to anticipate at contract formation. Even in these cases, the foreseeable amount of lost profits will be recoverable; courts reject only the unforeseeable excess.

Hadley v. Baxendale

The foreseeability rule derives from *Hadley v. Baxendale*, 9 Exch. 341, 156 Eng. Rep. 145 (1854), one of the most famous contract cases of all time. A mill shipped a broken part to a company that needed it in order to produce a replacement. The carrier did not deliver it as quickly as promised, causing the mill to remain closed (losing profits) for longer than necessary. The court refused to award lost profits on the ground that the carrier had no reason to know that the mill would remain closed. The facts are maddening. The carrier knew the mill was closed and that the mill wanted the part expedited. The court held that was not enough to inform the carrier that the mill would stay closed; maybe they had a spare part. In practice, you might persuade a judge to draw a different inference.

Proving Foreseeability

Parties may seek to prove foreseeability by showing one of two things:

1. the plaintiff provided defendant information that made losses foreseeable; or
2. the defendant should have realized for itself that losses were likely if a breach occurred.

Either will suffice.

A party can ensure that the other party foresees losses by mentioning them during negotiations. Especially if losses are unusual, either in amount or in the way they may arise, a party may wish to warn its contract partners of the type and magnitude of losses it may incur unless the other party performs. For instance, unless informed by the buyer, a retailer of car parts may not realize that the buyer intends to use the parts to repair a taxi cab (or a car used for Uber). Parties negotiating a contract may not discuss what might happen if a breach occurs. But during negotiation, parties may discuss the special needs or concerns one of them has — for example, concern for timely delivery in order to avoid some harmful consequence. That kind of information may make a loss foreseeable.

For many losses, however, specific communications will not be necessary. Losses that follow in the ordinary course of events will be foreseeable even without special notice. That will cover many consequential losses. For instance, the owner of a strip mall should realize that lessees will use the premises for retail shops, so that breaching the lease will cause lost profits in addition to loss of the premises themselves. In one case, a court ruled that a person selling an x-ray machine to a doctor should have realized the doctor would suffer lost profits if the machine was not powerful enough to produce useful plates.[25]

By encouraging disclosure, the foreseeability rule may encourage performance. Aware of the potential magnitude of the loss, the other party may take extra precautions to avoid inadvertent breaches or may obtain insurance against losses. Of course, mentioning the possible losses can lead to less favorable precautions. The potentially liable party might refuse the contract as too risky, might increase the price to make the risk worthwhile, or might add a contract term excluding some losses. All of these are legitimate things for the other party to request. To some extent, the foreseeability rule protects the parties' ability to negotiate over the losses that seem likely. If one party does not realize that negotiation is required (because the losses are unusual and hard to anticipate), the party that does recognize the risks must either raise them for discussion or bear the risks itself.

Foreseeability is not insurmountable, even when injuries are somewhat unusual. When an air conditioner failed, the elderly owner died of hyperthermia.[26] A court sent the case to a jury, holding that deaths of this sort were not so uncommon that it could dismiss a breach of warranty claim. However, not every claim succeeds. The seller of a used car breached a warranty of title when the car turned out to be stolen, but was not liable for damages buyer incurred after being arrested. That was unforeseeable.[27]

Case Preview

Sunnyland Farms v. Central New Mexico Electric Cooperative

When plaintiff failed to pay its electric bill, defendant cut the power — without the required advanced notice. That apparently minor error left plaintiff defenseless against fire, with disastrous results. The court employed the foreseeability doctrine to determine which party should bear the risk of these losses.

[25] *Manouchehri v. Heim*, 941 P.2d 978 (N.M. Ct. App. 1997).
[26] *Garavalia v. Heat Controller, Inc.*, 570 N.E.2d 1227 (Ill. App. Ct. 1991).
[27] *Marino v. Perna*, 629 N.Y.S.2d 669 (N.Y. Civ. Ct. 1995).

As you read *Sunnyland Farms v. Central New Mexico Electric Cooperative*, look for the following:

1. Why does the court reject a requirement of tacit agreement? Would that test work better in this case?
2. Does the court require special notice even if a loss arises in the natural course of events or only if it does not?
3. How specific must a communication be in order to put the other party on notice that losses of an unusual sort might arise from a breach?
4. Does the court require notice of the size of the loss or just the type of the loss?

Sunnyland Farms, Inc. v. Central New Mexico Electric Cooperative, Inc.

301 P.3d 387 (N.M. 2013)

CHÁVEZ, Justice.

...

Sunnyland purchased its electricity from [the Central New Mexico Electrical Cooperative] CNMEC. On September 8, 2003, CNMEC shut off electrical service to Sunnyland [for nonpayment, without providing the 15-day notice ordinarily given customers with overdue bills.]

On the morning of September 9, 2003, before electrical service was restored, several Sunnyland employees engaged in arc welding near flammable materials [negligently] started a fire that ultimately consumed Sunnyland Farms' packhouse and operations building. [The] employees . . . attempted to put it out using ordinary hoses, but without electricity, the Sunnyland facility had no running water, and the fire grew. [Use of hoses instead of a fire extinguisher also was negligent.]

[F]ire trucks arrived, but they were unable to access well water for firefighting because there was no electricity to power the pumps. Sunnyland had also failed to make alternative arrangements for emergency water in the event that power failed. Firefighters attempted to contact CNMEC to restore electricity to the water sources, but CNMEC employees expressed reservations to the emergency dispatcher, and the firefighters interpreted their statements as a threat that the fire department would have to assume liability. Firefighters attempted to use reservoir water and to preserve water by using foam and smaller hoses, but the buildings were nonetheless destroyed.

Sunnyland sued CNMEC in contract . . . alleging that if CNMEC had taken adequate care prior to disconnecting Sunnyland's electrical service, firefighters and Sunnyland employees would have had access to water and the fire could have been contained. The trial court found CNMEC liable both in contract and in tort. It calculated total consequential damages of over $21 million. . . .

...

[T]he Court of Appeals held that in New Mexico, awards of consequential damages in contract are governed by a "tacit agreement" test, which the trial court had failed to apply. [Citation omitted.] It therefore reversed the award of damages in contract. . . .

1. *Hadley v. Baxendale* and Restatement (Second) of Contracts state the proper test for consequential damages in New Mexico

This Court has previously stated that in an action for breach of contract, the breaching party "is justly responsible for all damages flowing naturally from the breach." *Camino Real Mobile Home Park P'ship v. Wolfe,* 119 N.M. 436, 443, 891 P.2d 1190, 1197 (1995). Damages "that arise naturally and necessarily as the result of the breach" are "general damages," which give the plaintiff whatever value he or she would have obtained from the breached contract. *Id.* In some circumstances, the plaintiff can also recover for "consequential damages" or "special damages," which "are not based on the capital or present value of the promised performance but upon benefits it can produce or losses that may be caused by its absence." *Id.* . . .

The classic test for whether a plaintiff may recover consequential damages comes from *Hadley v. Baxendale,* 156 Eng. Rep. 145, 9 Ex. 341 (1854). In that case, a mill was temporarily shut down due to a broken crankshaft. [Citations to *Hadley* omitted henceforth.] The defendants were common carriers who were supposed to ship the broken crankshaft to an engineering company to have a new one built, but the defendants "wholly neglected and refused so to do for the space of seven days," and the mill was shut down for five days longer than should have been necessary. The jury awarded the mill damages for the profits it lost due to the delay. The appellate court reversed, holding that in an action for breach of contract, recovery was permitted for consequential damages only "such as may reasonably be supposed to have been in the contemplation of both parties, at the time they made the contract, as the probable result of the breach of it."

The *Hadley* standard has been interpreted as an objective foreseeability test: A defendant is liable for losses that were foreseeable at the time of contracting, regardless of whether the defendant actually contemplated or foresaw the loss. Restatement (Second) of Contracts §351 cmt. a (1981); . . . This foreseeability standard is more stringent than "proximate cause" in tort law; the loss must have been foreseeable as the *probable* result of breach, not merely as a possibility. [Citations omitted.] The Restatement asks whether there were "special circumstances, beyond the ordinary course of events, that the party in breach had reason to know." *Id.* §351(2)(b); *see also* U.C.C. §2-715(2)(a) (2010) (allowing buyers consequential damages for "any loss resulting from general or particular requirements and needs of which the seller at the time of contracting had reason to know and which could not reasonably be prevented by cover or otherwise"). In the absence of such circumstances, the breaching party is liable only for general damages. [Citation omitted.]

This Court has cited the *Hadley* standard approvingly and described it as the appropriate rule of analysis in New Mexico cases dealing with consequential damages. [Citation omitted.] However, we have also stated that "the foreseeability . . . rule anticipates an explicit or tacit agreement by the defendant" that he or she will assume particular damages if he or she breaches. *Camino Real,* 119 N.M. at 446, 891 P.2d at 1200; *see also Wall v. Pate,* 104 N.M. 1, 2, 715 P.2d 449, 450 (1986) (suggesting that the conditions required for an award of special damages must include a "tacit agreement" (citing *Globe Ref. Co. v. Landa Cotton Oil Co.*, 190 U.S. 540, 543-44, 23 S. Ct. 754, 47 L. Ed. 1171 (1903))).

Engaging in an exhaustive analysis of *Camino Real, Wall*, and other cases in his well-written opinion, Judge Sutin synthesized a "New Mexico rule" of consequential damages. [Citation omitted.] This rule is similar to the test in Restatement (Second) of Contracts, but it incorporates the requirement that "the nonperforming party must explicitly or tacitly agree to respond in damages for the particular damages understood to be likely in the event of a breach." [Citations omitted.] This makes the "New Mexico rule . . . more limited and restrictive than the notion of foreseeability in . . . the Restatement or the UCC." [Citations omitted.]

We now abandon the "tacit agreement" test. While we suspect that there may not, in fact, be much space between a "tacit agreement" and the special circumstances required to render a defendant liable for consequential damages, our previous emphasis on the tacit agreement test from *Globe Refining* is confusing and antiquated. We hold that the proper test for consequential damages in New Mexico is the *Hadley* standard as interpreted in Restatement (Second) of Contracts Section 351. In a contract action, a defendant is liable only for those consequential damages that were objectively foreseeable as a probable result of his or her breach when the contract was made. To the extent our earlier cases suggest a different standard, they are overruled.

2. There were no special circumstances in this case warranting consequential damages

[T]he trial court in this case issued very limited conclusions of law regarding the issue of foreseeability and consequential damages. The trial court made one finding of fact stating that "the damages suffered by Plaintiff were foreseeable and a proximate cause [sic — should probably be "result"] of Defendant's Breach of Contract. . . ." However, in its findings, the trial court did not distinguish between the proximate cause required for tort liability and the more stringent foreseeability required for consequential damages in contract. [Citations omitted.] The trial transcript reveals that the trial court did consider the *Hadley* standard for special damages in contract [concluding] "I'm going to rule that the Co-op, in providing electricity and being the expert party to the contract should have been aware of the consequential damages of . . . failing to provide electricity if there was a breach of contract, that there would be consequential damages." However, despite this sign that the trial court contemplated the appropriate standard, we cannot say that the trial court actually applied the foreseeability standard correctly. To support the conclusion that Sunnyland's damages were foreseeable to CNMEC at the time of contracting, we would expect the trial court to find "special circumstances, beyond the ordinary course of events." [Citation omitted.] Despite the voluminous findings of fact by the trial court, there were no findings that special circumstances of this type existed.

Sunnyland suggests that it was sufficient that CNMEC knew that Sunnyland was a for-profit enterprise and it depended on electricity. Both of these factual statements are supported by the trial court's findings of fact. . . . [T]he trial court found that prior to disconnecting electricity, a CNMEC employee allowed a Sunnyland employee to open the windows in the greenhouse to allow venting, which suggests that CNMEC might have known that cutting off electricity could harm Sunnyland's tomato crop.

Taking these findings of fact to indicate the presence of special circumstances is problematic for three reasons. First, although this Court indulges reasonable inferences in favor of the trial court's judgment, [citation omitted], this is simply too speculative. This Court does not speculate about what the fact-finder might have meant to say but did not. [Citation omitted.]

Second, Sunnyland's injury was not directly caused by the lack of electricity. The actual harm was more attenuated: the lack of electricity interrupted Sunnyland's water supply, which, in conjunction with Sunnyland's lack of backup firefighting options, made it difficult for Sunnyland to respond to the fire its employees negligently started. There were no findings that CNMEC should have known that Sunnyland was likely to start fires or was depending on electricity in order to fight any fires that occurred. Even if some damage to the tomato crop was foreseeable from the disconnection of electricity, the particular damage that occurred was not, and consequential damages are only permissible if the particular damage that actually occurred was foreseeable. "The mere circumstance that some loss was foreseeable, or even that some loss of the same general kind was foreseeable, will not suffice if the loss that actually occurred was not foreseeable." Restatement (Second) of Contracts §351 cmt. (a).

Third, even if CNMEC had reason to know that Sunnyland depended on its electricity to power water in the event of a fire, CNMEC would still not be liable without the presence of additional special circumstances. *Hadley* provides a good example of what does and does not qualify as "special circumstances." In *Hadley*, the defendant knew that the crankshaft it was carrying was a broken part of a for-profit mill. However, the plaintiff never told the defendant exactly what was at stake, i.e., that there was no backup shaft or other alternative plan to keep the mill running. [Footnote omitted.] Similarly, in this case, CNMEC would have needed to know not only that Sunnyland depended on its electricity for access to water, but that there was no backup power source, or that there was a particularized need for uninterrupted water or power. There is no evidence that CNMEC had reason to know any of this. In particular, CNMEC could not have been expected to know that Sunnyland did not have a separate power source, independent of the power for the main building, for the well that was to be used in the event of a fire. A firefighter's trial testimony agreed that "if it's going to be an approved firefighting source of water, it has to have two separate sources of electricity . . . [a]nd one of them cannot come through the building that's being . . . protected by the pump," and the trial court found that "Sunnyland Farms was negligent in having only one source of power which ran through the support building to energize the exterior well pump." CNMEC cannot have been expected to anticipate Sunnyland's negligence in this regard.

Langley v. Pacific Gas & Electric Co., 41 Cal. 2d 655, 262 P.2d 846 (1953) (in bank), provides an instructive example of what a utility company would need to know to render it liable for consequential damages in the event of a power shutoff. The plaintiff ran a trout hatchery that required electricity to oxygenate the water and keep the trout alive. *Id.* at 847. If power was shut off, the fish could survive for only three and a half hours. *Id.* at 847-48. The plaintiff purchased electricity from the utility and explained his situation to its employees, asking whether the utility had 24-hour monitoring and would always be able to tell him before power was shut off.

Id. at 848. The plaintiff told the utility that if it was not able to make this guarantee, he would put in a backup pump. *Id.* The utility's employees assured the plaintiff that he would be notified any time the power was shut off. *Id.* Several years later, power to the fish hatchery was shut off for several hours, and the utility failed to warn or inform the plaintiff. *Id.* Nearly all of the plaintiff's fish died. *Id.* at 849. The plaintiff sued the utility for breach of contract, *id.* at 847, 849, and the California Supreme Court upheld a jury verdict in his favor, apparently including full consequential damages. *Id.* at 847; . . . The court found that the utility "knew that a continuous supply of electric current to plaintiff was imperative," and the utility had an obligation either to provide it or to give the plaintiff notice so that he could make alternative arrangements. *Id.* at 850.

The facts in *Langley* are starkly different from the facts in the present case. In *Langley,* the plaintiff had an unusual and pressing need for uninterrupted service, and he took steps to notify the utility of that need. *Id.* at 848. He also relied on the utility's assurances by choosing not to install backup power, and the utility knew of that fact as well. *Id.* Unlike in *Hadley* and the present case, the utility in *Langley* understood the particular consequences that would result from a breach, and it accepted the contract anyway.

There were no findings in this case that CNMEC should have known of a particular vulnerability to fire on Sunnyland's part, or that Sunnyland had no backup source of power or water. With neither findings nor evidence of special circumstances, we cannot uphold a judgment for consequential damages. Accordingly, we affirm the Court of Appeals' reversal of the trial court's award of contract damages to Sunnyland.

[Sunnyland recovered profits on its tort claims, reduced by 80 percent to account for its share of the negligence.]

Post-Case Follow-Up

In rejecting the tacit agreement test, New Mexico joined the mainstream of American contract law, though some vestiges of that test remain. Deciding whether silence included (or did not include) a promise to pay certain damages requires imagination more than analysis. The court applied the foreseeability rule more strenuously than some jurisdictions might. It probably would not matter that CNMEC did not know Sunnyland's employees would start fires if it had been told that Sunnyland needed electricity in order to protect itself from fires. Even failing to disclose the absence of a backup generator or pump might not matter to some courts willing to infer that the need for electricity to fight fires implied the lack of alternatives. But absent some warning that electricity was unusually important to Sunnyland, CNMEC lacked reason to know that breach might (let alone probably would) produce more than the usual harm to this client. One can only speculate whether, if the fire had resulted without Sunnyland's fault (say, from lightning), the court would have applied the rule with the same vigor.

Sunnyland Farms v. Central New Mexico Electric Cooperative: Real Life Applications

1. Oreco purchased a mine from a bankrupt competitor and began liquidating thousands of pieces of equipment in the mine. Sal, who dealt with Oreco regularly, paid Oreco $2,480 for 248 industrial circuit breakers that Oreco feared contained asbestos. Before Sal removed the goods, Oreco sold the mine to another party and included the circuit breakers in the sale. The breakers were worth about $27,000 each ($6.7 million). Can Sal recover the value of the goods? *See M.M. Silta, Inc. v. Cleveland Cliffs, Inc.*, 572 F.3d 632 (8th Cir. 2009). Would it matter if the goods were worth about $10 each when the contract was made, but appreciated rapidly when the manufacturer's factory was destroyed by an earthquake, creating an unexpected shortage of circuit breakers?
2. Bank promised to lend Chris $400,000 at 5 percent interest to buy a house from Leslie. Two weeks before closing, after learning that Chris posed a bigger credit risk than it originally thought, Bank repudiated the loan. Chris was unable to find a new lender in time to close the sale, even after Leslie agreed to postpone closing for ten days to allow Chris time to perform. Leslie canceled the contract and sold the house to a different buyer. Chris sued Bank. Bank claims that, at the time it entered the contract, it could not foresee that Chris would be unable to find a new loan. (It admits that when it breached the contract, it knew Chris probably would not find another loan.). Can Chris recover? How should a court measure Chris's damages?
3. Shelly, at 81, is in good health but has become more susceptible to heat as time passes. Shelly purchased an air conditioner from Big Al's and had it installed by a professional. During a prolonged period of unusually high heat, the air conditioner failed. Shelly died of hyperthermia. Shelly's estate sued Big Al's for breach of warranty. If it can prove liability, can the estate recover damages resulting from Shelly's death?

Classifying Losses

The foreseeability rule arguably applies to all losses. Market damages, however, are almost always foreseeable. Thus, defendants almost never raise foreseeability in that context. The UCC seems to assume that basic measures are foreseeable, including foreseeability only in the provision governing buyer's consequential damages.[28]

That clarification demonstrates the importance of finding ways to include more of the losses in the basic market measure, rather than treating them as consequential. For example, if a buyer of real estate entered a contract to resell the land at a profit, would the lost profit be included in damages? The buyer probably did not tell the seller (before the contract was entered) how large a profit it expected

---

[28]UCC §2-715(2)(a).

Consequential Damages or Direct Damages?

In a case similar to *Hadley v. Baxendale*, a carrier was paid to deliver ten packages containing the parts to a machine. Delay of one package prevented the use of the machine for some time. Plaintiff's claim to the lost profit on the rental of the machine was denied as unforeseeable. Yet depriving plaintiff of the use of the machine was a direct damage. The court awarded the fair rental value for the period the machine could not be used, rather than the actual rent the plaintiff would have received. *See Hector Martinez & Co. v. Southern Pacific Transportation Co.*, 606 F.2d 106 (5th Cir. 1979).

to generate by an immediate resale — or perhaps even that it intended to resell the land at all. If buyer had revealed that information, seller might have insisted on a higher price or tried to sell directly to the buyer's customer. Thus, foreseeability seems to fail. But recovery for the difference between the market value and the contract price remains available. If the market value is really the resale price buyer negotiated with another, not the contract price seller negotiated with buyer, buyer may recover the lost resale as part of the formula for general damages. The market value may not be quite as high as the resale contract. This specific resale contract represents the profit this buyer lost on this specific transaction, idiosyncratic losses that the foreseeability rule seeks to limit. Yet the market value might be even higher. (After all, the new buyer thinks the land is worth more than it is paying for it.) Even without foreseeability, a buyer might be able to recover some of the additional value it hoped to realize in the resale.

3. Certainty

Contract damages are not recoverable in an amount that exceeds what has been proven with reasonable certainty.[29] The rule technically applies to all damages, although market damages usually satisfy the rule without much difficulty. Consequential losses pose more difficulty.

Uncertainty does not preclude recovery, but sets a cap on recovery. Awards cannot exceed the amount that is reasonably certain. At some point, damage estimates become too speculative to award. But damages up to that point are recoverable.

Requiring certainty reduces the risk of overcompensation. Excessive recoveries pose as great a concern in contract damages as inadequate recoveries. Juries, however, may have a natural tendency to resolve doubts against the breaching party, perhaps granting more generous recoveries than the facts would warrant. The certainty doctrine allows courts to restrain that tendency. It reduces the amount of deference judges usually must show juries on issues of fact, such as the amount of damages. Thus, judges gain some leeway to grant motions for a new trial or a new trial on damages (or to use **remittitur**, a threat to grant a new trial unless plaintiff agrees to a smaller damage award).

Certainty can be applied to reject claims that seem very likely. For businesses with a track record, projecting future profits may be possible. But new businesses and unique events rely on projections that may or may not be as reliable. As courts

[29] Restatement (Second) of Contracts §352.

become increasingly comfortable with economic projections, plaintiffs may satisfy the certainty requirement in more cases in the future.

Case Preview

Advertising Specialty Institute v. Hall-Erickson

Defendant promised plaintiff the right to co-locate a trade show with defendant. When defendant breached, the plaintiff offered projections of how much it might have earned if it had been allowed to co-locate a show as promised. The court had to determine whether these projections offered enough confidence to justify a damage award.

As you read *Advertising Specialty Institute v. Hall-Erickson*, look for the following:

1. Did the rule applied here require certainty regarding the amount of loss suffered by the plaintiff or only certainty that the plaintiff suffered some losses?
2. Did the rule require a precise calculation of the amount of damages? Or would a reasonable estimate have satisfied the rule?
3. Did the court rule that plaintiff might have earned nothing if it had participated in the show? Did the evidence permit that inference?

Advertising Specialty Institute v. Hall-Erickson, Inc.

601 F.3d 683 (7th Cir. 2010)

CUDAHY, Circuit Judge.

In 2001, Advertising Specialty Institute (ASI) and The Motivation Show entered into a contract that purported to form a "strategic alliance" to "promote the professional use of promotional products and distributors." The parties agreed to provide "ASI with the right of first refusal concerning any activity, alliance, or opportunity concerning the promotional product/advertising specialty industry." The present dispute arises from The Motivation Show's co-locating a trade show in Chicago with Promotional Products Association International (PPAI), which is ASI's close competitor. The district court found that, in doing so, the defendants (collectively, "The Motivation Show") breached their contract with ASI by failing to honor the latter's right of first refusal. However, in light of ASI's failure to prove damages with reasonable certainty, the court awarded nominal damages in the amount of one dollar. ASI contends that the district court committed clear error in finding insufficient proof of damages. . . .

. . .

ASI is a trade-information publisher that facilitates the meeting of purveyors and purchasers of corporate promotional products.[1] ASI has approximately 21,000 distributor members and 3,300 supplier members. [It] holds roughly 80 shows per year throughout the United States [including a multi-day show in Chicago each May or July.]

Matthew Cohn (Mr. Cohn) is the vice chairman of ASI. . . .

The present case involves ASI's relationship with Hall-Erickson and National Premium Show, Inc. (NPS), the latter of which does business as The Motivation Show. Hall-Erickson is the exhibition manager for this show, which is held annually in the fall at McCormick Place in Chicago. Peter Erickson (Mr. Erickson) is [an officer and] sole shareholder of Hall-Erickson [and] NPS.

[Despite committing to give ASI] "the right of first refusal concerning any activity, alliance, or opportunity concerning the promotional product/advertising specialty industry," . . . Mr. Erickson "solicited and invited" PPAI [a close rival of ASI] to co-locate its trade show with The Motivation Show at McCormick Place in Chicago. This, the district court found, violated paragraph nine of the contract because The Motivation Show failed to grant ASI a right of first refusal over this co-location opportunity. . . .

. . .

The district court rejected Mr. Erickson's testimony [putting events in a more benign light], characterizing it as "just regrettably false" and further labeling certain of his explanations as "completely untruthful." . . .

However, despite concluding that the defendants were in breach of contract, the district court found that ASI had failed to prove damages with reasonable certainty. Although it reached this conclusion without addressing the factual record in great depth, the district court did note that "in view of [its] attitude toward the defendants' breach, [it] would not be reluctant to make a reasonable estimate of damages if [it] believed that [it] could do so."

II. DISCUSSION

. . .

B. The District Court Did Not Commit Clear Error in Determining That ASI Failed to Prove Damages with Reasonable Certainty

The district court concluded in no uncertain terms that ASI had failed to establish damages with reasonable certainty. Although its finding was not clearly erroneous, we are concerned that the court may have overstated the inadequacy of the proffered evidence. Having reviewed the record, we believe that the question whether ASI has made a sufficient showing of damages is a close one. Nevertheless, given our clear-error review, the question is not what we would find were we sitting at the trial level. [Citations omitted.] We must affirm if the district court's account of the

---

[1]Promotional products include corporate apparel, trophies, awards, mugs, pens, T-shirts, lighters, flashlights, Post-It notes, Coach-leather goods, barbeque grills and other items that can display the name or logo of a company.

evidence is plausible viewed in light of the record in its entirety. [Citations omitted.] Since a reasonable trier of fact could conclude that the proffered evidence falls short of proving damages with reasonable specificity, we affirm.

We begin by noting that the district court correctly identified relevant Pennsylvania law, which provides that contract "damages . . . are not recoverable for loss beyond an amount that the evidence permits to be established with reasonable certainty." *Spang & Co. v. U.S. Steel Corp.*, 519 Pa. 14, 545 A.2d 861, 866 (1988) (relying on Restatement (Second) of Contracts §352). In considering whether the district court clearly erred in finding that ASI failed to prove damages with reasonable certainty, we note that Pennsylvania law generally resolves doubts against the breaching party. *Id.* at 867 (citing Restatement, §352). We note too the Pennsylvania Supreme Court's pronouncement in 1979 that "mere uncertainty as to the amount of damages will not bar recovery where it is clear that damages were the certain result of the defendant's conduct." *Pugh v. Holmes*, 486 Pa. 272, 405 A.2d 897, 909-10 (1979). Notwithstanding this language, which might be read to relieve victims of contractual breach of the obligation of identifying actual damages with reasonable certainty, so long as they can demonstrate that they were in fact injured, "the law still requires a plaintiff to produce evidence which establishes, with a fair degree of probability, a basis for assessing damages." *Wujcik v. Yorktowne Dental Associates, Inc.*, 701 A.2d 581, 584 (Pa. Super. 1997).

We proceed by discussing the district court's analysis of the relevant testimony and explaining some of our concerns. [Footnote omitted.] In particular, we question the court's characterization of Mr. Cohn's testimony, which provided the plaintiff's primary evidence for establishing damages. The court declared:

> I do know that Mr. Cohn's testimony, which ranges from a half million to a million dollars without any specification whatever as to what would account for a difference between a half million and a million, is completely speculative and is not something that the Court could rely upon for an award of damages.

Tr. at 744.

We believe that three issues merit discussion here. First, having reviewed the transcript of Mr. Cohn's testimony, it is indeed true that the witness's estimation of damages ranged from $500,000 to $1,000,000 and even beyond. Mr. Cohn originally maintained that the relevant damages' range was $500,000 to $800,000. This, being a narrower band, may have been less troubling to the district court. Nevertheless, in light of the testimony of David Kordecki — a former employee of the CCTB [Chicago Convention and Tourism Bureau] — Mr. Cohn subsequently concluded that his original, estimated range was "extremely conservative." On cross-examination, Mr. Cohn clarified that the range of damages was linked to the number of booths ASI would have sold at the co-located event with The Motivation Show. He testified that 500 booths would have yielded a profit of half-a-million dollars. He also explained that 800 booths would correspond to over a million dollars' profit.

For this reason, we are troubled by the district court's assertion that Mr. Cohn failed to provide "any specification whatever" to explain the range of estimated damages. His testimony made clear that that range depended on the court's estimate as to the likely number of booths that ASI would have sold. Mr. Cohn also indicated that the low-end figure was based on the lowest level of profit that ASI had ever enjoyed when it sold the same number of booths that PPAI did at the co-located event. He testified that ASI's 2006 show in Philadelphia, which was a 600-booth show, yielded more than $500,000 in profit. He then explained that "frankly, we would have done better than that [in the co-located event with The Motivation Show] because we would have had shared costs that we would not have needed to spend the money on." He testified that ASI would not need to have spent as much money on a keynote speaker and that the $191,000 it spent on education in Philadelphia "mostly would have been saved."

Reviewing the transcript, we do not understand the district court's conclusion that Mr. Cohn's testimony did not provide "any specification whatever" about the range of damages. It seems clear to us that Mr. Cohn believed that $500,000 was an "extremely conservative" minimum and that a more accurate estimate of damages would be greater.

Our second concern is that the record suggests a (slight) possibility that the district court may have decided that Mr. Cohn's testimony on damages was speculative before it entertained the evidence. [We note the exchange] when the question of quantifying damages was first broached:

> Q. What would you have expected ASI to profit had it been given an opportunity to conduct a co-located show alongside of The Motivation Show in 2003?
>
> Mr. Kolman: Objection, Your Honor. That's completely speculative.
>
> The Court: I agree that it is, really, but I am going to let him answer, and I will take it for whatever it may be worth. But I concede your point. It's very speculative.

Mr. Cohn . . . had considerable experience in the industry. Unlike Mr. Erickson, his testimony was not found to be false or untruthful. In short, Mr. Cohn's testimony was likely to be an important source of evidence on ASI's damages. *See* Restatement (Second) of Contracts §352, Comment b (explaining that "[e]vidence of past performance will form the basis for a reasonable prediction as to the future" and explaining further that, if the business is a new one, "damages may be established with reasonable certainty with the aid of expert testimony"). We see no reason why his testimony on this subject would necessarily be "very speculative." Nor do we believe that it turned out to be. His subsequent explanation of why ASI's lost profit was between $500,000 and possibly more than a million dollars was neither arbitrary nor unsupported. Since ASI and PPAI are in the same market and have memberships that overlap to some extent, it is not wholly unreasonable to presume that the two companies would have sold a comparable number of booths. Had they done so, Mr. Cohn's testimony reveals that it would have yielded a minimum profit of $500,000. And, in fact, it would likely have yielded more, due to Chicago's higher profitability and the various cost savings associated with co-located events.

Our third, and final, concern is that the district court failed to address evidence of ASI's profitably holding major shows in the past and of the significant cost savings that co-location would have provided. Such evidence weighed on the question of damages and should have formed part of the district court's opinion.

Notwithstanding the district court's rather cursory, and at times inaccurate, assessment of Mr. Cohn's testimony, we cannot find that its ultimate conclusion was clearly erroneous. First, we take the district court at its word when it stated that it would hear Mr. Cohn's testimony and take it for whatever it was worth. In addition, there are facts in the record that render a direct comparison between the number of booths that PPAI sold and the number that ASI would have sold somewhat unreliable. Specifically, ASI had never held two major shows in the same city and in the same year before, and one can only speculate as to what the effect of holding two such events within four months would be on the respective demands for each event. The uncertainty injected by this fact renders a finding of clear error difficult.

Specifically, if the co-located event would have been as attractive to ASI's members as ASI contends, then presumably the demand for that event would have reduced demand for its May 2003 show. Indeed, some such effect would surely have occurred, given the evidence in the record that many distributors and suppliers will attend one trade show in a certain city in a year, but not more. In calculating damages for The Motivation Show's wrongly denying ASI the co-location opportunity in 2003, the damages awarded for that denial would have to be reduced by the profit that would otherwise have been lost by the diluted demand for the May 2003 show. [Footnote omitted.] We can do no more than speculate as to what the economic relationship between these two events would have been. And, as Pennsylvania law makes clear, such speculation is an inadequate basis for estimating damages. *See Spang*, 545 A.2d at 866.

This shortcoming is compounded by a number of other deficiencies. First, ASI did not identify companies that would have attended a co-located event with The Motivation Show in 2003. Such testimony from specific companies would have been helpful, especially if it could have been elicited from those of ASI's members that did not attend ASI's May 2003 show. ASI points out that 21 percent of its supplier members attended its May 2003 show, so it would have targeted the remaining 79 percent for the co-promoted event later that year. Specific evidence that certain of the latter group of members would have attended a co-located show in the fall of 2003 would have been highly relevant. Absent such evidence, some degree of speculation would be required as to the number of booths that ASI would have sold in a 2003 co-promotion with The Motivation Show.[4]

Second, [ASI] the appellant/cross-appellee did not obtain financial data from PPAI concerning the latter's revenue and profits from the co-promoted event it held with The Motivation Show in 2003.[5] Such information could have been helpful in crafting a reasonable estimate of the damages. Third, ASI did not introduce evidence of the identities of the specific companies that actually attended PPAI's co-promoted event in 2003. Such evidence would have enabled the district court to calculate damages with greater specificity. Fourth, had The Motivation Show offered ASI a right

[4][T]hat PPAI sold between 500 and 600 booths is certainly illuminative on the question of how many booths ASI would have sold, [but not] determinative. [T]he last time PPAI had held a show in Chicago was two years before the 2003 co-promoted event. That being the case, it is certainly possible that PPAI sold more booths than ASI would have [given ASI's] large show only four months previous.

[5]ASI sought the relevant documents from PPAI through a subpoena that issued from the U.S. District Court for the Northern District of Texas. However, that court refused to grant a motion to compel compliance by PPAI with the subpoena. ASI did not appeal this refusal to the United States Court of Appeals for the Fifth Circuit.

of first refusal, PPAI might still have held a separate show in July 2003. This would have resulted in three major shows being held in Chicago within four months, which complicates the proof of damages even further.

One inevitably sympathizes with ASI, which has been wronged by a company with which it hoped to enjoy a fruitful, strategic relationship. Proving damages from the improper denial of a future opportunity is a difficult endeavor, however, and ASI makes the strongest arguments it can with the evidence in the record. But in light of the preceding shortfalls in the proffered evidence, we cannot conclude that the district court clearly erred. This holds true even when the evidence is read in a manner favorable to the nonbreaching party. *See ATACS Corp. v. Trans World Communications, Inc.*, 155 F.3d 659, 669 (3d Cir. 1998). As explained, our review of the factual findings of the district court is highly deferential. Even if we would have been inclined to find some measure of damages reasonably certain in the present case, this fact alone does not allow us to reverse the district court's factual determination to the contrary. [Footnote omitted.]

Affirmed.

Post-Case Follow-Up

The rule stated here seems to favor the plaintiff: as long as it can demonstrate with reasonable certainty that it lost something, a court can decide that it should recover a reasonable estimate of the amount lost. The Seventh Circuit found the damage testimony more probative than the trial court did. It seems likely that if the trial court had awarded damages, that decision would have been affirmed. But given the trial court's skepticism concerning the projected losses, the gaps in plaintiff's proof precluded reversing the trial court.

Advertising Specialty Institute v. Hall-Erickson: Real Life Applications

1. City entered an exclusive development option agreement (DOA) with Golfco, agreeing not to entertain other nearby projects until it decided whether or not to proceed with the golf course and RV park Golfco proposed to develop. City later promised a different developer an exclusive DOA for a different RV project nearby, even though it was aware that this probably breached the DOA with Golfco. After Golfco invested considerable amounts in designing the project and obtaining necessary permissions (including City approval of all important aspects of the project), City reversed its approval of the RV park aspect. Golfco wants to sue. What damages would you advise it to seek? Does it matter that its rights to develop the golf course and RV park are assignable? *See Columbia Park Golf Course v. City of Kennewick*, 248 P.3d 1067 (Wash. Ct. App. 2011).

2. Flakeco agreed to remove from the ground and buy Grower's entire 2015 crop of grade no. 2 chipping potatoes (estimated at 20,000 cwt. (hundredweight)) for $18/cwt. Flakeco removed 4,000 cwt. of potatoes and paid for the 3,800 that satisfied grade no. 2. Flakeco then repudiated the contract and refused to remove any more potatoes. Grower found a buyer who removed 6,000 cwt. and paid $17/cwt. for the 5,400 cwt. that satisfied grade no. 2. Grower was unable to find a buyer for the remaining 10,000 cwt. of potatoes, which remained in the ground until they had to be removed and discarded. At trial the court awarded $5,400 as damages for the potatoes sold, but refused to award any damages for the unsold potatoes because the quantity that satisfied grade no. 2 could not be determined. Grower seeks your advice on whether to appeal this decision. Grower notes that prior to repudiation Grower complied with Flakeco's request that Grower apply heat to the fields, thus making harvesting easier but reducing the number of potatoes that would satisfy grade no. 2 and creating some of the uncertainty the court confronted.

3. Cunning Studios invested $50,000 preparing to make a short film in the hope that Cooper Brady would agree to play himself in the film. Shortly before production, Brady finally agreed to perform. Cunning incurred an additional $100,000 preparing for the shoot before Brady announced that he was double booked and could not perform after all. Total production budget for the film was $2 million. Because short films have a relatively small market, Cunning estimated that revenues might reach $5 million, but no higher. If a court determines that Brady breached a contract, how much should Cunning recover? *See Anglia Television Ltd. v. Reed*, [1971] 3 All E.R. 690.

Existence or Amount of Loss

The certainty requirement sometimes is stated in two parts: plaintiff must show both the existence and the amount of damages with reasonable certainty. As applied, the first part (certainty as to the existence of damages) dominates the rule. Once the plaintiff shows some damages with reasonable certainly, awarding zero damages becomes an error. The only question is how much to award. In that setting, courts usually allow the jury to award a reasonable estimate. If the jury awards an extravagant amount, a court still may reduce the award because the amount exceeded what the evidence established with reasonable certainty. But juries receive fairly wide latitude once the existence of damages is reasonably certain. Courts sometimes justify this on the ground that the defendant's misconduct caused the uncertainty by precluding the plaintiff from receiving the benefit promised under the contract. Thus, the onus of uncertainty should fall on the defendant. Sometimes called the wrongdoer rule, this argument applies only after the existence of damage has been established with reasonable certainty.

Recovery When Profits Are Uncertain

Certainty tends to be applied independently to each component of damages. Even if consequential damages are limited or denied based on uncertainty, other elements of damages will be awarded if they are reasonably certain. For example, in *Anglia Television Ltd. v. Reed*,[30] an actor's breach prevented completion of a film. The profit was speculative, but the costs incurred in trying to make it were reasonably certain and recoverable.

Some courts explain the recovery of costs as resort to the reliance interest. Recovery of costs puts the plaintiff in the position it would have occupied if the contract had not been made: no expenses incurred on the project, but no profits either. While awarding profits (expectation) would be speculative, costs (reliance) are certain. In many cases, even the recovery of costs is uncertain. In *Anglia Television*, the film might have lost money rather than covering all of the costs. Even under reliance rules, recovery of costs could be reduced by any losses the party in breach can show (with reasonable certainty) that the plaintiff would have suffered. (The uncertainty that prevents the plaintiff from proving the profits often prevents the defendant from proving the losses.) This suggests that courts really are choosing the break-even point, assuming that the contract, *if performed* (an expectation approach), would have generated zero profit. Either party may prove otherwise (with reasonable certainty), but the court will presume performance would have produced zero profit unless contrary evidence is produced.[31]

4. Emotional Distress

Generally, courts do not award recovery for emotional distress in contract cases. Contract law seeks to compensate people for the value they were entitled to receive, but does not address their peace of mind. In part this reflects the commercial origins of contract law. The stress of business is not for the courts to compensate, even if sometimes it results from a breach of contract. The rule also gives meaning to other limitations on damages, such as uncertainty. Allowing juries to award emotional distress recovery might permit very generous awards even where the plaintiff suffered relatively small financial losses as a result of the breach. The difficulty of measuring distress makes excessive awards hard to control.

Two exceptions have been recognized:

1. The breach caused physical injury to a person;
2. The type of contract or breach made serious emotional disturbance particularly likely.[32]

To some extent, the first is an example of the second. Both recognize that, in some settings, emotional components make up an important part of the performance promised.

Tort law generally awards distress resulting from physical injury. When physical injury results from breach of contract, there seems little reason to award a

[30] [1971] 3 All E.R. 690.
[31] *See* Restatement (Third) of Restitution and Unjust Enrichment §38 & cmt. a (2011).
[32] Restatement (Second) of Contracts §353.

different remedy. If a good malfunctions and causes physical harm, the resulting pain, suffering, and distress are a real component of the injury. Difficulty quantifying this component of damages does not alter the need for compensation. Despite this rule, lawyers tend to bring such claims in tort, removing any doubt about the availability of emotional distress recovery.

Physical injuries seem particularly likely to produce emotional disturbance. Occasionally, other cases in which distress seems particularly likely lead a court to allow recovery. Courts tend to apply the exception quite narrowly.

Early cases involved funerals: a casket fell apart as the deceased was being carried to or from the hearse. Distress to the survivors is understandable, especially given their recent loss. In addition, distress may be the only loss they suffered. A partial refund for the casket might apply, if the casket as warranted was worth more than the casket received. This recovery might be defeated by warranty disclaimers or limitations of remedy. Even if available, it may be small, failing to redress the real loss: the shock and horror of seeing the remains tumble to the ground (or worse).

However, courts are very reluctant to expand emotional distress into normal business activity, even where distress seems likely. For instance, some breaches in building or remodeling a home may distress residents, perhaps seriously. For example, poor work may cause a roof to blow off, exposing precious possessions to water damage. Courts have been reluctant to award distress even in this setting.[33]

Cases have allowed distress in other settings. In *Sullivan v. O'Connor*,[34] a plastic surgeon promised an entertainer he would enhance her beauty by improving her nose, but instead his surgery produced a nose the plaintiff found unsightly. Again, one might award the value of the nose as promised less the value of the nose as received. But the certainty doctrine is likely to limit the pecuniary difference (even to a plaintiff in show business). On the other hand, distress when looking into a mirror every day is particularly likely to result (even to plaintiffs who are not in show business). Distress seems the real damage in these cases.

Try your hand at applying the rule to the following situation. Plaintiff bought health insurance from defendant. Plaintiff required surgery following a serious accident. Defendant breached by denying the claim (though the denial was based on a plausible exclusion that ultimately proved inapplicable). The hospital treating plaintiff eventually refused to provide more care because plaintiff failed to pay the bills. Plaintiff obtained a second surgery at another hospital by appearing at a time when defendant's refusal of coverage would not be discovered until the surgery was over. Plaintiff agonized over how to pay for past care and whether additional care would be available when needed. Should the court award distress or limit recovery to the amount of coverage promised in the policy?

Because lawyers prefer to bring these cases in tort, efforts to explore the limits of emotional distress in contract have been slowed. If more courts decide to address these cases within contract law, the scope of this exception may expand.

---

[33]*Kishmarton v. William Bailey Construction, Inc.*, 754 N.E.2d 785 (Ohio 2001).
[34]296 N.E.2d 183 (Mass. 1973).

D. RELIANCE DAMAGES

Reliance and restitution offer measures of recovery that focus on the situation that would have existed if the contract never had been made. Neither allows the plaintiff the benefit of the bargain. Reliance seeks to prevent the *plaintiff* from being any *worse* off than if the bargain had not been made. Restitution seeks to prevent the *defendant* from being any *better* off than if the bargain had not been made. Each award creates a reason for parties not to make promises they cannot keep: they cannot benefit from breaching a promise (given restitution) and might be worse off if they breach (if damages for reliance or expectation exceed restitution). Restitution will be covered in Chapter 16.

Because reliance does not allow recovery for the promised performance, it fits uneasily with actions for breach of contract. Normally, remedies seek to put the plaintiff in the position she would have occupied if the wrong had not occurred. Breaching a contract is the wrong, so the position if the breach had not occurred fits the normal approach to damages. Making a contract is not a wrong (unless fraudulent, a matter for torts), so looking to the situation that would have occurred if the contract had not been made is counterintuitive.

Nonetheless, situations arise where a plaintiff prefers a remedy other than expectation. Reliance may be sought when plaintiff cannot recover the gains a contract would have produced, perhaps because the gains are uncertain or unforeseeable. Recovering the costs incurred in reliance on the contract allows the plaintiff to break even, although it does not include the gains the contract might have produced.

1. Measuring Reliance

Reliance recovery seeks to put the plaintiff in the position it would have occupied if the contract had never been made — but never a position better than if the contract had been performed. In theory, reliance includes two components:

1. recovery of any costs incurred in reliance on the promise;
2. recovery of any opportunities forgone in reliance on the promise.

Many cases award costs incurred. Most stop there. Lost opportunities are harder to prove, especially given the requirement of reasonable certainty.

Costs a party incurred in reliance on the contract include expenses incurred preparing to perform as well as the cost of any performance made before the contract failed — that is, before the other party's breach made further expenditure under the contract unreasonable.

Recoverable expenses are limited to net reliance. Where salvage or other actions may avoid or recapture some of the expenses, the recovery will be limited to the unavoidable portion of the reliance costs. This is an application of the avoidable consequences doctrine. For example, a carpenter who buys lumber to perform a remodeling contract cannot recover the full cost of the lumber under the reliance interest. The lumber can be resold to another. Only the net loss — the difference between the amount paid and the amount earned on resale (plus the cost of conducting the resale) — is lost in reliance on the breached contract.

Reliance expenses need not relate directly to the contract at issue. Incidental or consequential reliance is recoverable, at least if foreseeable. For example, in *Nurse v. Barnes*,[35] a plaintiff rented a mill for six months and purchased raw materials to process in the mill. That purchase was not directly related to the lease, but certainly was a foreseeable response to the lease. (Why lease a mill, if not to process raw materials in it?) The cost of the raw materials was an allowable reliance expense — offset by the amount the lessee realized by reselling the materials. (The cost to resell also is a recoverable incidental loss. If the contract had not been made, plaintiff would not have purchased the goods and, thus, would not have incurred any expense to resell them.)

Reliance damages cannot exceed expectation damages. Recoveries are limited to the expectation loss, if that is ascertainable. Reliance recovery will equal the expenses minus "any loss that the party in breach can prove with reasonable certainty the injured party would have suffered had the contract been performed."[36] This limitation makes reliance nearly useless as a way to avoid losing contracts. In theory, reliance would allow a party to break even by recovering all expenses. But if the other party can show that the contract would have involved losses for the plaintiff, those losses will be subtracted from the recovery. The result leaves plaintiff with the same loss whether it seeks recovery for reliance or expectation damages.

In theory, reliance recovery also includes any opportunities lost in reliance on the contract. To put plaintiff in the position she would have occupied if the contract had not been made, the court must consider any other opportunities she might have pursued if this contract had not been entered. For instance, if by entering one contract the plaintiff gave up the opportunity to enter a similar contract with another, reliance recovery should include compensation for that lost opportunity.

In practice, reliance recovery tends to be limited to proven expenditures. Lost opportunities are very hard to prove, especially if a party stopped looking for better deals when it entered this contract. To compensate for lost opportunities, courts generally award the expectation interest. The actual contract offers a reasonable approximation of the benefits another contract would have provided. (Thus, instead of asking what car insurance policy you would have bought if this insurer had not entered the contract, the court simply enforces the policy you did buy — perhaps assuming the other would have been nearly identical.)

In some cases, however, courts award lost opportunities directly. When an employee leaves a job to take another, breach by the new employer may be compensated by the income the plaintiff would have earned if she had not quit the first job. The prior job offers a fairly certain basis for estimating the wages the employee would have earned if the contract had not been made. It might be too low, if the employee had other job opportunities that offered more. But the defendant can hardly complain about this conservative estimate. And the plaintiff may

---

[35] Sir T. Raym. 77 (K.B. 1664).

[36] RESTATEMENT (SECOND) OF CONTRACTS §349.

have difficulty proving whether other offers would have worked out any better than the one she took.

Try your hand at applying this rule to the following situation. A developer agreed to lease space to a restaurateur. The restaurateur hired an architect, a chef, and a public relations firm, and halted negotiations for other locations. The developer repudiated the lease. Because other suitable locations were no longer available, the restaurateur canceled the project and paid $150,000 to terminate the contracts with the architect, chef, and public relations firm. Profits for the new restaurant are difficult to project. What recovery should the court award for the developer's breach?

2. Reliance Recovery Without Breach

Courts sometimes award reliance damages in cases where liability is difficult to justify. If a court cannot award either expectation or restitution, resort to reliance may avoid injustice. For example, technical impediments may preclude liability for breach of contract, while the lack of any benefit to the other party may preclude unjust enrichment. Rather than leave a nonbreaching party with no recovery, courts may resort to reliance—often without much effort to explain why liability attaches at all.

One common situation involves the statute of frauds. Absence of a writing allows defendant to avoid liability on the contract. If defendant received nothing from plaintiff, no unjust enrichment may exist. Courts sometimes award plaintiffs their out-of-pocket expenditures incurred in preparation for the contract. For example, when a lessor incurred expenses remodeling a building for a prospective tenant, the court awarded those expenses.[37] The tenant never signed a lease, so it had no contract liability, and never received the benefit of the remodeling because it never occupied the premises. Arguably, this is an exception to the statute of frauds, albeit one that the legislature did not create and that courts are coy about admitting they created.

Another situation involves employees promised a new job on an **at-will** basis: that is, the employment has no specified duration, allowing either the employee or the employer to terminate the contract at any time for any reason or no reason at all (but not an illegal reason), without obligation to the other party. When employment can be terminated at will, revoking the job offer may not be breach at all. There was no promise to retain the employee for any specific length of time. Even if discharge before the first day is a breach, expectation damages may be minuscule because the employer could have fired the employee soon after the new job commenced. Nonetheless, the employee may have resigned from a prior job in reliance on the new promise. Courts sometimes award recovery based on the income plaintiff would have earned had she kept the original job.

---

[37] *Farash v. Sykes Datatronics, Inc.*, 452 N.E.2d 1245, 1247 (N.Y. 1983).

Where no liability for breach of contract exists, reliance becomes a separate cause of action, not just an alternative way to measure recovery for breach of contract. Reliance is not a reason to enforce a promise; the promise is unenforceable despite reliance. But reliance becomes a separate, unnamed tort, something we might call "wrongful promise." In some cases, courts argue that §90 of the Restatement (Second) of Contracts created a separate cause of action,[38] although the drafters clearly intended to create no more than a means to satisfy the consideration requirement. Other courts award reliance without explaining how liability attaches.

E. AGREED REMEDIES

A contract may contain a provision governing the recovery either party can obtain in the event of breach. Just as the parties can agree to the terms governing performance, the parties may agree to the terms governing nonperformance.

This simple principle has met with considerable resistance over the years. Originally, courts were unwilling to cede to the parties the judicial function of determining the appropriate remedy. They crafted doctrines that rejected or limited the effect of remedies agreed upon by the parties. Even today, the parties' ability to dictate appropriate remedies remains subject to some limitations. This section addresses the most common types of agreements affecting the remedy and the doctrines that limit their enforcement in court.

Agreements affecting remedies seek to do one of four things:

1. substitute a different remedy for the usual damage rules;
2. exclude an element of damages courts might award;
3. add an element of damages the courts might not award; or
4. specify the appropriate amount of damages, usually by a formula for calculating damages.

In some cases, parties will go further and specify that courts should not hear their cases at all, specifying a different forum (such as arbitration) in which to resolve their contract dispute. The last type of provision differs slightly from the others and will be addressed in section F below.

While these situations arise in many contexts, the rules for sales of goods often are clearer. Some of the subsections below will focus on the UCC approach.

1. UCC: Substitute Recovery

Some contract terms may specify an entirely different remedy for breach. For instance, some clauses may limit recovery to a refund or a partial refund. (When

---

[38] *See Hoffman v. Red Owl Stores*, 133 N.W.2d 267 (Wis. 1965).

car batteries fail before their guaranteed life, a pro rata refund is a common remedy.) Where performance falls short of the quality promised, a clause might limit recovery to the cost to repair the goods or to bring the services up to the quality promised. These remedies do not start with the principle that the nonbreaching party should be made whole for any losses suffered. Rather, they specify a different approach.

Clauses providing substitute remedies typically are enforceable. Aside from contract defenses (such as public policy or unconscionability), the UCC offers courts two ways to limit the application of substitute remedies:

1. a substitute remedy may be treated as optional; or
2. a substitute remedy may be negated if it "fails of its essential purpose."[39]

A substitute remedy is optional unless the contract expressly provides that it is the exclusive remedy.[40] If optional, the aggrieved party may elect either the substitute remedy or the usual remedy (damages). For example, if a clause allows repair or replacement, but does not specify that it is the exclusive remedy, it does not supplant the usual damage rules. Parties drafting substitute remedies typically intend the substitute to be the exclusive remedy and are careful to say so in the contract.

A substitute remedy will not be enforced if it "fails of its essential purpose."[41] A substitute remedy fails of its essential purpose if it fails to provide the aggrieved party with a minimally adequate degree of relief from the consequences of the breach. The substitute need not be as good as the relief plaintiff might expect under damage rules; one point of the substitute is to specify relief that falls short of expectation recovery. On the other hand, a remedy that leaves the plaintiff with no relief whatsoever is unlikely to survive. A substitute remedy is supposed to provide some remedy, even if not complete relief.

For example, a clause may call for defendant to repair the performance if it proves defective. If, after efforts to repair the property, it cannot be brought up to the promised quality, the remedy may fail of its essential purpose. The clause seems to promise that the plaintiff (eventually) will receive performance that lives up to the promised quality. When that does not happen, limiting recovery to repair in effect deprives the plaintiff of even the minimal remedy the substitute envisions. If repair fails, courts may refuse to enforce the substitute remedy clause and allow plaintiff to resort to the usual damages rules.

A remedy does not fail of its essential purpose merely because it does not fully satisfy the expectation interest. Repairing goods may not put the plaintiff in the position she would have occupied if the contract had been performed. Repairs, even if effective, generally provide the plaintiff the promised quality much later than if the performance had been adequate from the start. In addition, any consequential losses the plaintiff suffers while waiting for the performance to be repaired are not included in the substitute remedy. Rather, once the defendant repairs the

[39]UCC §2-719.
[40]*Id.* §2-719(1)(b).
[41]*Id.* §2-719(2).

goods, the remedy is complete, without any compensation for the harmful side effects of the initial nonperformance. Nonetheless, if repairs are effective within a reasonable time, the clause will not fail of its essential purpose. Plaintiff receives the remedy that it was promised: repairs. The remedy achieved its essential purpose.

2. UCC: Limitations on Recovery

Some clauses exclude certain elements of recovery that courts normally would award. The most common provision excludes consequential damages. The possibility that consequential damages will greatly exceed the value of the contract leads many contracts to exclude them. These clauses leave the other party to insure against or take precautions to avoid consequential losses, rather than seeking their recovery as part of a lawsuit.

Generally, an exclusion of consequential losses is enforceable. Like any clause, excluding consequential damages will be unenforceable if unconscionable. Where the clause would exclude recovery for physical injury to a person, the UCC presumes it is unconscionable.[42] Courts generally enforce clauses that limit recovery of commercial consequential losses.

3. Augmenting Recovery

Occasionally, parties drafting a contract seek to augment the damages allowed by the general rules governing damages. In some cases, the parties seek to draft around specific limitations on damages, such as foreseeability, certainty, or avoidable consequences. Those efforts usually produce a **liquidated damages clause**, a term that specifies the amount of damages a party may recover in the event of a breach. In some cases, however, parties seek to include an element of damages that courts generally do not allow. Other clauses may attempt to clarify that the parties intend for consequential damages to include certain specific items, such as the recall costs specified in the *QVC* contract.

Courts generally enforce an express provision indicating that the parties agree to include an element in the recovery, even if courts would not award that element without the clause. For example, contracts commonly allow recovery of attorneys' fees. As a matter of law, parties generally bear their own costs of suit, including attorneys' fees. However, the parties may agree in the contract that the **prevailing party** (the one who wins in court) may recover attorneys' fees from the losing party. This provision is common in loan agreements, where the lender seeks to recover not only the amount of the debt (with interest), but also any costs involved in collecting the debt, including attorneys' fees.

[42] *Id.* §2-719(3).

4. Liquidated Damage Clauses

Liquidation refers to fixing a specific dollar amount. A liquidated damage clause seeks to specify the amount of damages a party may recover in the event of a breach. The amount may be specified as a specific sum or, more commonly, a formula for determining the amount of damages. For example, a clause might specify damages for late performance as a certain amount per day until completion.

Liquidated damage clauses are enforceable. **Penalty clauses**—amounts due upon breach that seek to deter or punish the breaching party—are void as against public policy. The line between them depends on the substance of the clause, not the form. Thus, courts will treat a clause as a penalty even if the heading for that provision reads "liquidated damages." The court examines instead whether the clause would provide an excessively large recovery. Conversely, a court might enforce a clause the contract labeled a penalty if the amount provided was not excessive. (Calling a clause a penalty is a bad idea, even if it might be enforced anyway.)

In order to qualify as a liquidated damage provision, the amount a clause specifies must be "reasonable in the light of the anticipated or actual harm caused by the breach, the difficulties of proof of loss, and the inconvenience or non-feasibility of otherwise obtaining an adequate remedy."[42] The basic rule here requires that the clause be reasonable. The factors listed suggest reasons the clause might be reasonable. No one factor or combination of factors is determinative; reasonableness might be established by only one factor or defeated by only one factor.

Evaluating Reasonableness

The first (and most important) factor considers the relationship between the amount the clause allows and the "actual or anticipated harm caused by the breach." **Anticipated harm** refers to the harm the parties expected at the time the contract was made. **Actual harm** refers to the harm that actually resulted from the breach. Generally, reasonableness requires that the clause approximate either one of those two amounts (anticipated harm or actual harm), not necessarily both. Thus, a clause that allows much more than the parties expected the loss to be may survive if the actual harm turns out to be about as large as the amount the clause allows. Similarly, a clause that produces an award much larger than the actual harm may survive as long as the amount is reasonably close to the amount of harm the parties expected when they made the contract. Despite the UCC's language, courts sometimes resist awarding liquidated damages that exceed actual loss.

For example, suppose a business lease gave a tenant the exclusive right to operate a restaurant in the building, but the lessor later leased a portion of the building to a small bakery that served food on the premises. A term allowing the tenant to deduct half the rent for any period during which the lessor violated the restrictive covenant in the lease might be challenged as a penalty. The competition may have negligible effects on the restaurant, so half the rent may greatly exceed any loss the

---

[42]UCC §2-718(2)(a); *see also* Restatement (Second) of Contracts §356 (similar, but omitting the final phrase referring to inconvenience or nonfeasibility of other remedies).

tenant actually suffered. But at the time of contract formation, it was unpredictable how much harm a competitor might cause the tenant. One court held that half the rent was reasonable in light of the anticipated harm.[43]

When damages are easily determined, a court is less likely to find a liquidated damage clause reasonable. A liquidated damage clause saves parties the expense of proving the loss and uncertainty over whose evidence will prevail. Where damages are relatively easy to prove, however, the value of liquidating them in the contract diminishes, raising the possibility that the clause was designed to impose a penalty.

Finally, courts consider the availability of other remedies. Specific performance or restitution might avoid the difficulty of proving damages. A party's effort to recover liquidated damages instead of specific performance suggests damages under the clause are better than performance, perhaps unreasonably high. While other problems may explain the choice, courts may consider the adequacy of other remedies in evaluating whether the liquidation clause is a reasonable estimate of the harm.

Case Preview

Karimi v. 401 North Wabash Venture

The loss the parties anticipate at the time they make the contract may exceed the loss that the parties actually suffer. In these cases, a liquidated damage clause may seem to overcompensate the nonbreaching party. Calling the clause a penalty will allow the court to limit the nonbreaching party to the actual loss suffered, but also reduces the usefulness of liquidated damage clauses by encouraging challenges based on hindsight. This case confronts a fairly common situation in which a seller agrees to accept a deposit as liquidated damages, but appears not to suffer any loss after buyer's breach.

Trump Tower from ground level
Basil D. Soufi/Wikimedia Commons

As you read *Karimi v. 401 North Wabash Venture*, look for the following:

1. Was the deposit an estimate of actual losses or just a convenient amount that seller could keep?
2. Did seller suffer any loss at all? Is retaining the deposit an unjust enrichment?
3. Would a clause that allowed the seller to choose between actual damages and liquidated damages work better in this case? Why did prior courts reject those clauses?

[43] *Red Sage Limited Partnership v. DESPA Deutsche Sparkassen Immobilien-Anlage-Gasellschaft mbH*, 254 F.3d 1120 (D.C. Cir. 2001).

Karimi v. 401 North Wabash Venture

952 N.E.2d 1278 (Ill. App. Ct. 2011)

Justice HARRIS delivered the judgment of the court, with opinion.

[Plaintiffs entered a contract to buy a condominium and three parking spaces in Trump International Hotel and Tower for about $2.2 million, paying a deposit of 15 percent (about $330,000). At plaintiffs' request, closing was postponed from October 6, 2008, to May 15, 2009, to provide more time to obtain financing.] Plaintiffs failed to close on May 15, 2009, and in a letter dated July 6, 2009, defendants declared:

> "The time and date for closing and the applicable cure period per the default notice has elapsed and Purchaser has not closed on the unit. Therefore, Purchaser is in breach of and in default under the Purchase Agreement. Consequently, Seller hereby terminates the Purchase Agreement."

Whereupon, defendants retained the earnest money and earned interest as liquidated damages. In November 2009, defendants subsequently sold the unit and one less parking space to a third party for $2.5 million.

. . .

The dismissal of count IV presents a more complicated issue as it concerns the validity and enforceability of the liquidated damages clause contained in paragraph 12(a) of the purchase agreement[:

> Time is of the essence with regard to Purchaser's obligations and covenants hereunder. In the event of a default or breach of this Purchase Agreement by Purchaser, Seller shall notify Purchaser of such breach or default and of the opportunity, which shall be given the Purchaser, to remedy such breach or default within twenty (20) days after the date such notice was received. If Purchaser fails to remedy such breach or default within twenty (20) days after receipt of Seller's notice, then, subject to the limitations set forth below, Seller may terminate this Purchase Agreement and, as its sole and exclusive remedy upon termination, retain as liquidated damages from Purchaser an amount equal to the sum of (i) the amount set forth . . . required to be paid as an Earnest Money deposit and (ii) all amounts paid or to be paid by Purchaser to Seller for any other services or work performed or to be performed by Seller. . . . In accordance with Section 1703(d) of the Interstate Land Sales Full Disclosure Act, if Seller is otherwise entitled to the liquidated damages described above, Seller shall return to Purchaser amounts paid to Seller (excluding interest paid under the Purchase Agreement) in excess of: (x) 15% of the Purchase Price (excluding any interest owed under the Purchase Agreement) or (y) the amount of Seller's actual damages, whichever is greater.]

In general, under Illinois law a liquidated damages provision is "valid and enforceable in a real estate contract, when: (1) the parties intended to agree in advance to the settlement of damages that might arise from the breach; (2) the amount of liquidated damages was reasonable at the time of contracting, bearing some relation to the damages which might be sustained; and (3) actual damages would be uncertain in amount and difficult to prove." *Grossinger Motorcorp, Inc. v. American National Bank & Trust Co.*, 240 Ill. App. 3d 737, 749-50, 180 Ill. Dec. 824, 607 N.E.2d 1337 (1992). Parties often include liquidated damages provisions in real estate transactions "to avoid the difficulty of ascertaining and proving damages by such methods as market value, resale value or otherwise." *Siegel v. Levy Organization Development Co.*, 182 Ill. App. 3d 859, 861, 131 Ill. Dec. 340, 538 N.E.2d 715 (1989).

In *Siegel*, we upheld as enforceable a clause in the purchase agreement providing that in case of buyer default all sums theretofore paid by the buyer, including earnest money, would be forfeited as liquidated damages. [Citation omitted.] We found that damages in the amount of $320,000 earnest money paid toward the purchase of a $1.6 million condominium was reasonable in light of losses that might have been anticipated at the time of contracting and the difficulty of ascertaining losses in the event of a breach. *Id.*

Plaintiffs first contend that paragraph 12(a) is unenforceable because it fails to set a certain sum as liquidated damages. Plaintiffs argue that a set sum evidences the parties' agreement on the settlement of damages, and paragraph 12(a)'s reference to amounts paid for other services or work performed by defendants, in addition to the earnest money, shows that they did not agree to a liquidated sum. However, in a real estate contract liquidated damages specified as "'all sums theretofore paid to Seller'" including earnest money and payment for extras, have been upheld as "reasonable in light of any losses that could have been anticipated at the time of the contract." *Siegel*, 182 Ill. App. 3d at 862, 131 Ill. Dec. 340, 538 N.E.2d 715. See also *Morris v. Flores*, 174 Ill. App. 3d 504, 507, 124 Ill. Dec. 122, 528 N.E.2d 1013 (1988) (enforceable liquidated damages clause provided that plaintiff would forfeit all money deposited under the contract, including earnest money). In their brief, plaintiffs acknowledge that "[a]t the time of contracting, it remained possible that Plaintiffs would, during the more than five-year period from execution of the Purchase Agreement to completion of the construction of the Unit, pay additional deposits for other services or work" performed by defendants. Plaintiffs, then, understood and agreed that the earnest money and additional deposits were the amount designated as liquidated damages in paragraph 12(a) when they executed the purchase agreement, and their argument that the parties did not agree to a set sum is not persuasive.

. . .

Plaintiffs' final contention is that the liquidated damages provision is an unenforceable penalty. Unlike the provisions upheld in *Siegel* and *Morris* discussed above, paragraph 12(a) refers to actual damages in determining the liquidated damages amount. The question is whether that reference is fatal to the enforcement of the liquidated damages provision. A provision that allows defendants the option to receive liquidated damages or seek actual damages is unenforceable as a penalty. *Grossinger*, 240 Ill. App. 3d at 752, 180 Ill. Dec. 824, 607 N.E.2d 1337. In *Grossinger*, the purchase contract provided that if the plaintiff caused the contract to terminate, "'the earnest money shall be forfeited to the [defendant] to be retained by the [defendant] as liquidated damages, or at [defendant]'s option, [defendant] may exercise any other remedy available at law.'" [Citation omitted.] This court held that the provision was unenforceable because it penalized the plaintiff by giving defendants a minimum recovery regardless of actual damages, and also allowed defendants to disregard liquidated damages if actual damages exceeded the specified amount. [Citations omitted.] Such a provision negates the purpose of liquidated damages, which is to provide parties with an agreed upon, predetermined damages amount when actual damages may be difficult to ascertain. *Hickox v. Bell*, 195 Ill. App. 3d 976, 987-88, 142 Ill. Dec. 392, 552 N.E.2d 1133 (1990).

Despite its reference to actual damages, paragraph 12(a) does not give defendants the option to seek actual damages. Although a calculation of actual damages may be necessary to determine a liquidated damages amount, defendants can receive no more than the amount plaintiffs have deposited pursuant to the agreement, even if actual damages prove greater than the sum deposited. Furthermore, unlike the clauses in *Grossinger* and *Catholic Charities*, no provision in the agreement allows defendants the option to pursue actual damages in case of plaintiffs' breach. . . . The liquidated damages provision at issue here is not an unenforceable penalty.

Plaintiffs also argue that paragraph 12(a) operates as a penalty because defendants suffered no actual damages. Instead, defendants sold the unit for approximately $400,000 more than the contract price contained in the purchase agreement with plaintiffs. Citing *Penske Truck Leasing Co. v. Chemetco, Inc.*, 311 Ill. App. 3d 447, 244 Ill. Dec. 218, 725 N.E.2d 13 (2000), plaintiffs argue that "when a party receives both substantial liquidated damages and windfall profits, the court will consider the damages unreasonable." *Penske*, however, concerned a provision with alternate methods of computing liquidated damages dependent on whether the nondefaulting party retained or sold the leased trucks at issue in the contract [citation omitted]. The court in *Penske* held that allowing the plaintiffs to retain the trucks, calculate liquidated damages based on that retention, then shortly thereafter sell the trucks at a profit would constitute unreasonable damages. [Citation omitted.] It reasoned that "it was never the intention of the parties to permit plaintiff to proceed under the method of recovery used when plaintiff decides to retain the vehicles but later sells the vehicles and reaps a windfall in the process." [Citation omitted.] Unlike the liquidated damages provision in *Penske*, paragraph 12(a) does not contain alternate methods for computing damages depending on whether defendants retain or sell the condominium unit at issue. Defendants here properly claimed liquidated damages for plaintiffs' default pursuant to the purchase agreement. Furthermore, unlike the provision in *Penske*, under the terms of this agreement whether defendants eventually sold the unit, and any proceeds from a sale, are irrelevant to the liquidated damages issue.

A term fixing unreasonably large liquidated damages, however, may be unenforceable as a penalty on public policy grounds. The reasonableness of the amount, though, depends not on the actual damages suffered by the nonbreaching party, but on whether the amount reasonably forecasts and bears some relation to the parties' potential loss as determined at the time of contracting. *Jameson*, 351 Ill. App. 3d at 423, 286 Ill. Dec. 431, 813 N.E.2d 1124. Courts have considered earnest money representing up to 20% of the purchase price a reasonable sum as liquidated damages. [Citation omitted.] Here, the earnest money represented 15% of the purchase price, and plaintiffs acknowledge they did not make further payments for other services or work. Liquidated damages in the amount of 15% of the purchase price is a reasonable amount considering the potential loss each party faced at the time of contracting. [Citation omitted.] Furthermore, plaintiffs' argument concerning defendant's sale of the unit for $400,000 more than the contract price proves the validity of the liquidated damages provision because it shows how uncertain and difficult it was for the parties to ascertain actual damages at the time of contracting. [Citation omitted.]

Finally, plaintiffs contend that in a case such as the one at bar, where the non-breaching party suffered no actual damages but instead reaped a handsome profit, enforcing the liquidated damages clause would be "obnoxious." As support, plaintiffs cite *Radloff v. Haase*, 196 Ill. 365, 63 N.E. 729 (1902). *Radloff* concerned a liquidated damages provision contained within a covenant not to compete. [Citation omitted.] The defendant sold his bakery to the plaintiff and in the contract promised not to engage in the bakery business within a five-block radius. *Id.* The contract further stated that the defendant agreed to pay a sum of $2,000 if he violated the agreement. *Id.* The plaintiff subsequently sold the bakery to a third party and moved out of Illinois. *Id.* at 366-67. Approximately one year later, the defendant opened a bakery business across the street from his former business without the plaintiff's consent. *Id.* at 367. The plaintiff brought suit, seeking damages from defendant's violation of the initial contract although he presented no evidence of actual damages from the breach. [Citation omitted.] Our supreme court noted that the terms of the contract in *Radloff* did not make clear whether the damages provision contained therein was a liquidated damages provision or a penalty. *Id.* In determining whether or not the amount specified was liquidated damages, the court in *Radloff* reasoned that "the idea of the courts is to ascertain, if possible, the actual damages sustained, and if it is possible to ascertain the actual damages, or if the amount of liquidated damages mentioned in the contract is exorbitant, the court will construe the amount as a penalty, rather than as liquidated damages." [Citation omitted.] It found that the plaintiff "has not been engaged in the bakery business at Chicago a single day since [the defendant] re-entered the restricted territory, nor has he been in any way injured by the action of [the defendant] . . . and to construe this contract as liquidated damages would work absurdity and oppression."

Unlike the contract in *Radloff*, the purchase agreement here concerns a real estate transaction with a provision explicitly designating an amount as liquidated damages. Where damages for breach of contract would be uncertain or difficult to calculate, our supreme court has upheld a reasonable amount stipulated at the time of contracting as liquidated damages without regard to actual damages. See *Weiss v. United States Fidelity & Guaranty Co.*, 300 Ill. 11, 17, 132 N.E. 749 (1921). In *Weiss*, the plaintiff contracted with the defendant to remodel a three-story building he owned. [Citation omitted.] The contract provided that the project would be completed no later than January 15, 1917, and defendant would pay as liquidated damages $15 per day for each day thereafter until completion. [Citation omitted.] The defendant subsequently failed to complete the project and the plaintiff hired another contractor who finished the job on July 10, 1917, at an additional cost of $872.64. [Citation omitted.] The supreme court held that under the terms of the contract, the plaintiff was entitled to $2,625 in liquidated damages. [Citation omitted.] It reasoned that at the time of contracting, the parties reasonably presumed that any delay that might occur would be minor and the amount of $15 per day was not excessive in light of that time frame. [Citation omitted.] It acknowledged that a liquidated damages provision specifying a certain amount per day "'could be extended to such length of time as to become grossly excessive,'" but the "'fact that the delay in the particular case was long continued to a time that may be said to be unreasonable or unusual cannot be looked to'" in determining whether to enforce a liquidated damages provision. [Citation omitted.]

The purpose of a liquidated damages provision is to provide parties with a reasonable predetermined damages amount where actual damages may be difficult to ascertain. *Hickox*, 195 Ill. App. 3d at 987-88, 142 Ill. Dec. 392, 552 N.E.2d 1133. Courts generally give effect to such provisions "if the parties have expressed their agreement in clear and explicit terms and there is no evidence of fraud or unconscionable oppression." *Hartford Fire Insurance Co. v. Architectural Management, Inc.*, 194 Ill. App. 3d 110, 115, 141 Ill. Dec. 64, 550 N.E.2d 1110 (1990). As discussed above, plaintiffs here understood and agreed to the explicit terms of paragraph 12(a) when they entered into the purchase agreement, and they make no claim that fraud or unconscionable oppression played a role in inducing them to sign the contract. The nature of a liquidated damages provision is such that the set amount may at times exceed actual damages, and other times actual damages may exceed the set amount. In entering into the purchase agreement, both parties here agreed to accept this inherent risk. *Newcastle Properties, Inc. v. Shalowitz*, 221 Ill. App. 3d 716, 725, 164 Ill. Dec. 221, 582 N.E.2d 1165 (1991). Although defendants could have elected not to seek liquidated damages given the circumstances here, they have the right to pursue such damages under paragraph 12(a), and the provision is valid and enforceable. The trial court properly dismissed plaintiffs' complaint.

...

Affirmed.

Post-Case Follow-Up

Keeping the deposit may undercompensate a seller if real estate prices fall significantly. That was possible here: prices fell sharply after 2007, but apparently had not quite fallen below the price in this 2003 contract. The possibility that the clause might undercompensate seller makes the clause seem less punitive, even when it produces a windfall in a particular case. The court suggests this when noting that clauses that allow a seller to choose actual damages would be punitive, allowing the seller the best of both worlds. The even-handed provision here did not violate the public policy against penalty clauses.

Karimi v. 401 North Wabash Venture: Real Life Applications

1. Would the case come out the same way in a state that followed the Restatement (Second) of Contracts? If this were a sale of goods, would the UCC produce a different result?

2. Gail had rented a condominium for years before Freddie Mac obtained it in a foreclosure. Freddie Mac agreed to sell the condominium to Gail for a modest price (little more than enough to cover the loan on which the owners defaulted). The contract provided that if either party failed to complete the deal, the other would receive $1,000 as liquidated damages. Before Gail could obtain financing,

Freddie Mac sold the property to another buyer. The other buyer offered the property to Gail for a much higher price. Gail sued Freddie Mac for specific performance or damages. Freddie Mac argued that the liquidated damage clause limited Gail's remedy to $1,000. Should Freddie Mac prevail? *See Slinski v. Bank of America*, 981 F. Supp. 2d 19 (2013); *see also Orr v. Goodwin*, 953 A.2d 1190 (N.H. 2008); *Avery v. Hughes*, 661 F.3d 690 (1st Cir. 2011) (sellers sought actual damages despite liquidated damages clause).

3. To induce Retailer to lease space in mall, Mall Owner agreed that if Anchor (a large store that draws many buyers to the mall) was not a tenant at the mall on the day Retailer's lease begins, Retailer need not pay rent until a suitable substitute opened a store in mall of similar size to Anchor's store. Anchor went bankrupt, closing its store in mall. Retailer offered to pay lower rent despite Anchor's closure, but Mall Owner refused. Retailer accepted the premises but refused to pay rent, as the lease provided. Mall Owner sued Retailer, arguing that the provision allowing Retailer to pay no rent is a penalty. Should Mall Owner prevail? How would you argue the case for Mall Owner? For Retailer? Does it matter that Retailer, at the time the lease takes effect, believes its sales may be unaffected by the absence of Anchor? *See Grand Prospect Partners v. Ross Dress for Less*, 232 Cal. App. 4th 1332 (Cal. Ct. App. 2015).

Evaluating Intent

Concern for punitive intent may lurk just beneath (and sometimes above) the surface of these rules and cases. At one time, courts displayed serious hostility to liquidated damage clauses. Cases exist in which the court completely ignores the breach that did occur. Instead, it imagines breaches that did not occur, determines that the clause would have been unreasonably large in those situations, and concludes that the clause is unenforceable as a penalty. These courts seem to attribute a punitive motive to the parties: they intended a penalty, or else they would not have drafted a clause that would be unreasonable in this other situation. That approach produced one useful response: drafters now produce clauses that vary the recovery with the magnitude of the breach. More recently, courts treated the reasonableness factors noted above as elements, requiring the party seeking to enforce the clause to establish both that damages were hard to ascertain and that the clause was reasonable in light of the loss (anticipated or actual).[44]

Today, courts are more receptive to liquidated damage clauses. This is particularly true of clauses that seem like a compromise. If a clause might undercompensate in some circumstances, the fact that it overcompensates in others is not a sign of unreasonableness. Rather, the choice of a middle ground is some indication that the parties were agreeing to a reasonable estimate. In contrast, a clause that will overcompensate the plaintiff in any conceivable breach is unlikely to be treated as a reasonable estimate of the loss. For example, in *Lake River Corp. v.*

---

[44] *See* Restatement of Contracts §339.

Carborundum Co.,[45] a clause would overcompensate the plaintiff no matter when or how the breach occurred, although for some breaches the overcompensation would be modest. A court held the clause was a penalty.

5. Other Agreed Remedies

Careful drafting can produce clauses that do not fall within the provisions governing liquidated damages. Techniques such as alternative performances or bonuses can produce provisions that have the effect of deterring nonperformance without violating the public policy against penalty clauses.

Some contracts define performance to give the other party two options, one of which is more onerous than the other. The decision to opt for the more onerous way to perform is not a breach. Thus, rules governing clauses liquidating damages for (or penalizing) a breach have no application in this setting. One example involves prepayment fees on loans. Loan documents may allow a borrower to choose between repaying the loan over the full term or repaying the loan earlier, with an additional fee. The borrower who chooses to prepay is not in breach and the fee is not a clause liquidating the damages for a breach. Similarly, **take or pay clauses** give buyer a choice: it may take the goods (and pay for them) or may pay for them (and not take them). These terms are common in contracts involving oil and gas. Under the terms of the contract, neither is breach, so the clause is not about liquidating damages for breach.

Bonus pay also may be drafted in a way that avoids the policy against penalties. Properly structured, any due date with a bonus for finishing early can produce exactly the same results as an earlier due date with liquidated damages for late performance. But the bonus does not involve a breach: neither finishing early nor finishing on time is a breach. So the public policy against penalties does not seem to apply.

Some argue that the policy against penalties should apply even when the penalties are disguised as bonuses or alternative performance. In fact, it is very difficult to treat these clauses as something other than what they say they are, leading to very few decisions seeking to extend this doctrine.

Bonus or Penalty

Consider two ways to draft a construction contract:

- $20 million to complete a building by September 1, with damages of $100,000 per day for late completion (up to a maximum of $2 million);
- $18 million to complete a building by September 21, plus $100,000 bonus for each day completion is early (up to a maximum of $2 million).

No matter what day completion occurs, the amount due will be the same under either clause. But the first clause might be challenged as a penalty. A party seeking to enforce it will need to defend its reasonableness as an estimate of actual or anticipated losses. The second clause cannot be a penalty for breach because no breach occurs until after September 20 — by which point the bonus clause is irrelevant.

[45] 769 F.2d 1284 (7th Cir. 1985).

F. ARBITRATION

Instead of litigating in courts, parties sometimes agree to submit their disputes to an **arbitrator**: a person (or a panel) they chose to resolve their dispute. Arbitration is not really a remedy, but a procedure. Clauses providing for arbitration resemble **forum selection clauses** specifying where suits should be brought or, to a lesser extent, **choice of law clauses** specifying which state's law should apply to any disputes.

Arbitration can be the subject of an entire course. The brief introduction possible here will resort to generalizations that would benefit from further elaboration.

Generally, courts enforce agreements by parties to submit their disputes to arbitration. Like any clause, it might be challenged as unconscionable. A growing number of cases find arbitration in consumer contracts to be unconscionable. That understandable result competes with statutes favoring arbitration, such as the Federal Arbitration Act.[46] Other cases involve clauses that may not extend to all disputes, forcing courts to interpret the scope of the clause.

If an agreement to arbitrate governs the dispute, then courts (at the request of one party) will **abate** or **stay** their proceedings (temporarily stop work on the case) until the parties conclude the arbitration. Thus, a party cannot avoid the arbitration clause simply by filing suit — unless the other party waives the right to arbitration by not seeking a stay and requesting arbitration.

When the arbitration is concluded, the court usually accepts the arbitration judgment as final. It will not reexamine the case independently unless

1. the arbitrator exceeded its authority (for example, resolved a dispute that the parties did not agree to submit to arbitration);
2. the arbitrator was guilty of serious misconduct, such as fraud, corruption, or bribery;
3. the result was completely irrational, falling beyond any reasonable resolution of the dispute; or
4. the result violated public policy.

An arbitrator need not produce the same result a court would produce — or even follow the same legal rules that a court would follow. As long as the result is not completely irrational or against public policy, the arbitrator remains free to resolve the situation in any manner she deems appropriate.

The ability to deviate from existing rules explains part of the appeal of arbitration. Arbitration may streamline procedures, reducing the delay that might result from lengthy discovery or motion practice. Arbitrators are not bound to follow the same rules of civil procedure and evidence that govern courts. Arbitrators also may have some expertise that helps resolve the dispute, perhaps experience in the industry involved or expertise in that area of the law. This may reduce the need to produce evidence concerning industry practice and produce a result that will seem

---

[46] 9 U.S.C. §§1-14.

fair to those involved in similar transactions. In addition, arbitration may allow parties to seek or to avoid some remedies that a court might consider. Arbitration, however, comes at a cost. Unlike judges paid by the state or federal government, the parties must pay arbitrators. Thus, the cost of arbitration often exceeds the cost of litigation in court.

Chapter Summary

- Contract damages usually seek to place the nonbreaching party in the position she would have occupied if the contract had been performed, including any gains she would have realized by using the performance as part of a larger venture.
- Direct loss covers the value of the performance itself, comparing what the party would have received if the contract had been performed (the price, services, goods, etc.) with what she actually received, including any savings (such as not paying for the performance) or other benefits that resulted from the breach.
- Incidental loss includes costs reacting to the breach, such as finding a substitute transaction, and shipping, storing, insuring, or otherwise dealing with a defective or rejected performance.
- Consequential loss involves how a party would have used the performance, if it had been received, such as the inability to resell or otherwise profit from the performance.
- Damages cannot include losses that plaintiff could have avoided by reasonable conduct.
- Damages cannot include losses that the other party, at the time the contract was formed, had no reason to foresee as a probable result of the breach. Direct damages usually are foreseeable, but consequential damages may not be.
- Damages cannot exceed the amount that can be proven with reasonable certainty. Reliance damages, which seek to place the plaintiff in the position it would have occupied if the contract had not been made, may allow recovery of costs incurred even if profits cannot be proven with reasonable certainty.
- Clauses limiting or expanding remedies usually are enforceable, with some limits. Most important, liquidated damage clauses are enforceable unless they are unreasonably large, in which case they are void penalty clauses.

Applying the Rules

1. Buyer agreed to pay Farmer $15/cwt. for 5,000 cwt. of chipping potatoes ($75,000 total). Buyer accepted and paid for 1,000 cwt. When the price of potatoes fell to $13/cwt., Buyer repudiated the contract with Farmer and started buying other, cheaper potatoes. At that time, Farmer had 6,000 cwt. of potatoes in the field available for delivery. Farmer sold 2,000 cwt. to a different buyer at $13.00 per cwt. Despite diligent efforts, Farmer could not find any Buyer willing

to purchase the remaining 4,000 cwt. of the potatoes. In an action against Buyer, Farmer should recover:

a. $60,000, the price of the potatoes Buyer refused to accept.
b. $34,000, the price of potatoes minus the amount Farmer received by reselling some of the potatoes to others.
c. $8,000, the price of the potatoes minus the fair market value of the unsold potatoes.
d. Nothing, because Farmer failed to minimize the loss by trying harder to sell the remaining potatoes.

2. A long-term contract (entered in 2000) requires Alex to sell all the grapes grown on Acher Vineyard to Mad Rigel Winery for $1,500 per ton, about the average price per ton for grapes of this varietal. Mad Rigel uses the grapes to make its very expensive Special Reserve wine. In breach of contract, Alex sold the grapes (80 tons) to Foxbreath Winery for $2,000 per ton ($160,000). Without these grapes, Mad Rigel decided not to make Special Reserve this year. It feared different grapes might produce a disappointing wine, hurting its ability to charge high prices in the future. In addition, grapes of this quality usually are committed to wineries long before the growing season ends, making it unlikely that Mad Rigel could locate suitable grapes even if it tried. Given the size of the harvest and the price of similar wines, Mad Rigel estimates that it would have grossed $1 million on sales of Special Reserve. By not bottling Special Reserve, Mad Rigel saved the cost of the grapes ($120,000) plus about $150,000 in other expenses (corks, bottles, labels, etc.), but did not save any personnel costs because it needed all of its employees to make its other wines. As counsel for Alex, what arguments would you raise to resist liability for Mad Rigel's lost profits? Do you expect the argument to succeed?

3. Builder sought a $2.5 million construction loan from Lender. Lender's standard terms included a $125,000 fee for paying off the loan early. Builder asked Lender to waive this fee. Lender agreed to waive the fee if Builder made all of its payments on time. Builder fell behind in payments, but subsequently sought to pay the loan off early. Lender sought to collect the prepayment fee. What is Lender's best argument against paying the fee? Should the argument succeed?

4. Utility owns a nuclear power plant. Fed agreed to take, process, and store all spent radioactive fuel produced by the plant. Fed breached the contract, forcing Utility to find alternative ways to store the fuel. Utility spent $2 million to build suitable facilities to store the fuel safely until Fed resumed accepting delivery of the spent fuel. Utility spent $1 million lobbying the State legislature to approve its plan to store the fuel on site at the power plant. State eventually passed a law permitting on-site storage of spent fuel, but only after Utility agreed to pay $3 million to a nonprofit organization created by State to promote environmental safety. Utility sued Fed, claiming all $6 million as damages. What is Fed's

strongest argument to defeat Utility's claim to some or all of these damages? Should that argument succeed?

5. University hired Visitor to teach at University for one year in exchange for $200,000. Before the year began, University repudiated the contract. Visitor obtained a tenured position at College, earning $175,000 in the first year. If Visitor sues University for breach of contract, what damages can Visitor recover? What additional information would you need in order to fully evaluate Visitor's damages?

6. Government awarded Lab a $5 million research grant to investigate promising new treatment for Ebola. Lab spent $1 million building suitable isolation facilities to ensure safe handling of the Ebola virus. Congress passed a law prohibiting research using Ebola virus in private facilities. Government therefore refused to pay any of the grant money to Lab. Lab sues, seeking to recover the full amount of the grant, plus the profit it lost because it will be unable to sell the treatment it would have discovered to health care providers in regions affected by Ebola. What, if any, damages can Lab recover from Government?

7. Buyer ordered two tons of heirloom tomatoes from Broker for $15,000. Broker delivered two tons of beefsteak tomatoes, worth only $11,000. Upon receipt and inspection (which cost $100), Buyer notified Broker that it rejected the tomatoes. Buyer immediately ordered heirloom tomatoes from another supplier for the same price, an effort that required about ten minutes of an employee's time, worth perhaps $10. The replacement tomatoes arrived before Buyer exhausted its supply of heirloom tomatoes from a previous order. To preserve the beefsteak tomatoes until Broker could take possession of them, Buyer paid Teamster $400 to move the tomatoes to a cool, underground facility to prevent deterioration. Buyer promised the owner of the facility $200/week to store the tomatoes and paid for one week in advance. Buyer notified Broker where it could reclaim its tomatoes. How much, if anything, may Buyer collect from Broker as damages for Broker's breach of contract? What other losses might you ask Buyer about in order to ensure that no loss goes uncompensated?

Contract Law in Practice

1. On December 26, Chas consults you concerning recovery against LineAir, an airline that ruined Chas's holiday vacation. Chas paid $2,000 for tickets to fly to Vail, Colorado on December 25 (returning January 1) for a ski vacation with Sean, Chas's teenage child. LineAir had overbooked the flight and bumped Chas and Sean involuntarily. LineAir offered the next available flight that was not overbooked (December 30) and a $400 voucher for future air travel. Chas declined this offer. LineAir immediately refunded the $2,000 purchase price

of the tickets. Chas found no other commercial airline willing to fly them to Vail earlier than December 30. People who bought tickets earlier that week paid about $1,500 per person for round trip coach seats. Chas considered chartering a flight, but lacked enough credit to charge $17,000, the lowest bid for an outbound flight. Chas did not check the price of a return trip. Other modes (train, car) would take too long to permit any skiing before starting the return trip. Chas considered driving to a (distinctly inferior) ski resort nearby, but their luggage was already on the plane (skis, ski clothing, toothbrushes, etc.); LineAir believed, but was not sure, that it could return the luggage on December 27. Chas had prepaid $3,500 (nonrefundable) for accommodations at a ski resort and $1,200 (nonrefundable) for a seven-day pass to several slopes in the area.

While trying not to set a bad example for Sean (who, to say the least, was disappointed), Chas was inwardly fuming. They took a cab ($60) to a nice restaurant for dinner ($120, including cocktails), took another cab home ($30), and plan to spend the rest of the week on activities such as games, movies, and other ordinary vacation activities — unless LineAir surprises them with an early return of their luggage, in which case they still might pursue local skiing.

a. Are there any steps Chas should take today in order to preserve any rights against LineAir or to improve the prospects for proving damages, if that becomes necessary? Take 15 minutes (all the time you have before Chas needs to hang up) and write down your suggestions.
b. If Chas pursues the plan to vacation at home with Sean, what damages can Chas recover from LineAir? Prepare a spreadsheet showing each element of loss and how much Chas should recover for that item. Include a column for highest, lowest, and most likely amount if any item poses difficulties.
c. If your response to part a suggested a different way for Chas to spend the week, what damages can Chas recover from LineAir if Chas follows that advice? Prepare a second spreadsheet showing each element of loss and how much Chas should recover for that item. (If your advice in part a would produce the same spreadsheet you prepared for part b, consider how much Chas should recover if Chas and Sean instead go skiing locally, filling any gaps left by the missing luggage as well as they can.)
d. Prepare a demand letter itemizing the amount Chas seeks from LineAir and explaining to the (reluctant) company why that amount is reasonable and should be paid without further delay.
e. Exchange demand letters with a classmate. You now represent LineAir. Prepare a response to Chas's demand. What grade would you give your classmate's demand letter? What grade would you give your classmate's response to your demand letter? Draft an improved version of one of the documents (your demand letter, your classmate's demand letter, or your classmate's response to your demand letter).

2. How does your state decide whether to award cost of repair or diminution in value when a construction contractor fails to perform as required by the

contract? Under that approach, how would a court decide the case of *Landis v. William Fannin Builders, Inc.*?

3. How does your state determine whether an employee discharged in breach of contract has made a reasonable effort to find substitute employment? Does it apply the same standard to discharge in violation of civil rights laws and tortious discharge from employment?

4. How does your state determine whether to refuse to enforce a liquidated damage clause? Applying that test, how would your state decide the case of *Karimi v. 401 North Wabash Venture*?

5. Go shopping online. Whether or not you buy anything, examine the terms of at least three websites from which you might buy something. Do their terms contain any provisions affecting the amount you could recover if they breached their obligations under the contract? Do these terms affect your willingness to buy from this site in the future?

16

Equitable Remedies

Money damages compensate a victim for the loss suffered from breach. But in some cases, money will be a poor substitute for performance. Your client or your opponent may request the specific performance promised or some key part of it, not just money damages. A court can award an injunction, ordering a breaching party to perform. The court can employ some serious coercive power to encourage performance, including jailing a defiant defendant. That escalation makes courts reluctant to issue injunctions.

Courts are less reluctant to issue other equitable relief, such as restitution. Where a party prefers to cancel a transaction altogether, rather than collect the damages for breach, a court can unwind the transaction. Restitution generally involves the return of any performance already provided or the monetary equivalent. The chapters on defenses included examples where parties avoiding a contract could recover their partial performance. Restitution is available for other forms of unjust enrichment, where defendant received a benefit that she cannot justly retain without compensating the provider. Because courts would prefer parties negotiated their own terms for an exchange, they are slow to award remedies for unjust enrichment where bargaining was possible.

This chapter addresses the special problems that arise when parties ask courts to award equitable injunctions and restitution. These remedies are available in appropriate cases. But you need to understand the limitations on these remedies so you can help a client obtain (or defeat) this relief and, equally important, avoid wasting time seeking a remedy you cannot obtain.

Key Concepts

- The irreparable injury rule
- Injunctions for personal service contracts
- Liability for unjust enrichment
- Measuring restitution

A. BACKGROUND: LAW AND EQUITY

The rules discussed in this chapter use language that will be easier to understand if you know the context in which it originated.

1. History

At one time, England maintained two separate court systems. **Courts of law** handled lawsuits, as they do today. Dissatisfaction with the rigidity of the law courts led many people to petition the monarch (by way of the Chancellor, the monarch's primary religious adviser) to help them redress injustices that the law courts failed to correct. **Courts of equity** (or **Chancery Courts**) were created to handle these petitions. Courts of equity were courts of conscience, trying to avoid injustice that law courts failed to correct. **Equitable relief** refers to the remedies available from courts of equity. While courts of law generally provided damage awards, courts of equity could issue **injunctions** — orders to individuals to do or refrain from doing some specific act(s). Courts of equity also could order a party to return money or property to a plaintiff, a form of restitution. While courts of law sometimes awarded restitution, equity courts applied it to situations where law courts would refuse to act. Thus, restitution was both legal and equitable, depending on the circumstances. The two systems also followed different procedures. For example, trial by jury was available in law courts but not in chancery.

Courts of equity were created to handle petitions to the monarch.
Lordprice Collection / Alamy Stock Photo

With two court systems operating side by side, inconsistent results were inevitable. To reduce the overlap between the two court systems, Parliament tried to keep courts of equity from interfering in cases that belonged in courts of law. By legislation, they decreed that courts of equity could not act unless the **remedy at law** — the remedy a court of law could award — was inadequate. This is called the **irreparable injury rule**. If courts of law could repair the wrong, then courts of equity should not interfere. However, if the remedy at law was inadequate, the injury was irreparable, and courts of equity could redress the injustice.

The American colonies inherited this system of dual (sometimes dueling) courts. The bifurcation retained general acceptance until the 1930s. Even today, some states maintain the distinction. In most states, however, both damages and injunctions are now available from the same court.

Dueling Courts

Think of courts of law and courts of equity as competing companies. Courts of equity were wooing away law courts' customers (litigants), enhancing profits and influence. Parliament divided the market, regulating competition.

2. Types of Specific Relief

Instead of awarding money as a substitute for a party's performance, a court may grant various forms of **specific relief**, awarding a party something closer to what the contract entitled it to receive. The most common specific relief involves injunctions.

Specific Performance

An injunction that orders a party to perform as promised is called **specific performance**. For example, the seller of land may be ordered to deliver a signed deed to the property to buyer — exactly what seller promised to do under the contract. An order of specific performance may compel a person to perform some or all of the duties undertaken in the contract. The order depends on the willingness of the party seeking it to fulfill its promises, such as paying for the land.

Specific performance is an **expectation** remedy; that is, it seeks to place the plaintiff in the position she would have occupied if the contract had been performed. Most injunctions (including specific performance) are **preventive injunctions**, seeking to prevent harm to the plaintiff. (**Reparative injunctions**, seeking to undo harm that already has been done, are rare in contract cases.) Ideally, specific performance can prevent the harm from occurring in the first place by preventing the breach or by curing it (ending the breach by completing performance) before any harm results. Performance following the injunction should place plaintiff in the position she would have occupied if the contract had been performed. If so, damages will be unnecessary.

In some cases, damages may be awarded in addition to specific performance. Complying with the order will not prevent all of the harm. Some harm may already have occurred or become inevitable. The injunction may be valuable to prevent additional harm from occurring. But the court may need to award money damages to compensate for any harm the injunction did not prevent. For example, an order to convey real estate may be issued after the date when performance should have occurred. Any loss suffered between the date performance should have occurred and the date performance does occur (say, renting substitute property) requires compensation by money damages. The combination of specific performance (to prevent future harms) and damages (to compensate for harms that could not be prevented) should leave the plaintiff in the position she would have occupied if the contract had been performed.

Negative Injunctions

A **negative injunction** orders a party not to do something that would be inconsistent with the performance it promised. For example, a person who had promised to work full time for one employer might be ordered not to work for its competitors, at least for a period of time. Some negative injunctions are based on implied obligations. Even without an express promise not to compete, full-time work for one employer implicitly promises not to work for its competitors at the same time.

Negative injunctions that enforce express duties are indistinguishable from partial specific performance. For instance, if the employee had promised not to work for competitors as part of the contract, the order not to do so specifically enforces that promise. It does not matter which label you attach. The limitations on these injunctions will be identical whether called negative injunctions or partial specific performance. The substance of the injunction, not the label, will determine any disputes.

Similar to specific performance, negative injunctions are a form of expectation remedy. They seek to preserve the benefit a party would have obtained if the contract had been performed, primarily by preventing the harms that breach might cause. By their nature, negative injunctions are partial. They do not order full performance and thus may not prevent all of the harm. Their goal is to leave the nonbreaching party in the position it would have occupied if the promise had been performed, to the extent possible.

As with specific performance, damages can be awarded to supplement negative injunctions. If the negative injunction cannot prevent all of the harm, damages are available to compensate for the portions not prevented.

Specific Restitution and Replevin

Specific relief may be useful when contracts are canceled (called off for breach) or terminated (called off for other reasons), not just when enforcing them. For example, if the purchase of a new car is rescinded, the buyer may want to recover the vehicle she traded in as part of the exchange. A court can grant **specific restitution**, ordering a party to return property to the original owner. Similarly, **replevin** is a cause of action that allows the true owner of property to recover it from others who have possession of it. This remedy is most useful when others take or keep property without permission. In some cases, replevin can be used to recover property after it leaves the seller's possession. Historically, replevin was available from courts of law; courts of equity awarded restitution.

Preliminary and Permanent Injunctions

An injunction granted after a full trial on the merits is called a **permanent injunction**. Permanent does not mean perpetual. Orders may be as long or as short as necessary to provide the plaintiff with the relief to which it is entitled. This may be as brief as ordering defendant to deliver a single shipment of goods or turn over a deed to land. It might take longer, such as ordering a defendant not to reveal plaintiff's **trade secrets** (business information legally protected from unauthorized disclosure). Permanent simply means that the injunction is the court's final judgment. (Even that is misleading; courts can revisit and modify injunctions later.)

Courts can issue **preliminary injunctions** at or near the beginning of a case. Preliminary injunctions usually offer partial or temporary relief. Preliminary injunctions remain in effect until the court finishes trial on the merits and enters final judgment (which may or may not include a permanent injunction). Where the plaintiff faces an immediate irreparable harm, a preliminary injunction may prevent that harm from happening until the court can resolve the dispute. Because trial on the merits of the claimed breach has not yet occurred, a court might not know which party breached a contract or even whether an enforceable contract existed. A court may be reluctant to grant complete relief, especially if that order will be hard to reverse if the **enjoined** party (the party the court orders to do something) prevails at the trial. As a result, preliminary injunctions may offer partial measures. For instance, rather than compelling the alleged seller to deliver a unique painting to the alleged buyer, the court may order the seller not to dispose of the painting. This is not specific performance; it merely prevents the sale of the painting to another person until the court can decide whether the contract requires its delivery to the plaintiff. Selling the painting (or any unique item) to another would make a later injunction harder, if not impossible, to enforce. The preliminary injunction protects the court's jurisdiction to grant a useful remedy at the end of the case.

B. THE IRREPARABLE INJURY RULE

Courts refuse to issue injunctions unless the injury is irreparable — that is, unless the remedy at law is inadequate. Where damages (or other remedies at law, such as replevin) are sufficient to satisfy the plaintiff's expectation interest, an injunction will be denied. (Even if the injury is irreparable, other factors may lead a court to deny an injunction, as discussed below.) Generally, a remedy at law is inadequate unless it is as complete, as practical, and as efficient as the equitable remedy. If injunctions are even slightly better than damages on any of these criteria, a court may decide to issue the injunction instead of forcing the plaintiff to settle for a less complete, less practical, or less efficient damage remedy.

In contract law, the irreparable injury rule may be stated in a slightly simpler form: specific performance is available if the promised performance is "unique or in other proper circumstances."[1] When performance is unique, damages may not allow the plaintiff to replace the performance with an adequate substitute. The rule, however, does not limit specific performance to uniqueness; other circumstances may justify an injunction.

While helpful, this rule does not replace the more general approach described above. First, uniqueness itself is not always a clear test. Minor differences may matter in some settings but not others. No two electronic devices have the same serial number. Each is unique, but not in any way that matters when thousands of the same model are available. In contrast, two identical houses on adjacent lots will each be treated as unique, because their location differs, albeit slightly.

Second, "other proper circumstances" says nothing about what makes circumstances proper. By contrast, asking whether damages are as complete, as practical, and as efficient as an injunction provides some help in deciding which "other proper circumstances" justify an injunction. While uniqueness usually forms the backbone of any argument for specific performance, the general rule puts meat on the bones.

[1] UCC §2-716.

Damages will be inadequate in several situations:

1. if the performance is unique, so no substitute is available;
2. if shortages make it difficult to find a substitute, even if not impossible;
3. if damages are hard to prove with reasonable certainty;
4. if the defendant is **insolvent** (cannot pay all its debts in full).

The range of reasons suggests that courts award specific performance much more often than believed. The rhetoric courts use, describing injunctions as extraordinary relief available only in unusual cases, overstates their reluctance to grant injunctions. If the buyer has a good reason for preferring specific performance, courts often will order performance.

Whether the remedy at law is adequate will be determined by the judge on a case-by-case basis. In some settings, however, the results are very consistent over time. For example, courts routinely order sellers of real estate to provide buyers a deed to the property because land is unique. For sales of goods, however, courts start with the presumption that plaintiff can find a substitute. The following sections discuss how judges apply the irreparable injury rule to different kinds of promises. Exceptions can be found. To persuade a court to grant an exception, focus on the reasons courts grant or deny injunctions, not just the pattern of results.

Case Preview

Sedmak v. Charlie's Chevrolet, Inc.

1978 Corvette Special Pace Car Model
AP Photo

This case involves the sale of a limited edition sports car. The court applied the irreparable injury rule to a case in which the property sold was not literally unique, but was rare and difficult to obtain. Shortages of this type arise more often than truly unique items. The court needed to decide whether to extend specific performance to these situations.

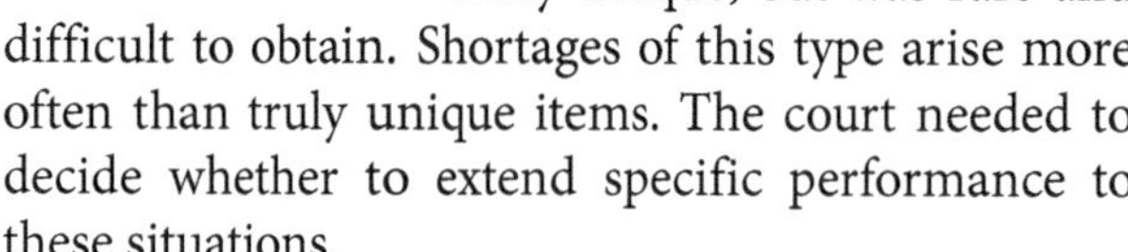

As you read *Sedmak v. Charlie's Chevrolet*, look for the following:

1. What would make property unique in "the traditional legal sense," mentioned by the court?
2. How did the court evaluate the remedy at law—the damages plaintiff might recover if the court denied specific performance? Why was that remedy insufficient?
3. Did the UCC require this result or does it flow from Missouri's more generous history under the common law?

Sedmak v. Charlie's Chevrolet, Inc.

622 S.W.2d 694 (Mo. Ct. App. 1981)

SATZ, Judge.

This is an appeal from a decree of specific performance. We affirm.

[D]r. and Mrs. Sedmak (Sedmaks) . . . entered into a contract with defendant, Charlie's Chevrolet, Inc. (Charlie's), to purchase a Corvette automobile for approximately $15,000.00. The Corvette was one of a limited number manufactured to commemorate the selection of the Corvette as the Pace Car for the Indianapolis 500. Charlie's breached the contract . . . when, after the automobile was delivered, an agent for Charlie's told the Sedmaks they could not purchase the automobile for $15,000.00 but would have to bid on it.

The trial court found the parties entered into an oral contract and also found the contract was excepted from the Statute of Frauds. The court then ordered Charlie's to make the automobile "available for delivery" to the Sedmaks.

[The court concluded that sufficient evidence supported the trial court's ruling that an oral contract existed and that partial payment satisfied the UCC exception to the statute of frauds.]

Finally, Charlie's contends the Sedmaks failed to show they were entitled to specific performance of the contract. We disagree. Although it has been stated that the determination whether to order specific performance lies within the discretion of the trial court, *Landau v. St. Louis Public Service Co.*, 273 S.W.2d 255, 259 (Mo. 1954), this discretion is, in fact, quite narrow. When the relevant equitable principles have been met and the contract is fair and plain, "'specific performance goes as a matter of right.'" *Miller v. Coffeen*, 280 S.W.2d 100, 102 (Mo. 1955). Here, the trial court ordered specific performance because it concluded the Sedmaks "have no adequate remedy at law for the reason that they cannot go upon the open market and purchase an automobile of this kind with the same mileage, condition, ownership and appearance as the automobile involved in this case, except, if at all, with considerable expense, trouble, loss, great delay and inconvenience." Contrary to defendant's complaint, this is a correct expression of the relevant law and it is supported by the evidence.

Under the Code, the court may decree specific performance as a buyer's remedy for breach of contract to sell goods "where the goods are unique or in other proper circumstances." §400.2-716(1) RSMo 1978. The general term "in other proper circumstances" expresses the drafters' intent to "further a more liberal attitude than some courts have shown in connection with the specific performance of contracts of sale." §400.2-716, U.C.C., Comment 1. This Comment was not directed to the courts of this state, for long before the Code, we, in Missouri, took a practical approach in determining whether specific performance would lie for the breach of contract for the sale of goods and did not limit this relief only to the sale of "unique" goods. *Boeving v. Vandover*, 240 Mo. App. 117, 218 S.W.2d 175 (1949). In *Boeving*, plaintiff contracted to buy a car from defendant. When the car arrived, defendant refused to sell. The car was not unique in the traditional legal sense but, at that time, all cars were difficult to obtain because of war-time shortages. The court held specific

performance was the proper remedy for plaintiff because a new car "could not be obtained elsewhere except at considerable expense, trouble or loss, which cannot be estimated in advance and under such circumstances (plaintiff) did not have an adequate remedy at law." ***Id.*** **at 177-178. Thus,** ***Boeving*** **presaged the broad and liberalized language of §400.2-716(1) and exemplifies one of the "other proper circumstances" contemplated by this subsection for ordering specific performance. §400.2-716, Missouri Code Comment 1. The present facts track those in** ***Boeving.***

The Pace Car, like the car in ***Boeving,*** **was not unique in the traditional legal sense. It was not an heirloom or, arguably, not one of a kind. However, its "mileage, condition, ownership and appearance" did make it difficult, if not impossible, to obtain its replication without considerable expense, delay and inconvenience. Admittedly, 6,000 Pace Cars were produced by Chevrolet. However, . . . this is limited production. In addition, only one of these cars was available to each dealer, and only a limited number of these were equipped with the specific options ordered by plaintiffs. Charlie's had not received a car like the Pace Car in the previous two years. The sticker price for the car was $14,284.21. Yet Charlie's received offers from individuals in Hawaii and Florida to buy the Pace Car for $24,000.00 and $28,000.00 respectively. As sensibly inferred by the trial court, the location and size of these offers demonstrated this limited edition was in short supply and great demand. We agree, with the trial court. This case was a "proper circumstance" for ordering specific performance.**

Judgment affirmed.

Deciding when a shortage justifies specific performance remains difficult to predict. *Boeving*, relied on by the court, was somewhat unusual. Many cases held that the post-WWII shortage of cars did not justify specific performance because there was nothing special about the car sold compared to thousands of similar cars being sold at the time. *See, e.g., McCallister v. Patton*, 215 S.W.2d 701 (Ark. 1948). In *Klein v. PepsiCo, Inc.*, 845 F.2d 76 (4th Cir. 1988), decided under the UCC, the court applied this reasoning to a jet, even though only three similar aircraft were available. It might matter that buyer wanted the jet to resell it for a profit — which money damages might compensate. The special aspects of the Pace Car might justify a different result even in other states. Shortage will not always justify specific performance. But in cases like *Sedmak*, where the damages would be very difficult to calculate (unless the buyer actually buys a substitute), specific performance seems the right result.

Sedmak v. Charlie's Chevrolet, Inc.: Real Life Applications

1. Soupson uses only Chantenay red-cored carrots in the soups it produces because they have a uniform color from the outer edge to the core. Soupson supplied

seed to Farmer, who promised to sell the carrots to Soupson at $30 per ton. At harvest, Chantenay red-cored carrots were selling for $90 per ton. Farmer delivered some carrots to Soupson but sold some to another buyer. Soupson sued Farmer, seeking an injunction ordering Farmer to deliver all the carrots promised in the contract. Are the carrots unique? Is the remedy at law adequate? *See Campbell Soup Co. v. Wentz*, 172 F.2d 80 (3d Cir. 1948).

2. Rancher hired Cowboy to tend the ranch in exchange for $400 and a horse named Blackjack. Cowboy performed and, in his spare time, trained Blackjack to be a top quality roping horse. Rancher paid Cowboy the money but refused to deliver Blackjack. A roping horse of equivalent quality could be obtained on the market. If Cowboy seeks specific performance, would a court find the remedy at law adequate?

3. Owner gave Tenant an option to buy land for $210,000. In anticipation of buying the land, Tenant built a barn on it. Tenant, however, was unable to find a loan, making it impossible for Tenant to pay for the land. In exchange for Angel providing the money needed to exercise the option, Tenant agreed to sell the land to Angel for $222,000 if Tenant obtained the land. Tenant exercised the option, but Owner breached the promise to sell the land. If Tenant seeks specific performance, will a court find the remedy at law adequate?

4. Buyer agreed to purchase land as is from Seller for $500,000. After discovering toxic chemicals on the land, Buyer breached the contract. Seller sought specific performance. Is Seller's remedy at law adequate? Even if no one else will buy the land at any price?

---

1. Irreparable Injury in Context

Some implications of the irreparable injury rule require relatively little comment. Sellers rarely get an injunction ordering a buyer to pay the price. Why not? Because money is no less adequate when part of a damage award than it is when provided by an injunction. The injunction might encourage payment to avoid contempt of court and jail time, but also raises the specter of debtor's prisons, an institution society has no interest in reviving. Similarly, the uniqueness of land makes specific performance the normal remedy when sellers refuse to deliver a deed. In contrast, goods frequently are fungible; one brick is about as good as another. So money usually will allow a buyer to find a substitute—subject to exceptions like the one in *Sedmak*.

2. Uncertainty, Insolvency, and Irreparable Injury

Money damages may seem better in theory than in practice. Money may suffice if plaintiff actually obtains the right amount of money damages. But plaintiff may encounter problems obtaining a sufficient judgment and collecting it from the defendant.

When damages are difficult to calculate, the remedy at law may be inadequate. This commonly arises when nondelivery causes lost profits. Uncertainty regarding the amount of lost profit makes it likely that damages will not fully compensate plaintiff for the loss. The certainty doctrine is designed to preclude overcompensation, while tolerating undercompensation. Specific performance may counteract the tendency to undercompensate. By ordering performance when damages are difficult to prove, the court allows the plaintiff to make the profit (or loss) rather than trying to predict how much that would been. If it is relatively easy to provide plaintiff with exactly what was promised (and thus avoid some or all of the losses), that may be a more complete or more practical remedy than forcing the plaintiff to suffer the losses and try to recover them in litigation.

Defendant's insolvency makes it difficult for the plaintiff to collect damages. Obtaining the goods may be possible, but suing for money later might be meaningless. A buyer's insolvency sometimes allows a seller to stop delivery of goods.[2] For buyers, a seller's insolvency may justify specific performance. Insolvency also may affect the adequacy of remedies beyond sales of goods. Regardless of the performance promised, compelling performance might be more complete than relegating plaintiff to damages that it may never receive.

3. Services

Services, like goods, often can be replaced. Damages may compensate completely for the difference in price between two providers of the same service. If one subcontractor refuses to finish the excavation, hiring another and collecting the difference in price (plus any consequential losses) may solve the problem. But in some situations, damages might not be as complete, practical, and efficient as an order to perform the promise.

Sometimes a substitute provider may be unavailable. For instance, cable television services often have a local monopoly. If the cable company breaches a promise to provide service, no substitute cable service may be available. Damages might allow a party to obtain an inexact substitute, such as satellite television service, but differences may make that a less desirable alternative. (Buyer probably had a reason to choose one over the other in the first place.) Specific performance might be a more complete remedy. Even if the differences could be measured and included in a damage award, the difficulty of those calculations might make it more efficient to award specific performance. Some differences might defy calculation, such as cable's greater reliability in severe weather conditions. Specific performance may be a more practical remedy, providing an easier way to deliver a complete remedy.

Even when several providers offer the same service, providers may differ in ways people find important, preferring to deal with the one that best suits their needs. When choosing a law school or a caterer for a wedding, people rarely conclude that all the competitors are equally good. That people sometimes choose a

---

[2] UCC §2-702.

service provider for reasons other than price suggests that the competitors differ in an important way. Damages might provide a substitute, but not necessarily an equally good substitute. If damages cannot accurately account for those differences, specific performance may be a more complete or a more practical remedy.

A right to receive a service may not include a right to receive a service from a particular individual. Hiring a contractor allows the contractor to choose which employees it sends to do the work. In these situations, it is harder to argue that the personal characteristics of the provider make that provider unique. Thus, if one contractor breaches, damages to hire a different contractor may be adequate. Where the characteristics of the contractor are unique, specific performance still might be available. For example, a government contract might require the use of a specific subcontractor. Alternatively, patent protection may make performance available from only one provider. If specific performance would not require a particular individual to perform services personally, the court might grant that relief.

C. PERSONAL SERVICE CONTRACTS

Personal service contracts — those that require a specific individual to perform the service — present special problems for courts. They reveal two interesting aspects of injunctions:

1. injunctions may be denied even if the remedy at law is inadequate; and
2. injunctions may be limited in scope.

Each issue is addressed below.

Not all service contracts call for personal services. If the contract requires an individual to perform, it involves personal services. But many services are provided by someone who can send any individual to perform. Hiring Merry Maids (the agency) differs from hiring Marian (the individual). One way to probe whether a contract involves personal services to ask whether the other party may delegate the duty to perform. Where the other party may select the individuals who perform the service, it does not call for personal services. Specific performance would not impinge on any individual's freedom; the other party could simply find another willing to perform and delegate the duty to that person. Where delegation would be impermissible, the contract requires some services from a specific individual. In those situations, specific performance would involve ordering an individual to perform a service she no longer wants to perform. That situation raises potential problems courts prefer to avoid.

1. Specific Performance

Courts refuse to award specific performance for contracts involving personal services. The irreparable injury rule explains relatively few of these decisions.

Irreparable Injury

Personal services frequently are unique. No one seriously maintains that wide receivers, leading ladies, or CEOs are fungible. Even for less elite positions, unique qualities often explain why one person is hired instead of another. An abundant supply of nannies would not make nannies fungible. A number of intangible factors enter into employment decisions, even when (objectively) equivalent applicants abound. In fact, it demeans human dignity to suggest that people are as interchangeable as ball bearings, not even as different as two identical houses in the same subdivision. The argument usually is deployed by individuals demeaning themselves in order to persuade a court not to issue an injunction against them. In that context, people seem willing to accept a certain amount of indignity to advance their immediate goal of winning the suit.

The individuality of employees permits courts to issue an appropriate injunction, often a negative injunction if the facts justify that relief. Consider the following example of negative injunctions.

Case Preview

Mission Independent School District v. Diserens

Courts frequently order breaching employees not to work for their employers' competitors. The rationale and scope for these decisions vary rather broadly. The court here relies on decisions enjoining Napoleon Lajoie (now in the Baseball Hall of Fame) and Johanna Wagner (a famous opera singer, niece of composer Richard Wagner) to support enjoining a music teacher from breaching her contract with one school district by teaching for another nearby school district in Texas.

As you read *Mission Independent School District v. Diserens*, look for the following:

1. What reasons did the court give for refusing to grant specific performance in personal service contracts?
2. Do those reasons apply to injunctions against working for competitors in breach of a promise not to do so?
3. Did the injunction decrease the harm plaintiff suffered? What purpose did the injunction serve?

Mission Independent School District v. Diserens

144 Tex. 107 (1945) (reh'g denied)

SIMPSON, Justice.

Mission Independent School District [hired] Ethel Diserens . . . to teach in the . . . public schools . . . for one year . . . and further agreed she would not teach anywhere

else in the State of Texas during the contract period. She was a musician and teacher of extraordinary and unique talents and abilities and it was a difficult matter for the employing school district to obtain any other teacher with her qualifications. On [her first day,] she . . . asked [to] be released and upon this request being refused she breached her contract and in violation of its terms went to Cisco, Texas, where she took up teaching music and directing a band in the public schools. Mission Independent School District has been willing at all times to offer Ethel Diserens employment under the terms of the contract she breached.

With matters in this attitude, Mission Independent School District sued . . . seeking to enjoin her from breaching the negative promise in the contract not to teach during the contract period elsewhere in the State of Texas. . . . The district court [found no] injury to the plaintiff school district incident to the defendant's "teaching at Cisco separate from her failure to teach at Mission," [concluding] the injunction should not issue. The Court of Civil Appeals . . . affirmed [denial of] the injunction. In this we conclude there was error.

. . .

[I]t is true that chancery courts have refused to grant mandatory injunction specifically enforcing contracts for the performance of personal services. It has been said that this refusal is based in part upon the difficulty of enforcement and of passing judgment upon the quality of performance and in part upon the undesirability of compelling the continuance of personal association after disputes have arisen and confidence and loyalty are gone. And in some cases, it has been observed, the decree would seem like the enforcement of an involuntary servitude. But to the contrary, it has also been pointed out that there may be negative promises in personal service contracts and within certain limits these may be enforced by injunction. Restatement of the Law, American Law Institute, Volume II of Contracts, Section 379; *E. M. Goodwin, Inc., v. Stuart*, Tex. Civ. App., 52 S.W.2d 311, affirmed 125 Tex. 212, 82 S.W.2d 632. These limits are well defined in the decisions, notably beginning with the leading case of *Lumley v. Wagner*, 1852, 1 De G. M. & G. 604, 42 English Rep. 687, and later in this country, in *McCaull v. Braham*, C.C.S.D.N.Y.1883, 16 F. 37; *Philadelphia Ball Club v. Lajoie*, 1902, 202 Pa. 210, 51 A. 973 [1901]; [citations omitted].

In *Lumley v. Wagner*, supra, a famous singer agreed to appear in the complainant's opera house for a certain time during which she was not to sing for anyone else. The court held that the services were of such a character that damages would be inadequate and that therefore an injunction was proper to restrain the defendant from singing elsewhere. A comment in 4 Pomeroy's Equity Jurisprudence, 4th Ed., section 1711, states that in the *Lumley v. Wagner* case, the opinion "fully reviews the previous authorities, and has been generally accepted, both in England and in this country, upon a similar state of facts." In the course of the opinion, the Lord Chancellor remarked that "wherever this Court has not proper jurisdiction to enforce specific performance, it operates to bind men's consciences, as far as they can be bound, to a true and literal performance of their agreements; and it will not suffer them to depart from their contracts at their pleasure, leaving the party with whom they have contracted to the mere chance of any damages which a jury may give."

And among the authorities in this country which have followed this doctrine, we note that United States Circuit Judge Walter H. Sanborn, in deciding the *Marsans* case, supra, declared it a settled rule "that where a person agrees to render services that are unique and extraordinary, and which may not be rendered by another, and has made a negative covenant in his agreement whereby he promises not to render such service to others, the court may issue an injunction to prevent him from violating the negative covenant in order to induce him to perform his contract."

The defendant comes fairly within the rule announced in these cases. She is a music teacher of extraordinary and unique talents and has engaged herself to devote those talents to teaching in the schools at Mission and not elsewhere in Texas during the contract period. The plaintiff school district finds difficulty in getting another teacher of her qualifications. It offers to extend to the defendant the benefits of the contract of employment she has breached. She ought not to be allowed to breach her contract at her pleasure and affirmatively violate the promise she made not to teach anywhere else in this State during the time embraced by the agreement. Accordingly, we conclude she should have been enjoined from violating the negative covenant in her contract.

We are not willing to restrict the doctrine laid down in the decisions so narrowly that it will include only such situations as obtained in *Patterson v. Crabb*, Tex. Civ. App., 51 S.W. 570, writ dismissed, where the parties were competitors and loss of business would have resulted if the injunction had not issued. The principles involved have a broader scope. They should properly be applied "to bind men's consciences, as far as they can be bound, to a true and literal performance of their agreements." We conclude they are properly applicable to the situation of the plaintiff and defendant here.

[The court then rejected two procedural challenges to granting injunctive relief.]

The judgments of the Court of Civil Appeals and district court are reversed, and this cause is remanded to the district court with instructions that the injunction issue as prayed.

Post-Case Follow-Up

This case stands at one extreme, enforcing a negative covenant specifically to encourage a plaintiff to return to her original employer. At the other extreme, some courts will refuse an injunction because it might have that effect, even if the injunction also reduces losses the plaintiff might suffer if the defendant works for a competitor. *See Ford v. Jermon*, 6 Phila. 6 (Pa. Dist. Ct. 1865). In between are cases involving athletes, actors, singers, and others whose performance for competitors seems likely to increase the harm caused by not working for the plaintiff. Today, courts tend to issue injunctions when the injunction will prevent part of the harm a plaintiff might suffer even if plaintiff does not return to work for defendant.

Mission Independent School District v. Diserens: Real Life Applications

1. In *Diserens*, if there was a higher court to which you could appeal, would you ask it to reverse this decision? What is the strongest argument you could raise in favor of reversal? Map out your strategy on appeal.

2. Partner's contract with Firm provides that if Partner leaves the firm, she must refrain from soliciting firm clients for ten years and refrain from opening a law office within 50 miles of the firm's three existing offices for five years. Partner resigned and set up a law office outside the restricted area. Partner did not solicit existing clients, but did advertise in general publications that existing clients might see. Firm seeks to enjoin Partner from soliciting or accepting any business from an existing client of Firm. Should a court grant that relief? Does it matter that Partner's primary skill involves drawing clients in (rainmaking), with no special talent for actually representing clients? *See Smith, Waters, Kuehn, Burnett & Hughes, Ltd. v. Burnett*, 192 Ill. App. 3d 693 (1989).

3. Harris is a good cornerback in the NFL, with skills about average for NFL cornerbacks. Harris's NFL contract entitles the Dallas Cowboys to Harris's exclusive services relating to professional football. Harris prefers to play for the Dallas Texans, a team in a rival football league. If the Cowboys seek to enjoin Harris from playing for the other team, should a court issue the injunction? Would it matter if the team were not in Texas? If it were not in the United States? What if Harris were the first person picked in the NFL draft last year? Consider *Dallas Cowboys Football Club, Inc. v. Harris*, 348 S.W.2d 37, 42 (Tex. Civ. 1961), and *Matuszak v. Houston Oilers*, 515 S.W.2d 725 (Tex. Civ. 1974).

Other Policies

As mentioned in *Diserens*, specific performance in personal service contracts borders on involuntary servitude, forbidden by the Thirteenth Amendment. The shadow of involuntary servitude helps explain modern judicial attitudes, but may not completely justify denying specific performance. For one thing, contractual obligations arise voluntarily, by assent of the individual. The service was voluntary at the time of contract formation, but has become involuntary because the person changed her mind. That change of heart need not preclude enforcement. Moreover, the Constitution tolerates involuntary servitude in some settings, such as the military or the merchant marine, where specific performance is granted.

The court in *Diserens* also identified several pragmatic concerns that make specific performance of questionable value in personal service contracts. These issues may explain judicial reluctance better than the constitutional question.

First, an employee ordered to resume work for an employer is unlikely to be a very enthusiastic employee. The intangible qualities that make the employee unique are unlikely to be as evident after the injunction.

Second, enforcing specific performance of personal service contracts threatens to burden courts. If the employee's morale produces substandard performance, the employer may seek contempt sanctions for the employee's failure to do the work, as ordered by the court. An order clarifying what is expected of the employee may lead to another request for contempt, leading to a series of additional clarifications of the injunction and additional contempt hearings. If courts can dispose of the case with a single damage award, they need not become embroiled in every subsequent dispute between the employer and employee over the quality of services provided.

Third, plaintiffs may request specific performance for strategic reasons. They may not want the performance, but want to use the threat of contempt to extract a more favorable settlement agreement from the employee. The court order does not preclude the employer and employee from settling the dispute on different terms. The injunction gives the employer considerable leverage to demand more in exchange for waiving any further right to the employee's services. This sounds a little like an employee buying his freedom, which may explain why concerns for involuntary servitude continue to arise in this context.

These same concerns may prevent an employee from obtaining specific performance against an employer. Some statutes, such as antidiscrimination laws, authorize courts to compel employers to hire, retain, or promote employees. But in contract settings specific performance against employers is rare. A court has enforced an arbitration award ordering reinstatement of an employee.[3] Employees often prefer damages, which provides reasonable relief and avoids the aggravation of continuing to work for a hostile employer. Some courts may require **mutuality of remedy**—neither party may obtain specific performance unless a court can order both parties to perform. Because the employer cannot obtain specific performance, neither should the employee. This ancient doctrine is losing favor,[4] but retains vitality in some jurisdictions.

2. Scope of Negative Injunctions

As *Diserens* shows, courts will enforce personal service contracts using negative injunctions. Courts routinely issue injunctions ordering former employees not to reveal trade secrets. Courts also enjoin performing for a competitor in appropriate cases. For example, a star athlete who promised to play for one team might be enjoined from playing for a cross-town rival.

An order limiting competition seeks to reduce the harm the first employer suffers as a result of the employee's breach. In any case where the employer can avoid all losses by hiring a suitable substitute, no injunction would issue. Preventing the employee from working for another would serve no remedial purpose. (It may satisfy the employer's desire for spite, but that is not a purpose the law should advance.) This may apply to the vast majority of employees.

Some employees, however, may play a more significant role. Their value is sufficiently great that their work for a competitor harms the former employer, even if the employee has been replaced. The employer's benefit from the new employee

[3]*Staklinski v. Pyramid Elec. Co.*, 6 N.Y.2d 159 (1959).
[4]Restatement (Third) of Restitution and Unjust Enrichment §363 cmt. c.

will be less if the former employee is competing than if the former employee is prevented from working elsewhere.

Consider a famous performer who breaks a contract to sing in one Broadway show in order to take a job with another Broadway show. Courts cannot order him to sing for the original employer. Damages can compensate for the sales lost if fewer people buy tickets to the show because the star is gone. But courts might prevent the sales from being even lower by ordering him not to sing for the competitor. This prevents losing sales to people who are drawn to the second show because the star is there, but might have seen the first show if the star were in neither show. See Exhibit 16.1.

EXHIBIT 16.1 Sales Results Based on Performance

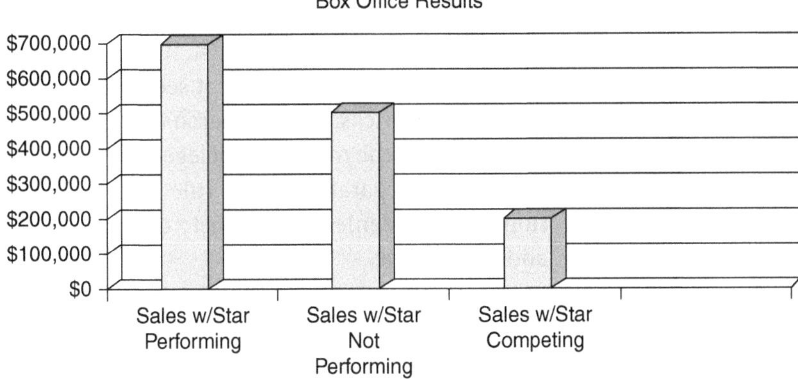

The bars represent the profits of the nonbreaching employer. An injunction preventing the star form appearing for a competitor will prevent some losses (the difference between the third column and the second). Specific performance would prevent the entrie loss, but is not available in personal service contracts. If there would be no difference between the second and third columns, the justification for a negative injuction would diminish; it would not prevent any harm to plaintiff.

The problem is not limited to entertainers, athletes, and newscasters. A skilled salesman, if working for a competitor, may affect the former employer's sales. A skilled researcher, if working for a competitor, may harm the former employer's ability to exploit a technological advantage before competitors can catch up. In other settings, an employee's service to a competitor may harm the former employer's profits in ways that they would not have been harmed if the employee were not working for either company.

If too broad, a negative injunction may create problems. Ordering a former employee not to work for competitors may impair her ability to earn a living. This hardship might induce an employee to return to the employer, something the court could not order directly. While the court in *Diserens* considered this the purpose of the injunction, most courts view this as a problem. You may recall from Chapter 8 that contract clauses limiting a party's subsequent employment too strictly violate public policy.

Courts try to draft injunctions that provide relief to plaintiff without unduly burdening the defendant. Thus, a negative injunction typically lasts a relatively short time—usually the duration of the contract, though some express terms limit competition for longer periods—and affect only positions that would harm the plaintiff. Thus, if jobs in other places or in other industries would not detract from plaintiff's business, the injunction should not preclude those jobs. Where a negative injunction cannot be limited to prevent undue hardship to the defendant, courts may refuse to issue the injunction.[5]

Injunctions That Prohibit Work

A duty not to work for a competitor may arise in several ways:

a. Express promises. Contract language may include a promise not to work for others during the contract period. A general promise that employees will devote all of their professional time to the employer may suffice.
b. Implied promises. If an employee devoting full-time service to an employer (in good faith) would be unable to work for a competitor, noncompetition is implicit in the promise to work.
c. Express promises limiting employment after the contract ends. Public policy may limit noncompetition clauses, especially if they preclude a person from earning a living. Some states reject these clauses, but most will enforce a reasonable noncompetition term.

D. OTHER LIMITATIONS

Equitable relief had its origins in the monarch's conscience. It was an effort to produce justice where the law was unable to do so. But justice is a difficult concept to define. Equitable relief relied on the discretion of the judges implementing it. It was not available mechanically, but only where it seemed necessary and appropriate to ease the monarch's conscience (or the conscience of the monarch's delegees). As a result, even when the irreparable injury rule is satisfied, injunctions may be denied for a variety of reasons. Some are addressed here.

1. Impossible to Comply

Equity will not order the impossible. If an injunction cannot be obeyed, there is no point in issuing the order. Violation is inevitable, forcing the court either to punish a person for contempt of court (even though she could not have obeyed the order no matter how hard she tried) or to attach no consequences to the failure to obey. The latter threatens to make the court look ineffectual, perhaps encouraging others (who could obey injunctions) to test the court's resolve by noncompliance. An injunction that cannot be obeyed provides no remedy at all. The remedy at law, no matter how inadequate, is still better than a futile injunction.

2. Undue Hardship

Undue hardship justifies denying an injunction if the harm of an injunction to the defendant is disproportionate to the benefit of an injunction to the plaintiff. Recall the discussion in Chapter 11 of *Jacob & Youngs v. Kent*,[6] where a builder used

[5] *Id.* §367(2).
[6] 230 N.Y. 239 (1921).

the wrong pipe in constructing a house. An order of specific performance could compel the builder to tear down the walls, insert the correct pipe, and rebuild the house. The cost to the builder would have been enormous, while the benefit to the plaintiff was slight, adding no value to the house. Even if the owner had serious reasons for preferring that pipe, those reasons might be dwarfed by the costs the contractor would incur to obey the injunction. The disproportionate hardship the contractor would suffer justifies denying an injunction.

Limiting Damages for Undue Hardship

Undue hardship can affect damage awards, not just equitable relief. Denying cost of repair when it is disproportionate to the loss in value resembles undue hardship. The breaching party can avoid the more onerous remedy, but only if it is significantly more wasteful than justified under the circumstances.

Undue hardship is not a mere cost-benefit analysis. If the cost to the defendant is a little higher than the benefit to the plaintiff, the injunction will be issued. The breaching party deserves less consideration than the nonbreaching party. Thus, the harm the enjoined party would suffer must be disproportionate to — that is, it must significantly outweigh — the benefit the injunction would have for the other party.

Undue hardship may not be available to intentional wrongdoers. Those who know they are risking an injunction and decide to breach anyway may find the court unwilling to exercise its discretion to relieve them of the consequences of their decision, even if the cost seems outrageous relative to the benefit. The cost of complying in the first place would have been much lower, but was waived by the party in breach.

Case Preview

Tierney v. Four H Land Company

To induce plaintiff to allow defendant to remove gravel from plaintiff's land, defendant promised to reclaim the land upon completion. Defendant breached because reclamation proved very expensive — much more than the decrease in the value of the land. Recall from Chapter 15 that courts may refuse to award damages based on the cost of repair when those costs are disproportionate to the benefits repairs produce — such as paying $10,000 to repair a car that, once fixed, will be worth $2,000. Specific performance would order the party to perform, regardless of the cost. This case raises the same objection: that the court should not compel wasteful performance for the same reasons it would not award damages based on the cost of wasteful repairs.

As you read *Tierney v. Four H Land Company*, look for the following:

1. How did the court define undue hardship?
2. Did defendants intentionally violate the terms of the agreement? Did the defendants' intent matter to the court?
3. Did the court determine that the plaintiffs deserved specific performance?

Tierney v. Four H Land Company

288 Neb. 586 (2014)

Wright, J.

In 1998, James Tierney and Jeffrey Tierney entered into an agreement with Four H Land Company Limited Partnership (Four H) and Western Engineering Company, Inc. (Western), regarding operation of a sand and gravel pit on property owned by Four H. In this agreement, the Tierneys agreed to waive their right to contest the issuance of a conditional use permit (CUP) for operation of the sand and gravel pit. In return, Four H and Western accepted various conditions regarding operation of the sand and gravel pit, including reclamation of the property after expiration of the CUP.

. . .

The relevant terms of the agreement provided:

> As the operation in one phase is completed and the operation moves to the next phase, [Four H] and [Western] shall reclaim the land in the phase of prior operations by filling to at least its approximate original topography, covered with a minimum of four (4) inches of top soil and seeded with appropriate native grasses to prevent erosion and to visually restore the site, except the area to be used for a lake. This shall be done within one (1) year of termination of operations on the phase. . . . In any event, reclamation and restoration of the property shall be completed by October 31, 2008. . . .

. . .

In April 2009, the Tierneys filed an action for specific performance against Four H (prior owner of the property), Western (operator of the sand and gravel pit), and the Aloi Living Trust and its trustee (current owners of the property). The Tierneys alleged that Four H and Western had "failed to meet . . . their obligations under the agreement." . . .

. . .

[After] a bench trial [held] over 4 trial days[,] the district court dismissed the Tierneys' complaint. . . .

. . .

The district court . . . stated that specific performance "would appear to be the only adequate remedy" due to the fact that damages "would be uncertain and difficult, if not impossible, to prove." However, the court ultimately concluded that specific performance was not an appropriate remedy, because . . . the burden upon Four H and Western outweighed the benefits to the Tierneys; [in fact, they] were "so out of balance" with the benefits to the Tierneys that the "overall result would be more spiteful than just." [P]erformance of the . . . agreement would be a project "massive in both scope and expense." Conversely, it concluded that the benefits to the Tierneys from specific performance would "essentially be aesthetic ones" and that even if specific performance were ordered, the Tierneys' "rural living circumstances [were] by no means guaranteed."

[The court considered defendants' claim that the agreement required filling in the pit, but did not require lowering the hill of sand. Admitting that the language, read literally, might support defendants' interpretation, the court concluded that in context the most reasonable reading of the language favored returning the land to its original topography.]

Because specific performance must be granted or denied according to general equitable principles, concepts of fairness and equity can be considered. In particular, "[e]xoneration from specific performance may be available when specific performance would be inequitable or unjust due to hardship on the one from whom performance is sought." *Mohrlang v. Draper*, 219 Neb. 630, 633, 365 N.W.2d 443, 447 (1985).

But to the extent hardship enters into the equation, it is not compared to the benefits accruing to the party seeking performance. In analyzing whether hardship is sufficient to excuse performance under a contract, the question is whether the hardship complained of was foreseeable at entry into the contract. Hardship arising from a "circumstance unforeseeable at entry into the contract" may excuse specific performance of a contract, provided that the hardship is not "self-inflicted or caused through inexcusable neglect on the part of the person seeking to be excused or exonerated from specific performance." [Citation omitted.] It is inconsequential to this analysis how the hardship compares to the benefits that would be obtained by the party seeking performance.

We adopted the foregoing approach to hardship, because under a contrary rule, "one would derive a benefit from his or her own inexcusable neglect." [Citation omitted.] For the same reasons, we decline to depart from our precedent and adopt the cost-benefit analysis used by the district court — that is, comparing the cost of performance to the benefits that would accrue to the party seeking specific performance.

Under an approach that weighs burdens and benefits of performance without considering the origins of those burdens, a party could be excused from specific performance due to the exact burdens it willingly and legally assumed under the contract. Furthermore, if the only relevant factor were the degree of hardship, a party could derive positive benefits from creating impediments to its own performance, such as by engaging in compounded breaches of the contract, and would thereby be encouraged to do so.

The instant case illustrates the potential problems of the district court's approach to hardship. The court excused Four H and Western from their contractual obligations, because performance would require them to "shove a huge amount of earth back into" the lake created by the sand and gravel pit operation in order to return the property to its original topography. [I]t would be a project "massive in both scope and expense," would require "pushing approximately 25 *acres* of fill material into the lake," and might require Four H and Western to obtain permits and licenses. (Emphasis in original.) We find it significant that these burdens were required by the . . . agreement and were the result of Four H's and Western's own actions.

The parties contemplated that performance by Four H and Western would require filling in a lake created by the sand and gravel pit operation. Indeed, the . . . agreement specifically required the lake to be filled in according to the site plan after each phase of the operation. . . . Thus, Four H and Western entered into . . . the agreement with knowledge that they would be taking on such burdens. They received the benefits of removing gravel from the property for 10 years and cannot now be excused from fulfilling their contractual obligations to restore the property due to the very burdens they intended to assume under the CUP and the agreement.

[By failing to] engage in . . . incremental restoration [as promised,] Four H and Western continually enlarged the lake until it covered 30 acres instead of 11 acres, which, in turn, created an increased burden of performance. They cannot claim that increased burden as justification for excusing specific performance. . . .

The approach of the district court rewarded Four H and Western for failing to perform their obligations under . . . the agreement. Such a result is neither just nor equitable. Generally speaking, contracts must be enforced even when performance works hardship. . . . """"If a party by his own contract creates a duty or imposes a charge on himself, he must under any and all conditions substantially comply with the undertaking."""" [Citation omitted.]

The district court erred in engaging in a comparison of the benefits and burdens of performance. Its consideration of burdens should have extended no further than a determination whether the burdens were foreseeable or self-inflicted. Such an analysis of hardship would have revealed that Four H's and Western's burdens were both foreseeable and self-inflicted, and therefore did not provide a reason to excuse Four H and Western from their obligation to restore the property to its original topography. See *Mohrlang v. Draper, supra.*

CONCLUSION

For the foregoing reasons, we reverse the judgment of the district court denying specific performance and remand the cause with direction to enter an order of specific performance.

Post-Case Follow-Up

In evaluating undue hardship, the court started with whether the hardships were expected. Where the party knew in advance what the cost would be, it could take those costs into account in deciding whether to make the promise. Having decided to enter the deal with eyes open, complaining that it will actually have to perform as promised seems disingenuous.

The court did not discuss what to do if the burdens were not apparent from the start. The court said it would not compare the burdens to the plaintiff's benefit, but did not say how it would decide whether the burdens were so large that they would justify denying specific performance and relegating the plaintiffs to damages. It seems unlikely that a court could make that judgment by evaluating only the burdens, without comparing them to something, such as the harm plaintiff would suffer if the injunction was denied.

Tierney v. Four H Land Company: Real Life Applications

1. The Sellers entered a contract to sell a beachfront house to Buyers. Thereafter, Mrs. Sellers was diagnosed with spinal muscular atrophy, an untreatable disease that gradually kills her nerve cells. The day before closing, Sellers repudiated the contract, in part because moving might exacerbate Mrs. Sellers' condition. In addition, Mrs. Sellers prefers to spend her remaining years in the comfort of her familiar home. Should the court grant Buyers specific performance? If not, what remedy should the court grant? *See Kilarjian v. Vastola*, 379N.J. Super. 277 (2004).
2. Owner purchased land in a subdivision subject to restrictive covenants designed to ensure that all homes built in the subdivision were complementary. Owner complied with the requirement to submit plans to the review committee, but neglected to submit revisions to those plans that reduced the amount of brick facade. After the committee approved the original plans, Owner started building according to the revised plans. The committee objected and sought a court order compelling Owner to build according to the original plans. Owner completed the house before a ruling. The house is of good quality and consistent with other houses in the subdivision. Should the court grant specific performance compelling Owner to comply with the original plans? *See Dossey v. Hanover, Inc.*, 48 Ark. App. 108 (1995).

Undue hardship sometimes takes a slightly different twist: the court may consider the hardship it would face in enforcing an injunction before deciding whether to grant it. For example, if a court foresees an endless stream of additional hearings to clarify the order and consider sanctions for alleged violations of it, the court may decline to enter the order in the first place. The hardship involved affects the court, not the parties. If damages seem reasonably close to an adequate remedy, the court may decide its hardship outweighs the benefits of issuing an injunction. This may help explain *Northern Delaware Industrial Development Corp. v. E. W. Bliss Co.*,[7] in which the court refused to order a contractor to add a second shift to speed completion of a project, despite a contract provision promising two shifts. The entanglement of addressing every dispute about the adequacy of a second shift seemed to deter the court.

3. Equitable Defenses

Over the years, courts of equity have identified several **equitable defenses**, reasons to use their discretion to withhold equitable relief. In contract cases, impossibility and undue hardship arise more often than other equitable defenses. Awareness of other equitable defenses may help you decide when to avoid seeking injunctive

[7] 245 A.2d 431 (Del. Ch. 1968).

relief. For example, **laches** precludes relief if plaintiff's unreasonable delay in filing a claim causes prejudice (harm) to the defendant. **Unclean hands** precludes equitable relief if the person seeking it has behaved inequitably himself, at least in relation to the transaction at issue. These doctrines receive fuller discussion in courses on Remedies or Equity. Be alert to these and other similar defenses when seeking an injunction.

E. RESTITUTION AND UNJUST ENRICHMENT

Restitution involves compensation for the benefits a defendant received. As a measure of recovery, restitution seeks to put the defendant (the party that received a benefit) in the position she would have occupied if the benefit had not been received. Often this means returning things received from another party, such as refunding a deposit or returning a shipment of goods.

In contract cases, claims of unjust enrichment primarily arise in three basic situations:

1. when a contract is unenforceable;
2. when a breaching party seeks compensation for partial performance of a contract;
3. when a nonbreaching party requests restitution instead of expectation or reliance damages.

In the first two cases, restitution usually is the only option. Breach of contract will be unavailable.

Restitution is the normal remedy for unjust enrichment, a cause of action introduced in Chapter 1. You may recall it has other names, such as quasi-contract, contract-implied-in-law, quantum meruit, quantum valebat, and money had and received. The section below reviews and expands on the elements necessary to establish liability for unjust enrichment. The following section discusses calculating the amount of restitution awarded.

1. Liability for Unjust Enrichment

Unjust enrichment requires a person who received benefits from another to compensate the provider, even if she never asked for or promised to pay for the performance. Liability for unjust enrichment depends on two elements: that the defendant received a benefit (typically from the plaintiff); and retaining the benefit would be unjust unless the recipient compensates the provider of the benefit. Even in cases where it was not unjust for the recipient to receive a benefit, it may be unjust to keep it without compensating the provider.

Unjust enrichment does not require a promise. In this way it differs dramatically from liability for breach of contract. A benefit a party never requested or even wanted may support a claim for unjust enrichment, if keeping it is unjust.

Often, keeping a benefit poses no injustice. A gift, almost by definition, does not require compensation to the donor. Keeping the benefit is just. Similarly, a right obtained under a contract can be retained without injustice, though the recipient must perform its side of the contract in order to justify keeping the benefit. In addition, benefits received from a volunteer may be kept without injustice. The definition of volunteer will vary, but primarily it refers to persons who provide a benefit before asking to be compensated for the benefit. Ideally, a party that wants compensation should mention this before performing, giving the other party a chance to reject the benefit or to negotiate how much she is willing to pay for the benefit. A party that bypasses negotiations by performing first is a volunteer.

Before exploring the application of unjust enrichment in contract settings, consider a case of unjust enrichment that does not involve any promises.

Case Preview

K.A.L. v. Southern Medical Business Services

K.A.L. involves medical services provided to an unconscious patient. Although the services saved her life, the patient objected to paying for them. Unable to find a promise made by the patient, the court considers whether liability attaches despite the absence of an express contract.

As you read *K.A.L. v. Southern Medical Business Services*, look for the following:

1. What does the court mean by an implied contract? Is that the same as quasi-contract?
2. Is *Odem*, where a teenaged mother agreed to pay for her child's care, similar to this case?
3. How did the court determine the amount the patient should pay for the services?

K.A.L. v. Southern Medical Business Services

854 So. 2d 106 (Ala. Civ. App. 2003)

PITTMAN, Judge.

[K.A.L.] attempted suicide by hanging herself . . . with a bedsheet. When jail personnel found her, K.A.L. had no pulse, and cardiopulmonary resuscitation was begun. . . . Upon her arrival at [Springhill Memorial Hospital] K.A.L. was comatose. . . . She was intubated and admitted to the intensive-care unit for treatment.

K.A.L. . . . was discharged [after nine days]. Residual symptoms [because] her brain was deprived of oxygen consisted of speech difficulties and tremors in her upper extremities. The costs [of treatment] have not been paid.

Southern Medical Business Services ("Southern Medical"), as Springhill Memorial Hospital's assignee, sued K.A.L. and the City of Saraland ("the City") to obtain payment. . . . The trial court entered a summary judgment in favor of the City. . . .

[Later] the trial court entered a summary judgment in favor of Southern Medical and against K.A.L. for $21,562. K.A.L. appeals from that judgment.

On appeal, K.A.L. does not . . . claim that the services for which recovery is sought were not reasonable and necessary; rather, her sole contention is that she is not liable for any charges pertaining to the December 1998 hospitalization because she did not consent to the services rendered.

K.A.L. . . . argues on appeal that she could not have expressly consented to the December 1998 medical treatment because she was unconscious at the time of her admission to the hospital. She further contends that there is not substantial evidence to support a finding of an implied contract between her and the hospital for the December 1998 treatment. . . .

[W]e find closely analogous a case in which a minor parent was held responsible for medical "necessaries" rendered to her seriously ill infant. *See Ex parte Odem*, 537 So. 2d 919 (Ala. 1988). In that case, our supreme court, citing *Flexner v. Dickerson*, 72 Ala. 318 (1882), noted the general rule of law in Alabama under which contracts executed by minors are voidable. The *Odem* court explained that a "voidable" contract could either be ratified or avoided at the election of the minor. After entering into a contract with Children's Hospital of Birmingham for treatment of her sick infant, the mother in *Odem* subsequently elected to avoid that contract.

Our supreme court concluded that even though the minor mother had elected to avoid her express contract, the minor mother nonetheless had an obligation to pay for her infant son's medical services; according to the Supreme Court, that obligation arose not from the express contract, but instead "from a quasi-contractual relationship created by operation of law which enforces the implied contract to pay." *Odem*, 537 So. 2d at 920. Using this rationale, the *Odem* court imposed upon the mother an obligation to pay for the reasonably necessary medical services, which it found to be the outstanding balance owed to Children's Hospital. [Footnote omitted.]

Although the *Odem* case involved a minor who had avoided an express contract for medically necessary treatment for her infant, the resulting circumstances in *Odem* are quite similar to the facts in the present case. In both *Odem* and this case, medically necessary treatment was rendered that was not covered by an express contract concerning financial responsibility. We conclude that our supreme court made it clear in *Odem* that the doctrine of quasi-contract would apply under such circumstances to enforce an implied contract between a provider of medical services and the patient (or the patient's legal representative) to pay the reasonable cost of those services.

Further, . . . this court held in *Shellnutt v. Randolph County Hospital*, 469 So. 2d 632 (Ala. App. 1985), that "[w]here . . . there is no evidence of an express contract, an agreement is implied that a hospital will render services and in return receive a reasonable fee for those services." 469 So. 2d at 633. In the present case, the evidence demonstrates that . . . the hospital rendered necessary medical services to enable her to recover. Southern Medical is clearly entitled to a reasonable fee from K.A.L. for the services rendered during that admission. *Accord, Restatement of Restitution* §116 (1937) (person who has supplied services to another, although acting without the other's knowledge or consent, is entitled to restitution if, among other things, the services were necessary to prevent the other from suffering serious bodily harm or pain and it was impossible for the other to give consent).[1]

The record reflects that the total charges assessed by Springhill Memorial Hospital for the medical services rendered to K.A.L. . . . were $17,969.12. . . . [T]he trial court awarded Southern Medical $21,562. . . .

The record contains a written objection filed by K.A.L. opposing the [additional award and seeking] a full accounting for the additional amount. The trial court denied the objection. . . . Although *Odem* indicates that an award of an attorney fee or of collection costs, in addition to the value of necessary medical services, would be erroneous, K.A.L. did not raise this issue in her brief to this court; therefore, this issue is not properly before us on appeal. . . .

AFFIRMED.

Post-Case Follow-Up

Without any words or conduct to signal assent by the patient, the court found liability based on quasi-contract, a term referring to unjust enrichment. Having received the services, which saved her life, she must pay for them. By assessing the amount that the hospital billed, the court reached the same result that would have applied if there had been an express contract.

K.A.L. v. Southern Medical Business Services: Real Life Applications

1. In *K.A.L.*, jail personnel provided CPR immediately upon discovering the suicide attempt. If the guards submit a claim for unjust enrichment, should they recover? Does it matter that guards receive training in CPR as a required part of their job? *See* RESTATEMENT (THIRD) OF RESTITUTION AND UNJUST ENRICHMENT §20 (2011).

2. Shaun, while reading a textbook, recognized that substantial portions of the book were identical to another book Shaun had read. Shaun prepared a highlighted version of the book, annotating the duplications. Shaun then called the original book's publisher and informed it of the apparent copying. The publisher asked to see the highlighted version and Shaun complied. Later, the publisher expressed its gratitude by sending Shaun a check for $300. Shaun did not cash the check. Instead, Shaun asked the publisher for one-third of any recovery the publisher obtained from the infringer. If the publisher resists, should a court

[1][The new Restatement states the rule a little differently, allowing a recovery to prevent unjust enrichment if a person provides a benefit that protects "another's life or health" and, under the circumstances, intervening without a request for help was justified. RESTATEMENT (THIRD) OF RESTITUTION AND UNJUST ENRICHMENT §20 (2011). —EDS.]

award Shaun compensation for unjust enrichment? *See Martin v. Little, Brown & Co.*, 304 Pa. Super. 424 (1981).

3. Chris was unconscious and bleeding after being hit by a car. Dr. Hu stopped and provided emergency medical care to Chris. Despite Dr. Hu's diligent efforts, Chris died before reaching the hospital. Dr. Hu seeks compensation for the services rendered to Chris (involving both time and medical supplies). If the estate resists paying the claim, should a court award compensation based on unjust enrichment? *See Cotnam v. Wisdom*, 83 Ark. 601 (1907).

4. Gail and Shelly decided to form a family. Without marriage or contract, they moved into a house Shelly purchased and held themselves out as a married couple. Shelly knew Gail expected that they would share any wealth they accumulated together equally. Shelly operated a small retail store. Gail helped at the store and offered ideas for improving it. Gail spent more time caring for the house and the family's needs outside the business. This freed Shelly to focus on the business. Over their 15 years together, the business grew in value from $300,000 to $1.8 million. At that time, their relationship had deteriorated to the point that Shelly asked Gail to move out. What advice would you offer Gail concerning the prospects for recovering from Shelly half of the gains they accumulated during their relationship?

Restitution and Unenforceable Contracts

Whenever a contract either did not exist or is rescinded, neither party may collect contract damages. This situation includes all the contract defenses (such as misrepresentation and duress), the technicalities of contract recognition (such as the statute of frauds), and the rules on enforceability (such as consideration and definiteness). These doctrines conclude that the contract should not be enforced. Thus, expectation damages (for the value promised in the contract) would be an inappropriate recovery.

When one party has already partially performed under an unenforceable contract, the recipient has no just claim to retain the performance. The unenforceable contract does not establish a right to keep it. The provider was not making a gift, but intended the performance as part of a bargained-for exchange. And the negotiations that produced the unenforceable agreement suggest she did not bypass negotiations, but tried to enter a bargain before performing. Unjust enrichment allows the court to sort out partial performance of an unenforceable contract, allowing a party (sometimes both parties) to recover the value of the performance.

Restitution for a Breaching Party

Even when a contract is enforceable, a breaching party typically cannot recover for breach of contract. If both parties breach, at least one is likely to have a claim under the contract. But a party's own breach does not necessarily allow the other party to keep partial performance already rendered without any compensation for it. As in the preceding section, the breaching plaintiff was not a donor or a volunteer. The nonbreaching party has a contract right to keep the performance if it paid for the performance—and may even be able to collect damages for the breach. But where the benefit bestowed exceeds the amount the nonbreaching party can claim under the contract, the breaching party may bring an action claiming the excess unjustly enriched the nonbreaching party. For example, in *Neri v. Retail Marine*[8] buyer made a down payment on a boat, then breached the promise to buy. Neri sued to recover the down payment as unjust enrichment. Seller was entitled to keep enough to cover the damages caused by this breach, but needed to refund the remainder to buyer.

Some courts are tempted to deny a breaching party any recovery at all, using a particularly strict application of the defense of ***in pari delicto*** (denying recovery to a plaintiff who is equally in the wrong). But unjust enrichment does not reward the breaching party; it merely limits the loss suffered by the breaching party to the damages the nonbreaching party has a right to claim. Without an action for unjust enrichment, the nonbreaching party's retention of the breaching party's performance might leave the nonbreaching party better off than if the contract had been performed. Contract remedies try to avoid recoveries that make the other party's breach more beneficial than performance would have been. Unjust enrichment, by limiting the breaching party's loss to the damages it would have owed, achieves the contract damage goal of avoiding overcompensation.

Restitution as an Alternative to Damages

In some cases, parties who could seek damages for breach of contract prefer to seek restitution. Usually, this reflects a bad deal: expectation damages will produce a loss, leading a party to prefer to recover based on restitution. Consider, for example, the sale of a house. The buyers discover that the house does not live up to a warranty. The buyers could sue for expectation: typically, the cost to cure the problem, bringing the house up to the quality promised. But if the breach of warranty is material, the buyer might choose to cancel the contract (see Chapter 11) and seek restitution instead. Restitution would permit buyers to return the property (and deed) to the sellers and receive a refund of the purchase price.

The option to rescind gives buyers a powerful choice. Rescission benefits buyers if real estate prices are falling. The buyer recovers the price, which today may buy an even better house. That is more profitable than fixing this house, which now may be worth less than the purchase price. If the market in real estate is rising, damages for the cost of repair offers a better choice. Rescission would leave the parties with the original price, but it will not buy as good a house today as it did when the contract was formed. Instead, buyers will seek damages to repair the house at the seller's expense.

The choice exists if restitution is not limited by expectation. Traditionally, courts may remove the benefit to the defendant even if it leaves the plaintiff in a better position than if performance had occurred. That occurred in *United States ex*

[8] 285 N.E.2d 311 (N.Y. 1972).

rel. Coastal Steel Erectors v. Algernon Blair, Inc.[9] A contractor's material breach justified a subcontractor's decision to cancel a contract. The subcontractor would have lost money if the contract had been completed. Yet the breaching contractor had no right to keep the partial performance without compensating the subcontractor for the fair market value of the services. This situation allowed the subcontractor to break even on the work done so far instead of losing money on the entire contract. Having materially breached the contract, the contractor had no right to insist on keeping the benefit of the good price the contract contained.

A different approach may be emerging in light of the Restatement (Third) of Restitution and Unjust Enrichment. It suggests that recovery following material breach generally should not exceed expectation. It calls the recovery performance-based damages, defined as either (a) reliance recovery (studied in Chapter 15) or (b) the market value of the performance, not exceeding the contract price of that performance.[10] Applied to *Algernon Blair*, the value of the subcontractor's services would have been limited to a pro rata share of the contract price, rather than how much defendant would have had to pay to obtain the services from a different provider. The subcontractor would have lost less than if it had performed the entire contract, but still incurs a loss on the portion performed. If courts are persuaded by this approach, defendants will retain some of the benefits the contract permitted despite their material breach.

Under the Restatement (Third), restitution remains an appropriate remedy for rescission,[11] but rescission may be limited unless a plaintiff seeks a return of property (as opposed to services) conveyed to the defendant and can make restitution of any benefits plaintiff received from the defendant.[12] This encompasses seeking a refund while offering to return the goods or other property, or vice versa (offering a refund while seeking the return of property). Rescission becomes less useful for construction or service contracts, where performance cannot be returned.

Even when return is possible, a plaintiff may not seek restitution if (a) it has already performed all of its duties under the contract; and (b) the only remaining duty of the other party is to pay a definite sum of money.[13] Courts easily can award damages based on the remaining payment. Restitution would require the court to assess the value of the performance already rendered — a much more difficult task. In effect, the party seeking restitution asks the court to change the contract price from the negotiated amount to the fair market value. This limitation reflects the unwillingness of courts to change the contract price after the performance has been completed.

2. Measuring Restitution

At its root, restitution seeks to restore the person unjustly enriched (defendant) to the position that person would have occupied if the benefit had not been bestowed.

[9]439 F.2d 638 (4th Cir. 1973).
[10]Restatement (Third) of Restitution and Unjust Enrichment §38 (2011).
[11]*Id.* §37.
[12]*Id.* §54 cmt. c.
[13]*Id.* §37(2); Restatement (Second) of Contracts §373.

In contract cases, that usually means the position she would have occupied if the promise had never been made and, thus, had never been performed even in part. Because restitution arises in a variety of circumstances, courts have applied a variety of measures for restitution. The goal remains the same, but the methods for calculating recovery vary.

In some cases, defendant can return property to the defendant. If a buyer is not entitled to keep a car or land, returning the property to the seller avoids unjust enrichment. Similarly, if a party receives a money payment, returning the money avoids unjust enrichment.[14] Recovery may need to include some supplementary remedies, such as the fair rental value of property or interest on money during the time defendant possessed it. Courts also may need to adjust recovery to account for any damage or improvements to the property — say, a building defendant added to or removed from real estate, or damage or repairs to a car.[15]

If return of property is not practical, courts need to estimate the value of the benefit to the defendant, awarding that value to the plaintiff. Courts measure value to the defendant in several ways:

(a) the value of the benefit to the defendant,
(b) plaintiff's cost to provide the benefit,
(c) the benefit's fair market value, or
(d) in some cases, the amount the defendant agreed to pay for the benefit.[16]

The choice between these measures will depend on a number of circumstances, primarily whether the recipient requested the benefit and whether she is an innocent recipient or a wrongdoer. Restitution for rescission (as opposed to performance-based damages) sometimes can exceed the amount a party would have received if the contract had been performed. Restitution, unlike the reliance interest, is not expressly limited to the amount of the expectation interest.

The differences between these formulations may be easier to explain in the context of an example. Assume that plaintiff built a fence on defendant's property, but the contract was unenforceable for failure to comply with state statutes. Defendant has been enriched by receiving the fence. The court must determine the value of the fence.

The value of the fence might equal the fair market value of the services provided by the plaintiff[17] (subpart (c) above) or, put another way, the amount it would have cost the defendant to obtain it from another source.[18] In effect, this approach asks how much the defendant saved by not having to pay someone else to provide the benefit. The amount another would have charged measures those savings. This measure applies very well to cases where the defendant requested plaintiff to provide the benefit, as here.

[14] RESTATEMENT (THIRD) OF RESTITUTION AND UNJUST ENRICHMENT §49(2) (2011).
[15] *Id.* §49(5).
[16] *Id.* §49(3).
[17] *Id.* §49(3)(c).
[18] RESTATEMENT (SECOND) OF CONTRACTS §371(a).

The value of the fence might be measured by the value to the defendant: the amount by which defendant's interests have been advanced[19] (subpart (a) above) or, put another way, the increase in the defendant's wealth (or utility, if that can be measured).[20] This might be measured by the increase in value of the defendant's property: the value of the house with the fence minus the value it would have without it. Defendant's net worth has increased by that much, on paper. Whether or not defendant likes the fence, defendant gained value. In a case where defendant did not ask for the fence, he could argue that the fence did not advance his purposes: that the fence is an eyesore, impedes free movement, makes it harder to mow the lawn, or otherwise contributes no benefit to defendant. This argument does not fit the example, where defendant hired the plaintiff to provide the fence, but it might apply to restitution cases where a plaintiff built the fence on defendant's land by mistake.

The value of the fence might be measured by the cost to the plaintiff to build it (subpart (b) above).[21] At its roots, this looks like a measure of reliance (loss to plaintiff) rather than restitution (value to defendant). But in cases where a benefit has no established market value, cost may offer an approximation of value. Cost may also provide a useful measure in cases where value seems inappropriate — such as where the cost of a benefit exceeds the value and defendant bears some fault in the transaction.

Finally, the value of the fence might have been agreed by the parties, as in a contract (subpart (d) above).[22] Of course, a price fixed in a contract induced by fraud probably will not reflect the value of fence, as the fraud may have influenced the price. But a contract unenforceable because of a technical flaw (say, lack of a writing) may nonetheless provide a reasonable estimate of the value — one that might fairly be imposed upon either party given that they agreed to the price at the outset. Where assent to the price seems valid, using the estimate of value the parties created seems apt.[23]

3. Choosing Among Measures of Restitution

In many cases, these measures will be very close. The price agreed by the parties (if any) may be very close to the price others would have charged (fair market value), especially where competition keeps prices from getting too high. Neither contract price nor market price can exceed the value to purchasers generally or no one will agree to pay the price — though price might exceed the value to an individual who does not share the general taste for this particular benefit. Of course, prices (market and contract) are likely to exceed cost in most contracts, as providers typically build overhead and profit into their bids. But exceptions to this also will arise, both intentional (such as loss leaders) and unintentional (such as miscalculation).

[19] Restatement (Third) of Restitution and Unjust Enrichment §49(3)(a) (2011).
[20] Restatement (Second) of Contracts §371(b).
[21] Restatement (Third) of Restitution and Unjust Enrichment §49(3)(b) (2011).
[22] *Id.* §49(3)(d).
[23] *See Walpole Woodworkers, Inc. v. Manning*, 307 Conn. 582 (2012).

The choice between these measures depends on the facts of each case. Some guidelines are fairly specific and reliable: medical professionals who provide unrequested service protecting a recipient's health collect a reasonable charge for the services (fair market value);[24] persons who provide unrequested services that protect defendant's property collect the loss prevented (the amount defendant's interests advanced) or a reasonable charge, whichever is less.[25] (Other guidelines are more general and applied less uniformly: an innocent recipient of unrequested services pays the smallest of the four measures;[26] an innocent recipient of requested services pays the "reasonable value to the recipient," which may equal the amount the recipient agreed to pay (if applicable) or the fair market value of the services, whichever is less.")[27]

These specific guidelines are helpful starting points. In practice, you will want to find the one that applies to your specific situation. Memorizing them now probably serves little use. But you should consider some of the reasons that generate these guidelines. Those reasons often will help you argue for an appropriate measure of restitution even without a guideline as your starting point. To this end, consider five questions that recur in discussions of how to measure restitution.

1. Would one measure produce absurd results?
2. Would one measure be more difficult to assess?
3. Did the party paying restitution seek the benefit?
4. Did the party seeking restitution breach the contract?
5. Did the recipient of the benefit act wrongfully, whether consciously or negligently?

You can see these factors at work in some of the choices already discussed.

Absurd Results

Consider alternative measures of restitution in *K.A.L. v. Southern Medical Business Services*, *supra*. Having saved the patient's life, should the hospital be entitled to recover based on the "value of the benefit in advancing the purposes of the defendant"? That is one suggestion for an innocent recipient of unrequested services. But the benefit of a saved life would be enormous: every dollar earned in the future, every future moment of joy, stems from these services. Allowing the doctor to recover on that basis would be absurd. The special rule limiting medical care to a reasonable charge avoids absurd results.

Practical Measurement

While ease of measurement should not be an excuse for an unjust measure, a practical measure may aid predictability, enhance settlement, and reduce litigation costs. Thus, where contract price provides a fair estimate of value, adopting that price

---

[24] RESTATEMENT (THIRD) OF RESTITUTION AND UNJUST ENRICHMENT §20 (2011).
[25] *Id.* §21.
[26] *Id.* §50(2)(a).
[27] *Id.* §50(2)(b).

instead trying to appraise the value of benefits seems both fair and efficient. This explains the rule rejecting restitution when a party has completed performance and is merely awaiting payment of a fixed sum. It also may explain why medical professionals (who have established charges for life-saving services) may recover for protecting health, but others (who have no established charges) cannot.

Unrequested Benefits

Valuing unrequested benefits poses a problem that does not arise for requested benefits: whether the service is a benefit at all. A homeowner who asks for a fence fairly can be charged for it at fair market value or agreed price. A homeowner who did not ask for a fence may argue that the fence actually makes the property less valuable. At the least, someone who had not sought a fence can object to being compelled to make this the next benefit for which she pays instead of being able to decide for herself when to build a fence (in what style, for how much). While enrichment may require some compensation, less generous measures such as the cost to the provider or the benefit to the recipient (even if less than cost to provider) may serve justice better. For another example, consider a patient who had specifically requested that the hospital not use extraordinary measures to prevent death—a DNR order (Do Not Resuscitate). Concluding the services benefit the patient seems to contradict the patient's own judgment.

Breaching Plaintiff

Similarly, a breaching party seeking restitution sits in a different position than a nonbreaching party. In part this results from the breaching party's obligation to pay damages to the nonbreaching party. In part it reflects a concern that a party should not be made better off by breaching than she would have been following performance. Thus, rules limit recovery by breaching parties to a pro rata share of contract price.

Recipient's Misconduct

When the recipient of a benefit has engaged in wrongdoing, courts gravitate toward more generous measures of restitution. In some situations, the importance of stripping the benefit away from the recipient may justify an award to plaintiff well in excess of the amount he actually provided to the defendant. In these settings, restitution takes on a somewhat punitive role, deterring misconduct by removing every last vestige of gain generated by the misconduct.

4. The Restatement (Third) and Disgorgement for Opportunistic Breach

The Restatement (Third) of Restitution and Unjust Enrichment proposes to create a new recovery: disgorgement. Disgorgement asks the defendant to pay the amount of any gain it would not have received if it had performed as promised. The gain need not have been provided by the plaintiff. Rather, disgorgement reaches out to capture profits a defendant makes by breaking a contract.

Disgorgement is available only if a breach is opportunistic, which applies when

- the breach is deliberate;
- the breach is profitable; and
- the damage recovery is inadequate to protect plaintiff's entitlement.[28]

Consider an example. A pharmaceutical company receives an offer to buy insulin at a price that would produce an extraordinary profit. In order to perform this contract, it must sell insulin that it had already promised to a previous buyer. The company breaches the contract, collects the extraordinary profit, and offers to pay the previous buyer its damages. If disgorgement is allowed, the previous buyer may recover the profit the pharmaceutical company earned by breaching, not just the expectation damages.

Where a defendant tries to perform but fails, breach will not be deliberate and, thus, not opportunistic. Where a breach does not leave the defendant better off than if the contract had been performed, the breach is not opportunistic because it is not profitable. (Besides, without a profit there is no profit to disgorge.) When damages offer a plaintiff adequate protection of its contract rights, courts need not impose disgorgement. Damages will make plaintiff whole, leaving plaintiff no worse off despite the breach. Allowing plaintiff to capture defendant's gain seems pointless—and might discourage defendants from making some breaches that would produce net benefits for society. But where defendant can take advantage of inadequate legal remedies to avoid compensating plaintiff for the full loss, allowing plaintiff a disgorgement recovery may help discourage inappropriate breaches.

Damages are inadequate when they will not leave plaintiff in as good a position as ordering the defendant to perform. Thus, if damages will allow the plaintiff to obtain the full equivalent of the promised performance (for example, by entering a substitute transaction), they seem an adequate recovery. In the insulin example above, if the previous buyer's need was not as urgent as the new buyer's need, perhaps damages will allow it to obtain a substitute supply of insulin in a timely manner, an adequate remedy. On the other hand, where performance by the defendant is irreplaceable in some important way, damages may not be adequate. To some extent, the rule here resembles the rule allowing plaintiff to obtain an injunction ordering the defendant to perform if the damage remedy is inadequate. The rule appears to authorize disgorgement after the breach if the court would have ordered specific performance had the case been resolved in time to prevent the breach.

Disgorgement is at odds with long-standing contract dogma. Normally, breach is considered acceptable, provided the breaching party compensates plaintiff for any losses. No moral outrage compels punishing the breach or siphoning off the profits. While courts occasionally choose a more generous measure of damages when faced with misconduct, they rarely discard the expectation interest as the guiding principle. Disgorgement, if limited to cases when expectation cannot be

[28] *Id.* §39.

compensated, may fit within this framework. On the other hand, disgorgement may be a square peg in the round hold of contract law. Whether courts will embrace or shun this proposal remains to be seen.

Chapter Summary

- Specific performance is an injunction that orders a party to perform all (or sometimes part) of the duties it promised under the contract.
- Negative injunctions order a party not to do something that it could not have done if it had performed the contract. Negative injunctions seek to prevent harm to the plaintiff.
- Injunctions will not be awarded if the remedy at law (usually damages) is adequate. The remedy at law is adequate if it is as complete, as practical, and as efficient as the injunction.
- Where injunctive relief cannot prevent all of the plaintiff's losses, damages may compensate for any remaining loss.
- Even when the remedy at law is inadequate, other reasons may justify rejecting requests for injunctive relief, such as the policy against specific performance of personal service contracts. Irreparable injury is necessary, but not sufficient, to get an injunction.
- Several equitable defenses justify denying an injunctions even if the injury might be irreparable, including undue hardship and impossibility of compliance.
- Restitution is available where the defendant was unjustly enriched: where it received a benefit from the plaintiff and keeping the benefit without compensating the plaintiff would be unjust. Restitution places the defendant in the position it would have occupied if the contract had not been made.
- Measures of restitution vary with the circumstances, particularly whether the benefit was requested and whether either party engaged in misconduct.

Applying the Rules

University agreed to pay Professor Cant $300,000 to fill the Wood Chair in Law and Sociology for one year. The job duties are relatively modest, involving a public lecture series, participation in faculty colloquia, and offering six two-hour master classes to advanced students at some point during the year. While living near the university is expected, it is not technically required by the contract. With the few exceptions noted, Professor Cant could, almost literally, phone it in. After University paid $50,000 to Professor Cant to cover relocation and start-up costs, Professor Cant repudiated the contract. University believes that, even at this late date, it can persuade Professor Wildew to fill the chair at a cost of only $220,000. But

University would rather have Professor Cant, a truly unique superstar in the field of Law and Sociology. Discuss University's options, including the following questions.

1. Can University obtain an injunction ordering Professor Cant to serve as promised?

2. Can University obtain a negative injunction ordering Professor Cant not to serve for any other university during this year? Is there any negative injunctive relief that University could obtain?

3. If the state where University is located decided to follow the Restatement (Third) of Restitution and Unjust Enrichment, would it be permitted to rescind the contract and seek restitution from Professor Cant? Or would it be limited to performance-based damages? If restitution, how would that restitution be measured? Would your answer be different if this state applied the restitution rules from the Restatement (Second) of Contracts?

4. Do your answers depend on why Professor Cant decided not to serve at University? Consider three possibilities: (a) Harvard offered Professor Cant $500,000 to spend the year in residence there instead; (b) Professor Cant's only child was diagnosed with a serious illness that requires medical attention in Boston and Professor Cant does not want to be so far away for the year; (c) Professor Cant was confused, thinking that the offer was from another University with a similar name and repudiated the contract immediately upon recognizing the difference.

Contract Law in Practice

1. Jurisdictions vary in the way they treat some bases for arguing that an injury is irreparable. Examine the statutes and cases of your state to determine whether a defendant's insolvency makes an injury irreparable (because defendant cannot pay damages even if plaintiff obtains a judgment for them). Does the difficulty of proving losses make an injury irreparable in your state?

2. Your friend Alex owns a house, but would like to sell it. The market has been weak but shows signs of improving. Alex would like to retain flexibility to accept better offers, even if they arrive after an earlier offer has been accepted. To this end, Alex hopes that a liquidated damage provision specifying a relatively small amount as buyer's damages for seller's breach will allow acceptance of a better offer (as long as the offer exceeds the earlier contract by more than the liquidated damage amount). An order of specific performance would prevent this strategy from working. Alex wants the contract to preclude a buyer from obtaining specific performance instead of liquidated damages. In your jurisdiction, will courts treat the liquidated damage provision as agreeing to waive equitable

relief? If not, can you draft a clause precluding specific performance in a way that courts in your jurisdiction will honor?

3. Instead of a new house, Alex intends to buy a boat large enough to serve as living quarters. When buying the boat, Alex would like to be sure the seller does not take the same approach. Can you prepare a term Alex could insert in the offer that ensures the court will grant specific performance of the contract in the event seller breaches? Is the clause unnecessary because your jurisdiction treats contracts for the sale of boats that size as if they are real estate, not goods?

4. Jurisdictions vary in the extent to which they are willing to enforce negative covenants, even if expressed in a contract. Examine the statutes and cases in your state to determine the extent to which it will enforce an employee's promise not to compete with the employer for a reasonable period after the employment ends. Do the rules differ depending on the plaintiff's profession or specialty? Does the same rule apply to noncompetition clauses in agreements for the sale of a business, where the former owner agrees not to compete with the new owner?

5. You represent DNAT, a medical research company. DNAT is negotiating to hire Singha, a brilliant researcher currently working in India. The contract includes substantial relocation expenses and a signing bonus, which DNAT is willing to pay. DNAT, however, wants to ensure that Singha will work for DNAT long enough to allow DNAT to benefit from these expenses — or, at least, that the expenses will not benefit a competitor that hires Singha away after only a few months. Draft a clause that will protect DNAT's interests in this regard. Provide DNAT the maximum protection that you believe your jurisdiction's law will permit. Be prepared to discuss where you might make concessions (and more importantly, where you cannot make concessions) in order to persuade Singha to sign the agreement.

Glossary

abate Temporarily stop work on the case. (Ch. Fifteen)

abuse of process Tort that allows remedies against people who file civil pleadings (claims or defenses) when they know they have no chance to succeed. (Ch. Six)

accelerate Allows a demand for repayment of an entire outstanding balance immediately. (Ch. Thirteen)

acceptance An expression of assent to the terms of an offer in a manner authorized by the offer. (Chs. Two, Three)

actual harm Harm that actually resulted from the breach. (Ch. Fifteen)

actual notice Subjective knowledge of what the other party intended. (Ch. Nine)

actual reliance Element of promissory estoppel where the promisee must actually rely upon this promise; may take the form of action or forbearance. (Ch. Five)

adequacy of consideration Compensation which is equal in value for an act or a thing for which it is given. (Ch. Four)

affirmative defenses See *defenses*. (Ch. Six)

agent A person authorized to act on behalf of another. (Chs. Two, Eight)

ambiguous Term that, in context, could mean at least two different things. (Ch. Nine)

answer Defendant's pleading, denying, or admitting the allegations in a complaint. (Ch. Eight)

anticipated harm Harm the parties expected at the time the contract was made. (Ch. Fifteen)

antitrust laws Laws governing monopolies and other anticompetitive practices; expressly ban contracts that unfairly restrict trade and marketplace competition. (Ch. Eight)

arbitrator Person (or panel) chosen to resolve a dispute. (Ch. Fifteen)

arm's-length transaction Contract negotiated between unrelated parties, each looking out for its own best interest. (Ch. Fifteen)

assent Agreement. (Ch. Fifteen)

assignee Receives rights from another party. (Ch. Fourteen)

assignment Voluntarily transferring any benefits under the contract to another party. (Ch. Fourteen)

assignor Gives rights to another party. (Ch. Fourteen)

at will Employment that has no specified duration, allowing either the employee or the employer to terminate the contract at any time for any reason or no reason at all (but not an illegal reason), without obligation to the other party. (Ch. Fifteen)

avoidable consequences doctrine Precludes recovery for losses the plaintiff could have avoided by reasonable conduct. (Ch. Fifteen)

bargain An exchange of performances. (Ch. Two)

bargain at arm's length See *arm's length transaction.* (Ch. Seven)

bargain theory Theory based on the notion of reciprocal conventional inducement; each party's promise induces the other to respond with a return promise, action, or forbearance. (Ch. Four)

bargained-for exchange Exists if a party making a promise seeks a performance or a return promise to be given by another in exchange for that promise. (Ch. Four)

beneficiary The person whose interests the trustee protects. (Ch. Six)

benefit rule Permits restitution against a person, despite the incapacity defense. (Ch. Six)

benefit-detriment theory Approach that asks whether or not the promisor receives a benefit or the promisee suffers a detriment, loss, or forbearance. (Ch. Four)

bilateral contract A contract where the parties are exchanging a promise for a promise. (Ch. Four)

boilerplate Terms governing details, typically ones that don't vary from deal to deal and, thus, don't justify time to renegotiate or redraft with each deal. (Ch. Three)

breach Failure to perform without an excuse. (Ch. One, Ch. Two, Ch. Eleven)

business goodwill The value of a business's existing reputation and customer satisfaction. (Ch. Eight)

business reality Justified commercial need for questioned contract term(s). (Ch. Eight)

cancel Refuse to perform any more duties. (Ch. Eleven)

canons of interpretation Rules of thumb courts sometimes use to find the meaning of contract language. (Ch. Nine)

caveat emptor Let the buyer beware. (Ch. Ten)

certainty See definiteness. (Ch. Two)

certainty requirement Rejects damages that exceed the amount proven with reasonable certainty. (Ch. Fifteen)

chancery courts See *courts of equity.* (Ch. Sixteen)

chattels Personal property; things not attached to the land. (Ch. Nine)

choice of law clauses Specify which state's law should apply to any disputes. (Ch. Fifteen)

clean hands Not having acted inequitably regarding a transaction. (Ch. Six)

cognitive disorders Conditions that may affect a person's ability to understand the nature and consequences of a proposed transaction proposed. (Ch. Six)

cognitive test Determines incapacity, focusing on whether the metal illness or defect was so serious that the party is unable to reasonably comprehend the nature and consequences of the contract. (Ch. Six)

complaint Pleading beginning a lawsuit by alleging defendant's wrongs. (Ch. Eight)

complete knockout rule Terms do not become part of the contract if notification of objection to them has already been given. (Ch. Three)

completely integrated A writing that provides the parties' final and exclusive agreement. (Ch. Nine)

concealment Conduct intended to prevent another from learning a fact. (Ch. Seven)

condition An event that must occur before performance is due. (Chs. One, Three, Four, Five, Seven, Eleven)

condition precedent See *condition*. (Ch. Eleven)

condition subsequent Describes events that discharge a duty after performance has already come due. (Ch. Eleven)

conditional gifts A gift that is subject to or dependent on a condition; often arise in instances of charitable pledges. (Ch. Four)

conscious ignorance When a party realizes it lacks information, but treats that limited knowledge as sufficient. (Ch. Seven)

consequential damages Damages that arise from the way the buyer intended to use the goods (such as lost profits on reselling them.) (Ch. Twelve)

consequential loss Involves the way the party would have used the performance promised. (Ch. Fifteen)

consideration The doctrine requiring a legally recognized exchange in order to justify enforcement of a promise. (Chs. One, Two, Four)

constructive notice Notice imputed to a party with no actual knowledge because that party had reason to know of the other's meaning. (Ch. Nine)

consumer surplus Additional satisfaction a consumer receives over and above the satisfaction of keeping the price. (Ch. Fifteen)

contract A promise that the law will enforce or, at least, that creates a duty the law will recognize. (Ch. One)

contract implied-in-fact An actual promise a party makes, but one inferred from conduct that signals a promise instead of from words expressing a promise. (Ch. One)

contract implied-in-law See *unjust enrichment*. (Ch. One)

contracts of adhesion Standardized contracts offered on a "take it or leave it" basis with little or no negotiation. (Chs. Two, Four, Eight)

Convention on Contracts for the International Sale of Goods (CISG) The treaty governing sales of goods between parties from different nations. (Ch. Four)

conversion A property tort; deprives an owner of personal property without his or her consent. (Ch. Six)

copyright Exclusive right to creative works, such as books, music, photographs, computer programs, and so on. (Ch. Ten)

counteroffer A proposal to deal on different terms. (Chs. Two, Three)

course of dealing The way parties' prior contracts have been interpreted by the parties themselves. (Ch. Nine)

course of performance The way parties have interpreted a contract, as inferred from their acceptance of prior conduct under the contract. (Ch. Nine)

courts of equity Historically, in England, petitions to the monarchy. (Ch. Sixteen)

courts of law Historically, in England, handled lawsuits. (Ch. Sixteen)

cover Substitute performance. (Ch. One, Twelve, Fifteen)

creditor beneficiaries Parties to whom a promisee owes money and wants the promisor's performance or payment to satisfy that debt in whole or in part. (Ch. Fourteen)

cure To promptly correct any problems with performance by adjusting the price or supplying the missing goods in a timely manner. (Ch. Twelve)

damages An amount of money necessary to produce the equivalent of performance; may be awarded in a lawsuit. (Chs. One, Six)

defenses Arguments raised by a party accused of breaching a contract that, if established, negate the enforceability of the contract. (Chs. One, Six)

definiteness Requirement that the promise be sufficiently detailed to allow a court to identify a breach and to formulate a suitable remedy. (Chs. One, Two, Ten)

delegated party Person to whom a duty is delegated. (Ch. Fourteen)

delegation Designation in a contract for someone else to perform some or all of another's contract duties. (Ch. Fourteen)

dependent promise A promise that need not be performed unless the other party has performed first. (Ch. Eleven)

depositions Oral responses to questions transcribed under oath. (Ch. Eight)

detrimental reliance Reliance that leaves the promisee worse off than if the promise had not been made; element of promissory estoppel. (Ch. Five)

direct loss Loss relating to the thing promised. (Ch. Fifteen)

disaffirm To repudiate a voidable contract. (Ch. Six)

discharge To treat as if fully performed. (Chs. Eleven, Fourteen)

disclaim Agree to terms that exclude implied promises. (Ch. Ten)

divisible Contract that can fairly be divided into two parts, one performed and one not performed. (Ch. Eleven)

doctrine of necessaries Allows children to make contracts for the essentials of life; require a showing that the child needed the benefits of the contract, not just that she wanted them. (Ch. Six)

donee beneficiaries Those whom a promisee intended to receive a gift under an agreement with a promisor. (Ch. Fourteen)

due diligence Verifying the other's accounts and objectively determining business value. (Ch. Seven)

duress Improper threat that induces assent to a contract. (Ch. Twelve)

duress Improper pressure (including threats) others apply that impairs a person's ability to make or to express a rational decision. (Ch. One)

duty to mitigate damages See *avoidable consequences doctrine.* (Ch. Fifteen)

economic duress Unlawful use of wrongful or improper financial or commercial threats. (Chs. Five, Six)

efficient breach Occurs if the breaching party can gain enough from the breach to compensate the other party's loss and still come out ahead. (Ch. Fifteen)

enjoined Party the court orders to do something. (Ch. Sixteen)

equitable defenses Reasons for courts to use their discretion to withhold equitable relief. (Ch. Sixteen)

equitable relief Remedies available from courts of equity. (Ch. Sixteen)

estopped Legally barred or precluded. (Ch. Five, Six)

executory gift A promised gift that is not yet delivered. (Ch. Four)

exemplary damages See *punitive damages.* (Ch. Fifteen)

expectation interest When the victim of a breach is placed in the position that she would have occupied if the breach had not occurred. (Ch. One)

expectation interest An amount that will put the plaintiff in the position that she would have occupied if the promise had been performed. (Chs. Five, Fifteen)

expectation remedy Seeks to place the plaintiff in the position she would have occupied if the contract had been performed. (Ch. Sixteen)

express repudiation Occurs when a party communicates an unequivocal intention not to perform when performance is due. (Ch. Twelve)

express warranties Promises that arise from statements or conduct of the seller that suggest a promise relating to the quality of performance. (Ch. Ten)

extrinsic evidence Any evidence, written or oral, other than the contract documents themselves. (Ch. Nine)

fair market value See *value.* (Ch. Fifteen)

fiduciary One who must put the interests of the ward ahead of the guardian's own interests in making decisions for the ward. (Ch. Six)

first shot rule Description of the effect of applying §2-207. An acceptance, even one with different or additional terms, accepts all the terms of the offer. (Ch. Three)

force majeure Clauses that excuse performance for extreme events, such as tornadoes or fires. (Chs. Three, Thirteen)

foreseeability A contract party's ability to anticipate, at the time a contract is made, the type (and perhaps the amount) of loss the other party might suffer if a breach occurs. (Ch. Fifteen)

foreseeable reliance Applies when the promisor reasonably should have expected the promisee's reliance on the promise; element of promissory estoppel. (Ch. Five)

forfeiture Occurs if a party does not receive the benefit of a contract and cannot recover what she invested in the contract. (Ch. Eleven)

formal emancipation Legal proceedings allowing a court to decree that the minor should be treated as an adult, despite not having reached age eighteen. (Ch. Six)

forum selection clauses Specify where suits should be brought. (Ch. Fifteen)

fraud Intentional deception; lies. (Ch. Seven)

fraud in the execution Deception as to the very nature of the document; a form of misrepresentation. (Ch. Seven)

fraud in the inducement Misrepresentations concerning the underlying subject matter of the deal. (Ch. Seven)

fraudulent Dishonest. (Ch. Seven)

frustration Occurs when unanticipated circumstances arise that make the other party's performance nearly useless. (Chs. One, Thirteen)

fully executed Completely performed. (Ch. Eight)

gap-filler UCC provisions which add in terms such as price, delivery, and warranties if not specified in the contract. (Ch. Eight)

gift promises Promise that seeks nothing in exchange. Gifts are excluded from the doctrine of consideration because promises are being made without requiring anything in return. (Ch. Four)

good faith Honestly and without notice of the error. (Ch. Nine)

goods Things which are moveable. (Ch. Four)

gratuitous promises See *gift promises*. (Ch. Four)

guaranty See *suretyship*. (Ch. Eight)

guardian Someone who manages the affairs of another. (Ch. Six)

illegality defense Defense against contracts to commit crimes or to undertake tortious activities. (Ch. Eight)

Illusory promise A promise that is unenforceable due to indefiniteness or lack of mutuality. (Ch. Ten)

implied ratification Applies to people who have discovered a defense, but do not invoke it promptly. Failure to disaffirm within a reasonable time or to plead the defense in an answer to a complaint usually waives the defense. (Ch. Six)

implied repudiation Occurs when a party's voluntary acts make it seem impossible for that party to perform when performance is due. (Ch. Twelve)

implied warranties Arise by operation of law unless the parties agree otherwise. (Ch. Ten)

impossibility Excuse indicating that changed circumstances have made it literally impossible for a party to perform its contract duties. (Ch. Thirteen)

impracticability Excuse for nonperformance that occurs when unexpected disasters beyond a party's control preclude performance. (Ch. One, Twelve, Thirteen)

in pari delicto In equal wrong. (Ch. Eight, Sixteen)

incapacity Applies to people who lack the ability to exercise the necessary legal judgment to assent to and carry out the terms of a contract. (Chs. One, Six)

incidental beneficiary Party not intended to receive a benefit under the contract; has no right to sue. (Ch. Fourteen)

incidental loss Costs involved in reacting to the breach. (Ch. Fifteen)

indemnify To compensate for loss or damage. (Ch. Nine)

independent promise A promise that must be performed regardless of whether the other party performs first. (Ch. Eleven)

induced Substantially contributed to a party's decision to enter into a deal on particular terms. (Ch. Seven)

infancy doctrine Views children as lacking capacity; seeks to protect minors from adults who might take advantage of their lack of maturity in contract situations and determined that such agreements were void. (Ch. Six)

injunction Compels or stops certain conduct. (Ch. Six, Sixteen)

injunctive relief Court orders compelling a party to perform the specific act promised. (Ch. Fifteen)

innocent misrepresentation A misrepresentation that the speaker honestly and reasonably believes to be true. (Ch. Seven)

insolvent Cannot pay all debts in full. (Ch. Sixteen)

installment contracts Contracts permitting or requiring a seller to deliver in more than one lot (for example, monthly deliveries). (Ch. Twelve)

intangibles Personal property that has no physical existence. (Ch. Two)

integrated agreements What the parties adopt as the final expression of their agreement (or part of their agreement). (Ch. Nine)

intended beneficiary A person who is not a party to a contract, but for whom the contract is intended to benefit; has the legal right to enforce the contract. (Ch. Fourteen)

interpretation Determining the meaning and effect of people's communications, expressed by words or by conduct. (Ch. Nine)

interrogatories Written responses to questions under oath. (Ch. Eight)

intoxication Applies to people who are under the influence of substances that impair a person's ability to make good decisions. (Ch. Six)

irreparable injury rule Rule that courts of equity could not act unless the remedy at law was inadequate. (Ch. Sixteen)

jest Arises when one party claims to be joking and did not intend for a deal to be taken seriously. (Ch. Two)

justifiable Reasonable. (Ch. Seven)

laches Precludes relief if plaintiff's unreasonable delay in filing a claim causes prejudice (harm) to the defendant. (Ch. Sixteen)

last shot rule Result reached by rigid application of the mirror image rule. Delivery of goods or payment accepts rather than rejects the most recent proposed terms and conditions, unless objected to by the receiving party. (Ch. Three)

legal sufficiency Principle that something of legally recognized value must be the foundation of the agreement between the contracting parties. (Ch. Four)

liquidated Reduced to a specific number or formula in the agreement. (Ch. Ten, Fifteen)

liquidated damages clause Specifies the amount of damages a party may recover in the event of a breach. (Chs. Two, Fifteen)

mailbox rule Rule that in many circumstances acceptances take effect before receipt; the moment it is put out of the offeree's possession, whether or not the acceptance reaches the offeror. (Ch. Three)

malice Intent to harm. (Ch. One)

malicious prosecution Tort that allow remedies against people who file civil pleadings (claims or defenses) when they know they have no chance to succeed. (Ch. Six)

manifestations Words or actions. (Ch. One)

market damages Damages based on the market value of the performance, the loss of which flows directly from the breach. (Ch. Fifteen)

material Significant. (Ch. Seven, Eleven)

material benefit rule Under promissory restitution, a court may enforce a subsequent promise. (Ch. Five)

material breach Failure to perform a significant part of the work. (Ch. One, Eleven)

merchant One who regularly deals in goods of a particular type. (Ch. Ten)

meretricious relationships Relationships where sexual relations are rewarded with money, property, or other valuable consideration. (Ch. Eight)

merger clause Clause that combines all prior discussions into the writing. (Ch. Nine)

minors Those under the age of eighteen. (Ch. Six)

mirror image rule Rule that requires the terms of the acceptance match the terms of the offer exactly. (Ch. Three)

misrepresentation Applies when one party has misled another into entering the contract. (Chs. One, Seven)

mistake When a party, without being misled by others, enters an agreement under an erroneous belief about some key aspect of the exchange. (Chs. One, Seven)

mistake of integration Occurs when writings are inaccurately recorded in the agreement. (Ch. Nine)

misunderstanding Arises when parties use the same words, but mean significantly different things. (Ch. Nine)

modification A change or revision to the terms of an existing contract. (Chs. Two, Five, Twelve)

money had and received An action seeking to recover payments made. (Ch. One)

moral hazard Temptation to take fewer precautions when someone else will pay the cost of that decision. (Ch. Fifteen)

motion to dismiss Throw a case out before discovery. (Ch. Nine)

motivational test Determines the severity of a disorder by examining whether the mental illness or defect creates a compulsion that the party is unable to control themselves and cannot act or perform the contract in a reasonable manner. (Ch. Six)

mutual Something both parties share. (Ch. Seven)

mutual assent Where both parties (or all of the parties) have agreed to the terms. (Ch. One)

mutual mistake Defense allowing rescission when both parties were mistaken about basic assumptions on which they agreed to the contract. (Ch. Five)

mutual mistake of integration Occurs when both parties believed, when signing the document, that it accurately reflected their agreement. (Ch. Nine)

mutuality of remedy Neither party may obtain specific performance unless a court can order both parties to perform. (Ch. Sixteen)

negative injunction Orders a party not to do something that would be inconsistent with the performance it promised. (Ch. Sixteen)

nominal damages Modest amount (such as $1) awarded where a breach caused no measurable harm. (Chs. One, Fifteen)

nondisclosure When a person omits information that should have been shared. (Ch. Seven)

novation New contract between the obligee and the delegated party in which the obligee agrees to discharge any duties owed by the delegating party. (Ch. Fourteen)

objective Refers to what reasonable people under the circumstances would have understood; focused on words and actions, as opposed to thoughts. (Ch. One, Nine)

obligee The party who is entitled to receive the obligor's performance of duties. (Ch. Fourteen)

obligor Person with an obligation to perform. (Ch. Fourteen)

offer Proposes an agreement on specific terms, giving another person the power to conclude the transaction by agreeing to those terms. (Ch. Two)

offeree The person to whom the proposal is made. (Ch. Two)

offeror The person making a proposal. (Ch. Two)

offsets Counteract; be subtracted from. (Ch. Fifteen)

option contracts Contracts that involve an enforceable promise to keep the offer open for a period of time. (Ch. Two)

output contract Contract where a seller agrees to sell all of some performance to a single buyer, who agrees to take the entire output. (Ch. Ten)

parol evidence Oral evidence; may also include extrinsic evidence. (Ch. Nine)

parol evidence rule Makes evidence of prior or contemporaneous agreements or negotiations inadmissible to vary or to contradict (or, in some cases, to supplement) the promises recorded in integrated agreements. (Ch. Nine)

partially integrated A writing that states the parties' final expression as to the terms that it contains, even if it is not necessarily the parties' exclusive agreement concerning their relationship. (Ch. Nine)

party to be charged Person resisting enforcement of a contract. (Ch. Eight)

past consideration Implies treating a performance received in the past as if it is the consideration for a subsequent promise. (Ch. Five)

patent Inventor's exclusive right to her invention. (Ch. Ten)

penalty clauses Specifies amounts due upon breach that seek to deter or punish the breaching party. (Ch. Fifteen)

perfect tender rule Allows buyers the right to reject, accept, or accept part and reject the rest of a delivery of goods. (Ch. Twelve)

permanent injunction Injunction granted after a full trial on the merits. (Ch. Sixteen)

physical compulsion Duress focusing on threats to life, limb, or liberty. (Ch. Six)

preexisting duty Refers to conduct or actions that a person already has a legal obligation to do. (Ch. Five)

preliminary injunctions Injunctions issued at or near the beginning of a case; usually offer partial or temporary relief. (Ch. Sixteen)

preliminary negotiations A communication where the person does not intend to conclude a bargain until he has made a further manifestation of assent. (Ch. Two)

preponderance of the evidence When something is more likely than not or 50% plus an iota. (Ch. Nine, Fifteen)

prevailing party One who wins in court. (Ch. Fifteen)

preventive injunctions Seek to prevent harm to the plaintiff. (Ch. Sixteen)

principal Person employing the agent. (Ch. Two)

privity When courts recognize only the rights and duties of the parties who entered into a contract. (Ch. Fourteen)

procedural unconscionability Refers to defects in the negotiation process. (Ch. Eight)

promise Expressed commitment to act. (Ch. Two)

promissory estoppel The doctrine that provides that if a party changes his or her position substantially either by acting or forbearing from acting in reliance upon a gratuitous promise, then that party can enforce the promise although the essential elements of a contract are not present. (Ch. Four)

promissory note A written, signed, unconditional promise to pay a certain amount of money on demand at a specified time, typically used in debtor-creditor situations. (Ch. Four)

promissory restitution Legal theory that allows compensation for services rendered even if no contract was formed; applied in situations where a promise to pay or compensate is made after a benefit is received. (Ch. Five)

public policy Applies primarily to contracts that require conduct that is illegal or violates well-established policies embodied in constitutional law, statutory law, and case precedent. (Ch. Eight)

puffing Putting one's product in the best light, even if that involves exaggeration. (Ch. Seven)

punitive damages Recovery over and above the amount plaintiff lost, imposed to punish or to make an example of the breaching defendant. (Chs. One, Fifteen)

quantum meruit An action seeking to recover the value of services rendered. (Ch. One)

quantum valebat An action seeking to recover the value of goods delivered. (Ch. One)

quasi-contract See *unjust enrichment*. (Ch. One)

quasi-fiduciary Describes situations where a person may need to compromise his or her own self-interest, in order to protect the interests of another. (Ch. Six)

ratify To elect to treat a voidable contract as enforceable. (Ch. Six)

reasonable grounds for insecurity Justifiable concerns or fear that the other party may not perform, but do not establish a repudiation. (Ch. Twelve)

recover restitution An amount needed to place the party that received the benefit (typically the defendant, a party who did not perform the alleged contract) in the position it would have occupied if the contract had not been made. (Ch. One, Fifteen)

reform Rewrite. (Ch. Seven)

reformation Action that requests the court to correct the writing to reflect the parties' actual agreement. (Ch. Nine)

rejection A refusal to enter the agreement. (Ch. Two)

relation of trust and confidence Includes fiduciaries, who have a legal obligation to put the interest of others ahead of their own interests, and other relationships in which one party has a right to expect another to treat their interests equally or, in some cases, put the others' interests ahead of their own. (Ch. Seven)

release Extinguish the obligation. (Ch. Fourteen)

reliance Acting upon another's statement of alledged fact, claim, or knowledge. (Ch. Seven)

reliance interest Seeks to place the victim in the position that she would have occupied if the promise had never been made. (Chs. One, Fifteen)

remedy at law Remedy a court of law could award. (Ch. Sixteen)

remittitur Threat to grant a new trial unless plaintiff agrees to a smaller damage award. (Ch. Fifteen)

reparative injunctions Seek to undo harm that already has been done; rare in contract cases. (Ch. Sixteen)

replevin Cause of action that allows the true owner of property to recover it from others who have possession of it. (Ch. Sixteen)

repudiation Notice that buyer will not perform contract duties. (Ch. Eight)

requirements contract Contract where a buyer agrees to buy all of its needs of some good from the seller. (Ch. Ten)

rescind To cancel. (Ch. Three, Fourteen)

rescission A contract that is canceled or torn up, as if it never had been made. (Ch. Two, Six, Twelve)

restitution Compensation for the benefits a defendant received. (Ch. Sixteen)

restitution interest See *recover restitution.* (Ch. One, Fifteen)

retraction Withdrawal. (Ch. Twelve)

revocation Withdrawing and offer. (Ch. Two)

sales puffery Self-promoting sales talk and statements of opinion about intangible qualities of products. (Ch. Ten)

security interest Right to foreclose on or to repossess goods. (Ch. Ten)

sham consideration Consideration that appears to have no true value. (Ch. Four)

single delivery contracts One-time, voluntary transfer of the possession of goods. (Ch. Twelve)

specific performance An injunction compelling a breaching party to perform the promise. (Ch. One, Fifteen)

specific relief Awarding a party something closer to what it is entitled to receive. (Ch. Sixteen)

specific restitution Forfeits gains obtained from the plaintiff, such as ordering a party to return property to the original owner. (Ch. Sixteen)

spin See *puffing*. (Ch. Seven)

standing Legal right to bring the lawsuit. (Ch. Fourteen)

statute of frauds Bars enforcement of certain oral promises if not contained in a proper signed writing. (Chs. Five, Eight)

statute of limitations Law which sets out the maximum time that parties have to initiate legal proceedings from the date of an alleged offense. (Ch. Five)

stay See *abate*. (Ch. Fifteen)

strike suits Suits brought in the hope of obtaining a settlement, with no real expectation that the suit ever could prevail. (Ch. Six)

subjective Refers to what a person actually thought. (Ch. One)

substantial performance Providing the recipient with the important aspects of performance, even if some details of performance fall short. (Chs. One, Eleven)

substantive unconscionability Analyzes whether the contract terms themselves are too harsh or one-sided to be legally enforceable. (Ch. Eight)

summary judgment Grants judgment before trial to one party because the other party lacked even minimal evidence to show a genuine issue as to a material fact. (Ch. Nine)

suretyship Situation where an individual undertakes an obligation to pay a sum of money or to perform some duty or promise for another in the event that person fails to act. (Ch. Eight)

suspended On hold until the condition occurs. (Ch. Eleven)

take or pay clauses Gives a buyer a choice to take the goods (and pay for them) or pay for them (and not take them). (Ch. Fifteen)

tender An offer to perform immediately with the demonstrated ability to do so. (Chs. Three, Eleven)

third party beneficiary Another person or entity, not a party to the contract, to whom a contract may specify that some or all of the consideration will be provided. (Ch. Fourteen)

trade secrets Business information legally protected from unauthorized disclosure. (Ch. Sixteen)

trademark Exclusive right to use identifying packaging or symbols, such as corporate logos. (Ch. Ten)

trust A special relationship between the trustee and the beneficiary. (Ch. Six)

trustee One who manages another's affairs. (Ch. Six)

unclean hands Precludes equitable relief if the person seeking it has behaved inequitably himself, at least in relation to the transaction at issue. (Ch. Sixteen)

unconscionability Addresses issues of flaws in the negotiation stage of the contract as well as contract terms considered harsh and one-sided; covers situations where oppressive contract terms pose serious and unexpected hardships for a party. (Chs. One, Seven, Eight)

uncured Not yet corrected by subsequent performance. (Ch. Eleven)

undue influence Addresses issues of unfair persuasion brought to bear against a party in a lessened capacity to exercise free will in making a contract. (Ch. Six)

Uniform Commercial Code (UCC) A body of law governing common business contracts. (Ch. Two)

unilateral Involving only one party. (Ch. Seven)

unilateral contract A contract that becomes binding after one party has already completed performance, and acceptance occurs when performance is complete. (Ch. Three, Four)

unilateral mistake Situations where only one party was mistaken. (Ch. Seven)

unilateral mistake of integration Occurs if one party believes that the written agreement includes a term, but the other believes that it does not. (Ch. Nine)

United Nations Convention on Contracts for the International Sale of Goods (CISG), A treaty governing sales of goods between parties in different nations. (Ch. Two)

unjust enrichment Occurs when two elements are met: 1) Defendant received a benefit (usually at the expense of plaintiff); and 2) Retaining the benefit would be unjust, unless plaintiff is compensated for the benefit. (Ch. One)

usage of trade Terms that, within a particular type of business, have taken on a meaning that everyone (or nearly everyone) in the trade knows. (Ch. Nine)

usury Excessive interest rates on loans. (Ch. Eight)

value The amount a willing buyer would pay and a willing seller would accept if neither was under compulsion to deal and each was reasonably informed. (Ch. Fifteen)

void A void contract is unenforceable because no valid contract ever existed. Courts will refuse to enforce a void contract, even if both parties want the contract enforced. (Ch. Six)

voidable Something declared void by the promisor, usually based on a defense to contract formation. (Ch. Five, Six)

volitional disorders Conditions that may impact a person's ability to act reasonably in relation to a contract—even though the person might understand the transaction and reasonable performance of their contract obligations. (Ch. Six)

volunteers Those who provide unsolicited benefits in circumstances where they should bargain before performing. (Ch. One)

waive To intentionally relinquish a known right. (Ch. Eleven)

waiver An intentional relinquishment of a known right. (Ch. Five)

ward A person who suffers an incapacity. (Ch. Six)

warrant A promise related to quality. (Chs. Ten, Fifteen)

warranty See *warrant*. (Ch. Fifteen)

warranty of merchantability Promises that the goods satisfy a minimal level of quality. (Ch. Ten)

willful ignorance See *conscious ignorance*. (Ch. Seven)

with reserve A right to remove items from the sale if bids are unsatisfactory. (Ch. Two)

without reserve Items for sale cannot be withdrawn unless no bids are made within a reasonable time. (Ch. Two)

Table of Cases

Principal cases are indicated by italics.

Table of Restatements, Uniform Commercial Code (UCC), and UN Convention on Contracts for the International Sale of Goods (CISG)

Restatement (Second) of Contracts

Restatement (Third) of Restitution and Unjust Enrichment

Uniform Commercial Code (UCC)

United Nations Convention on Contracts for the International Sale of Goods (CISG)

Index